STATE RANKINGS
2006

A Statistical View of the 50 United States

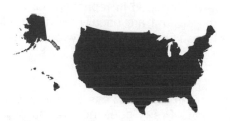

Kathleen O'Leary Morgan and Scott Morgan, Editors

MORGAN QUITNO

Morgan Quitno Press
©.Copyright 2006, All Rights Reserved
512 East 9th Street, P.O. Box 1656
Lawrence, KS 66044-8656
USA
800-457-0742 or 785-841-3534
www.statestats.com

Seventeenth Edition

© Copyright 2006 by
Morgan Quitno Corporation
512 East 9th Street, P.O. Box 1656
Lawrence, Kansas 66044-8656
USA
800-457-0742 or 785-841-3534
www.statestats.com

Cover Photo: photos.com

Limitation of Liability: While Morgan Quitno Press uses its best efforts to deliver accurate and complete information, Morgan Quitno Press does not warrant accuracy or completeness, is not responsible for errors and omissions and is not liable for any direct, indirect or consequential damages arising out of or in connection with the information presented.

ISBN: 0-7401-0742-9
ISSN: 1057-3623

State Rankings 2006 sells for $59.95 ($6 shipping) and is only available in paper binding. For those who prefer ranking information tailored to a particular state, we also offer *State Perspectives*, state-specific reports for each of the 50 states. These individual guides provide information on a state's data and rank for each of the categories featured in the national *State Rankings* volume. Perspectives sell for $19 or $9.50 if ordered with *State Rankings*. We also offer an annual that looks at states over time: *State Trends* ($59.95 paper). If crime statistics are your interest, please ask about our annual *Crime State Rankings* ($59.95 paper). If you are interested in city and metropolitan crime data, we offer *City Crime Rankings* ($49.95 paper). If you are interested in health statistics for states, please ask about our annual *Health Care State Rankings* ($59.95 paper). Also available is *Education State Rankings*. This view of preK-12 education at the state level is $49.95. All of our books are available on CD-ROM in PDF format (same price as printed book) or with both PDF format and data sets in various database formats ($99.95). Shipping and handling is $6 per order. For information, please visit our website at www.statestats.com.

Seventeenth Edition
Printed in the United States of America
March 2006

PREFACE

How does your state compare? *State Rankings 2006* makes it easy to learn how your state stacks up in taxes, housing, health care, education, crime, government spending, transportation, income and so much more. Find out how much your state's teachers are paid, what the homeownership rate is in your state and what percentage of your state's citizens have no health insurance coverage. In all, this newly revised 17th edition provides more than 550 tables of meaningful state comparisons.

Important Notes About *State Rankings 2006*

Our mission in publishing *State Rankings* is to translate complicated and often convoluted statistics into meaningful, easy-to-understand state comparisons. Each year, we review our books, update the majority of tables add a few new ones and remove others that no longer are pertinent. In this 2006 edition of *State Rankings,* you'll find 569 tables of state comparisons.

While there are a number of changes in this updated edition of *State Rankings,* its organization and other popular features remain the same. Source information and footnotes clearly are shown at the bottom of each page, while national totals, rates and percentages are prominently displayed at the top of each table. Every other line is shaded in gray for easier reading. Numerous information-finding tools are provided: a thorough table of contents, table listings at the beginning of each chapter, a detailed index and a chapter thumb index. In addition, a roster of sources, with addresses, phone numbers and Internet websites is found in the back of the book.

Designed to ease the job of researchers, the numbers shown in *State Rankings* require no additional calculations to convert them from millions, thousands, etc. All states are ranked on a high to low basis, with any ties among the states listed alphabetically for a given ranking. Negative numbers are shown in parentheses "( )." For tables displaying national totals (as opposed to rates, per capita, etc.) a separate column is included that shows what percent of the national total each individual state's total represents. This column is headed by "% of USA." This percentage figure is particularly interesting when compared with a state's population in a given year.

For basic information about states, check out the "State Fast Facts" section. Here you can quiz yourself on state capitals, songs, flowers, trees and birds. In addition, find out which state is the winner of our "Most Livable State Award," Morgan Quitno's annual honor based on 44 key quality of life factors.

For those of you needing information for just one state, we once again are offering our *State Perspective* series of publications. These 26-page comb bound reports feature data and ranking information for an individual state, pulled from the national *State Rankings 2006* book. (For example *New York in Perspective* features information about the state of New York only.) They serve as great timesavers for researchers who do not want to page through the entire *State Rankings* volume searching for information for their particular state. Purchased individually, *State Perspectives* sell for $19. When purchased with a copy of *State Rankings 2006,* these handy, quick reference guides are just $9.50.

Other Books From Morgan Quitno Press

In addition to *State Rankings 2006,* our company offers five other rankings reference books. *Education State Rankings 2005-2006* compares states in teachers' salaries, class sizes, graduation rates and more than 400 other categories relating to preK-12 education. *Health Care State Rankings 2006* provides an in-depth view of health care by state. Included in this 552-page annual volume are statistics on health care facilities, providers, insurance and finance, incidence of disease, mortality, physical fitness, natality and reproductive health. An annual compilation of state crime data is featured in *Crime State Rankings.* In its 13th edition for 2006, this reference volume examines state law enforcement personnel and expenditures, juvenile crime, corrections, arrests and offenses. Our *City Crime Rankings* reference book compares U.S. metropolitan areas and cities of 75,000+ population in all major crime categories. Numbers of crimes, crime rates and crime trends over one and five years are presented for all major crime categories reported by the FBI (features 2004 data). *State Trends* is our newest reference book. Now in its second edition, this annual volume has earned praise for providing a quick and easy way to track important quality of life changes in the 50 United States. One, five, 10 and 20-year trends are measured in health care, taxes, crime, education and more.

The data in all our reference books also are available on CD-ROM. These electronic editions feature a searchable PDF version of each book as well as the raw data in .dbf, Excel and ASCII formats. Additional information about all of our publications, including prices and ISBN numbers, is available online at www.statestats.com or by calling us toll-free at 1-800-457-0742.

Finally, we sincerely appreciate the assistance of those people who help to make this book possible year after year. To the librarians, government statisticians and other information keepers we extend a huge "thank you."

Our special thanks goes to Joe and Joan Williams of Lincoln, Nebraska, the original editors and creators of *State Rankings.* Many years ago, the Williams saw the need for a book that provided meaningful and interesting state information in an easy-to-understand format. We are honored to carry on their mission of creating books of statistics that all of us can understand and enjoy.

Many thanks also to you, our readers. We appreciate your comments and feedback that help keep our books relevant. Please continue to send your thoughts our way via email (information@morganquitno.com) or by phone at 1-800-457-0742. We look forward to hearing from you.

-THE EDITORS

WHICH STATE IS THE MOST LIVABLE?

 New Hampshire enjoys the view from the top and apparently plans on staying there. For the third consecutive year, the Granite State is the winner of Morgan Quitno's Most Livable State Award. Rounding out the top five states with New Hampshire are Minnesota, Iowa, Vermont and New Jersey.

At the opposite end of the rankings scale, Louisiana sinks to last place for the first time in eight years. Mississippi rose to 49th place. Preceding Louisiana and Mississippi are Arkansas, Kentucky and South Carolina.

Now in its 16th year, the Most Livable State Award is issued in conjunction with the publication of each year's new edition of *State Rankings*. Annually we reexamine our collection of data and select the factors that reflect a state's basic quality of life.

The 2006 award is based on 44 factors. The factors used for this year's award are the same as those used last year, however general electricity prices were replaced with statistics showing the price of residential electricity.

Unique among the various rankings of states, our Most Livable State Award does not focus on any one category of data. Instead it takes into account a broad range of economic, educational, health-oriented, public safety and environmental statistics.

The Most Livable State Award is one of six such designations announced each year by Morgan Quitno. The Safest City/Metro Area Award is based on data from our *City Crime Rankings* volume. The Most Dangerous and Safest State designations are announced with our *Crime State Rankings* volume. The Healthiest State Award is based on factors derived from *Health Care State Rankings*. The Smartest State Award is determined using data from *Education State Rankings* and the Most Improved State Award is based on statistics from our newest annual volume, *State Trends*.

While we strive to make our books as objective as possible, these awards give us the opportunity to choose the factors we think tell an interesting story about quality of life in the 50 United States. Congratulations once again to the citizens of New Hampshire!
                                            - THE EDITORS

Negative Factors
1. Percent Change in Number of Crimes: 2003 to 2004 (Table 27)
2. Crime Rate (Table 28)
3. State Prisoner Incarceration Rate (Table 58)
4. Personal Bankruptcy Rate (Table 98)
5. Estimated Pupil-Teacher Ratio in Public Elementary and Secondary Schools (Table 120)
6. Rate of Public Libraries and Branches (Table 152)
7. Unemployment Rate (Table 175)
8. Percent of Nonfarm Employees in Government (Table 189)
9. Average Monthly Electric Bill for Residential Customers (Table 207)
10. Hazardous Waste Sites on the National Priority List per 10,000 Square Miles (Table 219)
11. State & Local Taxes as a Percent of Personal Income (Table 290)
12. Per Capita State and Local Government Debt Outstanding (Table 304)
13. Percent of Population Not Covered by Health Insurance (Table 367)
14. Births of Low Birthweight as a Percent of All Births (Table 377)
15. Teenage Birth Rate (Table 378)
16. Infant Mortality Rate (Table 384)
17. Age-Adjusted Death Rate by Suicide (Table 398)
18. Population per Square Mile (Table 436)
19. Poverty Rate (Table 495)
20. Percent of Female-Headed Families with Children Living in Poverty (Table 499)
21. State and Local Government Spending for Welfare Programs as a Percent of All Spending (Table 502)
22. Percent of Households Receiving Food Stamps (Table 529)
23. Deficient Bridges as a Percent of Total Bridges (Table 544)
24. Highway Fatality Rate (Table 547)
25. Fatalities in Alcohol-Related Crashes as a Percent of All Highway Fatalities (Table 554)

Positive Factors
26. Per Capita Gross State Product (Table 89)
27. Percent Change in Per Capita Gross State Product: 2000 to 2004 (Adjusted to Constant 2000 Dollars) (Table 90)
28. Per Capita Personal Income (Table 93)
29. Change in Per Capita Personal Income: 2003 to 2004 (Table 94)
30. Median Household Income (Table 96)
31. Public High School Graduation Rate (Table 128)
32. Percent of Population Graduated from High School (Table 129)
33. Expenditures for Education as a Percent of All State and Local Government Expenditures (Table 137)
34. Percent of Population With a Bachelor's Degree or More (Table 150)
35. Books in Public Libraries Per Capita (Table 153)
36. Per Capita State Art Agencies' Legislative Appropriations (Table 156)
37. Average Weekly Earnings of Production Workers on Manufacturing Payrolls (Table 165)
38. Job Growth: 2003 to 2004 (Table 180)
39. Normal Daily Mean Temperature (Table 231)
40. Percent of Days That Are Sunny (Table 232)
41. Homeownership Rate (Table 424)
42. Domestic Migration of Population: 2003 to 2004 (Table 475)
43 Marriage Rate (Table 481)
44. Percent of Eligible Population Reported Voting (Table 494)

The 2006 Most Livable State Award:

New Hampshire Still on Top

ALPHA ORDER

RANK	STATE	LIVABILITY RATING	05 RANK	CHANGE
39	Alabama	20.50	39	0
23	Alaska	25.32	27	4
29	Arizona	24.39	36	7
48	Arkansas	18.45	48	0
34	California	23.59	35	1
20	Colorado	27.25	16	-4
10	Connecticut	30.61	14	4
18	Delaware	28.43	17	-1
18	Idaho	28.43	18	0
28	Illinois	24.41	31	3
36	Indiana	23.50	21	-15
3	Iowa	32.39	6	3
15	Kansas	28.84	20	5
47	Kentucky	18.66	41	-6
50	Louisiana	15.00	49	-1
17	Maine	28.50	15	-2
16	Maryland	28.61	12	-4
7	Massachusetts	31.14	7	0
35	Michigan	23.57	28	-7
2	Minnesota	34.68	2	0
49	Mississippi	15.43	50	1
27	Missouri	24.66	22	-5
21	Montana	26.57	24	3
9	Nebraska	30.70	10	1
24	Nevada	25.18	29	5
1	New Hampshire	35.84	1	0
5	New Jersey	31.30	8	3
41	New Mexico	20.30	42	1
32	New York	23.98	30	-2
40	North Carolina	20.39	40	0
12	North Dakota	29.80	11	-1
37	Ohio	22.48	32	-5
43	Oklahoma	19.67	43	0
33	Oregon	23.61	34	1
30	Pennsylvania	24.30	32	2
26	Rhode Island	25.09	23	-3
46	South Carolina	19.11	44	-2
13	South Dakota	29.52	9	-4
45	Tennessee	19.41	47	2
41	Texas	20.30	45	4
11	Utah	30.43	19	8
4	Vermont	31.89	3	-1
8	Virginia	30.84	5	-3
25	Washington	25.16	25	0
44	West Virginia	19.57	46	2
14	Wisconsin	29.30	13	-1
6	Wyoming	31.16	4	-2

RANK ORDER

RANK	STATE	LIVABILITY RATING	05 RANK	CHANGE
1	New Hampshire	35.84	1	0
2	Minnesota	34.68	2	0
3	Iowa	32.39	6	3
4	Vermont	31.89	3	-1
5	New Jersey	31.30	8	3
6	Wyoming	31.16	4	-2
7	Massachusetts	31.14	7	0
8	Virginia	30.84	5	-3
9	Nebraska	30.70	10	1
10	Connecticut	30.61	14	4
11	Utah	30.43	19	8
12	North Dakota	29.80	11	-1
13	South Dakota	29.52	9	-4
14	Wisconsin	29.30	13	-1
15	Kansas	28.84	20	5
16	Maryland	28.61	12	-4
17	Maine	28.50	15	-2
18	Delaware	28.43	17	-1
18	Idaho	28.43	18	0
20	Colorado	27.25	16	-4
21	Montana	26.57	24	3
22	Hawaii	26.39	26	4
23	Alaska	25.32	27	4
24	Nevada	25.18	29	5
25	Washington	25.16	25	0
26	Rhode Island	25.09	23	-3
27	Missouri	24.66	22	-5
28	Illinois	24.41	31	3
29	Arizona	24.39	36	7
30	Pennsylvania	24.30	32	2
31	Florida	24.02	37	6
32	New York	23.98	30	-2
33	Oregon	23.61	34	1
34	California	23.59	35	1
35	Michigan	23.57	28	-7
36	Indiana	23.50	21	15
37	Ohio	22.48	32	-5
38	Georgia	20.86	38	0
39	Alabama	20.50	39	0
40	North Carolina	20.39	40	0
41	New Mexico	20.30	42	1
41	Texas	20.30	45	4
43	Oklahoma	19.67	43	0
44	West Virginia	19.57	46	2
45	Tennessee	19.41	47	2
46	South Carolina	19.11	44	-2
47	Kentucky	18.66	41	-6
48	Arkansas	18.45	48	0
49	Mississippi	15.43	50	1
50	Louisiana	15.00	49	-1

METHODOLOGY: To determine a state's "Livability Rating," each state's rankings for 44 categories were averaged. The scale is 1 to 50, the higher the number, the better. Data used are for the most recent year in which comparable numbers are available from most states. All factors were given equal weight. States with no data available for a given category were ranked based only on the remaining factors. In our book, data are listed from highest to lowest. However, for purposes of this award, we inverted rankings for those factors we determined to be "positive." Thus the state with the highest median income in the book (ranking 1st) would be given a number 50 ranking for this award.

38	Georgia	20.86	38	0
22	Hawaii	26.39	26	4
31	Florida	24.02	37	6

STATE FAST FACTS

STATE	NICKNAME	CAPITAL	POPULATION*	AREA**
Alabama	Heart of Dixie	Montgomery	4,557,808	52,419
Alaska	The Last Frontier	Juneau	663,661	663,267
Arizona	Grand Canyon State	Phoenix	5,939,292	113,998
Arkansas	The Natural State	Little Rock	2,779,154	53,179
California	Golden State	Sacramento	36,132,147	163,696
Colorado	Centennial State	Denver	4,665,177	104,094
Connecticut	Constitution State	Hartford	3,510,297	5,543
Delaware	First State	Dover	843,524	2,489
Florida	Sunshine State	Tallahassee	17,789,864	65,755
Georgia	Peach State	Atlanta	9,072,576	59,425
Hawaii	Aloha State	Honolulu	1,275,194	10,931
Idaho	Gem State	Boise	1,429,096	83,570
Illinois	Land of Lincoln	Springfield	12,763,371	57,914
Indiana	Hoosier State	Indianapolis	6,271,973	36,418
Iowa	Hawkeye State	Des Moines	2,966,334	56,272
Kansas	Sunflower State	Topeka	2,744,687	82,277
Kentucky	Bluegrass State	Frankfort	4,173,405	40,409
Louisiana	Pelican State	Baton Rouge	4,523,628	51,840
Maine	Pine Tree State	Augusta	1,321,505	35,385
Maryland	Free State	Annapolis	5,600,388	12,407
Massachusetts	Bay State	Boston	6,398,743	10,555
Michigan	Great Lake State	Lansing	10,120,860	96,716
Minnesota	North Star State	St. Paul	5,132,799	86,939
Mississippi	Magnolia State	Jackson	2,921,088	48,430
Missouri	Show Me State	Jefferson City	5,800,310	69,704
Montana	Treasure State	Helena	935,670	147,042
Nebraska	Cornhusker State	Lincoln	1,758,787	77,354
Nevada	Sagebrush State	Carson City	2,414,807	110,561
New Hampshire	Granite State	Concord	1,309,940	9,350
New Jersey	Garden State	Trenton	8,717,925	8,721
New Mexico	Land of Enchantment	Santa Fe	1,928,384	121,590
New York	Empire State	Albany	19,254,630	54,556
North Carolina	Tar Heel State	Raleigh	8,683,242	53,819
North Dakota	Peace Garden State	Bismarck	636,677	70,700
Ohio	Buckeye State	Columbus	11,464,042	44,825
Oklahoma	Sooner State	Oklahoma City	3,547,884	69,898
Oregon	Beaver State	Salem	3,641,056	98,381
Pennsylvania	Keystone State	Harrisburg	12,429,616	46,055
Rhode Island	Ocean State	Providence	1,076,189	1,545
South Carolina	Palmetto State	Columbia	4,255,083	32,020
South Dakota	Mount Rushmore State	Pierre	775,933	77,117
Tennessee	Volunteer State	Nashville	5,962,959	42,143
Texas	Lone Star State	Austin	22,859,968	268,581
Utah	Beehive State	Salt Lake City	2,469,585	84,899
Vermont	Green Mountain State	Montpelier	623,050	9,614
Virginia	Old Dominion	Richmond	7,567,465	42,774
Washington	Evergreen State	Olympia	6,287,759	71,300
West Virginia	Mountain State	Charleston	1,816,856	24,230
Wisconsin	Badger State	Madison	5,536,201	65,498
Wyoming	Equality State	Cheyenne	509,294	97,814

*2005 Census resident population estimates.
**Total of land and water area in square miles.

STATE SONG	STATE FLOWER	STATE TREE	STATE BIRD
Alabama	Camellia	Southern Pine	Yellowhammer
Alaska's Flag	Forget-Me-Not	Sitka Spruce	Willow Ptarmigan
Arizona	Saguaro Cactus Blossom	Palo Verde	Cactus Wren
Arkansas	Apple Blossom	Pine	Mockingbird
I Love You, California	Golden Poppy	California Redwood	California Valley Quail
Where the Columbines Grow	Rocky Mountain Columbine	Colorado Blue Spruce	Lark Bunting
Yankee Doodle Dandy	Mountain Laurel	White Oak	American Robin
Our Delaware	Peach Blossom	American Holly	Blue Hen Chicken
Swanee River	Orange Blossom	Sabal Palmetto Palm	Mockingbird
Georgia On My Mind	Cherokee Rose	Live Oak	Brown Thrasher
Hawaii Ponol	Yellow Hibiscus	Candlenut	Nene
Here We Have Idaho	Syringa	White Pine	Mountain Bluebird
Illinois	Purple Violet	White Oak	Cardinal
On the Banks of the Wabash, Far Away	Peony	Tulip Poplar	Cardinal
The Song of Iowa	Wild Rose	Oak	Eastern Goldfinch
Home on the Range	Sunflower	Cottonwood	Western Meadowlark
My Old Kentucky Home	Goldenrod	Tulip Tree	Cardinal
Give Me Louisiana	Magnolia	Cypress	Eastern Brown Pelican
State of Maine Song	White Pine Cone and Tassel	Eastern White Pine	Chickadee
Maryland, My Maryland	Black-eyed Susan	White Oak	Baltimore Oriole
All Hail to Massachusetts	Mayflower	American Elm	Chickadee
Michigan, My Michigan	Apple Blossom	White Pine	Robin
Hail! Minnesota	Pink and White Lady's Slipper	Red Pine	Common Loon
Go, Mississippi!	Magnolia	Magnolia	Mockingbird
Missouri Waltz	Hawthorn	Dogwood	Bluebird
Montana	Bitterroot	Ponderosa Pine	Western Meadowlark
Beautiful Nebraska	Goldenrod	Cottonwood	Western Meadowlark
Home Means Nevada	Sagebrush	Single-Leaf Pinon	Mountain Bluebird
Old New Hampshire	Purple Lilac	White Birch	Purple Finch
Ode to New Jersey	Purple Violet	Red Oak	Eastern Goldfinch
O Fair New Mexico	Yucca	Pinon	Roadrunner
I Love New York	Rose	Sugar Maple	Bluebird
The Old North State	Dogwood	Pine	Cardinal
North Dakota Hymn	Wild Prairie Rose	American Elm	Western Meadowlark
Beautiful Ohio	Scarlet Carnation	Buckeye	Cardinal
Oklahoma!	Mistletoe	Redbud	Scissortailed Flycatcher
Oregon, My Oregon	Oregon Grape	Douglas Fir	Western Meadowlark
Hail! Pennsylvania	Mountain Laurel	Hemlock	Ruffed Grouse
Rhode Island	Violet	Red Maple	Rhode Island Red
Carolina	Yellow Jessamine	Palmetto	Carolina Wren
Hail, South Dakota	Pasque Flower	Black Hills Spruce	Ringnecked Pheasant
The Tennessee Waltz	Iris	Tulip Poplar	Mockingbird
Texas, Our Texas	Bluebonnet	Pecan	Mockingbird
Utah, We Love Thee	Sego Lily	Blue Spruce	Seagull
Hail, Vermont	Red Clover	Sugar Maple	Hermit Thrush
Carry Me Back to Old Virginia	Dogwood	Dogwood	Cardinal
Washington, My Home	Western Rhododendron	Western Hemlock	Willow Goldfinch
The West Virginia Hills; This Is My West Virginia; and West Virginia, My Home, Sweet Home	Big Rhododendron	Sugar Maple	Cardinal
On Wisconsin!	Wood Violet	Sugar Maple	Robin
Wyoming	Indian Paintbrush	Cottonwood	Meadowlark

TABLE OF CONTENTS

TABLE OF CONTENTS (continued)

TABLE OF CONTENTS (continued)

V. Education

VI. Employment and Labor

TABLE OF CONTENTS (continued)

VII. Energy and Environment

TABLE OF CONTENTS (continued)

VIII. Geography

IX. Government Finance: Federal

TABLE OF CONTENTS (continued)

X. Government Finance: State and Local

TABLE OF CONTENTS (continued)

XI. Health

TABLE OF CONTENTS (continued)

TABLE OF CONTENTS (continued)

XIV. Social Welfare

TABLE OF CONTENTS (continued)

Date Each State Admitted to Statehood*

RANK	STATE	DATE OF ADMISSION
22	Alabama	December 14, 1819
49	Alaska	January 3, 1959
48	Arizona	February 14, 1912
25	Arkansas	June 15, 1836
31	California	September 9, 1850
38	Colorado	August 1, 1876
5	Connecticut	January 9, 1788
1	Delaware	December 7, 1787
27	Florida	March 3, 1845
4	Georgia	January 2, 1788
50	Hawaii	August 21, 1959
43	Idaho	July 3, 1890
21	Illinois	December 3, 1818
19	Indiana	December 11, 1816
29	Iowa	December 28, 1846
34	Kansas	January 29, 1861
15	Kentucky	June 1, 1792
18	Louisiana	April 30, 1812
23	Maine	March 15, 1820
7	Maryland	April 28, 1788
6	Massachusetts	February 6, 1788
26	Michigan	January 26, 1837
32	Minnesota	May 11, 1858
20	Mississippi	December 10, 1817
24	Missouri	August 10, 1821
41	Montana	November 8, 1889
37	Nebraska	March 1, 1867
36	Nevada	October 31, 1864
9	New Hampshire	June 21, 1788
3	New Jersey	December 18, 1787
47	New Mexico	January 6, 1912
11	New York	July 26, 1788
12	North Carolina	November 21, 1789
39	North Dakota	November 2, 1889
17	Ohio	March 1, 1803
46	Oklahoma	November 16, 1907
33	Oregon	February 14, 1859
2	Pennsylvania	December 12, 1787
13	Rhode Island	May 29, 1790
8	South Carolina	May 23, 1788
39	South Dakota	November 2, 1889
16	Tennessee	June 1, 1796
28	Texas	December 29, 1845
45	Utah	January 4, 1896
14	Vermont	March 4, 1791
10	Virginia	June 26, 1788
42	Washington	November 11, 1889
35	West Virginia	June 20, 1863
30	Wisconsin	May 29, 1848
44	Wyoming	July 10, 1890

RANK	STATE	DATE OF ADMISSION
1	Delaware	December 7, 1787
2	Pennsylvania	December 12, 1787
3	New Jersey	December 18, 1787
4	Georgia	January 2, 1788
5	Connecticut	January 9, 1788
6	Massachusetts	February 6, 1788
7	Maryland	April 28, 1788
8	South Carolina	May 23, 1788
9	New Hampshire	June 21, 1788
10	Virginia	June 26, 1788
11	New York	July 26, 1788
12	North Carolina	November 21, 1789
13	Rhode Island	May 29, 1790
14	Vermont	March 4, 1791
15	Kentucky	June 1, 1792
16	Tennessee	June 1, 1796
17	Ohio	March 1, 1803
18	Louisiana	April 30, 1812
19	Indiana	December 11, 1816
20	Mississippi	December 10, 1817
21	Illinois	December 3, 1818
22	Alabama	December 14, 1819
23	Maine	March 15, 1820
24	Missouri	August 10, 1821
25	Arkansas	June 15, 1836
26	Michigan	January 26, 1837
27	Florida	March 3, 1845
28	Texas	December 29, 1845
29	Iowa	December 28, 1846
30	Wisconsin	May 29, 1848
31	California	September 9, 1850
32	Minnesota	May 11, 1858
33	Oregon	February 14, 1859
34	Kansas	January 29, 1861
35	West Virginia	June 20, 1863
36	Nevada	October 31, 1864
37	Nebraska	March 1, 1867
38	Colorado	August 1, 1876
39	North Dakota	November 2, 1889
39	South Dakota	November 2, 1889
41	Montana	November 8, 1889
42	Washington	November 11, 1889
43	Idaho	July 3, 1890
44	Wyoming	July 10, 1890
45	Utah	January 4, 1896
46	Oklahoma	November 16, 1907
47	New Mexico	January 6, 1912
48	Arizona	February 14, 1912
49	Alaska	January 3, 1959
50	Hawaii	August 21, 1959

Source: U.S. Bureau of the Census
    "1980 Census of Population" (vol. 1, part A, PC80-1-A)
First thirteen states show date of ratification of Constitution.

I. AGRICULTURE

Number of Farms in 2004

National Total = 2,113,470 Farms*

ALPHA ORDER				RANK ORDER			
RANK	STATE	FARMS	% of USA	RANK	STATE	FARMS	% of USA
21	Alabama	44,000	2.1%	1	Texas	229,000	10.8%
50	Alaska	620	0.0%	2	Missouri	106,000	5.0%
38	Arizona	10,200	0.5%	3	Iowa	89,700	4.2%
19	Arkansas	47,500	2.2%	4	Kentucky	85,000	4.0%
9	California	77,000	3.6%	4	Tennessee	85,000	4.0%
28	Colorado	30,900	1.5%	6	Oklahoma	83,500	4.0%
45	Connecticut	4,200	0.2%	7	Minnesota	79,800	3.8%
48	Delaware	2,300	0.1%	8	Ohio	77,300	3.7%
22	Florida	43,000	2.0%	9	California	77,000	3.6%
17	Georgia	49,000	2.3%	10	Wisconsin	76,500	3.6%
44	Hawaii	5,500	0.3%	11	Illinois	73,000	3.5%
32	Idaho	25,000	1.2%	12	Kansas	64,500	3.1%
11	Illinois	73,000	3.5%	13	Indiana	59,300	2.8%
13	Indiana	59,300	2.8%	14	Pennsylvania	58,200	2.8%
3	Iowa	89,700	4.2%	15	Michigan	53,200	2.5%
12	Kansas	64,500	3.1%	16	North Carolina	52,000	2.5%
4	Kentucky	85,000	4.0%	17	Georgia	49,000	2.3%
31	Louisiana	27,200	1.3%	18	Nebraska	48,300	2.3%
41	Maine	7,200	0.3%	19	Arkansas	47,500	2.2%
37	Maryland	12,100	0.6%	19	Virginia	47,500	2.2%
43	Massachusetts	6,100	0.3%	21	Alabama	44,000	2.1%
15	Michigan	53,200	2.5%	22	Florida	43,000	2.0%
7	Minnesota	79,800	3.8%	23	Mississippi	42,200	2.0%
23	Mississippi	42,200	2.0%	24	Oregon	40,000	1.9%
2	Missouri	106,000	5.0%	25	New York	36,000	1.7%
30	Montana	28,000	1.3%	26	Washington	35,000	1.7%
18	Nebraska	48,300	2.3%	27	South Dakota	31,600	1.5%
47	Nevada	3,000	0.1%	28	Colorado	30,900	1.5%
46	New Hampshire	3,400	0.2%	29	North Dakota	30,300	1.4%
39	New Jersey	9,900	0.5%	30	Montana	28,000	1.3%
35	New Mexico	17,500	0.8%	31	Louisiana	27,200	1.3%
25	New York	36,000	1.7%	32	Idaho	25,000	1.2%
16	North Carolina	52,000	2.5%	33	South Carolina	24,400	1.2%
29	North Dakota	30,300	1.4%	34	West Virginia	20,800	1.0%
8	Ohio	77,300	3.7%	35	New Mexico	17,500	0.8%
6	Oklahoma	83,500	4.0%	36	Utah	15,300	0.7%
24	Oregon	40,000	1.9%	37	Maryland	12,100	0.6%
14	Pennsylvania	58,200	2.8%	38	Arizona	10,200	0.5%
49	Rhode Island	850	0.0%	39	New Jersey	9,900	0.5%
33	South Carolina	24,400	1.2%	40	Wyoming	9,200	0.4%
27	South Dakota	31,600	1.5%	41	Maine	7,200	0.3%
4	Tennessee	85,000	4.0%	42	Vermont	6,400	0.3%
1	Texas	229,000	10.8%	43	Massachusetts	6,100	0.3%
36	Utah	15,300	0.7%	44	Hawaii	5,500	0.3%
42	Vermont	6,400	0.3%	45	Connecticut	4,200	0.2%
19	Virginia	47,500	2.2%	46	New Hampshire	3,400	0.2%
26	Washington	35,000	1.7%	47	Nevada	3,000	0.1%
34	West Virginia	20,800	1.0%	48	Delaware	2,300	0.1%
10	Wisconsin	76,500	3.6%	49	Rhode Island	850	0.0%
40	Wyoming	9,200	0.4%	50	Alaska	620	0.0%
					District of Columbia	0	0.0%

Source: U.S. Department of Agriculture, National Agricultural Statistics Service
    "Farms and Land in Farms" (http://usda.mannlib.cornell.edu/reports/nassr/other/zfl-bb/fnlo0105.pdf)
*A farm is any establishment from which $1,000 or more of agricultural products were sold or would normally be sold
during the year. This includes places with five or more horses, except horses in boarding stables or racetracks.

Land in Farms in 2004

National Total = 936,600,000 Acres*

ALPHA ORDER					RANK ORDER			
RANK	**STATE**	**ACRES**	**% of USA**		**RANK**	**STATE**	**ACRES**	**% of USA**
32	Alabama	8,700,000	0.9%		1	Texas	130,000,000	13.9%
44	Alaska	900,000	0.1%		2	Montana	60,100,000	6.4%
16	Arizona	26,400,000	2.8%		3	Kansas	47,200,000	5.0%
22	Arkansas	14,400,000	1.5%		4	Nebraska	45,900,000	4.9%
15	California	26,700,000	2.9%		5	New Mexico	44,700,000	4.8%
11	Colorado	30,900,000	3.3%		6	South Dakota	43,800,000	4.7%
49	Connecticut	360,000	0.0%		7	North Dakota	39,400,000	4.2%
46	Delaware	530,000	0.1%		8	Wyoming	34,440,000	3.7%
29	Florida	10,100,000	1.1%		9	Oklahoma	33,700,000	3.6%
28	Georgia	10,700,000	1.1%		10	Iowa	31,700,000	3.4%
42	Hawaii	1,300,000	0.1%		11	Colorado	30,900,000	3.3%
24	Idaho	11,800,000	1.3%		12	Missouri	30,100,000	3.2%
14	Illinois	27,500,000	2.9%		13	Minnesota	27,600,000	2.9%
20	Indiana	15,000,000	1.6%		14	Illinois	27,500,000	2.9%
10	Iowa	31,700,000	3.4%		15	California	26,700,000	2.9%
3	Kansas	47,200,000	5.0%		16	Arizona	26,400,000	2.8%
23	Kentucky	13,800,000	1.5%		17	Oregon	17,200,000	1.8%
34	Louisiana	7,850,000	0.8%		18	Wisconsin	15,500,000	1.7%
41	Maine	1,370,000	0.1%		19	Washington	15,200,000	1.6%
40	Maryland	2,050,000	0.2%		20	Indiana	15,000,000	1.6%
47	Massachusetts	520,000	0.1%		21	Ohio	14,600,000	1.6%
29	Michigan	10,100,000	1.1%		22	Arkansas	14,400,000	1.5%
13	Minnesota	27,600,000	2.9%		23	Kentucky	13,800,000	1.5%
27	Mississippi	11,050,000	1.2%		24	Idaho	11,800,000	1.3%
12	Missouri	30,100,000	3.2%		25	Tennessee	11,600,000	1.2%
2	Montana	60,100,000	6.4%		25	Utah	11,600,000	1.2%
4	Nebraska	45,900,000	4.9%		27	Mississippi	11,050,000	1.2%
37	Nevada	6,300,000	0.7%		28	Georgia	10,700,000	1.1%
48	New Hampshire	450,000	0.0%		29	Florida	10,100,000	1.1%
45	New Jersey	820,000	0.1%		29	Michigan	10,100,000	1.1%
5	New Mexico	44,700,000	4.8%		31	North Carolina	9,000,000	1.0%
36	New York	7,600,000	0.8%		32	Alabama	8,700,000	0.9%
31	North Carolina	9,000,000	1.0%		33	Virginia	8,600,000	0.9%
7	North Dakota	39,400,000	4.2%		34	Louisiana	7,850,000	0.8%
21	Ohio	14,600,000	1.6%		35	Pennsylvania	7,700,000	0.8%
9	Oklahoma	33,700,000	3.6%		36	New York	7,600,000	0.8%
17	Oregon	17,200,000	1.8%		37	Nevada	6,300,000	0.7%
35	Pennsylvania	7,700,000	0.8%		38	South Carolina	4,850,000	0.5%
50	Rhode Island	60,000	0.0%		39	West Virginia	3,600,000	0.4%
38	South Carolina	4,850,000	0.5%		40	Maryland	2,050,000	0.2%
6	South Dakota	43,800,000	4.7%		41	Maine	1,370,000	0.1%
25	Tennessee	11,600,000	1.2%		42	Hawaii	1,300,000	0.1%
1	Texas	130,000,000	13.9%		43	Vermont	1,250,000	0.1%
25	Utah	11,600,000	1.2%		44	Alaska	900,000	0.1%
43	Vermont	1,250,000	0.1%		45	New Jersey	820,000	0.1%
33	Virginia	8,600,000	0.9%		46	Delaware	530,000	0.1%
19	Washington	15,200,000	1.6%		47	Massachusetts	520,000	0.1%
39	West Virginia	3,600,000	0.4%		48	New Hampshire	450,000	0.0%
18	Wisconsin	15,500,000	1.7%		49	Connecticut	360,000	0.0%
8	Wyoming	34,440,000	3.7%		50	Rhode Island	60,000	0.0%
						District of Columbia	0	0.0%

Source: U.S. Department of Agriculture, National Agricultural Statistics Service
"Farms and Land in Farms" (http://usda.mannlib.cornell.edu/reports/nassr/other/zfl-bb/fnlo0105.pdf)
*A farm is any establishment from which $1,000 or more of agricultural products were sold or would normally be sold during the year. This includes places with five or more horses, except horses in boarding stables or racetracks.

Average Number of Acres per Farm in 2004

National Average = 443 Acres*

ALPHA ORDER

RANK	STATE	ACRES
34	Alabama	198
6	Alaska	1,452
2	Arizona	2,588
22	Arkansas	303
20	California	347
9	Colorado	1,000
47	Connecticut	86
29	Delaware	230
28	Florida	235
30	Georgia	218
27	Hawaii	236
14	Idaho	472
18	Illinois	377
26	Indiana	253
19	Iowa	353
12	Kansas	732
43	Kentucky	162
23	Louisiana	289
36	Maine	190
42	Maryland	169
48	Massachusetts	85
36	Michigan	190
21	Minnesota	346
25	Mississippi	262
24	Missouri	284
4	Montana	2,146
10	Nebraska	950
5	Nevada	2,100
45	New Hampshire	132
49	New Jersey	83
3	New Mexico	2,554
31	New York	211
40	North Carolina	173
8	North Dakota	1,300
38	Ohio	189
17	Oklahoma	404
16	Oregon	430
45	Pennsylvania	132
50	Rhode Island	71
33	South Carolina	199
7	South Dakota	1,386
44	Tennessee	136
13	Texas	568
11	Utah	758
35	Vermont	195
39	Virginia	181
15	Washington	434
40	West Virginia	173
32	Wisconsin	203
1	Wyoming	3,743

RANK ORDER

RANK	STATE	ACRES
1	Wyoming	3,743
2	Arizona	2,588
3	New Mexico	2,554
4	Montana	2,146
5	Nevada	2,100
6	Alaska	1,452
7	South Dakota	1,386
8	North Dakota	1,300
9	Colorado	1,000
10	Nebraska	950
11	Utah	758
12	Kansas	732
13	Texas	568
14	Idaho	472
15	Washington	434
16	Oregon	430
17	Oklahoma	404
18	Illinois	377
19	Iowa	353
20	California	347
21	Minnesota	346
22	Arkansas	303
23	Louisiana	289
24	Missouri	284
25	Mississippi	262
26	Indiana	253
27	Hawaii	236
28	Florida	235
29	Delaware	230
30	Georgia	218
31	New York	211
32	Wisconsin	203
33	South Carolina	199
34	Alabama	198
35	Vermont	195
36	Maine	190
36	Michigan	190
38	Ohio	189
39	Virginia	181
40	North Carolina	173
40	West Virginia	173
42	Maryland	169
43	Kentucky	162
44	Tennessee	136
45	New Hampshire	132
45	Pennsylvania	132
47	Connecticut	86
48	Massachusetts	85
49	New Jersey	83
50	Rhode Island	71
	District of Columbia**	NA

Source: U.S. Department of Agriculture, National Agricultural Statistics Service
"Farms and Land in Farms" (http://usda.mannlib.cornell.edu/reports/nassr/other/zfl-bb/fnlo0105.pdf)
A farm is any establishment from which $1,000 or more of agricultural products were sold or would normally be sold during the year. This includes places with five or more horses, except horses in boarding stables or racetracks.
**Not applicable.*

Average per Acre Value of Farmland and Buildings in 2005

National Average = $1,510 per Acre*

ALPHA ORDER

RANK	STATE	PER ACRE VALUE
24	Alabama	$2,050
NA	Alaska**	NA
29	Arizona	1,750
28	Arkansas	1,820
7	California	4,160
40	Colorado	845
2	Connecticut	10,800
5	Delaware	8,400
10	Florida	3,700
19	Georgia	2,590
NA	Hawaii**	NA
35	Idaho	1,480
16	Illinois	2,900
15	Indiana	3,050
20	Iowa	2,490
42	Kansas	800
23	Kentucky	2,200
31	Louisiana	1,680
26	Maine	1,950
6	Maryland	7,900
3	Massachusetts	10,500
14	Michigan	3,150
25	Minnesota	2,030
34	Mississippi	1,580
30	Missouri	1,740
46	Montana	445
39	Nebraska	910
44	Nevada	550
12	New Hampshire	3,450
4	New Jersey	10,300
48	New Mexico	290
27	New York	1,880
11	North Carolina	3,570
45	North Dakota	500
13	Ohio	3,180
41	Oklahoma	805
36	Oregon	1,350
8	Pennsylvania	4,000
1	Rhode Island	11,200
21	South Carolina	2,330
43	South Dakota	570
18	Tennessee	2,700
38	Texas	925
37	Utah	1,230
22	Vermont	2,300
9	Virginia	3,900
32	Washington	1,650
33	West Virginia	1,600
17	Wisconsin	2,850
47	Wyoming	350

RANK ORDER

RANK	STATE	PER ACRE VALUE
1	Rhode Island	$11,200
2	Connecticut	10,800
3	Massachusetts	10,500
4	New Jersey	10,300
5	Delaware	8,400
6	Maryland	7,900
7	California	4,160
8	Pennsylvania	4,000
9	Virginia	3,900
10	Florida	3,700
11	North Carolina	3,570
12	New Hampshire	3,450
13	Ohio	3,180
14	Michigan	3,150
15	Indiana	3,050
16	Illinois	2,900
17	Wisconsin	2,850
18	Tennessee	2,700
19	Georgia	2,590
20	Iowa	2,490
21	South Carolina	2,330
22	Vermont	2,300
23	Kentucky	2,200
24	Alabama	2,050
25	Minnesota	2,030
26	Maine	1,950
27	New York	1,880
28	Arkansas	1,820
29	Arizona	1,750
30	Missouri	1,740
31	Louisiana	1,680
32	Washington	1,650
33	West Virginia	1,600
34	Mississippi	1,580
35	Idaho	1,480
36	Oregon	1,350
37	Utah	1,230
38	Texas	925
39	Nebraska	910
40	Colorado	845
41	Oklahoma	805
42	Kansas	800
43	South Dakota	570
44	Nevada	550
45	North Dakota	500
46	Montana	445
47	Wyoming	350
48	New Mexico	290
NA	Alaska**	NA
NA	Hawaii**	NA
	District of Columbia**	NA

Source: U.S. Department of Agriculture, National Agricultural Statistics Service
    "Land Values and Cash Rents" (http://usda.mannlib.cornell.edu/reports/nassr/other/plr-bb/)
*As of January 1, 2005. Value of farmland and buildings in nominal dollars.
**Not applicable or available.

Percent Change in Average per Acre Value of Farmland: 2004 to 2005

National Percent Change = 11.0% Increase*

ALPHA ORDER				RANK ORDER		
RANK	STATE	PERCENT CHANGE		RANK	STATE	PERCENT CHANGE
14	Alabama	10.2		1	Delaware	40.0
NA	Alaska**	NA		2	Maryland	38.6
24	Arizona	9.4		3	Virginia	21.9
12	Arkansas	10.3		4	Florida	19.4
23	California	9.5		5	South Dakota	14.0
26	Colorado	9.0		5	Wisconsin	14.0
45	Connecticut	5.9		7	Iowa	13.2
1	Delaware	40.0		8	Minnesota	12.8
4	Florida	19.4		9	Kansas	11.9
14	Georgia	10.2		10	Illinois	11.1
NA	Hawaii**	NA		10	Wyoming	11.1
27	Idaho	8.8		12	Arkansas	10.3
10	Illinois	11.1		12	Nebraska	10.3
16	Indiana	10.1		14	Alabama	10.2
7	Iowa	13.2		14	Georgia	10.2
9	Kansas	11.9		16	Indiana	10.1
18	Kentucky	10.0		16	Missouri	10.1
42	Louisiana	6.3		18	Kentucky	10.0
48	Maine	5.4		18	Nevada	10.0
2	Maryland	38.6		20	North Dakota	9.9
44	Massachusetts	6.1		21	Rhode Island	9.8
36	Michigan	7.9		22	Pennsylvania	9.6
8	Minnesota	12.8		23	California	9.5
40	Mississippi	6.8		24	Arizona	9.4
16	Missouri	10.1		24	New Mexico	9.4
28	Montana	8.5		26	Colorado	9.0
12	Nebraska	10.3		27	Idaho	8.8
18	Nevada	10.0		28	Montana	8.5
43	New Hampshire	6.2		28	Ohio	8.5
46	New Jersey	5.6		30	South Carolina	8.4
24	New Mexico	9.4		31	North Carolina	8.2
46	New York	5.6		31	Texas	8.2
31	North Carolina	8.2		33	Oklahoma	8.1
20	North Dakota	9.9		34	Oregon	8.0
28	Ohio	8.5		34	Tennessee	8.0
33	Oklahoma	8.1		36	Michigan	7.9
34	Oregon	8.0		37	Washington	7.8
22	Pennsylvania	9.6		38	Utah	7.0
21	Rhode Island	9.8		38	Vermont	7.0
30	South Carolina	8.4		40	Mississippi	6.8
5	South Dakota	14.0		41	West Virginia	6.7
34	Tennessee	8.0		42	Louisiana	6.3
31	Texas	8.2		43	New Hampshire	6.2
38	Utah	7.0		44	Massachusetts	6.1
38	Vermont	7.0		45	Connecticut	5.9
3	Virginia	21.9		46	New Jersey	5.6
37	Washington	7.8		46	New York	5.6
41	West Virginia	6.7		48	Maine	5.4
5	Wisconsin	14.0		NA	Alaska**	NA
10	Wyoming	11.1		NA	Hawaii**	NA
					District of Columbia**	NA

Source: U.S. Department of Agriculture, National Agricultural Statistics Service
    "Land Values and Cash Rents" (http://usda.mannlib.cornell.edu/reports/nassr/other/plr-bb/)
As of January 1, 2005. Value of farmland and buildings in nominal dollars.
**Not applicable or available.*

6

Net Farm Income in 2004

National Total = $82,539,640,000*

ALPHA ORDER

RANK	STATE	FARM INCOME	% of USA
13	Alabama	$2,034,115,868	2.5%
50	Alaska	15,789,741	0.0%
22	Arizona	1,399,446,209	1.7%
6	Arkansas	3,242,643,381	3.9%
1	California	12,249,635,545	14.8%
23	Colorado	1,298,831,582	1.6%
45	Connecticut	102,285,671	0.1%
38	Delaware	349,789,737	0.4%
11	Florida	2,373,157,748	2.9%
8	Georgia	2,844,609,632	3.4%
42	Hawaii	121,942,711	0.1%
18	Idaho	1,536,467,816	1.9%
4	Illinois	4,022,264,113	4.9%
12	Indiana	2,360,080,694	2.9%
3	Iowa	5,683,116,623	6.9%
19	Kansas	1,466,321,166	1.8%
26	Kentucky	1,083,228,664	1.3%
30	Louisiana	822,428,464	1.0%
44	Maine	111,361,582	0.1%
35	Maryland	587,940,025	0.7%
46	Massachusetts	75,715,276	0.1%
27	Michigan	1,056,863,024	1.3%
9	Minnesota	2,645,304,868	3.2%
17	Mississippi	1,801,652,541	2.2%
10	Missouri	2,491,979,919	3.0%
32	Montana	721,730,227	0.9%
5	Nebraska	3,459,063,658	4.2%
41	Nevada	127,663,809	0.2%
48	New Hampshire	36,669,707	0.0%
40	New Jersey	157,785,623	0.2%
29	New Mexico	862,414,139	1.0%
33	New York	638,475,321	0.8%
7	North Carolina	2,989,725,144	3.6%
28	North Dakota	971,069,270	1.2%
21	Ohio	1,417,298,589	1.7%
20	Oklahoma	1,451,902,510	1.8%
24	Oregon	1,293,221,961	1.6%
25	Pennsylvania	1,272,525,535	1.5%
49	Rhode Island	18,424,297	0.0%
31	South Carolina	772,535,654	0.9%
14	South Dakota	2,012,435,469	2.4%
36	Tennessee	457,656,315	0.6%
2	Texas	6,722,369,167	8.1%
37	Utah	381,756,837	0.5%
43	Vermont	117,822,775	0.1%
34	Virginia	627,643,214	0.8%
15	Washington	2,012,079,880	2.4%
47	West Virginia	37,539,645	0.0%
16	Wisconsin	1,979,477,996	2.4%
39	Wyoming	223,380,515	0.3%

RANK ORDER

RANK	STATE	FARM INCOME	% of USA
1	California	$12,249,635,545	14.8%
2	Texas	6,722,369,167	8.1%
3	Iowa	5,683,116,623	6.9%
4	Illinois	4,022,264,113	4.9%
5	Nebraska	3,459,063,658	4.2%
6	Arkansas	3,242,643,381	3.9%
7	North Carolina	2,989,725,144	3.6%
8	Georgia	2,844,609,632	3.4%
9	Minnesota	2,645,304,868	3.2%
10	Missouri	2,491,979,919	3.0%
11	Florida	2,373,157,748	2.9%
12	Indiana	2,360,080,694	2.9%
13	Alabama	2,034,115,868	2.5%
14	South Dakota	2,012,435,469	2.4%
15	Washington	2,012,079,880	2.4%
16	Wisconsin	1,979,477,996	2.4%
17	Mississippi	1,801,652,541	2.2%
18	Idaho	1,536,467,816	1.9%
19	Kansas	1,466,321,166	1.8%
20	Oklahoma	1,451,902,510	1.8%
21	Ohio	1,417,298,589	1.7%
22	Arizona	1,399,446,209	1.7%
23	Colorado	1,298,831,582	1.6%
24	Oregon	1,293,221,961	1.6%
25	Pennsylvania	1,272,525,535	1.5%
26	Kentucky	1,083,228,664	1.3%
27	Michigan	1,056,863,024	1.3%
28	North Dakota	971,069,270	1.2%
29	New Mexico	862,414,139	1.0%
30	Louisiana	822,428,464	1.0%
31	South Carolina	772,535,654	0.0%
32	Montana	721,730,227	0.9%
33	New York	638,475,321	0.8%
34	Virginia	627,643,214	0.8%
35	Maryland	587,940,025	0.7%
36	Tennessee	457,656,315	0.6%
37	Utah	381,756,837	0.5%
38	Delaware	349,789,737	0.4%
39	Wyoming	223,380,515	0.3%
40	New Jersey	157,785,623	0.2%
41	Nevada	127,663,809	0.2%
42	Hawaii	121,942,711	0.1%
43	Vermont	117,822,775	0.1%
44	Maine	111,361,582	0.1%
45	Connecticut	102,285,671	0.1%
46	Massachusetts	75,715,276	0.1%
47	West Virginia	37,539,645	0.0%
48	New Hampshire	36,669,707	0.0%
49	Rhode Island	18,424,297	0.0%
50	Alaska	15,789,741	0.0%
	District of Columbia	0	0.0%

Source: U.S. Department of Agriculture, Economic Research Service
   "Net Farm Income and Value of Production per Acre for States, 2004"
*Net farm income is a measure of the net value of production in a given year. It is determined by subtracting total production expenses from gross farm income.

Net Farm Income per Operation in 2004

National Average = $27,848 per Operation

RANK	STATE	PER OPERATION		RANK	STATE	PER OPERATION
14	Alabama	$35,654		1	California	$107,959
36	Alaska	16,491		2	Arizona	104,635
2	Arizona	104,635		3	Delaware	67,686
11	Arkansas	40,301		4	Nebraska	66,554
1	California	107,959		5	Georgia	60,265
12	Colorado	37,313		6	Idaho	48,708
28	Connecticut	22,118		7	North Dakota	43,410
3	Delaware	67,686		8	South Dakota	41,801
9	Florida	41,614		9	Florida	41,614
5	Georgia	60,265		10	New Mexico	40,894
27	Hawaii	22,170		11	Arkansas	40,301
6	Idaho	48,708		12	Colorado	37,313
24	Illinois	22,699		13	Nevada	37,093
26	Indiana	22,315		14	Alabama	35,654
25	Iowa	22,474		15	Wyoming	31,679
29	Kansas	21,502		16	North Carolina	30,444
45	Kentucky	9,928		17	South Carolina	27,894
20	Louisiana	26,138		18	Maryland	27,009
42	Maine	11,724		19	Mississippi	26,832
18	Maryland	27,009		20	Louisiana	26,138
47	Massachusetts	6,577		21	Texas	25,935
46	Michigan	8,340		22	Oklahoma	24,391
32	Minnesota	19,605		23	Utah	24,044
19	Mississippi	26,832		24	Illinois	22,699
39	Missouri	14,519		25	Iowa	22,474
31	Montana	20,571		26	Indiana	22,315
4	Nebraska	66,554		27	Hawaii	22,170
13	Nevada	37,093		28	Connecticut	22,118
49	New Hampshire	4,855		29	Kansas	21,502
40	New Jersey	12,861		30	Wisconsin	21,255
10	New Mexico	40,894		31	Montana	20,571
37	New York	16,141		32	Minnesota	19,605
16	North Carolina	30,444		33	Washington	19,166
7	North Dakota	43,410		34	Pennsylvania	19,017
35	Ohio	18,948		35	Ohio	18,948
22	Oklahoma	24,391		36	Alaska	16,491
41	Oregon	12,330		37	New York	16,141
34	Pennsylvania	19,017		38	Vermont	15,733
43	Rhode Island	11,516		39	Missouri	14,519
17	South Carolina	27,894		40	New Jersey	12,861
8	South Dakota	41,801		41	Oregon	12,330
48	Tennessee	5,519		42	Maine	11,724
21	Texas	25,935		43	Rhode Island	11,516
23	Utah	24,044		44	Virginia	11,129
38	Vermont	15,733		45	Kentucky	9,928
44	Virginia	11,129		46	Michigan	8,340
33	Washington	19,166		47	Massachusetts	6,577
50	West Virginia	713		48	Tennessee	5,519
30	Wisconsin	21,255		49	New Hampshire	4,855
15	Wyoming	31,679		50	West Virginia	713
					District of Columbia*	NA

Source: U.S. Department of Agriculture, Economic Research Service
   "Net Farm Income and Value of Production per Acre for States, 2004"
*Not applicable.

Net Farm Income per Acre in 2004

National Average = $88 per Acre

ALPHA ORDER				RANK ORDER		
RANK	STATE	PER ACRE		RANK	STATE	PER ACRE
9	Alabama	$234		1	Delaware	$660
47	Alaska	18		2	California	459
36	Arizona	53		3	North Carolina	332
10	Arkansas	225		4	Rhode Island	307
2	California	459		5	Maryland	287
40	Colorado	42		6	Connecticut	284
6	Connecticut	284		7	Georgia	266
1	Delaware	660		8	Florida	235
8	Florida	235		9	Alabama	234
7	Georgia	266		10	Arkansas	225
26	Hawaii	94		11	New Jersey	192
20	Idaho	130		12	Iowa	179
17	Illinois	146		13	Pennsylvania	165
16	Indiana	157		14	Mississippi	163
12	Iowa	179		15	South Carolina	159
43	Kansas	31		16	Indiana	157
32	Kentucky	78		17	Illinois	146
22	Louisiana	105		17	Massachusetts	146
30	Maine	81		19	Washington	132
5	Maryland	287		20	Idaho	130
17	Massachusetts	146		21	Wisconsin	128
22	Michigan	105		22	Louisiana	105
25	Minnesota	96		22	Michigan	105
14	Mississippi	163		24	Ohio	97
29	Missouri	83		25	Minnesota	96
48	Montana	12		26	Hawaii	94
33	Nebraska	75		26	Vermont	94
45	Nevada	20		28	New York	84
30	New Hampshire	81		29	Missouri	83
11	New Jersey	192		30	Maine	81
46	New Mexico	19		30	New Hampshire	81
28	New York	84		32	Kentucky	78
3	North Carolina	332		33	Nebraska	75
44	North Dakota	25		33	Oregon	75
24	Ohio	97		35	Virginia	73
39	Oklahoma	43		36	Arizona	53
33	Oregon	75		37	Texas	52
13	Pennsylvania	165		38	South Dakota	46
4	Rhode Island	307		39	Oklahoma	43
15	South Carolina	159		40	Colorado	42
38	South Dakota	46		41	Tennessee	39
41	Tennessee	39		42	Utah	33
37	Texas	52		43	Kansas	31
42	Utah	33		44	North Dakota	25
26	Vermont	94		45	Nevada	20
35	Virginia	73		46	New Mexico	19
19	Washington	132		47	Alaska	18
49	West Virginia	10		48	Montana	12
21	Wisconsin	128		49	West Virginia	10
50	Wyoming	6		50	Wyoming	6
				District of Columbia*		NA

Source: U.S. Department of Agriculture, Economic Research Service
    "Net Farm Income and Value of Production per Acre for States, 2004"
Not applicable.

Farm Income: Cash Receipts from Commodities in 2004

National Total = $241,241,403,000*

ALPHA ORDER

RANK	STATE	FARM INCOME	% of USA
24	Alabama	$4,103,235,000	1.7%
50	Alaska	52,987,000	0.0%
29	Arizona	3,065,604,000	1.3%
11	Arkansas	6,604,401,000	2.7%
1	California	31,835,183,000	13.2%
16	Colorado	5,501,154,000	2.3%
44	Connecticut	526,580,000	0.2%
39	Delaware	933,842,000	0.4%
10	Florida	6,843,731,000	2.8%
12	Georgia	6,107,025,000	2.5%
43	Hawaii	549,830,000	0.2%
21	Idaho	4,349,255,000	1.8%
6	Illinois	9,708,305,000	4.0%
13	Indiana	6,043,191,000	2.5%
3	Iowa	14,652,945,000	6.1%
7	Kansas	9,502,727,000	3.9%
23	Kentucky	4,126,186,000	1.7%
34	Louisiana	2,225,802,000	0.9%
42	Maine	553,830,000	0.2%
36	Maryland	1,743,357,000	0.7%
47	Massachusetts	413,954,000	0.2%
22	Michigan	4,312,320,000	1.8%
5	Minnesota	9,794,911,000	4.1%
26	Mississippi	4,089,158,000	1.7%
15	Missouri	5,818,728,000	2.4%
33	Montana	2,238,980,000	0.9%
4	Nebraska	11,779,728,000	4.9%
45	Nevada	454,343,000	0.2%
48	New Hampshire	168,871,000	0.1%
40	New Jersey	866,719,000	0.4%
31	New Mexico	2,564,862,000	1.1%
28	New York	3,653,430,000	1.5%
8	North Carolina	8,210,496,000	3.4%
25	North Dakota	4,090,863,000	1.7%
17	Ohio	5,459,380,000	2.3%
18	Oklahoma	5,054,570,000	2.1%
27	Oregon	3,691,554,000	1.5%
20	Pennsylvania	4,859,335,000	2.0%
49	Rhode Island	63,826,000	0.0%
35	South Carolina	1,909,098,000	0.8%
19	South Dakota	4,877,484,000	2.0%
32	Tennessee	2,561,984,000	1.1%
2	Texas	16,498,398,000	6.8%
37	Utah	1,253,154,000	0.5%
41	Vermont	581,773,000	0.2%
30	Virginia	2,684,392,000	1.1%
14	Washington	5,868,195,000	2.4%
46	West Virginia	422,872,000	0.2%
9	Wisconsin	6,864,150,000	2.8%
38	Wyoming	1,104,702,000	0.5%

RANK ORDER

RANK	STATE	FARM INCOME	% of USA
1	California	$31,835,183,000	13.2%
2	Texas	16,498,398,000	6.8%
3	Iowa	14,652,945,000	6.1%
4	Nebraska	11,779,728,000	4.9%
5	Minnesota	9,794,911,000	4.1%
6	Illinois	9,708,305,000	4.0%
7	Kansas	9,502,727,000	3.9%
8	North Carolina	8,210,496,000	3.4%
9	Wisconsin	6,864,150,000	2.8%
10	Florida	6,843,731,000	2.8%
11	Arkansas	6,604,401,000	2.7%
12	Georgia	6,107,025,000	2.5%
13	Indiana	6,043,191,000	2.5%
14	Washington	5,868,195,000	2.4%
15	Missouri	5,818,728,000	2.4%
16	Colorado	5,501,154,000	2.3%
17	Ohio	5,459,380,000	2.3%
18	Oklahoma	5,054,570,000	2.1%
19	South Dakota	4,877,484,000	2.0%
20	Pennsylvania	4,859,335,000	2.0%
21	Idaho	4,349,255,000	1.8%
22	Michigan	4,312,320,000	1.8%
23	Kentucky	4,126,186,000	1.7%
24	Alabama	4,103,235,000	1.7%
25	North Dakota	4,090,863,000	1.7%
26	Mississippi	4,089,158,000	1.7%
27	Oregon	3,691,554,000	1.5%
28	New York	3,653,430,000	1.5%
29	Arizona	3,065,604,000	1.3%
30	Virginia	2,684,392,000	1.1%
31	New Mexico	2,564,862,000	1.1%
32	Tennessee	2,561,984,000	1.1%
33	Montana	2,238,980,000	0.9%
34	Louisiana	2,225,802,000	0.9%
35	South Carolina	1,909,098,000	0.8%
36	Maryland	1,743,357,000	0.7%
37	Utah	1,253,154,000	0.5%
38	Wyoming	1,104,702,000	0.5%
39	Delaware	933,842,000	0.4%
40	New Jersey	866,719,000	0.4%
41	Vermont	581,773,000	0.2%
42	Maine	553,830,000	0.2%
43	Hawaii	549,830,000	0.2%
44	Connecticut	526,580,000	0.2%
45	Nevada	454,343,000	0.2%
46	West Virginia	422,872,000	0.2%
47	Massachusetts	413,954,000	0.2%
48	New Hampshire	168,871,000	0.1%
49	Rhode Island	63,826,000	0.0%
50	Alaska	52,987,000	0.0%
	District of Columbia	0	0.0%

Source: U.S. Department of Agriculture, Economic Research Service
    "Farm Marketings"
*Commodities include crops and livestock.

Farm Income: Crops in 2004

National Total = $117,760,414,000

ALPHA ORDER

RANK	STATE	FARM INCOME	% of USA
34	Alabama	$734,696,000	0.6%
50	Alaska	24,329,000	0.0%
22	Arizona	1,628,576,000	1.4%
18	Arkansas	2,431,732,000	2.1%
1	California	23,212,043,000	19.7%
28	Colorado	1,345,001,000	1.1%
39	Connecticut	348,651,000	0.3%
43	Delaware	191,185,000	0.2%
5	Florida	5,359,595,000	4.6%
19	Georgia	2,036,173,000	1.7%
38	Hawaii	457,079,000	0.4%
20	Idaho	1,818,681,000	1.5%
2	Illinois	7,769,390,000	6.6%
9	Indiana	3,978,204,000	3.4%
3	Iowa	7,368,773,000	6.3%
12	Kansas	3,082,658,000	2.6%
24	Kentucky	1,387,682,000	1.2%
27	Louisiana	1,347,809,000	1.1%
42	Maine	223,221,000	0.2%
35	Maryland	732,691,000	0.6%
40	Massachusetts	319,810,000	0.3%
16	Michigan	2,566,437,000	2.2%
6	Minnesota	4,860,595,000	4.1%
25	Mississippi	1,377,005,000	1.2%
14	Missouri	2,756,149,000	2.3%
31	Montana	960,935,000	0.8%
7	Nebraska	4,441,545,000	3.8%
45	Nevada	147,274,000	0.1%
46	New Hampshire	95,222,000	0.1%
36	New Jersey	680,053,000	0.6%
37	New Mexico	565,345,000	0.5%
26	New York	1,351,115,000	1.1%
13	North Carolina	2,859,152,000	2.4%
11	North Dakota	3,152,582,000	2.7%
10	Ohio	3,387,276,000	2.9%
30	Oklahoma	1,172,866,000	1.0%
15	Oregon	2,647,919,000	2.2%
23	Pennsylvania	1,544,652,000	1.3%
49	Rhode Island	54,014,000	0.0%
33	South Carolina	833,134,000	0.7%
17	South Dakota	2,455,300,000	2.1%
29	Tennessee	1,263,003,000	1.1%
4	Texas	5,391,411,000	4.6%
41	Utah	270,028,000	0.2%
47	Vermont	84,927,000	0.1%
32	Virginia	902,271,000	0.8%
8	Washington	4,132,390,000	3.5%
48	West Virginia	74,359,000	0.1%
21	Wisconsin	1,781,723,000	1.5%
44	Wyoming	153,746,000	0.1%

RANK ORDER

RANK	STATE	FARM INCOME	% of USA
1	California	$23,212,043,000	19.7%
2	Illinois	7,769,390,000	6.6%
3	Iowa	7,368,773,000	6.3%
4	Texas	5,391,411,000	4.6%
5	Florida	5,359,595,000	4.6%
6	Minnesota	4,860,595,000	4.1%
7	Nebraska	4,441,545,000	3.8%
8	Washington	4,132,390,000	3.5%
9	Indiana	3,978,204,000	3.4%
10	Ohio	3,387,276,000	2.9%
11	North Dakota	3,152,582,000	2.7%
12	Kansas	3,082,658,000	2.6%
13	North Carolina	2,859,152,000	2.4%
14	Missouri	2,756,149,000	2.3%
15	Oregon	2,647,919,000	2.2%
16	Michigan	2,566,437,000	2.2%
17	South Dakota	2,455,300,000	2.1%
18	Arkansas	2,431,732,000	2.1%
19	Georgia	2,036,173,000	1.7%
20	Idaho	1,818,681,000	1.5%
21	Wisconsin	1,781,723,000	1.5%
22	Arizona	1,628,576,000	1.4%
23	Pennsylvania	1,544,652,000	1.3%
24	Kentucky	1,387,682,000	1.2%
25	Mississippi	1,377,005,000	1.2%
26	New York	1,351,115,000	1.1%
27	Louisiana	1,347,809,000	1.1%
28	Colorado	1,345,001,000	1.1%
29	Tennessee	1,263,003,000	1.1%
30	Oklahoma	1,172,866,000	1.0%
31	Montana	960,935,000	0.8%
32	Virginia	902,271,000	0.8%
33	South Carolina	833,134,000	0.7%
34	Alabama	734,696,000	0.6%
35	Maryland	732,691,000	0.6%
36	New Jersey	680,053,000	0.6%
37	New Mexico	565,345,000	0.5%
38	Hawaii	457,079,000	0.4%
39	Connecticut	348,651,000	0.3%
40	Massachusetts	319,810,000	0.3%
41	Utah	270,028,000	0.2%
42	Maine	223,221,000	0.2%
43	Delaware	191,185,000	0.2%
44	Wyoming	153,746,000	0.1%
45	Nevada	147,274,000	0.1%
46	New Hampshire	95,222,000	0.1%
47	Vermont	84,927,000	0.1%
48	West Virginia	74,359,000	0.1%
49	Rhode Island	54,014,000	0.0%
50	Alaska	24,329,000	0.0%
	District of Columbia	0	0.0%

Source: U.S. Department of Agriculture, Economic Research Service
"Farm Marketings"

Farm Income: Livestock in 2004

National Total = $123,480,989,000*

ALPHA ORDER

RANK	STATE	FARM INCOME	% of USA
13	Alabama	$3,368,539,000	2.7%
49	Alaska	28,658,000	0.0%
29	Arizona	1,437,028,000	1.2%
9	Arkansas	4,172,669,000	3.4%
2	California	8,623,140,000	7.0%
10	Colorado	4,156,153,000	3.4%
45	Connecticut	177,929,000	0.1%
39	Delaware	742,657,000	0.6%
28	Florida	1,484,136,000	1.2%
11	Georgia	4,070,852,000	3.3%
47	Hawaii	92,751,000	0.1%
18	Idaho	2,530,574,000	2.0%
24	Illinois	1,938,915,000	1.6%
22	Indiana	2,064,987,000	1.7%
4	Iowa	7,284,172,000	5.9%
5	Kansas	6,420,069,000	5.2%
16	Kentucky	2,738,504,000	2.2%
38	Louisiana	877,993,000	0.7%
42	Maine	330,609,000	0.3%
34	Maryland	1,010,666,000	0.8%
46	Massachusetts	94,144,000	0.1%
26	Michigan	1,745,883,000	1.4%
8	Minnesota	4,934,316,000	4.0%
17	Mississippi	2,712,153,000	2.2%
15	Missouri	3,062,579,000	2.5%
31	Montana	1,278,045,000	1.0%
3	Nebraska	7,338,183,000	5.9%
43	Nevada	307,069,000	0.2%
48	New Hampshire	73,649,000	0.1%
44	New Jersey	186,666,000	0.2%
23	New Mexico	1,999,517,000	1.6%
20	New York	2,302,315,000	1.9%
6	North Carolina	5,351,344,000	4.3%
37	North Dakota	938,281,000	0.8%
21	Ohio	2,072,104,000	1.7%
12	Oklahoma	3,881,704,000	3.1%
33	Oregon	1,043,635,000	0.8%
14	Pennsylvania	3,314,683,000	2.7%
50	Rhode Island	9,812,000	0.0%
32	South Carolina	1,075,964,000	0.9%
19	South Dakota	2,422,184,000	2.0%
30	Tennessee	1,298,981,000	1.1%
1	Texas	11,106,987,000	9.0%
35	Utah	983,126,000	0.8%
40	Vermont	496,846,000	0.4%
25	Virginia	1,782,121,000	1.4%
27	Washington	1,735,805,000	1.4%
41	West Virginia	348,513,000	0.3%
7	Wisconsin	5,082,427,000	4.1%
36	Wyoming	950,956,000	0.8%

RANK ORDER

RANK	STATE	FARM INCOME	% of USA
1	Texas	$11,106,987,000	9.0%
2	California	8,623,140,000	7.0%
3	Nebraska	7,338,183,000	5.9%
4	Iowa	7,284,172,000	5.9%
5	Kansas	6,420,069,000	5.2%
6	North Carolina	5,351,344,000	4.3%
7	Wisconsin	5,082,427,000	4.1%
8	Minnesota	4,934,316,000	4.0%
9	Arkansas	4,172,669,000	3.4%
10	Colorado	4,156,153,000	3.4%
11	Georgia	4,070,852,000	3.3%
12	Oklahoma	3,881,704,000	3.1%
13	Alabama	3,368,539,000	2.7%
14	Pennsylvania	3,314,683,000	2.7%
15	Missouri	3,062,579,000	2.5%
16	Kentucky	2,738,504,000	2.2%
17	Mississippi	2,712,153,000	2.2%
18	Idaho	2,530,574,000	2.0%
19	South Dakota	2,422,184,000	2.0%
20	New York	2,302,315,000	1.9%
21	Ohio	2,072,104,000	1.7%
22	Indiana	2,064,987,000	1.7%
23	New Mexico	1,999,517,000	1.6%
24	Illinois	1,938,915,000	1.6%
25	Virginia	1,782,121,000	1.4%
26	Michigan	1,745,883,000	1.4%
27	Washington	1,735,805,000	1.4%
28	Florida	1,484,136,000	1.2%
29	Arizona	1,437,028,000	1.2%
30	Tennessee	1,298,981,000	1.1%
31	Montana	1,278,045,000	1.0%
32	South Carolina	1,075,964,000	0.9%
33	Oregon	1,043,635,000	0.8%
34	Maryland	1,010,666,000	0.8%
35	Utah	983,126,000	0.8%
36	Wyoming	950,956,000	0.8%
37	North Dakota	938,281,000	0.8%
38	Louisiana	877,993,000	0.7%
39	Delaware	742,657,000	0.6%
40	Vermont	496,846,000	0.4%
41	West Virginia	348,513,000	0.3%
42	Maine	330,609,000	0.3%
43	Nevada	307,069,000	0.2%
44	New Jersey	186,666,000	0.2%
45	Connecticut	177,929,000	0.1%
46	Massachusetts	94,144,000	0.1%
47	Hawaii	92,751,000	0.1%
48	New Hampshire	73,649,000	0.1%
49	Alaska	28,658,000	0.0%
50	Rhode Island	9,812,000	0.0%
	District of Columbia	0	0.0%

Source: U.S. Department of Agriculture, Economic Research Service
    "Farm Marketings"
*Includes livestock products.

Farm Income: Government Payments in 2004

National Total = $13,303,598,000*

ALPHA ORDER

RANK	STATE	PAYMENTS	% of USA
25	Alabama	$155,508,000	1.2%
47	Alaska	5,723,000	0.0%
29	Arizona	99,959,000	0.8%
7	Arkansas	599,457,000	4.5%
9	California	506,591,000	3.8%
19	Colorado	220,900,000	1.7%
45	Connecticut	6,834,000	0.1%
40	Delaware	16,135,000	0.1%
22	Florida	214,409,000	1.6%
14	Georgia	344,290,000	2.6%
49	Hawaii	2,392,000	0.0%
27	Idaho	153,028,000	1.2%
2	Illinois	1,163,440,000	8.7%
8	Indiana	529,630,000	4.0%
1	Iowa	1,264,138,000	9.5%
6	Kansas	645,081,000	4.8%
28	Kentucky	147,021,000	1.1%
16	Louisiana	320,038,000	2.4%
41	Maine	10,713,000	0.1%
36	Maryland	52,286,000	0.4%
44	Massachusetts	6,942,000	0.1%
21	Michigan	215,232,000	1.6%
5	Minnesota	704,496,000	5.3%
12	Mississippi	401,413,000	3.0%
10	Missouri	470,259,000	3.5%
18	Montana	282,404,000	2.1%
4	Nebraska	728,310,000	5.5%
46	Nevada	6,531,000	0.0%
48	New Hampshire	4,590,000	0.0%
42	New Jersey	10,301,000	0.1%
34	New Mexico	80,649,000	0.6%
31	New York	82,064,000	0.6%
23	North Carolina	212,611,000	1.6%
11	North Dakota	466,546,000	3.5%
15	Ohio	332,574,000	2.5%
20	Oklahoma	220,307,000	1.7%
33	Oregon	80,760,000	0.6%
30	Pennsylvania	91,232,000	0.7%
50	Rhode Island	1,499,000	0.0%
32	South Carolina	81,299,000	0.6%
13	South Dakota	398,540,000	3.0%
26	Tennessee	153,214,000	1.2%
3	Texas	1,152,040,000	8.7%
37	Utah	36,853,000	0.3%
39	Vermont	18,153,000	0.1%
35	Virginia	68,052,000	0.5%
24	Washington	197,011,000	1.5%
43	West Virginia	7,615,000	0.1%
17	Wisconsin	298,182,000	2.2%
38	Wyoming	36,343,000	0.3%

RANK ORDER

RANK	STATE	PAYMENTS	% of USA
1	Iowa	$1,264,138,000	9.5%
2	Illinois	1,163,440,000	8.7%
3	Texas	1,152,040,000	8.7%
4	Nebraska	728,310,000	5.5%
5	Minnesota	704,496,000	5.3%
6	Kansas	645,081,000	4.8%
7	Arkansas	599,457,000	4.5%
8	Indiana	529,630,000	4.0%
9	California	506,591,000	3.8%
10	Missouri	470,259,000	3.5%
11	North Dakota	466,546,000	3.5%
12	Mississippi	401,413,000	3.0%
13	South Dakota	398,540,000	3.0%
14	Georgia	344,290,000	2.6%
15	Ohio	332,574,000	2.5%
16	Louisiana	320,038,000	2.4%
17	Wisconsin	298,182,000	2.2%
18	Montana	282,404,000	2.1%
19	Colorado	220,900,000	1.7%
20	Oklahoma	220,307,000	1.7%
21	Michigan	215,232,000	1.6%
22	Florida	214,409,000	1.6%
23	North Carolina	212,611,000	1.6%
24	Washington	197,011,000	1.5%
25	Alabama	155,508,000	1.2%
26	Tennessee	153,214,000	1.2%
27	Idaho	153,028,000	1.2%
28	Kentucky	147,021,000	1.1%
29	Arizona	99,959,000	0.8%
30	Pennsylvania	91,232,000	0.7%
31	New York	82,064,000	0.0%
32	South Carolina	81,299,000	0.6%
33	Oregon	80,760,000	0.6%
34	New Mexico	80,649,000	0.6%
35	Virginia	68,052,000	0.5%
36	Maryland	52,286,000	0.4%
37	Utah	36,853,000	0.3%
38	Wyoming	36,343,000	0.3%
39	Vermont	18,153,000	0.1%
40	Delaware	16,135,000	0.1%
41	Maine	10,713,000	0.1%
42	New Jersey	10,301,000	0.1%
43	West Virginia	7,615,000	0.1%
44	Massachusetts	6,942,000	0.1%
45	Connecticut	6,834,000	0.1%
46	Nevada	6,531,000	0.0%
47	Alaska	5,723,000	0.0%
48	New Hampshire	4,590,000	0.0%
49	Hawaii	2,392,000	0.0%
50	Rhode Island	1,499,000	0.0%
	District of Columbia	0	0.0%

Source: U.S. Department of Agriculture, Economic Research Service
"Farm Marketings"
Government payments made directly to farmers in cash.

Acres Planted in 2005

National Total = 317,739,000 Acres*

ALPHA ORDER

RANK	STATE	ACRES	% of USA
31	Alabama	2,037,000	0.6%
NA	Alaska**	NA	NA
38	Arizona	730,000	0.2%
15	Arkansas	7,559,000	2.4%
21	California	4,397,000	1.4%
17	Colorado	6,245,000	2.0%
46	Connecticut	93,000	0.0%
41	Delaware	443,000	0.1%
36	Florida	1,061,000	0.3%
25	Georgia	3,656,000	1.2%
48	Hawaii	24,000	0.0%
23	Idaho	4,219,000	1.3%
2	Illinois	23,110,000	7.3%
10	Indiana	12,330,000	3.9%
1	Iowa	24,730,000	7.8%
3	Kansas	22,710,000	7.1%
18	Kentucky	5,425,000	1.7%
27	Louisiana	3,365,000	1.1%
44	Maine	290,000	0.1%
34	Maryland	1,345,000	0.4%
45	Massachusetts	113,000	0.0%
16	Michigan	6,533,000	2.1%
6	Minnesota	19,377,000	6.1%
22	Mississippi	4,305,000	1.4%
9	Missouri	13,523,000	4.3%
13	Montana	9,495,000	3.0%
7	Nebraska	18,867,000	5.9%
40	Nevada	479,000	0.2%
47	New Hampshire	72,000	0.0%
43	New Jersey	323,000	0.1%
35	New Mexico	1,138,000	0.4%
28	New York	3,088,000	1.0%
19	North Carolina	4,635,000	1.5%
5	North Dakota	21,317,000	6.7%
12	Ohio	10,103,000	3.2%
11	Oklahoma	10,150,000	3.2%
30	Oregon	2,169,000	0.7%
24	Pennsylvania	3,753,000	1.2%
49	Rhode Island	12,000	0.0%
33	South Carolina	1,584,000	0.5%
8	South Dakota	16,998,000	5.3%
20	Tennessee	4,590,000	1.4%
4	Texas	22,216,000	7.0%
37	Utah	1,003,000	0.3%
42	Vermont	335,000	0.1%
29	Virginia	2,732,000	0.9%
26	Washington	3,615,000	1.1%
39	West Virginia	645,000	0.2%
14	Wisconsin	8,191,000	2.6%
32	Wyoming	1,589,000	0.5%

RANK ORDER

RANK	STATE	ACRES	% of USA
1	Iowa	24,730,000	7.8%
2	Illinois	23,110,000	7.3%
3	Kansas	22,710,000	7.1%
4	Texas	22,216,000	7.0%
5	North Dakota	21,317,000	6.7%
6	Minnesota	19,377,000	6.1%
7	Nebraska	18,867,000	5.9%
8	South Dakota	16,998,000	5.3%
9	Missouri	13,523,000	4.3%
10	Indiana	12,330,000	3.9%
11	Oklahoma	10,150,000	3.2%
12	Ohio	10,103,000	3.2%
13	Montana	9,495,000	3.0%
14	Wisconsin	8,191,000	2.6%
15	Arkansas	7,559,000	2.4%
16	Michigan	6,533,000	2.1%
17	Colorado	6,245,000	2.0%
18	Kentucky	5,425,000	1.7%
19	North Carolina	4,635,000	1.5%
20	Tennessee	4,590,000	1.4%
21	California	4,397,000	1.4%
22	Mississippi	4,305,000	1.4%
23	Idaho	4,219,000	1.3%
24	Pennsylvania	3,753,000	1.2%
25	Georgia	3,656,000	1.2%
26	Washington	3,615,000	1.1%
27	Louisiana	3,365,000	1.1%
28	New York	3,088,000	1.0%
29	Virginia	2,732,000	0.9%
30	Oregon	2,169,000	0.7%
31	Alabama	2,037,000	0.6%
32	Wyoming	1,589,000	0.5%
33	South Carolina	1,584,000	0.5%
34	Maryland	1,345,000	0.4%
35	New Mexico	1,138,000	0.4%
36	Florida	1,061,000	0.3%
37	Utah	1,003,000	0.3%
38	Arizona	730,000	0.2%
39	West Virginia	645,000	0.2%
40	Nevada	479,000	0.2%
41	Delaware	443,000	0.1%
42	Vermont	335,000	0.1%
43	New Jersey	323,000	0.1%
44	Maine	290,000	0.1%
45	Massachusetts	113,000	0.0%
46	Connecticut	93,000	0.0%
47	New Hampshire	72,000	0.0%
48	Hawaii	24,000	0.0%
49	Rhode Island	12,000	0.0%
NA	Alaska**	NA	NA
	District of Columbia**	NA	NA

Source: U.S. Department of Agriculture, National Agricultural Statistics Service
"Crop Production: 2005 Summary" (Cr Pr 2-1 (06), January 2006)
(http://usda.mannlib.cornell.edu/reports/nassr/field/pcp-bban/)
*Estimated totals.
**No acreage or not available.

Acres Harvested in 2005

National Total = 303,616,000 Acres*

ALPHA ORDER

RANK	STATE	ACRES	% of USA
31	Alabama	1,932,000	0.6%
NA	Alaska**	NA	NA
38	Arizona	719,000	0.2%
15	Arkansas	7,444,000	2.5%
23	California	3,895,000	1.3%
17	Colorado	5,727,000	1.9%
46	Connecticut	91,000	0.0%
41	Delaware	436,000	0.1%
35	Florida	1,032,000	0.3%
27	Georgia	3,193,000	1.1%
48	Hawaii	24,000	0.0%
22	Idaho	4,048,000	1.3%
2	Illinois	22,973,000	7.6%
10	Indiana	12,249,000	4.0%
1	Iowa	24,520,000	8.1%
3	Kansas	21,936,000	7.2%
18	Kentucky	5,318,000	1.8%
26	Louisiana	3,303,000	1.1%
44	Maine	281,000	0.1%
34	Maryland	1,309,000	0.4%
45	Massachusetts	110,000	0.0%
16	Michigan	6,478,000	2.1%
5	Minnesota	18,943,000	6.2%
21	Mississippi	4,261,000	1.4%
9	Missouri	13,392,000	4.4%
12	Montana	9,124,000	3.0%
7	Nebraska	18,508,000	6.1%
40	Nevada	471,000	0.2%
47	New Hampshire	71,000	0.0%
43	New Jersey	312,000	0.1%
36	New Mexico	942,000	0.3%
28	New York	3,046,000	1.0%
20	North Carolina	4,435,000	1.5%
4	North Dakota	20,445,000	6.7%
11	Ohio	9,992,000	3.3%
13	Oklahoma	8,109,000	2.7%
30	Oregon	2,067,000	0.7%
24	Pennsylvania	3,687,000	1.2%
49	Rhode Island	12,000	0.0%
32	South Carolina	1,547,000	0.5%
8	South Dakota	16,407,000	5.4%
19	Tennessee	4,459,000	1.5%
6	Texas	18,521,000	6.1%
37	Utah	928,000	0.3%
42	Vermont	330,000	0.1%
29	Virginia	2,659,000	0.9%
25	Washington	3,532,000	1.2%
39	West Virginia	641,000	0.2%
14	Wisconsin	7,905,000	2.6%
33	Wyoming	1,512,000	0.5%

RANK ORDER

RANK	STATE	ACRES	% of USA
1	Iowa	24,520,000	8.1%
2	Illinois	22,973,000	7.6%
3	Kansas	21,936,000	7.2%
4	North Dakota	20,445,000	6.7%
5	Minnesota	18,943,000	6.2%
6	Texas	18,521,000	6.1%
7	Nebraska	18,508,000	6.1%
8	South Dakota	16,407,000	5.4%
9	Missouri	13,392,000	4.4%
10	Indiana	12,249,000	4.0%
11	Ohio	9,992,000	3.3%
12	Montana	9,124,000	3.0%
13	Oklahoma	8,109,000	2.7%
14	Wisconsin	7,905,000	2.6%
15	Arkansas	7,444,000	2.5%
16	Michigan	6,478,000	2.1%
17	Colorado	5,727,000	1.9%
18	Kentucky	5,318,000	1.8%
19	Tennessee	4,459,000	1.5%
20	North Carolina	4,435,000	1.5%
21	Mississippi	4,261,000	1.4%
22	Idaho	4,048,000	1.3%
23	California	3,895,000	1.3%
24	Pennsylvania	3,687,000	1.2%
25	Washington	3,532,000	1.2%
26	Louisiana	3,303,000	1.1%
27	Georgia	3,193,000	1.1%
28	New York	3,046,000	1.0%
29	Virginia	2,659,000	0.9%
30	Oregon	2,067,000	0.7%
31	Alabama	1,932,000	0.6%
32	South Carolina	1,547,000	0.5%
33	Wyoming	1,512,000	0.5%
34	Maryland	1,309,000	0.4%
35	Florida	1,032,000	0.3%
36	New Mexico	942,000	0.3%
37	Utah	928,000	0.3%
38	Arizona	719,000	0.2%
39	West Virginia	641,000	0.2%
40	Nevada	471,000	0.2%
41	Delaware	436,000	0.1%
42	Vermont	330,000	0.1%
43	New Jersey	312,000	0.1%
44	Maine	281,000	0.1%
45	Massachusetts	110,000	0.0%
46	Connecticut	91,000	0.0%
47	New Hampshire	71,000	0.0%
48	Hawaii	24,000	0.0%
49	Rhode Island	12,000	0.0%
NA	Alaska**	NA	NA
	District of Columbia**	NA	NA

Source: U.S. Department of Agriculture, National Agricultural Statistics Service
    "Crop Production: 2005 Summary" (Cr Pr 2-1 (06), January 2006)
        (http://usda.mannlib.cornell.edu/reports/nassr/field/pcp-bban/)
Estimated totals.
**No acreage or not available.*

Acres Harvested: Corn in 2005

National Total = 81,027,000 Acres*

ALPHA ORDER					RANK ORDER			
RANK	STATE		ACRES	% of USA	RANK	STATE	ACRES	% of USA
30	Alabama		215,000	0.3%	1	Iowa	12,730,000	15.7%
NA	Alaska**		NA	NA	2	Illinois	12,065,000	14.9%
41	Arizona		49,000	0.1%	3	Nebraska	8,450,000	10.4%
28	Arkansas		235,000	0.3%	4	Minnesota	7,250,000	8.9%
20	California		535,000	0.7%	5	Indiana	5,870,000	7.2%
16	Colorado		1,060,000	1.3%	6	South Dakota	4,370,000	5.4%
43	Connecticut		26,000	0.0%	7	Wisconsin	3,780,000	4.7%
31	Delaware		159,000	0.2%	8	Kansas	3,600,000	4.4%
38	Florida		56,000	0.1%	9	Ohio	3,410,000	4.2%
27	Georgia		265,000	0.3%	10	Missouri	3,080,000	3.8%
NA	Hawaii**		NA	NA	11	Michigan	2,240,000	2.8%
29	Idaho		230,000	0.3%	12	Texas	1,980,000	2.4%
2	Illinois		12,065,000	14.9%	13	North Dakota	1,370,000	1.7%
5	Indiana		5,870,000	7.2%	14	Pennsylvania	1,340,000	1.7%
1	Iowa		12,730,000	15.7%	15	Kentucky	1,245,000	1.5%
8	Kansas		3,600,000	4.4%	16	Colorado	1,060,000	1.3%
15	Kentucky		1,245,000	1.5%	17	New York	980,000	1.2%
24	Louisiana		335,000	0.4%	18	North Carolina	745,000	0.9%
44	Maine		24,000	0.0%	19	Tennessee	645,000	0.8%
22	Maryland		465,000	0.6%	20	California	535,000	0.7%
45	Massachusetts		17,000	0.0%	21	Virginia	485,000	0.6%
11	Michigan		2,240,000	2.8%	22	Maryland	465,000	0.6%
4	Minnesota		7,250,000	8.9%	23	Mississippi	375,000	0.5%
23	Mississippi		375,000	0.5%	24	Louisiana	335,000	0.4%
10	Missouri		3,080,000	3.8%	25	South Carolina	297,000	0.4%
37	Montana		63,000	0.1%	26	Oklahoma	277,000	0.3%
3	Nebraska		8,450,000	10.4%	27	Georgia	265,000	0.3%
47	Nevada		5,000	0.0%	28	Arkansas	235,000	0.3%
46	New Hampshire		14,000	0.0%	29	Idaho	230,000	0.3%
35	New Jersey		79,000	0.1%	30	Alabama	215,000	0.3%
33	New Mexico		139,000	0.2%	31	Delaware	159,000	0.2%
17	New York		980,000	1.2%	32	Washington	150,000	0.2%
18	North Carolina		745,000	0.9%	33	New Mexico	139,000	0.2%
13	North Dakota		1,370,000	1.7%	34	Vermont	90,000	0.1%
9	Ohio		3,410,000	4.2%	35	New Jersey	79,000	0.1%
26	Oklahoma		277,000	0.3%	35	Wyoming	79,000	0.1%
40	Oregon		53,000	0.1%	37	Montana	63,000	0.1%
14	Pennsylvania		1,340,000	1.7%	38	Florida	56,000	0.1%
48	Rhode Island		2,000	0.0%	39	Utah	54,000	0.1%
25	South Carolina		297,000	0.4%	40	Oregon	53,000	0.1%
6	South Dakota		4,370,000	5.4%	41	Arizona	49,000	0.1%
19	Tennessee		645,000	0.8%	42	West Virginia	44,000	0.1%
12	Texas		1,980,000	2.4%	43	Connecticut	26,000	0.0%
39	Utah		54,000	0.1%	44	Maine	24,000	0.0%
34	Vermont		90,000	0.1%	45	Massachusetts	17,000	0.0%
21	Virginia		485,000	0.6%	46	New Hampshire	14,000	0.0%
32	Washington		150,000	0.2%	47	Nevada	5,000	0.0%
42	West Virginia		44,000	0.1%	48	Rhode Island	2,000	0.0%
7	Wisconsin		3,780,000	4.7%	NA	Alaska**	NA	NA
35	Wyoming		79,000	0.1%	NA	Hawaii**	NA	NA
						District of Columbia**	NA	NA

Source: U.S. Department of Agriculture, National Agricultural Statistics Service
"Crop Production: 2005 Summary" (Cr Pr 2-1 (06), January 2006)
(http://usda.mannlib.cornell.edu/reports/nassr/field/pcp-bban/)
*Estimated totals. Acres harvested for grain and silage. There were 75,107,000 acres harvested for grain.
**No acreage or not available.

Acres Harvested: Soybeans in 2005

National Total = 71,361,000 Acres*

RANK	STATE	ACRES	% of USA		RANK	STATE	ACRES	% of USA
28	Alabama	145,000	0.2%		1	Iowa	10,050,000	14.1%
NA	Alaska**	NA	NA		2	Illinois	9,450,000	13.2%
NA	Arizona**	NA	NA		3	Minnesota	6,800,000	9.5%
9	Arkansas	3,000,000	4.2%		4	Indiana	5,380,000	7.5%
NA	California**	NA	NA		5	Missouri	4,960,000	7.0%
NA	Colorado**	NA	NA		6	Nebraska	4,660,000	6.5%
NA	Connecticut**	NA	NA		7	Ohio	4,480,000	6.3%
26	Delaware	182,000	0.3%		8	South Dakota	3,850,000	5.4%
31	Florida	8,000	0.0%		9	Arkansas	3,000,000	4.2%
27	Georgia	175,000	0.2%		10	North Dakota	2,900,000	4.1%
NA	Hawaii**	NA	NA		11	Kansas	2,850,000	4.0%
NA	Idaho**	NA	NA		12	Michigan	1,990,000	2.8%
2	Illinois	9,450,000	13.2%		13	Mississippi	1,590,000	2.2%
4	Indiana	5,380,000	7.5%		14	Wisconsin	1,580,000	2.2%
1	Iowa	10,050,000	14.1%		15	North Carolina	1,460,000	2.0%
11	Kansas	2,850,000	4.0%		16	Kentucky	1,250,000	1.8%
16	Kentucky	1,250,000	1.8%		17	Tennessee	1,100,000	1.5%
18	Louisiana	850,000	1.2%		18	Louisiana	850,000	1.2%
NA	Maine**	NA	NA		19	Virginia	510,000	0.7%
20	Maryland	470,000	0.7%		20	Maryland	470,000	0.7%
NA	Massachusetts**	NA	NA		21	Pennsylvania	420,000	0.6%
12	Michigan	1,990,000	2.8%		21	South Carolina	420,000	0.6%
3	Minnesota	6,800,000	9.5%		23	Oklahoma	305,000	0.4%
13	Mississippi	1,590,000	2.2%		24	Texas	230,000	0.3%
5	Missouri	4,960,000	7.0%		25	New York	188,000	0.3%
NA	Montana**	NA	NA		26	Delaware	182,000	0.3%
6	Nebraska	4,660,000	6.5%		27	Georgia	175,000	0.2%
NA	Nevada**	NA	NA		28	Alabama	145,000	0.2%
NA	New Hampshire**	NA	NA		29	New Jersey	91,000	0.1%
29	New Jersey	91,000	0.1%		30	West Virginia	17,000	0.0%
NA	New Mexico**	NA	NA		31	Florida	8,000	0.0%
25	New York	188,000	0.3%		NA	Alaska**	NA	NA
15	North Carolina	1,460,000	2.0%		NA	Arizona**	NA	NA
10	North Dakota	2,900,000	4.1%		NA	California**	NA	NA
7	Ohio	4,480,000	6.3%		NA	Colorado**	NA	NA
23	Oklahoma	305,000	0.4%		NA	Connecticut**	NA	NA
NA	Oregon**	NA	NA		NA	Hawaii**	NA	NA
21	Pennsylvania	420,000	0.6%		NA	Idaho**	NA	NA
NA	Rhode Island**	NA	NA		NA	Maine**	NA	NA
21	South Carolina	420,000	0.6%		NA	Massachusetts**	NA	NA
8	South Dakota	3,850,000	5.4%		NA	Montana**	NA	NA
17	Tennessee	1,100,000	1.5%		NA	Nevada**	NA	NA
24	Texas	230,000	0.3%		NA	New Hampshire**	NA	NA
NA	Utah**	NA	NA		NA	New Mexico**	NA	NA
NA	Vermont**	NA	NA		NA	Oregon**	NA	NA
19	Virginia	510,000	0.7%		NA	Rhode Island**	NA	NA
NA	Washington**	NA	NA		NA	Utah**	NA	NA
30	West Virginia	17,000	0.0%		NA	Vermont**	NA	NA
14	Wisconsin	1,580,000	2.2%		NA	Washington**	NA	NA
NA	Wyoming**	NA	NA		NA	Wyoming**	NA	NA
						District of Columbia**	NA	NA

ALPHA ORDER — RANK ORDER

Source: U.S. Department of Agriculture, National Agricultural Statistics Service
    "Crop Production: 2005 Summary" (Cr Pr 2-1 (06), January 2006)
    (http://usda.mannlib.cornell.edu/reports/nassr/field/pcp-bban/)
Estimated totals.
**No acreage or not available.*

Acres Harvested: Wheat in 2005

National Total = 50,119,000 Acres*

ALPHA ORDER

RANK	STATE	ACRES	% of USA
37	Alabama	45,000	0.1%
NA	Alaska**	NA	NA
34	Arizona	81,000	0.2%
24	Arkansas	160,000	0.3%
18	California	369,000	0.7%
8	Colorado	2,219,000	4.4%
NA	Connecticut**	NA	NA
36	Delaware	51,000	0.1%
40	Florida	8,000	0.0%
30	Georgia	140,000	0.3%
NA	Hawaii**	NA	NA
11	Idaho	1,200,000	2.4%
14	Illinois	600,000	1.2%
19	Indiana	340,000	0.7%
39	Iowa	15,000	0.0%
1	Kansas	9,500,000	19.0%
20	Kentucky	300,000	0.6%
32	Louisiana	100,000	0.2%
NA	Maine**	NA	NA
30	Maryland	140,000	0.3%
NA	Massachusetts**	NA	NA
15	Michigan	590,000	1.2%
10	Minnesota	1,745,000	3.5%
35	Mississippi	65,000	0.1%
16	Missouri	540,000	1.1%
3	Montana	5,235,000	10.4%
9	Nebraska	1,760,000	3.5%
40	Nevada	8,000	0.0%
NA	New Hampshire**	NA	NA
38	New Jersey	23,000	0.0%
21	New Mexico	270,000	0.5%
33	New York	95,000	0.2%
17	North Carolina	435,000	0.9%
2	North Dakota	8,835,000	17.6%
13	Ohio	830,000	1.7%
4	Oklahoma	4,000,000	8.0%
12	Oregon	895,000	1.8%
29	Pennsylvania	145,000	0.3%
NA	Rhode Island**	NA	NA
23	South Carolina	165,000	0.3%
5	South Dakota	3,193,000	6.4%
27	Tennessee	150,000	0.3%
6	Texas	3,000,000	6.0%
28	Utah	148,000	0.3%
NA	Vermont**	NA	NA
24	Virginia	160,000	0.3%
7	Washington	2,225,000	4.4%
42	West Virginia	5,000	0.0%
22	Wisconsin	182,000	0.4%
26	Wyoming	152,000	0.3%

RANK ORDER

RANK	STATE	ACRES	% of USA
1	Kansas	9,500,000	19.0%
2	North Dakota	8,835,000	17.6%
3	Montana	5,235,000	10.4%
4	Oklahoma	4,000,000	8.0%
5	South Dakota	3,193,000	6.4%
6	Texas	3,000,000	6.0%
7	Washington	2,225,000	4.4%
8	Colorado	2,219,000	4.4%
9	Nebraska	1,760,000	3.5%
10	Minnesota	1,745,000	3.5%
11	Idaho	1,200,000	2.4%
12	Oregon	895,000	1.8%
13	Ohio	830,000	1.7%
14	Illinois	600,000	1.2%
15	Michigan	590,000	1.2%
16	Missouri	540,000	1.1%
17	North Carolina	435,000	0.9%
18	California	369,000	0.7%
19	Indiana	340,000	0.7%
20	Kentucky	300,000	0.6%
21	New Mexico	270,000	0.5%
22	Wisconsin	182,000	0.4%
23	South Carolina	165,000	0.3%
24	Arkansas	160,000	0.3%
24	Virginia	160,000	0.3%
26	Wyoming	152,000	0.3%
27	Tennessee	150,000	0.3%
28	Utah	148,000	0.3%
29	Pennsylvania	145,000	0.3%
30	Georgia	140,000	0.3%
30	Maryland	140,000	0.3%
32	Louisiana	100,000	0.2%
33	New York	95,000	0.2%
34	Arizona	81,000	0.2%
35	Mississippi	65,000	0.1%
36	Delaware	51,000	0.1%
37	Alabama	45,000	0.1%
38	New Jersey	23,000	0.0%
39	Iowa	15,000	0.0%
40	Florida	8,000	0.0%
40	Nevada	8,000	0.0%
42	West Virginia	5,000	0.0%
NA	Alaska**	NA	NA
NA	Connecticut**	NA	NA
NA	Hawaii**	NA	NA
NA	Maine**	NA	NA
NA	Massachusetts**	NA	NA
NA	New Hampshire**	NA	NA
NA	Rhode Island**	NA	NA
NA	Vermont**	NA	NA
	District of Columbia**	NA	NA

Source: U.S. Department of Agriculture, National Agricultural Statistics Service
"Crop Production: 2005 Summary" (Cr Pr 2-1 (06), January 2006)
(http://usda.mannlib.cornell.edu/reports/nassr/field/pcp-bban/)
*Estimated totals.
**No acreage or not available.

Cattle on Farms in 2006

National Total = 97,101,500 Cattle*

ALPHA ORDER				RANK ORDER			
RANK	STATE	CATTLE	% of USA	RANK	STATE	CATTLE	% of USA
26	Alabama	1,280,000	1.3%	1	Texas	14,100,000	14.5%
49	Alaska	15,500	0.0%	2	Kansas	6,650,000	6.8%
32	Arizona	940,000	1.0%	3	Nebraska	6,550,000	6.7%
16	Arkansas	1,750,000	1.8%	4	California	5,500,000	5.7%
4	California	5,500,000	5.7%	5	Oklahoma	5,450,000	5.6%
10	Colorado	2,650,000	2.7%	6	Missouri	4,550,000	4.7%
44	Connecticut	52,000	0.1%	7	Iowa	3,800,000	3.9%
48	Delaware	23,000	0.0%	8	South Dakota	3,750,000	3.9%
18	Florida	1,690,000	1.7%	9	Wisconsin	3,400,000	3.5%
28	Georgia	1,180,000	1.2%	10	Colorado	2,650,000	2.7%
42	Hawaii	161,000	0.2%	11	Kentucky	2,400,000	2.5%
15	Idaho	2,120,000	2.2%	11	Montana	2,400,000	2.5%
25	Illinois	1,340,000	1.4%	13	Minnesota	2,350,000	2.4%
33	Indiana	900,000	0.9%	14	Tennessee	2,240,000	2.3%
7	Iowa	3,800,000	3.9%	15	Idaho	2,120,000	2.2%
2	Kansas	6,650,000	6.8%	16	Arkansas	1,750,000	1.8%
11	Kentucky	2,400,000	2.5%	17	North Dakota	1,720,000	1.8%
35	Louisiana	820,000	0.8%	18	Florida	1,690,000	1.7%
43	Maine	92,000	0.1%	18	Virginia	1,690,000	1.7%
41	Maryland	230,000	0.2%	20	Pennsylvania	1,610,000	1.7%
45	Massachusetts	47,000	0.0%	21	New Mexico	1,550,000	1.6%
30	Michigan	1,040,000	1.1%	22	Oregon	1,440,000	1.5%
13	Minnesota	2,350,000	2.4%	22	Wyoming	1,440,000	1.5%
31	Mississippi	1,000,000	1.0%	24	New York	1,410,000	1.5%
6	Missouri	4,550,000	4.7%	25	Illinois	1,340,000	1.4%
11	Montana	2,400,000	2.5%	26	Alabama	1,280,000	1.3%
3	Nebraska	6,550,000	6.7%	26	Ohio	1,280,000	1.3%
37	Nevada	500,000	0.5%	28	Georgia	1,180,000	1.2%
47	New Hampshire	39,000	0.0%	29	Washington	1,120,000	1.2%
46	New Jersey	42,000	0.0%	30	Michigan	1,040,000	1.1%
21	New Mexico	1,550,000	1.6%	31	Mississippi	1,000,000	1.0%
24	New York	1,410,000	1.5%	32	Arizona	940,000	1.0%
34	North Carolina	860,000	0.9%	33	Indiana	900,000	0.9%
17	North Dakota	1,720,000	1.8%	34	North Carolina	860,000	0.9%
26	Ohio	1,280,000	1.3%	35	Louisiana	820,000	0.8%
5	Oklahoma	5,450,000	5.6%	35	Utah	820,000	0.8%
22	Oregon	1,440,000	1.5%	37	Nevada	500,000	0.5%
20	Pennsylvania	1,610,000	1.7%	38	South Carolina	415,000	0.4%
50	Rhode Island	5,000	0.0%	39	West Virginia	410,000	0.4%
38	South Carolina	415,000	0.4%	40	Vermont	280,000	0.3%
8	South Dakota	3,750,000	3.9%	41	Maryland	230,000	0.2%
14	Tennessee	2,240,000	2.3%	42	Hawaii	161,000	0.2%
1	Texas	14,100,000	14.5%	43	Maine	92,000	0.1%
35	Utah	820,000	0.8%	44	Connecticut	52,000	0.1%
40	Vermont	280,000	0.3%	45	Massachusetts	47,000	0.0%
18	Virginia	1,690,000	1.7%	46	New Jersey	42,000	0.0%
29	Washington	1,120,000	1.2%	47	New Hampshire	39,000	0.0%
39	West Virginia	410,000	0.4%	48	Delaware	23,000	0.0%
9	Wisconsin	3,400,000	3.5%	49	Alaska	15,500	0.0%
22	Wyoming	1,440,000	1.5%	50	Rhode Island	5,000	0.0%
					District of Columbia	0	0.0%

Source: U.S. Department of Agriculture, National Agricultural Statistics Service
  "Cattle" (http://usda.mannlib.cornell.edu/reports/nassr/livestock/pct-bb/)
*As of January 1, 2006.

Milk Cows on Farms in 2004

National Total = 9,010,000 Milk Cows*

ALPHA ORDER

RANK	STATE	MILK COWS	% of USA
40	Alabama	17,000	0.2%
49	Alaska	1,200	0.0%
13	Arizona	160,000	1.8%
37	Arkansas	24,000	0.3%
1	California	1,725,000	19.1%
23	Colorado	102,000	1.1%
38	Connecticut	20,000	0.2%
46	Delaware	7,400	0.1%
16	Florida	138,000	1.5%
25	Georgia	84,000	0.9%
47	Hawaii	6,100	0.1%
6	Idaho	424,000	4.7%
21	Illinois	107,000	1.2%
14	Indiana	150,000	1.7%
12	Iowa	193,000	2.1%
19	Kansas	113,000	1.3%
20	Kentucky	110,000	1.2%
32	Louisiana	38,000	0.4%
33	Maine	34,000	0.4%
29	Maryland	74,000	0.8%
40	Massachusetts	17,000	0.2%
9	Michigan	303,000	3.4%
5	Minnesota	463,000	5.1%
35	Mississippi	27,000	0.3%
17	Missouri	122,000	1.4%
39	Montana	18,000	0.2%
30	Nebraska	61,000	0.7%
36	Nevada	25,000	0.3%
43	New Hampshire	16,000	0.2%
45	New Jersey	12,000	0.1%
7	New Mexico	326,000	3.6%
3	New York	655,000	7.3%
31	North Carolina	57,000	0.6%
33	North Dakota	34,000	0.4%
10	Ohio	263,000	2.9%
27	Oklahoma	78,000	0.9%
18	Oregon	120,000	1.3%
4	Pennsylvania	562,000	6.2%
49	Rhode Island	1,200	0.0%
40	South Carolina	17,000	0.2%
26	South Dakota	80,000	0.9%
28	Tennessee	75,000	0.8%
8	Texas	319,000	3.5%
24	Utah	88,000	1.0%
15	Vermont	145,000	1.6%
22	Virginia	105,000	1.2%
11	Washington	237,000	2.6%
44	West Virginia	13,000	0.1%
2	Wisconsin	1,241,000	13.8%
48	Wyoming	4,300	0.0%

RANK ORDER

RANK	STATE	MILK COWS	% of USA
1	California	1,725,000	19.1%
2	Wisconsin	1,241,000	13.8%
3	New York	655,000	7.3%
4	Pennsylvania	562,000	6.2%
5	Minnesota	463,000	5.1%
6	Idaho	424,000	4.7%
7	New Mexico	326,000	3.6%
8	Texas	319,000	3.5%
9	Michigan	303,000	3.4%
10	Ohio	263,000	2.9%
11	Washington	237,000	2.6%
12	Iowa	193,000	2.1%
13	Arizona	160,000	1.8%
14	Indiana	150,000	1.7%
15	Vermont	145,000	1.6%
16	Florida	138,000	1.5%
17	Missouri	122,000	1.4%
18	Oregon	120,000	1.3%
19	Kansas	113,000	1.3%
20	Kentucky	110,000	1.2%
21	Illinois	107,000	1.2%
22	Virginia	105,000	1.2%
23	Colorado	102,000	1.1%
24	Utah	88,000	1.0%
25	Georgia	84,000	0.9%
26	South Dakota	80,000	0.9%
27	Oklahoma	78,000	0.9%
28	Tennessee	75,000	0.8%
29	Maryland	74,000	0.8%
30	Nebraska	61,000	0.7%
31	North Carolina	57,000	0.6%
32	Louisiana	38,000	0.4%
33	Maine	34,000	0.4%
33	North Dakota	34,000	0.4%
35	Mississippi	27,000	0.3%
36	Nevada	25,000	0.3%
37	Arkansas	24,000	0.3%
38	Connecticut	20,000	0.2%
39	Montana	18,000	0.2%
40	Alabama	17,000	0.2%
40	Massachusetts	17,000	0.2%
40	South Carolina	17,000	0.2%
43	New Hampshire	16,000	0.2%
44	West Virginia	13,000	0.1%
45	New Jersey	12,000	0.1%
46	Delaware	7,400	0.1%
47	Hawaii	6,100	0.1%
48	Wyoming	4,300	0.0%
49	Alaska	1,200	0.0%
49	Rhode Island	1,200	0.0%
	District of Columbia	0	0.0%

Source: U.S. Department of Agriculture, National Agricultural Statistics Service
  "Milk Production, Disposition and Income: 2004 Summary" (April 2005)
    (http://usda.mannlib.cornell.edu/reports/nassr/dairy/pmp-bbm/)
*Average number during year. Excludes heifers not yet fresh.

Milk Production in 2004

National Total = 170,805,000,000 Pounds of Milk*

ALPHA ORDER

RANK	STATE	POUNDS	% of USA
43	Alabama	245,000,000	0.1%
50	Alaska	14,600,000	0.0%
13	Arizona	3,646,000,000	2.1%
39	Arkansas	318,000,000	0.2%
1	California	36,465,000,000	21.3%
19	Colorado	2,184,000,000	1.3%
36	Connecticut	392,000,000	0.2%
46	Delaware	127,500,000	0.1%
17	Florida	2,253,000,000	1.3%
25	Georgia	1,416,000,000	0.8%
47	Hawaii	80,500,000	0.0%
5	Idaho	9,093,000,000	5.3%
20	Illinois	1,978,000,000	1.2%
14	Indiana	2,962,000,000	1.7%
12	Iowa	3,843,000,000	2.2%
18	Kansas	2,216,000,000	1.3%
24	Kentucky	1,423,000,000	0.8%
35	Louisiana	479,000,000	0.3%
32	Maine	612,000,000	0.4%
28	Maryland	1,162,000,000	0.7%
41	Massachusetts	296,000,000	0.2%
8	Michigan	6,315,000,000	3.7%
6	Minnesota	8,102,000,000	4.7%
37	Mississippi	379,000,000	0.2%
21	Missouri	1,847,000,000	1.1%
38	Montana	347,000,000	0.2%
30	Nebraska	1,051,000,000	0.6%
34	Nevada	509,000,000	0.3%
40	New Hampshire	302,000,000	0.2%
44	New Jersey	200,000,000	0.1%
7	New Mexico	6,710,000,000	3.9%
3	New York	11,650,000,000	6.8%
31	North Carolina	1,006,000,000	0.6%
33	North Dakota	526,000,000	0.3%
11	Ohio	4,560,000,000	2.7%
27	Oklahoma	1,263,000,000	0.7%
16	Oregon	2,270,000,000	1.3%
4	Pennsylvania	10,062,000,000	5.9%
49	Rhode Island	19,600,000	0.0%
42	South Carolina	287,000,000	0.2%
26	South Dakota	1,347,000,000	0.8%
29	Tennessee	1,155,000,000	0.7%
9	Texas	6,009,000,000	3.5%
23	Utah	1,609,000,000	0.9%
15	Vermont	2,584,000,000	1.5%
22	Virginia	1,731,000,000	1.0%
10	Washington	5,416,000,000	3.2%
45	West Virginia	194,000,000	0.1%
2	Wisconsin	22,085,000,000	12.9%
48	Wyoming	63,400,000	0.0%

RANK ORDER

RANK	STATE	POUNDS	% of USA
1	California	36,465,000,000	21.3%
2	Wisconsin	22,085,000,000	12.9%
3	New York	11,650,000,000	6.8%
4	Pennsylvania	10,062,000,000	5.9%
5	Idaho	9,093,000,000	5.3%
6	Minnesota	8,102,000,000	4.7%
7	New Mexico	6,710,000,000	3.9%
8	Michigan	6,315,000,000	3.7%
9	Texas	6,009,000,000	3.5%
10	Washington	5,416,000,000	3.2%
11	Ohio	4,560,000,000	2.7%
12	Iowa	3,843,000,000	2.2%
13	Arizona	3,646,000,000	2.1%
14	Indiana	2,962,000,000	1.7%
15	Vermont	2,584,000,000	1.5%
16	Oregon	2,270,000,000	1.3%
17	Florida	2,253,000,000	1.3%
18	Kansas	2,216,000,000	1.3%
19	Colorado	2,184,000,000	1.3%
20	Illinois	1,978,000,000	1.2%
21	Missouri	1,847,000,000	1.1%
22	Virginia	1,731,000,000	1.0%
23	Utah	1,609,000,000	0.9%
24	Kentucky	1,423,000,000	0.8%
25	Georgia	1,416,000,000	0.8%
26	South Dakota	1,347,000,000	0.8%
27	Oklahoma	1,263,000,000	0.7%
28	Maryland	1,162,000,000	0.7%
29	Tennessee	1,155,000,000	0.7%
30	Nebraska	1,051,000,000	0.6%
31	North Carolina	1,006,000,000	0.6%
32	Maine	612,000,000	0.4%
33	North Dakota	526,000,000	0.3%
34	Nevada	509,000,000	0.3%
35	Louisiana	479,000,000	0.3%
36	Connecticut	392,000,000	0.2%
37	Mississippi	379,000,000	0.2%
38	Montana	347,000,000	0.2%
39	Arkansas	318,000,000	0.2%
40	New Hampshire	302,000,000	0.2%
41	Massachusetts	296,000,000	0.2%
42	South Carolina	287,000,000	0.2%
43	Alabama	245,000,000	0.1%
44	New Jersey	200,000,000	0.1%
45	West Virginia	194,000,000	0.1%
46	Delaware	127,500,000	0.1%
47	Hawaii	80,500,000	0.0%
48	Wyoming	63,400,000	0.0%
49	Rhode Island	19,600,000	0.0%
50	Alaska	14,600,000	0.0%
	District of Columbia	0	0.0%

Source: U.S. Department of Agriculture, National Agricultural Statistics Service
"Milk Production, Disposition and Income: 2004 Summary" (April 2005)
(http://usda.mannlib.cornell.edu/reports/nassr/dairy/pmp-bbm/)
*Excludes milk sucked by calves.

Milk Production per Milk Cow in 2004

National Average = 18,957 Pounds of Milk per Cow*

ALPHA ORDER

RANK	STATE	POUNDS
44	Alabama	14,412
50	Alaska	12,167
2	Arizona	22,788
46	Arkansas	13,250
5	California	21,139
4	Colorado	21,412
12	Connecticut	19,600
28	Delaware	17,230
36	Florida	16,326
31	Georgia	16,857
47	Hawaii	13,197
3	Idaho	21,446
17	Illinois	18,486
10	Indiana	19,747
9	Iowa	19,912
11	Kansas	19,611
48	Kentucky	12,936
49	Louisiana	12,605
19	Maine	18,000
38	Maryland	15,703
26	Massachusetts	17,412
6	Michigan	20,842
25	Minnesota	17,499
45	Mississippi	14,037
41	Missouri	15,139
13	Montana	19,278
28	Nebraska	17,230
8	Nevada	20,360
15	New Hampshire	18,875
33	New Jersey	16,667
7	New Mexico	20,583
23	New York	17,786
24	North Carolina	17,649
39	North Dakota	15,471
27	Ohio	17,338
37	Oklahoma	16,192
14	Oregon	18,917
20	Pennsylvania	17,904
35	Rhode Island	16,333
30	South Carolina	16,882
32	South Dakota	16,838
40	Tennessee	15,400
16	Texas	18,837
18	Utah	18,284
21	Vermont	17,821
34	Virginia	16,486
1	Washington	22,852
42	West Virginia	14,923
22	Wisconsin	17,796
43	Wyoming	14,744

RANK ORDER

RANK	STATE	POUNDS
1	Washington	22,852
2	Arizona	22,788
3	Idaho	21,446
4	Colorado	21,412
5	California	21,139
6	Michigan	20,842
7	New Mexico	20,583
8	Nevada	20,360
9	Iowa	19,912
10	Indiana	19,747
11	Kansas	19,611
12	Connecticut	19,600
13	Montana	19,278
14	Oregon	18,917
15	New Hampshire	18,875
16	Texas	18,837
17	Illinois	18,486
18	Utah	18,284
19	Maine	18,000
20	Pennsylvania	17,904
21	Vermont	17,821
22	Wisconsin	17,796
23	New York	17,786
24	North Carolina	17,649
25	Minnesota	17,499
26	Massachusetts	17,412
27	Ohio	17,338
28	Delaware	17,230
28	Nebraska	17,230
30	South Carolina	16,882
31	Georgia	16,857
32	South Dakota	16,838
33	New Jersey	16,667
34	Virginia	16,486
35	Rhode Island	16,333
36	Florida	16,326
37	Oklahoma	16,192
38	Maryland	15,703
39	North Dakota	15,471
40	Tennessee	15,400
41	Missouri	15,139
42	West Virginia	14,923
43	Wyoming	14,744
44	Alabama	14,412
45	Mississippi	14,037
46	Arkansas	13,250
47	Hawaii	13,197
48	Kentucky	12,936
49	Louisiana	12,605
50	Alaska	12,167

District of Columbia**   NA

Source: U.S. Department of Agriculture, National Agricultural Statistics Service
    "Milk Production, Disposition and Income: 2004 Summary" (April 2005)
        (http://usda.mannlib.cornell.edu/reports/nassr/dairy/pmp-bbm/)
*Excludes milk sucked by calves.
**Not applicable.

Hogs and Pigs on Farms in 2005

National Total = 61,197,000 Hogs and Pigs*

ALPHA ORDER					RANK ORDER			
RANK	STATE	HOGS AND PIGS	% of USA		RANK	STATE	HOGS AND PIGS	% of USA
26	Alabama	160,000	0.3%		1	Iowa	16,400,000	26.8%
50	Alaska	1,600	0.0%		2	North Carolina	9,800,000	16.0%
29	Arizona	142,000	0.2%		3	Minnesota	6,600,000	10.8%
22	Arkansas	270,000	0.4%		4	Illinois	4,000,000	6.5%
28	California	145,000	0.2%		5	Indiana	3,200,000	5.2%
15	Colorado	840,000	1.4%		6	Nebraska	2,850,000	4.7%
45	Connecticut	3,500	0.0%		7	Missouri	2,750,000	4.5%
38	Delaware	16,500	0.0%		8	Oklahoma	2,370,000	3.9%
36	Florida	20,000	0.0%		9	Kansas	1,780,000	2.9%
22	Georgia	270,000	0.4%		10	Ohio	1,550,000	2.5%
37	Hawaii	19,000	0.0%		11	South Dakota	1,480,000	2.4%
35	Idaho	21,000	0.0%		12	Pennsylvania	1,090,000	1.8%
4	Illinois	4,000,000	6.5%		13	Michigan	950,000	1.6%
5	Indiana	3,200,000	5.2%		14	Texas	930,000	1.5%
1	Iowa	16,400,000	26.8%		15	Colorado	840,000	1.4%
9	Kansas	1,780,000	2.9%		16	Utah	690,000	1.1%
20	Kentucky	370,000	0.6%		17	Virginia	490,000	0.8%
39	Louisiana	14,000	0.0%		18	Wisconsin	430,000	0.7%
43	Maine	5,000	0.0%		19	Mississippi	375,000	0.6%
32	Maryland	35,000	0.1%		20	Kentucky	370,000	0.6%
40	Massachusetts	13,000	0.0%		21	South Carolina	315,000	0.5%
13	Michigan	950,000	1.6%		22	Arkansas	270,000	0.4%
3	Minnesota	6,600,000	10.8%		22	Georgia	270,000	0.4%
19	Mississippi	375,000	0.6%		24	Tennessee	190,000	0.3%
7	Missouri	2,750,000	4.5%		25	Montana	175,000	0.3%
25	Montana	175,000	0.3%		26	Alabama	160,000	0.3%
6	Nebraska	2,850,000	4.7%		27	North Dakota	157,000	0.3%
44	Nevada	4,000	0.0%		28	California	145,000	0.2%
46	New Hampshire	3,200	0.0%		29	Arizona	142,000	0.2%
41	New Jersey	9,000	0.0%		30	Wyoming	113,000	0.2%
48	New Mexico	2,000	0.0%		31	New York	83,000	0.1%
31	New York	83,000	0.1%		32	Maryland	35,000	0.1%
2	North Carolina	9,800,000	16.0%		33	Washington	30,000	0.0%
27	North Dakota	157,000	0.3%		34	Oregon	23,000	0.0%
10	Ohio	1,550,000	2.5%		35	Idaho	21,000	0.0%
8	Oklahoma	2,370,000	3.9%		36	Florida	20,000	0.0%
34	Oregon	23,000	0.0%		37	Hawaii	19,000	0.0%
12	Pennsylvania	1,090,000	1.8%		38	Delaware	16,500	0.0%
49	Rhode Island	1,800	0.0%		39	Louisiana	14,000	0.0%
21	South Carolina	315,000	0.5%		40	Massachusetts	13,000	0.0%
11	South Dakota	1,480,000	2.4%		41	New Jersey	9,000	0.0%
24	Tennessee	190,000	0.3%		42	West Virginia	8,000	0.0%
14	Texas	930,000	1.5%		43	Maine	5,000	0.0%
16	Utah	690,000	1.1%		44	Nevada	4,000	0.0%
47	Vermont	2,300	0.0%		45	Connecticut	3,500	0.0%
17	Virginia	490,000	0.8%		46	New Hampshire	3,200	0.0%
33	Washington	30,000	0.0%		47	Vermont	2,300	0.0%
42	West Virginia	8,000	0.0%		48	New Mexico	2,000	0.0%
18	Wisconsin	430,000	0.7%		49	Rhode Island	1,800	0.0%
30	Wyoming	113,000	0.2%		50	Alaska	1,600	0.0%
						District of Columbia	0	0.0%

Source: U.S. Department of Agriculture, National Agricultural Statistics Service
    "Quarterly Hogs and Pigs" (http://usda.mannlib.cornell.edu/reports/nassr/livestock/php-bb/)
*As of December 1, 2005.

Chickens in 2004 (Leading States Only)

National Total = 8,505,200,000 Chickens*

ALPHA ORDER

RANK	STATE	CHICKENS	% of USA
3	Alabama	1,052,000,000	12.4%
NA	Alaska***	NA	NA
NA	Arizona***	NA	NA
2	Arkansas	1,241,500,000	14.6%
NA	California**	NA	NA
NA	Colorado***	NA	NA
NA	Connecticut***	NA	NA
11	Delaware	240,700,000	2.8%
16	Florid	78,500,000	0.9%
1	Georgia	1,298,900,000	15.3%
NA	Hawaii**	NA	NA
NA	Idaho***	NA	NA
NA	Illinois***	NA	NA
NA	Indiana**	NA	NA
NA	Iowa**	NA	NA
NA	Kansas***	NA	NA
7	Kentucky	290,800,000	3.4%
NA	Louisiana**	NA	NA
NA	Maine***	NA	NA
8	Maryland	284,600,000	3.3%
NA	Massachusetts***	NA	NA
NA	Michigan**	NA	NA
17	Minnesota	46,300,000	0.5%
4	Mississippi	827,800,000	9.7%
NA	Missouri**	NA	NA
NA	Montana***	NA	NA
20	Nebraska	4,300,000	0.1%
NA	Nevada***	NA	NA
NA	New Hampshire***	NA	NA
NA	New Jersey***	NA	NA
NA	New Mexico***	NA	NA
21	New York	2,600,000	0.0%
5	North Carolina	720,200,000	8.5%
NA	North Dakota***	NA	NA
18	Ohio	41,600,000	0.5%
10	Oklahoma	243,800,000	2.9%
NA	Oregon**	NA	NA
14	Pennsylvania	133,500,000	1.6%
NA	Rhode Island***	NA	NA
12	South Carolina	204,500,000	2.4%
NA	South Dakota***	NA	NA
13	Tennessee	195,900,000	2.3%
6	Texas	620,700,000	7.3%
NA	Utah***	NA	NA
NA	Vermont***	NA	NA
9	Virginia	263,000,000	3.1%
NA	Washington**	NA	NA
15	West Virginia	86,400,000	1.0%
19	Wisconsin	33,800,000	0.4%
NA	Wyoming***	NA	NA

RANK ORDER

RANK	STATE	CHICKENS	% of USA
1	Georgia	1,298,900,000	15.3%
2	Arkansas	1,241,500,000	14.6%
3	Alabama	1,052,000,000	12.4%
4	Mississippi	827,800,000	9.7%
5	North Carolina	720,200,000	8.5%
6	Texas	620,700,000	7.3%
7	Kentucky	290,800,000	3.4%
8	Maryland	284,600,000	3.3%
9	Virginia	263,000,000	3.1%
10	Oklahoma	243,800,000	2.9%
11	Delaware	240,700,000	2.8%
12	South Carolina	204,500,000	2.4%
13	Tennessee	195,900,000	2.3%
14	Pennsylvania	133,500,000	1.6%
15	West Virginia	86,400,000	1.0%
16	Florid	78,500,000	0.9%
17	Minnesota	46,300,000	0.5%
18	Ohio	41,600,000	0.5%
19	Wisconsin	33,800,000	0.4%
20	Nebraska	4,300,000	0.1%
21	New York	2,600,000	0.0%
NA	Alaska***	NA	NA
NA	Arizona***	NA	NA
NA	California**	NA	NA
NA	Colorado***	NA	NA
NA	Connecticut***	NA	NA
NA	Hawaii**	NA	NA
NA	Idaho***	NA	NA
NA	Illinois***	NA	NA
NA	Indiana**	NA	NA
NA	Iowa**	NA	NA
NA	Kansas***	NA	NA
NA	Louisiana**	NA	NA
NA	Maine***	NA	NA
NA	Massachusetts***	NA	NA
NA	Michigan**	NA	NA
NA	Missouri**	NA	NA
NA	Montana***	NA	NA
NA	Nevada***	NA	NA
NA	New Hampshire***	NA	NA
NA	New Jersey***	NA	NA
NA	New Mexico***	NA	NA
NA	North Dakota***	NA	NA
NA	Oregon**	NA	NA
NA	Rhode Island***	NA	NA
NA	South Dakota***	NA	NA
NA	Utah***	NA	NA
NA	Vermont***	NA	NA
NA	Washington**	NA	NA
NA	Wyoming***	NA	NA
	District of Columbia	0	0.0%

Source: U.S. Department of Agriculture, National Agricultural Statistics Service
    "Poultry - Production and Value: 2004 Summary"
        (http://usda.mannlib.cornell.edu/reports/nassr/poultry/pbh-bbp/)
*Broilers. Total includes numbers for states not shown separately but excludes states producing less than 500,000 birds. **These states produced a combined total of 829,250,000 chickens. They are combined to avoid disclosing individual operations. National total does not include chickens used for egg production. ***Not available.

Eggs Produced in 2004

National Total = 89,131,000,000 Eggs

<table>
<tr><th colspan="4">ALPHA ORDER</th></tr>
<tr><th>RANK</th><th>STATE</th><th>EGGS</th><th>% of USA</th></tr>
<tr><td>13</td><td>Alabama</td><td>2,099,000,000</td><td>2.4%</td></tr>
<tr><td>NA</td><td>Alaska*</td><td>NA</td><td>NA</td></tr>
<tr><td>NA</td><td>Arizona*</td><td>NA</td><td>NA</td></tr>
<tr><td>8</td><td>Arkansas</td><td>3,565,000,000</td><td>4.0%</td></tr>
<tr><td>5</td><td>California</td><td>5,380,000,000</td><td>6.0%</td></tr>
<tr><td>22</td><td>Colorado</td><td>1,105,000,000</td><td>1.2%</td></tr>
<tr><td>29</td><td>Connecticut</td><td>818,000,000</td><td>0.9%</td></tr>
<tr><td>NA</td><td>Delaware*</td><td>NA</td><td>NA</td></tr>
<tr><td>10</td><td>Florida</td><td>3,068,000,000</td><td>3.4%</td></tr>
<tr><td>6</td><td>Georgia</td><td>5,038,000,000</td><td>5.7%</td></tr>
<tr><td>37</td><td>Hawaii</td><td>118,500,000</td><td>0.1%</td></tr>
<tr><td>36</td><td>Idaho</td><td>238,000,000</td><td>0.3%</td></tr>
<tr><td>23</td><td>Illinois</td><td>1,044,000,000</td><td>1.2%</td></tr>
<tr><td>4</td><td>Indiana</td><td>6,256,000,000</td><td>7.0%</td></tr>
<tr><td>1</td><td>Iowa</td><td>11,613,000,000</td><td>13.0%</td></tr>
<tr><td>NA</td><td>Kansas*</td><td>NA</td><td>NA</td></tr>
<tr><td>19</td><td>Kentucky</td><td>1,231,000,000</td><td>1.4%</td></tr>
<tr><td>33</td><td>Louisiana</td><td>465,000,000</td><td>0.5%</td></tr>
<tr><td>24</td><td>Maine</td><td>957,000,000</td><td>1.1%</td></tr>
<tr><td>27</td><td>Maryland</td><td>843,000,000</td><td>0.9%</td></tr>
<tr><td>39</td><td>Massachusetts</td><td>74,000,000</td><td>0.1%</td></tr>
<tr><td>14</td><td>Michigan</td><td>2,009,000,000</td><td>2.3%</td></tr>
<tr><td>11</td><td>Minnesota</td><td>2,930,000,000</td><td>3.3%</td></tr>
<tr><td>16</td><td>Mississippi</td><td>1,606,000,000</td><td>1.8%</td></tr>
<tr><td>15</td><td>Missouri</td><td>1,865,000,000</td><td>2.1%</td></tr>
<tr><td>38</td><td>Montana</td><td>107,000,000</td><td>0.1%</td></tr>
<tr><td>9</td><td>Nebraska</td><td>3,174,000,000</td><td>3.6%</td></tr>
<tr><td>NA</td><td>Nevada*</td><td>NA</td><td>NA</td></tr>
<tr><td>41</td><td>New Hampshire</td><td>43,000,000</td><td>0.0%</td></tr>
<tr><td>32</td><td>New Jersey</td><td>558,000,000</td><td>0.6%</td></tr>
<tr><td>NA</td><td>New Mexico*</td><td>NA</td><td>NA</td></tr>
<tr><td>21</td><td>New York</td><td>1,163,000,000</td><td>1.3%</td></tr>
<tr><td>12</td><td>North Carolina</td><td>2,522,000,000</td><td>2.8%</td></tr>
<tr><td>NA</td><td>North Dakota*</td><td>NA</td><td>NA</td></tr>
<tr><td>2</td><td>Ohio</td><td>7,355,000,000</td><td>8.3%</td></tr>
<tr><td>25</td><td>Oklahoma</td><td>937,000,000</td><td>1.1%</td></tr>
<tr><td>29</td><td>Oregon</td><td>818,000,000</td><td>0.9%</td></tr>
<tr><td>3</td><td>Pennsylvania</td><td>6,585,000,000</td><td>7.4%</td></tr>
<tr><td>NA</td><td>Rhode Island*</td><td>NA</td><td>NA</td></tr>
<tr><td>17</td><td>South Carolina</td><td>1,351,000,000</td><td>1.5%</td></tr>
<tr><td>26</td><td>South Dakota</td><td>933,000,000</td><td>1.0%</td></tr>
<tr><td>34</td><td>Tennessee</td><td>319,000,000</td><td>0.4%</td></tr>
<tr><td>7</td><td>Texas</td><td>4,825,000,000</td><td>5.4%</td></tr>
<tr><td>28</td><td>Utah</td><td>831,000,000</td><td>0.9%</td></tr>
<tr><td>40</td><td>Vermont</td><td>55,000,000</td><td>0.1%</td></tr>
<tr><td>31</td><td>Virginia</td><td>761,000,000</td><td>0.9%</td></tr>
<tr><td>18</td><td>Washington</td><td>1,332,000,000</td><td>1.5%</td></tr>
<tr><td>35</td><td>West Virginia</td><td>273,000,000</td><td>0.3%</td></tr>
<tr><td>20</td><td>Wisconsin</td><td>1,206,000,000</td><td>1.4%</td></tr>
<tr><td>42</td><td>Wyoming</td><td>3,600,000</td><td>0.0%</td></tr>
</table>

<table>
<tr><th colspan="4">RANK ORDER</th></tr>
<tr><th>RANK</th><th>STATE</th><th>EGGS</th><th>% of USA</th></tr>
<tr><td>1</td><td>Iowa</td><td>11,613,000,000</td><td>13.0%</td></tr>
<tr><td>2</td><td>Ohio</td><td>7,355,000,000</td><td>8.3%</td></tr>
<tr><td>3</td><td>Pennsylvania</td><td>6,585,000,000</td><td>7.4%</td></tr>
<tr><td>4</td><td>Indiana</td><td>6,256,000,000</td><td>7.0%</td></tr>
<tr><td>5</td><td>California</td><td>5,380,000,000</td><td>6.0%</td></tr>
<tr><td>6</td><td>Georgia</td><td>5,038,000,000</td><td>5.7%</td></tr>
<tr><td>7</td><td>Texas</td><td>4,825,000,000</td><td>5.4%</td></tr>
<tr><td>8</td><td>Arkansas</td><td>3,565,000,000</td><td>4.0%</td></tr>
<tr><td>9</td><td>Nebraska</td><td>3,174,000,000</td><td>3.6%</td></tr>
<tr><td>10</td><td>Florida</td><td>3,068,000,000</td><td>3.4%</td></tr>
<tr><td>11</td><td>Minnesota</td><td>2,930,000,000</td><td>3.3%</td></tr>
<tr><td>12</td><td>North Carolina</td><td>2,522,000,000</td><td>2.8%</td></tr>
<tr><td>13</td><td>Alabama</td><td>2,099,000,000</td><td>2.4%</td></tr>
<tr><td>14</td><td>Michigan</td><td>2,009,000,000</td><td>2.3%</td></tr>
<tr><td>15</td><td>Missouri</td><td>1,865,000,000</td><td>2.1%</td></tr>
<tr><td>16</td><td>Mississippi</td><td>1,606,000,000</td><td>1.8%</td></tr>
<tr><td>17</td><td>South Carolina</td><td>1,351,000,000</td><td>1.5%</td></tr>
<tr><td>18</td><td>Washington</td><td>1,332,000,000</td><td>1.5%</td></tr>
<tr><td>19</td><td>Kentucky</td><td>1,231,000,000</td><td>1.4%</td></tr>
<tr><td>20</td><td>Wisconsin</td><td>1,206,000,000</td><td>1.4%</td></tr>
<tr><td>21</td><td>New York</td><td>1,163,000,000</td><td>1.3%</td></tr>
<tr><td>22</td><td>Colorado</td><td>1,105,000,000</td><td>1.2%</td></tr>
<tr><td>23</td><td>Illinois</td><td>1,044,000,000</td><td>1.2%</td></tr>
<tr><td>24</td><td>Maine</td><td>957,000,000</td><td>1.1%</td></tr>
<tr><td>25</td><td>Oklahoma</td><td>937,000,000</td><td>1.1%</td></tr>
<tr><td>26</td><td>South Dakota</td><td>933,000,000</td><td>1.0%</td></tr>
<tr><td>27</td><td>Maryland</td><td>843,000,000</td><td>0.9%</td></tr>
<tr><td>28</td><td>Utah</td><td>831,000,000</td><td>0.9%</td></tr>
<tr><td>29</td><td>Connecticut</td><td>818,000,000</td><td>0.9%</td></tr>
<tr><td>29</td><td>Oregon</td><td>818,000,000</td><td>0.9%</td></tr>
<tr><td>31</td><td>Virginia</td><td>761,000,000</td><td>0.9%</td></tr>
<tr><td>32</td><td>New Jersey</td><td>558,000,000</td><td>0.6%</td></tr>
<tr><td>33</td><td>Louisiana</td><td>465,000,000</td><td>0.5%</td></tr>
<tr><td>34</td><td>Tennessee</td><td>319,000,000</td><td>0.4%</td></tr>
<tr><td>35</td><td>West Virginia</td><td>273,000,000</td><td>0.3%</td></tr>
<tr><td>36</td><td>Idaho</td><td>238,000,000</td><td>0.3%</td></tr>
<tr><td>37</td><td>Hawaii</td><td>118,500,000</td><td>0.1%</td></tr>
<tr><td>38</td><td>Montana</td><td>107,000,000</td><td>0.1%</td></tr>
<tr><td>39</td><td>Massachusetts</td><td>74,000,000</td><td>0.1%</td></tr>
<tr><td>40</td><td>Vermont</td><td>55,000,000</td><td>0.1%</td></tr>
<tr><td>41</td><td>New Hampshire</td><td>43,000,000</td><td>0.0%</td></tr>
<tr><td>42</td><td>Wyoming</td><td>3,600,000</td><td>0.0%</td></tr>
<tr><td>NA</td><td>Alaska*</td><td>NA</td><td>NA</td></tr>
<tr><td>NA</td><td>Arizona*</td><td>NA</td><td>NA</td></tr>
<tr><td>NA</td><td>Delaware*</td><td>NA</td><td>NA</td></tr>
<tr><td>NA</td><td>Kansas*</td><td>NA</td><td>NA</td></tr>
<tr><td>NA</td><td>Nevada*</td><td>NA</td><td>NA</td></tr>
<tr><td>NA</td><td>New Mexico*</td><td>NA</td><td>NA</td></tr>
<tr><td>NA</td><td>North Dakota*</td><td>NA</td><td>NA</td></tr>
<tr><td>NA</td><td>Rhode Island*</td><td>NA</td><td>NA</td></tr>
<tr><td></td><td>District of Columbia</td><td>0</td><td>0.0%</td></tr>
</table>

Source: U.S. Department of Agriculture, National Agricultural Statistics Service
*   "Poultry - Production and Value: 2004 Summary"*
*   (http://usda.mannlib.cornell.edu/reports/nassr/poultry/pbh-bbp/)*
These states produced a combined 1,657,000,000 eggs. They are combined to avoid disclosing individual operations.

II. CRIME AND LAW ENFORCEMENT

Crimes in 2004

National Total = 11,695,264 Crimes*

ALPHA ORDER				RANK ORDER			
RANK	STATE	CRIMES	% of USA	RANK	STATE	CRIMES	% of USA
21	Alabama	201,664	1.7%	1	California	1,425,264	12.2%
46	Alaska	26,331	0.2%	2	Texas	1,132,256	9.7%
11	Arizona	335,699	2.9%	3	Florida	850,895	7.3%
28	Arkansas	124,201	1.1%	4	New York	507,648	4.3%
1	California	1,425,264	12.2%	5	Illinois	474,096	4.1%
22	Colorado	197,527	1.7%	6	Ohio	460,073	3.9%
34	Connecticut	102,078	0.9%	7	Georgia	416,873	3.6%
43	Delaware	30,992	0.3%	8	North Carolina	393,572	3.4%
3	Florida	850,895	7.3%	9	Michigan	358,785	3.1%
7	Georgia	416,873	3.6%	10	Pennsylvania	350,609	3.0%
38	Hawaii	63,738	0.5%	11	Arizona	335,699	2.9%
40	Idaho	42,345	0.4%	12	Washington	322,167	2.8%
5	Illinois	474,096	4.1%	13	Tennessee	295,147	2.5%
17	Indiana	232,223	2.0%	14	Missouri	252,855	2.2%
35	Iowa	93,839	0.8%	15	New Jersey	242,256	2.1%
29	Kansas	118,939	1.0%	16	Maryland	241,258	2.1%
30	Kentucky	115,361	1.0%	17	Indiana	232,223	2.0%
18	Louisiana	227,997	1.9%	18	Louisiana	227,997	1.9%
42	Maine	33,104	0.3%	19	South Carolina	222,035	1.9%
16	Maryland	241,258	2.1%	20	Virginia	220,227	1.9%
23	Massachusetts	187,262	1.6%	21	Alabama	201,664	1.7%
9	Michigan	358,785	3.1%	22	Colorado	197,527	1.7%
25	Minnesota	168,770	1.4%	23	Massachusetts	187,262	1.6%
32	Mississippi	109,548	0.9%	24	Oregon	177,199	1.5%
14	Missouri	252,855	2.2%	25	Minnesota	168,770	1.4%
44	Montana	29,938	0.3%	26	Oklahoma	167,107	1.4%
37	Nebraska	66,905	0.6%	27	Wisconsin	158,258	1.4%
31	Nevada	112,594	1.0%	28	Arkansas	124,201	1.1%
45	New Hampshire	28,681	0.2%	29	Kansas	118,939	1.0%
15	New Jersey	242,256	2.1%	30	Kentucky	115,361	1.0%
36	New Mexico	92,976	0.8%	31	Nevada	112,594	1.0%
4	New York	507,648	4.3%	32	Mississippi	109,548	0.9%
8	North Carolina	393,572	3.4%	33	Utah	103,246	0.9%
50	North Dakota	12,662	0.1%	34	Connecticut	102,078	0.9%
6	Ohio	460,073	3.9%	35	Iowa	93,839	0.8%
26	Oklahoma	167,107	1.4%	36	New Mexico	92,976	0.8%
24	Oregon	177,199	1.5%	37	Nebraska	66,905	0.6%
10	Pennsylvania	350,609	3.0%	38	Hawaii	63,738	0.5%
41	Rhode Island	33,839	0.3%	39	West Virginia	50,421	0.4%
19	South Carolina	222,035	1.9%	40	Idaho	42,345	0.4%
48	South Dakota	16,227	0.1%	41	Rhode Island	33,839	0.3%
13	Tennessee	295,147	2.5%	42	Maine	33,104	0.3%
2	Texas	1,132,256	9.7%	43	Delaware	30,992	0.3%
33	Utah	103,246	0.9%	44	Montana	29,938	0.3%
49	Vermont	15,039	0.1%	45	New Hampshire	28,681	0.2%
20	Virginia	220,227	1.9%	46	Alaska	26,331	0.2%
12	Washington	322,167	2.8%	47	Wyoming	18,052	0.2%
39	West Virginia	50,421	0.4%	48	South Dakota	16,227	0.1%
27	Wisconsin	158,258	1.4%	49	Vermont	15,039	0.1%
47	Wyoming	18,052	0.2%	50	North Dakota	12,662	0.1%
					District of Columbia	34,486	0.3%

Source: Morgan Quitno Press using data from Federal Bureau of Investigation
   "Crime in the United States 2004" (Uniform Crime Reports, October 17, 2005)
Includes murder, rape, robbery, aggravated assault, burglary, larceny-theft and motor vehicle theft.

Percent Change in Number of Crimes: 2003 to 2004

National Percent Change = 1.1% Decrease*

ALPHA ORDER

RANK	STATE	PERCENT CHANGE
18	Alabama	0.0
46	Alaska	(6.8)
30	Arizona	(2.1)
1	Arkansas	11.4
16	California	0.3
10	Colorado	1.1
28	Connecticut	(1.9)
48	Delaware	(7.4)
38	Florida	(3.5)
8	Georgia	1.9
49	Hawaii	(8.0)
31	Idaho	(2.4)
32	Illinois	(2.5)
11	Indiana	1.0
29	Iowa	(2.0)
22	Kansas	(1.0)
9	Kentucky	1.5
6	Louisiana	2.6
25	Maine	(1.2)
36	Maryland	(2.8)
40	Massachusetts	(3.9)
45	Michigan	(6.1)
26	Minnesota	(1.3)
43	Mississippi	(5.7)
37	Missouri	(3.4)
44	Montana	(5.8)
42	Nebraska	(4.8)
7	Nevada	2.4
11	New Hampshire	1.0
39	New Jersey	(3.8)
3	New Mexico	4.1
35	New York	(2.7)
23	North Carolina	(1.1)
50	North Dakota	(8.7)
11	Ohio	1.0
23	Oklahoma	(1.1)
27	Oregon	(1.8)
17	Pennsylvania	0.2
41	Rhode Island	(4.2)
15	South Carolina	0.4
33	South Dakota	(2.6)
20	Tennessee	(0.6)
20	Texas	(0.6)
33	Utah	(2.6)
4	Vermont	3.6
19	Virginia	(0.3)
5	Washington	3.0
2	West Virginia	7.3
46	Wisconsin	(6.8)
14	Wyoming	0.5

RANK ORDER

RANK	STATE	PERCENT CHANGE
1	Arkansas	11.4
2	West Virginia	7.3
3	New Mexico	4.1
4	Vermont	3.6
5	Washington	3.0
6	Louisiana	2.6
7	Nevada	2.4
8	Georgia	1.9
9	Kentucky	1.5
10	Colorado	1.1
11	Indiana	1.0
11	New Hampshire	1.0
11	Ohio	1.0
14	Wyoming	0.5
15	South Carolina	0.4
16	California	0.3
17	Pennsylvania	0.2
18	Alabama	0.0
19	Virginia	(0.3)
20	Tennessee	(0.6)
20	Texas	(0.6)
22	Kansas	(1.0)
23	North Carolina	(1.1)
23	Oklahoma	(1.1)
25	Maine	(1.2)
26	Minnesota	(1.3)
27	Oregon	(1.8)
28	Connecticut	(1.9)
29	Iowa	(2.0)
30	Arizona	(2.1)
31	Idaho	(2.4)
32	Illinois	(2.5)
33	South Dakota	(2.6)
33	Utah	(2.6)
35	New York	(2.7)
36	Maryland	(2.8)
37	Missouri	(3.4)
38	Florida	(3.5)
39	New Jersey	(3.8)
40	Massachusetts	(3.9)
41	Rhode Island	(4.2)
42	Nebraska	(4.8)
43	Mississippi	(5.7)
44	Montana	(5.8)
45	Michigan	(6.1)
46	Alaska	(6.8)
46	Wisconsin	(6.8)
48	Delaware	(7.4)
49	Hawaii	(8.0)
50	North Dakota	(8.7)

| | District of Columbia | (17.4) |

Source: Morgan Quitno Press using data from Federal Bureau of Investigation
    "Crime in the United States 2004" (Uniform Crime Reports, October 17, 2005)
Includes murder, rape, robbery, aggravated assault, burglary, larceny-theft and motor vehicle theft.

Crime Rate in 2004

National Rate = 3,982.6 Crimes per 100,000 Population*

ALPHA ORDER

RANK	STATE	RATE
16	Alabama	4,451.6
22	Alaska	4,017.3
1	Arizona	5,844.6
15	Arkansas	4,512.1
24	California	3,970.8
21	Colorado	4,292.8
39	Connecticut	2,913.5
27	Delaware	3,732.3
9	Florida	4,891.0
13	Georgia	4,721.4
5	Hawaii	5,047.2
36	Idaho	3,039.3
28	Illinois	3,729.0
29	Indiana	3,723.0
34	Iowa	3,176.2
18	Kansas	4,348.0
43	Kentucky	2,782.6
4	Louisiana	5,048.9
46	Maine	2,513.1
19	Maryland	4,340.7
38	Massachusetts	2,918.5
31	Michigan	3,547.8
32	Minnesota	3,308.6
26	Mississippi	3,773.6
17	Missouri	4,394.0
33	Montana	3,230.0
25	Nebraska	3,829.3
11	Nevada	4,822.5
48	New Hampshire	2,207.1
42	New Jersey	2,784.9
10	New Mexico	4,885.0
45	New York	2,640.2
14	North Carolina	4,608.0
50	North Dakota	1,996.0
23	Ohio	4,015.0
12	Oklahoma	4,742.6
8	Oregon	4,929.6
41	Pennsylvania	2,826.1
35	Rhode Island	3,131.5
2	South Carolina	5,289.0
49	South Dakota	2,105.0
7	Tennessee	5,001.7
6	Texas	5,034.5
20	Utah	4,321.6
47	Vermont	2,420.2
37	Virginia	2,952.2
3	Washington	5,193.0
44	West Virginia	2,777.4
40	Wisconsin	2,872.7
30	Wyoming	3,563.9

RANK ORDER

RANK	STATE	RATE
1	Arizona	5,844.6
2	South Carolina	5,289.0
3	Washington	5,193.0
4	Louisiana	5,048.9
5	Hawaii	5,047.2
6	Texas	5,034.5
7	Tennessee	5,001.7
8	Oregon	4,929.6
9	Florida	4,891.0
10	New Mexico	4,885.0
11	Nevada	4,822.5
12	Oklahoma	4,742.6
13	Georgia	4,721.4
14	North Carolina	4,608.0
15	Arkansas	4,512.1
16	Alabama	4,451.6
17	Missouri	4,394.0
18	Kansas	4,348.0
19	Maryland	4,340.7
20	Utah	4,321.6
21	Colorado	4,292.8
22	Alaska	4,017.3
23	Ohio	4,015.0
24	California	3,970.8
25	Nebraska	3,829.3
26	Mississippi	3,773.6
27	Delaware	3,732.3
28	Illinois	3,729.0
29	Indiana	3,723.0
30	Wyoming	3,563.9
31	Michigan	3,547.8
32	Minnesota	3,308.6
33	Montana	3,230.0
34	Iowa	3,176.2
35	Rhode Island	3,131.5
36	Idaho	3,039.3
37	Virginia	2,952.2
38	Massachusetts	2,918.5
39	Connecticut	2,913.5
40	Wisconsin	2,872.7
41	Pennsylvania	2,826.1
42	New Jersey	2,784.9
43	Kentucky	2,782.6
44	West Virginia	2,777.4
45	New York	2,640.2
46	Maine	2,513.1
47	Vermont	2,420.2
48	New Hampshire	2,207.1
49	South Dakota	2,105.0
50	North Dakota	1,996.0
	District of Columbia	6,230.3

Source: Morgan Quitno Press using data from Federal Bureau of Investigation
    "Crime in the United States 2004" (Uniform Crime Reports, October 17, 2005)
*Includes murder, rape, robbery, aggravated assault, burglary, larceny-theft and motor vehicle theft.

Percent Change in Crime Rate: 2003 to 2004

National Percent Change = 2.1% Decrease*

ALPHA ORDER				RANK ORDER		
RANK	STATE	PERCENT CHANGE		RANK	STATE	PERCENT CHANGE
15	Alabama	(0.5)		1	Arkansas	10.4
47	Alaska	(7.9)		2	West Virginia	7.1
40	Arizona	(4.9)		3	Vermont	3.3
1	Arkansas	10.4		4	New Mexico	2.7
17	California	(0.9)		5	Louisiana	2.1
12	Colorado	(0.1)		6	Washington	1.8
25	Connecticut	(2.3)		7	Kentucky	0.9
48	Delaware	(8.8)		8	Ohio	0.8
42	Florida	(5.7)		9	Indiana	0.4
10	Georgia	0.2		10	Georgia	0.2
50	Hawaii	(9.0)		10	New Hampshire	0.2
37	Idaho	(4.3)		12	Colorado	(0.1)
31	Illinois	(3.0)		12	Pennsylvania	(0.1)
9	Indiana	0.4		14	Wyoming	(0.4)
27	Iowa	(2.4)		15	Alabama	(0.5)
18	Kansas	(1.4)		16	South Carolina	(0.7)
7	Kentucky	0.9		17	California	(0.9)
5	Louisiana	2.1		18	Kansas	(1.4)
23	Maine	(1.8)		19	Nevada	(1.6)
33	Maryland	(3.6)		19	Oklahoma	(1.6)
34	Massachusetts	(3.9)		19	Tennessee	(1.6)
43	Michigan	(6.4)		19	Virginia	(1.6)
24	Minnesota	(2.0)		23	Maine	(1.8)
43	Mississippi	(6.4)		24	Minnesota	(2.0)
34	Missouri	(3.9)		25	Connecticut	(2.3)
45	Montana	(6.7)		25	Texas	(2.3)
41	Nebraska	(5.3)		27	Iowa	(2.4)
19	Nevada	(1.6)		28	North Carolina	(2.5)
10	New Hampshire	0.2		29	Oregon	(2.6)
38	New Jersey	(4.4)		30	New York	(2.7)
4	New Mexico	2.7		31	Illinois	(3.0)
30	New York	(2.7)		32	South Dakota	(3.3)
28	North Carolina	(2.5)		33	Maryland	(3.6)
49	North Dakota	(8.9)		34	Massachusetts	(3.9)
8	Ohio	0.8		34	Missouri	(3.9)
19	Oklahoma	(1.6)		36	Utah	(4.1)
29	Oregon	(2.6)		37	Idaho	(4.3)
12	Pennsylvania	(0.1)		38	New Jersey	(4.4)
39	Rhode Island	(4.6)		39	Rhode Island	(4.6)
16	South Carolina	(0.7)		40	Arizona	(4.9)
32	South Dakota	(3.3)		41	Nebraska	(5.3)
19	Tennessee	(1.6)		42	Florida	(5.7)
25	Texas	(2.3)		43	Michigan	(6.4)
36	Utah	(4.1)		43	Mississippi	(6.4)
3	Vermont	3.3		45	Montana	(6.7)
19	Virginia	(1.6)		46	Wisconsin	(7.4)
6	Washington	1.8		47	Alaska	(7.9)
2	West Virginia	7.1		48	Delaware	(8.8)
46	Wisconsin	(7.4)		49	North Dakota	(8.9)
14	Wyoming	(0.4)		50	Hawaii	(9.0)

District of Columbia (16.8)

Source: Morgan Quitno Press using data from Federal Bureau of Investigation
"Crime in the United States 2004" (Uniform Crime Reports, October 17, 2005)
*Includes murder, rape, robbery, aggravated assault, burglary, larceny-theft and motor vehicle theft.

Violent Crimes in 2004

National Total = 1,367,009 Violent Crimes*

ALPHA ORDER

RANK ORDER

RANK	STATE	CRIMES	% of USA
22	Alabama	19,324	1.4%
40	Alaska	4,159	0.3%
16	Arizona	28,952	2.1%
27	Arkansas	13,737	1.0%
1	California	198,070	14.5%
24	Colorado	17,185	1.3%
33	Connecticut	10,032	0.7%
39	Delaware	4,720	0.3%
2	Florida	123,754	9.1%
9	Georgia	40,217	2.9%
42	Hawaii	3,213	0.2%
41	Idaho	3,412	0.2%
5	Illinois	69,026	5.0%
21	Indiana	20,294	1.5%
35	Iowa	8,003	0.6%
31	Kansas	10,245	0.7%
32	Kentucky	10,152	0.7%
17	Louisiana	28,844	2.1%
46	Maine	1,364	0.1%
11	Maryland	38,932	2.8%
15	Massachusetts	29,437	2.2%
7	Michigan	49,577	3.6%
26	Minnesota	13,751	1.0%
34	Mississippi	8,568	0.6%
18	Missouri	28,226	2.1%
43	Montana	2,723	0.2%
37	Nebraska	5,393	0.4%
25	Nevada	14,379	1.1%
45	New Hampshire	2,170	0.2%
14	New Jersey	30,943	2.3%
28	New Mexico	13,081	1.0%
4	New York	84,914	6.2%
12	North Carolina	38,244	2.8%
50	North Dakota	504	0.0%
10	Ohio	39,163	2.9%
23	Oklahoma	17,635	1.3%
30	Oregon	10,724	0.8%
6	Pennsylvania	50,998	3.7%
44	Rhode Island	2,673	0.2%
13	South Carolina	32,922	2.4%
47	South Dakota	1,322	0.1%
8	Tennessee	41,024	3.0%
3	Texas	121,554	8.9%
36	Utah	5,639	0.4%
49	Vermont	696	0.1%
20	Virginia	20,559	1.5%
19	Washington	21,330	1.6%
38	West Virginia	4,924	0.4%
29	Wisconsin	11,548	0.8%
48	Wyoming	1,163	0.1%

RANK	STATE	CRIMES	% of USA
1	California	198,070	14.5%
2	Florida	123,754	9.1%
3	Texas	121,554	8.9%
4	New York	84,914	6.2%
5	Illinois	69,026	5.0%
6	Pennsylvania	50,998	3.7%
7	Michigan	49,577	3.6%
8	Tennessee	41,024	3.0%
9	Georgia	40,217	2.9%
10	Ohio	39,163	2.9%
11	Maryland	38,932	2.8%
12	North Carolina	38,244	2.8%
13	South Carolina	32,922	2.4%
14	New Jersey	30,943	2.3%
15	Massachusetts	29,437	2.2%
16	Arizona	28,952	2.1%
17	Louisiana	28,844	2.1%
18	Missouri	28,226	2.1%
19	Washington	21,330	1.6%
20	Virginia	20,559	1.5%
21	Indiana	20,294	1.5%
22	Alabama	19,324	1.4%
23	Oklahoma	17,635	1.3%
24	Colorado	17,185	1.3%
25	Nevada	14,379	1.1%
26	Minnesota	13,751	1.0%
27	Arkansas	13,737	1.0%
28	New Mexico	13,081	1.0%
29	Wisconsin	11,548	0.8%
30	Oregon	10,724	0.8%
31	Kansas	10,245	0.7%
32	Kentucky	10,152	0.7%
33	Connecticut	10,032	0.7%
34	Mississippi	8,568	0.6%
35	Iowa	8,003	0.6%
36	Utah	5,639	0.4%
37	Nebraska	5,393	0.4%
38	West Virginia	4,924	0.4%
39	Delaware	4,720	0.3%
40	Alaska	4,159	0.3%
41	Idaho	3,412	0.2%
42	Hawaii	3,213	0.2%
43	Montana	2,723	0.2%
44	Rhode Island	2,673	0.2%
45	New Hampshire	2,170	0.2%
46	Maine	1,364	0.1%
47	South Dakota	1,322	0.1%
48	Wyoming	1,163	0.1%
49	Vermont	696	0.1%
50	North Dakota	504	0.0%
	District of Columbia	7,590	0.6%

Source: Federal Bureau of Investigation
"Crime in the United States 2004" (Uniform Crime Reports, October 17, 2005)
Violent crimes are offenses of murder, forcible rape, robbery and aggravated assault.

Percent Change in Number of Violent Crimes: 2003 to 2004

National Percent Change = 1.2% Decrease*

RANK	STATE	PERCENT CHANGE
22	Alabama	0.0
4	Alaska	7.3
16	Arizona	1.1
2	Arkansas	10.3
36	California	(3.6)
3	Colorado	9.1
46	Connecticut	(9.2)
49	Delaware	(14.6)
24	Florida	(0.4)
13	Georgia	2.0
43	Hawaii	(5.5)
14	Idaho	1.5
33	Illinois	(1.9)
44	Indiana	(7.1)
34	Iowa	(2.1)
42	Kansas	(5.4)
28	Kentucky	(0.8)
17	Louisiana	0.8
38	Maine	(4.1)
19	Maryland	0.4
35	Massachusetts	(3.1)
37	Michigan	(3.8)
10	Minnesota	3.3
45	Mississippi	(8.2)
18	Missouri	0.6
50	Montana	(18.7)
6	Nebraska	5.6
8	Nevada	4.1
1	New Hampshire	12.0
32	New Jersey	(1.7)
7	New Mexico	4.4
41	New York	(5.1)
22	North Carolina	0.0
28	North Dakota	(0.8)
11	Ohio	2.6
27	Oklahoma	(0.7)
12	Oregon	2.1
9	Pennsylvania	3.6
48	Rhode Island	(13.0)
30	South Carolina	(1.6)
25	South Dakota	(0.5)
14	Tennessee	1.5
26	Texas	(0.6)
39	Utah	(4.2)
30	Vermont	(1.6)
20	Virginia	0.3
20	Washington	0.3
5	West Virginia	6.4
40	Wisconsin	(4.6)
47	Wyoming	(11.5)

RANK	STATE	PERCENT CHANGE
1	New Hampshire	12.0
2	Arkansas	10.3
3	Colorado	9.1
4	Alaska	7.3
5	West Virginia	6.4
6	Nebraska	5.6
7	New Mexico	4.4
8	Nevada	4.1
9	Pennsylvania	3.6
10	Minnesota	3.3
11	Ohio	2.6
12	Oregon	2.1
13	Georgia	2.0
14	Idaho	1.5
14	Tennessee	1.5
16	Arizona	1.1
17	Louisiana	0.8
18	Missouri	0.6
19	Maryland	0.4
20	Virginia	0.3
20	Washington	0.3
22	Alabama	0.0
22	North Carolina	0.0
24	Florida	(0.4)
25	South Dakota	(0.5)
26	Texas	(0.6)
27	Oklahoma	(0.7)
28	Kentucky	(0.8)
28	North Dakota	(0.8)
30	South Carolina	(1.6)
30	Vermont	(1.6)
32	New Jersey	(1.7)
33	Illinois	(1.9)
34	Iowa	(2.1)
35	Massachusetts	(3.1)
36	California	(3.6)
37	Michigan	(3.8)
38	Maine	(4.1)
39	Utah	(4.2)
40	Wisconsin	(4.6)
41	New York	(5.1)
42	Kansas	(5.4)
43	Hawaii	(5.5)
44	Indiana	(7.1)
45	Mississippi	(8.2)
46	Connecticut	(9.2)
47	Wyoming	(11.5)
48	Rhode Island	(13.0)
49	Delaware	(14.6)
50	Montana	(18.7)

| | District of Columbia | (16.2) |

*Source: Morgan Quitno Press using data from Federal Bureau of Investigation
    "Crime in the United States 2004" (Uniform Crime Reports, October 17, 2005)*
Violent crimes are offenses of murder, forcible rape, robbery and aggravated assault.

Violent Crime Rate in 2004

National Rate = 465.5 Violent Crimes per 100,000 Population*

ALPHA ORDER

RANK ORDER

RANK	STATE	RATE		RANK	STATE	RATE
22	Alabama	426.6		1	South Carolina	784.2
7	Alaska	634.5		2	Florida	711.3
13	Arizona	504.1		3	Maryland	700.5
15	Arkansas	499.1		4	Tennessee	695.2
10	California	551.8		5	New Mexico	687.3
25	Colorado	373.5		6	Louisiana	638.7
34	Connecticut	286.3		7	Alaska	634.5
9	Delaware	568.4		8	Nevada	615.9
2	Florida	711.3		9	Delaware	568.4
19	Georgia	455.5		10	California	551.8
39	Hawaii	254.4		11	Illinois	542.9
41	Idaho	244.9		12	Texas	540.5
11	Illinois	542.9		13	Arizona	504.1
29	Indiana	325.4		14	Oklahoma	500.5
37	Iowa	270.9		15	Arkansas	499.1
24	Kansas	374.5		16	Missouri	490.5
41	Kentucky	244.9		17	Michigan	490.2
6	Louisiana	638.7		18	Massachusetts	458.8
49	Maine	103.5		19	Georgia	455.5
3	Maryland	700.5		20	North Carolina	447.8
18	Massachusetts	458.8		21	New York	441.6
17	Michigan	490.2		22	Alabama	426.6
38	Minnesota	269.6		23	Pennsylvania	411.1
32	Mississippi	295.1		24	Kansas	374.5
16	Missouri	490.5		25	Colorado	373.5
33	Montana	293.8		26	New Jersey	355.7
30	Nebraska	308.7		27	Washington	343.8
8	Nevada	615.9		28	Ohio	341.8
47	New Hampshire	167.0		29	Indiana	325.4
26	New Jersey	355.7		30	Nebraska	308.7
5	New Mexico	687.3		31	Oregon	298.3
21	New York	441.6		32	Mississippi	295.1
20	North Carolina	447.8		33	Montana	293.8
50	North Dakota	79.4		34	Connecticut	286.3
28	Ohio	341.8		35	Virginia	275.6
14	Oklahoma	500.5		36	West Virginia	271.2
31	Oregon	298.3		37	Iowa	270.9
23	Pennsylvania	411.1		38	Minnesota	269.6
40	Rhode Island	247.4		39	Hawaii	254.4
1	South Carolina	784.2		40	Rhode Island	247.4
46	South Dakota	171.5		41	Idaho	244.9
4	Tennessee	695.2		41	Kentucky	244.9
12	Texas	540.5		43	Utah	236.0
43	Utah	236.0		44	Wyoming	229.6
48	Vermont	112.0		45	Wisconsin	209.6
35	Virginia	275.6		46	South Dakota	171.5
27	Washington	343.8		47	New Hampshire	167.0
36	West Virginia	271.2		48	Vermont	112.0
45	Wisconsin	209.6		49	Maine	103.5
44	Wyoming	229.6		50	North Dakota	79.4

District of Columbia   1,371.2

Source: Federal Bureau of Investigation
"Crime in the United States 2004" (Uniform Crime Reports, October 17, 2005)
*Violent crimes are offenses of murder, forcible rape, robbery and aggravated assault.

Percent Change in Violent Crime Rate: 2003 to 2004

National Percent Change = 2.2% Decrease*

ALPHA ORDER

RANK	STATE	PERCENT CHANGE	RANK	STATE	PERCENT CHANGE
19	Alabama	(0.6)	1	New Hampshire	11.1
5	Alaska	6.1	2	Arkansas	9.3
27	Arizona	(1.8)	3	Colorado	7.8
2	Arkansas	9.3	4	West Virginia	6.2
38	California	(4.8)	5	Alaska	6.1
3	Colorado	7.8	6	Nebraska	5.1
46	Connecticut	(9.6)	7	Pennsylvania	3.3
49	Delaware	(15.8)	8	New Mexico	3.0
33	Florida	(2.7)	9	Minnesota	2.5
14	Georgia	0.2	10	Ohio	2.4
43	Hawaii	(6.6)	11	Oregon	1.2
17	Idaho	(0.4)	12	Tennessee	0.6
30	Illinois	(2.4)	13	Louisiana	0.3
44	Indiana	(7.7)	14	Georgia	0.2
32	Iowa	(2.5)	15	Nevada	0.0
42	Kansas	(5.8)	16	Missouri	(0.1)
25	Kentucky	(1.4)	17	Idaho	(0.4)
13	Louisiana	0.3	17	Maryland	(0.4)
37	Maine	(4.7)	19	Alabama	(0.6)
17	Maryland	(0.4)	20	North Dakota	(0.9)
35	Massachusetts	(3.0)	20	Virginia	(0.9)
36	Michigan	(4.1)	20	Washington	(0.9)
9	Minnesota	2.5	23	Oklahoma	(1.2)
45	Mississippi	(8.9)	24	South Dakota	(1.3)
16	Missouri	(0.1)	25	Kentucky	(1.4)
50	Montana	(19.5)	25	North Carolina	(1.4)
6	Nebraska	5.1	27	Arizona	(1.8)
15	Nevada	0.0	28	Vermont	(1.9)
1	New Hampshire	11.1	29	Texas	(2.3)
30	New Jersey	(2.4)	30	Illinois	(2.4)
8	New Mexico	3.0	30	New Jersey	(2.4)
39	New York	(5.2)	32	Iowa	(2.5)
25	North Carolina	(1.4)	33	Florida	(2.7)
20	North Dakota	(0.9)	33	South Carolina	(2.7)
10	Ohio	2.4	35	Massachusetts	(3.0)
23	Oklahoma	(1.2)	36	Michigan	(4.1)
11	Oregon	1.2	37	Maine	(4.7)
7	Pennsylvania	3.3	38	California	(4.8)
48	Rhode Island	(13.4)	39	New York	(5.2)
33	South Carolina	(2.7)	39	Wisconsin	(5.2)
24	South Dakota	(1.3)	41	Utah	(5.7)
12	Tennessee	0.6	42	Kansas	(5.8)
29	Texas	(2.3)	43	Hawaii	(6.6)
41	Utah	(5.7)	44	Indiana	(7.7)
28	Vermont	(1.9)	45	Mississippi	(8.9)
20	Virginia	(0.9)	46	Connecticut	(9.6)
20	Washington	(0.9)	47	Wyoming	(12.3)
4	West Virginia	6.2	48	Rhode Island	(13.4)
39	Wisconsin	(5.2)	49	Delaware	(15.8)
47	Wyoming	(12.3)	50	Montana	(19.5)

RANK ORDER

	District of Columbia	(15.6)

Source: Morgan Quitno Press using data from Federal Bureau of Investigation
   "Crime in the United States 2004" (Uniform Crime Reports, October 17, 2005)
*Violent crimes are offenses of murder, forcible rape, robbery and aggravated assault.

Murders in 2004

National Total = 16,137 Murders*

	ALPHA ORDER				RANK ORDER		
RANK	STATE	MURDERS	% of USA	RANK	STATE	MURDERS	% of USA
20	Alabama	254	1.6%	1	California	2,392	14.8%
39	Alaska	37	0.2%	2	Texas	1,364	8.5%
13	Arizona	414	2.6%	3	Florida	946	5.9%
26	Arkansas	176	1.1%	4	New York	889	5.5%
1	California	2,392	14.8%	5	Illinois	776	4.8%
23	Colorado	203	1.3%	6	Pennsylvania	650	4.0%
33	Connecticut	91	0.6%	7	Michigan	643	4.0%
47	Delaware	17	0.1%	8	Georgia	613	3.8%
3	Florida	946	5.9%	9	Louisiana	574	3.6%
8	Georgia	613	3.8%	10	North Carolina	532	3.3%
40	Hawaii	33	0.2%	11	Maryland	521	3.2%
41	Idaho	30	0.2%	12	Ohio	517	3.2%
5	Illinois	776	4.8%	13	Arizona	414	2.6%
18	Indiana	316	2.0%	14	New Jersey	392	2.4%
36	Iowa	46	0.3%	15	Virginia	391	2.4%
31	Kansas	123	0.8%	16	Missouri	354	2.2%
21	Kentucky	236	1.5%	17	Tennessee	351	2.2%
9	Louisiana	574	3.6%	18	Indiana	316	2.0%
44	Maine	18	0.1%	19	South Carolina	288	1.8%
11	Maryland	521	3.2%	20	Alabama	254	1.6%
28	Massachusetts	169	1.0%	21	Kentucky	236	1.5%
7	Michigan	643	4.0%	22	Mississippi	227	1.4%
32	Minnesota	113	0.7%	23	Colorado	203	1.3%
22	Mississippi	227	1.4%	24	Washington	190	1.2%
16	Missouri	354	2.2%	25	Oklahoma	186	1.2%
41	Montana	30	0.2%	26	Arkansas	176	1.1%
38	Nebraska	40	0.2%	27	Nevada	172	1.1%
27	Nevada	172	1.1%	28	Massachusetts	169	1.0%
44	New Hampshire	18	0.1%	28	New Mexico	169	1.0%
14	New Jersey	392	2.4%	30	Wisconsin	154	1.0%
28	New Mexico	169	1.0%	31	Kansas	123	0.8%
4	New York	889	5.5%	32	Minnesota	113	0.7%
10	North Carolina	532	3.3%	33	Connecticut	91	0.6%
50	North Dakota	9	0.1%	34	Oregon	90	0.6%
12	Ohio	517	3.2%	35	West Virginia	68	0.4%
25	Oklahoma	186	1.2%	36	Iowa	46	0.3%
34	Oregon	90	0.6%	36	Utah	46	0.3%
6	Pennsylvania	650	4.0%	38	Nebraska	40	0.2%
43	Rhode Island	26	0.2%	39	Alaska	37	0.2%
19	South Carolina	288	1.8%	40	Hawaii	33	0.2%
44	South Dakota	18	0.1%	41	Idaho	30	0.2%
17	Tennessee	351	2.2%	41	Montana	30	0.2%
2	Texas	1,364	8.5%	43	Rhode Island	26	0.2%
36	Utah	46	0.3%	44	Maine	18	0.1%
48	Vermont	16	0.1%	44	New Hampshire	18	0.1%
15	Virginia	391	2.4%	44	South Dakota	18	0.1%
24	Washington	190	1.2%	47	Delaware	17	0.1%
35	West Virginia	68	0.4%	48	Vermont	16	0.1%
30	Wisconsin	154	1.0%	49	Wyoming	11	0.1%
49	Wyoming	11	0.1%	50	North Dakota	9	0.1%
					District of Columbia	198	1.2%

Source: Federal Bureau of Investigation
"Crime in the United States 2004" (Uniform Crime Reports, October 17, 2005)
*Includes nonnegligent manslaughter.

Murder Rate in 2004

National Rate = 5.5 Murders per 100,000 Population*

ALPHA ORDER

RANK	STATE	RATE
18	Alabama	5.6
18	Alaska	5.6
6	Arizona	7.2
10	Arkansas	6.4
9	California	6.7
29	Colorado	4.4
34	Connecticut	2.6
45	Delaware	2.0
20	Florida	5.4
7	Georgia	6.9
34	Hawaii	2.6
42	Idaho	2.2
14	Illinois	6.1
24	Indiana	5.1
47	Iowa	1.6
26	Kansas	4.5
17	Kentucky	5.7
1	Louisiana	12.7
48	Maine	1.4
2	Maryland	9.4
34	Massachusetts	2.6
10	Michigan	6.4
42	Minnesota	2.2
4	Mississippi	7.8
12	Missouri	6.2
31	Montana	3.2
40	Nebraska	2.3
5	Nevada	7.4
48	New Hampshire	1.4
26	New Jersey	4.5
3	New Mexico	8.9
25	New York	4.6
12	North Carolina	6.2
48	North Dakota	1.4
26	Ohio	4.5
21	Oklahoma	5.3
38	Oregon	2.5
22	Pennsylvania	5.2
39	Rhode Island	2.4
7	South Carolina	6.9
40	South Dakota	2.3
16	Tennessee	5.9
14	Texas	6.1
46	Utah	1.9
34	Vermont	2.6
22	Virginia	5.2
32	Washington	3.1
30	West Virginia	3.7
33	Wisconsin	2.8
42	Wyoming	2.2

RANK ORDER

RANK	STATE	RATE
1	Louisiana	12.7
2	Maryland	9.4
3	New Mexico	8.9
4	Mississippi	7.8
5	Nevada	7.4
6	Arizona	7.2
7	Georgia	6.9
7	South Carolina	6.9
9	California	6.7
10	Arkansas	6.4
10	Michigan	6.4
12	Missouri	6.2
12	North Carolina	6.2
14	Illinois	6.1
14	Texas	6.1
16	Tennessee	5.9
17	Kentucky	5.7
18	Alabama	5.6
18	Alaska	5.6
20	Florida	5.4
21	Oklahoma	5.3
22	Pennsylvania	5.2
22	Virginia	5.2
24	Indiana	5.1
25	New York	4.6
26	Kansas	4.5
26	New Jersey	4.5
26	Ohio	4.5
29	Colorado	4.4
30	West Virginia	3.7
31	Montana	3.2
32	Washington	3.1
33	Wisconsin	2.8
34	Connecticut	2.6
34	Hawaii	2.6
34	Massachusetts	2.6
34	Vermont	2.6
38	Oregon	2.5
39	Rhode Island	2.4
40	Nebraska	2.3
40	South Dakota	2.3
42	Idaho	2.2
42	Minnesota	2.2
42	Wyoming	2.2
45	Delaware	2.0
46	Utah	1.9
47	Iowa	1.6
48	Maine	1.4
48	New Hampshire	1.4
48	North Dakota	1.4
	District of Columbia	35.8

Source: Federal Bureau of Investigation
    "Crime in the United States 2004" (Uniform Crime Reports, October 17, 2005)
*Includes nonnegligent manslaughter.

Percent of Murders Involving Firearms in 2004

National Percent = 66.0% of Murders*

ALPHA ORDER				RANK ORDER		
RANK	**STATE**	**PERCENT**		**RANK**	**STATE**	**PERCENT**
18	Alabama	64.0		1	Louisiana	79.4
44	Alaska	45.9		2	Illinois*	75.2
4	Arizona	72.1		3	Maryland	74.2
23	Arkansas	62.5		4	Arizona	72.1
4	California	72.1		4	California	72.1
28	Colorado	58.3		6	Michigan	71.5
35	Connecticut	54.7		7	Pennsylvania	71.0
16	Delaware	64.3		8	Mississippi	70.9
NA	Florida**	NA		9	Indiana	69.6
14	Georgia	64.8		10	Virginia	69.2
48	Hawaii	19.4		11	Missouri	68.8
33	Idaho	56.7		12	South Carolina	67.6
2	Illinois*	75.2		13	Minnesota	66.4
9	Indiana	69.6		14	Georgia	64.8
43	Iowa	47.5		14	Texas	64.8
25	Kansas	60.0		16	Delaware	64.3
22	Kentucky	62.7		16	Wisconsin	64.3
1	Louisiana	79.4		18	Alabama	64.0
37	Maine	52.9		18	Nevada	64.0
3	Maryland	74.2		20	Tennessee	63.1
29	Massachusetts	58.1		21	Nebraska	63.0
6	Michigan	71.5		22	Kentucky	62.7
13	Minnesota	66.4		23	Arkansas	62.5
8	Mississippi	70.9		24	Rhode Island	61.5
11	Missouri	68.8		25	Kansas	60.0
42	Montana	47.8		26	North Carolina	59.5
21	Nebraska	63.0		27	New Jersey	58.8
18	Nevada	64.0		28	Colorado	58.3
46	New Hampshire	30.8		29	Massachusetts	58.1
27	New Jersey	58.8		30	New York	57.9
39	New Mexico	50.0		31	Utah	57.1
30	New York	57.9		32	Oklahoma	57.0
26	North Carolina	59.5		33	Idaho	56.7
39	North Dakota	50.0		34	Washington	56.1
38	Ohio	52.8		35	Connecticut	54.7
32	Oklahoma	57.0		36	Oregon	53.3
36	Oregon	53.3		37	Maine	52.9
7	Pennsylvania	71.0		38	Ohio	52.8
24	Rhode Island	61.5		39	New Mexico	50.0
12	South Carolina	67.6		39	North Dakota	50.0
45	South Dakota	31.3		39	West Virginia	50.0
20	Tennessee	63.1		42	Montana	47.8
14	Texas	64.8		43	Iowa	47.5
31	Utah	57.1		44	Alaska	45.9
49	Vermont	18.8		45	South Dakota	31.3
10	Virginia	69.2		46	New Hampshire	30.8
34	Washington	56.1		47	Wyoming	27.3
39	West Virginia	50.0		48	Hawaii	19.4
16	Wisconsin	64.3		49	Vermont	18.8
47	Wyoming	27.3		NA	Florida**	NA
					District of Columbia**	NA

*Source: Morgan Quitno Press using data from Federal Bureau of Investigation
    "Crime in the United States 2004" (Uniform Crime Reports, October 17, 2005)*
*Of the 14,121 murders in 2004 for which supplemental data were received by the F.B.I. There were an additional
2,016 murders for which the type of murder weapon was not reported to the F.B.I. Includes nonnegligent
manslaughter. National and state rates based on population for reporting jurisdictions only. Illinois' rate is for
Chicago only. **Not available.*

Rapes in 2004

National Total = 94,635 Rapes*

RANK	STATE	RAPES	% of USA
19	Alabama	1,742	1.8%
39	Alaska	558	0.6%
15	Arizona	1,896	2.0%
28	Arkansas	1,166	1.2%
1	California	9,615	10.2%
14	Colorado	1,956	2.1%
36	Connecticut	724	0.8%
41	Delaware	345	0.4%
3	Florida	6,612	7.0%
10	Georgia	2,387	2.5%
43	Hawaii	333	0.4%
38	Idaho	570	0.6%
6	Illinois	4,216	4.5%
16	Indiana	1,803	1.9%
35	Iowa	790	0.8%
31	Kansas	1,104	1.2%
27	Kentucky	1,238	1.3%
21	Louisiana	1,616	1.7%
46	Maine	315	0.3%
25	Maryland	1,316	1.4%
17	Massachusetts	1,799	1.9%
4	Michigan	5,486	5.8%
13	Minnesota	2,123	2.2%
29	Mississippi	1,161	1.2%
23	Missouri	1,479	1.6%
47	Montana	273	0.3%
37	Nebraska	620	0.7%
33	Nevada	954	1.0%
40	New Hampshire	459	0.5%
24	New Jersey	1,331	1.4%
32	New Mexico	1,039	1.1%
7	New York	3,608	3.8%
11	North Carolina	2,339	2.5%
48	North Dakota	159	0.2%
5	Ohio	4,646	4.9%
22	Oklahoma	1,557	1.6%
26	Oregon	1,283	1.4%
8	Pennsylvania	3,535	3.7%
44	Rhode Island	320	0.3%
20	South Carolina	1,718	1.8%
42	South Dakota	338	0.4%
12	Tennessee	2,220	2.3%
2	Texas	8,388	8.9%
34	Utah	933	1.0%
49	Vermont	152	0.2%
18	Virginia	1,766	1.9%
9	Washington	2,857	3.0%
44	West Virginia	320	0.3%
30	Wisconsin	1,136	1.2%
50	Wyoming	112	0.1%

ALPHA ORDER

RANK ORDER

RANK	STATE	RAPES	% of USA
1	California	9,615	10.2%
2	Texas	8,388	8.9%
3	Florida	6,612	7.0%
4	Michigan	5,486	5.8%
5	Ohio	4,646	4.9%
6	Illinois	4,216	4.5%
7	New York	3,608	3.8%
8	Pennsylvania	3,535	3.7%
9	Washington	2,857	3.0%
10	Georgia	2,387	2.5%
11	North Carolina	2,339	2.5%
12	Tennessee	2,220	2.3%
13	Minnesota	2,123	2.2%
14	Colorado	1,956	2.1%
15	Arizona	1,896	2.0%
16	Indiana	1,803	1.9%
17	Massachusetts	1,799	1.9%
18	Virginia	1,766	1.9%
19	Alabama	1,742	1.8%
20	South Carolina	1,718	1.8%
21	Louisiana	1,616	1.7%
22	Oklahoma	1,557	1.6%
23	Missouri	1,479	1.6%
24	New Jersey	1,331	1.4%
25	Maryland	1,316	1.4%
26	Oregon	1,283	1.4%
27	Kentucky	1,238	1.3%
28	Arkansas	1,166	1.2%
29	Mississippi	1,161	1.2%
30	Wisconsin	1,136	1.2%
31	Kansas	1,104	1.2%
32	New Mexico	1,039	1.1%
33	Nevada	954	1.0%
34	Utah	933	1.0%
35	Iowa	790	0.8%
36	Connecticut	724	0.8%
37	Nebraska	620	0.7%
38	Idaho	570	0.6%
39	Alaska	558	0.6%
40	New Hampshire	459	0.5%
41	Delaware	345	0.4%
42	South Dakota	338	0.4%
43	Hawaii	333	0.4%
44	Rhode Island	320	0.3%
44	West Virginia	320	0.3%
46	Maine	315	0.3%
47	Montana	273	0.3%
48	North Dakota	159	0.2%
49	Vermont	152	0.2%
50	Wyoming	112	0.1%
	District of Columbia	222	0.2%

Source: Federal Bureau of Investigation
"Crime in the United States 2004" (Uniform Crime Reports, October 17, 2005)
*Forcible rape is the carnal knowledge of a female forcibly and against her will. Assaults or attempts to commit rape by force or threat of force are included. However, statutory rape without force and other sex offenses are excluded.

Rape Rate in 2004

National Rate = 32.2 Rapes per 100,000 Population*

ALPHA ORDER				RANK ORDER		
RANK	STATE	RATE		RANK	STATE	RATE
18	Alabama	38.5		1	Alaska	85.1
1	Alaska	85.1		2	New Mexico	54.6
27	Arizona	33.0		3	Michigan	54.2
8	Arkansas	42.4		4	Washington	46.1
36	California	26.8		5	Oklahoma	44.2
7	Colorado	42.5		6	South Dakota	43.8
46	Connecticut	20.7		7	Colorado	42.5
10	Delaware	41.5		8	Arkansas	42.4
19	Florida	38.0		9	Minnesota	41.6
35	Georgia	27.0		10	Delaware	41.5
38	Hawaii	26.4		11	Idaho	40.9
11	Idaho	40.9		11	Nevada	40.9
26	Illinois	33.2		11	South Carolina	40.9
31	Indiana	28.9		14	Ohio	40.5
37	Iowa	26.7		15	Kansas	40.4
15	Kansas	40.4		16	Mississippi	40.0
28	Kentucky	29.9		17	Utah	39.1
22	Louisiana	35.8		18	Alabama	38.5
42	Maine	23.9		19	Florida	38.0
43	Maryland	23.7		20	Tennessee	37.6
33	Massachusetts	28.0		21	Texas	37.3
3	Michigan	54.2		22	Louisiana	35.8
9	Minnesota	41.6		23	Oregon	35.7
16	Mississippi	40.0		24	Nebraska	35.5
39	Missouri	25.7		25	New Hampshire	35.3
30	Montana	29.5		26	Illinois	33.2
24	Nebraska	35.5		27	Arizona	33.0
11	Nevada	40.9		28	Kentucky	29.9
25	New Hampshire	35.3		29	Rhode Island	29.6
50	New Jersey	15.3		30	Montana	29.5
2	New Mexico	54.6		31	Indiana	28.9
48	New York	18.8		32	Pennsylvania	28.5
34	North Carolina	27.4		33	Massachusetts	28.0
40	North Dakota	25.1		34	North Carolina	27.4
14	Ohio	40.5		35	Georgia	27.0
5	Oklahoma	44.2		36	California	26.8
23	Oregon	35.7		37	Iowa	26.7
32	Pennsylvania	28.5		38	Hawaii	26.4
29	Rhode Island	29.6		39	Missouri	25.7
11	South Carolina	40.9		40	North Dakota	25.1
6	South Dakota	43.8		41	Vermont	24.5
20	Tennessee	37.6		42	Maine	23.9
21	Texas	37.3		43	Maryland	23.7
17	Utah	39.1		43	Virginia	23.7
41	Vermont	24.5		45	Wyoming	22.1
43	Virginia	23.7		46	Connecticut	20.7
4	Washington	46.1		47	Wisconsin	20.6
49	West Virginia	17.6		48	New York	18.8
47	Wisconsin	20.6		49	West Virginia	17.6
45	Wyoming	22.1		50	New Jersey	15.3
					District of Columbia	40.1

Source: Federal Bureau of Investigation
    "Crime in the United States 2004" (Uniform Crime Reports, October 17, 2005)
*Forcible rape is the carnal knowledge of a female forcibly and against her will. Assaults or attempts to commit rape by force or threat of force are included. However, statutory rape without force and other sex offenses are excluded.

Robberies in 2004

National Total = 401,326 Robberies*

ALPHA ORDER

RANK	STATE	ROBBERIES	% of USA
20	Alabama	6,042	1.5%
43	Alaska	447	0.1%
14	Arizona	7,721	1.9%
32	Arkansas	2,372	0.6%
1	California	61,768	15.4%
27	Colorado	3,750	0.9%
24	Connecticut	4,222	1.1%
36	Delaware	1,218	0.3%
4	Florida	29,997	7.5%
8	Georgia	13,656	3.4%
39	Hawaii	944	0.2%
45	Idaho	240	0.1%
5	Illinois	22,532	5.6%
19	Indiana	6,373	1.6%
38	Iowa	1,124	0.3%
34	Kansas	1,813	0.5%
28	Kentucky	3,268	0.8%
18	Louisiana	6,564	1.6%
44	Maine	289	0.1%
10	Maryland	12,761	3.2%
15	Massachusetts	7,467	1.9%
12	Michigan	11,320	2.8%
25	Minnesota	4,070	1.0%
31	Mississippi	2,503	0.6%
17	Missouri	6,630	1.7%
46	Montana	233	0.1%
37	Nebraska	1,138	0.3%
23	Nevada	4,905	1.2%
42	New Hampshire	500	0.1%
9	New Jersey	13,076	3.3%
33	New Mexico	2,062	0.5%
3	New York	33,506	8.3%
11	North Carolina	11,782	2.9%
50	North Dakota	39	0.0%
7	Ohio	17,543	4.4%
29	Oklahoma	3,090	0.8%
30	Oregon	2,751	0.7%
6	Pennsylvania	18,474	4.6%
41	Rhode Island	731	0.2%
22	South Carolina	5,446	1.4%
47	South Dakota	114	0.0%
13	Tennessee	8,840	2.2%
2	Texas	35,817	8.9%
35	Utah	1,236	0.3%
48	Vermont	76	0.0%
16	Virginia	6,906	1.7%
21	Washington	5,866	1.5%
40	West Virginia	768	0.2%
26	Wisconsin	4,067	1.0%
49	Wyoming	67	0.0%

RANK ORDER

RANK	STATE	ROBBERIES	% of USA
1	California	61,768	15.4%
2	Texas	35,817	8.9%
3	New York	33,506	8.3%
4	Florida	29,997	7.5%
5	Illinois	22,532	5.6%
6	Pennsylvania	18,474	4.6%
7	Ohio	17,543	4.4%
8	Georgia	13,656	3.4%
9	New Jersey	13,076	3.3%
10	Maryland	12,761	3.2%
11	North Carolina	11,782	2.9%
12	Michigan	11,320	2.8%
13	Tennessee	8,840	2.2%
14	Arizona	7,721	1.9%
15	Massachusetts	7,467	1.9%
16	Virginia	6,906	1.7%
17	Missouri	6,630	1.7%
18	Louisiana	6,564	1.6%
19	Indiana	6,373	1.6%
20	Alabama	6,042	1.5%
21	Washington	5,866	1.5%
22	South Carolina	5,446	1.4%
23	Nevada	4,905	1.2%
24	Connecticut	4,222	1.1%
25	Minnesota	4,070	1.0%
26	Wisconsin	4,067	1.0%
27	Colorado	3,750	0.9%
28	Kentucky	3,268	0.8%
29	Oklahoma	3,090	0.8%
30	Oregon	2,751	0.7%
31	Mississippi	2,503	0.6%
32	Arkansas	2,372	0.6%
33	New Mexico	2,062	0.5%
34	Kansas	1,813	0.5%
35	Utah	1,236	0.3%
36	Delaware	1,218	0.3%
37	Nebraska	1,138	0.3%
38	Iowa	1,124	0.3%
39	Hawaii	944	0.2%
40	West Virginia	768	0.2%
41	Rhode Island	731	0.2%
42	New Hampshire	500	0.1%
43	Alaska	447	0.1%
44	Maine	289	0.1%
45	Idaho	240	0.1%
46	Montana	233	0.1%
47	South Dakota	114	0.0%
48	Vermont	76	0.0%
49	Wyoming	67	0.0%
50	North Dakota	39	0.0%
	District of Columbia	3,202	0.8%

Source: Federal Bureau of Investigation
   "Crime in the United States 2004" (Uniform Crime Reports, October 17, 2005)
*Robbery is the taking or attempting to take anything of value by force or threat of force.

Robbery Rate in 2004

National Rate = 136.7 Robberies per 100,000 Population*

ALPHA ORDER			RANK ORDER		
RANK	STATE	RATE	RANK	STATE	RATE
17	Alabama	133.4	1	Maryland	229.6
36	Alaska	68.2	2	Nevada	210.1
16	Arizona	134.4	3	Illinois	177.2
28	Arkansas	86.2	4	New York	174.3
6	California	172.1	5	Florida	172.4
30	Colorado	81.5	6	California	172.1
19	Connecticut	120.5	7	Texas	159.3
13	Delaware	146.7	8	Georgia	154.7
5	Florida	172.4	9	Ohio	153.1
8	Georgia	154.7	10	New Jersey	150.3
34	Hawaii	74.8	11	Tennessee	149.8
46	Idaho	17.2	12	Pennsylvania	148.9
3	Illinois	177.2	13	Delaware	146.7
24	Indiana	102.2	14	Louisiana	145.4
43	Iowa	38.0	15	North Carolina	137.9
38	Kansas	66.3	16	Arizona	134.4
32	Kentucky	78.8	17	Alabama	133.4
14	Louisiana	145.4	18	South Carolina	129.7
45	Maine	21.9	19	Connecticut	120.5
1	Maryland	229.6	20	Massachusetts	116.4
20	Massachusetts	116.4	21	Missouri	115.2
22	Michigan	111.9	22	Michigan	111.9
31	Minnesota	79.8	23	New Mexico	108.3
28	Mississippi	86.2	24	Indiana	102.2
21	Missouri	115.2	25	Washington	94.6
44	Montana	25.1	26	Virginia	92.6
39	Nebraska	65.1	27	Oklahoma	87.7
2	Nevada	210.1	28	Arkansas	86.2
42	New Hampshire	38.5	28	Mississippi	86.2
10	New Jersey	150.3	30	Colorado	81.5
23	New Mexico	108.3	31	Minnesota	79.8
4	New York	174.3	32	Kentucky	78.8
15	North Carolina	137.9	33	Oregon	76.5
50	North Dakota	6.1	34	Hawaii	74.8
9	Ohio	153.1	35	Wisconsin	73.8
27	Oklahoma	87.7	36	Alaska	68.2
33	Oregon	76.5	37	Rhode Island	67.6
12	Pennsylvania	148.9	38	Kansas	66.3
37	Rhode Island	67.6	39	Nebraska	65.1
18	South Carolina	129.7	40	Utah	51.7
47	South Dakota	14.8	41	West Virginia	42.3
11	Tennessee	149.8	42	New Hampshire	38.5
7	Texas	159.3	43	Iowa	38.0
40	Utah	51.7	44	Montana	25.1
49	Vermont	12.2	45	Maine	21.9
26	Virginia	92.6	46	Idaho	17.2
25	Washington	94.6	47	South Dakota	14.8
41	West Virginia	42.3	48	Wyoming	13.2
35	Wisconsin	73.8	49	Vermont	12.2
48	Wyoming	13.2	50	North Dakota	6.1
				District of Columbia	578.5

Source: Federal Bureau of Investigation
    "Crime in the United States 2004" (Uniform Crime Reports, October 17, 2005)
*Robbery is the taking or attempting to take anything of value by force or threat of force.

Aggravated Assaults in 2004

National Total = 854,911 Aggravated Assaults*

ALPHA ORDER

RANK	STATE	ASSAULTS	% of USA
23	Alabama	11,286	1.3%
40	Alaska	3,117	0.4%
16	Arizona	18,921	2.2%
25	Arkansas	10,023	1.2%
1	California	124,295	14.5%
24	Colorado	11,276	1.3%
34	Connecticut	4,995	0.6%
39	Delaware	3,140	0.4%
2	Florida	86,199	10.1%
12	Georgia	23,561	2.8%
43	Hawaii	1,903	0.2%
41	Idaho	2,572	0.3%
5	Illinois	41,502	4.9%
21	Indiana	11,802	1.4%
32	Iowa	6,043	0.7%
29	Kansas	7,205	0.8%
33	Kentucky	5,410	0.6%
13	Louisiana	20,090	2.3%
48	Maine	742	0.1%
10	Maryland	24,334	2.8%
14	Massachusetts	20,002	2.3%
6	Michigan	32,128	3.8%
28	Minnesota	7,445	0.9%
35	Mississippi	4,677	0.5%
15	Missouri	19,763	2.3%
42	Montana	2,187	0.3%
37	Nebraska	3,595	0.4%
27	Nevada	8,348	1.0%
45	New Hampshire	1,193	0.1%
18	New Jersey	16,144	1.9%
26	New Mexico	9,811	1.1%
4	New York	46,911	5.5%
11	North Carolina	23,591	2.8%
50	North Dakota	297	0.0%
17	Ohio	16,457	1.9%
19	Oklahoma	12,802	1.5%
30	Oregon	6,600	0.8%
8	Pennsylvania	28,339	3.3%
44	Rhode Island	1,596	0.2%
9	South Carolina	25,470	3.0%
47	South Dakota	852	0.1%
7	Tennessee	29,613	3.5%
3	Texas	75,985	8.9%
38	Utah	3,424	0.4%
49	Vermont	452	0.1%
22	Virginia	11,496	1.3%
20	Washington	12,417	1.5%
36	West Virginia	3,768	0.4%
31	Wisconsin	6,191	0.7%
46	Wyoming	973	0.1%

RANK ORDER

RANK	STATE	ASSAULTS	% of USA
1	California	124,295	14.5%
2	Florida	86,199	10.1%
3	Texas	75,985	8.9%
4	New York	46,911	5.5%
5	Illinois	41,502	4.9%
6	Michigan	32,128	3.8%
7	Tennessee	29,613	3.5%
8	Pennsylvania	28,339	3.3%
9	South Carolina	25,470	3.0%
10	Maryland	24,334	2.8%
11	North Carolina	23,591	2.8%
12	Georgia	23,561	2.8%
13	Louisiana	20,090	2.3%
14	Massachusetts	20,002	2.3%
15	Missouri	19,763	2.3%
16	Arizona	18,921	2.2%
17	Ohio	16,457	1.9%
18	New Jersey	16,144	1.9%
19	Oklahoma	12,802	1.5%
20	Washington	12,417	1.5%
21	Indiana	11,802	1.4%
22	Virginia	11,496	1.3%
23	Alabama	11,286	1.3%
24	Colorado	11,276	1.3%
25	Arkansas	10,023	1.2%
26	New Mexico	9,811	1.1%
27	Nevada	8,348	1.0%
28	Minnesota	7,445	0.9%
29	Kansas	7,205	0.8%
30	Oregon	6,600	0.8%
31	Wisconsin	6,191	0.7%
32	Iowa	6,043	0.7%
33	Kentucky	5,410	0.6%
34	Connecticut	4,995	0.6%
35	Mississippi	4,677	0.5%
36	West Virginia	3,768	0.4%
37	Nebraska	3,595	0.4%
38	Utah	3,424	0.4%
39	Delaware	3,140	0.4%
40	Alaska	3,117	0.4%
41	Idaho	2,572	0.3%
42	Montana	2,187	0.3%
43	Hawaii	1,903	0.2%
44	Rhode Island	1,596	0.2%
45	New Hampshire	1,193	0.1%
46	Wyoming	973	0.1%
47	South Dakota	852	0.1%
48	Maine	742	0.1%
49	Vermont	452	0.1%
50	North Dakota	297	0.0%
	District of Columbia	3,968	0.5%

Source: Federal Bureau of Investigation
    "Crime in the United States 2004" (Uniform Crime Reports, October 17, 2005)
*Aggravated assault is an attack for the purpose of inflicting severe bodily injury.

Aggravated Assault Rate in 2004

National Rate = 291.1 Aggravated Assaults per 100,000 Population*

ALPHA ORDER

RANK	STATE	RATE
22	Alabama	249.1
5	Alaska	475.6
15	Arizona	329.4
9	Arkansas	364.1
12	California	346.3
23	Colorado	245.1
43	Connecticut	142.6
8	Delaware	378.1
4	Florida	495.5
20	Georgia	266.8
38	Hawaii	150.7
34	Idaho	184.6
16	Illinois	326.4
32	Indiana	189.2
29	Iowa	204.5
21	Kansas	263.4
44	Kentucky	130.5
6	Louisiana	444.9
49	Maine	56.3
7	Maryland	437.8
18	Massachusetts	311.7
17	Michigan	317.7
40	Minnesota	146.0
36	Mississippi	161.1
13	Missouri	343.4
25	Montana	236.0
28	Nebraska	205.8
11	Nevada	357.6
47	New Hampshire	91.8
33	New Jersey	185.6
2	New Mexico	515.5
24	New York	244.0
19	North Carolina	276.2
50	North Dakota	46.8
41	Ohio	143.6
10	Oklahoma	363.3
35	Oregon	183.6
26	Pennsylvania	228.4
39	Rhode Island	147.7
1	South Carolina	606.7
46	South Dakota	110.5
3	Tennessee	501.8
14	Texas	337.9
42	Utah	143.3
48	Vermont	72.7
37	Virginia	154.1
30	Washington	200.2
27	West Virginia	207.6
45	Wisconsin	112.4
31	Wyoming	192.1

RANK ORDER

RANK	STATE	RATE
1	South Carolina	606.7
2	New Mexico	515.5
3	Tennessee	501.8
4	Florida	495.5
5	Alaska	475.6
6	Louisiana	444.9
7	Maryland	437.8
8	Delaware	378.1
9	Arkansas	364.1
10	Oklahoma	363.3
11	Nevada	357.6
12	California	346.3
13	Missouri	343.4
14	Texas	337.9
15	Arizona	329.4
16	Illinois	326.4
17	Michigan	317.7
18	Massachusetts	311.7
19	North Carolina	276.2
20	Georgia	266.8
21	Kansas	263.4
22	Alabama	249.1
23	Colorado	245.1
24	New York	244.0
25	Montana	236.0
26	Pennsylvania	228.4
27	West Virginia	207.6
28	Nebraska	205.8
29	Iowa	204.5
30	Washington	200.2
31	Wyoming	192.1
32	Indiana	189.2
33	New Jersey	185.6
34	Idaho	184.6
35	Oregon	183.6
36	Mississippi	161.1
37	Virginia	154.1
38	Hawaii	150.7
39	Rhode Island	147.7
40	Minnesota	146.0
41	Ohio	143.6
42	Utah	143.3
43	Connecticut	142.6
44	Kentucky	130.5
45	Wisconsin	112.4
46	South Dakota	110.5
47	New Hampshire	91.8
48	Vermont	72.7
49	Maine	56.3
50	North Dakota	46.8
	District of Columbia	716.9

Source: Federal Bureau of Investigation
   "Crime in the United States 2004" (Uniform Crime Reports, October 17, 2005)
*Aggravated assault is an attack for the purpose of inflicting severe bodily injury.

Property Crimes in 2004

National Total = 10,328,255 Property Crimes*

<table>
<tr><td colspan="4">ALPHA ORDER</td><td colspan="4">RANK ORDER</td></tr>
<tr><th>RANK</th><th>STATE</th><th>CRIMES</th><th>% of USA</th><th>RANK</th><th>STATE</th><th>CRIMES</th><th>% of USA</th></tr>
<tr><td>21</td><td>Alabama</td><td>182,340</td><td>1.8%</td><td>1</td><td>California</td><td>1,227,194</td><td>11.9%</td></tr>
<tr><td>46</td><td>Alaska</td><td>22,172</td><td>0.2%</td><td>2</td><td>Texas</td><td>1,010,702</td><td>9.8%</td></tr>
<tr><td>10</td><td>Arizona</td><td>306,747</td><td>3.0%</td><td>3</td><td>Florida</td><td>727,141</td><td>7.0%</td></tr>
<tr><td>28</td><td>Arkansas</td><td>110,464</td><td>1.1%</td><td>4</td><td>New York</td><td>422,734</td><td>4.1%</td></tr>
<tr><td>1</td><td>California</td><td>1,227,194</td><td>11.9%</td><td>5</td><td>Ohio</td><td>420,910</td><td>4.1%</td></tr>
<tr><td>22</td><td>Colorado</td><td>180,342</td><td>1.7%</td><td>6</td><td>Illinois</td><td>405,070</td><td>3.9%</td></tr>
<tr><td>34</td><td>Connecticut</td><td>92,046</td><td>0.9%</td><td>7</td><td>Georgia</td><td>376,656</td><td>3.6%</td></tr>
<tr><td>45</td><td>Delaware</td><td>26,272</td><td>0.3%</td><td>8</td><td>North Carolina</td><td>355,328</td><td>3.4%</td></tr>
<tr><td>3</td><td>Florida</td><td>727,141</td><td>7.0%</td><td>9</td><td>Michigan</td><td>309,208</td><td>3.0%</td></tr>
<tr><td>7</td><td>Georgia</td><td>376,656</td><td>3.6%</td><td>10</td><td>Arizona</td><td>306,747</td><td>3.0%</td></tr>
<tr><td>38</td><td>Hawaii</td><td>60,525</td><td>0.6%</td><td>11</td><td>Washington</td><td>300,837</td><td>2.9%</td></tr>
<tr><td>40</td><td>Idaho</td><td>38,933</td><td>0.4%</td><td>12</td><td>Pennsylvania</td><td>299,611</td><td>2.9%</td></tr>
<tr><td>6</td><td>Illinois</td><td>405,070</td><td>3.9%</td><td>13</td><td>Tennessee</td><td>254,123</td><td>2.5%</td></tr>
<tr><td>15</td><td>Indiana</td><td>211,929</td><td>2.1%</td><td>14</td><td>Missouri</td><td>224,620</td><td>2.2%</td></tr>
<tr><td>35</td><td>Iowa</td><td>85,836</td><td>0.8%</td><td>15</td><td>Indiana</td><td>211,929</td><td>2.1%</td></tr>
<tr><td>29</td><td>Kansas</td><td>108,694</td><td>1.1%</td><td>16</td><td>New Jersey</td><td>211,313</td><td>2.0%</td></tr>
<tr><td>30</td><td>Kentucky</td><td>105,209</td><td>1.0%</td><td>17</td><td>Maryland</td><td>202,326</td><td>2.0%</td></tr>
<tr><td>19</td><td>Louisiana</td><td>199,153</td><td>1.9%</td><td>18</td><td>Virginia</td><td>199,668</td><td>1.9%</td></tr>
<tr><td>41</td><td>Maine</td><td>31,740</td><td>0.3%</td><td>19</td><td>Louisiana</td><td>199,153</td><td>1.9%</td></tr>
<tr><td>17</td><td>Maryland</td><td>202,326</td><td>2.0%</td><td>20</td><td>South Carolina</td><td>189,113</td><td>1.8%</td></tr>
<tr><td>24</td><td>Massachusetts</td><td>157,825</td><td>1.5%</td><td>21</td><td>Alabama</td><td>182,340</td><td>1.8%</td></tr>
<tr><td>9</td><td>Michigan</td><td>309,208</td><td>3.0%</td><td>22</td><td>Colorado</td><td>180,342</td><td>1.7%</td></tr>
<tr><td>25</td><td>Minnesota</td><td>155,019</td><td>1.5%</td><td>23</td><td>Oregon</td><td>166,475</td><td>1.6%</td></tr>
<tr><td>31</td><td>Mississippi</td><td>100,980</td><td>1.0%</td><td>24</td><td>Massachusetts</td><td>157,825</td><td>1.5%</td></tr>
<tr><td>14</td><td>Missouri</td><td>224,629</td><td>2.2%</td><td>25</td><td>Minnesota</td><td>155,019</td><td>1.5%</td></tr>
<tr><td>43</td><td>Montana</td><td>27,215</td><td>0.3%</td><td>26</td><td>Oklahoma</td><td>149,472</td><td>1.4%</td></tr>
<tr><td>37</td><td>Nebraska</td><td>61,512</td><td>0.6%</td><td>27</td><td>Wisconsin</td><td>146,710</td><td>1.4%</td></tr>
<tr><td>32</td><td>Nevada</td><td>98,215</td><td>1.0%</td><td>28</td><td>Arkansas</td><td>110,464</td><td>1.1%</td></tr>
<tr><td>44</td><td>New Hampshire</td><td>26,511</td><td>0.3%</td><td>29</td><td>Kansas</td><td>108,694</td><td>1.1%</td></tr>
<tr><td>16</td><td>New Jersey</td><td>211,313</td><td>2.0%</td><td>30</td><td>Kentucky</td><td>105,209</td><td>1.0%</td></tr>
<tr><td>36</td><td>New Mexico</td><td>79,895</td><td>0.8%</td><td>31</td><td>Mississippi</td><td>100,980</td><td>1.0%</td></tr>
<tr><td>4</td><td>New York</td><td>422,734</td><td>4.1%</td><td>32</td><td>Nevada</td><td>98,215</td><td>1.0%</td></tr>
<tr><td>8</td><td>North Carolina</td><td>355,328</td><td>3.4%</td><td>33</td><td>Utah</td><td>97,607</td><td>0.9%</td></tr>
<tr><td>50</td><td>North Dakota</td><td>12,158</td><td>0.1%</td><td>34</td><td>Connecticut</td><td>92,046</td><td>0.9%</td></tr>
<tr><td>5</td><td>Ohio</td><td>420,910</td><td>4.1%</td><td>35</td><td>Iowa</td><td>85,836</td><td>0.8%</td></tr>
<tr><td>26</td><td>Oklahoma</td><td>149,472</td><td>1.4%</td><td>36</td><td>New Mexico</td><td>79,895</td><td>0.8%</td></tr>
<tr><td>23</td><td>Oregon</td><td>166,475</td><td>1.6%</td><td>37</td><td>Nebraska</td><td>61,512</td><td>0.6%</td></tr>
<tr><td>12</td><td>Pennsylvania</td><td>299,611</td><td>2.9%</td><td>38</td><td>Hawaii</td><td>60,525</td><td>0.6%</td></tr>
<tr><td>42</td><td>Rhode Island</td><td>31,166</td><td>0.3%</td><td>39</td><td>West Virginia</td><td>45,497</td><td>0.4%</td></tr>
<tr><td>20</td><td>South Carolina</td><td>189,113</td><td>1.8%</td><td>40</td><td>Idaho</td><td>38,933</td><td>0.4%</td></tr>
<tr><td>48</td><td>South Dakota</td><td>14,905</td><td>0.1%</td><td>41</td><td>Maine</td><td>31,740</td><td>0.3%</td></tr>
<tr><td>13</td><td>Tennessee</td><td>254,123</td><td>2.5%</td><td>42</td><td>Rhode Island</td><td>31,166</td><td>0.3%</td></tr>
<tr><td>2</td><td>Texas</td><td>1,010,702</td><td>9.8%</td><td>43</td><td>Montana</td><td>27,215</td><td>0.3%</td></tr>
<tr><td>33</td><td>Utah</td><td>97,607</td><td>0.9%</td><td>44</td><td>New Hampshire</td><td>26,511</td><td>0.3%</td></tr>
<tr><td>49</td><td>Vermont</td><td>14,343</td><td>0.1%</td><td>45</td><td>Delaware</td><td>26,272</td><td>0.3%</td></tr>
<tr><td>18</td><td>Virginia</td><td>199,668</td><td>1.9%</td><td>46</td><td>Alaska</td><td>22,172</td><td>0.2%</td></tr>
<tr><td>11</td><td>Washington</td><td>300,837</td><td>2.9%</td><td>47</td><td>Wyoming</td><td>16,889</td><td>0.2%</td></tr>
<tr><td>39</td><td>West Virginia</td><td>45,497</td><td>0.4%</td><td>48</td><td>South Dakota</td><td>14,905</td><td>0.1%</td></tr>
<tr><td>27</td><td>Wisconsin</td><td>146,710</td><td>1.4%</td><td>49</td><td>Vermont</td><td>14,343</td><td>0.1%</td></tr>
<tr><td>47</td><td>Wyoming</td><td>16,889</td><td>0.2%</td><td>50</td><td>North Dakota</td><td>12,158</td><td>0.1%</td></tr>
<tr><td></td><td></td><td></td><td></td><td></td><td>District of Columbia</td><td>26,896</td><td>0.3%</td></tr>
</table>

Source: Federal Bureau of Investigation
   "Crime in the United States 2004" (Uniform Crime Reports, October 17, 2005)
*Property crimes are offenses of burglary, larceny-theft and motor vehicle theft.

Percent Change in Number of Property Crimes: 2003 to 2004

National Percent Change = 1.1% Decrease*

ALPHA ORDER				RANK ORDER		
RANK	STATE	PERCENT CHANGE		RANK	STATE	PERCENT CHANGE
17	Alabama	0.1		1	Arkansas	11.5
50	Alaska	(9.1)		2	West Virginia	7.4
31	Arizona	(2.4)		3	New Mexico	4.0
1	Arkansas	11.5		4	Vermont	3.9
12	California	1.0		5	Washington	3.2
15	Colorado	0.4		6	Louisiana	2.8
22	Connecticut	(1.0)		7	Nevada	2.2
45	Delaware	(6.0)		8	Georgia	1.9
39	Florida	(4.0)		8	Indiana	1.9
8	Georgia	1.9		10	Kentucky	1.8
48	Hawaii	(8.1)		11	Wyoming	1.4
35	Idaho	(2.8)		12	California	1.0
33	Illinois	(2.6)		13	Ohio	0.8
8	Indiana	1.9		13	South Carolina	0.8
28	Iowa	(2.0)		15	Colorado	0.4
20	Kansas	(0.5)		16	New Hampshire	0.2
10	Kentucky	1.8		17	Alabama	0.1
6	Louisiana	2.8		18	Pennsylvania	(0.3)
24	Maine	(1.1)		19	Virginia	(0.4)
37	Maryland	(3.4)		20	Kansas	(0.5)
40	Massachusetts	(4.1)		21	Texas	(0.6)
46	Michigan	(6.5)		22	Connecticut	(1.0)
27	Minnesota	(1.7)		22	Tennessee	(1.0)
43	Mississippi	(5.5)		24	Maine	(1.1)
38	Missouri	(3.8)		24	Oklahoma	(1.1)
42	Montana	(4.3)		26	North Carolina	(1.2)
44	Nebraska	(5.6)		27	Minnesota	(1.7)
7	Nevada	2.2		28	Iowa	(2.0)
16	New Hampshire	0.2		28	Oregon	(2.0)
40	New Jersey	(4.1)		30	New York	(2.2)
3	New Mexico	4.0		31	Arizona	(2.4)
30	New York	(2.2)		32	Utah	(2.5)
26	North Carolina	(1.2)		33	Illinois	(2.6)
49	North Dakota	(9.0)		34	South Dakota	(2.7)
13	Ohio	0.8		35	Idaho	(2.8)
24	Oklahoma	(1.1)		36	Rhode Island	(3.3)
28	Oregon	(2.0)		37	Maryland	(3.4)
18	Pennsylvania	(0.3)		38	Missouri	(3.8)
36	Rhode Island	(3.3)		39	Florida	(4.0)
13	South Carolina	0.8		40	Massachusetts	(4.1)
34	South Dakota	(2.7)		40	New Jersey	(4.1)
22	Tennessee	(1.0)		42	Montana	(4.3)
21	Texas	(0.6)		43	Mississippi	(5.5)
32	Utah	(2.5)		44	Nebraska	(5.6)
4	Vermont	3.9		45	Delaware	(6.0)
19	Virginia	(0.4)		46	Michigan	(6.5)
5	Washington	3.2		47	Wisconsin	(7.0)
2	West Virginia	7.4		48	Hawaii	(8.1)
47	Wisconsin	(7.0)		49	North Dakota	(9.0)
11	Wyoming	1.4		50	Alaska	(9.1)

	District of Columbia	(17.7)

Source: Federal Bureau of Investigation
"Crime in the United States 2004" (Uniform Crime Reports, October 17, 2005)
*Property crimes are offenses of burglary, larceny-theft and motor vehicle theft.

Property Crime Rate in 2004

National Rate = 3,517.1 Property Crimes per 100,000 Population*

ALPHA ORDER

RANK	STATE	RATE
16	Alabama	4,025.0
27	Alaska	3,382.8
1	Arizona	5,340.5
17	Arkansas	4,013.0
25	California	3,419.0
19	Colorado	3,919.3
39	Connecticut	2,627.2
30	Delaware	3,163.9
13	Florida	4,179.7
9	Georgia	4,265.9
3	Hawaii	4,792.8
36	Idaho	2,794.4
29	Illinois	3,186.1
26	Indiana	3,397.6
34	Iowa	2,905.3
18	Kansas	3,973.5
40	Kentucky	2,537.7
7	Louisiana	4,410.2
45	Maine	2,409.6
22	Maryland	3,640.2
42	Massachusetts	2,459.7
31	Michigan	3,057.6
32	Minnesota	3,039.0
24	Mississippi	3,478.5
20	Missouri	3,903.5
33	Montana	2,936.2
23	Nebraska	3,520.6
11	Nevada	4,206.6
48	New Hampshire	2,040.1
43	New Jersey	2,429.2
12	New Mexico	4,197.7
47	New York	2,198.6
14	North Carolina	4,160.2
50	North Dakota	1,916.6
21	Ohio	3,673.2
10	Oklahoma	4,242.1
4	Oregon	4,631.3
44	Pennsylvania	2,415.0
35	Rhode Island	2,884.1
5	South Carolina	4,504.8
49	South Dakota	1,933.5
8	Tennessee	4,306.5
6	Texas	4,494.0
15	Utah	4,085.6
46	Vermont	2,308.2
37	Virginia	2,676.6
2	Washington	4,849.2
41	West Virginia	2,506.2
38	Wisconsin	2,663.1
28	Wyoming	3,334.3

RANK ORDER

RANK	STATE	RATE
1	Arizona	5,340.5
2	Washington	4,849.2
3	Hawaii	4,792.8
4	Oregon	4,631.3
5	South Carolina	4,504.8
6	Texas	4,494.0
7	Louisiana	4,410.2
8	Tennessee	4,306.5
9	Georgia	4,265.9
10	Oklahoma	4,242.1
11	Nevada	4,206.6
12	New Mexico	4,197.7
13	Florida	4,179.7
14	North Carolina	4,160.2
15	Utah	4,085.6
16	Alabama	4,025.0
17	Arkansas	4,013.0
18	Kansas	3,973.5
19	Colorado	3,919.3
20	Missouri	3,903.5
21	Ohio	3,673.2
22	Maryland	3,640.2
23	Nebraska	3,520.6
24	Mississippi	3,478.5
25	California	3,419.0
26	Indiana	3,397.6
27	Alaska	3,382.8
28	Wyoming	3,334.3
29	Illinois	3,186.1
30	Delaware	3,163.9
31	Michigan	3,057.6
32	Minnesota	3,039.0
33	Montana	2,936.2
34	Iowa	2,905.3
35	Rhode Island	2,884.1
36	Idaho	2,794.4
37	Virginia	2,676.6
38	Wisconsin	2,663.1
39	Connecticut	2,627.2
40	Kentucky	2,537.7
41	West Virginia	2,506.2
42	Massachusetts	2,459.7
43	New Jersey	2,429.2
44	Pennsylvania	2,415.0
45	Maine	2,409.6
46	Vermont	2,308.2
47	New York	2,198.6
48	New Hampshire	2,040.1
49	South Dakota	1,933.5
50	North Dakota	1,916.6
	District of Columbia	4,859.1

Source: Federal Bureau of Investigation
   "Crime in the United States 2004" (Uniform Crime Reports, October 17, 2005)
*Property crimes are offenses of burglary, larceny-theft and motor vehicle theft.

Percent Change in Property Crime Rate: 2003 to 2004

National Percent Change = 2.1% Decrease*

ALPHA ORDER

RANK	STATE	PERCENT CHANGE
14	Alabama	(0.5)
50	Alaska	(10.1)
40	Arizona	(5.2)
1	Arkansas	10.5
12	California	(0.2)
17	Colorado	(0.8)
19	Connecticut	(1.5)
46	Delaware	(7.4)
42	Florida	(6.2)
11	Georgia	0.1
48	Hawaii	(9.1)
38	Idaho	(4.6)
31	Illinois	(3.1)
7	Indiana	1.2
27	Iowa	(2.4)
18	Kansas	(0.9)
8	Kentucky	1.1
5	Louisiana	2.3
21	Maine	(1.7)
36	Maryland	(4.2)
34	Massachusetts	(4.0)
45	Michigan	(6.7)
27	Minnesota	(2.4)
42	Mississippi	(6.2)
37	Missouri	(4.4)
40	Montana	(5.2)
42	Nebraska	(6.2)
23	Nevada	(1.9)
15	New Hampshire	(0.6)
39	New Jersey	(4.7)
4	New Mexico	2.7
25	New York	(2.2)
29	North Carolina	(2.6)
49	North Dakota	(9.2)
9	Ohio	0.6
20	Oklahoma	(1.6)
30	Oregon	(2.8)
15	Pennsylvania	(0.6)
33	Rhode Island	(3.7)
13	South Carolina	(0.4)
32	South Dakota	(3.5)
23	Tennessee	(1.9)
26	Texas	(2.3)
34	Utah	(4.0)
3	Vermont	3.6
21	Virginia	(1.7)
6	Washington	2.0
2	West Virginia	7.1
47	Wisconsin	(7.5)
9	Wyoming	0.6

RANK ORDER

RANK	STATE	PERCENT CHANGE
1	Arkansas	10.5
2	West Virginia	7.1
3	Vermont	3.6
4	New Mexico	2.7
5	Louisiana	2.3
6	Washington	2.0
7	Indiana	1.2
8	Kentucky	1.1
9	Ohio	0.6
9	Wyoming	0.6
11	Georgia	0.1
12	California	(0.2)
13	South Carolina	(0.4)
14	Alabama	(0.5)
15	New Hampshire	(0.6)
15	Pennsylvania	(0.6)
17	Colorado	(0.8)
18	Kansas	(0.9)
19	Connecticut	(1.5)
20	Oklahoma	(1.6)
21	Maine	(1.7)
21	Virginia	(1.7)
23	Nevada	(1.9)
23	Tennessee	(1.9)
25	New York	(2.2)
26	Texas	(2.3)
27	Iowa	(2.4)
27	Minnesota	(2.4)
29	North Carolina	(2.6)
30	Oregon	(2.8)
31	Illinois	(3.1)
32	South Dakota	(3.5)
33	Rhode Island	(3.7)
34	Massachusetts	(4.0)
34	Utah	(4.0)
36	Maryland	(4.2)
37	Missouri	(4.4)
38	Idaho	(4.6)
39	New Jersey	(4.7)
40	Arizona	(5.2)
40	Montana	(5.2)
42	Florida	(6.2)
42	Mississippi	(6.2)
42	Nebraska	(6.2)
45	Michigan	(6.7)
46	Delaware	(7.4)
47	Wisconsin	(7.5)
48	Hawaii	(9.1)
49	North Dakota	(9.2)
50	Alaska	(10.1)
	District of Columbia	(17.1)

Source: Federal Bureau of Investigation
   "Crime in the United States 2004" (Uniform Crime Reports, October 17, 2005)
*Property crimes are offenses of burglary, larceny-theft and motor vehicle theft.

Burglaries in 2004

National Total = 2,143,456 Burglaries*

ALPHA ORDER

RANK	STATE	BURGLARIES	% of USA
15	Alabama	44,666	2.1%
45	Alaska	3,773	0.2%
12	Arizona	56,885	2.7%
24	Arkansas	30,099	1.4%
1	California	245,903	11.5%
23	Colorado	33,008	1.5%
35	Connecticut	15,570	0.7%
43	Delaware	5,383	0.3%
3	Florida	166,332	7.8%
6	Georgia	82,992	3.9%
38	Hawaii	10,827	0.5%
40	Idaho	7,626	0.4%
7	Illinois	75,944	3.5%
17	Indiana	42,168	2.0%
34	Iowa	18,174	0.8%
32	Kansas	19,999	0.9%
29	Kentucky	25,902	1.2%
14	Louisiana	45,359	2.1%
41	Maine	6,341	0.3%
20	Maryland	36,682	1.7%
22	Massachusetts	34,469	1.6%
9	Michigan	64,394	3.0%
27	Minnesota	28,048	1.3%
28	Mississippi	27,661	1.3%
19	Missouri	40,472	1.9%
46	Montana	3,515	0.2%
39	Nebraska	9,826	0.5%
31	Nevada	23,142	1.1%
44	New Hampshire	4,966	0.2%
18	New Jersey	41,030	1.9%
33	New Mexico	19,924	0.9%
8	New York	70,696	3.3%
4	North Carolina	101,193	4.7%
50	North Dakota	1,910	0.1%
5	Ohio	96,954	4.5%
21	Oklahoma	35,244	1.6%
25	Oregon	30,072	1.4%
13	Pennsylvania	54,443	2.5%
42	Rhode Island	5,465	0.3%
16	South Carolina	43,425	2.0%
48	South Dakota	3,149	0.1%
11	Tennessee	60,205	2.8%
2	Texas	220,118	10.3%
36	Utah	15,221	0.7%
47	Vermont	3,386	0.2%
26	Virginia	28,793	1.3%
10	Washington	60,632	2.8%
37	West Virginia	10,932	0.5%
30	Wisconsin	23,854	1.1%
49	Wyoming	2,738	0.1%

RANK ORDER

RANK	STATE	BURGLARIES	% of USA
1	California	245,903	11.5%
2	Texas	220,118	10.3%
3	Florida	166,332	7.8%
4	North Carolina	101,193	4.7%
5	Ohio	96,954	4.5%
6	Georgia	82,992	3.9%
7	Illinois	75,944	3.5%
8	New York	70,696	3.3%
9	Michigan	64,394	3.0%
10	Washington	60,632	2.8%
11	Tennessee	60,205	2.8%
12	Arizona	56,885	2.7%
13	Pennsylvania	54,443	2.5%
14	Louisiana	45,359	2.1%
15	Alabama	44,666	2.1%
16	South Carolina	43,425	2.0%
17	Indiana	42,168	2.0%
18	New Jersey	41,030	1.9%
19	Missouri	40,472	1.9%
20	Maryland	36,682	1.7%
21	Oklahoma	35,244	1.6%
22	Massachusetts	34,469	1.6%
23	Colorado	33,008	1.5%
24	Arkansas	30,099	1.4%
25	Oregon	30,072	1.4%
26	Virginia	28,793	1.3%
27	Minnesota	28,048	1.3%
28	Mississippi	27,661	1.3%
29	Kentucky	25,902	1.2%
30	Wisconsin	23,854	1.1%
31	Nevada	23,142	1.1%
32	Kansas	19,999	0.9%
33	New Mexico	19,924	0.9%
34	Iowa	18,174	0.8%
35	Connecticut	15,570	0.7%
36	Utah	15,221	0.7%
37	West Virginia	10,932	0.5%
38	Hawaii	10,827	0.5%
39	Nebraska	9,826	0.5%
40	Idaho	7,626	0.4%
41	Maine	6,341	0.3%
42	Rhode Island	5,465	0.3%
43	Delaware	5,383	0.3%
44	New Hampshire	4,966	0.2%
45	Alaska	3,773	0.2%
46	Montana	3,515	0.2%
47	Vermont	3,386	0.2%
48	South Dakota	3,149	0.1%
49	Wyoming	2,738	0.1%
50	North Dakota	1,910	0.1%
	District of Columbia	3,946	0.2%

Source: Federal Bureau of Investigation
    "Crime in the United States 2004" (Uniform Crime Reports, October 17, 2005)
*Burglary is the unlawful entry of a structure to commit a felony or theft. Attempts are included.

Burglary Rate in 2004

National Rate = 729.9 Burglaries per 100,000 Population*

ALPHA ORDER			RANK ORDER		
RANK	STATE	RATE	RANK	STATE	RATE
10	Alabama	986.0	1	North Carolina	1,184.8
32	Alaska	575.6	2	Arkansas	1,093.5
9	Arizona	990.4	3	New Mexico	1,046.8
2	Arkansas	1,093.5	4	South Carolina	1,034.4
22	California	685.1	5	Tennessee	1,020.3
20	Colorado	717.3	6	Louisiana	1,004.5
42	Connecticut	444.4	7	Oklahoma	1,000.2
25	Delaware	648.3	8	Nevada	991.2
13	Florida	956.1	9	Arizona	990.4
15	Georgia	940.0	10	Alabama	986.0
16	Hawaii	857.4	11	Texas	978.7
35	Idaho	547.3	12	Washington	977.3
31	Illinois	597.3	13	Florida	956.1
23	Indiana	676.0	14	Mississippi	952.9
29	Iowa	615.1	15	Georgia	940.0
19	Kansas	731.1	16	Hawaii	857.4
28	Kentucky	624.8	17	Ohio	846.1
6	Louisiana	1,004.5	18	Oregon	836.6
40	Maine	481.4	19	Kansas	731.1
24	Maryland	660.0	20	Colorado	717.3
38	Massachusetts	537.2	21	Missouri	703.3
27	Michigan	636.8	22	California	685.1
34	Minnesota	549.9	23	Indiana	676.0
14	Mississippi	952.9	24	Maryland	660.0
21	Missouri	703.3	25	Delaware	648.3
48	Montana	379.2	26	Utah	637.1
33	Nebraska	562.4	27	Michigan	636.8
8	Nevada	991.2	28	Kentucky	624.8
47	New Hampshire	382.1	29	Iowa	615.1
41	New Jersey	471.7	30	West Virginia	602.2
3	New Mexico	1,046.8	31	Illinois	597.3
49	New York	367.7	32	Alaska	575.6
1	North Carolina	1,184.8	33	Nebraska	562.4
50	North Dakota	301.1	34	Minnesota	549.9
17	Ohio	846.1	35	Idaho	547.3
7	Oklahoma	1,000.2	36	Vermont	544.9
18	Oregon	836.6	37	Wyoming	540.5
43	Pennsylvania	438.8	38	Massachusetts	537.2
39	Rhode Island	505.7	39	Rhode Island	505.7
4	South Carolina	1,034.4	40	Maine	481.4
45	South Dakota	408.5	41	New Jersey	471.7
5	Tennessee	1,020.3	42	Connecticut	444.4
11	Texas	978.7	43	Pennsylvania	438.8
26	Utah	637.1	44	Wisconsin	433.0
36	Vermont	544.9	45	South Dakota	408.5
46	Virginia	386.0	46	Virginia	386.0
12	Washington	977.3	47	New Hampshire	382.1
30	West Virginia	602.2	48	Montana	379.2
44	Wisconsin	433.0	49	New York	367.7
37	Wyoming	540.5	50	North Dakota	301.1
				District of Columbia	712.9

Source: Federal Bureau of Investigation
"Crime in the United States 2004" (Uniform Crime Reports, October 17, 2005)
*Burglary is the unlawful entry of a structure to commit a felony or theft. Attempts are included.

Larcenies and Thefts in 2004

National Total = 6,947,685 Larcenies and Thefts*

<table>
<tr><td colspan="4">ALPHA ORDER</td><td colspan="4">RANK ORDER</td></tr>
<tr><td>RANK</td><td>STATE</td><td>THEFTS</td><td>% of USA</td><td>RANK</td><td>STATE</td><td>THEFTS</td><td>% of USA</td></tr>
<tr><td>21</td><td>Alabama</td><td>123,650</td><td>1.8%</td><td>1</td><td>California</td><td>728,687</td><td>10.5%</td></tr>
<tr><td>46</td><td>Alaska</td><td>16,159</td><td>0.2%</td><td>2</td><td>Texas</td><td>696,507</td><td>10.0%</td></tr>
<tr><td>11</td><td>Arizona</td><td>194,556</td><td>2.8%</td><td>3</td><td>Florida</td><td>482,484</td><td>6.9%</td></tr>
<tr><td>30</td><td>Arkansas</td><td>73,874</td><td>1.1%</td><td>4</td><td>New York</td><td>311,036</td><td>4.5%</td></tr>
<tr><td>1</td><td>California</td><td>728,687</td><td>10.5%</td><td>5</td><td>Illinois</td><td>288,771</td><td>4.2%</td></tr>
<tr><td>22</td><td>Colorado</td><td>123,271</td><td>1.8%</td><td>6</td><td>Ohio</td><td>283,103</td><td>4.1%</td></tr>
<tr><td>32</td><td>Connecticut</td><td>65,451</td><td>0.9%</td><td>7</td><td>Georgia</td><td>249,426</td><td>3.6%</td></tr>
<tr><td>45</td><td>Delaware</td><td>18,742</td><td>0.3%</td><td>8</td><td>North Carolina</td><td>227,147</td><td>3.3%</td></tr>
<tr><td>3</td><td>Florida</td><td>482,484</td><td>6.9%</td><td>9</td><td>Pennsylvania</td><td>214,199</td><td>3.1%</td></tr>
<tr><td>7</td><td>Georgia</td><td>249,426</td><td>3.6%</td><td>10</td><td>Washington</td><td>196,972</td><td>2.8%</td></tr>
<tr><td>38</td><td>Hawaii</td><td>41,078</td><td>0.6%</td><td>11</td><td>Arizona</td><td>194,556</td><td>2.8%</td></tr>
<tr><td>40</td><td>Idaho</td><td>28,583</td><td>0.4%</td><td>12</td><td>Michigan</td><td>194,259</td><td>2.8%</td></tr>
<tr><td>5</td><td>Illinois</td><td>288,771</td><td>4.2%</td><td>13</td><td>Tennessee</td><td>169,169</td><td>2.4%</td></tr>
<tr><td>16</td><td>Indiana</td><td>148,670</td><td>2.1%</td><td>14</td><td>Missouri</td><td>158,264</td><td>2.3%</td></tr>
<tr><td>34</td><td>Iowa</td><td>62,258</td><td>0.9%</td><td>15</td><td>Virginia</td><td>153,464</td><td>2.2%</td></tr>
<tr><td>28</td><td>Kansas</td><td>80,260</td><td>1.2%</td><td>16</td><td>Indiana</td><td>148,670</td><td>2.1%</td></tr>
<tr><td>31</td><td>Kentucky</td><td>70,535</td><td>1.0%</td><td>17</td><td>New Jersey</td><td>139,977</td><td>2.0%</td></tr>
<tr><td>18</td><td>Louisiana</td><td>134,080</td><td>1.9%</td><td>18</td><td>Louisiana</td><td>134,080</td><td>1.9%</td></tr>
<tr><td>41</td><td>Maine</td><td>24,096</td><td>0.3%</td><td>19</td><td>South Carolina</td><td>130,051</td><td>1.9%</td></tr>
<tr><td>20</td><td>Maryland</td><td>129,786</td><td>1.9%</td><td>20</td><td>Maryland</td><td>129,786</td><td>1.9%</td></tr>
<tr><td>26</td><td>Massachusetts</td><td>101,303</td><td>1.5%</td><td>21</td><td>Alabama</td><td>123,650</td><td>1.8%</td></tr>
<tr><td>12</td><td>Michigan</td><td>194,259</td><td>2.8%</td><td>22</td><td>Colorado</td><td>123,271</td><td>1.8%</td></tr>
<tr><td>24</td><td>Minnesota</td><td>113,453</td><td>1.6%</td><td>23</td><td>Oregon</td><td>117,868</td><td>1.7%</td></tr>
<tr><td>33</td><td>Mississippi</td><td>65,440</td><td>0.9%</td><td>24</td><td>Minnesota</td><td>113,453</td><td>1.6%</td></tr>
<tr><td>14</td><td>Missouri</td><td>158,264</td><td>2.3%</td><td>25</td><td>Wisconsin</td><td>111,482</td><td>1.6%</td></tr>
<tr><td>42</td><td>Montana</td><td>22,082</td><td>0.3%</td><td>26</td><td>Massachusetts</td><td>101,303</td><td>1.5%</td></tr>
<tr><td>37</td><td>Nebraska</td><td>46,399</td><td>0.7%</td><td>27</td><td>Oklahoma</td><td>101,271</td><td>1.5%</td></tr>
<tr><td>35</td><td>Nevada</td><td>52,438</td><td>0.8%</td><td>28</td><td>Kansas</td><td>80,260</td><td>1.2%</td></tr>
<tr><td>44</td><td>New Hampshire</td><td>19,603</td><td>0.3%</td><td>29</td><td>Utah</td><td>74,735</td><td>1.1%</td></tr>
<tr><td>17</td><td>New Jersey</td><td>139,977</td><td>2.0%</td><td>30</td><td>Arkansas</td><td>73,874</td><td>1.1%</td></tr>
<tr><td>36</td><td>New Mexico</td><td>52,069</td><td>0.7%</td><td>31</td><td>Kentucky</td><td>70,535</td><td>1.0%</td></tr>
<tr><td>4</td><td>New York</td><td>311,036</td><td>4.5%</td><td>32</td><td>Connecticut</td><td>65,451</td><td>0.9%</td></tr>
<tr><td>8</td><td>North Carolina</td><td>227,147</td><td>3.3%</td><td>33</td><td>Mississippi</td><td>65,440</td><td>0.9%</td></tr>
<tr><td>50</td><td>North Dakota</td><td>9,342</td><td>0.1%</td><td>34</td><td>Iowa</td><td>62,258</td><td>0.9%</td></tr>
<tr><td>6</td><td>Ohio</td><td>283,103</td><td>4.1%</td><td>35</td><td>Nevada</td><td>52,438</td><td>0.8%</td></tr>
<tr><td>27</td><td>Oklahoma</td><td>101,271</td><td>1.5%</td><td>36</td><td>New Mexico</td><td>52,069</td><td>0.7%</td></tr>
<tr><td>23</td><td>Oregon</td><td>117,868</td><td>1.7%</td><td>37</td><td>Nebraska</td><td>46,399</td><td>0.7%</td></tr>
<tr><td>9</td><td>Pennsylvania</td><td>214,199</td><td>3.1%</td><td>38</td><td>Hawaii</td><td>41,078</td><td>0.6%</td></tr>
<tr><td>43</td><td>Rhode Island</td><td>21,623</td><td>0.3%</td><td>39</td><td>West Virginia</td><td>30,826</td><td>0.4%</td></tr>
<tr><td>19</td><td>South Carolina</td><td>130,051</td><td>1.9%</td><td>40</td><td>Idaho</td><td>28,583</td><td>0.4%</td></tr>
<tr><td>48</td><td>South Dakota</td><td>10,910</td><td>0.2%</td><td>41</td><td>Maine</td><td>24,096</td><td>0.3%</td></tr>
<tr><td>13</td><td>Tennessee</td><td>169,169</td><td>2.4%</td><td>42</td><td>Montana</td><td>22,082</td><td>0.3%</td></tr>
<tr><td>2</td><td>Texas</td><td>696,507</td><td>10.0%</td><td>43</td><td>Rhode Island</td><td>21,623</td><td>0.3%</td></tr>
<tr><td>29</td><td>Utah</td><td>74,735</td><td>1.1%</td><td>44</td><td>New Hampshire</td><td>19,603</td><td>0.3%</td></tr>
<tr><td>49</td><td>Vermont</td><td>10,382</td><td>0.1%</td><td>45</td><td>Delaware</td><td>18,742</td><td>0.3%</td></tr>
<tr><td>15</td><td>Virginia</td><td>153,464</td><td>2.2%</td><td>46</td><td>Alaska</td><td>16,159</td><td>0.2%</td></tr>
<tr><td>10</td><td>Washington</td><td>196,972</td><td>2.8%</td><td>47</td><td>Wyoming</td><td>13,352</td><td>0.2%</td></tr>
<tr><td>39</td><td>West Virginia</td><td>30,826</td><td>0.4%</td><td>48</td><td>South Dakota</td><td>10,910</td><td>0.2%</td></tr>
<tr><td>25</td><td>Wisconsin</td><td>111,482</td><td>1.6%</td><td>49</td><td>Vermont</td><td>10,382</td><td>0.1%</td></tr>
<tr><td>47</td><td>Wyoming</td><td>13,352</td><td>0.2%</td><td>50</td><td>North Dakota</td><td>9,342</td><td>0.1%</td></tr>
<tr><td></td><td></td><td></td><td></td><td></td><td>District of Columbia</td><td>14,542</td><td>0.2%</td></tr>
</table>

Source: Federal Bureau of Investigation
   "Crime in the United States 2004" (Uniform Crime Reports, October 17, 2005)
*Larceny and theft is the unlawful taking of property without use of force, violence or fraud. Attempts are included. Motor vehicle thefts are excluded.

Larceny and Theft Rate in 2004

National Rate = 2,365.9 Larcenies and Thefts per 100,000 Population*

ALPHA ORDER			RANK ORDER		
RANK	STATE	RATE	RANK	STATE	RATE
16	Alabama	2,729.5	1	Arizona	3,387.2
23	Alaska	2,465.4	2	Oregon	3,279.0
1	Arizona	3,387.2	3	Hawaii	3,252.8
17	Arkansas	2,683.8	4	Washington	3,175.0
35	California	2,030.1	5	Utah	3,128.2
18	Colorado	2,679.0	6	South Carolina	3,097.9
39	Connecticut	1,868.1	7	Texas	3,097.0
28	Delaware	2,257.1	8	Louisiana	2,969.2
13	Florida	2,773.3	9	Kansas	2,934.0
12	Georgia	2,825.0	10	Oklahoma	2,874.1
3	Hawaii	3,252.8	11	Tennessee	2,866.8
34	Idaho	2,051.5	12	Georgia	2,825.0
27	Illinois	2,271.3	13	Florida	2,773.3
24	Indiana	2,383.5	14	Missouri	2,750.2
32	Iowa	2,107.3	15	New Mexico	2,735.7
9	Kansas	2,934.0	16	Alabama	2,729.5
42	Kentucky	1,701.3	17	Arkansas	2,683.8
8	Louisiana	2,969.2	18	Colorado	2,679.0
40	Maine	1,829.3	19	North Carolina	2,659.4
26	Maryland	2,335.1	20	Nebraska	2,655.6
47	Massachusetts	1,578.8	21	Wyoming	2,636.0
38	Michigan	1,921.0	22	Ohio	2,470.6
31	Minnesota	2,224.2	23	Alaska	2,465.4
29	Mississippi	2,254.2	24	Indiana	2,383.5
14	Missouri	2,750.2	25	Montana	2,382.4
25	Montana	2,382.4	26	Maryland	2,335.1
20	Nebraska	2,655.6	27	Illinois	2,271.3
30	Nevada	2,246.0	28	Delaware	2,257.1
48	New Hampshire	1,508.5	29	Mississippi	2,254.2
46	New Jersey	1,609.1	30	Nevada	2,246.0
15	New Mexico	2,735.7	31	Minnesota	2,224.2
45	New York	1,617.7	32	Iowa	2,107.3
19	North Carolina	2,659.4	33	Virginia	2,057.2
49	North Dakota	1,472.7	34	Idaho	2,051.5
22	Ohio	2,470.6	35	California	2,030.1
10	Oklahoma	2,874.1	36	Wisconsin	2,023.6
2	Oregon	3,279.0	37	Rhode Island	2,001.0
41	Pennsylvania	1,726.5	38	Michigan	1,921.0
37	Rhode Island	2,001.0	39	Connecticut	1,868.1
6	South Carolina	3,097.9	40	Maine	1,829.3
50	South Dakota	1,415.3	41	Pennsylvania	1,726.5
11	Tennessee	2,866.8	42	Kentucky	1,701.3
7	Texas	3,097.0	43	West Virginia	1,698.1
5	Utah	3,128.2	44	Vermont	1,670.8
44	Vermont	1,670.8	45	New York	1,617.7
33	Virginia	2,057.2	46	New Jersey	1,609.1
4	Washington	3,175.0	47	Massachusetts	1,578.8
43	West Virginia	1,698.1	48	New Hampshire	1,508.5
36	Wisconsin	2,023.6	49	North Dakota	1,472.7
21	Wyoming	2,636.0	50	South Dakota	1,415.3
				District of Columbia	2,627.2

Source: Federal Bureau of Investigation
  "Crime in the United States 2004" (Uniform Crime Reports, October 17, 2005)
*Larceny and theft is the unlawful taking of property without use of force, violence or fraud. Attempts are included.
Motor vehicle thefts are excluded.

Motor Vehicle Thefts in 2004

National Total = 1,237,114 Motor Vehicle Thefts*

ALPHA ORDER

RANK	STATE	THEFTS	% of USA
25	Alabama	14,024	1.1%
42	Alaska	2,240	0.2%
4	Arizona	55,306	4.5%
36	Arkansas	6,491	0.5%
1	California	252,604	20.4%
17	Colorado	24,063	1.9%
29	Connecticut	11,025	0.9%
43	Delaware	2,147	0.2%
3	Florida	78,325	6.3%
6	Georgia	44,238	3.6%
31	Hawaii	8,620	0.7%
41	Idaho	2,724	0.2%
10	Illinois	40,355	3.3%
20	Indiana	21,091	1.7%
37	Iowa	5,404	0.4%
32	Kansas	8,435	0.7%
30	Kentucky	8,772	0.7%
21	Louisiana	19,714	1.6%
46	Maine	1,303	0.1%
11	Maryland	35,858	2.9%
19	Massachusetts	22,053	1.8%
5	Michigan	50,555	4.1%
26	Minnesota	13,518	1.1%
34	Mississippi	7,879	0.6%
15	Missouri	25,893	2.1%
45	Montana	1,618	0.1%
38	Nebraska	5,287	0.4%
18	Nevada	22,635	1.8%
44	New Hampshire	1,942	0.2%
13	New Jersey	30,306	2.4%
33	New Mexico	7,902	0.6%
8	New York	41,002	3.3%
14	North Carolina	26,988	2.2%
47	North Dakota	906	0.1%
9	Ohio	40,853	3.3%
27	Oklahoma	12,957	1.0%
22	Oregon	18,535	1.5%
12	Pennsylvania	30,969	2.5%
39	Rhode Island	4,078	0.3%
24	South Carolina	15,637	1.3%
48	South Dakota	846	0.1%
16	Tennessee	24,749	2.0%
2	Texas	94,077	7.6%
35	Utah	7,651	0.6%
50	Vermont	575	0.0%
23	Virginia	17,411	1.4%
7	Washington	43,233	3.5%
40	West Virginia	3,739	0.3%
28	Wisconsin	11,374	0.9%
49	Wyoming	799	0.1%

RANK ORDER

RANK	STATE	THEFTS	% of USA
1	California	252,604	20.4%
2	Texas	94,077	7.6%
3	Florida	78,325	6.3%
4	Arizona	55,306	4.5%
5	Michigan	50,555	4.1%
6	Georgia	44,238	3.6%
7	Washington	43,233	3.5%
8	New York	41,002	3.3%
9	Ohio	40,853	3.3%
10	Illinois	40,355	3.3%
11	Maryland	35,858	2.9%
12	Pennsylvania	30,969	2.5%
13	New Jersey	30,306	2.4%
14	North Carolina	26,988	2.2%
15	Missouri	25,893	2.1%
16	Tennessee	24,749	2.0%
17	Colorado	24,063	1.9%
18	Nevada	22,635	1.8%
19	Massachusetts	22,053	1.8%
20	Indiana	21,091	1.7%
21	Louisiana	19,714	1.6%
22	Oregon	18,535	1.5%
23	Virginia	17,411	1.4%
24	South Carolina	15,637	1.3%
25	Alabama	14,024	1.1%
26	Minnesota	13,518	1.1%
27	Oklahoma	12,957	1.0%
28	Wisconsin	11,374	0.9%
29	Connecticut	11,025	0.9%
30	Kentucky	8,772	0.7%
31	Hawaii	8,620	0.7%
32	Kansas	8,435	0.7%
33	New Mexico	7,902	0.6%
34	Mississippi	7,879	0.6%
35	Utah	7,651	0.6%
36	Arkansas	6,491	0.5%
37	Iowa	5,404	0.4%
38	Nebraska	5,287	0.4%
39	Rhode Island	4,078	0.3%
40	West Virginia	3,739	0.3%
41	Idaho	2,724	0.2%
42	Alaska	2,240	0.2%
43	Delaware	2,147	0.2%
44	New Hampshire	1,942	0.2%
45	Montana	1,618	0.1%
46	Maine	1,303	0.1%
47	North Dakota	906	0.1%
48	South Dakota	846	0.1%
49	Wyoming	799	0.1%
50	Vermont	575	0.0%
	District of Columbia	8,408	0.7%

Source: Federal Bureau of Investigation
   "Crime in the United States 2004" (Uniform Crime Reports, October 17, 2005)
*Includes the theft or attempted theft of a self-propelled vehicle. Excludes motorboats, construction equipment,
airplanes and farming equipment.

Motor Vehicle Theft Rate in 2004

National Rate = 421.3 Motor Vehicle Thefts per 100,000 Population*

ALPHA ORDER				RANK ORDER		
RANK	STATE	RATE		RANK	STATE	RATE
29	Alabama	309.6		1	Nevada	969.5
23	Alaska	341.8		2	Arizona	962.9
2	Arizona	962.9		3	California	703.8
36	Arkansas	235.8		4	Washington	696.9
3	California	703.8		5	Hawaii	682.6
7	Colorado	522.9		6	Maryland	645.2
28	Connecticut	314.7		7	Colorado	522.9
34	Delaware	258.6		8	Oregon	515.6
11	Florida	450.2		9	Georgia	501.0
9	Georgia	501.0		10	Michigan	499.9
5	Hawaii	682.6		11	Florida	450.2
42	Idaho	195.5		12	Missouri	450.0
26	Illinois	317.4		13	Louisiana	436.6
24	Indiana	338.1		14	Tennessee	419.4
43	Iowa	182.9		15	Texas	418.3
30	Kansas	308.4		16	New Mexico	415.2
39	Kentucky	211.6		17	Rhode Island	377.4
13	Louisiana	436.6		18	South Carolina	372.5
49	Maine	98.9		19	Oklahoma	367.7
6	Maryland	645.2		20	Ohio	356.5
22	Massachusetts	343.7		21	New Jersey	348.4
10	Michigan	499.9		22	Massachusetts	343.7
33	Minnesota	265.0		23	Alaska	341.8
32	Mississippi	271.4		24	Indiana	338.1
12	Missouri	450.0		25	Utah	320.3
44	Montana	174.6		26	Illinois	317.4
31	Nebraska	302.6		27	North Carolina	316.0
1	Nevada	969.5		28	Connecticut	314.7
46	New Hampshire	149.4		29	Alabama	309.6
21	New Jersey	348.4		30	Kansas	308.4
16	New Mexico	415.2		31	Nebraska	302.6
38	New York	213.3		32	Mississippi	271.4
27	North Carolina	316.0		33	Minnesota	265.0
47	North Dakota	142.8		34	Delaware	258.6
20	Ohio	356.5		35	Pennsylvania	249.6
19	Oklahoma	367.7		36	Arkansas	235.8
8	Oregon	515.6		37	Virginia	233.4
35	Pennsylvania	249.6		38	New York	213.3
17	Rhode Island	377.4		39	Kentucky	211.6
18	South Carolina	372.5		40	Wisconsin	206.5
48	South Dakota	109.7		41	West Virginia	206.0
14	Tennessee	419.4		42	Idaho	195.5
15	Texas	418.3		43	Iowa	182.9
25	Utah	320.3		44	Montana	174.6
50	Vermont	92.5		45	Wyoming	157.7
37	Virginia	233.4		46	New Hampshire	149.4
4	Washington	696.9		47	North Dakota	142.8
41	West Virginia	206.0		48	South Dakota	109.7
40	Wisconsin	206.5		49	Maine	98.9
45	Wyoming	157.7		50	Vermont	92.5
				District of Columbia		1,519.0

Source: Federal Bureau of Investigation
   "Crime in the United States 2004" (Uniform Crime Reports, October 17, 2005)
Includes the theft or attempted theft of a self-propelled vehicle. Excludes motorboats, construction equipment, airplanes and farming equipment.

Rate of Consumer Fraud Complaints in 2005

National Rate = 125.3 Complaints per 100,000 Population*

ALPHA ORDER			RANK ORDER		
RANK	STATE	RATE	RANK	STATE	RATE
38	Alabama	106.2	1	Alaska	249.2
1	Alaska	249.2	2	Washington	175.1
3	Arizona	164.8	3	Arizona	164.8
49	Arkansas	77.5	4	Oregon	163.1
16	California	134.8	5	Colorado	161.9
5	Colorado	161.9	6	Nevada	156.1
18	Connecticut	133.5	7	Utah	155.0
24	Delaware	129.3	8	New Hampshire	153.3
14	Florida	139.4	9	Indiana	152.6
33	Georgia	113.4	10	Maryland	150.2
13	Hawaii	145.2	11	Virginia	148.5
20	Idaho	132.9	12	South Carolina	148.3
30	Illinois	116.6	13	Hawaii	145.2
9	Indiana	152.6	14	Florida	139.4
44	Iowa	100.5	15	Missouri	136.4
28	Kansas	121.1	16	California	134.8
45	Kentucky	99.4	17	Montana	133.9
48	Louisiana	82.3	18	Connecticut	133.5
22	Maine	129.7	19	Wyoming	133.3
10	Maryland	150.2	20	Idaho	132.9
31	Massachusetts	115.1	21	Wisconsin	130.3
32	Michigan	114.8	22	Maine	129.7
27	Minnesota	121.3	23	Nebraska	129.5
50	Mississippi	72.4	24	Delaware	129.3
15	Missouri	136.4	25	Pennsylvania	128.7
17	Montana	133.9	26	Ohio	122.8
23	Nebraska	129.5	27	Minnesota	121.3
6	Nevada	156.1	28	Kansas	121.1
8	New Hampshire	153.3	29	New Jersey	116.8
29	New Jersey	116.8	30	Illinois	116.6
35	New Mexico	112.4	31	Massachusetts	115.1
37	New York	108.4	32	Michigan	114.8
34	North Carolina	112.5	33	Georgia	113.4
46	North Dakota	99.3	34	North Carolina	112.5
26	Ohio	122.8	35	New Mexico	112.4
36	Oklahoma	110.4	36	Oklahoma	110.4
4	Oregon	163.1	37	New York	108.4
25	Pennsylvania	128.7	38	Alabama	106.2
40	Rhode Island	104.7	39	Tennessee	105.0
12	South Carolina	148.3	40	Rhode Island	104.7
47	South Dakota	91.4	41	Vermont	104.5
39	Tennessee	105.0	42	West Virginia	101.8
43	Texas	101.4	43	Texas	101.4
7	Utah	155.0	44	Iowa	100.5
41	Vermont	104.5	45	Kentucky	99.4
11	Virginia	148.5	46	North Dakota	99.3
2	Washington	175.1	47	South Dakota	91.4
42	West Virginia	101.8	48	Louisiana	82.3
21	Wisconsin	130.3	49	Arkansas	77.5
19	Wyoming	133.3	50	Mississippi	72.4
				District of Columbia	225.8

Source: Federal Trade Commission, Consumer Sentinel
   "Consumer Fraud and Identify Theft Complaint Data (January 2006)
*Figures are for individuals filing complaints. Some complaints result in multiple infractions. Does not include identity theft or "Do Not Call" registry complaints.

Rate of Identity Theft Complaints in 2005

National Rate = 83.8 Complaints per 100,000 Population*

RANK	STATE	RATE
30	Alabama	58.7
26	Alaska	63.4
1	Arizona	156.9
33	Arkansas	58.2
3	California	125.0
5	Colorado	97.2
23	Connecticut	65.9
16	Delaware	69.1
6	Florida	95.8
9	Georgia	87.3
25	Hawaii	63.5
38	Idaho	52.1
9	Illinois	87.3
22	Indiana	67.0
47	Iowa	36.7
32	Kansas	58.5
43	Kentucky	43.5
27	Louisiana	62.6
46	Maine	37.2
11	Maryland	86.6
28	Massachusetts	62.5
15	Michigan	70.5
30	Minnesota	58.7
40	Mississippi	49.9
19	Missouri	67.6
44	Montana	42.5
37	Nebraska	52.3
2	Nevada	130.2
41	New Hampshire	49.2
14	New Jersey	75.5
12	New Mexico	84.7
8	New York	90.3
21	North Carolina	67.1
50	North Dakota	24.8
29	Ohio	62.4
18	Oklahoma	67.7
13	Oregon	81.7
24	Pennsylvania	63.6
33	Rhode Island	58.2
36	South Carolina	56.8
49	South Dakota	30.0
35	Tennessee	57.2
4	Texas	116.5
20	Utah	67.5
48	Vermont	32.3
17	Virginia	68.2
7	Washington	92.4
45	West Virginia	37.3
39	Wisconsin	50.3
42	Wyoming	44.0

RANK	STATE	RATE
1	Arizona	156.9
2	Nevada	130.2
3	California	125.0
4	Texas	116.5
5	Colorado	97.2
6	Florida	95.8
7	Washington	92.4
8	New York	90.3
9	Georgia	87.3
9	Illinois	87.3
11	Maryland	86.6
12	New Mexico	84.7
13	Oregon	81.7
14	New Jersey	75.5
15	Michigan	70.5
16	Delaware	69.1
17	Virginia	68.2
18	Oklahoma	67.7
19	Missouri	67.6
20	Utah	67.5
21	North Carolina	67.1
22	Indiana	67.0
23	Connecticut	65.9
24	Pennsylvania	63.6
25	Hawaii	63.5
26	Alaska	63.4
27	Louisiana	62.6
28	Massachusetts	62.5
29	Ohio	62.4
30	Alabama	58.7
30	Minnesota	58.7
32	Kansas	58.5
33	Arkansas	58.2
33	Rhode Island	58.2
35	Tennessee	57.2
36	South Carolina	56.8
37	Nebraska	52.3
38	Idaho	52.1
39	Wisconsin	50.3
40	Mississippi	49.9
41	New Hampshire	49.2
42	Wyoming	44.0
43	Kentucky	43.5
44	Montana	42.5
45	West Virginia	37.3
46	Maine	37.2
47	Iowa	36.7
48	Vermont	32.3
49	South Dakota	30.0
50	North Dakota	24.8

	District of Columbia	152.9

Source: Federal Trade Commission, Consumer Sentinel
   "Consumer Fraud and Identify Theft Complaint Data (January 2006)
*Figures are for individuals filing complaints. Some complaints result in multiple infractions. Does not include consumer fraud or "Do Not Call" registry complaints.

Reported Arrest Rate in 2004

National Rate = 4,865.4 Reported Arrests per 100,000 Population*

<table>
<tr><td colspan="3">ALPHA ORDER</td><td colspan="3">RANK ORDER</td></tr>
<tr><th>RANK</th><th>STATE</th><th>RATE</th><th>RANK</th><th>STATE</th><th>RATE</th></tr>
<tr><td>21</td><td>Alabama</td><td>5,207.6</td><td>1</td><td>Wisconsin</td><td>8,441.4</td></tr>
<tr><td>14</td><td>Alaska</td><td>5,784.0</td><td>2</td><td>Mississippi</td><td>7,609.7</td></tr>
<tr><td>18</td><td>Arizona</td><td>5,631.4</td><td>3</td><td>Louisiana</td><td>7,400.8</td></tr>
<tr><td>5</td><td>Arkansas</td><td>6,673.2</td><td>4</td><td>Wyoming</td><td>7,276.1</td></tr>
<tr><td>32</td><td>California</td><td>4,215.4</td><td>5</td><td>Arkansas</td><td>6,673.2</td></tr>
<tr><td>12</td><td>Colorado</td><td>5,834.1</td><td>6</td><td>Nevada</td><td>6,607.1</td></tr>
<tr><td>39</td><td>Connecticut</td><td>4,003.3</td><td>7</td><td>Georgia</td><td>6,530.2</td></tr>
<tr><td>36</td><td>Delaware</td><td>4,126.9</td><td>8</td><td>North Carolina</td><td>6,502.0</td></tr>
<tr><td>11</td><td>Florida</td><td>5,916.3</td><td>9</td><td>New Mexico</td><td>6,421.8</td></tr>
<tr><td>7</td><td>Georgia</td><td>6,530.2</td><td>10</td><td>Utah</td><td>5,926.5</td></tr>
<tr><td>29</td><td>Hawaii</td><td>4,480.7</td><td>11</td><td>Florida</td><td>5,916.3</td></tr>
<tr><td>17</td><td>Idaho</td><td>5,711.6</td><td>12</td><td>Colorado</td><td>5,834.1</td></tr>
<tr><td>NA</td><td>Illinois**</td><td>NA</td><td>13</td><td>South Dakota</td><td>5,819.2</td></tr>
<tr><td>24</td><td>Indiana</td><td>4,707.2</td><td>14</td><td>Alaska</td><td>5,784.0</td></tr>
<tr><td>31</td><td>Iowa</td><td>4,397.8</td><td>15</td><td>Missouri</td><td>5,757.2</td></tr>
<tr><td>34</td><td>Kansas</td><td>4,139.5</td><td>16</td><td>Nebraska</td><td>5,737.9</td></tr>
<tr><td>NA</td><td>Kentucky**</td><td>NA</td><td>17</td><td>Idaho</td><td>5,711.6</td></tr>
<tr><td>3</td><td>Louisiana</td><td>7,400.8</td><td>18</td><td>Arizona</td><td>5,631.4</td></tr>
<tr><td>33</td><td>Maine</td><td>4,204.7</td><td>19</td><td>Maryland</td><td>5,574.6</td></tr>
<tr><td>19</td><td>Maryland</td><td>5,574.6</td><td>20</td><td>Tennessee</td><td>5,559.7</td></tr>
<tr><td>46</td><td>Massachusetts</td><td>2,208.3</td><td>21</td><td>Alabama</td><td>5,207.6</td></tr>
<tr><td>41</td><td>Michigan</td><td>3,525.1</td><td>22</td><td>North Dakota</td><td>5,086.4</td></tr>
<tr><td>40</td><td>Minnesota</td><td>3,722.2</td><td>23</td><td>Texas</td><td>5,013.0</td></tr>
<tr><td>2</td><td>Mississippi</td><td>7,609.7</td><td>24</td><td>Indiana</td><td>4,707.2</td></tr>
<tr><td>15</td><td>Missouri</td><td>5,757.2</td><td>25</td><td>Oklahoma</td><td>4,665.8</td></tr>
<tr><td>NA</td><td>Montana**</td><td>NA</td><td>26</td><td>Washington</td><td>4,572.7</td></tr>
<tr><td>16</td><td>Nebraska</td><td>5,737.9</td><td>27</td><td>Oregon</td><td>4,534.4</td></tr>
<tr><td>6</td><td>Nevada</td><td>6,607.1</td><td>28</td><td>New Jersey</td><td>4,496.5</td></tr>
<tr><td>30</td><td>New Hampshire</td><td>4,414.1</td><td>29</td><td>Hawaii</td><td>4,480.7</td></tr>
<tr><td>28</td><td>New Jersey</td><td>4,496.5</td><td>30</td><td>New Hampshire</td><td>4,414.1</td></tr>
<tr><td>9</td><td>New Mexico</td><td>6,421.8</td><td>31</td><td>Iowa</td><td>4,397.0</td></tr>
<tr><td>43</td><td>New York</td><td>3,221.0</td><td>32</td><td>California</td><td>4,215.4</td></tr>
<tr><td>8</td><td>North Carolina</td><td>6,502.0</td><td>33</td><td>Maine</td><td>4,204.7</td></tr>
<tr><td>22</td><td>North Dakota</td><td>5,086.4</td><td>34</td><td>Kansas</td><td>4,139.5</td></tr>
<tr><td>42</td><td>Ohio</td><td>3,477.8</td><td>35</td><td>Virginia</td><td>4,132.0</td></tr>
<tr><td>25</td><td>Oklahoma</td><td>4,665.8</td><td>36</td><td>Delaware</td><td>4,126.9</td></tr>
<tr><td>27</td><td>Oregon</td><td>4,534.4</td><td>37</td><td>Pennsylvania</td><td>4,119.7</td></tr>
<tr><td>37</td><td>Pennsylvania</td><td>4,119.7</td><td>38</td><td>Rhode Island</td><td>4,032.5</td></tr>
<tr><td>38</td><td>Rhode Island</td><td>4,032.5</td><td>39</td><td>Connecticut</td><td>4,003.3</td></tr>
<tr><td>NA</td><td>South Carolina**</td><td>NA</td><td>40</td><td>Minnesota</td><td>3,722.2</td></tr>
<tr><td>13</td><td>South Dakota</td><td>5,819.2</td><td>41</td><td>Michigan</td><td>3,525.1</td></tr>
<tr><td>20</td><td>Tennessee</td><td>5,559.7</td><td>42</td><td>Ohio</td><td>3,477.8</td></tr>
<tr><td>23</td><td>Texas</td><td>5,013.0</td><td>43</td><td>New York</td><td>3,221.0</td></tr>
<tr><td>10</td><td>Utah</td><td>5,926.5</td><td>44</td><td>West Virginia</td><td>2,873.0</td></tr>
<tr><td>45</td><td>Vermont</td><td>2,322.3</td><td>45</td><td>Vermont</td><td>2,322.3</td></tr>
<tr><td>35</td><td>Virginia</td><td>4,132.0</td><td>46</td><td>Massachusetts</td><td>2,208.3</td></tr>
<tr><td>26</td><td>Washington</td><td>4,572.7</td><td>NA</td><td>Illinois**</td><td>NA</td></tr>
<tr><td>44</td><td>West Virginia</td><td>2,873.0</td><td>NA</td><td>Kentucky**</td><td>NA</td></tr>
<tr><td>1</td><td>Wisconsin</td><td>8,441.4</td><td>NA</td><td>Montana**</td><td>NA</td></tr>
<tr><td>4</td><td>Wyoming</td><td>7,276.1</td><td>NA</td><td>South Carolina**</td><td>NA</td></tr>
<tr><td></td><td></td><td></td><td></td><td>District of Columbia**</td><td>NA</td></tr>
</table>

Source: Morgan Quitno Press using data from Federal Bureau of Investigation
"Crime in the United States 2004" (Uniform Crime Reports, October 17, 2005)
*By law enforcement agencies submitting complete reports to the F.B.I. for 12 months in 2004. These rates based on population estimates for areas under the jurisdiction of those agencies reporting. Arrest rate based on the F.B.I. estimate of total arrests is 4,769.0 reported and unreported arrests per 100,000 population. See important note at beginning of this chapter. **Not available.*

Reported Juvenile Arrest Rate in 2004

National Rate = 6,566.3 Reported Arrests per 100,000 Juvenile Population*

ALPHA ORDER				RANK ORDER		
RANK	STATE	RATE		RANK	STATE	RATE
42	Alabama	3,034.7		1	Wisconsin	19,558.5
37	Alaska	5,176.5		2	Wyoming	12,258.4
13	Arizona	8,013.4		3	North Dakota	11,799.9
33	Arkansas	5,684.5		4	Utah	11,144.3
38	California	4,997.1		5	Idaho	10,176.8
7	Colorado	9,651.7		6	South Dakota	9,703.0
32	Connecticut	5,966.4		7	Colorado	9,651.7
10	Delaware	8,406.3		8	Louisiana	9,448.0
25	Florida	6,571.8		9	Pennsylvania	8,761.9
NA	Georgia**	NA		10	Delaware	8,406.3
11	Hawaii	8,233.3		11	Hawaii	8,233.3
5	Idaho	10,176.8		12	Maryland	8,031.2
NA	Illinois**	NA		13	Arizona	8,013.4
26	Indiana	6,353.8		14	Oregon	7,997.0
19	Iowa	6,953.7		15	Nebraska	7,950.6
35	Kansas	5,621.7		16	Minnesota	7,629.8
NA	Kentucky**	NA		17	Texas	7,140.7
8	Louisiana	9,448.0		18	Mississippi	7,119.7
31	Maine	6,035.6		19	Iowa	6,953.7
12	Maryland	8,031.2		20	Missouri	6,944.0
43	Massachusetts	2,969.9		21	Nevada	6,897.7
41	Michigan	3,505.3		22	New Hampshire	6,733.7
16	Minnesota	7,629.8		23	Tennessee	6,648.1
18	Mississippi	7,119.7		24	Washington	6,593.9
20	Missouri	6,944.0		25	Florida	6,571.8
NA	Montana**	NA		26	Indiana	6,353.8
15	Nebraska	7,950.6		27	New Mexico	6,296.2
21	Nevada	6,897.7		28	New Jersey	6,280.1
22	New Hampshire	6,733.7		29	Oklahoma	6,171.5
28	New Jersey	6,280.1		30	Rhode Island	6,165.0
27	New Mexico	6,296.2		31	Maine	6,035.6
40	New York	4,432.8		32	Connecticut	5,966.4
34	North Carolina	5,632.8		33	Arkansas	5,684.5
3	North Dakota	11,799.9		34	North Carolina	5,632.8
36	Ohio	5,381.6		35	Kansas	5,621.7
29	Oklahoma	6,171.5		36	Ohio	5,381.6
14	Oregon	7,997.0		37	Alaska	5,176.5
9	Pennsylvania	8,761.9		38	California	4,997.1
30	Rhode Island	6,165.0		39	Virginia	4,710.2
NA	South Carolina**	NA		40	New York	4,432.8
6	South Dakota	9,703.0		41	Michigan	3,505.3
23	Tennessee	6,648.1		42	Alabama	3,034.7
17	Texas	7,140.7		43	Massachusetts	2,969.9
4	Utah	11,144.3		44	Vermont	2,427.7
44	Vermont	2,427.7		45	West Virginia	1,842.1
39	Virginia	4,710.2		NA	Georgia**	NA
24	Washington	6,593.9		NA	Illinois**	NA
45	West Virginia	1,842.1		NA	Kentucky**	NA
1	Wisconsin	19,558.5		NA	Montana**	NA
2	Wyoming	12,258.4		NA	South Carolina**	NA
					District of Columbia**	NA

Source: Morgan Quitno Press using data from Federal Bureau of Investigation
"Crime in the United States 2004" (Uniform Crime Reports, October 17, 2005)
*By law enforcement agencies submitting complete reports to the F.B.I. for 12 months in 2004. Arrests of youths 17 years and younger divided into population of 10 to 17 year olds. See important note at beginning of this chapter.
**Not available.

Prisoners in State Correctional Institutions: Year End 2004

National Total = 1,316,301 State Prisoners*

ALPHA ORDER

RANK	STATE	PRISONERS	% of USA
16	Alabama	25,887	2.0%
41	Alaska	4,554	0.3%
13	Arizona	32,515	2.5%
28	Arkansas	13,807	1.0%
2	California	166,556	12.7%
24	Colorado	20,293	1.5%
25	Connecticut	19,497	1.5%
35	Delaware	6,927	0.5%
3	Florida	85,533	6.5%
5	Georgia	51,104	3.9%
39	Hawaii	5,960	0.5%
37	Idaho	6,375	0.5%
8	Illinois	44,054	3.3%
18	Indiana	24,000	1.0%
34	Iowa	8,525	0.6%
32	Kansas	8,966	0.7%
26	Kentucky	17,814	1.4%
10	Louisiana	36,939	2.8%
47	Maine	2,024	0.2%
21	Maryland	23,285	1.8%
31	Massachusetts	10,144	0.8%
6	Michigan	48,883	3.7%
33	Minnesota	8,758	0.7%
23	Mississippi	20,983	1.6%
14	Missouri	31,081	2.4%
43	Montana	3,877	0.3%
42	Nebraska	4,130	0.3%
30	Nevada	11,365	0.9%
46	New Hampshire	2,448	0.2%
15	New Jersey	26,757	2.0%
36	New Mexico	6,379	0.5%
4	New York	63,751	4.8%
12	North Carolina	35,434	2.7%
50	North Dakota	1,327	0.1%
7	Ohio	44,806	3.4%
20	Oklahoma	23,319	1.8%
29	Oregon	13,183	1.0%
9	Pennsylvania	40,963	3.1%
44	Rhode Island	3,430	0.3%
19	South Carolina	23,428	1.8%
45	South Dakota	3,095	0.2%
17	Tennessee	25,884	2.0%
1	Texas	168,105	12.8%
38	Utah	5,989	0.5%
49	Vermont	1,968	0.1%
11	Virginia	35,564	2.7%
27	Washington	16,614	1.3%
40	West Virginia	5,067	0.4%
22	Wisconsin	22,966	1.7%
48	Wyoming	1,980	0.2%

RANK ORDER

RANK	STATE	PRISONERS	% of USA
1	Texas	168,105	12.8%
2	California	166,556	12.7%
3	Florida	85,533	6.5%
4	New York	63,751	4.8%
5	Georgia	51,104	3.9%
6	Michigan	48,883	3.7%
7	Ohio	44,806	3.4%
8	Illinois	44,054	3.3%
9	Pennsylvania	40,963	3.1%
10	Louisiana	36,939	2.8%
11	Virginia	35,564	2.7%
12	North Carolina	35,434	2.7%
13	Arizona	32,515	2.5%
14	Missouri	31,081	2.4%
15	New Jersey	26,757	2.0%
16	Alabama	25,887	2.0%
17	Tennessee	25,884	2.0%
18	Indiana	24,008	1.8%
19	South Carolina	23,428	1.8%
20	Oklahoma	23,319	1.8%
21	Maryland	23,285	1.8%
22	Wisconsin	22,966	1.7%
23	Mississippi	20,983	1.6%
24	Colorado	20,293	1.5%
25	Connecticut	19,497	1.5%
26	Kentucky	17,814	1.4%
27	Washington	16,614	1.3%
28	Arkansas	13,807	1.0%
29	Oregon	13,183	1.0%
30	Nevada	11,365	0.9%
31	Massachusetts	10,144	0.8%
32	Kansas	8,966	0.7%
33	Minnesota	8,758	0.7%
34	Iowa	8,525	0.6%
35	Delaware	6,927	0.5%
36	New Mexico	6,379	0.5%
37	Idaho	6,375	0.5%
38	Utah	5,989	0.5%
39	Hawaii	5,960	0.5%
40	West Virginia	5,067	0.4%
41	Alaska	4,554	0.3%
42	Nebraska	4,130	0.3%
43	Montana	3,877	0.3%
44	Rhode Island	3,430	0.3%
45	South Dakota	3,095	0.2%
46	New Hampshire	2,448	0.2%
47	Maine	2,024	0.2%
48	Wyoming	1,980	0.2%
49	Vermont	1,968	0.1%
50	North Dakota	1,327	0.1%
	District of Columbia**	NA	NA

Source: U.S. Department of Justice, Bureau of Justice Statistics
"Prisoners in 2004" (October 2005, NCJ-210677)
Advance figures as of December 31, 2004. Totals reflect all prisoners, including those sentenced to a year or less and those unsentenced. National total does not include 180,328 prisoners under federal jurisdiction. State and federal prisoners combined total 1,496,629.
**Responsibility for sentenced felons in D.C. was transferred to the Federal Bureau of Prisons in 2001.*

State Prisoner Incarceration Rate in 2004

National Rate = 432 State Prisoners per 100,000 Population*

ALPHA ORDER				RANK ORDER		
RANK	STATE	RATE		RANK	STATE	RATE
6	Alabama	556		1	Louisiana	816
24	Alaska	398		2	Texas	694
9	Arizona	534		3	Mississippi	669
10	Arkansas	495		4	Oklahoma	649
16	California	456		5	Georgia	574
18	Colorado	438		6	Alabama	556
29	Connecticut	377		7	South Carolina	539
11	Delaware	488		8	Missouri	538
12	Florida	486		9	Arizona	534
5	Georgia	574		10	Arkansas	495
34	Hawaii	329		11	Delaware	488
17	Idaho	454		12	Florida	486
32	Illinois	346		13	Michigan	483
28	Indiana	383		14	Nevada	474
39	Iowa	288		15	Virginia	473
36	Kansas	327		16	California	456
21	Kentucky	412		17	Idaho	454
1	Louisiana	816		18	Colorado	438
50	Maine	148		19	Tennessee	437
22	Maryland	406		20	Montana	416
44	Massachusetts	232		21	Kentucky	412
13	Michigan	483		22	Maryland	406
49	Minnesota	171		23	South Dakota	399
3	Mississippi	669		24	Alaska	398
8	Missouri	538		25	Ohio	391
20	Montana	416		26	Wisconsin	390
45	Nebraska	230		27	Wyoming	389
14	Nevada	474		28	Indiana	383
47	New Hampshire	187		29	Connecticut	377
38	New Jersey	306		30	Oregon	365
37	New Mexico	318		31	North Carolina	357
33	New York	331		32	Illinois	346
31	North Carolina	357		33	New York	331
46	North Dakota	195		34	Hawaii	329
25	Ohio	391		34	Pennsylvania	329
4	Oklahoma	649		36	Kansas	327
30	Oregon	365		37	New Mexico	318
34	Pennsylvania	329		38	New Jersey	306
48	Rhode Island	175		39	Iowa	288
7	South Carolina	539		40	West Virginia	277
23	South Dakota	399		41	Washington	264
19	Tennessee	437		42	Utah	246
2	Texas	694		43	Vermont	233
42	Utah	246		44	Massachusetts	232
43	Vermont	233		45	Nebraska	230
15	Virginia	473		46	North Dakota	195
41	Washington	264		47	New Hampshire	187
40	West Virginia	277		48	Rhode Island	175
26	Wisconsin	390		49	Minnesota	171
27	Wyoming	389		50	Maine	148
				District of Columbia**		NA

Source: U.S. Department of Justice, Bureau of Justice Statistics
   "Prisoners in 2004" (October 2005, NCJ-210677)
*As of December 31, 2004. Includes only inmates sentenced to more than one year. Does not include federal incarceration rate of 54 prisoners per 100,000 population. State and federal combined incarceration rate is 486 prisoners per 100,000 population.
**Responsibility for sentenced felons in D.C. was transferred to the Federal Bureau of Prisons in 2001.

Percent Change in Number of State Prisoners: 2003 to 2004

National Percent Change = 1.6% Increase*

ALPHA ORDER				RANK ORDER		
RANK	STATE	PERCENT CHANGE		RANK	STATE	PERCENT CHANGE
50	Alabama	(7.3)		1	Minnesota	11.4
35	Alaska	0.6		2	Idaho	11.1
11	Arizona	4.3		3	Georgia	8.3
15	Arkansas	3.7		4	Nevada	7.8
32	California	1.3		5	Kentucky	7.2
17	Colorado	3.2		6	Montana	7.1
44	Connecticut	(1.8)		6	North Dakota	7.1
26	Delaware	2.0		8	West Virginia	6.5
11	Florida	4.3		9	Wyoming	5.8
3	Georgia	8.3		10	North Carolina	5.6
22	Hawaii	2.3		11	Arizona	4.3
2	Idaho	11.1		11	Florida	4.3
30	Illinois	1.5		13	Indiana	4.1
13	Indiana	4.1		14	Utah	3.9
40	Iowa	(0.2)		15	Arkansas	3.7
46	Kansas	(1.8)		15	Oregon	3.7
5	Kentucky	7.2		17	Colorado	3.2
20	Louisiana	2.5		18	Washington	2.9
37	Maine	0.5		19	Missouri	2.6
47	Maryland	(2.1)		20	Louisiana	2.5
41	Massachusetts	(0.9)		20	New Mexico	2.5
42	Michigan	(1.0)		22	Hawaii	2.3
1	Minnesota	11.4		22	South Dakota	2.3
27	Mississippi	1.9		24	Nebraska	2.2
19	Missouri	2.6		24	Oklahoma	2.2
6	Montana	7.1		26	Delaware	2.0
24	Nebraska	2.2		27	Mississippi	1.9
4	Nevada	7.8		27	Tennessee	1.9
35	New Hampshire	0.6		29	Wisconsin	1.6
45	New Jersey	(1.8)		30	Illinois	1.5
20	New Mexico	2.5		31	Virginia	1.4
48	New York	(2.2)		32	California	1.3
10	North Carolina	5.6		33	Vermont	1.2
6	North Dakota	7.1		34	Texas	0.7
39	Ohio	0.1		35	Alaska	0.6
24	Oklahoma	2.2		35	New Hampshire	0.6
15	Oregon	3.7		37	Maine	0.5
38	Pennsylvania	0.2		38	Pennsylvania	0.2
49	Rhode Island	(2.8)		39	Ohio	0.1
43	South Carolina	(1.2)		40	Iowa	(0.2)
22	South Dakota	2.3		41	Massachusetts	(0.9)
27	Tennessee	1.9		42	Michigan	(1.0)
34	Texas	0.7		43	South Carolina	(1.2)
14	Utah	3.9		44	Connecticut	(1.8)
33	Vermont	1.2		45	New Jersey	(1.8)
31	Virginia	1.4		46	Kansas	(1.8)
18	Washington	2.9		47	Maryland	(2.1)
8	West Virginia	6.5		48	New York	(2.2)
29	Wisconsin	1.6		49	Rhode Island	(2.8)
9	Wyoming	5.8		50	Alabama	(7.3)
				District of Columbia**		NA

Source: U.S. Department of Justice, Bureau of Justice Statistics
   "Prisoners in 2004" (October 2005, NCJ-210677)
From December 31, 2003 to December 31, 2004. Includes inmates sentenced to more than one year and those sentenced to a year or less or with no sentence. The percent change in number of prisoners under federal jurisdiction during the same period was an 4.2% increase. The combined state and federal increase was 1.9%.
**Responsibility for sentenced felons in D.C. was transferred to the Federal Bureau of Prisons in 2001.*

Prisoners Under Sentence of Death in 2004

National Total = 3,282 State Prisoners*

ALPHA ORDER

RANK	STATE	PRISONERS	% of USA
6	Alabama	193	5.9%
NA	Alaska**	NA	NA
9	Arizona	105	3.2%
17	Arkansas	39	1.2%
1	California	637	19.4%
33	Colorado	3	0.1%
29	Connecticut	7	0.2%
23	Delaware	17	0.5%
3	Florida	364	11.1%
8	Georgia	109	3.3%
NA	Hawaii**	NA	NA
22	Idaho	22	0.7%
30	Illinois	6	0.2%
20	Indiana	27	0.8%
NA	Iowa**	NA	NA
37	Kansas	0	0.0%
18	Kentucky	34	1.0%
12	Louisiana	87	2.7%
NA	Maine**	NA	NA
27	Maryland	9	0.3%
NA	Massachusetts**	NA	NA
NA	Michigan**	NA	NA
NA	Minnesota**	NA	NA
15	Mississippi	70	2.1%
16	Missouri	52	1.6%
31	Montana	4	0.1%
28	Nebraska	8	0.2%
13	Nevada	83	2.5%
37	New Hampshire	0	0.0%
24	New Jersey	11	0.3%
34	New Mexico	2	0.1%
34	New York	2	0.1%
7	North Carolina	181	5.5%
NA	North Dakota**	NA	NA
5	Ohio	201	6.1%
11	Oklahoma	91	2.8%
19	Oregon	30	0.9%
4	Pennsylvania	222	6.8%
NA	Rhode Island**	NA	NA
14	South Carolina	71	2.2%
31	South Dakota	4	0.1%
10	Tennessee	99	3.0%
2	Texas	446	13.6%
26	Utah	10	0.3%
NA	Vermont**	NA	NA
21	Virginia	23	0.7%
24	Washington	11	0.3%
NA	West Virginia**	NA	NA
NA	Wisconsin**	NA	NA
34	Wyoming	2	0.1%

RANK ORDER

RANK	STATE	PRISONERS	% of USA
1	California	637	19.4%
2	Texas	446	13.6%
3	Florida	364	11.1%
4	Pennsylvania	222	6.8%
5	Ohio	201	6.1%
6	Alabama	193	5.9%
7	North Carolina	181	5.5%
8	Georgia	109	3.3%
9	Arizona	105	3.2%
10	Tennessee	99	3.0%
11	Oklahoma	91	2.8%
12	Louisiana	87	2.7%
13	Nevada	83	2.5%
14	South Carolina	71	2.2%
15	Mississippi	70	2.1%
16	Missouri	52	1.6%
17	Arkansas	39	1.2%
18	Kentucky	34	1.0%
19	Oregon	30	0.9%
20	Indiana	27	0.8%
21	Virginia	23	0.7%
22	Idaho	22	0.7%
23	Delaware	17	0.5%
24	New Jersey	11	0.3%
24	Washington	11	0.3%
26	Utah	10	0.3%
27	Maryland	9	0.3%
28	Nebraska	8	0.2%
29	Connecticut	7	0.2%
30	Illinois	6	0.2%
31	Montana	4	0.1%
31	South Dakota	4	0.1%
33	Colorado	3	0.1%
34	New Mexico	2	0.1%
34	New York	2	0.1%
34	Wyoming	2	0.1%
37	Kansas	0	0.0%
37	New Hampshire	0	0.0%
NA	Alaska**	NA	NA
NA	Hawaii**	NA	NA
NA	Iowa**	NA	NA
NA	Maine**	NA	NA
NA	Massachusetts**	NA	NA
NA	Michigan**	NA	NA
NA	Minnesota**	NA	NA
NA	North Dakota**	NA	NA
NA	Rhode Island**	NA	NA
NA	Vermont**	NA	NA
NA	West Virginia**	NA	NA
NA	Wisconsin**	NA	NA
	District of Columbia**	NA	NA

Source: U.S. Department of Justice, Bureau of Justice Statistics
   "Capital Punishment 2004" (Bulletin, November 2005, NCJ-211349)

*As of December 31, 2004. Does not include 33 federal prisoners under sentence of death. There were 59 executions in 2004.

**No death penalty as of 12/31/04.

Annual Operating Costs per State Prisoner in 2001

National Rate = $22,650 per Inmate*

ALPHA ORDER				RANK ORDER		
RANK	STATE	PER INMATE		RANK	STATE	PER INMATE
50	Alabama	$8,128		1	Maine	$44,379
6	Alaska	36,730		2	Rhode Island	38,503
28	Arizona	22,476		3	Massachusetts	37,718
43	Arkansas	15,619		4	Minnesota	36,836
23	California	25,053		5	New York	36,835
20	Colorado	25,408		6	Alaska	36,730
16	Connecticut	26,856		7	Oregon	36,060
27	Delaware	22,802		8	Michigan	32,525
35	Florida	20,190		9	Pennsylvania	31,900
36	Georgia	19,860		10	Washington	30,168
33	Hawaii	21,637		11	Wyoming	28,845
41	Idaho	16,319		12	Wisconsin	28,622
31	Illinois	21,844		13	New Mexico	28,035
32	Indiana	21,841		14	New Jersey	27,347
25	Iowa	22,997		15	North Carolina	26,984
34	Kansas	21,381		16	Connecticut	26,856
38	Kentucky	17,818		17	Maryland	26,398
47	Louisiana	12,951		18	Ohio	26,295
1	Maine	44,379		19	New Hampshire	25,949
17	Maryland	26,398		20	Colorado	25,408
3	Massachusetts	37,718		21	Nebraska	25,321
8	Michigan	32,525		22	Vermont	25,178
4	Minnesota	36,836		23	California	25,053
49	Mississippi	12,795		24	Utah	24,574
48	Missouri	12,867		25	Iowa	22,997
30	Montana	21,898		26	Virginia	22,942
21	Nebraska	25,321		27	Delaware	22,802
39	Nevada	17,572		28	Arizona	22,476
19	New Hampshire	25,949		29	North Dakota	22,425
14	New Jersey	27,347		30	Montana	21,898
13	New Mexico	28,035		31	Illinois	21,844
5	New York	36,835		32	Indiana	21,841
15	North Carolina	26,984		33	Hawaii	21,637
29	North Dakota	22,425		34	Kansas	21,381
18	Ohio	26,295		35	Florida	20,190
42	Oklahoma	16,309		36	Georgia	19,860
7	Oregon	36,060		37	Tennessee	18,206
9	Pennsylvania	31,900		38	Kentucky	17,818
2	Rhode Island	38,503		39	Nevada	17,572
40	South Carolina	16,762		40	South Carolina	16,762
45	South Dakota	13,853		41	Idaho	16,319
37	Tennessee	18,206		42	Oklahoma	16,309
46	Texas	13,808		43	Arkansas	15,619
24	Utah	24,574		44	West Virginia	14,817
22	Vermont	25,178		45	South Dakota	13,853
26	Virginia	22,942		46	Texas	13,808
10	Washington	30,168		47	Louisiana	12,951
44	West Virginia	14,817		48	Missouri	12,867
12	Wisconsin	28,622		49	Mississippi	12,795
11	Wyoming	28,845		50	Alabama	8,128
					District of Columbia	26,670

Source: U.S. Department of Justice, Bureau of Justice Statistics
    "State Prison Expenditures, 2001" (June 2004, NCJ-202949)
*Figures are net of amounts derived from revenue-generating activities such as farms.

Per Capita State & Local Government Expenditures for Police Protection: 2002

National Per Capita = $224*

ALPHA ORDER

RANK	STATE	PER CAPITA
40	Alabama	$159
1	Alaska	412
13	Arizona	231
43	Arkansas	149
4	California	290
10	Colorado	238
14	Connecticut	226
11	Delaware	237
6	Florida	263
27	Georgia	182
20	Hawaii	206
31	Idaho	179
7	Illinois	256
45	Indiana	145
41	Iowa	156
33	Kansas	176
48	Kentucky	133
22	Louisiana	199
46	Maine	139
8	Maryland	245
15	Massachusetts	225
24	Michigan	197
21	Minnesota	203
39	Mississippi	161
31	Missouri	179
26	Montana	187
42	Nebraska	155
3	Nevada	300
37	New Hampshire	166
5	New Jersey	282
17	New Mexico	221
2	New York	351
28	North Carolina	181
49	North Dakota	122
19	Ohio	212
38	Oklahoma	163
18	Oregon	219
22	Pennsylvania	199
16	Rhode Island	223
33	South Carolina	176
46	South Dakota	139
36	Tennessee	169
35	Texas	172
25	Utah	190
43	Vermont	149
29	Virginia	180
29	Washington	180
50	West Virginia	104
12	Wisconsin	234
9	Wyoming	243

RANK ORDER

RANK	STATE	PER CAPITA
1	Alaska	$412
2	New York	351
3	Nevada	300
4	California	290
5	New Jersey	282
6	Florida	263
7	Illinois	256
8	Maryland	245
9	Wyoming	243
10	Colorado	238
11	Delaware	237
12	Wisconsin	234
13	Arizona	231
14	Connecticut	226
15	Massachusetts	225
16	Rhode Island	223
17	New Mexico	221
18	Oregon	219
19	Ohio	212
20	Hawaii	206
21	Minnesota	203
22	Louisiana	199
22	Pennsylvania	199
24	Michigan	197
25	Utah	190
26	Montana	187
27	Georgia	182
28	North Carolina	181
29	Virginia	180
29	Washington	180
31	Idaho	179
31	Missouri	179
33	Kansas	176
33	South Carolina	176
35	Texas	172
36	Tennessee	169
37	New Hampshire	166
38	Oklahoma	163
39	Mississippi	161
40	Alabama	159
41	Iowa	156
42	Nebraska	155
43	Arkansas	149
43	Vermont	149
45	Indiana	145
46	Maine	139
46	South Dakota	139
48	Kentucky	133
49	North Dakota	122
50	West Virginia	104
	District of Columbia	681

Source: Morgan Quitno Press using data from U.S. Bureau of the Census, Governments Division
   "State and Local Government Finances: 2002 Census" (http://www.census.gov/govs/www/estimate02.html)
*Direct general expenditures.

Per Capita State and Local Government Expenditures for Corrections in 2002

National Per Capita = $190*

ALPHA ORDER				RANK ORDER		
RANK	STATE	PER CAPITA		RANK	STATE	PER CAPITA
48	Alabama	$103		1	Delaware	$304
2	Alaska	274		2	Alaska	274
12	Arizona	206		3	California	258
36	Arkansas	136		4	New York	243
3	California	258		5	Oregon	235
18	Colorado	190		6	Nevada	232
21	Connecticut	184		7	Maryland	231
1	Delaware	304		8	Wyoming	220
14	Florida	202		9	Wisconsin	216
11	Georgia	207		10	Michigan	210
41	Hawaii	127		11	Georgia	207
24	Idaho	171		12	Arizona	206
28	Illinois	149		13	Texas	203
35	Indiana	137		14	Florida	202
45	Iowa	112		15	New Mexico	200
38	Kansas	133		16	Pennsylvania	199
30	Kentucky	147		17	Virginia	191
23	Louisiana	173		18	Colorado	190
45	Maine	112		19	Washington	189
7	Maryland	231		20	New Jersey	187
22	Massachusetts	175		21	Connecticut	184
10	Michigan	210		22	Massachusetts	175
39	Minnesota	129		23	Louisiana	173
44	Mississippi	113		24	Idaho	171
32	Missouri	144		25	Utah	162
37	Montana	134		26	Oklahoma	161
28	Nebraska	149		27	Ohio	159
6	Nevada	232		28	Illinois	149
50	New Hampshire	90		28	Nebraska	149
20	New Jersey	187		30	Kentucky	147
15	New Mexico	200		30	Rhode Island	147
4	New York	243		32	Missouri	144
33	North Carolina	141		33	North Carolina	141
49	North Dakota	94		34	South Carolina	139
27	Ohio	159		35	Indiana	137
26	Oklahoma	161		36	Arkansas	136
5	Oregon	235		37	Montana	134
16	Pennsylvania	199		38	Kansas	133
30	Rhode Island	147		39	Minnesota	129
34	South Carolina	139		39	Vermont	129
42	South Dakota	123		41	Hawaii	127
43	Tennessee	119		42	South Dakota	123
13	Texas	203		43	Tennessee	119
25	Utah	162		44	Mississippi	113
39	Vermont	129		45	Iowa	112
17	Virginia	191		45	Maine	112
19	Washington	189		45	West Virginia	112
45	West Virginia	112		48	Alabama	103
9	Wisconsin	216		49	North Dakota	94
8	Wyoming	220		50	New Hampshire	90
					District of Columbia	308

Source: Morgan Quitno Press using data from U.S. Bureau of the Census, Governments Division
   "State and Local Government Finances: 2002 Census" (http://www.census.gov/govs/www/estimate02.html)
*Direct general expenditures.

Rate of Full-Time Sworn Officers in Law Enforcement Agencies in 2000

National Rate = 252 Officers per 100,000 Population*

ALPHA ORDER				RANK ORDER		
RANK	STATE	RATE		RANK	STATE	RATE
22	Alabama	240		1	Louisiana	415
34	Alaska	215		2	New York	384
29	Arizona	225		3	New Jersey	345
26	Arkansas	230		4	Illinois	321
33	California	217		5	Wyoming	299
22	Colorado	240		6	Maryland	287
16	Connecticut	245		7	Virginia	286
27	Delaware	226		8	Massachusetts	285
13	Florida	247		9	Nevada	263
10	Georgia	259		10	Georgia	259
21	Hawaii	241		11	Rhode Island	256
36	Idaho	212		12	Tennessee	255
4	Illinois	321		13	Florida	247
40	Indiana	196		13	Texas	247
45	Iowa	182		13	Wisconsin	247
18	Kansas	244		16	Connecticut	245
46	Kentucky	177		16	New Mexico	245
1	Louisiana	415		18	Kansas	244
44	Maine	186		18	Missouri	244
6	Maryland	287		20	South Carolina	243
8	Massachusetts	285		21	Hawaii	241
32	Michigan	218		22	Alabama	240
47	Minnesota	175		22	Colorado	240
25	Mississippi	231		24	North Carolina	235
18	Missouri	244		25	Mississippi	231
41	Montana	195		26	Arkansas	230
38	Nebraska	204		27	Delaware	226
9	Nevada	263		27	South Dakota	226
37	New Hampshire	206		29	Arizona	225
3	New Jersey	345		30	Ohio	221
16	New Mexico	245		30	Oklahoma	221
2	New York	384		32	Michigan	218
24	North Carolina	235		33	California	217
39	North Dakota	201		34	Alaska	215
30	Ohio	221		34	Pennsylvania	215
30	Oklahoma	221		36	Idaho	212
42	Oregon	190		37	New Hampshire	206
34	Pennsylvania	215		38	Nebraska	204
11	Rhode Island	256		39	North Dakota	201
20	South Carolina	243		40	Indiana	196
27	South Dakota	226		41	Montana	195
12	Tennessee	255		42	Oregon	190
13	Texas	247		43	Utah	187
43	Utah	187		44	Maine	186
49	Vermont	170		45	Iowa	182
7	Virginia	286		46	Kentucky	177
50	Washington	168		47	Minnesota	175
48	West Virginia	174		48	West Virginia	174
13	Wisconsin	247		49	Vermont	170
5	Wyoming	299		50	Washington	168
				District of Columbia		693

Source: U.S. Department of Justice, Bureau of Justice Statistics
    "Census of State and Local Law Enforcement Agencies, 2000" (Bulletin, October 2002, NCJ 194066)
Includes state and local police, sheriffs' departments and special police agencies.

III. DEFENSE

Homeland Security Grants in 2005

National Total = $2,518,763,000*

ALPHA ORDER

RANK	STATE	GRANTS	% of USA
28	Alabama	$28,153,000	1.1%
46	Alaska	14,879,000	0.6%
17	Arizona	41,705,000	1.7%
36	Arkansas	21,561,000	0.9%
2	California	282,622,000	11.2%
21	Colorado	36,799,000	1.5%
30	Connecticut	24,080,000	1.0%
45	Delaware	14,984,000	0.6%
5	Florida	101,285,000	4.0%
11	Georgia	54,918,000	2.2%
32	Hawaii	23,130,000	0.9%
40	Idaho	16,805,000	0.7%
4	Illinois	102,593,000	4.1%
18	Indiana	38,996,000	1.5%
33	Iowa	22,291,000	0.9%
35	Kansas	21,784,000	0.9%
25	Kentucky	31,419,000	1.2%
15	Louisiana	42,670,000	1.7%
42	Maine	16,609,000	0.7%
16	Maryland	42,250,000	1.7%
9	Massachusetts	62,436,000	2.5%
8	Michigan	64,075,000	2.5%
22	Minnesota	35,311,000	1.4%
34	Mississippi	22,081,000	0.9%
12	Missouri	46,952,000	1.9%
44	Montana	15,318,000	0.6%
31	Nebraska	23,656,000	0.9%
27	Nevada	28,386,000	1.1%
41	New Hampshire	16,776,000	0.7%
10	New Jersey	60,811,000	2.4%
38	New Mexico	18,499,000	0.7%
1	New York	298,351,000	11.8%
13	North Carolina	46,609,000	1.9%
48	North Dakota	14,376,000	0.6%
7	Ohio	77,823,000	3.1%
26	Oklahoma	29,974,000	1.2%
23	Oregon	34,820,000	1.4%
6	Pennsylvania	87,671,000	3.5%
43	Rhode Island	16,074,000	0.6%
29	South Carolina	26,284,000	1.0%
47	South Dakota	14,809,000	0.6%
24	Tennessee	32,605,000	1.3%
3	Texas	138,570,000	5.5%
37	Utah	20,308,000	0.8%
49	Vermont	14,326,000	0.6%
19	Virginia	38,185,000	1.5%
14	Washington	45,330,000	1.8%
39	West Virginia	18,289,000	0.7%
20	Wisconsin	37,251,000	1.5%
50	Wyoming	13,934,000	0.6%

RANK ORDER

RANK	STATE	GRANTS	% of USA
1	New York	$298,351,000	11.8%
2	California	282,622,000	11.2%
3	Texas	138,570,000	5.5%
4	Illinois	102,593,000	4.1%
5	Florida	101,285,000	4.0%
6	Pennsylvania	87,671,000	3.5%
7	Ohio	77,823,000	3.1%
8	Michigan	64,075,000	2.5%
9	Massachusetts	62,436,000	2.5%
10	New Jersey	60,811,000	2.4%
11	Georgia	54,918,000	2.2%
12	Missouri	46,952,000	1.9%
13	North Carolina	46,609,000	1.9%
14	Washington	45,330,000	1.8%
15	Louisiana	42,670,000	1.7%
16	Maryland	42,250,000	1.7%
17	Arizona	41,705,000	1.7%
18	Indiana	38,996,000	1.5%
19	Virginia	38,185,000	1.5%
20	Wisconsin	37,251,000	1.5%
21	Colorado	36,799,000	1.5%
22	Minnesota	35,311,000	1.4%
23	Oregon	34,820,000	1.4%
24	Tennessee	32,605,000	1.3%
25	Kentucky	31,419,000	1.2%
26	Oklahoma	29,974,000	1.2%
27	Nevada	28,386,000	1.1%
28	Alabama	28,153,000	1.1%
29	South Carolina	26,284,000	1.0%
30	Connecticut	24,080,000	1.0%
31	Nebraska	23,656,000	0.9%
32	Hawaii	23,130,000	0.9%
33	Iowa	22,291,000	0.9%
34	Mississippi	22,081,000	0.9%
35	Kansas	21,784,000	0.9%
36	Arkansas	21,561,000	0.9%
37	Utah	20,308,000	0.8%
38	New Mexico	18,499,000	0.7%
39	West Virginia	18,289,000	0.7%
40	Idaho	16,805,000	0.7%
41	New Hampshire	16,776,000	0.7%
42	Maine	16,609,000	0.7%
43	Rhode Island	16,074,000	0.6%
44	Montana	15,318,000	0.6%
45	Delaware	14,984,000	0.6%
46	Alaska	14,879,000	0.6%
47	South Dakota	14,809,000	0.6%
48	North Dakota	14,376,000	0.6%
49	Vermont	14,326,000	0.6%
50	Wyoming	13,934,000	0.6%
	District of Columbia	96,144,000	3.8%

Source: U.S. Department of Homeland Security, State and Local Government Coordination and Preparedness Unpublished data (reported in Census' Statistical Abstract of the United States: 2006)

*For fiscal year ending September 30. National total includes $43,199,000 in grants to U.S. territories. The Homeland Security Grant Program includes several sub-grant programs such as State Homeland Security, Urban Area Security Initiative, Law Enforcement Terrorism Prevention Program and Emergency Management Performance.

Per Capita Homeland Security Grants in 2005

National Per Capita = $8.35*

<table>
<tr><td colspan="3">ALPHA ORDER</td><td colspan="3">RANK ORDER</td></tr>
<tr><td>RANK</td><td>STATE</td><td>PER CAPITA</td><td>RANK</td><td>STATE</td><td>PER CAPITA</td></tr>
<tr><td>43</td><td>Alabama</td><td>$6.18</td><td>1</td><td>Wyoming</td><td>$27.36</td></tr>
<tr><td>4</td><td>Alaska</td><td>22.42</td><td>2</td><td>Vermont</td><td>22.99</td></tr>
<tr><td>35</td><td>Arizona</td><td>7.02</td><td>3</td><td>North Dakota</td><td>22.58</td></tr>
<tr><td>28</td><td>Arkansas</td><td>7.76</td><td>4</td><td>Alaska</td><td>22.42</td></tr>
<tr><td>27</td><td>California</td><td>7.82</td><td>5</td><td>South Dakota</td><td>19.09</td></tr>
<tr><td>26</td><td>Colorado</td><td>7.89</td><td>6</td><td>Hawaii</td><td>18.14</td></tr>
<tr><td>38</td><td>Connecticut</td><td>6.86</td><td>7</td><td>Delaware</td><td>17.76</td></tr>
<tr><td>7</td><td>Delaware</td><td>17.76</td><td>8</td><td>Montana</td><td>16.37</td></tr>
<tr><td>47</td><td>Florida</td><td>5.69</td><td>9</td><td>New York</td><td>15.50</td></tr>
<tr><td>46</td><td>Georgia</td><td>6.05</td><td>10</td><td>Rhode Island</td><td>14.94</td></tr>
<tr><td>6</td><td>Hawaii</td><td>18.14</td><td>11</td><td>Nebraska</td><td>13.45</td></tr>
<tr><td>14</td><td>Idaho</td><td>11.76</td><td>12</td><td>New Hampshire</td><td>12.81</td></tr>
<tr><td>24</td><td>Illinois</td><td>8.04</td><td>13</td><td>Maine</td><td>12.57</td></tr>
<tr><td>42</td><td>Indiana</td><td>6.22</td><td>14</td><td>Idaho</td><td>11.76</td></tr>
<tr><td>32</td><td>Iowa</td><td>7.51</td><td>15</td><td>Nevada</td><td>11.75</td></tr>
<tr><td>25</td><td>Kansas</td><td>7.94</td><td>16</td><td>West Virginia</td><td>10.07</td></tr>
<tr><td>31</td><td>Kentucky</td><td>7.53</td><td>17</td><td>Massachusetts</td><td>9.76</td></tr>
<tr><td>20</td><td>Louisiana</td><td>9.43</td><td>18</td><td>New Mexico</td><td>9.59</td></tr>
<tr><td>13</td><td>Maine</td><td>12.57</td><td>19</td><td>Oregon</td><td>9.56</td></tr>
<tr><td>30</td><td>Maryland</td><td>7.54</td><td>20</td><td>Louisiana</td><td>9.43</td></tr>
<tr><td>17</td><td>Massachusetts</td><td>9.76</td><td>21</td><td>Oklahoma</td><td>8.45</td></tr>
<tr><td>41</td><td>Michigan</td><td>6.33</td><td>22</td><td>Utah</td><td>8.22</td></tr>
<tr><td>37</td><td>Minnesota</td><td>6.88</td><td>23</td><td>Missouri</td><td>8.09</td></tr>
<tr><td>29</td><td>Mississippi</td><td>7.56</td><td>24</td><td>Illinois</td><td>8.04</td></tr>
<tr><td>23</td><td>Missouri</td><td>8.09</td><td>25</td><td>Kansas</td><td>7.94</td></tr>
<tr><td>8</td><td>Montana</td><td>16.37</td><td>26</td><td>Colorado</td><td>7.89</td></tr>
<tr><td>11</td><td>Nebraska</td><td>13.45</td><td>27</td><td>California</td><td>7.82</td></tr>
<tr><td>15</td><td>Nevada</td><td>11.75</td><td>28</td><td>Arkansas</td><td>7.76</td></tr>
<tr><td>12</td><td>New Hampshire</td><td>12.81</td><td>29</td><td>Mississippi</td><td>7.56</td></tr>
<tr><td>36</td><td>New Jersey</td><td>6.98</td><td>30</td><td>Maryland</td><td>7.54</td></tr>
<tr><td>18</td><td>New Mexico</td><td>9.59</td><td>31</td><td>Kentucky</td><td>7.53</td></tr>
<tr><td>9</td><td>New York</td><td>15.50</td><td>32</td><td>Iowa</td><td>7.51</td></tr>
<tr><td>49</td><td>North Carolina</td><td>5.37</td><td>33</td><td>Washington</td><td>7.21</td></tr>
<tr><td>3</td><td>North Dakota</td><td>22.58</td><td>34</td><td>Pennsylvania</td><td>7.05</td></tr>
<tr><td>39</td><td>Ohio</td><td>6.79</td><td>35</td><td>Arizona</td><td>7.02</td></tr>
<tr><td>21</td><td>Oklahoma</td><td>8.45</td><td>36</td><td>New Jersey</td><td>6.98</td></tr>
<tr><td>19</td><td>Oregon</td><td>9.56</td><td>37</td><td>Minnesota</td><td>6.88</td></tr>
<tr><td>34</td><td>Pennsylvania</td><td>7.05</td><td>38</td><td>Connecticut</td><td>6.86</td></tr>
<tr><td>10</td><td>Rhode Island</td><td>14.94</td><td>39</td><td>Ohio</td><td>6.79</td></tr>
<tr><td>43</td><td>South Carolina</td><td>6.18</td><td>40</td><td>Wisconsin</td><td>6.73</td></tr>
<tr><td>5</td><td>South Dakota</td><td>19.09</td><td>41</td><td>Michigan</td><td>6.33</td></tr>
<tr><td>48</td><td>Tennessee</td><td>5.47</td><td>42</td><td>Indiana</td><td>6.22</td></tr>
<tr><td>45</td><td>Texas</td><td>6.06</td><td>43</td><td>Alabama</td><td>6.18</td></tr>
<tr><td>22</td><td>Utah</td><td>8.22</td><td>43</td><td>South Carolina</td><td>6.18</td></tr>
<tr><td>2</td><td>Vermont</td><td>22.99</td><td>45</td><td>Texas</td><td>6.06</td></tr>
<tr><td>50</td><td>Virginia</td><td>5.05</td><td>46</td><td>Georgia</td><td>6.05</td></tr>
<tr><td>33</td><td>Washington</td><td>7.21</td><td>47</td><td>Florida</td><td>5.69</td></tr>
<tr><td>16</td><td>West Virginia</td><td>10.07</td><td>48</td><td>Tennessee</td><td>5.47</td></tr>
<tr><td>40</td><td>Wisconsin</td><td>6.73</td><td>49</td><td>North Carolina</td><td>5.37</td></tr>
<tr><td>1</td><td>Wyoming</td><td>27.36</td><td>50</td><td>Virginia</td><td>5.05</td></tr>
<tr><td></td><td></td><td></td><td></td><td>District of Columbia</td><td>174.64</td></tr>
</table>

Source: Morgan Quitno Press using data from U.S. Department of Homeland Security
Unpublished data (reported in Census' Statistical Abstract of the United States: 2006)
For fiscal year ending September 30. National per capita does not include grants to U.S. territories. The
Homeland Security Grant Program includes several sub-grant programs such as State Homeland Security, Urban
Area Security Initiative, Law Enforcement Terrorism Prevention Program and Emergency Management Performance.

U.S. Department of Defense Domestic Expenditures in 2004

National Total = $345,891,078,000*

ALPHA ORDER

RANK	STATE	EXPENDITURES	% of USA
10	Alabama	$9,172,422,000	2.7%
31	Alaska	2,581,282,000	0.7%
6	Arizona	11,199,538,000	3.2%
36	Arkansas	1,658,173,000	0.5%
1	California	43,276,557,000	12.5%
18	Colorado	6,225,635,000	1.8%
8	Connecticut	9,719,432,000	2.8%
48	Delaware	628,019,000	0.2%
4	Florida	17,802,719,000	5.1%
7	Georgia	10,587,001,000	3.1%
21	Hawaii	5,135,342,000	1.5%
44	Idaho	750,813,000	0.2%
20	Illinois	6,098,604,000	1.8%
24	Indiana	4,520,850,000	1.3%
40	Iowa	1,244,903,000	0.4%
30	Kansas	2,966,580,000	0.9%
17	Kentucky	6,567,905,000	1.9%
25	Louisiana	4,497,800,000	1.3%
34	Maine	2,392,993,000	0.7%
5	Maryland	14,367,595,000	4.2%
14	Massachusetts	8,207,663,000	2.4%
26	Michigan	3,973,048,000	1.1%
35	Minnesota	2,107,967,000	0.6%
28	Mississippi	3,740,404,000	1.1%
13	Missouri	8,662,259,000	2.5%
47	Montana	644,516,000	0.2%
38	Nebraska	1,349,466,000	0.4%
37	Nevada	1,621,028,000	0.5%
41	New Hampshire	1,123,135,000	0.3%
19	New Jersey	6,117,223,000	1.8%
32	New Mexico	2,550,615,000	0.7%
15	New York	7,825,403,000	2.3%
11	North Carolina	8,864,660,000	2.6%
43	North Dakota	841,302,000	0.2%
16	Ohio	7,599,834,000	2.2%
23	Oklahoma	4,532,829,000	1.3%
39	Oregon	1,345,559,000	0.4%
9	Pennsylvania	9,269,142,000	2.7%
42	Rhode Island	1,052,237,000	0.3%
22	South Carolina	4,950,022,000	1.4%
46	South Dakota	650,221,000	0.2%
27	Tennessee	3,764,744,000	1.1%
3	Texas	32,253,479,000	9.3%
29	Utah	3,451,209,000	1.0%
49	Vermont	603,141,000	0.2%
2	Virginia	39,603,822,000	11.4%
12	Washington	8,677,096,000	2.5%
45	West Virginia	728,233,000	0.2%
33	Wisconsin	2,434,144,000	0.7%
50	Wyoming	417,823,000	0.1%

RANK ORDER

RANK	STATE	EXPENDITURES	% of USA
1	California	$43,276,557,000	12.5%
2	Virginia	39,603,822,000	11.4%
3	Texas	32,253,479,000	9.3%
4	Florida	17,802,719,000	5.1%
5	Maryland	14,367,595,000	4.2%
6	Arizona	11,199,538,000	3.2%
7	Georgia	10,587,001,000	3.1%
8	Connecticut	9,719,432,000	2.8%
9	Pennsylvania	9,269,142,000	2.7%
10	Alabama	9,172,422,000	2.7%
11	North Carolina	8,864,660,000	2.6%
12	Washington	8,677,096,000	2.5%
13	Missouri	8,662,259,000	2.5%
14	Massachusetts	8,207,663,000	2.4%
15	New York	7,825,403,000	2.3%
16	Ohio	7,599,834,000	2.2%
17	Kentucky	6,567,905,000	1.9%
18	Colorado	6,225,635,000	1.8%
19	New Jersey	6,117,223,000	1.8%
20	Illinois	6,098,604,000	1.8%
21	Hawaii	5,135,342,000	1.5%
22	South Carolina	4,950,022,000	1.4%
23	Oklahoma	4,532,829,000	1.3%
24	Indiana	4,520,850,000	1.3%
25	Louisiana	4,497,800,000	1.3%
26	Michigan	3,973,048,000	1.1%
27	Tennessee	3,764,744,000	1.1%
28	Mississippi	3,740,404,000	1.1%
29	Utah	3,451,209,000	1.0%
30	Kansas	2,966,580,000	0.9%
31	Alaska	2,581,282,000	0.7%
32	New Mexico	2,550,615,000	0.7%
33	Wisconsin	2,434,144,000	0.7%
34	Maine	2,392,993,000	0.7%
35	Minnesota	2,107,967,000	0.6%
36	Arkansas	1,658,173,000	0.5%
37	Nevada	1,621,028,000	0.5%
38	Nebraska	1,349,466,000	0.4%
39	Oregon	1,345,559,000	0.4%
40	Iowa	1,244,903,000	0.4%
41	New Hampshire	1,123,135,000	0.3%
42	Rhode Island	1,052,237,000	0.3%
43	North Dakota	841,302,000	0.2%
44	Idaho	750,813,000	0.2%
45	West Virginia	728,233,000	0.2%
46	South Dakota	650,221,000	0.2%
47	Montana	644,516,000	0.2%
48	Delaware	628,019,000	0.2%
49	Vermont	603,141,000	0.2%
50	Wyoming	417,823,000	0.1%
	District of Columbia	5,534,691,000	1.6%

Source: U.S. Department of Defense
"Atlas/Data Abstract for the United States" (http://www.dior.whs.mil/mmid/l03/fy04/ATLAS_2004.pdf)
*Expenditures for payroll, grants and prime contracts ($25,000 or more) for civil and military functions. Does not include payroll, contracts or grants to U.S. territories and other countries.

Per Capita U.S. Department of Defense Domestic Expenditures in 2004

National Per Capita = $1,178*

ALPHA ORDER

RANK	STATE	PER CAPITA
6	Alabama	$2,027
3	Alaska	3,924
7	Arizona	1,951
41	Arkansas	603
20	California	1,207
14	Colorado	1,353
4	Connecticut	2,778
33	Delaware	757
25	Florida	1,024
21	Georgia	1,187
2	Hawaii	4,069
42	Idaho	538
43	Illinois	480
35	Indiana	726
45	Iowa	422
23	Kansas	1,085
9	Kentucky	1,586
26	Louisiana	998
8	Maine	1,820
5	Maryland	2,583
19	Massachusetts	1,281
49	Michigan	393
46	Minnesota	414
17	Mississippi	1,289
10	Missouri	1,504
37	Montana	695
32	Nebraska	772
37	Nevada	695
29	New Hampshire	865
36	New Jersey	704
15	New Mexico	1,340
47	New York	406
24	North Carolina	1,038
16	North Dakota	1,322
39	Ohio	664
18	Oklahoma	1,286
50	Oregon	375
34	Pennsylvania	748
27	Rhode Island	974
22	South Carolina	1,179
30	South Dakota	844
40	Tennessee	639
11	Texas	1,435
12	Utah	1,426
28	Vermont	971
1	Virginia	5,294
13	Washington	1,398
48	West Virginia	402
44	Wisconsin	442
31	Wyoming	826

RANK ORDER

RANK	STATE	PER CAPITA
1	Virginia	$5,294
2	Hawaii	4,069
3	Alaska	3,924
4	Connecticut	2,778
5	Maryland	2,583
6	Alabama	2,027
7	Arizona	1,951
8	Maine	1,820
9	Kentucky	1,586
10	Missouri	1,504
11	Texas	1,435
12	Utah	1,426
13	Washington	1,398
14	Colorado	1,353
15	New Mexico	1,340
16	North Dakota	1,322
17	Mississippi	1,289
18	Oklahoma	1,286
19	Massachusetts	1,281
20	California	1,207
21	Georgia	1,187
22	South Carolina	1,179
23	Kansas	1,085
24	North Carolina	1,038
25	Florida	1,024
26	Louisiana	998
27	Rhode Island	974
28	Vermont	971
29	New Hampshire	865
30	South Dakota	844
31	Wyoming	826
32	Nebraska	772
33	Delaware	757
34	Pennsylvania	748
35	Indiana	726
36	New Jersey	704
37	Montana	695
37	Nevada	695
39	Ohio	664
40	Tennessee	639
41	Arkansas	603
42	Idaho	538
43	Illinois	480
44	Wisconsin	442
45	Iowa	422
46	Minnesota	414
47	New York	406
48	West Virginia	402
49	Michigan	393
50	Oregon	375
	District of Columbia	9,986

Source: Morgan Quitno Press using data from U.S. Department of Defense
   "Atlas/Data Abstract for the United States" (http://www.dior.whs.mil/mmid/l03/fy04/ATLAS_2004.pdf)
Expenditures for payroll, grants and prime contracts ($25,000 or more) for civil and military functions. Does not include payroll, contracts or grants to U.S. territories and other countries.

U.S. Department of Defense Total Contracts in 2004

National Total = $203,388,706,000*

ALPHA ORDER

RANK	STATE	CONTRACTS	% of USA
11	Alabama	$5,849,355,000	2.9%
34	Alaska	1,262,101,000	0.6%
6	Arizona	8,430,013,000	4.1%
39	Arkansas	493,589,000	0.2%
1	California	27,875,260,000	13.7%
19	Colorado	3,151,274,000	1.5%
5	Connecticut	8,959,424,000	4.4%
48	Delaware	194,248,000	0.1%
7	Florida	8,385,549,000	4.1%
16	Georgia	3,905,216,000	1.9%
28	Hawaii	1,713,912,000	0.8%
49	Idaho	186,612,000	0.1%
20	Illinois	3,003,807,000	1.5%
18	Indiana	3,173,322,000	1.6%
36	Iowa	733,736,000	0.4%
32	Kansas	1,411,862,000	0.7%
15	Kentucky	4,118,662,000	2.0%
22	Louisiana	2,544,016,000	1.3%
30	Maine	1,555,537,000	0.8%
4	Maryland	9,206,239,000	4.5%
8	Massachusetts	6,961,412,000	3.4%
21	Michigan	2,611,682,000	1.3%
33	Minnesota	1,337,114,000	0.7%
26	Mississippi	1,866,809,000	0.9%
9	Missouri	6,502,128,000	3.2%
47	Montana	206,850,000	0.1%
43	Nebraska	401,296,000	0.2%
41	Nevada	439,062,000	0.2%
37	New Hampshire	715,773,000	0.4%
14	New Jersey	4,196,285,000	2.1%
35	New Mexico	1,070,808,000	0.5%
12	New York	5,243,889,000	2.6%
23	North Carolina	2,213,409,000	1.1%
44	North Dakota	309,564,000	0.2%
13	Ohio	4,636,572,000	2.3%
31	Oklahoma	1,524,233,000	0.7%
38	Oregon	529,559,000	0.3%
10	Pennsylvania	6,202,797,000	3.0%
42	Rhode Island	417,903,000	0.2%
29	South Carolina	1,598,654,000	0.8%
46	South Dakota	236,234,000	0.1%
24	Tennessee	2,115,771,000	1.0%
3	Texas	21,044,024,000	10.3%
25	Utah	1,877,914,000	0.9%
40	Vermont	452,321,000	0.2%
2	Virginia	23,542,542,000	11.6%
17	Washington	3,324,956,000	1.6%
45	West Virginia	279,585,000	0.1%
27	Wisconsin	1,745,612,000	0.9%
50	Wyoming	115,113,000	0.1%

RANK ORDER

RANK	STATE	CONTRACTS	% of USA
1	California	$27,875,260,000	13.7%
2	Virginia	23,542,542,000	11.6%
3	Texas	21,044,024,000	10.3%
4	Maryland	9,206,239,000	4.5%
5	Connecticut	8,959,424,000	4.4%
6	Arizona	8,430,013,000	4.1%
7	Florida	8,385,549,000	4.1%
8	Massachusetts	6,961,412,000	3.4%
9	Missouri	6,502,128,000	3.2%
10	Pennsylvania	6,202,797,000	3.0%
11	Alabama	5,849,355,000	2.9%
12	New York	5,243,889,000	2.6%
13	Ohio	4,636,572,000	2.3%
14	New Jersey	4,196,205,000	2.1%
15	Kentucky	4,118,662,000	2.0%
16	Georgia	3,905,216,000	1.9%
17	Washington	3,324,956,000	1.6%
18	Indiana	3,173,322,000	1.6%
19	Colorado	3,151,274,000	1.5%
20	Illinois	3,003,807,000	1.5%
21	Michigan	2,611,682,000	1.3%
22	Louisiana	2,544,016,000	1.3%
23	North Carolina	2,213,409,000	1.1%
24	Tennessee	2,115,771,000	1.0%
25	Utah	1,877,914,000	0.9%
26	Mississippi	1,866,809,000	0.9%
27	Wisconsin	1,745,612,000	0.9%
28	Hawaii	1,713,912,000	0.8%
29	South Carolina	1,598,654,000	0.8%
30	Maine	1,555,537,000	0.8%
31	Oklahoma	1,524,233,000	0.7%
32	Kansas	1,411,862,000	0.7%
33	Minnesota	1,337,114,000	0.7%
34	Alaska	1,262,101,000	0.6%
35	New Mexico	1,070,808,000	0.5%
36	Iowa	733,736,000	0.4%
37	New Hampshire	715,773,000	0.4%
38	Oregon	529,559,000	0.3%
39	Arkansas	493,589,000	0.2%
40	Vermont	452,321,000	0.2%
41	Nevada	439,062,000	0.2%
42	Rhode Island	417,903,000	0.2%
43	Nebraska	401,296,000	0.2%
44	North Dakota	309,564,000	0.2%
45	West Virginia	279,585,000	0.1%
46	South Dakota	236,234,000	0.1%
47	Montana	206,850,000	0.1%
48	Delaware	194,248,000	0.1%
49	Idaho	186,612,000	0.1%
50	Wyoming	115,113,000	0.1%
	District of Columbia	3,515,101,000	1.7%

Source: U.S. Department of Defense
   "Atlas/Data Abstract for the United States" (http://www.dior.whs.mil/mmid/l03/fy04/ATLAS_2004.pdf)
*Includes prime contracts ($25,000 or more) for civil and military functions. Does not include contracts to U.S. territories and other countries.

Per Capita U.S. Department of Defense Total Contracts in 2004

National Per Capita = $693*

ALPHA ORDER			RANK ORDER		
RANK	STATE	PER CAPITA	RANK	STATE	PER CAPITA
7	Alabama	$1,293	1	Virginia	$3,147
3	Alaska	1,919	2	Connecticut	2,561
5	Arizona	1,469	3	Alaska	1,919
47	Arkansas	179	4	Maryland	1,655
13	California	778	5	Arizona	1,469
16	Colorado	685	6	Hawaii	1,358
2	Connecticut	2,561	7	Alabama	1,293
42	Delaware	234	8	Maine	1,183
27	Florida	482	9	Missouri	1,129
28	Georgia	438	10	Massachusetts	1,086
6	Hawaii	1,358	11	Kentucky	994
50	Idaho	134	12	Texas	936
41	Illinois	236	13	California	778
23	Indiana	510	14	Utah	776
40	Iowa	248	15	Vermont	728
22	Kansas	516	16	Colorado	685
11	Kentucky	994	17	Mississippi	644
18	Louisiana	564	18	Louisiana	564
8	Maine	1,183	19	New Mexico	563
4	Maryland	1,655	20	New Hampshire	551
10	Massachusetts	1,086	21	Washington	536
39	Michigan	258	22	Kansas	516
37	Minnesota	262	23	Indiana	510
17	Mississippi	644	24	Pennsylvania	500
9	Missouri	1,129	25	North Dakota	487
45	Montana	223	26	New Jersey	483
43	Nebraska	230	27	Florida	482
46	Nevada	188	28	Georgia	438
20	New Hampshire	551	29	Oklahoma	433
26	New Jersey	483	30	Ohio	405
19	New Mexico	563	31	Rhode Island	387
36	New York	272	32	South Carolina	381
38	North Carolina	259	33	Tennessee	359
25	North Dakota	487	34	Wisconsin	317
30	Ohio	405	35	South Dakota	307
29	Oklahoma	433	36	New York	272
49	Oregon	147	37	Minnesota	262
24	Pennsylvania	500	38	North Carolina	259
31	Rhode Island	387	39	Michigan	258
32	South Carolina	381	40	Iowa	248
35	South Dakota	307	41	Illinois	236
33	Tennessee	359	42	Delaware	234
12	Texas	936	43	Nebraska	230
14	Utah	776	44	Wyoming	228
15	Vermont	728	45	Montana	223
1	Virginia	3,147	46	Nevada	188
21	Washington	536	47	Arkansas	179
48	West Virginia	154	48	West Virginia	154
34	Wisconsin	317	49	Oregon	147
44	Wyoming	228	50	Idaho	134
				District of Columbia	6,342

Source: Morgan Quitno Press using data from U.S. Department of Defense
   "Atlas/Data Abstract for the United States" (http://www.dior.whs.mil/mmid/l03/fy04/ATLAS_2004.pdf)
*Expenditures for payroll, grants and prime contracts ($25,000 or more) for civil and military functions. Does not include payroll, contracts or grants to U.S. territories and other countries.

U.S. Department of Defense Contracts for Military Functions in 2004

National Total = $200,127,015,000*

ALPHA ORDER

RANK	STATE	CONTRACTS	% of USA
11	Alabama	$5,766,101,000	2.9%
34	Alaska	1,215,161,000	0.6%
6	Arizona	8,401,595,000	4.2%
40	Arkansas	430,389,000	0.2%
1	California	27,706,619,000	13.8%
19	Colorado	3,125,208,000	1.6%
5	Connecticut	8,953,668,000	4.5%
48	Delaware	186,163,000	0.1%
7	Florida	8,112,378,000	4.1%
16	Georgia	3,802,163,000	1.9%
28	Hawaii	1,705,934,000	0.9%
49	Idaho	178,730,000	0.1%
20	Illinois	2,833,440,000	1.4%
18	Indiana	3,137,689,000	1.6%
36	Iowa	714,415,000	0.4%
32	Kansas	1,392,563,000	0.7%
14	Kentucky	4,012,662,000	2.0%
22	Louisiana	2,299,551,000	1.1%
30	Maine	1,547,736,000	0.8%
4	Maryland	9,163,770,000	4.6%
8	Massachusetts	6,897,538,000	3.4%
21	Michigan	2,576,468,000	1.3%
33	Minnesota	1,302,578,000	0.7%
26	Mississippi	1,740,654,000	0.9%
9	Missouri	6,357,333,000	3.2%
46	Montana	190,956,000	0.1%
43	Nebraska	376,926,000	0.2%
41	Nevada	418,738,000	0.2%
37	New Hampshire	711,978,000	0.4%
15	New Jersey	3,987,671,000	2.0%
35	New Mexico	1,029,812,000	0.5%
12	New York	5,154,326,000	2.6%
23	North Carolina	2,158,670,000	1.1%
44	North Dakota	272,015,000	0.1%
13	Ohio	4,575,115,000	2.3%
31	Oklahoma	1,493,649,000	0.7%
38	Oregon	449,529,000	0.2%
10	Pennsylvania	6,136,607,000	3.1%
42	Rhode Island	391,992,000	0.2%
29	South Carolina	1,550,533,000	0.8%
45	South Dakota	229,120,000	0.1%
24	Tennessee	2,052,643,000	1.0%
3	Texas	20,871,471,000	10.4%
25	Utah	1,871,200,000	0.9%
39	Vermont	440,813,000	0.2%
2	Virginia	23,470,137,000	11.7%
17	Washington	3,224,176,000	1.6%
47	West Virginia	190,427,000	0.1%
27	Wisconsin	1,732,739,000	0.9%
50	Wyoming	114,705,000	0.1%

RANK ORDER

RANK	STATE	CONTRACTS	% of USA
1	California	$27,706,619,000	13.8%
2	Virginia	23,470,137,000	11.7%
3	Texas	20,871,471,000	10.4%
4	Maryland	9,163,770,000	4.6%
5	Connecticut	8,953,668,000	4.5%
6	Arizona	8,401,595,000	4.2%
7	Florida	8,112,378,000	4.1%
8	Massachusetts	6,897,538,000	3.4%
9	Missouri	6,357,333,000	3.2%
10	Pennsylvania	6,136,607,000	3.1%
11	Alabama	5,766,101,000	2.9%
12	New York	5,154,326,000	2.6%
13	Ohio	4,575,115,000	2.3%
14	Kentucky	4,012,662,000	2.0%
15	New Jersey	3,987,671,000	2.0%
16	Georgia	3,802,163,000	1.9%
17	Washington	3,224,176,000	1.6%
18	Indiana	3,137,689,000	1.6%
19	Colorado	3,125,208,000	1.6%
20	Illinois	2,833,440,000	1.4%
21	Michigan	2,576,468,000	1.3%
22	Louisiana	2,299,551,000	1.1%
23	North Carolina	2,158,670,000	1.1%
24	Tennessee	2,052,643,000	1.0%
25	Utah	1,871,200,000	0.9%
26	Mississippi	1,740,654,000	0.9%
27	Wisconsin	1,732,739,000	0.9%
28	Hawaii	1,705,934,000	0.9%
29	South Carolina	1,550,533,000	0.8%
30	Maine	1,547,736,000	0.8%
31	Oklahoma	1,493,649,000	0.7%
32	Kansas	1,392,563,000	0.7%
33	Minnesota	1,302,578,000	0.7%
34	Alaska	1,215,161,000	0.6%
35	New Mexico	1,029,812,000	0.5%
36	Iowa	714,415,000	0.4%
37	New Hampshire	711,978,000	0.4%
38	Oregon	449,529,000	0.2%
39	Vermont	440,813,000	0.2%
40	Arkansas	430,389,000	0.2%
41	Nevada	418,738,000	0.2%
42	Rhode Island	391,992,000	0.2%
43	Nebraska	376,926,000	0.2%
44	North Dakota	272,015,000	0.1%
45	South Dakota	229,120,000	0.1%
46	Montana	190,956,000	0.1%
47	West Virginia	190,427,000	0.1%
48	Delaware	186,163,000	0.1%
49	Idaho	178,730,000	0.1%
50	Wyoming	114,705,000	0.1%
	District of Columbia	3,470,561,000	1.7%

Source: U.S. Department of Defense
   "Atlas/Data Abstract for the United States" (http://www.dior.whs.mil/mmid/l03/fy04/ATLAS_2004.pdf)
*Includes prime contracts ($25,000 or more). Does not include contracts to U.S. territories and other countries.

U.S. Department of Defense Contracts for Civil Functions in 2004

National Total = $3,261,691,000*

ALPHA ORDER

RANK	STATE	CONTRACTS	% of USA
14	Alabama	$83,254,000	2.6%
24	Alaska	46,940,000	1.4%
32	Arizona	28,418,000	0.9%
19	Arkansas	63,200,000	1.9%
6	California	168,641,000	5.2%
33	Colorado	26,066,000	0.8%
48	Connecticut	5,756,000	0.2%
42	Delaware	8,085,000	0.2%
1	Florida	273,171,000	8.4%
10	Georgia	103,053,000	3.2%
43	Hawaii	7,978,000	0.2%
44	Idaho	7,882,000	0.2%
5	Illinois	170,367,000	5.2%
28	Indiana	35,633,000	1.1%
37	Iowa	19,321,000	0.6%
38	Kansas	19,299,000	0.6%
9	Kentucky	106,000,000	3.2%
2	Louisiana	244,465,000	7.5%
45	Maine	7,801,000	0.2%
25	Maryland	42,469,000	1.3%
18	Massachusetts	63,874,000	2.0%
29	Michigan	35,214,000	1.1%
30	Minnesota	34,536,000	1.1%
8	Mississippi	126,155,000	3.9%
7	Missouri	144,795,000	4.4%
39	Montana	15,894,000	0.5%
35	Nebraska	24,370,000	0.7%
36	Nevada	20,324,000	0.6%
49	New Hampshire	3,795,000	0.1%
3	New Jersey	208,614,000	6.4%
26	New Mexico	40,996,000	1.3%
12	New York	89,563,000	2.7%
22	North Carolina	54,739,000	1.7%
27	North Dakota	37,549,000	1.2%
21	Ohio	61,457,000	1.9%
31	Oklahoma	30,584,000	0.9%
15	Oregon	80,030,000	2.5%
17	Pennsylvania	66,190,000	2.0%
34	Rhode Island	25,911,000	0.8%
23	South Carolina	48,121,000	1.5%
46	South Dakota	7,114,000	0.2%
20	Tennessee	63,128,000	1.9%
4	Texas	172,553,000	5.3%
47	Utah	6,714,000	0.2%
41	Vermont	11,508,000	0.4%
16	Virginia	72,405,000	2.2%
11	Washington	100,780,000	3.1%
13	West Virginia	89,158,000	2.7%
40	Wisconsin	12,873,000	0.4%
50	Wyoming	408,000	0.0%

RANK ORDER

RANK	STATE	CONTRACTS	% of USA
1	Florida	$273,171,000	8.4%
2	Louisiana	244,465,000	7.5%
3	New Jersey	208,614,000	6.4%
4	Texas	172,553,000	5.3%
5	Illinois	170,367,000	5.2%
6	California	168,641,000	5.2%
7	Missouri	144,795,000	4.4%
8	Mississippi	126,155,000	3.9%
9	Kentucky	106,000,000	3.2%
10	Georgia	103,053,000	3.2%
11	Washington	100,780,000	3.1%
12	New York	89,563,000	2.7%
13	West Virginia	89,158,000	2.7%
14	Alabama	83,254,000	2.6%
15	Oregon	80,030,000	2.5%
16	Virginia	72,405,000	2.2%
17	Pennsylvania	66,190,000	2.0%
18	Massachusetts	63,874,000	2.0%
19	Arkansas	63,200,000	1.9%
20	Tennessee	63,128,000	1.9%
21	Ohio	61,457,000	1.9%
22	North Carolina	54,739,000	1.7%
23	South Carolina	48,121,000	1.5%
24	Alaska	46,940,000	1.4%
25	Maryland	42,469,000	1.3%
26	New Mexico	40,996,000	1.3%
27	North Dakota	37,549,000	1.2%
28	Indiana	35,633,000	1.1%
29	Michigan	35,214,000	1.1%
30	Minnesota	34,536,000	1.1%
31	Oklahoma	30,584,000	0.9%
32	Arizona	28,418,000	0.9%
33	Colorado	26,066,000	0.8%
34	Rhode Island	25,911,000	0.8%
35	Nebraska	24,370,000	0.7%
36	Nevada	20,324,000	0.6%
37	Iowa	19,321,000	0.6%
38	Kansas	19,299,000	0.6%
39	Montana	15,894,000	0.5%
40	Wisconsin	12,873,000	0.4%
41	Vermont	11,508,000	0.4%
42	Delaware	8,085,000	0.2%
43	Hawaii	7,978,000	0.2%
44	Idaho	7,882,000	0.2%
45	Maine	7,801,000	0.2%
46	South Dakota	7,114,000	0.2%
47	Utah	6,714,000	0.2%
48	Connecticut	5,756,000	0.2%
49	New Hampshire	3,795,000	0.1%
50	Wyoming	408,000	0.0%
	District of Columbia	44,540,000	1.4%

Source: U.S. Department of Defense
"Atlas/Data Abstract for the United States" (http://www.dior.whs.mil/mmid/l03/fy04/ATLAS_2004.pdf)
*Includes prime contracts ($25,000 or more). Does not include contracts to U.S. territories and other countries.

U.S. Department of Defense Domestic Personnel in 2004

National Total = 2,763,823 Personnel*

ALPHA ORDER

RANK	STATE	PERSONNEL	% of USA
15	Alabama	63,343	2.3%
30	Alaska	27,602	1.0%
21	Arizona	49,449	1.8%
33	Arkansas	24,650	0.9%
1	California	275,224	10.0%
17	Colorado	59,765	2.2%
40	Connecticut	14,953	0.5%
45	Delaware	11,145	0.4%
6	Florida	126,646	4.6%
5	Georgia	134,260	4.9%
16	Hawaii	62,972	2.3%
42	Idaho	12,907	0.5%
10	Illinois	73,975	2.7%
27	Indiana	33,217	1.2%
38	Iowa	17,232	0.6%
24	Kansas	37,043	1.3%
18	Kentucky	59,239	2.1%
20	Louisiana	49,925	1.8%
39	Maine	14,963	0.5%
8	Maryland	84,006	3.0%
29	Massachusetts	28,534	1.0%
26	Michigan	33,558	1.2%
32	Minnesota	25,976	0.9%
22	Mississippi	43,071	1.6%
19	Missouri	51,539	1.9%
46	Montana	10,838	0.4%
35	Nebraska	20,032	0.7%
36	Nevada	17,716	0.6%
49	New Hampshire	6,305	0.2%
23	New Jersey	41,765	1.5%
31	New Mexico	26,187	0.9%
9	New York	77,597	2.8%
4	North Carolina	147,045	5.3%
41	North Dakota	14,914	0.5%
13	Ohio	66,744	2.4%
14	Oklahoma	64,530	2.3%
37	Oregon	17,509	0.6%
11	Pennsylvania	73,173	2.6%
44	Rhode Island	12,593	0.5%
12	South Carolina	70,084	2.5%
47	South Dakota	10,621	0.4%
28	Tennessee	31,773	1.1%
2	Texas	225,246	8.1%
25	Utah	33,875	1.2%
50	Vermont	5,160	0.2%
3	Virginia	205,602	7.4%
7	Washington	88,312	3.2%
43	West Virginia	12,898	0.5%
34	Wisconsin	24,137	0.9%
48	Wyoming	7,913	0.3%

RANK ORDER

RANK	STATE	PERSONNEL	% of USA
1	California	275,224	10.0%
2	Texas	225,246	8.1%
3	Virginia	205,602	7.4%
4	North Carolina	147,045	5.3%
5	Georgia	134,260	4.9%
6	Florida	126,646	4.6%
7	Washington	88,312	3.2%
8	Maryland	84,006	3.0%
9	New York	77,597	2.8%
10	Illinois	73,975	2.7%
11	Pennsylvania	73,173	2.6%
12	South Carolina	70,084	2.5%
13	Ohio	66,744	2.4%
14	Oklahoma	64,530	2.3%
15	Alabama	63,343	2.3%
16	Hawaii	62,972	2.3%
17	Colorado	59,765	2.2%
18	Kentucky	59,239	2.1%
19	Missouri	51,539	1.9%
20	Louisiana	49,925	1.8%
21	Arizona	49,449	1.8%
22	Mississippi	43,071	1.6%
23	New Jersey	41,765	1.5%
24	Kansas	37,043	1.3%
25	Utah	33,875	1.2%
26	Michigan	33,558	1.2%
27	Indiana	33,217	1.2%
28	Tennessee	31,773	1.1%
29	Massachusetts	28,534	1.0%
30	Alaska	27,602	1.0%
31	New Mexico	26,187	0.9%
32	Minnesota	25,976	0.9%
33	Arkansas	24,650	0.9%
34	Wisconsin	24,137	0.9%
35	Nebraska	20,032	0.7%
36	Nevada	17,716	0.6%
37	Oregon	17,509	0.6%
38	Iowa	17,232	0.6%
39	Maine	14,963	0.5%
40	Connecticut	14,953	0.5%
41	North Dakota	14,914	0.5%
42	Idaho	12,907	0.5%
43	West Virginia	12,898	0.5%
44	Rhode Island	12,593	0.5%
45	Delaware	11,145	0.4%
46	Montana	10,838	0.4%
47	South Dakota	10,621	0.4%
48	Wyoming	7,913	0.3%
49	New Hampshire	6,305	0.2%
50	Vermont	5,160	0.2%
	District of Columbia	36,114	1.3%

Source: U.S. Department of Defense

"Atlas/Data Abstract for the United States" (http://www.dior.whs.mil/mmid/l03/fy04/ATLAS_2004.pdf)

*Includes Active Duty Military, Civilian and Reserve and National Guard personnel. Does not include personnel in U.S. territories or in other countries.

U.S. Department of Defense Active Duty Military Personnel in 2004

National Total = 1,055,314 Personnel*

ALPHA ORDER

RANK	STATE	PERSONNEL	% of USA
23	Alabama	10,276	1.0%
17	Alaska	17,385	1.6%
15	Arizona	22,793	2.2%
30	Arkansas	5,257	0.5%
1	California	128,277	12.2%
11	Colorado	29,790	2.8%
35	Connecticut	3,467	0.3%
32	Delaware	3,949	0.4%
6	Florida	52,300	5.0%
5	Georgia	67,642	6.4%
10	Hawaii	35,061	3.3%
31	Idaho	4,619	0.4%
13	Illinois	26,650	2.5%
43	Indiana	988	0.1%
48	Iowa	364	0.0%
19	Kansas	16,294	1.5%
9	Kentucky	35,162	3.3%
18	Louisiana	17,380	1.6%
40	Maine	2,350	0.2%
12	Maryland	29,531	2.8%
38	Massachusetts	2,468	0.2%
42	Michigan	1,140	0.1%
44	Minnesota	667	0.1%
21	Mississippi	14,483	1.4%
20	Missouri	15,302	1.4%
33	Montana	3,789	0.4%
26	Nebraska	7,332	0.7%
24	Nevada	9,251	0.9%
49	New Hampshire	218	0.0%
28	New Jersey	6,392	0.6%
22	New Mexico	11,994	1.1%
16	New York	22,714	2.2%
3	North Carolina	101,033	9.6%
25	North Dakota	7,840	0.7%
27	Ohio	7,211	0.7%
14	Oklahoma	23,476	2.2%
44	Oregon	667	0.1%
37	Pennsylvania	2,837	0.3%
41	Rhode Island	2,336	0.2%
7	South Carolina	38,213	3.6%
34	South Dakota	3,698	0.4%
39	Tennessee	2,430	0.2%
2	Texas	109,760	10.4%
29	Utah	5,756	0.5%
50	Vermont	60	0.0%
4	Virginia	90,088	8.5%
8	Washington	37,906	3.6%
46	West Virginia	503	0.0%
47	Wisconsin	502	0.0%
36	Wyoming	3,447	0.3%

RANK ORDER

RANK	STATE	PERSONNEL	% of USA
1	California	128,277	12.2%
2	Texas	109,760	10.4%
3	North Carolina	101,033	9.6%
4	Virginia	90,088	8.5%
5	Georgia	67,642	6.4%
6	Florida	52,300	5.0%
7	South Carolina	38,213	3.6%
8	Washington	37,906	3.6%
9	Kentucky	35,162	3.3%
10	Hawaii	35,061	3.3%
11	Colorado	29,790	2.8%
12	Maryland	29,531	2.8%
13	Illinois	26,650	2.5%
14	Oklahoma	23,476	2.2%
15	Arizona	22,793	2.2%
16	New York	22,714	2.2%
17	Alaska	17,385	1.6%
18	Louisiana	17,380	1.6%
19	Kansas	16,294	1.5%
20	Missouri	15,302	1.4%
21	Mississippi	14,483	1.4%
22	New Mexico	11,994	1.1%
23	Alabama	10,276	1.0%
24	Nevada	9,251	0.9%
25	North Dakota	7,840	0.7%
26	Nebraska	7,332	0.7%
27	Ohio	7,211	0.7%
28	New Jersey	6,392	0.6%
29	Utah	5,756	0.5%
30	Arkansas	5,257	0.5%
31	Idaho	4,619	0.4%
32	Delaware	3,949	0.4%
33	Montana	3,789	0.4%
34	South Dakota	3,698	0.4%
35	Connecticut	3,467	0.3%
36	Wyoming	3,447	0.3%
37	Pennsylvania	2,837	0.3%
38	Massachusetts	2,468	0.2%
39	Tennessee	2,430	0.2%
40	Maine	2,350	0.2%
41	Rhode Island	2,336	0.2%
42	Michigan	1,140	0.1%
43	Indiana	988	0.1%
44	Minnesota	667	0.1%
44	Oregon	667	0.1%
46	West Virginia	503	0.0%
47	Wisconsin	502	0.0%
48	Iowa	364	0.0%
49	New Hampshire	218	0.0%
50	Vermont	60	0.0%
	District of Columbia	12,266	1.2%

Source: U.S. Department of Defense
  "Atlas/Data Abstract for the United States" (http://www.dior.whs.mil/mmid/l03/fy04/ATLAS_2004.pdf)
*Does not include active duty personnel in U.S. territories, in other countries or others undistributed.

U.S. Department of Defense Domestic Civilian Personnel in 2004

National Total = 634,185 Personnel*

ALPHA ORDER

RANK	STATE	PERSONNEL	% of USA
11	Alabama	21,155	3.3%
32	Alaska	4,536	0.7%
23	Arizona	9,002	1.4%
34	Arkansas	3,933	0.6%
2	California	58,062	9.2%
18	Colorado	10,345	1.6%
39	Connecticut	2,452	0.4%
45	Delaware	1,448	0.2%
6	Florida	27,076	4.3%
5	Georgia	30,623	4.8%
13	Hawaii	16,576	2.6%
43	Idaho	1,532	0.2%
16	Illinois	13,111	2.1%
21	Indiana	9,088	1.4%
44	Iowa	1,522	0.2%
30	Kansas	6,048	1.0%
24	Kentucky	8,314	1.3%
26	Louisiana	7,093	1.1%
29	Maine	6,290	1.0%
4	Maryland	31,611	5.0%
28	Massachusetts	6,707	1.1%
25	Michigan	8,110	1.3%
38	Minnesota	2,544	0.4%
21	Mississippi	9,088	1.4%
20	Missouri	9,208	1.5%
46	Montana	1,274	0.2%
35	Nebraska	3,769	0.6%
40	Nevada	2,089	0.3%
48	New Hampshire	1,059	0.2%
15	New Jersey	13,628	2.1%
27	New Mexico	6,805	1.1%
17	New York	11,409	1.8%
12	North Carolina	16,942	2.7%
42	North Dakota	1,706	0.3%
10	Ohio	21,704	3.4%
9	Oklahoma	21,860	3.4%
36	Oregon	3,276	0.5%
7	Pennsylvania	25,079	4.0%
33	Rhode Island	4,370	0.7%
19	South Carolina	9,382	1.5%
47	South Dakota	1,161	0.2%
31	Tennessee	5,390	0.8%
3	Texas	39,385	6.2%
14	Utah	14,715	2.3%
50	Vermont	613	0.1%
1	Virginia	78,792	12.4%
8	Washington	23,433	3.7%
41	West Virginia	1,810	0.3%
37	Wisconsin	2,847	0.4%
49	Wyoming	1,039	0.2%

RANK ORDER

RANK	STATE	PERSONNEL	% of USA
1	Virginia	78,792	12.4%
2	California	58,062	9.2%
3	Texas	39,385	6.2%
4	Maryland	31,611	5.0%
5	Georgia	30,623	4.8%
6	Florida	27,076	4.3%
7	Pennsylvania	25,079	4.0%
8	Washington	23,433	3.7%
9	Oklahoma	21,860	3.4%
10	Ohio	21,704	3.4%
11	Alabama	21,155	3.3%
12	North Carolina	16,942	2.7%
13	Hawaii	16,576	2.6%
14	Utah	14,715	2.3%
15	New Jersey	13,628	2.1%
16	Illinois	13,111	2.1%
17	New York	11,409	1.8%
18	Colorado	10,345	1.6%
19	South Carolina	9,382	1.5%
20	Missouri	9,208	1.5%
21	Indiana	9,088	1.4%
21	Mississippi	9,088	1.4%
23	Arizona	9,002	1.4%
24	Kentucky	8,314	1.3%
25	Michigan	8,110	1.3%
26	Louisiana	7,093	1.1%
27	New Mexico	6,805	1.1%
28	Massachusetts	6,707	1.1%
29	Maine	6,290	1.0%
30	Kansas	6,048	1.0%
31	Tennessee	5,390	0.8%
32	Alaska	4,536	0.7%
33	Rhode Island	4,370	0.7%
34	Arkansas	3,933	0.6%
35	Nebraska	3,769	0.6%
36	Oregon	3,276	0.5%
37	Wisconsin	2,847	0.4%
38	Minnesota	2,544	0.4%
39	Connecticut	2,452	0.4%
40	Nevada	2,089	0.3%
41	West Virginia	1,810	0.3%
42	North Dakota	1,706	0.3%
43	Idaho	1,532	0.2%
44	Iowa	1,522	0.2%
45	Delaware	1,448	0.2%
46	Montana	1,274	0.2%
47	South Dakota	1,161	0.2%
48	New Hampshire	1,059	0.2%
49	Wyoming	1,039	0.2%
50	Vermont	613	0.1%
	District of Columbia	15,174	2.4%

Source: U.S. Department of Defense
   "Atlas/Data Abstract for the United States" (http://www.dior.whs.mil/mmid/l03/fy04/ATLAS_2004.pdf)
*Does not include civilian personnel in U.S. territories or civilian personnel in other countries. Includes military and civil functions.

U.S. Department of Defense Reserve and National Guard Personnel in 2004

National Total = 1,074,324 Personnel*

ALPHA ORDER

ALPHA ORDER

RANK	STATE	PERSONNEL	% of USA
10	Alabama	31,912	3.0%
46	Alaska	5,681	0.5%
27	Arizona	17,654	1.6%
29	Arkansas	15,460	1.4%
1	California	88,885	8.3%
23	Colorado	19,630	1.8%
36	Connecticut	9,034	0.8%
45	Delaware	5,748	0.5%
3	Florida	47,270	4.4%
8	Georgia	35,995	3.4%
34	Hawaii	11,335	1.1%
39	Idaho	6,756	0.6%
9	Illinois	34,214	3.2%
17	Indiana	23,141	2.2%
30	Iowa	15,346	1.4%
31	Kansas	14,701	1.4%
28	Kentucky	15,763	1.5%
14	Louisiana	25,452	2.4%
41	Maine	6,323	0.6%
18	Maryland	22,864	2.1%
25	Massachusetts	19,359	1.8%
15	Michigan	24,308	2.3%
19	Minnesota	22,765	2.1%
24	Mississippi	19,446	1.8%
12	Missouri	27,029	2.5%
43	Montana	5,775	0.5%
37	Nebraska	8,931	0.8%
40	Nevada	6,376	0.6%
48	New Hampshire	5,028	0.5%
21	New Jersey	21,745	2.0%
38	New Mexico	7,388	0.7%
5	New York	43,474	4.0%
11	North Carolina	29,070	2.7%
47	North Dakota	5,368	0.5%
6	Ohio	37,829	3.5%
26	Oklahoma	19,194	1.8%
32	Oregon	13,566	1.3%
4	Pennsylvania	45,257	4.2%
42	Rhode Island	5,887	0.5%
20	South Carolina	22,489	2.1%
44	South Dakota	5,762	0.5%
16	Tennessee	23,953	2.2%
2	Texas	76,101	7.1%
33	Utah	13,404	1.2%
49	Vermont	4,487	0.4%
7	Virginia	36,722	3.4%
13	Washington	26,973	2.5%
35	West Virginia	10,585	1.0%
22	Wisconsin	20,788	1.9%
50	Wyoming	3,427	0.3%

RANK ORDER

RANK	STATE	PERSONNEL	% of USA
1	California	88,885	8.3%
2	Texas	76,101	7.1%
3	Florida	47,270	4.4%
4	Pennsylvania	45,257	4.2%
5	New York	43,474	4.0%
6	Ohio	37,829	3.5%
7	Virginia	36,722	3.4%
8	Georgia	35,995	3.4%
9	Illinois	34,214	3.2%
10	Alabama	31,912	3.0%
11	North Carolina	29,070	2.7%
12	Missouri	27,029	2.5%
13	Washington	26,973	2.5%
14	Louisiana	25,452	2.4%
15	Michigan	24,308	2.3%
16	Tennessee	23,953	2.2%
17	Indiana	23,141	2.2%
18	Maryland	22,864	2.1%
19	Minnesota	22,765	2.1%
20	South Carolina	22,489	2.1%
21	New Jersey	21,745	2.0%
22	Wisconsin	20,788	1.9%
23	Colorado	19,630	1.8%
24	Mississippi	19,446	1.8%
25	Massachusetts	19,359	1.8%
26	Oklahoma	19,194	1.8%
27	Arizona	17,654	1.6%
28	Kentucky	15,763	1.5%
29	Arkansas	15,460	1.4%
30	Iowa	15,346	1.4%
31	Kansas	14,701	1.4%
32	Oregon	13,566	1.3%
33	Utah	13,404	1.2%
34	Hawaii	11,335	1.1%
35	West Virginia	10,585	1.0%
36	Connecticut	9,034	0.8%
37	Nebraska	8,931	0.8%
38	New Mexico	7,388	0.7%
39	Idaho	6,756	0.6%
40	Nevada	6,376	0.6%
41	Maine	6,323	0.6%
42	Rhode Island	5,887	0.5%
43	Montana	5,775	0.5%
44	South Dakota	5,762	0.5%
45	Delaware	5,748	0.5%
46	Alaska	5,681	0.5%
47	North Dakota	5,368	0.5%
48	New Hampshire	5,028	0.5%
49	Vermont	4,487	0.4%
50	Wyoming	3,427	0.3%
	District of Columbia	8,674	0.8%

Source: U.S. Department of Defense
"Atlas/Data Abstract for the United States" (http://www.dior.whs.mil/mmid/l03/fy04/ATLAS_2004.pdf)
*Does not include reserve and national guard personnel in U.S. territories.

U.S. Department of Defense Total Compensation in 2004

National Total = $139,490,361,000*

ALPHA ORDER					RANK ORDER			

RANK	STATE	TOTAL PAY	% of USA		RANK	STATE	TOTAL PAY	% of USA
11	Alabama	$3,283,835,000	2.4%		1	Virginia	$15,992,369,000	11.5%
29	Alaska	1,281,538,000	0.9%		2	California	15,017,113,000	10.8%
17	Arizona	2,678,171,000	1.9%		3	Texas	11,082,032,000	7.9%
32	Arkansas	1,127,696,000	0.8%		4	Florida	9,333,981,000	6.7%
2	California	15,017,113,000	10.8%		5	Georgia	6,633,440,000	4.8%
13	Colorado	3,024,895,000	2.2%		6	North Carolina	6,569,452,000	4.7%
37	Connecticut	717,458,000	0.5%		7	Washington	5,300,771,000	3.8%
44	Delaware	417,218,000	0.3%		8	Maryland	4,999,382,000	3.6%
4	Florida	9,333,981,000	6.7%		9	Hawaii	3,374,038,000	2.4%
5	Georgia	6,633,440,000	4.8%		10	South Carolina	3,306,218,000	2.4%
9	Hawaii	3,374,038,000	2.4%		11	Alabama	3,283,835,000	2.4%
41	Idaho	535,099,000	0.4%		12	Illinois	3,025,482,000	2.2%
12	Illinois	3,025,482,000	2.2%		13	Colorado	3,024,895,000	2.2%
28	Indiana	1,298,906,000	0.9%		14	Oklahoma	2,975,918,000	2.1%
43	Iowa	480,640,000	0.3%		15	Pennsylvania	2,912,308,000	2.1%
26	Kansas	1,528,992,000	1.1%		16	Ohio	2,894,340,000	2.1%
19	Kentucky	2,431,603,000	1.7%		17	Arizona	2,678,171,000	1.9%
21	Louisiana	1,871,386,000	1.3%		18	New York	2,442,780,000	1.8%
35	Maine	805,481,000	0.6%		19	Kentucky	2,431,603,000	1.7%
8	Maryland	4,999,382,000	3.6%		20	Missouri	2,111,640,000	1.5%
33	Massachusetts	1,102,544,000	0.8%		21	Louisiana	1,871,386,000	1.3%
30	Michigan	1,240,876,000	0.9%		22	New Jersey	1,860,431,000	1.3%
38	Minnesota	708,113,000	0.5%		23	Mississippi	1,828,491,000	1.3%
23	Mississippi	1,828,491,000	1.3%		24	Tennessee	1,614,320,000	1.2%
20	Missouri	2,111,640,000	1.5%		25	Utah	1,548,035,000	1.1%
46	Montana	403,762,000	0.3%		26	Kansas	1,528,992,000	1.1%
34	Nebraska	925,249,000	0.7%		27	New Mexico	1,447,041,000	1.0%
31	Nevada	1,167,609,000	0.8%		28	Indiana	1,298,906,000	0.9%
40	New Hampshire	384,323,000	0.3%		29	Alaska	1,281,538,000	0.9%
22	New Jersey	1,860,431,000	1.3%		30	Michigan	1,240,876,000	0.9%
27	New Mexico	1,447,041,000	1.0%		31	Nevada	1,167,609,000	0.8%
18	New York	2,442,780,000	1.8%		32	Arkansas	1,127,696,000	0.8%
6	North Carolina	6,569,452,000	4.7%		33	Massachusetts	1,102,544,000	0.8%
42	North Dakota	498,241,000	0.4%		34	Nebraska	925,249,000	0.7%
16	Ohio	2,894,340,000	2.1%		35	Maine	805,481,000	0.6%
14	Oklahoma	2,975,918,000	2.1%		36	Oregon	804,895,000	0.6%
36	Oregon	804,895,000	0.6%		37	Connecticut	717,458,000	0.5%
15	Pennsylvania	2,912,308,000	2.1%		38	Minnesota	708,113,000	0.5%
40	Rhode Island	621,059,000	0.4%		39	Wisconsin	647,948,000	0.5%
10	South Carolina	3,306,218,000	2.4%		40	Rhode Island	621,059,000	0.4%
47	South Dakota	396,956,000	0.3%		41	Idaho	535,099,000	0.4%
24	Tennessee	1,614,320,000	1.2%		42	North Dakota	498,241,000	0.4%
3	Texas	11,082,032,000	7.9%		43	Iowa	480,640,000	0.3%
25	Utah	1,548,035,000	1.1%		44	Delaware	417,218,000	0.3%
50	Vermont	140,130,000	0.1%		45	West Virginia	410,585,000	0.3%
1	Virginia	15,992,369,000	11.5%		46	Montana	403,762,000	0.3%
7	Washington	5,300,771,000	3.8%		47	South Dakota	396,956,000	0.3%
45	West Virginia	410,585,000	0.3%		48	New Hampshire	384,323,000	0.3%
39	Wisconsin	647,948,000	0.5%		49	Wyoming	302,121,000	0.2%
49	Wyoming	302,121,000	0.2%		50	Vermont	140,130,000	0.1%
						District of Columbia	1,983,450,000	1.4%

Source: U.S. Department of Defense
   "Atlas/Data Abstract for the United States" (http://www.dior.whs.mil/mmid/l03/fy04/ATLAS_2004.pdf)
*Includes Civilian Pay, Military Active Duty Pay, Reserve and National Guard Pay and Retired Military Pay. Based on location of recipient. Does not include recipients in U.S. territories and other countries.

U.S. Department of Defense Military Active Duty Pay in 2004

National Total = $50,488,778,000*

ALPHA ORDER

RANK	STATE	PAYROLL	% of USA
22	Alabama	$506,833,000	1.0%
17	Alaska	812,168,000	1.6%
15	Arizona	933,896,000	1.8%
31	Arkansas	222,660,000	0.4%
2	California	6,497,680,000	12.9%
13	Colorado	1,166,830,000	2.3%
29	Connecticut	273,491,000	0.5%
34	Delaware	166,830,000	0.3%
6	Florida	2,845,392,000	5.6%
5	Georgia	2,924,648,000	5.8%
8	Hawaii	1,865,382,000	3.7%
32	Idaho	182,164,000	0.4%
12	Illinois	1,286,383,000	2.5%
43	Indiana	55,673,000	0.1%
49	Iowa	25,390,000	0.1%
19	Kansas	675,828,000	1.3%
11	Kentucky	1,417,239,000	2.8%
18	Louisiana	746,384,000	1.5%
40	Maine	137,016,000	0.3%
10	Maryland	1,487,904,000	2.9%
35	Massachusetts	153,443,000	0.3%
42	Michigan	80,509,000	0.2%
46	Minnesota	44,619,000	0.1%
20	Mississippi	657,363,000	1.3%
21	Missouri	619,075,000	1.2%
38	Montana	140,182,000	0.3%
26	Nebraska	358,968,000	0.7%
25	Nevada	407,761,000	0.8%
45	New Hampshire	47,561,000	0.1%
27	New Jersey	328,357,000	0.7%
23	New Mexico	503,538,000	1.0%
16	New York	860,036,000	1.7%
4	North Carolina	3,761,793,000	7.5%
28	North Dakota	280,630,000	0.6%
24	Ohio	425,820,000	0.8%
14	Oklahoma	988,368,000	2.0%
44	Oregon	52,544,000	0.1%
33	Pennsylvania	177,012,000	0.4%
36	Rhode Island	149,145,000	0.3%
9	South Carolina	1,489,952,000	3.0%
41	South Dakota	134,126,000	0.3%
37	Tennessee	142,606,000	0.3%
3	Texas	4,525,105,000	9.0%
30	Utah	242,647,000	0.5%
50	Vermont	8,738,000	0.0%
1	Virginia	6,652,246,000	13.2%
7	Washington	2,093,959,000	4.1%
48	West Virginia	31,690,000	0.1%
47	Wisconsin	40,201,000	0.1%
39	Wyoming	139,427,000	0.3%

RANK ORDER

RANK	STATE	PAYROLL	% of USA
1	Virginia	$6,652,246,000	13.2%
2	California	6,497,680,000	12.9%
3	Texas	4,525,105,000	9.0%
4	North Carolina	3,761,793,000	7.5%
5	Georgia	2,924,648,000	5.8%
6	Florida	2,845,392,000	5.6%
7	Washington	2,093,959,000	4.1%
8	Hawaii	1,865,382,000	3.7%
9	South Carolina	1,489,952,000	3.0%
10	Maryland	1,487,904,000	2.9%
11	Kentucky	1,417,239,000	2.8%
12	Illinois	1,286,383,000	2.5%
13	Colorado	1,166,830,000	2.3%
14	Oklahoma	988,368,000	2.0%
15	Arizona	933,896,000	1.8%
16	New York	860,036,000	1.7%
17	Alaska	812,168,000	1.6%
18	Louisiana	746,384,000	1.5%
19	Kansas	675,828,000	1.3%
20	Mississippi	657,363,000	1.3%
21	Missouri	619,075,000	1.2%
22	Alabama	506,833,000	1.0%
23	New Mexico	503,538,000	1.0%
24	Ohio	425,820,000	0.8%
25	Nevada	407,761,000	0.8%
26	Nebraska	358,968,000	0.7%
27	New Jersey	328,357,000	0.7%
28	North Dakota	280,630,000	0.6%
29	Connecticut	273,491,000	0.5%
30	Utah	242,647,000	0.5%
31	Arkansas	222,660,000	0.4%
32	Idaho	182,164,000	0.4%
33	Pennsylvania	177,012,000	0.4%
34	Delaware	166,830,000	0.3%
35	Massachusetts	153,443,000	0.3%
36	Rhode Island	149,145,000	0.3%
37	Tennessee	142,606,000	0.3%
38	Montana	140,182,000	0.3%
39	Wyoming	139,427,000	0.3%
40	Maine	137,016,000	0.3%
41	South Dakota	134,126,000	0.3%
42	Michigan	80,509,000	0.2%
43	Indiana	55,673,000	0.1%
44	Oregon	52,544,000	0.1%
45	New Hampshire	47,561,000	0.1%
46	Minnesota	44,619,000	0.1%
47	Wisconsin	40,201,000	0.1%
48	West Virginia	31,690,000	0.1%
49	Iowa	25,390,000	0.1%
50	Vermont	8,738,000	0.0%
	District of Columbia	721,566,000	1.4%

Source: U.S. Department of Defense
"Atlas/Data Abstract for the United States" (http://www.dior.whs.mil/mmid/l03/fy04/ATLAS_2004.pdf)
*Based on location of recipient. Does not include recipients in U.S. territories and other countries.

U.S. Department of Defense Civilian Pay in 2004

National Total = $36,233,796,000*

ALPHA ORDER

RANK	STATE	PAYROLL	% of USA
10	Alabama	$1,280,555,000	3.5%
32	Alaska	267,337,000	0.7%
22	Arizona	454,490,000	1.3%
35	Arkansas	177,387,000	0.5%
2	California	3,526,824,000	9.7%
18	Colorado	540,718,000	1.5%
37	Connecticut	133,203,000	0.4%
45	Delaware	59,590,000	0.2%
5	Florida	1,616,630,000	4.5%
6	Georgia	1,599,090,000	4.4%
12	Hawaii	1,042,127,000	2.9%
44	Idaho	61,468,000	0.2%
16	Illinois	747,090,000	2.1%
20	Indiana	510,805,000	1.4%
43	Iowa	63,511,000	0.2%
31	Kansas	274,001,000	0.8%
25	Kentucky	410,835,000	1.1%
29	Louisiana	332,144,000	0.9%
28	Maine	373,746,000	1.0%
3	Maryland	2,157,507,000	6.0%
26	Massachusetts	396,051,000	1.1%
19	Michigan	511,094,000	1.4%
39	Minnesota	115,498,000	0.3%
21	Mississippi	457,678,000	1.3%
24	Missouri	436,408,000	1.2%
46	Montana	54,753,000	0.2%
34	Nebraska	188,594,000	0.5%
40	Nevada	98,260,000	0.3%
47	New Hampshire	49,816,000	0.1%
13	New Jersey	949,781,000	2.6%
27	New Mexico	378,411,000	1.0%
17	New York	564,679,000	1.6%
15	North Carolina	795,709,000	2.2%
42	North Dakota	75,344,000	0.2%
9	Ohio	1,320,193,000	3.6%
11	Oklahoma	1,139,410,000	3.1%
36	Oregon	176,499,000	0.5%
7	Pennsylvania	1,402,708,000	3.9%
30	Rhode Island	281,939,000	0.8%
23	South Carolina	448,563,000	1.2%
48	South Dakota	48,751,000	0.1%
33	Tennessee	252,661,000	0.7%
4	Texas	1,889,321,000	5.2%
14	Utah	812,029,000	2.2%
50	Vermont	24,744,000	0.1%
1	Virginia	5,037,138,000	13.9%
8	Washington	1,346,659,000	3.7%
41	West Virginia	78,030,000	0.2%
38	Wisconsin	117,700,000	0.3%
49	Wyoming	45,464,000	0.1%

RANK ORDER

RANK	STATE	PAYROLL	% of USA
1	Virginia	$5,037,138,000	13.9%
2	California	3,526,824,000	9.7%
3	Maryland	2,157,507,000	6.0%
4	Texas	1,889,321,000	5.2%
5	Florida	1,616,630,000	4.5%
6	Georgia	1,599,090,000	4.4%
7	Pennsylvania	1,402,708,000	3.9%
8	Washington	1,346,659,000	3.7%
9	Ohio	1,320,193,000	3.6%
10	Alabama	1,280,555,000	3.5%
11	Oklahoma	1,139,410,000	3.1%
12	Hawaii	1,042,127,000	2.9%
13	New Jersey	949,781,000	2.6%
14	Utah	812,029,000	2.2%
15	North Carolina	795,709,000	2.2%
16	Illinois	747,090,000	2.1%
17	New York	564,679,000	1.6%
18	Colorado	540,718,000	1.5%
19	Michigan	511,094,000	1.4%
20	Indiana	510,805,000	1.4%
21	Mississippi	457,678,000	1.3%
22	Arizona	454,490,000	1.3%
23	South Carolina	448,563,000	1.2%
24	Missouri	436,408,000	1.2%
25	Kentucky	410,835,000	1.1%
26	Massachusetts	396,051,000	1.1%
27	New Mexico	378,411,000	1.0%
28	Maine	373,746,000	1.0%
29	Louisiana	332,144,000	0.9%
30	Rhode Island	281,939,000	0.8%
31	Kansas	274,001,000	0.8%
32	Alaska	267,337,000	0.7%
33	Tennessee	252,661,000	0.7%
34	Nebraska	188,594,000	0.5%
35	Arkansas	177,387,000	0.5%
36	Oregon	176,499,000	0.5%
37	Connecticut	133,203,000	0.4%
38	Wisconsin	117,700,000	0.3%
39	Minnesota	115,498,000	0.3%
40	Nevada	98,260,000	0.3%
41	West Virginia	78,030,000	0.2%
42	North Dakota	75,344,000	0.2%
43	Iowa	63,511,000	0.2%
44	Idaho	61,468,000	0.2%
45	Delaware	59,590,000	0.2%
46	Montana	54,753,000	0.2%
47	New Hampshire	49,816,000	0.1%
48	South Dakota	48,751,000	0.1%
49	Wyoming	45,464,000	0.1%
50	Vermont	24,744,000	0.1%
	District of Columbia	1,110,853,000	3.1%

Source: U.S. Department of Defense
   "Atlas/Data Abstract for the United States" (http://www.dior.whs.mil/mmid/l03/fy04/ATLAS_2004.pdf)
*Based on location of recipient. Does not include recipients in U.S. territories and other countries.

79

U.S. Department of Defense Reserve and National Guard Pay in 2004

National Total = $10,302,525,000*

ALPHA ORDER

ALPHA ORDER

RANK	STATE	PAYROLL	% of USA
5	Alabama	$387,172,000	3.8%
49	Alaska	27,748,000	0.3%
38	Arizona	84,303,000	0.8%
19	Arkansas	235,919,000	2.3%
1	California	645,750,000	6.3%
31	Colorado	134,080,000	1.3%
36	Connecticut	92,589,000	0.9%
48	Delaware	37,559,000	0.4%
7	Florida	361,003,000	3.5%
9	Georgia	329,491,000	3.2%
34	Hawaii	108,850,000	1.1%
45	Idaho	51,785,000	0.5%
13	Illinois	315,437,000	3.1%
10	Indiana	327,960,000	3.2%
21	Iowa	207,209,000	2.0%
29	Kansas	152,876,000	1.5%
32	Kentucky	129,109,000	1.3%
17	Louisiana	252,348,000	2.4%
42	Maine	65,853,000	0.6%
27	Maryland	183,851,000	1.8%
28	Massachusetts	178,293,000	1.7%
24	Michigan	188,457,000	1.8%
16	Minnesota	262,851,000	2.6%
22	Mississippi	205,710,000	2.0%
6	Missouri	378,522,000	3.7%
44	Montana	55,616,000	0.5%
37	Nebraska	92,321,000	0.9%
46	Nevada	44,353,000	0.4%
40	New Hampshire	72,309,000	0.7%
26	New Jersey	184,935,000	1.8%
39	New Mexico	80,165,000	0.8%
4	New York	416,633,000	4.0%
8	North Carolina	358,097,000	3.5%
41	North Dakota	69,429,000	0.7%
11	Ohio	320,328,000	3.1%
23	Oklahoma	196,481,000	1.9%
30	Oregon	141,517,000	1.4%
3	Pennsylvania	421,070,000	4.1%
43	Rhode Island	59,856,000	0.6%
18	South Carolina	242,593,000	2.4%
35	South Dakota	95,374,000	0.9%
15	Tennessee	275,563,000	2.7%
2	Texas	554,799,000	5.4%
20	Utah	212,157,000	2.1%
47	Vermont	41,914,000	0.4%
14	Virginia	285,505,000	2.8%
12	Washington	320,048,000	3.1%
33	West Virginia	123,023,000	1.2%
25	Wisconsin	186,345,000	1.8%
50	Wyoming	25,618,000	0.2%

RANK ORDER

RANK	STATE	PAYROLL	% of USA
1	California	$645,750,000	6.3%
2	Texas	554,799,000	5.4%
3	Pennsylvania	421,070,000	4.1%
4	New York	416,633,000	4.0%
5	Alabama	387,172,000	3.8%
6	Missouri	378,522,000	3.7%
7	Florida	361,003,000	3.5%
8	North Carolina	358,097,000	3.5%
9	Georgia	329,491,000	3.2%
10	Indiana	327,960,000	3.2%
11	Ohio	320,328,000	3.1%
12	Washington	320,048,000	3.1%
13	Illinois	315,437,000	3.1%
14	Virginia	285,505,000	2.8%
15	Tennessee	275,563,000	2.7%
16	Minnesota	262,851,000	2.6%
17	Louisiana	252,348,000	2.4%
18	South Carolina	242,593,000	2.4%
19	Arkansas	235,919,000	2.3%
20	Utah	212,157,000	2.1%
21	Iowa	207,209,000	2.0%
22	Mississippi	205,710,000	2.0%
23	Oklahoma	196,481,000	1.9%
24	Michigan	188,457,000	1.8%
25	Wisconsin	186,345,000	1.8%
26	New Jersey	184,935,000	1.8%
27	Maryland	183,851,000	1.8%
28	Massachusetts	178,293,000	1.7%
29	Kansas	152,876,000	1.5%
30	Oregon	141,517,000	1.4%
31	Colorado	134,080,000	1.3%
32	Kentucky	129,109,000	1.3%
33	West Virginia	123,023,000	1.2%
34	Hawaii	108,850,000	1.1%
35	South Dakota	95,374,000	0.9%
36	Connecticut	92,589,000	0.9%
37	Nebraska	92,321,000	0.9%
38	Arizona	84,303,000	0.8%
39	New Mexico	80,165,000	0.8%
40	New Hampshire	72,309,000	0.7%
41	North Dakota	69,429,000	0.7%
42	Maine	65,853,000	0.6%
43	Rhode Island	59,856,000	0.6%
44	Montana	55,616,000	0.5%
45	Idaho	51,785,000	0.5%
46	Nevada	44,353,000	0.4%
47	Vermont	41,914,000	0.4%
48	Delaware	37,559,000	0.4%
49	Alaska	27,748,000	0.3%
50	Wyoming	25,618,000	0.2%
	District of Columbia	81,751,000	0.8%

Source: U.S. Department of Defense
   "Atlas/Data Abstract for the United States" (http://www.dior.whs.mil/mmid/l03/fy04/ATLAS_2004.pdf)
   *Based on location of recipient. Does not include recipients in U.S. territories and other countries.

U.S. Department of Defense Retired Military Pay in 2004

National Total = $42,465,262,000*

ALPHA ORDER

RANK	STATE	PAYROLL	% of USA
12	Alabama	$1,109,275,000	2.6%
43	Alaska	174,285,000	0.4%
8	Arizona	1,205,482,000	2.8%
23	Arkansas	491,730,000	1.2%
2	California	4,346,859,000	10.2%
9	Colorado	1,183,267,000	2.8%
39	Connecticut	218,175,000	0.5%
44	Delaware	153,239,000	0.4%
1	Florida	4,510,956,000	10.6%
5	Georgia	1,780,211,000	4.2%
32	Hawaii	357,679,000	0.8%
37	Idaho	239,682,000	0.6%
17	Illinois	676,572,000	1.6%
29	Indiana	404,468,000	1.0%
41	Iowa	184,530,000	0.4%
28	Kansas	426,287,000	1.0%
25	Kentucky	474,420,000	1.1%
21	Louisiana	540,510,000	1.3%
38	Maine	228,866,000	0.5%
10	Maryland	1,170,120,000	2.8%
31	Massachusetts	374,757,000	0.9%
26	Michigan	460,816,000	1.1%
35	Minnesota	285,145,000	0.7%
22	Mississippi	507,740,000	1.2%
16	Missouri	677,635,000	1.6%
45	Montana	153,211,000	0.4%
34	Nebraska	285,366,000	0.7%
19	Nevada	617,235,000	1.5%
40	New Hampshire	214,637,000	0.5%
30	New Jersey	397,358,000	0.9%
24	New Mexico	484,927,000	1.1%
20	New York	601,432,000	1.4%
6	North Carolina	1,653,853,000	3.9%
49	North Dakota	72,838,000	0.2%
15	Ohio	827,999,000	1.9%
18	Oklahoma	651,659,000	1.5%
27	Oregon	434,335,000	1.0%
14	Pennsylvania	911,518,000	2.1%
46	Rhode Island	130,119,000	0.3%
11	South Carolina	1,125,110,000	2.6%
47	South Dakota	118,705,000	0.3%
13	Tennessee	943,490,000	2.2%
3	Texas	4,112,807,000	9.7%
36	Utah	281,202,000	0.7%
50	Vermont	64,734,000	0.2%
4	Virginia	4,017,480,000	9.5%
7	Washington	1,540,105,000	3.6%
42	West Virginia	177,842,000	0.4%
33	Wisconsin	303,702,000	0.7%
48	Wyoming	91,612,000	0.2%

RANK ORDER

RANK	STATE	PAYROLL	% of USA
1	Florida	$4,510,956,000	10.6%
2	California	4,346,859,000	10.2%
3	Texas	4,112,807,000	9.7%
4	Virginia	4,017,480,000	9.5%
5	Georgia	1,780,211,000	4.2%
6	North Carolina	1,653,853,000	3.9%
7	Washington	1,540,105,000	3.6%
8	Arizona	1,205,482,000	2.8%
9	Colorado	1,183,267,000	2.8%
10	Maryland	1,170,120,000	2.8%
11	South Carolina	1,125,110,000	2.6%
12	Alabama	1,109,275,000	2.6%
13	Tennessee	943,490,000	2.2%
14	Pennsylvania	911,518,000	2.1%
15	Ohio	827,999,000	1.9%
16	Missouri	677,635,000	1.6%
17	Illinois	676,572,000	1.6%
18	Oklahoma	651,659,000	1.5%
19	Nevada	617,235,000	1.5%
20	New York	601,432,000	1.4%
21	Louisiana	540,510,000	1.3%
22	Mississippi	507,740,000	1.2%
23	Arkansas	491,730,000	1.2%
24	New Mexico	484,927,000	1.1%
25	Kentucky	474,420,000	1.1%
26	Michigan	460,816,000	1.1%
27	Oregon	434,335,000	1.0%
28	Kansas	426,287,000	1.0%
29	Indiana	404,468,000	1.0%
30	New Jersey	397,358,000	0.9%
31	Massachusetts	374,757,000	0.9%
32	Hawaii	357,679,000	0.8%
33	Wisconsin	303,702,000	0.7%
34	Nebraska	285,366,000	0.7%
35	Minnesota	285,145,000	0.7%
36	Utah	281,202,000	0.7%
37	Idaho	239,682,000	0.6%
38	Maine	228,866,000	0.5%
39	Connecticut	218,175,000	0.5%
40	New Hampshire	214,637,000	0.5%
41	Iowa	184,530,000	0.4%
42	West Virginia	177,842,000	0.4%
43	Alaska	174,285,000	0.4%
44	Delaware	153,239,000	0.4%
45	Montana	153,211,000	0.4%
46	Rhode Island	130,119,000	0.3%
47	South Dakota	118,705,000	0.3%
48	Wyoming	91,612,000	0.2%
49	North Dakota	72,838,000	0.2%
50	Vermont	64,734,000	0.2%
	District of Columbia	69,280,000	0.2%

Source: U.S. Department of Defense
    "Atlas/Data Abstract for the United States" (http://www.dior.whs.mil/mmid/l03/fy04/ATLAS_2004.pdf)
*Based on location of recipient. Does not include recipients in U.S. territories and other countries.

Veterans in 2004

National Total = 24,793,336 Veterans*

ALPHA ORDER

RANK	STATE	VETERANS	% of USA
23	Alabama	426,322	1.7%
47	Alaska	67,299	0.3%
14	Arizona	555,223	2.2%
30	Arkansas	268,353	1.1%
1	California	2,310,968	9.3%
21	Colorado	427,956	1.7%
29	Connecticut	268,975	1.1%
45	Delaware	80,751	0.3%
2	Florida	1,788,496	7.2%
10	Georgia	760,323	3.1%
42	Hawaii	107,310	0.4%
40	Idaho	133,183	0.5%
7	Illinois	896,640	3.6%
16	Indiana	550,871	2.2%
31	Iowa	265,960	1.1%
32	Kansas	246,359	1.0%
27	Kentucky	359,845	1.5%
25	Louisiana	366,957	1.5%
39	Maine	143,726	0.6%
19	Maryland	486,298	2.0%
18	Massachusetts	490,882	2.0%
8	Michigan	836,950	3.4%
22	Minnesota	426,591	1.7%
34	Mississippi	240,109	1.0%
15	Missouri	554,531	2.2%
43	Montana	102,605	0.4%
37	Nebraska	159,487	0.6%
33	Nevada	243,716	1.0%
41	New Hampshire	131,074	0.5%
13	New Jersey	582,917	2.4%
36	New Mexico	180,172	0.7%
4	New York	1,171,900	4.7%
9	North Carolina	767,051	3.1%
49	North Dakota	55,374	0.2%
6	Ohio	1,051,683	4.2%
28	Oklahoma	355,312	1.4%
26	Oregon	366,780	1.5%
5	Pennsylvania	1,145,919	4.6%
44	Rhode Island	91,161	0.4%
24	South Carolina	413,551	1.7%
46	South Dakota	73,400	0.3%
17	Tennessee	540,778	2.2%
3	Texas	1,681,748	6.8%
38	Utah	151,129	0.6%
48	Vermont	57,802	0.2%
11	Virginia	750,950	3.0%
12	Washington	632,929	2.6%
35	West Virginia	188,101	0.8%
20	Wisconsin	474,594	1.9%
50	Wyoming	54,941	0.2%

RANK ORDER

RANK	STATE	VETERANS	% of USA
1	California	2,310,968	9.3%
2	Florida	1,788,496	7.2%
3	Texas	1,681,748	6.8%
4	New York	1,171,900	4.7%
5	Pennsylvania	1,145,919	4.6%
6	Ohio	1,051,683	4.2%
7	Illinois	896,640	3.6%
8	Michigan	836,950	3.4%
9	North Carolina	767,051	3.1%
10	Georgia	760,323	3.1%
11	Virginia	750,950	3.0%
12	Washington	632,929	2.6%
13	New Jersey	582,917	2.4%
14	Arizona	555,223	2.2%
15	Missouri	554,531	2.2%
16	Indiana	550,871	2.2%
17	Tennessee	540,778	2.2%
18	Massachusetts	490,882	2.0%
19	Maryland	486,298	2.0%
20	Wisconsin	474,594	1.9%
21	Colorado	427,956	1.7%
22	Minnesota	426,591	1.7%
23	Alabama	426,322	1.7%
24	South Carolina	413,551	1.7%
25	Louisiana	366,957	1.5%
26	Oregon	366,780	1.5%
27	Kentucky	359,845	1.5%
28	Oklahoma	355,312	1.4%
29	Connecticut	268,975	1.1%
30	Arkansas	268,353	1.1%
31	Iowa	265,960	1.1%
32	Kansas	246,359	1.0%
33	Nevada	243,716	1.0%
34	Mississippi	240,109	1.0%
35	West Virginia	188,101	0.8%
36	New Mexico	180,172	0.7%
37	Nebraska	159,487	0.6%
38	Utah	151,129	0.6%
39	Maine	143,726	0.6%
40	Idaho	133,183	0.5%
41	New Hampshire	131,074	0.5%
42	Hawaii	107,310	0.4%
43	Montana	102,605	0.4%
44	Rhode Island	91,161	0.4%
45	Delaware	80,751	0.3%
46	South Dakota	73,400	0.3%
47	Alaska	67,299	0.3%
48	Vermont	57,802	0.2%
49	North Dakota	55,374	0.2%
50	Wyoming	54,941	0.2%
	District of Columbia	37,377	0.2%

Source: U.S. Department of Veteran Affairs
    "Veteran Data and Information" (http://www.va.gov/vetdata/demographics/index.htm)
*Includes 270,007 veterans in U.S. territories or other countries.

Percent of Adult Population Who are Veterans: 2004

National Percent = 11.1%*

<table>
<tr><td colspan="3">ALPHA ORDER</td><td colspan="3">RANK ORDER</td></tr>
<tr><th>RANK</th><th>STATE</th><th>PERCENT</th><th>RANK</th><th>STATE</th><th>PERCENT</th></tr>
<tr><td>22</td><td>Alabama</td><td>12.4</td><td>1</td><td>Alaska</td><td>14.4</td></tr>
<tr><td>1</td><td>Alaska</td><td>14.4</td><td>2</td><td>Montana</td><td>14.3</td></tr>
<tr><td>11</td><td>Arizona</td><td>13.2</td><td>3</td><td>Nevada</td><td>14.1</td></tr>
<tr><td>16</td><td>Arkansas</td><td>12.9</td><td>3</td><td>Wyoming</td><td>14.1</td></tr>
<tr><td>49</td><td>California</td><td>8.8</td><td>5</td><td>Maine</td><td>13.9</td></tr>
<tr><td>21</td><td>Colorado</td><td>12.5</td><td>6</td><td>Florida</td><td>13.4</td></tr>
<tr><td>44</td><td>Connecticut</td><td>10.1</td><td>6</td><td>Oregon</td><td>13.4</td></tr>
<tr><td>18</td><td>Delaware</td><td>12.7</td><td>6</td><td>Washington</td><td>13.4</td></tr>
<tr><td>6</td><td>Florida</td><td>13.4</td><td>9</td><td>Oklahoma</td><td>13.3</td></tr>
<tr><td>31</td><td>Georgia</td><td>11.7</td><td>9</td><td>Virginia</td><td>13.3</td></tr>
<tr><td>38</td><td>Hawaii</td><td>11.1</td><td>11</td><td>Arizona</td><td>13.2</td></tr>
<tr><td>14</td><td>Idaho</td><td>13.0</td><td>11</td><td>New Hampshire</td><td>13.2</td></tr>
<tr><td>46</td><td>Illinois</td><td>9.5</td><td>13</td><td>West Virginia</td><td>13.1</td></tr>
<tr><td>28</td><td>Indiana</td><td>11.9</td><td>14</td><td>Idaho</td><td>13.0</td></tr>
<tr><td>31</td><td>Iowa</td><td>11.7</td><td>14</td><td>South Carolina</td><td>13.0</td></tr>
<tr><td>25</td><td>Kansas</td><td>12.0</td><td>16</td><td>Arkansas</td><td>12.9</td></tr>
<tr><td>34</td><td>Kentucky</td><td>11.4</td><td>17</td><td>New Mexico</td><td>12.8</td></tr>
<tr><td>39</td><td>Louisiana</td><td>11.0</td><td>18</td><td>Delaware</td><td>12.7</td></tr>
<tr><td>5</td><td>Maine</td><td>13.9</td><td>18</td><td>Missouri</td><td>12.7</td></tr>
<tr><td>31</td><td>Maryland</td><td>11.7</td><td>18</td><td>South Dakota</td><td>12.7</td></tr>
<tr><td>45</td><td>Massachusetts</td><td>9.9</td><td>21</td><td>Colorado</td><td>12.5</td></tr>
<tr><td>39</td><td>Michigan</td><td>11.0</td><td>22</td><td>Alabama</td><td>12.4</td></tr>
<tr><td>39</td><td>Minnesota</td><td>11.0</td><td>23</td><td>Nebraska</td><td>12.1</td></tr>
<tr><td>36</td><td>Mississippi</td><td>11.2</td><td>23</td><td>Ohio</td><td>12.1</td></tr>
<tr><td>18</td><td>Missouri</td><td>12.7</td><td>25</td><td>Kansas</td><td>12.0</td></tr>
<tr><td>2</td><td>Montana</td><td>14.3</td><td>25</td><td>Pennsylvania</td><td>12.0</td></tr>
<tr><td>23</td><td>Nebraska</td><td>12.1</td><td>25</td><td>Tennessee</td><td>12.0</td></tr>
<tr><td>3</td><td>Nevada</td><td>14.1</td><td>28</td><td>Indiana</td><td>11.9</td></tr>
<tr><td>11</td><td>New Hampshire</td><td>13.2</td><td>28</td><td>North Carolina</td><td>11.9</td></tr>
<tr><td>48</td><td>New Jersey</td><td>8.9</td><td>28</td><td>Vermont</td><td>11.9</td></tr>
<tr><td>17</td><td>New Mexico</td><td>12.8</td><td>31</td><td>Georgia</td><td>11.7</td></tr>
<tr><td>50</td><td>New York</td><td>8.0</td><td>31</td><td>Iowa</td><td>11.7</td></tr>
<tr><td>28</td><td>North Carolina</td><td>11.9</td><td>31</td><td>Maryland</td><td>11.7</td></tr>
<tr><td>36</td><td>North Dakota</td><td>11.2</td><td>34</td><td>Kentucky</td><td>11.4</td></tr>
<tr><td>23</td><td>Ohio</td><td>12.1</td><td>35</td><td>Wisconsin</td><td>11.3</td></tr>
<tr><td>9</td><td>Oklahoma</td><td>13.3</td><td>36</td><td>Mississippi</td><td>11.2</td></tr>
<tr><td>6</td><td>Oregon</td><td>13.4</td><td>36</td><td>North Dakota</td><td>11.2</td></tr>
<tr><td>25</td><td>Pennsylvania</td><td>12.0</td><td>38</td><td>Hawaii</td><td>11.1</td></tr>
<tr><td>42</td><td>Rhode Island</td><td>10.9</td><td>39</td><td>Louisiana</td><td>11.0</td></tr>
<tr><td>14</td><td>South Carolina</td><td>13.0</td><td>39</td><td>Michigan</td><td>11.0</td></tr>
<tr><td>18</td><td>South Dakota</td><td>12.7</td><td>39</td><td>Minnesota</td><td>11.0</td></tr>
<tr><td>25</td><td>Tennessee</td><td>12.0</td><td>42</td><td>Rhode Island</td><td>10.9</td></tr>
<tr><td>43</td><td>Texas</td><td>10.4</td><td>43</td><td>Texas</td><td>10.4</td></tr>
<tr><td>47</td><td>Utah</td><td>9.2</td><td>44</td><td>Connecticut</td><td>10.1</td></tr>
<tr><td>28</td><td>Vermont</td><td>11.9</td><td>45</td><td>Massachusetts</td><td>9.9</td></tr>
<tr><td>9</td><td>Virginia</td><td>13.3</td><td>46</td><td>Illinois</td><td>9.5</td></tr>
<tr><td>6</td><td>Washington</td><td>13.4</td><td>47</td><td>Utah</td><td>9.2</td></tr>
<tr><td>13</td><td>West Virginia</td><td>13.1</td><td>48</td><td>New Jersey</td><td>8.9</td></tr>
<tr><td>35</td><td>Wisconsin</td><td>11.3</td><td>49</td><td>California</td><td>8.8</td></tr>
<tr><td>3</td><td>Wyoming</td><td>14.1</td><td>50</td><td>New York</td><td>8.0</td></tr>
<tr><td></td><td></td><td></td><td></td><td>District of Columbia</td><td>8.4</td></tr>
</table>

Source: Morgan Quitno Press using data from U.S. Department of Veteran Affairs
   "Veteran Data and Information" (http://www.va.gov/vetdata/demographics/index.htm)
*National figures does not include veterans in U.S. territories or other countries.

U.S. Military Fatalities in Iraq as of January 25, 2006

National Total = 2,239 Fatalities*

ALPHA ORDER

RANK	STATE	FATALITIES	% of USA
19	Alabama	38	1.7%
46	Alaska	8	0.4%
11	Arizona	52	2.3%
28	Arkansas	30	1.3%
1	California	232	10.4%
28	Colorado	30	1.3%
34	Connecticut	18	0.8%
44	Delaware	9	0.4%
6	Florida	100	4.5%
9	Georgia	72	3.2%
44	Hawaii	9	0.4%
39	Idaho	14	0.6%
7	Illinois	90	4.0%
16	Indiana	44	2.0%
31	Iowa	27	1.2%
32	Kansas	23	1.0%
24	Kentucky	33	1.5%
12	Louisiana	50	2.2%
46	Maine	8	0.4%
23	Maryland	34	1.5%
24	Massachusetts	33	1.5%
8	Michigan	73	3.3%
28	Minnesota	30	1.3%
22	Mississippi	35	1.6%
24	Missouri	33	1.5%
42	Montana	10	0.4%
33	Nebraska	20	0.9%
36	Nevada	15	0.7%
49	New Hampshire	7	0.3%
18	New Jersey	42	1.9%
36	New Mexico	15	0.7%
5	New York	102	4.6%
14	North Carolina	49	2.2%
42	North Dakota	10	0.4%
4	Ohio	105	4.7%
19	Oklahoma	38	1.7%
21	Oregon	36	1.6%
3	Pennsylvania	111	5.0%
46	Rhode Island	8	0.4%
27	South Carolina	32	1.4%
40	South Dakota	13	0.6%
15	Tennessee	47	2.1%
2	Texas	201	9.0%
41	Utah	11	0.5%
36	Vermont	15	0.7%
10	Virginia	68	3.0%
17	Washington	43	1.9%
35	West Virginia	16	0.7%
12	Wisconsin	50	2.2%
50	Wyoming	6	0.3%

RANK ORDER

RANK	STATE	FATALITIES	% of USA
1	California	232	10.4%
2	Texas	201	9.0%
3	Pennsylvania	111	5.0%
4	Ohio	105	4.7%
5	New York	102	4.6%
6	Florida	100	4.5%
7	Illinois	90	4.0%
8	Michigan	73	3.3%
9	Georgia	72	3.2%
10	Virginia	68	3.0%
11	Arizona	52	2.3%
12	Louisiana	50	2.2%
12	Wisconsin	50	2.2%
14	North Carolina	49	2.2%
15	Tennessee	47	2.1%
16	Indiana	44	2.0%
17	Washington	43	1.9%
18	New Jersey	42	1.9%
19	Alabama	38	1.7%
19	Oklahoma	38	1.7%
21	Oregon	36	1.6%
22	Mississippi	35	1.6%
23	Maryland	34	1.5%
24	Kentucky	33	1.5%
24	Massachusetts	33	1.5%
24	Missouri	33	1.5%
27	South Carolina	32	1.4%
28	Arkansas	30	1.3%
28	Colorado	30	1.3%
28	Minnesota	30	1.3%
31	Iowa	27	1.2%
32	Kansas	23	1.0%
33	Nebraska	20	0.9%
34	Connecticut	18	0.8%
35	West Virginia	16	0.7%
36	Nevada	15	0.7%
36	New Mexico	15	0.7%
36	Vermont	15	0.7%
39	Idaho	14	0.6%
40	South Dakota	13	0.6%
41	Utah	11	0.5%
42	Montana	10	0.4%
42	North Dakota	10	0.4%
44	Delaware	9	0.4%
44	Hawaii	9	0.4%
46	Alaska	8	0.4%
46	Maine	8	0.4%
46	Rhode Island	8	0.4%
49	New Hampshire	7	0.3%
50	Wyoming	6	0.3%
	District of Columbia	3	0.1%

Source: Iraq Coalition Casualty Count
   "U.S. Fatalities by State" (http://icasualties.org/oif/Statecity.aspx)
*As of January 25, 2006. Total includes 41 deaths of soldiers from U.S. territories. Total does not include 98 deaths of United Kingdom soldiers or 103 deaths from other coalition nations. Includes combat and noncombat deaths. Does not include 259 U.S. military deaths from efforts in Afghanistan.

Rate of U.S. Military Fatalities in Iraq as of January 25, 2006

National Rate = 0.74 Fatalities per 100,000 Population*

ALPHA ORDER				RANK ORDER		
RANK	STATE	RATE		RANK	STATE	RATE
24	Alabama	0.83		1	Vermont	2.41
4	Alaska	1.21		2	South Dakota	1.68
20	Arizona	0.88		3	North Dakota	1.57
9	Arkansas	1.08		4	Alaska	1.21
36	California	0.64		5	Mississippi	1.20
36	Colorado	0.64		6	Wyoming	1.18
48	Connecticut	0.51		7	Nebraska	1.14
10	Delaware	1.07		8	Louisiana	1.11
43	Florida	0.56		9	Arkansas	1.08
25	Georgia	0.79		10	Delaware	1.07
32	Hawaii	0.71		10	Montana	1.07
14	Idaho	0.98		10	Oklahoma	1.07
32	Illinois	0.71		13	Oregon	0.99
34	Indiana	0.70		14	Idaho	0.98
16	Iowa	0.91		15	Ohio	0.92
23	Kansas	0.84		16	Iowa	0.91
25	Kentucky	0.79		17	Virginia	0.90
8	Louisiana	1.11		17	Wisconsin	0.90
39	Maine	0.61		19	Pennsylvania	0.89
39	Maryland	0.61		20	Arizona	0.88
47	Massachusetts	0.52		20	Texas	0.88
31	Michigan	0.72		20	West Virginia	0.88
41	Minnesota	0.58		23	Kansas	0.84
5	Mississippi	1.20		24	Alabama	0.83
42	Missouri	0.57		25	Georgia	0.79
10	Montana	1.07		25	Kentucky	0.79
7	Nebraska	1.14		25	Tennessee	0.79
38	Nevada	0.62		28	New Mexico	0.78
45	New Hampshire	0.53		29	South Carolina	0.75
49	New Jersey	0.40		30	Rhode Island	0.74
28	New Mexico	0.78		31	Michigan	0.72
45	New York	0.53		32	Hawaii	0.71
43	North Carolina	0.56		32	Illinois	0.71
3	North Dakota	1.57		34	Indiana	0.70
15	Ohio	0.92		35	Washington	0.68
10	Oklahoma	1.07		36	California	0.64
13	Oregon	0.99		36	Colorado	0.64
19	Pennsylvania	0.89		38	Nevada	0.62
30	Rhode Island	0.74		39	Maine	0.61
29	South Carolina	0.75		39	Maryland	0.61
2	South Dakota	1.68		41	Minnesota	0.58
25	Tennessee	0.79		42	Missouri	0.57
20	Texas	0.88		43	Florida	0.56
50	Utah	0.45		43	North Carolina	0.56
1	Vermont	2.41		45	New Hampshire	0.53
17	Virginia	0.90		45	New York	0.53
35	Washington	0.68		47	Massachusetts	0.52
20	West Virginia	0.88		48	Connecticut	0.51
17	Wisconsin	0.90		49	New Jersey	0.48
6	Wyoming	1.18		50	Utah	0.45
					District of Columbia	0.54

Source: Morgan Quitno Press using data from Iraq Coalition Casualty Count
   "U.S. Fatalities by State" (http://icasualties.org/oif/Statecity.aspx)
*As of January 25, 2006. National rate does not include deaths of soldiers from U.S. territories. Includes combat and noncombat deaths. Does not include U.S. military deaths from efforts in Afghanistan.

IV. ECONOMY

Gross State Product in 2004

National Total = $11,665,595,000,000*

ALPHA ORDER				RANK ORDER			
RANK	STATE	G.S.P.	% of USA	RANK	STATE	G.S.P.	% of USA
25	Alabama	$139,840,000,000	1.2%	1	California	$1,550,753,000,000	13.3%
45	Alaska	34,023,000,000	0.3%	2	New York	896,739,000,000	7.7%
22	Arizona	199,953,000,000	1.7%	3	Texas	884,136,000,000	7.6%
34	Arkansas	80,902,000,000	0.7%	4	Florida	599,068,000,000	5.1%
1	California	1,550,753,000,000	13.3%	5	Illinois	521,900,000,000	4.5%
21	Colorado	199,969,000,000	1.7%	6	Pennsylvania	468,089,000,000	4.0%
23	Connecticut	185,802,000,000	1.6%	7	Ohio	419,866,000,000	3.6%
38	Delaware	54,274,000,000	0.5%	8	New Jersey	416,053,000,000	3.6%
4	Florida	599,068,000,000	5.1%	9	Michigan	372,169,000,000	3.2%
10	Georgia	343,125,000,000	2.9%	10	Georgia	343,125,000,000	2.9%
40	Hawaii	50,322,000,000	0.4%	11	North Carolina	336,398,000,000	2.9%
42	Idaho	43,571,000,000	0.4%	12	Virginia	329,332,000,000	2.8%
5	Illinois	521,900,000,000	4.5%	13	Massachusetts	317,798,000,000	2.7%
16	Indiana	227,569,000,000	2.0%	14	Washington	261,549,000,000	2.2%
29	Iowa	111,114,000,000	1.0%	15	Maryland	227,991,000,000	2.0%
32	Kansas	98,946,000,000	0.8%	16	Indiana	227,569,000,000	2.0%
26	Kentucky	136,446,000,000	1.2%	17	Minnesota	223,822,000,000	1.9%
24	Louisiana	152,944,000,000	1.3%	18	Tennessee	217,626,000,000	1.9%
43	Maine	43,336,000,000	0.4%	19	Wisconsin	211,616,000,000	1.8%
15	Maryland	227,991,000,000	2.0%	20	Missouri	203,294,000,000	1.7%
13	Massachusetts	317,798,000,000	2.7%	21	Colorado	199,969,000,000	1.7%
9	Michigan	372,169,000,000	3.2%	22	Arizona	199,953,000,000	1.7%
17	Minnesota	223,822,000,000	1.9%	23	Connecticut	185,802,000,000	1.6%
35	Mississippi	76,166,000,000	0.7%	24	Louisiana	152,944,000,000	1.3%
20	Missouri	203,294,000,000	1.7%	25	Alabama	139,840,000,000	1.2%
47	Montana	27,482,000,000	0.2%	26	Kentucky	136,446,000,000	1.2%
36	Nebraska	68,183,000,000	0.6%	27	South Carolina	136,125,000,000	1.2%
31	Nevada	100,317,000,000	0.9%	28	Oregon	128,103,000,000	1.1%
39	New Hampshire	51,871,000,000	0.4%	29	Iowa	111,114,000,000	1.0%
8	New Jersey	416,053,000,000	3.6%	30	Oklahoma	107,600,000,000	0.9%
37	New Mexico	61,012,000,000	0.5%	31	Nevada	100,317,000,000	0.9%
2	New York	896,739,000,000	7.7%	32	Kansas	98,946,000,000	0.8%
11	North Carolina	336,398,000,000	2.9%	33	Utah	82,611,000,000	0.7%
49	North Dakota	22,687,000,000	0.2%	34	Arkansas	80,902,000,000	0.7%
7	Ohio	419,866,000,000	3.6%	35	Mississippi	76,166,000,000	0.7%
30	Oklahoma	107,600,000,000	0.9%	36	Nebraska	68,183,000,000	0.6%
28	Oregon	128,103,000,000	1.1%	37	New Mexico	61,012,000,000	0.5%
6	Pennsylvania	468,089,000,000	4.0%	38	Delaware	54,274,000,000	0.5%
44	Rhode Island	41,679,000,000	0.4%	39	New Hampshire	51,871,000,000	0.4%
27	South Carolina	136,125,000,000	1.2%	40	Hawaii	50,322,000,000	0.4%
46	South Dakota	29,386,000,000	0.3%	41	West Virginia	49,454,000,000	0.4%
18	Tennessee	217,626,000,000	1.9%	42	Idaho	43,571,000,000	0.4%
3	Texas	884,136,000,000	7.6%	43	Maine	43,336,000,000	0.4%
33	Utah	82,611,000,000	0.7%	44	Rhode Island	41,679,000,000	0.4%
50	Vermont	21,921,000,000	0.2%	45	Alaska	34,023,000,000	0.3%
12	Virginia	329,332,000,000	2.8%	46	South Dakota	29,386,000,000	0.3%
14	Washington	261,549,000,000	2.2%	47	Montana	27,482,000,000	0.2%
41	West Virginia	49,454,000,000	0.4%	48	Wyoming	23,979,000,000	0.2%
19	Wisconsin	211,616,000,000	1.8%	49	North Dakota	22,687,000,000	0.2%
48	Wyoming	23,979,000,000	0.2%	50	Vermont	21,921,000,000	0.2%
					District of Columbia	76,685,000,000	0.7%

Source: U.S. Department of Commerce, Bureau of Economic Analysis
    "Gross State Product Data" (http://www.bea.doc.gov/bea/regional/data.htm)
*G.S.P. is the market value of goods and services produced by the labor and property located in a state. It is the state counterpart to the nation's Gross Domestic Product.

Percent Change in Gross State Product: 2000 to 2004
(Adjusted to Constant 2000 Dollars)
National Percent Change = 10.1% Increase*

ALPHA ORDER

RANK ORDER

RANK	STATE	PERCENT CHANGE		RANK	STATE	PERCENT CHANGE
17	Alabama	12.0		1	Nevada	22.2
46	Alaska	5.3		2	Arizona	19.2
2	Arizona	19.2		3	Wyoming	18.1
25	Arkansas	10.9		4	Idaho	16.8
17	California	12.0		5	Florida	16.6
36	Colorado	8.2		6	Delaware	16.4
43	Connecticut	6.7		7	Virginia	15.9
6	Delaware	16.4		8	Vermont	15.8
5	Florida	16.6		9	Maryland	15.5
34	Georgia	8.8		10	South Dakota	15.2
13	Hawaii	13.4		11	Tennessee	14.8
4	Idaho	16.8		12	Montana	14.7
48	Illinois	3.2		13	Hawaii	13.4
41	Indiana	7.3		14	North Carolina	12.6
23	Iowa	11.1		15	North Dakota	12.5
37	Kansas	7.8		16	New Mexico	12.1
25	Kentucky	10.9		17	Alabama	12.0
50	Louisiana	(0.9)		17	California	12.0
25	Maine	10.9		19	New Jersey	11.8
9	Maryland	15.5		20	Rhode Island	11.7
39	Massachusetts	7.7		21	Texas	11.3
49	Michigan	2.3		22	Minnesota	11.2
22	Minnesota	11.2		23	Iowa	11.1
41	Mississippi	7.3		24	Utah	11.0
45	Missouri	5.4		25	Arkansas	10.9
12	Montana	14.7		25	Kentucky	10.9
30	Nebraska	10.5		25	Maine	10.9
1	Nevada	22.2		25	New Hampshire	10.9
25	New Hampshire	10.9		29	South Carolina	10.6
19	New Jersey	11.8		30	Nebraska	10.5
16	New Mexico	12.1		31	Wisconsin	10.0
33	New York	9.0		32	Pennsylvania	9.3
14	North Carolina	12.6		33	New York	9.0
15	North Dakota	12.5		34	Georgia	8.8
47	Ohio	3.8		35	Washington	8.4
37	Oklahoma	7.8		36	Colorado	8.2
40	Oregon	7.5		37	Kansas	7.8
32	Pennsylvania	9.3		37	Oklahoma	7.8
20	Rhode Island	11.7		39	Massachusetts	7.7
29	South Carolina	10.6		40	Oregon	7.5
10	South Dakota	15.2		41	Indiana	7.3
11	Tennessee	14.8		41	Mississippi	7.3
21	Texas	11.3		43	Connecticut	6.7
24	Utah	11.0		44	West Virginia	6.3
8	Vermont	15.8		45	Missouri	5.4
7	Virginia	15.9		46	Alaska	5.3
35	Washington	8.4		47	Ohio	3.8
44	West Virginia	6.3		48	Illinois	3.2
31	Wisconsin	10.0		49	Michigan	2.3
3	Wyoming	18.1		50	Louisiana	(0.9)

District of Columbia 16.6

Source: Morgan Quitno Press using data from U.S. Department of Commerce, Bureau of Economic Analysis "Gross State Product Data" (http://www.bea.doc.gov/bea/regional/data.htm)
*G.S.P. is the market value of goods and services produced by the labor and property located in a state. It is the state counterpart to the nation's Gross Domestic Product. Adjusted for inflation using chained 2000 dollars.

Average Annual Change in Gross State Product: 2000 to 2004
(Adjusted to Constant 2000 Dollars)
National Annual Percent Change = 1.9% Increase*

ALPHA ORDER

RANK	STATE	PERCENT CHANGE
16	Alabama	2.3
46	Alaska	1.0
2	Arizona	3.6
22	Arkansas	2.1
16	California	2.3
35	Colorado	1.6
43	Connecticut	1.3
4	Delaware	3.1
4	Florida	3.1
33	Georgia	1.7
13	Hawaii	2.5
4	Idaho	3.1
48	Illinois	0.6
40	Indiana	1.4
22	Iowa	2.1
37	Kansas	1.5
22	Kentucky	2.1
50	Louisiana	(0.2)
22	Maine	2.1
9	Maryland	2.9
37	Massachusetts	1.5
49	Michigan	0.5
22	Minnesota	2.1
40	Mississippi	1.4
45	Missouri	1.1
11	Montana	2.8
29	Nebraska	2.0
1	Nevada	4.1
22	New Hampshire	2.1
16	New Jersey	2.3
16	New Mexico	2.3
33	New York	1.7
14	North Carolina	2.4
14	North Dakota	2.4
47	Ohio	0.8
37	Oklahoma	1.5
40	Oregon	1.4
32	Pennsylvania	1.8
20	Rhode Island	2.2
29	South Carolina	2.0
9	South Dakota	2.9
11	Tennessee	2.8
20	Texas	2.2
22	Utah	2.1
7	Vermont	3.0
7	Virginia	3.0
35	Washington	1.6
44	West Virginia	1.2
31	Wisconsin	1.9
3	Wyoming	3.4

RANK ORDER

RANK	STATE	PERCENT CHANGE
1	Nevada	4.1
2	Arizona	3.6
3	Wyoming	3.4
4	Delaware	3.1
4	Florida	3.1
4	Idaho	3.1
7	Vermont	3.0
7	Virginia	3.0
9	Maryland	2.9
9	South Dakota	2.9
11	Montana	2.8
11	Tennessee	2.8
13	Hawaii	2.5
14	North Carolina	2.4
14	North Dakota	2.4
16	Alabama	2.3
16	California	2.3
16	New Jersey	2.3
16	New Mexico	2.3
20	Rhode Island	2.2
20	Texas	2.2
22	Arkansas	2.1
22	Iowa	2.1
22	Kentucky	2.1
22	Maine	2.1
22	Minnesota	2.1
22	New Hampshire	2.1
22	Utah	2.1
29	Nebraska	2.0
29	South Carolina	2.0
31	Wisconsin	1.9
32	Pennsylvania	1.8
33	Georgia	1.7
33	New York	1.7
35	Colorado	1.6
35	Washington	1.6
37	Kansas	1.5
37	Massachusetts	1.5
37	Oklahoma	1.5
40	Indiana	1.4
40	Mississippi	1.4
40	Oregon	1.4
43	Connecticut	1.3
44	West Virginia	1.2
45	Missouri	1.1
46	Alaska	1.0
47	Ohio	0.8
48	Illinois	0.6
49	Michigan	0.5
50	Louisiana	(0.2)

District of Columbia   3.1

*Source: Morgan Quitno Press using data from U.S. Department of Commerce, Bureau of Economic Analysis
"Gross State Product Data" (http://www.bea.doc.gov/bea/regional/data.htm)*
**G.S.P. is the market value of goods and services produced by the labor and property located in a state. It is the
state counterpart to the nation's Gross Domestic Product. Adjusted for inflation using chained 2000 dollars.*

Per Capita Gross State Product in 2004

National Per Capita = $39,725*

ALPHA ORDER

RANK ORDER

RANK	STATE	PER CAPITA		RANK	STATE	PER CAPITA
45	Alabama	$30,901		1	Delaware	$65,385
3	Alaska	51,726		2	Connecticut	53,102
36	Arizona	34,836		3	Alaska	51,726
48	Arkansas	29,419		4	Massachusetts	49,599
11	California	43,266		5	New Jersey	47,904
10	Colorado	43,454		6	Wyoming	47,400
2	Connecticut	53,102		7	New York	46,510
1	Delaware	65,385		8	Virginia	44,021
37	Florida	34,458		9	Minnesota	43,916
22	Georgia	38,475		10	Colorado	43,454
17	Hawaii	39,871		11	California	43,266
44	Idaho	31,231		12	Nevada	43,001
14	Illinois	41,056		13	Washington	42,137
30	Indiana	36,548		14	Illinois	41,056
26	Iowa	37,629		15	Maryland	40,996
31	Kansas	36,195		16	New Hampshire	39,926
41	Kentucky	32,943		17	Hawaii	39,871
39	Louisiana	33,937		18	North Carolina	39,389
40	Maine	32,956		19	Texas	39,345
15	Maryland	40,996		20	Nebraska	39,013
4	Massachusetts	49,599		21	Rhode Island	38,595
28	Michigan	36,833		22	Georgia	38,475
9	Minnesota	43,916		23	Wisconsin	38,451
50	Mississippi	26,257		24	South Dakota	38,133
34	Missouri	35,297		25	Pennsylvania	37,766
47	Montana	29,649		26	Iowa	37,629
20	Nebraska	39,013		27	Tennessee	36,928
12	Nevada	43,001		28	Michigan	36,833
16	New Hampshire	39,926		29	Ohio	36,669
5	New Jersey	47,904		30	Indiana	36,548
43	New Mexico	32,061		31	Kansas	36,195
7	New York	46,510		32	Oregon	35,670
18	North Carolina	39,389		33	North Dakota	35,654
33	North Dakota	35,654		34	Missouri	35,297
29	Ohio	36,669		35	Vermont	35,286
46	Oklahoma	30,537		36	Arizona	34,836
32	Oregon	35,670		37	Florida	34,458
25	Pennsylvania	37,766		38	Utah	34,127
21	Rhode Island	38,595		39	Louisiana	33,937
42	South Carolina	32,427		40	Maine	32,956
24	South Dakota	38,133		41	Kentucky	32,943
27	Tennessee	36,928		42	South Carolina	32,427
19	Texas	39,345		43	New Mexico	32,061
38	Utah	34,127		44	Idaho	31,231
35	Vermont	35,286		45	Alabama	30,901
8	Virginia	44,021		46	Oklahoma	30,537
13	Washington	42,137		47	Montana	29,649
49	West Virginia	27,284		48	Arkansas	29,419
23	Wisconsin	38,451		49	West Virginia	27,284
6	Wyoming	47,400		50	Mississippi	26,257
					District of Columbia	138,361

Source: Morgan Quitno Press using data from U.S. Department of Commerce, Bureau of Economic Analysis
   "Gross State Product Data" (http://www.bea.doc.gov/bea/regional/data.htm)
*G.S.P. is the market value of goods and services produced by the labor and property located in a state. It is the
state counterpart to the nation's Gross Domestic Product.

Percent Change in Per Capita Gross State Product: 2000 to 2004
(Adjusted to Constant 2000 Dollars)
National Percent Change = 5.8% Increase*

ALPHA ORDER

RANK	STATE	PERCENT CHANGE
8	Alabama	10.2
48	Alaska	0.4
25	Arizona	7.3
19	Arkansas	8.1
29	California	6.2
45	Colorado	1.7
38	Connecticut	4.1
8	Delaware	10.2
21	Florida	7.7
48	Georgia	0.4
12	Hawaii	8.9
13	Idaho	8.8
46	Illinois	1.0
37	Indiana	5.0
10	Iowa	10.1
29	Kansas	6.2
16	Kentucky	8.4
50	Louisiana	(1.7)
20	Maine	7.8
7	Maryland	10.3
27	Massachusetts	6.9
47	Michigan	0.8
21	Minnesota	7.7
36	Mississippi	5.4
44	Missouri	2.6
5	Montana	11.8
16	Nebraska	8.4
34	Nevada	5.7
33	New Hampshire	5.9
15	New Jersey	8.5
25	New Mexico	7.3
23	New York	7.4
28	North Carolina	6.5
3	North Dakota	13.4
41	Ohio	3.0
34	Oklahoma	5.7
43	Oregon	2.7
18	Pennsylvania	8.3
14	Rhode Island	8.7
31	South Carolina	6.0
4	South Dakota	13.0
6	Tennessee	11.1
39	Texas	3.8
42	Utah	2.8
2	Vermont	13.7
10	Virginia	10.1
40	Washington	3.2
31	West Virginia	6.0
23	Wisconsin	7.4
1	Wyoming	15.4

RANK ORDER

RANK	STATE	PERCENT CHANGE
1	Wyoming	15.4
2	Vermont	13.7
3	North Dakota	13.4
4	South Dakota	13.0
5	Montana	11.8
6	Tennessee	11.1
7	Maryland	10.3
8	Alabama	10.2
8	Delaware	10.2
10	Iowa	10.1
10	Virginia	10.1
12	Hawaii	8.9
13	Idaho	8.8
14	Rhode Island	8.7
15	New Jersey	8.5
16	Kentucky	8.4
16	Nebraska	8.4
18	Pennsylvania	8.3
19	Arkansas	8.1
20	Maine	7.8
21	Florida	7.7
21	Minnesota	7.7
23	New York	7.4
23	Wisconsin	7.4
25	Arizona	7.3
25	New Mexico	7.3
27	Massachusetts	6.9
28	North Carolina	6.5
29	California	6.2
29	Kansas	6.2
31	South Carolina	6.0
31	West Virginia	6.0
33	New Hampshire	5.9
34	Nevada	5.7
34	Oklahoma	5.7
36	Mississippi	5.4
37	Indiana	5.0
38	Connecticut	4.1
39	Texas	3.8
40	Washington	3.2
41	Ohio	3.0
42	Utah	2.8
43	Oregon	2.7
44	Missouri	2.6
45	Colorado	1.7
46	Illinois	1.0
47	Michigan	0.8
48	Alaska	0.4
48	Georgia	0.4
50	Louisiana	(1.7)

District of Columbia   20.1

Source: Morgan Quitno Press using data from U.S. Department of Commerce, Bureau of Economic Analysis "Gross State Product Data" (http://www.bea.doc.gov/bea/regional/data.htm)
*G.S.P. is the market value of goods and services produced by the labor and property located in a state. It is the state counterpart to the nation's Gross Domestic Product. Adjusted for inflation using chained 2000 dollars.

Personal Income in 2004

National Total = $9,702,525,000,000*

RANK	STATE	INCOME	% of USA
24	Alabama	$125,166,703,000	1.3%
47	Alaska	22,340,402,000	0.2%
22	Arizona	164,323,943,000	1.7%
33	Arkansas	70,809,895,000	0.7%
1	California	1,262,454,026,000	13.0%
21	Colorado	166,152,653,000	1.7%
23	Connecticut	159,435,002,000	1.6%
44	Delaware	29,527,185,000	0.3%
4	Florida	547,311,531,000	5.6%
12	Georgia	265,537,511,000	2.7%
40	Hawaii	41,175,569,000	0.4%
42	Idaho	37,393,570,000	0.4%
5	Illinois	441,485,267,000	4.6%
16	Indiana	187,565,068,000	1.9%
30	Iowa	91,499,771,000	0.9%
31	Kansas	84,809,871,000	0.9%
27	Kentucky	112,565,602,000	1.2%
25	Louisiana	122,913,214,000	1.3%
41	Maine	39,481,808,000	0.4%
14	Maryland	220,261,099,000	2.3%
10	Massachusetts	270,144,644,000	2.8%
9	Michigan	324,133,954,000	3.3%
17	Minnesota	184,514,849,000	1.9%
34	Mississippi	70,770,022,000	0.7%
20	Missouri	175,610,709,000	1.8%
45	Montana	25,642,844,000	0.3%
36	Nebraska	56,393,335,000	0.6%
32	Nevada	70,075,571,000	0.8%
38	New Hampshire	47,660,890,000	0.5%
7	New Jersey	362,189,814,000	3.7%
37	New Mexico	49,777,827,000	0.5%
2	New York	737,038,528,000	7.6%
13	North Carolina	250,285,714,000	2.6%
49	North Dakota	18,553,456,000	0.2%
8	Ohio	356,773,618,000	3.7%
29	Oklahoma	98,019,976,000	1.0%
28	Oregon	109,935,032,000	1.1%
6	Pennsylvania	412,590,849,000	4.3%
43	Rhode Island	36,935,647,000	0.4%
26	South Carolina	113,988,229,000	1.2%
46	South Dakota	23,602,399,000	0.2%
19	Tennessee	175,884,974,000	1.8%
3	Texas	690,376,069,000	7.1%
35	Utah	64,375,986,000	0.7%
48	Vermont	19,721,154,000	0.2%
11	Virginia	269,861,839,000	2.8%
15	Washington	217,240,119,000	2.2%
39	West Virginia	46,619,385,000	0.5%
18	Wisconsin	176,635,877,000	1.8%
50	Wyoming	17,322,645,000	0.2%

RANK ORDER

RANK	STATE	INCOME	% of USA
1	California	$1,262,454,026,000	13.0%
2	New York	737,038,528,000	7.6%
3	Texas	690,376,069,000	7.1%
4	Florida	547,311,531,000	5.6%
5	Illinois	441,485,267,000	4.6%
6	Pennsylvania	412,590,849,000	4.3%
7	New Jersey	362,189,814,000	3.7%
8	Ohio	356,773,618,000	3.7%
9	Michigan	324,133,954,000	3.3%
10	Massachusetts	270,144,644,000	2.8%
11	Virginia	269,861,839,000	2.8%
12	Georgia	265,537,511,000	2.7%
13	North Carolina	250,285,714,000	2.6%
14	Maryland	220,261,099,000	2.3%
15	Washington	217,240,119,000	2.2%
16	Indiana	187,565,068,000	1.9%
17	Minnesota	184,514,849,000	1.9%
18	Wisconsin	176,635,877,000	1.8%
19	Tennessee	175,884,974,000	1.8%
20	Missouri	175,610,709,000	1.8%
21	Colorado	166,152,653,000	1.7%
22	Arizona	164,323,943,000	1.7%
23	Connecticut	159,435,002,000	1.6%
24	Alabama	125,166,703,000	1.3%
25	Louisiana	122,913,214,000	1.3%
26	South Carolina	113,988,229,000	1.2%
27	Kentucky	112,565,602,000	1.2%
28	Oregon	109,935,032,000	1.1%
29	Oklahoma	98,019,976,000	1.0%
30	Iowa	91,499,771,000	0.9%
31	Kansas	84,809,871,000	0.9%
32	Nevada	78,875,571,000	0.8%
33	Arkansas	70,809,895,000	0.7%
34	Mississippi	70,770,022,000	0.7%
35	Utah	64,375,986,000	0.7%
36	Nebraska	56,393,335,000	0.6%
37	New Mexico	49,777,827,000	0.5%
38	New Hampshire	47,660,890,000	0.5%
39	West Virginia	46,619,385,000	0.5%
40	Hawaii	41,175,569,000	0.4%
41	Maine	39,481,808,000	0.4%
42	Idaho	37,393,570,000	0.4%
43	Rhode Island	36,935,647,000	0.4%
44	Delaware	29,527,185,000	0.3%
45	Montana	25,642,844,000	0.3%
46	South Dakota	23,602,399,000	0.2%
47	Alaska	22,340,402,000	0.2%
48	Vermont	19,721,154,000	0.2%
49	North Dakota	18,553,456,000	0.2%
50	Wyoming	17,322,645,000	0.2%
	District of Columbia	28,839,355,000	0.3%

Source: U.S. Department of Commerce, Bureau of Economic Analysis
    "Annual State Personal Income" (http://www.bea.doc.gov/bea/regional/spi/)
*The national total shown here is the sum of the state estimates. It differs from the national income and product accounts (NIPA) estimate of personal income because it omits the earnings of federal civilian and military personnel stationed abroad and of U.S. residents employed abroad temporarily by private U.S. firms.

Change in Personal Income: 2003 to 2004

National Percent Change = 6.0% Increase

ALPHA ORDER			RANK ORDER		
RANK	STATE	PERCENT CHANGE	RANK	STATE	PERCENT CHANGE
35	Alabama	5.6	1	Nevada	10.1
46	Alaska	4.4	2	Iowa	8.9
3	Arizona	8.3	3	Arizona	8.3
8	Arkansas	7.2	4	Hawaii	8.0
18	California	6.6	5	Idaho	7.9
29	Colorado	5.8	5	Washington	7.9
11	Connecticut	6.8	7	Virginia	7.8
14	Delaware	6.7	8	Arkansas	7.2
10	Florida	6.9	9	New Hampshire	7.1
26	Georgia	5.9	10	Florida	6.9
4	Hawaii	8.0	11	Connecticut	6.8
5	Idaho	7.9	11	New York	6.8
48	Illinois	3.3	11	Wyoming	6.8
45	Indiana	4.9	14	Delaware	6.7
2	Iowa	8.9	14	Maryland	6.7
44	Kansas	5.0	14	North Carolina	6.7
37	Kentucky	5.5	14	Utah	6.7
29	Louisiana	5.8	18	California	6.6
24	Maine	6.0	19	Minnesota	6.5
14	Maryland	6.7	20	Montana	6.4
29	Massachusetts	5.8	20	New Mexico	6.4
50	Michigan	1.8	22	Mississippi	6.2
19	Minnesota	6.5	22	South Dakota	6.2
22	Mississippi	6.2	24	Maine	6.0
42	Missouri	5.2	24	Texas	6.0
20	Montana	6.4	26	Georgia	5.9
35	Nebraska	5.6	26	South Carolina	5.9
1	Nevada	10.1	26	Tennessee	5.9
9	New Hampshire	7.1	29	Colorado	5.8
37	New Jersey	5.5	29	Louisiana	5.8
20	New Mexico	6.4	29	Massachusetts	5.8
11	New York	6.8	29	Rhode Island	5.8
14	North Carolina	6.7	29	Vermont	5.8
49	North Dakota	2.0	34	Oregon	5.7
47	Ohio	4.2	35	Alabama	5.6
40	Oklahoma	5.3	35	Nebraska	5.6
34	Oregon	5.7	37	Kentucky	5.5
43	Pennsylvania	5.1	37	New Jersey	5.5
29	Rhode Island	5.8	39	Wisconsin	5.4
26	South Carolina	5.9	40	Oklahoma	5.3
22	South Dakota	6.2	40	West Virginia	5.3
26	Tennessee	5.9	42	Missouri	5.2
24	Texas	6.0	43	Pennsylvania	5.1
14	Utah	6.7	44	Kansas	5.0
29	Vermont	5.8	45	Indiana	4.9
7	Virginia	7.8	46	Alaska	4.4
5	Washington	7.9	47	Ohio	4.2
40	West Virginia	5.3	48	Illinois	3.3
39	Wisconsin	5.4	49	North Dakota	2.0
11	Wyoming	6.8	50	Michigan	1.8
				District of Columbia	7.1

Source: Morgan Quitno Press using data from U.S. Department of Commerce, Bureau of Economic Analysis
"Annual State Personal Income" (http://www.bea.doc.gov/bea/regional/spi/)
*Based on revised 2003 figures.

Per Capita Personal Income in 2004

National Per Capita = $33,041*

<table>
<tr><td colspan="3">ALPHA ORDER</td><td colspan="3">RANK ORDER</td></tr>
<tr><th>RANK</th><th>STATE</th><th>PER CAPITA</th><th>RANK</th><th>STATE</th><th>PER CAPITA</th></tr>
<tr><td>41</td><td>Alabama</td><td>$27,630</td><td>1</td><td>Connecticut</td><td>$45,506</td></tr>
<tr><td>16</td><td>Alaska</td><td>34,085</td><td>2</td><td>Massachusetts</td><td>42,102</td></tr>
<tr><td>38</td><td>Arizona</td><td>28,609</td><td>3</td><td>New Jersey</td><td>41,636</td></tr>
<tr><td>48</td><td>Arkansas</td><td>25,724</td><td>4</td><td>Maryland</td><td>39,629</td></tr>
<tr><td>11</td><td>California</td><td>35,172</td><td>5</td><td>New York</td><td>38,333</td></tr>
<tr><td>9</td><td>Colorado</td><td>36,109</td><td>6</td><td>New Hampshire</td><td>36,676</td></tr>
<tr><td>1</td><td>Connecticut</td><td>45,506</td><td>7</td><td>Virginia</td><td>36,175</td></tr>
<tr><td>10</td><td>Delaware</td><td>35,559</td><td>8</td><td>Minnesota</td><td>36,173</td></tr>
<tr><td>24</td><td>Florida</td><td>31,460</td><td>9</td><td>Colorado</td><td>36,109</td></tr>
<tr><td>32</td><td>Georgia</td><td>30,074</td><td>10</td><td>Delaware</td><td>35,559</td></tr>
<tr><td>19</td><td>Hawaii</td><td>32,606</td><td>11</td><td>California</td><td>35,172</td></tr>
<tr><td>46</td><td>Idaho</td><td>26,839</td><td>12</td><td>Washington</td><td>35,017</td></tr>
<tr><td>13</td><td>Illinois</td><td>34,725</td><td>13</td><td>Illinois</td><td>34,725</td></tr>
<tr><td>33</td><td>Indiana</td><td>30,070</td><td>14</td><td>Wyoming</td><td>34,199</td></tr>
<tr><td>27</td><td>Iowa</td><td>30,970</td><td>15</td><td>Rhode Island</td><td>34,180</td></tr>
<tr><td>26</td><td>Kansas</td><td>31,003</td><td>16</td><td>Alaska</td><td>34,085</td></tr>
<tr><td>44</td><td>Kentucky</td><td>27,151</td><td>17</td><td>Nevada</td><td>33,783</td></tr>
<tr><td>42</td><td>Louisiana</td><td>27,219</td><td>18</td><td>Pennsylvania</td><td>33,257</td></tr>
<tr><td>34</td><td>Maine</td><td>29,973</td><td>19</td><td>Hawaii</td><td>32,606</td></tr>
<tr><td>4</td><td>Maryland</td><td>39,629</td><td>20</td><td>Nebraska</td><td>32,276</td></tr>
<tr><td>2</td><td>Massachusetts</td><td>42,102</td><td>21</td><td>Wisconsin</td><td>32,063</td></tr>
<tr><td>22</td><td>Michigan</td><td>32,052</td><td>22</td><td>Michigan</td><td>32,052</td></tr>
<tr><td>8</td><td>Minnesota</td><td>36,173</td><td>23</td><td>Vermont</td><td>31,737</td></tr>
<tr><td>50</td><td>Mississippi</td><td>24,379</td><td>24</td><td>Florida</td><td>31,460</td></tr>
<tr><td>31</td><td>Missouri</td><td>30,516</td><td>25</td><td>Ohio</td><td>31,135</td></tr>
<tr><td>40</td><td>Montana</td><td>27,666</td><td>26</td><td>Kansas</td><td>31,003</td></tr>
<tr><td>20</td><td>Nebraska</td><td>32,276</td><td>27</td><td>Iowa</td><td>30,970</td></tr>
<tr><td>17</td><td>Nevada</td><td>33,783</td><td>28</td><td>Texas</td><td>30,697</td></tr>
<tr><td>6</td><td>New Hampshire</td><td>36,676</td><td>29</td><td>South Dakota</td><td>30,617</td></tr>
<tr><td>3</td><td>New Jersey</td><td>41,636</td><td>30</td><td>Oregon</td><td>30,584</td></tr>
<tr><td>47</td><td>New Mexico</td><td>26,154</td><td>31</td><td>Missouri</td><td>30,516</td></tr>
<tr><td>5</td><td>New York</td><td>38,333</td><td>32</td><td>Georgia</td><td>30,074</td></tr>
<tr><td>36</td><td>North Carolina</td><td>29,303</td><td>33</td><td>Indiana</td><td>30,070</td></tr>
<tr><td>37</td><td>North Dakota</td><td>29,247</td><td>34</td><td>Maine</td><td>29,973</td></tr>
<tr><td>25</td><td>Ohio</td><td>31,135</td><td>35</td><td>Tennessee</td><td>29,806</td></tr>
<tr><td>39</td><td>Oklahoma</td><td>27,819</td><td>36</td><td>North Carolina</td><td>29,303</td></tr>
<tr><td>30</td><td>Oregon</td><td>30,584</td><td>37</td><td>North Dakota</td><td>29,247</td></tr>
<tr><td>18</td><td>Pennsylvania</td><td>33,257</td><td>38</td><td>Arizona</td><td>28,609</td></tr>
<tr><td>15</td><td>Rhode Island</td><td>34,180</td><td>39</td><td>Oklahoma</td><td>27,819</td></tr>
<tr><td>43</td><td>South Carolina</td><td>27,153</td><td>40</td><td>Montana</td><td>27,666</td></tr>
<tr><td>29</td><td>South Dakota</td><td>30,617</td><td>41</td><td>Alabama</td><td>27,630</td></tr>
<tr><td>35</td><td>Tennessee</td><td>29,806</td><td>42</td><td>Louisiana</td><td>27,219</td></tr>
<tr><td>28</td><td>Texas</td><td>30,697</td><td>43</td><td>South Carolina</td><td>27,153</td></tr>
<tr><td>45</td><td>Utah</td><td>26,946</td><td>44</td><td>Kentucky</td><td>27,151</td></tr>
<tr><td>23</td><td>Vermont</td><td>31,737</td><td>45</td><td>Utah</td><td>26,946</td></tr>
<tr><td>7</td><td>Virginia</td><td>36,175</td><td>46</td><td>Idaho</td><td>26,839</td></tr>
<tr><td>12</td><td>Washington</td><td>35,017</td><td>47</td><td>New Mexico</td><td>26,154</td></tr>
<tr><td>49</td><td>West Virginia</td><td>25,681</td><td>48</td><td>Arkansas</td><td>25,724</td></tr>
<tr><td>21</td><td>Wisconsin</td><td>32,063</td><td>49</td><td>West Virginia</td><td>25,681</td></tr>
<tr><td>14</td><td>Wyoming</td><td>34,199</td><td>50</td><td>Mississippi</td><td>24,379</td></tr>
<tr><td></td><td></td><td></td><td></td><td>District of Columbia</td><td>52,101</td></tr>
</table>

Source: U.S. Department of Commerce, Bureau of Economic Analysis
   "Annual State Personal Income" (http://www.bea.doc.gov/bea/regional/spi/)
*The national figure is based on the sum of the state estimates. It differs from the national income and product accounts (NIPA) estimate of personal income because it omits the earnings of federal civilian and military personnel stationed abroad and of U.S. residents employed abroad temporarily by private U.S. firms.

Change in Per Capita Personal Income: 2003 to 2004

National Percent Change = 4.9% Increase*

ALPHA ORDER			RANK ORDER		
RANK	STATE	PERCENT CHANGE	RANK	STATE	PERCENT CHANGE
27	Alabama	5.0	1	Iowa	8.4
47	Alaska	3.2	2	Hawaii	6.8
23	Arizona	5.2	3	New York	6.7
7	Arkansas	6.2	4	Washington	6.6
18	California	5.3	5	Virginia	6.4
40	Colorado	4.5	6	Connecticut	6.3
6	Connecticut	6.3	7	Arkansas	6.2
25	Delaware	5.1	7	New Hampshire	6.2
40	Florida	4.5	9	Idaho	5.9
45	Georgia	4.1	10	Maryland	5.8
2	Hawaii	6.8	10	Massachusetts	5.8
9	Idaho	5.9	10	Wyoming	5.8
48	Illinois	2.8	13	Minnesota	5.7
43	Indiana	4.3	13	Nevada	5.7
1	Iowa	8.4	15	Mississippi	5.4
38	Kansas	4.6	15	Montana	5.4
32	Kentucky	4.8	15	Vermont	5.4
18	Louisiana	5.3	18	California	5.3
18	Maine	5.3	18	Louisiana	5.3
10	Maryland	5.8	18	Maine	5.3
10	Massachusetts	5.8	18	Rhode Island	5.3
50	Michigan	1.5	18	South Dakota	5.3
13	Minnesota	5.7	23	Arizona	5.2
15	Mississippi	5.4	23	North Carolina	5.2
40	Missouri	4.5	25	Delaware	5.1
15	Montana	5.4	25	Utah	5.1
27	Nebraska	5.0	27	Alabama	5.0
13	Nevada	5.7	27	Nebraska	5.0
7	New Hampshire	6.2	27	New Mexico	5.0
32	New Jersey	4.8	27	West Virginia	5.0
27	New Mexico	5.0	31	Tennessee	4.9
3	New York	6.7	32	Kentucky	4.8
23	North Carolina	5.2	32	New Jersey	4.8
49	North Dakota	1.8	32	Oklahoma	4.8
46	Ohio	4.0	32	Oregon	4.8
32	Oklahoma	4.8	32	Pennsylvania	4.8
32	Oregon	4.8	37	Wisconsin	4.7
32	Pennsylvania	4.8	38	Kansas	4.6
18	Rhode Island	5.3	38	South Carolina	4.6
38	South Carolina	4.6	40	Colorado	4.5
18	South Dakota	5.3	40	Florida	4.5
31	Tennessee	4.9	40	Missouri	4.5
44	Texas	4.2	43	Indiana	4.3
25	Utah	5.1	44	Texas	4.2
15	Vermont	5.4	45	Georgia	4.1
5	Virginia	6.4	46	Ohio	4.0
4	Washington	6.6	47	Alaska	3.2
27	West Virginia	5.0	48	Illinois	2.8
37	Wisconsin	4.7	49	North Dakota	1.8
10	Wyoming	5.8	50	Michigan	1.5
				District of Columbia	7.9

Source: Morgan Quitno Press using data from U.S. Department of Commerce, Bureau of Economic Analysis "Annual State Personal Income" (http://www.bea.doc.gov/bea/regional/spi/)
Based on revised 2003 figures.

Per Capita Disposable Personal Income in 2004

National Per Capita = $29,472*

ALPHA ORDER

RANK	STATE	PER CAPITA
40	Alabama	$25,169
12	Alaska	31,066
38	Arizona	25,895
49	Arkansas	23,432
14	California	31,012
7	Colorado	32,273
1	Connecticut	38,790
11	Delaware	31,445
23	Florida	28,569
35	Georgia	26,889
20	Hawaii	29,174
44	Idaho	24,414
15	Illinois	30,931
33	Indiana	27,070
27	Iowa	28,164
28	Kansas	27,949
45	Kentucky	24,391
42	Louisiana	24,932
34	Maine	26,923
4	Maryland	34,518
2	Massachusetts	36,506
21	Michigan	28,845
8	Minnesota	31,904
50	Mississippi	22,560
30	Missouri	27,531
41	Montana	25,123
19	Nebraska	29,272
17	Nevada	30,345
5	New Hampshire	33,180
3	New Jersey	36,421
47	New Mexico	23,865
6	New York	32,922
37	North Carolina	26,246
36	North Dakota	26,859
29	Ohio	27,739
39	Oklahoma	25,236
32	Oregon	27,124
18	Pennsylvania	29,656
16	Rhode Island	30,420
43	South Carolina	24,678
24	South Dakota	28,507
31	Tennessee	27,523
26	Texas	28,176
46	Utah	24,366
22	Vermont	28,622
10	Virginia	31,751
9	Washington	31,860
48	West Virginia	23,488
25	Wisconsin	28,504
13	Wyoming	31,022

RANK ORDER

RANK	STATE	PER CAPITA
1	Connecticut	$38,790
2	Massachusetts	36,506
3	New Jersey	36,421
4	Maryland	34,518
5	New Hampshire	33,180
6	New York	32,922
7	Colorado	32,273
8	Minnesota	31,904
9	Washington	31,860
10	Virginia	31,751
11	Delaware	31,445
12	Alaska	31,066
13	Wyoming	31,022
14	California	31,012
15	Illinois	30,931
16	Rhode Island	30,420
17	Nevada	30,345
18	Pennsylvania	29,656
19	Nebraska	29,272
20	Hawaii	29,174
21	Michigan	28,845
22	Vermont	28,622
23	Florida	28,569
24	South Dakota	28,507
25	Wisconsin	28,504
26	Texas	28,176
27	Iowa	28,164
28	Kansas	27,949
29	Ohio	27,739
30	Missouri	27,531
31	Tennessee	27,523
32	Oregon	27,124
33	Indiana	27,070
34	Maine	26,923
35	Georgia	26,889
36	North Dakota	26,859
37	North Carolina	26,246
38	Arizona	25,895
39	Oklahoma	25,236
40	Alabama	25,169
41	Montana	25,123
42	Louisiana	24,932
43	South Carolina	24,678
44	Idaho	24,414
45	Kentucky	24,391
46	Utah	24,366
47	New Mexico	23,865
48	West Virginia	23,488
49	Arkansas	23,432
50	Mississippi	22,560
	District of Columbia	45,442

Source: U.S. Department of Commerce, Bureau of Economic Analysis
"Annual State Personal Income" (http://www.bea.doc.gov/bea/regional/spi/)
*Disposable personal income is personal income less personal tax and nontax payments. It is the income available
to persons for spending or saving.

Median Household Income in 2004

National Median = $44,473*

ALPHA ORDER

RANK	STATE	INCOME		RANK	STATE	INCOME
43	Alabama	$38,111		1	New Hampshire	$57,352
6	Alaska	54,627		2	New Jersey	56,772
32	Arizona	42,590		3	Maryland	56,763
48	Arkansas	33,948		4	Connecticut	55,970
13	California	49,894		5	Minnesota	55,914
10	Colorado	51,022		6	Alaska	54,627
4	Connecticut	55,970		7	Virginia	53,275
12	Delaware	50,152		8	Hawaii	53,123
36	Florida	40,171		9	Massachusetts	52,354
28	Georgia	43,217		10	Colorado	51,022
8	Hawaii	53,123		11	Utah	50,614
33	Idaho	42,519		12	Delaware	50,152
18	Illinois	45,787		13	California	49,894
30	Indiana	43,003		14	Washington	48,688
29	Iowa	43,042		15	Wisconsin	47,220
26	Kansas	43,725		16	Nevada	46,984
45	Kentucky	37,396		17	Rhode Island	46,199
46	Louisiana	35,523		18	Illinois	45,787
38	Maine	39,395		19	Vermont	45,692
3	Maryland	56,763		20	Nebraska	44,623
9	Massachusetts	52,354		21	Michigan	44,476
21	Michigan	44,476		22	Pennsylvania	44,286
5	Minnesota	55,914		23	New York	44,228
49	Mississippi	33,659		24	Ohio	44,160
25	Missouri	43,988		25	Missouri	43,988
47	Montana	35,201		26	Kansas	43,725
20	Nebraska	44,623		27	Wyoming	43,641
16	Nevada	46,984		28	Georgia	43,217
1	New Hampshire	57,352		29	Iowa	43,042
2	New Jersey	56,772		30	Indiana	43,003
44	New Mexico	37,587		31	Oregon	42,617
23	New York	44,228		32	Arizona	42,590
40	North Carolina	39,000		33	Idaho	42,519
37	North Dakota	39,594		34	Texas	41,275
24	Ohio	44,160		35	South Dakota	40,518
42	Oklahoma	38,281		36	Florida	40,171
31	Oregon	42,617		37	North Dakota	39,594
22	Pennsylvania	44,286		38	Maine	39,395
17	Rhode Island	46,199		39	South Carolina	39,326
39	South Carolina	39,326		40	North Carolina	39,000
35	South Dakota	40,518		41	Tennessee	38,550
41	Tennessee	38,550		42	Oklahoma	38,281
34	Texas	41,275		43	Alabama	38,111
11	Utah	50,614		44	New Mexico	37,587
19	Vermont	45,692		45	Kentucky	37,396
7	Virginia	53,275		46	Louisiana	35,523
14	Washington	48,688		47	Montana	35,201
50	West Virginia	32,589		48	Arkansas	33,948
15	Wisconsin	47,220		49	Mississippi	33,659
27	Wyoming	43,641		50	West Virginia	32,589
					District of Columbia	43,003

The left columns are headed **ALPHA ORDER** and the right columns **RANK ORDER**.

Source: U.S. Bureau of the Census
   "Income 2004" (http://www.census.gov/hhes/www/income/income04/statemhi.html)
*Three-year average: 2002-2004.

Bankruptcy Filings in 2005

National Total = 1,782,643 Bankruptcies*

ALPHA ORDER

RANK	STATE	BANKRUPTCIES	% of USA
12	Alabama	44,884	2.5%
50	Alaska	1,885	0.1%
18	Arizona	35,570	2.0%
26	Arkansas	27,608	1.5%
1	California	135,872	7.6%
19	Colorado	34,772	2.0%
36	Connecticut	12,777	0.7%
44	Delaware	3,798	0.2%
4	Florida	93,898	5.3%
7	Georgia	79,245	4.4%
45	Hawaii	3,716	0.2%
39	Idaho	10,462	0.6%
5	Illinois	91,160	5.1%
10	Indiana	63,158	3.5%
33	Iowa	16,083	0.9%
31	Kansas	18,936	1.1%
20	Kentucky	33,103	1.9%
22	Louisiana	32,134	1.8%
40	Maine	5,459	0.3%
24	Maryland	30,448	1.7%
28	Massachusetts	21,952	1.2%
8	Michigan	75,760	4.2%
27	Minnesota	22,025	1.2%
29	Mississippi	21,842	1.2%
13	Missouri	43,981	2.5%
42	Montana	4,929	0.3%
38	Nebraska	10,515	0.6%
32	Nevada	18,220	1.0%
41	New Hampshire	5,341	0.3%
14	New Jersey	42,829	2.4%
37	New Mexico	10,921	0.6%
6	New York	90,648	5.1%
17	North Carolina	39,917	2.2%
47	North Dakota	2,878	0.2%
2	Ohio	109,413	6.1%
23	Oklahoma	31,222	1.8%
25	Oregon	27,909	1.6%
9	Pennsylvania	67,087	3.8%
43	Rhode Island	4,855	0.3%
34	South Carolina	15,209	0.9%
46	South Dakota	3,530	0.2%
11	Tennessee	63,058	3.5%
3	Texas	104,815	5.9%
30	Utah	20,611	1.2%
49	Vermont	1,948	0.1%
15	Virginia	40,587	2.3%
16	Washington	40,536	2.3%
35	West Virginia	14,482	0.8%
21	Wisconsin	32,718	1.8%
48	Wyoming	2,733	0.2%

RANK ORDER

RANK	STATE	BANKRUPTCIES	% of USA
1	California	135,872	7.6%
2	Ohio	109,413	6.1%
3	Texas	104,815	5.9%
4	Florida	93,898	5.3%
5	Illinois	91,160	5.1%
6	New York	90,648	5.1%
7	Georgia	79,245	4.4%
8	Michigan	75,760	4.2%
9	Pennsylvania	67,087	3.8%
10	Indiana	63,158	3.5%
11	Tennessee	63,058	3.5%
12	Alabama	44,884	2.5%
13	Missouri	43,981	2.5%
14	New Jersey	42,829	2.4%
15	Virginia	40,587	2.3%
16	Washington	40,536	2.3%
17	North Carolina	39,917	2.2%
18	Arizona	35,570	2.0%
19	Colorado	34,772	2.0%
20	Kentucky	33,103	1.9%
21	Wisconsin	32,718	1.8%
22	Louisiana	32,134	1.8%
23	Oklahoma	31,222	1.8%
24	Maryland	30,448	1.7%
25	Oregon	27,909	1.6%
26	Arkansas	27,608	1.5%
27	Minnesota	22,025	1.2%
28	Massachusetts	21,952	1.2%
29	Mississippi	21,842	1.2%
30	Utah	20,611	1.2%
31	Kansas	18,936	1.1%
32	Nevada	18,220	1.0%
33	Iowa	16,083	0.9%
34	South Carolina	15,209	0.9%
35	West Virginia	14,482	0.8%
36	Connecticut	12,777	0.7%
37	New Mexico	10,921	0.6%
38	Nebraska	10,515	0.6%
39	Idaho	10,462	0.6%
40	Maine	5,459	0.3%
41	New Hampshire	5,341	0.3%
42	Montana	4,929	0.3%
43	Rhode Island	4,855	0.3%
44	Delaware	3,798	0.2%
45	Hawaii	3,716	0.2%
46	South Dakota	3,530	0.2%
47	North Dakota	2,878	0.2%
48	Wyoming	2,733	0.2%
49	Vermont	1,948	0.1%
50	Alaska	1,885	0.1%
	District of Columbia	1,951	0.1%

Source: Morgan Quitno Press using data from Administrative Office of the U.S. Courts
"Table F-2, U.S. Bankruptcy Courts" (press release, December 1, 2005)
For 12 months through September 2005. Includes business (34,222) and Non-Business (1,748,421) filings.
Includes all chapters of bankruptcy. National total includes 13,253 bankruptcies in U.S. territories.

Personal Bankruptcy Rate in 2005

National Rate = 586 Personal Bankruptcies per 100,000 Population*

ALPHA ORDER

RANK	STATE	RATE
4	Alabama	978
50	Alaska	273
22	Arizona	591
3	Arkansas	980
44	California	366
16	Colorado	727
45	Connecticut	361
40	Delaware	423
31	Florida	520
7	Georgia	849
49	Hawaii	286
17	Idaho	723
18	Illinois	707
2	Indiana	997
28	Iowa	529
20	Kansas	677
9	Kentucky	785
19	Louisiana	695
41	Maine	404
25	Maryland	533
47	Massachusetts	337
14	Michigan	740
42	Minnesota	398
12	Mississippi	742
11	Missouri	752
32	Montana	514
23	Nebraska	582
12	Nevada	742
43	New Hampshire	369
33	New Jersey	483
29	New Mexico	526
34	New York	463
35	North Carolina	453
38	North Dakota	440
5	Ohio	939
6	Oklahoma	857
14	Oregon	740
27	Pennsylvania	530
37	Rhode Island	443
46	South Carolina	354
39	South Dakota	434
1	Tennessee	1,049
36	Texas	444
8	Utah	818
48	Vermont	303
26	Virginia	531
21	Washington	633
10	West Virginia	784
24	Wisconsin	576
30	Wyoming	523

RANK ORDER

RANK	STATE	RATE
1	Tennessee	1,049
2	Indiana	997
3	Arkansas	980
4	Alabama	978
5	Ohio	939
6	Oklahoma	857
7	Georgia	849
8	Utah	818
9	Kentucky	785
10	West Virginia	784
11	Missouri	752
12	Mississippi	742
12	Nevada	742
14	Michigan	740
14	Oregon	740
16	Colorado	727
17	Idaho	723
18	Illinois	707
19	Louisiana	695
20	Kansas	677
21	Washington	633
22	Arizona	591
23	Nebraska	582
24	Wisconsin	576
25	Maryland	533
26	Virginia	531
27	Pennsylvania	530
28	Iowa	529
29	New Mexico	526
30	Wyoming	523
31	Florida	520
32	Montana	514
33	New Jersey	483
34	New York	463
35	North Carolina	453
36	Texas	444
37	Rhode Island	443
38	North Dakota	440
39	South Dakota	434
40	Delaware	423
41	Maine	404
42	Minnesota	398
43	New Hampshire	369
44	California	366
45	Connecticut	361
46	South Carolina	354
47	Massachusetts	337
48	Vermont	303
49	Hawaii	286
50	Alaska	273

District of Columbia 347

Source: Morgan Quitno Press using data from Administrative Office of the U.S. Courts
"Table F-2, U.S. Bankruptcy Courts" (press release, December 1, 2005)
*For 12 months through September 2005. National rate does not include bankruptcies or population in U.S. territories. Includes all nonbusiness bankruptcies.

Percent Change in Personal Bankruptcy Rate: 2004 to 2005

National Percent Change = 8.7% Increase*

RANK	STATE	PERCENT CHANGE		RANK	STATE	PERCENT CHANGE
36	Alabama	6.5		1	Alaska	28.2
1	Alaska	28.2		2	North Dakota	26.8
32	Arizona	8.8		3	West Virginia	26.5
26	Arkansas	12.4		4	Iowa	23.9
37	California	6.1		5	Colorado	23.4
5	Colorado	23.4		6	Massachusetts	22.1
31	Connecticut	10.1		7	South Dakota	20.9
40	Delaware	3.7		8	Ohio	20.7
39	Florida	3.8		9	Minnesota	18.8
47	Georgia	(2.9)		9	Wisconsin	18.8
20	Hawaii	13.5		11	Maine	18.5
33	Idaho	8.6		12	Michigan	18.4
22	Illinois	12.8		13	Nebraska	16.6
23	Indiana	12.7		14	Missouri	16.0
4	Iowa	23.9		14	New York	16.0
19	Kansas	14.7		16	Rhode Island	15.7
18	Kentucky	15.3		17	New Mexico	15.4
35	Louisiana	6.8		18	Kentucky	15.3
11	Maine	18.5		19	Kansas	14.7
45	Maryland	(1.3)		20	Hawaii	13.5
6	Massachusetts	22.1		21	Oklahoma	13.4
12	Michigan	18.4		22	Illinois	12.8
9	Minnesota	18.8		23	Indiana	12.7
43	Mississippi	1.8		24	Oregon	12.5
14	Missouri	16.0		24	Pennsylvania	12.5
28	Montana	11.5		26	Arkansas	12.4
13	Nebraska	16.6		27	Vermont	11.8
49	Nevada	(4.4)		28	Montana	11.5
34	New Hampshire	8.5		29	Wyoming	11.3
41	New Jersey	3.6		30	Texas	10.2
17	New Mexico	15.4		31	Connecticut	10.1
14	New York	16.0		32	Arizona	8.8
38	North Carolina	4.9		33	Idaho	8.6
2	North Dakota	26.8		34	New Hampshire	8.5
8	Ohio	20.7		35	Louisiana	6.8
21	Oklahoma	13.4		36	Alabama	6.5
24	Oregon	12.5		37	California	6.1
24	Pennsylvania	12.5		38	North Carolina	4.9
16	Rhode Island	15.7		39	Florida	3.8
48	South Carolina	(3.8)		40	Delaware	3.7
7	South Dakota	20.9		41	New Jersey	3.6
44	Tennessee	0.0		42	Washington	1.9
30	Texas	10.2		43	Mississippi	1.8
50	Utah	(6.2)		44	Tennessee	0.0
27	Vermont	11.8		45	Maryland	(1.3)
46	Virginia	(2.2)		46	Virginia	(2.2)
42	Washington	1.9		47	Georgia	(2.9)
3	West Virginia	26.5		48	South Carolina	(3.8)
9	Wisconsin	18.8		49	Nevada	(4.4)
29	Wyoming	11.3		50	Utah	(6.2)

ALPHA ORDER / RANK ORDER

District of Columbia (1.1)

Source: Morgan Quitno Press using data from Administrative Office of the U.S. Courts
"Table F-2, U.S. Bankruptcy Courts" (press release, December 1, 2005)
*Twelve months ending in September 2004 to 12 months ending in September 2005. National rate does not include bankruptcies or population in U.S. territories. Includes all nonbusiness bankruptcies.

Total Tax Burden as a Percentage of Income in 2005

National Percent = 29.1% of Income*

ALPHA ORDER			RANK ORDER		
RANK	STATE	PERCENT	RANK	STATE	PERCENT
49	Alabama	25.7	1	Connecticut	33.5
50	Alaska	25.0	2	New York	32.6
19	Arizona	28.6	3	New Jersey	31.4
31	Arkansas	27.8	4	Massachusetts	31.1
9	California	29.9	4	Wyoming	31.1
14	Colorado	29.3	6	Maine	30.8
1	Connecticut	33.5	7	Rhode Island	30.7
35	Delaware	27.5	8	Washington	30.1
19	Florida	28.6	9	California	29.9
25	Georgia	28.2	10	Wisconsin	29.8
22	Hawaii	28.4	11	Minnesota	29.6
42	Idaho	26.9	12	Vermont	29.5
16	Illinois	29.2	13	Nevada	29.4
28	Indiana	28.1	14	Colorado	29.3
39	Iowa	27.0	14	Maryland	29.3
28	Kansas	28.1	16	Illinois	29.2
35	Kentucky	27.5	17	Virginia	29.0
43	Louisiana	26.8	18	New Mexico	28.7
6	Maine	30.8	19	Arizona	28.6
14	Maryland	29.3	19	Florida	28.6
4	Massachusetts	31.1	19	Michigan	28.6
19	Michigan	28.6	22	Hawaii	28.4
11	Minnesota	29.6	22	Ohio	28.4
45	Mississippi	26.4	22	Texas	28.4
37	Missouri	27.2	25	Georgia	28.2
39	Montana	27.0	25	Nebraska	28.2
25	Nebraska	28.2	25	Utah	28.2
13	Nevada	29.4	28	Indiana	28.1
34	New Hampshire	27.7	28	Kansas	28.1
3	New Jersey	31.4	30	Pennsylvania	28.0
18	New Mexico	28.7	31	Arkansas	27.8
2	New York	32.6	31	North Carolina	27.8
31	North Carolina	27.8	31	Oregon	27.8
45	North Dakota	26.4	34	New Hampshire	27.7
22	Ohio	28.4	35	Delaware	27.5
44	Oklahoma	26.5	35	Kentucky	27.5
31	Oregon	27.8	37	Missouri	27.2
30	Pennsylvania	28.0	38	West Virginia	27.1
7	Rhode Island	30.7	39	Iowa	27.0
39	South Carolina	27.0	39	Montana	27.0
47	South Dakota	26.3	39	South Carolina	27.0
48	Tennessee	26.1	42	Idaho	26.9
22	Texas	28.4	43	Louisiana	26.8
25	Utah	28.2	44	Oklahoma	26.5
12	Vermont	29.5	45	Mississippi	26.4
17	Virginia	29.0	45	North Dakota	26.4
8	Washington	30.1	47	South Dakota	26.3
38	West Virginia	27.1	48	Tennessee	26.1
10	Wisconsin	29.8	49	Alabama	25.7
4	Wyoming	31.1	50	Alaska	25.0
				District of Columbia	32.8

Source: The Tax Foundation
   "America Celebrates Tax Freedom Day" (http://www.taxfoundation.org/publications/show/93.html)
*This table attempts to allocate federal tax revenue among the states based on who ultimately bears the burden of taxes as opposed to simply the states where taxes are collected. State and local taxes are then added to determine the "total tax burden."

Per Capita Total Tax Burden in 2005

National Per Capita = $10,834*

ALPHA ORDER				RANK ORDER		
RANK	STATE	PER CAPITA		RANK	STATE	PER CAPITA
48	Alabama	$7,858		1	Connecticut	$17,219
29	Alaska	9,617		2	New Jersey	15,038
36	Arizona	8,952		3	Massachusetts	14,648
47	Arkansas	7,903		4	New York	14,038
8	California	11,875		5	Maryland	12,761
12	Colorado	11,554		6	Minnesota	12,169
1	Connecticut	17,219		7	Washington	11,963
17	Delaware	10,686		8	California	11,875
24	Florida	10,122		9	Wyoming	11,691
27	Georgia	9,698		10	Illinois	11,680
22	Hawaii	10,327		11	Rhode Island	11,628
44	Idaho	8,135		12	Colorado	11,554
10	Illinois	11,680		13	New Hampshire	11,411
30	Indiana	9,575		14	Virginia	11,386
33	Iowa	9,391		15	Wisconsin	10,826
26	Kansas	9,837		16	Pennsylvania	10,817
39	Kentucky	8,567		17	Delaware	10,686
41	Louisiana	8,292		18	Vermont	10,645
20	Maine	10,414		19	Nevada	10,569
5	Maryland	12,761		20	Maine	10,414
3	Massachusetts	14,648		21	Michigan	10,391
21	Michigan	10,391		22	Hawaii	10,327
6	Minnesota	12,169		23	Nebraska	10,306
50	Mississippi	7,226		24	Florida	10,122
32	Missouri	9,462		25	Ohio	10,059
43	Montana	8,209		26	Kansas	9,837
23	Nebraska	10,306		27	Georgia	9,698
19	Nevada	10,569		28	Texas	9,646
13	New Hampshire	11,411		29	Alaska	9,617
2	New Jersey	15,038		30	Indiana	9,575
40	New Mexico	8,373		31	Oregon	9,486
4	New York	14,038		32	Missouri	9,462
34	North Carolina	9,128		33	Iowa	9,391
37	North Dakota	8,945		34	North Carolina	9,128
25	Ohio	10,059		35	South Dakota	8,955
46	Oklahoma	8,076		36	Arizona	8,952
31	Oregon	9,486		37	North Dakota	8,945
16	Pennsylvania	10,817		38	Tennessee	8,635
11	Rhode Island	11,628		39	Kentucky	8,567
42	South Carolina	8,252		40	New Mexico	8,373
35	South Dakota	8,955		41	Louisiana	8,292
38	Tennessee	8,635		42	South Carolina	8,252
28	Texas	9,646		43	Montana	8,209
45	Utah	8,123		44	Idaho	8,135
18	Vermont	10,645		45	Utah	8,123
14	Virginia	11,386		46	Oklahoma	8,076
7	Washington	11,963		47	Arkansas	7,903
49	West Virginia	7,739		48	Alabama	7,858
15	Wisconsin	10,826		49	West Virginia	7,739
9	Wyoming	11,691		50	Mississippi	7,226
					District of Columbia	17,455

Source: The Tax Foundation
    "America Celebrates Tax Freedom Day" (http://www.taxfoundation.org/publications/show/93.html)
*This table attempts to allocate federal tax revenue among the states based on who ultimately bears the burden of taxes as opposed to simply the states where taxes are collected. State and local taxes are then added to determine the "total tax burden."

State Business Tax Climate Index 2004

National Average Score = 5.00*

ALPHA ORDER			RANK ORDER		
RANK	**STATE**	**SCORE**	**RANK**	**STATE**	**SCORE**
16	Alabama	5.664	1	South Dakota	7.365
3	Alaska	6.846	2	Florida	6.925
19	Arizona	5.491	3	Alaska	6.846
43	Arkansas	4.441	4	Texas	6.798
38	California	4.607	5	New Hampshire	6.629
8	Colorado	6.352	6	Nevada	6.494
37	Connecticut	4.699	7	Wyoming	6.446
18	Delaware	5.570	8	Colorado	6.352
2	Florida	6.925	9	Washington	6.252
20	Georgia	5.443	10	Oregon	6.150
50	Hawaii	3.742	11	Missouri	5.840
31	Idaho	4.851	12	Indiana	5.737
23	Illinois	5.211	12	Virginia	5.737
12	Indiana	5.737	14	Oklahoma	5.682
28	Iowa	5.032	15	Tennessee	5.668
32	Kansas	4.822	16	Alabama	5.664
44	Kentucky	4.345	17	Montana	5.633
27	Louisiana	5.062	18	Delaware	5.570
42	Maine	4.444	19	Arizona	5.491
21	Maryland	5.422	20	Georgia	5.443
33	Massachusetts	4.803	21	Maryland	5.422
36	Michigan	4.703	22	Pennsylvania	5.311
48	Minnesota	4.063	23	Illinois	5.211
25	Mississippi	5.146	24	South Carolina	5.182
11	Missouri	5.840	25	Mississippi	5.146
17	Montana	5.633	26	Utah	5.095
35	Nebraska	4.767	27	Louisiana	5.062
6	Nevada	6.494	28	Iowa	5.032
5	New Hampshire	6.629	29	Ohio	4.866
34	New Jersey	4.782	30	North Carolina	4.861
40	New Mexico	4.502	31	Idaho	4.851
49	New York	4.043	32	Kansas	4.822
30	North Carolina	4.861	33	Massachusetts	4.803
39	North Dakota	4.504	34	New Jersey	4.782
29	Ohio	4.866	35	Nebraska	4.767
14	Oklahoma	5.682	36	Michigan	4.703
10	Oregon	6.150	37	Connecticut	4.699
22	Pennsylvania	5.311	38	California	4.607
46	Rhode Island	4.249	39	North Dakota	4.504
24	South Carolina	5.182	40	New Mexico	4.502
1	South Dakota	7.365	41	Wisconsin	4.460
15	Tennessee	5.668	42	Maine	4.444
4	Texas	6.798	43	Arkansas	4.441
26	Utah	5.095	44	Kentucky	4.345
45	Vermont	4.310	45	Vermont	4.310
12	Virginia	5.737	46	Rhode Island	4.249
9	Washington	6.252	47	West Virginia	4.240
47	West Virginia	4.240	48	Minnesota	4.063
41	Wisconsin	4.460	49	New York	4.043
7	Wyoming	6.446	50	Hawaii	3.742
				District of Columbia	3.702

Source: The Tax Foundation
   "State Business Tax Climate Index" (October 2004, http://www.taxfoundation.org/bp45.pdf)
*This index looks at levels of taxation and complexity of compliance to compare the states on how "business friendly" each state is compared to the others. The scale for each factor considered is one to ten, with ten being the "best."

Fortune 500 Companies in 2005

National Total = 500 Companies*

ALPHA ORDER

RANK	STATE	COMPANIES	% of USA
29	Alabama	2	0.4%
40	Alaska	0	0.0%
27	Arizona	3	0.6%
24	Arkansas	5	1.0%
2	California	52	10.4%
17	Colorado	10	2.0%
12	Connecticut	14	2.8%
29	Delaware	2	0.4%
12	Florida	14	2.8%
11	Georgia	17	3.4%
40	Hawaii	0	0.0%
29	Idaho	2	0.4%
4	Illinois	33	6.6%
21	Indiana	6	1.2%
29	Iowa	2	0.4%
29	Kansas	2	0.4%
21	Kentucky	6	1.2%
35	Louisiana	1	0.2%
40	Maine	0	0.0%
21	Maryland	6	1.2%
15	Massachusetts	11	2.2%
8	Michigan	22	4.4%
9	Minnesota	18	3.6%
40	Mississippi	0	0.0%
15	Missouri	11	2.2%
40	Montana	0	0.0%
26	Nebraska	4	0.8%
27	Nevada	3	0.6%
35	New Hampshire	1	0.2%
7	New Jersey	24	4.8%
40	New Mexico	0	0.0%
1	New York	54	10.8%
12	North Carolina	14	2.8%
40	North Dakota	0	0.0%
5	Ohio	30	6.0%
24	Oklahoma	5	1.0%
35	Oregon	1	0.2%
6	Pennsylvania	27	5.4%
29	Rhode Island	2	0.4%
35	South Carolina	1	0.2%
40	South Dakota	0	0.0%
20	Tennessee	7	1.4%
3	Texas	48	9.6%
35	Utah	1	0.2%
40	Vermont	0	0.0%
9	Virginia	18	3.6%
19	Washington	9	1.8%
40	West Virginia	0	0.0%
17	Wisconsin	10	2.0%
40	Wyoming	0	0.0%

RANK ORDER

RANK	STATE	COMPANIES	% of USA
1	New York	54	10.8%
2	California	52	10.4%
3	Texas	48	9.6%
4	Illinois	33	6.6%
5	Ohio	30	6.0%
6	Pennsylvania	27	5.4%
7	New Jersey	24	4.8%
8	Michigan	22	4.4%
9	Minnesota	18	3.6%
9	Virginia	18	3.6%
11	Georgia	17	3.4%
12	Connecticut	14	2.8%
12	Florida	14	2.8%
12	North Carolina	14	2.8%
15	Massachusetts	11	2.2%
15	Missouri	11	2.2%
17	Colorado	10	2.0%
17	Wisconsin	10	2.0%
19	Washington	9	1.8%
20	Tennessee	7	1.4%
21	Indiana	6	1.2%
21	Kentucky	6	1.2%
21	Maryland	6	1.2%
24	Arkansas	5	1.0%
24	Oklahoma	5	1.0%
26	Nebraska	4	0.8%
27	Arizona	3	0.6%
27	Nevada	3	0.6%
29	Alabama	2	0.4%
29	Delaware	2	0.4%
29	Idaho	2	0.4%
29	Iowa	2	0.4%
29	Kansas	2	0.4%
29	Rhode Island	2	0.4%
35	Louisiana	1	0.2%
35	New Hampshire	1	0.2%
35	Oregon	1	0.2%
35	South Carolina	1	0.2%
35	Utah	1	0.2%
40	Alaska	0	0.0%
40	Hawaii	0	0.0%
40	Maine	0	0.0%
40	Mississippi	0	0.0%
40	Montana	0	0.0%
40	New Mexico	0	0.0%
40	North Dakota	0	0.0%
40	South Dakota	0	0.0%
40	Vermont	0	0.0%
40	West Virginia	0	0.0%
40	Wyoming	0	0.0%
	District of Columbia	2	0.4%

Source: Fortune Magazine
   "Fortune 500 Ranked Within States" (April 18, 2005)
*By state where each company's headquarters is located.

Employer Firms in 2004

National Total = 5,683,700 Firms*

ALPHA ORDER

RANK	STATE	FIRMS	% of USA
27	Alabama	86,651	1.5%
50	Alaska	16,975	0.3%
21	Arizona	110,153	1.9%
32	Arkansas	61,778	1.1%
1	California	1,077,390	19.0%
15	Colorado	146,379	2.6%
24	Connecticut	97,311	1.7%
45	Delaware	25,833	0.5%
3	Florida	449,070	7.9%
10	Georgia	202,979	3.6%
44	Hawaii	29,791	0.5%
37	Idaho	43,675	0.8%
5	Illinois	285,208	5.0%
20	Indiana	125,746	2.2%
30	Iowa	69,354	1.2%
31	Kansas	69,241	1.2%
28	Kentucky	83,046	1.5%
25	Louisiana	96,084	1.7%
39	Maine	40,304	0.7%
16	Maryland	137,338	2.4%
13	Massachusetts	178,752	3.1%
9	Michigan	213,104	3.7%
18	Minnesota	134,438	2.4%
34	Mississippi	54,117	1.0%
17	Missouri	134,448	2.4%
42	Montana	34,570	0.6%
36	Nebraska	46,161	0.8%
35	Nevada	51,424	0.9%
40	New Hampshire	40,151	0.7%
7	New Jersey	256,863	4.5%
38	New Mexico	42,241	0.7%
2	New York	481,858	8.5%
12	North Carolina	182,598	3.2%
49	North Dakota	19,177	0.3%
8	Ohio	231,374	4.1%
29	Oklahoma	77,027	1.4%
23	Oregon	104,114	1.8%
6	Pennsylvania	275,853	4.9%
43	Rhode Island	33,253	0.6%
26	South Carolina	92,940	1.6%
46	South Dakota	23,713	0.4%
22	Tennessee	109,853	1.9%
4	Texas	404,683	7.1%
33	Utah	61,118	1.1%
47	Vermont	21,335	0.4%
14	Virginia	172,785	3.0%
11	Washington	198,635	3.5%
41	West Virginia	36,830	0.6%
19	Wisconsin	125,888	2.2%
48	Wyoming	20,071	0.4%

RANK ORDER

RANK	STATE	FIRMS	% of USA
1	California	1,077,390	19.0%
2	New York	481,858	8.5%
3	Florida	449,070	7.9%
4	Texas	404,683	7.1%
5	Illinois	285,208	5.0%
6	Pennsylvania	275,853	4.9%
7	New Jersey	256,863	4.5%
8	Ohio	231,374	4.1%
9	Michigan	213,104	3.7%
10	Georgia	202,979	3.6%
11	Washington	198,635	3.5%
12	North Carolina	182,598	3.2%
13	Massachusetts	178,752	3.1%
14	Virginia	172,785	3.0%
15	Colorado	146,379	2.6%
16	Maryland	137,338	2.4%
17	Missouri	134,448	2.4%
18	Minnesota	134,438	2.4%
19	Wisconsin	125,888	2.2%
20	Indiana	125,746	2.2%
21	Arizona	110,153	1.9%
22	Tennessee	109,853	1.9%
23	Oregon	104,114	1.8%
24	Connecticut	97,311	1.7%
25	Louisiana	96,084	1.7%
26	South Carolina	92,940	1.6%
27	Alabama	86,651	1.5%
28	Kentucky	83,046	1.5%
29	Oklahoma	77,027	1.4%
30	Iowa	69,354	1.2%
31	Kansas	69,241	1.2%
32	Arkansas	61,778	1.1%
33	Utah	61,118	1.1%
34	Mississippi	54,117	1.0%
35	Nevada	51,424	0.9%
36	Nebraska	46,161	0.8%
37	Idaho	43,675	0.8%
38	New Mexico	42,241	0.7%
39	Maine	40,304	0.7%
40	New Hampshire	40,151	0.7%
41	West Virginia	36,830	0.6%
42	Montana	34,570	0.6%
43	Rhode Island	33,253	0.6%
44	Hawaii	29,791	0.5%
45	Delaware	25,833	0.5%
46	South Dakota	23,713	0.4%
47	Vermont	21,335	0.4%
48	Wyoming	20,071	0.4%
49	North Dakota	19,177	0.3%
50	Alaska	16,975	0.3%
	District of Columbia	27,424	0.5%

Source: U.S. Small Business Administration
   "The Small Business Economy" (2005, http://www.sba.gov/advo/research/sb_econ2005.pdf)
*State totals do not add to the U.S. figure as firms can be in more than one state.

New Employer Firms in 2004

National Total = 580,900 New Firms*

ALPHA ORDER

RANK	STATE	FIRMS	% of USA
28	Alabama	9,413	1.6%
48	Alaska	1,848	0.3%
23	Arizona	12,421	2.1%
32	Arkansas	7,852	1.4%
1	California	117,016	20.1%
12	Colorado	23,694	4.1%
30	Connecticut	9,064	1.6%
45	Delaware	3,270	0.6%
2	Florida	77,754	13.4%
8	Georgia	29,547	5.1%
44	Hawaii	3,698	0.6%
33	Idaho	7,814	1.3%
9	Illinois	28,453	4.9%
20	Indiana	13,906	2.4%
36	Iowa	5,954	1.0%
34	Kansas	6,742	1.2%
31	Kentucky	8,807	1.5%
27	Louisiana	9,875	1.7%
41	Maine	4,300	0.7%
15	Maryland	21,751	3.7%
16	Massachusetts	18,822	3.2%
10	Michigan	24,625	4.2%
19	Minnesota	15,167	2.6%
35	Mississippi	6,141	1.1%
18	Missouri	16,155	2.8%
40	Montana	4,588	0.8%
39	Nebraska	4,849	0.8%
26	Nevada	10,183	1.8%
38	New Hampshire	4,865	0.8%
5	New Jersey	35,895	6.2%
37	New Mexico	5,683	1.0%
3	New York	62,854	10.8%
13	North Carolina	23,387	4.0%
49	North Dakota	1,747	0.3%
14	Ohio	22,725	3.9%
29	Oklahoma	9,263	1.6%
21	Oregon	13,481	2.3%
6	Pennsylvania	33,188	5.7%
43	Rhode Island	3,932	0.7%
24	South Carolina	11,745	2.0%
50	South Dakota	1,691	0.3%
17	Tennessee	17,415	3.0%
4	Texas	54,098	9.3%
25	Utah	11,357	2.0%
47	Vermont	2,322	0.4%
11	Virginia	24,134	4.2%
7	Washington	31,955	5.5%
42	West Virginia	3,937	0.7%
22	Wisconsin	13,093	2.3%
46	Wyoming	2,519	0.4%

RANK ORDER

RANK	STATE	FIRMS	% of USA
1	California	117,016	20.1%
2	Florida	77,754	13.4%
3	New York	62,854	10.8%
4	Texas	54,098	9.3%
5	New Jersey	35,895	6.2%
6	Pennsylvania	33,188	5.7%
7	Washington	31,955	5.5%
8	Georgia	29,547	5.1%
9	Illinois	28,453	4.9%
10	Michigan	24,625	4.2%
11	Virginia	24,134	4.2%
12	Colorado	23,694	4.1%
13	North Carolina	23,387	4.0%
14	Ohio	22,725	3.9%
15	Maryland	21,751	3.7%
16	Massachusetts	18,822	3.2%
17	Tennessee	17,415	3.0%
18	Missouri	16,155	2.8%
19	Minnesota	15,167	2.6%
20	Indiana	13,906	2.4%
21	Oregon	13,481	2.3%
22	Wisconsin	13,093	2.3%
23	Arizona	12,421	2.1%
24	South Carolina	11,745	2.0%
25	Utah	11,357	2.0%
26	Nevada	10,483	1.8%
27	Louisiana	9,875	1.7%
28	Alabama	9,413	1.6%
29	Oklahoma	9,263	1.6%
30	Connecticut	9,064	1.6%
31	Kentucky	8,807	1.5%
32	Arkansas	7,852	1.4%
33	Idaho	7,814	1.3%
34	Kansas	6,742	1.2%
35	Mississippi	6,141	1.1%
36	Iowa	5,954	1.0%
37	New Mexico	5,683	1.0%
38	New Hampshire	4,865	0.8%
39	Nebraska	4,849	0.8%
40	Montana	4,588	0.8%
41	Maine	4,300	0.7%
42	West Virginia	3,937	0.7%
43	Rhode Island	3,932	0.7%
44	Hawaii	3,698	0.6%
45	Delaware	3,270	0.6%
46	Wyoming	2,519	0.4%
47	Vermont	2,322	0.4%
48	Alaska	1,848	0.3%
49	North Dakota	1,747	0.3%
50	South Dakota	1,691	0.3%
	District of Columbia	4,393	0.8%

Source: U.S. Small Business Administration
"The Small Business Economy" (2005, http://www.sba.gov/advo/research/sb_econ2005.pdf)
State totals do not add to the U.S. figure as firms can be in more than one state.

Rate of New Employer Firms in 2004

National Rate = 10.2% of Existing Firms*

ALPHA ORDER				RANK ORDER		
RANK	STATE	RATE		RANK	STATE	RATE
34	Alabama	11.0		1	Nevada	21.4
34	Alaska	11.0		2	Utah	19.4
31	Arizona	11.3		3	Idaho	18.8
17	Arkansas	13.0		4	Florida	18.2
34	California	11.0		5	Colorado	16.5
5	Colorado	16.5		6	Maryland	16.2
47	Connecticut	9.4		7	Tennessee	15.8
19	Delaware	12.9		8	Washington	15.5
4	Florida	18.2		9	Georgia	15.0
9	Georgia	15.0		10	Virginia	14.4
22	Hawaii	12.7		11	New Mexico	13.6
3	Idaho	18.8		11	Texas	13.6
44	Illinois	10.1		13	Montana	13.5
32	Indiana	11.1		14	New Jersey	13.4
49	Iowa	8.7		15	New York	13.1
45	Kansas	9.9		15	Oregon	13.1
37	Kentucky	10.8		17	Arkansas	13.0
43	Louisiana	10.5		17	North Carolina	13.0
37	Maine	10.8		19	Delaware	12.9
6	Maryland	16.2		19	South Carolina	12.9
39	Massachusetts	10.7		21	Wyoming	12.8
28	Michigan	11.7		22	Hawaii	12.7
29	Minnesota	11.4		23	Missouri	12.3
29	Mississippi	11.4		23	New Hampshire	12.3
23	Missouri	12.3		23	Oklahoma	12.3
13	Montana	13.5		26	Pennsylvania	12.2
40	Nebraska	10.6		27	Rhode Island	12.1
1	Nevada	21.4		28	Michigan	11.7
23	New Hampshire	12.3		29	Minnesota	11.4
14	New Jersey	13.4		29	Mississippi	11.4
11	New Mexico	13.6		31	Arizona	11.3
15	New York	13.1		32	Indiana	11.1
17	North Carolina	13.0		32	Vermont	11.1
48	North Dakota	9.3		34	Alabama	11.0
45	Ohio	9.9		34	Alaska	11.0
23	Oklahoma	12.3		34	California	11.0
15	Oregon	13.1		37	Kentucky	10.8
26	Pennsylvania	12.2		37	Maine	10.8
27	Rhode Island	12.1		39	Massachusetts	10.7
19	South Carolina	12.9		40	Nebraska	10.6
50	South Dakota	7.3		40	West Virginia	10.6
7	Tennessee	15.8		40	Wisconsin	10.6
11	Texas	13.6		43	Louisiana	10.5
2	Utah	19.4		44	Illinois	10.1
32	Vermont	11.1		45	Kansas	9.9
10	Virginia	14.4		45	Ohio	9.9
8	Washington	15.5		47	Connecticut	9.4
40	West Virginia	10.6		48	North Dakota	9.3
40	Wisconsin	10.6		49	Iowa	8.7
21	Wyoming	12.8		50	South Dakota	7.3
					District of Columbia	16.5

Source: Morgan Quitno Press using data from U.S. Small Business Administration
   "The Small Business Economy" (2005, http://www.sba.gov/advo/research/sb_econ2005.pdf)
*Firms can be in more than one state. Rate figure represents the number of employer firms started in 2004 as a percent of existing firms at the beginning of 2004.

Employer Firm Terminations in 2004

National Total = 576,200 Terminations*

RANK	STATE	FIRMS	% of USA
26	Alabama	10,104	1.8%
47	Alaska	2,650	0.5%
17	Arizona	17,553	3.0%
35	Arkansas	6,481	1.1%
1	California	143,115	24.8%
27	Colorado	9,734	1.7%
24	Connecticut	11,018	1.9%
45	Delaware	3,362	0.6%
4	Florida	54,498	9.5%
9	Georgia	27,835	4.8%
44	Hawaii	3,754	0.7%
36	Idaho	5,716	1.0%
8	Illinois	33,472	5.8%
19	Indiana	15,282	2.7%
32	Iowa	7,391	1.3%
34	Kansas	7,250	1.3%
30	Kentucky	8,597	1.5%
28	Louisiana	9,668	1.7%
41	Maine	4,987	0.9%
13	Maryland	20,636	3.6%
14	Massachusetts	20,270	3.5%
10	Michigan	24,584	4.3%
20	Minnesota	15,209	2.6%
33	Mississippi	7,380	1.3%
16	Missouri	17,924	3.1%
42	Montana	4,896	0.8%
40	Nebraska	5,051	0.9%
29	Nevada	9,012	1.6%
38	New Hampshire	5,401	0.9%
5	New Jersey	50,034	8.7%
37	New Mexico	5,592	1.0%
2	New York	64,013	11.1%
11	North Carolina	22,055	3.8%
48	North Dakota	2,621	0.5%
12	Ohio	21,328	3.7%
31	Oklahoma	8,018	1.4%
21	Oregon	14,407	2.5%
7	Pennsylvania	34,507	6.0%
43	Rhode Island	4,250	0.7%
25	South Carolina	10,975	1.9%
50	South Dakota	2,251	0.4%
18	Tennessee	16,520	2.9%
3	Texas	55,792	9.7%
23	Utah	11,597	2.0%
49	Vermont	2,578	0.4%
15	Virginia	19,919	3.5%
6	Washington	47,141	8.2%
39	West Virginia	5,136	0.9%
22	Wisconsin	12,711	2.2%
46	Wyoming	2,737	0.5%

RANK	STATE	FIRMS	% of USA
1	California	143,115	24.8%
2	New York	64,013	11.1%
3	Texas	55,792	9.7%
4	Florida	54,498	9.5%
5	New Jersey	50,034	8.7%
6	Washington	47,141	8.2%
7	Pennsylvania	34,507	6.0%
8	Illinois	33,472	5.8%
9	Georgia	27,835	4.8%
10	Michigan	24,584	4.3%
11	North Carolina	22,055	3.8%
12	Ohio	21,328	3.7%
13	Maryland	20,636	3.6%
14	Massachusetts	20,270	3.5%
15	Virginia	19,919	3.5%
16	Missouri	17,924	3.1%
17	Arizona	17,553	3.0%
18	Tennessee	16,520	2.9%
19	Indiana	15,282	2.7%
20	Minnesota	15,209	2.6%
21	Oregon	14,407	2.5%
22	Wisconsin	12,711	2.2%
23	Utah	11,597	2.0%
24	Connecticut	11,018	1.9%
25	South Carolina	10,975	1.9%
26	Alabama	10,104	1.8%
27	Colorado	9,734	1.7%
28	Louisiana	9,668	1.7%
29	Nevada	9,012	1.6%
30	Kentucky	8,597	1.5%
31	Oklahoma	8,018	1.4%
32	Iowa	7,391	1.3%
33	Mississippi	7,380	1.3%
34	Kansas	7,250	1.3%
35	Arkansas	6,481	1.1%
36	Idaho	5,716	1.0%
37	New Mexico	5,592	1.0%
38	New Hampshire	5,401	0.9%
39	West Virginia	5,136	0.9%
40	Nebraska	5,051	0.9%
41	Maine	4,987	0.9%
42	Montana	4,896	0.8%
43	Rhode Island	4,250	0.7%
44	Hawaii	3,754	0.7%
45	Delaware	3,362	0.6%
46	Wyoming	2,737	0.5%
47	Alaska	2,650	0.5%
48	North Dakota	2,621	0.5%
49	Vermont	2,578	0.4%
50	South Dakota	2,251	0.4%
	District of Columbia	3,440	0.6%

Source: U.S. Small Business Administration
   "The Small Business Economy" (2005, http://www.sba.gov/advo/research/sb_econ2005.pdf)
*State totals do not add to the U.S. figure as firms can be in more than one state.

Rate of Employer Firm Terminations in 2004

National Rate = 10.1% of Existing Firms*

ALPHA ORDER				RANK ORDER		
RANK	STATE	RATE		RANK	STATE	RATE
35	Alabama	11.8		1	Washington	22.8
6	Alaska	15.8		2	Utah	19.8
5	Arizona	16.0		3	New Jersey	18.7
42	Arkansas	10.7		4	Nevada	18.4
20	California	13.5		5	Arizona	16.0
50	Colorado	6.8		6	Alaska	15.8
37	Connecticut	11.5		7	Maryland	15.3
23	Delaware	13.3		8	Tennessee	15.0
25	Florida	12.8		9	Montana	14.4
10	Georgia	14.1		10	Georgia	14.1
25	Hawaii	12.8		11	Oregon	14.0
15	Idaho	13.8		11	Texas	14.0
33	Illinois	11.9		11	Wyoming	14.0
31	Indiana	12.2		14	North Dakota	13.9
41	Iowa	10.8		15	Idaho	13.8
43	Kansas	10.6		15	Mississippi	13.8
43	Kentucky	10.6		15	West Virginia	13.8
47	Louisiana	10.2		18	New Hampshire	13.7
28	Maine	12.6		19	Missouri	13.6
7	Maryland	15.3		20	California	13.5
37	Massachusetts	11.5		21	New Mexico	13.4
36	Michigan	11.7		21	New York	13.4
39	Minnesota	11.4		23	Delaware	13.3
15	Mississippi	13.8		24	Rhode Island	13.0
19	Missouri	13.6		25	Florida	12.8
9	Montana	14.4		25	Hawaii	12.8
40	Nebraska	11.1		27	Pennsylvania	12.7
4	Nevada	18.4		28	Maine	12.6
18	New Hampshire	13.7		29	North Carolina	12.3
3	New Jersey	18.7		29	Vermont	12.3
21	New Mexico	13.4		31	Indiana	12.2
21	New York	13.4		32	South Carolina	12.1
29	North Carolina	12.3		33	Illinois	11.9
14	North Dakota	13.9		33	Virginia	11.9
49	Ohio	9.3		35	Alabama	11.8
43	Oklahoma	10.6		36	Michigan	11.7
11	Oregon	14.0		37	Connecticut	11.5
27	Pennsylvania	12.7		37	Massachusetts	11.5
24	Rhode Island	13.0		39	Minnesota	11.4
32	South Carolina	12.1		40	Nebraska	11.1
48	South Dakota	9.7		41	Iowa	10.8
8	Tennessee	15.0		42	Arkansas	10.7
11	Texas	14.0		43	Kansas	10.6
2	Utah	19.8		43	Kentucky	10.6
29	Vermont	12.3		43	Oklahoma	10.6
33	Virginia	11.9		46	Wisconsin	10.3
1	Washington	22.8		47	Louisiana	10.2
15	West Virginia	13.8		48	South Dakota	9.7
46	Wisconsin	10.3		49	Ohio	9.3
11	Wyoming	14.0		50	Colorado	6.8
					District of Columbia	12.9

Source: Morgan Quitno Press using data from U.S. Small Business Administration
    "The Small Business Economy" (2005, http://www.sba.gov/advo/research/sb_econ2005.pdf)
*Firms can be in more than one state. Firms with paid employees ceasing operations in 2004 as a percent of
employer firms existing in 2003. Some state terminations result in successor firms which are not listed as new firms,
thus making terminations higher than formations for most states.

Percent of Businesses Owned by Women in 2002

National Percent = 28.3% of Businesses*

ALPHA ORDER

RANK	STATE	PERCENT
28	Alabama	26.5
33	Alaska	26.2
13	Arizona	28.8
47	Arkansas	23.8
4	California	30.0
11	Colorado	29.1
22	Connecticut	27.2
45	Delaware	24.2
15	Florida	28.4
11	Georgia	29.1
3	Hawaii	30.1
48	Idaho	23.7
5	Illinois	29.8
20	Indiana	27.4
25	Iowa	27.0
22	Kansas	27.2
38	Kentucky	25.7
31	Louisiana	26.4
46	Maine	24.0
1	Maryland	31.0
14	Massachusetts	28.7
7	Michigan	29.6
18	Minnesota	27.9
40	Mississippi	25.1
20	Missouri	27.4
43	Montana	24.4
27	Nebraska	26.6
16	Nevada	28.1
42	New Hampshire	24.7
33	New Jersey	26.2
2	New Mexico	30.9
7	New York	29.6
24	North Carolina	27.1
49	North Dakota	23.2
16	Ohio	28.1
38	Oklahoma	25.7
9	Oregon	29.5
36	Pennsylvania	26.0
28	Rhode Island	26.5
33	South Carolina	26.2
50	South Dakota	22.4
36	Tennessee	26.0
25	Texas	27.0
40	Utah	25.1
32	Vermont	26.3
6	Virginia	29.7
10	Washington	29.4
19	West Virginia	27.7
28	Wisconsin	26.5
43	Wyoming	24.4

RANK ORDER

RANK	STATE	PERCENT
1	Maryland	31.0
2	New Mexico	30.9
3	Hawaii	30.1
4	California	30.0
5	Illinois	29.8
6	Virginia	29.7
7	Michigan	29.6
7	New York	29.6
9	Oregon	29.5
10	Washington	29.4
11	Colorado	29.1
11	Georgia	29.1
13	Arizona	28.8
14	Massachusetts	28.7
15	Florida	28.4
16	Nevada	28.1
16	Ohio	28.1
18	Minnesota	27.9
19	West Virginia	27.7
20	Indiana	27.4
20	Missouri	27.4
22	Connecticut	27.2
22	Kansas	27.2
24	North Carolina	27.1
25	Iowa	27.0
25	Texas	27.0
27	Nebraska	26.6
28	Alabama	26.5
28	Rhode Island	26.5
28	Wisconsin	26.5
31	Louisiana	26.4
32	Vermont	26.3
33	Alaska	26.2
33	New Jersey	26.2
33	South Carolina	26.2
36	Pennsylvania	26.0
36	Tennessee	26.0
38	Kentucky	25.7
38	Oklahoma	25.7
40	Mississippi	25.1
40	Utah	25.1
42	New Hampshire	24.7
43	Montana	24.4
43	Wyoming	24.4
45	Delaware	24.2
46	Maine	24.0
47	Arkansas	23.8
48	Idaho	23.7
49	North Dakota	23.2
50	South Dakota	22.4
	District of Columbia	33.2

Source: Morgan Quitno Press using data from U.S. Bureau of the Census
"2002 Survey of Business Owners" (http://www.census.gov/csd/sbo/index.html)
*Based on survey of firms with at least $1,000 in receipts. Ownership is defined as having 51 percent or more of the stock or equity in a business.

Percent of Businesses Owned by Minorities in 2002

National Percent = 17.9% of Businesses*

ALPHA ORDER

RANK	STATE	PERCENT
19	Alabama	12.4
15	Alaska	14.9
14	Arizona	15.4
29	Arkansas	7.4
2	California	33.0
24	Colorado	10.0
25	Connecticut	9.4
21	Delaware	11.6
5	Florida	27.4
8	Georgia	20.8
1	Hawaii	58.8
41	Idaho	4.5
12	Illinois	16.4
34	Indiana	6.4
48	Iowa	2.4
34	Kansas	6.4
38	Kentucky	4.7
10	Louisiana	17.9
49	Maine	1.9
7	Maryland	25.9
27	Massachusetts	8.8
23	Michigan	10.2
37	Minnesota	5.0
13	Mississippi	16.0
33	Missouri	6.9
43	Montana	3.7
42	Nebraska	4.1
15	Nevada	14.9
46	New Hampshire	2.8
9	New Jersey	19.9
3	New Mexico	29.6
6	New York	26.7
18	North Carolina	12.6
47	North Dakota	2.5
30	Ohio	7.3
20	Oklahoma	12.0
31	Oregon	7.0
31	Pennsylvania	7.0
28	Rhode Island	8.2
17	South Carolina	12.8
45	South Dakota	3.0
26	Tennessee	9.2
4	Texas	29.1
36	Utah	5.3
49	Vermont	1.9
11	Virginia	17.7
22	Washington	10.8
44	West Virginia	3.4
39	Wisconsin	4.6
39	Wyoming	4.6

RANK ORDER

RANK	STATE	PERCENT
1	Hawaii	58.8
2	California	33.0
3	New Mexico	29.6
4	Texas	29.1
5	Florida	27.4
6	New York	26.7
7	Maryland	25.9
8	Georgia	20.8
9	New Jersey	19.9
10	Louisiana	17.9
11	Virginia	17.7
12	Illinois	16.4
13	Mississippi	16.0
14	Arizona	15.4
15	Alaska	14.9
15	Nevada	14.9
17	South Carolina	12.8
18	North Carolina	12.6
19	Alabama	12.4
20	Oklahoma	12.0
21	Delaware	11.6
22	Washington	10.8
23	Michigan	10.2
24	Colorado	10.0
25	Connecticut	9.4
26	Tennessee	9.2
27	Massachusetts	8.8
28	Rhode Island	8.2
29	Arkansas	7.4
30	Ohio	7.3
31	Oregon	7.0
31	Pennsylvania	7.0
33	Missouri	6.9
34	Indiana	6.4
34	Kansas	6.4
36	Utah	5.3
37	Minnesota	5.0
38	Kentucky	4.7
39	Wisconsin	4.6
39	Wyoming	4.6
41	Idaho	4.5
42	Nebraska	4.1
43	Montana	3.7
44	West Virginia	3.4
45	South Dakota	3.0
46	New Hampshire	2.8
47	North Dakota	2.5
48	Iowa	2.4
49	Maine	1.9
49	Vermont	1.9
	District of Columbia	36.0

Source: Morgan Quitno Press using data from U.S. Bureau of the Census
   "2002 Survey of Business Owners" (http://www.census.gov/csd/sbo/index.html)
*Based on survey of firms with at least $1,000 in receipts. Ownership is defined as having 51 percent or more of the stock or equity in a business.

V. EDUCATION

School-Age Population as a Percent of Total Population in 2004

National Percent = 18.1% of Population is School-Age*

ALPHA ORDER

RANK	STATE	PERCENT
29	Alabama	17.6
2	Alaska	21.1
6	Arizona	19.1
24	Arkansas	17.8
4	California	19.4
16	Colorado	18.3
20	Connecticut	17.9
42	Delaware	16.8
44	Florida	16.7
9	Georgia	18.7
47	Hawaii	16.6
5	Idaho	19.3
14	Illinois	18.5
8	Indiana	18.8
40	Iowa	16.9
17	Kansas	18.1
36	Kentucky	17.2
10	Louisiana	18.6
48	Maine	16.3
15	Maryland	18.4
44	Massachusetts	16.7
10	Michigan	18.6
24	Minnesota	17.8
10	Mississippi	18.6
29	Missouri	17.6
42	Montana	16.8
20	Nebraska	17.9
10	Nevada	18.6
20	New Hampshire	17.9
17	New Jersey	18.1
7	New Mexico	18.9
35	New York	17.3
24	North Carolina	17.8
48	North Dakota	16.3
20	Ohio	17.9
32	Oklahoma	17.5
34	Oregon	17.4
37	Pennsylvania	17.1
40	Rhode Island	16.9
27	South Carolina	17.7
17	South Dakota	18.1
37	Tennessee	17.1
3	Texas	19.7
1	Utah	21.2
44	Vermont	16.7
32	Virginia	17.5
27	Washington	17.7
50	West Virginia	15.6
29	Wisconsin	17.6
39	Wyoming	17.0

RANK ORDER

RANK	STATE	PERCENT
1	Utah	21.2
2	Alaska	21.1
3	Texas	19.7
4	California	19.4
5	Idaho	19.3
6	Arizona	19.1
7	New Mexico	18.9
8	Indiana	18.8
9	Georgia	18.7
10	Louisiana	18.6
10	Michigan	18.6
10	Mississippi	18.6
10	Nevada	18.6
14	Illinois	18.5
15	Maryland	18.4
16	Colorado	18.3
17	Kansas	18.1
17	New Jersey	18.1
17	South Dakota	18.1
20	Connecticut	17.9
20	Nebraska	17.9
20	New Hampshire	17.9
20	Ohio	17.9
24	Arkansas	17.8
24	Minnesota	17.8
24	North Carolina	17.8
27	South Carolina	17.7
27	Washington	17.7
29	Alabama	17.6
29	Missouri	17.6
29	Wisconsin	17.6
32	Oklahoma	17.5
32	Virginia	17.5
34	Oregon	17.4
35	New York	17.3
36	Kentucky	17.2
37	Pennsylvania	17.1
37	Tennessee	17.1
39	Wyoming	17.0
40	Iowa	16.9
40	Rhode Island	16.9
42	Delaware	16.8
42	Montana	16.8
44	Florida	16.7
44	Massachusetts	16.7
44	Vermont	16.7
47	Hawaii	16.6
48	Maine	16.3
48	North Dakota	16.3
50	West Virginia	15.6
	District of Columbia	13.5

Source: Morgan Quitno Press using data from U.S. Bureau of the Census
"Table ST-EST2004-01res - State Characteristic Estimates" (February 25, 2005, www.census.gov/popest/states/)
*5 to 17-year-olds as of July 2004.

Regular Public Elementary and Secondary School Districts in 2004

National Total = 14,063 Districts*

ALPHA ORDER

RANK	STATE	DISTRICTS	% of USA
34	Alabama	130	0.9%
43	Alaska	53	0.4%
18	Arizona	298	2.1%
16	Arkansas	308	2.2%
2	California	989	7.0%
27	Colorado	178	1.3%
30	Connecticut	166	1.2%
48	Delaware	19	0.1%
41	Florida	67	0.5%
26	Georgia	180	1.3%
50	Hawaii	1	0.0%
37	Idaho	114	0.8%
3	Illinois	887	6.3%
20	Indiana	292	2.1%
14	Iowa	369	2.6%
17	Kansas	302	2.1%
28	Kentucky	176	1.3%
40	Louisiana	68	0.5%
23	Maine	224	1.6%
47	Maryland	24	0.2%
22	Massachusetts	244	1.7%
7	Michigan	553	3.9%
15	Minnesota	345	2.5%
32	Mississippi	152	1.1%
9	Missouri	523	3.7%
12	Montana	438	3.1%
11	Nebraska	495	3.5%
49	Nevada	17	0.1%
31	New Hampshire	164	1.2%
6	New Jersey	574	4.1%
38	New Mexico	89	0.6%
4	New York	724	5.1%
36	North Carolina	117	0.8%
24	North Dakota	211	1.5%
5	Ohio	612	4.4%
8	Oklahoma	541	3.8%
25	Oregon	198	1.4%
10	Pennsylvania	500	3.6%
46	Rhode Island	37	0.3%
38	South Carolina	89	0.6%
29	South Dakota	169	1.2%
33	Tennessee	136	1.0%
1	Texas	1,038	7.4%
45	Utah	40	0.3%
21	Vermont	245	1.7%
34	Virginia	130	0.9%
19	Washington	296	2.1%
42	West Virginia	55	0.4%
13	Wisconsin	437	3.1%
44	Wyoming	48	0.3%

RANK ORDER

RANK	STATE	DISTRICTS	% of USA
1	Texas	1,038	7.4%
2	California	989	7.0%
3	Illinois	887	6.3%
4	New York	724	5.1%
5	Ohio	612	4.4%
6	New Jersey	574	4.1%
7	Michigan	553	3.9%
8	Oklahoma	541	3.8%
9	Missouri	523	3.7%
10	Pennsylvania	500	3.6%
11	Nebraska	495	3.5%
12	Montana	438	3.1%
13	Wisconsin	437	3.1%
14	Iowa	369	2.6%
15	Minnesota	345	2.5%
16	Arkansas	308	2.2%
17	Kansas	302	2.1%
18	Arizona	298	2.1%
19	Washington	296	2.1%
20	Indiana	292	2.1%
21	Vermont	245	1.7%
22	Massachusetts	244	1.7%
23	Maine	224	1.6%
24	North Dakota	211	1.5%
25	Oregon	198	1.4%
26	Georgia	180	1.3%
27	Colorado	178	1.3%
28	Kentucky	176	1.3%
29	South Dakota	169	1.2%
30	Connecticut	166	1.2%
31	New Hampshire	164	1.2%
32	Mississippi	152	1.1%
33	Tennessee	136	1.0%
34	Alabama	130	0.9%
34	Virginia	130	0.9%
36	North Carolina	117	0.8%
37	Idaho	114	0.8%
38	New Mexico	89	0.6%
38	South Carolina	89	0.6%
40	Louisiana	68	0.5%
41	Florida	67	0.5%
42	West Virginia	55	0.4%
43	Alaska	53	0.4%
44	Wyoming	48	0.3%
45	Utah	40	0.3%
46	Rhode Island	37	0.3%
47	Maryland	24	0.2%
48	Delaware	19	0.1%
49	Nevada	17	0.1%
50	Hawaii	1	0.0%
	District of Columbia	1	0.0%

Source: U.S. Department of Education, National Center for Education Statistics
    "Common Core of Data (CCD) Database" (http://nces.ed.gov/ccd/)
*Preliminary data for school year 2003-2004. Regular school districts are agencies responsible for providing free
public education for school-age children residing within their jurisdiction. Excluded in these figures are 276
districts that reported having no students. This can occur when a small district has no pupils or contracts with
another district to educate the students under its jurisdiction.

Public Elementary and Secondary Schools in 2004

National Total = 92,816 Schools*

ALPHA ORDER

RANK	STATE	SCHOOLS	% of USA
26	Alabama	1,389	1.5%
44	Alaska	500	0.5%
16	Arizona	1,931	2.1%
31	Arkansas	1,128	1.2%
1	California	9,222	9.9%
21	Colorado	1,658	1.8%
32	Connecticut	1,099	1.2%
50	Delaware	200	0.2%
7	Florida	3,427	3.7%
15	Georgia	2,032	2.2%
49	Hawaii	284	0.3%
40	Idaho	664	0.7%
4	Illinois	4,267	4.6%
17	Indiana	1,911	2.1%
24	Iowa	1,491	1.6%
25	Kansas	1,410	1.5%
27	Kentucky	1,370	1.5%
23	Louisiana	1,519	1.6%
41	Maine	662	0.7%
28	Maryland	1,366	1.5%
18	Massachusetts	1,860	2.0%
5	Michigan	3,869	4.2%
14	Minnesota	2,187	2.4%
34	Mississippi	897	1.0%
10	Missouri	2,260	2.4%
36	Montana	858	0.9%
29	Nebraska	1,228	1.3%
42	Nevada	545	0.6%
45	New Hampshire	473	0.5%
9	New Jersey	2,428	2.6%
37	New Mexico	814	0.9%
3	New York	4,514	4.9%
10	North Carolina	2,260	2.4%
43	North Dakota	517	0.6%
6	Ohio	3,836	4.1%
20	Oklahoma	1,786	1.9%
30	Oregon	1,225	1.3%
8	Pennsylvania	3,189	3.4%
48	Rhode Island	328	0.4%
33	South Carolina	1,091	1.2%
39	South Dakota	734	0.8%
22	Tennessee	1,644	1.8%
2	Texas	7,843	8.5%
35	Utah	886	1.0%
47	Vermont	358	0.4%
19	Virginia	1,856	2.0%
12	Washington	2,241	2.4%
38	West Virginia	755	0.8%
13	Wisconsin	2,218	2.4%
46	Wyoming	380	0.4%

RANK ORDER

RANK	STATE	SCHOOLS	% of USA
1	California	9,222	9.9%
2	Texas	7,843	8.5%
3	New York	4,514	4.9%
4	Illinois	4,267	4.6%
5	Michigan	3,869	4.2%
6	Ohio	3,836	4.1%
7	Florida	3,427	3.7%
8	Pennsylvania	3,189	3.4%
9	New Jersey	2,428	2.6%
10	Missouri	2,260	2.4%
10	North Carolina	2,260	2.4%
12	Washington	2,241	2.4%
13	Wisconsin	2,218	2.4%
14	Minnesota	2,187	2.4%
15	Georgia	2,032	2.2%
16	Arizona	1,931	2.1%
17	Indiana	1,911	2.1%
18	Massachusetts	1,860	2.0%
19	Virginia	1,856	2.0%
20	Oklahoma	1,786	1.9%
21	Colorado	1,658	1.8%
22	Tennessee	1,644	1.8%
23	Louisiana	1,519	1.6%
24	Iowa	1,491	1.6%
25	Kansas	1,410	1.5%
26	Alabama	1,389	1.5%
27	Kentucky	1,370	1.5%
28	Maryland	1,366	1.5%
29	Nebraska	1,228	1.3%
30	Oregon	1,225	1.3%
31	Arkansas	1,128	1.2%
32	Connecticut	1,099	1.2%
33	South Carolina	1,091	1.2%
34	Mississippi	897	1.0%
35	Utah	886	1.0%
36	Montana	858	0.9%
37	New Mexico	814	0.9%
38	West Virginia	755	0.8%
39	South Dakota	734	0.8%
40	Idaho	664	0.7%
41	Maine	662	0.7%
42	Nevada	545	0.6%
43	North Dakota	517	0.6%
44	Alaska	500	0.5%
45	New Hampshire	473	0.5%
46	Wyoming	380	0.4%
47	Vermont	358	0.4%
48	Rhode Island	328	0.4%
49	Hawaii	284	0.3%
50	Delaware	200	0.2%
	District of Columbia	206	0.2%

Source: U.S. Department of Education, National Center for Education Statistics
    "Common Core of Data (CCD) Database" (http://nces.ed.gov/ccd/)
*Preliminary data for school year 2003-2004. Schools having membership.

Private Elementary and Secondary Schools in 2002

National Total = 29,273 Private Schools*

RANK	STATE	SCHOOLS	% of USA
22	Alabama	442	1.5%
48	Alaska	86	0.3%
28	Arizona	299	1.0%
34	Arkansas	202	0.7%
1	California	3,508	12.0%
24	Colorado	376	1.3%
27	Connecticut	341	1.2%
41	Delaware	121	0.4%
4	Florida	1,779	6.1%
15	Georgia	660	2.3%
39	Hawaii	137	0.5%
46	Idaho	108	0.4%
5	Illinois	1,375	4.7%
12	Indiana	750	2.6%
29	Iowa	284	1.0%
32	Kansas	226	0.8%
23	Kentucky	398	1.4%
21	Louisiana	444	1.5%
38	Maine	145	0.5%
11	Maryland	785	2.7%
14	Massachusetts	691	2.4%
8	Michigan	1,060	3.6%
19	Minnesota	590	2.0%
31	Mississippi	249	0.9%
16	Missouri	659	2.3%
45	Montana	109	0.4%
30	Nebraska	251	0.9%
43	Nevada	118	0.4%
37	New Hampshire	162	0.6%
10	New Jersey	989	3.4%
33	New Mexico	219	0.7%
2	New York	2,009	6.9%
13	North Carolina	706	2.4%
49	North Dakota	56	0.2%
9	Ohio	1,042	3.6%
35	Oklahoma	192	0.7%
25	Oregon	374	1.3%
3	Pennsylvania	1,971	6.7%
42	Rhode Island	119	0.4%
26	South Carolina	366	1.3%
47	South Dakota	97	0.3%
20	Tennessee	567	1.9%
6	Texas	1,362	4.7%
44	Utah	111	0.4%
40	Vermont	129	0.4%
17	Virginia	631	2.2%
18	Washington	606	2.1%
36	West Virginia	176	0.6%
7	Wisconsin	1,066	3.6%
50	Wyoming	41	0.1%

RANK	STATE	SCHOOLS	% of USA
1	California	3,508	12.0%
2	New York	2,009	6.9%
3	Pennsylvania	1,971	6.7%
4	Florida	1,779	6.1%
5	Illinois	1,375	4.7%
6	Texas	1,362	4.7%
7	Wisconsin	1,066	3.6%
8	Michigan	1,060	3.6%
9	Ohio	1,042	3.6%
10	New Jersey	989	3.4%
11	Maryland	785	2.7%
12	Indiana	750	2.6%
13	North Carolina	706	2.4%
14	Massachusetts	691	2.4%
15	Georgia	660	2.3%
16	Missouri	659	2.3%
17	Virginia	631	2.2%
18	Washington	606	2.1%
19	Minnesota	590	2.0%
20	Tennessee	567	1.9%
21	Louisiana	444	1.5%
22	Alabama	442	1.5%
23	Kentucky	398	1.4%
24	Colorado	376	1.3%
25	Oregon	374	1.3%
26	South Carolina	366	1.3%
27	Connecticut	341	1.2%
28	Arizona	299	1.0%
29	Iowa	284	1.0%
30	Nebraska	251	0.9%
31	Mississippi	249	0.9%
32	Kansas	226	0.8%
33	New Mexico	219	0.7%
34	Arkansas	202	0.7%
35	Oklahoma	192	0.7%
36	West Virginia	176	0.6%
37	New Hampshire	162	0.6%
38	Maine	145	0.5%
39	Hawaii	137	0.5%
40	Vermont	129	0.4%
41	Delaware	121	0.4%
42	Rhode Island	119	0.4%
43	Nevada	118	0.4%
44	Utah	111	0.4%
45	Montana	109	0.4%
46	Idaho	108	0.4%
47	South Dakota	97	0.3%
48	Alaska	86	0.3%
49	North Dakota	56	0.2%
50	Wyoming	41	0.1%
	District of Columbia	90	0.3%

Source: U.S. Department of Education, Institute of Education Sciences
   "Characteristics of Private Schools" (Private School Universe Survey, 2001-2002, NCES 2005-305)
*Estimate for 2001-2002.

Percent of Elementary/Secondary School Students in Private Schools in 2002

National Percent = 10.0% of Students*

ALPHA ORDER

RANK ORDER

RANK	STATE	PERCENT		RANK	STATE	PERCENT
21	Alabama	9.5		1	Delaware	19.0
45	Alaska	4.7		1	Hawaii	19.0
46	Arizona	4.2		3	Louisiana	15.9
41	Arkansas	5.9		4	Pennsylvania	15.4
21	California	9.5		5	Maryland	15.2
37	Colorado	6.6		6	Rhode Island	14.6
16	Connecticut	11.0		7	New York	14.5
1	Delaware	19.0		8	Wisconsin	14.2
19	Florida	10.6		9	New Jersey	14.0
34	Georgia	7.2		10	Nebraska	13.4
1	Hawaii	19.0		11	Massachusetts	13.1
48	Idaho	3.8		12	Illinois	12.4
12	Illinois	12.4		13	Missouri	12.1
21	Indiana	9.5		13	Ohio	12.1
26	Iowa	9.2		13	Vermont	12.1
31	Kansas	8.1		16	Connecticut	11.0
18	Kentucky	10.7		17	Minnesota	10.8
3	Louisiana	15.9		18	Kentucky	10.7
28	Maine	8.8		19	Florida	10.6
5	Maryland	15.2		20	New Hampshire	10.5
11	Massachusetts	13.1		21	Alabama	9.5
25	Michigan	9.3		21	California	9.5
17	Minnesota	10.8		21	Indiana	9.5
21	Mississippi	9.5		21	Mississippi	9.5
13	Missouri	12.1		25	Michigan	9.3
39	Montana	6.1		26	Iowa	9.2
10	Nebraska	13.4		27	Tennessee	9.0
47	Nevada	4.0		28	Maine	8.8
20	New Hampshire	10.5		29	Virginia	8.5
9	New Jersey	14.0		30	South Carolina	8.3
38	New Mexico	6.4		31	Kansas	8.1
7	New York	14.5		32	South Dakota	7.6
36	North Carolina	7.0		33	Washington	7.4
39	North Dakota	6.1		34	Georgia	7.2
13	Ohio	12.1		34	Oregon	7.2
44	Oklahoma	4.8		36	North Carolina	7.0
34	Oregon	7.2		37	Colorado	6.6
4	Pennsylvania	15.4		38	New Mexico	6.4
6	Rhode Island	14.6		39	Montana	6.1
30	South Carolina	8.3		39	North Dakota	6.1
32	South Dakota	7.6		41	Arkansas	5.9
27	Tennessee	9.0		42	Texas	5.5
42	Texas	5.5		43	West Virginia	5.4
49	Utah	3.4		44	Oklahoma	4.8
13	Vermont	12.1		45	Alaska	4.7
29	Virginia	8.5		46	Arizona	4.2
33	Washington	7.4		47	Nevada	4.0
43	West Virginia	5.4		48	Idaho	3.8
8	Wisconsin	14.2		49	Utah	3.4
50	Wyoming	2.4		50	Wyoming	2.4

District of Columbia   25.6

Source: Morgan Quitno Press using data from U.S. Department of Education, Institute of Education Sciences "Characteristics of Private Schools" (Private School Universe Survey, 2001-2002, NCES 2005-305)
*Estimate for 2001-2002. Calculated using 5-17 year old population estimates for 2002.

Estimated Enrollment in Public Elementary and Secondary Schools in 2005

National Total = 48,458,742 Students*

ALPHA ORDER

RANK	STATE	STUDENTS	% of USA
23	Alabama	727,829	1.5%
45	Alaska	132,970	0.3%
15	Arizona	986,221	2.0%
34	Arkansas	452,057	0.9%
1	California	6,322,142	13.0%
22	Colorado	766,707	1.6%
28	Connecticut	576,474	1.2%
47	Delaware	119,109	0.2%
4	Florida	2,628,429	5.4%
9	Georgia	1,553,437	3.2%
42	Hawaii	183,361	0.4%
39	Idaho	249,984	0.5%
5	Illinois	2,086,053	4.3%
14	Indiana	1,019,410	2.1%
32	Iowa	478,319	1.0%
33	Kansas	468,512	1.0%
26	Kentucky	631,989	1.3%
24	Louisiana	724,002	1.5%
41	Maine	200,649	0.4%
20	Maryland	865,836	1.8%
16	Massachusetts	976,674	2.0%
8	Michigan	1,730,897	3.6%
21	Minnesota	838,673	1.7%
31	Mississippi	485,094	1.0%
18	Missouri	892,194	1.8%
44	Montana	146,705	0.3%
37	Nebraska	284,559	0.6%
35	Nevada	400,671	0.8%
40	New Hampshire	206,852	0.4%
11	New Jersey	1,420,374	2.9%
36	New Mexico	322,800	0.7%
3	New York	2,822,000	5.8%
10	North Carolina	1,420,875	2.9%
48	North Dakota	99,324	0.2%
6	Ohio	1,843,555	3.8%
27	Oklahoma	629,134	1.3%
29	Oregon	558,956	1.2%
7	Pennsylvania	1,815,170	3.7%
43	Rhode Island	160,574	0.3%
25	South Carolina	670,080	1.4%
46	South Dakota	121,327	0.3%
17	Tennessee	929,428	1.9%
2	Texas	4,383,871	9.0%
30	Utah	494,100	1.0%
49	Vermont	95,187	0.2%
12	Virginia	1,204,808	2.5%
13	Washington	1,024,495	2.1%
38	West Virginia	279,457	0.6%
19	Wisconsin	881,480	1.8%
50	Wyoming	83,633	0.2%

RANK ORDER

RANK	STATE	STUDENTS	% of USA
1	California	6,322,142	13.0%
2	Texas	4,383,871	9.0%
3	New York	2,822,000	5.8%
4	Florida	2,628,429	5.4%
5	Illinois	2,086,053	4.3%
6	Ohio	1,843,555	3.8%
7	Pennsylvania	1,815,170	3.7%
8	Michigan	1,730,897	3.6%
9	Georgia	1,553,437	3.2%
10	North Carolina	1,420,875	2.9%
11	New Jersey	1,420,374	2.9%
12	Virginia	1,204,808	2.5%
13	Washington	1,024,495	2.1%
14	Indiana	1,019,410	2.1%
15	Arizona	986,221	2.0%
16	Massachusetts	976,674	2.0%
17	Tennessee	929,428	1.9%
18	Missouri	892,194	1.8%
19	Wisconsin	881,480	1.8%
20	Maryland	865,836	1.8%
21	Minnesota	838,673	1.7%
22	Colorado	766,707	1.6%
23	Alabama	727,829	1.5%
24	Louisiana	724,002	1.5%
25	South Carolina	670,080	1.4%
26	Kentucky	631,989	1.3%
27	Oklahoma	629,134	1.3%
28	Connecticut	576,474	1.2%
29	Oregon	558,956	1.2%
30	Utah	494,100	1.0%
31	Mississippi	485,094	1.0%
32	Iowa	478,319	1.0%
33	Kansas	468,512	1.0%
34	Arkansas	452,057	0.9%
35	Nevada	400,671	0.8%
36	New Mexico	322,800	0.7%
37	Nebraska	284,559	0.6%
38	West Virginia	279,457	0.6%
39	Idaho	249,984	0.5%
40	New Hampshire	206,852	0.4%
41	Maine	200,649	0.4%
42	Hawaii	183,361	0.4%
43	Rhode Island	160,574	0.3%
44	Montana	146,705	0.3%
45	Alaska	132,970	0.3%
46	South Dakota	121,327	0.3%
47	Delaware	119,109	0.2%
48	North Dakota	99,324	0.2%
49	Vermont	95,187	0.2%
50	Wyoming	83,633	0.2%
	District of Columbia	62,306	0.1%

Source: National Education Association, Washington, D.C.

"Rankings & Estimates, June 2005" (Copyright © 2005, NEA, used with permission)
Estimates for school year 2004-2005.

Average Class Size in Public Elementary Schools in 2000

National Average = 21.2 Students per Class*

ALPHA ORDER				RANK ORDER		
RANK	STATE	STUDENTS		RANK	STATE	STUDENTS
40	Alabama	18.7		1	Arizona	24.5
15	Alaska	22.0		2	Oregon	23.9
1	Arizona	24.5		2	Washington	23.9
33	Arkansas	19.8		4	Utah	23.7
8	California	22.7		5	Colorado	23.2
5	Colorado	23.2		6	Florida	23.1
29	Connecticut	20.0		6	Hawaii	23.1
25	Delaware	20.6		8	California	22.7
6	Florida	23.1		8	Ohio	22.7
34	Georgia	19.7		10	Illinois	22.3
6	Hawaii	23.1		10	New York	22.3
14	Idaho	22.1		12	Maryland	22.2
10	Illinois	22.3		12	Pennsylvania	22.2
18	Indiana	21.4		14	Idaho	22.1
28	Iowa	20.1		15	Alaska	22.0
43	Kansas	18.4		15	Michigan	22.0
22	Kentucky	20.8		15	Minnesota	22.0
38	Louisiana	18.9		18	Indiana	21.4
47	Maine	18.0		19	Massachusetts	21.0
12	Maryland	22.2		20	Missouri	20.9
19	Massachusetts	21.0		20	North Carolina	20.9
15	Michigan	22.0		22	Kentucky	20.8
15	Minnesota	22.0		22	Wisconsin	20.8
27	Mississippi	20.4		24	Nevada	20.7
20	Missouri	20.9		25	Delaware	20.6
44	Montana	18.2		26	New Jersey	20.5
50	Nebraska	17.5		27	Mississippi	20.4
24	Nevada	20.7		28	Iowa	20.1
29	New Hampshire	20.0		29	Connecticut	20.0
26	New Jersey	20.5		29	New Hampshire	20.0
32	New Mexico	19.9		29	Rhode Island	20.0
10	New York	22.3		32	New Mexico	19.9
20	North Carolina	20.9		33	Arkansas	19.8
49	North Dakota	17.8		34	Georgia	19.7
8	Ohio	22.7		34	Tennessee	19.7
41	Oklahoma	18.6		36	Virginia	19.4
2	Oregon	23.9		36	West Virginia	19.4
12	Pennsylvania	22.2		38	Louisiana	18.9
29	Rhode Island	20.0		39	South Dakota	18.8
48	South Carolina	17.9		40	Alabama	18.7
39	South Dakota	18.8		41	Oklahoma	18.6
34	Tennessee	19.7		42	Texas	18.5
42	Texas	18.5		43	Kansas	18.4
4	Utah	23.7		44	Montana	18.2
45	Vermont	18.1		45	Vermont	18.1
36	Virginia	19.4		45	Wyoming	18.1
2	Washington	23.9		47	Maine	18.0
36	West Virginia	19.4		48	South Carolina	17.9
22	Wisconsin	20.8		49	North Dakota	17.8
45	Wyoming	18.1		50	Nebraska	17.5
					District of Columbia	21.7

Source: U.S. Department of Education, National Center for Education Statistics
"Schools and Staffing Survey, 1999-2000" (NCES 2002-313)
*For school year 1999-2000.

117

Average Class Size in Public Secondary Schools in 2000

National Average = 23.4 Students per Class*

ALPHA ORDER				RANK ORDER		
RANK	STATE	STUDENTS		RANK	STATE	STUDENTS
29	Alabama	22.1		1	California	28.1
13	Alaska	23.9		2	Florida	27.3
6	Arizona	25.6		3	Utah	27.1
43	Arkansas	20.6		4	Nevada	27.0
1	California	28.1		5	Washington	26.6
12	Colorado	24.0		6	Arizona	25.6
45	Connecticut	20.1		7	Minnesota	25.5
18	Delaware	23.2		8	Oregon	25.4
2	Florida	27.3		9	Michigan	25.1
14	Georgia	23.7		10	Maryland	24.9
11	Hawaii	24.1		11	Hawaii	24.1
25	Idaho	22.8		12	Colorado	24.0
15	Illinois	23.6		13	Alaska	23.9
21	Indiana	23.0		14	Georgia	23.7
39	Iowa	21.0		15	Illinois	23.6
41	Kansas	20.8		16	Tennessee	23.5
21	Kentucky	23.0		17	New Mexico	23.4
24	Louisiana	22.9		18	Delaware	23.2
50	Maine	18.5		18	New York	23.2
10	Maryland	24.9		18	Wisconsin	23.2
39	Massachusetts	21.0		21	Indiana	23.0
9	Michigan	25.1		21	Kentucky	23.0
7	Minnesota	25.5		21	Ohio	23.0
30	Mississippi	22.0		24	Louisiana	22.9
38	Missouri	21.1		25	Idaho	22.8
47	Montana	19.5		26	Pennsylvania	22.4
36	Nebraska	21.2		27	South Carolina	22.2
4	Nevada	27.0		27	Texas	22.2
33	New Hampshire	21.4		29	Alabama	22.1
36	New Jersey	21.2		30	Mississippi	22.0
17	New Mexico	23.4		31	North Carolina	21.7
18	New York	23.2		32	Oklahoma	21.5
31	North Carolina	21.7		33	New Hampshire	21.4
49	North Dakota	18.9		33	Virginia	21.4
21	Ohio	23.0		35	West Virginia	21.3
32	Oklahoma	21.5		36	Nebraska	21.2
8	Oregon	25.4		36	New Jersey	21.2
26	Pennsylvania	22.4		38	Missouri	21.1
41	Rhode Island	20.8		39	Iowa	21.0
27	South Carolina	22.2		39	Massachusetts	21.0
48	South Dakota	19.4		41	Kansas	20.8
16	Tennessee	23.5		41	Rhode Island	20.8
27	Texas	22.2		43	Arkansas	20.6
3	Utah	27.1		44	Wyoming	20.5
46	Vermont	20.0		45	Connecticut	20.1
33	Virginia	21.4		46	Vermont	20.0
5	Washington	26.6		47	Montana	19.5
35	West Virginia	21.3		48	South Dakota	19.4
18	Wisconsin	23.2		49	North Dakota	18.9
44	Wyoming	20.5		50	Maine	18.5
					District of Columbia	20.8

Source: U.S. Department of Education, National Center for Education Statistics
    "Schools and Staffing Survey, 1999-2000" (NCES 2002-313)
*For school year 1999-2000.

Estimated Public Elementary and Secondary School Teachers in 2005

National Total = 3,105,783 Teachers*

ALPHA ORDER

RANK	STATE	TEACHERS	% of USA
22	Alabama	46,212	1.5%
48	Alaska	7,917	0.3%
24	Arizona	45,894	1.5%
31	Arkansas	32,732	1.1%
1	California	318,386	10.3%
25	Colorado	44,959	1.4%
26	Connecticut	43,426	1.4%
47	Delaware	7,974	0.3%
4	Florida	158,624	5.1%
9	Georgia	104,847	3.4%
43	Hawaii	11,365	0.4%
41	Idaho	14,190	0.5%
5	Illinois	133,255	4.3%
16	Indiana	61,169	2.0%
29	Iowa	34,693	1.1%
30	Kansas	32,831	1.1%
27	Kentucky	39,940	1.3%
21	Louisiana	50,955	1.6%
39	Maine	15,774	0.5%
18	Maryland	56,150	1.8%
14	Massachusetts	65,200	2.1%
11	Michigan	96,726	3.1%
20	Minnesota	52,218	1.7%
32	Mississippi	30,707	1.0%
13	Missouri	67,255	2.2%
44	Montana	10,224	0.3%
36	Nebraska	20,685	0.7%
37	Nevada	20,609	0.7%
40	New Hampshire	15,297	0.5%
8	New Jersey	111,679	3.6%
35	New Mexico	21,495	0.7%
3	New York	223,000	7.2%
12	North Carolina	90,657	2.9%
49	North Dakota	7,695	0.2%
6	Ohio	123,562	4.0%
28	Oklahoma	39,078	1.3%
33	Oregon	28,118	0.9%
7	Pennsylvania	118,300	3.8%
42	Rhode Island	14,171	0.5%
23	South Carolina	46,024	1.5%
45	South Dakota	8,926	0.3%
17	Tennessee	59,506	1.9%
2	Texas	294,547	9.5%
34	Utah	21,820	0.7%
46	Vermont	8,717	0.3%
10	Virginia	102,391	3.3%
19	Washington	53,082	1.7%
38	West Virginia	19,809	0.6%
15	Wisconsin	61,322	2.0%
50	Wyoming	6,660	0.2%

RANK ORDER

RANK	STATE	TEACHERS	% of USA
1	California	318,386	10.3%
2	Texas	294,547	9.5%
3	New York	223,000	7.2%
4	Florida	158,624	5.1%
5	Illinois	133,255	4.3%
6	Ohio	123,562	4.0%
7	Pennsylvania	118,300	3.8%
8	New Jersey	111,679	3.6%
9	Georgia	104,847	3.4%
10	Virginia	102,391	3.3%
11	Michigan	96,726	3.1%
12	North Carolina	90,657	2.9%
13	Missouri	67,255	2.2%
14	Massachusetts	65,200	2.1%
15	Wisconsin	61,322	2.0%
16	Indiana	61,169	2.0%
17	Tennessee	59,506	1.9%
18	Maryland	56,150	1.8%
19	Washington	53,082	1.7%
20	Minnesota	52,218	1.7%
21	Louisiana	50,955	1.6%
22	Alabama	46,212	1.5%
23	South Carolina	46,024	1.5%
24	Arizona	45,894	1.5%
25	Colorado	44,959	1.4%
26	Connecticut	43,426	1.4%
27	Kentucky	39,940	1.3%
28	Oklahoma	39,078	1.3%
29	Iowa	34,693	1.1%
30	Kansas	32,831	1.1%
31	Arkansas	32,732	1.1%
32	Mississippi	30,707	1.0%
33	Oregon	28,118	0.9%
34	Utah	21,820	0.7%
35	New Mexico	21,495	0.7%
36	Nebraska	20,685	0.7%
37	Nevada	20,609	0.7%
38	West Virginia	19,809	0.6%
39	Maine	15,774	0.5%
40	New Hampshire	15,297	0.5%
41	Idaho	14,190	0.5%
42	Rhode Island	14,171	0.5%
43	Hawaii	11,365	0.4%
44	Montana	10,224	0.3%
45	South Dakota	8,926	0.3%
46	Vermont	8,717	0.3%
47	Delaware	7,974	0.3%
48	Alaska	7,917	0.3%
49	North Dakota	7,695	0.2%
50	Wyoming	6,660	0.2%
	District of Columbia	5,011	0.2%

Source: National Education Association, Washington, D.C.
    "Rankings & Estimates" (Copyright © 2005, NEA, used with permission)
*Estimates for school year 2004-05.

Estimated Pupil-Teacher Ratio in
Public Elementary and Secondary Schools in 2005
National Ratio = 15.6 Pupils per Teacher*

ALPHA ORDER

RANK STATE | RATIO
--- | --- | ---
18 | Alabama | 15.7
10 | Alaska | 16.8
2 | Arizona | 21.5
36 | Arkansas | 13.8
3 | California | 19.9
9 | Colorado | 17.1
41 | Connecticut | 13.3
26 | Delaware | 14.9
12 | Florida | 16.6
29 | Georgia | 14.8
13 | Hawaii | 16.1
8 | Idaho | 17.6
18 | Illinois | 15.7
11 | Indiana | 16.7
36 | Iowa | 13.8
32 | Kansas | 14.3
16 | Kentucky | 15.8
34 | Louisiana | 14.2
44 | Maine | 12.7
22 | Maryland | 15.4
24 | Massachusetts | 15.0
7 | Michigan | 17.9
13 | Minnesota | 16.1
16 | Mississippi | 15.8
41 | Missouri | 13.3
32 | Montana | 14.3
36 | Nebraska | 13.8
5 | Nevada | 19.4
40 | New Hampshire | 13.5
44 | New Jersey | 12.7
24 | New Mexico | 15.0
44 | New York | 12.7
18 | North Carolina | 15.7
43 | North Dakota | 12.9
26 | Ohio | 14.9
13 | Oklahoma | 16.1
3 | Oregon | 19.9
23 | Pennsylvania | 15.3
49 | Rhode Island | 11.3
30 | South Carolina | 14.6
39 | South Dakota | 13.6
21 | Tennessee | 15.6
26 | Texas | 14.9
1 | Utah | 22.6
50 | Vermont | 10.9
48 | Virginia | 11.8
6 | Washington | 19.3
35 | West Virginia | 14.1
31 | Wisconsin | 14.4
47 | Wyoming | 12.6

RANK ORDER

RANK STATE | RATIO
--- | --- | ---
1 | Utah | 22.6
2 | Arizona | 21.5
3 | California | 19.9
3 | Oregon | 19.9
5 | Nevada | 19.4
6 | Washington | 19.3
7 | Michigan | 17.9
8 | Idaho | 17.6
9 | Colorado | 17.1
10 | Alaska | 16.8
11 | Indiana | 16.7
12 | Florida | 16.6
13 | Hawaii | 16.1
13 | Minnesota | 16.1
13 | Oklahoma | 16.1
16 | Kentucky | 15.8
16 | Mississippi | 15.8
18 | Alabama | 15.7
18 | Illinois | 15.7
18 | North Carolina | 15.7
21 | Tennessee | 15.6
22 | Maryland | 15.4
23 | Pennsylvania | 15.3
24 | Massachusetts | 15.0
24 | New Mexico | 15.0
26 | Delaware | 14.9
26 | Ohio | 14.9
26 | Texas | 14.9
29 | Georgia | 14.8
30 | South Carolina | 14.6
31 | Wisconsin | 14.4
32 | Kansas | 14.3
32 | Montana | 14.3
34 | Louisiana | 14.2
35 | West Virginia | 14.1
36 | Arkansas | 13.8
36 | Iowa | 13.8
36 | Nebraska | 13.8
39 | South Dakota | 13.6
40 | New Hampshire | 13.5
41 | Connecticut | 13.3
41 | Missouri | 13.3
43 | North Dakota | 12.9
44 | Maine | 12.7
44 | New Jersey | 12.7
44 | New York | 12.7
47 | Wyoming | 12.6
48 | Virginia | 11.8
49 | Rhode Island | 11.3
50 | Vermont | 10.9
| District of Columbia | 12.4

Source: Morgan Quitno Press using data from National Education Association, Washington, D.C.
    "Rankings & Estimates, June 2005" (Copyright © 2005, NEA, used with permission)
*Estimates for school year 2004-2005.

Estimated Average Salary of Public School Classroom Teachers in 2005
(National Education Association)
National Average = $47,750*

ALPHA ORDER

RANK	STATE	SALARY
44	Alabama	$38,863
10	Alaska	52,424
27	Arizona	42,905
35	Arkansas	40,495
2	California	57,876
22	Colorado	44,161
1	Connecticut	58,688
12	Delaware	50,869
31	Florida	41,081
17	Georgia	46,526
21	Hawaii	44,273
29	Idaho	42,122
6	Illinois	55,629
16	Indiana	46,851
37	Iowa	40,347
41	Kansas	39,190
33	Kentucky	41,002
43	Louisiana	38,880
34	Maine	40,940
11	Maryland	52,331
7	Massachusetts	54,596
5	Michigan	55,693
15	Minnesota	46,906
48	Mississippi	36,590
42	Missouri	38,971
45	Montana	38,485
39	Nebraska	39,456
25	Nevada	43,394
23	New Hampshire	43,941
3	New Jersey	56,600
40	New Mexico	39,328
4	New York	56,200
26	North Carolina	43,313
49	North Dakota	36,449
14	Ohio	48,692
47	Oklahoma	37,141
13	Oregon	50,790
9	Pennsylvania	52,700
8	Rhode Island	53,473
28	South Carolina	42,207
50	South Dakota	34,040
30	Tennessee	41,527
32	Texas	41,009
38	Utah	39,965
20	Vermont	44,535
19	Virginia	44,763
18	Washington	45,712
46	West Virginia	38,360
24	Wisconsin	43,466
36	Wyoming	40,392

RANK ORDER

RANK	STATE	SALARY
1	Connecticut	$58,688
2	California	57,876
3	New Jersey	56,600
4	New York	56,200
5	Michigan	55,693
6	Illinois	55,629
7	Massachusetts	54,596
8	Rhode Island	53,473
9	Pennsylvania	52,700
10	Alaska	52,424
11	Maryland	52,331
12	Delaware	50,869
13	Oregon	50,790
14	Ohio	48,692
15	Minnesota	46,906
16	Indiana	46,851
17	Georgia	46,526
18	Washington	45,712
19	Virginia	44,763
20	Vermont	44,535
21	Hawaii	44,273
22	Colorado	44,161
23	New Hampshire	43,941
24	Wisconsin	43,466
25	Nevada	43,394
26	North Carolina	43,313
27	Arizona	42,905
28	South Carolina	42,207
29	Idaho	42,122
30	Tennessee	41,527
31	Florida	41,081
32	Texas	41,009
33	Kentucky	41,002
34	Maine	40,940
35	Arkansas	40,495
36	Wyoming	40,392
37	Iowa	40,347
38	Utah	39,965
39	Nebraska	39,456
40	New Mexico	39,328
41	Kansas	39,190
42	Missouri	38,971
43	Louisiana	38,880
44	Alabama	38,863
45	Montana	38,485
46	West Virginia	38,360
47	Oklahoma	37,141
48	Mississippi	36,590
49	North Dakota	36,449
50	South Dakota	34,040
	District of Columbia	58,456

Source: National Education Association, Washington, D.C.
    "Rankings & Estimates" (Copyright © 2005, NEA, used with permission)
*Estimates for school year 2004-05.

Average Teacher's Salary as a Percent of Average Annual Wages in 2004

National Average = 120.1% of Average Annual Wages*

<table>
<tr><td colspan="3">ALPHA ORDER</td><td colspan="3">RANK ORDER</td></tr>
<tr><td>RANK</td><td>STATE</td><td>PERCENT</td><td>RANK</td><td>STATE</td><td>PERCENT</td></tr>
<tr><td>40</td><td>Alabama</td><td>115.5</td><td>1</td><td>Rhode Island</td><td>140.4</td></tr>
<tr><td>8</td><td>Alaska</td><td>133.3</td><td>2</td><td>Oregon</td><td>140.3</td></tr>
<tr><td>39</td><td>Arizona</td><td>115.6</td><td>3</td><td>Idaho</td><td>139.3</td></tr>
<tr><td>10</td><td>Arkansas</td><td>131.9</td><td>4</td><td>Michigan</td><td>136.4</td></tr>
<tr><td>14</td><td>California</td><td>128.0</td><td>5</td><td>Montana</td><td>135.9</td></tr>
<tr><td>49</td><td>Colorado</td><td>108.6</td><td>6</td><td>Pennsylvania</td><td>135.6</td></tr>
<tr><td>43</td><td>Connecticut</td><td>113.7</td><td>7</td><td>Indiana</td><td>133.5</td></tr>
<tr><td>33</td><td>Delaware</td><td>118.0</td><td>8</td><td>Alaska</td><td>133.3</td></tr>
<tr><td>37</td><td>Florida</td><td>116.1</td><td>9</td><td>Ohio</td><td>132.0</td></tr>
<tr><td>28</td><td>Georgia</td><td>122.2</td><td>10</td><td>Arkansas</td><td>131.9</td></tr>
<tr><td>16</td><td>Hawaii</td><td>127.5</td><td>11</td><td>South Carolina</td><td>130.9</td></tr>
<tr><td>3</td><td>Idaho</td><td>139.3</td><td>12</td><td>Vermont</td><td>130.0</td></tr>
<tr><td>13</td><td>Illinois</td><td>129.9</td><td>13</td><td>Illinois</td><td>129.9</td></tr>
<tr><td>7</td><td>Indiana</td><td>133.5</td><td>14</td><td>California</td><td>128.0</td></tr>
<tr><td>20</td><td>Iowa</td><td>124.3</td><td>14</td><td>Wyoming</td><td>128.0</td></tr>
<tr><td>32</td><td>Kansas</td><td>118.8</td><td>16</td><td>Hawaii</td><td>127.5</td></tr>
<tr><td>27</td><td>Kentucky</td><td>122.5</td><td>17</td><td>Maine</td><td>126.6</td></tr>
<tr><td>30</td><td>Louisiana</td><td>120.4</td><td>17</td><td>Mississippi</td><td>126.6</td></tr>
<tr><td>17</td><td>Maine</td><td>126.6</td><td>19</td><td>West Virginia</td><td>126.4</td></tr>
<tr><td>29</td><td>Maryland</td><td>120.5</td><td>20</td><td>Iowa</td><td>124.3</td></tr>
<tr><td>47</td><td>Massachusetts</td><td>110.2</td><td>20</td><td>North Carolina</td><td>124.3</td></tr>
<tr><td>4</td><td>Michigan</td><td>136.4</td><td>20</td><td>Wisconsin</td><td>124.3</td></tr>
<tr><td>42</td><td>Minnesota</td><td>114.2</td><td>23</td><td>North Dakota</td><td>124.0</td></tr>
<tr><td>17</td><td>Mississippi</td><td>126.6</td><td>24</td><td>Nebraska</td><td>123.5</td></tr>
<tr><td>46</td><td>Missouri</td><td>110.5</td><td>25</td><td>New Mexico</td><td>123.2</td></tr>
<tr><td>5</td><td>Montana</td><td>135.9</td><td>26</td><td>Utah</td><td>122.7</td></tr>
<tr><td>24</td><td>Nebraska</td><td>123.5</td><td>27</td><td>Kentucky</td><td>122.5</td></tr>
<tr><td>41</td><td>Nevada</td><td>115.4</td><td>28</td><td>Georgia</td><td>122.2</td></tr>
<tr><td>45</td><td>New Hampshire</td><td>110.6</td><td>29</td><td>Maryland</td><td>120.5</td></tr>
<tr><td>36</td><td>New Jersey</td><td>116.7</td><td>30</td><td>Louisiana</td><td>120.4</td></tr>
<tr><td>25</td><td>New Mexico</td><td>123.2</td><td>31</td><td>South Dakota</td><td>118.9</td></tr>
<tr><td>44</td><td>New York</td><td>111.5</td><td>32</td><td>Kansas</td><td>118.8</td></tr>
<tr><td>20</td><td>North Carolina</td><td>124.3</td><td>33</td><td>Delaware</td><td>118.0</td></tr>
<tr><td>23</td><td>North Dakota</td><td>124.0</td><td>34</td><td>Oklahoma</td><td>117.4</td></tr>
<tr><td>9</td><td>Ohio</td><td>132.0</td><td>35</td><td>Tennessee</td><td>117.2</td></tr>
<tr><td>34</td><td>Oklahoma</td><td>117.4</td><td>36</td><td>New Jersey</td><td>116.7</td></tr>
<tr><td>2</td><td>Oregon</td><td>140.3</td><td>37</td><td>Florida</td><td>116.1</td></tr>
<tr><td>6</td><td>Pennsylvania</td><td>135.6</td><td>38</td><td>Washington</td><td>115.8</td></tr>
<tr><td>1</td><td>Rhode Island</td><td>140.4</td><td>39</td><td>Arizona</td><td>115.6</td></tr>
<tr><td>11</td><td>South Carolina</td><td>130.9</td><td>40</td><td>Alabama</td><td>115.5</td></tr>
<tr><td>31</td><td>South Dakota</td><td>118.9</td><td>41</td><td>Nevada</td><td>115.4</td></tr>
<tr><td>35</td><td>Tennessee</td><td>117.2</td><td>42</td><td>Minnesota</td><td>114.2</td></tr>
<tr><td>50</td><td>Texas</td><td>105.8</td><td>43</td><td>Connecticut</td><td>113.7</td></tr>
<tr><td>26</td><td>Utah</td><td>122.7</td><td>44</td><td>New York</td><td>111.5</td></tr>
<tr><td>12</td><td>Vermont</td><td>130.0</td><td>45</td><td>New Hampshire</td><td>110.6</td></tr>
<tr><td>48</td><td>Virginia</td><td>109.1</td><td>46</td><td>Missouri</td><td>110.5</td></tr>
<tr><td>38</td><td>Washington</td><td>115.8</td><td>47</td><td>Massachusetts</td><td>110.2</td></tr>
<tr><td>19</td><td>West Virginia</td><td>126.4</td><td>48</td><td>Virginia</td><td>109.1</td></tr>
<tr><td>20</td><td>Wisconsin</td><td>124.3</td><td>49</td><td>Colorado</td><td>108.6</td></tr>
<tr><td>14</td><td>Wyoming</td><td>128.0</td><td>50</td><td>Texas</td><td>105.8</td></tr>
<tr><td></td><td></td><td></td><td></td><td>District of Columbia</td><td>90.4</td></tr>
</table>

Source: Morgan Quitno Press using data from National Education Association, Washington, D.C.
"Rankings & Estimates" (Copyright © 2004 and 2005, NEA, used with permission) and
"Quarterly Census of Employment and Wages: Annual Data Tables" (http://www.bls.gov/cew/cewsnote2.htm)
*Average of public elementary and secondary teacher salary for school years 2003-2004 and 2004-2005 compared
to each state's 2004 teacher average annual pay for all workers covered by federal unemployment.

Percent of Public School Fourth Graders
Proficient or Better in Reading in 2005
National Percent = 30%*

ALPHA ORDER

RANK	STATE	PERCENT
45	Alabama	22
37	Alaska	27
43	Arizona	24
29	Arkansas	30
46	California	21
6	Colorado	37
4	Connecticut	38
14	Delaware	34
29	Florida	30
39	Georgia	26
44	Hawaii	23
19	Idaho	33
33	Illinois	29
29	Indiana	30
19	Iowa	33
25	Kansas	32
28	Kentucky	31
48	Louisiana	20
12	Maine	35
25	Maryland	32
1	Massachusetts	44
25	Michigan	32
4	Minnesota	38
50	Mississippi	18
19	Missouri	33
9	Montana	36
14	Nebraska	34
46	Nevada	21
2	New Hampshire	39
6	New Jersey	37
48	New Mexico	20
19	New York	33
33	North Carolina	29
12	North Dakota	35
14	Ohio	34
42	Oklahoma	25
33	Oregon	29
9	Pennsylvania	36
29	Rhode Island	30
39	South Carolina	26
19	South Dakota	33
37	Tennessee	27
33	Texas	29
14	Utah	34
2	Vermont	39
6	Virginia	37
9	Washington	36
39	West Virginia	26
19	Wisconsin	33
14	Wyoming	34

RANK ORDER

RANK	STATE	PERCENT
1	Massachusetts	44
2	New Hampshire	39
2	Vermont	39
4	Connecticut	38
4	Minnesota	38
6	Colorado	37
6	New Jersey	37
6	Virginia	37
9	Montana	36
9	Pennsylvania	36
9	Washington	36
12	Maine	35
12	North Dakota	35
14	Delaware	34
14	Nebraska	34
14	Ohio	34
14	Utah	34
14	Wyoming	34
19	Idaho	33
19	Iowa	33
19	Missouri	33
19	New York	33
19	South Dakota	33
19	Wisconsin	33
25	Kansas	32
25	Maryland	32
25	Michigan	32
28	Kentucky	31
29	Arkansas	30
29	Florida	30
29	Indiana	30
29	Rhode Island	30
33	Illinois	29
33	North Carolina	29
33	Oregon	29
33	Texas	29
37	Alaska	27
37	Tennessee	27
39	Georgia	26
39	South Carolina	26
39	West Virginia	26
42	Oklahoma	25
43	Arizona	24
44	Hawaii	23
45	Alabama	22
46	California	21
46	Nevada	21
48	Louisiana	20
48	New Mexico	20
50	Mississippi	18

| | District of Columbia | 11 |

Source: U.S. Department of Education, National Center for Education Statistics
   "NAEP 2005: Reading Report Card for the Nation and the States" (NCES 2006-451)
*There are four achievement levels: Below Basic, Basic, Proficient and Advanced.   Proficient represents solid
academic mastery for 4th graders. Students reaching this level have demonstrated competency over challenging
subject matter, including subject matter knowledge, application of such knowledge to real-world situations and
analytical skills appropriate to the subject matter.

Percent of Public School Eighth Graders
Proficient or Better in Reading in 2005
National Percent = 29%*

ALPHA ORDER

RANK	STATE	PERCENT
43	Alabama	22
34	Alaska	26
42	Arizona	23
34	Arkansas	26
46	California	21
22	Colorado	32
17	Connecticut	34
27	Delaware	30
38	Florida	25
38	Georgia	25
49	Hawaii	18
22	Idaho	32
24	Illinois	31
31	Indiana	28
17	Iowa	34
13	Kansas	35
24	Kentucky	31
47	Louisiana	20
2	Maine	38
27	Maryland	30
1	Massachusetts	44
31	Michigan	28
5	Minnesota	37
49	Mississippi	18
24	Missouri	31
5	Montana	37
13	Nebraska	35
43	Nevada	22
2	New Hampshire	38
2	New Jersey	38
48	New Mexico	19
20	New York	33
33	North Carolina	27
5	North Dakota	37
9	Ohio	36
38	Oklahoma	25
20	Oregon	33
9	Pennsylvania	36
29	Rhode Island	29
38	South Carolina	25
13	South Dakota	35
34	Tennessee	26
34	Texas	26
29	Utah	29
5	Vermont	37
9	Virginia	36
17	Washington	34
43	West Virginia	22
13	Wisconsin	35
9	Wyoming	36

RANK ORDER

RANK	STATE	PERCENT
1	Massachusetts	44
2	Maine	38
2	New Hampshire	38
2	New Jersey	38
5	Minnesota	37
5	Montana	37
5	North Dakota	37
5	Vermont	37
9	Ohio	36
9	Pennsylvania	36
9	Virginia	36
9	Wyoming	36
13	Kansas	35
13	Nebraska	35
13	South Dakota	35
13	Wisconsin	35
17	Connecticut	34
17	Iowa	34
17	Washington	34
20	New York	33
20	Oregon	33
22	Colorado	32
22	Idaho	32
24	Illinois	31
24	Kentucky	31
24	Missouri	31
27	Delaware	30
27	Maryland	30
29	Rhode Island	29
29	Utah	29
31	Indiana	28
31	Michigan	28
33	North Carolina	27
34	Alaska	26
34	Arkansas	26
34	Tennessee	26
34	Texas	26
38	Florida	25
38	Georgia	25
38	Oklahoma	25
38	South Carolina	25
42	Arizona	23
43	Alabama	22
43	Nevada	22
43	West Virginia	22
46	California	21
47	Louisiana	20
48	New Mexico	19
49	Hawaii	18
49	Mississippi	18
	District of Columbia	12

Source: U.S. Department of Education, National Center for Education Statistics
   "NAEP 2005: Reading Report Card for the Nation and the States" (NCES 2006-451)
There are four achievement levels: Below Basic, Basic, Proficient and Advanced. Proficient represents solid academic mastery for 8th graders. Students reaching this level have demonstrated competency over challenging subject matter, including subject matter knowledge, application of such knowledge to real-world situations and analytical skills appropriate to the subject matter.

Percent of Public School Fourth Graders Proficient or Better in Mathematics in 2005
National Percent = 35%*

ALPHA ORDER

RANK	STATE	PERCENT
48	Alabama	21
33	Alaska	34
40	Arizona	28
33	Arkansas	34
40	California	28
18	Colorado	39
9	Connecticut	42
29	Delaware	36
25	Florida	37
38	Georgia	30
43	Hawaii	27
13	Idaho	40
35	Illinois	32
21	Indiana	38
25	Iowa	37
2	Kansas	47
44	Kentucky	26
47	Louisiana	24
18	Maine	39
21	Maryland	38
1	Massachusetts	49
21	Michigan	38
2	Minnesota	47
49	Mississippi	19
36	Missouri	31
21	Montana	38
29	Nebraska	36
44	Nevada	26
2	New Hampshire	47
5	New Jersey	45
49	New Mexico	19
29	New York	36
13	North Carolina	40
13	North Dakota	40
7	Ohio	43
39	Oklahoma	29
25	Oregon	37
11	Pennsylvania	41
36	Rhode Island	31
29	South Carolina	36
11	South Dakota	41
40	Tennessee	28
13	Texas	40
25	Utah	37
6	Vermont	44
18	Virginia	39
9	Washington	42
46	West Virginia	25
13	Wisconsin	40
7	Wyoming	43

RANK ORDER

RANK	STATE	PERCENT
1	Massachusetts	49
2	Kansas	47
2	Minnesota	47
2	New Hampshire	47
5	New Jersey	45
6	Vermont	44
7	Ohio	43
7	Wyoming	43
9	Connecticut	42
9	Washington	42
11	Pennsylvania	41
11	South Dakota	41
13	Idaho	40
13	North Carolina	40
13	North Dakota	40
13	Texas	40
13	Wisconsin	40
18	Colorado	39
18	Maine	39
18	Virginia	39
21	Indiana	38
21	Maryland	38
21	Michigan	38
21	Montana	38
25	Florida	37
25	Iowa	37
25	Oregon	37
25	Utah	37
29	Delaware	36
29	Nebraska	36
29	New York	36
29	South Carolina	36
33	Alaska	34
33	Arkansas	34
35	Illinois	32
36	Missouri	31
36	Rhode Island	31
38	Georgia	30
39	Oklahoma	29
40	Arizona	28
40	California	28
40	Tennessee	28
43	Hawaii	27
44	Kentucky	26
44	Nevada	26
46	West Virginia	25
47	Louisiana	24
48	Alabama	21
49	Mississippi	19
49	New Mexico	19
	District of Columbia	10

Source: U.S. Department of Education, National Center for Education Statistics
   "The Nation's Report Card, Mathematics 2005" (NCES 2006-453)
There are four achievement levels: Below Basic, Basic, Proficient and Advanced. Proficient represents solid academic mastery for 4th graders. Students reaching this level have demonstrated competency over challenging subject matter, including subject matter knowledge, application of such knowledge to real-world situations and analytical skills appropriate to the subject matter.

Percent of Public School Eighth Graders Proficient or Better in Mathematics in 2005
National Percent = 28%*

ALPHA ORDER

RANK	STATE	PERCENT	RANK	STATE	PERCENT
47	Alabama	15	1	Massachusetts	43
29	Alaska	29	1	Minnesota	43
33	Arizona	26	3	Vermont	38
39	Arkansas	22	4	Montana	36
39	California	22	4	New Jersey	36
NA	Colorado**	NA	4	South Dakota	36
9	Connecticut	35	4	Washington	36
22	Delaware	30	4	Wisconsin	36
33	Florida	26	9	Connecticut	35
37	Georgia	23	9	Nebraska	35
44	Hawaii	18	9	New Hampshire	35
22	Idaho	30	9	North Dakota	35
29	Illinois	29	13	Iowa	34
22	Indiana	30	13	Kansas	34
13	Iowa	34	13	Oregon	34
13	Kansas	34	16	Ohio	33
37	Kentucky	23	16	Virginia	33
46	Louisiana	16	18	North Carolina	32
22	Maine	30	19	New York	31
22	Maryland	30	19	Pennsylvania	31
1	Massachusetts	43	19	Texas	31
29	Michigan	29	22	Delaware	30
1	Minnesota	43	22	Idaho	30
48	Mississippi	14	22	Indiana	30
33	Missouri	26	22	Maine	30
4	Montana	36	22	Maryland	30
9	Nebraska	35	22	South Carolina	30
41	Nevada	21	22	Utah	30
9	New Hampshire	35	29	Alaska	29
4	New Jersey	36	29	Illinois	29
48	New Mexico	14	29	Michigan	29
19	New York	31	29	Wyoming	29
18	North Carolina	32	33	Arizona	26
9	North Dakota	35	33	Florida	26
16	Ohio	33	33	Missouri	26
41	Oklahoma	21	36	Rhode Island	24
13	Oregon	34	37	Georgia	23
19	Pennsylvania	31	37	Kentucky	23
36	Rhode Island	24	39	Arkansas	22
22	South Carolina	30	39	California	22
4	South Dakota	36	41	Nevada	21
41	Tennessee	21	41	Oklahoma	21
19	Texas	31	41	Tennessee	21
22	Utah	30	44	Hawaii	18
3	Vermont	38	44	West Virginia	18
16	Virginia	33	46	Louisiana	16
4	Washington	36	47	Alabama	15
44	West Virginia	18	48	Mississippi	14
4	Wisconsin	36	48	New Mexico	14
29	Wyoming	29	NA	Colorado**	NA
				District of Columbia	7

Source: U.S. Department of Education, National Center for Education Statistics
   "The Nation's Report Card, Mathematics 2005" (NCES 2006-453)
*There are four achievement levels: Below Basic, Basic, Proficient and Advanced. Proficient represents solid academic mastery for 8th graders. Students reaching this level have demonstrated competency over challenging subject matter, including subject matter knowledge, application of such knowledge to real-world situations and analytical skills appropriate to the subject matter. **Not available.

Estimated Public High School Graduates in 2005

National Total = 2,814,996 Graduates*

ALPHA ORDER					RANK ORDER			
RANK	STATE	GRADUATES	% of USA		RANK	STATE	GRADUATES	% of USA
25	Alabama	36,743	1.3%		1	California	359,414	12.8%
47	Alaska	7,540	0.3%		2	Texas	246,344	8.8%
16	Arizona	60,138	2.1%		3	New York	156,000	5.5%
33	Arkansas	28,144	1.0%		4	Florida	127,012	4.5%
1	California	359,414	12.8%		5	Pennsylvania	124,300	4.4%
22	Colorado	44,617	1.6%		6	Illinois	122,922	4.4%
28	Connecticut	35,430	1.3%		7	Ohio	114,558	4.1%
49	Delaware	7,066	0.3%		8	Michigan	101,888	3.6%
4	Florida	127,012	4.5%		9	New Jersey	84,287	3.0%
12	Georgia	73,724	2.6%		10	Virginia	74,276	2.6%
43	Hawaii	10,133	0.4%		11	North Carolina	74,221	2.6%
39	Idaho	15,937	0.6%		12	Georgia	73,724	2.6%
6	Illinois	122,922	4.4%		13	Wisconsin	63,741	2.3%
19	Indiana	54,277	1.9%		14	Washington	63,133	2.2%
29	Iowa	34,403	1.2%		15	Minnesota	60,886	2.2%
31	Kansas	30,000	1.1%		16	Arizona	60,138	2.1%
23	Kentucky	37,282	1.3%		17	Missouri	58,473	2.1%
24	Louisiana	37,022	1.3%		18	Massachusetts	57,894	2.1%
41	Maine	13,657	0.5%		19	Indiana	54,277	1.9%
20	Maryland	53,956	1.9%		20	Maryland	53,956	1.9%
18	Massachusetts	57,894	2.1%		21	Tennessee	48,838	1.7%
8	Michigan	101,888	3.6%		22	Colorado	44,617	1.6%
15	Minnesota	60,886	2.2%		23	Kentucky	37,282	1.3%
34	Mississippi	24,986	0.9%		24	Louisiana	37,022	1.3%
17	Missouri	58,473	2.1%		25	Alabama	36,743	1.3%
42	Montana	10,459	0.4%		26	Oklahoma	36,582	1.3%
35	Nebraska	19,419	0.7%		27	South Carolina	36,462	1.3%
37	Nevada	17,932	0.6%		28	Connecticut	35,430	1.3%
40	New Hampshire	13,876	0.5%		29	Iowa	34,403	1.2%
9	New Jersey	84,287	3.0%		30	Oregon	32,901	1.2%
36	New Mexico	17,996	0.6%		31	Kansas	30,000	1.1%
3	New York	156,000	5.5%		32	Utah	28,721	1.0%
11	North Carolina	74,221	2.6%		33	Arkansas	28,144	1.0%
46	North Dakota	7,850	0.3%		34	Mississippi	24,986	0.9%
7	Ohio	114,558	4.1%		35	Nebraska	19,419	0.7%
26	Oklahoma	36,582	1.3%		36	New Mexico	17,996	0.6%
30	Oregon	32,901	1.2%		37	Nevada	17,932	0.6%
5	Pennsylvania	124,300	4.4%		38	West Virginia	16,949	0.6%
44	Rhode Island	8,860	0.3%		39	Idaho	15,937	0.6%
27	South Carolina	36,462	1.3%		40	New Hampshire	13,876	0.5%
45	South Dakota	8,470	0.3%		41	Maine	13,657	0.5%
21	Tennessee	48,838	1.7%		42	Montana	10,459	0.4%
2	Texas	246,344	8.8%		43	Hawaii	10,133	0.4%
32	Utah	28,721	1.0%		44	Rhode Island	8,860	0.3%
48	Vermont	7,378	0.3%		45	South Dakota	8,470	0.3%
10	Virginia	74,276	2.6%		46	North Dakota	7,850	0.3%
14	Washington	63,133	2.2%		47	Alaska	7,540	0.3%
38	West Virginia	16,949	0.6%		48	Vermont	7,378	0.3%
13	Wisconsin	63,741	2.3%		49	Delaware	7,066	0.3%
50	Wyoming	5,453	0.2%		50	Wyoming	5,453	0.2%
						District of Columbia	2,449	0.1%

Source: National Education Association, Washington, D.C.
   "Rankings & Estimates" (Copyright © 2005, NEA, used with permission)
Estimates for school year 2004-05.

Estimated Public High School Graduation Rate in 2005

National Rate = 71.5% Graduated*

ALPHA ORDER

ALPHA ORDER | | | RANK ORDER | | |

RANK	STATE	PERCENT	RANK	STATE	PERCENT
46	Alabama	60.1	1	New Jersey	94.5
41	Alaska	65.2	2	Arizona	87.6
2	Arizona	87.6	3	Minnesota	85.5
18	Arkansas	76.8	4	Vermont	84.3
25	California	74.5	5	Iowa	83.1
20	Colorado	76.0	6	North Dakota	81.1
9	Connecticut	80.6	7	Pennsylvania	81.0
34	Delaware	69.6	8	Wisconsin	80.7
50	Florida	56.8	9	Connecticut	80.6
47	Georgia	58.8	10	Maine	80.2
42	Hawaii	64.8	11	Utah	79.9
12	Idaho	79.5	12	Idaho	79.5
24	Illinois	74.7	13	New Hampshire	79.2
37	Indiana	67.0	14	Virginia	78.2
5	Iowa	83.1	15	Nebraska	78.1
21	Kansas	75.6	16	Montana	77.3
39	Kentucky	65.8	17	Missouri	77.2
48	Louisiana	58.0	18	Arkansas	76.8
10	Maine	80.2	19	Maryland	76.7
19	Maryland	76.7	20	Colorado	76.0
25	Massachusetts	74.5	21	Kansas	75.6
23	Michigan	75.0	22	South Dakota	75.3
3	Minnesota	85.5	23	Michigan	75.0
43	Mississippi	63.4	24	Illinois	74.7
17	Missouri	77.2	25	California	74.5
16	Montana	77.3	25	Massachusetts	74.5
15	Nebraska	78.1	27	Ohio	73.2
29	Nevada	72.8	28	Washington	72.9
13	New Hampshire	79.2	29	Nevada	72.8
1	New Jersey	94.5	29	Oklahoma	72.8
45	New Mexico	61.4	31	Oregon	72.1
44	New York	61.7	32	West Virginia	71.0
38	North Carolina	66.6	33	Rhode Island	70.6
6	North Dakota	81.1	34	Delaware	69.6
27	Ohio	73.2	35	Texas	68.5
29	Oklahoma	72.8	36	Wyoming	67.7
31	Oregon	72.1	37	Indiana	67.0
7	Pennsylvania	81.0	38	North Carolina	66.6
33	Rhode Island	70.6	39	Kentucky	65.8
48	South Carolina	58.0	40	Tennessee	65.4
22	South Dakota	75.3	41	Alaska	65.2
40	Tennessee	65.4	42	Hawaii	64.8
35	Texas	68.5	43	Mississippi	63.4
11	Utah	79.9	44	New York	61.7
4	Vermont	84.3	45	New Mexico	61.4
14	Virginia	78.2	46	Alabama	60.1
28	Washington	72.9	47	Georgia	58.8
32	West Virginia	71.0	48	Louisiana	58.0
8	Wisconsin	80.7	48	South Carolina	58.0
36	Wyoming	67.7	50	Florida	56.8

| | | | | District of Columbia | 46.3 |

Source: Morgan Quitno Press using data from National Education Association, Washington, D.C.
"Rankings & Estimates" (Copyright © 2005, NEA, used with permission) and U.S. Department of Education, National Center for Education Statistics, "Common Core of Data (CCD) Database" (http://nces.ed.gov/ccd/)
Calculated by comparing estimated number of public high school graduates in 2005 with 9th grade enrollment in Fall 1999. Data exclude ungraded pupils and have not been adjusted for interstate migration or switching to private schools.

Percent of Population Graduated from High School in 2004

National Percent = 85.2%*

ALPHA ORDER

RANK	STATE	PERCENT
42	Alabama	82.4
8	Alaska	90.2
37	Arizona	84.4
48	Arkansas	79.2
44	California	81.3
16	Colorado	88.3
13	Connecticut	88.8
30	Delaware	86.5
33	Florida	85.9
35	Georgia	85.2
18	Hawaii	88.0
19	Idaho	87.9
29	Illinois	86.8
26	Indiana	87.2
9	Iowa	89.8
11	Kansas	89.6
43	Kentucky	81.8
49	Louisiana	78.7
27	Maine	87.1
24	Maryland	87.4
28	Massachusetts	86.9
19	Michigan	87.9
1	Minnesota	92.3
39	Mississippi	83.0
19	Missouri	87.9
2	Montana	91.9
4	Nebraska	91.3
32	Nevada	86.3
6	New Hampshire	90.8
22	New Jersey	87.6
40	New Mexico	82.9
34	New York	85.4
46	North Carolina	80.9
12	North Dakota	89.5
17	Ohio	88.1
35	Oklahoma	85.2
24	Oregon	87.4
30	Pennsylvania	86.5
45	Rhode Island	81.1
38	South Carolina	83.6
23	South Dakota	87.5
40	Tennessee	82.9
50	Texas	78.3
5	Utah	91.0
6	Vermont	90.8
15	Virginia	88.4
10	Washington	89.7
46	West Virginia	80.9
13	Wisconsin	88.8
2	Wyoming	91.9

RANK ORDER

RANK	STATE	PERCENT
1	Minnesota	92.3
2	Montana	91.9
2	Wyoming	91.9
4	Nebraska	91.3
5	Utah	91.0
6	New Hampshire	90.8
6	Vermont	90.8
8	Alaska	90.2
9	Iowa	89.8
10	Washington	89.7
11	Kansas	89.6
12	North Dakota	89.5
13	Connecticut	88.8
13	Wisconsin	88.8
15	Virginia	88.4
16	Colorado	88.3
17	Ohio	88.1
18	Hawaii	88.0
19	Idaho	87.9
19	Michigan	87.9
19	Missouri	87.9
22	New Jersey	87.6
23	South Dakota	87.5
24	Maryland	87.4
24	Oregon	87.4
26	Indiana	87.2
27	Maine	87.1
28	Massachusetts	86.9
29	Illinois	86.8
30	Delaware	86.5
30	Pennsylvania	86.5
32	Nevada	86.3
33	Florida	85.9
34	New York	85.4
35	Georgia	85.2
35	Oklahoma	85.2
37	Arizona	84.4
38	South Carolina	83.6
39	Mississippi	83.0
40	New Mexico	82.9
40	Tennessee	82.9
42	Alabama	82.4
43	Kentucky	81.8
44	California	81.3
45	Rhode Island	81.1
46	North Carolina	80.9
46	West Virginia	80.9
48	Arkansas	79.2
49	Louisiana	78.7
50	Texas	78.3

| | District of Columbia | 86.4 |

Source: U.S. Bureau of the Census
   "Educational Attainment in the United States" (March 2005)
     (http://www.census.gov/population/www/socdemo/educ-attn.html)
*Persons age 25 and older.

Public High School Drop Out Rate in 2001

National Median = 4.2%*

ALPHA ORDER				RANK ORDER		
RANK	STATE	RATE		RANK	STATE	RATE
27	Alabama	4.1		1	Arizona	10.9
3	Alaska	8.2		2	Louisiana	8.3
1	Arizona	10.9		3	Alaska	8.2
11	Arkansas	5.3		4	Georgia	7.2
NA	California**	NA		5	Wyoming	6.4
NA	Colorado**	NA		6	North Carolina	6.3
41	Connecticut	3.0		7	Illinois	6.0
22	Delaware	4.2		8	Hawaii	5.7
20	Florida	4.4		9	Idaho	5.6
4	Georgia	7.2		10	New Hampshire	5.4
8	Hawaii	5.7		11	Arkansas	5.3
9	Idaho	5.6		11	New Mexico	5.3
7	Illinois	6.0		11	Oregon	5.3
NA	Indiana**	NA		14	Nevada	5.2
43	Iowa	2.7		14	Oklahoma	5.2
39	Kansas	3.2		16	Rhode Island	5.0
18	Kentucky	4.6		17	Vermont	4.7
2	Louisiana	8.3		18	Kentucky	4.6
40	Maine	3.1		18	Mississippi	4.6
27	Maryland	4.1		20	Florida	4.4
37	Massachusetts	3.4		21	Tennessee	4.3
NA	Michigan**	NA		22	Delaware	4.2
29	Minnesota	4.0		22	Missouri	4.2
18	Mississippi	4.6		22	Montana	4.2
22	Missouri	4.2		22	Texas	4.2
22	Montana	4.2		22	West Virginia	4.2
29	Nebraska	4.0		27	Alabama	4.1
14	Nevada	5.2		27	Maryland	4.1
10	New Hampshire	5.4		29	Minnesota	4.0
42	New Jersey	2.8		29	Nebraska	4.0
11	New Mexico	5.3		31	Ohio	3.9
33	New York	3.8		31	South Dakota	3.9
6	North Carolina	6.3		33	New York	3.8
45	North Dakota	2.2		34	Utah	3.7
31	Ohio	3.9		35	Pennsylvania	3.6
14	Oklahoma	5.2		36	Virginia	3.5
11	Oregon	5.3		37	Massachusetts	3.4
35	Pennsylvania	3.6		38	South Carolina	3.3
16	Rhode Island	5.0		39	Kansas	3.2
38	South Carolina	3.3		40	Maine	3.1
31	South Dakota	3.9		41	Connecticut	3.0
21	Tennessee	4.3		42	New Jersey	2.8
22	Texas	4.2		43	Iowa	2.7
34	Utah	3.7		44	Wisconsin	2.3
17	Vermont	4.7		45	North Dakota	2.2
36	Virginia	3.5		NA	California**	NA
NA	Washington**	NA		NA	Colorado**	NA
22	West Virginia	4.2		NA	Indiana**	NA
44	Wisconsin	2.3		NA	Michigan**	NA
5	Wyoming	6.4		NA	Washington**	NA
					District of Columbia**	NA

Source: U.S. Department of Education, National Center for Educational Statistics
"Dropout Rates in the United States: 2001" (NCES 2005-046, October 2004)
**"Event" dropout rates showing the number of 9-12th grade dropouts divided by the number of students enrolled at the beginning of the school year in those grades. National rate is the median of reporting states.*
***Not available.*

ACT Average Composite Score in 2005

National Average = 20.9*

ALPHA ORDER

RANK	STATE	AVERAGE SCORE
42	Alabama	20.2
28	Alaska	21.3
21	Arizona	21.5
40	Arkansas	20.3
19	California	21.6
42	Colorado	20.2
1	Connecticut	22.8
33	Delaware	20.8
36	Florida	20.4
46	Georgia	20.0
12	Hawaii	21.9
28	Idaho	21.3
40	Illinois	20.3
16	Indiana	21.7
11	Iowa	22.0
16	Kansas	21.7
36	Kentucky	20.4
48	Louisiana	19.8
6	Maine	22.4
32	Maryland	21.0
1	Massachusetts	22.8
25	Michigan	21.4
8	Minnesota	22.3
50	Mississippi	18.7
19	Missouri	21.6
14	Montana	21.8
14	Nebraska	21.8
21	Nevada	21.5
8	New Hampshire	22.3
28	New Jersey	21.3
46	New Mexico	20.0
6	New York	22.4
42	North Carolina	20.2
28	North Dakota	21.3
25	Ohio	21.4
36	Oklahoma	20.4
4	Oregon	22.6
16	Pennsylvania	21.7
12	Rhode Island	21.9
49	South Carolina	19.4
21	South Dakota	21.5
35	Tennessee	20.5
42	Texas	20.2
21	Utah	21.5
4	Vermont	22.6
33	Virginia	20.8
3	Washington	22.7
36	West Virginia	20.4
10	Wisconsin	22.2
25	Wyoming	21.4

RANK ORDER

RANK	STATE	AVERAGE SCORE
1	Connecticut	22.8
1	Massachusetts	22.8
3	Washington	22.7
4	Oregon	22.6
4	Vermont	22.6
6	Maine	22.4
6	New York	22.4
8	Minnesota	22.3
8	New Hampshire	22.3
10	Wisconsin	22.2
11	Iowa	22.0
12	Hawaii	21.9
12	Rhode Island	21.9
14	Montana	21.8
14	Nebraska	21.8
16	Indiana	21.7
16	Kansas	21.7
16	Pennsylvania	21.7
19	California	21.6
19	Missouri	21.6
21	Arizona	21.5
21	Nevada	21.5
21	South Dakota	21.5
21	Utah	21.5
25	Michigan	21.4
25	Ohio	21.4
25	Wyoming	21.4
28	Alaska	21.3
28	Idaho	21.3
28	New Jersey	21.3
28	North Dakota	21.3
32	Maryland	21.0
33	Delaware	20.8
33	Virginia	20.8
35	Tennessee	20.5
36	Florida	20.4
36	Kentucky	20.4
36	Oklahoma	20.4
36	West Virginia	20.4
40	Arkansas	20.3
40	Illinois	20.3
42	Alabama	20.2
42	Colorado	20.2
42	North Carolina	20.2
42	Texas	20.2
46	Georgia	20.0
46	New Mexico	20.0
48	Louisiana	19.8
49	South Carolina	19.4
50	Mississippi	18.7
	District of Columbia	18.0

Source: The American College Testing Program (copyright 2005)
   "Average ACT Scores by State" (http://www.act.org/news/data/05/states.html)
*The ACT score range is 1 to 36. Almost 1.2 million 2005 U.S. high school graduates took the test. Caution should be used in using ACT scores to compare states. The percentage of high school students taking the test varies greatly from one state to another.

Education Expenditures by State and Local Governments in 2002

National Total = $594,590,671,000*

ALPHA ORDER

RANK	STATE	EXPENDITURES	% of USA
24	Alabama	$8,320,322,000	1.4%
44	Alaska	2,106,699,000	0.4%
22	Arizona	8,796,455,000	1.5%
34	Arkansas	4,783,305,000	0.8%
1	California	76,827,021,000	12.9%
21	Colorado	9,011,024,000	1.5%
26	Connecticut	7,852,255,000	1.3%
45	Delaware	1,936,589,000	0.3%
5	Florida	25,795,182,000	4.3%
10	Georgia	17,365,657,000	2.9%
42	Hawaii	2,257,427,000	0.4%
41	Idaho	2,422,610,000	0.4%
4	Illinois	25,952,978,000	4.4%
16	Indiana	12,192,513,000	2.1%
30	Iowa	6,467,435,000	1.1%
31	Kansas	5,501,024,000	0.9%
29	Kentucky	6,877,749,000	1.2%
25	Louisiana	7,994,460,000	1.3%
39	Maine	2,491,164,000	0.4%
17	Maryland	12,141,950,000	2.0%
13	Massachusetts	13,443,047,000	2.3%
7	Michigan	23,745,486,000	4.0%
18	Minnesota	11,266,335,000	1.9%
33	Mississippi	5,100,683,000	0.9%
19	Missouri	10,556,277,000	1.8%
46	Montana	1,792,025,000	0.3%
36	Nebraska	3,797,037,000	0.6%
37	Nevada	3,678,635,000	0.6%
40	New Hampshire	2,439,260,000	0.4%
9	New Jersey	20,543,653,000	3.5%
35	New Mexico	4,175,592,000	0.7%
2	New York	47,723,251,000	8.0%
11	North Carolina	15,261,615,000	2.6%
49	North Dakota	1,311,273,000	0.2%
8	Ohio	23,623,234,000	4.0%
28	Oklahoma	6,903,663,000	1.2%
27	Oregon	7,542,824,000	1.3%
6	Pennsylvania	24,295,573,000	4.1%
43	Rhode Island	2,180,271,000	0.4%
23	South Carolina	8,379,856,000	1.4%
48	South Dakota	1,360,120,000	0.2%
20	Tennessee	9,467,645,000	1.6%
3	Texas	45,702,517,000	7.7%
32	Utah	5,196,240,000	0.9%
47	Vermont	1,460,238,000	0.2%
12	Virginia	15,148,890,000	2.5%
14	Washington	12,865,672,000	2.2%
38	West Virginia	3,518,821,000	0.6%
15	Wisconsin	12,564,896,000	2.1%
50	Wyoming	1,277,482,000	0.2%

RANK ORDER

RANK	STATE	EXPENDITURES	% of USA
1	California	$76,827,021,000	12.9%
2	New York	47,723,251,000	8.0%
3	Texas	45,702,517,000	7.7%
4	Illinois	25,952,978,000	4.4%
5	Florida	25,795,182,000	4.3%
6	Pennsylvania	24,295,573,000	4.1%
7	Michigan	23,745,486,000	4.0%
8	Ohio	23,623,234,000	4.0%
9	New Jersey	20,543,653,000	3.5%
10	Georgia	17,365,657,000	2.9%
11	North Carolina	15,261,615,000	2.6%
12	Virginia	15,148,890,000	2.5%
13	Massachusetts	13,443,047,000	2.3%
14	Washington	12,865,672,000	2.2%
15	Wisconsin	12,564,896,000	2.1%
16	Indiana	12,192,513,000	2.1%
17	Maryland	12,141,950,000	2.0%
18	Minnesota	11,266,335,000	1.9%
19	Missouri	10,556,277,000	1.8%
20	Tennessee	9,467,645,000	1.6%
21	Colorado	9,011,024,000	1.5%
22	Arizona	8,796,455,000	1.5%
23	South Carolina	8,379,856,000	1.4%
24	Alabama	8,320,322,000	1.4%
25	Louisiana	7,994,460,000	1.3%
26	Connecticut	7,852,255,000	1.3%
27	Oregon	7,542,824,000	1.3%
28	Oklahoma	6,903,663,000	1.2%
29	Kentucky	6,877,749,000	1.2%
30	Iowa	6,467,435,000	1.1%
31	Kansas	5,501,024,000	0.9%
32	Utah	5,196,240,000	0.9%
33	Mississippi	5,100,683,000	0.9%
34	Arkansas	4,783,305,000	0.8%
35	New Mexico	4,175,592,000	0.7%
36	Nebraska	3,797,037,000	0.6%
37	Nevada	3,678,635,000	0.6%
38	West Virginia	3,518,821,000	0.6%
39	Maine	2,491,164,000	0.4%
40	New Hampshire	2,439,260,000	0.4%
41	Idaho	2,422,610,000	0.4%
42	Hawaii	2,257,427,000	0.4%
43	Rhode Island	2,180,271,000	0.4%
44	Alaska	2,106,699,000	0.4%
45	Delaware	1,936,589,000	0.3%
46	Montana	1,792,025,000	0.3%
47	Vermont	1,460,238,000	0.2%
48	South Dakota	1,360,120,000	0.2%
49	North Dakota	1,311,273,000	0.2%
50	Wyoming	1,277,482,000	0.2%
	District of Columbia	1,174,741,000	0.2%

Source: U.S. Bureau of the Census, Governments Division
   "State and Local Government Finances: 2002 Census" (http://www.census.gov/govs/www/estimate02.html)
*Direct general expenditures for higher, secondary, elementary and "other" education. Includes capital outlays.

Per Capita State and Local Government Expenditures for Education in 2002

National Per Capita = $2,065*

RANK	STATE	PER CAPITA
38	Alabama	$1,857
1	Alaska	3,287
49	Arizona	1,617
45	Arkansas	1,767
16	California	2,196
29	Colorado	2,003
9	Connecticut	2,270
4	Delaware	2,402
50	Florida	1,546
27	Georgia	2,034
40	Hawaii	1,829
41	Idaho	1,804
24	Illinois	2,062
30	Indiana	1,980
14	Iowa	2,204
28	Kansas	2,028
47	Kentucky	1,682
43	Louisiana	1,786
35	Maine	1,920
13	Maryland	2,231
20	Massachusetts	2,096
7	Michigan	2,365
11	Minnesota	2,242
44	Mississippi	1,779
37	Missouri	1,859
33	Montana	1,968
15	Nebraska	2,199
46	Nevada	1,697
36	New Hampshire	1,912
5	New Jersey	2,395
10	New Mexico	2,251
3	New York	2,492
39	North Carolina	1,836
23	North Dakota	2,069
22	Ohio	2,070
31	Oklahoma	1,979
17	Oregon	2,141
32	Pennsylvania	1,971
26	Rhode Island	2,040
25	South Carolina	2,041
42	South Dakota	1,789
48	Tennessee	1,635
19	Texas	2,104
12	Utah	2,240
6	Vermont	2,369
21	Virginia	2,083
18	Washington	2,121
34	West Virginia	1,949
8	Wisconsin	2,310
2	Wyoming	2,559

RANK	STATE	PER CAPITA
1	Alaska	$3,287
2	Wyoming	2,559
3	New York	2,492
4	Delaware	2,402
5	New Jersey	2,395
6	Vermont	2,369
7	Michigan	2,365
8	Wisconsin	2,310
9	Connecticut	2,270
10	New Mexico	2,251
11	Minnesota	2,242
12	Utah	2,240
13	Maryland	2,231
14	Iowa	2,204
15	Nebraska	2,199
16	California	2,196
17	Oregon	2,141
18	Washington	2,121
19	Texas	2,104
20	Massachusetts	2,096
21	Virginia	2,083
22	Ohio	2,070
23	North Dakota	2,069
24	Illinois	2,062
25	South Carolina	2,041
26	Rhode Island	2,040
27	Georgia	2,034
28	Kansas	2,028
29	Colorado	2,003
30	Indiana	1,980
31	Oklahoma	1,979
32	Pennsylvania	1,971
33	Montana	1,968
34	West Virginia	1,949
35	Maine	1,920
36	New Hampshire	1,912
37	Missouri	1,859
38	Alabama	1,857
39	North Carolina	1,836
40	Hawaii	1,829
41	Idaho	1,804
42	South Dakota	1,789
43	Louisiana	1,786
44	Mississippi	1,779
45	Arkansas	1,767
46	Nevada	1,697
47	Kentucky	1,682
48	Tennessee	1,635
49	Arizona	1,617
50	Florida	1,546

| | District of Columbia | 2,081 |

*Source: Morgan Quitno Press using data from U.S. Bureau of the Census, Governments Division
"State and Local Government Finances: 2002 Census" (http://www.census.gov/govs/www/estimate02.html)
Direct general expenditures for higher, secondary, elementary and "other" education. Includes capital outlays.

Expenditures for Education as a Percent of
All State and Local Government Expenditures in 2002
National Percent = 34.4%*

ALPHA ORDER

RANK	STATE	PERCENT
29	Alabama	33.8
50	Alaska	25.0
27	Arizona	34.8
16	Arkansas	36.6
39	California	32.6
31	Colorado	33.3
40	Connecticut	32.4
19	Delaware	36.2
47	Florida	29.6
5	Georgia	38.6
49	Hawaii	27.2
21	Idaho	35.6
23	Illinois	35.2
13	Indiana	37.2
12	Iowa	37.6
14	Kansas	37.0
43	Kentucky	31.9
36	Louisiana	32.9
45	Maine	31.3
9	Maryland	38.2
44	Massachusetts	31.7
3	Michigan	39.1
41	Minnesota	32.3
33	Mississippi	33.2
18	Missouri	36.3
22	Montana	35.5
4	Nebraska	39.0
45	Nevada	31.3
7	New Hampshire	38.5
11	New Jersey	37.8
17	New Mexico	36.5
47	New York	29.6
28	North Carolina	34.3
30	North Dakota	33.7
23	Ohio	35.2
10	Oklahoma	38.0
37	Oregon	32.8
35	Pennsylvania	33.1
41	Rhode Island	32.3
23	South Carolina	35.2
26	South Dakota	35.0
38	Tennessee	32.7
1	Texas	41.0
2	Utah	40.4
8	Vermont	38.4
5	Virginia	38.6
31	Washington	33.3
20	West Virginia	35.7
14	Wisconsin	37.0
33	Wyoming	33.2

RANK ORDER

RANK	STATE	PERCENT
1	Texas	41.0
2	Utah	40.4
3	Michigan	39.1
4	Nebraska	39.0
5	Georgia	38.6
5	Virginia	38.6
7	New Hampshire	38.5
8	Vermont	38.4
9	Maryland	38.2
10	Oklahoma	38.0
11	New Jersey	37.8
12	Iowa	37.6
13	Indiana	37.2
14	Kansas	37.0
14	Wisconsin	37.0
16	Arkansas	36.6
17	New Mexico	36.5
18	Missouri	36.3
19	Delaware	36.2
20	West Virginia	35.7
21	Idaho	35.6
22	Montana	35.5
23	Illinois	35.2
23	Ohio	35.2
23	South Carolina	35.2
26	South Dakota	35.0
27	Arizona	34.8
28	North Carolina	34.3
29	Alabama	33.8
30	North Dakota	33.7
31	Colorado	33.3
31	Washington	33.3
33	Mississippi	33.2
33	Wyoming	33.2
35	Pennsylvania	33.1
36	Louisiana	32.9
37	Oregon	32.8
38	Tennessee	32.7
39	California	32.6
40	Connecticut	32.4
41	Minnesota	32.3
41	Rhode Island	32.3
43	Kentucky	31.9
44	Massachusetts	31.7
45	Maine	31.3
45	Nevada	31.3
47	Florida	29.6
47	New York	29.6
49	Hawaii	27.2
50	Alaska	25.0
	District of Columbia	19.0

Source: Morgan Quitno Press using data from U.S. Bureau of the Census, Governments Division
"State and Local Government Finances: 2002 Census" (http://www.census.gov/govs/www/estimate02.html)
*Direct general expenditures for higher, secondary, elementary and "other" education as a percent of all direct general expenditures. Includes capital outlays.

Elementary and Secondary Education Expenditures by State and Local Governments in 2002
National Total = $411,072,926,000*

RANK	STATE	EXPENDITURES	% of USA
26	Alabama	$5,089,034,000	1.2%
43	Alaska	1,498,827,000	0.4%
23	Arizona	5,769,877,000	1.4%
33	Arkansas	2,951,007,000	0.7%
1	California	53,202,893,000	12.9%
22	Colorado	5,876,447,000	1.4%
21	Connecticut	5,959,827,000	1.4%
45	Delaware	1,203,692,000	0.3%
4	Florida	18,616,807,000	4.5%
10	Georgia	12,322,448,000	3.0%
44	Hawaii	1,442,094,000	0.4%
41	Idaho	1,630,585,000	0.4%
5	Illinois	17,940,444,000	4.4%
17	Indiana	7,988,381,000	1.9%
30	Iowa	3,803,645,000	0.9%
31	Kansas	3,454,002,000	0.8%
29	Kentucky	3,896,402,000	0.9%
25	Louisiana	5,223,210,000	1.3%
40	Maine	1,802,826,000	0.4%
16	Maryland	7,995,206,000	1.9%
12	Massachusetts	10,260,894,000	2.5%
9	Michigan	15,985,000,000	3.9%
18	Minnesota	7,770,097,000	1.9%
32	Mississippi	2,952,675,000	0.7%
19	Missouri	7,388,110,000	1.8%
46	Montana	1,132,350,000	0.3%
37	Nebraska	2,479,479,000	0.6%
35	Nevada	2,774,848,000	0.7%
39	New Hampshire	1,809,045,000	0.4%
8	New Jersey	16,009,247,000	3.9%
36	New Mexico	2,506,800,000	0.6%
2	New York	38,283,816,000	9.3%
13	North Carolina	9,600,354,000	2.3%
50	North Dakota	748,686,000	0.2%
6	Ohio	16,494,612,000	4.0%
28	Oklahoma	4,384,386,000	1.1%
27	Oregon	4,806,560,000	1.2%
7	Pennsylvania	16,451,546,000	4.0%
42	Rhode Island	1,574,975,000	0.4%
24	South Carolina	5,756,399,000	1.4%
47	South Dakota	941,262,000	0.2%
20	Tennessee	6,152,499,000	1.5%
3	Texas	32,071,684,000	7.8%
34	Utah	2,845,270,000	0.7%
48	Vermont	936,676,000	0.2%
11	Virginia	10,400,990,000	2.5%
15	Washington	8,190,612,000	2.0%
38	West Virginia	2,279,292,000	0.6%
14	Wisconsin	8,464,946,000	2.1%
49	Wyoming	856,713,000	0.2%

RANK ORDER

RANK	STATE	EXPENDITURES	% of USA
1	California	$53,202,893,000	12.9%
2	New York	38,283,816,000	9.3%
3	Texas	32,071,684,000	7.8%
4	Florida	18,616,807,000	4.5%
5	Illinois	17,940,444,000	4.4%
6	Ohio	16,494,612,000	4.0%
7	Pennsylvania	16,451,546,000	4.0%
8	New Jersey	16,009,247,000	3.9%
9	Michigan	15,985,000,000	3.9%
10	Georgia	12,322,448,000	3.0%
11	Virginia	10,400,990,000	2.5%
12	Massachusetts	10,260,894,000	2.5%
13	North Carolina	9,600,354,000	2.3%
14	Wisconsin	8,464,946,000	2.1%
15	Washington	8,190,612,000	2.0%
16	Maryland	7,995,206,000	1.9%
17	Indiana	7,988,381,000	1.9%
18	Minnesota	7,770,097,000	1.9%
19	Missouri	7,388,110,000	1.8%
20	Tennessee	6,152,499,000	1.5%
21	Connecticut	5,959,827,000	1.4%
22	Colorado	5,876,447,000	1.4%
23	Arizona	5,769,877,000	1.4%
24	South Carolina	5,756,399,000	1.4%
25	Louisiana	5,223,210,000	1.3%
26	Alabama	5,089,034,000	1.2%
27	Oregon	4,806,560,000	1.2%
28	Oklahoma	4,384,386,000	1.1%
29	Kentucky	3,896,402,000	0.9%
30	Iowa	3,803,645,000	0.9%
31	Kansas	3,454,002,000	0.8%
32	Mississippi	2,952,675,000	0.7%
33	Arkansas	2,951,007,000	0.7%
34	Utah	2,845,270,000	0.7%
35	Nevada	2,774,848,000	0.7%
36	New Mexico	2,506,800,000	0.6%
37	Nebraska	2,479,479,000	0.6%
38	West Virginia	2,279,292,000	0.6%
39	New Hampshire	1,809,045,000	0.4%
40	Maine	1,802,826,000	0.4%
41	Idaho	1,630,585,000	0.4%
42	Rhode Island	1,574,975,000	0.4%
43	Alaska	1,498,827,000	0.4%
44	Hawaii	1,442,094,000	0.4%
45	Delaware	1,203,692,000	0.3%
46	Montana	1,132,350,000	0.3%
47	South Dakota	941,262,000	0.2%
48	Vermont	936,676,000	0.2%
49	Wyoming	856,713,000	0.2%
50	North Dakota	748,686,000	0.2%
	District of Columbia	1,095,449,000	0.3%

ALPHA ORDER

Source: U.S. Bureau of the Census, Governments Division
"State and Local Government Finances: 2002 Census" (http://www.census.gov/govs/www/estimate02.html)
*Direct general expenditures. Includes capital outlays.

Per Capita State and Local Government Expenditures for Elementary and Secondary Education in 2002
National Per Capita = $1,428*

ALPHA ORDER

RANK	STATE	PER CAPITA
44	Alabama	$1,136
1	Alaska	2,339
48	Arizona	1,061
46	Arkansas	1,090
10	California	1,521
28	Colorado	1,306
4	Connecticut	1,723
12	Delaware	1,493
45	Florida	1,116
17	Georgia	1,443
41	Hawaii	1,168
39	Idaho	1,214
20	Illinois	1,426
30	Indiana	1,297
31	Iowa	1,296
33	Kansas	1,273
50	Kentucky	953
42	Louisiana	1,167
23	Maine	1,389
15	Maryland	1,469
6	Massachusetts	1,600
7	Michigan	1,592
9	Minnesota	1,546
49	Mississippi	1,030
29	Missouri	1,301
36	Montana	1,243
18	Nebraska	1,436
32	Nevada	1,280
21	New Hampshire	1,418
3	New Jersey	1,866
25	New Mexico	1,351
2	New York	1,999
43	North Carolina	1,155
40	North Dakota	1,181
16	Ohio	1,446
35	Oklahoma	1,257
24	Oregon	1,364
27	Pennsylvania	1,334
14	Rhode Island	1,473
22	South Carolina	1,402
37	South Dakota	1,238
47	Tennessee	1,062
13	Texas	1,476
38	Utah	1,227
11	Vermont	1,519
19	Virginia	1,430
26	Washington	1,350
34	West Virginia	1,263
8	Wisconsin	1,556
5	Wyoming	1,716

RANK ORDER

RANK	STATE	PER CAPITA
1	Alaska	$2,339
2	New York	1,999
3	New Jersey	1,866
4	Connecticut	1,723
5	Wyoming	1,716
6	Massachusetts	1,600
7	Michigan	1,592
8	Wisconsin	1,556
9	Minnesota	1,546
10	California	1,521
11	Vermont	1,519
12	Delaware	1,493
13	Texas	1,476
14	Rhode Island	1,473
15	Maryland	1,469
16	Ohio	1,446
17	Georgia	1,443
18	Nebraska	1,436
19	Virginia	1,430
20	Illinois	1,426
21	New Hampshire	1,418
22	South Carolina	1,402
23	Maine	1,389
24	Oregon	1,364
25	New Mexico	1,351
26	Washington	1,350
27	Pennsylvania	1,334
28	Colorado	1,306
29	Missouri	1,301
30	Indiana	1,297
31	Iowa	1,296
32	Nevada	1,280
33	Kansas	1,273
34	West Virginia	1,263
35	Oklahoma	1,257
36	Montana	1,243
37	South Dakota	1,238
38	Utah	1,227
39	Idaho	1,214
40	North Dakota	1,181
41	Hawaii	1,168
42	Louisiana	1,167
43	North Carolina	1,155
44	Alabama	1,136
45	Florida	1,116
46	Arkansas	1,090
47	Tennessee	1,062
48	Arizona	1,061
49	Mississippi	1,030
50	Kentucky	953
	District of Columbia	1,940

Source: Morgan Quitno Press using data from U.S. Bureau of the Census, Governments Division
    "State and Local Government Finances: 2002 Census" (http://www.census.gov/govs/www/estimate02.html)
*Direct general expenditures. Includes capital outlays.

Expenditures for Elementary and Secondary Education
As a Percent of All State and Local Government Expenditures in 2002
National Percent = 23.8%*

ALPHA ORDER

RANK	STATE	PERCENT
45	Alabama	20.7
49	Alaska	17.8
26	Arizona	22.8
28	Arkansas	22.6
28	California	22.6
38	Colorado	21.7
11	Connecticut	24.6
30	Delaware	22.5
41	Florida	21.4
4	Georgia	27.4
50	Hawaii	17.4
20	Idaho	24.0
15	Illinois	24.3
14	Indiana	24.4
35	Iowa	22.1
24	Kansas	23.2
48	Kentucky	18.0
40	Louisiana	21.5
27	Maine	22.7
9	Maryland	25.1
16	Massachusetts	24.2
6	Michigan	26.3
33	Minnesota	22.2
47	Mississippi	19.2
7	Missouri	25.4
31	Montana	22.4
7	Nebraska	25.4
22	Nevada	23.6
3	New Hampshire	28.5
1	New Jersey	29.4
37	New Mexico	21.9
21	New York	23.8
39	North Carolina	21.6
46	North Dakota	19.3
11	Ohio	24.6
16	Oklahoma	24.2
44	Oregon	20.9
31	Pennsylvania	22.4
23	Rhode Island	23.3
16	South Carolina	24.2
16	South Dakota	24.2
42	Tennessee	21.3
2	Texas	28.7
35	Utah	22.1
11	Vermont	24.6
5	Virginia	26.5
43	Washington	21.2
25	West Virginia	23.1
10	Wisconsin	24.9
33	Wyoming	22.2

RANK ORDER

RANK	STATE	PERCENT
1	New Jersey	29.4
2	Texas	28.7
3	New Hampshire	28.5
4	Georgia	27.4
5	Virginia	26.5
6	Michigan	26.3
7	Missouri	25.4
7	Nebraska	25.4
9	Maryland	25.1
10	Wisconsin	24.9
11	Connecticut	24.6
11	Ohio	24.6
11	Vermont	24.6
14	Indiana	24.4
15	Illinois	24.3
16	Massachusetts	24.2
16	Oklahoma	24.2
16	South Carolina	24.2
16	South Dakota	24.2
20	Idaho	24.0
21	New York	23.8
22	Nevada	23.6
23	Rhode Island	23.3
24	Kansas	23.2
25	West Virginia	23.1
26	Arizona	22.8
27	Maine	22.7
28	Arkansas	22.6
28	California	22.6
30	Delaware	22.5
31	Montana	22.4
31	Pennsylvania	22.4
33	Minnesota	22.2
33	Wyoming	22.2
35	Iowa	22.1
35	Utah	22.1
37	New Mexico	21.9
38	Colorado	21.7
39	North Carolina	21.6
40	Louisiana	21.5
41	Florida	21.4
42	Tennessee	21.3
43	Washington	21.2
44	Oregon	20.9
45	Alabama	20.7
46	North Dakota	19.3
47	Mississippi	19.2
48	Kentucky	18.0
49	Alaska	17.8
50	Hawaii	17.4

| | District of Columbia | 17.7 |

Source: Morgan Quitno Press using data from U.S. Bureau of the Census, Governments Division
     "State and Local Government Finances: 2002 Census" (http://www.census.gov/govs/www/estimate02.html)
*Direct general expenditures for elementary and secondary education as a percent of all direct general
expenditures. Includes capital outlays.

Estimated Per Pupil Public Elementary and Secondary School Current Expenditures in 2005
National Per Pupil = $8,554*

ALPHA ORDER

RANK	STATE	PER PUPIL
42	Alabama	$6,993
11	Alaska	10,042
49	Arizona	5,474
48	Arkansas	6,202
29	California	7,815
25	Colorado	8,095
2	Connecticut	11,893
9	Delaware	10,329
40	Florida	7,040
22	Georgia	8,500
23	Hawaii	8,356
44	Idaho	6,743
8	Illinois	10,439
21	Indiana	8,734
35	Iowa	7,477
33	Kansas	7,558
30	Kentucky	7,719
34	Louisiana	7,552
6	Maine	10,736
13	Maryland	9,762
5	Massachusetts	11,322
19	Michigan	8,909
18	Minnesota	9,239
46	Mississippi	6,452
36	Missouri	7,452
26	Montana	8,025
32	Nebraska	7,617
39	Nevada	7,098
16	New Hampshire	9,566
4	New Jersey	11,502
37	New Mexico	7,227
1	New York	12,879
43	North Carolina	6,958
41	North Dakota	7,033
15	Ohio	9,573
47	Oklahoma	6,269
27	Oregon	7,913
14	Pennsylvania	9,638
7	Rhode Island	10,641
24	South Carolina	8,161
31	South Dakota	7,636
45	Tennessee	6,725
38	Texas	7,140
50	Utah	5,245
3	Vermont	11,641
20	Virginia	8,847
28	Washington	7,858
17	West Virginia	9,448
12	Wisconsin	9,881
10	Wyoming	10,198

RANK ORDER

RANK	STATE	PER PUPIL
1	New York	$12,879
2	Connecticut	11,893
3	Vermont	11,641
4	New Jersey	11,502
5	Massachusetts	11,322
6	Maine	10,736
7	Rhode Island	10,641
8	Illinois	10,439
9	Delaware	10,329
10	Wyoming	10,198
11	Alaska	10,042
12	Wisconsin	9,881
13	Maryland	9,762
14	Pennsylvania	9,638
15	Ohio	9,573
16	New Hampshire	9,566
17	West Virginia	9,448
18	Minnesota	9,239
19	Michigan	8,909
20	Virginia	8,847
21	Indiana	8,734
22	Georgia	8,500
23	Hawaii	8,356
24	South Carolina	8,161
25	Colorado	8,095
26	Montana	8,025
27	Oregon	7,913
28	Washington	7,858
29	California	7,815
30	Kentucky	7,719
31	South Dakota	7,636
32	Nebraska	7,617
33	Kansas	7,558
34	Louisiana	7,552
35	Iowa	7,477
36	Missouri	7,452
37	New Mexico	7,227
38	Texas	7,140
39	Nevada	7,098
40	Florida	7,040
41	North Dakota	7,033
42	Alabama	6,993
43	North Carolina	6,958
44	Idaho	6,743
45	Tennessee	6,725
46	Mississippi	6,452
47	Oklahoma	6,269
48	Arkansas	6,202
49	Arizona	5,474
50	Utah	5,245
	District of Columbia	15,073

Source: National Education Association, Washington, D.C.
     "Rankings & Estimates" (Copyright © 2005, NEA, used with permission)
*Estimates for school year 2004-05. Based on student membership.

Higher Education Expenditures by State and Local Governments in 2002

National Total = $156,810,252,000*

ALPHA ORDER

RANK	STATE	EXPENDITURES	% of USA
20	Alabama	$2,720,196,000	1.7%
46	Alaska	487,283,000	0.3%
21	Arizona	2,702,906,000	1.7%
35	Arkansas	1,438,001,000	0.9%
1	California	20,375,753,000	13.0%
19	Colorado	2,856,236,000	1.8%
33	Connecticut	1,554,972,000	1.0%
41	Delaware	629,493,000	0.4%
7	Florida	5,791,614,000	3.7%
13	Georgia	3,890,955,000	2.5%
39	Hawaii	792,210,000	0.5%
40	Idaho	692,076,000	0.4%
5	Illinois	6,506,274,000	4.1%
15	Indiana	3,614,096,000	2.3%
26	Iowa	2,327,927,000	1.5%
32	Kansas	1,770,463,000	1.1%
25	Kentucky	2,402,629,000	1.5%
30	Louisiana	2,092,465,000	1.3%
43	Maine	559,307,000	0.4%
16	Maryland	3,531,280,000	2.3%
24	Massachusetts	2,516,945,000	1.6%
4	Michigan	7,296,108,000	4.7%
18	Minnesota	2,946,707,000	1.9%
31	Mississippi	1,841,358,000	1.2%
22	Missouri	2,645,247,000	1.7%
45	Montana	506,367,000	0.3%
36	Nebraska	1,192,051,000	0.8%
38	Nevada	810,417,000	0.5%
42	New Hampshire	560,879,000	0.4%
11	New Jersey	4,027,545,000	2.6%
34	New Mexico	1,461,831,000	0.9%
3	New York	7,982,926,000	5.1%
9	North Carolina	5,147,632,000	3.3%
44	North Dakota	510,270,000	0.3%
6	Ohio	5,833,807,000	3.7%
27	Oklahoma	2,227,866,000	1.4%
23	Oregon	2,538,085,000	1.6%
8	Pennsylvania	5,770,486,000	3.7%
47	Rhode Island	479,719,000	0.3%
29	South Carolina	2,130,103,000	1.4%
49	South Dakota	362,050,000	0.2%
17	Tennessee	2,957,768,000	1.9%
2	Texas	12,481,739,000	8.0%
28	Utah	2,131,325,000	1.4%
48	Vermont	428,518,000	0.3%
10	Virginia	4,154,135,000	2.6%
12	Washington	3,982,261,000	2.5%
37	West Virginia	1,000,161,000	0.6%
14	Wisconsin	3,710,116,000	2.4%
50	Wyoming	360,402,000	0.2%

RANK ORDER

RANK	STATE	EXPENDITURES	% of USA
1	California	$20,375,753,000	13.0%
2	Texas	12,481,739,000	8.0%
3	New York	7,982,926,000	5.1%
4	Michigan	7,296,108,000	4.7%
5	Illinois	6,506,274,000	4.1%
6	Ohio	5,833,807,000	3.7%
7	Florida	5,791,614,000	3.7%
8	Pennsylvania	5,770,486,000	3.7%
9	North Carolina	5,147,632,000	3.3%
10	Virginia	4,154,135,000	2.6%
11	New Jersey	4,027,545,000	2.6%
12	Washington	3,982,261,000	2.5%
13	Georgia	3,890,955,000	2.5%
14	Wisconsin	3,710,116,000	2.4%
15	Indiana	3,614,096,000	2.3%
16	Maryland	3,531,280,000	2.3%
17	Tennessee	2,957,768,000	1.9%
18	Minnesota	2,946,707,000	1.9%
19	Colorado	2,856,236,000	1.8%
20	Alabama	2,720,196,000	1.7%
21	Arizona	2,702,906,000	1.7%
22	Missouri	2,645,247,000	1.7%
23	Oregon	2,538,085,000	1.6%
24	Massachusetts	2,516,945,000	1.6%
25	Kentucky	2,402,629,000	1.5%
26	Iowa	2,327,927,000	1.5%
27	Oklahoma	2,227,866,000	1.4%
28	Utah	2,131,325,000	1.4%
29	South Carolina	2,130,103,000	1.4%
30	Louisiana	2,092,465,000	1.3%
31	Mississippi	1,841,358,000	1.2%
32	Kansas	1,770,463,000	1.1%
33	Connecticut	1,554,972,000	1.0%
34	New Mexico	1,461,831,000	0.9%
35	Arkansas	1,438,001,000	0.9%
36	Nebraska	1,192,051,000	0.8%
37	West Virginia	1,000,161,000	0.6%
38	Nevada	810,417,000	0.5%
39	Hawaii	792,210,000	0.5%
40	Idaho	692,076,000	0.4%
41	Delaware	629,493,000	0.4%
42	New Hampshire	560,879,000	0.4%
43	Maine	559,307,000	0.4%
44	North Dakota	510,270,000	0.3%
45	Montana	506,367,000	0.3%
46	Alaska	487,283,000	0.3%
47	Rhode Island	479,719,000	0.3%
48	Vermont	428,518,000	0.3%
49	South Dakota	362,050,000	0.2%
50	Wyoming	360,402,000	0.2%
	District of Columbia	79,292,000	0.1%

Source: U.S. Bureau of the Census, Governments Division
   "State and Local Government Finances: 2002 Census" (http://www.census.gov/govs/www/estimate02.html)
*Direct general expenditures. Includes capital outlays.

Per Capita State and Local Government Expenditures for Higher Education in 2002
National Per Capita = $545*

ALPHA ORDER

RANK	STATE	PER CAPITA
21	Alabama	$607
6	Alaska	760
36	Arizona	497
30	Arkansas	531
25	California	582
19	Colorado	635
43	Connecticut	450
5	Delaware	781
50	Florida	347
42	Georgia	456
16	Hawaii	642
33	Idaho	515
32	Illinois	517
22	Indiana	587
3	Iowa	793
14	Kansas	653
22	Kentucky	587
40	Louisiana	467
46	Maine	431
15	Maryland	649
48	Massachusetts	393
7	Michigan	727
24	Minnesota	586
16	Mississippi	642
41	Missouri	466
28	Montana	556
11	Nebraska	690
49	Nevada	374
45	New Hampshire	440
38	New Jersey	470
4	New Mexico	788
47	New York	417
20	North Carolina	619
2	North Dakota	805
34	Ohio	511
18	Oklahoma	639
9	Oregon	720
39	Pennsylvania	468
44	Rhode Island	449
31	South Carolina	519
37	South Dakota	476
34	Tennessee	511
26	Texas	575
1	Utah	919
10	Vermont	695
27	Virginia	571
13	Washington	656
29	West Virginia	554
12	Wisconsin	682
8	Wyoming	722

RANK ORDER

RANK	STATE	PER CAPITA
1	Utah	$919
2	North Dakota	805
3	Iowa	793
4	New Mexico	788
5	Delaware	781
6	Alaska	760
7	Michigan	727
8	Wyoming	722
9	Oregon	720
10	Vermont	695
11	Nebraska	690
12	Wisconsin	682
13	Washington	656
14	Kansas	653
15	Maryland	649
16	Hawaii	642
16	Mississippi	642
18	Oklahoma	639
19	Colorado	635
20	North Carolina	619
21	Alabama	607
22	Indiana	587
22	Kentucky	587
24	Minnesota	586
25	California	582
26	Texas	575
27	Virginia	571
28	Montana	556
29	West Virginia	554
30	Arkansas	531
31	South Carolina	519
32	Illinois	517
33	Idaho	515
34	Ohio	511
34	Tennessee	511
36	Arizona	497
37	South Dakota	476
38	New Jersey	470
39	Pennsylvania	468
40	Louisiana	467
41	Missouri	466
42	Georgia	456
43	Connecticut	450
44	Rhode Island	449
45	New Hampshire	440
46	Maine	431
47	New York	417
48	Massachusetts	393
49	Nevada	374
50	Florida	347
	District of Columbia	140

Source: Morgan Quitno Press using data from U.S. Bureau of the Census, Governments Division
   "State and Local Government Finances: 2002 Census" (http://www.census.gov/govs/www/estimate02.html)
*Direct general expenditures. Includes capital outlays.

Expenditures for Higher Education as a Percent
Of All State and Local Government Expenditures in 2002
National Percent = 9.1%*

ALPHA ORDER

RANK	STATE	PERCENT		RANK	STATE	PERCENT
14	Alabama	11.1		1	Utah	16.6
49	Alaska	5.8		2	Iowa	13.5
21	Arizona	10.7		3	North Dakota	13.1
17	Arkansas	11.0		4	New Mexico	12.8
38	California	8.6		5	Oklahoma	12.3
23	Colorado	10.5		6	Nebraska	12.2
47	Connecticut	6.4		7	Michigan	12.0
10	Delaware	11.8		7	Mississippi	12.0
46	Florida	6.7		9	Kansas	11.9
36	Georgia	8.7		10	Delaware	11.8
29	Hawaii	9.6		11	North Carolina	11.6
25	Idaho	10.2		12	Vermont	11.3
34	Illinois	8.8		13	Texas	11.2
17	Indiana	11.0		14	Alabama	11.1
2	Iowa	13.5		14	Kentucky	11.1
9	Kansas	11.9		14	Maryland	11.1
14	Kentucky	11.1		17	Arkansas	11.0
38	Louisiana	8.6		17	Indiana	11.0
44	Maine	7.0		17	Oregon	11.0
14	Maryland	11.1		20	Wisconsin	10.9
48	Massachusetts	5.9		21	Arizona	10.7
7	Michigan	12.0		22	Virginia	10.6
40	Minnesota	8.4		23	Colorado	10.5
7	Mississippi	12.0		24	Washington	10.3
32	Missouri	9.1		25	Idaho	10.2
28	Montana	10.0		25	Tennessee	10.2
6	Nebraska	12.2		25	West Virginia	10.2
45	Nevada	6.9		28	Montana	10.0
34	New Hampshire	8.8		29	Hawaii	9.6
42	New Jersey	7.4		30	Wyoming	9.4
4	New Mexico	12.8		31	South Dakota	9.3
50	New York	5.0		32	Missouri	9.1
11	North Carolina	11.6		33	South Carolina	8.9
3	North Dakota	13.1		34	Illinois	8.8
36	Ohio	8.7		34	New Hampshire	8.8
5	Oklahoma	12.3		36	Georgia	8.7
17	Oregon	11.0		36	Ohio	8.7
41	Pennsylvania	7.9		38	California	8.6
43	Rhode Island	7.1		38	Louisiana	8.6
33	South Carolina	8.9		40	Minnesota	8.4
31	South Dakota	9.3		41	Pennsylvania	7.9
25	Tennessee	10.2		42	New Jersey	7.4
13	Texas	11.2		43	Rhode Island	7.1
1	Utah	16.6		44	Maine	7.0
12	Vermont	11.3		45	Nevada	6.9
22	Virginia	10.6		46	Florida	6.7
24	Washington	10.3		47	Connecticut	6.4
25	West Virginia	10.2		48	Massachusetts	5.9
20	Wisconsin	10.9		49	Alaska	5.8
30	Wyoming	9.4		50	New York	5.0

RANK ORDER

	District of Columbia	1.3

Source: Morgan Quitno Press using data from U.S. Bureau of the Census, Governments Division
    "State and Local Government Finances: 2002 Census" (http://www.census.gov/govs/www/estimate02.html)
*Direct general expenditures for higher education as a percent of all direct general expenditures. Includes capital outlays.

Average Faculty Salary at Institutions of Higher Education in 2004

National Average = $62,615*

ALPHA ORDER

RANK	STATE	AVERAGE SALARY
42	Alabama	$51,513
34	Alaska	54,697
11	Arizona	64,448
49	Arkansas	47,079
2	California	75,179
24	Colorado	58,529
3	Connecticut	75,133
5	Delaware	71,490
23	Florida	58,537
22	Georgia	59,211
18	Hawaii	60,457
45	Idaho	49,272
10	Illinois	64,468
17	Indiana	60,502
27	Iowa	56,664
37	Kansas	53,028
40	Kentucky	52,665
39	Louisiana	52,666
28	Maine	56,619
14	Maryland	63,328
1	Massachusetts	76,676
9	Michigan	66,625
19	Minnesota	60,409
48	Mississippi	47,623
30	Missouri	56,277
44	Montana	49,332
33	Nebraska	54,715
12	Nevada	64,144
13	New Hampshire	63,882
4	New Jersey	74,707
38	New Mexico	52,860
7	New York	70,431
35	North Carolina	54,163
50	North Dakota	45,396
16	Ohio	61,088
43	Oklahoma	50,109
31	Oregon	55,343
8	Pennsylvania	67,676
6	Rhode Island	70,647
41	South Carolina	51,950
47	South Dakota	47,645
32	Tennessee	54,819
25	Texas	57,134
20	Utah	60,325
26	Vermont	56,765
21	Virginia	59,897
29	Washington	56,596
46	West Virginia	48,719
15	Wisconsin	61,629
36	Wyoming	53,363

RANK ORDER

RANK	STATE	AVERAGE SALARY
1	Massachusetts	$76,676
2	California	75,179
3	Connecticut	75,133
4	New Jersey	74,707
5	Delaware	71,490
6	Rhode Island	70,647
7	New York	70,431
8	Pennsylvania	67,676
9	Michigan	66,625
10	Illinois	64,468
11	Arizona	64,448
12	Nevada	64,144
13	New Hampshire	63,882
14	Maryland	63,328
15	Wisconsin	61,629
16	Ohio	61,088
17	Indiana	60,502
18	Hawaii	60,457
19	Minnesota	60,409
20	Utah	60,325
21	Virginia	59,897
22	Georgia	59,211
23	Florida	58,537
24	Colorado	58,529
25	Texas	57,134
26	Vermont	56,765
27	Iowa	56,664
28	Maine	56,619
29	Washington	56,596
30	Missouri	56,277
31	Oregon	55,343
32	Tennessee	54,819
33	Nebraska	54,715
34	Alaska	54,697
35	North Carolina	54,163
36	Wyoming	53,363
37	Kansas	53,028
38	New Mexico	52,860
39	Louisiana	52,666
40	Kentucky	52,665
41	South Carolina	51,950
42	Alabama	51,513
43	Oklahoma	50,109
44	Montana	49,332
45	Idaho	49,272
46	West Virginia	48,719
47	South Dakota	47,645
48	Mississippi	47,623
49	Arkansas	47,079
50	North Dakota	45,396
	District of Columbia	74,472

Source: U.S. Department of Education, National Center for Education Statistics
    "Digest of Education Statistics 2004" (NCES 2006005, October 2005)
*For 2003-2004 school year. For full-time instructional faculty on 9-month contracts at four-year and two-year public and private degree-granting institutions.

Average Student Costs at Public Institutions of Higher Education in 2004

National Average = $10,720*

ALPHA ORDER				RANK ORDER		
RANK	**STATE**	**AVERAGE COSTS**		**RANK**	**STATE**	**AVERAGE COSTS**
34	Alabama	$8,983		1	New Jersey	$15,109
26	Alaska	10,118		2	Vermont	14,766
25	Arizona	10,140		3	New Hampshire	13,852
44	Arkansas	8,349		4	Pennsylvania	13,754
11	California	12,275		5	Maryland	13,419
27	Colorado	9,751		6	Ohio	13,319
7	Connecticut	12,772		7	Connecticut	12,772
10	Delaware	12,496		8	Rhode Island	12,763
30	Florida	9,207		9	South Carolina	12,710
32	Georgia	9,090		10	Delaware	12,496
37	Hawaii	8,760		11	California	12,275
46	Idaho	8,091		12	Massachusetts	12,250
15	Illinois	11,804		13	Michigan	12,208
16	Indiana	11,637		14	New York	12,002
21	Iowa	10,878		15	Illinois	11,804
39	Kansas	8,604		16	Indiana	11,637
41	Kentucky	8,521		17	Oregon	11,626
50	Louisiana	7,494		18	Washington	11,353
19	Maine	11,010		19	Maine	11,010
5	Maryland	13,419		20	Virginia	10,900
12	Massachusetts	12,250		21	Iowa	10,878
13	Michigan	12,208		22	Minnesota	10,845
22	Minnesota	10,845		23	Nevada	10,333
40	Mississippi	8,547		24	Missouri	10,320
24	Missouri	10,320		25	Arizona	10,140
29	Montana	9,348		26	Alaska	10,118
28	Nebraska	9,620		27	Colorado	9,751
23	Nevada	10,333		28	Nebraska	9,620
3	New Hampshire	13,852		29	Montana	9,348
1	New Jersey	15,109		30	Florida	9,207
45	New Mexico	8,238		31	Texas	9,202
14	New York	12,002		32	Georgia	9,090
36	North Carolina	8,805		33	Wisconsin	9,066
47	North Dakota	8,028		34	Alabama	8,983
6	Ohio	13,319		35	Tennessee	8,936
48	Oklahoma	7,901		36	North Carolina	8,805
17	Oregon	11,626		37	Hawaii	8,760
4	Pennsylvania	13,754		38	West Virginia	8,751
8	Rhode Island	12,763		39	Kansas	8,604
9	South Carolina	12,710		40	Mississippi	8,547
43	South Dakota	8,379		41	Kentucky	8,521
35	Tennessee	8,936		42	Wyoming	8,485
31	Texas	9,202		43	South Dakota	8,379
49	Utah	7,865		44	Arkansas	8,349
2	Vermont	14,766		45	New Mexico	8,238
20	Virginia	10,900		46	Idaho	8,091
18	Washington	11,353		47	North Dakota	8,028
38	West Virginia	8,751		48	Oklahoma	7,901
33	Wisconsin	9,066		49	Utah	7,865
42	Wyoming	8,485		50	Louisiana	7,494
					District of Columbia**	NA

Source: U.S. Department of Education, National Center for Education Statistics
   "Digest of Education Statistics 2004" (NCES 2006005, October 2005)
*Data for 2003-2004 school year. Based on average in-state tuition, room and board and fees for full-time students in public four-year institutions for an entire academic year.
**Not available.

Average Student Costs at Private Institutions of Higher Education in 2004

National Average = $25,204*

ALPHA ORDER				RANK ORDER		
RANK	STATE	AVERAGE COSTS		RANK	STATE	AVERAGE COSTS
43	Alabama	$16,452		1	Massachusetts	$33,719
40	Alaska	17,941		2	Connecticut	32,383
31	Arizona	19,035		3	Rhode Island	29,376
45	Arkansas	16,001		4	New York	29,294
8	California	28,222		5	Pennsylvania	29,050
11	Colorado	26,260		6	Maryland	28,961
2	Connecticut	32,383		7	New Hampshire	28,410
44	Delaware	16,408		8	California	28,222
23	Florida	22,723		9	New Jersey	28,011
21	Georgia	23,309		10	Maine	27,131
38	Hawaii	18,041		11	Colorado	26,260
48	Idaho	10,905		12	Oregon	26,074
14	Illinois	25,666		13	Louisiana	25,677
16	Indiana	25,151		14	Illinois	25,666
25	Iowa	22,121		15	Vermont	25,567
33	Kansas	18,607		16	Indiana	25,151
37	Kentucky	18,142		17	Washington	24,767
13	Louisiana	25,677		18	Minnesota	24,635
10	Maine	27,131		19	Ohio	24,354
6	Maryland	28,961		20	Wisconsin	23,340
1	Massachusetts	33,719		21	Georgia	23,309
36	Michigan	18,232		22	North Carolina	23,169
18	Minnesota	24,635		23	Florida	22,723
46	Mississippi	15,973		24	Virginia	22,628
28	Missouri	20,837		25	Iowa	22,121
42	Montana	16,635		26	Tennessee	21,170
30	Nebraska	19,207		27	Texas	20,892
35	Nevada	18,354		28	Missouri	20,837
7	New Hampshire	28,410		29	South Carolina	20,189
9	New Jersey	28,011		30	Nebraska	19,207
34	New Mexico	18,501		31	Arizona	19,035
4	New York	29,294		32	West Virginia	19,029
22	North Carolina	23,169		33	Kansas	18,607
47	North Dakota	13,476		34	New Mexico	18,501
19	Ohio	24,354		35	Nevada	18,354
39	Oklahoma	17,999		36	Michigan	18,232
12	Oregon	26,074		37	Kentucky	18,142
5	Pennsylvania	29,050		38	Hawaii	18,041
3	Rhode Island	29,376		39	Oklahoma	17,999
29	South Carolina	20,189		40	Alaska	17,941
41	South Dakota	17,001		41	South Dakota	17,001
26	Tennessee	21,170		42	Montana	16,635
27	Texas	20,892		43	Alabama	16,452
49	Utah	9,993		44	Delaware	16,408
15	Vermont	25,567		45	Arkansas	16,001
24	Virginia	22,628		46	Mississippi	15,973
17	Washington	24,767		47	North Dakota	13,476
32	West Virginia	19,029		48	Idaho	10,905
20	Wisconsin	23,340		49	Utah	9,993
NA	Wyoming**	NA		NA	Wyoming**	NA
					District of Columbia	29,509

Source: U.S. Department of Education, National Center for Education Statistics
    "Digest of Education Statistics 2004" (NCES 2006005, October 2005)
*Data for 2003-2004 school year. Based on average in-state tuition, room and board and fees for full-time students
in private four-year institutions for an entire academic year.
**Not available or not applicable.

Institutions of Higher Education in 2004

National Total = 4,236 Institutions*

ALPHA ORDER

RANK	STATE	INSTITUTIONS	% of USA
20	Alabama	75	1.8%
50	Alaska	8	0.2%
21	Arizona	74	1.7%
31	Arkansas	47	1.1%
1	California	401	9.5%
21	Colorado	74	1.7%
32	Connecticut	45	1.1%
48	Delaware	10	0.2%
7	Florida	169	4.0%
9	Georgia	126	3.0%
44	Hawaii	20	0.5%
46	Idaho	14	0.3%
6	Illinois	173	4.1%
15	Indiana	101	2.4%
24	Iowa	63	1.5%
24	Kansas	63	1.5%
19	Kentucky	77	1.8%
17	Louisiana	90	2.1%
37	Maine	30	0.7%
27	Maryland	62	1.5%
11	Massachusetts	122	2.9%
13	Michigan	110	2.6%
12	Minnesota	113	2.7%
34	Mississippi	40	0.9%
10	Missouri	123	2.9%
42	Montana	23	0.5%
36	Nebraska	39	0.9%
45	Nevada	17	0.4%
41	New Hampshire	25	0.6%
29	New Jersey	58	1.4%
33	New Mexico	42	1.0%
2	New York	307	7.2%
8	North Carolina	130	3.1%
43	North Dakota	21	0.5%
5	Ohio	187	4.4%
30	Oklahoma	53	1.3%
28	Oregon	59	1.4%
3	Pennsylvania	262	6.2%
47	Rhode Island	13	0.3%
24	South Carolina	63	1.5%
40	South Dakota	26	0.6%
16	Tennessee	95	2.2%
4	Texas	208	4.9%
38	Utah	28	0.7%
39	Vermont	27	0.6%
14	Virginia	104	2.5%
18	Washington	81	1.9%
34	West Virginia	40	0.9%
23	Wisconsin	68	1.6%
49	Wyoming	9	0.2%

RANK ORDER

RANK	STATE	INSTITUTIONS	% of USA
1	California	401	9.5%
2	New York	307	7.2%
3	Pennsylvania	262	6.2%
4	Texas	208	4.9%
5	Ohio	187	4.4%
6	Illinois	173	4.1%
7	Florida	169	4.0%
8	North Carolina	130	3.1%
9	Georgia	126	3.0%
10	Missouri	123	2.9%
11	Massachusetts	122	2.9%
12	Minnesota	113	2.7%
13	Michigan	110	2.6%
14	Virginia	104	2.5%
15	Indiana	101	2.4%
16	Tennessee	95	2.2%
17	Louisiana	90	2.1%
18	Washington	81	1.9%
19	Kentucky	77	1.8%
20	Alabama	75	1.8%
21	Arizona	74	1.7%
21	Colorado	74	1.7%
23	Wisconsin	68	1.6%
24	Iowa	63	1.5%
24	Kansas	63	1.5%
24	South Carolina	63	1.5%
27	Maryland	62	1.5%
28	Oregon	59	1.4%
29	New Jersey	58	1.4%
30	Oklahoma	53	1.3%
31	Arkansas	47	1.1%
32	Connecticut	45	1.1%
33	New Mexico	42	1.0%
34	Mississippi	40	0.9%
34	West Virginia	40	0.9%
36	Nebraska	39	0.9%
37	Maine	30	0.7%
38	Utah	28	0.7%
39	Vermont	27	0.6%
40	South Dakota	26	0.6%
41	New Hampshire	25	0.6%
42	Montana	23	0.5%
43	North Dakota	21	0.5%
44	Hawaii	20	0.5%
45	Nevada	17	0.4%
46	Idaho	14	0.3%
47	Rhode Island	13	0.3%
48	Delaware	10	0.2%
49	Wyoming	9	0.2%
50	Alaska	8	0.2%
	District of Columbia	16	0.4%

*Source: U.S. Department of Education, National Center for Education Statistics
"Digest of Education Statistics 2004" (NCES 2006005, October 2005)*
For 2003-04 school year. Consists of 2,530 four-year and 1,706 two-year public and private degree-granting institutions. Includes five U.S. Service Schools not shown by state.

Enrollment in Institutions of Higher Education in 2002

National Total = 16,611,711 Students*

ALPHA ORDER

RANK	STATE	STUDENTS	% of USA
23	Alabama	246,414	1.5%
50	Alaska	29,546	0.2%
12	Arizona	401,605	2.4%
34	Arkansas	127,372	0.8%
1	California	2,474,024	14.9%
21	Colorado	282,343	1.7%
32	Connecticut	170,606	1.0%
44	Delaware	49,228	0.3%
4	Florida	792,079	4.8%
13	Georgia	397,604	2.4%
42	Hawaii	65,368	0.4%
40	Idaho	72,072	0.4%
5	Illinois	776,622	4.7%
16	Indiana	342,064	2.1%
27	Iowa	202,546	1.2%
30	Kansas	188,049	1.1%
25	Kentucky	225,489	1.4%
24	Louisiana	232,140	1.4%
43	Maine	63,308	0.4%
20	Maryland	300,269	1.8%
10	Massachusetts	431,224	2.6%
7	Michigan	605,835	3.6%
19	Minnesota	323,791	1.9%
33	Mississippi	147,077	0.9%
15	Missouri	348,146	2.1%
47	Montana	45,111	0.3%
36	Nebraska	116,737	0.7%
37	Nevada	95,671	0.6%
41	New Hampshire	68,523	0.4%
14	New Jersey	361,733	2.2%
35	New Mexico	120,997	0.7%
3	New York	1,107,270	6.7%
9	North Carolina	447,335	2.7%
46	North Dakota	45,800	0.3%
8	Ohio	587,996	3.5%
29	Oklahoma	198,423	1.2%
26	Oregon	204,565	1.2%
6	Pennsylvania	654,826	3.9%
39	Rhode Island	77,417	0.5%
28	South Carolina	202,007	1.2%
45	South Dakota	47,751	0.3%
22	Tennessee	261,899	1.6%
2	Texas	1,152,369	6.9%
31	Utah	178,932	1.1%
48	Vermont	36,537	0.2%
11	Virginia	404,966	2.4%
17	Washington	338,820	2.0%
38	West Virginia	93,723	0.6%
18	Wisconsin	329,443	2.0%
49	Wyoming	32,605	0.2%

RANK ORDER

RANK	STATE	STUDENTS	% of USA
1	California	2,474,024	14.9%
2	Texas	1,152,369	6.9%
3	New York	1,107,270	6.7%
4	Florida	792,079	4.8%
5	Illinois	776,622	4.7%
6	Pennsylvania	654,826	3.9%
7	Michigan	605,835	3.6%
8	Ohio	587,996	3.5%
9	North Carolina	447,335	2.7%
10	Massachusetts	431,224	2.6%
11	Virginia	404,966	2.4%
12	Arizona	401,605	2.4%
13	Georgia	397,604	2.4%
14	New Jersey	361,733	2.2%
15	Missouri	348,146	2.1%
16	Indiana	342,064	2.1%
17	Washington	338,820	2.0%
18	Wisconsin	329,443	2.0%
19	Minnesota	323,791	1.9%
20	Maryland	300,269	1.8%
21	Colorado	282,343	1.7%
22	Tennessee	261,899	1.6%
23	Alabama	246,414	1.5%
24	Louisiana	232,140	1.4%
25	Kentucky	225,489	1.4%
26	Oregon	204,565	1.2%
27	Iowa	202,546	1.2%
28	South Carolina	202,007	1.2%
29	Oklahoma	198,423	1.2%
30	Kansas	188,049	1.1%
31	Utah	178,932	1.1%
32	Connecticut	170,606	1.0%
33	Mississippi	147,077	0.9%
34	Arkansas	127,372	0.8%
35	New Mexico	120,997	0.7%
36	Nebraska	116,737	0.7%
37	Nevada	95,671	0.6%
38	West Virginia	93,723	0.6%
39	Rhode Island	77,417	0.5%
40	Idaho	72,072	0.4%
41	New Hampshire	68,523	0.4%
42	Hawaii	65,368	0.4%
43	Maine	63,308	0.4%
44	Delaware	49,228	0.3%
45	South Dakota	47,751	0.3%
46	North Dakota	45,800	0.3%
47	Montana	45,111	0.3%
48	Vermont	36,537	0.2%
49	Wyoming	32,605	0.2%
50	Alaska	29,546	0.2%
	District of Columbia	91,014	0.5%

Source: U.S. Department of Education, National Center for Education Statistics
   "Digest of Education Statistics 2004" (NCES 2006005, October 2005)
*Fall 2002 enrollment. Includes full-time and part-time students at Title IV eligible, degree-granting four-year and two-year institutions. National total includes 14,420 students at U.S. Service Schools.

Enrollment Rate in Institutions of Higher Education in 2002

National Rate = 586 Students per 1,000 Population 18 to 24 Years Old*

ALPHA ORDER

RANK	STATE	RATE
31	Alabama	545
42	Alaska	503
1	Arizona	744
47	Arkansas	468
3	California	697
11	Colorado	630
21	Connecticut	594
17	Delaware	604
27	Florida	564
49	Georgia	458
37	Hawaii	531
44	Idaho	484
8	Illinois	632
32	Indiana	544
6	Iowa	643
5	Kansas	645
34	Kentucky	537
47	Louisiana	468
35	Maine	536
13	Maryland	614
2	Massachusetts	721
12	Michigan	624
7	Minnesota	639
50	Mississippi	456
14	Missouri	613
43	Montana	486
8	Nebraska	632
40	Nevada	511
20	New Hampshire	597
39	New Jersey	522
10	New Mexico	631
15	New York	610
30	North Carolina	549
18	North Dakota	602
36	Ohio	535
38	Oklahoma	526
16	Oregon	605
26	Pennsylvania	568
4	Rhode Island	679
46	South Carolina	470
24	South Dakota	578
45	Tennessee	473
41	Texas	504
29	Utah	557
23	Vermont	588
28	Virginia	562
25	Washington	571
33	West Virginia	539
22	Wisconsin	592
19	Wyoming	601

RANK ORDER

RANK	STATE	RATE
1	Arizona	744
2	Massachusetts	721
3	California	697
4	Rhode Island	679
5	Kansas	645
6	Iowa	643
7	Minnesota	639
8	Illinois	632
8	Nebraska	632
10	New Mexico	631
11	Colorado	630
12	Michigan	624
13	Maryland	614
14	Missouri	613
15	New York	610
16	Oregon	605
17	Delaware	604
18	North Dakota	602
19	Wyoming	601
20	New Hampshire	597
21	Connecticut	594
22	Wisconsin	592
23	Vermont	588
24	South Dakota	578
25	Washington	571
26	Pennsylvania	568
27	Florida	564
28	Virginia	562
29	Utah	557
30	North Carolina	549
31	Alabama	545
32	Indiana	544
33	West Virginia	539
34	Kentucky	537
35	Maine	536
36	Ohio	535
37	Hawaii	531
38	Oklahoma	526
39	New Jersey	522
40	Nevada	511
41	Texas	504
42	Alaska	503
43	Montana	486
44	Idaho	484
45	Tennessee	473
46	South Carolina	470
47	Arkansas	468
47	Louisiana	468
49	Georgia	458
50	Mississippi	456

District of Columbia 1,379

Source: Morgan Quitno Press using data from U.S. Department of Education, National Center for Education Statistics "Digest of Education Statistics 2004" (NCES 2006005, October 2005)

*Based on fall 2002 enrollment. National rate includes U.S. Service Schools. Includes students at four-year and two-year public and private degree-granting institutions. Enrollment based on location of institution. Population based on residence.

Enrollment in Public Institutions of Higher Education in 2002

National Total = 12,751,993 Students*

ALPHA ORDER					RANK ORDER			
RANK	STATE		STUDENTS	% of USA	RANK	STATE	STUDENTS	% of USA
20	Alabama		217,883	1.7%	1	California	2,121,106	16.6%
49	Alaska		28,314	0.2%	2	Texas	1,006,549	7.9%
12	Arizona		307,496	2.4%	3	Florida	617,754	4.8%
33	Arkansas		113,509	0.9%	4	New York	610,756	4.8%
1	California		2,121,106	16.6%	5	Illinois	554,093	4.3%
19	Colorado		233,740	1.8%	6	Michigan	495,676	3.9%
35	Connecticut		108,522	0.9%	7	Ohio	441,738	3.5%
47	Delaware		37,344	0.3%	8	Pennsylvania	370,386	2.9%
3	Florida		617,754	4.8%	9	North Carolina	367,861	2.9%
11	Georgia		317,180	2.5%	10	Virginia	337,286	2.6%
40	Hawaii		48,163	0.4%	11	Georgia	317,180	2.5%
39	Idaho		57,996	0.5%	12	Arizona	307,496	2.4%
5	Illinois		554,093	4.3%	13	Washington	293,007	2.3%
16	Indiana		258,627	2.0%	14	New Jersey	289,275	2.3%
30	Iowa		145,798	1.1%	15	Wisconsin	268,010	2.1%
28	Kansas		167,741	1.3%	16	Indiana	258,627	2.0%
24	Kentucky		188,518	1.5%	17	Maryland	246,792	1.9%
22	Louisiana		197,547	1.5%	18	Minnesota	235,513	1.8%
41	Maine		44,850	0.4%	19	Colorado	233,740	1.8%
17	Maryland		246,792	1.9%	20	Alabama	217,883	1.7%
25	Massachusetts		187,874	1.5%	21	Missouri	214,022	1.7%
6	Michigan		495,676	3.9%	22	Louisiana	197,547	1.5%
18	Minnesota		235,513	1.8%	23	Tennessee	194,202	1.5%
32	Mississippi		134,130	1.1%	24	Kentucky	188,518	1.5%
21	Missouri		214,022	1.7%	25	Massachusetts	187,874	1.5%
44	Montana		40,615	0.3%	26	Oregon	173,698	1.4%
36	Nebraska		92,111	0.7%	27	Oklahoma	171,369	1.3%
37	Nevada		89,547	0.7%	28	Kansas	167,741	1.3%
43	New Hampshire		40,958	0.3%	29	South Carolina	167,563	1.3%
14	New Jersey		289,275	2.3%	30	Iowa	145,798	1.1%
34	New Mexico		111,667	0.9%	31	Utah	135,778	1.1%
4	New York		610,756	4.8%	32	Mississippi	134,130	1.1%
9	North Carolina		367,861	2.9%	33	Arkansas	113,509	0.9%
42	North Dakota		41,134	0.3%	34	New Mexico	111,667	0.9%
7	Ohio		441,738	3.5%	35	Connecticut	108,522	0.9%
27	Oklahoma		171,369	1.3%	36	Nebraska	92,111	0.7%
26	Oregon		173,698	1.4%	37	Nevada	89,547	0.7%
8	Pennsylvania		370,386	2.9%	38	West Virginia	79,741	0.6%
45	Rhode Island		38,867	0.3%	39	Idaho	57,996	0.5%
29	South Carolina		167,563	1.3%	40	Hawaii	48,163	0.4%
46	South Dakota		37,760	0.3%	41	Maine	44,850	0.4%
23	Tennessee		194,202	1.5%	42	North Dakota	41,134	0.3%
2	Texas		1,006,549	7.9%	43	New Hampshire	40,958	0.3%
31	Utah		135,778	1.1%	44	Montana	40,615	0.3%
50	Vermont		21,238	0.2%	45	Rhode Island	38,867	0.3%
10	Virginia		337,286	2.6%	46	South Dakota	37,760	0.3%
13	Washington		293,007	2.3%	47	Delaware	37,344	0.3%
38	West Virginia		79,741	0.6%	48	Wyoming	30,666	0.2%
15	Wisconsin		268,010	2.1%	49	Alaska	28,314	0.2%
48	Wyoming		30,666	0.2%	50	Vermont	21,238	0.2%
						District of Columbia	5,603	0.0%

Source: U.S. Department of Education, National Center for Education Statistics
"Digest of Education Statistics 2004" (NCES 2006005, October 2005)
*Fall 2002 enrollment. Includes full-time and part-time students at Title IV eligible, degree-granting four-year and two-year institutions. National total includes 14,420 students at U.S. Service Schools.

Enrollment in Private Institutions of Higher Education in 2002

National Total = 3,859,718 Students*

RANK	STATE	STUDENTS	% of USA
31	Alabama	28,531	0.7%
50	Alaska	1,232	0.0%
11	Arizona	94,109	2.4%
41	Arkansas	13,863	0.4%
2	California	352,918	9.1%
23	Colorado	48,603	1.3%
19	Connecticut	62,084	1.6%
43	Delaware	11,884	0.3%
6	Florida	174,325	4.5%
14	Georgia	80,424	2.1%
37	Hawaii	17,205	0.4%
39	Idaho	14,076	0.4%
5	Illinois	222,529	5.8%
13	Indiana	83,437	2.2%
21	Iowa	56,748	1.5%
35	Kansas	20,308	0.5%
27	Kentucky	36,971	1.0%
28	Louisiana	34,593	0.9%
36	Maine	18,458	0.5%
22	Maryland	53,477	1.4%
4	Massachusetts	243,350	6.3%
10	Michigan	110,159	2.9%
12	Minnesota	88,278	2.3%
42	Mississippi	12,947	0.3%
9	Missouri	134,124	3.5%
48	Montana	4,496	0.1%
34	Nebraska	24,626	0.6%
46	Nevada	6,124	0.2%
32	New Hampshire	27,565	0.7%
16	New Jersey	72,458	1.9%
45	New Mexico	9,330	0.2%
1	New York	496,514	12.9%
15	North Carolina	79,474	2.1%
47	North Dakota	4,666	0.1%
7	Ohio	146,258	3.8%
33	Oklahoma	27,054	0.7%
30	Oregon	30,867	0.8%
3	Pennsylvania	284,440	7.4%
26	Rhode Island	38,550	1.0%
29	South Carolina	34,444	0.9%
44	South Dakota	9,991	0.3%
17	Tennessee	67,697	1.8%
8	Texas	145,820	3.8%
25	Utah	43,154	1.1%
38	Vermont	15,299	0.4%
18	Virginia	67,680	1.8%
24	Washington	45,813	1.2%
40	West Virginia	13,982	0.4%
20	Wisconsin	61,433	1.6%
49	Wyoming	1,939	0.1%

RANK	STATE	STUDENTS	% of USA
1	New York	496,514	12.9%
2	California	352,918	9.1%
3	Pennsylvania	284,440	7.4%
4	Massachusetts	243,350	6.3%
5	Illinois	222,529	5.8%
6	Florida	174,325	4.5%
7	Ohio	146,258	3.8%
8	Texas	145,820	3.8%
9	Missouri	134,124	3.5%
10	Michigan	110,159	2.9%
11	Arizona	94,109	2.4%
12	Minnesota	88,278	2.3%
13	Indiana	83,437	2.2%
14	Georgia	80,424	2.1%
15	North Carolina	79,474	2.1%
16	New Jersey	72,458	1.9%
17	Tennessee	67,697	1.8%
18	Virginia	67,680	1.8%
19	Connecticut	62,084	1.6%
20	Wisconsin	61,433	1.6%
21	Iowa	56,748	1.5%
22	Maryland	53,477	1.4%
23	Colorado	48,603	1.3%
24	Washington	45,813	1.2%
25	Utah	43,154	1.1%
26	Rhode Island	38,550	1.0%
27	Kentucky	36,971	1.0%
28	Louisiana	34,593	0.9%
29	South Carolina	34,444	0.9%
30	Oregon	30,867	0.8%
31	Alabama	28,531	0.7%
32	New Hampshire	27,565	0.7%
33	Oklahoma	27,054	0.7%
34	Nebraska	24,626	0.6%
35	Kansas	20,308	0.5%
36	Maine	18,458	0.5%
37	Hawaii	17,205	0.4%
38	Vermont	15,299	0.4%
39	Idaho	14,076	0.4%
40	West Virginia	13,982	0.4%
41	Arkansas	13,863	0.4%
42	Mississippi	12,947	0.3%
43	Delaware	11,884	0.3%
44	South Dakota	9,991	0.3%
45	New Mexico	9,330	0.2%
46	Nevada	6,124	0.2%
47	North Dakota	4,666	0.1%
48	Montana	4,496	0.1%
49	Wyoming	1,939	0.1%
50	Alaska	1,232	0.0%
	District of Columbia	85,411	2.2%

Source: U.S. Department of Education, National Center for Education Statistics
    "Digest of Education Statistics 2004" (NCES 2006005, October 2005)
Fall 2002 enrollment. Includes full-time and part-time students at Title IV eligible, degree-granting four-year and two-year institutions.

Percent of Population With a Bachelor's Degree or More in 2004

National Percent = 27.7%*

	ALPHA ORDER			RANK ORDER	
RANK	STATE	PERCENT	RANK	STATE	PERCENT
45	Alabama	22.3	1	Massachusetts	36.7
25	Alaska	25.5	2	Colorado	35.5
16	Arizona	28.0	3	New Hampshire	35.4
49	Arkansas	18.8	4	Maryland	35.2
10	California	31.7	5	New Jersey	34.6
2	Colorado	35.5	6	Connecticut	34.5
6	Connecticut	34.5	7	Vermont	34.2
20	Delaware	26.9	8	Virginia	33.1
22	Florida	26.0	9	Minnesota	32.5
17	Georgia	27.6	10	California	31.7
21	Hawaii	26.6	11	Utah	30.8
40	Idaho	23.8	12	New York	30.6
18	Illinois	27.4	13	Kansas	30.0
46	Indiana	21.1	14	Washington	29.9
37	Iowa	24.3	15	Missouri	28.1
13	Kansas	30.0	16	Arizona	28.0
47	Kentucky	21.0	17	Georgia	27.6
44	Louisiana	22.4	18	Illinois	27.4
39	Maine	24.2	19	Rhode Island	27.2
4	Maryland	35.2	20	Delaware	26.9
1	Massachusetts	36.7	21	Hawaii	26.6
36	Michigan	24.4	22	Florida	26.0
9	Minnesota	32.5	23	Oregon	25.9
48	Mississippi	20.1	24	Wisconsin	25.6
15	Missouri	28.1	25	Alaska	25.5
25	Montana	25.5	25	Montana	25.5
32	Nebraska	24.8	25	South Dakota	25.5
34	Nevada	24.5	28	Pennsylvania	25.3
3	New Hampshire	35.4	29	North Dakota	25.2
5	New Jersey	34.6	30	New Mexico	25.1
30	New Mexico	25.1	31	South Carolina	24.9
12	New York	30.6	32	Nebraska	24.8
41	North Carolina	23.4	33	Ohio	24.6
29	North Dakota	25.2	34	Nevada	24.5
33	Ohio	24.6	34	Texas	24.5
42	Oklahoma	22.9	36	Michigan	24.4
23	Oregon	25.9	37	Iowa	24.3
28	Pennsylvania	25.3	37	Tennessee	24.3
19	Rhode Island	27.2	39	Maine	24.2
31	South Carolina	24.9	40	Idaho	23.8
25	South Dakota	25.5	41	North Carolina	23.4
37	Tennessee	24.3	42	Oklahoma	22.9
34	Texas	24.5	43	Wyoming	22.5
11	Utah	30.8	44	Louisiana	22.4
7	Vermont	34.2	45	Alabama	22.3
8	Virginia	33.1	46	Indiana	21.1
14	Washington	29.9	47	Kentucky	21.0
50	West Virginia	15.3	48	Mississippi	20.1
24	Wisconsin	25.6	49	Arkansas	18.8
43	Wyoming	22.5	50	West Virginia	15.3
				District of Columbia	45.7

Source: U.S. Bureau of the Census
   "Educational Attainment of the Population 25 Years and Over, By State"
      (http://www.census.gov/population/www/socdemo/education/cps2004.html)
*Persons age 25 and older.

Public Libraries and Branches in 2003

National Total = 16,541 Libraries and Branches*

ALPHA ORDER				RANK ORDER			
RANK	STATE	LIBRARIES	% of USA	RANK	STATE	LIBRARIES	% of USA
24	Alabama	284	1.7%	1	California	1,084	6.6%
44	Alaska	102	0.6%	2	New York	1,083	6.5%
35	Arizona	185	1.1%	3	Texas	841	5.1%
30	Arkansas	210	1.3%	4	Illinois	793	4.8%
1	California	1,084	6.6%	5	Ohio	720	4.4%
27	Colorado	242	1.5%	6	Michigan	661	4.0%
26	Connecticut	244	1.5%	7	Pennsylvania	630	3.8%
50	Delaware	33	0.2%	8	Iowa	563	3.4%
9	Florida	487	2.9%	9	Florida	487	2.9%
17	Georgia	369	2.2%	10	Massachusetts	483	2.9%
49	Hawaii	50	0.3%	11	Wisconsin	456	2.8%
40	Idaho	142	0.9%	12	New Jersey	455	2.8%
4	Illinois	793	4.8%	13	Indiana	434	2.6%
13	Indiana	434	2.6%	14	Missouri	388	2.3%
8	Iowa	563	3.4%	15	North Carolina	379	2.3%
16	Kansas	374	2.3%	16	Kansas	374	2.3%
34	Kentucky	190	1.1%	17	Georgia	369	2.2%
20	Louisiana	334	2.0%	18	Minnesota	357	2.2%
25	Maine	280	1.7%	19	Virginia	341	2.1%
37	Maryland	176	1.1%	20	Louisiana	334	2.0%
10	Massachusetts	483	2.9%	21	Washington	325	2.0%
6	Michigan	661	4.0%	22	Nebraska	291	1.8%
18	Minnesota	357	2.2%	23	Tennessee	286	1.7%
28	Mississippi	239	1.4%	24	Alabama	284	1.7%
14	Missouri	388	2.3%	25	Maine	280	1.7%
43	Montana	108	0.7%	26	Connecticut	244	1.5%
22	Nebraska	291	1.8%	27	Colorado	242	1.5%
46	Nevada	85	0.5%	28	Mississippi	239	1.4%
29	New Hampshire	237	1.4%	29	New Hampshire	237	1.4%
12	New Jersey	455	2.8%	30	Arkansas	210	1.3%
41	New Mexico	113	0.7%	30	Oregon	210	1.3%
2	New York	1,083	6.5%	32	Oklahoma	206	1.2%
15	North Carolina	379	2.3%	33	Vermont	191	1.2%
45	North Dakota	91	0.6%	34	Kentucky	190	1.1%
5	Ohio	720	4.4%	35	Arizona	185	1.1%
32	Oklahoma	206	1.2%	36	South Carolina	184	1.1%
30	Oregon	210	1.3%	37	Maryland	176	1.1%
7	Pennsylvania	630	3.8%	37	West Virginia	176	1.1%
48	Rhode Island	72	0.4%	39	South Dakota	144	0.9%
36	South Carolina	184	1.1%	40	Idaho	142	0.9%
39	South Dakota	144	0.9%	41	New Mexico	113	0.7%
23	Tennessee	286	1.7%	42	Utah	112	0.7%
3	Texas	841	5.1%	43	Montana	108	0.7%
42	Utah	112	0.7%	44	Alaska	102	0.6%
33	Vermont	191	1.2%	45	North Dakota	91	0.6%
19	Virginia	341	2.1%	46	Nevada	85	0.5%
21	Washington	325	2.0%	47	Wyoming	74	0.4%
37	West Virginia	176	1.1%	48	Rhode Island	72	0.4%
11	Wisconsin	456	2.8%	49	Hawaii	50	0.3%
47	Wyoming	74	0.4%	50	Delaware	33	0.2%
					District of Columbia	27	0.2%

Source: U.S. Dept. of Education, Office of Educational Research & Improvement
   "Public Libraries in the United States: FY 2003" (NCES 2005363, September 2005)
*For fiscal year 2003. Total of central and branch outlets. Does not include 729 bookmobiles. There are 9,211 public libraries.

Rate of Public Libraries and Branches in 2003

National Average = 17,584 Population per Library*

ALPHA ORDER				RANK ORDER		
RANK	STATE	RATE		RANK	STATE	RATE
26	Alabama	15,852		1	Florida	34,894
44	Alaska	6,358		2	California	32,709
4	Arizona	30,150		3	Maryland	31,321
35	Arkansas	12,982		4	Arizona	30,150
2	California	32,709		5	Nevada	26,373
19	Colorado	18,794		6	Texas	26,277
30	Connecticut	14,286		7	Hawaii	24,964
8	Delaware	24,783		8	Delaware	24,783
1	Florida	34,894		9	Georgia	23,704
9	Georgia	23,704		10	South Carolina	22,537
7	Hawaii	24,964		11	North Carolina	22,223
39	Idaho	9,635		12	Kentucky	21,667
24	Illinois	15,952		13	Virginia	21,652
31	Indiana	14,277		14	Utah	21,238
48	Iowa	5,224		15	Tennessee	20,425
41	Kansas	7,284		16	Pennsylvania	19,627
12	Kentucky	21,667		17	New Jersey	18,989
33	Louisiana	13,444		18	Washington	18,865
49	Maine	4,672		19	Colorado	18,794
3	Maryland	31,321		20	New York	17,754
34	Massachusetts	13,287		21	Oklahoma	17,014
27	Michigan	15,247		22	Oregon	16,965
32	Minnesota	14,178		23	New Mexico	16,631
36	Mississippi	12,054		24	Illinois	15,952
29	Missouri	14,739		25	Ohio	15,877
40	Montana	8,499		26	Alabama	15,852
45	Nebraska	5,973		27	Michigan	15,247
5	Nevada	26,373		28	Rhode Island	14,941
46	New Hampshire	5,433		29	Missouri	14,739
17	New Jersey	18,989		30	Connecticut	14,286
23	New Mexico	16,631		31	Indiana	14,277
20	New York	17,754		32	Minnesota	14,178
11	North Carolina	22,223		33	Louisiana	13,444
42	North Dakota	6,957		34	Massachusetts	13,287
25	Ohio	15,877		35	Arkansas	12,982
21	Oklahoma	17,014		36	Mississippi	12,054
22	Oregon	16,965		37	Wisconsin	12,000
16	Pennsylvania	19,627		38	West Virginia	10,286
28	Rhode Island	14,941		39	Idaho	9,635
10	South Carolina	22,537		40	Montana	8,499
47	South Dakota	5,310		41	Kansas	7,284
15	Tennessee	20,425		42	North Dakota	6,957
6	Texas	26,277		43	Wyoming	6,783
14	Utah	21,238		44	Alaska	6,358
50	Vermont	3,241		45	Nebraska	5,973
13	Virginia	21,652		46	New Hampshire	5,433
18	Washington	18,865		47	South Dakota	5,310
38	West Virginia	10,286		48	Iowa	5,224
37	Wisconsin	12,000		49	Maine	4,672
43	Wyoming	6,783		50	Vermont	3,241

District of Columbia   20,661

Source: Morgan Quitno Press using data from U.S. Dept. of Education, Office of Educational Research & Improvement "Public Libraries in the United States: FY 2003" (NCES 2005363, September 2005)

*For fiscal year 2003. Total of central and branch outlets. Does not include 729 bookmobiles. There are 9,211 public libraries.

Books in Public Libraries Per Capita in 2003

National Per Capita = 2.9 Books*

ALPHA ORDER

RANK	STATE	BOOKS PER CAPITA
38	Alabama	2.1
19	Alaska	3.5
48	Arizona	1.8
38	Arkansas	2.1
37	California	2.2
27	Colorado	2.7
10	Connecticut	4.2
41	Delaware	2.0
44	Florida	1.9
48	Georgia	1.8
32	Hawaii	2.6
22	Idaho	3.2
16	Illinois	3.8
10	Indiana	4.2
12	Iowa	4.1
6	Kansas	4.7
41	Kentucky	2.0
34	Louisiana	2.5
1	Maine	5.2
25	Maryland	2.9
4	Massachusetts	4.8
21	Michigan	3.3
23	Minnesota	3.1
41	Mississippi	2.0
18	Missouri	3.7
24	Montana	3.0
8	Nebraska	4.5
50	Nevada	1.7
7	New Hampshire	4.6
16	New Jersey	3.8
34	New Mexico	2.5
12	New York	4.1
44	North Carolina	1.9
12	North Dakota	4.1
9	Ohio	4.3
36	Oklahoma	2.3
27	Oregon	2.7
27	Pennsylvania	2.7
15	Rhode Island	3.9
38	South Carolina	2.1
1	South Dakota	5.2
44	Tennessee	1.9
44	Texas	1.9
27	Utah	2.7
4	Vermont	4.8
32	Virginia	2.6
25	Washington	2.9
27	West Virginia	2.7
19	Wisconsin	3.5
3	Wyoming	4.9

RANK ORDER

RANK	STATE	BOOKS PER CAPITA
1	Maine	5.2
1	South Dakota	5.2
3	Wyoming	4.9
4	Massachusetts	4.8
4	Vermont	4.8
6	Kansas	4.7
7	New Hampshire	4.6
8	Nebraska	4.5
9	Ohio	4.3
10	Connecticut	4.2
10	Indiana	4.2
12	Iowa	4.1
12	New York	4.1
12	North Dakota	4.1
15	Rhode Island	3.9
16	Illinois	3.8
16	New Jersey	3.8
18	Missouri	3.7
19	Alaska	3.5
19	Wisconsin	3.5
21	Michigan	3.3
22	Idaho	3.2
23	Minnesota	3.1
24	Montana	3.0
25	Maryland	2.9
25	Washington	2.9
27	Colorado	2.7
27	Oregon	2.7
27	Pennsylvania	2.7
27	Utah	2.7
27	West Virginia	2.7
32	Hawaii	2.6
32	Virginia	2.6
34	Louisiana	2.5
34	New Mexico	2.5
36	Oklahoma	2.3
37	California	2.2
38	Alabama	2.1
38	Arkansas	2.1
38	South Carolina	2.1
41	Delaware	2.0
41	Kentucky	2.0
41	Mississippi	2.0
44	Florida	1.9
44	North Carolina	1.9
44	Tennessee	1.9
44	Texas	1.9
48	Arizona	1.8
48	Georgia	1.8
50	Nevada	1.7
	District of Columbia	4.5

Source: U.S. Dept. of Education, Office of Educational Research & Improvement
   "Public Libraries in the United States: FY 2003" (NCES 2005363, September 2005)
*For fiscal year 2003. Includes serial volumes but not serial subscriptions.

Internet Terminals in Public Libraries: 2003

National Total = 156,563 Terminals*

ALPHA ORDER

RANK	STATE	TERMINALS	% of USA
18	Alabama	2,939	1.9%
45	Alaska	598	0.4%
23	Arizona	2,489	1.6%
36	Arkansas	1,078	0.7%
1	California	12,461	8.0%
24	Colorado	2,486	1.6%
27	Connecticut	2,213	1.4%
50	Delaware	274	0.2%
5	Florida	7,053	4.5%
10	Georgia	4,731	3.0%
49	Hawaii	303	0.2%
41	Idaho	760	0.5%
6	Illinois	6,847	4.4%
9	Indiana	4,866	3.1%
22	Iowa	2,539	1.6%
26	Kansas	2,256	1.4%
29	Kentucky	2,061	1.3%
25	Louisiana	2,380	1.5%
37	Maine	1,065	0.7%
20	Maryland	2,816	1.8%
13	Massachusetts	4,054	2.6%
7	Michigan	6,802	4.3%
19	Minnesota	2,907	1.9%
32	Mississippi	1,548	1.0%
17	Missouri	3,267	2.1%
46	Montana	518	0.3%
33	Nebraska	1,392	0.9%
40	Nevada	800	0.5%
35	New Hampshire	1,095	0.7%
11	New Jersey	4,626	3.0%
38	New Mexico	974	0.6%
3	New York	10,430	6.7%
12	North Carolina	4,165	2.7%
48	North Dakota	391	0.2%
4	Ohio	9,276	5.9%
31	Oklahoma	1,683	1.1%
30	Oregon	1,795	1.1%
8	Pennsylvania	6,710	4.3%
42	Rhode Island	742	0.5%
28	South Carolina	2,198	1.4%
43	South Dakota	738	0.5%
21	Tennessee	2,672	1.7%
2	Texas	10,909	7.0%
34	Utah	1,221	0.8%
44	Vermont	701	0.4%
15	Virginia	3,753	2.4%
16	Washington	3,525	2.3%
39	West Virginia	931	0.6%
14	Wisconsin	3,940	2.5%
47	Wyoming	432	0.3%

RANK ORDER

RANK	STATE	TERMINALS	% of USA
1	California	12,461	8.0%
2	Texas	10,909	7.0%
3	New York	10,430	6.7%
4	Ohio	9,276	5.9%
5	Florida	7,053	4.5%
6	Illinois	6,847	4.4%
7	Michigan	6,802	4.3%
8	Pennsylvania	6,710	4.3%
9	Indiana	4,866	3.1%
10	Georgia	4,731	3.0%
11	New Jersey	4,626	3.0%
12	North Carolina	4,165	2.7%
13	Massachusetts	4,054	2.6%
14	Wisconsin	3,940	2.5%
15	Virginia	3,753	2.4%
16	Washington	3,525	2.3%
17	Missouri	3,267	2.1%
18	Alabama	2,939	1.9%
19	Minnesota	2,907	1.9%
20	Maryland	2,816	1.8%
21	Tennessee	2,672	1.7%
22	Iowa	2,539	1.6%
23	Arizona	2,489	1.6%
24	Colorado	2,486	1.6%
25	Louisiana	2,380	1.5%
26	Kansas	2,256	1.4%
27	Connecticut	2,213	1.4%
28	South Carolina	2,198	1.4%
29	Kentucky	2,061	1.3%
30	Oregon	1,795	1.1%
31	Oklahoma	1,683	1.1%
32	Mississippi	1,548	1.0%
33	Nebraska	1,392	0.9%
34	Utah	1,221	0.8%
35	New Hampshire	1,095	0.7%
36	Arkansas	1,078	0.7%
37	Maine	1,065	0.7%
38	New Mexico	974	0.6%
39	West Virginia	931	0.6%
40	Nevada	800	0.5%
41	Idaho	760	0.5%
42	Rhode Island	742	0.5%
43	South Dakota	738	0.5%
44	Vermont	701	0.4%
45	Alaska	598	0.4%
46	Montana	518	0.3%
47	Wyoming	432	0.3%
48	North Dakota	391	0.2%
49	Hawaii	303	0.2%
50	Delaware	274	0.2%
	District of Columbia	153	0.1%

Source: U.S. Dept. of Education, Office of Educational Research & Improvement
    "Public Libraries in the United States: FY 2003" (NCES 2005363, September 2005)
*For fiscal year 2003. Total of public-use internet terminals in central and branch outlets.

Rate of Internet Terminals in Public Libraries: 2003

National Rate = 9.5 Terminals per Library*

RANK	STATE	RATE		RANK	STATE	RATE
16	Alabama	10.3		1	Maryland	16.0
38	Alaska	5.9		2	Florida	14.5
3	Arizona	13.5		3	Arizona	13.5
42	Arkansas	5.1		4	Texas	13.0
8	California	11.5		5	Ohio	12.9
16	Colorado	10.3		6	Georgia	12.8
24	Connecticut	9.1		7	South Carolina	11.9
31	Delaware	8.3		8	California	11.5
2	Florida	14.5		9	Indiana	11.2
6	Georgia	12.8		10	North Carolina	11.0
36	Hawaii	6.1		10	Virginia	11.0
40	Idaho	5.4		12	Utah	10.9
25	Illinois	8.6		13	Kentucky	10.8
9	Indiana	11.2		13	Washington	10.8
47	Iowa	4.5		15	Pennsylvania	10.7
37	Kansas	6.0		16	Alabama	10.3
13	Kentucky	10.8		16	Colorado	10.3
34	Louisiana	7.1		16	Michigan	10.3
49	Maine	3.8		16	Rhode Island	10.3
1	Maryland	16.0		20	New Jersey	10.2
29	Massachusetts	8.4		21	New York	9.6
16	Michigan	10.3		22	Nevada	9.4
33	Minnesota	8.1		23	Tennessee	9.3
35	Mississippi	6.5		24	Connecticut	9.1
29	Missouri	8.4		25	Illinois	8.6
44	Montana	4.8		25	New Mexico	8.6
44	Nebraska	4.8		25	Wisconsin	8.6
22	Nevada	9.4		28	Oregon	8.5
46	New Hampshire	4.6		29	Massachusetts	8.4
20	New Jersey	10.2		29	Missouri	8.4
25	New Mexico	8.6		31	Delaware	8.3
21	New York	9.6		32	Oklahoma	8.2
10	North Carolina	11.0		33	Minnesota	8.1
48	North Dakota	4.3		34	Louisiana	7.1
5	Ohio	12.9		35	Mississippi	6.5
32	Oklahoma	8.2		36	Hawaii	6.1
28	Oregon	8.5		37	Kansas	6.0
15	Pennsylvania	10.7		38	Alaska	5.9
16	Rhode Island	10.3		39	Wyoming	5.8
7	South Carolina	11.9		40	Idaho	5.4
42	South Dakota	5.1		41	West Virginia	5.3
23	Tennessee	9.3		42	Arkansas	5.1
4	Texas	13.0		42	South Dakota	5.1
12	Utah	10.9		44	Montana	4.8
50	Vermont	3.7		44	Nebraska	4.8
10	Virginia	11.0		46	New Hampshire	4.6
13	Washington	10.8		47	Iowa	4.5
41	West Virginia	5.3		48	North Dakota	4.3
25	Wisconsin	8.6		49	Maine	3.8
39	Wyoming	5.8		50	Vermont	3.7
					District of Columbia	5.7

ALPHA ORDER

RANK ORDER

Source: U.S. Dept. of Education, Office of Educational Research & Improvement
   "Public Libraries in the United States: FY 2003" (NCES 2005363, September 2005)
*For fiscal year 2003. Total of public-use internet terminals in central and branch outlets divided by the number of outlets.

Per Capita State Art Agencies' Legislative Appropriations in 2006

National Per Capita = $1.02*

ALPHA ORDER

RANK	STATE	PER CAPITA
24	Alabama	$0.86
26	Alaska	0.81
32	Arizona	0.61
38	Arkansas	0.54
50	California	0.06
48	Colorado	0.15
6	Connecticut	2.02
5	Delaware	2.11
9	Florida	1.65
42	Georgia	0.43
1	Hawaii	5.36
33	Idaho	0.59
10	Illinois	1.53
34	Indiana	0.58
44	Iowa	0.41
36	Kansas	0.56
19	Kentucky	1.01
16	Louisiana	1.11
34	Maine	0.58
7	Maryland	2.01
11	Massachusetts	1.51
22	Michigan	0.97
8	Minnesota	1.67
38	Mississippi	0.54
49	Missouri	0.08
42	Montana	0.43
29	Nebraska	0.78
31	Nevada	0.71
37	New Hampshire	0.55
2	New Jersey	3.42
19	New Mexico	1.01
4	New York	2.35
23	North Carolina	0.91
27	North Dakota	0.79
21	Ohio	0.98
14	Oklahoma	1.20
47	Oregon	0.17
15	Pennsylvania	1.17
3	Rhode Island	3.02
25	South Carolina	0.84
29	South Dakota	0.78
16	Tennessee	1.11
46	Texas	0.19
18	Utah	1.10
27	Vermont	0.79
40	Virginia	0.47
45	Washington	0.37
12	West Virginia	1.33
41	Wisconsin	0.44
13	Wyoming	1.27

RANK ORDER

RANK	STATE	PER CAPITA
1	Hawaii	$5.36
2	New Jersey	3.42
3	Rhode Island	3.02
4	New York	2.35
5	Delaware	2.11
6	Connecticut	2.02
7	Maryland	2.01
8	Minnesota	1.67
9	Florida	1.65
10	Illinois	1.53
11	Massachusetts	1.51
12	West Virginia	1.33
13	Wyoming	1.27
14	Oklahoma	1.20
15	Pennsylvania	1.17
16	Louisiana	1.11
16	Tennessee	1.11
18	Utah	1.10
19	Kentucky	1.01
19	New Mexico	1.01
21	Ohio	0.98
22	Michigan	0.97
23	North Carolina	0.91
24	Alabama	0.86
25	South Carolina	0.84
26	Alaska	0.81
27	North Dakota	0.79
27	Vermont	0.79
29	Nebraska	0.78
29	South Dakota	0.78
31	Nevada	0.71
32	Arizona	0.61
33	Idaho	0.59
34	Indiana	0.58
34	Maine	0.58
36	Kansas	0.56
37	New Hampshire	0.55
38	Arkansas	0.54
38	Mississippi	0.54
40	Virginia	0.47
41	Wisconsin	0.44
42	Georgia	0.43
42	Montana	0.43
44	Iowa	0.41
45	Washington	0.37
46	Texas	0.19
47	Oregon	0.17
48	Colorado	0.15
49	Missouri	0.08
50	California	0.06
	District of Columbia	15.53

Source: Morgan Quitno Press using data from National Assembly of State Arts Agencies
    "State Arts Spending Exhibits Modest Gains" (Press Release, January 17, 2006)
*Preliminary figures for fiscal year 2006. Includes line item appropriations. Line items are legislative appropriations that are not controlled by the state art agencies but are passed through their budgets directly to another entity. Calculated using 2005 census population estimates. National per capita does not include appropriations or population in U.S. territories.

156

Federal Allocations for Head Start Program in 2004

National Total = $6,542,292,000*

ALPHA ORDER

RANK	STATE	ALLOCATIONS	% of USA
18	Alabama	$105,500,307	1.6%
49	Alaska	12,352,697	0.2%
19	Arizona	102,022,603	1.6%
29	Arkansas	63,808,419	1.0%
1	California	823,694,368	12.6%
28	Colorado	67,676,158	1.0%
32	Connecticut	51,400,659	0.8%
48	Delaware	12,770,909	0.2%
5	Florida	260,307,421	4.0%
9	Georgia	166,837,016	2.6%
40	Hawaii	22,664,976	0.3%
41	Idaho	22,410,937	0.3%
4	Illinois	267,111,453	4.1%
22	Indiana	95,093,413	1.5%
33	Iowa	51,049,850	0.8%
34	Kansas	50,433,097	0.8%
17	Kentucky	106,799,358	1.6%
11	Louisiana	144,497,478	2.2%
38	Maine	27,343,732	0.4%
26	Maryland	77,277,126	1.2%
16	Massachusetts	107,298,837	1.6%
7	Michigan	232,214,668	3.5%
27	Minnesota	71,119,492	1.1%
10	Mississippi	160,120,548	2.4%
15	Missouri	117,837,078	1.8%
43	Montana	20,746,775	0.3%
37	Nebraska	35,709,352	0.5%
39	Nevada	23,698,194	0.4%
47	New Hampshire	13,257,126	0.2%
13	New Jersey	127,761,210	2.0%
31	New Mexico	51,789,732	0.8%
3	New York	430,086,285	6.6%
12	North Carolina	139,359,686	2.1%
45	North Dakota	17,009,140	0.3%
6	Ohio	244,101,839	3.7%
25	Oklahoma	80,249,056	1.2%
30	Oregon	58,892,507	0.9%
8	Pennsylvania	226,002,253	3.5%
42	Rhode Island	21,802,422	0.3%
24	South Carolina	81,718,067	1.2%
44	South Dakota	18,643,605	0.3%
14	Tennessee	118,216,822	1.8%
2	Texas	474,091,773	7.2%
36	Utah	37,398,515	0.6%
46	Vermont	13,428,786	0.2%
21	Virginia	98,142,388	1.5%
20	Washington	100,192,902	1.5%
35	West Virginia	50,152,151	0.8%
23	Wisconsin	89,783,879	1.4%
50	Wyoming	12,252,314	0.2%

RANK ORDER

RANK	STATE	ALLOCATIONS	% of USA
1	California	$823,694,368	12.6%
2	Texas	474,091,773	7.2%
3	New York	430,086,285	6.6%
4	Illinois	267,111,453	4.1%
5	Florida	260,307,421	4.0%
6	Ohio	244,101,839	3.7%
7	Michigan	232,214,668	3.5%
8	Pennsylvania	226,002,253	3.5%
9	Georgia	166,837,016	2.6%
10	Mississippi	160,120,548	2.4%
11	Louisiana	144,497,478	2.2%
12	North Carolina	139,359,686	2.1%
13	New Jersey	127,761,210	2.0%
14	Tennessee	118,216,822	1.8%
15	Missouri	117,837,078	1.8%
16	Massachusetts	107,298,837	1.6%
17	Kentucky	106,799,358	1.6%
18	Alabama	105,500,307	1.6%
19	Arizona	102,022,603	1.6%
20	Washington	100,192,902	1.5%
21	Virginia	98,142,388	1.5%
22	Indiana	95,093,413	1.5%
23	Wisconsin	89,783,879	1.4%
24	South Carolina	81,718,067	1.2%
25	Oklahoma	80,249,056	1.2%
26	Maryland	77,277,126	1.2%
27	Minnesota	71,119,492	1.1%
28	Colorado	67,676,158	1.0%
29	Arkansas	63,808,419	1.0%
30	Oregon	58,892,507	0.9%
31	New Mexico	51,789,732	0.8%
32	Connecticut	51,400,659	0.8%
33	Iowa	51,049,850	0.8%
34	Kansas	50,433,097	0.8%
35	West Virginia	50,152,151	0.8%
36	Utah	37,398,515	0.6%
37	Nebraska	35,709,352	0.5%
38	Maine	27,343,732	0.4%
39	Nevada	23,698,194	0.4%
40	Hawaii	22,664,976	0.3%
41	Idaho	22,410,937	0.3%
42	Rhode Island	21,802,422	0.3%
43	Montana	20,746,775	0.3%
44	South Dakota	18,643,605	0.3%
45	North Dakota	17,009,140	0.3%
46	Vermont	13,428,786	0.2%
47	New Hampshire	13,257,126	0.2%
48	Delaware	12,770,909	0.2%
49	Alaska	12,352,697	0.2%
50	Wyoming	12,252,314	0.2%
	District of Columbia	24,864,991	0.4%

Source: U.S. Department of Health and Human Services, Administration for Children and Families
   "2004 Head Start Fact Sheet" (http://www.acf.hhs.gov/programs/hsb/research/2005.htm)
*For fiscal year 2004. National total includes $451,325,089 to Migrant and Native American programs and
$261,972,950 to U.S. territories. Does not include $231,617,000 in "support activities" expenditures.

Head Start Enrollment in 2004

National Total = 905,970 Enrollees*

ALPHA ORDER

RANK	STATE	ENROLLEES	% of USA
15	Alabama	16,374	1.8%
48	Alaska	1,634	0.2%
22	Arizona	13,215	1.5%
26	Arkansas	10,879	1.2%
1	California	98,933	10.9%
29	Colorado	9,820	1.1%
35	Connecticut	7,148	0.8%
46	Delaware	2,197	0.2%
6	Florida	35,574	3.9%
10	Georgia	23,450	2.6%
40	Hawaii	3,063	0.3%
41	Idaho	2,957	0.3%
4	Illinois	39,672	4.4%
18	Indiana	14,234	1.6%
32	Iowa	7,775	0.9%
31	Kansas	7,949	0.9%
16	Kentucky	16,071	1.8%
11	Louisiana	21,982	2.4%
38	Maine	3,979	0.4%
27	Maryland	10,344	1.1%
23	Massachusetts	13,011	1.4%
7	Michigan	35,124	3.9%
28	Minnesota	10,339	1.1%
9	Mississippi	26,754	3.0%
13	Missouri	17,473	1.9%
42	Montana	2,945	0.3%
37	Nebraska	5,080	0.6%
44	Nevada	2,754	0.3%
49	New Hampshire	1,632	0.2%
17	New Jersey	15,130	1.7%
34	New Mexico	7,451	0.8%
3	New York	49,300	5.4%
12	North Carolina	19,098	2.1%
45	North Dakota	2,353	0.3%
5	Ohio	38,029	4.2%
21	Oklahoma	13,474	1.5%
30	Oregon	8,716	1.0%
8	Pennsylvania	30,868	3.4%
39	Rhode Island	3,150	0.3%
24	South Carolina	12,248	1.4%
43	South Dakota	2,827	0.3%
14	Tennessee	16,437	1.8%
2	Texas	67,785	7.5%
36	Utah	5,518	0.6%
50	Vermont	1,569	0.2%
19	Virginia	13,768	1.5%
25	Washington	11,118	1.2%
33	West Virginia	7,650	0.8%
20	Wisconsin	13,532	1.5%
47	Wyoming	1,793	0.2%

RANK ORDER

RANK	STATE	ENROLLEES	% of USA
1	California	98,933	10.9%
2	Texas	67,785	7.5%
3	New York	49,300	5.4%
4	Illinois	39,672	4.4%
5	Ohio	38,029	4.2%
6	Florida	35,574	3.9%
7	Michigan	35,124	3.9%
8	Pennsylvania	30,868	3.4%
9	Mississippi	26,754	3.0%
10	Georgia	23,450	2.6%
11	Louisiana	21,982	2.4%
12	North Carolina	19,098	2.1%
13	Missouri	17,473	1.9%
14	Tennessee	16,437	1.8%
15	Alabama	16,374	1.8%
16	Kentucky	16,071	1.8%
17	New Jersey	15,130	1.7%
18	Indiana	14,234	1.6%
19	Virginia	13,768	1.5%
20	Wisconsin	13,532	1.5%
21	Oklahoma	13,474	1.5%
22	Arizona	13,215	1.5%
23	Massachusetts	13,011	1.4%
24	South Carolina	12,248	1.4%
25	Washington	11,118	1.2%
26	Arkansas	10,879	1.2%
27	Maryland	10,344	1.1%
28	Minnesota	10,339	1.1%
29	Colorado	9,820	1.1%
30	Oregon	8,716	1.0%
31	Kansas	7,949	0.9%
32	Iowa	7,775	0.9%
33	West Virginia	7,650	0.8%
34	New Mexico	7,451	0.8%
35	Connecticut	7,148	0.8%
36	Utah	5,518	0.6%
37	Nebraska	5,080	0.6%
38	Maine	3,979	0.4%
39	Rhode Island	3,150	0.3%
40	Hawaii	3,063	0.3%
41	Idaho	2,957	0.3%
42	Montana	2,945	0.3%
43	South Dakota	2,827	0.3%
44	Nevada	2,754	0.3%
45	North Dakota	2,353	0.3%
46	Delaware	2,197	0.2%
47	Wyoming	1,793	0.2%
48	Alaska	1,634	0.2%
49	New Hampshire	1,632	0.2%
50	Vermont	1,569	0.2%
	District of Columbia	3,403	0.4%

Source: U.S. Department of Health and Human Services, Administration for Children and Families
   "2004 Head Start Fact Sheet" (http://www.acf.hhs.gov/programs/hsb/research/2005.htm)
*For fiscal year 2004. National total includes 56,891 enrollees in Migrant and Native American programs and 41,500 enrollees in U.S. territories.

VI. EMPLOYMENT AND LABOR

Average Annual Pay in 2004

National Average = $39,354*

ALPHA ORDER				RANK ORDER		
RANK	STATE	ANNUAL PAY		RANK	STATE	ANNUAL PAY
31	Alabama	$33,414		1	Connecticut	$51,007
15	Alaska	39,062		2	New York	49,941
21	Arizona	36,646		3	Massachusetts	48,916
45	Arkansas	30,245		4	New Jersey	48,064
5	California	44,641		5	California	44,641
12	Colorado	40,276		6	Maryland	42,579
1	Connecticut	51,007		7	Delaware	42,487
7	Delaware	42,487		8	Illinois	42,277
25	Florida	35,186		9	Virginia	40,534
18	Georgia	37,866		10	Minnesota	40,398
24	Hawaii	35,198		11	Michigan	40,373
46	Idaho	29,871		12	Colorado	40,276
8	Illinois	42,277		13	Washington	39,361
30	Indiana	34,694		14	New Hampshire	39,176
36	Iowa	32,097		15	Alaska	39,062
34	Kansas	32,738		16	Pennsylvania	38,555
33	Kentucky	33,165		17	Texas	38,511
38	Louisiana	31,880		18	Georgia	37,866
37	Maine	31,906		19	Rhode Island	37,651
6	Maryland	42,579		20	Nevada	37,106
3	Massachusetts	48,916		21	Arizona	36,646
11	Michigan	40,373		22	Ohio	36,441
10	Minnesota	40,398		23	Oregon	35,630
48	Mississippi	28,535		24	Hawaii	35,198
27	Missouri	34,845		25	Florida	35,186
50	Montana	27,830		26	Tennessee	34,925
40	Nebraska	31,507		27	Missouri	34,845
20	Nevada	37,106		28	North Carolina	34,791
14	New Hampshire	39,176		29	Wisconsin	34,743
4	New Jersey	40,064		30	Indiana	34,694
41	New Mexico	31,411		31	Alabama	33,414
2	New York	49,941		32	Vermont	33,274
28	North Carolina	34,791		33	Kentucky	33,165
47	North Dakota	28,987		34	Kansas	32,738
22	Ohio	36,441		35	Utah	32,171
43	Oklahoma	30,743		36	Iowa	32,097
23	Oregon	35,630		37	Maine	31,906
16	Pennsylvania	38,555		38	Louisiana	31,880
19	Rhode Island	37,651		39	South Carolina	31,839
39	South Carolina	31,839		40	Nebraska	31,507
49	South Dakota	28,281		41	New Mexico	31,411
26	Tennessee	34,925		42	Wyoming	31,210
17	Texas	38,511		43	Oklahoma	30,743
35	Utah	32,171		44	West Virginia	30,382
32	Vermont	33,274		45	Arkansas	30,245
9	Virginia	40,534		46	Idaho	29,871
13	Washington	39,361		47	North Dakota	28,987
44	West Virginia	30,382		48	Mississippi	28,535
29	Wisconsin	34,743		49	South Dakota	28,281
42	Wyoming	31,210		50	Montana	27,830
					District of Columbia	63,887

Source: U.S. Department of Labor, Bureau of Labor Statistics
   "Quarterly Census of Employment and Wages: Annual Data Tables" (http://www.bls.gov/cew/cewsnote2.htm)
*Computed by dividing total annual wages of employees covered by unemployment insurance programs by the average monthly number of these employees. Includes bonuses, cash value of meals and lodging, tips and, in many states, employer contributions to certain deferred compensation plans such as 401(k) plans.

Percent Change in Average Annual Pay: 2003 to 2004

National Percent Change = 4.2% Increase*

ALPHA ORDER				RANK ORDER		
RANK	**STATE**	**PERCENT CHANGE**		**RANK**	**STATE**	**PERCENT CHANGE**
30	Alabama	3.7		1	New York	5.7
47	Alaska	3.3		2	Massachusetts	5.6
13	Arizona	4.5		3	Connecticut	5.5
10	Arkansas	4.7		4	Virginia	5.1
9	California	4.8		5	Nevada	5.0
40	Colorado	3.4		5	New Hampshire	5.0
3	Connecticut	5.5		7	Florida	4.9
30	Delaware	3.7		7	North Dakota	4.9
7	Florida	4.9		9	California	4.8
40	Georgia	3.4		10	Arkansas	4.7
15	Hawaii	4.3		10	Maryland	4.7
18	Idaho	4.2		12	Minnesota	4.6
15	Illinois	4.3		13	Arizona	4.5
25	Indiana	3.9		13	Iowa	4.5
13	Iowa	4.5		15	Hawaii	4.3
22	Kansas	4.0		15	Illinois	4.3
21	Kentucky	4.1		15	Wyoming	4.3
37	Louisiana	3.6		18	Idaho	4.2
28	Maine	3.8		18	Pennsylvania	4.2
10	Maryland	4.7		18	Texas	4.2
2	Massachusetts	5.6		21	Kentucky	4.1
49	Michigan	2.4		22	Kansas	4.0
12	Minnesota	4.6		22	New Mexico	4.0
40	Mississippi	3.4		22	Tennessee	4.0
48	Missouri	3.1		25	Indiana	3.9
40	Montana	3.4		25	South Dakota	3.9
30	Nebraska	3.7		25	Wisconsin	3.9
5	Nevada	5.0		28	Maine	3.8
5	New Hampshire	5.0		28	North Carolina	3.8
30	New Jersey	3.7		30	Alabama	3.7
22	New Mexico	4.0		30	Delaware	3.7
1	New York	5.7		30	Nebraska	3.7
28	North Carolina	3.8		30	New Jersey	3.7
7	North Dakota	4.9		30	Ohio	3.7
30	Ohio	3.7		30	Vermont	3.7
38	Oklahoma	3.5		30	West Virginia	3.7
40	Oregon	3.4		37	Louisiana	3.6
18	Pennsylvania	4.2		38	Oklahoma	3.5
40	Rhode Island	3.4		38	South Carolina	3.5
38	South Carolina	3.5		40	Colorado	3.4
25	South Dakota	3.9		40	Georgia	3.4
22	Tennessee	4.0		40	Mississippi	3.4
18	Texas	4.2		40	Montana	3.4
40	Utah	3.4		40	Oregon	3.4
30	Vermont	3.7		40	Rhode Island	3.4
4	Virginia	5.1		40	Utah	3.4
50	Washington	0.9		47	Alaska	3.3
30	West Virginia	3.7		48	Missouri	3.1
25	Wisconsin	3.9		49	Michigan	2.4
15	Wyoming	4.3		50	Washington	0.9
					District of Columbia	5.7

Source: Morgan Quitno Press using data from U.S. Department of Labor, Bureau of Labor Statistics
   "Quarterly Census of Employment and Wages: Annual Data Tables" (http://www.bls.gov/cew/cewsnote2.htm)
*Includes bonuses, cash value of meals and lodging, tips and, in many states, employer contributions to certain deferred compensation plans such as 401(k) plans.

Median Earnings of Male Full-Time Workers in 2004

National Median = $41,194

<table>
<tr><th colspan="3">ALPHA ORDER</th><th colspan="3">RANK ORDER</th></tr>
<tr><th>RANK</th><th>STATE</th><th>EARNINGS</th><th>RANK</th><th>STATE</th><th>EARNINGS</th></tr>
<tr><td>34</td><td>Alabama</td><td>$36,874</td><td>1</td><td>Connecticut</td><td>$51,996</td></tr>
<tr><td>5</td><td>Alaska</td><td>47,115</td><td>2</td><td>New Jersey</td><td>51,855</td></tr>
<tr><td>32</td><td>Arizona</td><td>37,516</td><td>3</td><td>Massachusetts</td><td>50,406</td></tr>
<tr><td>49</td><td>Arkansas</td><td>33,131</td><td>4</td><td>Maryland</td><td>47,971</td></tr>
<tr><td>15</td><td>California</td><td>42,626</td><td>5</td><td>Alaska</td><td>47,115</td></tr>
<tr><td>14</td><td>Colorado</td><td>42,635</td><td>6</td><td>Washington</td><td>46,599</td></tr>
<tr><td>1</td><td>Connecticut</td><td>51,996</td><td>7</td><td>Michigan</td><td>46,475</td></tr>
<tr><td>10</td><td>Delaware</td><td>44,562</td><td>8</td><td>New Hampshire</td><td>45,373</td></tr>
<tr><td>38</td><td>Florida</td><td>36,434</td><td>9</td><td>Illinois</td><td>44,620</td></tr>
<tr><td>24</td><td>Georgia</td><td>39,707</td><td>10</td><td>Delaware</td><td>44,562</td></tr>
<tr><td>22</td><td>Hawaii</td><td>40,170</td><td>11</td><td>Minnesota</td><td>44,389</td></tr>
<tr><td>39</td><td>Idaho</td><td>36,412</td><td>12</td><td>New York</td><td>44,101</td></tr>
<tr><td>9</td><td>Illinois</td><td>44,620</td><td>13</td><td>Virginia</td><td>43,050</td></tr>
<tr><td>20</td><td>Indiana</td><td>40,573</td><td>14</td><td>Colorado</td><td>42,635</td></tr>
<tr><td>33</td><td>Iowa</td><td>36,894</td><td>15</td><td>California</td><td>42,626</td></tr>
<tr><td>30</td><td>Kansas</td><td>37,952</td><td>16</td><td>Rhode Island</td><td>42,040</td></tr>
<tr><td>42</td><td>Kentucky</td><td>36,222</td><td>17</td><td>Ohio</td><td>41,874</td></tr>
<tr><td>35</td><td>Louisiana</td><td>36,873</td><td>18</td><td>Pennsylvania</td><td>41,873</td></tr>
<tr><td>28</td><td>Maine</td><td>38,296</td><td>19</td><td>Wisconsin</td><td>41,223</td></tr>
<tr><td>4</td><td>Maryland</td><td>47,971</td><td>20</td><td>Indiana</td><td>40,573</td></tr>
<tr><td>3</td><td>Massachusetts</td><td>50,406</td><td>21</td><td>Utah</td><td>40,317</td></tr>
<tr><td>7</td><td>Michigan</td><td>46,475</td><td>22</td><td>Hawaii</td><td>40,170</td></tr>
<tr><td>11</td><td>Minnesota</td><td>44,389</td><td>23</td><td>Wyoming</td><td>40,113</td></tr>
<tr><td>48</td><td>Mississippi</td><td>33,753</td><td>24</td><td>Georgia</td><td>39,707</td></tr>
<tr><td>26</td><td>Missouri</td><td>38,637</td><td>25</td><td>Oregon</td><td>39,485</td></tr>
<tr><td>46</td><td>Montana</td><td>34,530</td><td>26</td><td>Missouri</td><td>38,637</td></tr>
<tr><td>37</td><td>Nebraska</td><td>36,702</td><td>27</td><td>South Carolina</td><td>38,443</td></tr>
<tr><td>31</td><td>Nevada</td><td>37,785</td><td>28</td><td>Maine</td><td>38,296</td></tr>
<tr><td>8</td><td>New Hampshire</td><td>45,373</td><td>29</td><td>Texas</td><td>38,200</td></tr>
<tr><td>2</td><td>New Jersey</td><td>51,855</td><td>30</td><td>Kansas</td><td>37,952</td></tr>
<tr><td>45</td><td>New Mexico</td><td>35,040</td><td>31</td><td>Nevada</td><td>37,785</td></tr>
<tr><td>12</td><td>New York</td><td>44,101</td><td>32</td><td>Arizona</td><td>37,516</td></tr>
<tr><td>43</td><td>North Carolina</td><td>36,159</td><td>33</td><td>Iowa</td><td>36,894</td></tr>
<tr><td>44</td><td>North Dakota</td><td>35,790</td><td>34</td><td>Alabama</td><td>36,874</td></tr>
<tr><td>17</td><td>Ohio</td><td>41,874</td><td>35</td><td>Louisiana</td><td>36,873</td></tr>
<tr><td>47</td><td>Oklahoma</td><td>34,503</td><td>36</td><td>Vermont</td><td>36,840</td></tr>
<tr><td>25</td><td>Oregon</td><td>39,485</td><td>37</td><td>Nebraska</td><td>36,702</td></tr>
<tr><td>18</td><td>Pennsylvania</td><td>41,873</td><td>38</td><td>Florida</td><td>36,434</td></tr>
<tr><td>16</td><td>Rhode Island</td><td>42,040</td><td>39</td><td>Idaho</td><td>36,412</td></tr>
<tr><td>27</td><td>South Carolina</td><td>38,443</td><td>40</td><td>Tennessee</td><td>36,369</td></tr>
<tr><td>50</td><td>South Dakota</td><td>32,413</td><td>41</td><td>West Virginia</td><td>36,243</td></tr>
<tr><td>40</td><td>Tennessee</td><td>36,369</td><td>42</td><td>Kentucky</td><td>36,222</td></tr>
<tr><td>29</td><td>Texas</td><td>38,200</td><td>43</td><td>North Carolina</td><td>36,159</td></tr>
<tr><td>21</td><td>Utah</td><td>40,317</td><td>44</td><td>North Dakota</td><td>35,790</td></tr>
<tr><td>36</td><td>Vermont</td><td>36,840</td><td>45</td><td>New Mexico</td><td>35,040</td></tr>
<tr><td>13</td><td>Virginia</td><td>43,050</td><td>46</td><td>Montana</td><td>34,530</td></tr>
<tr><td>6</td><td>Washington</td><td>46,599</td><td>47</td><td>Oklahoma</td><td>34,503</td></tr>
<tr><td>41</td><td>West Virginia</td><td>36,243</td><td>48</td><td>Mississippi</td><td>33,753</td></tr>
<tr><td>19</td><td>Wisconsin</td><td>41,223</td><td>49</td><td>Arkansas</td><td>33,131</td></tr>
<tr><td>23</td><td>Wyoming</td><td>40,113</td><td>50</td><td>South Dakota</td><td>32,413</td></tr>
<tr><td></td><td></td><td></td><td></td><td>District of Columbia</td><td>50,933</td></tr>
</table>

Source: U.S. Bureau of the Census
  "American Community Survey" (http://www.census.gov/acs/www/)

Median Earnings of Female Full-Time Workers in 2004

National Median = $31,374

<table>
<tr><td colspan="3">ALPHA ORDER</td><td colspan="3">RANK ORDER</td></tr>
<tr><td>RANK</td><td>STATE</td><td>EARNINGS</td><td>RANK</td><td>STATE</td><td>EARNINGS</td></tr>
<tr><td>42</td><td>Alabama</td><td>$26,801</td><td>1</td><td>New Jersey</td><td>$40,154</td></tr>
<tr><td>8</td><td>Alaska</td><td>34,444</td><td>2</td><td>Connecticut</td><td>40,147</td></tr>
<tr><td>23</td><td>Arizona</td><td>30,196</td><td>3</td><td>Maryland</td><td>39,546</td></tr>
<tr><td>49</td><td>Arkansas</td><td>24,346</td><td>4</td><td>Massachusetts</td><td>37,424</td></tr>
<tr><td>5</td><td>California</td><td>36,133</td><td>5</td><td>California</td><td>36,133</td></tr>
<tr><td>9</td><td>Colorado</td><td>34,063</td><td>6</td><td>Washington</td><td>35,324</td></tr>
<tr><td>2</td><td>Connecticut</td><td>40,147</td><td>7</td><td>New York</td><td>35,034</td></tr>
<tr><td>10</td><td>Delaware</td><td>33,801</td><td>8</td><td>Alaska</td><td>34,444</td></tr>
<tr><td>28</td><td>Florida</td><td>29,352</td><td>9</td><td>Colorado</td><td>34,063</td></tr>
<tr><td>22</td><td>Georgia</td><td>30,552</td><td>10</td><td>Delaware</td><td>33,801</td></tr>
<tr><td>16</td><td>Hawaii</td><td>32,098</td><td>11</td><td>Minnesota</td><td>33,712</td></tr>
<tr><td>43</td><td>Idaho</td><td>26,763</td><td>12</td><td>Illinois</td><td>33,451</td></tr>
<tr><td>12</td><td>Illinois</td><td>33,451</td><td>13</td><td>Rhode Island</td><td>33,437</td></tr>
<tr><td>33</td><td>Indiana</td><td>27,780</td><td>14</td><td>Virginia</td><td>33,303</td></tr>
<tr><td>36</td><td>Iowa</td><td>27,176</td><td>15</td><td>New Hampshire</td><td>32,658</td></tr>
<tr><td>31</td><td>Kansas</td><td>28,186</td><td>16</td><td>Hawaii</td><td>32,098</td></tr>
<tr><td>38</td><td>Kentucky</td><td>27,095</td><td>17</td><td>Michigan</td><td>31,808</td></tr>
<tr><td>46</td><td>Louisiana</td><td>25,028</td><td>18</td><td>Oregon</td><td>31,759</td></tr>
<tr><td>27</td><td>Maine</td><td>29,766</td><td>19</td><td>Pennsylvania</td><td>31,197</td></tr>
<tr><td>3</td><td>Maryland</td><td>39,546</td><td>20</td><td>Vermont</td><td>30,864</td></tr>
<tr><td>4</td><td>Massachusetts</td><td>37,424</td><td>21</td><td>Nevada</td><td>30,830</td></tr>
<tr><td>17</td><td>Michigan</td><td>31,808</td><td>22</td><td>Georgia</td><td>30,552</td></tr>
<tr><td>11</td><td>Minnesota</td><td>33,712</td><td>23</td><td>Arizona</td><td>30,196</td></tr>
<tr><td>48</td><td>Mississippi</td><td>24,415</td><td>24</td><td>Ohio</td><td>30,149</td></tr>
<tr><td>29</td><td>Missouri</td><td>29,108</td><td>25</td><td>Texas</td><td>30,139</td></tr>
<tr><td>50</td><td>Montana</td><td>23,180</td><td>26</td><td>Wisconsin</td><td>29,820</td></tr>
<tr><td>35</td><td>Nebraska</td><td>27,381</td><td>27</td><td>Maine</td><td>29,766</td></tr>
<tr><td>21</td><td>Nevada</td><td>30,830</td><td>28</td><td>Florida</td><td>29,352</td></tr>
<tr><td>15</td><td>New Hampshire</td><td>32,658</td><td>29</td><td>Missouri</td><td>29,108</td></tr>
<tr><td>1</td><td>New Jersey</td><td>40,154</td><td>30</td><td>North Carolina</td><td>28,426</td></tr>
<tr><td>41</td><td>New Mexico</td><td>26,935</td><td>31</td><td>Kansas</td><td>28,186</td></tr>
<tr><td>7</td><td>New York</td><td>35,034</td><td>32</td><td>Wyoming</td><td>28,179</td></tr>
<tr><td>30</td><td>North Carolina</td><td>28,426</td><td>33</td><td>Indiana</td><td>27,780</td></tr>
<tr><td>45</td><td>North Dakota</td><td>25,182</td><td>34</td><td>Utah</td><td>27,471</td></tr>
<tr><td>24</td><td>Ohio</td><td>30,149</td><td>35</td><td>Nebraska</td><td>27,381</td></tr>
<tr><td>39</td><td>Oklahoma</td><td>27,029</td><td>36</td><td>Iowa</td><td>27,176</td></tr>
<tr><td>18</td><td>Oregon</td><td>31,759</td><td>37</td><td>South Carolina</td><td>27,166</td></tr>
<tr><td>19</td><td>Pennsylvania</td><td>31,197</td><td>38</td><td>Kentucky</td><td>27,095</td></tr>
<tr><td>13</td><td>Rhode Island</td><td>33,437</td><td>39</td><td>Oklahoma</td><td>27,029</td></tr>
<tr><td>37</td><td>South Carolina</td><td>27,166</td><td>40</td><td>Tennessee</td><td>26,989</td></tr>
<tr><td>47</td><td>South Dakota</td><td>24,936</td><td>41</td><td>New Mexico</td><td>26,935</td></tr>
<tr><td>40</td><td>Tennessee</td><td>26,989</td><td>42</td><td>Alabama</td><td>26,801</td></tr>
<tr><td>25</td><td>Texas</td><td>30,139</td><td>43</td><td>Idaho</td><td>26,763</td></tr>
<tr><td>34</td><td>Utah</td><td>27,471</td><td>44</td><td>West Virginia</td><td>25,189</td></tr>
<tr><td>20</td><td>Vermont</td><td>30,864</td><td>45</td><td>North Dakota</td><td>25,182</td></tr>
<tr><td>14</td><td>Virginia</td><td>33,303</td><td>46</td><td>Louisiana</td><td>25,028</td></tr>
<tr><td>6</td><td>Washington</td><td>35,324</td><td>47</td><td>South Dakota</td><td>24,936</td></tr>
<tr><td>44</td><td>West Virginia</td><td>25,189</td><td>48</td><td>Mississippi</td><td>24,415</td></tr>
<tr><td>26</td><td>Wisconsin</td><td>29,820</td><td>49</td><td>Arkansas</td><td>24,346</td></tr>
<tr><td>32</td><td>Wyoming</td><td>28,179</td><td>50</td><td>Montana</td><td>23,180</td></tr>
<tr><td></td><td></td><td></td><td></td><td>District of Columbia</td><td>46,292</td></tr>
</table>

Source: U.S. Bureau of the Census
   "American Community Survey" (http://www.census.gov/acs/www/)

State Minimum Wage Rates in 2006

National Rate = $5.15 per Hour*

ALPHA ORDER

RANK	STATE	MINIMUM WAGE
NA	Alabama**	NA
5	Alaska	7.15
NA	Arizona**	NA
18	Arkansas	5.15
6	California	6.75
18	Colorado	5.15
3	Connecticut	7.40
14	Delaware	6.15
13	Florida	6.40
18	Georgia	5.15
6	Hawaii	6.75
18	Idaho	5.15
11	Illinois	6.50
10	Indiana	5.15
18	Iowa	5.15
44	Kansas	2.65
18	Kentucky	5.15
NA	Louisiana**	NA
11	Maine	6.50
18	Maryland	5.15
6	Massachusetts	6.75
18	Michigan	5.15
14	Minnesota	6.15
NA	Mississippi**	NA
18	Missouri	5.15
18	Montana	5.15
18	Nebraska	5.15
18	Nevada	5.15
18	New Hampshire	5.15
14	New Jersey	6.15
18	New Mexico	5.15
6	New York	6.75
18	North Carolina	5.15
18	North Dakota	5.15
43	Ohio	4.25
18	Oklahoma	5.15
2	Oregon	7.50
18	Pennsylvania	5.15
6	Rhode Island	6.75
NA	South Carolina**	NA
18	South Dakota	5.15
NA	Tennessee**	NA
18	Texas	5.15
18	Utah	5.15
4	Vermont	7.25
18	Virginia	5.15
1	Washington	7.63
18	West Virginia	5.15
17	Wisconsin	5.70
18	Wyoming	5.15

RANK ORDER

RANK	STATE	MINIMUM WAGE
1	Washington	$7.63
2	Oregon	7.50
3	Connecticut	7.40
4	Vermont	7.25
5	Alaska	7.15
6	California	6.75
6	Hawaii	6.75
6	Massachusetts	6.75
6	New York	6.75
6	Rhode Island	6.75
11	Illinois	6.50
11	Maine	6.50
13	Florida	6.40
14	Delaware	6.15
14	Minnesota	6.15
14	New Jersey	6.15
17	Wisconsin	5.70
18	Arkansas	5.15
18	Colorado	5.15
18	Georgia	5.15
18	Idaho	5.15
18	Indiana	5.15
18	Iowa	5.15
18	Kentucky	5.15
18	Maryland	5.15
18	Michigan	5.15
18	Missouri	5.15
18	Montana	5.15
18	Nebraska	5.15
18	Nevada	5.15
18	New Hampshire	5.15
18	New Mexico	5.15
18	North Carolina	5.15
18	North Dakota	5.15
18	Oklahoma	5.15
18	Pennsylvania	5.15
18	South Dakota	5.15
18	Texas	5.15
18	Utah	5.15
18	Virginia	5.15
18	West Virginia	5.15
18	Wyoming	5.15
43	Ohio	4.25
44	Kansas	2.65
NA	Alabama**	NA
NA	Arizona**	NA
NA	Louisiana**	NA
NA	Mississippi**	NA
NA	South Carolina**	NA
NA	Tennessee**	NA
	District of Columbia	7.00

Source: U.S. Department of Labor, Employment Standards Administration
   "Minimum Wage Laws in the States" (http://www.dol.gov/esa/minwage/america.htm)
*As of January 1, 2006. State minimum wage rates are for those employers and jobs not covered by the federal program.
**No separate state program.

Average Hourly Earnings of Production Workers
On Manufacturing Payrolls in 2005
National Average = $16.56*

ALPHA ORDER

RANK	STATE	HOURLY EARNINGS
30	Alabama	$15.44
20	Alaska	16.67
36	Arizona	14.75
49	Arkansas	13.68
27	California	15.89
22	Colorado	16.32
3	Connecticut	19.44
6	Delaware	18.34
48	Florida	13.78
38	Georgia	14.58
39	Hawaii	14.45
35	Idaho	15.01
28	Illinois	15.79
5	Indiana	18.81
21	Iowa	16.58
10	Kansas	17.65
18	Kentucky	16.83
9	Louisiana	17.69
14	Maine	17.52
13	Maryland	17.56
8	Massachusetts	17.84
1	Michigan	22.02
12	Minnesota	17.59
47	Mississippi	13.79
16	Missouri	17.37
29	Montana	15.55
32	Nebraska	15.26
34	Nevada	15.23
24	New Hampshire	16.25
26	New Jersey	15.93
46	New Mexico	13.96
7	New York	18.09
41	North Carolina	14.23
11	North Dakota	17.63
4	Ohio	19.39
43	Oklahoma	14.05
25	Oregon	16.03
32	Pennsylvania	15.26
50	Rhode Island	13.33
37	South Carolina	14.69
42	South Dakota	14.21
45	Tennessee	13.97
44	Texas	14.03
40	Utah	14.28
31	Vermont	15.31
19	Virginia	16.69
2	Washington	19.97
17	West Virginia	17.28
23	Wisconsin	16.27
15	Wyoming	17.44

RANK ORDER

RANK	STATE	HOURLY EARNINGS
1	Michigan	$22.02
2	Washington	19.97
3	Connecticut	19.44
4	Ohio	19.39
5	Indiana	18.81
6	Delaware	18.34
7	New York	18.09
8	Massachusetts	17.84
9	Louisiana	17.69
10	Kansas	17.65
11	North Dakota	17.63
12	Minnesota	17.59
13	Maryland	17.56
14	Maine	17.52
15	Wyoming	17.44
16	Missouri	17.37
17	West Virginia	17.28
18	Kentucky	16.83
19	Virginia	16.69
20	Alaska	16.67
21	Iowa	16.58
22	Colorado	16.32
23	Wisconsin	16.27
24	New Hampshire	16.25
25	Oregon	16.03
26	New Jersey	15.93
27	California	15.89
28	Illinois	15.79
29	Montana	15.55
30	Alabama	15.44
31	Vermont	15.31
32	Nebraska	15.26
32	Pennsylvania	15.26
34	Nevada	15.23
35	Idaho	15.01
36	Arizona	14.75
37	South Carolina	14.69
38	Georgia	14.58
39	Hawaii	14.45
40	Utah	14.28
41	North Carolina	14.23
42	South Dakota	14.21
43	Oklahoma	14.05
44	Texas	14.03
45	Tennessee	13.97
46	New Mexico	13.96
47	Mississippi	13.79
48	Florida	13.78
49	Arkansas	13.68
50	Rhode Island	13.33
	District of Columbia**	NA

Source: U.S. Department of Labor, Bureau of Labor Statistics
"Current Employment Statistics Survey" (http://www.bls.gov/sae/home.htm)
Preliminary data for December 2005. Not seasonally adjusted.
***Not available*

Average Weekly Earnings of Production Workers
On Manufacturing Payrolls in 2005
National Average = $673.20*

ALPHA ORDER

RANK	STATE	WEEKLY EARNINGS
27	Alabama	$648.48
50	Alaska	398.41
28	Arizona	641.63
45	Arkansas	559.51
29	California	634.01
26	Colorado	649.54
2	Connecticut	828.14
9	Delaware	728.10
39	Florida	581.52
42	Georgia	570.08
43	Hawaii	563.55
32	Idaho	612.41
25	Illinois	652.13
4	Indiana	793.78
16	Iowa	704.65
6	Kansas	737.77
19	Kentucky	683.30
11	Louisiana	723.52
14	Maine	713.06
15	Maryland	712.94
7	Massachusetts	733.22
1	Michigan	944.66
8	Minnesota	729.99
37	Mississippi	588.83
21	Missouri	679.17
31	Montana	622.00
33	Nebraska	607.35
34	Nevada	603.11
20	New Hampshire	682.50
22	New Jersey	672.25
48	New Mexico	544.44
10	New York	723.60
40	North Carolina	577.74
17	North Dakota	701.67
5	Ohio	791.11
44	Oklahoma	560.60
24	Oregon	660.44
30	Pennsylvania	622.61
49	Rhode Island	509.21
38	South Carolina	584.66
36	South Dakota	591.14
47	Tennessee	549.02
41	Texas	572.42
46	Utah	549.78
35	Vermont	597.09
18	Virginia	687.63
3	Washington	796.80
12	West Virginia	720.58
23	Wisconsin	671.95
13	Wyoming	713.30

RANK ORDER

RANK	STATE	WEEKLY EARNINGS
1	Michigan	$944.66
2	Connecticut	828.14
3	Washington	796.80
4	Indiana	793.78
5	Ohio	791.11
6	Kansas	737.77
7	Massachusetts	733.22
8	Minnesota	729.99
9	Delaware	728.10
10	New York	723.60
11	Louisiana	723.52
12	West Virginia	720.58
13	Wyoming	713.30
14	Maine	713.06
15	Maryland	712.94
16	Iowa	704.65
17	North Dakota	701.67
18	Virginia	687.63
19	Kentucky	683.30
20	New Hampshire	682.50
21	Missouri	679.17
22	New Jersey	672.25
23	Wisconsin	671.95
24	Oregon	660.44
25	Illinois	652.13
26	Colorado	649.54
27	Alabama	648.48
28	Arizona	641.63
29	California	634.01
30	Pennsylvania	622.61
31	Montana	622.00
32	Idaho	612.41
33	Nebraska	607.35
34	Nevada	603.11
35	Vermont	597.09
36	South Dakota	591.14
37	Mississippi	588.83
38	South Carolina	584.66
39	Florida	581.52
40	North Carolina	577.74
41	Texas	572.42
42	Georgia	570.08
43	Hawaii	563.55
44	Oklahoma	560.60
45	Arkansas	559.51
46	Utah	549.78
47	Tennessee	549.02
48	New Mexico	544.44
49	Rhode Island	509.21
50	Alaska	398.41

District of Columbia**   NA

Source: U.S. Department of Labor, Bureau of Labor Statistics
   "Current Employment Statistics Survey" (http://www.bls.gov/sae/home.htm)
*Preliminary data for December 2005. Not seasonally adjusted.
**Not available

Average Work Week of Production Workers
On Manufacturing Payrolls in 2005
National Average = 40.7 Hours per Week

ALPHA ORDER

RANK	STATE	WEEKLY HOURS
9	Alabama	42.0
50	Alaska	23.9
1	Arizona	43.5
20	Arkansas	40.9
33	California	39.9
36	Colorado	39.8
4	Connecticut	42.6
40	Delaware	39.7
6	Florida	42.2
43	Georgia	39.1
45	Hawaii	39.0
23	Idaho	40.8
15	Illinois	41.3
6	Indiana	42.2
5	Iowa	42.5
11	Kansas	41.8
28	Kentucky	40.6
20	Louisiana	40.9
27	Maine	40.7
28	Maryland	40.6
19	Massachusetts	41.1
2	Michigan	42.9
14	Minnesota	41.5
3	Mississippi	42.7
43	Missouri	39.1
31	Montana	40.0
36	Nebraska	39.8
41	Nevada	39.6
9	New Hampshire	42.0
6	New Jersey	42.2
45	New Mexico	39.0
31	New York	40.0
28	North Carolina	40.6
36	North Dakota	39.8
23	Ohio	40.8
33	Oklahoma	39.9
17	Oregon	41.2
23	Pennsylvania	40.8
49	Rhode Island	38.2
36	South Carolina	39.8
13	South Dakota	41.6
42	Tennessee	39.3
23	Texas	40.8
48	Utah	38.5
45	Vermont	39.0
17	Virginia	41.2
33	Washington	39.9
12	West Virginia	41.7
15	Wisconsin	41.3
20	Wyoming	40.9

RANK ORDER

RANK	STATE	WEEKLY HOURS
1	Arizona	43.5
2	Michigan	42.9
3	Mississippi	42.7
4	Connecticut	42.6
5	Iowa	42.5
6	Florida	42.2
6	Indiana	42.2
6	New Jersey	42.2
9	Alabama	42.0
9	New Hampshire	42.0
11	Kansas	41.8
12	West Virginia	41.7
13	South Dakota	41.6
14	Minnesota	41.5
15	Illinois	41.3
15	Wisconsin	41.3
17	Oregon	41.2
17	Virginia	41.2
19	Massachusetts	41.1
20	Arkansas	40.9
20	Louisiana	40.9
20	Wyoming	40.9
23	Idaho	40.8
23	Ohio	40.8
23	Pennsylvania	40.8
23	Texas	40.8
27	Maine	40.7
28	Kentucky	40.6
28	Maryland	40.6
28	North Carolina	40.6
31	Montana	40.0
31	New York	40.0
33	California	39.9
33	Oklahoma	39.9
33	Washington	39.9
36	Colorado	39.8
36	Nebraska	39.8
36	North Dakota	39.8
36	South Carolina	39.8
40	Delaware	39.7
41	Nevada	39.6
42	Tennessee	39.3
43	Georgia	39.1
43	Missouri	39.1
45	Hawaii	39.0
45	New Mexico	39.0
45	Vermont	39.0
48	Utah	38.5
49	Rhode Island	38.2
50	Alaska	23.9
	District of Columbia**	NA

Source: U.S. Department of Labor, Bureau of Labor Statistics
   "Current Employment Statistics Survey" (http://www.bls.gov/sae/home.htm)
Preliminary data for December 2005. Not seasonally adjusted.
**Not available*

Average Weekly Unemployment Benefit in 2005

National Average = $266.04 a Week

ALPHA ORDER

RANK	STATE	BENEFIT
49	Alabama	$182.07
47	Alaska	193.94
46	Arizona	195.08
35	Arkansas	229.69
13	California	278.14
6	Colorado	302.08
8	Connecticut	295.14
28	Delaware	247.35
36	Florida	226.44
30	Georgia	244.73
2	Hawaii	337.79
33	Idaho	234.50
11	Illinois	283.88
14	Indiana	277.54
16	Iowa	270.19
12	Kansas	278.35
21	Kentucky	259.72
48	Louisiana	193.13
32	Maine	240.84
24	Maryland	256.94
1	Massachusetts	356.53
10	Michigan	290.07
5	Minnesota	319.10
50	Mississippi	180.51
45	Missouri	205.78
41	Montana	217.14
38	Nebraska	223.94
22	Nevada	258.70
26	New Hampshire	252.50
4	New Jersey	335.95
40	New Mexico	218.07
15	New York	276.17
23	North Carolina	257.83
34	North Dakota	233.29
25	Ohio	256.73
39	Oklahoma	221.64
19	Oregon	261.42
9	Pennsylvania	291.43
3	Rhode Island	336.15
42	South Carolina	216.78
44	South Dakota	209.59
43	Tennessee	212.41
20	Texas	261.34
18	Utah	263.43
17	Vermont	265.78
29	Virginia	246.23
7	Washington	298.56
37	West Virginia	225.60
27	Wisconsin	251.33
31	Wyoming	241.34

RANK ORDER

RANK	STATE	BENEFIT
1	Massachusetts	$356.53
2	Hawaii	337.79
3	Rhode Island	336.15
4	New Jersey	335.95
5	Minnesota	319.10
6	Colorado	302.08
7	Washington	298.56
8	Connecticut	295.14
9	Pennsylvania	291.43
10	Michigan	290.07
11	Illinois	283.88
12	Kansas	278.35
13	California	278.14
14	Indiana	277.54
15	New York	276.17
16	Iowa	270.19
17	Vermont	265.78
18	Utah	263.43
19	Oregon	261.42
20	Texas	261.34
21	Kentucky	259.72
22	Nevada	258.70
23	North Carolina	257.83
24	Maryland	256.94
25	Ohio	256.73
26	New Hampshire	252.50
27	Wisconsin	251.33
28	Delaware	247.35
29	Virginia	246.23
30	Georgia	244.73
31	Wyoming	241.34
32	Maine	240.84
33	Idaho	234.50
34	North Dakota	233.29
35	Arkansas	229.69
36	Florida	226.44
37	West Virginia	225.60
38	Nebraska	223.94
39	Oklahoma	221.64
40	New Mexico	218.07
41	Montana	217.14
42	South Carolina	216.78
43	Tennessee	212.41
44	South Dakota	209.59
45	Missouri	205.78
46	Arizona	195.08
47	Alaska	193.94
48	Louisiana	193.13
49	Alabama	182.07
50	Mississippi	180.51

District of Columbia   266.45

Source: Morgan Quitno Press using data from U.S. Department of Labor, Bureau of Labor Statistics
"Unemployment Insurance Data Summary" (http://workforcesecurity.doleta.gov/unemploy/content/data.asp)

Workers' Compensation Benefit Payments in 2003

National Total = $54,870,813,000*

ALPHA ORDER

RANK	STATE	PAYMENTS	% of USA
26	Alabama	$623,315,000	1.1%
41	Alaska	199,364,000	0.4%
29	Arizona	458,790,000	0.8%
42	Arkansas	198,144,000	0.4%
1	California	13,021,785,000	23.7%
22	Colorado	693,316,000	1.3%
18	Connecticut	753,618,000	1.4%
45	Delaware	169,158,000	0.3%
5	Florida	2,201,435,000	4.0%
12	Georgia	1,120,886,000	2.0%
35	Hawaii	274,922,000	0.5%
44	Idaho	181,194,000	0.3%
6	Illinois	2,099,685,000	3.8%
27	Indiana	567,587,000	1.0%
32	Iowa	320,454,000	0.6%
33	Kansas	294,304,000	0.5%
19	Kentucky	717,196,000	1.3%
23	Louisiana	659,533,000	1.2%
37	Maine	260,845,000	0.5%
25	Maryland	628,510,000	1.1%
14	Massachusetts	890,044,000	1.6%
10	Michigan	1,476,850,000	2.7%
15	Minnesota	883,619,000	1.6%
36	Mississippi	271,677,000	0.5%
11	Missouri	1,257,962,000	2.3%
39	Montana	204,677,000	0.4%
34	Nebraska	290,901,000	0.5%
31	Nevada	369,747,000	0.7%
38	New Hampshire	224,407,000	0.4%
9	New Jersey	1,542,608,000	2.8%
43	New Mexico	197,026,000	0.4%
2	New York	3,220,398,000	5.9%
13	North Carolina	1,059,955,000	1.9%
50	North Dakota	77,524,000	0.1%
4	Ohio	2,442,165,000	4.5%
28	Oklahoma	561,643,000	1.0%
30	Oregon	446,887,000	0.8%
3	Pennsylvania	2,625,878,000	4.8%
47	Rhode Island	106,948,000	0.2%
24	South Carolina	656,935,000	1.2%
49	South Dakota	95,119,000	0.2%
20	Tennessee	710,475,000	1.3%
7	Texas	1,919,527,000	3.5%
40	Utah	201,557,000	0.4%
46	Vermont	140,534,000	0.3%
21	Virginia	701,464,000	1.3%
8	Washington	1,800,477,000	3.3%
17	West Virginia	828,913,000	1.5%
16	Wisconsin	839,829,000	1.5%
48	Wyoming	102,663,000	0.2%

RANK ORDER

RANK	STATE	PAYMENTS	% of USA
1	California	$13,021,785,000	23.7%
2	New York	3,220,398,000	5.9%
3	Pennsylvania	2,625,878,000	4.8%
4	Ohio	2,442,165,000	4.5%
5	Florida	2,201,435,000	4.0%
6	Illinois	2,099,685,000	3.8%
7	Texas	1,919,527,000	3.5%
8	Washington	1,800,477,000	3.3%
9	New Jersey	1,542,608,000	2.8%
10	Michigan	1,476,850,000	2.7%
11	Missouri	1,257,962,000	2.3%
12	Georgia	1,120,886,000	2.0%
13	North Carolina	1,059,955,000	1.9%
14	Massachusetts	890,044,000	1.6%
15	Minnesota	883,619,000	1.6%
16	Wisconsin	839,829,000	1.5%
17	West Virginia	828,913,000	1.5%
18	Connecticut	753,618,000	1.4%
19	Kentucky	717,196,000	1.3%
20	Tennessee	710,475,000	1.3%
21	Virginia	701,464,000	1.3%
22	Colorado	693,316,000	1.3%
23	Louisiana	659,533,000	1.2%
24	South Carolina	656,935,000	1.2%
25	Maryland	628,510,000	1.1%
26	Alabama	623,315,000	1.1%
27	Indiana	567,587,000	1.0%
28	Oklahoma	561,643,000	1.0%
29	Arizona	458,790,000	0.8%
30	Oregon	446,887,000	0.8%
31	Nevada	369,747,000	0.7%
32	Iowa	320,454,000	0.6%
33	Kansas	294,304,000	0.5%
34	Nebraska	290,901,000	0.5%
35	Hawaii	274,922,000	0.5%
36	Mississippi	271,677,000	0.5%
37	Maine	260,845,000	0.5%
38	New Hampshire	224,407,000	0.4%
39	Montana	204,677,000	0.4%
40	Utah	201,557,000	0.4%
41	Alaska	199,364,000	0.4%
42	Arkansas	198,144,000	0.4%
43	New Mexico	197,026,000	0.4%
44	Idaho	181,194,000	0.3%
45	Delaware	169,158,000	0.3%
46	Vermont	140,534,000	0.3%
47	Rhode Island	106,948,000	0.2%
48	Wyoming	102,663,000	0.2%
49	South Dakota	95,119,000	0.2%
50	North Dakota	77,524,000	0.1%
	District of Columbia	93,677,000	0.2%

Source: National Academy of Social Insurance (Washington, DC)
   "Workers' Compensation: Benefits, Coverage and Costs 2003" (http://www.nasi.org)
*Estimated payments from private insurance, state and federal funds and self insurance. National total includes
payments for federal civilian employee program, Black Lung Program and other federal programs.

Workers' Compensation Benefit Payment per Covered Worker in 2003

National Average = $438*

ALPHA ORDER

RANK	STATE	AVERAGE
22	Alabama	$367
3	Alaska	725
47	Arizona	206
50	Arkansas	187
2	California	895
28	Colorado	336
10	Connecticut	470
15	Delaware	427
30	Florida	322
32	Georgia	312
7	Hawaii	511
30	Idaho	322
21	Illinois	375
48	Indiana	205
45	Iowa	231
44	Kansas	235
14	Kentucky	429
23	Louisiana	362
12	Maine	452
38	Maryland	273
36	Massachusetts	288
24	Michigan	354
25	Minnesota	348
40	Mississippi	266
6	Missouri	514
5	Montana	539
27	Nebraska	342
25	Nevada	348
20	New Hampshire	377
17	New Jersey	407
37	New Mexico	286
18	New York	398
33	North Carolina	296
41	North Dakota	257
11	Ohio	469
16	Oklahoma	411
34	Oregon	292
8	Pennsylvania	490
43	Rhode Island	241
19	South Carolina	391
39	South Dakota	269
35	Tennessee	290
42	Texas	253
49	Utah	200
9	Vermont	488
46	Virginia	220
4	Washington	697
1	West Virginia	1,264
29	Wisconsin	323
13	Wyoming	443

RANK ORDER

RANK	STATE	AVERAGE
1	West Virginia	$1,264
2	California	895
3	Alaska	725
4	Washington	697
5	Montana	539
6	Missouri	514
7	Hawaii	511
8	Pennsylvania	490
9	Vermont	488
10	Connecticut	470
11	Ohio	469
12	Maine	452
13	Wyoming	443
14	Kentucky	429
15	Delaware	427
16	Oklahoma	411
17	New Jersey	407
18	New York	398
19	South Carolina	391
20	New Hampshire	377
21	Illinois	375
22	Alabama	367
23	Louisiana	362
24	Michigan	354
25	Minnesota	348
25	Nevada	348
27	Nebraska	342
28	Colorado	336
29	Wisconsin	323
30	Florida	322
30	Idaho	322
32	Georgia	312
33	North Carolina	296
34	Oregon	292
35	Tennessee	290
36	Massachusetts	288
37	New Mexico	286
38	Maryland	273
39	South Dakota	269
40	Mississippi	266
41	North Dakota	257
42	Texas	253
43	Rhode Island	241
44	Kansas	235
45	Iowa	231
46	Virginia	220
47	Arizona	206
48	Indiana	205
49	Utah	200
50	Arkansas	187

District of Columbia 204

Source: Morgan Quitno Press using data from National Academy of Social Insurance (Washington, DC)
    "Workers' Compensation: Benefits, Coverage and Costs 2003" (http://www.nasi.org)
*Estimated payments from private insurance, state and federal funds and self insurance. National rate includes
payments for federal civilian employee program, Black Lung Program and other federal programs. Total divided by
number of workers covered by workers' compensation.

Percent Change in Workers' Compensation Benefit Payments: 2002 to 2003

National Percent Change = 3.2% Increase*

ALPHA ORDER				RANK ORDER		
RANK	STATE	PERCENT CHANGE		RANK	STATE	PERCENT CHANGE
42	Alabama	(5.1)		1	Idaho	18.8
14	Alaska	6.3		2	Virginia	12.3
6	Arizona	9.9		3	Massachusetts	12.1
5	Arkansas	10.1		4	South Carolina	10.9
7	California	9.6		5	Arkansas	10.1
41	Colorado	(4.4)		6	Arizona	9.9
32	Connecticut	0.8		7	California	9.6
26	Delaware	2.1		8	Maryland	9.4
21	Florida	3.4		9	Oklahoma	7.8
20	Georgia	3.5		10	New Mexico	7.3
23	Hawaii	2.6		11	Montana	7.2
1	Idaho	18.8		12	Vermont	6.7
39	Illinois	(3.4)		13	North Carolina	6.5
33	Indiana	0.2		14	Alaska	6.3
35	Iowa	(0.3)		14	Tennessee	6.3
50	Kansas	(16.1)		16	Washington	5.0
18	Kentucky	4.2		17	New Jersey	4.8
30	Louisiana	1.1		18	Kentucky	4.2
47	Maine	(9.6)		19	Pennsylvania	3.7
8	Maryland	9.4		20	Georgia	3.5
3	Massachusetts	12.1		21	Florida	3.4
38	Michigan	(2.4)		22	New Hampshire	2.8
40	Minnesota	(4.1)		23	Hawaii	2.6
43	Mississippi	(5.2)		24	New York	2.5
28	Missouri	1.9		25	Ohio	2.3
11	Montana	7.2		26	Delaware	2.1
31	Nebraska	1.0		27	North Dakota	2.0
46	Nevada	(8.4)		28	Missouri	1.9
22	New Hampshire	2.8		29	South Dakota	1.6
17	New Jersey	4.8		30	Louisiana	1.1
10	New Mexico	7.3		31	Nebraska	1.0
24	New York	2.5		32	Connecticut	0.8
13	North Carolina	6.5		33	Indiana	0.2
27	North Dakota	2.0		34	Oregon	(0.2)
25	Ohio	2.3		35	Iowa	(0.3)
9	Oklahoma	7.8		36	West Virginia	(0.4)
34	Oregon	(0.2)		37	Wyoming	(1.5)
19	Pennsylvania	3.7		38	Michigan	(2.4)
47	Rhode Island	(9.6)		39	Illinois	(3.4)
4	South Carolina	10.9		40	Minnesota	(4.1)
29	South Dakota	1.6		41	Colorado	(4.4)
14	Tennessee	6.3		42	Alabama	(5.1)
44	Texas	(5.9)		43	Mississippi	(5.2)
49	Utah	(12.8)		44	Texas	(5.9)
12	Vermont	6.7		45	Wisconsin	(6.1)
2	Virginia	12.3		46	Nevada	(8.4)
16	Washington	5.0		47	Maine	(9.6)
36	West Virginia	(0.4)		47	Rhode Island	(9.6)
45	Wisconsin	(6.1)		49	Utah	(12.8)
37	Wyoming	(1.5)		50	Kansas	(16.1)
					District of Columbia	(6.6)

Source: National Academy of Social Insurance (Washington, DC)
    "Workers' Compensation: Benefits, Coverage and Costs 2003" (http://www.nasi.org)
*Estimated payments from private insurance, state and federal funds and self insurance. National rate includes payments for federal civilian employee program, Black Lung Program and other federal programs.

Civilian Labor Force in 2005

National Total = 150,153,000 Workers*

ALPHA ORDER

RANK ORDER

RANK	STATE	EMPLOYEES	% of USA		RANK	STATE	EMPLOYEES	% of USA
23	Alabama	2,161,700	1.4%		1	California	18,038,100	12.0%
49	Alaska	344,700	0.2%		2	Texas	11,310,200	7.5%
21	Arizona	2,855,000	1.9%		3	New York	9,473,100	6.3%
32	Arkansas	1,369,400	0.9%		4	Florida	8,765,500	5.8%
1	California	18,038,100	12.0%		5	Illinois	6,497,800	4.3%
22	Colorado	2,544,600	1.7%		6	Pennsylvania	6,306,100	4.2%
28	Connecticut	1,829,200	1.2%		7	Ohio	5,923,700	3.9%
45	Delaware	443,900	0.3%		8	Michigan	5,138,800	3.4%
4	Florida	8,765,500	5.8%		9	Georgia	4,562,700	3.0%
9	Georgia	4,562,700	3.0%		10	New Jersey	4,507,800	3.0%
42	Hawaii	650,100	0.4%		11	North Carolina	4,357,000	2.9%
40	Idaho	737,300	0.5%		12	Virginia	3,960,100	2.6%
5	Illinois	6,497,800	4.3%		13	Massachusetts	3,383,600	2.3%
15	Indiana	3,231,400	2.2%		14	Washington	3,325,900	2.2%
30	Iowa	1,655,400	1.1%		15	Indiana	3,231,400	2.2%
31	Kansas	1,471,700	1.0%		16	Wisconsin	3,058,700	2.0%
25	Kentucky	2,017,000	1.3%		17	Missouri	3,037,600	2.0%
27	Louisiana	1,834,900	1.2%		18	Maryland	2,972,200	2.0%
41	Maine	720,600	0.5%		19	Minnesota	2,949,400	2.0%
18	Maryland	2,972,200	2.0%		20	Tennessee	2,927,000	1.9%
13	Massachusetts	3,383,600	2.3%		21	Arizona	2,855,000	1.9%
8	Michigan	5,138,800	3.4%		22	Colorado	2,544,600	1.7%
19	Minnesota	2,949,400	2.0%		23	Alabama	2,161,700	1.4%
33	Mississippi	1,293,400	0.9%		24	South Carolina	2,104,600	1.4%
17	Missouri	3,037,600	2.0%		25	Kentucky	2,017,000	1.3%
44	Montana	495,200	0.3%		26	Oregon	1,861,100	1.2%
36	Nebraska	982,100	0.7%		27	Louisiana	1,834,900	1.2%
35	Nevada	1,235,500	0.8%		28	Connecticut	1,829,200	1.2%
39	New Hampshire	739,500	0.5%		29	Oklahoma	1,738,600	1.2%
10	New Jersey	4,507,800	3.0%		30	Iowa	1,655,400	1.1%
37	New Mexico	941,300	0.6%		31	Kansas	1,471,700	1.0%
3	New York	9,473,100	6.3%		32	Arkansas	1,369,400	0.9%
11	North Carolina	4,357,000	2.9%		33	Mississippi	1,293,400	0.9%
48	North Dakota	357,600	0.2%		34	Utah	1,242,700	0.8%
7	Ohio	5,923,700	3.9%		35	Nevada	1,235,500	0.8%
29	Oklahoma	1,738,600	1.2%		36	Nebraska	982,100	0.7%
26	Oregon	1,861,100	1.2%		37	New Mexico	941,300	0.6%
6	Pennsylvania	6,306,100	4.2%		38	West Virginia	802,400	0.5%
43	Rhode Island	580,600	0.4%		39	New Hampshire	739,500	0.5%
24	South Carolina	2,104,600	1.4%		40	Idaho	737,300	0.5%
46	South Dakota	433,000	0.3%		41	Maine	720,600	0.5%
20	Tennessee	2,927,000	1.9%		42	Hawaii	650,100	0.4%
2	Texas	11,310,200	7.5%		43	Rhode Island	580,600	0.4%
34	Utah	1,242,700	0.8%		44	Montana	495,200	0.3%
47	Vermont	360,500	0.2%		45	Delaware	443,900	0.3%
12	Virginia	3,960,100	2.6%		46	South Dakota	433,000	0.3%
14	Washington	3,325,900	2.2%		47	Vermont	360,500	0.2%
38	West Virginia	802,400	0.5%		48	North Dakota	357,600	0.2%
16	Wisconsin	3,058,700	2.0%		49	Alaska	344,700	0.2%
50	Wyoming	285,200	0.2%		50	Wyoming	285,200	0.2%
						District of Columbia	294,500	0.2%

Source: U.S. Department of Labor, Bureau of Labor Statistics
"Regional and State Employment and Unemployment" (press release, January 24, 2006)
*Seasonally adjusted preliminary data as of December 2005. National total calculated through a different formula.

Employed Civilian Labor Force in 2005

National Total = 142,779,000 Employed Workers*

ALPHA ORDER

RANK	STATE	EMPLOYED	% of USA
23	Alabama	2,085,600	1.5%
49	Alaska	320,800	0.2%
21	Arizona	2,723,800	1.9%
32	Arkansas	1,307,700	0.9%
1	California	17,117,600	12.0%
22	Colorado	2,426,500	1.7%
27	Connecticut	1,741,800	1.2%
45	Delaware	424,200	0.3%
4	Florida	8,476,400	5.9%
9	Georgia	4,326,200	3.0%
42	Hawaii	632,300	0.4%
40	Idaho	712,500	0.5%
5	Illinois	6,141,900	4.3%
15	Indiana	3,055,000	2.1%
30	Iowa	1,581,300	1.1%
31	Kansas	1,400,000	1.0%
25	Kentucky	1,889,800	1.3%
28	Louisiana	1,718,100	1.2%
41	Maine	686,000	0.5%
18	Maryland	2,856,300	2.0%
13	Massachusetts	3,218,400	2.3%
8	Michigan	4,794,700	3.4%
19	Minnesota	2,827,300	2.0%
35	Mississippi	1,165,700	0.8%
17	Missouri	2,882,100	2.0%
44	Montana	476,800	0.3%
36	Nebraska	945,800	0.7%
34	Nevada	1,189,100	0.8%
39	New Hampshire	713,500	0.5%
10	New Jersey	4,295,000	3.0%
37	New Mexico	896,200	0.6%
3	New York	8,986,000	6.3%
11	North Carolina	4,141,800	2.9%
48	North Dakota	345,700	0.2%
7	Ohio	5,576,800	3.9%
29	Oklahoma	1,666,900	1.2%
26	Oregon	1,754,500	1.2%
6	Pennsylvania	5,998,800	4.2%
43	Rhode Island	550,400	0.4%
24	South Carolina	1,957,200	1.4%
46	South Dakota	416,200	0.3%
20	Tennessee	2,769,300	1.9%
2	Texas	10,733,000	7.5%
33	Utah	1,194,900	0.8%
47	Vermont	347,400	0.2%
12	Virginia	3,830,700	2.7%
14	Washington	3,149,400	2.2%
38	West Virginia	765,000	0.5%
16	Wisconsin	2,910,900	2.0%
50	Wyoming	276,100	0.2%

RANK ORDER

RANK	STATE	EMPLOYED	% of USA
1	California	17,117,600	12.0%
2	Texas	10,733,000	7.5%
3	New York	8,986,000	6.3%
4	Florida	8,476,400	5.9%
5	Illinois	6,141,900	4.3%
6	Pennsylvania	5,998,800	4.2%
7	Ohio	5,576,800	3.9%
8	Michigan	4,794,700	3.4%
9	Georgia	4,326,200	3.0%
10	New Jersey	4,295,000	3.0%
11	North Carolina	4,141,800	2.9%
12	Virginia	3,830,700	2.7%
13	Massachusetts	3,218,400	2.3%
14	Washington	3,149,400	2.2%
15	Indiana	3,055,000	2.1%
16	Wisconsin	2,910,900	2.0%
17	Missouri	2,882,100	2.0%
18	Maryland	2,856,300	2.0%
19	Minnesota	2,827,300	2.0%
20	Tennessee	2,769,300	1.9%
21	Arizona	2,723,800	1.9%
22	Colorado	2,426,500	1.7%
23	Alabama	2,085,600	1.5%
24	South Carolina	1,957,200	1.4%
25	Kentucky	1,889,800	1.3%
26	Oregon	1,754,500	1.2%
27	Connecticut	1,741,800	1.2%
28	Louisiana	1,718,100	1.2%
29	Oklahoma	1,666,900	1.2%
30	Iowa	1,581,300	1.1%
31	Kansas	1,400,000	1.0%
32	Arkansas	1,307,700	0.9%
33	Utah	1,194,900	0.8%
34	Nevada	1,189,100	0.8%
35	Mississippi	1,165,700	0.8%
36	Nebraska	945,800	0.7%
37	New Mexico	896,200	0.6%
38	West Virginia	765,000	0.5%
39	New Hampshire	713,500	0.5%
40	Idaho	712,500	0.5%
41	Maine	686,000	0.5%
42	Hawaii	632,300	0.4%
43	Rhode Island	550,400	0.4%
44	Montana	476,800	0.3%
45	Delaware	424,200	0.3%
46	South Dakota	416,200	0.3%
47	Vermont	347,400	0.2%
48	North Dakota	345,700	0.2%
49	Alaska	320,800	0.2%
50	Wyoming	276,100	0.2%
	District of Columbia	276,800	0.2%

Source: Morgan Quitno Press using data from U.S. Department of Labor, Bureau of Labor Statistics
"Regional and State Employment and Unemployment" (press release, January 24, 2006)
*Seasonally adjusted preliminary data as of December 2005. National total calculated through a different formula.

Employment to Population Ratio in 2005

National Percent = 62.5% of Population 16 Years and Older Employed*

ALPHA ORDER

RANK	STATE	PERCENT
46	Alabama	58.6
16	Alaska	65.5
32	Arizona	62.5
40	Arkansas	60.7
31	California	62.6
7	Colorado	68.4
29	Connecticut	63.1
18	Delaware	64.4
37	Florida	61.2
20	Georgia	64.1
26	Hawaii	63.4
11	Idaho	67.0
32	Illinois	62.5
26	Indiana	63.4
10	Iowa	67.1
15	Kansas	65.7
47	Kentucky	57.7
50	Louisiana	49.3
21	Maine	63.9
14	Maryland	66.1
30	Massachusetts	62.9
39	Michigan	60.9
1	Minnesota	70.5
48	Mississippi	52.1
23	Missouri	63.6
21	Montana	63.9
2	Nebraska	69.4
13	Nevada	66.3
4	New Hampshire	69.1
28	New Jersey	63.3
38	New Mexico	61.0
45	New York	59.2
34	North Carolina	62.3
9	North Dakota	67.3
35	Ohio	61.9
42	Oklahoma	60.3
36	Oregon	61.8
41	Pennsylvania	60.5
23	Rhode Island	63.6
43	South Carolina	59.5
5	South Dakota	69.0
44	Tennessee	59.3
25	Texas	63.5
3	Utah	69.3
6	Vermont	68.8
17	Virginia	65.4
18	Washington	64.4
49	West Virginia	51.8
12	Wisconsin	66.7
8	Wyoming	68.2

RANK ORDER

RANK	STATE	PERCENT
1	Minnesota	70.5
2	Nebraska	69.4
3	Utah	69.3
4	New Hampshire	69.1
5	South Dakota	69.0
6	Vermont	68.8
7	Colorado	68.4
8	Wyoming	68.2
9	North Dakota	67.3
10	Iowa	67.1
11	Idaho	67.0
12	Wisconsin	66.7
13	Nevada	66.3
14	Maryland	66.1
15	Kansas	65.7
16	Alaska	65.5
17	Virginia	65.4
18	Delaware	64.4
18	Washington	64.4
20	Georgia	64.1
21	Maine	63.9
21	Montana	63.9
23	Missouri	63.6
23	Rhode Island	63.6
25	Texas	63.5
26	Hawaii	63.4
26	Indiana	63.4
28	New Jersey	63.3
29	Connecticut	63.1
30	Massachusetts	62.9
31	California	62.6
32	Arizona	62.5
32	Illinois	62.5
34	North Carolina	62.3
35	Ohio	61.9
36	Oregon	61.8
37	Florida	61.2
38	New Mexico	61.0
39	Michigan	60.9
40	Arkansas	60.7
41	Pennsylvania	60.5
42	Oklahoma	60.3
43	South Carolina	59.5
44	Tennessee	59.3
45	New York	59.2
46	Alabama	58.6
47	Kentucky	57.7
48	Mississippi	52.1
49	West Virginia	51.8
50	Louisiana	49.3

| | District of Columbia | 61.0 |

Source: Morgan Quitno Press using data from U.S. Department of Labor, Bureau of Labor Statistics
    "Regional and State Employment and Unemployment" (press release, January 24, 2006)
*Seasonally adjusted preliminary data as of December 2005.

Unemployed Civilian Labor Force in 2005

National Total = 7,375,000 Unemployed Workers*

ALPHA ORDER

RANK	STATE	UNEMPLOYED	% of USA
29	Alabama	76,100	1.0%
43	Alaska	23,900	0.3%
19	Arizona	131,200	1.8%
33	Arkansas	61,700	0.8%
1	California	920,500	12.5%
24	Colorado	118,100	1.6%
28	Connecticut	87,400	1.2%
44	Delaware	19,700	0.3%
8	Florida	289,100	3.9%
9	Georgia	236,500	3.2%
46	Hawaii	17,800	0.2%
42	Idaho	24,800	0.3%
4	Illinois	355,900	4.8%
13	Indiana	176,400	2.4%
30	Iowa	74,100	1.0%
31	Kansas	71,700	1.0%
22	Kentucky	127,200	1.7%
25	Louisiana	116,800	1.6%
39	Maine	34,600	0.5%
26	Maryland	115,900	1.6%
14	Massachusetts	165,200	2.2%
6	Michigan	344,100	4.7%
23	Minnesota	122,100	1.7%
21	Mississippi	127,700	1.7%
16	Missouri	155,500	2.1%
45	Montana	18,400	0.2%
38	Nebraska	36,300	0.5%
35	Nevada	46,400	0.6%
41	New Hampshire	26,000	0.4%
11	New Jersey	212,800	2.9%
36	New Mexico	45,100	0.6%
3	New York	487,100	6.6%
10	North Carolina	215,200	2.9%
49	North Dakota	11,900	0.2%
5	Ohio	346,900	4.7%
31	Oklahoma	71,700	1.0%
27	Oregon	106,600	1.4%
7	Pennsylvania	307,300	4.2%
40	Rhode Island	30,200	0.4%
18	South Carolina	147,400	2.0%
47	South Dakota	16,800	0.2%
15	Tennessee	157,700	2.1%
2	Texas	577,200	7.8%
34	Utah	47,800	0.6%
48	Vermont	13,100	0.2%
20	Virginia	129,400	1.8%
12	Washington	176,500	2.4%
37	West Virginia	37,400	0.5%
17	Wisconsin	147,800	2.0%
50	Wyoming	9,100	0.1%

RANK ORDER

RANK	STATE	UNEMPLOYED	% of USA
1	California	920,500	12.5%
2	Texas	577,200	7.8%
3	New York	487,100	6.6%
4	Illinois	355,900	4.8%
5	Ohio	346,900	4.7%
6	Michigan	344,100	4.7%
7	Pennsylvania	307,300	4.2%
8	Florida	289,100	3.9%
9	Georgia	236,500	3.2%
10	North Carolina	215,200	2.9%
11	New Jersey	212,800	2.9%
12	Washington	176,500	2.4%
13	Indiana	176,400	2.4%
14	Massachusetts	165,200	2.2%
15	Tennessee	157,700	2.1%
16	Missouri	155,500	2.1%
17	Wisconsin	147,800	2.0%
18	South Carolina	147,400	2.0%
19	Arizona	131,200	1.8%
20	Virginia	129,400	1.8%
21	Mississippi	127,700	1.7%
22	Kentucky	127,200	1.7%
23	Minnesota	122,100	1.7%
24	Colorado	118,100	1.6%
25	Louisiana	116,800	1.6%
26	Maryland	115,900	1.6%
27	Oregon	106,600	1.4%
28	Connecticut	87,400	1.2%
29	Alabama	76,100	1.0%
30	Iowa	74,100	1.0%
31	Kansas	71,700	1.0%
31	Oklahoma	71,700	1.0%
33	Arkansas	61,700	0.8%
34	Utah	47,800	0.6%
35	Nevada	46,400	0.6%
36	New Mexico	45,100	0.6%
37	West Virginia	37,400	0.5%
38	Nebraska	36,300	0.5%
39	Maine	34,600	0.5%
40	Rhode Island	30,200	0.4%
41	New Hampshire	26,000	0.4%
42	Idaho	24,800	0.3%
43	Alaska	23,900	0.3%
44	Delaware	19,700	0.3%
45	Montana	18,400	0.2%
46	Hawaii	17,800	0.2%
47	South Dakota	16,800	0.2%
48	Vermont	13,100	0.2%
49	North Dakota	11,900	0.2%
50	Wyoming	9,100	0.1%
	District of Columbia	17,700	0.2%

Source: U.S. Department of Labor, Bureau of Labor Statistics
    "Regional and State Employment and Unemployment" (press release, January 24, 2006)
*Seasonally adjusted preliminary data as of December 2005. National total calculated through a different formula.

Unemployment Rate in 2005

National Rate = 4.9% of Labor Force Unemployed*

ALPHA ORDER

RANK ORDER

RANK	STATE	PERCENT		RANK	STATE	PERCENT
43	Alabama	3.5		1	Mississippi	9.9
3	Alaska	6.9		2	South Carolina	7.0
29	Arizona	4.6		3	Alaska	6.9
31	Arkansas	4.5		4	Michigan	6.7
15	California	5.1		5	Louisiana	6.4
29	Colorado	4.6		6	Kentucky	6.3
23	Connecticut	4.8		7	Ohio	5.9
33	Delaware	4.4		8	Oregon	5.7
46	Florida	3.3		9	Illinois	5.5
13	Georgia	5.2		9	Indiana	5.5
50	Hawaii	2.7		11	Tennessee	5.4
45	Idaho	3.4		12	Washington	5.3
9	Illinois	5.5		13	Georgia	5.2
9	Indiana	5.5		13	Rhode Island	5.2
31	Iowa	4.5		15	California	5.1
19	Kansas	4.9		15	Missouri	5.1
6	Kentucky	6.3		15	New York	5.1
5	Louisiana	6.4		15	Texas	5.1
23	Maine	4.8		19	Kansas	4.9
36	Maryland	3.9		19	Massachusetts	4.9
19	Massachusetts	4.9		19	North Carolina	4.9
4	Michigan	6.7		19	Pennsylvania	4.9
34	Minnesota	4.1		23	Connecticut	4.8
1	Mississippi	9.9		23	Maine	4.8
15	Missouri	5.1		23	New Mexico	4.8
40	Montana	3.7		23	Wisconsin	4.8
40	Nebraska	3.7		27	New Jersey	4.7
38	Nevada	3.8		27	West Virginia	4.7
43	New Hampshire	3.5		29	Arizona	4.6
27	New Jersey	4.7		29	Colorado	4.6
23	New Mexico	4.8		31	Arkansas	4.5
15	New York	5.1		31	Iowa	4.5
19	North Carolina	4.9		33	Delaware	4.4
46	North Dakota	3.3		34	Minnesota	4.1
7	Ohio	5.9		34	Oklahoma	4.1
34	Oklahoma	4.1		36	Maryland	3.9
8	Oregon	5.7		36	South Dakota	3.9
19	Pennsylvania	4.9		38	Nevada	3.8
13	Rhode Island	5.2		38	Utah	3.8
2	South Carolina	7.0		40	Montana	3.7
36	South Dakota	3.9		40	Nebraska	3.7
11	Tennessee	5.4		42	Vermont	3.6
15	Texas	5.1		43	Alabama	3.5
38	Utah	3.8		43	New Hampshire	3.5
42	Vermont	3.6		45	Idaho	3.4
46	Virginia	3.3		46	Florida	3.3
12	Washington	5.3		46	North Dakota	3.3
27	West Virginia	4.7		46	Virginia	3.3
23	Wisconsin	4.8		49	Wyoming	3.2
49	Wyoming	3.2		50	Hawaii	2.7

District of Columbia   6.0

Source: U.S. Department of Labor, Bureau of Labor Statistics
    "Regional and State Employment and Unemployment" (press release, January 24, 2006)
*Seasonally adjusted preliminary data as of December 2005. National rate calculated through a different formula.

Women in Civilian Labor Force in 2004

National Total = 69,772,000 Women*

ALPHA ORDER					RANK ORDER			
RANK	STATE	WOMEN	% of USA		RANK	STATE	WOMEN	% of USA
23	Alabama	1,023,000	1.5%		1	California	7,860,000	11.3%
49	Alaska	152,000	0.2%		2	Texas	4,901,000	7.0%
21	Arizona	1,242,000	1.8%		3	New York	4,406,000	6.3%
33	Arkansas	601,000	0.9%		4	Florida	3,904,000	5.6%
1	California	7,860,000	11.3%		5	Illinois	2,979,000	4.3%
22	Colorado	1,142,000	1.6%		6	Pennsylvania	2,950,000	4.2%
27	Connecticut	848,000	1.2%		7	Ohio	2,778,000	4.0%
46	Delaware	206,000	0.3%		8	Michigan	2,394,000	3.4%
4	Florida	3,904,000	5.6%		9	New Jersey	2,032,000	2.9%
10	Georgia	2,010,000	2.9%		10	Georgia	2,010,000	2.9%
42	Hawaii	295,000	0.4%		11	North Carolina	1,973,000	2.8%
41	Idaho	323,000	0.5%		12	Virginia	1,791,000	2.6%
5	Illinois	2,979,000	4.3%		13	Massachusetts	1,629,000	2.3%
15	Indiana	1,486,000	2.1%		14	Washington	1,494,000	2.1%
30	Iowa	774,000	1.1%		15	Indiana	1,486,000	2.1%
31	Kansas	685,000	1.0%		16	Wisconsin	1,456,000	2.1%
26	Kentucky	920,000	1.3%		17	Missouri	1,445,000	2.1%
25	Louisiana	982,000	1.4%		18	Maryland	1,394,000	2.0%
40	Maine	334,000	0.5%		19	Minnesota	1,384,000	2.0%
18	Maryland	1,394,000	2.0%		20	Tennessee	1,365,000	2.0%
13	Massachusetts	1,629,000	2.3%		21	Arizona	1,242,000	1.8%
8	Michigan	2,394,000	3.4%		22	Colorado	1,142,000	1.6%
19	Minnesota	1,384,000	2.0%		23	Alabama	1,023,000	1.5%
32	Mississippi	637,000	0.9%		24	South Carolina	1,002,000	1.4%
17	Missouri	1,445,000	2.1%		25	Louisiana	982,000	1.4%
44	Montana	230,000	0.3%		26	Kentucky	920,000	1.3%
36	Nebraska	467,000	0.7%		27	Connecticut	848,000	1.2%
35	Nevada	518,000	0.7%		28	Oregon	840,000	1.2%
39	New Hampshire	337,000	0.5%		29	Oklahoma	798,000	1.1%
9	New Jersey	2,032,000	2.9%		30	Iowa	774,000	1.1%
37	New Mexico	427,000	0.6%		31	Kansas	685,000	1.0%
3	New York	4,406,000	6.3%		32	Mississippi	637,000	0.9%
11	North Carolina	1,973,000	2.8%		33	Arkansas	601,000	0.9%
47	North Dakota	170,000	0.2%		34	Utah	538,000	0.8%
7	Ohio	2,778,000	4.0%		35	Nevada	518,000	0.7%
29	Oklahoma	798,000	1.1%		36	Nebraska	467,000	0.7%
28	Oregon	840,000	1.2%		37	New Mexico	427,000	0.6%
6	Pennsylvania	2,950,000	4.2%		38	West Virginia	369,000	0.5%
43	Rhode Island	275,000	0.4%		39	New Hampshire	337,000	0.5%
24	South Carolina	1,002,000	1.4%		40	Maine	334,000	0.5%
45	South Dakota	207,000	0.3%		41	Idaho	323,000	0.5%
20	Tennessee	1,365,000	2.0%		42	Hawaii	295,000	0.4%
2	Texas	4,901,000	7.0%		43	Rhode Island	275,000	0.4%
34	Utah	538,000	0.8%		44	Montana	230,000	0.3%
48	Vermont	169,000	0.2%		45	South Dakota	207,000	0.3%
12	Virginia	1,791,000	2.6%		46	Delaware	206,000	0.3%
14	Washington	1,494,000	2.1%		47	North Dakota	170,000	0.2%
38	West Virginia	369,000	0.5%		48	Vermont	169,000	0.2%
16	Wisconsin	1,456,000	2.1%		49	Alaska	152,000	0.2%
50	Wyoming	130,000	0.2%		50	Wyoming	130,000	0.2%
						District of Columbia	149,000	0.2%

Source: U.S. Department of Labor, Bureau of Labor Statistics
   "Geographic Profiles of Employment and Unemployment, 2004" (http://www.bls.gov/gps/)
*Annual averages.

Percent of Women in the Civilian Labor Force in 2004

National Percent = 59.3% of Women*

ALPHA ORDER

RANK	STATE	PERCENT
44	Alabama	55.8
7	Alaska	65.6
41	Arizona	57.4
48	Arkansas	54.9
38	California	57.6
9	Colorado	65.3
27	Connecticut	60.0
21	Delaware	61.1
46	Florida	55.4
32	Georgia	59.2
26	Hawaii	60.1
19	Idaho	61.3
28	Illinois	59.7
22	Indiana	61.0
8	Iowa	65.4
12	Kansas	64.5
46	Kentucky	55.4
48	Louisiana	54.9
22	Maine	61.0
15	Maryland	62.3
17	Massachusetts	61.9
28	Michigan	59.7
2	Minnesota	69.0
45	Mississippi	55.5
13	Missouri	62.7
16	Montana	62.0
3	Nebraska	68.5
31	Nevada	59.3
11	New Hampshire	64.7
35	New Jersey	58.4
40	New Mexico	57.5
43	New York	56.2
34	North Carolina	58.8
4	North Dakota	67.6
25	Ohio	60.4
38	Oklahoma	57.6
33	Oregon	59.0
37	Pennsylvania	58.1
18	Rhode Island	61.7
30	South Carolina	59.5
1	South Dakota	69.4
41	Tennessee	57.4
36	Texas	58.2
13	Utah	62.7
6	Vermont	65.8
24	Virginia	60.8
20	Washington	61.2
50	West Virginia	49.1
5	Wisconsin	66.6
9	Wyoming	65.3

RANK ORDER

RANK	STATE	PERCENT
1	South Dakota	69.4
2	Minnesota	69.0
3	Nebraska	68.5
4	North Dakota	67.6
5	Wisconsin	66.6
6	Vermont	65.8
7	Alaska	65.6
8	Iowa	65.4
9	Colorado	65.3
9	Wyoming	65.3
11	New Hampshire	64.7
12	Kansas	64.5
13	Missouri	62.7
13	Utah	62.7
15	Maryland	62.3
16	Montana	62.0
17	Massachusetts	61.9
18	Rhode Island	61.7
19	Idaho	61.3
20	Washington	61.2
21	Delaware	61.1
22	Indiana	61.0
22	Maine	61.0
24	Virginia	60.8
25	Ohio	60.4
26	Hawaii	60.1
27	Connecticut	60.0
28	Illinois	59.7
28	Michigan	59.7
30	South Carolina	59.5
31	Nevada	59.3
32	Georgia	59.2
33	Oregon	59.0
34	North Carolina	58.8
35	New Jersey	58.4
36	Texas	58.2
37	Pennsylvania	58.1
38	California	57.6
38	Oklahoma	57.6
40	New Mexico	57.5
41	Arizona	57.4
41	Tennessee	57.4
43	New York	56.2
44	Alabama	55.8
45	Mississippi	55.5
46	Florida	55.4
46	Kentucky	55.4
48	Arkansas	54.9
48	Louisiana	54.9
50	West Virginia	49.1
	District of Columbia	62.3

Source: U.S. Department of Labor, Bureau of Labor Statistics
    "Geographic Profiles of Employment and Unemployment, 2004" (http://www.bls.gov/gps/)
*Annual averages.

Percent of Civilian Labor Force Comprised of Women in 2004

National Percent = 46.5% of Civilian Labor Force*

ALPHA ORDER

RANK	STATE	PERCENT
26	Alabama	46.9
40	Alaska	45.9
47	Arizona	44.7
40	Arkansas	45.9
46	California	44.8
45	Colorado	45.2
15	Connecticut	47.4
2	Delaware	48.4
35	Florida	46.4
43	Georgia	45.7
4	Hawaii	48.2
42	Idaho	45.8
30	Illinois	46.6
24	Indiana	47.0
11	Iowa	47.8
37	Kansas	46.3
32	Kentucky	46.5
12	Louisiana	47.7
6	Maine	48.0
2	Maryland	48.4
8	Massachusetts	47.9
28	Michigan	46.8
22	Minnesota	47.1
12	Mississippi	47.7
8	Missouri	47.9
18	Montana	47.3
19	Nebraska	47.2
50	Nevada	44.1
32	New Hampshire	46.5
28	New Jersey	46.8
26	New Mexico	46.9
24	New York	47.0
32	North Carolina	46.5
15	North Dakota	47.4
19	Ohio	47.2
30	Oklahoma	46.6
44	Oregon	45.4
22	Pennsylvania	47.1
1	Rhode Island	48.9
4	South Carolina	48.2
6	South Dakota	48.0
19	Tennessee	47.2
48	Texas	44.6
48	Utah	44.6
8	Vermont	47.9
14	Virginia	47.6
38	Washington	46.1
35	West Virginia	46.4
15	Wisconsin	47.4
38	Wyoming	46.1

RANK ORDER

RANK	STATE	PERCENT
1	Rhode Island	48.9
2	Delaware	48.4
2	Maryland	48.4
4	Hawaii	48.2
4	South Carolina	48.2
6	Maine	48.0
6	South Dakota	48.0
8	Massachusetts	47.9
8	Missouri	47.9
8	Vermont	47.9
11	Iowa	47.8
12	Louisiana	47.7
12	Mississippi	47.7
14	Virginia	47.6
15	Connecticut	47.4
15	North Dakota	47.4
15	Wisconsin	47.4
18	Montana	47.3
19	Nebraska	47.2
19	Ohio	47.2
19	Tennessee	47.2
22	Minnesota	47.1
22	Pennsylvania	47.1
24	Indiana	47.0
24	New York	47.0
26	Alabama	46.9
26	New Mexico	46.9
28	Michigan	46.8
28	New Jersey	46.8
30	Illinois	46.6
30	Oklahoma	46.6
32	Kentucky	46.5
32	New Hampshire	46.5
32	North Carolina	46.5
35	Florida	46.4
35	West Virginia	46.4
37	Kansas	46.3
38	Washington	46.1
38	Wyoming	46.1
40	Alaska	45.9
40	Arkansas	45.9
42	Idaho	45.8
43	Georgia	45.7
44	Oregon	45.4
45	Colorado	45.2
46	California	44.8
47	Arizona	44.7
48	Texas	44.6
48	Utah	44.6
50	Nevada	44.1

	District of Columbia	49.8

Source: Morgan Quitno Press using data from U.S. Department of Labor, Bureau of Labor Statistics
    "Geographic Profiles of Employment and Unemployment, 2004" (http://www.bls.gov/gps/)
*Annual averages.

Percent of Children Under 6 Years Old With All Parents Working: 2004

National Percent = 59.5%

ALPHA ORDER

RANK	STATE	PERCENT
14	Alabama	64.2
13	Alaska	64.4
47	Arizona	53.8
20	Arkansas	62.9
45	California	54.4
31	Colorado	59.8
28	Connecticut	61.0
1	Delaware	71.8
16	Florida	63.8
24	Georgia	61.7
22	Hawaii	62.5
49	Idaho	49.6
34	Illinois	50.2
34	Indiana	59.2
3	Iowa	71.0
7	Kansas	66.8
34	Kentucky	59.2
23	Louisiana	62.4
25	Maine	61.6
8	Maryland	66.3
18	Massachusetts	63.7
30	Michigan	60.4
12	Minnesota	64.9
6	Mississippi	67.0
16	Missouri	63.8
11	Montana	65.2
5	Nebraska	70.4
48	Nevada	52.2
44	New Hampshire	55.5
40	New Jersey	56.6
27	New Mexico	61.2
43	New York	55.6
29	North Carolina	60.8
2	North Dakota	71.6
14	Ohio	64.2
33	Oklahoma	59.4
42	Oregon	56.2
38	Pennsylvania	58.5
26	Rhode Island	61.5
10	South Carolina	65.5
4	South Dakota	70.6
31	Tennessee	59.8
41	Texas	56.4
50	Utah	47.5
19	Vermont	63.4
20	Virginia	62.9
46	Washington	54.0
39	West Virginia	57.1
9	Wisconsin	66.0
37	Wyoming	59.1

RANK ORDER

RANK	STATE	PERCENT
1	Delaware	71.8
2	North Dakota	71.6
3	Iowa	71.0
4	South Dakota	70.6
5	Nebraska	70.4
6	Mississippi	67.0
7	Kansas	66.8
8	Maryland	66.3
9	Wisconsin	66.0
10	South Carolina	65.5
11	Montana	65.2
12	Minnesota	64.9
13	Alaska	64.4
14	Alabama	64.2
14	Ohio	64.2
16	Florida	63.8
16	Missouri	63.8
18	Massachusetts	63.7
19	Vermont	63.4
20	Arkansas	62.9
20	Virginia	62.9
22	Hawaii	62.5
23	Louisiana	62.4
24	Georgia	61.7
25	Maine	61.6
26	Rhode Island	61.5
27	New Mexico	61.2
28	Connecticut	61.0
29	North Carolina	60.8
30	Michigan	60.4
31	Colorado	59.8
31	Tennessee	59.8
33	Oklahoma	59.4
34	Illinois	59.2
34	Indiana	59.2
34	Kentucky	59.2
37	Wyoming	59.1
38	Pennsylvania	58.5
39	West Virginia	57.1
40	New Jersey	56.6
41	Texas	56.4
42	Oregon	56.2
43	New York	55.6
44	New Hampshire	55.5
45	California	54.4
46	Washington	54.0
47	Arizona	53.8
48	Nevada	52.2
49	Idaho	49.6
50	Utah	47.5
	District of Columbia	67.2

Source: U.S. Bureau of the Census
   "American Community Survey" (http://www.census.gov/acs/www/)

Job Growth: 2004 to 2005

National Percent Change = 1.5% Increase*

ALPHA ORDER

RANK	STATE	PERCENT CHANGE
37	Alabama	0.9
14	Alaska	1.8
3	Arizona	4.5
31	Arkansas	1.1
17	California	1.6
14	Colorado	1.8
42	Connecticut	0.6
21	Delaware	1.5
6	Florida	3.3
17	Georgia	1.6
8	Hawaii	2.8
2	Idaho	4.7
31	Illinois	1.1
44	Indiana	0.4
11	Iowa	2.0
17	Kansas	1.6
29	Kentucky	1.2
50	Louisiana	(10.2)
44	Maine	0.4
26	Maryland	1.3
44	Massachusetts	0.4
48	Michigan	(0.6)
29	Minnesota	1.2
49	Mississippi	(2.2)
39	Missouri	0.8
11	Montana	2.0
26	Nebraska	1.3
1	Nevada	5.8
21	New Hampshire	1.5
37	New Jersey	0.9
10	New Mexico	2.2
41	New York	0.7
24	North Carolina	1.4
11	North Dakota	2.0
47	Ohio	0.1
21	Oklahoma	1.5
5	Oregon	3.5
31	Pennsylvania	1.1
39	Rhode Island	0.8
36	South Carolina	1.0
14	South Dakota	1.8
42	Tennessee	0.6
17	Texas	1.6
4	Utah	4.4
26	Vermont	1.3
31	Virginia	1.1
7	Washington	2.9
31	West Virginia	1.1
24	Wisconsin	1.4
9	Wyoming	2.4

RANK ORDER

RANK	STATE	PERCENT CHANGE
1	Nevada	5.8
2	Idaho	4.7
3	Arizona	4.5
4	Utah	4.4
5	Oregon	3.5
6	Florida	3.3
7	Washington	2.9
8	Hawaii	2.8
9	Wyoming	2.4
10	New Mexico	2.2
11	Iowa	2.0
11	Montana	2.0
11	North Dakota	2.0
14	Alaska	1.8
14	Colorado	1.8
14	South Dakota	1.8
17	California	1.6
17	Georgia	1.6
17	Kansas	1.6
17	Texas	1.6
21	Delaware	1.5
21	New Hampshire	1.5
21	Oklahoma	1.5
24	North Carolina	1.4
24	Wisconsin	1.4
26	Maryland	1.3
26	Nebraska	1.3
26	Vermont	1.3
29	Kentucky	1.2
29	Minnesota	1.2
31	Arkansas	1.1
31	Illinois	1.1
31	Pennsylvania	1.1
31	Virginia	1.1
31	West Virginia	1.1
36	South Carolina	1.0
37	Alabama	0.9
37	New Jersey	0.9
39	Missouri	0.8
39	Rhode Island	0.8
41	New York	0.7
42	Connecticut	0.6
42	Tennessee	0.6
44	Indiana	0.4
44	Maine	0.4
44	Massachusetts	0.4
47	Ohio	0.1
48	Michigan	(0.6)
49	Mississippi	(2.2)
50	Louisiana	(10.2)
	District of Columbia	1.7

Source: Morgan Quitno Press using data from U.S. Department of Labor, Bureau of Labor Statistics
   "Regional and State Employment and Unemployment" (press release, January 24, 2006)
*Nonfarm jobs. December 2004 to December 2005, seasonally adjusted. National figure based on nonfarm
employment from a different survey.

Employees on Nonfarm Payrolls in 2005

National Total = 134,468,000 Employees*

ALPHA ORDER

RANK	STATE	EMPLOYEES	% of USA
23	Alabama	1,931,600	1.4%
49	Alaska	309,900	0.2%
21	Arizona	2,523,700	1.9%
33	Arkansas	1,177,100	0.9%
1	California	14,879,200	11.1%
22	Colorado	2,243,600	1.7%
27	Connecticut	1,675,300	1.2%
44	Delaware	435,300	0.3%
4	Florida	7,856,700	5.8%
10	Georgia	3,970,700	3.0%
42	Hawaii	607,600	0.5%
40	Idaho	619,100	0.5%
5	Illinois	5,074,000	4.4%
14	Indiana	2,956,500	2.2%
30	Iowa	1,490,800	1.1%
31	Kansas	1,355,200	1.0%
25	Kentucky	1,823,600	1.4%
26	Louisiana	1,721,600	1.3%
41	Maine	618,700	0.5%
20	Maryland	2,575,100	1.9%
13	Massachusetts	3,202,200	2.4%
8	Michigan	4,362,600	3.2%
18	Minnesota	2,730,500	2.0%
35	Mississippi	1,103,300	0.8%
19	Missouri	2,729,300	2.0%
45	Montana	427,600	0.3%
36	Nebraska	937,700	0.7%
32	Nevada	1,255,800	0.9%
39	New Hampshire	642,200	0.5%
9	New Jersey	4,069,400	3.0%
37	New Mexico	816,400	0.6%
3	New York	8,553,900	6.4%
11	North Carolina	3,909,600	2.9%
47	North Dakota	344,700	0.3%
7	Ohio	5,418,200	4.0%
29	Oklahoma	1,505,700	1.1%
28	Oregon	1,672,600	1.2%
6	Pennsylvania	5,730,300	4.3%
43	Rhode Island	494,000	0.4%
24	South Carolina	1,850,500	1.4%
46	South Dakota	391,400	0.3%
17	Tennessee	2,732,300	2.0%
2	Texas	9,684,100	7.2%
34	Utah	1,165,700	0.9%
48	Vermont	310,700	0.2%
12	Virginia	3,664,700	2.7%
16	Washington	2,800,600	2.1%
38	West Virginia	744,600	0.6%
15	Wisconsin	2,851,000	2.1%
50	Wyoming	263,800	0.2%

RANK ORDER

RANK	STATE	EMPLOYEES	% of USA
1	California	14,879,200	11.1%
2	Texas	9,684,100	7.2%
3	New York	8,553,900	6.4%
4	Florida	7,856,700	5.8%
5	Illinois	5,874,000	4.4%
6	Pennsylvania	5,730,300	4.3%
7	Ohio	5,418,200	4.0%
8	Michigan	4,362,600	3.2%
9	New Jersey	4,069,400	3.0%
10	Georgia	3,970,700	3.0%
11	North Carolina	3,909,600	2.9%
12	Virginia	3,664,700	2.7%
13	Massachusetts	3,202,200	2.4%
14	Indiana	2,956,500	2.2%
15	Wisconsin	2,851,000	2.1%
16	Washington	2,800,600	2.1%
17	Tennessee	2,732,300	2.0%
18	Minnesota	2,730,500	2.0%
19	Missouri	2,729,300	2.0%
20	Maryland	2,575,100	1.9%
21	Arizona	2,523,700	1.9%
22	Colorado	2,243,600	1.7%
23	Alabama	1,931,600	1.4%
24	South Carolina	1,850,500	1.4%
25	Kentucky	1,823,600	1.4%
26	Louisiana	1,721,600	1.3%
27	Connecticut	1,675,300	1.2%
28	Oregon	1,672,600	1.2%
29	Oklahoma	1,505,700	1.1%
30	Iowa	1,490,800	1.1%
31	Kansas	1,355,200	1.0%
32	Nevada	1,255,800	0.9%
33	Arkansas	1,177,100	0.9%
34	Utah	1,165,700	0.9%
35	Mississippi	1,103,300	0.8%
36	Nebraska	937,700	0.7%
37	New Mexico	816,400	0.6%
38	West Virginia	744,600	0.6%
39	New Hampshire	642,200	0.5%
40	Idaho	619,100	0.5%
41	Maine	618,700	0.5%
42	Hawaii	607,600	0.5%
43	Rhode Island	494,000	0.4%
44	Delaware	435,300	0.3%
45	Montana	427,600	0.3%
46	South Dakota	391,400	0.3%
47	North Dakota	344,700	0.3%
48	Vermont	310,700	0.2%
49	Alaska	309,900	0.2%
50	Wyoming	263,800	0.2%
	District of Columbia	685,500	0.5%

Source: U.S. Department of Labor, Bureau of Labor Statistics
"Regional and State Employment and Unemployment" (press release, January 24, 2006)
*Seasonally adjusted preliminary data as of December 2005. National total calculated through a different formula.

Employees in Construction in 2005

National Total = 7,332,000 Employees*

ALPHA ORDER

RANK	STATE	EMPLOYEES	% of USA
25	Alabama	107,300	1.5%
48	Alaska	18,800	0.3%
10	Arizona	224,100	3.1%
35	Arkansas	53,800	0.7%
1	California	938,000	12.8%
16	Colorado	164,300	2.2%
30	Connecticut	70,900	1.0%
43	Delaware**	27,800	0.4%
3	Florida	529,800	7.2%
11	Georgia	204,700	2.8%
40	Hawaii**	34,200	0.5%
38	Idaho	47,100	0.6%
5	Illinois	269,100	3.7%
17	Indiana	152,400	2.1%
31	Iowa	70,100	1.0%
32	Kansas	64,400	0.9%
28	Kentucky	87,800	1.2%
27	Louisiana	94,300	1.3%
41	Maine	31,400	0.4%
14	Maryland**	179,900	2.5%
18	Massachusetts	142,300	1.9%
12	Michigan	187,500	2.6%
22	Minnesota	127,000	1.7%
36	Mississippi	49,400	0.7%
20	Missouri	140,100	1.9%
44	Montana	27,100	0.4%
37	Nebraska**	47,600	0.6%
19	Nevada	140,800	1.9%
42	New Hampshire	31,200	0.4%
15	New Jersey	168,500	2.3%
34	New Mexico	55,300	0.8%
4	New York	323,200	4.4%
9	North Carolina	227,000	3.1%
49	North Dakota	18,000	0.2%
8	Ohio	236,600	3.2%
33	Oklahoma	63,300	0.9%
26	Oregon	95,800	1.3%
6	Pennsylvania	254,700	3.5%
45	Rhode Island	21,500	0.3%
24	South Carolina	115,300	1.6%
46	South Dakota	21,300	0.3%
23	Tennessee	120,700	1.6%
2	Texas	560,100	7.6%
29	Utah	85,000	1.2%
50	Vermont	17,800	0.2%
7	Virginia	249,000	3.4%
13	Washington	180,100	2.5%
39	West Virginia	37,900	0.5%
21	Wisconsin	132,300	1.8%
47	Wyoming	19,700	0.3%

RANK ORDER

RANK	STATE	EMPLOYEES	% of USA
1	California	938,000	12.8%
2	Texas	560,100	7.6%
3	Florida	529,800	7.2%
4	New York	323,200	4.4%
5	Illinois	269,100	3.7%
6	Pennsylvania	254,700	3.5%
7	Virginia	249,000	3.4%
8	Ohio	236,600	3.2%
9	North Carolina	227,000	3.1%
10	Arizona	224,100	3.1%
11	Georgia	204,700	2.8%
12	Michigan	187,500	2.6%
13	Washington	180,100	2.5%
14	Maryland**	179,900	2.5%
15	New Jersey	168,500	2.3%
16	Colorado	164,300	2.2%
17	Indiana	152,400	2.1%
18	Massachusetts	142,300	1.9%
19	Nevada	140,800	1.9%
20	Missouri	140,100	1.9%
21	Wisconsin	132,300	1.8%
22	Minnesota	127,000	1.7%
23	Tennessee	120,700	1.6%
24	South Carolina	115,300	1.6%
25	Alabama	107,300	1.5%
26	Oregon	95,800	1.3%
27	Louisiana	94,300	1.3%
28	Kentucky	87,800	1.2%
29	Utah	85,000	1.2%
30	Connecticut	70,900	1.0%
31	Iowa	70,100	1.0%
32	Kansas	64,400	0.9%
33	Oklahoma	63,300	0.9%
34	New Mexico	55,300	0.8%
35	Arkansas	53,800	0.7%
36	Mississippi	49,400	0.7%
37	Nebraska**	47,600	0.6%
38	Idaho	47,100	0.6%
39	West Virginia	37,900	0.5%
40	Hawaii**	34,200	0.5%
41	Maine	31,400	0.4%
42	New Hampshire	31,200	0.4%
43	Delaware**	27,800	0.4%
44	Montana	27,100	0.4%
45	Rhode Island	21,500	0.3%
46	South Dakota	21,300	0.3%
47	Wyoming	19,700	0.3%
48	Alaska	18,800	0.3%
49	North Dakota	18,000	0.2%
50	Vermont	17,800	0.2%
	District of Columbia**	12,100	0.2%

Source: U.S. Department of Labor, Bureau of Labor Statistics
   "Regional and State Employment and Unemployment" (press release, January 25, 2005)
*Seasonally adjusted preliminary data as of December 2004. National total calculated through a different formula.
**Figures for Delaware, DC, Hawaii, Maryland and Nebraska include employees in natural resources and mining.

Percent of Nonfarm Employees in Construction in 2005

National Percent = 5.5% of Employees*

ALPHA ORDER

RANK	STATE	PERCENT
21	Alabama	5.6
16	Alaska	6.1
2	Arizona	8.9
37	Arkansas	4.6
13	California	6.3
5	Colorado	7.3
47	Connecticut	4.2
11	Delaware**	6.4
10	Florida	6.7
25	Georgia	5.2
21	Hawaii**	5.6
3	Idaho	7.6
37	Illinois	4.6
25	Indiana	5.2
35	Iowa	4.7
33	Kansas	4.8
33	Kentucky	4.8
23	Louisiana	5.5
28	Maine	5.1
7	Maryland**	7.0
41	Massachusetts	4.4
46	Michigan	4.3
35	Minnesota	4.7
40	Mississippi	4.5
28	Missouri	5.1
13	Montana	6.3
28	Nebraska**	5.1
1	Nevada	11.2
32	New Hampshire	4.9
49	New Jersey	4.1
8	New Mexico	6.8
50	New York	3.8
17	North Carolina	5.8
25	North Dakota	5.2
41	Ohio	4.4
47	Oklahoma	4.2
19	Oregon	5.7
41	Pennsylvania	4.4
41	Rhode Island	4.4
15	South Carolina	6.2
24	South Dakota	5.4
41	Tennessee	4.4
17	Texas	5.8
5	Utah	7.3
19	Vermont	5.7
8	Virginia	6.8
11	Washington	6.4
28	West Virginia	5.1
37	Wisconsin	4.6
4	Wyoming	7.5

RANK ORDER

RANK	STATE	PERCENT
1	Nevada	11.2
2	Arizona	8.9
3	Idaho	7.6
4	Wyoming	7.5
5	Colorado	7.3
5	Utah	7.3
7	Maryland**	7.0
8	New Mexico	6.8
8	Virginia	6.8
10	Florida	6.7
11	Delaware**	6.4
11	Washington	6.4
13	California	6.3
13	Montana	6.3
15	South Carolina	6.2
16	Alaska	6.1
17	North Carolina	5.8
17	Texas	5.8
19	Oregon	5.7
19	Vermont	5.7
21	Alabama	5.6
21	Hawaii**	5.6
23	Louisiana	5.5
24	South Dakota	5.4
25	Georgia	5.2
25	Indiana	5.2
25	North Dakota	5.2
28	Maine	5.1
28	Missouri	5.1
28	Nebraska**	5.1
28	West Virginia	5.1
32	New Hampshire	4.9
33	Kansas	4.8
33	Kentucky	4.8
35	Iowa	4.7
35	Minnesota	4.7
37	Arkansas	4.6
37	Illinois	4.6
37	Wisconsin	4.6
40	Mississippi	4.5
41	Massachusetts	4.4
41	Ohio	4.4
41	Pennsylvania	4.4
41	Rhode Island	4.4
41	Tennessee	4.4
46	Michigan	4.3
47	Connecticut	4.2
47	Oklahoma	4.2
49	New Jersey	4.1
50	New York	3.8
	District of Columbia**	1.8

Source: Morgan Quitno Press using data from U.S. Department of Labor, Bureau of Labor Statistics
   "Regional and State Employment and Unemployment" (press release, January 24, 2006)
*Seasonally adjusted preliminary data as of December 2005. National figure calculated through a different formula.
**Figures for Delaware, DC, Hawaii, Maryland and Nebraska include employees in natural resources and mining.

Employees in Education and Health Services in 2005

National Total = 17,505,000 Employees*

<table>
<tr><td colspan="4">ALPHA ORDER</td><td colspan="4">RANK ORDER</td></tr>
<tr><th>RANK</th><th>STATE</th><th>EMPLOYEES</th><th>% of USA</th><th>RANK</th><th>STATE</th><th>EMPLOYEES</th><th>% of USA</th></tr>
<tr><td>NA</td><td>Alabama**</td><td>NA</td><td>NA</td><td>1</td><td>California</td><td>1,596,300</td><td>9.1%</td></tr>
<tr><td>39</td><td>Alaska</td><td>36,100</td><td>0.2%</td><td>2</td><td>New York</td><td>1,562,600</td><td>8.9%</td></tr>
<tr><td>19</td><td>Arizona</td><td>281,300</td><td>1.6%</td><td>3</td><td>Texas</td><td>1,182,100</td><td>6.8%</td></tr>
<tr><td>27</td><td>Arkansas</td><td>149,000</td><td>0.9%</td><td>4</td><td>Pennsylvania</td><td>1,028,000</td><td>5.9%</td></tr>
<tr><td>1</td><td>California</td><td>1,596,300</td><td>9.1%</td><td>5</td><td>Florida</td><td>965,600</td><td>5.5%</td></tr>
<tr><td>21</td><td>Colorado</td><td>226,600</td><td>1.3%</td><td>6</td><td>Ohio</td><td>754,500</td><td>4.3%</td></tr>
<tr><td>NA</td><td>Connecticut**</td><td>NA</td><td>NA</td><td>7</td><td>Illinois</td><td>740,600</td><td>4.2%</td></tr>
<tr><td>37</td><td>Delaware</td><td>53,300</td><td>0.3%</td><td>8</td><td>Massachusetts</td><td>588,000</td><td>3.4%</td></tr>
<tr><td>5</td><td>Florida</td><td>965,600</td><td>5.5%</td><td>9</td><td>New Jersey</td><td>566,200</td><td>3.2%</td></tr>
<tr><td>NA</td><td>Georgia**</td><td>NA</td><td>NA</td><td>10</td><td>Michigan</td><td>554,200</td><td>3.2%</td></tr>
<tr><td>34</td><td>Hawaii</td><td>70,300</td><td>0.4%</td><td>11</td><td>North Carolina</td><td>465,100</td><td>2.7%</td></tr>
<tr><td>NA</td><td>Idaho**</td><td>NA</td><td>NA</td><td>12</td><td>Minnesota</td><td>394,500</td><td>2.3%</td></tr>
<tr><td>7</td><td>Illinois</td><td>740,600</td><td>4.2%</td><td>13</td><td>Virginia</td><td>393,000</td><td>2.2%</td></tr>
<tr><td>15</td><td>Indiana</td><td>381,500</td><td>2.2%</td><td>14</td><td>Wisconsin</td><td>387,700</td><td>2.2%</td></tr>
<tr><td>24</td><td>Iowa</td><td>196,300</td><td>1.1%</td><td>15</td><td>Indiana</td><td>381,500</td><td>2.2%</td></tr>
<tr><td>NA</td><td>Kansas**</td><td>NA</td><td>NA</td><td>16</td><td>Missouri</td><td>369,300</td><td>2.1%</td></tr>
<tr><td>20</td><td>Kentucky</td><td>236,500</td><td>1.4%</td><td>17</td><td>Maryland</td><td>360,900</td><td>2.1%</td></tr>
<tr><td>22</td><td>Louisiana</td><td>210,900</td><td>1.2%</td><td>18</td><td>Washington</td><td>332,900</td><td>1.9%</td></tr>
<tr><td>30</td><td>Maine</td><td>114,100</td><td>0.7%</td><td>19</td><td>Arizona</td><td>281,300</td><td>1.6%</td></tr>
<tr><td>17</td><td>Maryland</td><td>360,900</td><td>2.1%</td><td>20</td><td>Kentucky</td><td>236,500</td><td>1.4%</td></tr>
<tr><td>8</td><td>Massachusetts</td><td>588,000</td><td>3.4%</td><td>21</td><td>Colorado</td><td>226,600</td><td>1.3%</td></tr>
<tr><td>10</td><td>Michigan</td><td>554,200</td><td>3.2%</td><td>22</td><td>Louisiana</td><td>210,900</td><td>1.2%</td></tr>
<tr><td>12</td><td>Minnesota</td><td>394,500</td><td>2.3%</td><td>23</td><td>Oregon</td><td>207,700</td><td>1.2%</td></tr>
<tr><td>NA</td><td>Mississippi**</td><td>NA</td><td>NA</td><td>24</td><td>Iowa</td><td>196,300</td><td>1.1%</td></tr>
<tr><td>16</td><td>Missouri</td><td>369,300</td><td>2.1%</td><td>25</td><td>South Carolina</td><td>187,500</td><td>1.1%</td></tr>
<tr><td>36</td><td>Montana</td><td>56,500</td><td>0.3%</td><td>26</td><td>Oklahoma</td><td>183,200</td><td>1.0%</td></tr>
<tr><td>29</td><td>Nebraska</td><td>128,500</td><td>0.7%</td><td>27</td><td>Arkansas</td><td>149,000</td><td>0.9%</td></tr>
<tr><td>NA</td><td>Nevada**</td><td>NA</td><td>NA</td><td>28</td><td>Utah</td><td>131,100</td><td>0.7%</td></tr>
<tr><td>NA</td><td>New Hampshire**</td><td>NA</td><td>NA</td><td>29</td><td>Nebraska</td><td>128,500</td><td>0.7%</td></tr>
<tr><td>9</td><td>New Jersey</td><td>566,200</td><td>3.2%</td><td>30</td><td>Maine</td><td>114,100</td><td>0.7%</td></tr>
<tr><td>32</td><td>New Mexico</td><td>106,400</td><td>0.6%</td><td>31</td><td>West Virginia</td><td>113,600</td><td>0.6%</td></tr>
<tr><td>2</td><td>New York</td><td>1,562,600</td><td>8.9%</td><td>32</td><td>New Mexico</td><td>106,400</td><td>0.6%</td></tr>
<tr><td>11</td><td>North Carolina</td><td>465,100</td><td>2.7%</td><td>33</td><td>Rhode Island</td><td>96,300</td><td>0.6%</td></tr>
<tr><td>38</td><td>North Dakota</td><td>49,800</td><td>0.3%</td><td>34</td><td>Hawaii</td><td>70,300</td><td>0.4%</td></tr>
<tr><td>6</td><td>Ohio</td><td>754,500</td><td>4.3%</td><td>35</td><td>South Dakota</td><td>58,500</td><td>0.3%</td></tr>
<tr><td>26</td><td>Oklahoma</td><td>183,200</td><td>1.0%</td><td>36</td><td>Montana</td><td>56,500</td><td>0.3%</td></tr>
<tr><td>23</td><td>Oregon</td><td>207,700</td><td>1.2%</td><td>37</td><td>Delaware</td><td>53,300</td><td>0.3%</td></tr>
<tr><td>4</td><td>Pennsylvania</td><td>1,028,000</td><td>5.9%</td><td>38</td><td>North Dakota</td><td>49,800</td><td>0.3%</td></tr>
<tr><td>33</td><td>Rhode Island</td><td>96,300</td><td>0.6%</td><td>39</td><td>Alaska</td><td>36,100</td><td>0.2%</td></tr>
<tr><td>25</td><td>South Carolina</td><td>187,500</td><td>1.1%</td><td>NA</td><td>Alabama**</td><td>NA</td><td>NA</td></tr>
<tr><td>35</td><td>South Dakota</td><td>58,500</td><td>0.3%</td><td>NA</td><td>Connecticut**</td><td>NA</td><td>NA</td></tr>
<tr><td>NA</td><td>Tennessee**</td><td>NA</td><td>NA</td><td>NA</td><td>Georgia**</td><td>NA</td><td>NA</td></tr>
<tr><td>3</td><td>Texas</td><td>1,182,100</td><td>6.8%</td><td>NA</td><td>Idaho**</td><td>NA</td><td>NA</td></tr>
<tr><td>28</td><td>Utah</td><td>131,100</td><td>0.7%</td><td>NA</td><td>Kansas**</td><td>NA</td><td>NA</td></tr>
<tr><td>NA</td><td>Vermont**</td><td>NA</td><td>NA</td><td>NA</td><td>Mississippi**</td><td>NA</td><td>NA</td></tr>
<tr><td>13</td><td>Virginia</td><td>393,000</td><td>2.2%</td><td>NA</td><td>Nevada**</td><td>NA</td><td>NA</td></tr>
<tr><td>18</td><td>Washington</td><td>332,900</td><td>1.9%</td><td>NA</td><td>New Hampshire**</td><td>NA</td><td>NA</td></tr>
<tr><td>31</td><td>West Virginia</td><td>113,600</td><td>0.6%</td><td>NA</td><td>Tennessee**</td><td>NA</td><td>NA</td></tr>
<tr><td>14</td><td>Wisconsin</td><td>387,700</td><td>2.2%</td><td>NA</td><td>Vermont**</td><td>NA</td><td>NA</td></tr>
<tr><td>NA</td><td>Wyoming**</td><td>NA</td><td>NA</td><td>NA</td><td>Wyoming**</td><td>NA</td><td>NA</td></tr>
<tr><td></td><td></td><td></td><td></td><td></td><td>District of Columbia**</td><td>NA</td><td>NA</td></tr>
</table>

Source: U.S. Department of Labor, Bureau of Labor Statistics
   "Regional and State Employment and Unemployment" (press release, January 24, 2006)
*Seasonally adjusted preliminary data as of December 2005. National total calculated through a different formula.
**The Bureau of Labor Statistics does not publish seasonally adjusted figures in this category for these states.

Percent of Nonfarm Employees in Education and Health Services in 2005

National Percent = 13.0% of Employees*

ALPHA ORDER				RANK ORDER		
RANK	STATE	PERCENT		RANK	STATE	PERCENT
NA	Alabama**	NA		1	Rhode Island	19.5
32	Alaska	11.6		2	Maine	18.4
35	Arizona	11.1		2	Massachusetts	18.4
21	Arkansas	12.7		4	New York	18.3
36	California	10.7		5	Pennsylvania	17.9
38	Colorado	10.1		6	West Virginia	15.3
NA	Connecticut**	NA		7	South Dakota	14.9
27	Delaware	12.2		8	Minnesota	14.4
25	Florida	12.3		8	North Dakota	14.4
NA	Georgia**	NA		10	Maryland	14.0
32	Hawaii	11.6		11	New Jersey	13.9
NA	Idaho**	NA		11	Ohio	13.9
23	Illinois	12.6		13	Nebraska	13.7
20	Indiana	12.9		14	Wisconsin	13.6
16	Iowa	13.2		15	Missouri	13.5
NA	Kansas**	NA		16	Iowa	13.2
18	Kentucky	13.0		16	Montana	13.2
25	Louisiana	12.3		18	Kentucky	13.0
2	Maine	18.4		18	New Mexico	13.0
10	Maryland	14.0		20	Indiana	12.9
2	Massachusetts	18.4		21	Arkansas	12.7
21	Michigan	12.7		21	Michigan	12.7
8	Minnesota	14.4		23	Illinois	12.6
NA	Mississippi**	NA		24	Oregon	12.4
15	Missouri	13.5		25	Florida	12.3
16	Montana	13.2		25	Louisiana	12.3
13	Nebraska	13.7		27	Delaware	12.2
NA	Nevada**	NA		27	Oklahoma	12.2
NA	New Hampshire**	NA		27	Texas	12.2
11	New Jersey	13.9		30	North Carolina	11.9
18	New Mexico	13.0		30	Washington	11.9
4	New York	18.3		32	Alaska	11.6
30	North Carolina	11.9		32	Hawaii	11.6
8	North Dakota	14.4		34	Utah	11.2
11	Ohio	13.9		35	Arizona	11.1
27	Oklahoma	12.2		36	California	10.7
24	Oregon	12.4		36	Virginia	10.7
5	Pennsylvania	17.9		38	Colorado	10.1
1	Rhode Island	19.5		38	South Carolina	10.1
38	South Carolina	10.1		NA	Alabama**	NA
7	South Dakota	14.9		NA	Connecticut**	NA
NA	Tennessee**	NA		NA	Georgia**	NA
27	Texas	12.2		NA	Idaho**	NA
34	Utah	11.2		NA	Kansas**	NA
NA	Vermont**	NA		NA	Mississippi**	NA
36	Virginia	10.7		NA	Nevada**	NA
30	Washington	11.9		NA	New Hampshire**	NA
6	West Virginia	15.3		NA	Tennessee**	NA
14	Wisconsin	13.6		NA	Vermont**	NA
NA	Wyoming**	NA		NA	Wyoming**	NA
					District of Columbia**	NA

Source: Morgan Quitno Press using data from U.S. Department of Labor, Bureau of Labor Statistics
    "Regional and State Employment and Unemployment" (press release, January 24, 2006)
*Seasonally adjusted preliminary data as of December 2005. National figure calculated through a different formula.
**The Bureau of Labor Statistics does not publish seasonally adjusted figures in this category for these states.

Employees in Financial Activities in 2005

National Total = 8,316,000 Employees*

ALPHA ORDER					RANK ORDER			
RANK	STATE	EMPLOYEES	% of USA		RANK	STATE	EMPLOYEES	% of USA
26	Alabama	95,800	1.2%		1	California	927,800	11.2%
42	Alaska	14,800	0.2%		2	New York	717,200	8.6%
14	Arizona	173,400	2.1%		3	Texas	607,800	7.3%
32	Arkansas	52,500	0.6%		4	Florida	518,400	6.2%
1	California	927,800	11.2%		5	Illinois	406,300	4.9%
16	Colorado	161,900	1.9%		6	Pennsylvania	339,300	4.1%
21	Connecticut	142,200	1.7%		7	Ohio	314,100	3.8%
33	Delaware	46,200	0.6%		8	New Jersey	283,700	3.4%
4	Florida	518,400	6.2%		9	Georgia	223,700	2.7%
9	Georgia	223,700	2.7%		10	Massachusetts	220,000	2.6%
NA	Hawaii**	NA	NA		11	Michigan	218,800	2.6%
NA	Idaho**	NA	NA		12	Virginia	191,700	2.3%
5	Illinois	406,300	4.9%		13	Minnesota	181,200	2.2%
22	Indiana	141,900	1.7%		14	Arizona	173,400	2.1%
23	Iowa	100,900	1.2%		15	Missouri	169,100	2.0%
NA	Kansas**	NA	NA		16	Colorado	161,900	1.9%
29	Kentucky	84,800	1.0%		17	Wisconsin	158,400	1.9%
25	Louisiana	97,800	1.2%		18	Maryland	158,300	1.9%
37	Maine	34,200	0.4%		19	Washington	155,100	1.9%
18	Maryland	158,300	1.9%		20	Tennessee	144,800	1.7%
10	Massachusetts	220,000	2.6%		21	Connecticut	142,200	1.7%
11	Michigan	218,800	2.6%		22	Indiana	141,900	1.7%
13	Minnesota	181,200	2.2%		23	Iowa	100,900	1.2%
NA	Mississippi**	NA	NA		24	Oregon	99,300	1.2%
15	Missouri	169,100	2.0%		25	Louisiana	97,800	1.2%
40	Montana	21,300	0.3%		26	Alabama	95,800	1.2%
31	Nebraska	64,900	0.8%		27	South Carolina	94,700	1.1%
30	Nevada	67,500	0.8%		28	Oklahoma	86,500	1.0%
34	New Hampshire	38,800	0.5%		29	Kentucky	84,800	1.0%
8	New Jersey	283,700	3.4%		30	Nevada	67,500	0.8%
36	New Mexico	35,600	0.4%		31	Nebraska	64,900	0.8%
2	New York	717,200	8.6%		32	Arkansas	52,500	0.6%
NA	North Carolina**	NA	NA		33	Delaware	46,200	0.6%
41	North Dakota	19,000	0.2%		34	New Hampshire	38,800	0.5%
7	Ohio	314,100	3.8%		35	Rhode Island	35,700	0.4%
28	Oklahoma	86,500	1.0%		36	New Mexico	35,600	0.4%
24	Oregon	99,300	1.2%		37	Maine	34,200	0.4%
6	Pennsylvania	339,300	4.1%		38	West Virginia	30,500	0.4%
35	Rhode Island	35,700	0.4%		39	South Dakota	28,900	0.3%
27	South Carolina	94,700	1.1%		40	Montana	21,300	0.3%
39	South Dakota	28,900	0.3%		41	North Dakota	19,000	0.2%
20	Tennessee	144,800	1.7%		42	Alaska	14,800	0.2%
3	Texas	607,800	7.3%		NA	Hawaii**	NA	NA
NA	Utah**	NA	NA		NA	Idaho**	NA	NA
NA	Vermont**	NA	NA		NA	Kansas**	NA	NA
12	Virginia	191,700	2.3%		NA	Mississippi**	NA	NA
19	Washington	155,100	1.9%		NA	North Carolina**	NA	NA
38	West Virginia	30,500	0.4%		NA	Utah**	NA	NA
17	Wisconsin	158,400	1.9%		NA	Vermont**	NA	NA
NA	Wyoming**	NA	NA		NA	Wyoming**	NA	NA
					NA	District of Columbia**	NA	NA

Source: U.S. Department of Labor, Bureau of Labor Statistics
    "Regional and State Employment and Unemployment" (press release, January 24, 2006)
*Seasonally adjusted preliminary data as of December 2005. National total calculated through a different formula.
Financial activities include insurance and real estate.
**The Bureau of Labor Statistics does not publish seasonally adjusted figures in this category for these states.

Percent of Nonfarm Employees in Financial Activities in 2005

National Percent = 6.2% of Employees*

ALPHA ORDER

RANK ORDER

RANK	STATE	PERCENT		RANK	STATE	PERCENT
34	Alabama	5.0		1	Delaware	10.6
37	Alaska	4.8		2	Connecticut	8.5
8	Arizona	6.9		3	New York	8.4
40	Arkansas	4.5		4	South Dakota	7.4
16	California	6.2		5	Colorado	7.2
5	Colorado	7.2		5	Rhode Island	7.2
2	Connecticut	8.5		7	New Jersey	7.0
1	Delaware	10.6		8	Arizona	6.9
13	Florida	6.6		8	Illinois	6.9
25	Georgia	5.6		8	Massachusetts	6.9
NA	Hawaii**	NA		8	Nebraska	6.9
NA	Idaho**	NA		12	Iowa	6.8
8	Illinois	6.9		13	Florida	6.6
37	Indiana	4.8		13	Minnesota	6.6
12	Iowa	6.8		15	Texas	6.3
NA	Kansas**	NA		16	California	6.2
39	Kentucky	4.7		16	Missouri	6.2
23	Louisiana	5.7		18	Maryland	6.1
27	Maine	5.5		19	New Hampshire	6.0
18	Maryland	6.1		20	Oregon	5.9
8	Massachusetts	6.9		20	Pennsylvania	5.9
34	Michigan	5.0		22	Ohio	5.8
13	Minnesota	6.6		23	Louisiana	5.7
NA	Mississippi**	NA		23	Oklahoma	5.7
16	Missouri	6.2		25	Georgia	5.6
34	Montana	5.0		25	Wisconsin	5.6
8	Nebraska	6.9		27	Maine	5.5
30	Nevada	5.4		27	North Dakota	5.5
19	New Hampshire	6.0		27	Washington	5.5
7	New Jersey	7.0		30	Nevada	5.4
41	New Mexico	4.4		31	Tennessee	5.3
3	New York	8.4		32	Virginia	5.2
NA	North Carolina**	NA		33	South Carolina	5.1
27	North Dakota	5.5		34	Alabama	5.0
22	Ohio	5.8		34	Michigan	5.0
23	Oklahoma	5.7		34	Montana	5.0
20	Oregon	5.9		37	Alaska	4.8
20	Pennsylvania	5.9		37	Indiana	4.8
5	Rhode Island	7.2		39	Kentucky	4.7
33	South Carolina	5.1		40	Arkansas	4.5
4	South Dakota	7.4		41	New Mexico	4.4
31	Tennessee	5.3		42	West Virginia	4.1
15	Texas	6.3		NA	Hawaii**	NA
NA	Utah**	NA		NA	Idaho**	NA
NA	Vermont**	NA		NA	Kansas**	NA
32	Virginia	5.2		NA	Mississippi**	NA
27	Washington	5.5		NA	North Carolina**	NA
42	West Virginia	4.1		NA	Utah**	NA
25	Wisconsin	5.6		NA	Vermont**	NA
NA	Wyoming**	NA		NA	Wyoming**	NA
					District of Columbia**	NA

Source: Morgan Quitno Press using data from U.S. Department of Labor, Bureau of Labor Statistics
    "Regional and State Employment and Unemployment" (press release, January 24, 2006)
*Seasonally adjusted preliminary data as of December 2005. National figure calculated through a different formula.
Financial activities include insurance and real estate.
**The Bureau of Labor Statistics does not publish seasonally adjusted figures in this category for these states.

Employees in Government in 2005

National Total = 21,888,000 Employees*

ALPHA ORDER					RANK ORDER			
RANK	STATE	EMPLOYEES	% of USA		RANK	STATE	EMPLOYEES	% of USA
24	Alabama	359,200	1.6%		1	California	2,411,500	11.0%
44	Alaska	81,200	0.4%		2	Texas	1,674,800	7.7%
20	Arizona	409,600	1.9%		3	New York	1,486,800	6.8%
33	Arkansas	206,100	0.9%		4	Florida	1,098,200	5.0%
1	California	2,411,500	11.0%		5	Illinois	844,300	3.9%
23	Colorado	367,800	1.7%		6	Ohio	794,200	3.6%
31	Connecticut	243,100	1.1%		7	Pennsylvania	753,000	3.4%
49	Delaware	59,100	0.3%		8	Michigan	676,400	3.1%
4	Florida	1,098,200	5.0%		9	North Carolina	663,200	3.0%
11	Georgia	649,600	3.0%		10	Virginia	662,100	3.0%
39	Hawaii	120,000	0.5%		11	Georgia	649,600	3.0%
40	Idaho	114,900	0.5%		12	New Jersey	642,600	2.9%
5	Illinois	844,300	3.9%		13	Washington	525,300	2.4%
16	Indiana	421,900	1.9%		14	Maryland	464,700	2.1%
30	Iowa	245,800	1.1%		15	Missouri	425,100	1.9%
29	Kansas	259,700	1.2%		16	Indiana	421,900	1.9%
27	Kentucky	308,900	1.4%		17	Minnesota	416,600	1.9%
22	Louisiana	376,300	1.7%		18	Wisconsin	416,200	1.9%
41	Maine	105,800	0.5%		19	Tennessee	414,200	1.9%
14	Maryland	464,700	2.1%		20	Arizona	409,600	1.9%
21	Massachusetts	406,100	1.9%		21	Massachusetts	406,100	1.9%
8	Michigan	676,400	3.1%		22	Louisiana	376,300	1.7%
17	Minnesota	416,600	1.9%		23	Colorado	367,800	1.7%
32	Mississippi	242,100	1.1%		24	Alabama	359,200	1.6%
15	Missouri	425,100	1.9%		25	South Carolina	331,300	1.5%
43	Montana	88,500	0.4%		26	Oklahoma	314,500	1.4%
36	Nebraska	161,900	0.7%		27	Kentucky	308,900	1.4%
37	Nevada	146,100	0.7%		28	Oregon	273,100	1.2%
42	New Hampshire	89,700	0.4%		29	Kansas	259,700	1.2%
12	New Jersey	642,600	2.9%		30	Iowa	245,800	1.1%
35	New Mexico	202,800	0.9%		31	Connecticut	243,100	1.1%
3	New York	1,486,800	6.8%		32	Mississippi	242,100	1.1%
9	North Carolina	663,200	3.0%		33	Arkansas	206,100	0.9%
46	North Dakota	74,900	0.3%		34	Utah	203,700	0.9%
6	Ohio	794,200	3.6%		35	New Mexico	202,800	0.9%
26	Oklahoma	314,500	1.4%		36	Nebraska	161,900	0.7%
28	Oregon	273,100	1.2%		37	Nevada	146,100	0.7%
7	Pennsylvania	753,000	3.4%		38	West Virginia	143,000	0.7%
47	Rhode Island	65,600	0.3%		39	Hawaii	120,000	0.5%
25	South Carolina	331,300	1.5%		40	Idaho	114,900	0.5%
45	South Dakota	75,000	0.3%		41	Maine	105,800	0.5%
19	Tennessee	414,200	1.9%		42	New Hampshire	89,700	0.4%
2	Texas	1,674,800	7.7%		43	Montana	88,500	0.4%
34	Utah	203,700	0.9%		44	Alaska	81,200	0.4%
50	Vermont	52,700	0.2%		45	South Dakota	75,000	0.3%
10	Virginia	662,100	3.0%		46	North Dakota	74,900	0.3%
13	Washington	525,300	2.4%		47	Rhode Island	65,600	0.3%
38	West Virginia	143,000	0.7%		48	Wyoming	65,200	0.3%
18	Wisconsin	416,200	1.9%		49	Delaware	59,100	0.3%
48	Wyoming	65,200	0.3%		50	Vermont	52,700	0.2%
						District of Columbia	230,500	1.1%

Source: U.S. Department of Labor, Bureau of Labor Statistics
    "Regional and State Employment and Unemployment" (press release, January 24, 2006)
    *Seasonally adjusted preliminary data as of December 2005. National total calculated through a different formula.

Percent of Nonfarm Employees in Government in 2005

National Percent = 16.3% of Employees*

RANK	STATE	PERCENT	RANK	STATE	PERCENT
	ALPHA ORDER			**RANK ORDER**	
14	Alabama	18.6	1	Alaska	26.2
1	Alaska	26.2	2	New Mexico	24.8
32	Arizona	16.2	3	Wyoming	24.7
19	Arkansas	17.5	4	Louisiana	21.9
32	California	16.2	4	Mississippi	21.9
29	Colorado	16.4	6	North Dakota	21.7
41	Connecticut	14.5	7	Oklahoma	20.9
46	Delaware	13.6	8	Montana	20.7
44	Florida	14.0	9	Hawaii	19.7
29	Georgia	16.4	10	Kansas	19.2
9	Hawaii	19.7	10	South Dakota	19.2
14	Idaho	18.6	10	West Virginia	19.2
42	Illinois	14.4	13	Washington	18.8
43	Indiana	14.3	14	Alabama	18.6
28	Iowa	16.5	14	Idaho	18.6
10	Kansas	19.2	16	Virginia	18.1
27	Kentucky	16.9	17	Maryland	18.0
4	Louisiana	21.9	18	South Carolina	17.9
24	Maine	17.1	19	Arkansas	17.5
17	Maryland	18.0	19	Utah	17.5
49	Massachusetts	12.7	21	New York	17.4
36	Michigan	15.5	22	Nebraska	17.3
37	Minnesota	15.3	22	Texas	17.3
4	Mississippi	21.9	24	Maine	17.1
35	Missouri	15.6	25	North Carolina	17.0
8	Montana	20.7	25	Vermont	17.0
22	Nebraska	17.3	27	Kentucky	16.9
50	Nevada	11.6	28	Iowa	16.5
44	New Hampshire	14.0	29	Colorado	16.4
34	New Jersey	15.8	29	Georgia	16.4
2	New Mexico	24.8	31	Oregon	16.3
21	New York	17.4	32	Arizona	16.2
25	North Carolina	17.0	32	California	16.2
6	North Dakota	21.7	34	New Jersey	15.8
39	Ohio	14.7	35	Missouri	15.6
7	Oklahoma	20.9	36	Michigan	15.5
31	Oregon	16.3	37	Minnesota	15.3
48	Pennsylvania	13.1	38	Tennessee	15.2
47	Rhode Island	13.3	39	Ohio	14.7
18	South Carolina	17.9	40	Wisconsin	14.6
10	South Dakota	19.2	41	Connecticut	14.5
38	Tennessee	15.2	42	Illinois	14.4
22	Texas	17.3	43	Indiana	14.3
19	Utah	17.5	44	Florida	14.0
25	Vermont	17.0	44	New Hampshire	14.0
16	Virginia	18.1	46	Delaware	13.6
13	Washington	18.8	47	Rhode Island	13.3
10	West Virginia	19.2	48	Pennsylvania	13.1
40	Wisconsin	14.6	49	Massachusetts	12.7
3	Wyoming	24.7	50	Nevada	11.6
				District of Columbia	33.6

Source: Morgan Quitno Press using data from U.S. Department of Labor, Bureau of Labor Statistics
    "Regional and State Employment and Unemployment" (press release, January 24, 2006)
*Seasonally adjusted preliminary data as of December 2005. National figure calculated through a different formula.

Employees in Leisure and Hospitality in 2005

National Total = 12,831,000 Employees*

ALPHA ORDER

RANK	STATE	EMPLOYEES	% of USA
27	Alabama	162,400	1.3%
48	Alaska	30,900	0.2%
20	Arizona	257,900	2.0%
35	Arkansas	91,700	0.7%
1	California	1,489,800	11.6%
19	Colorado	258,000	2.0%
29	Connecticut	129,300	1.0%
44	Delaware	42,200	0.3%
3	Florida	904,600	7.1%
9	Georgia	372,800	2.9%
33	Hawaii	108,000	0.8%
42	Idaho	58,000	0.5%
5	Illinois	521,000	4.1%
15	Indiana	279,600	2.2%
NA	Iowa**	NA	NA
31	Kansas	112,200	0.9%
25	Kentucky	166,500	1.3%
26	Louisiana	165,700	1.3%
40	Maine	62,100	0.5%
23	Maryland	237,700	1.9%
14	Massachusetts	295,900	2.3%
8	Michigan	407,700	3.2%
22	Minnesota	245,600	1.9%
32	Mississippi	109,200	0.9%
16	Missouri	267,600	2.1%
41	Montana	59,900	0.5%
37	Nebraska	79,500	0.6%
12	Nevada	331,800	2.6%
38	New Hampshire	68,200	0.5%
11	New Jersey	348,000	2.7%
36	New Mexico	83,600	0.7%
4	New York	678,200	5.3%
10	North Carolina	356,800	2.8%
47	North Dakota	31,900	0.2%
6	Ohio	496,900	3.9%
30	Oklahoma	128,800	1.0%
28	Oregon	160,800	1.3%
7	Pennsylvania	493,200	3.8%
43	Rhode Island	52,500	0.4%
24	South Carolina	203,300	1.6%
45	South Dakota	41,900	0.3%
18	Tennessee	259,800	2.0%
2	Texas	910,000	7.1%
34	Utah	106,200	0.8%
NA	Vermont**	NA	NA
13	Virginia	325,100	2.5%
17	Washington	266,400	2.1%
39	West Virginia	68,100	0.5%
21	Wisconsin	257,400	2.0%
46	Wyoming	32,600	0.3%

RANK ORDER

RANK	STATE	EMPLOYEES	% of USA
1	California	1,489,800	11.6%
2	Texas	910,000	7.1%
3	Florida	904,600	7.1%
4	New York	678,200	5.3%
5	Illinois	521,000	4.1%
6	Ohio	496,900	3.9%
7	Pennsylvania	493,200	3.8%
8	Michigan	407,700	3.2%
9	Georgia	372,800	2.9%
10	North Carolina	356,800	2.8%
11	New Jersey	348,000	2.7%
12	Nevada	331,800	2.6%
13	Virginia	325,100	2.5%
14	Massachusetts	295,900	2.3%
15	Indiana	279,600	2.2%
16	Missouri	267,600	2.1%
17	Washington	266,400	2.1%
18	Tennessee	259,800	2.0%
19	Colorado	258,000	2.0%
20	Arizona	257,900	2.0%
21	Wisconsin	257,400	2.0%
22	Minnesota	245,600	1.9%
23	Maryland	237,700	1.9%
24	South Carolina	203,300	1.6%
25	Kentucky	166,500	1.3%
26	Louisiana	165,700	1.3%
27	Alabama	162,400	1.3%
28	Oregon	160,800	1.3%
29	Connecticut	129,300	1.0%
30	Oklahoma	128,800	1.0%
31	Kansas	112,200	0.9%
32	Mississippi	109,200	0.9%
33	Hawaii	108,000	0.8%
34	Utah	106,200	0.8%
35	Arkansas	91,700	0.7%
36	New Mexico	83,600	0.7%
37	Nebraska	79,500	0.6%
38	New Hampshire	68,200	0.5%
39	West Virginia	68,100	0.5%
40	Maine	62,100	0.5%
41	Montana	59,900	0.5%
42	Idaho	58,000	0.5%
43	Rhode Island	52,500	0.4%
44	Delaware	42,200	0.3%
45	South Dakota	41,900	0.3%
46	Wyoming	32,600	0.3%
47	North Dakota	31,900	0.2%
48	Alaska	30,900	0.2%
NA	Iowa**	NA	NA
NA	Vermont**	NA	NA
	District of Columbia	53,900	0.4%

Source: U.S. Department of Labor, Bureau of Labor Statistics
   "Regional and State Employment and Unemployment" (press release, January 24, 2006)
*Seasonally adjusted preliminary data as of December 2005. National total calculated through a different formula.
**The Bureau of Labor Statistics does not publish seasonally adjusted figures in this category for these states.

Percent of Nonfarm Employees in Leisure and Hospitality in 2005

National Percent = 9.5% of Employees*

ALPHA ORDER

RANK	STATE	PERCENT
44	Alabama	8.4
13	Alaska	10.0
11	Arizona	10.2
47	Arkansas	7.8
13	California	10.0
5	Colorado	11.5
48	Connecticut	7.7
18	Delaware	9.7
5	Florida	11.5
24	Georgia	9.4
2	Hawaii	17.8
24	Idaho	9.4
30	Illinois	8.9
21	Indiana	9.5
NA	Iowa**	NA
45	Kansas	8.3
32	Kentucky	9.1
19	Louisiana	9.6
13	Maine	10.0
29	Maryland	9.2
29	Massachusetts	9.2
27	Michigan	9.3
36	Minnesota	9.0
16	Mississippi	9.9
17	Missouri	9.8
3	Montana	14.0
43	Nebraska	8.5
1	Nevada	26.4
9	New Hampshire	10.6
40	New Jersey	8.6
11	New Mexico	10.2
46	New York	7.9
32	North Carolina	9.1
27	North Dakota	9.3
29	Ohio	9.2
40	Oklahoma	8.6
19	Oregon	9.6
40	Pennsylvania	8.6
9	Rhode Island	10.6
7	South Carolina	11.0
8	South Dakota	10.7
21	Tennessee	9.5
24	Texas	9.4
32	Utah	9.1
NA	Vermont**	NA
38	Virginia	8.9
21	Washington	9.5
32	West Virginia	9.1
36	Wisconsin	9.0
4	Wyoming	12.4

RANK ORDER

RANK	STATE	PERCENT
1	Nevada	26.4
2	Hawaii	17.8
3	Montana	14.0
4	Wyoming	12.4
5	Colorado	11.5
5	Florida	11.5
7	South Carolina	11.0
8	South Dakota	10.7
9	New Hampshire	10.6
9	Rhode Island	10.6
11	Arizona	10.2
11	New Mexico	10.2
13	Alaska	10.0
13	California	10.0
13	Maine	10.0
16	Mississippi	9.9
17	Missouri	9.8
18	Delaware	9.7
19	Louisiana	9.6
19	Oregon	9.6
21	Indiana	9.5
21	Tennessee	9.5
21	Washington	9.5
24	Georgia	9.4
24	Idaho	9.4
24	Texas	9.4
27	Michigan	9.3
27	North Dakota	9.3
29	Maryland	9.2
29	Massachusetts	9.2
29	Ohio	9.2
32	Kentucky	9.1
32	North Carolina	9.1
32	Utah	9.1
32	West Virginia	9.1
36	Minnesota	9.0
36	Wisconsin	9.0
38	Illinois	8.9
38	Virginia	8.9
40	New Jersey	8.6
40	Oklahoma	8.6
40	Pennsylvania	8.6
43	Nebraska	8.5
44	Alabama	8.4
45	Kansas	8.3
46	New York	7.9
47	Arkansas	7.8
48	Connecticut	7.7
NA	Iowa**	NA
NA	Vermont**	NA

District of Columbia   7.9

Source: Morgan Quitno Press using data from U.S. Department of Labor, Bureau of Labor Statistics
    "Regional and State Employment and Unemployment" (press release, January 24, 2006)
*Seasonally adjusted preliminary data as of December 2005. National figure calculated through a different formula.
**The Bureau of Labor Statistics does not publish seasonally adjusted figures in this category for these states.

Employees in Manufacturing in 2005

National Total = 14,283,000 Employees*

ALPHA ORDER

RANK	STATE	EMPLOYEES	% of USA
NA	Alabama**	NA	NA
NA	Alaska**	NA	NA
24	Arizona	176,200	1.2%
21	Arkansas	199,800	1.4%
1	California	1,538,700	10.8%
26	Colorado	151,800	1.1%
22	Connecticut	196,500	1.4%
NA	Delaware**	NA	NA
11	Florida	390,400	2.7%
NA	Georgia**	NA	NA
40	Hawaii	15,400	0.1%
32	Idaho	62,300	0.4%
4	Illinois	692,500	4.8%
8	Indiana	569,900	4.0%
19	Iowa	230,400	1.6%
23	Kansas	179,600	1.3%
18	Kentucky	265,200	1.9%
27	Louisiana	139,600	1.0%
34	Maine	61,600	0.4%
28	Maryland	137,600	1.0%
15	Massachusetts	312,900	2.2%
6	Michigan	669,900	4.7%
12	Minnesota	350,000	2.5%
25	Mississippi	175,200	1.2%
14	Missouri	316,700	2.2%
39	Montana	19,300	0.1%
30	Nebraska	100,700	0.7%
NA	Nevada**	NA	NA
31	New Hampshire	81,700	0.6%
13	New Jersey	322,900	2.3%
37	New Mexico	36,900	0.3%
7	New York	573,200	4.0%
9	North Carolina	565,800	4.0%
38	North Dakota	24,900	0.2%
3	Ohio	822,800	5.8%
NA	Oklahoma**	NA	NA
20	Oregon	211,200	1.5%
5	Pennsylvania	673,600	4.7%
35	Rhode Island	54,500	0.4%
NA	South Carolina**	NA	NA
NA	South Dakota**	NA	NA
NA	Tennessee**	NA	NA
2	Texas	892,200	6.2%
29	Utah	118,600	0.8%
36	Vermont	37,300	0.3%
16	Virginia	295,800	2.1%
17	Washington	272,900	1.9%
33	West Virginia	61,700	0.4%
10	Wisconsin	506,200	3.5%
NA	Wyoming**	NA	NA

RANK ORDER

RANK	STATE	EMPLOYEES	% of USA
1	California	1,538,700	10.8%
2	Texas	892,200	6.2%
3	Ohio	822,800	5.8%
4	Illinois	692,500	4.8%
5	Pennsylvania	673,600	4.7%
6	Michigan	669,900	4.7%
7	New York	573,200	4.0%
8	Indiana	569,900	4.0%
9	North Carolina	565,800	4.0%
10	Wisconsin	506,200	3.5%
11	Florida	390,400	2.7%
12	Minnesota	350,000	2.5%
13	New Jersey	322,900	2.3%
14	Missouri	316,700	2.2%
15	Massachusetts	312,900	2.2%
16	Virginia	295,800	2.1%
17	Washington	272,900	1.9%
18	Kentucky	265,200	1.9%
19	Iowa	230,400	1.6%
20	Oregon	211,200	1.5%
21	Arkansas	199,800	1.4%
22	Connecticut	196,500	1.4%
23	Kansas	179,600	1.3%
24	Arizona	176,200	1.2%
25	Mississippi	175,200	1.2%
26	Colorado	151,800	1.1%
27	Louisiana	139,600	1.0%
28	Maryland	137,600	1.0%
29	Utah	118,600	0.8%
30	Nebraska	100,700	0.7%
31	New Hampshire	81,700	0.6%
32	Idaho	62,300	0.4%
33	West Virginia	61,700	0.4%
34	Maine	61,600	0.4%
35	Rhode Island	54,500	0.4%
36	Vermont	37,300	0.3%
37	New Mexico	36,900	0.3%
38	North Dakota	24,900	0.2%
39	Montana	19,300	0.1%
40	Hawaii	15,400	0.1%
NA	Alabama**	NA	NA
NA	Alaska**	NA	NA
NA	Delaware**	NA	NA
NA	Georgia**	NA	NA
NA	Nevada**	NA	NA
NA	Oklahoma**	NA	NA
NA	South Carolina**	NA	NA
NA	South Dakota**	NA	NA
NA	Tennessee**	NA	NA
NA	Wyoming**	NA	NA
	District of Columbia**	NA	NA

Source: U.S. Department of Labor, Bureau of Labor Statistics
"Regional and State Employment and Unemployment" (press release, January 24, 2006)
*Seasonally adjusted preliminary data as of December 2005. National total calculated through a different formula.
**The Bureau of Labor Statistics does not publish seasonally adjusted figures in this category for these states.

Percent of Nonfarm Employees in Manufacturing in 2005

National Percent = 10.6% of Employees*

ALPHA ORDER				RANK ORDER		
RANK	**STATE**	**PERCENT**		**RANK**	**STATE**	**PERCENT**
NA	Alabama**	NA		1	Indiana	19.3
NA	Alaska**	NA		2	Wisconsin	17.8
33	Arizona	7.0		3	Arkansas	17.0
3	Arkansas	17.0		4	Mississippi	15.9
21	California	10.3		5	Iowa	15.5
34	Colorado	6.8		6	Michigan	15.4
17	Connecticut	11.7		7	Ohio	15.2
NA	Delaware**	NA		8	Kentucky	14.5
37	Florida	5.0		8	North Carolina	14.5
NA	Georgia**	NA		10	Kansas	13.3
40	Hawaii	2.5		11	Minnesota	12.8
23	Idaho	10.1		12	New Hampshire	12.7
15	Illinois	11.8		13	Oregon	12.6
1	Indiana	19.3		14	Vermont	12.0
5	Iowa	15.5		15	Illinois	11.8
10	Kansas	13.3		15	Pennsylvania	11.8
8	Kentucky	14.5		17	Connecticut	11.7
29	Louisiana	8.1		18	Missouri	11.6
24	Maine	10.0		19	Rhode Island	11.0
36	Maryland	5.3		20	Nebraska	10.7
25	Massachusetts	9.8		21	California	10.3
6	Michigan	15.4		22	Utah	10.2
11	Minnesota	12.8		23	Idaho	10.1
4	Mississippi	15.9		24	Maine	10.0
18	Missouri	11.6		25	Massachusetts	9.8
38	Montana	4.5		26	Washington	9.7
20	Nebraska	10.7		27	Texas	9.2
NA	Nevada**	NA		28	West Virginia	8.3
12	New Hampshire	12.7		29	Louisiana	8.1
31	New Jersey	7.9		29	Virginia	8.1
38	New Mexico	4.5		31	New Jersey	7.9
35	New York	6.7		32	North Dakota	7.2
8	North Carolina	14.5		33	Arizona	7.0
32	North Dakota	7.2		34	Colorado	6.8
7	Ohio	15.2		35	New York	6.7
NA	Oklahoma**	NA		36	Maryland	5.3
13	Oregon	12.6		37	Florida	5.0
15	Pennsylvania	11.8		38	Montana	4.5
19	Rhode Island	11.0		38	New Mexico	4.5
NA	South Carolina**	NA		40	Hawaii	2.5
NA	South Dakota**	NA		NA	Alabama**	NA
NA	Tennessee**	NA		NA	Alaska**	NA
27	Texas	9.2		NA	Delaware**	NA
22	Utah	10.2		NA	Georgia**	NA
14	Vermont	12.0		NA	Nevada**	NA
29	Virginia	8.1		NA	Oklahoma**	NA
26	Washington	9.7		NA	South Carolina**	NA
28	West Virginia	8.3		NA	South Dakota**	NA
2	Wisconsin	17.8		NA	Tennessee**	NA
NA	Wyoming**	NA		NA	Wyoming**	NA
					District of Columbia**	NA

Source: U.S. Department of Labor, Bureau of Labor Statistics
    "Regional and State Employment and Unemployment" (press release, January 24, 2006)
Seasonally adjusted preliminary data as of December 2005. National figure calculated through a different formula.
**The Bureau of Labor Statistics does not publish seasonally adjusted figures in this category for these states.*

Employees in Natural Resources and Mining in 2005

National Total = 647,000 Employees*

ALPHA ORDER

ALPHA ORDER

RANK	STATE	EMPLOYEES	% of USA
11	Alabama	13,000	2.0%
15	Alaska	10,700	1.7%
17	Arizona	9,700	1.5%
26	Arkansas	7,600	1.2%
6	California	23,200	3.6%
10	Colorado	16,800	2.6%
45	Connecticut	700	0.1%
NA	Delaware**	NA	NA
28	Florida	6,500	1.0%
12	Georgia	12,000	1.9%
NA	Hawaii**	NA	NA
33	Idaho	4,400	0.7%
18	Illinois	9,300	1.4%
27	Indiana	7,400	1.1%
39	Iowa	2,200	0.3%
21	Kansas	8,400	1.3%
7	Kentucky	21,000	3.2%
2	Louisiana	46,200	7.1%
38	Maine	2,700	0.4%
NA	Maryland**	NA	NA
40	Massachusetts	1,900	0.3%
24	Michigan	8,200	1.3%
30	Minnesota	6,100	0.9%
23	Mississippi	8,300	1.3%
32	Missouri	5,200	0.8%
25	Montana	8,100	1.3%
NA	Nebraska**	NA	NA
14	Nevada	10,800	1.7%
43	New Hampshire	1,000	0.2%
41	New Jersey	1,500	0.2%
9	New Mexico	17,100	2.6%
31	New York	5,900	0.9%
29	North Carolina	6,300	1.0%
34	North Dakota	4,200	0.6%
13	Ohio	11,800	1.8%
3	Oklahoma	32,600	5.0%
21	Oregon	8,400	1.3%
8	Pennsylvania	18,400	2.8%
46	Rhode Island	200	0.0%
36	South Carolina	3,800	0.6%
44	South Dakota	800	0.1%
34	Tennessee	4,200	0.6%
1	Texas	158,600	24.5%
20	Utah	8,600	1.3%
42	Vermont	1,100	0.2%
16	Virginia	10,400	1.6%
19	Washington	9,100	1.4%
4	West Virginia	25,700	4.0%
37	Wisconsin	3,300	0.5%
5	Wyoming	23,800	3.7%

RANK ORDER

RANK	STATE	EMPLOYEES	% of USA
1	Texas	158,600	24.5%
2	Louisiana	46,200	7.1%
3	Oklahoma	32,600	5.0%
4	West Virginia	25,700	4.0%
5	Wyoming	23,800	3.7%
6	California	23,200	3.6%
7	Kentucky	21,000	3.2%
8	Pennsylvania	18,400	2.8%
9	New Mexico	17,100	2.6%
10	Colorado	16,800	2.6%
11	Alabama	13,000	2.0%
12	Georgia	12,000	1.9%
13	Ohio	11,800	1.8%
14	Nevada	10,800	1.7%
15	Alaska	10,700	1.7%
16	Virginia	10,400	1.6%
17	Arizona	9,700	1.5%
18	Illinois	9,300	1.4%
19	Washington	9,100	1.4%
20	Utah	8,600	1.3%
21	Kansas	8,400	1.3%
21	Oregon	8,400	1.3%
23	Mississippi	8,300	1.3%
24	Michigan	8,200	1.3%
25	Montana	8,100	1.3%
26	Arkansas	7,600	1.2%
27	Indiana	7,400	1.1%
28	Florida	6,500	1.0%
29	North Carolina	6,300	1.0%
30	Minnesota	6,100	0.9%
31	New York	5,900	0.9%
32	Missouri	5,200	0.8%
33	Idaho	4,400	0.7%
34	North Dakota	4,200	0.6%
34	Tennessee	4,200	0.6%
36	South Carolina	3,800	0.6%
37	Wisconsin	3,300	0.5%
38	Maine	2,700	0.4%
39	Iowa	2,200	0.3%
40	Massachusetts	1,900	0.3%
41	New Jersey	1,500	0.2%
42	Vermont	1,100	0.2%
43	New Hampshire	1,000	0.2%
44	South Dakota	800	0.1%
45	Connecticut	700	0.1%
46	Rhode Island	200	0.0%
NA	Delaware**	NA	NA
NA	Hawaii**	NA	NA
NA	Maryland**	NA	NA
NA	Nebraska**	NA	NA
	District of Columbia**	NA	NA

Source: U.S. Department of Labor, Bureau of Labor Statistics
    "Regional and State Employment and Unemployment" (press release, January 24, 2006)
*Seasonally adjusted preliminary data as of December 2005. National total calculated through a different formula.
**The Bureau of Labor Statistics does not publish seasonally adjusted figures in this category for these states.

Percent of Nonfarm Employees in Natural Resources and Mining in 2005

National Percent = 0.5% of Employees*

ALPHA ORDER

RANK	STATE	PERCENT
13	Alabama	0.7
2	Alaska	3.5
20	Arizona	0.4
17	Arkansas	0.6
28	California	0.2
13	Colorado	0.7
44	Connecticut	0.0
NA	Delaware**	NA
39	Florida	0.1
23	Georgia	0.3
NA	Hawaii**	NA
13	Idaho	0.7
28	Illinois	0.2
23	Indiana	0.3
39	Iowa	0.1
17	Kansas	0.6
9	Kentucky	1.2
4	Louisiana	2.7
20	Maine	0.4
NA	Maryland**	NA
39	Massachusetts	0.1
28	Michigan	0.2
28	Minnesota	0.2
12	Mississippi	0.8
28	Missouri	0.2
7	Montana	1.9
NA	Nebraska**	NA
11	Nevada	0.9
28	New Hampshire	0.2
44	New Jersey	0.0
6	New Mexico	2.1
39	New York	0.1
28	North Carolina	0.2
9	North Dakota	1.2
28	Ohio	0.2
5	Oklahoma	2.2
19	Oregon	0.5
23	Pennsylvania	0.3
44	Rhode Island	0.0
28	South Carolina	0.2
28	South Dakota	0.2
28	Tennessee	0.2
8	Texas	1.6
13	Utah	0.7
20	Vermont	0.4
23	Virginia	0.3
23	Washington	0.3
2	West Virginia	3.5
39	Wisconsin	0.1
1	Wyoming	9.0

RANK ORDER

RANK	STATE	PERCENT
1	Wyoming	9.0
2	Alaska	3.5
2	West Virginia	3.5
4	Louisiana	2.7
5	Oklahoma	2.2
6	New Mexico	2.1
7	Montana	1.9
8	Texas	1.6
9	Kentucky	1.2
9	North Dakota	1.2
11	Nevada	0.9
12	Mississippi	0.8
13	Alabama	0.7
13	Colorado	0.7
13	Idaho	0.7
13	Utah	0.7
17	Arkansas	0.6
17	Kansas	0.6
19	Oregon	0.5
20	Arizona	0.4
20	Maine	0.4
20	Vermont	0.4
23	Georgia	0.3
23	Indiana	0.3
23	Pennsylvania	0.3
23	Virginia	0.3
23	Washington	0.3
28	California	0.2
28	Illinois	0.2
28	Michigan	0.2
28	Minnesota	0.2
28	Missouri	0.2
28	New Hampshire	0.2
28	North Carolina	0.2
28	Ohio	0.2
28	South Carolina	0.2
28	South Dakota	0.2
28	Tennessee	0.2
39	Florida	0.1
39	Iowa	0.1
39	Massachusetts	0.1
39	New York	0.1
39	Wisconsin	0.1
44	Connecticut	0.0
44	New Jersey	0.0
44	Rhode Island	0.0
NA	Delaware**	NA
NA	Hawaii**	NA
NA	Maryland**	NA
NA	Nebraska**	NA
	District of Columbia**	NA

Source: Morgan Quitno Press using data from U.S. Department of Labor, Bureau of Labor Statistics
    "Regional and State Employment and Unemployment" (press release, January 24, 2006)
*Seasonally adjusted preliminary data as of December 2005. National figure calculated through a different formula.
**The Bureau of Labor Statistics does not publish seasonally adjusted figures in this category for these states.

Employees in Professional and Business Services in 2005

National Total = 17,160,000 Employees*

ALPHA ORDER

RANK	STATE	EMPLOYEES	% of USA
NA	Alabama**	NA	NA
42	Alaska	24,100	0.1%
15	Arizona	363,600	2.1%
30	Arkansas	109,900	0.6%
1	California	2,163,700	12.6%
17	Colorado	315,500	1.8%
23	Connecticut	200,300	1.2%
35	Delaware	63,300	0.4%
2	Florida	1,402,200	8.2%
11	Georgia	529,500	3.1%
NA	Hawaii**	NA	NA
34	Idaho	78,800	0.5%
5	Illinois	824,500	4.8%
21	Indiana	272,300	1.6%
31	Iowa	106,200	0.6%
NA	Kansas**	NA	NA
25	Kentucky	170,200	1.0%
27	Louisiana	156,400	0.9%
39	Maine	49,400	0.3%
14	Maryland	386,000	2.2%
12	Massachusetts	462,700	2.7%
9	Michigan	592,500	3.5%
18	Minnesota	307,900	1.8%
NA	Mississippi**	NA	NA
19	Missouri	306,900	1.8%
40	Montana	34,400	0.2%
32	Nebraska	97,700	0.6%
29	Nevada	148,900	0.9%
37	New Hampshire	56,200	0.3%
10	New Jersey	589,400	3.4%
33	New Mexico	93,700	0.5%
4	New York	1,083,200	6.3%
13	North Carolina	454,700	2.6%
41	North Dakota	24,800	0.1%
7	Ohio	641,700	3.7%
26	Oklahoma	168,800	1.0%
24	Oregon	184,000	1.1%
6	Pennsylvania	655,400	3.8%
38	Rhode Island	55,500	0.3%
NA	South Carolina**	NA	NA
NA	South Dakota**	NA	NA
20	Tennessee	304,400	1.8%
3	Texas	1,126,300	6.6%
28	Utah	149,600	0.9%
43	Vermont	22,300	0.1%
8	Virginia	599,100	3.5%
16	Washington	320,000	1.9%
36	West Virginia	59,800	0.3%
22	Wisconsin	259,600	1.5%
44	Wyoming	15,600	0.1%

RANK ORDER

RANK	STATE	EMPLOYEES	% of USA
1	California	2,163,700	12.6%
2	Florida	1,402,200	8.2%
3	Texas	1,126,300	6.6%
4	New York	1,083,200	6.3%
5	Illinois	824,500	4.8%
6	Pennsylvania	655,400	3.8%
7	Ohio	641,700	3.7%
8	Virginia	599,100	3.5%
9	Michigan	592,500	3.5%
10	New Jersey	589,400	3.4%
11	Georgia	529,500	3.1%
12	Massachusetts	462,700	2.7%
13	North Carolina	454,700	2.6%
14	Maryland	386,000	2.2%
15	Arizona	363,600	2.1%
16	Washington	320,000	1.9%
17	Colorado	315,500	1.8%
18	Minnesota	307,900	1.8%
19	Missouri	306,900	1.8%
20	Tennessee	304,400	1.8%
21	Indiana	272,300	1.6%
22	Wisconsin	259,600	1.5%
23	Connecticut	200,300	1.2%
24	Oregon	184,000	1.1%
25	Kentucky	170,200	1.0%
26	Oklahoma	168,800	1.0%
27	Louisiana	156,400	0.9%
28	Utah	149,600	0.9%
29	Nevada	148,900	0.9%
30	Arkansas	109,900	0.6%
31	Iowa	106,200	0.6%
32	Nebraska	97,700	0.6%
33	New Mexico	93,700	0.5%
34	Idaho	78,800	0.5%
35	Delaware	63,300	0.4%
36	West Virginia	59,800	0.3%
37	New Hampshire	56,200	0.3%
38	Rhode Island	55,500	0.3%
39	Maine	49,400	0.3%
40	Montana	34,400	0.2%
41	North Dakota	24,800	0.1%
42	Alaska	24,100	0.1%
43	Vermont	22,300	0.1%
44	Wyoming	15,600	0.1%
NA	Alabama**	NA	NA
NA	Hawaii**	NA	NA
NA	Kansas**	NA	NA
NA	Mississippi**	NA	NA
NA	South Carolina**	NA	NA
NA	South Dakota**	NA	NA
	District of Columbia	147,600	0.9%

Source: U.S. Department of Labor, Bureau of Labor Statistics
"Regional and State Employment and Unemployment" (press release, January 24, 2006)
*Seasonally adjusted preliminary data as of December 2005. National total calculated through a different formula.
**The Bureau of Labor Statistics does not publish seasonally adjusted figures in this category for these states.

Percent of Nonfarm Employees in Professional and Business Services in 2005

National Percent = 12.8% of Employees*

ALPHA ORDER

RANK	STATE	PERCENT
NA	Alabama**	NA
40	Alaska	7.8
7	Arizona	14.4
31	Arkansas	9.3
4	California	14.5
9	Colorado	14.1
16	Connecticut	12.0
4	Delaware	14.5
1	Florida	17.8
12	Georgia	13.3
NA	Hawaii**	NA
14	Idaho	12.7
10	Illinois	14.0
33	Indiana	9.2
43	Iowa	7.1
NA	Kansas**	NA
31	Kentucky	9.3
34	Louisiana	9.1
37	Maine	8.0
3	Maryland	15.0
7	Massachusetts	14.4
11	Michigan	13.6
24	Minnesota	11.3
NA	Mississippi**	NA
25	Missouri	11.2
37	Montana	8.0
30	Nebraska	10.4
17	Nevada	11.9
36	New Hampshire	8.8
4	New Jersey	14.5
21	New Mexico	11.5
14	New York	12.7
19	North Carolina	11.6
41	North Dakota	7.2
18	Ohio	11.8
25	Oklahoma	11.2
29	Oregon	11.0
22	Pennsylvania	11.4
25	Rhode Island	11.2
NA	South Carolina**	NA
NA	South Dakota**	NA
28	Tennessee	11.1
19	Texas	11.6
13	Utah	12.8
41	Vermont	7.2
2	Virginia	16.3
22	Washington	11.4
37	West Virginia	8.0
34	Wisconsin	9.1
44	Wyoming	5.9

RANK ORDER

RANK	STATE	PERCENT
1	Florida	17.8
2	Virginia	16.3
3	Maryland	15.0
4	California	14.5
4	Delaware	14.5
4	New Jersey	14.5
7	Arizona	14.4
7	Massachusetts	14.4
9	Colorado	14.1
10	Illinois	14.0
11	Michigan	13.6
12	Georgia	13.3
13	Utah	12.8
14	Idaho	12.7
14	New York	12.7
16	Connecticut	12.0
17	Nevada	11.9
18	Ohio	11.8
19	North Carolina	11.6
19	Texas	11.6
21	New Mexico	11.5
22	Pennsylvania	11.4
22	Washington	11.4
24	Minnesota	11.3
25	Missouri	11.2
25	Oklahoma	11.2
25	Rhode Island	11.2
28	Tennessee	11.1
29	Oregon	11.0
30	Nebraska	10.4
31	Arkansas	9.3
31	Kentucky	9.3
33	Indiana	9.2
34	Louisiana	9.1
34	Wisconsin	9.1
36	New Hampshire	8.8
37	Maine	8.0
37	Montana	8.0
37	West Virginia	8.0
40	Alaska	7.8
41	North Dakota	7.2
41	Vermont	7.2
43	Iowa	7.1
44	Wyoming	5.9
NA	Alabama**	NA
NA	Hawaii**	NA
NA	Kansas**	NA
NA	Mississippi**	NA
NA	South Carolina**	NA
NA	South Dakota**	NA

District of Columbia   21.5

Source: Morgan Quitno Press using data from U.S. Department of Labor, Bureau of Labor Statistics
   "Regional and State Employment and Unemployment" (press release, January 24, 2006)
*Seasonally adjusted preliminary data as of December 2005. National figure calculated through a different formula.
**The Bureau of Labor Statistics does not publish seasonally adjusted figures in this category for these states.

Employees in Trade, Transportation and Public Utilities in 2005

National Total = 25,880,000 Employees*

ALPHA ORDER

RANK	STATE	EMPLOYEES	% of USA
22	Alabama	380,300	1.5%
47	Alaska	63,400	0.2%
NA	Arizona**	NA	NA
31	Arkansas	245,800	0.9%
1	California	2,794,400	10.8%
21	Colorado	416,500	1.6%
27	Connecticut	313,500	1.2%
43	Delaware	84,500	0.3%
3	Florida	1,543,900	6.0%
9	Georgia	834,700	3.2%
41	Hawaii	119,000	0.5%
40	Idaho	124,600	0.5%
5	Illinois	1,190,600	4.6%
14	Indiana	578,600	2.2%
28	Iowa	311,400	1.2%
30	Kansas	261,200	1.0%
23	Kentucky	375,300	1.5%
25	Louisiana	345,700	1.3%
39	Maine	127,500	0.5%
20	Maryland	476,700	1.8%
15	Massachusetts	572,700	2.2%
10	Michigan	800,800	3.1%
19	Minnesota	525,000	2.0%
33	Mississippi	218,600	0.8%
17	Missouri	543,600	2.1%
42	Montana	87,400	0.3%
35	Nebraska	199,900	0.8%
34	Nevada	218,000	0.8%
36	New Hampshire	144,300	0.6%
8	New Jersey	889,800	3.4%
37	New Mexico	140,200	0.5%
4	New York	1,496,100	5.8%
11	North Carolina	724,200	2.8%
46	North Dakota	74,000	0.3%
7	Ohio	1,027,400	4.0%
29	Oklahoma	278,600	1.1%
26	Oregon	336,600	1.3%
6	Pennsylvania	1,139,200	4.4%
45	Rhode Island	78,100	0.3%
24	South Carolina	361,600	1.4%
44	South Dakota	78,500	0.3%
13	Tennessee	592,200	2.3%
2	Texas	1,973,400	7.6%
32	Utah	228,600	0.9%
NA	Vermont**	NA	NA
12	Virginia	659,800	2.5%
18	Washington	539,800	2.1%
38	West Virginia	136,900	0.5%
16	Wisconsin	545,000	2.1%
48	Wyoming	51,100	0.2%

RANK ORDER

RANK	STATE	EMPLOYEES	% of USA
1	California	2,794,400	10.8%
2	Texas	1,973,400	7.6%
3	Florida	1,543,900	6.0%
4	New York	1,496,100	5.8%
5	Illinois	1,190,600	4.6%
6	Pennsylvania	1,139,200	4.4%
7	Ohio	1,027,400	4.0%
8	New Jersey	889,800	3.4%
9	Georgia	834,700	3.2%
10	Michigan	800,800	3.1%
11	North Carolina	724,200	2.8%
12	Virginia	659,800	2.5%
13	Tennessee	592,200	2.3%
14	Indiana	578,600	2.2%
15	Massachusetts	572,700	2.2%
16	Wisconsin	545,000	2.1%
17	Missouri	543,600	2.1%
18	Washington	539,800	2.1%
19	Minnesota	525,000	2.0%
20	Maryland	476,700	1.8%
21	Colorado	416,500	1.6%
22	Alabama	380,300	1.5%
23	Kentucky	375,300	1.5%
24	South Carolina	361,600	1.4%
25	Louisiana	345,700	1.3%
26	Oregon	336,600	1.3%
27	Connecticut	313,500	1.2%
28	Iowa	311,400	1.2%
29	Oklahoma	278,600	1.1%
30	Kansas	261,200	1.0%
31	Arkansas	245,800	0.9%
32	Utah	228,600	0.9%
33	Mississippi	218,600	0.8%
34	Nevada	218,000	0.8%
35	Nebraska	199,900	0.8%
36	New Hampshire	144,300	0.6%
37	New Mexico	140,200	0.5%
38	West Virginia	136,900	0.5%
39	Maine	127,500	0.5%
40	Idaho	124,600	0.5%
41	Hawaii	119,000	0.5%
42	Montana	87,400	0.3%
43	Delaware	84,500	0.3%
44	South Dakota	78,500	0.3%
45	Rhode Island	78,100	0.3%
46	North Dakota	74,000	0.3%
47	Alaska	63,400	0.2%
48	Wyoming	51,100	0.2%
NA	Arizona**	NA	NA
NA	Vermont**	NA	NA
	District of Columbia**	NA	NA

Source: U.S. Department of Labor, Bureau of Labor Statistics
    "Regional and State Employment and Unemployment" (press release, January 24, 2006)
*Seasonally adjusted preliminary data as of December 2005. National total calculated through a different formula.
**The Bureau of Labor Statistics does not publish seasonally adjusted figures in this category for these states.

Percent of Nonfarm Employees in
Trade, Transportation and Public Utilities in 2005
National Percent = 19.2% of Employees*

ALPHA ORDER				RANK ORDER		
RANK	STATE	PERCENT		RANK	STATE	PERCENT
22	Alabama	19.7		1	New Hampshire	22.5
11	Alaska	20.5		2	New Jersey	21.9
NA	Arizona**	NA		3	Tennessee	21.7
7	Arkansas	20.9		4	North Dakota	21.5
35	California	18.8		5	Nebraska	21.3
37	Colorado	18.6		6	Georgia	21.0
36	Connecticut	18.7		7	Arkansas	20.9
28	Delaware	19.4		7	Iowa	20.9
22	Florida	19.7		9	Kentucky	20.6
6	Georgia	21.0		9	Maine	20.6
24	Hawaii	19.6		11	Alaska	20.5
15	Idaho	20.1		12	Montana	20.4
14	Illinois	20.3		12	Texas	20.4
24	Indiana	19.6		14	Illinois	20.3
7	Iowa	20.9		15	Idaho	20.1
30	Kansas	19.3		15	Louisiana	20.1
9	Kentucky	20.6		15	Oregon	20.1
15	Louisiana	20.1		15	South Dakota	20.1
9	Maine	20.6		19	Missouri	19.9
38	Maryland	18.5		19	Pennsylvania	19.9
44	Massachusetts	17.9		21	Mississippi	19.8
41	Michigan	18.4		22	Alabama	19.7
32	Minnesota	19.2		22	Florida	19.7
21	Mississippi	19.8		24	Hawaii	19.6
19	Missouri	19.9		24	Indiana	19.6
12	Montana	20.4		24	Utah	19.6
5	Nebraska	21.3		27	South Carolina	19.5
46	Nevada	17.4		28	Delaware	19.4
1	New Hampshire	22.5		28	Wyoming	19.4
2	New Jersey	21.9		30	Kansas	19.3
47	New Mexico	17.2		30	Washington	19.3
45	New York	17.5		32	Minnesota	19.2
38	North Carolina	18.5		33	Wisconsin	19.1
4	North Dakota	21.5		34	Ohio	19.0
34	Ohio	19.0		35	California	18.8
38	Oklahoma	18.5		36	Connecticut	18.7
15	Oregon	20.1		37	Colorado	18.6
19	Pennsylvania	19.9		38	Maryland	18.5
48	Rhode Island	15.8		38	North Carolina	18.5
27	South Carolina	19.5		38	Oklahoma	18.5
15	South Dakota	20.1		41	Michigan	18.4
3	Tennessee	21.7		41	West Virginia	18.4
12	Texas	20.4		43	Virginia	18.0
24	Utah	19.6		44	Massachusetts	17.9
NA	Vermont**	NA		45	New York	17.5
43	Virginia	18.0		46	Nevada	17.4
30	Washington	19.3		47	New Mexico	17.2
41	West Virginia	18.4		48	Rhode Island	15.8
33	Wisconsin	19.1		NA	Arizona**	NA
28	Wyoming	19.4		NA	Vermont**	NA
					District of Columbia**	NA

Source: Morgan Quitno Press using data from U.S. Department of Labor, Bureau of Labor Statistics
    "Regional and State Employment and Unemployment" (press release, January 24, 2006)
*Seasonally adjusted preliminary data as of December 2005. National figure calculated through a different formula.

VII. ENERGY AND ENVIRONMENT

Energy Consumption in 2001

National Total = 96,275,334,860,000,000 BTUs*

ALPHA ORDER

RANK	STATE	BTUs	% of USA
17	Alabama	1,942,649,789,000,000	2.0%
35	Alaska	736,646,872,500,000	0.8%
26	Arizona	1,352,977,655,000,000	1.4%
30	Arkansas	1,106,348,749,000,000	1.1%
2	California	7,853,442,293,000,000	8.2%
27	Colorado	1,270,023,430,000,000	1.3%
33	Connecticut	853,080,720,000,000	0.9%
46	Delaware	292,493,468,600,000	0.3%
3	Florida	4,134,775,972,000,000	4.3%
10	Georgia	2,880,616,975,000,000	3.0%
47	Hawaii	282,163,186,600,000	0.3%
40	Idaho	501,019,071,600,000	0.5%
7	Illinois	3,870,147,875,000,000	4.0%
11	Indiana	2,801,668,658,000,000	2.9%
29	Iowa	1,150,674,775,000,000	1.2%
32	Kansas	1,043,701,106,000,000	1.1%
18	Kentucky	1,879,463,194,000,000	2.0%
8	Louisiana	3,499,523,752,000,000	3.6%
41	Maine	490,685,733,400,000	0.5%
25	Maryland	1,420,355,654,000,000	1.5%
23	Massachusetts	1,548,818,361,000,000	1.6%
9	Michigan	3,119,998,679,000,000	3.2%
21	Minnesota	1,744,512,168,000,000	1.8%
28	Mississippi	1,172,648,041,000,000	1.2%
20	Missouri	1,815,043,148,000,000	1.9%
44	Montana	365,570,740,700,000	0.4%
39	Nebraska	627,081,266,100,000	0.7%
38	Nevada	629,370,405,700,000	0.7%
45	New Hampshire	322,162,843,500,000	0.3%
13	New Jersey	2,500,366,051,000,000	2.6%
37	New Mexico	679,201,980,100,000	0.7%
4	New York	4,134,643,792,000,000	4.3%
12	North Carolina	2,590,457,096,000,000	2.7%
43	North Dakota	406,878,955,400,000	0.4%
5	Ohio	3,982,276,488,000,000	4.1%
24	Oklahoma	1,539,471,059,000,000	1.6%
31	Oregon	1,064,263,275,000,000	1.1%
6	Pennsylvania	3,922,516,160,000,000	4.1%
49	Rhode Island	227,337,513,100,000	0.2%
22	South Carolina	1,548,838,727,000,000	1.6%
48	South Dakota	247,994,295,700,000	0.3%
15	Tennessee	2,195,374,652,000,000	2.3%
1	Texas	12,028,829,470,000,000	12.5%
36	Utah	725,378,378,600,000	0.8%
50	Vermont	163,614,215,400,000	0.2%
14	Virginia	2,314,639,489,000,000	2.4%
16	Washington	2,033,893,719,000,000	2.1%
34	West Virginia	761,657,340,200,000	0.8%
19	Wisconsin	1,863,373,045,000,000	1.9%
42	Wyoming	439,141,719,200,000	0.5%

RANK ORDER

RANK	STATE	BTUs	% of USA
1	Texas	12,028,829,470,000,000	12.5%
2	California	7,853,442,293,000,000	8.2%
3	Florida	4,134,775,972,000,000	4.3%
4	New York	4,134,643,792,000,000	4.3%
5	Ohio	3,982,276,488,000,000	4.1%
6	Pennsylvania	3,922,516,160,000,000	4.1%
7	Illinois	3,870,147,875,000,000	4.0%
8	Louisiana	3,499,523,752,000,000	3.6%
9	Michigan	3,119,998,679,000,000	3.2%
10	Georgia	2,880,616,975,000,000	3.0%
11	Indiana	2,801,668,658,000,000	2.9%
12	North Carolina	2,590,457,096,000,000	2.7%
13	New Jersey	2,500,366,051,000,000	2.6%
14	Virginia	2,314,639,489,000,000	2.4%
15	Tennessee	2,195,374,652,000,000	2.3%
16	Washington	2,033,893,719,000,000	2.1%
17	Alabama	1,942,649,789,000,000	2.0%
18	Kentucky	1,879,463,194,000,000	2.0%
19	Wisconsin	1,863,373,045,000,000	1.9%
20	Missouri	1,815,043,148,000,000	1.9%
21	Minnesota	1,744,512,168,000,000	1.8%
22	South Carolina	1,548,838,727,000,000	1.6%
23	Massachusetts	1,548,818,361,000,000	1.6%
24	Oklahoma	1,539,471,059,000,000	1.6%
25	Maryland	1,420,355,654,000,000	1.5%
26	Arizona	1,352,977,655,000,000	1.4%
27	Colorado	1,270,023,430,000,000	1.3%
28	Mississippi	1,172,648,041,000,000	1.2%
29	Iowa	1,150,674,775,000,000	1.2%
30	Arkansas	1,106,348,749,000,000	1.1%
31	Oregon	1,064,263,275,000,000	1.1%
32	Kansas	1,043,701,106,000,000	1.1%
33	Connecticut	853,080,720,000,000	0.9%
34	West Virginia	761,657,340,200,000	0.8%
35	Alaska	736,646,872,500,000	0.8%
36	Utah	725,378,378,600,000	0.8%
37	New Mexico	679,201,980,100,000	0.7%
38	Nevada	629,370,405,700,000	0.7%
39	Nebraska	627,081,266,100,000	0.7%
40	Idaho	501,019,071,600,000	0.5%
41	Maine	490,685,733,400,000	0.5%
42	Wyoming	439,141,719,200,000	0.5%
43	North Dakota	406,878,955,400,000	0.4%
44	Montana	365,570,740,700,000	0.4%
45	New Hampshire	322,162,843,500,000	0.3%
46	Delaware	292,493,468,600,000	0.3%
47	Hawaii	282,163,186,600,000	0.3%
48	South Dakota	247,994,295,700,000	0.3%
49	Rhode Island	227,337,513,100,000	0.2%
50	Vermont	163,614,215,400,000	0.2%
	District of Columbia	168,230,583,900,000	0.2%

Source: U.S. Department of Energy, Energy Information Administration
"State Energy Data 2001: Consumption" (http://www.eia.doe.gov/emeu/states/_multi_states.html)
British Thermal Units: The amount of heat required to raise the temperature of one pound of water one degree.

Per Capita Energy Consumption in 2001

National Per Capita = 337,687,247 BTUs*

ALPHA ORDER

RANK	STATE	BTUs
9	Alabama	434,788,789
1	Alaska	1,164,863,514
43	Arizona	255,430,856
11	Arkansas	410,956,048
48	California	227,423,990
39	Colorado	286,862,619
45	Connecticut	248,476,650
21	Delaware	367,623,601
44	Florida	252,836,368
26	Georgia	343,286,875
47	Hawaii	230,900,693
19	Idaho	379,207,125
35	Illinois	309,155,739
7	Indiana	457,211,356
14	Iowa	392,508,365
15	Kansas	386,379,519
6	Kentucky	462,036,475
3	Louisiana	783,499,089
18	Maine	381,371,948
41	Maryland	264,033,619
46	Massachusetts	242,176,403
34	Michigan	311,852,985
23	Minnesota	349,905,543
12	Mississippi	410,257,070
30	Missouri	321,669,300
13	Montana	403,392,410
22	Nebraska	364,828,178
37	Nevada	300,381,774
42	New Hampshire	255,850,693
38	New Jersey	293,943,989
20	New Mexico	370,675,657
49	New York	216,633,851
33	North Carolina	315,976,605
4	North Dakota	639,419,033
24	Ohio	349,694,893
8	Oklahoma	444,095,313
36	Oregon	306,336,775
31	Pennsylvania	318,942,985
50	Rhode Island	214,752,177
17	South Carolina	381,373,804
28	South Dakota	327,075,620
16	Tennessee	381,934,610
5	Texas	563,811,166
32	Utah	317,986,490
40	Vermont	266,923,042
29	Virginia	322,125,447
27	Washington	339,391,423
10	West Virginia	422,714,616
25	Wisconsin	344,692,155
2	Wyoming	888,738,559

RANK ORDER

RANK	STATE	BTUs
1	Alaska	1,164,863,514
2	Wyoming	888,738,559
3	Louisiana	783,499,089
4	North Dakota	639,419,033
5	Texas	563,811,166
6	Kentucky	462,036,475
7	Indiana	457,211,356
8	Oklahoma	444,095,313
9	Alabama	434,788,789
10	West Virginia	422,714,616
11	Arkansas	410,956,048
12	Mississippi	410,257,070
13	Montana	403,392,410
14	Iowa	392,508,365
15	Kansas	386,379,519
16	Tennessee	381,934,610
17	South Carolina	381,373,804
18	Maine	381,371,948
19	Idaho	379,207,125
20	New Mexico	370,675,657
21	Delaware	367,623,601
22	Nebraska	364,828,178
23	Minnesota	349,905,543
24	Ohio	349,694,893
25	Wisconsin	344,692,155
26	Georgia	343,286,875
27	Washington	339,391,423
28	South Dakota	327,075,620
29	Virginia	322,125,447
30	Missouri	321,669,300
31	Pennsylvania	318,942,985
32	Utah	317,986,490
33	North Carolina	315,976,605
34	Michigan	311,852,985
35	Illinois	309,155,739
36	Oregon	306,336,775
37	Nevada	300,381,774
38	New Jersey	293,943,989
39	Colorado	286,862,619
40	Vermont	266,923,042
41	Maryland	264,033,619
42	New Hampshire	255,850,693
43	Arizona	255,430,856
44	Florida	252,836,368
45	Connecticut	248,476,650
46	Massachusetts	242,176,403
47	Hawaii	230,900,693
48	California	227,423,990
49	New York	216,633,851
50	Rhode Island	214,752,177
	District of Columbia	295,448,227

Source: Morgan Quitno Press using data from U.S. Department of Energy, Energy Information Administration
"State Energy Data 2001: Consumption" (http://www.eia.doe.gov/emeu/states/_multi_states.html)
*British Thermal Units: The amount of heat required to raise the temperature of one pound of water one degree.

Energy Prices in 2001

National Rate = $10.72 per Million BTUs*

ALPHA ORDER

RANK	STATE	RATE
41	Alabama	$9.31
49	Alaska	8.12
10	Arizona	12.68
36	Arkansas	9.94
8	California	13.04
21	Colorado	10.85
6	Connecticut	13.30
17	Delaware	11.11
11	Florida	12.48
33	Georgia	10.08
1	Hawaii	15.41
40	Idaho	9.63
18	Illinois	11.01
45	Indiana	8.78
35	Iowa	10.02
25	Kansas	10.58
42	Kentucky	9.29
48	Louisiana	8.19
34	Maine	10.05
12	Maryland	12.09
2	Massachusetts	14.18
39	Michigan	9.77
26	Minnesota	10.43
32	Mississippi	10.13
16	Missouri	11.12
31	Montana	10.23
29	Nebraska	10.25
9	Nevada	12.70
7	New Hampshire	13.29
19	New Jersey	11.00
14	New Mexico	11.24
5	New York	13.41
13	North Carolina	11.43
50	North Dakota	7.53
20	Ohio	10.92
30	Oklahoma	10.24
23	Oregon	10.81
15	Pennsylvania	11.20
4	Rhode Island	13.95
27	South Carolina	10.41
22	South Dakota	10.82
37	Tennessee	9.92
44	Texas	8.80
43	Utah	9.16
3	Vermont	14.08
24	Virginia	10.72
38	Washington	9.89
46	West Virginia	8.74
28	Wisconsin	10.30
47	Wyoming	8.46

RANK ORDER

RANK	STATE	RATE
1	Hawaii	$15.41
2	Massachusetts	14.18
3	Vermont	14.08
4	Rhode Island	13.95
5	New York	13.41
6	Connecticut	13.30
7	New Hampshire	13.29
8	California	13.04
9	Nevada	12.70
10	Arizona	12.68
11	Florida	12.48
12	Maryland	12.09
13	North Carolina	11.43
14	New Mexico	11.24
15	Pennsylvania	11.20
16	Missouri	11.12
17	Delaware	11.11
18	Illinois	11.01
19	New Jersey	11.00
20	Ohio	10.92
21	Colorado	10.85
22	South Dakota	10.82
23	Oregon	10.81
24	Virginia	10.72
25	Kansas	10.58
26	Minnesota	10.43
27	South Carolina	10.41
28	Wisconsin	10.30
29	Nebraska	10.25
30	Oklahoma	10.24
31	Montana	10.23
32	Mississippi	10.13
33	Georgia	10.08
34	Maine	10.05
35	Iowa	10.02
36	Arkansas	9.94
37	Tennessee	9.92
38	Washington	9.89
39	Michigan	9.77
40	Idaho	9.63
41	Alabama	9.31
42	Kentucky	9.29
43	Utah	9.16
44	Texas	8.80
45	Indiana	8.78
46	West Virginia	8.74
47	Wyoming	8.46
48	Louisiana	8.19
49	Alaska	8.12
50	North Dakota	7.53
	District of Columbia	15.57

Source: U.S. Department of Energy, Energy Information Administration
   "State Energy Data 2001: Prices and Expenditures" (http://www.eia.doe.gov/emeu/states/_multi_states.html)
*British Thermal Units: The amount of heat required to raise the temperature of one pound of water one degree.

Energy Expenditures in 2001

National Total = $693,599,000,000

ALPHA ORDER

RANK	STATE	EXPENDITURES	% of USA
21	Alabama	$11,579,800,000	1.7%
43	Alaska	2,780,000,000	0.4%
24	Arizona	10,671,800,000	1.5%
32	Arkansas	7,339,500,000	1.1%
1	California	72,923,700,000	10.5%
27	Colorado	9,279,400,000	1.3%
29	Connecticut	8,062,100,000	1.2%
48	Delaware	1,985,000,000	0.3%
4	Florida	31,605,300,000	4.6%
10	Georgia	19,361,300,000	2.8%
42	Hawaii	2,811,500,000	0.4%
40	Idaho	3,142,100,000	0.5%
6	Illinois	29,386,500,000	4.2%
13	Indiana	17,066,200,000	2.5%
28	Iowa	8,160,500,000	1.2%
33	Kansas	7,082,000,000	1.0%
23	Kentucky	11,017,800,000	1.6%
12	Louisiana	18,026,000,000	2.6%
39	Maine	3,625,000,000	0.5%
22	Maryland	11,445,500,000	1.7%
15	Massachusetts	15,956,700,000	2.3%
8	Michigan	21,912,700,000	3.2%
20	Minnesota	12,446,700,000	1.8%
30	Mississippi	7,458,700,000	1.1%
16	Missouri	13,821,700,000	2.0%
44	Montana	2,483,500,000	0.4%
36	Nebraska	4,412,300,000	0.6%
34	Nevada	5,126,900,000	0.7%
41	New Hampshire	3,127,900,000	0.5%
9	New Jersey	20,178,400,000	2.9%
37	New Mexico	4,312,600,000	0.6%
3	New York	39,903,200,000	5.8%
11	North Carolina	18,865,000,000	2.7%
47	North Dakota	2,243,200,000	0.3%
7	Ohio	29,070,500,000	4.2%
25	Oklahoma	10,180,700,000	1.5%
31	Oregon	7,411,100,000	1.1%
5	Pennsylvania	29,887,600,000	4.3%
46	Rhode Island	2,312,600,000	0.3%
26	South Carolina	9,867,100,000	1.4%
49	South Dakota	1,881,000,000	0.3%
17	Tennessee	13,808,400,000	2.0%
2	Texas	72,652,500,000	10.5%
35	Utah	4,533,000,000	0.7%
50	Vermont	1,660,300,000	0.2%
14	Virginia	16,290,200,000	2.3%
19	Washington	12,906,000,000	1.9%
38	West Virginia	4,297,200,000	0.6%
18	Wisconsin	13,357,800,000	1.9%
45	Wyoming	2,321,600,000	0.3%

RANK ORDER

RANK	STATE	EXPENDITURES	% of USA
1	California	$72,923,700,000	10.5%
2	Texas	72,652,500,000	10.5%
3	New York	39,903,200,000	5.8%
4	Florida	31,605,300,000	4.6%
5	Pennsylvania	29,887,600,000	4.3%
6	Illinois	29,386,500,000	4.2%
7	Ohio	29,070,500,000	4.2%
8	Michigan	21,912,700,000	3.2%
9	New Jersey	20,178,400,000	2.9%
10	Georgia	19,361,300,000	2.8%
11	North Carolina	18,865,000,000	2.7%
12	Louisiana	18,026,000,000	2.6%
13	Indiana	17,066,200,000	2.5%
14	Virginia	16,290,200,000	2.3%
15	Massachusetts	15,956,700,000	2.3%
16	Missouri	13,821,700,000	2.0%
17	Tennessee	13,808,400,000	2.0%
18	Wisconsin	13,357,800,000	1.9%
19	Washington	12,906,000,000	1.9%
20	Minnesota	12,446,700,000	1.8%
21	Alabama	11,579,800,000	1.7%
22	Maryland	11,445,500,000	1.7%
23	Kentucky	11,017,800,000	1.6%
24	Arizona	10,671,800,000	1.5%
25	Oklahoma	10,180,700,000	1.5%
26	South Carolina	9,867,100,000	1.4%
27	Colorado	9,279,400,000	1.3%
28	Iowa	8,160,500,000	1.2%
29	Connecticut	8,062,100,000	1.2%
30	Mississippi	7,458,700,000	1.1%
31	Oregon	7,411,100,000	1.1%
32	Arkansas	7,339,500,000	1.1%
33	Kansas	7,082,000,000	1.0%
34	Nevada	5,126,900,000	0.7%
35	Utah	4,533,000,000	0.7%
36	Nebraska	4,412,300,000	0.6%
37	New Mexico	4,312,600,000	0.6%
38	West Virginia	4,297,200,000	0.6%
39	Maine	3,625,000,000	0.5%
40	Idaho	3,142,100,000	0.5%
41	New Hampshire	3,127,900,000	0.5%
42	Hawaii	2,811,500,000	0.4%
43	Alaska	2,780,000,000	0.4%
44	Montana	2,483,500,000	0.4%
45	Wyoming	2,321,600,000	0.3%
46	Rhode Island	2,312,600,000	0.3%
47	North Dakota	2,243,200,000	0.3%
48	Delaware	1,985,000,000	0.3%
49	South Dakota	1,881,000,000	0.3%
50	Vermont	1,660,300,000	0.2%
	District of Columbia	1,479,300,000	0.2%

Source: U.S. Department of Energy, Energy Information Administration
    "State Energy Data 2001: Prices and Expenditures" (http://www.eia.doe.gov/emeu/states/_multi_states.html)

Per Capita Energy Expenditures in 2001

National Per Capita = $2,433

<table>
<tr><td colspan="3">ALPHA ORDER</td><td colspan="3">RANK ORDER</td></tr>
<tr><th>RANK</th><th>STATE</th><th>PER CAPITA</th><th>RANK</th><th>STATE</th><th>PER CAPITA</th></tr>
<tr><td>16</td><td>Alabama</td><td>$2,592</td><td>1</td><td>Wyoming</td><td>$4,698</td></tr>
<tr><td>2</td><td>Alaska</td><td>4,396</td><td>2</td><td>Alaska</td><td>4,396</td></tr>
<tr><td>48</td><td>Arizona</td><td>2,015</td><td>3</td><td>Louisiana</td><td>4,036</td></tr>
<tr><td>11</td><td>Arkansas</td><td>2,726</td><td>4</td><td>North Dakota</td><td>3,525</td></tr>
<tr><td>45</td><td>California</td><td>2,112</td><td>5</td><td>Texas</td><td>3,405</td></tr>
<tr><td>46</td><td>Colorado</td><td>2,096</td><td>6</td><td>Oklahoma</td><td>2,937</td></tr>
<tr><td>34</td><td>Connecticut</td><td>2,348</td><td>7</td><td>Maine</td><td>2,817</td></tr>
<tr><td>20</td><td>Delaware</td><td>2,495</td><td>8</td><td>Indiana</td><td>2,785</td></tr>
<tr><td>50</td><td>Florida</td><td>1,933</td><td>9</td><td>Iowa</td><td>2,784</td></tr>
<tr><td>36</td><td>Georgia</td><td>2,307</td><td>10</td><td>Montana</td><td>2,740</td></tr>
<tr><td>37</td><td>Hawaii</td><td>2,301</td><td>11</td><td>Arkansas</td><td>2,726</td></tr>
<tr><td>31</td><td>Idaho</td><td>2,378</td><td>12</td><td>Kentucky</td><td>2,709</td></tr>
<tr><td>35</td><td>Illinois</td><td>2,347</td><td>12</td><td>Vermont</td><td>2,709</td></tr>
<tr><td>8</td><td>Indiana</td><td>2,785</td><td>14</td><td>Kansas</td><td>2,622</td></tr>
<tr><td>9</td><td>Iowa</td><td>2,784</td><td>15</td><td>Mississippi</td><td>2,609</td></tr>
<tr><td>14</td><td>Kansas</td><td>2,622</td><td>16</td><td>Alabama</td><td>2,592</td></tr>
<tr><td>12</td><td>Kentucky</td><td>2,709</td><td>17</td><td>Nebraska</td><td>2,567</td></tr>
<tr><td>3</td><td>Louisiana</td><td>4,036</td><td>18</td><td>Ohio</td><td>2,553</td></tr>
<tr><td>7</td><td>Maine</td><td>2,817</td><td>19</td><td>Minnesota</td><td>2,496</td></tr>
<tr><td>44</td><td>Maryland</td><td>2,128</td><td>20</td><td>Delaware</td><td>2,495</td></tr>
<tr><td>20</td><td>Massachusetts</td><td>2,495</td><td>20</td><td>Massachusetts</td><td>2,495</td></tr>
<tr><td>40</td><td>Michigan</td><td>2,190</td><td>22</td><td>New Hampshire</td><td>2,484</td></tr>
<tr><td>19</td><td>Minnesota</td><td>2,496</td><td>23</td><td>South Dakota</td><td>2,481</td></tr>
<tr><td>15</td><td>Mississippi</td><td>2,609</td><td>24</td><td>Wisconsin</td><td>2,471</td></tr>
<tr><td>25</td><td>Missouri</td><td>2,450</td><td>25</td><td>Missouri</td><td>2,450</td></tr>
<tr><td>10</td><td>Montana</td><td>2,740</td><td>26</td><td>Nevada</td><td>2,447</td></tr>
<tr><td>17</td><td>Nebraska</td><td>2,567</td><td>27</td><td>Pennsylvania</td><td>2,430</td></tr>
<tr><td>26</td><td>Nevada</td><td>2,447</td><td>27</td><td>South Carolina</td><td>2,430</td></tr>
<tr><td>22</td><td>New Hampshire</td><td>2,484</td><td>29</td><td>Tennessee</td><td>2,402</td></tr>
<tr><td>32</td><td>New Jersey</td><td>2,372</td><td>30</td><td>West Virginia</td><td>2,385</td></tr>
<tr><td>33</td><td>New Mexico</td><td>2,354</td><td>31</td><td>Idaho</td><td>2,378</td></tr>
<tr><td>47</td><td>New York</td><td>2,091</td><td>32</td><td>New Jersey</td><td>2,372</td></tr>
<tr><td>37</td><td>North Carolina</td><td>2,301</td><td>33</td><td>New Mexico</td><td>2,354</td></tr>
<tr><td>4</td><td>North Dakota</td><td>3,525</td><td>34</td><td>Connecticut</td><td>2,348</td></tr>
<tr><td>18</td><td>Ohio</td><td>2,553</td><td>35</td><td>Illinois</td><td>2,347</td></tr>
<tr><td>6</td><td>Oklahoma</td><td>2,937</td><td>36</td><td>Georgia</td><td>2,307</td></tr>
<tr><td>43</td><td>Oregon</td><td>2,133</td><td>37</td><td>Hawaii</td><td>2,301</td></tr>
<tr><td>27</td><td>Pennsylvania</td><td>2,430</td><td>37</td><td>North Carolina</td><td>2,301</td></tr>
<tr><td>41</td><td>Rhode Island</td><td>2,185</td><td>39</td><td>Virginia</td><td>2,267</td></tr>
<tr><td>27</td><td>South Carolina</td><td>2,430</td><td>40</td><td>Michigan</td><td>2,190</td></tr>
<tr><td>23</td><td>South Dakota</td><td>2,481</td><td>41</td><td>Rhode Island</td><td>2,185</td></tr>
<tr><td>29</td><td>Tennessee</td><td>2,402</td><td>42</td><td>Washington</td><td>2,154</td></tr>
<tr><td>5</td><td>Texas</td><td>3,405</td><td>43</td><td>Oregon</td><td>2,133</td></tr>
<tr><td>49</td><td>Utah</td><td>1,987</td><td>44</td><td>Maryland</td><td>2,128</td></tr>
<tr><td>12</td><td>Vermont</td><td>2,709</td><td>45</td><td>California</td><td>2,112</td></tr>
<tr><td>39</td><td>Virginia</td><td>2,267</td><td>46</td><td>Colorado</td><td>2,096</td></tr>
<tr><td>42</td><td>Washington</td><td>2,154</td><td>47</td><td>New York</td><td>2,091</td></tr>
<tr><td>30</td><td>West Virginia</td><td>2,385</td><td>48</td><td>Arizona</td><td>2,015</td></tr>
<tr><td>24</td><td>Wisconsin</td><td>2,471</td><td>49</td><td>Utah</td><td>1,987</td></tr>
<tr><td>1</td><td>Wyoming</td><td>4,698</td><td>50</td><td>Florida</td><td>1,933</td></tr>
<tr><td></td><td></td><td></td><td></td><td>District of Columbia</td><td>2,598</td></tr>
</table>

Source: Morgan Quitno Press using data from U.S. Department of Energy, Energy Information Administration
"State Energy Data 2001: Prices and Expenditures" (http://www.eia.doe.gov/emeu/states/_multi_states.html)

Average Monthly Electric Bill for Industrial Customers in 2004

National Average = $5,981 a Month

ALPHA ORDER

RANK	STATE	MONTHLY BILL
8	Alabama	$14,495
25	Alaska	7,024
24	Arizona	7,160
48	Arkansas	1,893
35	California	4,782
36	Colorado	4,183
29	Connecticut	6,187
3	Delaware	30,809
39	Florida	3,465
17	Georgia	10,356
1	Hawaii	65,082
49	Idaho	1,163
18	Illinois	10,152
20	Indiana	8,992
16	Iowa	10,430
46	Kansas	2,551
7	Kentucky	17,927
22	Louisiana	7,536
23	Maine	7,168
27	Maryland	6,749
34	Massachusetts	4,791
19	Michigan	9,989
13	Minnesota	11,235
12	Mississippi	11,428
32	Missouri	5,123
40	Montana	3,424
50	Nebraska	915
4	Nevada	25,817
31	New Hampshire	5,990
26	New Jersey	6,933
28	New Mexico	6,480
11	New York	11,970
14	North Carolina	11,037
33	North Dakota	4,792
15	Ohio	10,916
41	Oklahoma	3,237
47	Oregon	2,244
21	Pennsylvania	8,227
37	Rhode Island	4,123
6	South Carolina	21,919
44	South Dakota	3,041
2	Tennessee	61,934
38	Texas	3,724
45	Utah	2,948
5	Vermont	23,148
9	Virginia	12,706
42	Washington	3,136
43	West Virginia	3,051
10	Wisconsin	12,449
30	Wyoming	6,002

RANK ORDER

RANK	STATE	MONTHLY BILL
1	Hawaii	$65,082
2	Tennessee	61,934
3	Delaware	30,809
4	Nevada	25,817
5	Vermont	23,148
6	South Carolina	21,919
7	Kentucky	17,927
8	Alabama	14,495
9	Virginia	12,706
10	Wisconsin	12,449
11	New York	11,970
12	Mississippi	11,428
13	Minnesota	11,235
14	North Carolina	11,037
15	Ohio	10,916
16	Iowa	10,430
17	Georgia	10,356
18	Illinois	10,152
19	Michigan	9,989
20	Indiana	8,992
21	Pennsylvania	8,227
22	Louisiana	7,536
23	Maine	7,168
24	Arizona	7,160
25	Alaska	7,024
26	New Jersey	6,933
27	Maryland	6,749
28	New Mexico	6,480
29	Connecticut	6,187
30	Wyoming	6,002
31	New Hampshire	5,990
32	Missouri	5,123
33	North Dakota	4,792
34	Massachusetts	4,791
35	California	4,782
36	Colorado	4,183
37	Rhode Island	4,123
38	Texas	3,724
39	Florida	3,465
40	Montana	3,424
41	Oklahoma	3,237
42	Washington	3,136
43	West Virginia	3,051
44	South Dakota	3,041
45	Utah	2,948
46	Kansas	2,551
47	Oregon	2,244
48	Arkansas	1,893
49	Idaho	1,163
50	Nebraska	915
	District of Columbia	556,583

Source: U.S. Department of Energy, Energy Information Administration
"Electric Sales and Revenue" (http://www.eia.doe.gov/cneaf/electricity/esr/esr_sum.html)

Average Monthly Electric Bill for Commercial Customers in 2004

National Average = $503 a Month

ALPHA ORDER

RANK	STATE	MONTHLY BILL
38	Alabama	$363
13	Alaska	541
7	Arizona	612
46	Arkansas	303
5	California	665
41	Colorado	326
3	Connecticut	732
9	Delaware	565
14	Florida	525
17	Georgia	485
2	Hawaii	789
49	Idaho	278
12	Illinois	546
36	Indiana	374
43	Iowa	306
39	Kansas	356
42	Kentucky	307
11	Louisiana	559
31	Maine	390
17	Maryland	485
6	Massachusetts	651
19	Michigan	483
24	Minnesota	421
28	Mississippi	401
30	Missouri	395
47	Montana	287
48	Nebraska	285
20	Nevada	479
25	New Hampshire	411
4	New Jersey	698
28	New Mexico	401
1	New York	819
27	North Carolina	403
40	North Dakota	347
15	Ohio	495
31	Oklahoma	390
35	Oregon	377
16	Pennsylvania	486
8	Rhode Island	585
37	South Carolina	373
44	South Dakota	305
34	Tennessee	385
21	Texas	454
22	Utah	447
26	Vermont	404
10	Virginia	561
23	Washington	438
50	West Virginia	256
33	Wisconsin	386
44	Wyoming	305

RANK ORDER

RANK	STATE	MONTHLY BILL
1	New York	$819
2	Hawaii	789
3	Connecticut	732
4	New Jersey	698
5	California	665
6	Massachusetts	651
7	Arizona	612
8	Rhode Island	585
9	Delaware	565
10	Virginia	561
11	Louisiana	559
12	Illinois	546
13	Alaska	541
14	Florida	525
15	Ohio	495
16	Pennsylvania	486
17	Georgia	485
17	Maryland	485
19	Michigan	483
20	Nevada	479
21	Texas	454
22	Utah	447
23	Washington	438
24	Minnesota	421
25	New Hampshire	411
26	Vermont	404
27	North Carolina	403
28	Mississippi	401
28	New Mexico	401
30	Missouri	395
31	Maine	390
31	Oklahoma	390
33	Wisconsin	386
34	Tennessee	385
35	Oregon	377
36	Indiana	374
37	South Carolina	373
38	Alabama	363
39	Kansas	356
40	North Dakota	347
41	Colorado	326
42	Kentucky	307
43	Iowa	306
44	South Dakota	305
44	Wyoming	305
46	Arkansas	303
47	Montana	287
48	Nebraska	285
49	Idaho	278
50	West Virginia	256
	District of Columbia	2,126

Source: U.S. Department of Energy, Energy Information Administration
"Electric Sales and Revenue" (http://www.eia.doe.gov/cneaf/electricity/esr/esr_sum.html)

Average Monthly Electric Bill for Residential Customers in 2004

National Average = $81.42 a Month

RANK	STATE	MONTHLY BILL
7	Alabama	$95.02
17	Alaska	85.08
11	Arizona	90.38
23	Arkansas	77.24
28	California	72.18
47	Colorado	55.38
12	Connecticut	90.14
16	Delaware	86.21
3	Florida	106.59
13	Georgia	89.21
1	Hawaii	122.24
42	Idaho	63.23
44	Illinois	61.61
30	Indiana	71.49
27	Iowa	73.32
36	Kansas	67.95
33	Kentucky	68.95
4	Louisiana	102.15
40	Maine	65.78
15	Maryland	87.12
25	Massachusetts	75.20
48	Michigan	54.10
45	Minnesota	61.40
5	Mississippi	100.20
31	Missouri	70.98
43	Montana	61.69
37	Nebraska	66.56
10	Nevada	92.29
22	New Hampshire	77.95
20	New Jersey	79.22
50	New Mexico	52.07
18	New York	84.50
9	North Carolina	94.69
35	North Dakota	68.03
26	Ohio	73.35
19	Oklahoma	80.74
32	Oregon	70.64
21	Pennsylvania	78.95
29	Rhode Island	72.06
6	South Carolina	99.80
34	South Dakota	68.35
14	Tennessee	87.52
2	Texas	113.93
49	Utah	52.41
24	Vermont	76.82
8	Virginia	94.97
39	Washington	66.19
38	West Virginia	66.38
41	Wisconsin	64.44
46	Wyoming	57.51

RANK	STATE	MONTHLY BILL
1	Hawaii	$122.24
2	Texas	113.93
3	Florida	106.59
4	Louisiana	102.15
5	Mississippi	100.20
6	South Carolina	99.80
7	Alabama	95.02
8	Virginia	94.97
9	North Carolina	94.69
10	Nevada	92.29
11	Arizona	90.38
12	Connecticut	90.14
13	Georgia	89.21
14	Tennessee	87.52
15	Maryland	87.12
16	Delaware	86.21
17	Alaska	85.08
18	New York	84.50
19	Oklahoma	80.74
20	New Jersey	79.22
21	Pennsylvania	78.95
22	New Hampshire	77.95
23	Arkansas	77.24
24	Vermont	76.82
25	Massachusetts	75.20
26	Ohio	73.35
27	Iowa	73.32
28	California	72.18
29	Rhode Island	72.06
30	Indiana	71.49
31	Missouri	70.98
32	Oregon	70.64
33	Kentucky	68.95
34	South Dakota	68.35
35	North Dakota	68.03
36	Kansas	67.95
37	Nebraska	66.56
38	West Virginia	66.38
39	Washington	66.19
40	Maine	65.78
41	Wisconsin	64.44
42	Idaho	63.23
43	Montana	61.69
44	Illinois	61.61
45	Minnesota	61.40
46	Wyoming	57.51
47	Colorado	55.38
48	Michigan	54.10
49	Utah	52.41
50	New Mexico	52.07
	District of Columbia	60.56

*Source: U.S. Department of Energy, Energy Information Administration
"Electric Sales and Revenue" (http://www.eia.doe.gov/cneaf/electricity/esr/esr_sum.html)*

Electricity Generated Through Renewable Sources in 2003

National Total = 363,216,799,000 Kilowatthours*

ALPHA ORDER

RANK	STATE	KWH	% of USA
5	Alabama	16,363,268,000	4.5%
33	Alaska	1,588,313,000	0.4%
11	Arizona	7,120,253,000	2.0%
17	Arkansas	4,498,507,000	1.2%
2	California	60,153,118,000	16.6%
36	Colorado	1,440,776,000	0.4%
29	Connecticut	2,130,358,000	0.6%
50	Delaware	0	0.0%
14	Florida	6,068,359,000	1.7%
10	Georgia	7,346,740,000	2.0%
43	Hawaii	787,271,000	0.2%
8	Idaho	8,894,987,000	2.4%
38	Illinois	1,112,995,000	0.3%
46	Indiana	557,983,000	0.2%
31	Iowa	1,894,358,000	0.5%
47	Kansas	378,374,000	0.1%
20	Kentucky	4,268,964,000	1.2%
22	Louisiana	4,066,755,000	1.1%
12	Maine	7,082,232,000	1.9%
23	Maryland	3,521,258,000	1.0%
26	Massachusetts	3,126,266,000	0.9%
21	Michigan	4,192,631,000	1.2%
24	Minnesota	3,225,489,000	0.9%
40	Mississippi	1,022,331,000	0.3%
44	Missouri	784,789,000	0.2%
9	Montana	8,772,940,000	2.4%
39	Nebraska	1,074,773,000	0.3%
27	Nevada	2,822,416,000	0.8%
28	New Hampshire	2,187,525,000	0.6%
37	New Jersey	1,437,423,000	0.4%
48	New Mexico	353,434,000	0.1%
4	New York	26,846,902,000	7.4%
7	North Carolina	9,232,366,000	2.5%
32	North Dakota	1,783,384,000	0.5%
42	Ohio	951,552,000	0.3%
30	Oklahoma	2,120,005,000	0.6%
3	Oregon	34,373,498,000	9.5%
13	Pennsylvania	6,155,723,000	1.7%
49	Rhode Island	107,789,000	0.0%
15	South Carolina	5,010,052,000	1.4%
19	South Dakota	4,320,552,000	1.2%
6	Tennessee	12,835,766,000	3.5%
16	Texas	4,862,275,000	1.3%
45	Utah	629,045,000	0.2%
34	Vermont	1,559,174,000	0.4%
18	Virginia	4,495,864,000	1.2%
1	Washington	73,941,095,000	20.4%
35	West Virginia	1,547,053,000	0.4%
25	Wisconsin	3,209,785,000	0.9%
41	Wyoming	960,033,000	0.3%

RANK ORDER

RANK	STATE	KWH	% of USA
1	Washington	73,941,095,000	20.4%
2	California	60,153,118,000	16.6%
3	Oregon	34,373,498,000	9.5%
4	New York	26,846,902,000	7.4%
5	Alabama	16,363,268,000	4.5%
6	Tennessee	12,835,766,000	3.5%
7	North Carolina	9,232,366,000	2.5%
8	Idaho	8,894,987,000	2.4%
9	Montana	8,772,940,000	2.4%
10	Georgia	7,346,740,000	2.0%
11	Arizona	7,120,253,000	2.0%
12	Maine	7,082,232,000	1.9%
13	Pennsylvania	6,155,723,000	1.7%
14	Florida	6,068,359,000	1.7%
15	South Carolina	5,010,052,000	1.4%
16	Texas	4,862,275,000	1.3%
17	Arkansas	4,498,507,000	1.2%
18	Virginia	4,495,864,000	1.2%
19	South Dakota	4,320,552,000	1.2%
20	Kentucky	4,268,964,000	1.2%
21	Michigan	4,192,631,000	1.2%
22	Louisiana	4,066,755,000	1.1%
23	Maryland	3,521,258,000	1.0%
24	Minnesota	3,225,489,000	0.9%
25	Wisconsin	3,209,785,000	0.9%
26	Massachusetts	3,126,266,000	0.9%
27	Nevada	2,822,416,000	0.8%
28	New Hampshire	2,187,525,000	0.6%
29	Connecticut	2,130,358,000	0.6%
30	Oklahoma	2,120,005,000	0.6%
31	Iowa	1,894,358,000	0.5%
32	North Dakota	1,783,384,000	0.5%
33	Alaska	1,588,313,000	0.4%
34	Vermont	1,559,174,000	0.4%
35	West Virginia	1,547,053,000	0.4%
36	Colorado	1,440,776,000	0.4%
37	New Jersey	1,437,423,000	0.4%
38	Illinois	1,112,995,000	0.3%
39	Nebraska	1,074,773,000	0.3%
40	Mississippi	1,022,331,000	0.3%
41	Wyoming	960,033,000	0.3%
42	Ohio	951,552,000	0.3%
43	Hawaii	787,271,000	0.2%
44	Missouri	784,789,000	0.2%
45	Utah	629,045,000	0.2%
46	Indiana	557,983,000	0.2%
47	Kansas	378,374,000	0.1%
48	New Mexico	353,434,000	0.1%
49	Rhode Island	107,789,000	0.0%
50	Delaware	0	0.0%
	District of Columbia	0	0.0%

Source: U.S. Department of Energy, Energy Information Administration
    "Renewable Energy Trends, 2004" (www.eia.doe.gov/cneaf/solar.renewables/page/trends/rentrends04.html)
Includes hydroelectric, geothermal, solar, wind, MSW/landfill gas, wood/wood waste and other biomass.

Percent of Electricity Generated Through Renewable Sources in 2003

National Percent = 9.4%*

ALPHA ORDER

RANK	STATE	PERCENT
12	Alabama	11.9
9	Alaska	25.1
16	Arizona	7.5
14	Arkansas	8.9
7	California	31.2
34	Colorado	3.1
17	Connecticut	7.2
50	Delaware	0.0
36	Florida	2.9
23	Georgia	5.9
17	Hawaii	7.2
1	Idaho	85.3
48	Illinois	0.6
49	Indiana	0.5
29	Iowa	4.5
46	Kansas	0.8
28	Kentucky	4.7
30	Louisiana	4.3
5	Maine	37.3
20	Maryland	6.7
21	Massachusetts	6.5
31	Michigan	3.8
23	Minnesota	5.9
37	Mississippi	2.6
45	Missouri	0.9
6	Montana	33.4
32	Nebraska	3.5
15	Nevada	8.5
13	New Hampshire	10.1
38	New Jersey	2.5
44	New Mexico	1.1
10	New York	19.5
17	North Carolina	7.2
25	North Dakota	5.7
47	Ohio	0.7
32	Oklahoma	3.5
3	Oregon	70.2
35	Pennsylvania	3.0
40	Rhode Island	1.9
26	South Carolina	5.3
4	South Dakota	54.4
11	Tennessee	13.9
43	Texas	1.3
41	Utah	1.7
8	Vermont	25.9
22	Virginia	6.0
2	Washington	73.9
42	West Virginia	1.6
26	Wisconsin	5.3
39	Wyoming	2.2

RANK ORDER

RANK	STATE	PERCENT
1	Idaho	85.3
2	Washington	73.9
3	Oregon	70.2
4	South Dakota	54.4
5	Maine	37.3
6	Montana	33.4
7	California	31.2
8	Vermont	25.9
9	Alaska	25.1
10	New York	19.5
11	Tennessee	13.9
12	Alabama	11.9
13	New Hampshire	10.1
14	Arkansas	8.9
15	Nevada	8.5
16	Arizona	7.5
17	Connecticut	7.2
17	Hawaii	7.2
17	North Carolina	7.2
20	Maryland	6.7
21	Massachusetts	6.5
22	Virginia	6.0
23	Georgia	5.9
23	Minnesota	5.9
25	North Dakota	5.7
26	South Carolina	5.3
26	Wisconsin	5.3
28	Kentucky	4.7
29	Iowa	4.5
30	Louisiana	4.3
31	Michigan	3.8
32	Nebraska	3.5
32	Oklahoma	3.5
34	Colorado	3.1
35	Pennsylvania	3.0
36	Florida	2.9
37	Mississippi	2.6
38	New Jersey	2.5
39	Wyoming	2.2
40	Rhode Island	1.9
41	Utah	1.7
42	West Virginia	1.6
43	Texas	1.3
44	New Mexico	1.1
45	Missouri	0.9
46	Kansas	0.8
47	Ohio	0.7
48	Illinois	0.6
49	Indiana	0.5
50	Delaware	0.0
	District of Columbia	0.0

Source: U.S. Department of Energy, Energy Information Administration
"Renewable Energy Trends, 2004" (www.eia.doe.gov/cneaf/solar.renewables/page/trends/rentrends04.html)
*Includes hydroelectric, geothermal, solar, wind, MSW/landfill gas, wood/wood waste and other biomass.

Average Price of Natural Gas Delivered to Industrial Customers in 2004

National Average = $6.56 per Thousand Cubic Feet

ALPHA ORDER

RANK	STATE	RATE
29	Alabama	$7.34
50	Alaska	3.62
33	Arizona	6.91
17	Arkansas	8.03
21	California	7.89
41	Colorado	6.54
7	Connecticut	9.32
23	Delaware	7.72
14	Florida	8.38
26	Georgia	7.56
1	Hawaii	13.22
32	Idaho	6.97
15	Illinois	8.07
18	Indiana	7.99
30	Iowa	7.33
42	Kansas	6.43
28	Kentucky	7.38
39	Louisiana	6.58
5	Maine	10.43
4	Maryland	11.14
2	Massachusetts	12.29
34	Michigan	6.88
40	Minnesota	6.57
37	Mississippi	6.67
10	Missouri	8.81
43	Montana	6.34
36	Nebraska	6.68
13	Nevada	8.57
3	New Hampshire	11.86
11	New Jersey	8.65
38	New Mexico	6.66
16	New York	8.05
31	North Carolina	7.20
49	North Dakota	5.70
9	Ohio	8.86
12	Oklahoma	8.63
44	Oregon	6.30
8	Pennsylvania	8.97
6	Rhode Island	9.63
24	South Carolina	7.69
45	South Dakota	6.26
27	Tennessee	7.44
47	Texas	5.91
48	Utah	5.90
46	Vermont	6.04
20	Virginia	7.91
22	Washington	7.83
25	West Virginia	7.59
19	Wisconsin	7.92
35	Wyoming	6.77

RANK ORDER

RANK	STATE	RATE
1	Hawaii	$13.22
2	Massachusetts	12.29
3	New Hampshire	11.86
4	Maryland	11.14
5	Maine	10.43
6	Rhode Island	9.63
7	Connecticut	9.32
8	Pennsylvania	8.97
9	Ohio	8.86
10	Missouri	8.81
11	New Jersey	8.65
12	Oklahoma	8.63
13	Nevada	8.57
14	Florida	8.38
15	Illinois	8.07
16	New York	8.05
17	Arkansas	8.03
18	Indiana	7.99
19	Wisconsin	7.92
20	Virginia	7.91
21	California	7.89
22	Washington	7.83
23	Delaware	7.72
24	South Carolina	7.69
25	West Virginia	7.59
26	Georgia	7.56
27	Tennessee	7.44
28	Kentucky	7.38
29	Alabama	7.34
30	Iowa	7.33
31	North Carolina	7.20
32	Idaho	6.97
33	Arizona	6.91
34	Michigan	6.88
35	Wyoming	6.77
36	Nebraska	6.68
37	Mississippi	6.67
38	New Mexico	6.66
39	Louisiana	6.58
40	Minnesota	6.57
41	Colorado	6.54
42	Kansas	6.43
43	Montana	6.34
44	Oregon	6.30
45	South Dakota	6.26
46	Vermont	6.04
47	Texas	5.91
48	Utah	5.90
49	North Dakota	5.70
50	Alaska	3.62
	District of Columbia*	NA

Source: U.S. Department of Energy, Energy Information Administration
"Natural Gas Annual 2004" (http://www.eia.doe.gov/oil_gas/natural_gas/info_glance/natural_gas.html)
Not applicable.

Average Price of Natural Gas Delivered to Commercial Customers in 2004

National Average = $9.41 per Thousand Cubic Feet

ALPHA ORDER

RANK	STATE	RATE
10	Alabama	$10.91
50	Alaska	4.14
37	Arizona	8.50
30	Arkansas	8.86
34	California	8.63
47	Colorado	7.48
8	Connecticut	11.31
13	Delaware	10.56
7	Florida	11.43
6	Georgia	11.45
1	Hawaii	21.42
40	Idaho	8.37
29	Illinois	9.10
35	Indiana	8.56
36	Iowa	8.51
19	Kansas	10.09
15	Kentucky	10.18
22	Louisiana	9.56
4	Maine	12.30
26	Maryland	9.30
3	Massachusetts	12.48
44	Michigan	7.98
38	Minnesota	8.43
31	Mississippi	8.84
20	Missouri	10.00
28	Montana	9.11
46	Nebraska	7.60
39	Nevada	8.38
2	New Hampshire	13.04
9	New Jersey	10.94
45	New Mexico	7.94
18	New York	10.11
14	North Carolina	10.45
42	North Dakota	8.21
27	Ohio	9.18
21	Oklahoma	9.68
25	Oregon	9.37
12	Pennsylvania	10.59
5	Rhode Island	11.77
11	South Carolina	10.81
43	South Dakota	8.09
23	Tennessee	9.51
41	Texas	8.23
49	Utah	6.75
33	Vermont	8.70
16	Virginia	10.13
24	Washington	9.40
16	West Virginia	10.13
32	Wisconsin	8.71
48	Wyoming	7.24

RANK ORDER

RANK	STATE	RATE
1	Hawaii	$21.42
2	New Hampshire	13.04
3	Massachusetts	12.48
4	Maine	12.30
5	Rhode Island	11.77
6	Georgia	11.45
7	Florida	11.43
8	Connecticut	11.31
9	New Jersey	10.94
10	Alabama	10.91
11	South Carolina	10.81
12	Pennsylvania	10.59
13	Delaware	10.56
14	North Carolina	10.45
15	Kentucky	10.18
16	Virginia	10.13
16	West Virginia	10.13
18	New York	10.11
19	Kansas	10.09
20	Missouri	10.00
21	Oklahoma	9.68
22	Louisiana	9.56
23	Tennessee	9.51
24	Washington	9.40
25	Oregon	9.37
26	Maryland	9.30
27	Ohio	9.18
28	Montana	9.11
29	Illinois	9.10
30	Arkansas	8.86
31	Mississippi	8.84
32	Wisconsin	8.71
33	Vermont	8.70
34	California	8.63
35	Indiana	8.56
36	Iowa	8.51
37	Arizona	8.50
38	Minnesota	8.43
39	Nevada	8.38
40	Idaho	8.37
41	Texas	8.23
42	North Dakota	8.21
43	South Dakota	8.09
44	Michigan	7.98
45	New Mexico	7.94
46	Nebraska	7.60
47	Colorado	7.48
48	Wyoming	7.24
49	Utah	6.75
50	Alaska	4.14
	District of Columbia	13.60

Source: U.S. Department of Energy, Energy Information Administration
   "Natural Gas Annual 2004" (http://www.eia.doe.gov/oil_gas/natural_gas/info_glance/natural_gas.html)

Average Price of Natural Gas Delivered to Residential Customers in 2004

National Average = $10.75 per Thousand Cubic Feet

ALPHA ORDER

RANK	STATE	RATE
8	Alabama	$13.34
50	Alaska	4.88
15	Arizona	12.16
18	Arkansas	11.73
37	California	9.86
48	Colorado	8.47
5	Connecticut	14.06
16	Delaware	12.08
2	Florida	17.75
7	Georgia	13.87
1	Hawaii	27.15
44	Idaho	9.04
41	Illinois	9.41
35	Indiana	9.98
33	Iowa	10.14
26	Kansas	10.72
24	Kentucky	10.97
20	Louisiana	11.21
6	Maine	14.00
13	Maryland	12.37
4	Massachusetts	14.41
47	Michigan	8.52
40	Minnesota	9.50
28	Mississippi	10.56
23	Missouri	11.02
42	Montana	9.19
43	Nebraska	9.06
34	Nevada	10.05
3	New Hampshire	14.52
19	New Jersey	11.56
38	New Mexico	9.57
12	New York	12.50
11	North Carolina	12.70
45	North Dakota	9.03
29	Ohio	10.46
31	Oklahoma	10.23
21	Oregon	11.11
14	Pennsylvania	12.27
9	Rhode Island	13.24
17	South Carolina	12.00
39	South Dakota	9.52
27	Tennessee	10.60
30	Texas	10.37
49	Utah	8.12
22	Vermont	11.03
10	Virginia	13.04
36	Washington	9.91
25	West Virginia	10.91
32	Wisconsin	10.16
46	Wyoming	8.65

RANK ORDER

RANK	STATE	RATE
1	Hawaii	$27.15
2	Florida	17.75
3	New Hampshire	14.52
4	Massachusetts	14.41
5	Connecticut	14.06
6	Maine	14.00
7	Georgia	13.87
8	Alabama	13.34
9	Rhode Island	13.24
10	Virginia	13.04
11	North Carolina	12.70
12	New York	12.50
13	Maryland	12.37
14	Pennsylvania	12.27
15	Arizona	12.16
16	Delaware	12.08
17	South Carolina	12.00
18	Arkansas	11.73
19	New Jersey	11.56
20	Louisiana	11.21
21	Oregon	11.11
22	Vermont	11.03
23	Missouri	11.02
24	Kentucky	10.97
25	West Virginia	10.91
26	Kansas	10.72
27	Tennessee	10.60
28	Mississippi	10.56
29	Ohio	10.46
30	Texas	10.37
31	Oklahoma	10.23
32	Wisconsin	10.16
33	Iowa	10.14
34	Nevada	10.05
35	Indiana	9.98
36	Washington	9.91
37	California	9.86
38	New Mexico	9.57
39	South Dakota	9.52
40	Minnesota	9.50
41	Illinois	9.41
42	Montana	9.19
43	Nebraska	9.06
44	Idaho	9.04
45	North Dakota	9.03
46	Wyoming	8.65
47	Michigan	8.52
48	Colorado	8.47
49	Utah	8.12
50	Alaska	4.88
	District of Columbia	14.31

Source: U.S. Department of Energy, Energy Information Administration
"Natural Gas Annual 2004" (http://www.eia.doe.gov/oil_gas/natural_gas/info_glance/natural_gas.html)

Natural Gas Consumption in 2004

National Total = 22,430,225,000,000 Cubic Feet*

ALPHA ORDER

RANK	STATE	CUBIC FEET	% of USA
16	Alabama	388,174,000,000	1.7%
14	Alaska	406,157,000,000	1.8%
20	Arizona	351,685,000,000	1.6%
32	Arkansas	219,648,000,000	1.0%
2	California	2,423,304,000,000	10.8%
13	Colorado	440,156,000,000	2.0%
36	Connecticut	162,642,000,000	0.7%
47	Delaware	48,057,000,000	0.2%
8	Florida	733,937,000,000	3.3%
15	Georgia	393,389,000,000	1.8%
50	Hawaii	2,772,000,000	0.0%
41	Idaho	75,335,000,000	0.3%
5	Illinois	956,167,000,000	4.3%
12	Indiana	526,701,000,000	2.3%
28	Iowa	226,779,000,000	1.0%
24	Kansas	262,832,000,000	1.2%
29	Kentucky	225,452,000,000	1.0%
3	Louisiana	1,281,135,000,000	5.7%
43	Maine	72,565,000,000	0.3%
34	Maryland	192,959,000,000	0.9%
18	Massachusetts	372,533,000,000	1.7%
6	Michigan	916,530,000,000	4.1%
19	Minnesota	359,685,000,000	1.6%
21	Mississippi	282,051,000,000	1.3%
23	Missouri	263,549,000,000	1.2%
44	Montana	66,829,000,000	0.3%
39	Nebraska	115,585,000,000	0.5%
33	Nevada	214,984,000,000	1.0%
45	New Hampshire	61,172,000,000	0.3%
10	New Jersey	622,839,000,000	2.8%
31	New Mexico	223,265,000,000	1.0%
4	New York	1,097,926,000,000	4.9%
30	North Carolina	224,796,000,000	1.0%
46	North Dakota	59,986,000,000	0.3%
7	Ohio	824,357,000,000	3.7%
11	Oklahoma	538,141,000,000	2.4%
26	Oregon	234,997,000,000	1.0%
9	Pennsylvania	696,258,000,000	3.1%
42	Rhode Island	72,609,000,000	0.3%
35	South Carolina	163,787,000,000	0.7%
48	South Dakota	41,678,000,000	0.2%
27	Tennessee	231,133,000,000	1.0%
1	Texas	3,916,433,000,000	17.5%
37	Utah	155,891,000,000	0.7%
49	Vermont	8,685,000,000	0.0%
22	Virginia	277,434,000,000	1.2%
25	Washington	262,485,000,000	1.2%
38	West Virginia	122,098,000,000	0.5%
17	Wisconsin	383,354,000,000	1.7%
40	Wyoming	107,060,000,000	0.5%

RANK ORDER

RANK	STATE	CUBIC FEET	% of USA
1	Texas	3,916,433,000,000	17.5%
2	California	2,423,304,000,000	10.8%
3	Louisiana	1,281,135,000,000	5.7%
4	New York	1,097,926,000,000	4.9%
5	Illinois	956,167,000,000	4.3%
6	Michigan	916,530,000,000	4.1%
7	Ohio	824,357,000,000	3.7%
8	Florida	733,937,000,000	3.3%
9	Pennsylvania	696,258,000,000	3.1%
10	New Jersey	622,839,000,000	2.8%
11	Oklahoma	538,141,000,000	2.4%
12	Indiana	526,701,000,000	2.3%
13	Colorado	440,156,000,000	2.0%
14	Alaska	406,157,000,000	1.8%
15	Georgia	393,389,000,000	1.8%
16	Alabama	388,174,000,000	1.7%
17	Wisconsin	383,354,000,000	1.7%
18	Massachusetts	372,533,000,000	1.7%
19	Minnesota	359,685,000,000	1.6%
20	Arizona	351,685,000,000	1.6%
21	Mississippi	282,051,000,000	1.3%
22	Virginia	277,434,000,000	1.2%
23	Missouri	263,549,000,000	1.2%
24	Kansas	262,832,000,000	1.2%
25	Washington	262,485,000,000	1.2%
26	Oregon	234,997,000,000	1.0%
27	Tennessee	231,133,000,000	1.0%
28	Iowa	226,779,000,000	1.0%
29	Kentucky	225,452,000,000	1.0%
30	North Carolina	224,796,000,000	1.0%
31	New Mexico	223,265,000,000	1.0%
32	Arkansas	219,648,000,000	1.0%
33	Nevada	214,984,000,000	1.0%
34	Maryland	192,959,000,000	0.9%
35	South Carolina	163,787,000,000	0.7%
36	Connecticut	162,642,000,000	0.7%
37	Utah	155,891,000,000	0.7%
38	West Virginia	122,098,000,000	0.5%
39	Nebraska	115,585,000,000	0.5%
40	Wyoming	107,060,000,000	0.5%
41	Idaho	75,335,000,000	0.3%
42	Rhode Island	72,609,000,000	0.3%
43	Maine	72,565,000,000	0.3%
44	Montana	66,829,000,000	0.3%
45	New Hampshire	61,172,000,000	0.3%
46	North Dakota	59,986,000,000	0.3%
47	Delaware	48,057,000,000	0.2%
48	South Dakota	41,678,000,000	0.2%
49	Vermont	8,685,000,000	0.0%
50	Hawaii	2,772,000,000	0.0%
	District of Columbia	32,227,000,000	0.1%

Source: U.S. Department of Energy, Energy Information Administration
"Natural Gas Annual 2004" (http://www.eia.doe.gov/oil_gas/natural_gas/info_glance/natural_gas.html)
National total includes 90,025,000,000 cubic feet of consumption in the Gulf of Mexico not shown by state.

213

Coal Production in 2004

National Total = 1,112,099,000 Short Tons*

ALPHA ORDER				RANK ORDER			
RANK	STATE	SHORT TONS	% of USA	RANK	STATE	SHORT TONS	% of USA
14	Alabama	22,271,000	2.0%	1	Wyoming	396,493,000	35.7%
23	Alaska	1,512,000	0.1%	2	West Virginia	147,993,000	13.3%
16	Arizona	12,731,000	1.1%	3	Kentucky	114,244,000	10.3%
26	Arkansas	7,000	0.0%	4	Pennsylvania	65,996,000	5.9%
NA	California**	NA	NA	5	Texas	45,863,000	4.1%
7	Colorado	39,870,000	3.6%	6	Montana	39,989,000	3.6%
NA	Connecticut**	NA	NA	7	Colorado	39,870,000	3.6%
NA	Delaware**	NA	NA	8	Indiana	35,110,000	3.2%
NA	Florida**	NA	NA	9	Illinois	31,853,000	2.9%
NA	Georgia**	NA	NA	10	Virginia	31,420,000	2.8%
NA	Hawaii**	NA	NA	11	North Dakota	29,943,000	2.7%
NA	Idaho**	NA	NA	12	New Mexico	27,250,000	2.5%
9	Illinois	31,853,000	2.9%	13	Ohio	23,222,000	2.1%
8	Indiana	35,110,000	3.2%	14	Alabama	22,271,000	2.0%
NA	Iowa**	NA	NA	15	Utah	21,746,000	2.0%
25	Kansas	71,000	0.0%	16	Arizona	12,731,000	1.1%
3	Kentucky	114,244,000	10.3%	17	Washington	5,653,000	0.5%
19	Louisiana	3,805,000	0.3%	18	Maryland	5,225,000	0.5%
NA	Maine**	NA	NA	19	Louisiana	3,805,000	0.3%
18	Maryland	5,225,000	0.5%	20	Mississippi	3,586,000	0.3%
NA	Massachusetts**	NA	NA	21	Tennessee	2,887,000	0.3%
NA	Michigan**	NA	NA	22	Oklahoma	1,792,000	0.2%
NA	Minnesota**	NA	NA	23	Alaska	1,512,000	0.1%
20	Mississippi	3,586,000	0.3%	24	Missouri	578,000	0.1%
24	Missouri	578,000	0.1%	25	Kansas	71,000	0.0%
6	Montana	39,989,000	3.6%	26	Arkansas	7,000	0.0%
NA	Nebraska**	NA	NA	NA	California**	NA	NA
NA	Nevada**	NA	NA	NA	Connecticut**	NA	NA
NA	New Hampshire**	NA	NA	NA	Delaware**	NA	NA
NA	New Jersey**	NA	NA	NA	Florida**	NA	NA
12	New Mexico	27,250,000	2.5%	NA	Georgia**	NA	NA
NA	New York**	NA	NA	NA	Hawaii**	NA	NA
NA	North Carolina**	NA	NA	NA	Idaho**	NA	NA
11	North Dakota	29,943,000	2.7%	NA	Iowa**	NA	NA
13	Ohio	23,222,000	2.1%	NA	Maine**	NA	NA
22	Oklahoma	1,792,000	0.2%	NA	Massachusetts**	NA	NA
NA	Oregon**	NA	NA	NA	Michigan**	NA	NA
4	Pennsylvania	65,996,000	5.9%	NA	Minnesota**	NA	NA
NA	Rhode Island**	NA	NA	NA	Nebraska**	NA	NA
NA	South Carolina**	NA	NA	NA	Nevada**	NA	NA
NA	South Dakota**	NA	NA	NA	New Hampshire**	NA	NA
21	Tennessee	2,887,000	0.3%	NA	New Jersey**	NA	NA
5	Texas	45,863,000	4.1%	NA	New York**	NA	NA
15	Utah	21,746,000	2.0%	NA	North Carolina**	NA	NA
NA	Vermont**	NA	NA	NA	Oregon**	NA	NA
10	Virginia	31,420,000	2.8%	NA	Rhode Island**	NA	NA
17	Washington	5,653,000	0.5%	NA	South Carolina**	NA	NA
2	West Virginia	147,993,000	13.3%	NA	South Dakota**	NA	NA
NA	Wisconsin**	NA	NA	NA	Vermont**	NA	NA
1	Wyoming	396,493,000	35.7%	NA	Wisconsin**	NA	NA
					District of Columbia**	NA	NA

Source: U.S. Department of Energy, Energy Information Administration
"Coal Production Report" (http://www.eia.doe.gov/cneaf/coal/page/acr/table6.pdf)
*National total includes 990,000 short tons from refuse recovery not shown by state.
**Not available or no production.

Gasoline Used in 2004

National Total = 141,181,942,000 Gallons*

ALPHA ORDER

RANK	STATE	GALLONS	% of USA
21	Alabama	2,629,731,000	1.9%
50	Alaska	302,912,000	0.2%
17	Arizona	2,766,367,000	2.0%
32	Arkansas	1,470,188,000	1.0%
1	California	15,921,644,000	11.3%
26	Colorado	2,154,468,000	1.5%
28	Connecticut	1,851,959,000	1.3%
45	Delaware	429,228,000	0.3%
3	Florida	8,546,039,000	6.1%
8	Georgia	5,114,432,000	3.6%
43	Hawaii	456,000,000	0.3%
41	Idaho	637,205,000	0.5%
5	Illinois	5,308,322,000	3.8%
13	Indiana	3,266,984,000	2.3%
29	Iowa	1,671,745,000	1.2%
33	Kansas	1,350,687,000	1.0%
25	Kentucky	2,339,758,000	1.7%
24	Louisiana	2,359,141,000	1.7%
40	Maine	720,497,000	0.5%
20	Maryland	2,693,114,000	1.9%
16	Massachusetts	2,889,431,000	2.0%
9	Michigan	5,032,812,000	3.6%
18	Minnesota	2,743,920,000	1.9%
30	Mississippi	1,663,020,000	1.2%
14	Missouri	3,262,774,000	2.3%
42	Montana	506,144,000	0.4%
37	Nebraska	883,764,000	0.6%
34	Nevada	1,105,368,000	0.8%
39	New Hampshire	725,008,000	0.5%
11	New Jersey	4,392,602,000	3.1%
36	New Mexico	987,226,000	0.7%
4	New York	5,818,967,000	4.1%
10	North Carolina	4,461,325,000	3.2%
47	North Dakota	366,879,000	0.3%
6	Ohio	5,284,114,000	3.7%
27	Oklahoma	1,925,980,000	1.4%
31	Oregon	1,562,741,000	1.1%
7	Pennsylvania	5,270,045,000	3.7%
46	Rhode Island	385,591,000	0.3%
22	South Carolina	2,611,987,000	1.9%
44	South Dakota	441,072,000	0.3%
15	Tennessee	3,089,062,000	2.2%
2	Texas	11,678,206,000	8.3%
35	Utah	1,049,891,000	0.7%
48	Vermont	356,443,000	0.3%
12	Virginia	4,015,323,000	2.8%
19	Washington	2,728,349,000	1.9%
38	West Virginia	861,321,000	0.6%
23	Wisconsin	2,592,179,000	1.8%
49	Wyoming	348,191,000	0.2%

RANK ORDER

RANK	STATE	GALLONS	% of USA
1	California	15,921,644,000	11.3%
2	Texas	11,678,206,000	8.3%
3	Florida	8,546,039,000	6.1%
4	New York	5,818,967,000	4.1%
5	Illinois	5,308,322,000	3.8%
6	Ohio	5,284,114,000	3.7%
7	Pennsylvania	5,270,045,000	3.7%
8	Georgia	5,114,432,000	3.6%
9	Michigan	5,032,812,000	3.6%
10	North Carolina	4,461,325,000	3.2%
11	New Jersey	4,392,602,000	3.1%
12	Virginia	4,015,323,000	2.8%
13	Indiana	3,266,984,000	2.3%
14	Missouri	3,262,774,000	2.3%
15	Tennessee	3,089,062,000	2.2%
16	Massachusetts	2,889,431,000	2.0%
17	Arizona	2,766,367,000	2.0%
18	Minnesota	2,743,920,000	1.9%
19	Washington	2,728,349,000	1.9%
20	Maryland	2,693,114,000	1.9%
21	Alabama	2,629,731,000	1.9%
22	South Carolina	2,611,987,000	1.9%
23	Wisconsin	2,592,179,000	1.8%
24	Louisiana	2,359,141,000	1.7%
25	Kentucky	2,339,758,000	1.7%
26	Colorado	2,154,468,000	1.5%
27	Oklahoma	1,925,980,000	1.4%
28	Connecticut	1,851,959,000	1.3%
29	Iowa	1,671,745,000	1.2%
30	Mississippi	1,663,020,000	1.2%
31	Oregon	1,562,741,000	1.1%
32	Arkansas	1,470,188,000	1.0%
33	Kansas	1,350,687,000	1.0%
34	Nevada	1,105,368,000	0.8%
35	Utah	1,049,891,000	0.7%
36	New Mexico	987,226,000	0.7%
37	Nebraska	883,764,000	0.6%
38	West Virginia	861,321,000	0.6%
39	New Hampshire	725,008,000	0.5%
40	Maine	720,497,000	0.5%
41	Idaho	637,205,000	0.5%
42	Montana	506,144,000	0.4%
43	Hawaii	456,000,000	0.3%
44	South Dakota	441,072,000	0.3%
45	Delaware	429,228,000	0.3%
46	Rhode Island	385,591,000	0.3%
47	North Dakota	366,879,000	0.3%
48	Vermont	356,443,000	0.3%
49	Wyoming	348,191,000	0.2%
50	Alaska	302,912,000	0.2%
	District of Columbia	151,786,000	0.1%

Source: U.S. Department of Transportation, Federal Highway Administration
"Highway Statistics 2004" (Table MF-21) (http://www.fhwa.dot.gov/policy/ohpi/hss/index.htm)
Includes gasoline for highway and nonhighway uses. "Gasoline" includes gasohol but excludes "special fuels" such as diesel.

Per Capita Gasoline Used in 2004

National Per Capita = 481 Gallons*

ALPHA ORDER				RANK ORDER		
RANK	STATE	GALLONS		RANK	STATE	GALLONS
3	Alabama	581		1	Wyoming	688
38	Alaska	461		2	South Carolina	622
33	Arizona	482		3	Alabama	581
18	Arkansas	535		4	North Dakota	577
42	California	444		5	Vermont	574
37	Colorado	468		6	Georgia	573
19	Connecticut	529		6	Mississippi	573
26	Delaware	517		8	South Dakota	572
31	Florida	492		9	Iowa	566
6	Georgia	573		9	Missouri	566
48	Hawaii	361		11	Kentucky	565
40	Idaho	457		12	New Hampshire	558
47	Illinois	418		13	Maine	548
20	Indiana	525		14	Oklahoma	547
9	Iowa	566		15	Montana	546
30	Kansas	494		16	Minnesota	538
11	Kentucky	565		17	Virginia	537
22	Louisiana	523		18	Arkansas	535
13	Maine	548		19	Connecticut	529
32	Maryland	484		20	Indiana	525
41	Massachusetts	451		21	Tennessee	524
29	Michigan	498		22	Louisiana	523
16	Minnesota	538		23	North Carolina	522
6	Mississippi	573		24	Texas	520
9	Missouri	566		25	New Mexico	519
15	Montana	546		26	Delaware	517
27	Nebraska	506		27	Nebraska	506
35	Nevada	474		27	New Jersey	506
12	New Hampshire	558		29	Michigan	498
27	New Jersey	506		30	Kansas	494
25	New Mexico	519		31	Florida	492
50	New York	302		32	Maryland	484
23	North Carolina	522		33	Arizona	482
4	North Dakota	577		34	West Virginia	475
38	Ohio	461		35	Nevada	474
14	Oklahoma	547		36	Wisconsin	471
44	Oregon	435		37	Colorado	468
46	Pennsylvania	425		38	Alaska	461
49	Rhode Island	357		38	Ohio	461
2	South Carolina	622		40	Idaho	457
8	South Dakota	572		41	Massachusetts	451
21	Tennessee	524		42	California	444
24	Texas	520		43	Washington	440
45	Utah	434		44	Oregon	435
5	Vermont	574		45	Utah	434
17	Virginia	537		46	Pennsylvania	425
43	Washington	440		47	Illinois	418
34	West Virginia	475		48	Hawaii	361
36	Wisconsin	471		49	Rhode Island	357
1	Wyoming	688		50	New York	302
					District of Columbia	274

Source: Morgan Quitno Press using data from U.S. Department of Transportation, Federal Highway Administration "Highway Statistics 2004" (Table MF-21) (http://www.fhwa.dot.gov/policy/ohpi/hss/index.htm)
*Includes gasoline for highway and nonhighway uses. "Gasoline" includes gasohol but excludes "special fuels" such as diesel.

Daily Production of Crude Oil in 2004

National Total = 5,418,858 Barrels a Day*

ALPHA ORDER				RANK ORDER			
RANK	STATE	BARRELS	% of USA	RANK	STATE	BARRELS	% of USA
15	Alabama	20,336	0.4%	1	Texas	1,073,407	19.8%
2	Alaska	908,374	16.8%	2	Alaska	908,374	16.8%
30	Arizona	142	0.0%	3	California	656,301	12.1%
16	Arkansas	18,393	0.3%	4	Louisiana	227,899	4.2%
3	California	656,301	12.1%	5	New Mexico	175,508	3.2%
11	Colorado	60,374	1.1%	6	Oklahoma	170,770	3.2%
NA	Connecticut**	NA	NA	7	Wyoming	141,036	2.6%
NA	Delaware**	NA	NA	8	Kansas	92,508	1.7%
19	Florida	7,855	0.1%	9	North Dakota	85,120	1.6%
NA	Georgia**	NA	NA	10	Montana	67,552	1.2%
NA	Hawaii**	NA	NA	11	Colorado	60,374	1.1%
NA	Idaho**	NA	NA	12	Mississippi	46,866	0.9%
14	Illinois	30,011	0.6%	13	Utah	39,970	0.7%
23	Indiana	4,795	0.1%	14	Illinois	30,011	0.6%
NA	Iowa**	NA	NA	15	Alabama	20,336	0.4%
8	Kansas	92,508	1.7%	16	Arkansas	18,393	0.3%
20	Kentucky	6,962	0.1%	17	Michigan	17,511	0.3%
4	Louisiana	227,899	4.2%	18	Ohio	15,806	0.3%
NA	Maine**	NA	NA	19	Florida	7,855	0.1%
NA	Maryland**	NA	NA	20	Kentucky	6,962	0.1%
NA	Massachusetts**	NA	NA	21	Pennsylvania	6,934	0.1%
17	Michigan	17,511	0.3%	22	Nebraska	6,850	0.1%
NA	Minnesota**	NA	NA	23	Indiana	4,795	0.1%
12	Mississippi	46,866	0.9%	24	South Dakota	3,708	0.1%
29	Missouri	240	0.0%	25	West Virginia	3,658	0.1%
10	Montana	67,552	1.2%	26	Nevada	1,265	0.0%
22	Nebraska	6,850	0.1%	27	Tennessee	986	0.0%
26	Nevada	1,265	0.0%	28	New York	464	0.0%
NA	New Hampshire**	NA	NA	29	Missouri	240	0.0%
NA	New Jersey**	NA	NA	30	Arizona	142	0.0%
5	New Mexico	175,508	3.2%	31	Virginia	52	0.0%
28	New York	464	0.0%	NA	Connecticut**	NA	NA
NA	North Carolina**	NA	NA	NA	Delaware**	NA	NA
9	North Dakota	85,120	1.6%	NA	Georgia**	NA	NA
18	Ohio	15,806	0.3%	NA	Hawaii**	NA	NA
6	Oklahoma	170,770	3.2%	NA	Idaho**	NA	NA
NA	Oregon**	NA	NA	NA	Iowa**	NA	NA
21	Pennsylvania	6,934	0.1%	NA	Maine**	NA	NA
NA	Rhode Island**	NA	NA	NA	Maryland**	NA	NA
NA	South Carolina**	NA	NA	NA	Massachusetts**	NA	NA
24	South Dakota	3,708	0.1%	NA	Minnesota**	NA	NA
27	Tennessee	986	0.0%	NA	New Hampshire**	NA	NA
1	Texas	1,073,407	19.8%	NA	New Jersey**	NA	NA
13	Utah	39,970	0.7%	NA	North Carolina**	NA	NA
NA	Vermont**	NA	NA	NA	Oregon**	NA	NA
31	Virginia	52	0.0%	NA	Rhode Island**	NA	NA
NA	Washington**	NA	NA	NA	South Carolina**	NA	NA
25	West Virginia	3,658	0.1%	NA	Vermont**	NA	NA
NA	Wisconsin**	NA	NA	NA	Washington**	NA	NA
7	Wyoming	141,036	2.6%	NA	Wisconsin**	NA	NA
					District of Columbia**	NA	NA

Source: Morgan Quitno Press using data from U.S. Department of Energy, Energy Information Administration
   "Production of Crude Oil by PAD District and State, 2004"
*National total includes 1,527,197 barrels in federal offshore production. Figures for Alaska, California, Louisiana and Texas include state offshore production.
**No reported production.

Hazardous Waste Sites on the National Priority List in 2005

National Total = 1,300 Sites*

<table>
<tr><td colspan="4">ALPHA ORDER</td><td colspan="4">RANK ORDER</td></tr>
<tr><td>RANK</td><td>STATE</td><td>SITES</td><td>% of USA</td><td>RANK</td><td>STATE</td><td>SITES</td><td>% of USA</td></tr>
<tr><td>24</td><td>Alabama</td><td>15</td><td>1.2%</td><td>1</td><td>New Jersey</td><td>115</td><td>8.8%</td></tr>
<tr><td>44</td><td>Alaska</td><td>6</td><td>0.5%</td><td>2</td><td>California</td><td>96</td><td>7.4%</td></tr>
<tr><td>41</td><td>Arizona</td><td>9</td><td>0.7%</td><td>2</td><td>Pennsylvania</td><td>96</td><td>7.4%</td></tr>
<tr><td>40</td><td>Arkansas</td><td>10</td><td>0.8%</td><td>4</td><td>New York</td><td>87</td><td>6.7%</td></tr>
<tr><td>2</td><td>California</td><td>96</td><td>7.4%</td><td>5</td><td>Michigan</td><td>68</td><td>5.2%</td></tr>
<tr><td>20</td><td>Colorado</td><td>19</td><td>1.5%</td><td>6</td><td>Florida</td><td>51</td><td>3.9%</td></tr>
<tr><td>24</td><td>Connecticut</td><td>15</td><td>1.2%</td><td>7</td><td>Illinois</td><td>47</td><td>3.6%</td></tr>
<tr><td>27</td><td>Delaware</td><td>14</td><td>1.1%</td><td>7</td><td>Washington</td><td>47</td><td>3.6%</td></tr>
<tr><td>6</td><td>Florida</td><td>51</td><td>3.9%</td><td>9</td><td>Texas</td><td>45</td><td>3.5%</td></tr>
<tr><td>23</td><td>Georgia</td><td>17</td><td>1.3%</td><td>10</td><td>Wisconsin</td><td>38</td><td>2.9%</td></tr>
<tr><td>46</td><td>Hawaii</td><td>3</td><td>0.2%</td><td>11</td><td>Ohio</td><td>37</td><td>2.8%</td></tr>
<tr><td>41</td><td>Idaho</td><td>9</td><td>0.7%</td><td>12</td><td>Massachusetts</td><td>33</td><td>2.5%</td></tr>
<tr><td>7</td><td>Illinois</td><td>47</td><td>3.6%</td><td>13</td><td>North Carolina</td><td>31</td><td>2.4%</td></tr>
<tr><td>14</td><td>Indiana</td><td>30</td><td>2.3%</td><td>14</td><td>Indiana</td><td>30</td><td>2.3%</td></tr>
<tr><td>33</td><td>Iowa</td><td>12</td><td>0.9%</td><td>15</td><td>Virginia</td><td>29</td><td>2.2%</td></tr>
<tr><td>33</td><td>Kansas</td><td>12</td><td>0.9%</td><td>16</td><td>Missouri</td><td>26</td><td>2.0%</td></tr>
<tr><td>27</td><td>Kentucky</td><td>14</td><td>1.1%</td><td>16</td><td>South Carolina</td><td>26</td><td>2.0%</td></tr>
<tr><td>27</td><td>Louisiana</td><td>14</td><td>1.1%</td><td>18</td><td>Minnesota</td><td>24</td><td>1.8%</td></tr>
<tr><td>33</td><td>Maine</td><td>12</td><td>0.9%</td><td>19</td><td>New Hampshire</td><td>21</td><td>1.6%</td></tr>
<tr><td>21</td><td>Maryland</td><td>18</td><td>1.4%</td><td>20</td><td>Colorado</td><td>19</td><td>1.5%</td></tr>
<tr><td>12</td><td>Massachusetts</td><td>33</td><td>2.5%</td><td>21</td><td>Maryland</td><td>18</td><td>1.4%</td></tr>
<tr><td>5</td><td>Michigan</td><td>68</td><td>5.2%</td><td>21</td><td>Utah</td><td>18</td><td>1.4%</td></tr>
<tr><td>18</td><td>Minnesota</td><td>24</td><td>1.8%</td><td>23</td><td>Georgia</td><td>17</td><td>1.3%</td></tr>
<tr><td>45</td><td>Mississippi</td><td>5</td><td>0.4%</td><td>24</td><td>Alabama</td><td>15</td><td>1.2%</td></tr>
<tr><td>16</td><td>Missouri</td><td>26</td><td>2.0%</td><td>24</td><td>Connecticut</td><td>15</td><td>1.2%</td></tr>
<tr><td>24</td><td>Montana</td><td>15</td><td>1.2%</td><td>24</td><td>Montana</td><td>15</td><td>1.2%</td></tr>
<tr><td>27</td><td>Nebraska</td><td>14</td><td>1.1%</td><td>27</td><td>Delaware</td><td>14</td><td>1.1%</td></tr>
<tr><td>49</td><td>Nevada</td><td>1</td><td>0.1%</td><td>27</td><td>Kentucky</td><td>14</td><td>1.1%</td></tr>
<tr><td>19</td><td>New Hampshire</td><td>21</td><td>1.6%</td><td>27</td><td>Louisiana</td><td>14</td><td>1.1%</td></tr>
<tr><td>1</td><td>New Jersey</td><td>115</td><td>8.8%</td><td>27</td><td>Nebraska</td><td>14</td><td>1.1%</td></tr>
<tr><td>32</td><td>New Mexico</td><td>13</td><td>1.0%</td><td>27</td><td>Tennessee</td><td>14</td><td>1.1%</td></tr>
<tr><td>4</td><td>New York</td><td>87</td><td>6.7%</td><td>32</td><td>New Mexico</td><td>13</td><td>1.0%</td></tr>
<tr><td>13</td><td>North Carolina</td><td>31</td><td>2.4%</td><td>33</td><td>Iowa</td><td>12</td><td>0.9%</td></tr>
<tr><td>50</td><td>North Dakota</td><td>0</td><td>0.0%</td><td>33</td><td>Kansas</td><td>12</td><td>0.9%</td></tr>
<tr><td>11</td><td>Ohio</td><td>37</td><td>2.8%</td><td>33</td><td>Maine</td><td>12</td><td>0.9%</td></tr>
<tr><td>37</td><td>Oklahoma</td><td>11</td><td>0.8%</td><td>33</td><td>Rhode Island</td><td>12</td><td>0.9%</td></tr>
<tr><td>37</td><td>Oregon</td><td>11</td><td>0.8%</td><td>37</td><td>Oklahoma</td><td>11</td><td>0.8%</td></tr>
<tr><td>2</td><td>Pennsylvania</td><td>96</td><td>7.4%</td><td>37</td><td>Oregon</td><td>11</td><td>0.8%</td></tr>
<tr><td>33</td><td>Rhode Island</td><td>12</td><td>0.9%</td><td>37</td><td>Vermont</td><td>11</td><td>0.8%</td></tr>
<tr><td>16</td><td>South Carolina</td><td>26</td><td>2.0%</td><td>40</td><td>Arkansas</td><td>10</td><td>0.8%</td></tr>
<tr><td>47</td><td>South Dakota</td><td>2</td><td>0.2%</td><td>41</td><td>Arizona</td><td>9</td><td>0.7%</td></tr>
<tr><td>27</td><td>Tennessee</td><td>14</td><td>1.1%</td><td>41</td><td>Idaho</td><td>9</td><td>0.7%</td></tr>
<tr><td>9</td><td>Texas</td><td>45</td><td>3.5%</td><td>41</td><td>West Virginia</td><td>9</td><td>0.7%</td></tr>
<tr><td>21</td><td>Utah</td><td>18</td><td>1.4%</td><td>44</td><td>Alaska</td><td>6</td><td>0.5%</td></tr>
<tr><td>37</td><td>Vermont</td><td>11</td><td>0.8%</td><td>45</td><td>Mississippi</td><td>5</td><td>0.4%</td></tr>
<tr><td>15</td><td>Virginia</td><td>29</td><td>2.2%</td><td>46</td><td>Hawaii</td><td>3</td><td>0.2%</td></tr>
<tr><td>7</td><td>Washington</td><td>47</td><td>3.6%</td><td>47</td><td>South Dakota</td><td>2</td><td>0.2%</td></tr>
<tr><td>41</td><td>West Virginia</td><td>9</td><td>0.7%</td><td>47</td><td>Wyoming</td><td>2</td><td>0.2%</td></tr>
<tr><td>10</td><td>Wisconsin</td><td>38</td><td>2.9%</td><td>49</td><td>Nevada</td><td>1</td><td>0.1%</td></tr>
<tr><td>47</td><td>Wyoming</td><td>2</td><td>0.2%</td><td>50</td><td>North Dakota</td><td>0</td><td>0.0%</td></tr>
<tr><td></td><td></td><td></td><td></td><td></td><td>District of Columbia</td><td>1</td><td>0.1%</td></tr>
</table>

Source: U.S. Environmental Protection Agency
    "National Priorities List (NPL) Sites in the United States" (www.epa.gov/superfund/sites/npl/npl.htm)
*As of November 29, 2005. Includes final and proposed General Superfund and Federal Facilities Sites. National total includes 13 sites in Puerto Rico, two in Guam and two in the Virgin Islands.

Hazardous Waste Sites on the National Priority List
Per 10,000 Square Miles in 2005
National Rate = 3.4 Sites per 10,000 Square Miles*

RANK	STATE	RATE		RANK	STATE	RATE
27	Alabama	2.9		1	New Jersey	131.9
48	Alaska	0.1		2	Rhode Island	77.7
45	Arizona	0.8		3	Delaware	56.2
34	Arkansas	1.9		4	Massachusetts	31.3
19	California	5.9		5	Connecticut	27.1
35	Colorado	1.8		6	New Hampshire	22.5
5	Connecticut	27.1		7	Pennsylvania	20.8
3	Delaware	56.2		8	New York	15.9
15	Florida	7.8		9	Maryland	14.5
27	Georgia	2.9		10	Vermont	11.4
30	Hawaii	2.7		11	Ohio	8.3
40	Idaho	1.1		12	Indiana	8.2
13	Illinois	8.1		13	Illinois	8.1
12	Indiana	8.2		13	South Carolina	8.1
32	Iowa	2.1		15	Florida	7.8
39	Kansas	1.5		16	Michigan	7.0
24	Kentucky	3.5		17	Virginia	6.8
30	Louisiana	2.7		18	Washington	6.6
25	Maine	3.4		19	California	5.9
9	Maryland	14.5		20	North Carolina	5.8
4	Massachusetts	31.3		20	Wisconsin	5.8
16	Michigan	7.0		22	Missouri	3.7
29	Minnesota	2.8		22	West Virginia	3.7
43	Mississippi	1.0		24	Kentucky	3.5
22	Missouri	3.7		25	Maine	3.4
43	Montana	1.0		26	Tennessee	3.3
35	Nebraska	1.8		27	Alabama	2.9
48	Nevada	0.1		27	Georgia	2.9
6	New Hampshire	22.5		29	Minnesota	2.8
1	New Jersey	131.9		30	Hawaii	2.7
40	New Mexico	1.1		30	Louisiana	2.7
8	New York	15.9		32	Iowa	2.1
20	North Carolina	5.8		32	Utah	2.1
50	North Dakota	0.0		34	Arkansas	1.9
11	Ohio	8.3		35	Colorado	1.8
38	Oklahoma	1.6		35	Nebraska	1.8
40	Oregon	1.1		37	Texas	1.7
7	Pennsylvania	20.8		38	Oklahoma	1.6
2	Rhode Island	77.7		39	Kansas	1.5
13	South Carolina	8.1		40	Idaho	1.1
46	South Dakota	0.3		40	New Mexico	1.1
26	Tennessee	3.3		40	Oregon	1.1
37	Texas	1.7		43	Mississippi	1.0
32	Utah	2.1		43	Montana	1.0
10	Vermont	11.4		45	Arizona	0.8
17	Virginia	6.8		46	South Dakota	0.3
18	Washington	6.6		47	Wyoming	0.2
22	West Virginia	3.7		48	Alaska	0.1
20	Wisconsin	5.8		48	Nevada	0.1
47	Wyoming	0.2		50	North Dakota	0.0
					District of Columbia**	NA

Source: Morgan Quitno Press using data from U.S. Environmental Protection Agency
    "National Priorities List (NPL) Sites in the United States"
*As of November 29, 2005. Includes final and proposed General Superfund and Federal Facilities Sites. National rate excludes sites and square miles in Puerto Rico, Guam and the Virgin Islands. Based on land and water area of states.
**The District of Columbia has one site in its 68 square miles.

Hazardous Waste Sites Deleted from the National Priorities List as of 2005

National Total = 309 Sites*

ALPHA ORDER

RANK	STATE	SITES	% of USA
42	Alabama	1	0.3%
34	Alaska	2	0.6%
34	Arizona	2	0.6%
18	Arkansas	5	1.6%
8	California	10	3.2%
26	Colorado	3	1.0%
26	Connecticut	3	1.0%
14	Delaware	6	1.9%
5	Florida	20	6.5%
26	Georgia	3	1.0%
42	Hawaii	1	0.3%
26	Idaho	3	1.0%
34	Illinois	2	0.6%
11	Indiana	8	2.6%
8	Iowa	10	3.2%
18	Kansas	5	1.6%
14	Kentucky	6	1.9%
10	Louisiana	9	2.9%
34	Maine	2	0.6%
21	Maryland	4	1.3%
26	Massachusetts	3	1.0%
7	Michigan	16	5.2%
4	Minnesota	21	6.8%
26	Mississippi	3	1.0%
18	Missouri	5	1.6%
47	Montana	0	0.0%
47	Nebraska	0	0.0%
47	Nevada	0	0.0%
47	New Hampshire	0	0.0%
2	New Jersey	23	7.4%
21	New Mexico	4	1.3%
2	New York	23	7.4%
42	North Carolina	1	0.3%
34	North Dakota	2	0.6%
12	Ohio	7	2.3%
26	Oklahoma	3	1.0%
21	Oregon	4	1.3%
1	Pennsylvania	26	8.4%
42	Rhode Island	1	0.3%
26	South Carolina	3	1.0%
34	South Dakota	2	0.6%
14	Tennessee	6	1.9%
12	Texas	7	2.3%
21	Utah	4	1.3%
34	Vermont	2	0.6%
21	Virginia	4	1.3%
6	Washington	17	5.5%
34	West Virginia	2	0.6%
14	Wisconsin	6	1.9%
42	Wyoming	1	0.3%

RANK ORDER

RANK	STATE	SITES	% of USA
1	Pennsylvania	26	8.4%
2	New Jersey	23	7.4%
2	New York	23	7.4%
4	Minnesota	21	6.8%
5	Florida	20	6.5%
6	Washington	17	5.5%
7	Michigan	16	5.2%
8	California	10	3.2%
8	Iowa	10	3.2%
10	Louisiana	9	2.9%
11	Indiana	8	2.6%
12	Ohio	7	2.3%
12	Texas	7	2.3%
14	Delaware	6	1.9%
14	Kentucky	6	1.9%
14	Tennessee	6	1.9%
14	Wisconsin	6	1.9%
18	Arkansas	5	1.6%
18	Kansas	5	1.6%
18	Missouri	5	1.6%
21	Maryland	4	1.3%
21	New Mexico	4	1.3%
21	Oregon	4	1.3%
21	Utah	4	1.3%
21	Virginia	4	1.3%
26	Colorado	3	1.0%
26	Connecticut	3	1.0%
26	Georgia	3	1.0%
26	Idaho	3	1.0%
26	Massachusetts	3	1.0%
26	Mississippi	3	1.0%
26	Oklahoma	3	1.0%
26	South Carolina	3	1.0%
34	Alaska	2	0.6%
34	Arizona	2	0.6%
34	Illinois	2	0.6%
34	Maine	2	0.6%
34	North Dakota	2	0.6%
34	South Dakota	2	0.6%
34	Vermont	2	0.6%
34	West Virginia	2	0.6%
42	Alabama	1	0.3%
42	Hawaii	1	0.3%
42	North Carolina	1	0.3%
42	Rhode Island	1	0.3%
42	Wyoming	1	0.3%
47	Montana	0	0.0%
47	Nebraska	0	0.0%
47	Nevada	0	0.0%
47	New Hampshire	0	0.0%
	District of Columbia	0	0.0%

Source: U.S. Environmental Protection Agency
   "National Priorities List (NPL) Sites in the United States" (www.epa.gov/superfund/sites/npl/npl.htm)
*Cumulative total as of November 29, 2005. National total includes five sites in Puerto Rico, one in American Samoa and one in the Northern Mariana Islands.

Toxic Releases: Total Pollution Released in 2003

National Total = 4,432,782,410 Pounds of Toxins*

ALPHA ORDER

RANK	STATE	POUNDS	% of USA
14	Alabama	118,449,143	2.7%
1	Alaska	539,644,265	12.2%
26	Arizona	48,264,484	1.1%
31	Arkansas	40,602,821	0.9%
23	California	57,858,347	1.3%
38	Colorado	22,518,627	0.5%
47	Connecticut	5,426,304	0.1%
42	Delaware	13,594,799	0.3%
11	Florida	126,489,800	2.9%
13	Georgia	126,197,045	2.8%
48	Hawaii	3,117,568	0.1%
22	Idaho	61,327,809	1.4%
9	Illinois	132,421,988	3.0%
6	Indiana	234,713,210	5.3%
32	Iowa	37,433,853	0.8%
35	Kansas	29,064,869	0.7%
18	Kentucky	90,534,417	2.0%
12	Louisiana	126,350,144	2.9%
44	Maine	9,334,055	0.2%
28	Maryland	45,499,979	1.0%
45	Massachusetts	8,983,284	0.2%
15	Michigan	104,334,602	2.4%
33	Minnesota	31,438,324	0.7%
21	Mississippi	63,077,058	1.4%
16	Missouri	102,475,425	2.3%
27	Montana	45,650,733	1.0%
24	Nebraska	51,471,736	1.2%
2	Nevada	403,353,335	9.1%
46	New Hampshire	5,944,216	0.1%
37	New Jersey	23,077,884	0.5%
41	New Mexico	17,899,251	0.4%
29	New York	44,079,924	1.0%
10	North Carolina	129,845,723	2.9%
36	North Dakota	23,638,798	0.5%
4	Ohio	250,096,685	5.6%
34	Oklahoma	29,939,161	0.7%
30	Oregon	42,128,922	1.0%
7	Pennsylvania	166,938,547	3.8%
49	Rhode Island	892,279	0.0%
19	South Carolina	86,150,278	1.9%
43	South Dakota	10,332,613	0.2%
8	Tennessee	142,611,914	3.2%
3	Texas	268,408,959	6.1%
5	Utah	241,992,559	5.5%
50	Vermont	346,702	0.0%
20	Virginia	74,266,389	1.7%
39	Washington	22,386,266	0.5%
17	West Virginia	102,165,281	2.3%
25	Wisconsin	50,733,525	1.1%
40	Wyoming	19,264,722	0.4%

RANK ORDER

RANK	STATE	POUNDS	% of USA
1	Alaska	539,644,265	12.2%
2	Nevada	403,353,335	9.1%
3	Texas	268,408,959	6.1%
4	Ohio	250,096,685	5.6%
5	Utah	241,992,559	5.5%
6	Indiana	234,713,210	5.3%
7	Pennsylvania	166,938,547	3.8%
8	Tennessee	142,611,914	3.2%
9	Illinois	132,421,988	3.0%
10	North Carolina	129,845,723	2.9%
11	Florida	126,489,800	2.9%
12	Louisiana	126,350,144	2.9%
13	Georgia	126,197,045	2.8%
14	Alabama	118,449,143	2.7%
15	Michigan	104,334,602	2.4%
16	Missouri	102,475,425	2.3%
17	West Virginia	102,165,281	2.3%
18	Kentucky	90,534,417	2.0%
19	South Carolina	86,150,278	1.9%
20	Virginia	74,266,389	1.7%
21	Mississippi	63,077,058	1.4%
22	Idaho	61,327,809	1.4%
23	California	57,858,347	1.3%
24	Nebraska	51,471,736	1.2%
25	Wisconsin	50,733,525	1.1%
26	Arizona	48,264,484	1.1%
27	Montana	45,650,733	1.0%
28	Maryland	45,499,979	1.0%
29	New York	44,079,924	1.0%
30	Oregon	42,128,922	1.0%
31	Arkansas	40,602,821	0.9%
32	Iowa	37,433,853	0.8%
33	Minnesota	31,438,324	0.7%
34	Oklahoma	29,939,161	0.7%
35	Kansas	29,064,869	0.7%
36	North Dakota	23,638,798	0.5%
37	New Jersey	23,077,884	0.5%
38	Colorado	22,518,627	0.5%
39	Washington	22,386,266	0.5%
40	Wyoming	19,264,722	0.4%
41	New Mexico	17,899,251	0.4%
42	Delaware	13,594,799	0.3%
43	South Dakota	10,332,613	0.2%
44	Maine	9,334,055	0.2%
45	Massachusetts	8,983,284	0.2%
46	New Hampshire	5,944,216	0.1%
47	Connecticut	5,426,304	0.1%
48	Hawaii	3,117,568	0.1%
49	Rhode Island	892,279	0.0%
50	Vermont	346,702	0.0%
	District of Columbia	13,788	0.0%

Source: U.S. Environmental Protection Agency, Office of Pollution Prevention and Toxics Information Management
"2003 Toxics Release Inventory" (http://www.epa.gov/tri/tridata/tri03/)
*National total does not include 10,384,283 pounds of toxins in U.S. territories. Includes discharges to air, surface water, underground injection and surface land. Includes both original (or manufacturing) industries and those added by EPA since it began tracking releases.

Toxic Releases: Total Air Emissions in 2003

National Total = 1,576,754,145 Pounds*

ALPHA ORDER

RANK	STATE	POUNDS	% of USA
10	Alabama	58,079,863	3.7%
44	Alaska	2,085,117	0.1%
37	Arizona	4,691,083	0.3%
23	Arkansas	20,297,313	1.3%
24	California	18,170,890	1.2%
42	Colorado	2,958,778	0.2%
41	Connecticut	3,051,680	0.2%
32	Delaware	7,266,780	0.5%
8	Florida	77,329,650	4.9%
3	Georgia	98,828,132	6.3%
45	Hawaii	2,081,773	0.1%
40	Idaho	4,033,349	0.3%
12	Illinois	56,037,306	3.6%
9	Indiana	73,627,764	4.7%
22	Iowa	22,132,690	1.4%
28	Kansas	13,201,814	0.8%
11	Kentucky	57,895,672	3.7%
13	Louisiana	54,908,229	3.5%
39	Maine	4,297,731	0.3%
17	Maryland	35,862,849	2.3%
34	Massachusetts	6,048,627	0.4%
16	Michigan	50,783,015	3.2%
26	Minnesota	13,622,582	0.9%
18	Mississippi	31,798,664	2.0%
19	Missouri	27,666,721	1.8%
38	Montana	4,299,020	0.3%
33	Nebraska	6,873,702	0.4%
46	Nevada	1,841,524	0.1%
35	New Hampshire	5,374,269	0.3%
30	New Jersey	12,271,032	0.8%
48	New Mexico	947,742	0.1%
20	New York	27,153,439	1.7%
2	North Carolina	100,658,655	6.4%
36	North Dakota	4,872,462	0.3%
1	Ohio	131,744,722	8.4%
25	Oklahoma	15,902,001	1.0%
27	Oregon	13,322,437	0.8%
5	Pennsylvania	90,992,569	5.8%
49	Rhode Island	626,806	0.0%
14	South Carolina	52,405,655	3.3%
47	South Dakota	1,476,032	0.1%
6	Tennessee	88,790,182	5.6%
4	Texas	91,779,636	5.8%
31	Utah	9,123,840	0.6%
50	Vermont	64,849	0.0%
15	Virginia	50,961,444	3.2%
29	Washington	12,838,947	0.8%
7	West Virginia	78,923,743	5.0%
21	Wisconsin	24,595,225	1.6%
43	Wyoming	2,152,801	0.1%

RANK ORDER

RANK	STATE	POUNDS	% of USA
1	Ohio	131,744,722	8.4%
2	North Carolina	100,658,655	6.4%
3	Georgia	98,828,132	6.3%
4	Texas	91,779,636	5.8%
5	Pennsylvania	90,992,569	5.8%
6	Tennessee	88,790,182	5.6%
7	West Virginia	78,923,743	5.0%
8	Florida	77,329,650	4.9%
9	Indiana	73,627,764	4.7%
10	Alabama	58,079,863	3.7%
11	Kentucky	57,895,672	3.7%
12	Illinois	56,037,306	3.6%
13	Louisiana	54,908,229	3.5%
14	South Carolina	52,405,655	3.3%
15	Virginia	50,961,444	3.2%
16	Michigan	50,783,015	3.2%
17	Maryland	35,862,849	2.3%
18	Mississippi	31,798,664	2.0%
19	Missouri	27,666,721	1.8%
20	New York	27,153,439	1.7%
21	Wisconsin	24,595,225	1.6%
22	Iowa	22,132,690	1.4%
23	Arkansas	20,297,313	1.3%
24	California	18,170,890	1.2%
25	Oklahoma	15,902,001	1.0%
26	Minnesota	13,622,582	0.9%
27	Oregon	13,322,437	0.8%
28	Kansas	13,201,814	0.8%
29	Washington	12,838,947	0.8%
30	New Jersey	12,271,032	0.8%
31	Utah	9,123,840	0.6%
32	Delaware	7,266,780	0.5%
33	Nebraska	6,873,702	0.4%
34	Massachusetts	6,048,627	0.4%
35	New Hampshire	5,374,269	0.3%
36	North Dakota	4,872,462	0.3%
37	Arizona	4,691,083	0.3%
38	Montana	4,299,020	0.3%
39	Maine	4,297,731	0.3%
40	Idaho	4,033,349	0.3%
41	Connecticut	3,051,680	0.2%
42	Colorado	2,958,778	0.2%
43	Wyoming	2,152,801	0.1%
44	Alaska	2,085,117	0.1%
45	Hawaii	2,081,773	0.1%
46	Nevada	1,841,524	0.1%
47	South Dakota	1,476,032	0.1%
48	New Mexico	947,742	0.1%
49	Rhode Island	626,806	0.0%
50	Vermont	64,849	0.0%
	District of Columbia	3,339	0.0%

Source: U.S. Environmental Protection Agency, Office of Pollution Prevention and Toxics Information Management
"2003 Toxics Release Inventory" (http://www.epa.gov/tri/tridata/tri03/)
*National total does not include 9,159,551 pounds of emissions in U.S. territories. Includes both original (or manufacturing) industries and those added by EPA since it began tracking releases.

Toxic Releases: Total Surface Water Discharges in 2003

National Total = 221,358,914 Pounds*

RANK	STATE (ALPHA ORDER)	POUNDS	% of USA	RANK	STATE (RANK ORDER)	POUNDS	% of USA
10	Alabama	7,805,767	3.5%	1	Indiana	23,296,145	10.5%
38	Alaska	541,992	0.2%	2	Texas	20,392,228	9.2%
49	Arizona	7,215	0.0%	3	Nebraska	18,177,388	8.2%
14	Arkansas	5,419,186	2.4%	4	Louisiana	11,303,517	5.1%
16	California	4,618,030	2.1%	5	Pennsylvania	9,684,373	4.4%
27	Colorado	2,955,073	1.3%	6	Georgia	9,573,195	4.3%
37	Connecticut	722,325	0.3%	7	North Carolina	8,676,036	3.9%
36	Delaware	918,650	0.4%	8	Virginia	8,198,927	3.7%
30	Florida	2,507,602	1.1%	9	New York	7,940,065	3.6%
6	Georgia	9,573,195	4.3%	10	Alabama	7,805,767	3.5%
39	Hawaii	364,067	0.2%	11	Mississippi	7,751,466	3.5%
15	Idaho	4,642,166	2.1%	12	Illinois	7,221,382	3.3%
12	Illinois	7,221,382	3.3%	13	Ohio	6,716,440	3.0%
1	Indiana	23,296,145	10.5%	14	Arkansas	5,419,186	2.4%
24	Iowa	3,274,619	1.5%	15	Idaho	4,642,166	2.1%
20	Kansas	4,021,427	1.8%	16	California	4,618,030	2.1%
26	Kentucky	3,014,776	1.4%	17	Wisconsin	4,595,311	2.1%
4	Louisiana	11,303,517	5.1%	18	West Virginia	4,194,526	1.9%
23	Maine	3,363,311	1.5%	19	New Jersey	4,148,648	1.9%
28	Maryland	2,704,113	1.2%	20	Kansas	4,021,427	1.8%
44	Massachusetts	68,806	0.0%	21	South Carolina	3,777,536	1.7%
35	Michigan	1,218,195	0.6%	22	Oklahoma	3,450,036	1.6%
34	Minnesota	1,246,533	0.6%	23	Maine	3,363,311	1.5%
11	Mississippi	7,751,466	3.5%	24	Iowa	3,274,619	1.5%
29	Missouri	2,620,282	1.2%	25	South Dakota	3,199,143	1.4%
47	Montana	49,172	0.0%	26	Kentucky	3,014,776	1.4%
3	Nebraska	18,177,388	8.2%	27	Colorado	2,955,073	1.3%
42	Nevada	102,551	0.0%	28	Maryland	2,704,113	1.2%
43	New Hampshire	86,194	0.0%	29	Missouri	2,620,282	1.2%
19	New Jersey	4,148,648	1.9%	30	Florida	2,507,602	1.1%
45	New Mexico	62,237	0.0%	31	Oregon	2,452,054	1.1%
9	New York	7,940,065	3.6%	32	Tennessee	2,410,358	1.1%
7	North Carolina	8,676,036	3.9%	33	Washington	1,397,187	0.6%
40	North Dakota	248,831	0.1%	34	Minnesota	1,246,533	0.6%
13	Ohio	6,716,440	3.0%	35	Michigan	1,218,195	0.6%
22	Oklahoma	3,450,036	1.6%	36	Delaware	918,650	0.4%
31	Oregon	2,452,054	1.1%	37	Connecticut	722,325	0.3%
5	Pennsylvania	9,684,373	4.4%	38	Alaska	541,992	0.2%
50	Rhode Island	6,947	0.0%	39	Hawaii	364,067	0.2%
21	South Carolina	3,777,536	1.7%	40	North Dakota	248,831	0.1%
25	South Dakota	3,199,143	1.4%	41	Vermont	136,856	0.1%
32	Tennessee	2,410,358	1.1%	42	Nevada	102,551	0.0%
2	Texas	20,392,228	9.2%	43	New Hampshire	86,194	0.0%
46	Utah	56,978	0.0%	44	Massachusetts	68,806	0.0%
41	Vermont	136,856	0.1%	45	New Mexico	62,237	0.0%
8	Virginia	8,198,927	3.7%	46	Utah	56,978	0.0%
33	Washington	1,397,187	0.6%	47	Montana	49,172	0.0%
18	West Virginia	4,194,526	1.9%	48	Wyoming	10,990	0.0%
17	Wisconsin	4,595,311	2.1%	49	Arizona	7,215	0.0%
48	Wyoming	10,990	0.0%	50	Rhode Island	6,947	0.0%
					District of Columbia	8,062	0.0%

Source: U.S. Environmental Protection Agency, Office of Pollution Prevention and Toxics Information Management
   "2003 Toxics Release Inventory" (http://www.epa.gov/tri/tridata/tri03/)
*National total does not include 451,863 pounds of discharges in U.S. territories. Includes both original (or manufacturing) industries and those added by EPA since it began tracking releases.

Pollution Released by Manufacturing Plants in 2003

National Total = 1,936,459,718 Pounds of Toxins*

ALPHA ORDER

RANK	STATE	POUNDS	% of USA
8	Alabama	73,996,558	3.8%
44	Alaska	2,615,076	0.1%
31	Arizona	15,390,905	0.8%
19	Arkansas	38,019,646	2.0%
23	California	32,236,249	1.7%
38	Colorado	5,628,580	0.3%
40	Connecticut	4,424,838	0.2%
37	Delaware	7,505,967	0.4%
14	Florida	54,521,185	2.8%
11	Georgia	59,633,048	3.1%
47	Hawaii	1,320,014	0.1%
32	Idaho	15,246,562	0.8%
6	Illinois	84,624,915	4.4%
2	Indiana	173,112,088	8.9%
22	Iowa	34,664,766	1.8%
27	Kansas	20,463,609	1.1%
20	Kentucky	37,715,084	1.9%
4	Louisiana	114,385,194	5.9%
36	Maine	9,250,568	0.5%
34	Maryland	11,918,865	0.6%
41	Massachusetts	4,395,592	0.2%
10	Michigan	60,986,340	3.1%
28	Minnesota	18,414,179	1.0%
13	Mississippi	54,954,424	2.8%
17	Missouri	46,784,502	2.4%
42	Montana	4,070,431	0.2%
21	Nebraska	36,192,350	1.9%
45	Nevada	1,953,368	0.1%
46	New Hampshire	1,470,746	0.1%
33	New Jersey	14,426,415	0.7%
48	New Mexico	1,169,709	0.1%
24	New York	24,505,140	1.3%
12	North Carolina	56,844,071	2.9%
43	North Dakota	3,904,409	0.2%
3	Ohio	126,301,883	6.5%
26	Oklahoma	22,573,199	1.2%
25	Oregon	23,306,703	1.2%
7	Pennsylvania	80,988,403	4.2%
49	Rhode Island	807,522	0.0%
9	South Carolina	68,599,932	3.5%
39	South Dakota	4,542,929	0.2%
5	Tennessee	85,345,093	4.4%
1	Texas	214,357,655	11.1%
16	Utah	48,677,190	2.5%
50	Vermont	347,326	0.0%
15	Virginia	49,197,097	2.5%
30	Washington	16,630,761	0.9%
29	West Virginia	17,490,719	0.9%
18	Wisconsin	41,172,282	2.1%
35	Wyoming	9,361,846	0.5%

RANK ORDER

RANK	STATE	POUNDS	% of USA
1	Texas	214,357,655	11.1%
2	Indiana	173,112,088	8.9%
3	Ohio	126,301,883	6.5%
4	Louisiana	114,385,194	5.9%
5	Tennessee	85,345,093	4.4%
6	Illinois	84,624,915	4.4%
7	Pennsylvania	80,988,403	4.2%
8	Alabama	73,996,558	3.8%
9	South Carolina	68,599,932	3.5%
10	Michigan	60,986,340	3.1%
11	Georgia	59,633,048	3.1%
12	North Carolina	56,844,071	2.9%
13	Mississippi	54,954,424	2.8%
14	Florida	54,521,185	2.8%
15	Virginia	49,197,097	2.5%
16	Utah	48,677,190	2.5%
17	Missouri	46,784,502	2.4%
18	Wisconsin	41,172,282	2.1%
19	Arkansas	38,019,646	2.0%
20	Kentucky	37,715,084	1.9%
21	Nebraska	36,192,350	1.9%
22	Iowa	34,664,766	1.8%
23	California	32,236,249	1.7%
24	New York	24,505,140	1.3%
25	Oregon	23,306,703	1.2%
26	Oklahoma	22,573,199	1.2%
27	Kansas	20,463,609	1.1%
28	Minnesota	18,414,179	1.0%
29	West Virginia	17,490,719	0.9%
30	Washington	16,630,761	0.9%
31	Arizona	15,390,905	0.8%
32	Idaho	15,246,562	0.8%
33	New Jersey	14,426,415	0.7%
34	Maryland	11,918,865	0.6%
35	Wyoming	9,361,846	0.5%
36	Maine	9,250,568	0.5%
37	Delaware	7,505,967	0.4%
38	Colorado	5,628,580	0.3%
39	South Dakota	4,542,929	0.2%
40	Connecticut	4,424,838	0.2%
41	Massachusetts	4,395,592	0.2%
42	Montana	4,070,431	0.2%
43	North Dakota	3,904,409	0.2%
44	Alaska	2,615,076	0.1%
45	Nevada	1,953,368	0.1%
46	New Hampshire	1,470,746	0.1%
47	Hawaii	1,320,014	0.1%
48	New Mexico	1,169,709	0.1%
49	Rhode Island	807,522	0.0%
50	Vermont	347,326	0.0%
	District of Columbia	13,785	0.0%

Source: U.S. Environmental Protection Agency, Office of Pollution Prevention and Toxics Information Management
    "2003 Toxics Release Inventory" (http://www.epa.gov/tri/tridata/tri03/)
*National total does not include 3,515,177 pounds of toxins in U.S. territories. Includes discharges to air, surface water, underground injection and surface land by what are labeled by the EPA as "original industries" for which data have been collected since 1988. An additional 2,496,322,692 pounds (excluding territories) of toxins were released by industries that have been added by EPA (see table 221).

VIII. GEOGRAPHY

Total Area of States in Square Miles in 2005

National Total = 3,794,083 Square Miles*

ALPHA ORDER					RANK ORDER			
RANK	STATE	MILES	% of USA		RANK	STATE	MILES	% of USA
30	Alabama	52,419	1.4%		1	Alaska	663,267	17.5%
1	Alaska	663,267	17.5%		2	Texas	268,581	7.1%
6	Arizona	113,998	3.0%		3	California	163,696	4.3%
29	Arkansas	53,179	1.4%		4	Montana	147,042	3.9%
3	California	163,696	4.3%		5	New Mexico	121,590	3.2%
8	Colorado	104,094	2.7%		6	Arizona	113,998	3.0%
48	Connecticut	5,543	0.1%		7	Nevada	110,561	2.9%
49	Delaware	2,489	0.1%		8	Colorado	104,094	2.7%
22	Florida	65,755	1.7%		9	Oregon	98,381	2.6%
24	Georgia	59,425	1.6%		10	Wyoming	97,814	2.6%
43	Hawaii	10,931	0.3%		11	Michigan	96,716	2.5%
14	Idaho	83,570	2.2%		12	Minnesota	86,939	2.3%
25	Illinois	57,914	1.5%		13	Utah	84,899	2.2%
38	Indiana	36,418	1.0%		14	Idaho	83,570	2.2%
26	Iowa	56,272	1.5%		15	Kansas	82,277	2.2%
15	Kansas	82,277	2.2%		16	Nebraska	77,354	2.0%
37	Kentucky	40,409	1.1%		17	South Dakota	77,117	2.0%
31	Louisiana	51,840	1.4%		18	Washington	71,300	1.9%
39	Maine	35,385	0.9%		19	North Dakota	70,700	1.9%
42	Maryland	12,407	0.3%		20	Oklahoma	69,898	1.8%
44	Massachusetts	10,555	0.3%		21	Missouri	69,704	1.8%
11	Michigan	96,716	2.5%		22	Florida	65,755	1.7%
12	Minnesota	86,939	2.3%		23	Wisconsin	65,498	1.7%
32	Mississippi	48,430	1.3%		24	Georgia	59,425	1.6%
21	Missouri	69,704	1.8%		25	Illinois	57,914	1.5%
4	Montana	147,042	3.9%		26	Iowa	56,272	1.5%
16	Nebraska	77,354	2.0%		27	New York	54,556	1.4%
7	Nevada	110,561	2.9%		28	North Carolina	53,819	1.4%
46	New Hampshire	9,350	0.2%		29	Arkansas	53,179	1.4%
47	New Jersey	8,721	0.2%		30	Alabama	52,419	1.4%
5	New Mexico	121,590	3.2%		31	Louisiana	51,840	1.4%
27	New York	54,556	1.4%		32	Mississippi	48,430	1.3%
28	North Carolina	53,819	1.4%		33	Pennsylvania	46,055	1.2%
19	North Dakota	70,700	1.9%		34	Ohio	44,825	1.2%
34	Ohio	44,825	1.2%		35	Virginia	42,774	1.1%
20	Oklahoma	69,898	1.8%		36	Tennessee	42,143	1.1%
9	Oregon	98,381	2.6%		37	Kentucky	40,409	1.1%
33	Pennsylvania	46,055	1.2%		38	Indiana	36,418	1.0%
50	Rhode Island	1,545	0.0%		39	Maine	35,385	0.9%
40	South Carolina	32,020	0.8%		40	South Carolina	32,020	0.8%
17	South Dakota	77,117	2.0%		41	West Virginia	24,230	0.6%
36	Tennessee	42,143	1.1%		42	Maryland	12,407	0.3%
2	Texas	268,581	7.1%		43	Hawaii	10,931	0.3%
13	Utah	84,899	2.2%		44	Massachusetts	10,555	0.3%
45	Vermont	9,614	0.3%		45	Vermont	9,614	0.3%
35	Virginia	42,774	1.1%		46	New Hampshire	9,350	0.2%
18	Washington	71,300	1.9%		47	New Jersey	8,721	0.2%
41	West Virginia	24,230	0.6%		48	Connecticut	5,543	0.1%
23	Wisconsin	65,498	1.7%		49	Delaware	2,489	0.1%
10	Wyoming	97,814	2.6%		50	Rhode Island	1,545	0.0%
						District of Columbia	68	0.0%

Source: U.S. Bureau of the Census
  "2000 Census of Population and Housing" (Series PHC-1)
*Total of land and water area. Revised.

Land Area of States in Square Miles in 2005

National Total = 3,537,438 Square Miles of Land Area*

ALPHA ORDER					RANK ORDER			
RANK	STATE	MILES	% of USA		RANK	STATE	MILES	% of USA
28	Alabama	50,744	1.4%		1	Alaska	571,951	16.2%
1	Alaska	571,951	16.2%		2	Texas	261,797	7.4%
6	Arizona	113,635	3.2%		3	California	155,959	4.4%
27	Arkansas	52,068	1.5%		4	Montana	145,552	4.1%
3	California	155,959	4.4%		5	New Mexico	121,356	3.4%
8	Colorado	103,718	2.9%		6	Arizona	113,635	3.2%
48	Connecticut	4,845	0.1%		7	Nevada	109,826	3.1%
49	Delaware	1,954	0.1%		8	Colorado	103,718	2.9%
26	Florida	53,927	1.5%		9	Wyoming	97,100	2.7%
21	Georgia	57,906	1.6%		10	Oregon	95,997	2.7%
47	Hawaii	6,423	0.2%		11	Idaho	82,747	2.3%
11	Idaho	82,747	2.3%		12	Utah	82,144	2.3%
24	Illinois	55,584	1.6%		13	Kansas	81,815	2.3%
38	Indiana	35,867	1.0%		14	Minnesota	79,610	2.3%
23	Iowa	55,869	1.6%		15	Nebraska	76,872	2.2%
13	Kansas	81,815	2.3%		16	South Dakota	75,885	2.1%
36	Kentucky	39,728	1.1%		17	North Dakota	68,976	1.9%
33	Louisiana	43,562	1.2%		18	Missouri	68,886	1.9%
39	Maine	30,862	0.9%		19	Oklahoma	68,667	1.9%
42	Maryland	9,774	0.3%		20	Washington	66,544	1.9%
45	Massachusetts	7,840	0.2%		21	Georgia	57,906	1.6%
22	Michigan	56,804	1.6%		22	Michigan	56,804	1.6%
14	Minnesota	79,610	2.3%		23	Iowa	55,869	1.6%
31	Mississippi	46,907	1.3%		24	Illinois	55,584	1.6%
18	Missouri	68,886	1.9%		25	Wisconsin	54,310	1.5%
4	Montana	145,552	4.1%		26	Florida	53,927	1.5%
15	Nebraska	76,872	2.2%		27	Arkansas	52,068	1.5%
7	Nevada	109,826	3.1%		28	Alabama	50,744	1.4%
44	New Hampshire	8,968	0.3%		29	North Carolina	48,711	1.4%
46	New Jersey	7,417	0.2%		30	New York	47,214	1.3%
5	New Mexico	121,356	3.4%		31	Mississippi	46,907	1.3%
30	New York	47,214	1.3%		32	Pennsylvania	44,817	1.3%
29	North Carolina	48,711	1.4%		33	Louisiana	43,562	1.2%
17	North Dakota	68,976	1.9%		34	Tennessee	41,217	1.2%
35	Ohio	40,948	1.2%		35	Ohio	40,948	1.2%
19	Oklahoma	68,667	1.9%		36	Kentucky	39,728	1.1%
10	Oregon	95,997	2.7%		37	Virginia	39,594	1.1%
32	Pennsylvania	44,817	1.3%		38	Indiana	35,867	1.0%
50	Rhode Island	1,045	0.0%		39	Maine	30,862	0.9%
40	South Carolina	30,110	0.9%		40	South Carolina	30,110	0.9%
16	South Dakota	75,885	2.1%		41	West Virginia	24,078	0.7%
34	Tennessee	41,217	1.2%		42	Maryland	9,774	0.3%
2	Texas	261,797	7.4%		43	Vermont	9,250	0.3%
12	Utah	82,144	2.3%		44	New Hampshire	8,968	0.3%
43	Vermont	9,250	0.3%		45	Massachusetts	7,840	0.2%
37	Virginia	39,594	1.1%		46	New Jersey	7,417	0.2%
20	Washington	66,544	1.9%		47	Hawaii	6,423	0.2%
41	West Virginia	24,078	0.7%		48	Connecticut	4,845	0.1%
25	Wisconsin	54,310	1.5%		49	Delaware	1,954	0.1%
9	Wyoming	97,100	2.7%		50	Rhode Island	1,045	0.0%
						District of Columbia	61	0.0%

Source: U.S. Bureau of the Census
   "2000 Census of Population and Housing" (Series PHC-1)
Revised. Includes dry land temporarily or partially covered by water, such as marshland, swamps, etc.; streams and canals under one-eighth mile wide; and lakes, reservoirs and ponds under 40 acres.

Water Area of States in Square Miles in 2005

National Total = 256,645 Square Miles of Water*

ALPHA ORDER

RANK	STATE	MILES	% of USA
23	Alabama	1,675	0.7%
1	Alaska	91,316	35.6%
48	Arizona	364	0.1%
31	Arkansas	1,110	0.4%
6	California	7,736	3.0%
46	Colorado	376	0.1%
37	Connecticut	699	0.3%
40	Delaware	536	0.2%
3	Florida	11,828	4.6%
25	Georgia	1,519	0.6%
13	Hawaii	4,508	1.8%
33	Idaho	823	0.3%
20	Illinois	2,331	0.9%
39	Indiana	551	0.2%
44	Iowa	402	0.2%
43	Kansas	462	0.2%
38	Kentucky	681	0.3%
5	Louisiana	8,278	3.2%
12	Maine	4,523	1.8%
18	Maryland	2,633	1.0%
17	Massachusetts	2,715	1.1%
2	Michigan	39,912	15.6%
8	Minnesota	7,329	2.9%
24	Mississippi	1,523	0.6%
34	Missouri	818	0.3%
26	Montana	1,490	0.6%
42	Nebraska	481	0.2%
35	Nevada	735	0.3%
45	New Hampshire	382	0.1%
27	New Jersey	1,304	0.5%
49	New Mexico	234	0.1%
7	New York	7,342	2.9%
10	North Carolina	5,108	2.0%
22	North Dakota	1,724	0.7%
14	Ohio	3,877	1.5%
30	Oklahoma	1,231	0.5%
19	Oregon	2,384	0.9%
28	Pennsylvania	1,239	0.5%
41	Rhode Island	500	0.2%
21	South Carolina	1,911	0.7%
29	South Dakota	1,232	0.5%
32	Tennessee	926	0.4%
9	Texas	6,784	2.6%
16	Utah	2,755	1.1%
47	Vermont	365	0.1%
15	Virginia	3,180	1.2%
11	Washington	4,756	1.9%
50	West Virginia	152	0.1%
4	Wisconsin	11,188	4.4%
36	Wyoming	713	0.3%

RANK ORDER

RANK	STATE	MILES	% of USA
1	Alaska	91,316	35.6%
2	Michigan	39,912	15.6%
3	Florida	11,828	4.6%
4	Wisconsin	11,188	4.4%
5	Louisiana	8,278	3.2%
6	California	7,736	3.0%
7	New York	7,342	2.9%
8	Minnesota	7,329	2.9%
9	Texas	6,784	2.6%
10	North Carolina	5,108	2.0%
11	Washington	4,756	1.9%
12	Maine	4,523	1.8%
13	Hawaii	4,508	1.8%
14	Ohio	3,877	1.5%
15	Virginia	3,180	1.2%
16	Utah	2,755	1.1%
17	Massachusetts	2,715	1.1%
18	Maryland	2,633	1.0%
19	Oregon	2,384	0.9%
20	Illinois	2,331	0.9%
21	South Carolina	1,911	0.7%
22	North Dakota	1,724	0.7%
23	Alabama	1,675	0.7%
24	Mississippi	1,523	0.6%
25	Georgia	1,519	0.6%
26	Montana	1,490	0.6%
27	New Jersey	1,304	0.5%
28	Pennsylvania	1,239	0.5%
29	South Dakota	1,232	0.5%
30	Oklahoma	1,231	0.5%
31	Arkansas	1,110	0.4%
32	Tennessee	926	0.4%
33	Idaho	823	0.3%
34	Missouri	818	0.3%
35	Nevada	735	0.3%
36	Wyoming	713	0.3%
37	Connecticut	699	0.3%
38	Kentucky	681	0.3%
39	Indiana	551	0.2%
40	Delaware	536	0.2%
41	Rhode Island	500	0.2%
42	Nebraska	481	0.2%
43	Kansas	462	0.2%
44	Iowa	402	0.2%
45	New Hampshire	382	0.1%
46	Colorado	376	0.1%
47	Vermont	365	0.1%
48	Arizona	364	0.1%
49	New Mexico	234	0.1%
50	West Virginia	152	0.1%
	District of Columbia	7	0.0%

Source: U.S. Bureau of the Census
"2000 Census of Population and Housing" (Series PHC-1)
*Revised. Includes permanent inland water surface, such as lakes, reservoirs, and ponds having an area of 40 acres or more, canals one-eighth mile or more in width; coastal waters behind or sheltered by headlands or islands separated by less than 1 nautical mile of water, and islands under 40 acres in area. Excludes areas of oceans, bays, etc., lying within U.S. jurisdiction but not defined as inland water.

Highest Point of Elevation in Feet

National High Point = 20,320 Feet Above Sea Level (Mt. McKinley, Alaska)

ALPHA ORDER

RANK ORDER

RANK	STATE	HIGHEST POINT		RANK	STATE	HIGHEST POINT
35	Alabama	2,405		1	Alaska	20,320
1	Alaska	20,320		2	California	14,494
12	Arizona	12,633		3	Colorado	14,433
34	Arkansas	2,753		4	Washington	14,410
2	California	14,494		5	Wyoming	13,804
3	Colorado	14,433		6	Hawaii	13,796
36	Connecticut	2,380		7	Utah	13,528
49	Delaware	448		8	New Mexico	13,161
50	Florida	345		9	Nevada	13,140
25	Georgia	4,784		10	Montana	12,799
6	Hawaii	13,796		11	Idaho	12,662
11	Idaho	12,662		12	Arizona	12,633
45	Illinois	1,235		13	Oregon	11,239
44	Indiana	1,257		14	Texas	8,749
42	Iowa	1,670		15	South Dakota	7,242
28	Kansas	4,039		16	North Carolina	6,684
27	Kentucky	4,139		17	Tennessee	6,643
48	Louisiana	535		18	New Hampshire	6,288
22	Maine	5,267		19	Virginia	5,729
32	Maryland	3,360		20	Nebraska	5,424
31	Massachusetts	3,487		21	New York	5,344
38	Michigan	1,979		22	Maine	5,267
37	Minnesota	2,301		23	Oklahoma	4,973
47	Mississippi	806		24	West Virginia	4,861
41	Missouri	1,772		25	Georgia	4,784
10	Montana	12,799		26	Vermont	4,393
20	Nebraska	5,424		27	Kentucky	4,139
9	Nevada	13,140		28	Kansas	4,039
18	New Hampshire	6,288		29	South Carolina	3,560
40	New Jersey	1,803		30	North Dakota	3,506
8	New Mexico	13,161		31	Massachusetts	3,487
21	New York	5,344		32	Maryland	3,360
16	North Carolina	6,684		33	Pennsylvania	3,213
30	North Dakota	3,506		34	Arkansas	2,753
43	Ohio	1,549		35	Alabama	2,405
23	Oklahoma	4,973		36	Connecticut	2,380
13	Oregon	11,239		37	Minnesota	2,301
33	Pennsylvania	3,213		38	Michigan	1,979
46	Rhode Island	812		39	Wisconsin	1,951
29	South Carolina	3,560		40	New Jersey	1,803
15	South Dakota	7,242		41	Missouri	1,772
17	Tennessee	6,643		42	Iowa	1,670
14	Texas	8,749		43	Ohio	1,549
7	Utah	13,528		44	Indiana	1,257
26	Vermont	4,393		45	Illinois	1,235
19	Virginia	5,729		46	Rhode Island	812
4	Washington	14,410		47	Mississippi	806
24	West Virginia	4,861		48	Louisiana	535
39	Wisconsin	1,951		49	Delaware	448
5	Wyoming	13,804		50	Florida	345
					District of Columbia	410

Source: U.S. Department of Interior, U.S. Geological Survey
"Elevations and Distances in the United States" (http://erg.usgs.gov/isb/pubs/booklets/elvadist/elvadist.html)

Lowest Point of Elevation in Feet

National Low Point = 282 Feet Below Sea Level (Death Valley, California)*

ALPHA ORDER

RANK	STATE	LOWEST POINT
3	Alabama	0
3	Alaska	0
26	Arizona	70
25	Arkansas	55
1	California	(282)
50	Colorado	3,350
3	Connecticut	0
3	Delaware	0
3	Florida	0
3	Georgia	0
3	Hawaii	0
42	Idaho	710
32	Illinois	279
34	Indiana	320
37	Iowa	480
41	Kansas	679
31	Kentucky	257
2	Louisiana	(8)
3	Maine	0
3	Maryland	0
3	Massachusetts	0
38	Michigan	571
40	Minnesota	601
3	Mississippi	0
29	Missouri	230
46	Montana	1,800
44	Nebraska	840
36	Nevada	479
3	New Hampshire	0
3	New Jersey	0
48	New Mexico	2,842
3	New York	0
3	North Carolina	0
43	North Dakota	750
35	Ohio	455
33	Oklahoma	289
3	Oregon	0
3	Pennsylvania	0
3	Rhode Island	0
3	South Carolina	0
45	South Dakota	966
28	Tennessee	178
3	Texas	0
47	Utah	2,000
27	Vermont	95
3	Virginia	0
3	Washington	0
30	West Virginia	240
39	Wisconsin	579
49	Wyoming	3,099

RANK ORDER

RANK	STATE	LOWEST POINT
1	California	(282)
2	Louisiana	(8)
3	Alabama*	0
3	Alaska	0
3	Connecticut	0
3	Delaware	0
3	Florida	0
3	Georgia	0
3	Hawaii	0
3	Maine	0
3	Maryland	0
3	Massachusetts	0
3	Mississippi	0
3	New Hampshire	0
3	New Jersey	0
3	New York	0
3	North Carolina	0
3	Oregon	0
3	Pennsylvania	0
3	Rhode Island	0
3	South Carolina	0
3	Texas	0
3	Virginia	0
3	Washington	0
25	Arkansas	55
26	Arizona	70
27	Vermont	95
28	Tennessee	178
29	Missouri	230
30	West Virginia	240
31	Kentucky	257
32	Illinois	279
33	Oklahoma	289
34	Indiana	320
35	Ohio	455
36	Nevada	479
37	Iowa	480
38	Michigan	571
39	Wisconsin	579
40	Minnesota	601
41	Kansas	679
42	Idaho	710
43	North Dakota	750
44	Nebraska	840
45	South Dakota	966
46	Montana	1,800
47	Utah	2,000
48	New Mexico	2,842
49	Wyoming	3,099
50	Colorado	3,350
	District of Columbia	1

Source: U.S. Department of Interior, U.S. Geological Survey
"Elevations and Distances in the United States" (http://erg.usgs.gov/isb/pubs/booklets/elvadist/elvadist.html)
States with "0" have sea level as lowest point.

Approximate Mean Elevation in Feet

Approximate National Mean Elevation = 2,500 Feet Above Sea Level

ALPHA ORDER

RANK	STATE	MEAN ELEVATION
40	Alabama	500
15	Alaska	1,900
7	Arizona	4,100
36	Arkansas	650
11	California	2,900
1	Colorado	6,800
40	Connecticut	500
50	Delaware	60
48	Florida	100
37	Georgia	600
10	Hawaii	3,030
6	Idaho	5,000
37	Illinois	600
34	Indiana	700
22	Iowa	1,100
14	Kansas	2,000
33	Kentucky	750
48	Louisiana	100
37	Maine	600
43	Maryland	350
40	Massachusetts	500
29	Michigan	900
21	Minnesota	1,200
45	Mississippi	300
32	Missouri	800
8	Montana	3,400
12	Nebraska	2,600
5	Nevada	5,500
25	New Hampshire	1,000
46	New Jersey	250
4	New Mexico	5,700
25	New York	1,000
34	North Carolina	700
15	North Dakota	1,900
31	Ohio	850
20	Oklahoma	1,300
9	Oregon	3,300
22	Pennsylvania	1,100
47	Rhode Island	200
43	South Carolina	350
13	South Dakota	2,200
29	Tennessee	900
17	Texas	1,700
3	Utah	6,100
25	Vermont	1,000
28	Virginia	950
17	Washington	1,700
19	West Virginia	1,500
24	Wisconsin	1,050
2	Wyoming	6,700

RANK ORDER

RANK	STATE	MEAN ELEVATION
1	Colorado	6,800
2	Wyoming	6,700
3	Utah	6,100
4	New Mexico	5,700
5	Nevada	5,500
6	Idaho	5,000
7	Arizona	4,100
8	Montana	3,400
9	Oregon	3,300
10	Hawaii	3,030
11	California	2,900
12	Nebraska	2,600
13	South Dakota	2,200
14	Kansas	2,000
15	Alaska	1,900
15	North Dakota	1,900
17	Texas	1,700
17	Washington	1,700
19	West Virginia	1,500
20	Oklahoma	1,300
21	Minnesota	1,200
22	Iowa	1,100
22	Pennsylvania	1,100
24	Wisconsin	1,050
25	New Hampshire	1,000
25	New York	1,000
25	Vermont	1,000
28	Virginia	950
29	Michigan	900
29	Tennessee	900
31	Ohio	850
32	Missouri	800
33	Kentucky	750
34	Indiana	700
34	North Carolina	700
36	Arkansas	650
37	Georgia	600
37	Illinois	600
37	Maine	600
40	Alabama	500
40	Connecticut	500
40	Massachusetts	500
43	Maryland	350
43	South Carolina	350
45	Mississippi	300
46	New Jersey	250
47	Rhode Island	200
48	Florida	100
48	Louisiana	100
50	Delaware	60
	District of Columbia	150

Source: U.S. Department of Interior, U.S. Geological Survey
"Elevations and Distances in the United States" (http://erg.usgs.gov/isb/pubs/booklets/elvadist/elvadist.html)

Normal Daily Mean Temperature*

<table>
<tr><td colspan="3">ALPHA ORDER</td><td colspan="3">RANK ORDER</td></tr>
<tr><th>RANK</th><th>STATE</th><th>MEAN TEMPERATURE</th><th>RANK</th><th>STATE</th><th>MEAN TEMPERATURE</th></tr>
<tr><td>5</td><td>Alabama</td><td>66.8</td><td>1</td><td>Hawaii</td><td>77.5</td></tr>
<tr><td>50</td><td>Alaska</td><td>41.5</td><td>2</td><td>Arizona</td><td>72.9</td></tr>
<tr><td>2</td><td>Arizona</td><td>72.9</td><td>3</td><td>Florida**</td><td>72.4</td></tr>
<tr><td>10</td><td>Arkansas</td><td>62.1</td><td>4</td><td>Louisiana</td><td>68.8</td></tr>
<tr><td>11</td><td>California**</td><td>61.5</td><td>5</td><td>Alabama</td><td>66.8</td></tr>
<tr><td>35</td><td>Colorado</td><td>50.1</td><td>6</td><td>Texas**</td><td>66.3</td></tr>
<tr><td>34</td><td>Connecticut</td><td>50.2</td><td>7</td><td>Mississippi</td><td>64.1</td></tr>
<tr><td>22</td><td>Delaware</td><td>54.4</td><td>8</td><td>South Carolina</td><td>63.6</td></tr>
<tr><td>3</td><td>Florida**</td><td>72.4</td><td>9</td><td>Georgia</td><td>62.2</td></tr>
<tr><td>9</td><td>Georgia</td><td>62.2</td><td>10</td><td>Arkansas</td><td>62.1</td></tr>
<tr><td>1</td><td>Hawaii</td><td>77.5</td><td>11</td><td>California**</td><td>61.5</td></tr>
<tr><td>28</td><td>Idaho</td><td>52.0</td><td>12</td><td>Tennessee**</td><td>60.7</td></tr>
<tr><td>37</td><td>Illinois**</td><td>50.0</td><td>13</td><td>North Carolina**</td><td>60.5</td></tr>
<tr><td>26</td><td>Indiana</td><td>52.5</td><td>14</td><td>Oklahoma</td><td>60.1</td></tr>
<tr><td>37</td><td>Iowa</td><td>50.0</td><td>15</td><td>Virginia**</td><td>58.6</td></tr>
<tr><td>18</td><td>Kansas</td><td>56.4</td><td>16</td><td>Kentucky</td><td>57.0</td></tr>
<tr><td>16</td><td>Kentucky</td><td>57.0</td><td>17</td><td>New Mexico</td><td>56.8</td></tr>
<tr><td>4</td><td>Louisiana</td><td>68.8</td><td>18</td><td>Kansas</td><td>56.4</td></tr>
<tr><td>42</td><td>Maine</td><td>45.8</td><td>19</td><td>Missouri**</td><td>55.3</td></tr>
<tr><td>20</td><td>Maryland</td><td>54.6</td><td>20</td><td>Maryland</td><td>54.6</td></tr>
<tr><td>30</td><td>Massachusetts</td><td>51.6</td><td>21</td><td>West Virginia</td><td>54.5</td></tr>
<tr><td>45</td><td>Michigan**</td><td>45.0</td><td>22</td><td>Delaware</td><td>54.4</td></tr>
<tr><td>48</td><td>Minnesota**</td><td>42.3</td><td>23</td><td>New Jersey</td><td>53.5</td></tr>
<tr><td>7</td><td>Mississippi</td><td>64.1</td><td>23</td><td>Oregon</td><td>53.5</td></tr>
<tr><td>19</td><td>Missouri**</td><td>55.3</td><td>25</td><td>Pennsylvania**</td><td>53.2</td></tr>
<tr><td>47</td><td>Montana</td><td>43.8</td><td>26</td><td>Indiana</td><td>52.5</td></tr>
<tr><td>33</td><td>Nebraska</td><td>50.7</td><td>27</td><td>Ohio**</td><td>52.3</td></tr>
<tr><td>31</td><td>Nevada</td><td>51.3</td><td>28</td><td>Idaho</td><td>52.0</td></tr>
<tr><td>41</td><td>New Hampshire</td><td>45.9</td><td>28</td><td>Utah</td><td>52.0</td></tr>
<tr><td>23</td><td>New Jersey</td><td>53.5</td><td>30</td><td>Massachusetts</td><td>51.6</td></tr>
<tr><td>17</td><td>New Mexico</td><td>56.8</td><td>31</td><td>Nevada</td><td>51.3</td></tr>
<tr><td>35</td><td>New York**</td><td>50.1</td><td>32</td><td>Rhode Island</td><td>51.1</td></tr>
<tr><td>13</td><td>North Carolina**</td><td>60.5</td><td>33</td><td>Nebraska</td><td>50.7</td></tr>
<tr><td>48</td><td>North Dakota</td><td>42.3</td><td>34</td><td>Connecticut</td><td>50.2</td></tr>
<tr><td>27</td><td>Ohio**</td><td>52.3</td><td>35</td><td>Colorado</td><td>50.1</td></tr>
<tr><td>14</td><td>Oklahoma</td><td>60.1</td><td>35</td><td>New York**</td><td>50.1</td></tr>
<tr><td>23</td><td>Oregon</td><td>53.5</td><td>37</td><td>Illinois**</td><td>50.0</td></tr>
<tr><td>25</td><td>Pennsylvania**</td><td>53.2</td><td>37</td><td>Iowa</td><td>50.0</td></tr>
<tr><td>32</td><td>Rhode Island</td><td>51.1</td><td>39</td><td>Washington**</td><td>49.8</td></tr>
<tr><td>8</td><td>South Carolina</td><td>63.6</td><td>40</td><td>Wisconsin</td><td>47.5</td></tr>
<tr><td>44</td><td>South Dakota</td><td>45.1</td><td>41</td><td>New Hampshire</td><td>45.9</td></tr>
<tr><td>12</td><td>Tennessee**</td><td>60.7</td><td>42</td><td>Maine</td><td>45.8</td></tr>
<tr><td>6</td><td>Texas**</td><td>66.3</td><td>43</td><td>Vermont</td><td>45.2</td></tr>
<tr><td>28</td><td>Utah</td><td>52.0</td><td>44</td><td>South Dakota</td><td>45.1</td></tr>
<tr><td>43</td><td>Vermont</td><td>45.2</td><td>45</td><td>Michigan**</td><td>45.0</td></tr>
<tr><td>15</td><td>Virginia**</td><td>58.6</td><td>45</td><td>Wyoming</td><td>45.0</td></tr>
<tr><td>39</td><td>Washington**</td><td>49.8</td><td>47</td><td>Montana</td><td>43.8</td></tr>
<tr><td>21</td><td>West Virginia</td><td>54.5</td><td>48</td><td>Minnesota**</td><td>42.3</td></tr>
<tr><td>40</td><td>Wisconsin</td><td>47.5</td><td>48</td><td>North Dakota</td><td>42.3</td></tr>
<tr><td>45</td><td>Wyoming</td><td>45.0</td><td>50</td><td>Alaska</td><td>41.5</td></tr>
<tr><td></td><td></td><td></td><td></td><td>District of Columbia</td><td>57.5</td></tr>
</table>

Source: U.S. Department of Commerce, National Oceanic and Atmospheric Administration
   "Climatography of the United States" (No. 81)
*Based on standard 30 year period, 1971-2000.
**Temperatures from multiple reporting cities within one state were averaged to determine a state's mean temperature.

Percent of Days That Are Sunny*

ALPHA ORDER

ALPHA ORDER

RANK	STATE	PERCENT OF DAYS SUNNY
12	Alabama	60
50	Alaska	23
1	Arizona	81
12	Arkansas	60
4	California**	72
6	Colorado	67
37	Connecticut	52
28	Delaware	55
8	Florida**	65
16	Georgia	59
3	Hawaii	74
20	Idaho	58
35	Illinois**	53
41	Indiana	51
28	Iowa	55
20	Kansas	58
35	Kentucky	53
12	Louisiana	60
28	Maine	55
20	Maryland	58
28	Massachusetts	55
46	Michigan**	46
37	Minnesota**	52
16	Mississippi	59
24	Missouri**	57
41	Montana	51
16	Nebraska	59
5	Nevada	69
28	New Hampshire	55
27	New Jersey	56
2	New Mexico	76
37	New York**	52
16	North Carolina**	59
28	North Dakota	55
45	Ohio**	47
9	Oklahoma	64
49	Oregon	39
43	Pennsylvania**	50
28	Rhode Island	55
12	South Carolina	60
24	South Dakota	57
20	Tennessee**	58
6	Texas**	67
11	Utah	62
47	Vermont	44
24	Virginia**	57
48	Washington**	43
44	West Virginia	48
37	Wisconsin	52
9	Wyoming	64

RANK ORDER

RANK	STATE	PERCENT OF DAYS SUNNY
1	Arizona	81
2	New Mexico	76
3	Hawaii	74
4	California**	72
5	Nevada	69
6	Colorado	67
6	Texas**	67
8	Florida**	65
9	Oklahoma	64
9	Wyoming	64
11	Utah	62
12	Alabama	60
12	Arkansas	60
12	Louisiana	60
12	South Carolina	60
16	Georgia	59
16	Mississippi	59
16	Nebraska	59
16	North Carolina**	59
20	Idaho	58
20	Kansas	58
20	Maryland	58
20	Tennessee**	58
24	Missouri**	57
24	South Dakota	57
24	Virginia**	57
27	New Jersey	56
28	Delaware	55
28	Iowa	55
28	Maine	55
28	Massachusetts	55
28	New Hampshire	55
28	North Dakota	55
28	Rhode Island	55
35	Illinois**	53
35	Kentucky	53
37	Connecticut	52
37	Minnesota**	52
37	New York**	52
37	Wisconsin	52
41	Indiana	51
41	Montana	51
43	Pennsylvania**	50
44	West Virginia	48
45	Ohio**	47
46	Michigan**	46
47	Vermont	44
48	Washington**	43
49	Oregon	39
50	Alaska	23
	District of Columbia	55

Source: U.S. Department of Commerce, National Oceanic and Atmospheric Administration
    "Comparative Climatic Data" (annual)
*Averages over various years.
**Percentages from multiple reporting cities within one state were averaged to determine a state's average percentage of sunny days.

Average Wind Speed (M.P.H.)*

ALPHA ORDER

RANK	STATE	MILES PER HOUR
29	Alabama	8.8
39	Alaska	8.2
49	Arizona	6.2
43	Arkansas	7.8
39	California**	8.2
34	Colorado	8.6
36	Connecticut	8.4
24	Delaware	9.0
35	Florida**	8.5
22	Georgia	9.1
7	Hawaii	11.3
32	Idaho	8.7
14	Illinois**	10.1
19	Indiana	9.6
10	Iowa	10.7
4	Kansas	12.2
38	Kentucky	8.3
39	Louisiana	8.2
32	Maine	8.7
29	Maryland	8.8
3	Massachusetts	12.4
18	Michigan**	9.7
9	Minnesota**	10.8
45	Mississippi	7.0
14	Missouri**	10.1
2	Montana	12.5
11	Nebraska	10.5
48	Nevada	6.6
47	New Hampshire	6.7
17	New Jersey	9.8
27	New Mexico	8.9
16	New York**	10.0
44	North Carolina**	7.5
13	North Dakota	10.2
20	Ohio**	9.3
4	Oklahoma	12.2
42	Oregon	7.9
20	Pennsylvania**	9.3
12	Rhode Island	10.4
46	South Carolina	6.8
8	South Dakota	11.0
36	Tennessee**	8.4
24	Texas**	9.0
29	Utah	8.8
24	Vermont	9.0
22	Virginia**	9.1
27	Washington**	8.9
50	West Virginia	5.8
6	Wisconsin	11.5
1	Wyoming	12.9

RANK ORDER

RANK	STATE	MILES PER HOUR
1	Wyoming	12.9
2	Montana	12.5
3	Massachusetts	12.4
4	Kansas	12.2
4	Oklahoma	12.2
6	Wisconsin	11.5
7	Hawaii	11.3
8	South Dakota	11.0
9	Minnesota**	10.8
10	Iowa	10.7
11	Nebraska	10.5
12	Rhode Island	10.4
13	North Dakota	10.2
14	Illinois**	10.1
14	Missouri**	10.1
16	New York**	10.0
17	New Jersey	9.8
18	Michigan**	9.7
19	Indiana	9.6
20	Ohio**	9.3
20	Pennsylvania**	9.3
22	Georgia	9.1
22	Virginia**	9.1
24	Delaware	9.0
24	Texas**	9.0
24	Vermont	9.0
27	New Mexico	8.9
27	Washington**	8.9
29	Alabama	8.8
29	Maryland	8.8
29	Utah	8.8
32	Idaho	8.7
32	Maine	8.7
34	Colorado	8.6
35	Florida**	8.5
36	Connecticut	8.4
36	Tennessee**	8.4
38	Kentucky	8.3
39	Alaska	8.2
39	California**	8.2
39	Louisiana	8.2
42	Oregon	7.9
43	Arkansas	7.8
44	North Carolina**	7.5
45	Mississippi	7.0
46	South Carolina	6.8
47	New Hampshire	6.7
48	Nevada	6.6
49	Arizona	6.2
50	West Virginia	5.8

	District of Columbia	9.4

Source: U.S. Department of Commerce, National Oceanic and Atmospheric Administration
     "Comparative Climatic Data" (annual)

*Averages over various years.

**Wind speeds from multiple reporting cities within one state were averaged to determine a state's average wind speed.

Tornadoes in 2004

National Total = 1,819 Tornadoes*

ALPHA ORDER

RANK	STATE	TORNADOES	% of USA
14	Alabama	55	3.0%
41	Alaska	2	0.1%
39	Arizona	3	0.2%
16	Arkansas	48	2.6%
29	California	10	0.5%
7	Colorado	84	4.6%
41	Connecticut	2	0.1%
41	Delaware	2	0.1%
5	Florida	104	5.7%
18	Georgia	45	2.5%
39	Hawaii	3	0.2%
36	Idaho	5	0.3%
9	Illinois	80	4.4%
17	Indiana	47	2.6%
3	Iowa	120	6.6%
2	Kansas	124	6.8%
25	Kentucky	22	1.2%
22	Louisiana	28	1.5%
45	Maine	1	0.1%
26	Maryland	18	1.0%
45	Massachusetts	1	0.1%
24	Michigan	23	1.3%
13	Minnesota	57	3.1%
15	Mississippi	54	3.0%
10	Missouri	71	3.9%
33	Montana	6	0.3%
4	Nebraska	111	6.1%
36	Nevada	5	0.3%
45	New Hampshire	1	0.1%
41	New Jersey	2	0.1%
28	New Mexico	11	0.6%
31	New York	8	0.4%
11	North Carolina	66	3.6%
19	North Dakota	38	2.1%
31	Ohio	8	0.4%
12	Oklahoma	62	3.4%
33	Oregon	6	0.3%
23	Pennsylvania	26	1.4%
49	Rhode Island	0	0.0%
6	South Carolina	85	4.7%
21	South Dakota	35	1.9%
27	Tennessee	15	0.8%
1	Texas	178	9.8%
45	Utah	1	0.1%
49	Vermont	0	0.0%
8	Virginia	83	4.6%
30	Washington	9	0.5%
36	West Virginia	5	0.3%
20	Wisconsin	36	2.0%
33	Wyoming	6	0.3%

RANK ORDER

RANK	STATE	TORNADOES	% of USA
1	Texas	178	9.8%
2	Kansas	124	6.8%
3	Iowa	120	6.6%
4	Nebraska	111	6.1%
5	Florida	104	5.7%
6	South Carolina	85	4.7%
7	Colorado	84	4.6%
8	Virginia	83	4.6%
9	Illinois	80	4.4%
10	Missouri	71	3.9%
11	North Carolina	66	3.6%
12	Oklahoma	62	3.4%
13	Minnesota	57	3.1%
14	Alabama	55	3.0%
15	Mississippi	54	3.0%
16	Arkansas	48	2.6%
17	Indiana	47	2.6%
18	Georgia	45	2.5%
19	North Dakota	38	2.1%
20	Wisconsin	36	2.0%
21	South Dakota	35	1.9%
22	Louisiana	28	1.5%
23	Pennsylvania	26	1.4%
24	Michigan	23	1.3%
25	Kentucky	22	1.2%
26	Maryland	18	1.0%
27	Tennessee	15	0.8%
28	New Mexico	11	0.6%
29	California	10	0.5%
30	Washington	9	0.5%
31	New York	8	0.4%
31	Ohio	8	0.4%
33	Montana	6	0.3%
33	Oregon	6	0.3%
33	Wyoming	6	0.3%
36	Idaho	5	0.3%
36	Nevada	5	0.3%
36	West Virginia	5	0.3%
39	Arizona	3	0.2%
39	Hawaii	3	0.2%
41	Alaska	2	0.1%
41	Connecticut	2	0.1%
41	Delaware	2	0.1%
41	New Jersey	2	0.1%
45	Maine	1	0.1%
45	Massachusetts	1	0.1%
45	New Hampshire	1	0.1%
45	Utah	1	0.1%
49	Rhode Island	0	0.0%
49	Vermont	0	0.0%
	District of Columbia	0	0.0%

Source: National Weather Service, Storm Prediction Center
unpublished data
Preliminary data.

Hazardous Weather Fatalities in 2004

National Total = 333 Fatalities*

ALPHA ORDER

RANK ORDER

RANK	STATE	FATALITIES	% of USA		RANK	STATE	FATALITIES	% of USA
17	Alabama	5	1.5%		1	Florida	61	18.3%
27	Alaska	3	0.9%		2	Illinois	28	8.4%
27	Arizona	3	0.9%		3	Texas	25	7.5%
27	Arkansas	3	0.9%		4	North Carolina	23	6.9%
6	California	18	5.4%		5	Pennsylvania	20	6.0%
10	Colorado	7	2.1%		6	California	18	5.4%
43	Connecticut	0	0.0%		7	Virginia	17	5.1%
35	Delaware	1	0.3%		8	Missouri	11	3.3%
1	Florida	61	18.3%		9	South Carolina	9	2.7%
10	Georgia	7	2.1%		10	Colorado	7	2.1%
21	Hawaii	4	1.2%		10	Georgia	7	2.1%
14	Idaho	6	1.8%		10	Kentucky	7	2.1%
2	Illinois	28	8.4%		10	New York	7	2.1%
14	Indiana	6	1.8%		14	Idaho	6	1.8%
35	Iowa	1	0.3%		14	Indiana	6	1.8%
17	Kansas	5	1.5%		14	Mississippi	6	1.8%
10	Kentucky	7	2.1%		17	Alabama	5	1.5%
27	Louisiana	3	0.9%		17	Kansas	5	1.5%
43	Maine	0	0.0%		17	Nebraska	5	1.5%
21	Maryland	4	1.2%		17	West Virginia	5	1.5%
35	Massachusetts	1	0.3%		21	Hawaii	4	1.2%
27	Michigan	3	0.9%		21	Maryland	4	1.2%
35	Minnesota	1	0.3%		21	Ohio	4	1.2%
14	Mississippi	6	1.8%		21	Oklahoma	4	1.2%
8	Missouri	11	3.3%		21	Tennessee	4	1.2%
35	Montana	1	0.3%		21	Utah	4	1.2%
17	Nebraska	5	1.5%		27	Alaska	3	0.9%
43	Nevada	0	0.0%		27	Arizona	3	0.9%
43	New Hampshire	0	0.0%		27	Arkansas	3	0.9%
34	New Jersey	2	0.6%		27	Louisiana	3	0.9%
43	New Mexico	0	0.0%		27	Michigan	3	0.9%
10	New York	7	2.1%		27	Vermont	3	0.9%
4	North Carolina	23	6.9%		27	Wisconsin	3	0.9%
43	North Dakota	0	0.0%		34	New Jersey	2	0.6%
21	Ohio	4	1.2%		35	Delaware	1	0.3%
21	Oklahoma	4	1.2%		35	Iowa	1	0.3%
35	Oregon	1	0.3%		35	Massachusetts	1	0.3%
5	Pennsylvania	20	6.0%		35	Minnesota	1	0.3%
35	Rhode Island	1	0.3%		35	Montana	1	0.3%
9	South Carolina	9	2.7%		35	Oregon	1	0.3%
43	South Dakota	0	0.0%		35	Rhode Island	1	0.3%
21	Tennessee	4	1.2%		35	Washington	1	0.3%
3	Texas	25	7.5%		43	Connecticut	0	0.0%
21	Utah	4	1.2%		43	Maine	0	0.0%
27	Vermont	3	0.9%		43	Nevada	0	0.0%
7	Virginia	17	5.1%		43	New Hampshire	0	0.0%
35	Washington	1	0.3%		43	New Mexico	0	0.0%
17	West Virginia	5	1.5%		43	North Dakota	0	0.0%
27	Wisconsin	3	0.9%		43	South Dakota	0	0.0%
43	Wyoming	0	0.0%		43	Wyoming	0	0.0%
						District of Columbia	0	0.0%

Source: National Weather Service, Water and Weather Services
*   "2004 Summary of Hazardous Weather Fatalities" (http://www.nws.noaa.gov/om/severe_weather/state04.pdf)*
Includes lightning, tornado, thunderstorm, extreme temperature, flood, coastal storm, rip current, hurricane, winter
storm, fog, avalanche and other weather events. National total does not include 30 fatalities in U.S. territories.

Cost of Damage from Hazardous Weather in 2004

National Total = $26,510,800,000*

	ALPHA ORDER					RANK ORDER		
RANK	STATE	DAMAGE	% of USA		RANK	STATE	DAMAGE	% of USA
2	Alabama	$2,627,800,000	9.9%		1	Florida	$20,165,500,000	76.1%
31	Alaska	21,700,000	0.1%		2	Alabama	2,627,800,000	9.9%
40	Arizona	3,100,000	0.0%		3	Pennsylvania	484,200,000	1.8%
30	Arkansas	25,900,000	0.1%		4	Wisconsin	338,400,000	1.3%
22	California	55,200,000	0.2%		5	Texas	309,500,000	1.2%
9	Colorado	154,600,000	0.6%		6	North Carolina	289,100,000	1.1%
50	Connecticut	100,000	0.0%		7	Ohio	274,400,000	1.0%
41	Delaware	2,500,000	0.0%		8	Nebraska	239,700,000	0.9%
1	Florida	20,165,500,000	76.1%		9	Colorado	154,600,000	0.6%
12	Georgia	137,000,000	0.5%		10	Michigan	143,900,000	0.5%
16	Hawaii	81,400,000	0.3%		11	West Virginia	141,100,000	0.5%
45	Idaho	1,000,000	0.0%		12	Georgia	137,000,000	0.5%
29	Illinois	27,600,000	0.1%		13	New York	115,600,000	0.4%
21	Indiana	57,300,000	0.2%		14	Virginia	104,300,000	0.4%
18	Iowa	73,600,000	0.3%		15	New Jersey	88,400,000	0.3%
24	Kansas	54,300,000	0.2%		16	Hawaii	81,400,000	0.3%
16	Kentucky	81,400,000	0.3%		16	Kentucky	81,400,000	0.3%
26	Louisiana	39,200,000	0.1%		18	Iowa	73,600,000	0.3%
46	Maine	700,000	0.0%		19	South Carolina	72,400,000	0.3%
36	Maryland	10,000,000	0.0%		20	Mississippi	57,600,000	0.2%
39	Massachusetts	3,800,000	0.0%		21	Indiana	57,300,000	0.2%
10	Michigan	143,900,000	0.5%		22	California	55,200,000	0.2%
25	Minnesota	42,500,000	0.2%		23	New Mexico	54,500,000	0.2%
20	Mississippi	57,600,000	0.2%		24	Kansas	54,300,000	0.2%
27	Missouri	30,700,000	0.1%		25	Minnesota	42,500,000	0.2%
38	Montana	3,900,000	0.0%		26	Louisiana	39,200,000	0.1%
8	Nebraska	239,700,000	0.9%		27	Missouri	30,700,000	0.1%
49	Nevada	200,000	0.0%		28	Oklahoma	29,400,000	0.1%
44	New Hampshire	1,200,000	0.0%		29	Illinois	27,600,000	0.1%
15	New Jersey	88,400,000	0.3%		30	Arkansas	25,900,000	0.1%
23	New Mexico	54,500,000	0.2%		31	Alaska	21,700,000	0.1%
13	New York	115,600,000	0.4%		32	South Dakota	18,500,000	0.1%
6	North Carolina	289,100,000	1.1%		33	Tennessee	15,700,000	0.1%
35	North Dakota	11,000,000	0.0%		34	Washington	11,900,000	0.0%
7	Ohio	274,400,000	1.0%		35	North Dakota	11,000,000	0.0%
28	Oklahoma	29,400,000	0.1%		36	Maryland	10,000,000	0.0%
47	Oregon	600,000	0.0%		37	Vermont	4,200,000	0.0%
3	Pennsylvania	484,200,000	1.8%		38	Montana	3,900,000	0.0%
47	Rhode Island	600,000	0.0%		39	Massachusetts	3,800,000	0.0%
19	South Carolina	72,400,000	0.3%		40	Arizona	3,100,000	0.0%
32	South Dakota	18,500,000	0.1%		41	Delaware	2,500,000	0.0%
33	Tennessee	15,700,000	0.1%		42	Utah	2,200,000	0.0%
5	Texas	309,500,000	1.2%		43	Wyoming	1,400,000	0.0%
42	Utah	2,200,000	0.0%		44	New Hampshire	1,200,000	0.0%
37	Vermont	4,200,000	0.0%		45	Idaho	1,000,000	0.0%
14	Virginia	104,300,000	0.4%		46	Maine	700,000	0.0%
34	Washington	11,900,000	0.0%		47	Oregon	600,000	0.0%
11	West Virginia	141,100,000	0.5%		47	Rhode Island	600,000	0.0%
4	Wisconsin	338,400,000	1.3%		49	Nevada	200,000	0.0%
43	Wyoming	1,400,000	0.0%		50	Connecticut	100,000	0.0%
						District of Columbia	0	0.0%

Source: National Weather Service, Water and Weather Services
"2004 Summary of Hazardous Weather Fatalities" (http://www.nws.noaa.gov/om/severe_weather/state04.pdf)
*Includes lightning, tornado, thunderstorm, extreme temperature, flood, coastal storm, rip current, hurricane, winter storm, fog, avalanche and other weather events. National total does not include damage costs in U.S. territories

Acres Owned by the Federal Government in 2004

National Total = 653,299,090 Acres*

	ALPHA ORDER					RANK ORDER		
RANK	**STATE**	**ACRES**	**% of USA**		**RANK**	**STATE**	**ACRES**	**% of USA**
38	Alabama	513,913	0.1%		1	Alaska	252,495,811	38.6%
1	Alaska	252,495,811	38.6%		2	Nevada	59,362,643	9.1%
4	Arizona	34,933,236	5.3%		3	California	45,393,238	6.9%
20	Arkansas	2,407,948	0.4%		4	Arizona	34,933,236	5.3%
3	California	45,393,238	6.9%		5	Oregon	32,715,514	5.0%
11	Colorado	24,354,713	3.7%		6	New Mexico	32,483,877	5.0%
49	Connecticut	13,938	0.0%		7	Utah	30,271,905	4.6%
48	Delaware	25,874	0.0%		8	Montana	27,910,152	4.3%
18	Florida	2,858,782	0.4%		9	Idaho	26,565,412	4.1%
26	Georgia	1,409,406	0.2%		10	Wyoming	26,391,487	4.0%
31	Hawaii	796,726	0.1%		11	Colorado	24,354,713	3.7%
9	Idaho	26,565,412	4.1%		12	Washington	12,949,662	2.0%
35	Illinois	641,959	0.1%		13	North Carolina	3,710,338	0.6%
39	Indiana	463,245	0.1%		14	Michigan	3,637,873	0.6%
42	Iowa	273,954	0.0%		15	Texas	3,130,345	0.5%
36	Kansas	631,351	0.1%		16	South Dakota	3,028,003	0.5%
27	Kentucky	1,378,677	0.2%		17	Minnesota	2,873,517	0.4%
25	Louisiana	1,474,788	0.2%		18	Florida	2,858,782	0.4%
44	Maine	208,422	0.0%		19	Virginia	2,534,178	0.4%
45	Maryland	178,527	0.0%		20	Arkansas	2,407,948	0.4%
47	Massachusetts	93,950	0.0%		21	Missouri	2,224,788	0.3%
14	Michigan	3,637,873	0.6%		22	Mississippi	2,196,940	0.3%
17	Minnesota	2,873,517	0.4%		23	Wisconsin	1,971,902	0.3%
22	Mississippi	2,196,940	0.3%		24	Oklahoma	1,586,148	0.2%
21	Missouri	2,224,788	0.3%		25	Louisiana	1,474,788	0.2%
8	Montana	27,910,152	4.3%		26	Georgia	1,409,406	0.2%
34	Nebraska	665,481	0.1%		27	Kentucky	1,378,677	0.2%
2	Nevada	59,362,643	9.1%		28	North Dakota	1,185,777	0.2%
32	New Hampshire	775,665	0.1%		29	West Virginia	1,146,211	0.2%
46	New Jersey	148,441	0.0%		30	Tennessee	865,837	0.1%
6	New Mexico	32,483,877	5.0%		31	Hawaii	796,726	0.1%
43	New York	233,533	0.0%		32	New Hampshire	775,665	0.1%
13	North Carolina	3,710,338	0.6%		33	Pennsylvania	719,864	0.1%
28	North Dakota	1,185,777	0.2%		34	Nebraska	665,481	0.1%
40	Ohio	448,381	0.1%		35	Illinois	641,959	0.1%
24	Oklahoma	1,586,148	0.2%		36	Kansas	631,351	0.1%
5	Oregon	32,715,514	5.0%		37	South Carolina	560,956	0.1%
33	Pennsylvania	719,864	0.1%		38	Alabama	513,913	0.1%
50	Rhode Island	2,923	0.0%		39	Indiana	463,245	0.1%
37	South Carolina	560,956	0.1%		40	Ohio	448,381	0.1%
16	South Dakota	3,028,003	0.5%		41	Vermont	443,249	0.1%
30	Tennessee	865,837	0.1%		42	Iowa	273,954	0.0%
15	Texas	3,130,345	0.5%		43	New York	233,533	0.0%
7	Utah	30,271,905	4.6%		44	Maine	208,422	0.0%
41	Vermont	443,249	0.1%		45	Maryland	178,527	0.0%
19	Virginia	2,534,178	0.4%		46	New Jersey	148,441	0.0%
12	Washington	12,949,662	2.0%		47	Massachusetts	93,950	0.0%
29	West Virginia	1,146,211	0.2%		48	Delaware	25,874	0.0%
23	Wisconsin	1,971,902	0.3%		49	Connecticut	13,938	0.0%
10	Wyoming	26,391,487	4.0%		50	Rhode Island	2,923	0.0%
						District of Columbia	9,631	0.0%

Source: Government Services Administration, Office of Governmentwide Real Property Policy
  "Federal Real Property Profile" (http://www.gsa.gov/realpropertyprofile)
As of September 30, 2004. Does not include land owned by the federal government in U.S. territories or in foreign countries.

Percent of Land Owned by the Federal Government in 2004

National Percent = 28.8%*

<table>
<thead>
<tr><th colspan="3">ALPHA ORDER</th><th colspan="3">RANK ORDER</th></tr>
<tr><th>RANK</th><th>STATE</th><th>PERCENT</th><th>RANK</th><th>STATE</th><th>PERCENT</th></tr>
</thead>
<tbody>
<tr><td>43</td><td>Alabama</td><td>1.6</td><td>1</td><td>Nevada</td><td>84.5</td></tr>
<tr><td>2</td><td>Alaska</td><td>69.1</td><td>2</td><td>Alaska</td><td>69.1</td></tr>
<tr><td>6</td><td>Arizona</td><td>48.1</td><td>3</td><td>Utah</td><td>57.5</td></tr>
<tr><td>22</td><td>Arkansas</td><td>7.2</td><td>4</td><td>Oregon</td><td>53.1</td></tr>
<tr><td>7</td><td>California</td><td>45.3</td><td>5</td><td>Idaho</td><td>50.2</td></tr>
<tr><td>10</td><td>Colorado</td><td>36.6</td><td>6</td><td>Arizona</td><td>48.1</td></tr>
<tr><td>49</td><td>Connecticut</td><td>0.4</td><td>7</td><td>California</td><td>45.3</td></tr>
<tr><td>37</td><td>Delaware</td><td>2.0</td><td>8</td><td>Wyoming</td><td>42.3</td></tr>
<tr><td>18</td><td>Florida</td><td>8.2</td><td>9</td><td>New Mexico</td><td>41.8</td></tr>
<tr><td>29</td><td>Georgia</td><td>3.8</td><td>10</td><td>Colorado</td><td>36.6</td></tr>
<tr><td>13</td><td>Hawaii</td><td>19.4</td><td>11</td><td>Washington</td><td>30.3</td></tr>
<tr><td>5</td><td>Idaho</td><td>50.2</td><td>12</td><td>Montana</td><td>29.9</td></tr>
<tr><td>41</td><td>Illinois</td><td>1.8</td><td>13</td><td>Hawaii</td><td>19.4</td></tr>
<tr><td>37</td><td>Indiana</td><td>2.0</td><td>14</td><td>New Hampshire</td><td>13.5</td></tr>
<tr><td>47</td><td>Iowa</td><td>0.8</td><td>15</td><td>North Carolina</td><td>11.8</td></tr>
<tr><td>45</td><td>Kansas</td><td>1.2</td><td>16</td><td>Michigan</td><td>10.0</td></tr>
<tr><td>26</td><td>Kentucky</td><td>5.4</td><td>17</td><td>Virginia</td><td>9.9</td></tr>
<tr><td>27</td><td>Louisiana</td><td>5.1</td><td>18</td><td>Florida</td><td>8.2</td></tr>
<tr><td>46</td><td>Maine</td><td>1.1</td><td>19</td><td>Vermont</td><td>7.5</td></tr>
<tr><td>34</td><td>Maryland</td><td>2.8</td><td>20</td><td>West Virginia</td><td>7.4</td></tr>
<tr><td>39</td><td>Massachusetts</td><td>1.9</td><td>21</td><td>Mississippi</td><td>7.3</td></tr>
<tr><td>16</td><td>Michigan</td><td>10.0</td><td>22</td><td>Arkansas</td><td>7.2</td></tr>
<tr><td>24</td><td>Minnesota</td><td>5.6</td><td>23</td><td>South Dakota</td><td>6.2</td></tr>
<tr><td>21</td><td>Mississippi</td><td>7.3</td><td>24</td><td>Minnesota</td><td>5.6</td></tr>
<tr><td>28</td><td>Missouri</td><td>5.0</td><td>24</td><td>Wisconsin</td><td>5.6</td></tr>
<tr><td>12</td><td>Montana</td><td>29.9</td><td>26</td><td>Kentucky</td><td>5.4</td></tr>
<tr><td>44</td><td>Nebraska</td><td>1.4</td><td>27</td><td>Louisiana</td><td>5.1</td></tr>
<tr><td>1</td><td>Nevada</td><td>84.5</td><td>28</td><td>Missouri</td><td>5.0</td></tr>
<tr><td>14</td><td>New Hampshire</td><td>13.5</td><td>29</td><td>Georgia</td><td>3.8</td></tr>
<tr><td>32</td><td>New Jersey</td><td>3.1</td><td>30</td><td>Oklahoma</td><td>3.6</td></tr>
<tr><td>9</td><td>New Mexico</td><td>41.8</td><td>31</td><td>Tennessee</td><td>3.2</td></tr>
<tr><td>47</td><td>New York</td><td>0.8</td><td>32</td><td>New Jersey</td><td>3.1</td></tr>
<tr><td>15</td><td>North Carolina</td><td>11.8</td><td>33</td><td>South Carolina</td><td>2.9</td></tr>
<tr><td>35</td><td>North Dakota</td><td>2.7</td><td>34</td><td>Maryland</td><td>2.8</td></tr>
<tr><td>42</td><td>Ohio</td><td>1.7</td><td>35</td><td>North Dakota</td><td>2.7</td></tr>
<tr><td>30</td><td>Oklahoma</td><td>3.6</td><td>36</td><td>Pennsylvania</td><td>2.5</td></tr>
<tr><td>4</td><td>Oregon</td><td>53.1</td><td>37</td><td>Delaware</td><td>2.0</td></tr>
<tr><td>36</td><td>Pennsylvania</td><td>2.5</td><td>37</td><td>Indiana</td><td>2.0</td></tr>
<tr><td>49</td><td>Rhode Island</td><td>0.4</td><td>39</td><td>Massachusetts</td><td>1.9</td></tr>
<tr><td>33</td><td>South Carolina</td><td>2.9</td><td>39</td><td>Texas</td><td>1.9</td></tr>
<tr><td>23</td><td>South Dakota</td><td>6.2</td><td>41</td><td>Illinois</td><td>1.8</td></tr>
<tr><td>31</td><td>Tennessee</td><td>3.2</td><td>42</td><td>Ohio</td><td>1.7</td></tr>
<tr><td>39</td><td>Texas</td><td>1.9</td><td>43</td><td>Alabama</td><td>1.6</td></tr>
<tr><td>3</td><td>Utah</td><td>57.5</td><td>44</td><td>Nebraska</td><td>1.4</td></tr>
<tr><td>19</td><td>Vermont</td><td>7.5</td><td>45</td><td>Kansas</td><td>1.2</td></tr>
<tr><td>17</td><td>Virginia</td><td>9.9</td><td>46</td><td>Maine</td><td>1.1</td></tr>
<tr><td>11</td><td>Washington</td><td>30.3</td><td>47</td><td>Iowa</td><td>0.8</td></tr>
<tr><td>20</td><td>West Virginia</td><td>7.4</td><td>47</td><td>New York</td><td>0.8</td></tr>
<tr><td>24</td><td>Wisconsin</td><td>5.6</td><td>49</td><td>Connecticut</td><td>0.4</td></tr>
<tr><td>8</td><td>Wyoming</td><td>42.3</td><td>49</td><td>Rhode Island</td><td>0.4</td></tr>
<tr><td></td><td></td><td></td><td></td><td>District of Columbia</td><td>24.7</td></tr>
</tbody>
</table>

Source: Government Services Administration, Office of Governmentwide Real Property Policy
    "Federal Real Property Profile" (http://www.gsa.gov/realpropertyprofile)
*As of September 30, 2004. Does not include land owned by the federal government in U.S. territories or in foreign countries.

National Park Service Land in 2005

National Total = 84,552,445 Acres*

ALPHA ORDER				RANK ORDER			
RANK	STATE	ACRES	% of USA	RANK	STATE	ACRES	% of USA
41	Alabama	21,081	0.0%	1	Alaska	54,638,794	64.6%
1	Alaska	54,638,794	64.6%	2	California	8,093,122	9.6%
3	Arizona	2,962,821	3.5%	3	Arizona	2,962,821	3.5%
25	Arkansas	104,976	0.1%	4	Florida	2,637,762	3.1%
2	California	8,093,122	9.6%	5	Wyoming	2,396,340	2.8%
13	Colorado	673,296	0.8%	6	Utah	2,117,196	2.5%
46	Connecticut	7,782	0.0%	7	Washington	1,964,486	2.3%
50	Delaware	0	0.0%	8	Montana	1,273,443	1.5%
4	Florida	2,637,762	3.1%	9	Texas	1,236,404	1.5%
34	Georgia	62,885	0.1%	10	Nevada	778,512	0.9%
17	Hawaii	364,999	0.4%	11	Idaho	767,133	0.9%
11	Idaho	767,133	0.9%	12	Michigan	718,186	0.8%
48	Illinois	13	0.0%	13	Colorado	673,296	0.8%
43	Indiana	15,293	0.0%	14	North Carolina	405,832	0.5%
47	Iowa	2,713	0.0%	15	New Mexico	391,029	0.5%
44	Kansas	11,792	0.0%	16	Tennessee	382,554	0.5%
27	Kentucky	94,997	0.1%	17	Hawaii	364,999	0.4%
40	Louisiana	21,130	0.0%	18	Virginia	361,312	0.4%
29	Maine	90,258	0.1%	19	South Dakota	307,746	0.4%
33	Maryland	72,150	0.1%	20	Minnesota	301,333	0.4%
35	Massachusetts	57,897	0.1%	21	Oregon	199,085	0.2%
12	Michigan	718,186	0.8%	22	Pennsylvania	135,734	0.2%
20	Minnesota	301,333	0.4%	23	Wisconsin	133,754	0.2%
24	Mississippi	117,141	0.1%	24	Mississippi	117,141	0.1%
30	Missouri	83,467	0.1%	25	Arkansas	104,976	0.1%
8	Montana	1,273,443	1.5%	26	New Jersey	99,100	0.1%
38	Nebraska	29,376	0.0%	27	Kentucky	94,997	0.1%
10	Nevada	778,512	0.9%	28	West Virginia	92,606	0.1%
42	New Hampshire	15,856	0.0%	29	Maine	90,258	0.1%
26	New Jersey	99,100	0.1%	30	Missouri	83,467	0.1%
15	New Mexico	391,029	0.5%	31	North Dakota	72,581	0.1%
32	New York	72,558	0.1%	32	New York	72,558	0.1%
14	North Carolina	405,832	0.5%	33	Maryland	72,150	0.1%
31	North Dakota	72,581	0.1%	34	Georgia	62,885	0.1%
36	Ohio	34,154	0.0%	35	Massachusetts	57,897	0.1%
45	Oklahoma	10,202	0.0%	36	Ohio	34,154	0.0%
21	Oregon	199,085	0.2%	37	South Carolina	32,583	0.0%
22	Pennsylvania	135,734	0.2%	38	Nebraska	29,376	0.0%
49	Rhode Island	5	0.0%	39	Vermont	22,178	0.0%
37	South Carolina	32,583	0.0%	40	Louisiana	21,130	0.0%
19	South Dakota	307,746	0.4%	41	Alabama	21,081	0.0%
16	Tennessee	382,554	0.5%	42	New Hampshire	15,856	0.0%
9	Texas	1,236,404	1.5%	43	Indiana	15,293	0.0%
6	Utah	2,117,196	2.5%	44	Kansas	11,792	0.0%
39	Vermont	22,178	0.0%	45	Oklahoma	10,202	0.0%
18	Virginia	361,312	0.4%	46	Connecticut	7,782	0.0%
7	Washington	1,964,486	2.3%	47	Iowa	2,713	0.0%
28	West Virginia	92,606	0.1%	48	Illinois	13	0.0%
23	Wisconsin	133,754	0.2%	49	Rhode Island	5	0.0%
5	Wyoming	2,396,340	2.8%	50	Delaware	0	0.0%
					District of Columbia	7,083	0.0%

Source: National Park Service
   "Listing of Acreage by State" (unpublished data)
*As of December 31, 2005. Includes federal and nonfederal land in national parks, monuments, historic sites, recreation areas, preserves, battlefields, grasslands, seashores, parkways, trails and rivers. Does not include land in national forest or wildlife areas. Includes 59,712 acres in U.S. territories.

Recreation Visits to National Park Service Areas in 2004

National Total = 276,908,337 Visits*

ALPHA ORDER					RANK ORDER			

RANK	STATE	VISITS	% of USA		RANK	STATE	VISITS	% of USA
36	Alabama	726,238	0.3%		1	California	33,054,222	11.9%
27	Alaska	2,296,834	0.8%		2	Virginia	23,092,142	8.3%
5	Arizona	10,681,922	3.9%		3	North Carolina	19,179,280	6.9%
26	Arkansas	2,816,668	1.0%		4	New York	15,204,609	5.5%
1	California	33,054,222	11.9%		5	Arizona	10,681,922	3.9%
17	Colorado	5,374,920	1.9%		6	Massachusetts	9,454,225	3.4%
49	Connecticut	11,333	0.0%		7	Pennsylvania	9,100,357	3.3%
50	Delaware	0	0.0%		8	Florida	9,064,585	3.3%
8	Florida	9,064,585	3.3%		9	Utah	7,952,719	2.9%
14	Georgia	5,918,030	2.1%		10	Tennessee	7,741,291	2.8%
16	Hawaii	5,403,073	2.0%		11	Washington	7,019,800	2.5%
40	Idaho	468,708	0.2%		12	Mississippi	6,569,735	2.4%
41	Illinois	361,349	0.1%		13	Nevada	5,944,867	2.1%
29	Indiana	2,073,250	0.7%		14	Georgia	5,918,030	2.1%
43	Iowa	276,120	0.1%		15	New Jersey	5,542,863	2.0%
45	Kansas	160,285	0.1%		16	Hawaii	5,403,073	2.0%
25	Kentucky	3,305,085	1.2%		17	Colorado	5,374,920	1.9%
37	Louisiana	652,287	0.2%		18	Wyoming	5,363,178	1.9%
28	Maine	2,207,847	0.8%		19	Texas	5,018,588	1.8%
24	Maryland	3,413,476	1.2%		20	Missouri	4,358,468	1.6%
6	Massachusetts	9,454,225	3.4%		21	Montana	4,004,824	1.4%
32	Michigan	1,513,745	0.5%		22	South Dakota	3,729,748	1.3%
38	Minnesota	550,581	0.2%		23	Ohio	3,575,432	1.3%
12	Mississippi	6,569,735	2.4%		24	Maryland	3,413,476	1.2%
20	Missouri	4,358,468	1.6%		25	Kentucky	3,305,085	1.2%
21	Montana	4,004,824	1.4%		26	Arkansas	2,816,668	1.0%
44	Nebraska	226,111	0.1%		27	Alaska	2,296,834	0.8%
13	Nevada	5,944,867	2.1%		28	Maine	2,207,847	0.8%
47	New Hampshire	30,725	0.0%		29	Indiana	2,073,250	0.7%
15	New Jersey	5,542,863	2.0%		30	West Virginia	1,782,442	0.6%
31	New Mexico	1,733,165	0.6%		31	New Mexico	1,733,165	0.6%
4	New York	15,204,609	5.5%		32	Michigan	1,513,745	0.5%
3	North Carolina	19,179,280	6.9%		33	South Carolina	1,438,241	0.5%
39	North Dakota	536,266	0.2%		34	Oklahoma	1,290,466	0.5%
23	Ohio	3,575,432	1.3%		35	Oregon	837,572	0.3%
34	Oklahoma	1,290,466	0.5%		36	Alabama	726,238	0.3%
35	Oregon	837,572	0.3%		37	Louisiana	652,287	0.2%
7	Pennsylvania	9,100,357	3.3%		38	Minnesota	550,581	0.2%
46	Rhode Island	50,677	0.0%		39	North Dakota	536,266	0.2%
33	South Carolina	1,438,241	0.5%		40	Idaho	468,708	0.2%
22	South Dakota	3,729,748	1.3%		41	Illinois	361,349	0.1%
10	Tennessee	7,741,291	2.8%		42	Wisconsin	308,833	0.1%
19	Texas	5,018,588	1.8%		43	Iowa	276,120	0.1%
9	Utah	7,952,719	2.9%		44	Nebraska	226,111	0.1%
48	Vermont	29,205	0.0%		45	Kansas	160,285	0.1%
2	Virginia	23,092,142	8.3%		46	Rhode Island	50,677	0.0%
11	Washington	7,019,800	2.5%		47	New Hampshire	30,725	0.0%
30	West Virginia	1,782,442	0.6%		48	Vermont	29,205	0.0%
42	Wisconsin	308,833	0.1%		49	Connecticut	11,333	0.0%
18	Wyoming	5,363,178	1.9%		50	Delaware	0	0.0%
						District of Columbia	33,429,861	12.1%

Source: National Park Service, Public Use Statistics Office
"National Park Service Statistical Abstract 2004" (http://www2.nature.nps.gov/stats/abst2004.pdf)
*National total includes 2,032,091 visits in U.S. territories.

State Parks, Recreation Areas and Natural Areas in 2004

National Total = 5,793 Areas*

ALPHA ORDER

RANK	STATE	AREAS	% of USA
49	Alabama	24	0.4%
11	Alaska	139	2.4%
44	Arizona	31	0.5%
35	Arkansas	50	0.9%
4	California	278	4.8%
18	Colorado	114	2.0%
12	Connecticut	133	2.3%
41	Delaware	33	0.6%
10	Florida	157	2.7%
26	Georgia	72	1.2%
27	Hawaii	68	1.2%
43	Idaho	32	0.6%
3	Illinois	296	5.1%
41	Indiana	33	0.6%
9	Iowa	182	3.1%
48	Kansas	25	0.4%
35	Kentucky	50	0.9%
30	Louisiana	57	1.0%
13	Maine	131	2.3%
34	Maryland	51	0.9%
6	Massachusetts	241	4.2%
19	Michigan	103	1.8%
8	Minnesota	198	3.4%
47	Mississippi	28	0.5%
23	Missouri	83	1.4%
2	Montana	396	6.8%
22	Nebraska	85	1.5%
49	Nevada	24	0.4%
21	New Hampshire	89	1.5%
17	New Jersey	116	2.0%
44	New Mexico	31	0.5%
1	New York	867	15.0%
29	North Carolina	62	1.1%
46	North Dakota	30	0.5%
24	Ohio	74	1.3%
35	Oklahoma	50	0.9%
7	Oregon	233	4.0%
16	Pennsylvania	119	2.1%
24	Rhode Island	74	1.3%
31	South Carolina	55	0.9%
14	South Dakota	129	2.2%
32	Tennessee	53	0.9%
15	Texas	125	2.2%
33	Utah	52	0.9%
19	Vermont	103	1.8%
39	Virginia	38	0.7%
5	Washington	252	4.4%
38	West Virginia	47	0.8%
27	Wisconsin	68	1.2%
40	Wyoming	36	0.6%

RANK ORDER

RANK	STATE	AREAS	% of USA
1	New York	867	15.0%
2	Montana	396	6.8%
3	Illinois	296	5.1%
4	California	278	4.8%
5	Washington	252	4.4%
6	Massachusetts	241	4.2%
7	Oregon	233	4.0%
8	Minnesota	198	3.4%
9	Iowa	182	3.1%
10	Florida	157	2.7%
11	Alaska	139	2.4%
12	Connecticut	133	2.3%
13	Maine	131	2.3%
14	South Dakota	129	2.2%
15	Texas	125	2.2%
16	Pennsylvania	119	2.1%
17	New Jersey	116	2.0%
18	Colorado	114	2.0%
19	Michigan	103	1.8%
19	Vermont	103	1.8%
21	New Hampshire	89	1.5%
22	Nebraska	85	1.5%
23	Missouri	83	1.4%
24	Ohio	74	1.3%
24	Rhode Island	74	1.3%
26	Georgia	72	1.2%
27	Hawaii	68	1.2%
27	Wisconsin	68	1.2%
29	North Carolina	62	1.1%
30	Louisiana	57	1.0%
31	South Carolina	55	0.9%
32	Tennessee	53	0.9%
33	Utah	52	0.9%
34	Maryland	51	0.9%
35	Arkansas	50	0.9%
35	Kentucky	50	0.9%
35	Oklahoma	50	0.9%
38	West Virginia	47	0.8%
39	Virginia	38	0.7%
40	Wyoming	36	0.6%
41	Delaware	33	0.6%
41	Indiana	33	0.6%
43	Idaho	32	0.6%
44	Arizona	31	0.5%
44	New Mexico	31	0.5%
46	North Dakota	30	0.5%
47	Mississippi	28	0.5%
48	Kansas	25	0.4%
49	Alabama	24	0.4%
49	Nevada	24	0.4%
	District of Columbia**	NA	NA

Source: The National Association of State Parks Directors
    "The 2005 Annual Information Exchange" (http://www.naspd.org/)
*For the period July 1, 2003 through June 30, 2004. Includes operating and nonoperating state parks, recreation areas, natural areas and other areas.
**Not available.

Visitors to State Parks and Recreation Areas in 2004

National Total = 718,858,489 Visitors*

ALPHA ORDER

RANK	STATE	VISITORS	% of USA
35	Alabama	4,397,182	0.6%
37	Alaska	4,002,570	0.6%
46	Arizona	2,195,917	0.3%
23	Arkansas	9,804,639	1.4%
1	California	82,031,611	11.4%
18	Colorado	12,145,561	1.7%
32	Connecticut	6,573,381	0.9%
38	Delaware	3,927,146	0.5%
10	Florida	19,117,944	2.7%
17	Georgia	12,764,864	1.8%
25	Hawaii	9,221,298	1.3%
43	Idaho	2,782,272	0.4%
5	Illinois	43,327,764	6.0%
11	Indiana	18,341,243	2.6%
14	Iowa	14,628,428	2.0%
31	Kansas	7,280,720	1.0%
29	Kentucky	7,597,611	1.1%
47	Louisiana	2,086,735	0.3%
45	Maine	2,226,262	0.3%
20	Maryland	10,742,810	1.5%
21	Massachusetts	10,050,913	1.4%
9	Michigan	20,451,534	2.8%
28	Minnesota	7,819,666	1.1%
40	Mississippi	3,128,072	0.4%
12	Missouri	17,046,931	2.4%
48	Montana	1,485,489	0.2%
22	Nebraska	9,885,628	1.4%
36	Nevada	4,148,777	0.6%
42	New Hampshire	2,850,965	0.4%
15	New Jersey	14,123,509	2.0%
39	New Mexico	3,840,234	0.5%
2	New York	53,524,966	7.4%
19	North Carolina	11,275,117	1.6%
49	North Dakota	1,048,530	0.1%
3	Ohio	53,371,001	7.4%
16	Oklahoma	14,085,522	2.0%
4	Oregon	45,144,475	6.3%
7	Pennsylvania	34,692,235	4.8%
41	Rhode Island	3,071,536	0.4%
30	South Carolina	7,367,371	1.0%
26	South Dakota	9,216,721	1.3%
8	Tennessee	28,161,581	3.9%
24	Texas	9,715,728	1.4%
34	Utah	5,867,074	0.8%
50	Vermont	679,614	0.1%
33	Virginia	6,125,745	0.9%
6	Washington	40,409,572	5.6%
27	West Virginia	7,833,092	1.1%
13	Wisconsin	14,967,419	2.1%
44	Wyoming	2,273,514	0.3%

RANK ORDER

RANK	STATE	VISITORS	% of USA
1	California	82,031,611	11.4%
2	New York	53,524,966	7.4%
3	Ohio	53,371,001	7.4%
4	Oregon	45,144,475	6.3%
5	Illinois	43,327,764	6.0%
6	Washington	40,409,572	5.6%
7	Pennsylvania	34,692,235	4.8%
8	Tennessee	28,161,581	3.9%
9	Michigan	20,451,534	2.8%
10	Florida	19,117,944	2.7%
11	Indiana	18,341,243	2.6%
12	Missouri	17,046,931	2.4%
13	Wisconsin	14,967,419	2.1%
14	Iowa	14,628,428	2.0%
15	New Jersey	14,123,509	2.0%
16	Oklahoma	14,085,522	2.0%
17	Georgia	12,764,864	1.8%
18	Colorado	12,145,561	1.7%
19	North Carolina	11,275,117	1.6%
20	Maryland	10,742,810	1.5%
21	Massachusetts	10,050,913	1.4%
22	Nebraska	9,885,628	1.4%
23	Arkansas	9,804,639	1.4%
24	Texas	9,715,728	1.4%
25	Hawaii	9,221,298	1.3%
26	South Dakota	9,216,721	1.3%
27	West Virginia	7,833,092	1.1%
28	Minnesota	7,819,666	1.1%
29	Kentucky	7,597,611	1.1%
30	South Carolina	7,367,371	1.0%
31	Kansas	7,280,720	1.0%
32	Connecticut	6,573,381	0.9%
33	Virginia	6,125,745	0.9%
34	Utah	5,867,074	0.8%
35	Alabama	4,397,182	0.6%
36	Nevada	4,148,777	0.6%
37	Alaska	4,002,570	0.6%
38	Delaware	3,927,146	0.5%
39	New Mexico	3,840,234	0.5%
40	Mississippi	3,128,072	0.4%
41	Rhode Island	3,071,536	0.4%
42	New Hampshire	2,850,965	0.4%
43	Idaho	2,782,272	0.4%
44	Wyoming	2,273,514	0.3%
45	Maine	2,226,262	0.3%
46	Arizona	2,195,917	0.3%
47	Louisiana	2,086,735	0.3%
48	Montana	1,485,489	0.2%
49	North Dakota	1,048,530	0.1%
50	Vermont	679,614	0.1%
	District of Columbia**	NA	NA

Source: The National Association of State Parks Directors
   "The 2005 Annual Information Exchange" (http://www.naspd.org/)
For the period July 1, 2003 through June 30, 2004. Includes operating and nonoperating state parks, recreation areas, natural areas and other areas. Includes day and overnight visitors.
**Not available.*

IX. GOVERNMENT FINANCE: FEDERAL

Internal Revenue Service Gross Collections in 2004

National Total = $2,018,502,103,000*

<table>
<tr><td colspan="4">ALPHA ORDER</td><td colspan="4">RANK ORDER</td></tr>
<tr><th>RANK</th><th>STATE</th><th>COLLECTIONS</th><th>% of USA</th><th>RANK</th><th>STATE</th><th>COLLECTIONS</th><th>% of USA</th></tr>
<tr><td>28</td><td>Alabama</td><td>$18,489,339,000</td><td>0.9%</td><td>1</td><td>California</td><td>$237,931,491,000</td><td>11.8%</td></tr>
<tr><td>46</td><td>Alaska</td><td>3,267,127,000</td><td>0.2%</td><td>2</td><td>New York</td><td>171,948,716,000</td><td>8.5%</td></tr>
<tr><td>23</td><td>Arizona</td><td>25,344,852,000</td><td>1.3%</td><td>3</td><td>Texas</td><td>152,691,189,000</td><td>7.6%</td></tr>
<tr><td>24</td><td>Arkansas</td><td>20,576,284,000</td><td>1.0%</td><td>4</td><td>Illinois</td><td>108,476,636,000</td><td>5.4%</td></tr>
<tr><td>1</td><td>California</td><td>237,931,491,000</td><td>11.8%</td><td>5</td><td>Florida</td><td>94,277,725,000</td><td>4.7%</td></tr>
<tr><td>21</td><td>Colorado</td><td>34,660,999,000</td><td>1.7%</td><td>6</td><td>New Jersey</td><td>91,082,077,000</td><td>4.5%</td></tr>
<tr><td>16</td><td>Connecticut</td><td>41,909,468,000</td><td>2.1%</td><td>7</td><td>Ohio</td><td>87,853,784,000</td><td>4.4%</td></tr>
<tr><td>35</td><td>Delaware</td><td>11,151,222,000</td><td>0.6%</td><td>8</td><td>Pennsylvania</td><td>87,841,245,000</td><td>4.4%</td></tr>
<tr><td>5</td><td>Florida</td><td>94,277,725,000</td><td>4.7%</td><td>9</td><td>Michigan</td><td>63,744,637,000</td><td>3.2%</td></tr>
<tr><td>10</td><td>Georgia</td><td>59,083,748,000</td><td>2.9%</td><td>10</td><td>Georgia</td><td>59,083,748,000</td><td>2.9%</td></tr>
<tr><td>39</td><td>Hawaii</td><td>8,394,777,000</td><td>0.4%</td><td>11</td><td>Massachusetts</td><td>59,060,000,000</td><td>2.9%</td></tr>
<tr><td>41</td><td>Idaho</td><td>6,479,611,000</td><td>0.3%</td><td>12</td><td>Minnesota</td><td>58,068,156,000</td><td>2.9%</td></tr>
<tr><td>4</td><td>Illinois</td><td>108,476,636,000</td><td>5.4%</td><td>13</td><td>North Carolina</td><td>53,979,373,000</td><td>2.7%</td></tr>
<tr><td>22</td><td>Indiana</td><td>32,192,435,000</td><td>1.6%</td><td>14</td><td>Virginia</td><td>47,016,582,000</td><td>2.3%</td></tr>
<tr><td>32</td><td>Iowa</td><td>14,543,095,000</td><td>0.7%</td><td>15</td><td>Washington</td><td>42,167,997,000</td><td>2.1%</td></tr>
<tr><td>30</td><td>Kansas</td><td>15,897,378,000</td><td>0.8%</td><td>16</td><td>Connecticut</td><td>41,909,468,000</td><td>2.1%</td></tr>
<tr><td>29</td><td>Kentucky</td><td>17,515,169,000</td><td>0.9%</td><td>17</td><td>Maryland</td><td>40,893,427,000</td><td>2.0%</td></tr>
<tr><td>26</td><td>Louisiana</td><td>20,340,779,000</td><td>1.0%</td><td>18</td><td>Missouri</td><td>38,326,485,000</td><td>1.9%</td></tr>
<tr><td>43</td><td>Maine</td><td>5,486,728,000</td><td>0.3%</td><td>19</td><td>Tennessee</td><td>36,802,257,000</td><td>1.8%</td></tr>
<tr><td>17</td><td>Maryland</td><td>40,893,427,000</td><td>2.0%</td><td>20</td><td>Wisconsin</td><td>34,711,183,000</td><td>1.7%</td></tr>
<tr><td>11</td><td>Massachusetts</td><td>59,060,000,000</td><td>2.9%</td><td>21</td><td>Colorado</td><td>34,660,999,000</td><td>1.7%</td></tr>
<tr><td>9</td><td>Michigan</td><td>63,744,637,000</td><td>3.2%</td><td>22</td><td>Indiana</td><td>32,192,435,000</td><td>1.6%</td></tr>
<tr><td>12</td><td>Minnesota</td><td>58,068,156,000</td><td>2.9%</td><td>23</td><td>Arizona</td><td>25,344,852,000</td><td>1.3%</td></tr>
<tr><td>37</td><td>Mississippi</td><td>8,951,397,000</td><td>0.4%</td><td>24</td><td>Arkansas</td><td>20,576,284,000</td><td>1.0%</td></tr>
<tr><td>18</td><td>Missouri</td><td>38,326,485,000</td><td>1.9%</td><td>25</td><td>Oklahoma</td><td>20,418,765,000</td><td>1.0%</td></tr>
<tr><td>47</td><td>Montana</td><td>3,134,044,000</td><td>0.2%</td><td>26</td><td>Louisiana</td><td>20,340,779,000</td><td>1.0%</td></tr>
<tr><td>33</td><td>Nebraska</td><td>14,392,629,000</td><td>0.7%</td><td>27</td><td>Oregon</td><td>18,880,258,000</td><td>0.9%</td></tr>
<tr><td>34</td><td>Nevada</td><td>13,293,706,000</td><td>0.7%</td><td>28</td><td>Alabama</td><td>18,489,339,000</td><td>0.9%</td></tr>
<tr><td>40</td><td>New Hampshire</td><td>7,183,339,000</td><td>0.4%</td><td>29</td><td>Kentucky</td><td>17,515,169,000</td><td>0.9%</td></tr>
<tr><td>6</td><td>New Jersey</td><td>91,082,077,000</td><td>4.5%</td><td>30</td><td>Kansas</td><td>15,897,378,000</td><td>0.8%</td></tr>
<tr><td>42</td><td>New Mexico</td><td>6,050,390,000</td><td>0.3%</td><td>31</td><td>South Carolina</td><td>15,357,129,000</td><td>0.8%</td></tr>
<tr><td>2</td><td>New York</td><td>171,948,716,000</td><td>8.5%</td><td>32</td><td>Iowa</td><td>14,543,095,000</td><td>0.7%</td></tr>
<tr><td>13</td><td>North Carolina</td><td>53,979,373,000</td><td>2.7%</td><td>33</td><td>Nebraska</td><td>14,392,629,000</td><td>0.7%</td></tr>
<tr><td>50</td><td>North Dakota</td><td>2,825,077,000</td><td>0.1%</td><td>34</td><td>Nevada</td><td>13,293,706,000</td><td>0.7%</td></tr>
<tr><td>7</td><td>Ohio</td><td>87,853,784,000</td><td>4.4%</td><td>35</td><td>Delaware</td><td>11,151,222,000</td><td>0.6%</td></tr>
<tr><td>25</td><td>Oklahoma</td><td>20,418,765,000</td><td>1.0%</td><td>36</td><td>Utah</td><td>9,593,606,000</td><td>0.5%</td></tr>
<tr><td>27</td><td>Oregon</td><td>18,880,258,000</td><td>0.9%</td><td>37</td><td>Mississippi</td><td>8,951,397,000</td><td>0.4%</td></tr>
<tr><td>8</td><td>Pennsylvania</td><td>87,841,245,000</td><td>4.4%</td><td>38</td><td>Rhode Island</td><td>8,544,847,000</td><td>0.4%</td></tr>
<tr><td>38</td><td>Rhode Island</td><td>8,544,847,000</td><td>0.4%</td><td>39</td><td>Hawaii</td><td>8,394,777,000</td><td>0.4%</td></tr>
<tr><td>31</td><td>South Carolina</td><td>15,357,129,000</td><td>0.8%</td><td>40</td><td>New Hampshire</td><td>7,183,339,000</td><td>0.4%</td></tr>
<tr><td>45</td><td>South Dakota</td><td>3,293,837,000</td><td>0.2%</td><td>41</td><td>Idaho</td><td>6,479,611,000</td><td>0.3%</td></tr>
<tr><td>19</td><td>Tennessee</td><td>36,802,257,000</td><td>1.8%</td><td>42</td><td>New Mexico</td><td>6,050,390,000</td><td>0.3%</td></tr>
<tr><td>3</td><td>Texas</td><td>152,691,189,000</td><td>7.6%</td><td>43</td><td>Maine</td><td>5,486,728,000</td><td>0.3%</td></tr>
<tr><td>36</td><td>Utah</td><td>9,593,606,000</td><td>0.5%</td><td>44</td><td>West Virginia</td><td>5,226,420,000</td><td>0.3%</td></tr>
<tr><td>48</td><td>Vermont</td><td>3,079,343,000</td><td>0.2%</td><td>45</td><td>South Dakota</td><td>3,293,837,000</td><td>0.2%</td></tr>
<tr><td>14</td><td>Virginia</td><td>47,016,582,000</td><td>2.3%</td><td>46</td><td>Alaska</td><td>3,267,127,000</td><td>0.2%</td></tr>
<tr><td>15</td><td>Washington</td><td>42,167,997,000</td><td>2.1%</td><td>47</td><td>Montana</td><td>3,134,044,000</td><td>0.2%</td></tr>
<tr><td>44</td><td>West Virginia</td><td>5,226,420,000</td><td>0.3%</td><td>48</td><td>Vermont</td><td>3,079,343,000</td><td>0.2%</td></tr>
<tr><td>20</td><td>Wisconsin</td><td>34,711,183,000</td><td>1.7%</td><td>49</td><td>Wyoming</td><td>2,933,993,000</td><td>0.1%</td></tr>
<tr><td>49</td><td>Wyoming</td><td>2,933,993,000</td><td>0.1%</td><td>50</td><td>North Dakota</td><td>2,825,077,000</td><td>0.1%</td></tr>
<tr><td></td><td></td><td></td><td></td><td></td><td>District of Columbia</td><td>16,930,784,000</td><td>0.8%</td></tr>
</table>

Source: U.S. Department of the Treasury, Internal Revenue Service
   "Tax Collections" (http://www.irs.gov/)
*Total includes $27,971,167,000 from U.S. citizens abroad and other miscellaneous returns not shown separately.

Per Capita Internal Revenue Service Gross Collections in 2004

National Per Capita = $6,818*

ALPHA ORDER

ALPHA ORDER

RANK	STATE	PER CAPITA
44	Alabama	$4,086
34	Alaska	4,967
40	Arizona	4,416
12	Arkansas	7,482
19	California	6,638
11	Colorado	7,532
2	Connecticut	11,978
1	Delaware	13,434
31	Florida	5,423
20	Georgia	6,625
18	Hawaii	6,651
37	Idaho	4,644
7	Illinois	8,533
33	Indiana	5,170
36	Iowa	4,925
26	Kansas	5,815
42	Kentucky	4,229
38	Louisiana	4,513
43	Maine	4,172
13	Maryland	7,353
5	Massachusetts	9,217
22	Michigan	6,309
3	Minnesota	11,394
49	Mississippi	3,086
17	Missouri	6,654
47	Montana	3,381
8	Nebraska	8,235
29	Nevada	5,698
30	New Hampshire	5,529
4	New Jersey	10,487
48	New Mexico	3,179
6	New York	8,918
21	North Carolina	6,320
39	North Dakota	4,440
10	Ohio	7,673
28	Oklahoma	5,795
32	Oregon	5,257
14	Pennsylvania	7,087
9	Rhode Island	7,913
46	South Carolina	3,658
41	South Dakota	4,274
25	Tennessee	6,245
15	Texas	6,795
45	Utah	3,963
35	Vermont	4,957
24	Virginia	6,285
16	Washington	6,794
50	West Virginia	2,883
23	Wisconsin	6,307
27	Wyoming	5,800

RANK ORDER

RANK	STATE	PER CAPITA
1	Delaware	$13,434
2	Connecticut	11,978
3	Minnesota	11,394
4	New Jersey	10,487
5	Massachusetts	9,217
6	New York	8,918
7	Illinois	8,533
8	Nebraska	8,235
9	Rhode Island	7,913
10	Ohio	7,673
11	Colorado	7,532
12	Arkansas	7,482
13	Maryland	7,353
14	Pennsylvania	7,087
15	Texas	6,795
16	Washington	6,794
17	Missouri	6,654
18	Hawaii	6,651
19	California	6,638
20	Georgia	6,625
21	North Carolina	6,320
22	Michigan	6,309
23	Wisconsin	6,307
24	Virginia	6,285
25	Tennessee	6,245
26	Kansas	5,815
27	Wyoming	5,800
28	Oklahoma	5,795
29	Nevada	5,698
30	New Hampshire	5,529
31	Florida	5,423
32	Oregon	5,257
33	Indiana	5,170
34	Alaska	4,967
35	Vermont	4,957
36	Iowa	4,925
37	Idaho	4,644
38	Louisiana	4,513
39	North Dakota	4,440
40	Arizona	4,416
41	South Dakota	4,274
42	Kentucky	4,229
43	Maine	4,172
44	Alabama	4,086
45	Utah	3,963
46	South Carolina	3,658
47	Montana	3,381
48	New Mexico	3,179
49	Mississippi	3,086
50	West Virginia	2,883
	District of Columbia	30,548

Source: Morgan Quitno Press using data from U.S. Department of the Treasury, Internal Revenue Service
     "Tax Collections" (http://www.irs.gov/)
*National per capita does not include collections from U.S. citizens abroad and other miscellaneous returns not
shown separately.

Federal Individual Income Tax Collections in 2004

National Total = $1,707,496,056,000*

ALPHA ORDER

RANK	STATE	COLLECTIONS	% of USA
26	Alabama	$16,205,117,000	0.9%
45	Alaska	3,077,947,000	0.2%
23	Arizona	22,687,926,000	1.3%
28	Arkansas	14,657,385,000	0.9%
1	California	202,345,010,000	11.9%
20	Colorado	30,621,321,000	1.8%
19	Connecticut	32,560,865,000	1.9%
38	Delaware	7,086,221,000	0.4%
4	Florida	86,738,693,000	5.1%
12	Georgia	46,401,995,000	2.7%
37	Hawaii	7,746,147,000	0.5%
41	Idaho	6,134,461,000	0.4%
5	Illinois	86,357,840,000	5.1%
22	Indiana	29,079,537,000	1.7%
32	Iowa	12,661,060,000	0.7%
30	Kansas	12,954,523,000	0.8%
27	Kentucky	15,849,995,000	0.9%
24	Louisiana	19,133,840,000	1.1%
43	Maine	4,927,343,000	0.3%
15	Maryland	37,772,869,000	2.2%
10	Massachusetts	53,699,352,000	3.1%
9	Michigan	58,754,149,000	3.4%
11	Minnesota	48,050,665,000	2.8%
36	Mississippi	8,005,741,000	0.5%
18	Missouri	32,579,102,000	1.9%
47	Montana	2,939,876,000	0.2%
34	Nebraska	10,036,235,000	0.6%
33	Nevada	11,142,062,000	0.7%
40	New Hampshire	6,695,993,000	0.4%
6	New Jersey	77,076,938,000	4.5%
42	New Mexico	5,740,363,000	0.3%
2	New York	147,210,379,000	8.6%
13	North Carolina	41,910,144,000	2.5%
49	North Dakota	2,603,011,000	0.2%
8	Ohio	73,909,457,000	4.3%
31	Oklahoma	12,843,853,000	0.8%
25	Oregon	17,140,695,000	1.0%
7	Pennsylvania	76,223,055,000	4.5%
39	Rhode Island	6,949,536,000	0.4%
29	South Carolina	14,179,633,000	0.8%
46	South Dakota	3,048,862,000	0.2%
17	Tennessee	32,601,321,000	1.9%
3	Texas	118,410,514,000	6.9%
35	Utah	8,677,321,000	0.5%
48	Vermont	2,767,214,000	0.2%
14	Virginia	41,381,186,000	2.4%
16	Washington	35,247,916,000	2.1%
44	West Virginia	4,818,131,000	0.3%
21	Wisconsin	30,394,876,000	1.8%
50	Wyoming	2,357,056,000	0.1%

RANK ORDER

RANK	STATE	COLLECTIONS	% of USA
1	California	$202,345,010,000	11.9%
2	New York	147,210,379,000	8.6%
3	Texas	118,410,514,000	6.9%
4	Florida	86,738,693,000	5.1%
5	Illinois	86,357,840,000	5.1%
6	New Jersey	77,076,938,000	4.5%
7	Pennsylvania	76,223,055,000	4.5%
8	Ohio	73,909,457,000	4.3%
9	Michigan	58,754,149,000	3.4%
10	Massachusetts	53,699,352,000	3.1%
11	Minnesota	48,050,665,000	2.8%
12	Georgia	46,401,995,000	2.7%
13	North Carolina	41,910,144,000	2.5%
14	Virginia	41,381,186,000	2.4%
15	Maryland	37,772,869,000	2.2%
16	Washington	35,247,916,000	2.1%
17	Tennessee	32,601,321,000	1.9%
18	Missouri	32,579,102,000	1.9%
19	Connecticut	32,560,865,000	1.9%
20	Colorado	30,621,321,000	1.8%
21	Wisconsin	30,394,876,000	1.8%
22	Indiana	29,079,537,000	1.7%
23	Arizona	22,687,926,000	1.3%
24	Louisiana	19,133,840,000	1.1%
25	Oregon	17,140,695,000	1.0%
26	Alabama	16,205,117,000	0.9%
27	Kentucky	15,849,995,000	0.9%
28	Arkansas	14,657,385,000	0.9%
29	South Carolina	14,179,633,000	0.8%
30	Kansas	12,954,523,000	0.8%
31	Oklahoma	12,843,853,000	0.8%
32	Iowa	12,661,060,000	0.7%
33	Nevada	11,142,062,000	0.7%
34	Nebraska	10,036,235,000	0.6%
35	Utah	8,677,321,000	0.5%
36	Mississippi	8,005,741,000	0.5%
37	Hawaii	7,746,147,000	0.5%
38	Delaware	7,086,221,000	0.4%
39	Rhode Island	6,949,536,000	0.4%
40	New Hampshire	6,695,993,000	0.4%
41	Idaho	6,134,461,000	0.4%
42	New Mexico	5,740,363,000	0.3%
43	Maine	4,927,343,000	0.3%
44	West Virginia	4,818,131,000	0.3%
45	Alaska	3,077,947,000	0.2%
46	South Dakota	3,048,862,000	0.2%
47	Montana	2,939,876,000	0.2%
48	Vermont	2,767,214,000	0.2%
49	North Dakota	2,603,011,000	0.2%
50	Wyoming	2,357,056,000	0.1%
	District of Columbia	14,296,490,000	0.8%

Source: U.S. Department of the Treasury, Internal Revenue Service
   "Tax Collections" (http://www.irs.gov/)
*Total includes $119,515,751,000 from U.S. citizens abroad and other miscellaneous returns not shown separately.

Average Revenue Collection per Federal Individual Income Tax Return in 2004

National Average = $13,004 per Return*

ALPHA ORDER

RANK	STATE	AVERAGE
43	Alabama	$8,581
40	Alaska	8,947
34	Arizona	9,953
15	Arkansas	13,067
12	California	13,361
8	Colorado	14,752
2	Connecticut	19,707
4	Delaware	18,256
26	Florida	10,986
21	Georgia	12,528
14	Hawaii	13,125
30	Idaho	10,624
7	Illinois	15,094
32	Indiana	10,330
36	Iowa	9,560
29	Kansas	10,636
38	Kentucky	9,103
33	Louisiana	10,150
45	Maine	8,001
9	Maryland	14,524
5	Massachusetts	17,619
16	Michigan	12,928
1	Minnesota	20,164
48	Mississippi	6,844
19	Missouri	12,702
49	Montana	6,790
22	Nebraska	12,510
28	Nevada	10,701
31	New Hampshire	10,556
3	New Jersey	18,901
47	New Mexico	7,050
6	New York	17,164
25	North Carolina	11,411
42	North Dakota	8,605
11	Ohio	13,569
41	Oklahoma	8,795
27	Oregon	10,919
13	Pennsylvania	13,205
10	Rhode Island	13,962
46	South Carolina	7,866
44	South Dakota	8,528
18	Tennessee	12,719
17	Texas	12,745
39	Utah	8,975
37	Vermont	9,160
23	Virginia	12,050
20	Washington	12,564
50	West Virginia	6,475
24	Wisconsin	11,740
35	Wyoming	9,785

RANK ORDER

RANK	STATE	AVERAGE
1	Minnesota	$20,164
2	Connecticut	19,707
3	New Jersey	18,901
4	Delaware	18,256
5	Massachusetts	17,619
6	New York	17,164
7	Illinois	15,094
8	Colorado	14,752
9	Maryland	14,524
10	Rhode Island	13,962
11	Ohio	13,569
12	California	13,361
13	Pennsylvania	13,205
14	Hawaii	13,125
15	Arkansas	13,067
16	Michigan	12,928
17	Texas	12,745
18	Tennessee	12,719
19	Missouri	12,702
20	Washington	12,564
21	Georgia	12,528
22	Nebraska	12,510
23	Virginia	12,050
24	Wisconsin	11,740
25	North Carolina	11,411
26	Florida	10,986
27	Oregon	10,919
28	Nevada	10,701
29	Kansas	10,636
30	Idaho	10,624
31	New Hampshire	10,556
32	Indiana	10,330
33	Louisiana	10,150
34	Arizona	9,953
35	Wyoming	9,785
36	Iowa	9,560
37	Vermont	9,160
38	Kentucky	9,103
39	Utah	8,975
40	Alaska	8,947
41	Oklahoma	8,795
42	North Dakota	8,605
43	Alabama	8,581
44	South Dakota	8,528
45	Maine	8,001
46	South Carolina	7,866
47	New Mexico	7,050
48	Mississippi	6,844
49	Montana	6,790
50	West Virginia	6,475

District of Columbia   51,821

Source: Morgan Quitno Press using data from U.S. Department of the Treasury, Internal Revenue Service
"Tax Collections" and "Number of Returns" (http://www.irs.gov/)
*Total includes collections and returns from U.S. citizens abroad and other miscellaneous returns not shown separately.

Adjusted Gross Income in 2003

National Total = $6,199,925,184,000*

ALPHA ORDER

RANK	STATE	A.G.I.	% of USA
24	Alabama	$74,842,665,000	1.2%
46	Alaska	14,832,589,000	0.2%
23	Arizona	102,846,339,000	1.7%
33	Arkansas	41,364,084,000	0.7%
1	California	803,511,651,000	13.0%
22	Colorado	105,024,784,000	1.7%
19	Connecticut	111,028,777,000	1.8%
44	Delaware	19,284,435,000	0.3%
4	Florida	350,664,124,000	5.7%
12	Georgia	168,864,213,000	2.7%
40	Hawaii	25,718,250,000	0.4%
43	Idaho	22,254,112,000	0.4%
5	Illinois	290,425,049,000	4.7%
17	Indiana	119,764,629,000	1.9%
30	Iowa	54,107,442,000	0.9%
31	Kansas	52,503,139,000	0.8%
27	Kentucky	68,275,688,000	1.1%
26	Louisiana	70,865,204,000	1.1%
41	Maine	24,727,190,000	0.4%
14	Maryland	145,388,987,000	2.3%
11	Massachusetts	178,243,921,000	2.9%
9	Michigan	209,645,953,000	3.4%
16	Minnesota	119,929,752,000	1.9%
35	Mississippi	40,609,782,000	0.7%
20	Missouri	107,992,455,000	1.7%
45	Montana	15,198,027,000	0.2%
36	Nebraska	33,043,454,000	0.5%
32	Nevada	52,306,616,000	0.8%
37	New Hampshire	32,337,174,000	0.5%
7	New Jersey	247,077,300,000	4.0%
38	New Mexico	29,959,183,000	0.5%
2	New York	465,511,760,000	7.5%
13	North Carolina	157,402,225,000	2.5%
49	North Dakota	11,284,748,000	0.2%
8	Ohio	227,753,519,000	3.7%
29	Oklahoma	56,019,101,000	0.9%
28	Oregon	67,955,934,000	1.1%
6	Pennsylvania	261,845,583,000	4.2%
42	Rhode Island	23,700,505,000	0.4%
25	South Carolina	70,930,507,000	1.1%
47	South Dakota	13,475,212,000	0.2%
21	Tennessee	105,526,051,000	1.7%
3	Texas	415,647,089,000	6.7%
34	Utah	41,014,757,000	0.7%
48	Vermont	12,524,941,000	0.2%
10	Virginia	180,639,507,000	2.9%
15	Washington	141,431,438,000	2.3%
39	West Virginia	26,629,491,000	0.4%
18	Wisconsin	117,029,363,000	1.9%
50	Wyoming	11,092,479,000	0.2%

RANK ORDER

RANK	STATE	A.G.I.	% of USA
1	California	$803,511,651,000	13.0%
2	New York	465,511,760,000	7.5%
3	Texas	415,647,089,000	6.7%
4	Florida	350,664,124,000	5.7%
5	Illinois	290,425,049,000	4.7%
6	Pennsylvania	261,845,583,000	4.2%
7	New Jersey	247,077,300,000	4.0%
8	Ohio	227,753,519,000	3.7%
9	Michigan	209,645,953,000	3.4%
10	Virginia	180,639,507,000	2.9%
11	Massachusetts	178,243,921,000	2.9%
12	Georgia	168,864,213,000	2.7%
13	North Carolina	157,402,225,000	2.5%
14	Maryland	145,388,987,000	2.3%
15	Washington	141,431,438,000	2.3%
16	Minnesota	119,929,752,000	1.9%
17	Indiana	119,764,629,000	1.9%
18	Wisconsin	117,029,363,000	1.9%
19	Connecticut	111,028,777,000	1.8%
20	Missouri	107,992,455,000	1.7%
21	Tennessee	105,526,051,000	1.7%
22	Colorado	105,024,784,000	1.7%
23	Arizona	102,846,339,000	1.7%
24	Alabama	74,842,665,000	1.2%
25	South Carolina	70,930,507,000	1.1%
26	Louisiana	70,865,204,000	1.1%
27	Kentucky	68,275,688,000	1.1%
28	Oregon	67,955,934,000	1.1%
29	Oklahoma	56,019,101,000	0.9%
30	Iowa	54,107,442,000	0.9%
31	Kansas	52,503,139,000	0.8%
32	Nevada	52,306,616,000	0.8%
33	Arkansas	41,364,084,000	0.7%
34	Utah	41,014,757,000	0.7%
35	Mississippi	40,609,782,000	0.7%
36	Nebraska	33,043,454,000	0.5%
37	New Hampshire	32,337,174,000	0.5%
38	New Mexico	29,959,183,000	0.5%
39	West Virginia	26,629,491,000	0.4%
40	Hawaii	25,718,250,000	0.4%
41	Maine	24,727,190,000	0.4%
42	Rhode Island	23,700,505,000	0.4%
43	Idaho	22,254,112,000	0.4%
44	Delaware	19,284,435,000	0.3%
45	Montana	15,198,027,000	0.2%
46	Alaska	14,832,589,000	0.2%
47	South Dakota	13,475,212,000	0.2%
48	Vermont	12,524,941,000	0.2%
49	North Dakota	11,284,748,000	0.2%
50	Wyoming	11,092,479,000	0.2%
	District of Columbia	16,145,339,000	0.3%

Source: U.S. Department of the Treasury, Internal Revenue Service
   "Individual Tax Statistics, State Income" (http://www.irs.gov/)
*Total includes $43,728,667,000 from U.S. citizens abroad and other miscellaneous returns not shown separately.

Per Capita Adjusted Gross Income in 2003

National Per Capita = $21,166*

ALPHA ORDER

RANK	STATE	PER CAPITA
41	Alabama	$16,625
14	Alaska	22,872
34	Arizona	18,439
48	Arkansas	15,173
15	California	22,662
11	Colorado	23,092
1	Connecticut	31,851
9	Delaware	23,580
21	Florida	20,635
26	Georgia	19,306
22	Hawaii	20,604
44	Idaho	16,266
13	Illinois	22,959
25	Indiana	19,329
35	Iowa	18,395
27	Kansas	19,273
42	Kentucky	16,585
47	Louisiana	15,782
30	Maine	18,901
4	Maryland	26,375
3	Massachusetts	27,774
20	Michigan	20,802
8	Minnesota	23,694
50	Mississippi	14,097
31	Missouri	18,884
43	Montana	16,558
29	Nebraska	19,012
10	Nevada	23,333
5	New Hampshire	25,114
2	New Jersey	28,597
46	New Mexico	15,942
7	New York	24,210
33	North Carolina	18,689
37	North Dakota	17,826
24	Ohio	19,923
45	Oklahoma	15,983
28	Oregon	19,074
19	Pennsylvania	21,176
17	Rhode Island	22,032
40	South Carolina	17,105
38	South Dakota	17,624
36	Tennessee	18,065
32	Texas	18,808
39	Utah	17,243
23	Vermont	20,231
6	Virginia	24,466
12	Washington	23,068
49	West Virginia	14,710
18	Wisconsin	21,388
16	Wyoming	22,100

RANK ORDER

RANK	STATE	PER CAPITA
1	Connecticut	$31,851
2	New Jersey	28,597
3	Massachusetts	27,774
4	Maryland	26,375
5	New Hampshire	25,114
6	Virginia	24,466
7	New York	24,210
8	Minnesota	23,694
9	Delaware	23,580
10	Nevada	23,333
11	Colorado	23,092
12	Washington	23,068
13	Illinois	22,959
14	Alaska	22,872
15	California	22,662
16	Wyoming	22,100
17	Rhode Island	22,032
18	Wisconsin	21,388
19	Pennsylvania	21,176
20	Michigan	20,802
21	Florida	20,635
22	Hawaii	20,604
23	Vermont	20,231
24	Ohio	19,923
25	Indiana	19,329
26	Georgia	19,306
27	Kansas	19,273
28	Oregon	19,074
29	Nebraska	19,012
30	Maine	18,901
31	Missouri	18,884
32	Texas	18,808
33	North Carolina	18,689
34	Arizona	18,439
35	Iowa	18,395
36	Tennessee	18,065
37	North Dakota	17,826
38	South Dakota	17,624
39	Utah	17,243
40	South Carolina	17,105
41	Alabama	16,625
42	Kentucky	16,585
43	Montana	16,558
44	Idaho	16,266
45	Oklahoma	15,983
46	New Mexico	15,942
47	Louisiana	15,782
48	Arkansas	15,173
49	West Virginia	14,710
50	Mississippi	14,097
	District of Columbia	28,942

Source: Morgan Quitno Press using data from U.S. Department of the Treasury, Internal Revenue Service "Individual Tax Statistics, State Income" (http://www.irs.gov/)

National per capita does not include income from U.S. citizens abroad and other miscellaneous returns not shown separately.

Federal Corporate Income Tax Collections in 2004

National Total = $230,619,359,000*

ALPHA ORDER

RANK	STATE	COLLECTIONS	% of USA
27	Alabama	$1,931,414,000	0.8%
48	Alaska	124,599,000	0.1%
28	Arizona	1,894,886,000	0.8%
13	Arkansas	5,204,945,000	2.3%
1	California	28,252,413,000	12.3%
26	Colorado	2,131,191,000	0.9%
11	Connecticut	8,107,681,000	3.5%
20	Delaware	3,922,315,000	1.7%
15	Florida	4,447,784,000	1.9%
8	Georgia	9,195,080,000	4.0%
39	Hawaii	460,777,000	0.2%
42	Idaho	261,352,000	0.1%
3	Illinois	17,581,098,000	7.6%
25	Indiana	2,270,997,000	1.0%
30	Iowa	1,626,888,000	0.7%
34	Kansas	1,036,076,000	0.4%
33	Kentucky	1,217,679,000	0.5%
35	Louisiana	854,664,000	0.4%
41	Maine	326,757,000	0.1%
23	Maryland	2,361,572,000	1.0%
19	Massachusetts	3,955,703,000	1.7%
16	Michigan	4,163,750,000	1.8%
10	Minnesota	8,485,882,000	3.7%
38	Mississippi	583,703,000	0.3%
18	Missouri	4,124,336,000	1.8%
49	Montana	120,677,000	0.1%
17	Nebraska	4,124,398,000	1.8%
29	Nevada	1,767,895,000	0.8%
40	New Hampshire	355,208,000	0.2%
5	New Jersey	11,535,032,000	5.0%
46	New Mexico	171,491,000	0.1%
2	New York	20,399,783,000	8.8%
6	North Carolina	11,251,342,000	4.9%
47	North Dakota	158,334,000	0.1%
7	Ohio	9,912,042,000	4.3%
24	Oklahoma	2,303,842,000	1.0%
32	Oregon	1,262,025,000	0.5%
9	Pennsylvania	8,741,526,000	3.8%
31	Rhode Island	1,493,266,000	0.6%
36	South Carolina	839,709,000	0.4%
45	South Dakota	174,084,000	0.1%
22	Tennessee	3,292,517,000	1.4%
4	Texas	17,127,574,000	7.4%
37	Utah	648,792,000	0.3%
44	Vermont	226,227,000	0.1%
14	Virginia	4,895,573,000	2.1%
12	Washington	5,544,468,000	2.4%
43	West Virginia	249,566,000	0.1%
21	Wisconsin	3,727,712,000	1.6%
50	Wyoming	108,409,000	0.0%

RANK ORDER

RANK	STATE	COLLECTIONS	% of USA
1	California	$28,252,413,000	12.3%
2	New York	20,399,783,000	8.8%
3	Illinois	17,581,098,000	7.6%
4	Texas	17,127,574,000	7.4%
5	New Jersey	11,535,032,000	5.0%
6	North Carolina	11,251,342,000	4.9%
7	Ohio	9,912,042,000	4.3%
8	Georgia	9,195,080,000	4.0%
9	Pennsylvania	8,741,526,000	3.8%
10	Minnesota	8,485,882,000	3.7%
11	Connecticut	8,107,681,000	3.5%
12	Washington	5,544,468,000	2.4%
13	Arkansas	5,204,945,000	2.3%
14	Virginia	4,895,573,000	2.1%
15	Florida	4,447,784,000	1.9%
16	Michigan	4,163,750,000	1.8%
17	Nebraska	4,124,398,000	1.8%
18	Missouri	4,124,336,000	1.8%
19	Massachusetts	3,955,703,000	1.7%
20	Delaware	3,922,315,000	1.7%
21	Wisconsin	3,727,712,000	1.6%
22	Tennessee	3,292,517,000	1.4%
23	Maryland	2,361,572,000	1.0%
24	Oklahoma	2,303,842,000	1.0%
25	Indiana	2,270,997,000	1.0%
26	Colorado	2,131,191,000	0.9%
27	Alabama	1,931,414,000	0.8%
28	Arizona	1,894,886,000	0.8%
29	Nevada	1,767,895,000	0.8%
30	Iowa	1,626,888,000	0.7%
31	Rhode Island	1,493,266,000	0.6%
32	Oregon	1,262,025,000	0.5%
33	Kentucky	1,217,679,000	0.5%
34	Kansas	1,036,076,000	0.4%
35	Louisiana	854,664,000	0.4%
36	South Carolina	839,709,000	0.4%
37	Utah	648,792,000	0.3%
38	Mississippi	583,703,000	0.3%
39	Hawaii	460,777,000	0.2%
40	New Hampshire	355,208,000	0.2%
41	Maine	326,757,000	0.1%
42	Idaho	261,352,000	0.1%
43	West Virginia	249,566,000	0.1%
44	Vermont	226,227,000	0.1%
45	South Dakota	174,084,000	0.1%
46	New Mexico	171,491,000	0.1%
47	North Dakota	158,334,000	0.1%
48	Alaska	124,599,000	0.1%
49	Montana	120,677,000	0.1%
50	Wyoming	108,409,000	0.0%
	District of Columbia	2,322,763,000	1.0%

Source: U.S. Department of the Treasury, Internal Revenue Service
   "Tax Collections" (http://www.irs.gov/)
*Total includes collections and returns from international sources and others not distributed by state.

Average Revenue Collection per Federal Corporate Income Tax Return in 2004

National Average = $38,152 per Return*

ALPHA ORDER				RANK ORDER		
RANK	STATE	AVERAGE		RANK	STATE	AVERAGE
22	Alabama	$29,907		1	Delaware	$164,079
40	Alaska	11,596		2	Connecticut	137,365
30	Arizona	18,963		3	Nebraska	106,318
4	Arkansas	100,805		4	Arkansas	100,805
11	California	49,646		5	Minnesota	72,303
34	Colorado	16,303		6	North Carolina	68,340
2	Connecticut	137,365		7	Illinois	59,546
1	Delaware	164,079		8	Rhode Island	57,486
48	Florida	7,102		9	Ohio	52,031
13	Georgia	47,787		10	Tennessee	49,870
33	Hawaii	17,212		11	California	49,646
46	Idaho	9,150		12	New Jersey	48,513
7	Illinois	59,546		13	Georgia	47,787
28	Indiana	20,284		14	Washington	47,659
23	Iowa	29,029		15	Texas	47,099
27	Kansas	20,984		16	Pennsylvania	42,001
31	Kentucky	17,841		17	Missouri	41,551
45	Louisiana	9,779		18	Wisconsin	40,400
44	Maine	10,905		19	New York	36,009
29	Maryland	19,685		20	Oklahoma	35,172
25	Massachusetts	27,852		21	Virginia	33,094
26	Michigan	22,565		22	Alabama	29,907
5	Minnesota	72,303		23	Iowa	29,029
35	Mississippi	14,378		24	Nevada	27,991
17	Missouri	41,551		25	Massachusetts	27,852
50	Montana	4,426		26	Michigan	22,565
3	Nebraska	106,318		27	Kansas	20,984
24	Nevada	27,991		28	Indiana	20,284
36	New Hampshire	14,101		29	Maryland	19,685
12	New Jersey	48,513		30	Arizona	18,963
49	New Mexico	6,170		31	Kentucky	17,841
19	New York	36,009		32	Oregon	17,784
6	North Carolina	68,340		33	Hawaii	17,212
38	North Dakota	13,245		34	Colorado	16,303
9	Ohio	52,031		35	Mississippi	14,378
20	Oklahoma	35,172		36	New Hampshire	14,101
32	Oregon	17,784		37	Vermont	13,540
16	Pennsylvania	42,001		38	North Dakota	13,245
8	Rhode Island	57,486		39	Utah	12,148
43	South Carolina	10,957		40	Alaska	11,596
42	South Dakota	11,141		41	West Virginia	11,523
10	Tennessee	49,870		42	South Dakota	11,141
15	Texas	47,099		43	South Carolina	10,957
39	Utah	12,148		44	Maine	10,905
37	Vermont	13,540		45	Louisiana	9,779
21	Virginia	33,094		46	Idaho	9,150
14	Washington	47,659		47	Wyoming	7,846
41	West Virginia	11,523		48	Florida	7,102
18	Wisconsin	40,400		49	New Mexico	6,170
47	Wyoming	7,846		50	Montana	4,426
					District of Columbia	153,348

Source: Morgan Quitno Press using data from U.S. Department of the Treasury, Internal Revenue Service
    "Tax Collections" and "Number of Returns" (http://www.irs.gov/)
*National rate includes collections and returns from U.S. citizens abroad and other miscellaneous returns not shown
separately.

Federal Tax Returns Filed in 2004

National Total = 224,392,821 Returns*

ALPHA ORDER

RANK	STATE	RETURNS	% of USA	RANK	STATE	RETURNS	% of USA
24	Alabama	3,009,327	1.3%	1	California	26,586,857	11.8%
47	Alaska	578,309	0.3%	2	Texas	15,549,146	6.9%
22	Arizona	3,506,766	1.6%	3	New York	14,733,912	6.6%
32	Arkansas	1,901,734	0.8%	4	Florida	14,491,187	6.5%
1	California	26,586,857	11.8%	5	Illinois	9,677,073	4.3%
21	Colorado	3,903,595	1.7%	6	Pennsylvania	9,553,066	4.3%
25	Connecticut	2,965,529	1.3%	7	Ohio	8,835,420	3.9%
45	Delaware	700,335	0.3%	8	Michigan	7,333,008	3.3%
4	Florida	14,491,187	6.5%	9	New Jersey	7,278,405	3.2%
10	Georgia	6,120,985	2.7%	10	Georgia	6,120,985	2.7%
41	Hawaii	1,034,878	0.5%	11	North Carolina	6,099,340	2.7%
42	Idaho	1,014,145	0.5%	12	Virginia	5,764,740	2.6%
5	Illinois	9,677,073	4.3%	13	Massachusetts	5,462,506	2.4%
15	Indiana	4,535,104	2.0%	14	Washington	4,939,463	2.2%
30	Iowa	2,323,421	1.0%	15	Indiana	4,535,104	2.0%
31	Kansas	2,142,212	1.0%	16	Maryland	4,423,050	2.0%
28	Kentucky	2,806,986	1.3%	17	Wisconsin	4,364,704	1.9%
23	Louisiana	3,082,706	1.4%	18	Missouri	4,329,864	1.9%
39	Maine	1,047,025	0.5%	19	Minnesota	4,178,398	1.9%
16	Maryland	4,423,050	2.0%	20	Tennessee	4,069,383	1.8%
13	Massachusetts	5,462,506	2.4%	21	Colorado	3,903,595	1.7%
8	Michigan	7,333,008	3.3%	22	Arizona	3,506,766	1.6%
19	Minnesota	4,178,398	1.9%	23	Louisiana	3,082,706	1.4%
33	Mississippi	1,823,160	0.8%	24	Alabama	3,009,327	1.3%
18	Missouri	4,329,864	1.9%	25	Connecticut	2,965,529	1.3%
44	Montana	843,931	0.4%	26	South Carolina	2,905,999	1.3%
36	Nebraska	1,409,381	0.6%	27	Oregon	2,878,468	1.3%
34	Nevada	1,772,093	0.8%	28	Kentucky	2,806,986	1.3%
40	New Hampshire	1,044,457	0.5%	29	Oklahoma	2,593,181	1.2%
9	New Jersey	7,278,405	3.2%	30	Iowa	2,323,421	1.0%
37	New Mexico	1,340,769	0.6%	31	Kansas	2,142,212	1.0%
3	New York	14,733,912	6.6%	32	Arkansas	1,901,734	0.8%
11	North Carolina	6,099,340	2.7%	33	Mississippi	1,823,160	0.8%
48	North Dakota	559,204	0.2%	34	Nevada	1,772,093	0.8%
7	Ohio	8,835,420	3.9%	35	Utah	1,577,571	0.7%
29	Oklahoma	2,593,181	1.2%	36	Nebraska	1,409,381	0.6%
27	Oregon	2,878,468	1.3%	37	New Mexico	1,340,769	0.6%
6	Pennsylvania	9,553,066	4.3%	38	West Virginia	1,183,011	0.5%
43	Rhode Island	910,742	0.4%	39	Maine	1,047,025	0.5%
26	South Carolina	2,905,999	1.3%	40	New Hampshire	1,044,457	0.5%
46	South Dakota	662,688	0.3%	41	Hawaii	1,034,878	0.5%
20	Tennessee	4,069,383	1.8%	42	Idaho	1,014,145	0.5%
2	Texas	15,549,146	6.9%	43	Rhode Island	910,742	0.4%
35	Utah	1,577,571	0.7%	44	Montana	843,931	0.4%
49	Vermont	540,585	0.2%	45	Delaware	700,335	0.3%
12	Virginia	5,764,740	2.6%	46	South Dakota	662,688	0.3%
14	Washington	4,939,463	2.2%	47	Alaska	578,309	0.3%
38	West Virginia	1,183,011	0.5%	48	North Dakota	559,204	0.2%
17	Wisconsin	4,364,704	1.9%	49	Vermont	540,585	0.2%
50	Wyoming	465,694	0.2%	50	Wyoming	465,694	0.2%
					District of Columbia	947,682	0.4%

Source: U.S. Department of the Treasury, Internal Revenue Service
"Number of Returns" (http://www.irs.gov/)
Total includes returns from international sources and other miscellaneous returns not shown separately.

Federal Individual Income Tax Returns Filed in 2004

National Total = 131,301,697 Returns*

RANK	STATE	RETURNS	% of USA
23	Alabama	1,888,500	1.4%
47	Alaska	344,025	0.3%
21	Arizona	2,279,505	1.7%
33	Arkansas	1,121,717	0.9%
1	California	15,144,971	11.5%
22	Colorado	2,075,681	1.6%
27	Connecticut	1,652,224	1.3%
45	Delaware	388,157	0.3%
4	Florida	7,895,518	6.0%
10	Georgia	3,704,005	2.8%
41	Hawaii	590,168	0.4%
42	Idaho	577,428	0.4%
6	Illinois	5,721,222	4.4%
14	Indiana	2,815,040	2.1%
30	Iowa	1,324,353	1.0%
31	Kansas	1,217,939	0.9%
26	Kentucky	1,741,155	1.3%
24	Louisiana	1,885,108	1.4%
40	Maine	615,847	0.5%
16	Maryland	2,600,801	2.0%
13	Massachusetts	3,047,797	2.3%
8	Michigan	4,544,642	3.5%
20	Minnesota	2,382,954	1.8%
32	Mississippi	1,169,752	0.9%
18	Missouri	2,564,924	2.0%
44	Montana	432,967	0.3%
37	Nebraska	802,231	0.6%
34	Nevada	1,041,194	0.8%
39	New Hampshire	634,309	0.5%
9	New Jersey	4,077,830	3.1%
36	New Mexico	814,286	0.6%
3	New York	8,576,821	6.5%
11	North Carolina	3,672,896	2.8%
48	North Dakota	302,502	0.2%
7	Ohio	5,446,774	4.1%
29	Oklahoma	1,460,379	1.1%
28	Oregon	1,569,785	1.2%
5	Pennsylvania	5,772,233	4.4%
43	Rhode Island	497,745	0.4%
25	South Carolina	1,802,691	1.4%
46	South Dakota	357,511	0.3%
19	Tennessee	2,563,181	2.0%
2	Texas	9,290,654	7.1%
35	Utah	966,843	0.7%
49	Vermont	302,089	0.2%
12	Virginia	3,434,062	2.6%
15	Washington	2,805,383	2.1%
38	West Virginia	744,148	0.6%
17	Wisconsin	2,588,919	2.0%
50	Wyoming	240,892	0.2%

RANK	STATE	RETURNS	% of USA
1	California	15,144,971	11.5%
2	Texas	9,290,654	7.1%
3	New York	8,576,821	6.5%
4	Florida	7,895,518	6.0%
5	Pennsylvania	5,772,233	4.4%
6	Illinois	5,721,222	4.4%
7	Ohio	5,446,774	4.1%
8	Michigan	4,544,642	3.5%
9	New Jersey	4,077,830	3.1%
10	Georgia	3,704,005	2.8%
11	North Carolina	3,672,896	2.8%
12	Virginia	3,434,062	2.6%
13	Massachusetts	3,047,797	2.3%
14	Indiana	2,815,040	2.1%
15	Washington	2,805,383	2.1%
16	Maryland	2,600,801	2.0%
17	Wisconsin	2,588,919	2.0%
18	Missouri	2,564,924	2.0%
19	Tennessee	2,563,181	2.0%
20	Minnesota	2,382,954	1.8%
21	Arizona	2,279,505	1.7%
22	Colorado	2,075,681	1.6%
23	Alabama	1,888,500	1.4%
24	Louisiana	1,885,108	1.4%
25	South Carolina	1,802,691	1.4%
26	Kentucky	1,741,155	1.3%
27	Connecticut	1,652,224	1.3%
28	Oregon	1,569,785	1.2%
29	Oklahoma	1,460,379	1.1%
30	Iowa	1,324,353	1.0%
31	Kansas	1,217,939	0.9%
32	Mississippi	1,169,752	0.9%
33	Arkansas	1,121,717	0.9%
34	Nevada	1,041,194	0.8%
35	Utah	966,843	0.7%
36	New Mexico	814,286	0.6%
37	Nebraska	802,231	0.6%
38	West Virginia	744,148	0.6%
39	New Hampshire	634,309	0.5%
40	Maine	615,847	0.5%
41	Hawaii	590,168	0.4%
42	Idaho	577,428	0.4%
43	Rhode Island	497,745	0.4%
44	Montana	432,967	0.3%
45	Delaware	388,157	0.3%
46	South Dakota	357,511	0.3%
47	Alaska	344,025	0.3%
48	North Dakota	302,502	0.2%
49	Vermont	302,089	0.2%
50	Wyoming	240,892	0.2%
	District of Columbia	275,884	0.2%

Source: U.S. Department of the Treasury, Internal Revenue Service
    "Number of Returns" (http://www.irs.gov/)
Total includes returns from international sources and other miscellaneous returns not shown separately.

Federal Corporate Income Tax Returns Filed in 2004

National Total = 6,044,821 Returns*

ALPHA ORDER

RANK	STATE	RETURNS	% of USA
28	Alabama	64,581	1.1%
50	Alaska	10,745	0.2%
19	Arizona	99,925	1.7%
33	Arkansas	51,634	0.9%
2	California	569,074	9.4%
14	Colorado	130,727	2.2%
30	Connecticut	59,023	1.0%
44	Delaware	23,905	0.4%
1	Florida	626,266	10.4%
8	Georgia	192,418	3.2%
41	Hawaii	26,770	0.4%
38	Idaho	28,563	0.5%
5	Illinois	295,253	4.9%
18	Indiana	111,961	1.9%
31	Iowa	56,043	0.9%
34	Kansas	49,375	0.8%
25	Kentucky	68,252	1.1%
22	Louisiana	87,396	1.4%
37	Maine	29,964	0.5%
15	Maryland	119,970	2.0%
13	Massachusetts	142,025	2.3%
10	Michigan	184,520	3.1%
16	Minnesota	117,365	1.9%
35	Mississippi	40,596	0.7%
20	Missouri	99,259	1.6%
40	Montana	27,263	0.5%
36	Nebraska	38,793	0.6%
29	Nevada	63,159	1.0%
43	New Hampshire	25,191	0.4%
6	New Jersey	237,774	3.9%
39	New Mexico	27,794	0.5%
3	New York	566,512	9.4%
11	North Carolina	164,638	2.7%
49	North Dakota	11,954	0.2%
9	Ohio	190,504	3.2%
27	Oklahoma	65,502	1.1%
24	Oregon	70,966	1.2%
7	Pennsylvania	208,129	3.4%
42	Rhode Island	25,976	0.4%
23	South Carolina	76,634	1.3%
47	South Dakota	15,626	0.3%
26	Tennessee	66,022	1.1%
4	Texas	363,648	6.0%
32	Utah	53,409	0.9%
46	Vermont	16,708	0.3%
12	Virginia	147,930	2.4%
17	Washington	116,337	1.9%
45	West Virginia	21,659	0.4%
21	Wisconsin	92,270	1.5%
48	Wyoming	13,817	0.2%

RANK ORDER

RANK	STATE	RETURNS	% of USA
1	Florida	626,266	10.4%
2	California	569,074	9.4%
3	New York	566,512	9.4%
4	Texas	363,648	6.0%
5	Illinois	295,253	4.9%
6	New Jersey	237,774	3.9%
7	Pennsylvania	208,129	3.4%
8	Georgia	192,418	3.2%
9	Ohio	190,504	3.2%
10	Michigan	184,520	3.1%
11	North Carolina	164,638	2.7%
12	Virginia	147,930	2.4%
13	Massachusetts	142,025	2.3%
14	Colorado	130,727	2.2%
15	Maryland	119,970	2.0%
16	Minnesota	117,365	1.9%
17	Washington	116,337	1.9%
18	Indiana	111,961	1.9%
19	Arizona	99,925	1.7%
20	Missouri	99,259	1.6%
21	Wisconsin	92,270	1.5%
22	Louisiana	87,396	1.4%
23	South Carolina	76,634	1.3%
24	Oregon	70,966	1.2%
25	Kentucky	68,252	1.1%
26	Tennessee	66,022	1.1%
27	Oklahoma	65,502	1.1%
28	Alabama	64,581	1.1%
29	Nevada	63,159	1.0%
30	Connecticut	59,023	1.0%
31	Iowa	56,043	0.9%
32	Utah	53,409	0.9%
33	Arkansas	51,634	0.9%
34	Kansas	49,375	0.8%
35	Mississippi	40,596	0.7%
36	Nebraska	38,793	0.6%
37	Maine	29,964	0.5%
38	Idaho	28,563	0.5%
39	New Mexico	27,794	0.5%
40	Montana	27,263	0.5%
41	Hawaii	26,770	0.4%
42	Rhode Island	25,976	0.4%
43	New Hampshire	25,191	0.4%
44	Delaware	23,905	0.4%
45	West Virginia	21,659	0.4%
46	Vermont	16,708	0.3%
47	South Dakota	15,626	0.3%
48	Wyoming	13,817	0.2%
49	North Dakota	11,954	0.2%
50	Alaska	10,745	0.2%
	District of Columbia	15,147	0.3%

Source: U.S. Department of the Treasury, Internal Revenue Service
 "Number of Returns" (http://www.irs.gov/)
*Total includes returns from international sources and other miscellaneous returns not shown separately.

Federal Tax Refunds in 2004

National Total = 108,543,272 Refunds*

RANK	STATE	REFUNDS	% of USA
24	Alabama	1,586,943	1.5%
47	Alaska	255,416	0.2%
21	Arizona	1,826,666	1.7%
33	Arkansas	928,499	0.9%
1	California	12,085,278	11.1%
22	Colorado	1,665,759	1.5%
27	Connecticut	1,353,261	1.2%
45	Delaware	328,021	0.3%
4	Florida	6,505,752	6.0%
10	Georgia	3,045,431	2.8%
41	Hawaii	477,749	0.4%
42	Idaho	466,228	0.4%
6	Illinois	4,813,917	4.4%
14	Indiana	2,425,949	2.2%
30	Iowa	1,072,000	1.0%
31	Kansas	996,414	0.9%
26	Kentucky	1,478,589	1.4%
23	Louisiana	1,608,350	1.5%
40	Maine	509,721	0.5%
16	Maryland	2,164,094	2.0%
13	Massachusetts	2,496,584	2.3%
8	Michigan	3,856,520	3.6%
20	Minnesota	1,929,045	1.8%
32	Mississippi	981,972	0.9%
19	Missouri	2,134,790	2.0%
44	Montana	341,809	0.3%
38	Nebraska	654,338	0.6%
34	Nevada	848,595	0.8%
39	New Hampshire	531,343	0.5%
9	New Jersey	3,353,386	3.1%
36	New Mexico	678,571	0.6%
3	New York	7,088,504	6.5%
11	North Carolina	3,020,844	2.8%
49	North Dakota	237,063	0.2%
7	Ohio	4,669,557	4.3%
29	Oklahoma	1,203,987	1.1%
28	Oregon	1,226,406	1.1%
5	Pennsylvania	4,874,729	4.5%
43	Rhode Island	424,039	0.4%
25	South Carolina	1,510,797	1.4%
46	South Dakota	287,108	0.3%
17	Tennessee	2,159,469	2.0%
2	Texas	7,874,175	7.3%
35	Utah	812,248	0.7%
48	Vermont	249,073	0.2%
12	Virginia	2,844,120	2.6%
15	Washington	2,306,918	2.1%
37	West Virginia	654,763	0.6%
18	Wisconsin	2,140,136	2.0%
50	Wyoming	200,992	0.2%

RANK	STATE	REFUNDS	% of USA
1	California	12,085,278	11.1%
2	Texas	7,874,175	7.3%
3	New York	7,088,504	6.5%
4	Florida	6,505,752	6.0%
5	Pennsylvania	4,874,729	4.5%
6	Illinois	4,813,917	4.4%
7	Ohio	4,669,557	4.3%
8	Michigan	3,856,520	3.6%
9	New Jersey	3,353,386	3.1%
10	Georgia	3,045,431	2.8%
11	North Carolina	3,020,844	2.8%
12	Virginia	2,844,120	2.6%
13	Massachusetts	2,496,584	2.3%
14	Indiana	2,425,949	2.2%
15	Washington	2,306,918	2.1%
16	Maryland	2,164,094	2.0%
17	Tennessee	2,159,469	2.0%
18	Wisconsin	2,140,136	2.0%
19	Missouri	2,134,790	2.0%
20	Minnesota	1,929,045	1.8%
21	Arizona	1,826,666	1.7%
22	Colorado	1,665,759	1.5%
23	Louisiana	1,608,350	1.5%
24	Alabama	1,586,943	1.5%
25	South Carolina	1,510,797	1.4%
26	Kentucky	1,478,589	1.4%
27	Connecticut	1,353,261	1.2%
28	Oregon	1,226,406	1.1%
29	Oklahoma	1,203,987	1.1%
30	Iowa	1,072,000	1.0%
31	Kansas	996,414	0.9%
32	Mississippi	981,972	0.9%
33	Arkansas	928,499	0.9%
34	Nevada	848,595	0.8%
35	Utah	812,248	0.7%
36	New Mexico	678,571	0.6%
37	West Virginia	654,763	0.6%
38	Nebraska	654,338	0.6%
39	New Hampshire	531,343	0.5%
40	Maine	509,721	0.5%
41	Hawaii	477,749	0.4%
42	Idaho	466,228	0.4%
43	Rhode Island	424,039	0.4%
44	Montana	341,809	0.3%
45	Delaware	328,021	0.3%
46	South Dakota	287,108	0.3%
47	Alaska	255,416	0.2%
48	Vermont	249,073	0.2%
49	North Dakota	237,063	0.2%
50	Wyoming	200,992	0.2%
	District of Columbia	224,750	0.2%

Source: U.S. Department of the Treasury, Internal Revenue Service
   "Tax Refunds" (http://www.irs.gov/)
*Total includes refunds to international sources and other miscellaneous refunds not shown separately.

Value of Federal Tax Refunds in 2004

National Total = $279,799,934,000*

ALPHA ORDER

RANK	STATE	REFUNDS	% of USA
26	Alabama	$3,468,399,000	1.2%
47	Alaska	532,479,000	0.2%
22	Arizona	3,993,161,000	1.4%
34	Arkansas	1,898,292,000	0.7%
1	California	31,169,773,000	11.1%
23	Colorado	3,847,565,000	1.4%
21	Connecticut	4,260,914,000	1.5%
37	Delaware	1,345,736,000	0.5%
4	Florida	15,059,920,000	5.4%
10	Georgia	7,957,276,000	2.8%
44	Hawaii	902,878,000	0.3%
43	Idaho	915,256,000	0.3%
6	Illinois	13,680,273,000	4.9%
16	Indiana	5,469,142,000	2.0%
30	Iowa	2,408,378,000	0.9%
32	Kansas	2,098,996,000	0.8%
28	Kentucky	2,975,939,000	1.1%
24	Louisiana	3,783,244,000	1.4%
42	Maine	938,224,000	0.3%
14	Maryland	6,003,540,000	2.1%
13	Massachusetts	6,340,449,000	2.3%
8	Michigan	11,463,168,000	4.1%
19	Minnesota	4,748,178,000	1.7%
31	Mississippi	2,108,265,000	0.8%
17	Missouri	4,965,594,000	1.8%
45	Montana	588,163,000	0.2%
36	Nebraska	1,514,884,000	0.5%
33	Nevada	1,998,884,000	0.7%
40	New Hampshire	1,192,784,000	0.4%
9	New Jersey	9,789,873,000	3.5%
38	New Mexico	1,297,534,000	0.5%
3	New York	21,936,704,000	7.8%
11	North Carolina	7,570,288,000	2.7%
49	North Dakota	422,575,000	0.2%
5	Ohio	14,000,167,000	5.0%
29	Oklahoma	2,580,661,000	0.9%
25	Oregon	3,634,080,000	1.3%
7	Pennsylvania	11,515,592,000	4.1%
41	Rhode Island	1,128,580,000	0.4%
27	South Carolina	3,066,402,000	1.1%
46	South Dakota	561,411,000	0.2%
18	Tennessee	4,907,023,000	1.8%
2	Texas	22,034,323,000	7.9%
35	Utah	1,572,199,000	0.6%
48	Vermont	483,676,000	0.2%
12	Virginia	6,354,226,000	2.3%
15	Washington	5,818,698,000	2.1%
39	West Virginia	1,200,787,000	0.4%
20	Wisconsin	4,498,078,000	1.6%
50	Wyoming	397,722,000	0.1%

RANK ORDER

RANK	STATE	REFUNDS	% of USA
1	California	$31,169,773,000	11.1%
2	Texas	22,034,323,000	7.9%
3	New York	21,936,704,000	7.8%
4	Florida	15,059,920,000	5.4%
5	Ohio	14,000,167,000	5.0%
6	Illinois	13,680,273,000	4.9%
7	Pennsylvania	11,515,592,000	4.1%
8	Michigan	11,463,168,000	4.1%
9	New Jersey	9,789,873,000	3.5%
10	Georgia	7,957,276,000	2.8%
11	North Carolina	7,570,288,000	2.7%
12	Virginia	6,354,226,000	2.3%
13	Massachusetts	6,340,449,000	2.3%
14	Maryland	6,003,540,000	2.1%
15	Washington	5,818,698,000	2.1%
16	Indiana	5,469,142,000	2.0%
17	Missouri	4,965,594,000	1.8%
18	Tennessee	4,907,023,000	1.8%
19	Minnesota	4,748,178,000	1.7%
20	Wisconsin	4,498,078,000	1.6%
21	Connecticut	4,260,914,000	1.5%
22	Arizona	3,993,161,000	1.4%
23	Colorado	3,847,565,000	1.4%
24	Louisiana	3,783,244,000	1.4%
25	Oregon	3,634,080,000	1.3%
26	Alabama	3,468,399,000	1.2%
27	South Carolina	3,066,402,000	1.1%
28	Kentucky	2,975,939,000	1.1%
29	Oklahoma	2,580,661,000	0.9%
30	Iowa	2,408,378,000	0.9%
31	Mississippi	2,108,265,000	0.8%
32	Kansas	2,098,996,000	0.8%
33	Nevada	1,998,884,000	0.7%
34	Arkansas	1,898,292,000	0.7%
35	Utah	1,572,199,000	0.6%
36	Nebraska	1,514,884,000	0.5%
37	Delaware	1,345,736,000	0.5%
38	New Mexico	1,297,534,000	0.5%
39	West Virginia	1,200,787,000	0.4%
40	New Hampshire	1,192,784,000	0.4%
41	Rhode Island	1,128,580,000	0.4%
42	Maine	938,224,000	0.3%
43	Idaho	915,256,000	0.3%
44	Hawaii	902,878,000	0.3%
45	Montana	588,163,000	0.2%
46	South Dakota	561,411,000	0.2%
47	Alaska	532,479,000	0.2%
48	Vermont	483,676,000	0.2%
49	North Dakota	422,575,000	0.2%
50	Wyoming	397,722,000	0.1%
	District of Columbia	620,705,000	0.2%

Source: U.S. Department of the Treasury, Internal Revenue Service
    "Tax Refunds" (http://www.irs.gov/)
*Total includes refunds to international sources and other miscellaneous refunds not shown separately.

Average Value of Federal Tax Refunds in 2004

National Average = $2,578*

ALPHA ORDER

RANK	STATE	REFUNDS
30	Alabama	$2,186
36	Alaska	2,085
30	Arizona	2,186
37	Arkansas	2,044
13	California	2,579
24	Colorado	2,310
2	Connecticut	3,149
1	Delaware	4,103
22	Florida	2,315
12	Georgia	2,613
46	Hawaii	1,890
41	Idaho	1,963
8	Illinois	2,842
26	Indiana	2,254
27	Iowa	2,247
34	Kansas	2,107
39	Kentucky	2,013
20	Louisiana	2,352
47	Maine	1,841
10	Maryland	2,774
14	Massachusetts	2,540
5	Michigan	2,972
17	Minnesota	2,461
32	Mississippi	2,147
21	Missouri	2,326
50	Montana	1,721
22	Nebraska	2,315
19	Nevada	2,356
28	New Hampshire	2,245
7	New Jersey	2,919
45	New Mexico	1,912
3	New York	3,095
16	North Carolina	2,506
49	North Dakota	1,783
4	Ohio	2,998
33	Oklahoma	2,143
6	Oregon	2,963
18	Pennsylvania	2,362
11	Rhode Island	2,662
38	South Carolina	2,030
42	South Dakota	1,955
25	Tennessee	2,272
9	Texas	2,798
44	Utah	1,936
43	Vermont	1,942
29	Virginia	2,234
15	Washington	2,522
48	West Virginia	1,834
35	Wisconsin	2,102
40	Wyoming	1,979

RANK ORDER

RANK	STATE	REFUNDS
1	Delaware	$4,103
2	Connecticut	3,149
3	New York	3,095
4	Ohio	2,998
5	Michigan	2,972
6	Oregon	2,963
7	New Jersey	2,919
8	Illinois	2,842
9	Texas	2,798
10	Maryland	2,774
11	Rhode Island	2,662
12	Georgia	2,613
13	California	2,579
14	Massachusetts	2,540
15	Washington	2,522
16	North Carolina	2,506
17	Minnesota	2,461
18	Pennsylvania	2,362
19	Nevada	2,356
20	Louisiana	2,352
21	Missouri	2,326
22	Florida	2,315
22	Nebraska	2,315
24	Colorado	2,310
25	Tennessee	2,272
26	Indiana	2,254
27	Iowa	2,247
28	New Hampshire	2,245
29	Virginia	2,234
30	Alabama	2,186
30	Arizona	2,186
32	Mississippi	2,147
33	Oklahoma	2,143
34	Kansas	2,107
35	Wisconsin	2,102
36	Alaska	2,085
37	Arkansas	2,044
38	South Carolina	2,030
39	Kentucky	2,013
40	Wyoming	1,979
41	Idaho	1,963
42	South Dakota	1,955
43	Vermont	1,942
44	Utah	1,936
45	New Mexico	1,912
46	Hawaii	1,890
47	Maine	1,841
48	West Virginia	1,834
49	North Dakota	1,783
50	Montana	1,721

	District of Columbia	2,762

Source: Morgan Quitno Press using data from U.S. Department of the Treasury, Internal Revenue Service
"Tax Refunds" (http://www.irs.gov/)
*National average includes refunds to international sources and other miscellaneous refunds not shown separately.

Value of Federal Individual Income Tax Refunds in 2004

National Total = $227,573,835,000*

ALPHA ORDER

RANK	STATE	REFUNDS	% of USA
24	Alabama	$3,292,846,000	1.4%
47	Alaska	495,857,000	0.2%
20	Arizona	3,590,151,000	1.6%
34	Arkansas	1,799,181,000	0.8%
1	California	26,972,818,000	11.9%
23	Colorado	3,383,858,000	1.5%
25	Connecticut	3,237,065,000	1.4%
44	Delaware	656,915,000	0.3%
4	Florida	13,807,389,000	6.1%
10	Georgia	6,599,296,000	2.9%
42	Hawaii	831,053,000	0.4%
43	Idaho	792,633,000	0.3%
5	Illinois	10,917,562,000	4.8%
14	Indiana	4,815,947,000	2.1%
31	Iowa	1,845,136,000	0.8%
32	Kansas	1,825,710,000	0.8%
27	Kentucky	2,810,257,000	1.2%
22	Louisiana	3,451,665,000	1.5%
40	Maine	859,037,000	0.4%
15	Maryland	4,766,911,000	2.1%
13	Massachusetts	5,613,205,000	2.5%
9	Michigan	7,982,330,000	3.5%
21	Minnesota	3,502,142,000	1.5%
30	Mississippi	2,026,246,000	0.9%
18	Missouri	4,055,852,000	1.8%
45	Montana	538,922,000	0.2%
38	Nebraska	1,140,941,000	0.5%
33	Nevada	1,818,888,000	0.8%
39	New Hampshire	1,084,308,000	0.5%
8	New Jersey	8,112,949,000	3.6%
36	New Mexico	1,230,605,000	0.5%
3	New York	16,560,401,000	7.3%
11	North Carolina	5,901,142,000	2.6%
50	North Dakota	368,021,000	0.2%
7	Ohio	8,991,941,000	4.0%
28	Oklahoma	2,237,720,000	1.0%
29	Oregon	2,170,372,000	1.0%
6	Pennsylvania	9,559,191,000	4.2%
41	Rhode Island	836,350,000	0.4%
26	South Carolina	2,905,692,000	1.3%
46	South Dakota	512,410,000	0.2%
17	Tennessee	4,326,725,000	1.9%
2	Texas	17,261,476,000	7.6%
35	Utah	1,470,036,000	0.6%
48	Vermont	429,166,000	0.2%
12	Virginia	5,814,902,000	2.6%
16	Washington	4,573,810,000	2.0%
37	West Virginia	1,155,948,000	0.5%
19	Wisconsin	3,775,458,000	1.7%
49	Wyoming	378,369,000	0.2%

RANK ORDER

RANK	STATE	REFUNDS	% of USA
1	California	$26,972,818,000	11.9%
2	Texas	17,261,476,000	7.6%
3	New York	16,560,401,000	7.3%
4	Florida	13,807,389,000	6.1%
5	Illinois	10,917,562,000	4.8%
6	Pennsylvania	9,559,191,000	4.2%
7	Ohio	8,991,941,000	4.0%
8	New Jersey	8,112,949,000	3.6%
9	Michigan	7,982,330,000	3.5%
10	Georgia	6,599,296,000	2.9%
11	North Carolina	5,901,142,000	2.6%
12	Virginia	5,814,902,000	2.6%
13	Massachusetts	5,613,205,000	2.5%
14	Indiana	4,815,947,000	2.1%
15	Maryland	4,766,911,000	2.1%
16	Washington	4,573,810,000	2.0%
17	Tennessee	4,326,725,000	1.9%
18	Missouri	4,055,852,000	1.8%
19	Wisconsin	3,775,458,000	1.7%
20	Arizona	3,590,151,000	1.6%
21	Minnesota	3,502,142,000	1.5%
22	Louisiana	3,451,665,000	1.5%
23	Colorado	3,383,858,000	1.5%
24	Alabama	3,292,846,000	1.4%
25	Connecticut	3,237,065,000	1.4%
26	South Carolina	2,905,692,000	1.3%
27	Kentucky	2,810,257,000	1.2%
28	Oklahoma	2,237,720,000	1.0%
29	Oregon	2,170,372,000	1.0%
30	Mississippi	2,026,246,000	0.9%
31	Iowa	1,845,136,000	0.8%
32	Kansas	1,825,710,000	0.8%
33	Nevada	1,818,888,000	0.8%
34	Arkansas	1,799,181,000	0.8%
35	Utah	1,470,036,000	0.6%
36	New Mexico	1,230,605,000	0.5%
37	West Virginia	1,155,948,000	0.5%
38	Nebraska	1,140,941,000	0.5%
39	New Hampshire	1,084,308,000	0.5%
40	Maine	859,037,000	0.4%
41	Rhode Island	836,350,000	0.4%
42	Hawaii	831,053,000	0.4%
43	Idaho	792,633,000	0.3%
44	Delaware	656,915,000	0.3%
45	Montana	538,922,000	0.2%
46	South Dakota	512,410,000	0.2%
47	Alaska	495,857,000	0.2%
48	Vermont	429,166,000	0.2%
49	Wyoming	378,369,000	0.2%
50	North Dakota	368,021,000	0.2%
	District of Columbia	526,086,000	0.2%

Source: U.S. Department of the Treasury, Internal Revenue Service
   "Tax Refunds" (http://www.irs.gov/)
*Total includes refunds to international sources and other miscellaneous refunds not shown separately.

Average Value of Federal Individual Income Tax Refunds in 2004

National Average = $2,143*

ALPHA ORDER

RANK	STATE	REFUNDS
13	Alabama	$2,116
23	Alaska	2,006
24	Arizona	2,005
28	Arkansas	1,985
6	California	2,282
17	Colorado	2,086
2	Connecticut	2,444
20	Delaware	2,045
12	Florida	2,175
9	Georgia	2,213
44	Hawaii	1,776
47	Idaho	1,752
4	Illinois	2,313
22	Indiana	2,019
46	Iowa	1,764
35	Kansas	1,877
33	Kentucky	1,935
10	Louisiana	2,199
48	Maine	1,722
8	Maryland	2,245
5	Massachusetts	2,291
14	Michigan	2,111
36	Minnesota	1,855
15	Mississippi	2,109
32	Missouri	1,940
49	Montana	1,638
43	Nebraska	1,791
11	Nevada	2,193
16	New Hampshire	2,090
1	New Jersey	2,474
37	New Mexico	1,854
3	New York	2,386
26	North Carolina	1,994
50	North Dakota	1,601
29	Ohio	1,980
34	Oklahoma	1,902
40	Oregon	1,814
26	Pennsylvania	1,994
25	Rhode Island	2,002
30	South Carolina	1,961
39	South Dakota	1,842
19	Tennessee	2,046
7	Texas	2,246
38	Utah	1,852
45	Vermont	1,773
17	Virginia	2,086
21	Washington	2,037
42	West Virginia	1,800
41	Wisconsin	1,801
31	Wyoming	1,955

RANK ORDER

RANK	STATE	REFUNDS
1	New Jersey	$2,474
2	Connecticut	2,444
3	New York	2,386
4	Illinois	2,313
5	Massachusetts	2,291
6	California	2,282
7	Texas	2,246
8	Maryland	2,245
9	Georgia	2,213
10	Louisiana	2,199
11	Nevada	2,193
12	Florida	2,175
13	Alabama	2,116
14	Michigan	2,111
15	Mississippi	2,109
16	New Hampshire	2,090
17	Colorado	2,086
17	Virginia	2,086
19	Tennessee	2,046
20	Delaware	2,045
21	Washington	2,037
22	Indiana	2,019
23	Alaska	2,006
24	Arizona	2,005
25	Rhode Island	2,002
26	North Carolina	1,994
26	Pennsylvania	1,994
28	Arkansas	1,985
29	Ohio	1,980
30	South Carolina	1,961
31	Wyoming	1,955
32	Missouri	1,940
33	Kentucky	1,935
34	Oklahoma	1,902
35	Kansas	1,877
36	Minnesota	1,855
37	New Mexico	1,854
38	Utah	1,852
39	South Dakota	1,842
40	Oregon	1,814
41	Wisconsin	1,801
42	West Virginia	1,800
43	Nebraska	1,791
44	Hawaii	1,776
45	Vermont	1,773
46	Iowa	1,764
47	Idaho	1,752
48	Maine	1,722
49	Montana	1,638
50	North Dakota	1,601

District of Columbia   2,397

Source: Morgan Quitno Press using data from U.S. Department of the Treasury, Internal Revenue Service
"Tax Refunds" (http://www.irs.gov/)
*National average includes refunds to international sources and other miscellaneous refunds not shown separately.

Value of Federal Corporate Income Tax Refunds in 2004

National Total = $45,849,884,000*

ALPHA ORDER

RANK	STATE	REFUNDS	% of USA
33	Alabama	$141,742,000	0.3%
49	Alaska	28,744,000	0.1%
26	Arizona	350,673,000	0.8%
39	Arkansas	82,489,000	0.2%
4	California	3,732,361,000	8.1%
27	Colorado	336,528,000	0.7%
16	Connecticut	963,643,000	2.1%
19	Delaware	680,413,000	1.5%
15	Florida	1,050,373,000	2.3%
11	Georgia	1,292,002,000	2.8%
42	Hawaii	62,467,000	0.1%
36	Idaho	109,843,000	0.2%
6	Illinois	2,607,056,000	5.7%
21	Indiana	551,668,000	1.2%
22	Iowa	546,241,000	1.2%
31	Kansas	256,239,000	0.6%
35	Kentucky	132,324,000	0.3%
29	Louisiana	289,536,000	0.6%
40	Maine	70,998,000	0.2%
13	Maryland	1,157,659,000	2.5%
20	Massachusetts	636,831,000	1.4%
5	Michigan	3,363,458,000	7.3%
12	Minnesota	1,160,927,000	2.5%
41	Mississippi	69,383,000	0.2%
17	Missouri	853,035,000	1.9%
47	Montana	40,073,000	0.1%
25	Nebraska	355,596,000	0.8%
32	Nevada	160,546,000	0.4%
37	New Hampshire	98,977,000	0.2%
9	New Jersey	1,530,471,000	3.3%
43	New Mexico	56,053,000	0.1%
1	New York	5,039,048,000	11.0%
8	North Carolina	1,605,916,000	3.5%
44	North Dakota	50,296,000	0.1%
2	Ohio	4,594,168,000	10.0%
28	Oklahoma	300,221,000	0.7%
10	Oregon	1,425,047,000	3.1%
7	Pennsylvania	1,857,076,000	4.1%
30	Rhode Island	278,763,000	0.6%
34	South Carolina	139,305,000	0.3%
46	South Dakota	41,913,000	0.1%
23	Tennessee	519,216,000	1.1%
3	Texas	4,498,392,000	9.8%
38	Utah	83,586,000	0.2%
45	Vermont	49,028,000	0.1%
24	Virginia	424,939,000	0.9%
14	Washington	1,123,521,000	2.5%
48	West Virginia	30,152,000	0.1%
18	Wisconsin	686,186,000	1.5%
50	Wyoming	16,609,000	0.0%

RANK ORDER

RANK	STATE	REFUNDS	% of USA
1	New York	$5,039,048,000	11.0%
2	Ohio	4,594,168,000	10.0%
3	Texas	4,498,392,000	9.8%
4	California	3,732,361,000	8.1%
5	Michigan	3,363,458,000	7.3%
6	Illinois	2,607,056,000	5.7%
7	Pennsylvania	1,857,076,000	4.1%
8	North Carolina	1,605,916,000	3.5%
9	New Jersey	1,530,471,000	3.3%
10	Oregon	1,425,047,000	3.1%
11	Georgia	1,292,002,000	2.8%
12	Minnesota	1,160,927,000	2.5%
13	Maryland	1,157,659,000	2.5%
14	Washington	1,123,521,000	2.5%
15	Florida	1,050,373,000	2.3%
16	Connecticut	963,643,000	2.1%
17	Missouri	853,035,000	1.9%
18	Wisconsin	686,186,000	1.5%
19	Delaware	680,413,000	1.5%
20	Massachusetts	636,831,000	1.4%
21	Indiana	551,668,000	1.2%
22	Iowa	546,241,000	1.2%
23	Tennessee	519,216,000	1.1%
24	Virginia	424,939,000	0.9%
25	Nebraska	355,596,000	0.8%
26	Arizona	350,673,000	0.8%
27	Colorado	336,528,000	0.7%
28	Oklahoma	300,221,000	0.7%
29	Louisiana	289,536,000	0.6%
30	Rhode Island	278,763,000	0.6%
31	Kansas	256,239,000	0.6%
32	Nevada	160,546,000	0.4%
33	Alabama	141,742,000	0.3%
34	South Carolina	139,305,000	0.3%
35	Kentucky	132,324,000	0.3%
36	Idaho	109,843,000	0.2%
37	New Hampshire	98,977,000	0.2%
38	Utah	83,586,000	0.2%
39	Arkansas	82,489,000	0.2%
40	Maine	70,998,000	0.2%
41	Mississippi	69,383,000	0.2%
42	Hawaii	62,467,000	0.1%
43	New Mexico	56,053,000	0.1%
44	North Dakota	50,296,000	0.1%
45	Vermont	49,028,000	0.1%
46	South Dakota	41,913,000	0.1%
47	Montana	40,073,000	0.1%
48	West Virginia	30,152,000	0.1%
49	Alaska	28,744,000	0.1%
50	Wyoming	16,609,000	0.0%
	District of Columbia	70,187,000	0.2%

Source: U.S. Department of the Treasury, Internal Revenue Service
    "Tax Refunds" (http://www.irs.gov/)
*Total includes refunds to international sources and other miscellaneous refunds not shown separately.

Average Value of Federal Corporate Income Tax Refunds in 2004

National Average = $94,917*

RANK	STATE	REFUNDS
36	Alabama	$33,367
42	Alaska	27,323
26	Arizona	59,893
45	Arkansas	23,302
20	California	71,545
31	Colorado	41,424
5	Connecticut	183,132
1	Delaware	432,283
27	Florida	51,850
12	Georgia	120,388
43	Hawaii	25,383
28	Idaho	48,029
9	Illinois	144,539
17	Indiana	82,228
22	Iowa	65,075
32	Kansas	40,660
37	Kentucky	32,900
29	Louisiana	46,445
40	Maine	29,374
8	Maryland	145,563
25	Massachusetts	61,193
6	Michigan	174,444
13	Minnesota	119,241
46	Mississippi	20,911
16	Missouri	90,642
49	Montana	10,816
19	Nebraska	76,720
33	Nevada	40,593
35	New Hampshire	37,505
15	New Jersey	103,438
44	New Mexico	24,868
4	New York	212,001
10	North Carolina	144,274
41	North Dakota	28,272
21	Ohio	68,774
24	Oklahoma	61,282
3	Oregon	215,037
7	Pennsylvania	155,847
2	Rhode Island	224,990
38	South Carolina	32,187
47	South Dakota	20,287
18	Tennessee	78,101
11	Texas	130,593
39	Utah	29,756
30	Vermont	42,633
34	Virginia	40,351
14	Washington	103,665
48	West Virginia	16,334
23	Wisconsin	61,930
50	Wyoming	10,329

RANK	STATE	REFUNDS
1	Delaware	$432,283
2	Rhode Island	224,990
3	Oregon	215,037
4	New York	212,001
5	Connecticut	183,132
6	Michigan	174,444
7	Pennsylvania	155,847
8	Maryland	145,563
9	Illinois	144,539
10	North Carolina	144,274
11	Texas	130,593
12	Georgia	120,388
13	Minnesota	119,241
14	Washington	103,665
15	New Jersey	103,438
16	Missouri	90,642
17	Indiana	82,228
18	Tennessee	78,101
19	Nebraska	76,720
20	California	71,545
21	Ohio	68,774
22	Iowa	65,075
23	Wisconsin	61,930
24	Oklahoma	61,282
25	Massachusetts	61,193
26	Arizona	59,893
27	Florida	51,850
28	Idaho	48,029
29	Louisiana	46,445
30	Vermont	42,633
31	Colorado	41,424
32	Kansas	40,660
33	Nevada	40,593
34	Virginia	40,351
35	New Hampshire	37,505
36	Alabama	33,367
37	Kentucky	32,900
38	South Carolina	32,187
39	Utah	29,756
40	Maine	29,374
41	North Dakota	28,272
42	Alaska	27,323
43	Hawaii	25,383
44	New Mexico	24,868
45	Arkansas	23,302
46	Mississippi	20,911
47	South Dakota	20,287
48	West Virginia	16,334
49	Montana	10,816
50	Wyoming	10,329
	District of Columbia	69,977

Source: Morgan Quitno Press using data from U.S. Department of the Treasury, Internal Revenue Service
    "Tax Refunds" (http://www.irs.gov/)
*National average includes refunds to international sources and other miscellaneous refunds not shown separately.

Federal Tax Burden as a Percentage of Income in 2005

National Percent = 19.0% of Income*

ALPHA ORDER				RANK ORDER		
RANK	STATE	PERCENT		RANK	STATE	PERCENT
43	Alabama	17.0		1	Connecticut	23.0
20	Alaska	18.6		2	Massachusetts	21.3
22	Arizona	18.4		3	New Jersey	21.1
38	Arkansas	17.3		4	Wyoming	21.0
10	California	19.6		5	New York	20.6
9	Colorado	19.8		6	New Hampshire	20.3
1	Connecticut	23.0		7	Washington	20.0
11	Delaware	19.4		8	Nevada	19.9
11	Florida	19.4		9	Colorado	19.8
22	Georgia	18.4		10	California	19.6
43	Hawaii	17.0		11	Delaware	19.4
47	Idaho	16.9		11	Florida	19.4
11	Illinois	19.4		11	Illinois	19.4
29	Indiana	17.8		14	Rhode Island	19.3
43	Iowa	17.0		15	Virginia	19.2
32	Kansas	17.7		16	Texas	19.1
41	Kentucky	17.2		17	Maryland	18.9
49	Louisiana	16.5		17	Minnesota	18.9
29	Maine	17.8		19	New Mexico	18.8
17	Maryland	18.9		20	Alaska	18.6
2	Massachusetts	21.3		21	Michigan	18.5
21	Michigan	18.5		22	Arizona	18.4
17	Minnesota	18.9		22	Georgia	18.4
50	Mississippi	16.4		22	Vermont	18.4
32	Missouri	17.7		22	Wisconsin	18.4
35	Montana	17.5		26	Pennsylvania	18.3
38	Nebraska	17.3		27	Oregon	18.2
8	Nevada	19.9		28	North Carolina	17.9
6	New Hampshire	20.3		29	Indiana	17.8
3	New Jersey	21.1		29	Maine	17.8
19	New Mexico	18.8		29	Tennessee	17.8
5	New York	20.6		32	Kansas	17.7
28	North Carolina	17.9		32	Missouri	17.7
43	North Dakota	17.0		34	South Dakota	17.6
36	Ohio	17.4		35	Montana	17.5
42	Oklahoma	17.1		36	Ohio	17.4
27	Oregon	18.2		36	Utah	17.4
26	Pennsylvania	18.3		38	Arkansas	17.3
14	Rhode Island	19.3		38	Nebraska	17.3
38	South Carolina	17.3		38	South Carolina	17.3
34	South Dakota	17.6		41	Kentucky	17.2
29	Tennessee	17.8		42	Oklahoma	17.1
16	Texas	19.1		43	Alabama	17.0
36	Utah	17.4		43	Hawaii	17.0
22	Vermont	18.4		43	Iowa	17.0
15	Virginia	19.2		43	North Dakota	17.0
7	Washington	20.0		47	Idaho	16.9
48	West Virginia	16.6		48	West Virginia	16.6
22	Wisconsin	18.4		49	Louisiana	16.5
4	Wyoming	21.0		50	Mississippi	16.4
					District of Columbia	20.6

Source: The Tax Foundation
"America Celebrates Tax Freedom Day" (http://www.taxfoundation.org/publications/show/93.html)
*This table attempts to allocate federal tax revenue among the states based on who ultimately bears the burden of taxes as opposed to simply the states where taxes are collected.

Per Capita Federal Tax Burden in 2005

National Per Capita = $7,071*

ALPHA ORDER			RANK ORDER		
RANK	**STATE**	**PER CAPITA**	**RANK**	**STATE**	**PER CAPITA**
43	Alabama	$5,202	1	Connecticut	$11,819
16	Alaska	7,165	2	New Jersey	10,067
38	Arizona	5,768	3	Massachusetts	10,040
48	Arkansas	4,911	4	New York	8,868
9	California	7,798	5	New Hampshire	8,372
10	Colorado	7,797	6	Maryland	8,260
1	Connecticut	11,819	7	Washington	7,973
14	Delaware	7,559	8	Wyoming	7,890
19	Florida	6,851	9	California	7,798
25	Georgia	6,321	10	Colorado	7,797
29	Hawaii	6,166	11	Illinois	7,760
45	Idaho	5,122	11	Minnesota	7,760
11	Illinois	7,760	13	Virginia	7,566
31	Indiana	6,072	14	Delaware	7,559
34	Iowa	5,913	15	Rhode Island	7,301
27	Kansas	6,208	16	Alaska	7,165
40	Kentucky	5,368	17	Nevada	7,147
46	Louisiana	5,092	18	Pennsylvania	7,071
32	Maine	6,023	19	Florida	6,851
6	Maryland	8,260	20	Michigan	6,705
3	Massachusetts	10,040	21	Wisconsin	6,684
20	Michigan	6,705	22	Vermont	6,640
11	Minnesota	7,760	23	Texas	6,479
50	Mississippi	4,487	24	Nebraska	6,322
28	Missouri	6,180	25	Georgia	6,321
41	Montana	5,332	26	Oregon	6,215
24	Nebraska	6,322	27	Kansas	6,208
17	Nevada	7,147	28	Missouri	6,180
5	New Hampshire	8,372	29	Hawaii	6,166
2	New Jersey	10,067	30	Ohio	6,154
39	New Mexico	5,491	31	Indiana	6,072
4	New York	8,868	32	Maine	6,023
36	North Carolina	5,859	33	South Dakota	5,979
37	North Dakota	5,775	34	Iowa	5,913
30	Ohio	6,154	35	Tennessee	5,877
44	Oklahoma	5,200	36	North Carolina	5,859
26	Oregon	6,215	37	North Dakota	5,775
18	Pennsylvania	7,071	38	Arizona	5,768
15	Rhode Island	7,301	39	New Mexico	5,491
42	South Carolina	5,276	40	Kentucky	5,368
33	South Dakota	5,979	41	Montana	5,332
35	Tennessee	5,877	42	South Carolina	5,276
23	Texas	6,479	43	Alabama	5,202
47	Utah	5,001	44	Oklahoma	5,200
22	Vermont	6,640	45	Idaho	5,122
13	Virginia	7,566	46	Louisiana	5,092
7	Washington	7,973	47	Utah	5,001
49	West Virginia	4,744	48	Arkansas	4,911
21	Wisconsin	6,684	49	West Virginia	4,744
8	Wyoming	7,890	50	Mississippi	4,487
				District of Columbia	10,975

Source: The Tax Foundation
"America Celebrates Tax Freedom Day" (http://www.taxfoundation.org/publications/show/93.html)
*This table attempts to allocate federal tax revenue among the states based on who ultimately bears the burden of taxes as opposed to simply the states where taxes are collected.

Federal Expenditures per Dollar of Federal Taxes in 2004

National Median = $1.13 Received for Each Dollar Sent*

RANK	STATE	PER DOLLAR
6	Alabama	$1.69
2	Alaska	1.89
21	Arizona	1.23
13	Arkansas	1.47
43	California	0.78
41	Colorado	0.80
48	Connecticut	0.65
40	Delaware	0.82
32	Florida	1.00
36	Georgia	0.95
8	Hawaii	1.58
18	Idaho	1.32
45	Illinois	0.73
35	Indiana	0.96
28	Iowa	1.06
24	Kansas	1.13
10	Kentucky	1.52
13	Louisiana	1.47
15	Maine	1.36
17	Maryland	1.34
43	Massachusetts	0.78
38	Michigan	0.86
46	Minnesota	0.70
3	Mississippi	1.83
19	Missouri	1.31
7	Montana	1.60
28	Nebraska	1.06
46	Nevada	0.70
49	New Hampshire	0.64
50	New Jersey	0.57
1	New Mexico	1.99
41	New York	0.80
26	North Carolina	1.09
5	North Dakota	1.75
31	Ohio	1.02
12	Oklahoma	1.48
32	Oregon	1.00
27	Pennsylvania	1.08
28	Rhode Island	1.06
15	South Carolina	1.36
11	South Dakota	1.49
20	Tennessee	1.29
34	Texas	0.98
22	Utah	1.19
23	Vermont	1.14
8	Virginia	1.58
37	Washington	0.90
4	West Virginia	1.82
39	Wisconsin	0.84
24	Wyoming	1.13

RANK	STATE	PER DOLLAR
1	New Mexico	$1.99
2	Alaska	1.89
3	Mississippi	1.83
4	West Virginia	1.82
5	North Dakota	1.75
6	Alabama	1.69
7	Montana	1.60
8	Hawaii	1.58
8	Virginia	1.58
10	Kentucky	1.52
11	South Dakota	1.49
12	Oklahoma	1.48
13	Arkansas	1.47
13	Louisiana	1.47
15	Maine	1.36
15	South Carolina	1.36
17	Maryland	1.34
18	Idaho	1.32
19	Missouri	1.31
20	Tennessee	1.29
21	Arizona	1.23
22	Utah	1.19
23	Vermont	1.14
24	Kansas	1.13
24	Wyoming	1.13
26	North Carolina	1.09
27	Pennsylvania	1.08
28	Iowa	1.06
28	Nebraska	1.06
28	Rhode Island	1.06
31	Ohio	1.02
32	Florida	1.00
32	Oregon	1.00
34	Texas	0.98
35	Indiana	0.96
36	Georgia	0.95
37	Washington	0.90
38	Michigan	0.86
39	Wisconsin	0.84
40	Delaware	0.82
41	Colorado	0.80
41	New York	0.80
43	California	0.78
43	Massachusetts	0.78
45	Illinois	0.73
46	Minnesota	0.70
46	Nevada	0.70
48	Connecticut	0.65
49	New Hampshire	0.64
50	New Jersey	0.57

District of Columbia 6.59

Source: The Tax Foundation
   "Federal Spending in Each State Per Dollar of Federal Taxes, 2003" (http://www.taxfoundation.org/taxdata/)
*This table shows how much the federal government spent in each state compared to how much the federal government receives from each state.

Per Capita Cost of Complying with Federal Income Tax Requirements: 2005

National Per Capita = $897*

RANK	STATE	PER CAPITA
47	Alabama	$711
35	Alaska	837
44	Arizona	768
40	Arkansas	791
45	California	762
3	Colorado	1,167
12	Connecticut	1,013
2	Delaware	1,181
9	Florida	1,071
36	Georgia	820
31	Hawaii	866
25	Idaho	891
19	Illinois	936
37	Indiana	816
23	Iowa	899
28	Kansas	877
43	Kentucky	771
41	Louisiana	777
17	Maine	955
18	Maryland	945
14	Massachusetts	984
33	Michigan	841
22	Minnesota	901
50	Mississippi	658
29	Missouri	876
4	Montana	1,155
13	Nebraska	993
7	Nevada	1,090
21	New Hampshire	922
6	New Jersey	1,097
46	New Mexico	746
8	New York	1,088
38	North Carolina	813
16	North Dakota	974
27	Ohio	883
20	Oklahoma	927
24	Oregon	894
32	Pennsylvania	844
5	Rhode Island	1,125
41	South Carolina	777
15	South Dakota	976
48	Tennessee	705
39	Texas	797
10	Utah	1,046
11	Vermont	1,030
33	Virginia	841
30	Washington	875
49	West Virginia	689
26	Wisconsin	887
1	Wyoming	1,242

RANK	STATE	PER CAPITA
1	Wyoming	$1,242
2	Delaware	1,181
3	Colorado	1,167
4	Montana	1,155
5	Rhode Island	1,125
6	New Jersey	1,097
7	Nevada	1,090
8	New York	1,088
9	Florida	1,071
10	Utah	1,046
11	Vermont	1,030
12	Connecticut	1,013
13	Nebraska	993
14	Massachusetts	984
15	South Dakota	976
16	North Dakota	974
17	Maine	955
18	Maryland	945
19	Illinois	936
20	Oklahoma	927
21	New Hampshire	922
22	Minnesota	901
23	Iowa	899
24	Oregon	894
25	Idaho	891
26	Wisconsin	887
27	Ohio	883
28	Kansas	877
29	Missouri	876
30	Washington	875
31	Hawaii	866
32	Pennsylvania	844
33	Michigan	841
33	Virginia	841
35	Alaska	837
36	Georgia	820
37	Indiana	816
38	North Carolina	813
39	Texas	797
40	Arkansas	791
41	Louisiana	777
41	South Carolina	777
43	Kentucky	771
44	Arizona	768
45	California	762
46	New Mexico	746
47	Alabama	711
48	Tennessee	705
49	West Virginia	689
50	Mississippi	658

| | District of Columbia | 5,476 |

Source: The Tax Foundation
"The Rising Cost of Complying with the Federal Income Tax" (www.taxfoundation.org/press/show/1282.html)
*This estimate is based on the number and types of tax forms filed by state and the estimated paper work burden generated by the IRS. Does not include costs of the IRS, the Tax Court and any litigation regarding disputed tax returns. Also does not include the productive value of what people might have been doing with their time instead of filling out forms.

Federal Government Expenditures in 2004

National Total = $2,162,204,000,000*

ALPHA ORDER

RANK	STATE	EXPENDITURES	% of USA
19	Alabama	$39,047,000,000	1.8%
42	Alaska	8,445,000,000	0.4%
18	Arizona	41,979,000,000	1.9%
32	Arkansas	19,489,000,000	0.9%
1	California	232,387,000,000	10.7%
25	Colorado	30,060,000,000	1.4%
24	Connecticut	30,304,000,000	1.4%
48	Delaware	5,253,000,000	0.2%
4	Florida	121,934,000,000	5.6%
13	Georgia	55,153,000,000	2.6%
38	Hawaii	12,187,000,000	0.6%
41	Idaho	8,968,000,000	0.4%
7	Illinois	76,828,000,000	3.6%
20	Indiana	37,918,000,000	1.8%
33	Iowa	19,473,000,000	0.9%
34	Kansas	19,131,000,000	0.9%
22	Kentucky	31,714,000,000	1.5%
21	Louisiana	32,954,000,000	1.5%
40	Maine	10,865,000,000	0.5%
9	Maryland	64,726,000,000	3.0%
14	Massachusetts	53,120,000,000	2.5%
10	Michigan	60,488,000,000	2.8%
27	Minnesota	28,791,000,000	1.3%
29	Mississippi	22,338,000,000	1.0%
15	Missouri	45,730,000,000	2.1%
45	Montana	7,494,000,000	0.3%
39	Nebraska	11,795,000,000	0.5%
37	Nevada	12,769,000,000	0.6%
44	New Hampshire	7,959,000,000	0.4%
11	New Jersey	55,264,000,000	2.6%
31	New Mexico	19,864,000,000	0.9%
2	New York	143,903,000,000	6.7%
12	North Carolina	55,233,000,000	2.6%
47	North Dakota	6,035,000,000	0.3%
8	Ohio	73,195,000,000	3.4%
28	Oklahoma	26,644,000,000	1.2%
30	Oregon	21,871,000,000	1.0%
5	Pennsylvania	94,900,000,000	4.4%
43	Rhode Island	8,245,000,000	0.4%
26	South Carolina	30,051,000,000	1.4%
46	South Dakota	6,602,000,000	0.3%
16	Tennessee	45,441,000,000	2.1%
3	Texas	141,858,000,000	6.6%
36	Utah	13,684,000,000	0.6%
49	Vermont	4,633,000,000	0.2%
6	Virginia	90,638,000,000	4.2%
17	Washington	44,841,000,000	2.1%
35	West Virginia	15,183,000,000	0.7%
23	Wisconsin	31,554,000,000	1.5%
50	Wyoming	4,393,000,000	0.2%

RANK ORDER

RANK	STATE	EXPENDITURES	% of USA
1	California	$232,387,000,000	10.7%
2	New York	143,903,000,000	6.7%
3	Texas	141,858,000,000	6.6%
4	Florida	121,934,000,000	5.6%
5	Pennsylvania	94,900,000,000	4.4%
6	Virginia	90,638,000,000	4.2%
7	Illinois	76,828,000,000	3.6%
8	Ohio	73,195,000,000	3.4%
9	Maryland	64,726,000,000	3.0%
10	Michigan	60,488,000,000	2.8%
11	New Jersey	55,264,000,000	2.6%
12	North Carolina	55,233,000,000	2.6%
13	Georgia	55,153,000,000	2.6%
14	Massachusetts	53,120,000,000	2.5%
15	Missouri	45,730,000,000	2.1%
16	Tennessee	45,441,000,000	2.1%
17	Washington	44,841,000,000	2.1%
18	Arizona	41,979,000,000	1.9%
19	Alabama	39,047,000,000	1.8%
20	Indiana	37,918,000,000	1.8%
21	Louisiana	32,954,000,000	1.5%
22	Kentucky	31,714,000,000	1.5%
23	Wisconsin	31,554,000,000	1.5%
24	Connecticut	30,304,000,000	1.4%
25	Colorado	30,060,000,000	1.4%
26	South Carolina	30,051,000,000	1.4%
27	Minnesota	28,791,000,000	1.3%
28	Oklahoma	26,644,000,000	1.2%
29	Mississippi	22,338,000,000	1.0%
30	Oregon	21,871,000,000	1.0%
31	New Mexico	19,864,000,000	0.9%
32	Arkansas	19,489,000,000	0.9%
33	Iowa	19,473,000,000	0.9%
34	Kansas	19,131,000,000	0.9%
35	West Virginia	15,183,000,000	0.7%
36	Utah	13,684,000,000	0.6%
37	Nevada	12,769,000,000	0.6%
38	Hawaii	12,187,000,000	0.6%
39	Nebraska	11,795,000,000	0.5%
40	Maine	10,865,000,000	0.5%
41	Idaho	8,968,000,000	0.4%
42	Alaska	8,445,000,000	0.4%
43	Rhode Island	8,245,000,000	0.4%
44	New Hampshire	7,959,000,000	0.4%
45	Montana	7,494,000,000	0.3%
46	South Dakota	6,602,000,000	0.3%
47	North Dakota	6,035,000,000	0.3%
48	Delaware	5,253,000,000	0.2%
49	Vermont	4,633,000,000	0.2%
50	Wyoming	4,393,000,000	0.2%
	District of Columbia	37,630,000,000	1.7%

Source: U.S. Bureau of the Census
   "Consolidated Federal Funds Report: 2004" (CFFR/04, Dec 2005, http://www.census.gov/govs/www/cffr04.html)
*Total includes $18,167,000,000 in U.S. territories ($15,479,000,000 in Puerto Rico) and $23,075,000,000 in expenditures not distributed by state.

Per Capita Federal Government Expenditures in 2004

National Per Capita = $7,223*

ALPHA ORDER				RANK ORDER		
RANK	STATE	PER CAPITA		RANK	STATE	PER CAPITA
9	Alabama	$8,628		1	Alaska	$12,839
1	Alaska	12,839		2	Virginia	12,115
24	Arizona	7,314		3	Maryland	11,639
28	Arkansas	7,087		4	New Mexico	10,438
34	California	6,484		5	Hawaii	9,656
33	Colorado	6,532		6	North Dakota	9,484
8	Connecticut	8,661		7	Wyoming	8,684
39	Delaware	6,328		8	Connecticut	8,661
29	Florida	7,014		9	Alabama	8,628
41	Georgia	6,184		10	South Dakota	8,567
5	Hawaii	9,656		11	West Virginia	8,377
36	Idaho	6,428		12	Massachusetts	8,290
45	Illinois	6,044		13	Maine	8,262
43	Indiana	6,090		14	Montana	8,085
32	Iowa	6,595		15	Missouri	7,940
30	Kansas	6,998		16	Tennessee	7,711
18	Kentucky	7,657		17	Mississippi	7,701
25	Louisiana	7,312		18	Kentucky	7,657
13	Maine	8,262		18	Pennsylvania	7,657
3	Maryland	11,639		20	Rhode Island	7,635
12	Massachusetts	8,290		21	Oklahoma	7,562
46	Michigan	5,986		22	New York	7,464
49	Minnesota	5,649		23	Vermont	7,458
17	Mississippi	7,701		24	Arizona	7,314
15	Missouri	7,940		25	Louisiana	7,312
14	Montana	8,085		26	Washington	7,224
31	Nebraska	6,749		27	South Carolina	7,159
50	Nevada	5,473		28	Arkansas	7,087
42	New Hampshire	6,126		29	Florida	7,014
38	New Jersey	6,363		30	Kansas	6,998
4	New Mexico	10,438		31	Nebraska	6,749
22	New York	7,464		32	Iowa	6,595
35	North Carolina	6,467		33	Colorado	6,532
6	North Dakota	9,484		34	California	6,484
37	Ohio	6,392		35	North Carolina	6,467
21	Oklahoma	7,562		36	Idaho	6,428
43	Oregon	6,090		37	Ohio	6,392
18	Pennsylvania	7,657		38	New Jersey	6,363
20	Rhode Island	7,635		39	Delaware	6,328
27	South Carolina	7,159		40	Texas	6,313
10	South Dakota	8,567		41	Georgia	6,184
16	Tennessee	7,711		42	New Hampshire	6,126
40	Texas	6,313		43	Indiana	6,090
48	Utah	5,653		43	Oregon	6,090
23	Vermont	7,458		45	Illinois	6,044
2	Virginia	12,115		46	Michigan	5,986
26	Washington	7,224		47	Wisconsin	5,733
11	West Virginia	8,377		48	Utah	5,653
47	Wisconsin	5,733		49	Minnesota	5,649
7	Wyoming	8,684		50	Nevada	5,473
					District of Columbia	67,895

Source: Morgan Quitno Press using data from U.S. Bureau of the Census
"Consolidated Federal Funds Report: 2004" (CFFR/04, Dec 2005, http://www.census.gov/govs/www/cffr04.html)
*National per capita excludes expenditures and population for territories and undistributed amounts.

Federal Government Grants in 2004

National Total = $460,152,000,000*

ALPHA ORDER

RANK	STATE	EXPENDITURES	% of USA
23	Alabama	$7,008,000,000	1.5%
36	Alaska	3,217,000,000	0.7%
17	Arizona	8,364,000,000	1.8%
31	Arkansas	4,683,000,000	1.0%
1	California	54,534,000,000	11.9%
26	Colorado	5,643,000,000	1.2%
27	Connecticut	5,556,000,000	1.2%
50	Delaware	1,241,000,000	0.3%
5	Florida	19,610,000,000	4.3%
11	Georgia	11,759,000,000	2.6%
42	Hawaii	2,158,000,000	0.5%
44	Idaho	1,995,000,000	0.4%
6	Illinois	16,531,000,000	3.6%
21	Indiana	7,436,000,000	1.6%
33	Iowa	4,039,000,000	0.9%
35	Kansas	3,469,000,000	0.8%
24	Kentucky	6,743,000,000	1.5%
19	Louisiana	7,787,000,000	1.7%
38	Maine	2,758,000,000	0.6%
15	Maryland	8,837,000,000	1.9%
8	Massachusetts	13,876,000,000	3.0%
9	Michigan	13,227,000,000	2.9%
22	Minnesota	7,209,000,000	1.6%
28	Mississippi	5,379,000,000	1.2%
16	Missouri	8,734,000,000	1.9%
43	Montana	1,997,000,000	0.4%
39	Nebraska	2,531,000,000	0.6%
41	Nevada	2,322,000,000	0.5%
45	New Hampshire	1,879,000,000	0.4%
12	New Jersey	11,333,000,000	2.5%
32	New Mexico	4,663,000,000	1.0%
2	New York	50,009,000,000	10.9%
10	North Carolina	12,574,000,000	2.7%
48	North Dakota	1,515,000,000	0.3%
7	Ohio	16,514,000,000	3.6%
29	Oklahoma	5,271,000,000	1.1%
30	Oregon	5,185,000,000	1.1%
4	Pennsylvania	19,916,000,000	4.3%
40	Rhode Island	2,329,000,000	0.5%
25	South Carolina	6,145,000,000	1.3%
47	South Dakota	1,620,000,000	0.4%
13	Tennessee	9,863,000,000	2.1%
3	Texas	27,792,000,000	6.0%
37	Utah	2,948,000,000	0.6%
49	Vermont	1,423,000,000	0.3%
18	Virginia	7,991,000,000	1.7%
14	Washington	9,083,000,000	2.0%
34	West Virginia	3,701,000,000	0.8%
20	Wisconsin	7,484,000,000	1.6%
46	Wyoming	1,636,000,000	0.4%

RANK ORDER

RANK	STATE	EXPENDITURES	% of USA
1	California	$54,534,000,000	11.9%
2	New York	50,009,000,000	10.9%
3	Texas	27,792,000,000	6.0%
4	Pennsylvania	19,916,000,000	4.3%
5	Florida	19,610,000,000	4.3%
6	Illinois	16,531,000,000	3.6%
7	Ohio	16,514,000,000	3.6%
8	Massachusetts	13,876,000,000	3.0%
9	Michigan	13,227,000,000	2.9%
10	North Carolina	12,574,000,000	2.7%
11	Georgia	11,759,000,000	2.6%
12	New Jersey	11,333,000,000	2.5%
13	Tennessee	9,863,000,000	2.1%
14	Washington	9,083,000,000	2.0%
15	Maryland	8,837,000,000	1.9%
16	Missouri	8,734,000,000	1.9%
17	Arizona	8,364,000,000	1.8%
18	Virginia	7,991,000,000	1.7%
19	Louisiana	7,787,000,000	1.7%
20	Wisconsin	7,484,000,000	1.6%
21	Indiana	7,436,000,000	1.6%
22	Minnesota	7,209,000,000	1.6%
23	Alabama	7,008,000,000	1.5%
24	Kentucky	6,743,000,000	1.5%
25	South Carolina	6,145,000,000	1.3%
26	Colorado	5,643,000,000	1.2%
27	Connecticut	5,556,000,000	1.2%
28	Mississippi	5,379,000,000	1.2%
29	Oklahoma	5,271,000,000	1.1%
30	Oregon	5,185,000,000	1.1%
31	Arkansas	4,683,000,000	1.0%
32	New Mexico	4,663,000,000	1.0%
33	Iowa	4,039,000,000	0.9%
34	West Virginia	3,701,000,000	0.8%
35	Kansas	3,469,000,000	0.8%
36	Alaska	3,217,000,000	0.7%
37	Utah	2,948,000,000	0.6%
38	Maine	2,758,000,000	0.6%
39	Nebraska	2,531,000,000	0.6%
40	Rhode Island	2,329,000,000	0.5%
41	Nevada	2,322,000,000	0.5%
42	Hawaii	2,158,000,000	0.5%
43	Montana	1,997,000,000	0.4%
44	Idaho	1,995,000,000	0.4%
45	New Hampshire	1,879,000,000	0.4%
46	Wyoming	1,636,000,000	0.4%
47	South Dakota	1,620,000,000	0.4%
48	North Dakota	1,515,000,000	0.3%
49	Vermont	1,423,000,000	0.3%
50	Delaware	1,241,000,000	0.3%
	District of Columbia	4,205,000,000	0.9%

Source: U.S. Bureau of the Census
    "Consolidated Federal Funds Report: 2004" (CFFR/04, Dec 2005, http://www.census.gov/govs/www/cffr04.html)
*Total includes $6,387,000,000 in U.S. territories ($5,324,000,000 in Puerto Rico) and $44,000,000 in expenditures not distributed by state.

Per Capita Expenditures for Federal Government Grants in 2004

National Per Capita = $1,545*

ALPHA ORDER

RANK	STATE	PER CAPITA
22	Alabama	$1,549
1	Alaska	4,891
30	Arizona	1,457
16	Arkansas	1,703
23	California	1,522
45	Colorado	1,226
21	Connecticut	1,588
26	Delaware	1,495
48	Florida	1,128
39	Georgia	1,319
15	Hawaii	1,710
35	Idaho	1,430
42	Illinois	1,300
47	Indiana	1,194
37	Iowa	1,368
43	Kansas	1,269
18	Kentucky	1,628
14	Louisiana	1,728
11	Maine	2,097
20	Maryland	1,589
7	Massachusetts	2,166
40	Michigan	1,309
36	Minnesota	1,414
13	Mississippi	1,854
24	Missouri	1,516
9	Montana	2,154
31	Nebraska	1,448
50	Nevada	995
32	New Hampshire	1,446
41	New Jersey	1,305
4	New Mexico	2,450
3	New York	2,594
27	North Carolina	1,472
5	North Dakota	2,381
34	Ohio	1,442
25	Oklahoma	1,496
33	Oregon	1,444
19	Pennsylvania	1,607
8	Rhode Island	2,157
28	South Carolina	1,464
10	South Dakota	2,102
17	Tennessee	1,674
44	Texas	1,237
46	Utah	1,218
6	Vermont	2,291
49	Virginia	1,068
29	Washington	1,463
12	West Virginia	2,042
38	Wisconsin	1,360
2	Wyoming	3,234

RANK ORDER

RANK	STATE	PER CAPITA
1	Alaska	$4,891
2	Wyoming	3,234
3	New York	2,594
4	New Mexico	2,450
5	North Dakota	2,381
6	Vermont	2,291
7	Massachusetts	2,166
8	Rhode Island	2,157
9	Montana	2,154
10	South Dakota	2,102
11	Maine	2,097
12	West Virginia	2,042
13	Mississippi	1,854
14	Louisiana	1,728
15	Hawaii	1,710
16	Arkansas	1,703
17	Tennessee	1,674
18	Kentucky	1,628
19	Pennsylvania	1,607
20	Maryland	1,589
21	Connecticut	1,588
22	Alabama	1,549
23	California	1,522
24	Missouri	1,516
25	Oklahoma	1,496
26	Delaware	1,495
27	North Carolina	1,472
28	South Carolina	1,464
29	Washington	1,463
30	Arizona	1,457
31	Nebraska	1,448
32	New Hampshire	1,446
33	Oregon	1,444
34	Ohio	1,442
35	Idaho	1,430
36	Minnesota	1,414
37	Iowa	1,368
38	Wisconsin	1,360
39	Georgia	1,319
40	Michigan	1,309
41	New Jersey	1,305
42	Illinois	1,300
43	Kansas	1,269
44	Texas	1,237
45	Colorado	1,226
46	Utah	1,218
47	Indiana	1,194
48	Florida	1,128
49	Virginia	1,068
50	Nevada	995

District of Columbia 7,587

Source: Morgan Quitno Press using data from U.S. Bureau of the Census
"Consolidated Federal Funds Report: 2004" (CFFR/04, Dec 2005, http://www.census.gov/govs/www/cffr04.html)
*National per capita excludes expenditures and population for territories and undistributed amounts.

Federal Government Procurement Contract Awards in 2004

National Total = $339,681,000,000*

ALPHA ORDER					RANK ORDER			
RANK	STATE	EXPENDITURES	% of USA		RANK	STATE	EXPENDITURES	% of USA
13	Alabama	$7,600,000,000	2.2%		1	California	$40,254,000,000	11.9%
35	Alaska	1,700,000,000	0.5%		2	Virginia	35,325,000,000	10.4%
6	Arizona	9,797,000,000	2.9%		3	Texas	26,969,000,000	7.9%
42	Arkansas	848,000,000	0.2%		4	Maryland	20,804,000,000	6.1%
1	California	40,254,000,000	11.9%		5	Florida	11,447,000,000	3.4%
20	Colorado	5,747,000,000	1.7%		6	Arizona	9,797,000,000	2.9%
7	Connecticut	9,509,000,000	2.8%		7	Connecticut	9,509,000,000	2.8%
50	Delaware	265,000,000	0.1%		8	Pennsylvania	9,311,000,000	2.7%
5	Florida	11,447,000,000	3.4%		9	Massachusetts	9,127,000,000	2.7%
19	Georgia	5,813,000,000	1.7%		10	New York	8,889,000,000	2.6%
33	Hawaii	2,066,000,000	0.6%		11	Tennessee	8,118,000,000	2.4%
38	Idaho	1,373,000,000	0.4%		12	Missouri	7,991,000,000	2.4%
16	Illinois	6,583,000,000	1.9%		13	Alabama	7,600,000,000	2.2%
24	Indiana	4,002,000,000	1.2%		14	Washington	6,946,000,000	2.0%
37	Iowa	1,599,000,000	0.5%		15	Ohio	6,936,000,000	2.0%
32	Kansas	2,242,000,000	0.7%		16	Illinois	6,583,000,000	1.9%
21	Kentucky	4,637,000,000	1.4%		17	New Jersey	6,132,000,000	1.8%
26	Louisiana	3,418,000,000	1.0%		18	New Mexico	5,973,000,000	1.8%
34	Maine	1,711,000,000	0.5%		19	Georgia	5,813,000,000	1.7%
4	Maryland	20,804,000,000	6.1%		20	Colorado	5,747,000,000	1.7%
9	Massachusetts	9,127,000,000	2.7%		21	Kentucky	4,637,000,000	1.4%
23	Michigan	4,119,000,000	1.2%		22	South Carolina	4,193,000,000	1.2%
30	Minnesota	2,329,000,000	0.7%		23	Michigan	4,119,000,000	1.2%
29	Mississippi	2,372,000,000	0.7%		24	Indiana	4,002,000,000	1.2%
12	Missouri	7,991,000,000	2.4%		25	North Carolina	3,933,000,000	1.2%
44	Montana	587,000,000	0.2%		26	Louisiana	3,418,000,000	1.0%
43	Nebraska	697,000,000	0.2%		27	Oklahoma	2,804,000,000	0.8%
36	Nevada	1,600,000,000	0.5%		28	Wisconsin	2,641,000,000	0.8%
41	New Hampshire	985,000,000	0.3%		29	Mississippi	2,372,000,000	0.7%
17	New Jersey	6,132,000,000	1.8%		30	Minnesota	2,329,000,000	0.7%
18	New Mexico	5,973,000,000	1.8%		31	Utah	2,304,000,000	0.7%
10	New York	8,889,000,000	2.6%		32	Kansas	2,242,000,000	0.7%
25	North Carolina	3,933,000,000	1.2%		33	Hawaii	2,066,000,000	0.6%
47	North Dakota	503,000,000	0.1%		34	Maine	1,711,000,000	0.5%
15	Ohio	6,936,000,000	2.0%		35	Alaska	1,700,000,000	0.5%
27	Oklahoma	2,804,000,000	0.8%		36	Nevada	1,600,000,000	0.5%
39	Oregon	1,283,000,000	0.4%		37	Iowa	1,599,000,000	0.5%
8	Pennsylvania	9,311,000,000	2.7%		38	Idaho	1,373,000,000	0.4%
45	Rhode Island	559,000,000	0.2%		39	Oregon	1,283,000,000	0.4%
22	South Carolina	4,193,000,000	1.2%		40	West Virginia	1,041,000,000	0.3%
48	South Dakota	438,000,000	0.1%		41	New Hampshire	985,000,000	0.3%
11	Tennessee	8,118,000,000	2.4%		42	Arkansas	848,000,000	0.2%
3	Texas	26,969,000,000	7.9%		43	Nebraska	697,000,000	0.2%
31	Utah	2,304,000,000	0.7%		44	Montana	587,000,000	0.2%
46	Vermont	541,000,000	0.2%		45	Rhode Island	559,000,000	0.2%
2	Virginia	35,325,000,000	10.4%		46	Vermont	541,000,000	0.2%
14	Washington	6,946,000,000	2.0%		47	North Dakota	503,000,000	0.1%
40	West Virginia	1,041,000,000	0.3%		48	South Dakota	438,000,000	0.1%
28	Wisconsin	2,641,000,000	0.8%		49	Wyoming	403,000,000	0.1%
49	Wyoming	403,000,000	0.1%		50	Delaware	265,000,000	0.1%
						District of Columbia	13,347,000,000	3.9%

Source: U.S. Bureau of the Census
"Consolidated Federal Funds Report: 2004" (CFFR/04, Dec 2005, http://www.census.gov/govs/www/cffr04.html)
*Total includes $1,022,000,000 in U.S. territories ($462,000,000 in Puerto Rico) and $18,851,000,000 in expenditures not distributed by state.

Per Capita Expenditures for Federal Government Procurement Contract Awards in 2004
National Per Capita = $1,089*

ALPHA ORDER

RANK	STATE	PER CAPITA
7	Alabama	$1,679
5	Alaska	2,585
6	Arizona	1,707
50	Arkansas	308
15	California	1,123
13	Colorado	1,249
4	Connecticut	2,718
49	Delaware	319
32	Florida	658
33	Georgia	652
8	Hawaii	1,637
19	Idaho	984
40	Illinois	518
34	Indiana	643
39	Iowa	542
22	Kansas	820
16	Kentucky	1,120
27	Louisiana	758
12	Maine	1,301
2	Maryland	3,741
9	Massachusetts	1,424
46	Michigan	408
45	Minnesota	457
23	Mississippi	818
10	Missouri	1,387
35	Montana	633
47	Nebraska	399
31	Nevada	686
27	New Hampshire	758
30	New Jersey	706
3	New Mexico	3,139
43	New York	461
43	North Carolina	461
26	North Dakota	790
36	Ohio	606
25	Oklahoma	796
48	Oregon	357
29	Pennsylvania	751
40	Rhode Island	518
18	South Carolina	999
38	South Dakota	568
11	Tennessee	1,377
14	Texas	1,200
20	Utah	952
21	Vermont	871
1	Virginia	4,722
17	Washington	1,119
37	West Virginia	574
42	Wisconsin	480
24	Wyoming	797

RANK ORDER

RANK	STATE	PER CAPITA
1	Virginia	$4,722
2	Maryland	3,741
3	New Mexico	3,139
4	Connecticut	2,718
5	Alaska	2,585
6	Arizona	1,707
7	Alabama	1,679
8	Hawaii	1,637
9	Massachusetts	1,424
10	Missouri	1,387
11	Tennessee	1,377
12	Maine	1,301
13	Colorado	1,249
14	Texas	1,200
15	California	1,123
16	Kentucky	1,120
17	Washington	1,119
18	South Carolina	999
19	Idaho	984
20	Utah	952
21	Vermont	871
22	Kansas	820
23	Mississippi	818
24	Wyoming	797
25	Oklahoma	796
26	North Dakota	790
27	Louisiana	758
27	New Hampshire	758
29	Pennsylvania	751
30	New Jersey	706
31	Nevada	686
32	Florida	658
33	Georgia	652
34	Indiana	643
35	Montana	633
36	Ohio	606
37	West Virginia	574
38	South Dakota	568
39	Iowa	542
40	Illinois	518
40	Rhode Island	518
42	Wisconsin	480
43	New York	461
43	North Carolina	461
45	Minnesota	457
46	Michigan	408
47	Nebraska	399
48	Oregon	357
49	Delaware	319
50	Arkansas	308

District of Columbia — 24,082

Source: Morgan Quitno Press using data from U.S. Bureau of the Census
"Consolidated Federal Funds Report: 2004" (CFFR/04, Dec 2005, http://www.census.gov/govs/www/cffr04.html)
*National per capita excludes expenditures and population for territories and undistributed amounts.

Federal Government Direct Payments for Retirement and Disability in 2004
National Total = $666,969,000,000*

ALPHA ORDER

RANK	STATE	PAYMENTS	% of USA
20	Alabama	$12,930,000,000	1.9%
50	Alaska	1,135,000,000	0.2%
19	Arizona	12,942,000,000	1.9%
30	Arkansas	7,404,000,000	1.1%
1	California	64,078,000,000	9.6%
27	Colorado	8,918,000,000	1.3%
29	Connecticut	7,809,000,000	1.2%
45	Delaware	2,085,000,000	0.3%
2	Florida	48,050,000,000	7.2%
12	Georgia	17,748,000,000	2.7%
40	Hawaii	3,202,000,000	0.5%
41	Idaho	3,053,000,000	0.5%
7	Illinois	25,597,000,000	3.8%
18	Indiana	14,019,000,000	2.1%
32	Iowa	6,971,000,000	1.0%
33	Kansas	6,412,000,000	1.0%
23	Kentucky	10,579,000,000	1.6%
25	Louisiana	9,981,000,000	1.5%
39	Maine	3,587,000,000	0.5%
15	Maryland	14,190,000,000	2.1%
16	Massachusetts	14,186,000,000	2.1%
8	Michigan	22,916,000,000	3.4%
24	Minnesota	10,059,000,000	1.5%
31	Mississippi	7,297,000,000	1.1%
17	Missouri	14,071,000,000	2.1%
44	Montana	2,394,000,000	0.4%
38	Nebraska	4,070,000,000	0.6%
35	Nevada	5,149,000,000	0.8%
42	New Hampshire	3,028,000,000	0.5%
11	New Jersey	18,922,000,000	2.8%
36	New Mexico	4,681,000,000	0.7%
4	New York	41,209,000,000	6.2%
10	North Carolina	20,131,000,000	3.0%
47	North Dakota	1,477,000,000	0.2%
6	Ohio	26,251,000,000	3.9%
26	Oklahoma	9,169,000,000	1.4%
28	Oregon	8,452,000,000	1.3%
5	Pennsylvania	33,147,000,000	5.0%
43	Rhode Island	2,627,000,000	0.4%
22	South Carolina	10,812,000,000	1.6%
46	South Dakota	1,842,000,000	0.3%
13	Tennessee	14,517,000,000	2.2%
3	Texas	41,765,000,000	6.3%
37	Utah	4,123,000,000	0.6%
48	Vermont	1,417,000,000	0.2%
9	Virginia	20,982,000,000	3.1%
14	Washington	14,472,000,000	2.2%
34	West Virginia	5,835,000,000	0.9%
21	Wisconsin	12,065,000,000	1.8%
49	Wyoming	1,192,000,000	0.2%

RANK ORDER

RANK	STATE	PAYMENTS	% of USA
1	California	$64,078,000,000	9.6%
2	Florida	48,050,000,000	7.2%
3	Texas	41,765,000,000	6.3%
4	New York	41,209,000,000	6.2%
5	Pennsylvania	33,147,000,000	5.0%
6	Ohio	26,251,000,000	3.9%
7	Illinois	25,597,000,000	3.8%
8	Michigan	22,916,000,000	3.4%
9	Virginia	20,982,000,000	3.1%
10	North Carolina	20,131,000,000	3.0%
11	New Jersey	18,922,000,000	2.8%
12	Georgia	17,748,000,000	2.7%
13	Tennessee	14,517,000,000	2.2%
14	Washington	14,472,000,000	2.2%
15	Maryland	14,190,000,000	2.1%
16	Massachusetts	14,186,000,000	2.1%
17	Missouri	14,071,000,000	2.1%
18	Indiana	14,019,000,000	2.1%
19	Arizona	12,942,000,000	1.9%
20	Alabama	12,930,000,000	1.9%
21	Wisconsin	12,065,000,000	1.8%
22	South Carolina	10,812,000,000	1.6%
23	Kentucky	10,579,000,000	1.6%
24	Minnesota	10,059,000,000	1.5%
25	Louisiana	9,981,000,000	1.5%
26	Oklahoma	9,169,000,000	1.4%
27	Colorado	8,918,000,000	1.3%
28	Oregon	8,452,000,000	1.3%
29	Connecticut	7,809,000,000	1.2%
30	Arkansas	7,404,000,000	1.1%
31	Mississippi	7,297,000,000	1.1%
32	Iowa	6,971,000,000	1.0%
33	Kansas	6,412,000,000	1.0%
34	West Virginia	5,835,000,000	0.9%
35	Nevada	5,149,000,000	0.8%
36	New Mexico	4,681,000,000	0.7%
37	Utah	4,123,000,000	0.6%
38	Nebraska	4,070,000,000	0.6%
39	Maine	3,587,000,000	0.5%
40	Hawaii	3,202,000,000	0.5%
41	Idaho	3,053,000,000	0.5%
42	New Hampshire	3,028,000,000	0.5%
43	Rhode Island	2,627,000,000	0.4%
44	Montana	2,394,000,000	0.4%
45	Delaware	2,085,000,000	0.3%
46	South Dakota	1,842,000,000	0.3%
47	North Dakota	1,477,000,000	0.2%
48	Vermont	1,417,000,000	0.2%
49	Wyoming	1,192,000,000	0.2%
50	Alaska	1,135,000,000	0.2%
	District of Columbia	1,882,000,000	0.3%

Source: U.S. Bureau of the Census
"Consolidated Federal Funds Report: 2004" (CFFR/04, Dec 2005, http://www.census.gov/govs/www/cffr04.html)
*Total includes $6,113,000,000 in U.S. territories ($5,668,000,000 in Puerto Rico) and $26,000,000 in expenditures not distributed by state. "Direct Payments for Retirement and Disability" include Social Security, federal retirement and disability payments and veterans benefits.

Per Capita Federal Government Direct Payments for Retirement and Disability in 2004
National Per Capita = $2,250*

ALPHA ORDER

RANK	STATE	PER CAPITA
2	Alabama	$2,857
49	Alaska	1,726
33	Arizona	2,255
6	Arkansas	2,692
48	California	1,788
46	Colorado	1,938
35	Connecticut	2,232
15	Delaware	2,512
4	Florida	2,764
44	Georgia	1,990
13	Hawaii	2,537
40	Idaho	2,188
43	Illinois	2,014
34	Indiana	2,251
21	Iowa	2,361
25	Kansas	2,346
11	Kentucky	2,554
36	Louisiana	2,215
5	Maine	2,728
12	Maryland	2,552
37	Massachusetts	2,214
32	Michigan	2,268
45	Minnesota	1,974
14	Mississippi	2,516
18	Missouri	2,443
9	Montana	2,583
28	Nebraska	2,329
38	Nevada	2,207
27	New Hampshire	2,331
41	New Jersey	2,179
17	New Mexico	2,460
42	New York	2,137
22	North Carolina	2,357
29	North Dakota	2,321
30	Ohio	2,293
8	Oklahoma	2,602
24	Oregon	2,353
7	Pennsylvania	2,674
19	Rhode Island	2,433
10	South Carolina	2,576
20	South Dakota	2,390
16	Tennessee	2,463
47	Texas	1,859
50	Utah	1,703
31	Vermont	2,281
3	Virginia	2,805
26	Washington	2,332
1	West Virginia	3,219
39	Wisconsin	2,192
23	Wyoming	2,356

RANK ORDER

RANK	STATE	PER CAPITA
1	West Virginia	$3,219
2	Alabama	2,857
3	Virginia	2,805
4	Florida	2,764
5	Maine	2,728
6	Arkansas	2,692
7	Pennsylvania	2,674
8	Oklahoma	2,602
9	Montana	2,583
10	South Carolina	2,576
11	Kentucky	2,554
12	Maryland	2,552
13	Hawaii	2,537
14	Mississippi	2,516
15	Delaware	2,512
16	Tennessee	2,463
17	New Mexico	2,460
18	Missouri	2,443
19	Rhode Island	2,433
20	South Dakota	2,390
21	Iowa	2,361
22	North Carolina	2,357
23	Wyoming	2,356
24	Oregon	2,353
25	Kansas	2,346
26	Washington	2,332
27	New Hampshire	2,331
28	Nebraska	2,329
29	North Dakota	2,321
30	Ohio	2,293
31	Vermont	2,281
32	Michigan	2,268
33	Arizona	2,255
34	Indiana	2,251
35	Connecticut	2,232
36	Louisiana	2,215
37	Massachusetts	2,214
38	Nevada	2,207
39	Wisconsin	2,192
40	Idaho	2,188
41	New Jersey	2,179
42	New York	2,137
43	Illinois	2,014
44	Georgia	1,990
45	Minnesota	1,974
46	Colorado	1,938
47	Texas	1,859
48	California	1,788
49	Alaska	1,726
50	Utah	1,703

District of Columbia 3,396

Source: Morgan Quitno Press using data from U.S. Bureau of the Census
"Consolidated Federal Funds Report: 2004" (CFFR/04, Dec 2005, http://www.census.gov/govs/www/cffr04.html)
*National per capita excludes expenditures and population for territories and undistributed amounts. "Direct Payments for Retirement and Disability" include Social Security, federal retirement and disability payments and terans benefits.

Federal Government "Other" Direct Payments in 2004

National Total = $469,800,000,000*

ALPHA ORDER

RANK	STATE	PAYMENTS	% of USA
20	Alabama	$8,017,000,000	1.7%
49	Alaska	665,000,000	0.1%
22	Arizona	7,269,000,000	1.5%
32	Arkansas	5,045,000,000	1.1%
1	California	51,492,000,000	11.0%
29	Colorado	5,295,000,000	1.1%
26	Connecticut	5,828,000,000	1.2%
47	Delaware	1,168,000,000	0.2%
3	Florida	32,432,000,000	6.9%
11	Georgia	11,509,000,000	2.4%
45	Hawaii	1,607,000,000	0.3%
43	Idaho	1,649,000,000	0.4%
6	Illinois	21,111,000,000	4.5%
15	Indiana	10,004,000,000	2.1%
28	Iowa	5,615,000,000	1.2%
33	Kansas	4,801,000,000	1.0%
24	Kentucky	6,523,000,000	1.4%
18	Louisiana	8,950,000,000	1.9%
41	Maine	1,852,000,000	0.4%
14	Maryland	10,372,000,000	2.2%
10	Massachusetts	12,374,000,000	2.6%
8	Michigan	16,616,000,000	3.5%
23	Minnesota	6,891,000,000	1.5%
30	Mississippi	5,196,000,000	1.1%
13	Missouri	10,892,000,000	2.3%
44	Montana	1,629,000,000	0.3%
35	Nebraska	3,199,000,000	0.7%
37	Nevada	2,352,000,000	0.5%
46	New Hampshire	1,412,000,000	0.3%
9	New Jersey	14,549,000,000	3.1%
36	New Mexico	2,476,000,000	0.5%
2	New York	34,726,000,000	7.4%
12	North Carolina	11,398,000,000	2.4%
42	North Dakota	1,753,000,000	0.4%
7	Ohio	17,918,000,000	3.8%
25	Oklahoma	5,938,000,000	1.3%
31	Oregon	5,048,000,000	1.1%
5	Pennsylvania	25,917,000,000	5.5%
40	Rhode Island	1,902,000,000	0.4%
27	South Carolina	5,746,000,000	1.2%
39	South Dakota	1,937,000,000	0.4%
17	Tennessee	9,467,000,000	2.0%
4	Texas	30,642,000,000	6.5%
38	Utah	2,158,000,000	0.5%
48	Vermont	847,000,000	0.2%
16	Virginia	9,997,000,000	2.1%
19	Washington	8,282,000,000	1.8%
34	West Virginia	3,249,000,000	0.7%
21	Wisconsin	7,469,000,000	1.6%
50	Wyoming	641,000,000	0.1%

RANK ORDER

RANK	STATE	PAYMENTS	% of USA
1	California	$51,492,000,000	11.0%
2	New York	34,726,000,000	7.4%
3	Florida	32,432,000,000	6.9%
4	Texas	30,642,000,000	6.5%
5	Pennsylvania	25,917,000,000	5.5%
6	Illinois	21,111,000,000	4.5%
7	Ohio	17,918,000,000	3.8%
8	Michigan	16,616,000,000	3.5%
9	New Jersey	14,549,000,000	3.1%
10	Massachusetts	12,374,000,000	2.6%
11	Georgia	11,509,000,000	2.4%
12	North Carolina	11,398,000,000	2.4%
13	Missouri	10,892,000,000	2.3%
14	Maryland	10,372,000,000	2.2%
15	Indiana	10,004,000,000	2.1%
16	Virginia	9,997,000,000	2.1%
17	Tennessee	9,467,000,000	2.0%
18	Louisiana	8,950,000,000	1.9%
19	Washington	8,282,000,000	1.8%
20	Alabama	8,017,000,000	1.7%
21	Wisconsin	7,469,000,000	1.6%
22	Arizona	7,269,000,000	1.5%
23	Minnesota	6,891,000,000	1.5%
24	Kentucky	6,523,000,000	1.4%
25	Oklahoma	5,938,000,000	1.3%
26	Connecticut	5,828,000,000	1.2%
27	South Carolina	5,746,000,000	1.2%
28	Iowa	5,615,000,000	1.2%
29	Colorado	5,295,000,000	1.1%
30	Mississippi	5,196,000,000	1.1%
31	Oregon	5,048,000,000	1.1%
32	Arkansas	5,045,000,000	1.1%
33	Kansas	4,801,000,000	1.0%
34	West Virginia	3,249,000,000	0.7%
35	Nebraska	3,199,000,000	0.7%
36	New Mexico	2,476,000,000	0.5%
37	Nevada	2,352,000,000	0.5%
38	Utah	2,158,000,000	0.5%
39	South Dakota	1,937,000,000	0.4%
40	Rhode Island	1,902,000,000	0.4%
41	Maine	1,852,000,000	0.4%
42	North Dakota	1,753,000,000	0.4%
43	Idaho	1,649,000,000	0.4%
44	Montana	1,629,000,000	0.3%
45	Hawaii	1,607,000,000	0.3%
46	New Hampshire	1,412,000,000	0.3%
47	Delaware	1,168,000,000	0.2%
48	Vermont	847,000,000	0.2%
49	Alaska	665,000,000	0.1%
50	Wyoming	641,000,000	0.1%
	District of Columbia	2,670,000,000	0.6%

Source: U.S. Bureau of the Census
    "Consolidated Federal Funds Report: 2004" (CFFR/04, Dec 2005, http://www.census.gov/govs/www/cffr04.html)
*Total includes $3,216,000,000 in U.S. territories ($2,999,000,000 in Puerto Rico) and $89,000,000 in
expenditures not distributed by state. "Other Direct Payments" include direct payments for programs other than
retirement and disability. These include Medicare, excess earned income tax credits, unemployment compensation,
food stamps, housing assistance and agricultural assistance.

Per Capita Expenditures for Federal Government
"Other" Direct Payments in 2004
National Per Capita = $1,589*

ALPHA ORDER

RANK	STATE	PER CAPITA
15	Alabama	$1,772
48	Alaska	1,011
44	Arizona	1,266
10	Arkansas	1,835
28	California	1,437
46	Colorado	1,151
21	Connecticut	1,666
30	Delaware	1,407
8	Florida	1,865
41	Georgia	1,291
42	Hawaii	1,273
45	Idaho	1,182
22	Illinois	1,661
24	Indiana	1,607
6	Iowa	1,902
18	Kansas	1,756
26	Kentucky	1,575
4	Louisiana	1,986
29	Maine	1,408
8	Maryland	1,865
5	Massachusetts	1,931
23	Michigan	1,644
36	Minnesota	1,352
14	Mississippi	1,791
7	Missouri	1,891
17	Montana	1,757
11	Nebraska	1,830
49	Nevada	1,008
47	New Hampshire	1,087
20	New Jersey	1,675
40	New Mexico	1,301
12	New York	1,801
38	North Carolina	1,335
1	North Dakota	2,755
27	Ohio	1,565
19	Oklahoma	1,685
31	Oregon	1,406
3	Pennsylvania	2,091
16	Rhode Island	1,761
32	South Carolina	1,369
2	South Dakota	2,514
25	Tennessee	1,606
33	Texas	1,364
50	Utah	891
34	Vermont	1,363
37	Virginia	1,336
39	Washington	1,334
13	West Virginia	1,793
35	Wisconsin	1,357
43	Wyoming	1,267

RANK ORDER

RANK	STATE	PER CAPITA
1	North Dakota	$2,755
2	South Dakota	2,514
3	Pennsylvania	2,091
4	Louisiana	1,986
5	Massachusetts	1,931
6	Iowa	1,902
7	Missouri	1,891
8	Florida	1,865
8	Maryland	1,865
10	Arkansas	1,835
11	Nebraska	1,830
12	New York	1,801
13	West Virginia	1,793
14	Mississippi	1,791
15	Alabama	1,772
16	Rhode Island	1,761
17	Montana	1,757
18	Kansas	1,756
19	Oklahoma	1,685
20	New Jersey	1,675
21	Connecticut	1,666
22	Illinois	1,661
23	Michigan	1,644
24	Indiana	1,607
25	Tennessee	1,606
26	Kentucky	1,575
27	Ohio	1,565
28	California	1,437
29	Maine	1,408
30	Delaware	1,407
31	Oregon	1,406
32	South Carolina	1,369
33	Texas	1,364
34	Vermont	1,363
35	Wisconsin	1,357
36	Minnesota	1,352
37	Virginia	1,336
38	North Carolina	1,335
39	Washington	1,334
40	New Mexico	1,301
41	Georgia	1,291
42	Hawaii	1,273
43	Wyoming	1,267
44	Arizona	1,266
45	Idaho	1,182
46	Colorado	1,151
47	New Hampshire	1,087
48	Alaska	1,011
49	Nevada	1,008
50	Utah	891

District of Columbia   4,817

Source: Morgan Quitno Press using data from U.S. Bureau of the Census
    "Consolidated Federal Funds Report: 2004" (CFFR/04, Dec 2005, http://www.census.gov/govs/www/cffr04.html)
*National per capita excludes expenditures and population for territories and undistributed amounts. "Other Direct Payments" include direct payments for programs other than retirement and disability. These include Medicare, excess earned income tax credits, unemployment compensation, food stamps, housing assistance and agricultural assistance.

Federal Government Expenditures for Salaries and Wages in 2004

National Total = $225,601,000,000*

ALPHA ORDER

RANK	STATE	SALARIES	% of USA
19	Alabama	$3,492,000,000	1.5%
34	Alaska	1,728,000,000	0.8%
17	Arizona	3,608,000,000	1.6%
36	Arkansas	1,509,000,000	0.7%
1	California	22,029,000,000	9.8%
13	Colorado	4,457,000,000	2.0%
35	Connecticut	1,602,000,000	0.7%
49	Delaware	494,000,000	0.2%
5	Florida	10,395,000,000	4.6%
7	Georgia	8,324,000,000	3.7%
24	Hawaii	3,154,000,000	1.4%
42	Idaho	898,000,000	0.4%
9	Illinois	7,007,000,000	3.1%
26	Indiana	2,457,000,000	1.1%
40	Iowa	1,249,000,000	0.6%
28	Kansas	2,208,000,000	1.0%
22	Kentucky	3,231,000,000	1.4%
25	Louisiana	2,818,000,000	1.2%
41	Maine	957,000,000	0.4%
4	Maryland	10,523,000,000	4.7%
18	Massachusetts	3,557,000,000	1.6%
16	Michigan	3,610,000,000	1.6%
27	Minnesota	2,302,000,000	1.0%
30	Mississippi	2,094,000,000	0.9%
15	Missouri	4,042,000,000	1.8%
43	Montana	886,000,000	0.4%
39	Nebraska	1,298,000,000	0.6%
38	Nevada	1,347,000,000	0.6%
47	New Hampshire	654,000,000	0.3%
14	New Jersey	4,328,000,000	1.9%
31	New Mexico	2,072,000,000	0.9%
6	New York	9,070,000,000	4.0%
8	North Carolina	7,197,000,000	3.2%
45	North Dakota	787,000,000	0.3%
12	Ohio	5,576,000,000	2.5%
21	Oklahoma	3,463,000,000	1.5%
32	Oregon	1,903,000,000	0.8%
10	Pennsylvania	6,609,000,000	2.9%
44	Rhode Island	829,000,000	0.4%
23	South Carolina	3,156,000,000	1.4%
46	South Dakota	765,000,000	0.3%
20	Tennessee	3,476,000,000	1.5%
3	Texas	14,690,000,000	6.5%
29	Utah	2,150,000,000	1.0%
50	Vermont	405,000,000	0.2%
2	Virginia	16,342,000,000	7.2%
11	Washington	6,058,000,000	2.7%
37	West Virginia	1,358,000,000	0.6%
33	Wisconsin	1,895,000,000	0.8%
48	Wyoming	521,000,000	0.2%

RANK ORDER

RANK	STATE	SALARIES	% of USA
1	California	$22,029,000,000	9.8%
2	Virginia	16,342,000,000	7.2%
3	Texas	14,690,000,000	6.5%
4	Maryland	10,523,000,000	4.7%
5	Florida	10,395,000,000	4.6%
6	New York	9,070,000,000	4.0%
7	Georgia	8,324,000,000	3.7%
8	North Carolina	7,197,000,000	3.2%
9	Illinois	7,007,000,000	3.1%
10	Pennsylvania	6,609,000,000	2.9%
11	Washington	6,058,000,000	2.7%
12	Ohio	5,576,000,000	2.5%
13	Colorado	4,457,000,000	2.0%
14	New Jersey	4,328,000,000	1.9%
15	Missouri	4,042,000,000	1.8%
16	Michigan	3,610,000,000	1.6%
17	Arizona	3,608,000,000	1.6%
18	Massachusetts	3,557,000,000	1.6%
19	Alabama	3,492,000,000	1.5%
20	Tennessee	3,476,000,000	1.5%
21	Oklahoma	3,463,000,000	1.5%
22	Kentucky	3,231,000,000	1.4%
23	South Carolina	3,156,000,000	1.4%
24	Hawaii	3,154,000,000	1.4%
25	Louisiana	2,818,000,000	1.2%
26	Indiana	2,457,000,000	1.1%
27	Minnesota	2,302,000,000	1.0%
28	Kansas	2,208,000,000	1.0%
29	Utah	2,150,000,000	1.0%
30	Mississippi	2,094,000,000	0.9%
31	New Mexico	2,072,000,000	0.9%
32	Oregon	1,903,000,000	0.8%
33	Wisconsin	1,895,000,000	0.8%
34	Alaska	1,728,000,000	0.8%
35	Connecticut	1,602,000,000	0.7%
36	Arkansas	1,509,000,000	0.7%
37	West Virginia	1,358,000,000	0.6%
38	Nevada	1,347,000,000	0.6%
39	Nebraska	1,298,000,000	0.6%
40	Iowa	1,249,000,000	0.6%
41	Maine	957,000,000	0.4%
42	Idaho	898,000,000	0.4%
43	Montana	886,000,000	0.4%
44	Rhode Island	829,000,000	0.4%
45	North Dakota	787,000,000	0.3%
46	South Dakota	765,000,000	0.3%
47	New Hampshire	654,000,000	0.3%
48	Wyoming	521,000,000	0.2%
49	Delaware	494,000,000	0.2%
50	Vermont	405,000,000	0.2%
	District of Columbia	15,526,000,000	6.9%

Source: U.S. Bureau of the Census
   "Consolidated Federal Funds Report: 2004" (CFFR/04, Dec 2005, http://www.census.gov/govs/www/cffr04.html)
Total includes $1,427,000,000 in U.S. territories ($1,026,000,000 in Puerto Rico) and $4,065,000,000 in expenditures not distributed by state.

Per Capita Expenditures for Federal Government Salaries and Wages in 2004

National Per Capita = $750*

ALPHA ORDER				RANK ORDER		
RANK	STATE	PER CAPITA		RANK	STATE	PER CAPITA
18	Alabama	$772		1	Alaska	$2,627
1	Alaska	2,627		2	Hawaii	2,499
29	Arizona	629		3	Virginia	2,184
38	Arkansas	549		4	Maryland	1,892
31	California	615		5	North Dakota	1,237
11	Colorado	969		6	New Mexico	1,089
45	Connecticut	458		7	Wyoming	1,030
33	Delaware	595		8	South Dakota	993
32	Florida	598		9	Oklahoma	983
13	Georgia	933		10	Washington	976
2	Hawaii	2,499		11	Colorado	969
28	Idaho	644		12	Montana	956
37	Illinois	551		13	Georgia	933
48	Indiana	395		14	Utah	888
47	Iowa	423		15	North Carolina	843
16	Kansas	808		16	Kansas	808
17	Kentucky	780		17	Kentucky	780
30	Louisiana	625		18	Alabama	772
23	Maine	728		19	Rhode Island	768
4	Maryland	1,092		20	South Carolina	752
36	Massachusetts	555		21	West Virginia	749
49	Michigan	357		22	Nebraska	743
46	Minnesota	452		23	Maine	728
24	Mississippi	722		24	Mississippi	722
25	Missouri	702		25	Missouri	702
12	Montana	956		26	Texas	654
22	Nebraska	743		27	Vermont	652
35	Nevada	577		28	Idaho	644
41	New Hampshire	503		29	Arizona	629
42	New Jersey	498		30	Louisiana	625
6	New Mexico	1,089		31	California	615
44	New York	470		32	Florida	598
15	North Carolina	843		33	Delaware	595
5	North Dakota	1,237		34	Tennessee	590
43	Ohio	487		35	Nevada	577
9	Oklahoma	983		36	Massachusetts	555
40	Oregon	530		37	Illinois	551
39	Pennsylvania	533		38	Arkansas	549
19	Rhode Island	768		39	Pennsylvania	533
20	South Carolina	752		40	Oregon	530
8	South Dakota	993		41	New Hampshire	503
34	Tennessee	590		42	New Jersey	498
26	Texas	654		43	Ohio	487
14	Utah	888		44	New York	470
27	Vermont	652		45	Connecticut	458
3	Virginia	2,184		46	Minnesota	452
10	Washington	976		47	Iowa	423
21	West Virginia	749		48	Indiana	395
50	Wisconsin	344		49	Michigan	357
7	Wyoming	1,030		50	Wisconsin	344
					District of Columbia	28,013

Source: Morgan Quitno Press using data from U.S. Bureau of the Census
    "Consolidated Federal Funds Report: 2004" (CFFR/04, Dec 2005, http://www.census.gov/govs/www/cffr04.html)
*National per capita excludes expenditures and population for territories and undistributed amounts.

Average Salary of Federal Civilian Employees in 2003

National Average = $57,704*

ALPHA ORDER

RANK	STATE	SALARY
10	Alabama	$58,150
28	Alaska	51,391
43	Arizona	49,323
45	Arkansas	48,755
12	California	57,552
7	Colorado	58,871
11	Connecticut	57,955
29	Delaware	51,230
20	Florida	53,136
17	Georgia	54,298
41	Hawaii	49,757
31	Idaho	51,133
8	Illinois	58,864
19	Indiana	53,307
40	Iowa	49,927
27	Kansas	52,022
50	Kentucky	46,831
34	Louisiana	50,848
32	Maine	51,053
1	Maryland	68,831
9	Massachusetts	58,420
13	Michigan	57,177
16	Minnesota	55,327
35	Mississippi	50,827
33	Missouri	50,851
42	Montana	49,446
36	Nebraska	50,813
26	Nevada	52,111
2	New Hampshire	64,223
5	New Jersey	62,458
25	New Mexico	52,218
14	New York	55,850
39	North Carolina	50,271
47	North Dakota	48,396
6	Ohio	59,553
38	Oklahoma	50,691
18	Oregon	53,426
24	Pennsylvania	52,271
4	Rhode Island	63,303
30	South Carolina	51,183
49	South Dakota	47,417
23	Tennessee	52,819
21	Texas	53,074
48	Utah	47,871
44	Vermont	49,044
3	Virginia	63,623
15	Washington	55,498
22	West Virginia	52,931
37	Wisconsin	50,717
46	Wyoming	48,641

RANK ORDER

RANK	STATE	SALARY
1	Maryland	$68,831
2	New Hampshire	64,223
3	Virginia	63,623
4	Rhode Island	63,303
5	New Jersey	62,458
6	Ohio	59,553
7	Colorado	58,871
8	Illinois	58,864
9	Massachusetts	58,420
10	Alabama	58,150
11	Connecticut	57,955
12	California	57,552
13	Michigan	57,177
14	New York	55,850
15	Washington	55,498
16	Minnesota	55,327
17	Georgia	54,298
18	Oregon	53,426
19	Indiana	53,307
20	Florida	53,136
21	Texas	53,074
22	West Virginia	52,931
23	Tennessee	52,819
24	Pennsylvania	52,271
25	New Mexico	52,218
26	Nevada	52,111
27	Kansas	52,022
28	Alaska	51,391
29	Delaware	51,230
30	South Carolina	51,183
31	Idaho	51,133
32	Maine	51,053
33	Missouri	50,851
34	Louisiana	50,848
35	Mississippi	50,827
36	Nebraska	50,813
37	Wisconsin	50,717
38	Oklahoma	50,691
39	North Carolina	50,271
40	Iowa	49,927
41	Hawaii	49,757
42	Montana	49,446
43	Arizona	49,323
44	Vermont	49,044
45	Arkansas	48,755
46	Wyoming	48,641
47	North Dakota	48,396
48	Utah	47,871
49	South Dakota	47,417
50	Kentucky	46,831
	District of Columbia	75,925

Source: Office of Personnel Management
   "The Fact Book: 2004 Edition" (http://www.opm.gov/feddata/04factbk.pdf)
*Full-time employees. National average includes employees not shown by state.

Federal Civilian Employees in 2003

National Total = 1,700,319 Full-Time Employees*

RANK	STATE	EMPLOYEES	% of USA
12	Alabama	35,223	2.1%
34	Alaska	12,323	0.7%
18	Arizona	32,076	1.9%
36	Arkansas	11,646	0.7%
1	California	145,996	8.6%
14	Colorado	33,893	2.0%
44	Connecticut	6,994	0.4%
50	Delaware	2,563	0.2%
5	Florida	70,901	4.2%
6	Georgia	64,931	3.8%
24	Hawaii	21,241	1.2%
41	Idaho	8,190	0.5%
10	Illinois	43,602	2.6%
27	Indiana	19,093	1.1%
42	Iowa	7,475	0.4%
31	Kansas	15,043	0.9%
25	Kentucky	20,814	1.2%
26	Louisiana	20,540	1.2%
39	Maine	9,001	0.5%
4	Maryland	105,702	6.2%
21	Massachusetts	25,304	1.5%
22	Michigan	23,862	1.4%
32	Minnesota	14,431	0.8%
29	Mississippi	17,021	1.0%
15	Missouri	33,310	2.0%
38	Montana	9,086	0.5%
40	Nebraska	8,578	0.5%
37	Nevada	9,441	0.6%
49	New Hampshire	3,309	0.2%
19	New Jersey	27,443	1.6%
23	New Mexico	21,848	1.3%
8	New York	60,794	3.6%
17	North Carolina	32,178	1.9%
46	North Dakota	5,355	0.3%
11	Ohio	42,495	2.5%
16	Oklahoma	33,261	2.0%
28	Oregon	18,661	1.1%
7	Pennsylvania	63,138	3.7%
45	Rhode Island	6,191	0.4%
30	South Carolina	16,509	1.0%
43	South Dakota	7,158	0.4%
13	Tennessee	35,177	2.1%
3	Texas	106,501	6.3%
20	Utah	27,422	1.6%
48	Vermont	3,586	0.2%
2	Virginia	116,012	6.8%
9	Washington	45,767	2.7%
33	West Virginia	12,625	0.7%
35	Wisconsin	11,786	0.7%
47	Wyoming	4,886	0.3%

RANK	STATE	EMPLOYEES	% of USA
1	California	145,996	8.6%
2	Virginia	116,012	6.8%
3	Texas	106,501	6.3%
4	Maryland	105,702	6.2%
5	Florida	70,901	4.2%
6	Georgia	64,931	3.8%
7	Pennsylvania	63,138	3.7%
8	New York	60,794	3.6%
9	Washington	45,767	2.7%
10	Illinois	43,602	2.6%
11	Ohio	42,495	2.5%
12	Alabama	35,223	2.1%
13	Tennessee	35,177	2.1%
14	Colorado	33,893	2.0%
15	Missouri	33,310	2.0%
16	Oklahoma	33,261	2.0%
17	North Carolina	32,178	1.9%
18	Arizona	32,076	1.9%
19	New Jersey	27,443	1.6%
20	Utah	27,422	1.6%
21	Massachusetts	25,304	1.5%
22	Michigan	23,862	1.4%
23	New Mexico	21,848	1.3%
24	Hawaii	21,241	1.2%
25	Kentucky	20,814	1.2%
26	Louisiana	20,540	1.2%
27	Indiana	19,093	1.1%
28	Oregon	18,661	1.1%
29	Mississippi	17,021	1.0%
30	South Carolina	16,509	1.0%
31	Kansas	15,043	0.9%
32	Minnesota	14,431	0.8%
33	West Virginia	12,625	0.7%
34	Alaska	12,323	0.7%
35	Wisconsin	11,786	0.7%
36	Arkansas	11,646	0.7%
37	Nevada	9,441	0.6%
38	Montana	9,086	0.5%
39	Maine	9,001	0.5%
40	Nebraska	8,578	0.5%
41	Idaho	8,190	0.5%
42	Iowa	7,475	0.4%
43	South Dakota	7,158	0.4%
44	Connecticut	6,994	0.4%
45	Rhode Island	6,191	0.4%
46	North Dakota	5,355	0.3%
47	Wyoming	4,886	0.3%
48	Vermont	3,586	0.2%
49	New Hampshire	3,309	0.2%
50	Delaware	2,563	0.2%
	District of Columbia	151,338	8.9%

Source: Office of Personnel Management
"The Fact Book: 2004 Edition" (http://www.opm.gov/feddata/04factbk.pdf)
*Full-time employees. National total includes 18,308 employees not shown by state.

Rate of Federal Civilian Employees in 2003

National Rate = 58 Full-Time Employees per 10,000 Population*

ALPHA ORDER

RANK	STATE	RATE
12	Alabama	78
2	Alaska	190
21	Arizona	58
32	Arkansas	43
35	California	41
13	Colorado	75
50	Connecticut	20
43	Delaware	31
33	Florida	42
15	Georgia	74
3	Hawaii	170
18	Idaho	60
40	Illinois	34
43	Indiana	31
47	Iowa	25
25	Kansas	55
27	Kentucky	51
31	Louisiana	46
17	Maine	69
1	Maryland	192
37	Massachusetts	39
48	Michigan	24
45	Minnesota	29
20	Mississippi	59
21	Missouri	58
7	Montana	99
29	Nebraska	49
33	Nevada	42
46	New Hampshire	26
41	New Jersey	32
5	New Mexico	116
41	New York	32
38	North Carolina	30
11	North Dakota	85
39	Ohio	37
9	Oklahoma	95
26	Oregon	52
27	Pennsylvania	51
21	Rhode Island	58
36	South Carolina	40
10	South Dakota	94
18	Tennessee	60
30	Texas	48
6	Utah	115
21	Vermont	58
4	Virginia	157
13	Washington	75
16	West Virginia	70
49	Wisconsin	22
8	Wyoming	97

RANK ORDER

RANK	STATE	RATE
1	Maryland	192
2	Alaska	190
3	Hawaii	170
4	Virginia	157
5	New Mexico	116
6	Utah	115
7	Montana	99
8	Wyoming	97
9	Oklahoma	95
10	South Dakota	94
11	North Dakota	85
12	Alabama	78
13	Colorado	75
13	Washington	75
15	Georgia	74
16	West Virginia	70
17	Maine	69
18	Idaho	60
18	Tennessee	60
20	Mississippi	59
21	Arizona	58
21	Missouri	58
21	Rhode Island	58
21	Vermont	58
25	Kansas	55
26	Oregon	52
27	Kentucky	51
27	Pennsylvania	51
29	Nebraska	49
30	Texas	48
31	Louisiana	46
32	Arkansas	43
33	Florida	42
33	Nevada	42
35	California	41
36	South Carolina	40
37	Massachusetts	39
38	North Carolina	38
39	Ohio	37
40	Illinois	34
41	New Jersey	32
41	New York	32
43	Delaware	31
43	Indiana	31
45	Minnesota	29
46	New Hampshire	26
47	Iowa	25
48	Michigan	24
49	Wisconsin	22
50	Connecticut	20

District of Columbia — 2,713

Source: Morgan Quitno Press using data from Office of Personnel Management
"The Fact Book: 2004 Edition" (http://www.opm.gov/feddata/04factbk.pdf)
*Full-time employees. National rate includes employees not shown by state.

X. GOVERNMENT FINANCE: STATE AND LOCAL

X. GOVERNMENT FINANCE: STATE AND LOCAL

A Note About Fiscal Years:

State and Local:

Data in these tables relate to the state and local governments' 12-month fiscal years. The data reflect individual government fiscal years that ended between July 1 and the following June 30.

State:

The statistics show state government data for fiscal years that end on June 30, 2003, except for four states with other ending dates: Alabama and Michigan (September 30, 2003), New York (March 31, 2003) and Texas (August 31, 2003).

State and Local Government Total Revenue in 2002

National Total = $1,807,573,045,000*

ALPHA ORDER

RANK	STATE	REVENUE	% of USA
26	Alabama	$24,739,824,000	1.4%
41	Alaska	6,992,884,000	0.4%
21	Arizona	30,083,389,000	1.7%
34	Arkansas	13,616,364,000	0.8%
1	California	250,724,771,000	13.9%
23	Colorado	25,656,651,000	1.4%
25	Connecticut	24,831,156,000	1.4%
45	Delaware	5,972,101,000	0.3%
4	Florida	92,630,871,000	5.1%
11	Georgia	46,166,078,000	2.6%
40	Hawaii	7,451,684,000	0.4%
42	Idaho	6,872,684,000	0.4%
6	Illinois	73,587,675,000	4.1%
16	Indiana	34,220,921,000	1.9%
30	Iowa	17,601,402,000	1.0%
31	Kansas	15,985,150,000	0.9%
28	Kentucky	22,474,542,000	1.2%
22	Louisiana	27,372,666,000	1.5%
39	Maine	8,019,443,000	0.4%
18	Maryland	33,468,019,000	1.9%
13	Massachusetts	41,925,472,000	2.3%
8	Michigan	63,098,683,000	3.5%
15	Minnesota	35,131,055,000	1.9%
32	Mississippi	15,905,116,000	0.9%
20	Missouri	30,620,582,000	1.7%
46	Montana	5,510,513,000	0.3%
36	Nebraska	12,030,515,000	0.7%
35	Nevada	12,809,362,000	0.7%
44	New Hampshire	6,728,627,000	0.4%
9	New Jersey	54,835,385,000	3.0%
37	New Mexico	11,503,161,000	0.6%
2	New York	170,981,866,000	9.5%
10	North Carolina	48,596,900,000	2.7%
48	North Dakota	4,226,558,000	0.2%
7	Ohio	72,627,137,000	4.0%
29	Oklahoma	19,160,982,000	1.1%
27	Oregon	23,201,119,000	1.3%
5	Pennsylvania	73,694,315,000	4.1%
43	Rhode Island	6,861,649,000	0.4%
24	South Carolina	24,984,750,000	1.4%
50	South Dakota	3,964,187,000	0.2%
17	Tennessee	33,483,212,000	1.9%
3	Texas	114,018,046,000	6.3%
33	Utah	13,788,726,000	0.8%
49	Vermont	4,045,603,000	0.2%
14	Virginia	38,780,385,000	2.1%
12	Washington	42,123,922,000	2.3%
38	West Virginia	11,344,643,000	0.6%
19	Wisconsin	31,424,054,000	1.7%
47	Wyoming	4,346,263,000	0.2%

RANK ORDER

RANK	STATE	REVENUE	% of USA
1	California	$250,724,771,000	13.9%
2	New York	170,981,866,000	9.5%
3	Texas	114,018,046,000	6.3%
4	Florida	92,630,871,000	5.1%
5	Pennsylvania	73,694,315,000	4.1%
6	Illinois	73,587,675,000	4.1%
7	Ohio	72,627,137,000	4.0%
8	Michigan	63,098,683,000	3.5%
9	New Jersey	54,835,385,000	3.0%
10	North Carolina	48,596,900,000	2.7%
11	Georgia	46,166,078,000	2.6%
12	Washington	42,123,922,000	2.3%
13	Massachusetts	41,925,472,000	2.3%
14	Virginia	38,780,385,000	2.1%
15	Minnesota	35,131,055,000	1.9%
16	Indiana	34,220,921,000	1.9%
17	Tennessee	33,483,212,000	1.9%
18	Maryland	33,468,019,000	1.9%
19	Wisconsin	31,424,054,000	1.7%
20	Missouri	30,620,582,000	1.7%
21	Arizona	30,083,389,000	1.7%
22	Louisiana	27,372,666,000	1.5%
23	Colorado	25,656,651,000	1.4%
24	South Carolina	24,984,750,000	1.4%
25	Connecticut	24,831,156,000	1.4%
26	Alabama	24,739,824,000	1.4%
27	Oregon	23,201,119,000	1.3%
28	Kentucky	22,474,542,000	1.2%
29	Oklahoma	19,160,982,000	1.1%
30	Iowa	17,601,402,000	1.0%
31	Kansas	15,985,150,000	0.9%
32	Mississippi	15,905,116,000	0.9%
33	Utah	13,788,726,000	0.8%
34	Arkansas	13,616,364,000	0.8%
35	Nevada	12,809,362,000	0.7%
36	Nebraska	12,030,515,000	0.7%
37	New Mexico	11,503,161,000	0.6%
38	West Virginia	11,344,643,000	0.6%
39	Maine	8,019,443,000	0.4%
40	Hawaii	7,451,684,000	0.4%
41	Alaska	6,992,884,000	0.4%
42	Idaho	6,872,684,000	0.4%
43	Rhode Island	6,861,649,000	0.4%
44	New Hampshire	6,728,627,000	0.4%
45	Delaware	5,972,101,000	0.3%
46	Montana	5,510,513,000	0.3%
47	Wyoming	4,346,263,000	0.2%
48	North Dakota	4,226,558,000	0.2%
49	Vermont	4,045,603,000	0.2%
50	South Dakota	3,964,187,000	0.2%
	District of Columbia	7,351,982,000	0.4%

Source: U.S. Bureau of the Census, Governments Division
"State and Local Government Finances: 2002 Census" (http://www.census.gov/govs/www/estimate02.html)
Total revenue includes all money received from external sources. This includes taxes, intergovernmental transfers and insurance trust revenue and revenue from government owned utilities and other commercial or auxiliary enterprise.

Per Capita State and Local Government Revenue in 2002

National Per Capita = $6,278*

ALPHA ORDER

ALPHA ORDER

RANK	STATE	PER CAPITA
40	Alabama	$5,521
1	Alaska	10,912
39	Arizona	5,531
50	Arkansas	5,029
6	California	7,166
35	Colorado	5,704
5	Connecticut	7,179
4	Delaware	7,409
37	Florida	5,553
43	Georgia	5,406
25	Hawaii	6,036
49	Idaho	5,117
31	Illinois	5,847
36	Indiana	5,557
26	Iowa	5,990
30	Kansas	5,892
41	Kentucky	5,495
22	Louisiana	6,114
20	Maine	6,179
21	Maryland	6,150
13	Massachusetts	6,538
18	Michigan	6,283
7	Minnesota	6,991
38	Mississippi	5,546
44	Missouri	5,391
24	Montana	6,051
8	Nebraska	6,968
29	Nevada	5,908
46	New Hampshire	5,275
15	New Jersey	6,393
19	New Mexico	6,201
2	New York	8,928
31	North Carolina	5,847
10	North Dakota	6,669
16	Ohio	6,365
42	Oklahoma	5,493
11	Oregon	6,585
27	Pennsylvania	5,978
14	Rhode Island	6,419
23	South Carolina	6,085
48	South Dakota	5,213
33	Tennessee	5,781
47	Texas	5,249
28	Utah	5,944
12	Vermont	6,562
45	Virginia	5,332
9	Washington	6,943
17	West Virginia	6,284
34	Wisconsin	5,776
3	Wyoming	8,707

RANK ORDER

RANK	STATE	PER CAPITA
1	Alaska	$10,912
2	New York	8,928
3	Wyoming	8,707
4	Delaware	7,409
5	Connecticut	7,179
6	California	7,166
7	Minnesota	6,991
8	Nebraska	6,968
9	Washington	6,943
10	North Dakota	6,669
11	Oregon	6,585
12	Vermont	6,562
13	Massachusetts	6,538
14	Rhode Island	6,419
15	New Jersey	6,393
16	Ohio	6,365
17	West Virginia	6,284
18	Michigan	6,283
19	New Mexico	6,201
20	Maine	6,179
21	Maryland	6,150
22	Louisiana	6,114
23	South Carolina	6,085
24	Montana	6,051
25	Hawaii	6,036
26	Iowa	5,998
27	Pennsylvania	5,978
28	Utah	5,944
29	Nevada	5,908
30	Kansas	5,892
31	Illinois	5,847
31	North Carolina	5,847
33	Tennessee	5,781
34	Wisconsin	5,776
35	Colorado	5,704
36	Indiana	5,557
37	Florida	5,553
38	Mississippi	5,546
39	Arizona	5,531
40	Alabama	5,521
41	Kentucky	5,495
42	Oklahoma	5,493
43	Georgia	5,406
44	Missouri	5,391
45	Virginia	5,332
46	New Hampshire	5,275
47	Texas	5,249
48	South Dakota	5,213
49	Idaho	5,117
50	Arkansas	5,029

	District of Columbia	13,021

Source: Morgan Quitno Press using data from U.S. Bureau of the Census, Governments Division
"State and Local Government Finances: 2002 Census" (http://www.census.gov/govs/www/estimate02.html)
*Total revenue includes all money received from external sources. This includes taxes, intergovernmental transfers and insurance trust revenue and revenue from government owned utilities and other commercial or auxiliary enterprise.

State and Local Government Revenue from the Federal Government in 2002

National Total = $360,534,307,000

ALPHA ORDER

RANK	STATE	REVENUE	% of USA
19	Alabama	$6,263,380,000	1.7%
39	Alaska	1,789,266,000	0.5%
24	Arizona	5,718,580,000	1.6%
31	Arkansas	3,645,274,000	1.0%
1	California	48,249,715,000	13.4%
29	Colorado	4,268,690,000	1.2%
30	Connecticut	4,039,357,000	1.1%
50	Delaware	959,029,000	0.3%
5	Florida	14,956,257,000	4.1%
10	Georgia	9,357,310,000	2.6%
43	Hawaii	1,547,487,000	0.4%
44	Idaho	1,415,152,000	0.4%
7	Illinois	12,716,518,000	3.5%
18	Indiana	6,282,589,000	1.7%
32	Iowa	3,626,235,000	1.0%
34	Kansas	3,098,044,000	0.9%
25	Kentucky	5,413,584,000	1.5%
15	Louisiana	6,484,806,000	1.8%
38	Maine	1,900,585,000	0.5%
23	Maryland	5,927,446,000	1.6%
21	Massachusetts	6,175,943,000	1.7%
8	Michigan	12,543,078,000	3.5%
22	Minnesota	6,088,091,000	1.7%
27	Mississippi	4,625,225,000	1.3%
13	Missouri	7,328,511,000	2.0%
42	Montana	1,590,402,000	0.4%
37	Nebraska	1,973,494,000	0.5%
41	Nevada	1,632,438,000	0.5%
45	New Hampshire	1,295,929,000	0.4%
11	New Jersey	8,948,972,000	2.5%
33	New Mexico	3,123,522,000	0.9%
2	New York	36,185,629,000	10.0%
9	North Carolina	10,240,822,000	2.8%
47	North Dakota	1,156,195,000	0.3%
6	Ohio	13,863,196,000	3.8%
28	Oklahoma	4,412,993,000	1.2%
17	Oregon	6,437,869,000	1.8%
4	Pennsylvania	16,026,341,000	4.4%
40	Rhode Island	1,766,157,000	0.5%
26	South Carolina	5,332,695,000	1.5%
48	South Dakota	1,150,293,000	0.3%
12	Tennessee	7,604,069,000	2.1%
3	Texas	22,914,707,000	6.4%
36	Utah	2,613,020,000	0.7%
49	Vermont	1,087,106,000	0.3%
20	Virginia	6,234,846,000	1.7%
14	Washington	7,041,596,000	2.0%
35	West Virginia	2,998,971,000	0.8%
16	Wisconsin	6,455,616,000	1.8%
46	Wyoming	1,187,183,000	0.3%

RANK ORDER

RANK	STATE	REVENUE	% of USA
1	California	$48,249,715,000	13.4%
2	New York	36,185,629,000	10.0%
3	Texas	22,914,707,000	6.4%
4	Pennsylvania	16,026,341,000	4.4%
5	Florida	14,956,257,000	4.1%
6	Ohio	13,863,196,000	3.8%
7	Illinois	12,716,518,000	3.5%
8	Michigan	12,543,078,000	3.5%
9	North Carolina	10,240,822,000	2.8%
10	Georgia	9,357,310,000	2.6%
11	New Jersey	8,948,972,000	2.5%
12	Tennessee	7,604,069,000	2.1%
13	Missouri	7,328,511,000	2.0%
14	Washington	7,041,596,000	2.0%
15	Louisiana	6,484,806,000	1.8%
16	Wisconsin	6,455,616,000	1.8%
17	Oregon	6,437,869,000	1.8%
18	Indiana	6,282,589,000	1.7%
19	Alabama	6,263,380,000	1.7%
20	Virginia	6,234,846,000	1.7%
21	Massachusetts	6,175,943,000	1.7%
22	Minnesota	6,088,091,000	1.7%
23	Maryland	5,927,446,000	1.6%
24	Arizona	5,718,580,000	1.6%
25	Kentucky	5,413,584,000	1.5%
26	South Carolina	5,332,695,000	1.5%
27	Mississippi	4,625,225,000	1.3%
28	Oklahoma	4,412,993,000	1.2%
29	Colorado	4,268,690,000	1.2%
30	Connecticut	4,039,357,000	1.1%
31	Arkansas	3,645,274,000	1.0%
32	Iowa	3,626,235,000	1.0%
33	New Mexico	3,123,522,000	0.9%
34	Kansas	3,098,044,000	0.9%
35	West Virginia	2,998,971,000	0.8%
36	Utah	2,613,020,000	0.7%
37	Nebraska	1,973,494,000	0.5%
38	Maine	1,900,585,000	0.5%
39	Alaska	1,789,266,000	0.5%
40	Rhode Island	1,766,157,000	0.5%
41	Nevada	1,632,438,000	0.5%
42	Montana	1,590,402,000	0.4%
43	Hawaii	1,547,487,000	0.4%
44	Idaho	1,415,152,000	0.4%
45	New Hampshire	1,295,929,000	0.4%
46	Wyoming	1,187,183,000	0.3%
47	North Dakota	1,156,195,000	0.3%
48	South Dakota	1,150,293,000	0.3%
49	Vermont	1,087,106,000	0.3%
50	Delaware	959,029,000	0.3%
	District of Columbia	2,840,094,000	0.8%

Source: U.S. Bureau of the Census, Governments Division
"State and Local Government Finances: 2002 Census" (http://www.census.gov/govs/www/estimate02.html)

Per Capita State and Local Government Revenue
From the Federal Government in 2002
National Per Capita = $1,252

ALPHA ORDER

RANK	STATE	PER CAPITA
15	Alabama	$1,398
1	Alaska	2,792
41	Arizona	1,051
17	Arkansas	1,346
16	California	1,379
47	Colorado	949
32	Connecticut	1,168
30	Delaware	1,190
48	Florida	897
37	Georgia	1,096
24	Hawaii	1,254
40	Idaho	1,054
45	Illinois	1,010
43	Indiana	1,020
26	Iowa	1,236
35	Kansas	1,142
18	Kentucky	1,324
14	Louisiana	1,448
13	Maine	1,465
38	Maryland	1,089
46	Massachusetts	963
25	Michigan	1,249
29	Minnesota	1,212
11	Mississippi	1,613
22	Missouri	1,290
7	Montana	1,746
34	Nebraska	1,143
50	Nevada	753
44	New Hampshire	1,016
42	New Jersey	1,043
8	New Mexico	1,684
3	New York	1,889
27	North Carolina	1,232
5	North Dakota	1,824
28	Ohio	1,215
23	Oklahoma	1,265
4	Oregon	1,827
20	Pennsylvania	1,300
10	Rhode Island	1,652
21	South Carolina	1,299
12	South Dakota	1,513
19	Tennessee	1,313
39	Texas	1,055
36	Utah	1,126
6	Vermont	1,763
49	Virginia	857
33	Washington	1,161
9	West Virginia	1,661
31	Wisconsin	1,187
2	Wyoming	2,378

RANK ORDER

RANK	STATE	PER CAPITA
1	Alaska	$2,792
2	Wyoming	2,378
3	New York	1,889
4	Oregon	1,827
5	North Dakota	1,824
6	Vermont	1,763
7	Montana	1,746
8	New Mexico	1,684
9	West Virginia	1,661
10	Rhode Island	1,652
11	Mississippi	1,613
12	South Dakota	1,513
13	Maine	1,465
14	Louisiana	1,448
15	Alabama	1,398
16	California	1,379
17	Arkansas	1,346
18	Kentucky	1,324
19	Tennessee	1,313
20	Pennsylvania	1,300
21	South Carolina	1,299
22	Missouri	1,290
23	Oklahoma	1,265
24	Hawaii	1,254
25	Michigan	1,249
26	Iowa	1,236
27	North Carolina	1,232
28	Ohio	1,215
29	Minnesota	1,212
30	Delaware	1,190
31	Wisconsin	1,187
32	Connecticut	1,168
33	Washington	1,161
34	Nebraska	1,143
35	Kansas	1,142
36	Utah	1,126
37	Georgia	1,096
38	Maryland	1,089
39	Texas	1,055
40	Idaho	1,054
41	Arizona	1,051
42	New Jersey	1,043
43	Indiana	1,020
44	New Hampshire	1,016
45	Illinois	1,010
46	Massachusetts	963
47	Colorado	949
48	Florida	897
49	Virginia	857
50	Nevada	753

District of Columbia   5,030

Source: Morgan Quitno Press using data from U.S. Bureau of the Census, Governments Division
"State and Local Government Finances: 2002 Census" (http://www.census.gov/govs/www/estimate02.html)

Percent of State and Local Government Revenue
From the Federal Government in 2002
National Percent = 19.9%*

ALPHA ORDER

RANK	STATE	PERCENT
13	Alabama	25.3
12	Alaska	25.6
35	Arizona	19.0
9	Arkansas	26.8
33	California	19.2
42	Colorado	16.6
44	Connecticut	16.3
46	Delaware	16.1
46	Florida	16.1
28	Georgia	20.3
24	Hawaii	20.8
25	Idaho	20.6
39	Illinois	17.3
37	Indiana	18.4
25	Iowa	20.6
31	Kansas	19.4
14	Kentucky	24.1
16	Louisiana	23.7
16	Maine	23.7
38	Maryland	17.7
49	Massachusetts	14.7
30	Michigan	19.9
39	Minnesota	17.3
1	Mississippi	29.1
15	Missouri	23.9
3	Montana	28.9
43	Nebraska	16.4
50	Nevada	12.7
32	New Hampshire	19.3
44	New Jersey	16.3
7	New Mexico	27.2
22	New York	21.2
23	North Carolina	21.1
5	North Dakota	27.4
34	Ohio	19.1
18	Oklahoma	23.0
4	Oregon	27.7
20	Pennsylvania	21.7
11	Rhode Island	25.7
21	South Carolina	21.3
2	South Dakota	29.0
19	Tennessee	22.7
29	Texas	20.1
35	Utah	19.0
8	Vermont	26.9
46	Virginia	16.1
41	Washington	16.7
10	West Virginia	26.4
27	Wisconsin	20.5
6	Wyoming	27.3

RANK ORDER

RANK	STATE	PERCENT
1	Mississippi	29.1
2	South Dakota	29.0
3	Montana	28.9
4	Oregon	27.7
5	North Dakota	27.4
6	Wyoming	27.3
7	New Mexico	27.2
8	Vermont	26.9
9	Arkansas	26.8
10	West Virginia	26.4
11	Rhode Island	25.7
12	Alaska	25.6
13	Alabama	25.3
14	Kentucky	24.1
15	Missouri	23.9
16	Louisiana	23.7
16	Maine	23.7
18	Oklahoma	23.0
19	Tennessee	22.7
20	Pennsylvania	21.7
21	South Carolina	21.3
22	New York	21.2
23	North Carolina	21.1
24	Hawaii	20.8
25	Idaho	20.6
25	Iowa	20.6
27	Wisconsin	20.5
28	Georgia	20.3
29	Texas	20.1
30	Michigan	19.9
31	Kansas	19.4
32	New Hampshire	19.3
33	California	19.2
34	Ohio	19.1
35	Arizona	19.0
35	Utah	19.0
37	Indiana	18.4
38	Maryland	17.7
39	Illinois	17.3
39	Minnesota	17.3
41	Washington	16.7
42	Colorado	16.6
43	Nebraska	16.4
44	Connecticut	16.3
44	New Jersey	16.3
46	Delaware	16.1
46	Florida	16.1
46	Virginia	16.1
49	Massachusetts	14.7
50	Nevada	12.7

District of Columbia   38.6

Source: Morgan Quitno Press using data from U.S. Bureau of the Census, Governments Division
"State and Local Government Finances: 2002 Census" (http://www.census.gov/govs/www/estimate02.html)
*As a percent of total revenue.

State and Local Government Own Source Revenue in 2002

National Total = $1,324,241,223,000*

ALPHA ORDER

RANK	STATE	REVENUE	% of USA
25	Alabama	$17,477,607,000	1.3%
41	Alaska	5,419,599,000	0.4%
22	Arizona	19,804,935,000	1.5%
35	Arkansas	9,614,278,000	0.7%
1	California	178,394,306,000	13.5%
19	Colorado	21,772,406,000	1.6%
24	Connecticut	18,765,835,000	1.4%
45	Delaware	4,641,006,000	0.4%
4	Florida	71,707,132,000	5.4%
10	Georgia	35,002,321,000	2.6%
40	Hawaii	5,881,217,000	0.4%
42	Idaho	5,204,475,000	0.4%
5	Illinois	56,381,620,000	4.3%
18	Indiana	26,080,099,000	2.0%
30	Iowa	13,244,933,000	1.0%
31	Kansas	11,537,216,000	0.9%
27	Kentucky	15,817,489,000	1.2%
23	Louisiana	19,562,758,000	1.5%
39	Maine	6,176,108,000	0.5%
16	Maryland	26,391,429,000	2.0%
12	Massachusetts	32,825,907,000	2.5%
9	Michigan	45,398,497,000	3.4%
15	Minnesota	27,105,143,000	2.0%
32	Mississippi	10,667,364,000	0.8%
20	Missouri	21,733,074,000	1.6%
46	Montana	3,531,689,000	0.3%
36	Nebraska	7,847,901,000	0.6%
34	Nevada	9,784,738,000	0.7%
43	New Hampshire	5,109,904,000	0.4%
8	New Jersey	46,306,696,000	3.5%
37	New Mexico	7,744,141,000	0.6%
2	New York	119,355,529,000	9.0%
11	North Carolina	33,924,004,000	2.6%
48	North Dakota	2,837,897,000	0.2%
7	Ohio	51,704,415,000	3.9%
29	Oklahoma	13,648,023,000	1.0%
28	Oregon	15,187,403,000	1.1%
6	Pennsylvania	55,935,071,000	4.2%
44	Rhode Island	4,870,229,000	0.4%
26	South Carolina	15,906,729,000	1.2%
50	South Dakota	2,751,679,000	0.2%
21	Tennessee	19,879,580,000	1.5%
3	Texas	86,213,786,000	6.5%
33	Utah	9,886,410,000	0.7%
49	Vermont	2,770,283,000	0.2%
13	Virginia	32,791,325,000	2.5%
14	Washington	29,303,365,000	2.2%
38	West Virginia	7,111,968,000	0.5%
17	Wisconsin	26,099,770,000	2.0%
47	Wyoming	3,049,692,000	0.2%

RANK ORDER

RANK	STATE	REVENUE	% of USA
1	California	$178,394,306,000	13.5%
2	New York	119,355,529,000	9.0%
3	Texas	86,213,786,000	6.5%
4	Florida	71,707,132,000	5.4%
5	Illinois	56,381,620,000	4.3%
6	Pennsylvania	55,935,071,000	4.2%
7	Ohio	51,704,415,000	3.9%
8	New Jersey	46,306,696,000	3.5%
9	Michigan	45,398,497,000	3.4%
10	Georgia	35,002,321,000	2.6%
11	North Carolina	33,924,004,000	2.6%
12	Massachusetts	32,825,907,000	2.5%
13	Virginia	32,791,325,000	2.5%
14	Washington	29,303,365,000	2.2%
15	Minnesota	27,105,143,000	2.0%
16	Maryland	26,391,429,000	2.0%
17	Wisconsin	26,099,770,000	2.0%
18	Indiana	26,080,099,000	2.0%
19	Colorado	21,772,406,000	1.6%
20	Missouri	21,733,074,000	1.6%
21	Tennessee	19,879,580,000	1.5%
22	Arizona	19,804,935,000	1.5%
23	Louisiana	19,562,758,000	1.5%
24	Connecticut	18,765,835,000	1.4%
25	Alabama	17,477,607,000	1.3%
26	South Carolina	15,906,729,000	1.2%
27	Kentucky	15,817,489,000	1.2%
28	Oregon	15,187,403,000	1.1%
29	Oklahoma	13,648,023,000	1.0%
30	Iowa	13,244,933,000	1.0%
31	Kansas	11,537,216,000	0.9%
32	Mississippi	10,667,364,000	0.8%
33	Utah	9,886,410,000	0.7%
34	Nevada	9,784,738,000	0.7%
35	Arkansas	9,614,278,000	0.7%
36	Nebraska	7,847,901,000	0.6%
37	New Mexico	7,744,141,000	0.6%
38	West Virginia	7,111,968,000	0.5%
39	Maine	6,176,108,000	0.5%
40	Hawaii	5,881,217,000	0.4%
41	Alaska	5,419,599,000	0.4%
42	Idaho	5,204,475,000	0.4%
43	New Hampshire	5,109,904,000	0.4%
44	Rhode Island	4,870,229,000	0.4%
45	Delaware	4,641,006,000	0.4%
46	Montana	3,531,689,000	0.3%
47	Wyoming	3,049,692,000	0.2%
48	North Dakota	2,837,897,000	0.2%
49	Vermont	2,770,283,000	0.2%
50	South Dakota	2,751,679,000	0.2%
	District of Columbia	4,082,242,000	0.3%

Source: U.S. Bureau of the Census, Governments Division
   "State and Local Government Finances: 2002 Census" (http://www.census.gov/govs/www/estimate02.html)
*Own source revenue includes taxes, current charges and miscellaneous general revenue. Excluded are intergovernmental transfers, insurance trust revenue and revenue from government owned utilities and other commercial or auxiliary enterprise.

Per Capita State and Local Government Own Source Revenue in 2002

National Per Capita = $4,599*

ALPHA ORDER				RANK ORDER		
RANK	STATE	PER CAPITA		RANK	STATE	PER CAPITA
40	Alabama	$3,900		1	Alaska	$8,457
1	Alaska	8,457		2	New York	6,232
47	Arizona	3,641		3	Wyoming	6,109
49	Arkansas	3,551		4	Delaware	5,757
9	California	5,099		5	Connecticut	5,425
11	Colorado	4,840		6	New Jersey	5,399
5	Connecticut	5,425		7	Minnesota	5,394
4	Delaware	5,757		8	Massachusetts	5,119
29	Florida	4,299		9	California	5,099
34	Georgia	4,099		10	Maryland	4,850
14	Hawaii	4,764		11	Colorado	4,840
42	Idaho	3,875		12	Washington	4,830
25	Illinois	4,480		13	Wisconsin	4,797
32	Indiana	4,235		14	Hawaii	4,764
21	Iowa	4,513		15	Maine	4,759
31	Kansas	4,253		16	Rhode Island	4,556
44	Kentucky	3,867		17	Nebraska	4,546
27	Louisiana	4,370		18	Pennsylvania	4,537
15	Maine	4,759		19	Ohio	4,531
10	Maryland	4,850		20	Michigan	4,521
8	Massachusetts	5,119		21	Iowa	4,513
20	Michigan	4,521		21	Nevada	4,513
7	Minnesota	5,394		23	Virginia	4,508
46	Mississippi	3,720		24	Vermont	4,494
45	Missouri	3,826		25	Illinois	4,480
41	Montana	3,878		26	North Dakota	4,478
17	Nebraska	4,546		27	Louisiana	4,370
21	Nevada	4,513		28	Oregon	4,311
36	New Hampshire	4,006		29	Florida	4,299
6	New Jersey	5,399		30	Utah	4,262
33	New Mexico	4,174		31	Kansas	4,253
2	New York	6,232		32	Indiana	4,235
35	North Carolina	4,081		33	New Mexico	4,174
26	North Dakota	4,478		34	Georgia	4,099
19	Ohio	4,531		35	North Carolina	4,081
39	Oklahoma	3,913		36	New Hampshire	4,006
28	Oregon	4,311		37	Texas	3,969
18	Pennsylvania	4,537		38	West Virginia	3,940
16	Rhode Island	4,556		39	Oklahoma	3,913
43	South Carolina	3,874		40	Alabama	3,900
48	South Dakota	3,618		41	Montana	3,878
50	Tennessee	3,432		42	Idaho	3,875
37	Texas	3,969		43	South Carolina	3,874
30	Utah	4,262		44	Kentucky	3,867
24	Vermont	4,494		45	Missouri	3,826
23	Virginia	4,508		46	Mississippi	3,720
12	Washington	4,830		47	Arizona	3,641
38	West Virginia	3,940		48	South Dakota	3,618
13	Wisconsin	4,797		49	Arkansas	3,551
3	Wyoming	6,109		50	Tennessee	3,432
					District of Columbia	7,230

Source: Morgan Quitno Press using data from U.S. Bureau of the Census, Governments Division
    "State and Local Government Finances: 2002 Census" (http://www.census.gov/govs/www/estimate02.html)
*Own source revenue includes taxes, current charges and miscellaneous general revenue. Excluded are
intergovernmental transfers, insurance trust revenue and revenue from government owned utilities and other
commercial or auxiliary enterprise.

State and Local Government Tax Revenue in 2002

National Total = $904,971,370,000

<table>
<tr><td colspan="4">ALPHA ORDER</td><td colspan="4">RANK ORDER</td></tr>
<tr><td>RANK</td><td>STATE</td><td>TAX REVENUE</td><td>% of USA</td><td>RANK</td><td>STATE</td><td>TAX REVENUE</td><td>% of USA</td></tr>
<tr><td>27</td><td>Alabama</td><td>$9,718,827,000</td><td>1.1%</td><td>1</td><td>California</td><td>$120,424,066,000</td><td>13.3%</td></tr>
<tr><td>46</td><td>Alaska</td><td>2,069,908,000</td><td>0.2%</td><td>2</td><td>New York</td><td>88,878,112,000</td><td>9.8%</td></tr>
<tr><td>21</td><td>Arizona</td><td>14,420,322,000</td><td>1.6%</td><td>3</td><td>Texas</td><td>58,980,508,000</td><td>6.5%</td></tr>
<tr><td>33</td><td>Arkansas</td><td>6,460,855,000</td><td>0.7%</td><td>4</td><td>Florida</td><td>44,840,449,000</td><td>5.0%</td></tr>
<tr><td>1</td><td>California</td><td>120,424,066,000</td><td>13.3%</td><td>5</td><td>Illinois</td><td>41,569,580,000</td><td>4.6%</td></tr>
<tr><td>22</td><td>Colorado</td><td>13,900,024,000</td><td>1.5%</td><td>6</td><td>Pennsylvania</td><td>37,626,620,000</td><td>4.2%</td></tr>
<tr><td>19</td><td>Connecticut</td><td>15,124,928,000</td><td>1.7%</td><td>7</td><td>Ohio</td><td>36,165,190,000</td><td>4.0%</td></tr>
<tr><td>44</td><td>Delaware</td><td>2,687,098,000</td><td>0.3%</td><td>8</td><td>New Jersey</td><td>34,628,804,000</td><td>3.8%</td></tr>
<tr><td>4</td><td>Florida</td><td>44,840,449,000</td><td>5.0%</td><td>9</td><td>Michigan</td><td>30,644,184,000</td><td>3.4%</td></tr>
<tr><td>10</td><td>Georgia</td><td>24,058,380,000</td><td>2.7%</td><td>10</td><td>Georgia</td><td>24,058,380,000</td><td>2.7%</td></tr>
<tr><td>40</td><td>Hawaii</td><td>4,239,557,000</td><td>0.5%</td><td>11</td><td>Massachusetts</td><td>23,895,436,000</td><td>2.6%</td></tr>
<tr><td>43</td><td>Idaho</td><td>3,291,095,000</td><td>0.4%</td><td>12</td><td>North Carolina</td><td>22,576,419,000</td><td>2.5%</td></tr>
<tr><td>5</td><td>Illinois</td><td>41,569,580,000</td><td>4.6%</td><td>13</td><td>Virginia</td><td>22,131,246,000</td><td>2.4%</td></tr>
<tr><td>18</td><td>Indiana</td><td>16,986,637,000</td><td>1.9%</td><td>14</td><td>Maryland</td><td>19,874,281,000</td><td>2.2%</td></tr>
<tr><td>30</td><td>Iowa</td><td>8,330,414,000</td><td>0.0%</td><td>15</td><td>Washington</td><td>19,513,503,000</td><td>2.2%</td></tr>
<tr><td>31</td><td>Kansas</td><td>7,974,975,000</td><td>0.9%</td><td>16</td><td>Wisconsin</td><td>18,609,916,000</td><td>2.1%</td></tr>
<tr><td>25</td><td>Kentucky</td><td>10,780,757,000</td><td>1.2%</td><td>17</td><td>Minnesota</td><td>18,456,409,000</td><td>2.0%</td></tr>
<tr><td>24</td><td>Louisiana</td><td>12,182,065,000</td><td>1.3%</td><td>18</td><td>Indiana</td><td>16,986,637,000</td><td>1.9%</td></tr>
<tr><td>39</td><td>Maine</td><td>4,541,146,000</td><td>0.5%</td><td>19</td><td>Connecticut</td><td>15,124,928,000</td><td>1.7%</td></tr>
<tr><td>14</td><td>Maryland</td><td>19,874,281,000</td><td>2.2%</td><td>20</td><td>Missouri</td><td>15,123,432,000</td><td>1.7%</td></tr>
<tr><td>11</td><td>Massachusetts</td><td>23,895,436,000</td><td>2.6%</td><td>21</td><td>Arizona</td><td>14,420,322,000</td><td>1.6%</td></tr>
<tr><td>9</td><td>Michigan</td><td>30,644,184,000</td><td>3.4%</td><td>22</td><td>Colorado</td><td>13,900,024,000</td><td>1.5%</td></tr>
<tr><td>17</td><td>Minnesota</td><td>18,456,409,000</td><td>2.0%</td><td>23</td><td>Tennessee</td><td>12,973,768,000</td><td>1.4%</td></tr>
<tr><td>32</td><td>Mississippi</td><td>6,523,722,000</td><td>0.7%</td><td>24</td><td>Louisiana</td><td>12,182,065,000</td><td>1.3%</td></tr>
<tr><td>20</td><td>Missouri</td><td>15,123,432,000</td><td>1.7%</td><td>25</td><td>Kentucky</td><td>10,780,757,000</td><td>1.2%</td></tr>
<tr><td>45</td><td>Montana</td><td>2,135,182,000</td><td>0.2%</td><td>26</td><td>South Carolina</td><td>9,751,701,000</td><td>1.1%</td></tr>
<tr><td>36</td><td>Nebraska</td><td>5,316,341,000</td><td>0.6%</td><td>27</td><td>Alabama</td><td>9,718,827,000</td><td>1.1%</td></tr>
<tr><td>34</td><td>Nevada</td><td>6,432,564,000</td><td>0.7%</td><td>28</td><td>Oregon</td><td>9,003,237,000</td><td>1.0%</td></tr>
<tr><td>42</td><td>New Hampshire</td><td>3,598,862,000</td><td>0.4%</td><td>29</td><td>Oklahoma</td><td>8,781,889,000</td><td>1.0%</td></tr>
<tr><td>8</td><td>New Jersey</td><td>34,628,804,000</td><td>3.8%</td><td>30</td><td>Iowa</td><td>8,330,414,000</td><td>0.9%</td></tr>
<tr><td>37</td><td>New Mexico</td><td>4,877,614,000</td><td>0.5%</td><td>31</td><td>Kansas</td><td>7,974,975,000</td><td>0.9%</td></tr>
<tr><td>2</td><td>New York</td><td>88,878,112,000</td><td>9.8%</td><td>32</td><td>Mississippi</td><td>6,523,722,000</td><td>0.7%</td></tr>
<tr><td>12</td><td>North Carolina</td><td>22,576,419,000</td><td>2.5%</td><td>33</td><td>Arkansas</td><td>6,460,855,000</td><td>0.7%</td></tr>
<tr><td>50</td><td>North Dakota</td><td>1,728,755,000</td><td>0.2%</td><td>34</td><td>Nevada</td><td>6,432,564,000</td><td>0.7%</td></tr>
<tr><td>7</td><td>Ohio</td><td>36,165,190,000</td><td>4.0%</td><td>35</td><td>Utah</td><td>6,026,142,000</td><td>0.7%</td></tr>
<tr><td>29</td><td>Oklahoma</td><td>8,781,889,000</td><td>1.0%</td><td>36</td><td>Nebraska</td><td>5,316,341,000</td><td>0.6%</td></tr>
<tr><td>28</td><td>Oregon</td><td>9,003,237,000</td><td>1.0%</td><td>37</td><td>New Mexico</td><td>4,877,614,000</td><td>0.5%</td></tr>
<tr><td>6</td><td>Pennsylvania</td><td>37,626,620,000</td><td>4.2%</td><td>38</td><td>West Virginia</td><td>4,641,349,000</td><td>0.5%</td></tr>
<tr><td>41</td><td>Rhode Island</td><td>3,622,244,000</td><td>0.4%</td><td>39</td><td>Maine</td><td>4,541,146,000</td><td>0.5%</td></tr>
<tr><td>26</td><td>South Carolina</td><td>9,751,701,000</td><td>1.1%</td><td>40</td><td>Hawaii</td><td>4,239,557,000</td><td>0.5%</td></tr>
<tr><td>48</td><td>South Dakota</td><td>1,841,448,000</td><td>0.2%</td><td>41</td><td>Rhode Island</td><td>3,622,244,000</td><td>0.4%</td></tr>
<tr><td>23</td><td>Tennessee</td><td>12,973,768,000</td><td>1.4%</td><td>42</td><td>New Hampshire</td><td>3,598,862,000</td><td>0.4%</td></tr>
<tr><td>3</td><td>Texas</td><td>58,980,508,000</td><td>6.5%</td><td>43</td><td>Idaho</td><td>3,291,095,000</td><td>0.4%</td></tr>
<tr><td>35</td><td>Utah</td><td>6,026,142,000</td><td>0.7%</td><td>44</td><td>Delaware</td><td>2,687,098,000</td><td>0.3%</td></tr>
<tr><td>47</td><td>Vermont</td><td>1,965,132,000</td><td>0.2%</td><td>45</td><td>Montana</td><td>2,135,182,000</td><td>0.2%</td></tr>
<tr><td>13</td><td>Virginia</td><td>22,131,246,000</td><td>2.4%</td><td>46</td><td>Alaska</td><td>2,069,908,000</td><td>0.2%</td></tr>
<tr><td>15</td><td>Washington</td><td>19,513,503,000</td><td>2.2%</td><td>47</td><td>Vermont</td><td>1,965,132,000</td><td>0.2%</td></tr>
<tr><td>38</td><td>West Virginia</td><td>4,641,349,000</td><td>0.5%</td><td>48</td><td>South Dakota</td><td>1,841,448,000</td><td>0.2%</td></tr>
<tr><td>16</td><td>Wisconsin</td><td>18,609,916,000</td><td>2.1%</td><td>49</td><td>Wyoming</td><td>1,818,368,000</td><td>0.2%</td></tr>
<tr><td>49</td><td>Wyoming</td><td>1,818,368,000</td><td>0.2%</td><td>50</td><td>North Dakota</td><td>1,728,755,000</td><td>0.2%</td></tr>
<tr><td></td><td></td><td></td><td></td><td></td><td>District of Columbia</td><td>3,227,909,000</td><td>0.4%</td></tr>
</table>

Source: U.S. Bureau of the Census, Governments Division
    "State and Local Government Finances: 2002 Census" (http://www.census.gov/govs/www/estimate02.html)

Per Capita State and Local Government Tax Revenue in 2002

National Per Capita = $3,143

ALPHA ORDER

RANK ORDER

RANK	STATE	PER CAPITA		RANK	STATE	PER CAPITA
50	Alabama	$2,169		1	New York	$4,641
15	Alaska	3,230		2	Connecticut	4,373
36	Arizona	2,651		3	New Jersey	4,037
45	Arkansas	2,386		4	Massachusetts	3,726
9	California	3,442		5	Minnesota	3,673
19	Colorado	3,090		6	Maryland	3,652
2	Connecticut	4,373		7	Wyoming	3,643
13	Delaware	3,333		8	Maine	3,499
34	Florida	2,688		9	California	3,442
28	Georgia	2,817		10	Hawaii	3,434
10	Hawaii	3,434		11	Wisconsin	3,421
43	Idaho	2,450		12	Rhode Island	3,389
14	Illinois	3,303		13	Delaware	3,333
29	Indiana	2,758		14	Illinois	3,303
26	Iowa	2,839		15	Alaska	3,230
25	Kansas	2,940		16	Washington	3,216
37	Kentucky	2,636		17	Vermont	3,188
31	Louisiana	2,721		18	Ohio	3,169
8	Maine	3,499		19	Colorado	3,090
6	Maryland	3,652		20	Nebraska	3,079
4	Massachusetts	3,726		21	Pennsylvania	3,052
22	Michigan	3,051		22	Michigan	3,051
5	Minnesota	3,673		23	Virginia	3,043
48	Mississippi	2,275		24	Nevada	2,967
35	Missouri	2,663		25	Kansas	2,940
47	Montana	2,345		26	Iowa	2,839
20	Nebraska	3,079		27	New Hampshire	2,821
24	Nevada	2,967		28	Georgia	2,817
27	New Hampshire	2,821		29	Indiana	2,758
3	New Jersey	4,037		30	North Dakota	2,728
38	New Mexico	2,629		31	Louisiana	2,721
1	New York	4,641		32	North Carolina	2,716
32	North Carolina	2,716		33	Texas	2,715
30	North Dakota	2,728		34	Florida	2,688
18	Ohio	3,169		35	Missouri	2,663
42	Oklahoma	2,518		36	Arizona	2,651
41	Oregon	2,555		37	Kentucky	2,636
21	Pennsylvania	3,052		38	New Mexico	2,629
12	Rhode Island	3,389		39	Utah	2,598
46	South Carolina	2,375		40	West Virginia	2,571
44	South Dakota	2,422		41	Oregon	2,555
49	Tennessee	2,240		42	Oklahoma	2,518
33	Texas	2,715		43	Idaho	2,450
39	Utah	2,598		44	South Dakota	2,422
17	Vermont	3,188		45	Arkansas	2,386
23	Virginia	3,043		46	South Carolina	2,375
16	Washington	3,216		47	Montana	2,345
40	West Virginia	2,571		48	Mississippi	2,275
11	Wisconsin	3,421		49	Tennessee	2,240
7	Wyoming	3,643		50	Alabama	2,169

District of Columbia   5,717

Source: Morgan Quitno Press using data from U.S. Bureau of the Census, Governments Division
"State and Local Government Finances: 2002 Census" (http://www.census.gov/govs/www/estimate02.html)

Percent of State and Local Government Revenue from Taxes in 2002

National Percent = 50.1%

ALPHA ORDER

RANK	STATE	PERCENT
45	Alabama	39.3
50	Alaska	29.6
28	Arizona	47.9
30	Arkansas	47.4
26	California	48.0
10	Colorado	54.2
2	Connecticut	60.9
36	Delaware	45.0
25	Florida	48.4
14	Georgia	52.1
7	Hawaii	56.9
28	Idaho	47.9
9	Illinois	56.5
21	Indiana	49.6
31	Iowa	47.3
19	Kansas	49.9
26	Kentucky	48.0
37	Louisiana	44.5
8	Maine	56.6
3	Maryland	59.4
6	Massachusetts	57.0
23	Michigan	48.6
13	Minnesota	52.5
42	Mississippi	41.0
22	Missouri	49.4
48	Montana	38.7
38	Nebraska	44.2
18	Nevada	50.2
11	New Hampshire	53.5
1	New Jersey	63.2
40	New Mexico	42.4
15	New York	52.0
32	North Carolina	46.5
43	North Dakota	40.9
20	Ohio	49.8
35	Oklahoma	45.8
47	Oregon	38.8
17	Pennsylvania	51.1
12	Rhode Island	52.8
46	South Carolina	39.0
32	South Dakota	46.5
48	Tennessee	38.7
16	Texas	51.7
39	Utah	43.7
23	Vermont	48.6
5	Virginia	57.1
34	Washington	46.3
43	West Virginia	40.9
4	Wisconsin	59.2
41	Wyoming	41.8

RANK ORDER

RANK	STATE	PERCENT
1	New Jersey	63.2
2	Connecticut	60.9
3	Maryland	59.4
4	Wisconsin	59.2
5	Virginia	57.1
6	Massachusetts	57.0
7	Hawaii	56.9
8	Maine	56.6
9	Illinois	56.5
10	Colorado	54.2
11	New Hampshire	53.5
12	Rhode Island	52.8
13	Minnesota	52.5
14	Georgia	52.1
15	New York	52.0
16	Texas	51.7
17	Pennsylvania	51.1
18	Nevada	50.2
19	Kansas	49.9
20	Ohio	49.8
21	Indiana	49.6
22	Missouri	49.4
23	Michigan	48.6
23	Vermont	48.6
25	Florida	48.4
26	California	48.0
26	Kentucky	48.0
28	Arizona	47.9
28	Idaho	47.9
30	Arkansas	47.4
31	Iowa	47.3
32	North Carolina	46.5
32	South Dakota	46.5
34	Washington	46.3
35	Oklahoma	45.8
36	Delaware	45.0
37	Louisiana	44.5
38	Nebraska	44.2
39	Utah	43.7
40	New Mexico	42.4
41	Wyoming	41.8
42	Mississippi	41.0
43	North Dakota	40.9
43	West Virginia	40.9
45	Alabama	39.3
46	South Carolina	39.0
47	Oregon	38.8
48	Montana	38.7
48	Tennessee	38.7
50	Alaska	29.6

| | District of Columbia | 43.9 |

Source: Morgan Quitno Press using data from U.S. Bureau of the Census, Governments Division
"State and Local Government Finances: 2002 Census" (http://www.census.gov/govs/www/estimate02.html)

State and Local Government Tax Revenue
As a Percent of Personal Income in 2002
National Percent = 10.2% of Personal Income*

ALPHA ORDER

RANK STATE | PERCENT
--- | --- | ---
48 | Alabama | 8.6
29 | Alaska | 9.9
27 | Arizona | 10.0
19 | Arkansas | 10.2
14 | California | 10.5
46 | Colorado | 9.0
19 | Connecticut | 10.2
17 | Delaware | 10.3
44 | Florida | 9.1
34 | Georgia | 9.7
4 | Hawaii | 11.5
34 | Idaho | 9.7
24 | Illinois | 10.1
29 | Indiana | 9.9
19 | Iowa | 10.2
19 | Kansas | 10.2
15 | Kentucky | 10.4
9 | Louisiana | 10.8
2 | Maine | 12.5
27 | Maryland | 10.0
38 | Massachusetts | 9.6
24 | Michigan | 10.1
6 | Minnesota | 11.1
24 | Mississippi | 10.1
41 | Missouri | 9.4
39 | Montana | 9.5
11 | Nebraska | 10.7
34 | Nevada | 9.7
49 | New Hampshire | 8.3
19 | New Jersey | 10.2
13 | New Mexico | 10.6
1 | New York | 13.1
32 | North Carolina | 9.8
17 | North Dakota | 10.3
7 | Ohio | 10.9
34 | Oklahoma | 9.7
46 | Oregon | 9.0
29 | Pennsylvania | 9.9
7 | Rhode Island | 10.9
42 | South Carolina | 9.3
44 | South Dakota | 9.1
50 | Tennessee | 8.1
39 | Texas | 9.5
15 | Utah | 10.4
9 | Vermont | 10.8
43 | Virginia | 9.2
32 | Washington | 9.8
11 | West Virginia | 10.7
5 | Wisconsin | 11.4
3 | Wyoming | 11.8

RANK ORDER

RANK STATE | PERCENT
--- | --- | ---
1 | New York | 13.1
2 | Maine | 12.5
3 | Wyoming | 11.8
4 | Hawaii | 11.5
5 | Wisconsin | 11.4
6 | Minnesota | 11.1
7 | Ohio | 10.9
7 | Rhode Island | 10.9
9 | Louisiana | 10.8
9 | Vermont | 10.8
11 | Nebraska | 10.7
11 | West Virginia | 10.7
13 | New Mexico | 10.6
14 | California | 10.5
15 | Kentucky | 10.4
15 | Utah | 10.4
17 | Delaware | 10.3
17 | North Dakota | 10.3
19 | Arkansas | 10.2
19 | Connecticut | 10.2
19 | Iowa | 10.2
19 | Kansas | 10.2
19 | New Jersey | 10.2
24 | Illinois | 10.1
24 | Michigan | 10.1
24 | Mississippi | 10.1
27 | Arizona | 10.0
27 | Maryland | 10.0
29 | Alaska | 9.9
29 | Indiana | 9.9
29 | Pennsylvania | 9.9
32 | North Carolina | 9.8
32 | Washington | 9.8
34 | Georgia | 9.7
34 | Idaho | 9.7
34 | Nevada | 9.7
34 | Oklahoma | 9.7
38 | Massachusetts | 9.6
39 | Montana | 9.5
39 | Texas | 9.5
41 | Missouri | 9.4
42 | South Carolina | 9.3
43 | Virginia | 9.2
44 | Florida | 9.1
44 | South Dakota | 9.1
46 | Colorado | 9.0
46 | Oregon | 9.0
48 | Alabama | 8.6
49 | New Hampshire | 8.3
50 | Tennessee | 8.1

District of Columbia | 12.4

Source: Morgan Quitno Press using data from Bureau of Economic Analysis and U.S. Census Bureau
"State Personal Income" and "State and Local Government Finances: 2002 Census"
*The personal income total used for this table is the sum of state estimates. This total differs from the national income and product accounts (NIPA) estimate of personal income because it omits the earnings of federal civilian and military personnel stationed abroad and of U.S. residents employed abroad temporarily by private U.S. firms.

State and Local Government General Sales Tax Revenue in 2002

National Total = $222,986,687,000*

ALPHA ORDER

ALPHA ORDER

RANK	STATE	REVENUE	% of USA
24	Alabama	$2,968,306,000	1.3%
46	Alaska	121,944,000	0.1%
13	Arizona	5,783,197,000	2.6%
27	Arkansas	2,540,788,000	1.1%
1	California	31,292,794,000	14.0%
17	Colorado	4,127,711,000	1.9%
23	Connecticut	3,043,971,000	1.4%
47	Delaware	0	0.0%
4	Florida	15,034,278,000	6.7%
10	Georgia	7,493,304,000	3.4%
36	Hawaii	1,612,333,000	0.7%
40	Idaho	796,373,000	0.4%
8	Illinois	7,528,462,000	3.4%
19	Indiana	3,798,490,000	1.7%
33	Iowa	2,016,193,000	0.9%
31	Kansas	2,294,733,000	1.0%
30	Kentucky	2,312,322,000	1.0%
15	Louisiana	4,838,025,000	2.2%
39	Maine	836,134,000	0.4%
25	Maryland	2,690,434,000	1.2%
21	Massachusetts	3,695,874,000	1.7%
6	Michigan	7,784,308,000	3.5%
20	Minnesota	3,782,249,000	1.7%
29	Mississippi	2,341,447,000	1.1%
16	Missouri	4,246,139,000	1.9%
47	Montana	0	0.0%
37	Nebraska	1,287,487,000	0.6%
32	Nevada	2,216,779,000	1.0%
47	New Hampshire	0	0.0%
11	New Jersey	5,996,839,000	2.7%
35	New Mexico	1,764,879,000	0.8%
3	New York	16,630,208,000	7.5%
14	North Carolina	4,909,217,000	2.2%
44	North Dakota	394,508,000	0.2%
7	Ohio	7,686,517,000	3.4%
26	Oklahoma	2,600,204,000	1.2%
47	Oregon	0	0.0%
9	Pennsylvania	7,500,034,000	3.4%
41	Rhode Island	731,597,000	0.3%
28	South Carolina	2,435,404,000	1.1%
42	South Dakota	671,952,000	0.3%
12	Tennessee	5,841,589,000	2.6%
2	Texas	18,321,523,000	8.2%
34	Utah	1,970,374,000	0.9%
45	Vermont	214,746,000	0.1%
22	Virginia	3,586,938,000	1.6%
5	Washington	9,231,321,000	4.1%
38	West Virginia	962,756,000	0.4%
18	Wisconsin	3,913,811,000	1.8%
43	Wyoming	579,715,000	0.3%

RANK ORDER

RANK	STATE	REVENUE	% of USA
1	California	$31,292,794,000	14.0%
2	Texas	18,321,523,000	8.2%
3	New York	16,630,208,000	7.5%
4	Florida	15,034,278,000	6.7%
5	Washington	9,231,321,000	4.1%
6	Michigan	7,784,308,000	3.5%
7	Ohio	7,686,517,000	3.4%
8	Illinois	7,528,462,000	3.4%
9	Pennsylvania	7,500,034,000	3.4%
10	Georgia	7,493,304,000	3.4%
11	New Jersey	5,996,839,000	2.7%
12	Tennessee	5,841,589,000	2.6%
13	Arizona	5,783,197,000	2.6%
14	North Carolina	4,909,217,000	2.2%
15	Louisiana	4,838,025,000	2.2%
16	Missouri	4,246,139,000	1.9%
17	Colorado	4,127,711,000	1.9%
18	Wisconsin	3,913,811,000	1.8%
19	Indiana	3,798,490,000	1.7%
20	Minnesota	3,782,249,000	1.7%
21	Massachusetts	3,695,874,000	1.7%
22	Virginia	3,586,938,000	1.6%
23	Connecticut	3,043,971,000	1.4%
24	Alabama	2,968,306,000	1.3%
25	Maryland	2,690,434,000	1.2%
26	Oklahoma	2,600,204,000	1.2%
27	Arkansas	2,540,788,000	1.1%
28	South Carolina	2,435,404,000	1.1%
29	Mississippi	2,341,447,000	1.1%
30	Kentucky	2,312,322,000	1.0%
31	Kansas	2,294,733,000	1.0%
32	Nevada	2,216,779,000	1.0%
33	Iowa	2,016,193,000	0.9%
34	Utah	1,970,374,000	0.9%
35	New Mexico	1,764,879,000	0.8%
36	Hawaii	1,612,333,000	0.7%
37	Nebraska	1,287,487,000	0.6%
38	West Virginia	962,756,000	0.4%
39	Maine	836,134,000	0.4%
40	Idaho	796,373,000	0.4%
41	Rhode Island	731,597,000	0.3%
42	South Dakota	671,952,000	0.3%
43	Wyoming	579,715,000	0.3%
44	North Dakota	394,508,000	0.2%
45	Vermont	214,746,000	0.1%
46	Alaska	121,944,000	0.1%
47	Delaware	0	0.0%
47	Montana	0	0.0%
47	New Hampshire	0	0.0%
47	Oregon	0	0.0%
	District of Columbia	558,480,000	0.3%

Source: U.S. Bureau of the Census, Governments Division
"State and Local Government Finances: 2002 Census" (http://www.census.gov/govs/www/estimate02.html)
*Does not include special sales taxes such as those on sale of alcohol, gasoline or tobacco.

Per Capita State and Local Government General Sales Tax Revenue in 2002

National Per Capita = $774*

ALPHA ORDER

RANK	STATE	PER CAPITA
31	Alabama	$662
46	Alaska	190
5	Arizona	1,063
9	Arkansas	938
12	California	894
10	Colorado	918
14	Connecticut	880
47	Delaware	0
11	Florida	901
15	Georgia	877
2	Hawaii	1,306
37	Idaho	593
36	Illinois	598
34	Indiana	617
28	Iowa	687
18	Kansas	846
41	Kentucky	565
4	Louisiana	1,081
32	Maine	644
43	Maryland	494
40	Massachusetts	576
21	Michigan	775
22	Minnesota	753
20	Mississippi	817
23	Missouri	748
47	Montana	0
24	Nebraska	746
6	Nevada	1,022
47	New Hampshire	0
27	New Jersey	699
8	New Mexico	951
16	New York	868
39	North Carolina	591
33	North Dakota	622
30	Ohio	674
25	Oklahoma	745
47	Oregon	0
35	Pennsylvania	608
29	Rhode Island	684
37	South Carolina	593
13	South Dakota	884
7	Tennessee	1,009
19	Texas	843
17	Utah	849
45	Vermont	348
44	Virginia	493
1	Washington	1,522
42	West Virginia	533
26	Wisconsin	719
3	Wyoming	1,161

RANK ORDER

RANK	STATE	PER CAPITA
1	Washington	$1,522
2	Hawaii	1,306
3	Wyoming	1,161
4	Louisiana	1,081
5	Arizona	1,063
6	Nevada	1,022
7	Tennessee	1,009
8	New Mexico	951
9	Arkansas	938
10	Colorado	918
11	Florida	901
12	California	894
13	South Dakota	884
14	Connecticut	880
15	Georgia	877
16	New York	868
17	Utah	849
18	Kansas	846
19	Texas	843
20	Mississippi	817
21	Michigan	775
22	Minnesota	753
23	Missouri	748
24	Nebraska	746
25	Oklahoma	745
26	Wisconsin	719
27	New Jersey	699
28	Iowa	687
29	Rhode Island	684
30	Ohio	674
31	Alabama	662
32	Maine	644
33	North Dakota	622
34	Indiana	617
35	Pennsylvania	608
36	Illinois	598
37	Idaho	593
37	South Carolina	593
39	North Carolina	591
40	Massachusetts	576
41	Kentucky	565
42	West Virginia	533
43	Maryland	494
44	Virginia	493
45	Vermont	348
46	Alaska	190
47	Delaware	0
47	Montana	0
47	New Hampshire	0
47	Oregon	0

District of Columbia	989

Source: Morgan Quitno Press using data from U.S. Bureau of the Census, Governments Division
"State and Local Government Finances: 2002 Census" (http://www.census.gov/govs/www/estimate02.html)
*Does not include special sales taxes such as those on sale of alcohol, gasoline or tobacco.

State and Local Government Property Tax Revenue in 2002

National Total = $279,121,680,000

ALPHA ORDER

RANK	STATE	REVENUE	% of USA
36	Alabama	$1,473,554,000	0.5%
43	Alaska	830,011,000	0.3%
20	Arizona	4,254,395,000	1.5%
39	Arkansas	1,003,909,000	0.4%
1	California	30,242,523,000	10.8%
21	Colorado	4,162,161,000	1.5%
14	Connecticut	5,995,482,000	2.1%
50	Delaware	399,939,000	0.1%
6	Florida	15,754,214,000	5.6%
12	Georgia	6,640,041,000	2.4%
48	Hawaii	614,930,000	0.2%
40	Idaho	958,763,000	0.3%
5	Illinois	15,872,667,000	5.7%
15	Indiana	5,976,203,000	2.1%
26	Iowa	2,877,921,000	1.0%
27	Kansas	2,524,888,000	0.9%
29	Kentucky	1,977,011,000	0.7%
30	Louisiana	1,940,420,000	0.7%
31	Maine	1,912,158,000	0.7%
18	Maryland	5,412,209,000	1.9%
10	Massachusetts	8,721,832,000	3.1%
9	Michigan	9,793,418,000	3.5%
19	Minnesota	5,214,735,000	1.9%
34	Mississippi	1,646,563,000	0.6%
22	Missouri	3,880,344,000	1.4%
42	Montana	852,399,000	0.3%
32	Nebraska	1,748,841,000	0.6%
33	Nevada	1,702,186,000	0.6%
28	New Hampshire	2,169,494,000	0.8%
4	New Jersey	16,049,550,000	5.8%
45	New Mexico	755,948,000	0.3%
2	New York	26,825,697,000	9.6%
17	North Carolina	5,421,740,000	1.9%
49	North Dakota	532,340,000	0.2%
8	Ohio	10,643,420,000	3.8%
35	Oklahoma	1,482,139,000	0.5%
24	Oregon	3,138,875,000	1.1%
7	Pennsylvania	10,910,756,000	3.9%
37	Rhode Island	1,462,064,000	0.5%
25	South Carolina	3,096,431,000	1.1%
47	South Dakota	668,048,000	0.2%
23	Tennessee	3,453,047,000	1.2%
3	Texas	24,520,989,000	8.8%
38	Utah	1,419,769,000	0.5%
44	Vermont	823,610,000	0.3%
11	Virginia	6,710,588,000	2.4%
16	Washington	5,790,556,000	2.1%
41	West Virginia	900,999,000	0.3%
13	Wisconsin	6,466,173,000	2.3%
46	Wyoming	692,341,000	0.2%

RANK ORDER

RANK	STATE	REVENUE	% of USA
1	California	$30,242,523,000	10.8%
2	New York	26,825,697,000	9.6%
3	Texas	24,520,989,000	8.8%
4	New Jersey	16,049,550,000	5.8%
5	Illinois	15,872,667,000	5.7%
6	Florida	15,754,214,000	5.6%
7	Pennsylvania	10,910,756,000	3.9%
8	Ohio	10,643,420,000	3.8%
9	Michigan	9,793,418,000	3.5%
10	Massachusetts	8,721,832,000	3.1%
11	Virginia	6,710,588,000	2.4%
12	Georgia	6,640,041,000	2.4%
13	Wisconsin	6,466,173,000	2.3%
14	Connecticut	5,995,482,000	2.1%
15	Indiana	5,976,203,000	2.1%
16	Washington	5,790,556,000	2.1%
17	North Carolina	5,421,740,000	1.9%
18	Maryland	5,412,209,000	1.9%
19	Minnesota	5,214,735,000	1.9%
20	Arizona	4,254,395,000	1.5%
21	Colorado	4,162,161,000	1.5%
22	Missouri	3,880,344,000	1.4%
23	Tennessee	3,453,047,000	1.2%
24	Oregon	3,138,875,000	1.1%
25	South Carolina	3,096,431,000	1.1%
26	Iowa	2,877,921,000	1.0%
27	Kansas	2,524,888,000	0.9%
28	New Hampshire	2,169,494,000	0.8%
29	Kentucky	1,977,011,000	0.7%
30	Louisiana	1,940,420,000	0.7%
31	Maine	1,912,158,000	0.7%
32	Nebraska	1,748,841,000	0.6%
33	Nevada	1,702,186,000	0.6%
34	Mississippi	1,646,563,000	0.6%
35	Oklahoma	1,482,139,000	0.5%
36	Alabama	1,473,554,000	0.5%
37	Rhode Island	1,462,064,000	0.5%
38	Utah	1,419,769,000	0.5%
39	Arkansas	1,003,909,000	0.4%
40	Idaho	958,763,000	0.3%
41	West Virginia	900,999,000	0.3%
42	Montana	852,399,000	0.3%
43	Alaska	830,011,000	0.3%
44	Vermont	823,610,000	0.3%
45	New Mexico	755,948,000	0.3%
46	Wyoming	692,341,000	0.2%
47	South Dakota	668,048,000	0.2%
48	Hawaii	614,930,000	0.2%
49	North Dakota	532,340,000	0.2%
50	Delaware	399,939,000	0.1%
	District of Columbia	803,389,000	0.3%

Source: U.S. Bureau of the Census, Governments Division
"State and Local Government Finances: 2002 Census" (http://www.census.gov/govs/www/estimate02.html)

293

Per Capita State and Local Government Property Tax Revenue in 2002

National Per Capita = $969

ALPHA ORDER

RANK	STATE	PER CAPITA
50	Alabama	$329
10	Alaska	1,295
33	Arizona	782
49	Arkansas	371
30	California	864
25	Colorado	925
2	Connecticut	1,733
44	Delaware	496
21	Florida	944
34	Georgia	778
43	Hawaii	498
36	Idaho	714
11	Illinois	1,261
19	Indiana	970
17	Iowa	981
24	Kansas	931
45	Kentucky	483
46	Louisiana	433
4	Maine	1,473
16	Maryland	995
8	Massachusetts	1,360
18	Michigan	975
14	Minnesota	1,038
41	Mississippi	574
37	Missouri	683
22	Montana	936
15	Nebraska	1,013
32	Nevada	785
3	New Hampshire	1,701
1	New Jersey	1,871
48	New Mexico	407
5	New York	1,401
38	North Carolina	652
31	North Dakota	840
23	Ohio	933
47	Oklahoma	425
27	Oregon	891
28	Pennsylvania	885
7	Rhode Island	1,368
35	South Carolina	754
29	South Dakota	878
40	Tennessee	596
13	Texas	1,129
39	Utah	612
9	Vermont	1,336
26	Virginia	923
20	Washington	954
42	West Virginia	499
12	Wisconsin	1,189
6	Wyoming	1,387

RANK ORDER

RANK	STATE	PER CAPITA
1	New Jersey	$1,871
2	Connecticut	1,733
3	New Hampshire	1,701
4	Maine	1,473
5	New York	1,401
6	Wyoming	1,387
7	Rhode Island	1,368
8	Massachusetts	1,360
9	Vermont	1,336
10	Alaska	1,295
11	Illinois	1,261
12	Wisconsin	1,189
13	Texas	1,129
14	Minnesota	1,038
15	Nebraska	1,013
16	Maryland	995
17	Iowa	981
18	Michigan	975
19	Indiana	970
20	Washington	954
21	Florida	944
22	Montana	936
23	Ohio	933
24	Kansas	931
25	Colorado	925
26	Virginia	923
27	Oregon	891
28	Pennsylvania	885
29	South Dakota	878
30	California	864
31	North Dakota	840
32	Nevada	785
33	Arizona	782
34	Georgia	778
35	South Carolina	754
36	Idaho	714
37	Missouri	683
38	North Carolina	652
39	Utah	612
40	Tennessee	596
41	Mississippi	574
42	West Virginia	499
43	Hawaii	498
44	Delaware	496
45	Kentucky	483
46	Louisiana	433
47	Oklahoma	425
48	New Mexico	407
49	Arkansas	371
50	Alabama	329

District of Columbia 1,423

Source: Morgan Quitno Press using data from U.S. Bureau of the Census, Governments Division
"State and Local Government Finances: 2002 Census" (http://www.census.gov/govs/www/estimate02.html)

State and Local Government Property Tax as a Percent
Of State and Local Government Total Revenue in 2002
National Percent = 15.4%

ALPHA ORDER

RANK	STATE	PERCENT
50	Alabama	6.0
37	Alaska	11.9
28	Arizona	14.1
46	Arkansas	7.4
36	California	12.1
16	Colorado	16.2
3	Connecticut	24.1
48	Delaware	6.7
13	Florida	17.0
27	Georgia	14.4
43	Hawaii	8.3
29	Idaho	14.0
5	Illinois	21.6
11	Indiana	17.5
15	Iowa	16.4
19	Kansas	15.8
42	Kentucky	8.8
47	Louisiana	7.1
4	Maine	23.8
16	Maryland	16.2
8	Massachusetts	20.8
21	Michigan	15.5
23	Minnesota	14.8
39	Mississippi	10.4
33	Missouri	12.7
21	Montana	15.5
26	Nebraska	14.5
32	Nevada	13.3
1	New Hampshire	32.2
2	New Jersey	29.3
49	New Mexico	6.6
20	New York	15.7
38	North Carolina	11.2
34	North Dakota	12.6
25	Ohio	14.7
45	Oklahoma	7.7
31	Oregon	13.5
23	Pennsylvania	14.8
7	Rhode Island	21.3
35	South Carolina	12.4
14	South Dakota	16.9
40	Tennessee	10.3
6	Texas	21.5
40	Utah	10.3
10	Vermont	20.4
12	Virginia	17.3
30	Washington	13.7
44	West Virginia	7.9
9	Wisconsin	20.6
18	Wyoming	15.9

RANK ORDER

RANK	STATE	PERCENT
1	New Hampshire	32.2
2	New Jersey	29.3
3	Connecticut	24.1
4	Maine	23.8
5	Illinois	21.6
6	Texas	21.5
7	Rhode Island	21.3
8	Massachusetts	20.8
9	Wisconsin	20.6
10	Vermont	20.4
11	Indiana	17.5
12	Virginia	17.3
13	Florida	17.0
14	South Dakota	16.9
15	Iowa	16.4
16	Colorado	16.2
16	Maryland	16.2
18	Wyoming	15.9
19	Kansas	15.8
20	New York	15.7
21	Michigan	15.5
21	Montana	15.5
23	Minnesota	14.8
23	Pennsylvania	14.8
25	Ohio	14.7
26	Nebraska	14.5
27	Georgia	14.4
28	Arizona	14.1
29	Idaho	14.0
30	Washington	13.7
31	Oregon	13.5
32	Nevada	13.3
33	Missouri	12.7
34	North Dakota	12.6
35	South Carolina	12.4
36	California	12.1
37	Alaska	11.9
38	North Carolina	11.2
39	Mississippi	10.4
40	Tennessee	10.3
40	Utah	10.3
42	Kentucky	8.8
43	Hawaii	8.3
44	West Virginia	7.9
45	Oklahoma	7.7
46	Arkansas	7.4
47	Louisiana	7.1
48	Delaware	6.7
49	New Mexico	6.6
50	Alabama	6.0

District of Columbia 10.9

Source: Morgan Quitno Press using data from U.S. Bureau of the Census, Governments Division
"State and Local Government Finances: 2002 Census" (http://www.census.gov/govs/www/estimate02.html)

State and Local Government Property Tax Revenue as a Percent Of State and Local Government Own Source Revenue in 2002
National Percent = 21.1%*

ALPHA ORDER

RANK	STATE	PERCENT
50	Alabama	8.4
40	Alaska	15.3
21	Arizona	21.5
46	Arkansas	10.4
37	California	17.0
30	Colorado	19.1
3	Connecticut	31.9
49	Delaware	8.6
17	Florida	22.0
31	Georgia	19.0
45	Hawaii	10.5
33	Idaho	18.4
8	Illinois	28.2
13	Indiana	22.9
19	Iowa	21.7
18	Kansas	21.9
43	Kentucky	12.5
47	Louisiana	9.9
4	Maine	31.0
24	Maryland	20.5
9	Massachusetts	26.6
20	Michigan	21.6
29	Minnesota	19.2
39	Mississippi	15.4
34	Missouri	17.9
12	Montana	24.1
16	Nebraska	22.3
35	Nevada	17.4
1	New Hampshire	42.5
2	New Jersey	34.7
48	New Mexico	9.8
15	New York	22.5
38	North Carolina	16.0
32	North Dakota	18.8
23	Ohio	20.6
44	Oklahoma	10.9
22	Oregon	20.7
27	Pennsylvania	19.5
5	Rhode Island	30.0
27	South Carolina	19.5
11	South Dakota	24.3
35	Tennessee	17.4
7	Texas	28.4
41	Utah	14.4
6	Vermont	29.7
24	Virginia	20.5
26	Washington	19.8
42	West Virginia	12.7
10	Wisconsin	24.8
14	Wyoming	22.7

RANK ORDER

RANK	STATE	PERCENT
1	New Hampshire	42.5
2	New Jersey	34.7
3	Connecticut	31.9
4	Maine	31.0
5	Rhode Island	30.0
6	Vermont	29.7
7	Texas	28.4
8	Illinois	28.2
9	Massachusetts	26.6
10	Wisconsin	24.8
11	South Dakota	24.3
12	Montana	24.1
13	Indiana	22.9
14	Wyoming	22.7
15	New York	22.5
16	Nebraska	22.3
17	Florida	22.0
18	Kansas	21.9
19	Iowa	21.7
20	Michigan	21.6
21	Arizona	21.5
22	Oregon	20.7
23	Ohio	20.6
24	Maryland	20.5
24	Virginia	20.5
26	Washington	19.8
27	Pennsylvania	19.5
27	South Carolina	19.5
29	Minnesota	19.2
30	Colorado	19.1
31	Georgia	19.0
32	North Dakota	18.8
33	Idaho	18.4
34	Missouri	17.9
35	Nevada	17.4
35	Tennessee	17.4
37	California	17.0
38	North Carolina	16.0
39	Mississippi	15.4
40	Alaska	15.3
41	Utah	14.4
42	West Virginia	12.7
43	Kentucky	12.5
44	Oklahoma	10.9
45	Hawaii	10.5
46	Arkansas	10.4
47	Louisiana	9.9
48	New Mexico	9.8
49	Delaware	8.6
50	Alabama	8.4
	District of Columbia	19.7

Source: Morgan Quitno Press using data from U.S. Bureau of the Census, Governments Division
"State and Local Government Finances: 2002 Census" (http://www.census.gov/govs/www/estimate02.html)
*Own source revenue includes taxes, current charges and miscellaneous general revenue. Excluded are intergovernmental transfers, insurance trust revenue and revenue from government owned utilities and other commercial or auxiliary enterprise.

State and Local Tax Burden as a Percentage of Income in 2005

National Percent = 10.1% of Income*

ALPHA ORDER			RANK ORDER		
RANK	STATE	PERCENT	RANK	STATE	PERCENT
46	Alabama	8.7	1	Maine	13.0
50	Alaska	6.4	2	New York	12.0
21	Arizona	10.2	3	Hawaii	11.5
11	Arkansas	10.5	4	Rhode Island	11.4
17	California	10.3	4	Wisconsin	11.4
37	Colorado	9.5	6	Vermont	11.1
11	Connecticut	10.5	7	Ohio	11.0
48	Delaware	8.0	8	Nebraska	10.9
44	Florida	9.2	8	Utah	10.9
30	Georgia	9.8	10	Minnesota	10.7
3	Hawaii	11.5	11	Arkansas	10.5
24	Idaho	10.0	11	Connecticut	10.5
30	Illinois	9.8	11	West Virginia	10.5
17	Indiana	10.3	14	Kansas	10.4
24	Iowa	10.0	14	Louisiana	10.4
14	Kansas	10.4	14	New Jersey	10.4
17	Kentucky	10.3	17	California	10.3
14	Louisiana	10.4	17	Indiana	10.3
1	Maine	13.0	17	Kentucky	10.3
17	Maryland	10.3	17	Maryland	10.3
30	Massachusetts	9.8	21	Arizona	10.2
22	Michigan	10.1	22	Michigan	10.1
10	Minnesota	10.7	22	Wyoming	10.1
24	Mississippi	10.0	24	Idaho	10.0
40	Missouri	9.4	24	Iowa	10.0
37	Montana	9.5	24	Mississippi	10.0
8	Nebraska	10.9	24	North Carolina	10.0
37	Nevada	9.5	24	Washington	10.0
49	New Hampshire	7.4	29	New Mexico	9.9
14	New Jersey	10.4	30	Georgia	9.8
29	New Mexico	9.9	30	Illinois	9.8
2	New York	12.0	30	Massachusetts	9.8
24	North Carolina	10.0	33	Pennsylvania	9.7
40	North Dakota	9.4	33	South Carolina	9.7
7	Ohio	11.0	33	Virginia	9.7
40	Oklahoma	9.4	36	Oregon	9.6
36	Oregon	9.6	37	Colorado	9.5
33	Pennsylvania	9.7	37	Montana	9.5
4	Rhode Island	11.4	37	Nevada	9.5
33	South Carolina	9.7	40	Missouri	9.4
45	South Dakota	8.8	40	North Dakota	9.4
47	Tennessee	8.3	40	Oklahoma	9.4
43	Texas	9.3	43	Texas	9.3
8	Utah	10.9	44	Florida	9.2
6	Vermont	11.1	45	South Dakota	8.8
33	Virginia	9.7	46	Alabama	8.7
24	Washington	10.0	47	Tennessee	8.3
11	West Virginia	10.5	48	Delaware	8.0
4	Wisconsin	11.4	49	New Hampshire	7.4
22	Wyoming	10.1	50	Alaska	6.4

	District of Columbia	12.2

Source: The Tax Foundation
  "America Celebrates Tax Freedom Day" (http://www.taxfoundation.org/publications/show/93.html)
*All state and local taxes.

Per Capita State and Local Tax Burden in 2005

National Per Capita = $3,763*

ALPHA ORDER

RANK	STATE	PER CAPITA
49	Alabama	$2,656
50	Alaska	2,452
33	Arizona	3,184
41	Arkansas	2,993
11	California	4,078
19	Colorado	3,758
1	Connecticut	5,400
36	Delaware	3,128
28	Florida	3,271
26	Georgia	3,377
9	Hawaii	4,161
39	Idaho	3,014
15	Illinois	3,920
23	Indiana	3,503
24	Iowa	3,479
22	Kansas	3,629
32	Kentucky	3,199
31	Louisiana	3,200
7	Maine	4,390
5	Maryland	4,501
4	Massachusetts	4,608
21	Michigan	3,686
6	Minnesota	4,409
48	Mississippi	2,739
27	Missouri	3,282
45	Montana	2,878
14	Nebraska	3,984
25	Nevada	3,423
38	New Hampshire	3,040
3	New Jersey	4,971
44	New Mexico	2,882
2	New York	5,170
30	North Carolina	3,268
34	North Dakota	3,170
16	Ohio	3,906
46	Oklahoma	2,876
28	Oregon	3,271
20	Pennsylvania	3,747
8	Rhode Island	4,327
42	South Carolina	2,976
42	South Dakota	2,976
47	Tennessee	2,757
35	Texas	3,167
37	Utah	3,122
12	Vermont	4,005
17	Virginia	3,820
13	Washington	3,990
40	West Virginia	2,996
10	Wisconsin	4,141
18	Wyoming	3,802

RANK ORDER

RANK	STATE	PER CAPITA
1	Connecticut	$5,400
2	New York	5,170
3	New Jersey	4,971
4	Massachusetts	4,608
5	Maryland	4,501
6	Minnesota	4,409
7	Maine	4,390
8	Rhode Island	4,327
9	Hawaii	4,161
10	Wisconsin	4,141
11	California	4,078
12	Vermont	4,005
13	Washington	3,990
14	Nebraska	3,984
15	Illinois	3,920
16	Ohio	3,906
17	Virginia	3,820
18	Wyoming	3,802
19	Colorado	3,758
20	Pennsylvania	3,747
21	Michigan	3,686
22	Kansas	3,629
23	Indiana	3,503
24	Iowa	3,479
25	Nevada	3,423
26	Georgia	3,377
27	Missouri	3,282
28	Florida	3,271
28	Oregon	3,271
30	North Carolina	3,268
31	Louisiana	3,200
32	Kentucky	3,199
33	Arizona	3,184
34	North Dakota	3,170
35	Texas	3,167
36	Delaware	3,128
37	Utah	3,122
38	New Hampshire	3,040
39	Idaho	3,014
40	West Virginia	2,996
41	Arkansas	2,993
42	South Carolina	2,976
42	South Dakota	2,976
44	New Mexico	2,882
45	Montana	2,878
46	Oklahoma	2,876
47	Tennessee	2,757
48	Mississippi	2,739
49	Alabama	2,656
50	Alaska	2,452
	District of Columbia	6,479

Source: The Tax Foundation
"America Celebrates Tax Freedom Day" (http://www.taxfoundation.org/publications/show/93.html)
*All state and local taxes.

State and Local Government Total Expenditures in 2002

National Total = $2,048,718,695,000*

ALPHA ORDER

RANK	STATE	EXPENDITURES	% of USA
23	Alabama	$28,530,974,000	1.4%
40	Alaska	9,397,434,000	0.5%
22	Arizona	31,308,193,000	1.5%
34	Arkansas	14,570,002,000	0.7%
1	California	293,424,276,000	14.3%
21	Colorado	31,890,729,000	1.6%
27	Connecticut	27,591,660,000	1.3%
45	Delaware	5,947,349,000	0.3%
4	Florida	99,307,092,000	4.8%
10	Georgia	52,310,112,000	2.6%
39	Hawaii	9,402,041,000	0.5%
43	Idaho	7,564,676,000	0.4%
5	Illinois	87,401,299,000	4.3%
18	Indiana	36,302,060,000	1.8%
30	Iowa	10,293,784,000	0.0%
32	Kansas	16,718,097,000	0.8%
28	Kentucky	24,839,062,000	1.2%
26	Louisiana	27,667,539,000	1.4%
41	Maine	8,677,113,000	0.4%
19	Maryland	35,576,810,000	1.7%
12	Massachusetts	51,146,058,000	2.5%
8	Michigan	69,533,498,000	3.4%
15	Minnesota	40,515,667,000	2.0%
31	Mississippi	17,284,802,000	0.8%
20	Missouri	33,036,367,000	1.6%
46	Montana	5,616,294,000	0.3%
37	Nebraska	12,492,121,000	0.6%
35	Nevada	13,970,658,000	0.7%
44	New Hampshire	7,065,915,000	0.3%
9	New Jersey	64,289,465,000	3.1%
36	New Mexico	12,688,548,000	0.6%
2	New York	198,535,830,000	9.7%
11	North Carolina	51,838,538,000	2.5%
50	North Dakota	4,190,494,000	0.2%
7	Ohio	79,971,645,000	3.9%
29	Oklahoma	20,776,022,000	1.0%
25	Oregon	27,731,191,000	1.4%
6	Pennsylvania	86,261,928,000	4.2%
42	Rhode Island	7,938,761,000	0.4%
24	South Carolina	28,105,735,000	1.4%
48	South Dakota	4,275,780,000	0.2%
17	Tennessee	36,638,052,000	1.8%
3	Texas	129,873,711,000	6.3%
33	Utah	15,523,271,000	0.8%
49	Vermont	4,218,112,000	0.2%
14	Virginia	43,687,513,000	2.1%
13	Washington	50,431,244,000	2.5%
38	West Virginia	11,929,874,000	0.6%
16	Wisconsin	39,261,767,000	1.9%
47	Wyoming	4,337,409,000	0.2%

RANK ORDER

RANK	STATE	EXPENDITURES	% of USA
1	California	$293,424,276,000	14.3%
2	New York	198,535,830,000	9.7%
3	Texas	129,873,711,000	6.3%
4	Florida	99,307,092,000	4.8%
5	Illinois	87,401,299,000	4.3%
6	Pennsylvania	86,261,928,000	4.2%
7	Ohio	79,971,645,000	3.9%
8	Michigan	69,533,498,000	3.4%
9	New Jersey	64,289,465,000	3.1%
10	Georgia	52,310,112,000	2.6%
11	North Carolina	51,838,538,000	2.5%
12	Massachusetts	51,146,058,000	2.5%
13	Washington	50,431,244,000	2.5%
14	Virginia	43,687,513,000	2.1%
15	Minnesota	40,515,667,000	2.0%
16	Wisconsin	39,261,767,000	1.9%
17	Tennessee	36,638,052,000	1.8%
18	Indiana	36,302,060,000	1.8%
19	Maryland	35,576,810,000	1.7%
20	Missouri	33,036,367,000	1.6%
21	Colorado	31,890,729,000	1.6%
22	Arizona	31,308,193,000	1.5%
23	Alabama	28,530,974,000	1.4%
24	South Carolina	28,105,735,000	1.4%
25	Oregon	27,731,191,000	1.4%
26	Louisiana	27,667,539,000	1.4%
27	Connecticut	27,591,660,000	1.3%
28	Kentucky	24,839,062,000	1.2%
29	Oklahoma	20,776,022,000	1.0%
30	Iowa	19,293,784,000	0.9%
31	Mississippi	17,284,802,000	0.8%
32	Kansas	16,718,097,000	0.8%
33	Utah	15,523,271,000	0.8%
34	Arkansas	14,570,002,000	0.7%
35	Nevada	13,970,658,000	0.7%
36	New Mexico	12,688,548,000	0.6%
37	Nebraska	12,492,121,000	0.6%
38	West Virginia	11,929,874,000	0.6%
39	Hawaii	9,402,041,000	0.5%
40	Alaska	9,397,434,000	0.5%
41	Maine	8,677,113,000	0.4%
42	Rhode Island	7,938,761,000	0.4%
43	Idaho	7,564,676,000	0.4%
44	New Hampshire	7,065,915,000	0.3%
45	Delaware	5,947,349,000	0.3%
46	Montana	5,616,294,000	0.3%
47	Wyoming	4,337,409,000	0.2%
48	South Dakota	4,275,780,000	0.2%
49	Vermont	4,218,112,000	0.2%
50	North Dakota	4,190,494,000	0.2%
	District of Columbia	7,832,123,000	0.4%

Source: U.S. Bureau of the Census, Governments Division
    "State and Local Government Finances: 2002 Census" (http://www.census.gov/govs/www/estimate02.html)
*Total expenditures includes all money paid other than for retirement of debt and extension of loans. Includes payments from all sources of funds including current revenues and proceeds from borrowing and prior year fund balances. Includes intergovernmental transfers and expenditures for government owned utilities and other commercial or auxiliary enterprise and insurance trust expenditures.

Per Capita State and Local Government Total Expenditures in 2002

National Per Capita = $7,115*

ALPHA ORDER

RANK	STATE	PER CAPITA
31	Alabama	$6,367
1	Alaska	14,664
46	Arizona	5,756
50	Arkansas	5,381
4	California	8,386
16	Colorado	7,090
7	Connecticut	7,977
13	Delaware	7,378
43	Florida	5,953
37	Georgia	6,125
10	Hawaii	7,616
47	Idaho	5,632
19	Illinois	6,945
44	Indiana	5,895
28	Iowa	6,574
36	Kansas	6,162
38	Kentucky	6,073
34	Louisiana	6,180
25	Maine	6,686
29	Maryland	6,538
8	Massachusetts	7,976
20	Michigan	6,924
6	Minnesota	8,063
39	Mississippi	6,028
45	Missouri	5,816
35	Montana	6,167
14	Nebraska	7,236
30	Nevada	6,443
49	New Hampshire	5,539
11	New Jersey	7,495
23	New Mexico	6,840
2	New York	10,367
33	North Carolina	6,237
26	North Dakota	6,612
17	Ohio	7,009
42	Oklahoma	5,956
9	Oregon	7,871
18	Pennsylvania	6,997
12	Rhode Island	7,427
21	South Carolina	6,845
48	South Dakota	5,623
32	Tennessee	6,325
41	Texas	5,979
24	Utah	6,692
22	Vermont	6,842
40	Virginia	6,006
5	Washington	8,312
27	West Virginia	6,609
15	Wisconsin	7,217
3	Wyoming	8,689

RANK ORDER

RANK	STATE	PER CAPITA
1	Alaska	$14,664
2	New York	10,367
3	Wyoming	8,689
4	California	8,386
5	Washington	8,312
6	Minnesota	8,063
7	Connecticut	7,977
8	Massachusetts	7,976
9	Oregon	7,871
10	Hawaii	7,616
11	New Jersey	7,495
12	Rhode Island	7,427
13	Delaware	7,378
14	Nebraska	7,236
15	Wisconsin	7,217
16	Colorado	7,090
17	Ohio	7,009
18	Pennsylvania	6,997
19	Illinois	6,945
20	Michigan	6,924
21	South Carolina	6,845
22	Vermont	6,842
23	New Mexico	6,840
24	Utah	6,692
25	Maine	6,686
26	North Dakota	6,612
27	West Virginia	6,609
28	Iowa	6,574
29	Maryland	6,538
30	Nevada	6,443
31	Alabama	6,367
32	Tennessee	6,325
33	North Carolina	6,237
34	Louisiana	6,180
35	Montana	6,167
36	Kansas	6,162
37	Georgia	6,125
38	Kentucky	6,073
39	Mississippi	6,028
40	Virginia	6,006
41	Texas	5,979
42	Oklahoma	5,956
43	Florida	5,953
44	Indiana	5,895
45	Missouri	5,816
46	Arizona	5,756
47	Idaho	5,632
48	South Dakota	5,623
49	New Hampshire	5,539
50	Arkansas	5,381

	District of Columbia	13,871

Source: Morgan Quitno Press using data from U.S. Bureau of the Census, Governments Division
    "State and Local Government Finances: 2002 Census" (http://www.census.gov/govs/www/estimate02.html)
*Total expenditures includes all money paid other than for retirement of debt and extension of loans. Includes payments from all sources of funds including current revenues and proceeds from borrowing and prior year fund balances. Includes intergovernmental transfers and expenditures for government owned utilities and other commercial or auxiliary enterprise and insurance trust expenditures.

State and Local Government Direct General Expenditures in 2002

National Total = $1,730,808,887,000*

ALPHA ORDER

RANK	STATE	EXPENDITURES	% of USA
23	Alabama	$24,604,802,000	1.4%
39	Alaska	8,443,238,000	0.5%
22	Arizona	25,252,471,000	1.5%
33	Arkansas	13,067,988,000	0.8%
1	California	235,626,698,000	13.6%
21	Colorado	27,098,646,000	1.6%
25	Connecticut	24,198,952,000	1.4%
45	Delaware	5,356,760,000	0.3%
4	Florida	87,081,941,000	5.0%
10	Georgia	44,950,898,000	2.6%
40	Hawaii	8,289,459,000	0.5%
42	Idaho	6,803,725,000	0.4%
5	Illinois	73,818,552,000	4.3%
17	Indiana	32,796,487,000	1.9%
30	Iowa	17,100,430,000	1.0%
32	Kansas	14,875,765,000	0.9%
28	Kentucky	21,591,680,000	1.2%
24	Louisiana	24,320,549,000	1.4%
41	Maine	7,948,044,000	0.5%
18	Maryland	31,796,384,000	1.8%
12	Massachusetts	42,346,880,000	2.4%
8	Michigan	60,722,940,000	3.5%
15	Minnesota	34,933,058,000	2.0%
31	Mississippi	15,384,166,000	0.9%
19	Missouri	29,044,682,000	1.7%
46	Montana	5,050,712,000	0.3%
38	Nebraska	9,745,328,000	0.6%
35	Nevada	11,766,368,000	0.7%
44	New Hampshire	6,343,015,000	0.4%
9	New Jersey	54,387,436,000	3.1%
36	New Mexico	11,435,993,000	0.7%
2	New York	161,129,758,000	9.3%
11	North Carolina	44,539,961,000	2.6%
47	North Dakota	3,886,155,000	0.2%
7	Ohio	67,047,030,000	3.9%
29	Oklahoma	18,154,361,000	1.0%
27	Oregon	22,989,775,000	1.3%
6	Pennsylvania	73,311,585,000	4.2%
43	Rhode Island	6,756,404,000	0.4%
26	South Carolina	23,819,949,000	1.4%
48	South Dakota	3,884,676,000	0.2%
20	Tennessee	28,952,456,000	1.7%
3	Texas	111,603,861,000	6.4%
34	Utah	12,860,641,000	0.7%
50	Vermont	3,804,994,000	0.2%
13	Virginia	39,266,925,000	2.3%
14	Washington	38,645,719,000	2.2%
37	West Virginia	9,848,116,000	0.6%
16	Wisconsin	34,003,403,000	2.0%
49	Wyoming	3,853,458,000	0.2%

RANK ORDER

RANK	STATE	EXPENDITURES	% of USA
1	California	$235,626,698,000	13.6%
2	New York	161,129,758,000	9.3%
3	Texas	111,603,861,000	6.4%
4	Florida	87,081,941,000	5.0%
5	Illinois	73,818,552,000	4.3%
6	Pennsylvania	73,311,585,000	4.2%
7	Ohio	67,047,030,000	3.9%
8	Michigan	60,722,940,000	3.5%
9	New Jersey	54,387,436,000	3.1%
10	Georgia	44,950,898,000	2.6%
11	North Carolina	44,539,961,000	2.6%
12	Massachusetts	42,346,880,000	2.4%
13	Virginia	39,266,925,000	2.3%
14	Washington	38,645,719,000	2.2%
15	Minnesota	34,933,058,000	2.0%
16	Wisconsin	34,003,403,000	2.0%
17	Indiana	32,796,487,000	1.9%
18	Maryland	31,796,384,000	1.8%
19	Missouri	29,044,682,000	1.7%
20	Tennessee	28,952,456,000	1.7%
21	Colorado	27,098,646,000	1.6%
22	Arizona	25,252,471,000	1.5%
23	Alabama	24,604,802,000	1.4%
24	Louisiana	24,320,549,000	1.4%
25	Connecticut	24,198,952,000	1.4%
26	South Carolina	23,819,949,000	1.4%
27	Oregon	22,989,775,000	1.3%
28	Kentucky	21,591,680,000	1.2%
29	Oklahoma	18,154,361,000	1.0%
30	Iowa	17,186,430,000	1.0%
31	Mississippi	15,384,166,000	0.9%
32	Kansas	14,875,765,000	0.9%
33	Arkansas	13,067,988,000	0.8%
34	Utah	12,860,641,000	0.7%
35	Nevada	11,766,368,000	0.7%
36	New Mexico	11,435,993,000	0.7%
37	West Virginia	9,848,116,000	0.6%
38	Nebraska	9,745,328,000	0.6%
39	Alaska	8,443,238,000	0.5%
40	Hawaii	8,289,459,000	0.5%
41	Maine	7,948,044,000	0.5%
42	Idaho	6,803,725,000	0.4%
43	Rhode Island	6,756,404,000	0.4%
44	New Hampshire	6,343,015,000	0.4%
45	Delaware	5,356,760,000	0.3%
46	Montana	5,050,712,000	0.3%
47	North Dakota	3,886,155,000	0.2%
48	South Dakota	3,884,676,000	0.2%
49	Wyoming	3,853,458,000	0.2%
50	Vermont	3,804,994,000	0.2%
	District of Columbia	6,179,613,000	0.4%

Source: U.S. Bureau of the Census, Governments Division
   "State and Local Government Finances: 2002 Census" (http://www.census.gov/govs/www/estimate02.html)
*Direct general expenditures include expenditures for current operations, assistance and subsidies, interest on debt and capital outlay. Excludes intergovernmental transfers, expenditures for government owned utilities and other commercial or auxiliary enterprise and insurance trust expenditures.

Per Capita State and Local Government Direct General Expenditures in 2002

National Per Capita = $6,011*

ALPHA ORDER			RANK ORDER		
RANK	**STATE**	**PER CAPITA**	**RANK**	**STATE**	**PER CAPITA**
30	Alabama	$5,491	1	Alaska	$13,175
1	Alaska	13,175	2	New York	8,414
50	Arizona	4,643	3	Wyoming	7,719
49	Arkansas	4,827	4	Connecticut	6,996
6	California	6,734	5	Minnesota	6,952
20	Colorado	6,024	6	California	6,734
4	Connecticut	6,996	7	Hawaii	6,715
8	Delaware	6,645	8	Delaware	6,645
41	Florida	5,220	9	Massachusetts	6,604
40	Georgia	5,264	10	Oregon	6,525
7	Hawaii	6,715	11	Washington	6,370
46	Idaho	5,065	12	New Jersey	6,341
23	Illinois	5,866	13	Rhode Island	6,321
38	Indiana	5,326	14	Wisconsin	6,250
24	Iowa	5,856	15	Vermont	6,172
31	Kansas	5,483	16	New Mexico	6,164
39	Kentucky	5,279	17	North Dakota	6,132
33	Louisiana	5,432	18	Maine	6,124
18	Maine	6,124	19	Michigan	6,047
25	Maryland	5,843	20	Colorado	6,024
9	Massachusetts	6,604	21	Pennsylvania	5,947
19	Michigan	6,047	22	Ohio	5,876
5	Minnesota	6,952	23	Illinois	5,866
36	Mississippi	5,365	24	Iowa	5,856
44	Missouri	5,114	25	Maryland	5,843
28	Montana	5,546	26	South Carolina	5,801
27	Nebraska	5,645	27	Nebraska	5,645
34	Nevada	5,427	28	Montana	5,546
48	New Hampshire	4,973	29	Utah	5,544
12	New Jersey	6,341	30	Alabama	5,491
16	New Mexico	6,164	31	Kansas	5,483
2	New York	8,414	32	West Virginia	5,455
37	North Carolina	5,359	33	Louisiana	5,432
17	North Dakota	6,132	34	Nevada	5,427
22	Ohio	5,876	35	Virginia	5,399
42	Oklahoma	5,205	36	Mississippi	5,365
10	Oregon	6,525	37	North Carolina	5,359
21	Pennsylvania	5,947	38	Indiana	5,326
13	Rhode Island	6,321	39	Kentucky	5,279
26	South Carolina	5,801	40	Georgia	5,264
45	South Dakota	5,108	41	Florida	5,220
47	Tennessee	4,998	42	Oklahoma	5,205
43	Texas	5,138	43	Texas	5,138
29	Utah	5,544	44	Missouri	5,114
15	Vermont	6,172	45	South Dakota	5,108
35	Virginia	5,399	46	Idaho	5,065
11	Washington	6,370	47	Tennessee	4,998
32	West Virginia	5,455	48	New Hampshire	4,973
14	Wisconsin	6,250	49	Arkansas	4,827
3	Wyoming	7,719	50	Arizona	4,643

District of Columbia   10,944

Source: Morgan Quitno Press using data from U.S. Bureau of the Census, Governments Division
"State and Local Government Finances: 2002 Census" (http://www.census.gov/govs/www/estimate02.html)
*Direct general expenditures include expenditures for current operations, assistance and subsidies, interest on debt and capital outlay. Excludes intergovernmental transfers, expenditures for government owned utilities and other commercial or auxiliary enterprise and insurance trust expenditures.

State and Local Government Debt Outstanding in 2002

National Total = $1,686,106,158,000*

ALPHA ORDER

RANK	STATE	DEBT	% of USA
27	Alabama	$19,056,995,000	1.1%
36	Alaska	8,645,562,000	0.5%
20	Arizona	26,606,401,000	1.6%
35	Arkansas	8,753,923,000	0.5%
1	California	209,299,330,000	12.4%
19	Colorado	26,718,356,000	1.6%
18	Connecticut	27,767,247,000	1.6%
44	Delaware	5,532,722,000	0.3%
4	Florida	90,275,844,000	5.4%
13	Georgia	34,300,600,000	2.0%
38	Hawaii	8,448,272,000	0.5%
45	Idaho	3,985,310,000	0.2%
6	Illinois	80,936,138,000	4.8%
23	Indiana	24,070,857,000	1.4%
34	Iowa	9,494,328,000	0.6%
32	Kansas	12,313,015,000	0.7%
17	Kentucky	28,993,629,000	1.7%
26	Louisiana	20,985,667,000	1.2%
43	Maine	6,346,249,000	0.4%
21	Maryland	25,663,252,000	1.5%
7	Massachusetts	65,322,342,000	3.9%
9	Michigan	54,194,825,000	3.2%
15	Minnesota	32,010,125,000	1.9%
33	Mississippi	9,933,625,000	0.6%
22	Missouri	24,244,237,000	1.4%
46	Montana	3,962,884,000	0.2%
40	Nebraska	7,905,990,000	0.5%
29	Nevada	15,772,823,000	0.9%
42	New Hampshire	7,221,258,000	0.4%
8	New Jersey	57,590,436,000	3.4%
37	New Mexico	8,603,278,000	0.5%
2	New York	197,194,861,000	11.7%
14	North Carolina	33,460,541,000	2.0%
49	North Dakota	2,904,992,000	0.2%
10	Ohio	51,343,613,000	3.0%
31	Oklahoma	12,508,160,000	0.7%
28	Oregon	18,827,113,000	1.1%
5	Pennsylvania	83,809,049,000	5.0%
41	Rhode Island	7,344,889,000	0.4%
24	South Carolina	22,872,515,000	1.4%
47	South Dakota	3,450,753,000	0.2%
25	Tennessee	21,128,046,000	1.3%
3	Texas	122,809,828,000	7.3%
30	Utah	13,249,622,000	0.8%
48	Vermont	3,027,741,000	0.2%
12	Virginia	35,422,294,000	2.1%
11	Washington	45,560,550,000	2.7%
39	West Virginia	8,084,701,000	0.5%
16	Wisconsin	30,327,288,000	1.8%
50	Wyoming	2,387,995,000	0.1%

RANK ORDER

RANK	STATE	DEBT	% of USA
1	California	$209,299,330,000	12.4%
2	New York	197,194,861,000	11.7%
3	Texas	122,809,828,000	7.3%
4	Florida	90,275,844,000	5.4%
5	Pennsylvania	83,809,049,000	5.0%
6	Illinois	80,936,138,000	4.8%
7	Massachusetts	65,322,342,000	3.9%
8	New Jersey	57,590,436,000	3.4%
9	Michigan	54,194,825,000	3.2%
10	Ohio	51,343,613,000	3.0%
11	Washington	45,560,550,000	2.7%
12	Virginia	35,422,294,000	2.1%
13	Georgia	34,300,600,000	2.0%
14	North Carolina	33,460,541,000	2.0%
15	Minnesota	32,010,125,000	1.9%
16	Wisconsin	30,327,288,000	1.8%
17	Kentucky	28,993,629,000	1.7%
18	Connecticut	27,767,247,000	1.6%
19	Colorado	26,718,356,000	1.6%
20	Arizona	26,606,401,000	1.6%
21	Maryland	25,663,252,000	1.5%
22	Missouri	24,244,237,000	1.4%
23	Indiana	24,070,857,000	1.4%
24	South Carolina	22,872,515,000	1.4%
25	Tennessee	21,128,046,000	1.3%
26	Louisiana	20,985,667,000	1.2%
27	Alabama	19,056,995,000	1.1%
28	Oregon	18,827,113,000	1.1%
29	Nevada	15,772,823,000	0.9%
30	Utah	13,249,622,000	0.8%
31	Oklahoma	12,508,160,000	0.7%
32	Kansas	12,313,015,000	0.7%
33	Mississippi	9,933,625,000	0.6%
34	Iowa	9,494,328,000	0.6%
35	Arkansas	8,753,923,000	0.5%
36	Alaska	8,645,562,000	0.5%
37	New Mexico	8,603,278,000	0.5%
38	Hawaii	8,448,272,000	0.5%
39	West Virginia	8,084,701,000	0.5%
40	Nebraska	7,905,990,000	0.5%
41	Rhode Island	7,344,889,000	0.4%
42	New Hampshire	7,221,258,000	0.4%
43	Maine	6,346,249,000	0.4%
44	Delaware	5,532,722,000	0.3%
45	Idaho	3,985,310,000	0.2%
46	Montana	3,962,884,000	0.2%
47	South Dakota	3,450,753,000	0.2%
48	Vermont	3,027,741,000	0.2%
49	North Dakota	2,904,992,000	0.2%
50	Wyoming	2,387,995,000	0.1%
	District of Columbia	5,436,087,000	0.3%

Source: U.S. Bureau of the Census, Governments Division
   "State and Local Government Finances: 2002 Census" (http://www.census.gov/govs/www/estimate02.html)
*Includes short-term, long-term, full faith and credit, nonguaranteed and public debt for private purposes.

Per Capita State and Local Government Debt Outstanding in 2002

National Per Capita = $5,856*

ALPHA ORDER

RANK	STATE	PER CAPITA
41	Alabama	$4,253
1	Alaska	13,491
26	Arizona	4,892
49	Arkansas	3,233
15	California	5,982
16	Colorado	5,940
4	Connecticut	8,028
9	Delaware	6,864
22	Florida	5,412
43	Georgia	4,017
10	Hawaii	6,843
50	Idaho	2,967
13	Illinois	6,431
44	Indiana	3,909
48	Iowa	3,235
35	Kansas	4,539
7	Kentucky	7,089
31	Louisiana	4,687
27	Maine	4,890
30	Maryland	4,716
3	Massachusetts	10,187
23	Michigan	5,397
14	Minnesota	6,370
47	Mississippi	3,464
40	Missouri	4,269
39	Montana	4,352
34	Nebraska	4,579
6	Nevada	7,274
18	New Hampshire	5,661
12	New Jersey	6,714
32	New Mexico	4,638
2	New York	10,297
42	North Carolina	4,026
33	North Dakota	4,583
37	Ohio	4,500
46	Oklahoma	3,586
24	Oregon	5,344
11	Pennsylvania	6,798
8	Rhode Island	6,871
21	South Carolina	5,571
36	South Dakota	4,538
45	Tennessee	3,648
19	Texas	5,653
17	Utah	5,712
25	Vermont	4,911
28	Virginia	4,870
5	Washington	7,509
38	West Virginia	4,478
20	Wisconsin	5,574
29	Wyoming	4,784

RANK ORDER

RANK	STATE	PER CAPITA
1	Alaska	$13,491
2	New York	10,297
3	Massachusetts	10,187
4	Connecticut	8,028
5	Washington	7,509
6	Nevada	7,274
7	Kentucky	7,089
8	Rhode Island	6,871
9	Delaware	6,864
10	Hawaii	6,843
11	Pennsylvania	6,798
12	New Jersey	6,714
13	Illinois	6,431
14	Minnesota	6,370
15	California	5,982
16	Colorado	5,940
17	Utah	5,712
18	New Hampshire	5,661
19	Texas	5,653
20	Wisconsin	5,574
21	South Carolina	5,571
22	Florida	5,412
23	Michigan	5,397
24	Oregon	5,344
25	Vermont	4,911
26	Arizona	4,892
27	Maine	4,890
28	Virginia	4,870
29	Wyoming	4,784
30	Maryland	4,716
31	Louisiana	4,687
32	New Mexico	4,638
33	North Dakota	4,583
34	Nebraska	4,579
35	Kansas	4,539
36	South Dakota	4,538
37	Ohio	4,500
38	West Virginia	4,478
39	Montana	4,352
40	Missouri	4,269
41	Alabama	4,253
42	North Carolina	4,026
43	Georgia	4,017
44	Indiana	3,909
45	Tennessee	3,648
46	Oklahoma	3,586
47	Mississippi	3,464
48	Iowa	3,235
49	Arkansas	3,233
50	Idaho	2,967

	District of Columbia	9,627

Source: Morgan Quitno Press using data from U.S. Bureau of the Census, Governments Division
"State and Local Government Finances: 2002 Census" (http://www.census.gov/govs/www/estimate02.html)
*Includes short-term, long-term, full faith and credit, nonguaranteed and public debt for private purposes.

State and Local Government Full-Time Equivalent Employees in 2004

National Total = 15,788,784 FTE Employees*

ALPHA ORDER					RANK ORDER			
RANK	STATE	EMPLOYEES	% of USA		RANK	STATE	EMPLOYEES	% of USA
23	Alabama	270,632	1.7%		1	California	1,776,132	11.2%
44	Alaska	50,841	0.3%		2	Texas	1,271,164	8.1%
22	Arizona	270,719	1.7%		3	New York	1,184,394	7.5%
33	Arkansas	151,938	1.0%		4	Florida	824,337	5.2%
1	California	1,776,132	11.2%		5	Illinois	635,760	4.0%
24	Colorado	248,404	1.6%		6	Ohio	623,226	3.9%
30	Connecticut	181,617	1.2%		7	Pennsylvania	570,379	3.6%
46	Delaware	47,879	0.3%		8	Michigan	504,272	3.2%
4	Florida	824,337	5.2%		9	Georgia	500,305	3.2%
9	Georgia	500,305	3.2%		10	New Jersey	495,189	3.1%
41	Hawaii	70,932	0.4%		11	North Carolina	453,940	2.9%
39	Idaho	78,310	0.5%		12	Virginia	410,885	2.6%
5	Illinois	635,760	4.0%		13	Indiana	329,581	2.1%
13	Indiana	329,581	2.1%		14	Massachusetts	323,067	2.0%
29	Iowa	184,552	1.2%		15	Washington	322,991	2.0%
32	Kansas	179,546	1.1%		16	Tennessee	317,514	2.0%
26	Kentucky	237,217	1.5%		17	Missouri	311,206	2.0%
20	Louisiana	282,311	1.8%		18	Wisconsin	287,256	1.8%
40	Maine	77,055	0.5%		19	Maryland	282,362	1.8%
19	Maryland	282,362	1.8%		20	Louisiana	282,311	1.8%
14	Massachusetts	323,067	2.0%		21	Minnesota	275,067	1.7%
8	Michigan	504,272	3.2%		22	Arizona	270,719	1.7%
21	Minnesota	275,067	1.7%		23	Alabama	270,632	1.7%
28	Mississippi	188,369	1.2%		24	Colorado	248,404	1.6%
17	Missouri	311,206	2.0%		25	South Carolina	243,004	1.5%
43	Montana	54,272	0.3%		26	Kentucky	237,217	1.5%
36	Nebraska	114,767	0.7%		27	Oklahoma	200,939	1.3%
38	Nevada	96,376	0.6%		28	Mississippi	188,369	1.2%
42	New Hampshire	68,484	0.4%		29	Iowa	184,552	1.2%
10	New Jersey	495,189	3.1%		30	Connecticut	181,617	1.2%
35	New Mexico	124,642	0.8%		31	Oregon	179,817	1.1%
3	New York	1,184,394	7.5%		32	Kansas	179,546	1.1%
11	North Carolina	453,940	2.9%		33	Arkansas	151,938	1.0%
49	North Dakota	40,884	0.3%		34	Utah	127,595	0.8%
6	Ohio	623,226	3.9%		35	New Mexico	124,642	0.8%
27	Oklahoma	200,939	1.3%		36	Nebraska	114,767	0.7%
31	Oregon	179,817	1.1%		37	West Virginia	98,232	0.6%
7	Pennsylvania	570,379	3.6%		38	Nevada	96,376	0.6%
45	Rhode Island	50,521	0.3%		39	Idaho	78,310	0.5%
25	South Carolina	243,004	1.5%		40	Maine	77,055	0.5%
47	South Dakota	43,549	0.3%		41	Hawaii	70,932	0.4%
16	Tennessee	317,514	2.0%		42	New Hampshire	68,484	0.4%
2	Texas	1,271,164	8.1%		43	Montana	54,272	0.3%
34	Utah	127,595	0.8%		44	Alaska	50,841	0.3%
50	Vermont	38,149	0.2%		45	Rhode Island	50,521	0.3%
12	Virginia	410,885	2.6%		46	Delaware	47,879	0.3%
15	Washington	322,991	2.0%		47	South Dakota	43,549	0.3%
37	West Virginia	98,232	0.6%		48	Wyoming	43,533	0.3%
18	Wisconsin	287,256	1.8%		49	North Dakota	40,884	0.3%
48	Wyoming	43,533	0.3%		50	Vermont	38,149	0.2%
						District of Columbia	44,671	0.3%

Source: U.S. Bureau of the Census, Governments Division
    "State and Local Employment and Payroll - March 2004" (http://www.census.gov/govs/www/apesstl04.html)
*As of March 2004.

Rate of State and Local Government Full-Time Equivalent Employees in 2004

National Rate = 538 State/Local Government Employees per 10,000 Population*

ALPHA ORDER			RANK ORDER		
RANK	STATE	RATE	RANK	STATE	RATE
12	Alabama	598	1	Wyoming	861
2	Alaska	773	2	Alaska	773
47	Arizona	472	3	Kansas	657
25	Arkansas	553	3	Nebraska	657
45	California	496	5	New Mexico	655
29	Colorado	540	6	Mississippi	649
39	Connecticut	519	7	North Dakota	643
16	Delaware	577	8	Louisiana	626
46	Florida	474	9	Iowa	625
23	Georgia	561	10	New York	614
22	Hawaii	562	10	Vermont	614
23	Idaho	561	12	Alabama	598
43	Illinois	500	13	Maine	586
34	Indiana	529	13	Montana	586
9	Iowa	625	15	South Carolina	579
3	Kansas	657	16	Delaware	577
17	Kentucky	573	17	Kentucky	573
8	Louisiana	626	18	New Jersey	570
13	Maine	586	18	Oklahoma	570
40	Maryland	508	20	Texas	566
41	Massachusetts	504	21	South Dakota	565
44	Michigan	499	22	Hawaii	562
29	Minnesota	540	23	Georgia	561
6	Mississippi	649	23	Idaho	561
29	Missouri	540	25	Arkansas	553
13	Montana	586	26	Virginia	549
3	Nebraska	657	27	Ohio	544
50	Nevada	413	28	West Virginia	542
35	New Hampshire	527	29	Colorado	540
18	New Jersey	570	29	Minnesota	540
5	New Mexico	655	29	Missouri	540
10	New York	614	32	Tennessee	539
33	North Carolina	532	33	North Carolina	532
7	North Dakota	643	34	Indiana	529
27	Ohio	544	35	New Hampshire	527
18	Oklahoma	570	35	Utah	527
42	Oregon	501	37	Wisconsin	522
49	Pennsylvania	460	38	Washington	520
48	Rhode Island	468	39	Connecticut	519
15	South Carolina	579	40	Maryland	508
21	South Dakota	565	41	Massachusetts	504
32	Tennessee	539	42	Oregon	501
20	Texas	566	43	Illinois	500
35	Utah	527	44	Michigan	499
10	Vermont	614	45	California	496
26	Virginia	549	46	Florida	474
38	Washington	520	47	Arizona	472
28	West Virginia	542	48	Rhode Island	468
37	Wisconsin	522	49	Pennsylvania	460
1	Wyoming	861	50	Nevada	413
				District of Columbia	806

Source: Morgan Quitno Press using data from U.S. Bureau of the Census, Governments Division
   "State and Local Employment and Payroll - March 2004" (http://www.census.gov/govs/www/apesstl04.html)
*Full-time equivalent as of March 2004.

Average Annual Earnings of Full-Time State and Local Government Employees in 2004
National Average = $43,998*

<table>
<tr><td colspan="3">ALPHA ORDER</td><td colspan="3">RANK ORDER</td></tr>
<tr><th>RANK</th><th>STATE</th><th>EARNINGS</th><th>RANK</th><th>STATE</th><th>EARNINGS</th></tr>
<tr><td>38</td><td>Alabama</td><td>$35,624</td><td>1</td><td>California</td><td>$58,400</td></tr>
<tr><td>7</td><td>Alaska</td><td>49,543</td><td>2</td><td>New Jersey</td><td>54,829</td></tr>
<tr><td>21</td><td>Arizona</td><td>41,988</td><td>3</td><td>New York</td><td>53,525</td></tr>
<tr><td>48</td><td>Arkansas</td><td>32,507</td><td>4</td><td>Connecticut</td><td>53,188</td></tr>
<tr><td>1</td><td>California</td><td>58,400</td><td>5</td><td>Washington</td><td>50,991</td></tr>
<tr><td>14</td><td>Colorado</td><td>45,845</td><td>6</td><td>Rhode Island</td><td>50,403</td></tr>
<tr><td>4</td><td>Connecticut</td><td>53,188</td><td>7</td><td>Alaska</td><td>49,543</td></tr>
<tr><td>18</td><td>Delaware</td><td>43,854</td><td>8</td><td>Massachusetts</td><td>49,181</td></tr>
<tr><td>22</td><td>Florida</td><td>40,457</td><td>9</td><td>Nevada</td><td>48,774</td></tr>
<tr><td>34</td><td>Georgia</td><td>36,579</td><td>10</td><td>Maryland</td><td>48,086</td></tr>
<tr><td>20</td><td>Hawaii</td><td>42,244</td><td>11</td><td>Michigan</td><td>47,755</td></tr>
<tr><td>37</td><td>Idaho</td><td>36,031</td><td>12</td><td>Minnesota</td><td>46,940</td></tr>
<tr><td>13</td><td>Illinois</td><td>46,197</td><td>13</td><td>Illinois</td><td>46,197</td></tr>
<tr><td>29</td><td>Indiana</td><td>38,004</td><td>14</td><td>Colorado</td><td>45,845</td></tr>
<tr><td>23</td><td>Iowa</td><td>40,029</td><td>15</td><td>Pennsylvania</td><td>45,459</td></tr>
<tr><td>36</td><td>Kansas</td><td>36,339</td><td>16</td><td>Wisconsin</td><td>44,714</td></tr>
<tr><td>39</td><td>Kentucky</td><td>35,391</td><td>17</td><td>Oregon</td><td>44,020</td></tr>
<tr><td>47</td><td>Louisiana</td><td>33,296</td><td>18</td><td>Delaware</td><td>43,854</td></tr>
<tr><td>35</td><td>Maine</td><td>36,408</td><td>19</td><td>Ohio</td><td>42,539</td></tr>
<tr><td>10</td><td>Maryland</td><td>48,086</td><td>20</td><td>Hawaii</td><td>42,244</td></tr>
<tr><td>8</td><td>Massachusetts</td><td>49,181</td><td>21</td><td>Arizona</td><td>41,988</td></tr>
<tr><td>11</td><td>Michigan</td><td>47,755</td><td>22</td><td>Florida</td><td>40,457</td></tr>
<tr><td>12</td><td>Minnesota</td><td>46,940</td><td>23</td><td>Iowa</td><td>40,029</td></tr>
<tr><td>50</td><td>Mississippi</td><td>31,567</td><td>24</td><td>Virginia</td><td>39,925</td></tr>
<tr><td>41</td><td>Missouri</td><td>35,147</td><td>25</td><td>New Hampshire</td><td>39,185</td></tr>
<tr><td>43</td><td>Montana</td><td>34,645</td><td>26</td><td>Vermont</td><td>39,125</td></tr>
<tr><td>30</td><td>Nebraska</td><td>37,866</td><td>27</td><td>Utah</td><td>38,916</td></tr>
<tr><td>9</td><td>Nevada</td><td>48,774</td><td>28</td><td>North Dakota</td><td>38,457</td></tr>
<tr><td>25</td><td>New Hampshire</td><td>39,185</td><td>29</td><td>Indiana</td><td>38,004</td></tr>
<tr><td>2</td><td>New Jersey</td><td>54,829</td><td>30</td><td>Nebraska</td><td>37,866</td></tr>
<tr><td>46</td><td>New Mexico</td><td>33,910</td><td>31</td><td>North Carolina</td><td>37,753</td></tr>
<tr><td>3</td><td>New York</td><td>53,525</td><td>32</td><td>Wyoming</td><td>37,528</td></tr>
<tr><td>31</td><td>North Carolina</td><td>37,753</td><td>33</td><td>Texas</td><td>36,822</td></tr>
<tr><td>28</td><td>North Dakota</td><td>38,457</td><td>34</td><td>Georgia</td><td>36,579</td></tr>
<tr><td>19</td><td>Ohio</td><td>42,539</td><td>35</td><td>Maine</td><td>36,408</td></tr>
<tr><td>49</td><td>Oklahoma</td><td>32,440</td><td>36</td><td>Kansas</td><td>36,339</td></tr>
<tr><td>17</td><td>Oregon</td><td>44,020</td><td>37</td><td>Idaho</td><td>36,031</td></tr>
<tr><td>15</td><td>Pennsylvania</td><td>45,459</td><td>38</td><td>Alabama</td><td>35,624</td></tr>
<tr><td>6</td><td>Rhode Island</td><td>50,403</td><td>39</td><td>Kentucky</td><td>35,391</td></tr>
<tr><td>42</td><td>South Carolina</td><td>35,074</td><td>40</td><td>Tennessee</td><td>35,378</td></tr>
<tr><td>45</td><td>South Dakota</td><td>34,111</td><td>41</td><td>Missouri</td><td>35,147</td></tr>
<tr><td>40</td><td>Tennessee</td><td>35,378</td><td>42</td><td>South Carolina</td><td>35,074</td></tr>
<tr><td>33</td><td>Texas</td><td>36,822</td><td>43</td><td>Montana</td><td>34,645</td></tr>
<tr><td>27</td><td>Utah</td><td>38,916</td><td>44</td><td>West Virginia</td><td>34,207</td></tr>
<tr><td>26</td><td>Vermont</td><td>39,125</td><td>45</td><td>South Dakota</td><td>34,111</td></tr>
<tr><td>24</td><td>Virginia</td><td>39,925</td><td>46</td><td>New Mexico</td><td>33,910</td></tr>
<tr><td>5</td><td>Washington</td><td>50,991</td><td>47</td><td>Louisiana</td><td>33,296</td></tr>
<tr><td>44</td><td>West Virginia</td><td>34,207</td><td>48</td><td>Arkansas</td><td>32,507</td></tr>
<tr><td>16</td><td>Wisconsin</td><td>44,714</td><td>49</td><td>Oklahoma</td><td>32,440</td></tr>
<tr><td>32</td><td>Wyoming</td><td>37,528</td><td>50</td><td>Mississippi</td><td>31,567</td></tr>
<tr><td></td><td></td><td></td><td></td><td>District of Columbia</td><td>56,782</td></tr>
</table>

Source: Morgan Quitno Press using data from U.S. Bureau of the Census, Governments Division
   "State and Local Employment and Payroll - March 2004" (http://www.census.gov/govs/www/apesstl04.html)
*March 2004 full-time payroll (multiplied by 12) divided by full-time employees.

State Government Total Revenue in 2003

National Total = $1,295,658,820,000*

ALPHA ORDER

RANK	STATE	REVENUE	% of USA
24	Alabama	$19,098,788,000	1.5%
39	Alaska	6,924,221,000	0.5%
27	Arizona	17,927,436,000	1.4%
32	Arkansas	11,805,012,000	0.9%
1	California	195,545,076,000	15.1%
29	Colorado	13,805,946,000	1.1%
26	Connecticut	18,240,537,000	1.4%
45	Delaware	5,040,703,000	0.4%
4	Florida	55,212,605,000	4.3%
12	Georgia	29,874,373,000	2.3%
40	Hawaii	6,808,157,000	0.5%
43	Idaho	5,492,993,000	0.4%
9	Illinois	44,422,828,000	3.4%
17	Indiana	24,553,393,000	1.9%
31	Iowa	12,972,701,000	1.0%
34	Kansas	10,401,734,000	0.8%
25	Kentucky	18,377,403,000	1.4%
22	Louisiana	19,437,629,000	1.5%
41	Maine	6,801,191,000	0.5%
19	Maryland	21,801,442,000	1.7%
10	Massachusetts	30,371,289,000	2.3%
5	Michigan	50,076,603,000	3.9%
15	Minnesota	25,596,307,000	2.0%
30	Mississippi	13,393,021,000	1.0%
18	Missouri	22,023,719,000	1.7%
46	Montana	4,608,118,000	0.4%
38	Nebraska	7,285,210,000	0.6%
37	Nevada	8,351,343,000	0.6%
44	New Hampshire	5,206,836,000	0.4%
8	New Jersey	46,077,610,000	3.6%
35	New Mexico	9,847,659,000	0.8%
2	New York	118,274,576,000	9.1%
11	North Carolina	30,042,985,000	2.3%
49	North Dakota	3,359,107,000	0.3%
6	Ohio	49,904,580,000	3.9%
28	Oklahoma	14,918,730,000	1.2%
23	Oregon	19,252,091,000	1.5%
7	Pennsylvania	49,459,403,000	3.8%
42	Rhode Island	5,855,988,000	0.5%
21	South Carolina	19,669,246,000	1.5%
50	South Dakota	2,999,838,000	0.2%
20	Tennessee	20,564,361,000	1.6%
3	Texas	82,621,328,000	6.4%
33	Utah	11,534,161,000	0.9%
47	Vermont	3,639,339,000	0.3%
14	Virginia	28,185,448,000	2.2%
13	Washington	29,661,378,000	2.3%
36	West Virginia	9,766,188,000	0.8%
16	Wisconsin	25,165,038,000	1.9%
48	Wyoming	3,403,152,000	0.3%

RANK ORDER

RANK	STATE	REVENUE	% of USA
1	California	$195,545,076,000	15.1%
2	New York	118,274,576,000	9.1%
3	Texas	82,621,328,000	6.4%
4	Florida	55,212,605,000	4.3%
5	Michigan	50,076,603,000	3.9%
6	Ohio	49,904,580,000	3.9%
7	Pennsylvania	49,459,403,000	3.8%
8	New Jersey	46,077,610,000	3.6%
9	Illinois	44,422,828,000	3.4%
10	Massachusetts	30,371,289,000	2.3%
11	North Carolina	30,042,985,000	2.3%
12	Georgia	29,874,373,000	2.3%
13	Washington	29,661,378,000	2.3%
14	Virginia	28,185,448,000	2.2%
15	Minnesota	25,596,307,000	2.0%
16	Wisconsin	25,165,038,000	1.9%
17	Indiana	24,553,393,000	1.9%
18	Missouri	22,023,719,000	1.7%
19	Maryland	21,801,442,000	1.7%
20	Tennessee	20,564,361,000	1.6%
21	South Carolina	19,669,246,000	1.5%
22	Louisiana	19,437,629,000	1.5%
23	Oregon	19,252,091,000	1.5%
24	Alabama	19,098,788,000	1.5%
25	Kentucky	18,377,403,000	1.4%
26	Connecticut	18,240,537,000	1.4%
27	Arizona	17,927,436,000	1.4%
28	Oklahoma	14,918,730,000	1.2%
29	Colorado	13,805,946,000	1.1%
30	Mississippi	13,393,021,000	1.0%
31	Iowa	12,972,701,000	1.0%
32	Arkansas	11,805,012,000	0.9%
33	Utah	11,534,161,000	0.9%
34	Kansas	10,401,734,000	0.8%
35	New Mexico	9,847,659,000	0.8%
36	West Virginia	9,766,188,000	0.8%
37	Nevada	8,351,343,000	0.6%
38	Nebraska	7,285,210,000	0.6%
39	Alaska	6,924,221,000	0.5%
40	Hawaii	6,808,157,000	0.5%
41	Maine	6,801,191,000	0.5%
42	Rhode Island	5,855,988,000	0.5%
43	Idaho	5,492,993,000	0.4%
44	New Hampshire	5,206,836,000	0.4%
45	Delaware	5,040,703,000	0.4%
46	Montana	4,608,118,000	0.4%
47	Vermont	3,639,339,000	0.3%
48	Wyoming	3,403,152,000	0.3%
49	North Dakota	3,359,107,000	0.3%
50	South Dakota	2,999,838,000	0.2%

District of Columbia**   NA   NA

Source: U.S. Bureau of the Census, Governments Division
"2003 State Government Finances" (http://www.census.gov/govs/www/state03.html)
Total revenue includes all money received from external sources. This includes taxes, intergovernmental transfers and insurance trust revenue and revenue from government owned utilities and other commercial or auxiliary enterprise.
***Not applicable.*

Per Capita State Government Total Revenue in 2003

National Per Capita = $4,463*

ALPHA ORDER

RANK	STATE	PER CAPITA
31	Alabama	$4,242
1	Alaska	10,677
49	Arizona	3,214
28	Arkansas	4,330
6	California	5,515
50	Colorado	3,036
14	Connecticut	5,233
3	Delaware	6,164
48	Florida	3,249
47	Georgia	3,415
7	Hawaii	5,454
34	Idaho	4,015
46	Illinois	3,512
36	Indiana	3,963
26	Iowa	4,410
40	Kansas	3,818
25	Kentucky	4,464
29	Louisiana	4,329
15	Maine	5,199
37	Maryland	3,955
22	Massachusetts	4,733
18	Michigan	4,969
16	Minnesota	5,057
23	Mississippi	4,649
39	Missouri	3,851
17	Montana	5,020
32	Nebraska	4,192
43	Nevada	3,725
33	New Hampshire	4,044
11	New Jersey	5,333
13	New Mexico	5,240
4	New York	6,151
44	North Carolina	3,567
12	North Dakota	5,306
27	Ohio	4,365
30	Oklahoma	4,257
9	Oregon	5,404
35	Pennsylvania	4,000
8	Rhode Island	5,444
21	South Carolina	4,743
38	South Dakota	3,923
45	Tennessee	3,520
42	Texas	3,739
19	Utah	4,849
5	Vermont	5,879
41	Virginia	3,817
20	Washington	4,838
10	West Virginia	5,395
24	Wisconsin	4,599
2	Wyoming	6,780

RANK ORDER

RANK	STATE	PER CAPITA
1	Alaska	$10,677
2	Wyoming	6,780
3	Delaware	6,164
4	New York	6,151
5	Vermont	5,879
6	California	5,515
7	Hawaii	5,454
8	Rhode Island	5,444
9	Oregon	5,404
10	West Virginia	5,395
11	New Jersey	5,333
12	North Dakota	5,306
13	New Mexico	5,240
14	Connecticut	5,233
15	Maine	5,199
16	Minnesota	5,057
17	Montana	5,020
18	Michigan	4,969
19	Utah	4,849
20	Washington	4,838
21	South Carolina	4,743
22	Massachusetts	4,733
23	Mississippi	4,649
24	Wisconsin	4,599
25	Kentucky	4,464
26	Iowa	4,410
27	Ohio	4,365
28	Arkansas	4,330
29	Louisiana	4,329
30	Oklahoma	4,257
31	Alabama	4,242
32	Nebraska	4,192
33	New Hampshire	4,044
34	Idaho	4,015
35	Pennsylvania	4,000
36	Indiana	3,963
37	Maryland	3,955
38	South Dakota	3,923
39	Missouri	3,851
40	Kansas	3,818
41	Virginia	3,817
42	Texas	3,739
43	Nevada	3,725
44	North Carolina	3,567
45	Tennessee	3,520
46	Illinois	3,512
47	Georgia	3,415
48	Florida	3,249
49	Arizona	3,214
50	Colorado	3,036

District of Columbia**   NA

Source: Morgan Quitno Press using data from U.S. Bureau of the Census, Governments Division
    "2003 State Government Finances" (http://www.census.gov/govs/www/state03.html)

*Total revenue includes all money received from external sources. This includes taxes, intergovernmental transfers and insurance trust revenue and revenue from government owned utilities and other commercial or auxiliary enterprise.
**Not applicable.

State Government Intergovernmental Revenue in 2003

National Total = $361,617,049,000*

ALPHA ORDER

RANK	STATE	REVENUE	% of USA
16	Alabama	$6,668,784,000	1.8%
39	Alaska	1,997,175,000	0.6%
19	Arizona	6,092,557,000	1.7%
31	Arkansas	3,685,249,000	1.0%
1	California	48,245,951,000	13.3%
29	Colorado	4,178,537,000	1.2%
30	Connecticut	4,020,036,000	1.1%
50	Delaware	994,952,000	0.3%
6	Florida	12,850,982,000	3.6%
11	Georgia	9,028,114,000	2.5%
43	Hawaii	1,537,997,000	0.4%
46	Idaho	1,455,705,000	0.4%
8	Illinois	12,027,338,000	3.3%
18	Indiana	6,346,679,000	1.8%
32	Iowa	3,534,400,000	1.0%
33	Kansas	3,266,719,000	0.9%
24	Kentucky	5,330,212,000	1.5%
17	Louisiana	6,501,978,000	1.8%
38	Maine	2,062,560,000	0.6%
21	Maryland	5,829,817,000	1.6%
25	Massachusetts	5,130,127,000	1.4%
7	Michigan	12,221,555,000	3.4%
20	Minnesota	5,982,225,000	1.7%
26	Mississippi	5,086,417,000	1.4%
13	Missouri	7,172,806,000	2.0%
42	Montana	1,582,665,000	0.4%
37	Nebraska	2,139,810,000	0.6%
44	Nevada	1,498,008,000	0.4%
45	New Hampshire	1,464,454,000	0.4%
10	New Jersey	9,064,614,000	2.5%
34	New Mexico	3,220,765,000	0.9%
2	New York	43,442,351,000	12.0%
9	North Carolina	10,278,725,000	2.8%
48	North Dakota	1,128,029,000	0.3%
5	Ohio	14,058,065,000	3.9%
27	Oklahoma	4,255,172,000	1.2%
28	Oregon	4,215,696,000	1.2%
4	Pennsylvania	14,466,919,000	4.0%
40	Rhode Island	1,855,350,000	0.5%
22	South Carolina	5,738,966,000	1.6%
49	South Dakota	1,111,450,000	0.3%
12	Tennessee	8,292,209,000	2.3%
3	Texas	24,349,595,000	6.7%
36	Utah	2,493,503,000	0.7%
47	Vermont	1,152,305,000	0.3%
23	Virginia	5,679,471,000	1.6%
15	Washington	7,012,389,000	1.9%
35	West Virginia	2,975,382,000	0.8%
14	Wisconsin	7,094,092,000	2.0%
41	Wyoming	1,798,192,000	0.5%

RANK ORDER

RANK	STATE	REVENUE	% of USA
1	California	$48,245,951,000	13.3%
2	New York	43,442,351,000	12.0%
3	Texas	24,349,595,000	6.7%
4	Pennsylvania	14,466,919,000	4.0%
5	Ohio	14,058,065,000	3.9%
6	Florida	12,850,982,000	3.6%
7	Michigan	12,221,555,000	3.4%
8	Illinois	12,027,338,000	3.3%
9	North Carolina	10,278,725,000	2.8%
10	New Jersey	9,064,614,000	2.5%
11	Georgia	9,028,114,000	2.5%
12	Tennessee	8,292,209,000	2.3%
13	Missouri	7,172,806,000	2.0%
14	Wisconsin	7,094,092,000	2.0%
15	Washington	7,012,389,000	1.9%
16	Alabama	6,668,784,000	1.8%
17	Louisiana	6,501,978,000	1.8%
18	Indiana	6,346,679,000	1.8%
19	Arizona	6,092,557,000	1.7%
20	Minnesota	5,982,225,000	1.7%
21	Maryland	5,829,817,000	1.6%
22	South Carolina	5,738,966,000	1.6%
23	Virginia	5,679,471,000	1.6%
24	Kentucky	5,330,212,000	1.5%
25	Massachusetts	5,130,127,000	1.4%
26	Mississippi	5,086,417,000	1.4%
27	Oklahoma	4,255,172,000	1.2%
28	Oregon	4,215,696,000	1.2%
29	Colorado	4,178,537,000	1.2%
30	Connecticut	4,020,036,000	1.1%
31	Arkansas	3,685,249,000	1.0%
32	Iowa	3,534,400,000	1.0%
33	Kansas	3,266,719,000	0.9%
34	New Mexico	3,220,765,000	0.9%
35	West Virginia	2,975,382,000	0.8%
36	Utah	2,493,503,000	0.7%
37	Nebraska	2,139,810,000	0.6%
38	Maine	2,062,560,000	0.6%
39	Alaska	1,997,175,000	0.6%
40	Rhode Island	1,855,350,000	0.5%
41	Wyoming	1,798,192,000	0.5%
42	Montana	1,582,665,000	0.4%
43	Hawaii	1,537,997,000	0.4%
44	Nevada	1,498,008,000	0.4%
45	New Hampshire	1,464,454,000	0.4%
46	Idaho	1,455,705,000	0.4%
47	Vermont	1,152,305,000	0.3%
48	North Dakota	1,128,029,000	0.3%
49	South Dakota	1,111,450,000	0.3%
50	Delaware	994,952,000	0.3%
	District of Columbia**	NA	NA

Source: U.S. Bureau of the Census, Governments Division
   "2003 State Government Finances" (http://www.census.gov/govs/www/state03.html)
Includes revenue from federal and local government sources.
**Not applicable.*

Per Capita State Government Intergovernmental Revenue in 2003

National Per Capita = $1,246*

ALPHA ORDER

RANK	STATE	PER CAPITA
12	Alabama	$1,481
2	Alaska	3,080
38	Arizona	1,092
18	Arkansas	1,352
17	California	1,361
46	Colorado	919
34	Connecticut	1,153
26	Delaware	1,217
49	Florida	756
43	Georgia	1,032
22	Hawaii	1,232
39	Idaho	1,064
45	Illinois	951
44	Indiana	1,024
29	Iowa	1,202
30	Kansas	1,199
20	Kentucky	1,295
14	Louisiana	1,448
11	Maine	1,577
40	Maryland	1,058
47	Massachusetts	799
28	Michigan	1,213
32	Minnesota	1,182
6	Mississippi	1,766
21	Missouri	1,254
8	Montana	1,724
23	Nebraska	1,231
50	Nevada	668
36	New Hampshire	1,137
41	New Jersey	1,049
9	New Mexico	1,714
3	New York	2,259
25	North Carolina	1,220
5	North Dakota	1,782
24	Ohio	1,230
27	Oklahoma	1,214
31	Oregon	1,183
33	Pennsylvania	1,170
7	Rhode Island	1,725
16	South Carolina	1,384
13	South Dakota	1,454
15	Tennessee	1,420
37	Texas	1,102
42	Utah	1,048
4	Vermont	1,861
48	Virginia	769
35	Washington	1,144
10	West Virginia	1,644
19	Wisconsin	1,296
1	Wyoming	3,583

RANK ORDER

RANK	STATE	PER CAPITA
1	Wyoming	$3,583
2	Alaska	3,080
3	New York	2,259
4	Vermont	1,861
5	North Dakota	1,782
6	Mississippi	1,766
7	Rhode Island	1,725
8	Montana	1,724
9	New Mexico	1,714
10	West Virginia	1,644
11	Maine	1,577
12	Alabama	1,481
13	South Dakota	1,454
14	Louisiana	1,448
15	Tennessee	1,420
16	South Carolina	1,384
17	California	1,361
18	Arkansas	1,352
19	Wisconsin	1,296
20	Kentucky	1,295
21	Missouri	1,254
22	Hawaii	1,232
23	Nebraska	1,231
24	Ohio	1,230
25	North Carolina	1,220
26	Delaware	1,217
27	Oklahoma	1,214
28	Michigan	1,213
29	Iowa	1,202
30	Kansas	1,199
31	Oregon	1,183
32	Minnesota	1,182
33	Pennsylvania	1,170
34	Connecticut	1,153
35	Washington	1,144
36	New Hampshire	1,137
37	Texas	1,102
38	Arizona	1,092
39	Idaho	1,064
40	Maryland	1,058
41	New Jersey	1,049
42	Utah	1,048
43	Georgia	1,032
44	Indiana	1,024
45	Illinois	951
46	Colorado	919
47	Massachusetts	799
48	Virginia	769
49	Florida	756
50	Nevada	668
	District of Columbia**	NA

Source: Morgan Quitno Press using data from U.S. Bureau of the Census, Governments Division
   "2003 State Government Finances" (http://www.census.gov/govs/www/state03.html)
*Includes revenue from federal and local government sources.
**Not applicable.

State Government Own Source Revenue in 2003

National Total = $750,731,975,000*

ALPHA ORDER

RANK	STATE	REVENUE	% of USA
25	Alabama	$9,905,972,000	1.3%
40	Alaska	4,101,494,000	0.5%
24	Arizona	10,797,789,000	1.4%
31	Arkansas	7,045,292,000	0.9%
1	California	99,752,298,000	13.3%
26	Colorado	9,820,051,000	1.3%
19	Connecticut	12,196,506,000	1.6%
42	Delaware	3,726,166,000	0.5%
4	Florida	36,733,297,000	4.9%
13	Georgia	17,292,027,000	2.3%
38	Hawaii	4,839,454,000	0.6%
44	Idaho	3,160,894,000	0.4%
8	Illinois	28,788,375,000	3.8%
17	Indiana	15,328,075,000	2.0%
30	Iowa	7,562,504,000	1.0%
33	Kansas	6,485,359,000	0.9%
22	Kentucky	11,195,558,000	1.5%
21	Louisiana	11,774,133,000	1.6%
41	Maine	4,030,824,000	0.5%
18	Maryland	14,708,723,000	2.0%
10	Massachusetts	21,882,311,000	2.9%
6	Michigan	30,788,685,000	4.1%
15	Minnesota	17,090,264,000	2.3%
32	Mississippi	6,786,616,000	0.9%
20	Missouri	11,962,273,000	1.6%
46	Montana	2,385,123,000	0.3%
39	Nebraska	4,609,990,000	0.6%
37	Nevada	5,050,488,000	0.7%
45	New Hampshire	3,101,853,000	0.4%
7	New Jersey	29,754,841,000	4.0%
35	New Mexico	5,786,507,000	0.8%
2	New York	55,399,749,000	7.4%
11	North Carolina	19,892,309,000	2.6%
48	North Dakota	1,907,497,000	0.3%
9	Ohio	28,364,072,000	3.8%
29	Oklahoma	8,648,012,000	1.2%
28	Oregon	9,066,830,000	1.2%
5	Pennsylvania	32,437,851,000	4.3%
43	Rhode Island	3,316,582,000	0.4%
27	South Carolina	9,669,559,000	1.3%
50	South Dakota	1,571,402,000	0.2%
23	Tennessee	10,986,093,000	1.5%
3	Texas	42,108,137,000	5.6%
34	Utah	6,265,426,000	0.8%
47	Vermont	2,199,943,000	0.3%
12	Virginia	19,848,590,000	2.6%
14	Washington	17,121,159,000	2.3%
36	West Virginia	5,341,185,000	0.7%
16	Wisconsin	16,339,063,000	2.2%
49	Wyoming	1,804,774,000	0.2%

RANK ORDER

RANK	STATE	REVENUE	% of USA
1	California	$99,752,298,000	13.3%
2	New York	55,399,749,000	7.4%
3	Texas	42,108,137,000	5.6%
4	Florida	36,733,297,000	4.9%
5	Pennsylvania	32,437,851,000	4.3%
6	Michigan	30,788,685,000	4.1%
7	New Jersey	29,754,841,000	4.0%
8	Illinois	28,788,375,000	3.8%
9	Ohio	28,364,072,000	3.8%
10	Massachusetts	21,882,311,000	2.9%
11	North Carolina	19,892,309,000	2.6%
12	Virginia	19,848,590,000	2.6%
13	Georgia	17,292,027,000	2.3%
14	Washington	17,121,159,000	2.3%
15	Minnesota	17,090,264,000	2.3%
16	Wisconsin	16,339,063,000	2.2%
17	Indiana	15,328,075,000	2.0%
18	Maryland	14,708,723,000	2.0%
19	Connecticut	12,196,506,000	1.6%
20	Missouri	11,962,273,000	1.6%
21	Louisiana	11,774,133,000	1.6%
22	Kentucky	11,195,558,000	1.5%
23	Tennessee	10,986,093,000	1.5%
24	Arizona	10,797,789,000	1.4%
25	Alabama	9,905,972,000	1.3%
26	Colorado	9,820,051,000	1.3%
27	South Carolina	9,669,559,000	1.3%
28	Oregon	9,066,830,000	1.2%
29	Oklahoma	8,648,012,000	1.2%
30	Iowa	7,562,504,000	1.0%
31	Arkansas	7,045,292,000	0.9%
32	Mississippi	6,786,616,000	0.9%
33	Kansas	6,485,359,000	0.9%
34	Utah	6,265,426,000	0.8%
35	New Mexico	5,786,507,000	0.8%
36	West Virginia	5,341,185,000	0.7%
37	Nevada	5,050,488,000	0.7%
38	Hawaii	4,839,454,000	0.6%
39	Nebraska	4,609,990,000	0.6%
40	Alaska	4,101,494,000	0.5%
41	Maine	4,030,824,000	0.5%
42	Delaware	3,726,166,000	0.5%
43	Rhode Island	3,316,582,000	0.4%
44	Idaho	3,160,894,000	0.4%
45	New Hampshire	3,101,853,000	0.4%
46	Montana	2,385,123,000	0.3%
47	Vermont	2,199,943,000	0.3%
48	North Dakota	1,907,497,000	0.3%
49	Wyoming	1,804,774,000	0.2%
50	South Dakota	1,571,402,000	0.2%
	District of Columbia**	NA	NA

Source: U.S. Bureau of the Census, Governments Division
    "2003 State Government Finances" (http://www.census.gov/govs/www/state03.html)
*Own source revenue includes taxes, current charges and miscellaneous general revenue. Excluded are intergovernmental transfers, insurance trust revenue and revenue from government owned utilities and other commercial or auxiliary enterprise.
**Not applicable.

312

Per Capita State Government Own Source Revenue in 2003

National Per Capita = $2,586*

ALPHA ORDER

RANK	STATE	PER CAPITA
42	Alabama	$2,200
1	Alaska	6,324
48	Arizona	1,936
28	Arkansas	2,584
18	California	2,813
44	Colorado	2,159
6	Connecticut	3,499
2	Delaware	4,556
43	Florida	2,162
47	Georgia	1,977
3	Hawaii	3,877
39	Idaho	2,310
40	Illinois	2,276
32	Indiana	2,474
29	Iowa	2,571
35	Kansas	2,381
20	Kentucky	2,719
26	Louisiana	2,622
11	Maine	3,081
22	Maryland	2,668
8	Massachusetts	3,410
13	Michigan	3,055
9	Minnesota	3,376
37	Mississippi	2,356
45	Missouri	2,092
27	Montana	2,598
23	Nebraska	2,652
41	Nevada	2,253
34	New Hampshire	2,409
7	New Jersey	3,444
12	New Mexico	3,079
17	New York	2,881
36	North Carolina	2,362
14	North Dakota	3,013
31	Ohio	2,481
33	Oklahoma	2,467
30	Oregon	2,545
25	Pennsylvania	2,623
10	Rhode Island	3,083
38	South Carolina	2,332
46	South Dakota	2,055
50	Tennessee	1,881
49	Texas	1,905
24	Utah	2,634
5	Vermont	3,553
21	Virginia	2,688
19	Washington	2,792
16	West Virginia	2,950
15	Wisconsin	2,986
4	Wyoming	3,596

RANK ORDER

RANK	STATE	PER CAPITA
1	Alaska	$6,324
2	Delaware	4,556
3	Hawaii	3,877
4	Wyoming	3,596
5	Vermont	3,553
6	Connecticut	3,499
7	New Jersey	3,444
8	Massachusetts	3,410
9	Minnesota	3,376
10	Rhode Island	3,083
11	Maine	3,081
12	New Mexico	3,079
13	Michigan	3,055
14	North Dakota	3,013
15	Wisconsin	2,986
16	West Virginia	2,950
17	New York	2,881
18	California	2,813
19	Washington	2,792
20	Kentucky	2,719
21	Virginia	2,688
22	Maryland	2,668
23	Nebraska	2,652
24	Utah	2,634
25	Pennsylvania	2,623
26	Louisiana	2,622
27	Montana	2,598
28	Arkansas	2,584
29	Iowa	2,571
30	Oregon	2,545
31	Ohio	2,481
32	Indiana	2,474
33	Oklahoma	2,467
34	New Hampshire	2,409
35	Kansas	2,381
36	North Carolina	2,362
37	Mississippi	2,356
38	South Carolina	2,332
39	Idaho	2,310
40	Illinois	2,276
41	Nevada	2,253
42	Alabama	2,200
43	Florida	2,162
44	Colorado	2,159
45	Missouri	2,092
46	South Dakota	2,055
47	Georgia	1,977
48	Arizona	1,936
49	Texas	1,905
50	Tennessee	1,881
	District of Columbia**	NA

Source: Morgan Quitno Press using data from U.S. Bureau of the Census, Governments Division
   "2003 State Government Finances" (http://www.census.gov/govs/www/state03.html)
*Own source revenue includes taxes, current charges and miscellaneous general revenue. Excluded are intergovernmental transfers, insurance trust revenue and revenue from government owned utilities and other commercial or auxiliary enterprise.
**Not applicable.

State Government Net Revenue from Lotteries in 2003

National Total = $13,254,500,000*

ALPHA ORDER

RANK	STATE	REVENUE	% of USA
NA	Alabama**	NA	NA
NA	Alaska**	NA	NA
23	Arizona	96,300,000	0.7%
NA	Arkansas**	NA	NA
3	California	1,121,900,000	8.5%
22	Colorado	105,000,000	0.8%
14	Connecticut	260,300,000	2.0%
32	Delaware	32,500,000	0.2%
2	Florida	1,153,500,000	8.7%
7	Georgia	767,200,000	5.8%
NA	Hawaii**	NA	NA
34	Idaho	22,000,000	0.2%
11	Illinois	536,100,000	4.0%
18	Indiana	178,900,000	1.3%
29	Iowa	47,400,000	0.4%
27	Kansas	63,800,000	0.5%
17	Kentucky	198,200,000	1.5%
21	Louisiana	111,000,000	0.8%
30	Maine	40,300,000	0.3%
12	Maryland	438,500,000	3.3%
5	Massachusetts	889,500,000	6.7%
10	Michigan	564,200,000	4.3%
24	Minnesota	79,400,000	0.6%
NA	Mississippi**	NA	NA
16	Missouri	209,300,000	1.6%
37	Montana	7,500,000	0.1%
35	Nebraska	20,000,000	0.2%
NA	Nevada**	NA	NA
26	New Hampshire	66,600,000	0.5%
8	New Jersey	754,000,000	5.7%
31	New Mexico	33,100,000	0.2%
1	New York	1,910,600,000	14.4%
NA	North Carolina**	NA	NA
NA	North Dakota**	NA	NA
9	Ohio	708,000,000	5.3%
NA	Oklahoma**	NA	NA
28	Oregon	62,500,000	0.5%
6	Pennsylvania	787,700,000	5.9%
25	Rhode Island	67,200,000	0.5%
15	South Carolina	219,300,000	1.7%
38	South Dakota	6,900,000	0.1%
NA	Tennessee**	NA	NA
4	Texas	937,700,000	7.1%
NA	Utah**	NA	NA
36	Vermont	16,200,000	0.1%
13	Virginia	375,200,000	2.8%
20	Washington	130,100,000	1.0%
33	West Virginia	31,600,000	0.2%
19	Wisconsin	133,100,000	1.0%
NA	Wyoming**	NA	NA

RANK ORDER

RANK	STATE	REVENUE	% of USA
1	New York	$1,910,600,000	14.4%
2	Florida	1,153,500,000	8.7%
3	California	1,121,900,000	8.5%
4	Texas	937,700,000	7.1%
5	Massachusetts	889,500,000	6.7%
6	Pennsylvania	787,700,000	5.9%
7	Georgia	767,200,000	5.8%
8	New Jersey	754,000,000	5.7%
9	Ohio	708,000,000	5.3%
10	Michigan	564,200,000	4.3%
11	Illinois	536,100,000	4.0%
12	Maryland	438,500,000	3.3%
13	Virginia	375,200,000	2.8%
14	Connecticut	260,300,000	2.0%
15	South Carolina	219,300,000	1.7%
16	Missouri	209,300,000	1.6%
17	Kentucky	198,200,000	1.5%
18	Indiana	178,900,000	1.3%
19	Wisconsin	133,100,000	1.0%
20	Washington	130,100,000	1.0%
21	Louisiana	111,000,000	0.8%
22	Colorado	105,000,000	0.8%
23	Arizona	96,300,000	0.7%
24	Minnesota	79,400,000	0.6%
25	Rhode Island	67,200,000	0.5%
26	New Hampshire	66,600,000	0.5%
27	Kansas	63,800,000	0.5%
28	Oregon	62,500,000	0.5%
29	Iowa	47,400,000	0.4%
30	Maine	40,300,000	0.3%
31	New Mexico	33,100,000	0.2%
32	Delaware	32,500,000	0.2%
33	West Virginia	31,600,000	0.2%
34	Idaho	22,000,000	0.2%
35	Nebraska	20,000,000	0.2%
36	Vermont	16,200,000	0.1%
37	Montana	7,500,000	0.1%
38	South Dakota	6,900,000	0.1%
NA	Alabama**	NA	NA
NA	Alaska**	NA	NA
NA	Arkansas**	NA	NA
NA	Hawaii**	NA	NA
NA	Mississippi**	NA	NA
NA	Nevada**	NA	NA
NA	North Carolina**	NA	NA
NA	North Dakota**	NA	NA
NA	Oklahoma**	NA	NA
NA	Tennessee**	NA	NA
NA	Utah**	NA	NA
NA	Wyoming**	NA	NA
	District of Columbia	72,100,000	0.5%

Source: The Tax Foundation
    "Lotteries and State Fiscal Policy" (October 2004, http://www.taxfoundation.org/bp46.pdf)
*This is total lottery sales minus payments for prizes and operating expenses. This calculation results in "operating income." Amounts from various other funds including unclaimed prizes in many states are then added back in to calculate the "government revenue" shown here.
**No lottery as of fiscal year 2003.

314

Per Capita State Government Net Revenue from Lotteries in 2003

National Per Capita = $51.92*

ALPHA ORDER

RANK	STATE	PER CAPITA
NA	Alabama**	NA
NA	Alaska**	NA
32	Arizona	17.26
NA	Arkansas**	NA
20	California	31.64
27	Colorado	23.09
6	Connecticut	74.65
18	Delaware	39.72
7	Florida	67.86
3	Georgia	88.42
NA	Hawaii**	NA
34	Idaho	16.09
17	Illinois	42.38
22	Indiana	28.86
33	Iowa	16.11
26	Kansas	23.41
15	Kentucky	48.13
24	Louisiana	24.70
21	Maine	30.78
5	Maryland	79.55
1	Massachusetts	138.54
11	Michigan	55.96
35	Minnesota	15.68
NA	Mississippi**	NA
19	Missouri	36.60
38	Montana	8.17
36	Nebraska	11.51
NA	Nevada**	NA
13	New Hampshire	51.68
4	New Jersey	87.24
29	New Mexico	17.62
2	New York	99.45
NA	North Carolina**	NA
NA	North Dakota**	NA
10	Ohio	61.90
NA	Oklahoma**	NA
30	Oregon	17.53
8	Pennsylvania	63.67
9	Rhode Island	62.45
12	South Carolina	52.86
37	South Dakota	9.02
NA	Tennessee**	NA
16	Texas	42.42
NA	Utah**	NA
23	Vermont	26.16
14	Virginia	50.94
28	Washington	21.22
31	West Virginia	17.44
25	Wisconsin	24.31
NA	Wyoming**	NA

RANK ORDER

RANK	STATE	PER CAPITA
1	Massachusetts	$138.54
2	New York	99.45
3	Georgia	88.42
4	New Jersey	87.24
5	Maryland	79.55
6	Connecticut	74.65
7	Florida	67.86
8	Pennsylvania	63.67
9	Rhode Island	62.45
10	Ohio	61.90
11	Michigan	55.96
12	South Carolina	52.86
13	New Hampshire	51.68
14	Virginia	50.94
15	Kentucky	48.13
16	Texas	42.42
17	Illinois	42.38
18	Delaware	39.72
19	Missouri	36.60
20	California	31.64
21	Maine	30.78
22	Indiana	28.86
23	Vermont	26.16
24	Louisiana	24.70
25	Wisconsin	24.31
26	Kansas	23.41
27	Colorado	23.09
28	Washington	21.22
29	New Mexico	17.62
30	Oregon	17.53
31	West Virginia	17.44
32	Arizona	17.26
33	Iowa	16.11
34	Idaho	16.09
35	Minnesota	15.68
36	Nebraska	11.51
37	South Dakota	9.02
38	Montana	8.17
NA	Alabama**	NA
NA	Alaska**	NA
NA	Arkansas**	NA
NA	Hawaii**	NA
NA	Mississippi**	NA
NA	Nevada**	NA
NA	North Carolina**	NA
NA	North Dakota**	NA
NA	Oklahoma**	NA
NA	Tennessee**	NA
NA	Utah**	NA
NA	Wyoming**	NA

District of Columbia 129.30

Source: Morgan Quitno Press using data from The Tax Foundation
"Lotteries and State Fiscal Policy" (October 2004, http://www.taxfoundation.org/bp46.pdf)
*This is total lottery sales minus payments for prizes and operating expenses. This calculation results in "operating income." Amounts from various other funds including unclaimed prizes in many states are then added back in to calculate the "government revenue" shown here. National rate is based on population of states with a lottery.
**No lottery as of fiscal year 2003.

Projected vs. Actual State Tax Collections in 2005

National Percent = 104.2% of Projected Taxes*

ALPHA ORDER

RANK	STATE	PERCENT
15	Alabama	108.0
1	Alaska	174.4
25	Arizona	105.0
18	Arkansas	107.7
27	California	104.5
29	Colorado	103.8
20	Connecticut	106.6
12	Delaware	108.4
15	Florida	108.0
37	Georgia	101.5
6	Hawaii	111.8
17	Idaho	107.8
22	Illinois	106.0
33	Indiana	102.7
25	Iowa	105.0
39	Kansas	100.8
43	Kentucky	100.0
NA	Louisiana**	NA
38	Maine	100.9
12	Maryland	108.4
8	Massachusetts	108.9
46	Michigan	98.5
34	Minnesota	102.6
31	Mississippi	103.3
35	Missouri	102.4
2	Montana	123.9
7	Nebraska	109.4
4	Nevada	115.5
NA	New Hampshire**	NA
36	New Jersey	102.1
10	New Mexico	108.5
28	New York	104.0
23	North Carolina	105.5
12	North Dakota	108.4
30	Ohio	103.6
19	Oklahoma	107.3
47	Oregon	97.0
40	Pennsylvania	100.7
NA	Rhode Island**	NA
10	South Carolina	108.5
43	South Dakota	100.0
32	Tennessee	103.1
24	Texas	105.3
21	Utah	106.4
5	Vermont	112.3
3	Virginia	119.2
41	Washington	100.6
9	West Virginia	108.6
42	Wisconsin	100.4
43	Wyoming	100.0

RANK ORDER

RANK	STATE	PERCENT
1	Alaska	174.4
2	Montana	123.9
3	Virginia	119.2
4	Nevada	115.5
5	Vermont	112.3
6	Hawaii	111.8
7	Nebraska	109.4
8	Massachusetts	108.9
9	West Virginia	108.6
10	New Mexico	108.5
10	South Carolina	108.5
12	Delaware	108.4
12	Maryland	108.4
12	North Dakota	108.4
15	Alabama	108.0
15	Florida	108.0
17	Idaho	107.8
18	Arkansas	107.7
19	Oklahoma	107.3
20	Connecticut	106.6
21	Utah	106.4
22	Illinois	106.0
23	North Carolina	105.5
24	Texas	105.3
25	Arizona	105.0
25	Iowa	105.0
27	California	104.5
28	New York	104.0
29	Colorado	103.8
30	Ohio	103.6
31	Mississippi	103.3
32	Tennessee	103.1
33	Indiana	102.7
34	Minnesota	102.6
35	Missouri	102.4
36	New Jersey	102.1
37	Georgia	101.5
38	Maine	100.9
39	Kansas	100.8
40	Pennsylvania	100.7
41	Washington	100.6
42	Wisconsin	100.4
43	Kentucky	100.0
43	South Dakota	100.0
43	Wyoming	100.0
46	Michigan	98.5
47	Oregon	97.0
NA	Louisiana**	NA
NA	New Hampshire**	NA
NA	Rhode Island**	NA
	District of Columbia**	NA

Source: Morgan Quitno Press using data from National Association of State Budget Officers
"The Fiscal Survey of States" (December 2005, www.nasbo.org/Publications/fiscalsurvey/fsfall2005.pdf)
*For fiscal year 2005. This table compares sales, personal and corporate income tax collections projected in adopting budgets with the amount collected.
**Not available.

State Government Tax Revenue in 2004

National Total = $593,488,853,000

ALPHA ORDER

RANK	STATE	STATE TAXES	% of USA
26	Alabama	$7,018,242,000	1.2%
48	Alaska	1,288,164,000	0.2%
20	Arizona	9,606,318,000	1.6%
30	Arkansas	5,580,678,000	0.9%
1	California	85,721,483,000	14.4%
25	Colorado	7,051,457,000	1.2%
19	Connecticut	10,291,289,000	1.7%
43	Delaware	2,375,482,000	0.4%
3	Florida	30,767,561,000	5.2%
13	Georgia	14,570,573,000	2.5%
37	Hawaii	3,849,135,000	0.6%
41	Idaho	2,647,790,000	0.4%
5	Illinois	25,490,593,000	4.3%
18	Indiana	11,957,470,000	2.0%
32	Iowa	5,133,126,000	0.9%
31	Kansas	5,283,676,000	0.9%
23	Kentucky	8,463,400,000	1.4%
24	Louisiana	8,025,507,000	1.4%
40	Maine	2,896,759,000	0.5%
17	Maryland	12,314,799,000	2.1%
10	Massachusetts	16,698,723,000	2.8%
7	Michigan	24,061,065,000	4.1%
12	Minnesota	14,734,921,000	2.5%
33	Mississippi	5,124,730,000	0.9%
22	Missouri	9,119,664,000	1.5%
46	Montana	1,625,692,000	0.3%
39	Nebraska	3,639,811,000	0.6%
34	Nevada	4,738,877,000	0.8%
44	New Hampshire	2,005,389,000	0.3%
9	New Jersey	20,981,428,000	3.5%
36	New Mexico	4,001,780,000	0.7%
2	New York	45,833,652,000	7.7%
11	North Carolina	16,576,316,000	2.8%
49	North Dakota	1,228,890,000	0.2%
8	Ohio	22,475,528,000	3.8%
28	Oklahoma	6,426,713,000	1.1%
29	Oregon	6,103,071,000	1.0%
6	Pennsylvania	25,346,869,000	4.3%
42	Rhode Island	2,408,861,000	0.4%
27	South Carolina	6,803,568,000	1.1%
50	South Dakota	1,062,722,000	0.2%
21	Tennessee	9,536,031,000	1.6%
4	Texas	30,751,860,000	5.2%
35	Utah	4,189,172,000	0.7%
45	Vermont	1,766,719,000	0.3%
14	Virginia	14,233,065,000	2.4%
15	Washington	13,895,346,000	2.3%
38	West Virginia	3,749,013,000	0.6%
16	Wisconsin	12,531,098,000	2.1%
47	Wyoming	1,504,777,000	0.3%

RANK ORDER

RANK	STATE	STATE TAXES	% of USA
1	California	$85,721,483,000	14.4%
2	New York	45,833,652,000	7.7%
3	Florida	30,767,561,000	5.2%
4	Texas	30,751,860,000	5.2%
5	Illinois	25,490,593,000	4.3%
6	Pennsylvania	25,346,869,000	4.3%
7	Michigan	24,061,065,000	4.1%
8	Ohio	22,475,528,000	3.8%
9	New Jersey	20,981,428,000	3.5%
10	Massachusetts	16,698,723,000	2.8%
11	North Carolina	16,576,316,000	2.8%
12	Minnesota	14,734,921,000	2.5%
13	Georgia	14,570,573,000	2.5%
14	Virginia	14,233,065,000	2.4%
15	Washington	13,895,346,000	2.3%
16	Wisconsin	12,531,098,000	2.1%
17	Maryland	12,314,799,000	2.1%
18	Indiana	11,957,470,000	2.0%
19	Connecticut	10,291,289,000	1.7%
20	Arizona	9,606,318,000	1.6%
21	Tennessee	9,536,031,000	1.6%
22	Missouri	9,119,664,000	1.5%
23	Kentucky	8,463,400,000	1.4%
24	Louisiana	8,025,507,000	1.4%
25	Colorado	7,051,457,000	1.2%
26	Alabama	7,018,242,000	1.2%
27	South Carolina	6,803,568,000	1.1%
28	Oklahoma	6,426,713,000	1.1%
29	Oregon	6,103,071,000	1.0%
30	Arkansas	5,580,678,000	0.9%
31	Kansas	5,283,676,000	0.9%
32	Iowa	5,133,126,000	0.9%
33	Mississippi	5,124,730,000	0.9%
34	Nevada	4,738,877,000	0.8%
35	Utah	4,189,172,000	0.7%
36	New Mexico	4,001,780,000	0.7%
37	Hawaii	3,849,135,000	0.6%
38	West Virginia	3,749,013,000	0.6%
39	Nebraska	3,639,811,000	0.6%
40	Maine	2,896,759,000	0.5%
41	Idaho	2,647,790,000	0.4%
42	Rhode Island	2,408,861,000	0.4%
43	Delaware	2,375,482,000	0.4%
44	New Hampshire	2,005,389,000	0.3%
45	Vermont	1,766,719,000	0.3%
46	Montana	1,625,692,000	0.3%
47	Wyoming	1,504,777,000	0.3%
48	Alaska	1,288,164,000	0.2%
49	North Dakota	1,228,890,000	0.2%
50	South Dakota	1,062,722,000	0.2%
	District of Columbia*	NA	NA

Source: U.S. Bureau of the Census, Governments Division
 "2004 State Government Tax Collections" (http://www.census.gov/govs/www/statetax04.html)
*Not applicable.

Per Capita State Government Tax Revenue in 2004

National Per Capita = $2,025

ALPHA ORDER

RANK	STATE	PER CAPITA
46	Alabama	$1,551
26	Alaska	1,958
41	Arizona	1,674
23	Arkansas	2,029
9	California	2,392
48	Colorado	1,532
3	Connecticut	2,941
5	Delaware	2,862
35	Florida	1,770
42	Georgia	1,634
1	Hawaii	3,050
32	Idaho	1,898
24	Illinois	2,005
30	Indiana	1,920
38	Iowa	1,738
28	Kansas	1,933
21	Kentucky	2,043
34	Louisiana	1,781
16	Maine	2,203
15	Maryland	2,214
7	Massachusetts	2,606
10	Michigan	2,381
4	Minnesota	2,891
36	Mississippi	1,767
45	Missouri	1,583
37	Montana	1,754
18	Nebraska	2,083
22	Nevada	2,031
47	New Hampshire	1,544
8	New Jersey	2,416
17	New Mexico	2,103
11	New York	2,377
27	North Carolina	1,941
29	North Dakota	1,931
25	Ohio	1,963
33	Oklahoma	1,824
40	Oregon	1,699
20	Pennsylvania	2,045
14	Rhode Island	2,231
43	South Carolina	1,621
49	South Dakota	1,379
44	Tennessee	1,618
50	Texas	1,368
39	Utah	1,731
6	Vermont	2,844
31	Virginia	1,902
13	Washington	2,239
19	West Virginia	2,068
12	Wisconsin	2,277
2	Wyoming	2,975

RANK ORDER

RANK	STATE	PER CAPITA
1	Hawaii	$3,050
2	Wyoming	2,975
3	Connecticut	2,941
4	Minnesota	2,891
5	Delaware	2,862
6	Vermont	2,844
7	Massachusetts	2,606
8	New Jersey	2,416
9	California	2,392
10	Michigan	2,381
11	New York	2,377
12	Wisconsin	2,277
13	Washington	2,239
14	Rhode Island	2,231
15	Maryland	2,214
16	Maine	2,203
17	New Mexico	2,103
18	Nebraska	2,083
19	West Virginia	2,068
20	Pennsylvania	2,045
21	Kentucky	2,043
22	Nevada	2,031
23	Arkansas	2,029
24	Illinois	2,005
25	Ohio	1,963
26	Alaska	1,958
27	North Carolina	1,941
28	Kansas	1,933
29	North Dakota	1,931
30	Indiana	1,920
31	Virginia	1,902
32	Idaho	1,898
33	Oklahoma	1,824
34	Louisiana	1,781
35	Florida	1,770
36	Mississippi	1,767
37	Montana	1,754
38	Iowa	1,738
39	Utah	1,731
40	Oregon	1,699
41	Arizona	1,674
42	Georgia	1,634
43	South Carolina	1,621
44	Tennessee	1,618
45	Missouri	1,583
46	Alabama	1,551
47	New Hampshire	1,544
48	Colorado	1,532
49	South Dakota	1,379
50	Texas	1,368

District of Columbia* NA

Source: Morgan Quitno Press using data from U.S. Bureau of the Census, Governments Division
    "2004 State Government Tax Collections" (http://www.census.gov/govs/www/statetax04.html)
*Not applicable.

State Government Tax Revenue as a Percent of Personal Income in 2004

National Percent = 6.1% of Personal Income*

ALPHA ORDER

RANK	STATE	PERCENT
38	Alabama	5.6
34	Alaska	5.8
34	Arizona	5.8
8	Arkansas	7.9
15	California	6.8
49	Colorado	4.2
19	Connecticut	6.5
4	Delaware	8.0
38	Florida	5.6
43	Georgia	5.5
1	Hawaii	9.3
13	Idaho	7.1
34	Illinois	5.8
24	Indiana	6.4
38	Iowa	5.6
28	Kansas	6.2
9	Kentucky	7.5
19	Louisiana	6.5
11	Maine	7.3
38	Maryland	5.6
28	Massachusetts	6.2
10	Michigan	7.4
4	Minnesota	8.0
12	Mississippi	7.2
46	Missouri	5.2
26	Montana	6.3
19	Nebraska	6.5
32	Nevada	6.0
49	New Hampshire	4.2
34	New Jersey	5.8
4	New Mexico	8.0
28	New York	6.2
16	North Carolina	6.6
16	North Dakota	6.6
26	Ohio	6.3
16	Oklahoma	6.6
38	Oregon	5.6
31	Pennsylvania	6.1
19	Rhode Island	6.5
32	South Carolina	6.0
47	South Dakota	4.5
44	Tennessee	5.4
47	Texas	4.5
19	Utah	6.5
2	Vermont	9.0
45	Virginia	5.3
24	Washington	6.4
4	West Virginia	8.0
13	Wisconsin	7.1
3	Wyoming	8.7

RANK ORDER

RANK	STATE	PERCENT
1	Hawaii	9.3
2	Vermont	9.0
3	Wyoming	8.7
4	Delaware	8.0
4	Minnesota	8.0
4	New Mexico	8.0
4	West Virginia	8.0
8	Arkansas	7.9
9	Kentucky	7.5
10	Michigan	7.4
11	Maine	7.3
12	Mississippi	7.2
13	Idaho	7.1
13	Wisconsin	7.1
15	California	6.8
16	North Carolina	6.6
16	North Dakota	6.6
16	Oklahoma	6.6
19	Connecticut	6.5
19	Louisiana	6.5
19	Nebraska	6.5
19	Rhode Island	6.5
19	Utah	6.5
24	Indiana	6.4
24	Washington	6.4
26	Montana	6.3
26	Ohio	6.3
28	Kansas	6.2
28	Massachusetts	6.2
28	New York	6.2
31	Pennsylvania	6.1
32	Nevada	6.0
32	South Carolina	6.0
34	Alaska	5.8
34	Arizona	5.8
34	Illinois	5.8
34	New Jersey	5.8
38	Alabama	5.6
38	Florida	5.6
38	Iowa	5.6
38	Maryland	5.6
38	Oregon	5.6
43	Georgia	5.5
44	Tennessee	5.4
45	Virginia	5.3
46	Missouri	5.2
47	South Dakota	4.5
47	Texas	4.5
49	Colorado	4.2
49	New Hampshire	4.2
	District of Columbia**	NA

Source: Morgan Quitno Press using data from U.S. Bureau of the Census, Governments Division
"2004 State Government Tax Collections" (http://www.census.gov/govs/www/statetax04.html)
U.S. Department of Commerce, Bureau of Economic Analysis
"Annual State Personal Income" (http://www.bea.doc.gov/bea/regional/spi/)
*National figure does not include personal income or taxes from the District of Columbia.
**Not applicable.

State Government Individual Income Tax Revenue in 2004

National Total = $197,421,360,000

ALPHA ORDER

RANK	STATE	INCOME TAX	% of USA
24	Alabama	$2,243,537,000	1.1%
44	Alaska	0	0.0%
23	Arizona	2,315,865,000	1.2%
29	Arkansas	1,685,585,000	0.9%
1	California	36,398,983,000	18.4%
19	Colorado	3,413,891,000	1.7%
15	Connecticut	4,319,546,000	2.2%
38	Delaware	781,212,000	0.4%
44	Florida	0	0.0%
10	Georgia	6,830,486,000	3.5%
31	Hawaii	1,169,205,000	0.6%
36	Idaho	907,795,000	0.5%
5	Illinois	8,139,558,000	4.1%
17	Indiana	3,807,861,000	1.9%
26	Iowa	1,958,697,000	1.0%
27	Kansas	1,915,530,000	1.0%
20	Kentucky	2,819,393,000	1.4%
25	Louisiana	2,187,050,000	1.1%
32	Maine	1,160,028,000	0.6%
13	Maryland	5,277,844,000	2.7%
3	Massachusetts	8,830,334,000	4.5%
11	Michigan	6,576,065,000	3.3%
12	Minnesota	5,709,584,000	2.9%
34	Mississippi	1,061,704,000	0.5%
18	Missouri	3,720,749,000	1.9%
39	Montana	605,582,000	0.3%
30	Nebraska	1,242,603,000	0.6%
44	Nevada	0	0.0%
43	New Hampshire	54,769,000	0.0%
7	New Jersey	7,400,733,000	3.7%
35	New Mexico	1,007,248,000	0.5%
2	New York	24,647,225,000	12.5%
9	North Carolina	7,250,837,000	3.7%
41	North Dakota	213,982,000	0.1%
4	Ohio	8,705,161,000	4.4%
22	Oklahoma	2,319,123,000	1.2%
16	Oregon	4,270,740,000	2.2%
8	Pennsylvania	7,323,364,000	3.7%
37	Rhode Island	899,939,000	0.5%
21	South Carolina	2,438,712,000	1.2%
44	South Dakota	0	0.0%
42	Tennessee	146,851,000	0.1%
44	Texas	0	0.0%
28	Utah	1,692,277,000	0.9%
40	Vermont	429,817,000	0.2%
6	Virginia	7,422,071,000	3.8%
44	Washington	0	0.0%
33	West Virginia	1,068,212,000	0.5%
14	Wisconsin	5,051,612,000	2.6%
44	Wyoming	0	0.0%

RANK ORDER

RANK	STATE	INCOME TAX	% of USA
1	California	$36,398,983,000	18.4%
2	New York	24,647,225,000	12.5%
3	Massachusetts	8,830,334,000	4.5%
4	Ohio	8,705,161,000	4.4%
5	Illinois	8,139,558,000	4.1%
6	Virginia	7,422,071,000	3.8%
7	New Jersey	7,400,733,000	3.7%
8	Pennsylvania	7,323,364,000	3.7%
9	North Carolina	7,250,837,000	3.7%
10	Georgia	6,830,486,000	3.5%
11	Michigan	6,576,065,000	3.3%
12	Minnesota	5,709,584,000	2.9%
13	Maryland	5,277,844,000	2.7%
14	Wisconsin	5,051,612,000	2.6%
15	Connecticut	4,319,546,000	2.2%
16	Oregon	4,270,740,000	2.2%
17	Indiana	3,807,861,000	1.9%
18	Missouri	3,720,749,000	1.9%
19	Colorado	3,413,891,000	1.7%
20	Kentucky	2,819,393,000	1.4%
21	South Carolina	2,438,712,000	1.2%
22	Oklahoma	2,319,123,000	1.2%
23	Arizona	2,315,865,000	1.2%
24	Alabama	2,243,537,000	1.1%
25	Louisiana	2,187,050,000	1.1%
26	Iowa	1,958,697,000	1.0%
27	Kansas	1,915,530,000	1.0%
28	Utah	1,692,277,000	0.9%
29	Arkansas	1,685,585,000	0.9%
30	Nebraska	1,242,603,000	0.6%
31	Hawaii	1,169,205,000	0.6%
32	Maine	1,160,028,000	0.6%
33	West Virginia	1,068,212,000	0.5%
34	Mississippi	1,061,704,000	0.5%
35	New Mexico	1,007,248,000	0.5%
36	Idaho	907,795,000	0.5%
37	Rhode Island	899,939,000	0.5%
38	Delaware	781,212,000	0.4%
39	Montana	605,582,000	0.3%
40	Vermont	429,817,000	0.2%
41	North Dakota	213,982,000	0.1%
42	Tennessee	146,851,000	0.1%
43	New Hampshire	54,769,000	0.0%
44	Alaska	0	0.0%
44	Florida	0	0.0%
44	Nevada	0	0.0%
44	South Dakota	0	0.0%
44	Texas	0	0.0%
44	Washington	0	0.0%
44	Wyoming	0	0.0%
	District of Columbia*	NA	NA

Source: U.S. Bureau of the Census, Governments Division
"2004 State Government Tax Collections" (http://www.census.gov/govs/www/statetax04.html)
*Not applicable.

Per Capita State Government Individual Income Tax Revenue in 2004

National Per Capita = $674

RANK	STATE	PER CAPITA
37	Alabama	$496
44	Alaska	0
39	Arizona	403
31	Arkansas	613
6	California	1,016
18	Colorado	742
3	Connecticut	1,235
9	Delaware	941
44	Florida	0
16	Georgia	766
10	Hawaii	926
27	Idaho	651
30	Illinois	640
32	Indiana	612
24	Iowa	663
20	Kansas	701
23	Kentucky	681
38	Louisiana	485
12	Maine	882
8	Maryland	949
1	Massachusetts	1,378
27	Michigan	651
5	Minnesota	1,120
40	Mississippi	366
29	Missouri	646
26	Montana	653
19	Nebraska	711
44	Nevada	0
42	New Hampshire	42
13	New Jersey	852
36	New Mexico	529
2	New York	1,278
14	North Carolina	849
41	North Dakota	336
17	Ohio	760
25	Oklahoma	658
4	Oregon	1,189
33	Pennsylvania	591
15	Rhode Island	833
35	South Carolina	581
44	South Dakota	0
43	Tennessee	25
44	Texas	0
21	Utah	699
22	Vermont	692
7	Virginia	992
44	Washington	0
34	West Virginia	589
11	Wisconsin	918
44	Wyoming	0

RANK	STATE	PER CAPITA
1	Massachusetts	$1,378
2	New York	1,278
3	Connecticut	1,235
4	Oregon	1,189
5	Minnesota	1,120
6	California	1,016
7	Virginia	992
8	Maryland	949
9	Delaware	941
10	Hawaii	926
11	Wisconsin	918
12	Maine	882
13	New Jersey	852
14	North Carolina	849
15	Rhode Island	833
16	Georgia	766
17	Ohio	760
18	Colorado	742
19	Nebraska	711
20	Kansas	701
21	Utah	699
22	Vermont	692
23	Kentucky	681
24	Iowa	663
25	Oklahoma	658
26	Montana	653
27	Idaho	651
27	Michigan	651
29	Missouri	646
30	Illinois	640
31	Arkansas	613
32	Indiana	612
33	Pennsylvania	591
34	West Virginia	589
35	South Carolina	581
36	New Mexico	529
37	Alabama	496
38	Louisiana	485
39	Arizona	403
40	Mississippi	366
41	North Dakota	336
42	New Hampshire	42
43	Tennessee	25
44	Alaska	0
44	Florida	0
44	Nevada	0
44	South Dakota	0
44	Texas	0
44	Washington	0
44	Wyoming	0
	District of Columbia*	NA

Source: Morgan Quitno Press using data from U.S. Bureau of the Census, Governments Division
"2004 State Government Tax Collections" (http://www.census.gov/govs/www/statetax04.html)
*Not applicable.

State Government Corporation Net Income Tax Revenue in 2004

National Total = $30,801,302,000

ALPHA ORDER

RANK	STATE	REVENUE	% of USA
24	Alabama	$292,051,000	0.9%
22	Alaska	339,564,000	1.1%
15	Arizona	525,650,000	1.7%
31	Arkansas	181,830,000	0.6%
1	California	6,925,916,000	22.5%
26	Colorado	239,591,000	0.8%
21	Connecticut	379,822,000	1.2%
29	Delaware	217,768,000	0.7%
7	Florida	1,345,780,000	4.4%
16	Georgia	494,701,000	1.6%
44	Hawaii	58,119,000	0.2%
39	Idaho	103,784,000	0.3%
2	Illinois	2,068,574,000	6.7%
13	Indiana	644,787,000	2.1%
40	Iowa	89,826,000	0.3%
34	Kansas	166,609,000	0.5%
20	Kentucky	381,538,000	1.2%
27	Louisiana	236,745,000	0.8%
38	Maine	111,616,000	0.4%
17	Maryland	447,487,000	1.5%
8	Massachusetts	1,301,076,000	4.2%
5	Michigan	1,841,010,000	6.0%
14	Minnesota	637,183,000	2.1%
25	Mississippi	243,846,000	0.8%
28	Missouri	224,366,000	0.7%
42	Montana	67,723,000	0.2%
33	Nebraska	167,429,000	0.5%
47	Nevada	0	0.0%
19	New Hampshire	407,603,000	1.3%
4	New Jersey	1,896,998,000	6.2%
36	New Mexico	138,196,000	0.4%
3	New York	2,044,504,000	6.6%
10	North Carolina	837,085,000	2.7%
45	North Dakota	49,807,000	0.2%
9	Ohio	1,060,594,000	3.4%
37	Oklahoma	133,309,000	0.4%
23	Oregon	320,065,000	1.0%
6	Pennsylvania	1,677,998,000	5.4%
41	Rhode Island	69,479,000	0.2%
30	South Carolina	196,510,000	0.6%
46	South Dakota	47,108,000	0.2%
11	Tennessee	694,798,000	2.3%
47	Texas	0	0.0%
35	Utah	145,005,000	0.5%
43	Vermont	62,228,000	0.2%
18	Virginia	422,119,000	1.4%
47	Washington	0	0.0%
32	West Virginia	181,515,000	0.6%
12	Wisconsin	681,990,000	2.2%
47	Wyoming	0	0.0%

RANK ORDER

RANK	STATE	REVENUE	% of USA
1	California	$6,925,916,000	22.5%
2	Illinois	2,068,574,000	6.7%
3	New York	2,044,504,000	6.6%
4	New Jersey	1,896,998,000	6.2%
5	Michigan	1,841,010,000	6.0%
6	Pennsylvania	1,677,998,000	5.4%
7	Florida	1,345,780,000	4.4%
8	Massachusetts	1,301,076,000	4.2%
9	Ohio	1,060,594,000	3.4%
10	North Carolina	837,085,000	2.7%
11	Tennessee	694,798,000	2.3%
12	Wisconsin	681,990,000	2.2%
13	Indiana	644,787,000	2.1%
14	Minnesota	637,183,000	2.1%
15	Arizona	525,650,000	1.7%
16	Georgia	494,701,000	1.6%
17	Maryland	447,487,000	1.5%
18	Virginia	422,119,000	1.4%
19	New Hampshire	407,603,000	1.3%
20	Kentucky	381,538,000	1.2%
21	Connecticut	379,822,000	1.2%
22	Alaska	339,564,000	1.1%
23	Oregon	320,065,000	1.0%
24	Alabama	292,051,000	0.9%
25	Mississippi	243,846,000	0.8%
26	Colorado	239,591,000	0.8%
27	Louisiana	236,745,000	0.8%
28	Missouri	224,366,000	0.7%
29	Delaware	217,768,000	0.7%
30	South Carolina	196,510,000	0.6%
31	Arkansas	181,830,000	0.6%
32	West Virginia	181,515,000	0.6%
33	Nebraska	167,429,000	0.5%
34	Kansas	166,609,000	0.5%
35	Utah	145,005,000	0.5%
36	New Mexico	138,196,000	0.4%
37	Oklahoma	133,309,000	0.4%
38	Maine	111,616,000	0.4%
39	Idaho	103,784,000	0.3%
40	Iowa	89,826,000	0.3%
41	Rhode Island	69,479,000	0.2%
42	Montana	67,723,000	0.2%
43	Vermont	62,228,000	0.2%
44	Hawaii	58,119,000	0.2%
45	North Dakota	49,807,000	0.2%
46	South Dakota	47,108,000	0.2%
47	Nevada	0	0.0%
47	Texas	0	0.0%
47	Washington	0	0.0%
47	Wyoming	0	0.0%
	District of Columbia*	NA	NA

Source: U.S. Bureau of the Census, Governments Division
"2004 State Government Tax Collections" (http://www.census.gov/govs/www/statetax04.html)
*Not applicable.

Per Capita State Government Corporation Net Income Tax Revenue in 2004

National Per Capita = $105

ALPHA ORDER

RANK	STATE	PER CAPITA
33	Alabama	$65
1	Alaska	516
21	Arizona	92
32	Arkansas	66
6	California	193
41	Colorado	52
13	Connecticut	109
3	Delaware	262
28	Florida	77
39	Georgia	55
43	Hawaii	46
29	Idaho	74
8	Illinois	163
15	Indiana	104
46	Iowa	30
35	Kansas	61
21	Kentucky	92
40	Louisiana	53
24	Maine	85
26	Maryland	80
5	Massachusetts	203
7	Michigan	182
10	Minnesota	125
25	Mississippi	84
44	Missouri	39
30	Montana	73
19	Nebraska	96
47	Nevada	0
2	New Hampshire	314
4	New Jersey	218
30	New Mexico	73
14	New York	106
18	North Carolina	98
27	North Dakota	78
20	Ohio	93
45	Oklahoma	38
23	Oregon	89
9	Pennsylvania	135
34	Rhode Island	64
42	South Carolina	47
35	South Dakota	61
12	Tennessee	118
47	Texas	0
37	Utah	60
16	Vermont	100
38	Virginia	56
47	Washington	0
16	West Virginia	100
11	Wisconsin	124
47	Wyoming	0

RANK ORDER

RANK	STATE	PER CAPITA
1	Alaska	$516
2	New Hampshire	314
3	Delaware	262
4	New Jersey	218
5	Massachusetts	203
6	California	193
7	Michigan	182
8	Illinois	163
9	Pennsylvania	135
10	Minnesota	125
11	Wisconsin	124
12	Tennessee	118
13	Connecticut	109
14	New York	106
15	Indiana	104
16	Vermont	100
16	West Virginia	100
18	North Carolina	98
19	Nebraska	96
20	Ohio	93
21	Arizona	92
21	Kentucky	92
23	Oregon	89
24	Maine	85
25	Mississippi	84
26	Maryland	80
27	North Dakota	78
28	Florida	77
29	Idaho	74
30	Montana	73
30	New Mexico	73
32	Arkansas	66
33	Alabama	65
34	Rhode Island	64
35	Kansas	61
35	South Dakota	61
37	Utah	60
38	Virginia	56
39	Georgia	55
40	Louisiana	53
41	Colorado	52
42	South Carolina	47
43	Hawaii	46
44	Missouri	39
45	Oklahoma	38
46	Iowa	30
47	Nevada	0
47	Texas	0
47	Washington	0
47	Wyoming	0

District of Columbia*   NA

Source: Morgan Quitno Press using data from U.S. Bureau of the Census, Governments Division
    "2004 State Government Tax Collections" (http://www.census.gov/govs/www/statetax04.html)
*Not applicable.

State Government General Sales Tax Revenue in 2004

National Total = $198,431,303,000*

ALPHA ORDER

ALPHA ORDER

RANK ORDER

RANK	STATE	SALES TAX	% of USA		RANK	STATE	SALES TAX	% of USA
32	Alabama	$1,892,560,000	1.0%		1	California	$26,506,911,000	13.4%
46	Alaska	0	0.0%		2	Florida	17,355,404,000	8.7%
14	Arizona	4,719,642,000	2.4%		3	Texas	15,460,221,000	7.8%
28	Arkansas	2,149,527,000	1.1%		4	New York	10,050,291,000	5.1%
1	California	26,506,911,000	13.4%		5	Washington	8,423,160,000	4.2%
30	Colorado	1,909,246,000	1.0%		6	Michigan	7,894,458,000	4.0%
19	Connecticut	3,127,221,000	1.6%		7	Ohio	7,881,510,000	4.0%
46	Delaware	0	0.0%		8	Pennsylvania	7,773,131,000	3.9%
2	Florida	17,355,404,000	8.7%		9	Illinois	6,922,587,000	3.5%
12	Georgia	4,921,337,000	2.5%		10	New Jersey	6,261,700,000	3.2%
31	Hawaii	1,900,377,000	1.0%		11	Tennessee	5,845,206,000	2.9%
38	Idaho	1,036,924,000	0.5%		12	Georgia	4,921,337,000	2.5%
9	Illinois	6,922,587,000	3.5%		13	Indiana	4,759,445,000	2.4%
13	Indiana	4,759,445,000	2.4%		14	Arizona	4,719,642,000	2.4%
33	Iowa	1,617,505,000	0.8%		15	North Carolina	4,351,823,000	2.2%
29	Kansas	1,932,927,000	1.0%		16	Minnesota	4,066,790,000	2.0%
26	Kentucky	2,466,033,000	1.2%		17	Wisconsin	3,899,395,000	2.0%
24	Louisiana	2,680,716,000	1.4%		18	Massachusetts	3,743,204,000	1.9%
40	Maine	917,248,000	0.5%		19	Connecticut	3,127,221,000	1.6%
22	Maryland	2,945,060,000	1.5%		20	Virginia	2,977,401,000	1.5%
18	Massachusetts	3,743,204,000	1.9%		21	Missouri	2,950,055,000	1.5%
6	Michigan	7,894,458,000	4.0%		22	Maryland	2,945,060,000	1.5%
16	Minnesota	4,066,790,000	2.0%		23	South Carolina	2,726,657,000	1.4%
25	Mississippi	2,482,908,000	1.3%		24	Louisiana	2,680,716,000	1.4%
21	Missouri	2,950,055,000	1.5%		25	Mississippi	2,482,908,000	1.3%
46	Montana	0	0.0%		26	Kentucky	2,466,033,000	1.2%
36	Nebraska	1,524,591,000	0.8%		27	Nevada	2,264,749,000	1.1%
27	Nevada	2,264,749,000	1.1%		28	Arkansas	2,149,527,000	1.1%
46	New Hampshire	0	0.0%		29	Kansas	1,932,927,000	1.0%
10	New Jersey	6,261,700,000	3.2%		30	Colorado	1,909,246,000	1.0%
37	New Mexico	1,443,300,000	0.7%		31	Hawaii	1,900,377,000	1.0%
4	New York	10,050,291,000	5.1%		32	Alabama	1,892,560,000	1.0%
15	North Carolina	4,351,823,000	2.2%		33	Iowa	1,617,505,000	0.8%
44	North Dakota	367,304,000	0.2%		34	Oklahoma	1,594,246,000	0.8%
7	Ohio	7,881,510,000	4.0%		35	Utah	1,556,332,000	0.8%
34	Oklahoma	1,594,246,000	0.8%		36	Nebraska	1,524,591,000	0.8%
46	Oregon	0	0.0%		37	New Mexico	1,443,300,000	0.7%
8	Pennsylvania	7,773,131,000	3.9%		38	Idaho	1,036,924,000	0.5%
41	Rhode Island	804,647,000	0.4%		39	West Virginia	1,021,365,000	0.5%
23	South Carolina	2,726,657,000	1.4%		40	Maine	917,248,000	0.5%
42	South Dakota	586,389,000	0.3%		41	Rhode Island	804,647,000	0.4%
11	Tennessee	5,845,206,000	2.9%		42	South Dakota	586,389,000	0.3%
3	Texas	15,460,221,000	7.8%		43	Wyoming	462,842,000	0.2%
35	Utah	1,556,332,000	0.8%		44	North Dakota	367,304,000	0.2%
45	Vermont	256,958,000	0.1%		45	Vermont	256,958,000	0.1%
20	Virginia	2,977,401,000	1.5%		46	Alaska	0	0.0%
5	Washington	8,423,160,000	4.2%		46	Delaware	0	0.0%
39	West Virginia	1,021,365,000	0.5%		46	Montana	0	0.0%
17	Wisconsin	3,899,395,000	2.0%		46	New Hampshire	0	0.0%
43	Wyoming	462,842,000	0.2%		46	Oregon	0	0.0%
						District of Columbia**	NA	NA

Source: U.S. Bureau of the Census, Governments Division
   "2004 State Government Tax Collections" (http://www.census.gov/govs/www/statetax04.html)
*Does not include special sales taxes such as those on sale of alcohol, gasoline or tobacco.
**Not applicable.

Per Capita State Government General Sales Tax Revenue in 2004

National Per Capita = $677*

ALPHA ORDER

RANK	STATE	PER CAPITA
42	Alabama	$418
46	Alaska	0
10	Arizona	822
12	Arkansas	782
19	California	740
43	Colorado	415
7	Connecticut	894
46	Delaware	0
3	Florida	998
34	Georgia	552
1	Hawaii	1,506
18	Idaho	743
36	Illinois	545
14	Indiana	764
35	Iowa	548
22	Kansas	707
29	Kentucky	595
29	Louisiana	595
23	Maine	698
37	Maryland	530
31	Massachusetts	584
13	Michigan	781
11	Minnesota	798
9	Mississippi	856
39	Missouri	512
46	Montana	0
8	Nebraska	872
5	Nevada	971
46	New Hampshire	0
20	New Jersey	721
16	New Mexico	758
38	New York	521
40	North Carolina	510
32	North Dakota	577
24	Ohio	688
41	Oklahoma	452
46	Oregon	0
28	Pennsylvania	627
17	Rhode Island	745
26	South Carolina	650
15	South Dakota	761
4	Tennessee	992
24	Texas	688
27	Utah	643
44	Vermont	414
45	Virginia	398
2	Washington	1,357
33	West Virginia	563
21	Wisconsin	709
6	Wyoming	915

RANK ORDER

RANK	STATE	PER CAPITA
1	Hawaii	$1,506
2	Washington	1,357
3	Florida	998
4	Tennessee	992
5	Nevada	971
6	Wyoming	915
7	Connecticut	894
8	Nebraska	872
9	Mississippi	856
10	Arizona	822
11	Minnesota	798
12	Arkansas	782
13	Michigan	781
14	Indiana	764
15	South Dakota	761
16	New Mexico	758
17	Rhode Island	745
18	Idaho	743
19	California	740
20	New Jersey	721
21	Wisconsin	709
22	Kansas	707
23	Maine	698
24	Ohio	688
24	Texas	688
26	South Carolina	650
27	Utah	643
28	Pennsylvania	627
29	Kentucky	595
29	Louisiana	595
31	Massachusetts	584
32	North Dakota	577
33	West Virginia	563
34	Georgia	552
35	Iowa	548
36	Illinois	545
37	Maryland	530
38	New York	521
39	Missouri	512
40	North Carolina	510
41	Oklahoma	452
42	Alabama	418
43	Colorado	415
44	Vermont	414
45	Virginia	398
46	Alaska	0
46	Delaware	0
46	Montana	0
46	New Hampshire	0
46	Oregon	0

District of Columbia**   NA

Source: Morgan Quitno Press using data from U.S. Bureau of the Census, Governments Division
    "2004 State Government Tax Collections" (http://www.census.gov/govs/www/statetax04.html)
*Does not include special sales taxes such as those on sale of alcohol, gasoline or tobacco.
**Not applicable.

State Government Motor Fuels Sales Tax Revenue in 2004

National Total = $33,605,402,000

RANK	STATE	FUEL TAX	% of USA
23	Alabama	$535,493,000	1.6%
50	Alaska	40,660,000	0.1%
18	Arizona	671,765,000	2.0%
29	Arkansas	453,148,000	1.3%
1	California	3,324,883,000	9.9%
20	Colorado	597,558,000	1.8%
28	Connecticut	456,805,000	1.4%
46	Delaware	112,435,000	0.3%
3	Florida	1,823,349,000	5.4%
14	Georgia	755,994,000	2.2%
48	Hawaii	84,378,000	0.3%
39	Idaho	218,019,000	0.6%
6	Illinois	1,421,927,000	4.2%
13	Indiana	802,168,000	2.4%
33	Iowa	357,835,000	1.1%
30	Kansas	428,985,000	1.3%
26	Kentucky	476,605,000	1.4%
21	Louisiana	560,769,000	1.7%
38	Maine	220,410,000	0.7%
15	Maryland	746,044,000	2.2%
17	Massachusetts	684,242,000	2.0%
8	Michigan	1,081,259,000	3.2%
19	Minnesota	648,428,000	1.9%
27	Mississippi	464,748,000	1.4%
16	Missouri	726,705,000	2.2%
41	Montana	197,605,000	0.6%
36	Nebraska	302,899,000	0.9%
37	Nevada	293,595,000	0.9%
43	New Hampshire	129,913,000	0.4%
22	New Jersey	546,952,000	1.6%
40	New Mexico	210,863,000	0.6%
24	New York	518,557,000	1.5%
7	North Carolina	1,272,611,000	3.8%
45	North Dakota	118,744,000	0.4%
5	Ohio	1,541,151,000	4.6%
31	Oklahoma	415,318,000	1.2%
32	Oregon	404,547,000	1.2%
4	Pennsylvania	1,785,200,000	5.3%
42	Rhode Island	133,415,000	0.4%
25	South Carolina	489,322,000	1.5%
44	South Dakota	126,017,000	0.4%
12	Tennessee	832,168,000	2.5%
2	Texas	2,918,842,000	8.7%
34	Utah	344,121,000	1.0%
47	Vermont	85,994,000	0.3%
11	Virginia	909,468,000	2.7%
10	Washington	925,723,000	2.8%
35	West Virginia	309,274,000	0.9%
9	Wisconsin	1,028,516,000	3.1%
49	Wyoming	69,975,000	0.2%

RANK	STATE	FUEL TAX	% of USA
1	California	$3,324,883,000	9.9%
2	Texas	2,918,842,000	8.7%
3	Florida	1,823,349,000	5.4%
4	Pennsylvania	1,785,200,000	5.3%
5	Ohio	1,541,151,000	4.6%
6	Illinois	1,421,927,000	4.2%
7	North Carolina	1,272,611,000	3.8%
8	Michigan	1,081,259,000	3.2%
9	Wisconsin	1,028,516,000	3.1%
10	Washington	925,723,000	2.8%
11	Virginia	909,468,000	2.7%
12	Tennessee	832,168,000	2.5%
13	Indiana	802,168,000	2.4%
14	Georgia	755,994,000	2.2%
15	Maryland	746,044,000	2.2%
16	Missouri	726,705,000	2.2%
17	Massachusetts	684,242,000	2.0%
18	Arizona	671,765,000	2.0%
19	Minnesota	648,428,000	1.9%
20	Colorado	597,558,000	1.8%
21	Louisiana	560,769,000	1.7%
22	New Jersey	546,952,000	1.6%
23	Alabama	535,493,000	1.6%
24	New York	518,557,000	1.5%
25	South Carolina	489,322,000	1.5%
26	Kentucky	476,605,000	1.4%
27	Mississippi	464,748,000	1.4%
28	Connecticut	456,805,000	1.4%
29	Arkansas	453,148,000	1.3%
30	Kansas	428,985,000	1.3%
31	Oklahoma	415,318,000	1.2%
32	Oregon	404,547,000	1.2%
33	Iowa	357,835,000	1.1%
34	Utah	344,121,000	1.0%
35	West Virginia	309,274,000	0.9%
36	Nebraska	302,899,000	0.9%
37	Nevada	293,595,000	0.9%
38	Maine	220,410,000	0.7%
39	Idaho	218,019,000	0.6%
40	New Mexico	210,863,000	0.6%
41	Montana	197,605,000	0.6%
42	Rhode Island	133,415,000	0.4%
43	New Hampshire	129,913,000	0.4%
44	South Dakota	126,017,000	0.4%
45	North Dakota	118,744,000	0.4%
46	Delaware	112,435,000	0.3%
47	Vermont	85,994,000	0.3%
48	Hawaii	84,378,000	0.3%
49	Wyoming	69,975,000	0.2%
50	Alaska	40,660,000	0.1%
	District of Columbia*	NA	NA

Source: U.S. Bureau of the Census, Governments Division
"2004 State Government Tax Collections" (http://www.census.gov/govs/www/statetax04.html)
*Not applicable.

Per Capita State Government Motor Fuel Sales Tax Revenue in 2004

National Per Capita = $115

ALPHA ORDER

RANK	STATE	PER CAPITA
33	Alabama	$118
49	Alaska	62
35	Arizona	117
7	Arkansas	165
45	California	93
23	Colorado	130
22	Connecticut	131
19	Delaware	135
43	Florida	105
46	Georgia	85
47	Hawaii	67
11	Idaho	156
39	Illinois	112
25	Indiana	129
32	Iowa	121
10	Kansas	157
37	Kentucky	115
29	Louisiana	124
6	Maine	168
21	Maryland	134
41	Massachusetts	107
41	Michigan	107
26	Minnesota	127
9	Mississippi	160
27	Missouri	126
1	Montana	213
4	Nebraska	173
27	Nevada	126
44	New Hampshire	100
48	New Jersey	63
40	New Mexico	111
50	New York	27
12	North Carolina	149
2	North Dakota	187
19	Ohio	135
33	Oklahoma	118
38	Oregon	113
14	Pennsylvania	144
29	Rhode Island	124
35	South Carolina	117
8	South Dakota	164
16	Tennessee	141
23	Texas	130
15	Utah	142
17	Vermont	138
31	Virginia	122
12	Washington	149
5	West Virginia	171
2	Wisconsin	187
17	Wyoming	138

RANK ORDER

RANK	STATE	PER CAPITA
1	Montana	$213
2	North Dakota	187
2	Wisconsin	187
4	Nebraska	173
5	West Virginia	171
6	Maine	168
7	Arkansas	165
8	South Dakota	164
9	Mississippi	160
10	Kansas	157
11	Idaho	156
12	North Carolina	149
12	Washington	149
14	Pennsylvania	144
15	Utah	142
16	Tennessee	141
17	Vermont	138
17	Wyoming	138
19	Delaware	135
19	Ohio	135
21	Maryland	134
22	Connecticut	131
23	Colorado	130
23	Texas	130
25	Indiana	129
26	Minnesota	127
27	Missouri	126
27	Nevada	126
29	Louisiana	124
29	Rhode Island	124
31	Virginia	122
32	Iowa	121
33	Alabama	118
33	Oklahoma	118
35	Arizona	117
35	South Carolina	117
37	Kentucky	115
38	Oregon	113
39	Illinois	112
40	New Mexico	111
41	Massachusetts	107
41	Michigan	107
43	Florida	105
44	New Hampshire	100
45	California	93
46	Georgia	85
47	Hawaii	67
48	New Jersey	63
49	Alaska	62
50	New York	27

District of Columbia*   NA

Source: Morgan Quitno Press using data from U.S. Bureau of the Census, Governments Division
    "2004 State Government Tax Collections" (http://www.census.gov/govs/www/statetax04.html)
*Not applicable.

State Tax Rates on Gasoline in 2005

National Median = 21.00 Cents per Gallon*

ALPHA ORDER

RANK	STATE	CENTS PER GALLON
36	Alabama	18.00
49	Alaska	8.00
36	Arizona	18.00
22	Arkansas	21.50
36	California	18.00
20	Colorado	22.00
11	Connecticut	25.00
18	Delaware	23.00
46	Florida	14.50
50	Georgia	7.50
44	Hawaii	16.00
11	Idaho	25.00
27	Illinois	20.10
36	Indiana	18.00
26	Iowa	20.50
14	Kansas	24.00
41	Kentucky	17.40
28	Louisiana	20.00
10	Maine	25.20
16	Maryland	23.50
24	Massachusetts	21.00
33	Michigan	19.00
28	Minnesota	20.00
35	Mississippi	18.40
42	Missouri	17.03
5	Montana	27.00
8	Nebraska	26.30
18	Nevada	23.00
32	New Hampshire	19.50
46	New Jersey	14.50
34	New Mexico	18.90
17	New York	23.20
7	North Carolina	26.85
24	North Dakota	21.00
9	Ohio	26.00
43	Oklahoma	17.00
14	Oregon	24.00
2	Pennsylvania	30.00
1	Rhode Island	31.00
44	South Carolina	16.00
20	South Dakota	22.00
23	Tennessee	21.40
28	Texas	20.00
13	Utah	24.50
28	Vermont	20.00
40	Virginia	17.50
4	Washington	28.00
5	West Virginia	27.00
3	Wisconsin	29.10
48	Wyoming	14.00

RANK ORDER

RANK	STATE	CENTS PER GALLON
1	Rhode Island	31.00
2	Pennsylvania	30.00
3	Wisconsin	29.10
4	Washington	28.00
5	Montana	27.00
5	West Virginia	27.00
7	North Carolina	26.85
8	Nebraska	26.30
9	Ohio	26.00
10	Maine	25.20
11	Connecticut	25.00
11	Idaho	25.00
13	Utah	24.50
14	Kansas	24.00
14	Oregon	24.00
16	Maryland	23.50
17	New York	23.20
18	Delaware	23.00
18	Nevada	23.00
20	Colorado	22.00
20	South Dakota	22.00
22	Arkansas	21.50
23	Tennessee	21.40
24	Massachusetts	21.00
24	North Dakota	21.00
26	Iowa	20.50
27	Illinois	20.10
28	Louisiana	20.00
28	Minnesota	20.00
28	Texas	20.00
28	Vermont	20.00
32	New Hampshire	19.50
33	Michigan	19.00
34	New Mexico	18.90
35	Mississippi	18.40
36	Alabama	18.00
36	Arizona	18.00
36	California	18.00
36	Indiana	18.00
40	Virginia	17.50
41	Kentucky	17.40
42	Missouri	17.03
43	Oklahoma	17.00
44	Hawaii	16.00
44	South Carolina	16.00
46	Florida	14.50
46	New Jersey	14.50
48	Wyoming	14.00
49	Alaska	8.00
50	Georgia	7.50
	District of Columbia	22.50

Source: Federation of Tax Administrators
   "Motor Fuel Excise Tax Rates" (http://www.taxadmin.org/fta/rate/motor_fl.html)
*As of January 1, 2005. Federal gasoline tax rate is an additional 18.4 cents per gallon. Many states also allow additional local option taxes on gasoline.

State Government Motor Vehicle and Operators' License Tax Revenue in 2004

National Total = $19,287,571,000

<table>
<tr><th colspan="4">ALPHA ORDER</th><th colspan="4">RANK ORDER</th></tr>
<tr><th>RANK</th><th>STATE</th><th>REVENUE</th><th>% of USA</th><th>RANK</th><th>STATE</th><th>REVENUE</th><th>% of USA</th></tr>
<tr><td>27</td><td>Alabama</td><td>$189,527,000</td><td>1.0%</td><td>1</td><td>California</td><td>$2,342,437,000</td><td>12.1%</td></tr>
<tr><td>49</td><td>Alaska</td><td>43,782,000</td><td>0.2%</td><td>2</td><td>Illinois</td><td>1,447,814,000</td><td>7.5%</td></tr>
<tr><td>28</td><td>Arizona</td><td>177,467,000</td><td>0.9%</td><td>3</td><td>Texas</td><td>1,328,693,000</td><td>6.9%</td></tr>
<tr><td>35</td><td>Arkansas</td><td>125,706,000</td><td>0.7%</td><td>4</td><td>Florida</td><td>1,276,625,000</td><td>6.6%</td></tr>
<tr><td>1</td><td>California</td><td>2,342,437,000</td><td>12.1%</td><td>5</td><td>Michigan</td><td>1,131,408,000</td><td>5.9%</td></tr>
<tr><td>26</td><td>Colorado</td><td>207,216,000</td><td>1.1%</td><td>6</td><td>New York</td><td>913,822,000</td><td>4.7%</td></tr>
<tr><td>24</td><td>Connecticut</td><td>235,622,000</td><td>1.2%</td><td>7</td><td>Pennsylvania</td><td>852,639,000</td><td>4.4%</td></tr>
<tr><td>50</td><td>Delaware</td><td>33,797,000</td><td>0.2%</td><td>8</td><td>Ohio</td><td>780,653,000</td><td>4.0%</td></tr>
<tr><td>4</td><td>Florida</td><td>1,276,625,000</td><td>6.6%</td><td>9</td><td>Oklahoma</td><td>566,838,000</td><td>2.9%</td></tr>
<tr><td>20</td><td>Georgia</td><td>316,898,000</td><td>1.6%</td><td>10</td><td>Minnesota</td><td>555,399,000</td><td>2.9%</td></tr>
<tr><td>41</td><td>Hawaii</td><td>89,457,000</td><td>0.5%</td><td>11</td><td>North Carolina</td><td>515,552,000</td><td>2.7%</td></tr>
<tr><td>37</td><td>Idaho</td><td>114,311,000</td><td>0.6%</td><td>12</td><td>Oregon</td><td>450,655,000</td><td>2.3%</td></tr>
<tr><td>2</td><td>Illinois</td><td>1,447,814,000</td><td>7.5%</td><td>13</td><td>New Jersey</td><td>433,360,000</td><td>2.2%</td></tr>
<tr><td>18</td><td>Indiana</td><td>370,541,000</td><td>1.9%</td><td>14</td><td>Iowa</td><td>396,772,000</td><td>2.1%</td></tr>
<tr><td>14</td><td>Iowa</td><td>396,772,000</td><td>2.1%</td><td>15</td><td>Virginia</td><td>385,911,000</td><td>2.0%</td></tr>
<tr><td>29</td><td>Kansas</td><td>176,338,000</td><td>0.9%</td><td>16</td><td>Massachusetts</td><td>383,293,000</td><td>2.0%</td></tr>
<tr><td>25</td><td>Kentucky</td><td>216,519,000</td><td>1.1%</td><td>17</td><td>Washington</td><td>382,056,000</td><td>2.0%</td></tr>
<tr><td>36</td><td>Louisiana</td><td>125,326,000</td><td>0.6%</td><td>18</td><td>Indiana</td><td>370,541,000</td><td>1.9%</td></tr>
<tr><td>42</td><td>Maine</td><td>88,849,000</td><td>0.5%</td><td>19</td><td>Wisconsin</td><td>361,050,000</td><td>1.9%</td></tr>
<tr><td>21</td><td>Maryland</td><td>311,232,000</td><td>1.6%</td><td>20</td><td>Georgia</td><td>316,898,000</td><td>1.6%</td></tr>
<tr><td>16</td><td>Massachusetts</td><td>383,293,000</td><td>2.0%</td><td>21</td><td>Maryland</td><td>311,232,000</td><td>1.6%</td></tr>
<tr><td>5</td><td>Michigan</td><td>1,131,408,000</td><td>5.9%</td><td>22</td><td>Tennessee</td><td>296,874,000</td><td>1.5%</td></tr>
<tr><td>10</td><td>Minnesota</td><td>555,399,000</td><td>2.9%</td><td>23</td><td>Missouri</td><td>271,299,000</td><td>1.4%</td></tr>
<tr><td>33</td><td>Mississippi</td><td>140,655,000</td><td>0.7%</td><td>24</td><td>Connecticut</td><td>235,622,000</td><td>1.2%</td></tr>
<tr><td>23</td><td>Missouri</td><td>271,299,000</td><td>1.4%</td><td>25</td><td>Kentucky</td><td>216,519,000</td><td>1.1%</td></tr>
<tr><td>32</td><td>Montana</td><td>149,733,000</td><td>0.8%</td><td>26</td><td>Colorado</td><td>207,216,000</td><td>1.1%</td></tr>
<tr><td>40</td><td>Nebraska</td><td>96,990,000</td><td>0.5%</td><td>27</td><td>Alabama</td><td>189,527,000</td><td>1.0%</td></tr>
<tr><td>31</td><td>Nevada</td><td>154,013,000</td><td>0.8%</td><td>28</td><td>Arizona</td><td>177,467,000</td><td>0.9%</td></tr>
<tr><td>39</td><td>New Hampshire</td><td>97,482,000</td><td>0.5%</td><td>29</td><td>Kansas</td><td>176,338,000</td><td>0.9%</td></tr>
<tr><td>13</td><td>New Jersey</td><td>433,360,000</td><td>2.2%</td><td>30</td><td>South Carolina</td><td>158,150,000</td><td>0.8%</td></tr>
<tr><td>34</td><td>New Mexico</td><td>127,101,000</td><td>0.7%</td><td>31</td><td>Nevada</td><td>154,013,000</td><td>0.8%</td></tr>
<tr><td>6</td><td>New York</td><td>913,822,000</td><td>4.7%</td><td>32</td><td>Montana</td><td>149,733,000</td><td>0.8%</td></tr>
<tr><td>11</td><td>North Carolina</td><td>515,552,000</td><td>2.7%</td><td>33</td><td>Mississippi</td><td>140,655,000</td><td>0.7%</td></tr>
<tr><td>45</td><td>North Dakota</td><td>58,596,000</td><td>0.3%</td><td>34</td><td>New Mexico</td><td>127,101,000</td><td>0.7%</td></tr>
<tr><td>8</td><td>Ohio</td><td>780,653,000</td><td>4.0%</td><td>35</td><td>Arkansas</td><td>125,706,000</td><td>0.7%</td></tr>
<tr><td>9</td><td>Oklahoma</td><td>566,838,000</td><td>2.9%</td><td>36</td><td>Louisiana</td><td>125,326,000</td><td>0.6%</td></tr>
<tr><td>12</td><td>Oregon</td><td>450,655,000</td><td>2.3%</td><td>37</td><td>Idaho</td><td>114,311,000</td><td>0.6%</td></tr>
<tr><td>7</td><td>Pennsylvania</td><td>852,639,000</td><td>4.4%</td><td>38</td><td>Utah</td><td>100,605,000</td><td>0.5%</td></tr>
<tr><td>46</td><td>Rhode Island</td><td>57,563,000</td><td>0.3%</td><td>39</td><td>New Hampshire</td><td>97,482,000</td><td>0.5%</td></tr>
<tr><td>30</td><td>South Carolina</td><td>158,150,000</td><td>0.8%</td><td>40</td><td>Nebraska</td><td>96,990,000</td><td>0.5%</td></tr>
<tr><td>48</td><td>South Dakota</td><td>44,042,000</td><td>0.2%</td><td>41</td><td>Hawaii</td><td>89,457,000</td><td>0.5%</td></tr>
<tr><td>22</td><td>Tennessee</td><td>296,874,000</td><td>1.5%</td><td>42</td><td>Maine</td><td>88,849,000</td><td>0.5%</td></tr>
<tr><td>3</td><td>Texas</td><td>1,328,693,000</td><td>6.9%</td><td>43</td><td>West Virginia</td><td>87,471,000</td><td>0.5%</td></tr>
<tr><td>38</td><td>Utah</td><td>100,605,000</td><td>0.5%</td><td>44</td><td>Vermont</td><td>66,741,000</td><td>0.3%</td></tr>
<tr><td>44</td><td>Vermont</td><td>66,741,000</td><td>0.3%</td><td>45</td><td>North Dakota</td><td>58,596,000</td><td>0.3%</td></tr>
<tr><td>15</td><td>Virginia</td><td>385,911,000</td><td>2.0%</td><td>46</td><td>Rhode Island</td><td>57,563,000</td><td>0.3%</td></tr>
<tr><td>17</td><td>Washington</td><td>382,056,000</td><td>2.0%</td><td>47</td><td>Wyoming</td><td>52,691,000</td><td>0.3%</td></tr>
<tr><td>43</td><td>West Virginia</td><td>87,471,000</td><td>0.5%</td><td>48</td><td>South Dakota</td><td>44,042,000</td><td>0.2%</td></tr>
<tr><td>19</td><td>Wisconsin</td><td>361,050,000</td><td>1.9%</td><td>49</td><td>Alaska</td><td>43,782,000</td><td>0.2%</td></tr>
<tr><td>47</td><td>Wyoming</td><td>52,691,000</td><td>0.3%</td><td>50</td><td>Delaware</td><td>33,797,000</td><td>0.2%</td></tr>
<tr><td></td><td></td><td></td><td></td><td></td><td>District of Columbia*</td><td>NA</td><td>NA</td></tr>
</table>

Source: U.S. Bureau of the Census, Governments Division
  "2004 State Government Tax Collections" (http://www.census.gov/govs/www/statetax04.html)
*Not applicable.

Per Capita State Government Motor Vehicle and Operators' License Tax Revenue in 2004
National Per Capita = $65.80

ALPHA ORDER

RANK	STATE	PER CAPITA
44	Alabama	$41.88
20	Alaska	66.56
49	Arizona	30.92
42	Arkansas	45.71
23	California	65.35
43	Colorado	45.03
18	Connecticut	67.34
46	Delaware	40.72
13	Florida	73.43
48	Georgia	35.53
14	Hawaii	70.88
11	Idaho	81.94
5	Illinois	113.89
28	Indiana	59.51
3	Iowa	134.37
24	Kansas	64.51
34	Kentucky	52.28
50	Louisiana	27.81
17	Maine	67.57
31	Maryland	55.96
27	Massachusetts	59.82
6	Michigan	111.97
7	Minnesota	108.98
38	Mississippi	48.49
41	Missouri	47.10
1	Montana	161.54
32	Nebraska	55.50
21	Nevada	66.02
12	New Hampshire	75.03
37	New Jersey	49.90
19	New Mexico	66.79
40	New York	47.40
26	North Carolina	60.37
10	North Dakota	92.09
16	Ohio	68.18
2	Oklahoma	160.87
4	Oregon	125.48
15	Pennsylvania	68.79
33	Rhode Island	53.30
47	South Carolina	37.67
30	South Dakota	57.15
36	Tennessee	50.37
29	Texas	59.13
45	Utah	41.56
8	Vermont	107.43
35	Virginia	51.58
25	Washington	61.55
39	West Virginia	48.26
22	Wisconsin	65.60
9	Wyoming	104.16

RANK ORDER

RANK	STATE	PER CAPITA
1	Montana	$161.54
2	Oklahoma	160.87
3	Iowa	134.37
4	Oregon	125.48
5	Illinois	113.89
6	Michigan	111.97
7	Minnesota	108.98
8	Vermont	107.43
9	Wyoming	104.16
10	North Dakota	92.09
11	Idaho	81.94
12	New Hampshire	75.03
13	Florida	73.43
14	Hawaii	70.88
15	Pennsylvania	68.79
16	Ohio	68.18
17	Maine	67.57
18	Connecticut	67.34
19	New Mexico	66.79
20	Alaska	66.56
21	Nevada	66.02
22	Wisconsin	65.60
23	California	65.35
24	Kansas	64.51
25	Washington	61.55
26	North Carolina	60.37
27	Massachusetts	59.82
28	Indiana	59.51
29	Texas	59.13
30	South Dakota	57.15
31	Maryland	55.96
32	Nebraska	55.50
33	Rhode Island	53.30
34	Kentucky	52.28
35	Virginia	51.58
36	Tennessee	50.37
37	New Jersey	49.90
38	Mississippi	48.49
39	West Virginia	48.26
40	New York	47.40
41	Missouri	47.10
42	Arkansas	45.71
43	Colorado	45.03
44	Alabama	41.88
45	Utah	41.56
46	Delaware	40.72
47	South Carolina	37.67
48	Georgia	35.53
49	Arizona	30.92
50	Louisiana	27.81

District of Columbia* — NA

Source: Morgan Quitno Press using data from U.S. Bureau of the Census, Governments Division
"2004 State Government Tax Collections" (http://www.census.gov/govs/www/statetax04.html)
*Not applicable.

State Government Tobacco Product Sales Tax Revenue in 2004

National Total = $12,300,310,000

ALPHA ORDER

RANK	STATE	REVENUE	% of USA
30	Alabama	$93,270,000	0.8%
44	Alaska	43,222,000	0.4%
15	Arizona	274,716,000	2.2%
20	Arkansas	146,485,000	1.2%
1	California	1,081,588,000	8.8%
35	Colorado	65,144,000	0.5%
14	Connecticut	277,333,000	2.3%
33	Delaware	75,479,000	0.6%
9	Florida	446,406,000	3.6%
18	Georgia	227,348,000	1.8%
32	Hawaii	79,387,000	0.6%
40	Idaho	52,271,000	0.4%
6	Illinois	760,226,000	6.2%
12	Indiana	338,716,000	2.8%
29	Iowa	94,282,000	0.8%
22	Kansas	124,586,000	1.0%
48	Kentucky	20,627,000	0.2%
27	Louisiana	101,040,000	0.8%
31	Maine	92,626,000	0.8%
16	Maryland	272,066,000	2.2%
10	Massachusetts	425,421,000	3.5%
3	Michigan	992,793,000	8.1%
19	Minnesota	190,116,000	1.5%
38	Mississippi	55,587,000	0.5%
25	Missouri	109,653,000	0.9%
42	Montana	45,209,000	0.4%
34	Nebraska	71,220,000	0.6%
21	Nevada	129,055,000	1.0%
28	New Hampshire	100,014,000	0.8%
5	New Jersey	777,512,000	6.3%
39	New Mexico	52,718,000	0.4%
2	New York	1,009,505,000	8.2%
43	North Carolina	43,733,000	0.4%
47	North Dakota	21,167,000	0.2%
7	Ohio	557,569,000	4.5%
36	Oklahoma	63,398,000	0.5%
17	Oregon	265,348,000	2.2%
4	Pennsylvania	981,253,000	8.0%
24	Rhode Island	115,503,000	0.9%
45	South Carolina	29,742,000	0.2%
46	South Dakota	27,644,000	0.2%
23	Tennessee	119,482,000	1.0%
8	Texas	534,577,000	4.3%
37	Utah	61,663,000	0.5%
41	Vermont	51,182,000	0.4%
50	Virginia	16,199,000	0.1%
11	Washington	352,527,000	2.9%
26	West Virginia	107,609,000	0.9%
13	Wisconsin	307,425,000	2.5%
49	Wyoming	18,578,000	0.2%

RANK ORDER

RANK	STATE	REVENUE	% of USA
1	California	$1,081,588,000	8.8%
2	New York	1,009,595,000	8.2%
3	Michigan	992,793,000	8.1%
4	Pennsylvania	981,253,000	8.0%
5	New Jersey	777,512,000	6.3%
6	Illinois	760,226,000	6.2%
7	Ohio	557,569,000	4.5%
8	Texas	534,577,000	4.3%
9	Florida	446,406,000	3.6%
10	Massachusetts	425,421,000	3.5%
11	Washington	352,527,000	2.9%
12	Indiana	338,716,000	2.8%
13	Wisconsin	307,425,000	2.5%
14	Connecticut	277,333,000	2.3%
15	Arizona	274,716,000	2.2%
16	Maryland	272,066,000	2.2%
17	Oregon	265,348,000	2.2%
18	Georgia	227,348,000	1.8%
19	Minnesota	190,116,000	1.5%
20	Arkansas	146,485,000	1.2%
21	Nevada	129,055,000	1.0%
22	Kansas	124,586,000	1.0%
23	Tennessee	119,482,000	1.0%
24	Rhode Island	115,503,000	0.9%
25	Missouri	109,653,000	0.9%
26	West Virginia	107,609,000	0.9%
27	Louisiana	101,040,000	0.8%
28	New Hampshire	100,014,000	0.8%
29	Iowa	94,282,000	0.8%
30	Alabama	93,270,000	0.8%
31	Maine	92,626,000	0.8%
32	Hawaii	79,387,000	0.6%
33	Delaware	75,479,000	0.6%
34	Nebraska	71,220,000	0.6%
35	Colorado	65,144,000	0.5%
36	Oklahoma	63,398,000	0.5%
37	Utah	61,663,000	0.5%
38	Mississippi	55,587,000	0.5%
39	New Mexico	52,718,000	0.4%
40	Idaho	52,271,000	0.4%
41	Vermont	51,182,000	0.4%
42	Montana	45,209,000	0.4%
43	North Carolina	43,733,000	0.4%
44	Alaska	43,222,000	0.4%
45	South Carolina	29,742,000	0.2%
46	South Dakota	27,644,000	0.2%
47	North Dakota	21,167,000	0.2%
48	Kentucky	20,627,000	0.2%
49	Wyoming	18,578,000	0.2%
50	Virginia	16,199,000	0.1%
	District of Columbia*	NA	NA

Source: U.S. Bureau of the Census, Governments Division
    "2004 State Government Tax Collections" (http://www.census.gov/govs/www/statetax04.html)
*Not applicable.

Per Capita State Government Tobacco Sales Tax Revenue in 2004

National Per Capita = $41.97

RANK	STATE	PER CAPITA
41	Alabama	$20.61
12	Alaska	65.71
25	Arizona	47.86
20	Arkansas	53.27
34	California	30.18
46	Colorado	14.16
6	Connecticut	79.26
3	Delaware	90.93
36	Florida	25.68
37	Georgia	25.49
13	Hawaii	62.90
28	Idaho	37.47
14	Illinois	59.80
19	Indiana	54.40
33	Iowa	31.93
26	Kansas	45.57
49	Kentucky	4.98
40	Louisiana	22.42
10	Maine	70.44
22	Maryland	48.92
11	Massachusetts	66.40
2	Michigan	98.26
29	Minnesota	37.30
43	Mississippi	19.16
44	Missouri	19.04
23	Montana	48.77
27	Nebraska	40.75
18	Nevada	55.32
8	New Hampshire	76.98
4	New Jersey	89.52
35	New Mexico	27.70
21	New York	52.36
48	North Carolina	5.12
32	North Dakota	33.27
24	Ohio	48.70
45	Oklahoma	17.99
9	Oregon	73.89
7	Pennsylvania	79.17
1	Rhode Island	106.96
47	South Carolina	7.08
31	South Dakota	35.87
42	Tennessee	20.27
39	Texas	23.79
38	Utah	25.47
5	Vermont	82.39
50	Virginia	2.17
16	Washington	56.79
15	West Virginia	59.37
17	Wisconsin	55.86
30	Wyoming	36.72

RANK	STATE	PER CAPITA
1	Rhode Island	$106.96
2	Michigan	98.26
3	Delaware	90.93
4	New Jersey	89.52
5	Vermont	82.39
6	Connecticut	79.26
7	Pennsylvania	79.17
8	New Hampshire	76.98
9	Oregon	73.89
10	Maine	70.44
11	Massachusetts	66.40
12	Alaska	65.71
13	Hawaii	62.90
14	Illinois	59.80
15	West Virginia	59.37
16	Washington	56.79
17	Wisconsin	55.86
18	Nevada	55.32
19	Indiana	54.40
20	Arkansas	53.27
21	New York	52.36
22	Maryland	48.92
23	Montana	48.77
24	Ohio	48.70
25	Arizona	47.86
26	Kansas	45.57
27	Nebraska	40.75
28	Idaho	37.47
29	Minnesota	37.30
30	Wyoming	36.72
31	South Dakota	35.87
32	North Dakota	33.27
33	Iowa	31.93
34	California	30.18
35	New Mexico	27.70
36	Florida	25.68
37	Georgia	25.49
38	Utah	25.47
39	Texas	23.79
40	Louisiana	22.42
41	Alabama	20.61
42	Tennessee	20.27
43	Mississippi	19.16
44	Missouri	19.04
45	Oklahoma	17.99
46	Colorado	14.16
47	South Carolina	7.08
48	North Carolina	5.12
49	Kentucky	4.98
50	Virginia	2.17
	District of Columbia*	NA

Source: Morgan Quitno Press using data from U.S. Bureau of the Census, Governments Division
"2004 State Government Tax Collections" (http://www.census.gov/govs/www/statetax04.html)
Not applicable.

State Tax on a Pack of Cigarettes in 2005

National Median = 69.5 Cents per Pack*

ALPHA ORDER

RANK	STATE	CENTS PER PACK
38	Alabama	42.5
5	Alaska	160.0
13	Arizona	118.0
28	Arkansas	59.0
20	California	87.0
20	Colorado	87.0
6	Connecticut	151.0
31	Delaware	55.0
43	Florida	33.9
40	Georgia	37.0
10	Hawaii	140.0
29	Idaho	57.0
18	Illinois	98.0
30	Indiana	55.5
41	Iowa	36.0
23	Kansas	79.0
50	Kentucky	3.0
41	Louisiana	36.0
16	Maine	100.0
16	Maryland	100.0
6	Massachusetts	151.0
3	Michigan	200.0
36	Minnesota	48.0
46	Mississippi	18.0
47	Missouri	17.0
4	Montana	170.0
26	Nebraska	64.0
22	Nevada	80.0
35	New Hampshire	52.0
2	New Jersey	240.0
19	New Mexico	91.0
8	New York	150.0
49	North Carolina	5.0
37	North Dakota	44.0
31	Ohio	55.0
15	Oklahoma	103.0
13	Oregon	118.0
11	Pennsylvania	135.0
1	Rhode Island	246.0
48	South Carolina	7.0
34	South Dakota	53.0
44	Tennessee	20.0
39	Texas	41.0
25	Utah	69.5
12	Vermont	119.0
44	Virginia**	20.0
9	Washington	142.5
31	West Virginia	55.0
24	Wisconsin	77.0
27	Wyoming	60.0

RANK ORDER

RANK	STATE	CENTS PER PACK
1	Rhode Island	246.0
2	New Jersey	240.0
3	Michigan	200.0
4	Montana	170.0
5	Alaska	160.0
6	Connecticut	151.0
6	Massachusetts	151.0
8	New York	150.0
9	Washington	142.5
10	Hawaii	140.0
11	Pennsylvania	135.0
12	Vermont	119.0
13	Arizona	118.0
13	Oregon	118.0
15	Oklahoma	103.0
16	Maine	100.0
16	Maryland	100.0
18	Illinois	98.0
19	New Mexico	91.0
20	California	87.0
20	Colorado	87.0
22	Nevada	80.0
23	Kansas	79.0
24	Wisconsin	77.0
25	Utah	69.5
26	Nebraska	64.0
27	Wyoming	60.0
28	Arkansas	59.0
29	Idaho	57.0
30	Indiana	55.5
31	Delaware	55.0
31	Ohio	55.0
31	West Virginia	55.0
34	South Dakota	53.0
35	New Hampshire	52.0
36	Minnesota	48.0
37	North Dakota	44.0
38	Alabama	42.5
39	Texas	41.0
40	Georgia	37.0
41	Iowa	36.0
41	Louisiana	36.0
43	Florida	33.9
44	Tennessee	20.0
44	Virginia**	20.0
46	Mississippi	18.0
47	Missouri	17.0
48	South Carolina	7.0
49	North Carolina	5.0
50	Kentucky	3.0

	District of Columbia	100.0

Source: Federation of Tax Administrators
  "State Cigarette Excise Tax Rates" (http://www.taxadmin.org/fta/rate/cigarett.html)
*As of January 1, 2005. Many states also allow additional local option taxes on cigarettes.
**On July 1, 2005, the rate per pack was scheduled to rise in Virginia to $0.50.

State Government Alcoholic Beverage Sales Tax Revenue in 2004

National Total = $4,614,804,000

ALPHA ORDER

RANK	STATE	LIQUOR TAX	% of USA
13	Alabama	$137,222,000	3.0%
34	Alaska	28,262,000	0.6%
22	Arizona	55,954,000	1.2%
27	Arkansas	41,240,000	0.9%
3	California	312,826,000	6.8%
33	Colorado	31,317,000	0.7%
25	Connecticut	44,026,000	1.0%
41	Delaware	13,385,000	0.3%
2	Florida	591,551,000	12.8%
8	Georgia	149,801,000	3.2%
26	Hawaii	41,250,000	0.9%
48	Idaho	6,609,000	0.1%
10	Illinois	147,883,000	3.2%
30	Indiana	38,509,000	0.8%
43	Iowa	12,709,000	0.3%
16	Kansas	87,637,000	1.9%
18	Kentucky	79,104,000	1.7%
23	Louisiana	53,422,000	1.2%
29	Maine	39,279,000	0.9%
37	Maryland	26,863,000	0.6%
20	Massachusetts	68,522,000	1.5%
9	Michigan	149,424,000	3.2%
19	Minnesota	69,497,000	1.5%
28	Mississippi	39,793,000	0.9%
36	Missouri	28,026,000	0.6%
39	Montana	20,570,000	0.4%
38	Nebraska	23,159,000	0.5%
32	Nevada	33,867,000	0.7%
45	New Hampshire	12,239,000	0.3%
17	New Jersey	87,357,000	1.9%
31	New Mexico	37,503,000	0.8%
7	New York	191,128,000	4.1%
5	North Carolina	212,224,000	4.6%
49	North Dakota	5,910,000	0.1%
15	Ohio	88,267,000	1.9%
21	Oklahoma	68,420,000	1.5%
42	Oregon	13,306,000	0.3%
4	Pennsylvania	221,408,000	4.8%
46	Rhode Island	10,607,000	0.2%
11	South Carolina	146,658,000	3.2%
44	South Dakota	12,435,000	0.3%
14	Tennessee	92,062,000	2.0%
1	Texas	601,841,000	13.0%
35	Utah	28,174,000	0.6%
40	Vermont	16,894,000	0.4%
12	Virginia	146,019,000	3.2%
6	Washington	192,618,000	4.2%
47	West Virginia	8,624,000	0.2%
24	Wisconsin	48,071,000	1.0%
50	Wyoming	1,332,000	0.0%

RANK ORDER

RANK	STATE	LIQUOR TAX	% of USA
1	Texas	$601,841,000	13.0%
2	Florida	591,551,000	12.8%
3	California	312,826,000	6.8%
4	Pennsylvania	221,408,000	4.8%
5	North Carolina	212,224,000	4.6%
6	Washington	192,618,000	4.2%
7	New York	191,128,000	4.1%
8	Georgia	149,801,000	3.2%
9	Michigan	149,424,000	3.2%
10	Illinois	147,883,000	3.2%
11	South Carolina	146,658,000	3.2%
12	Virginia	146,019,000	3.2%
13	Alabama	137,222,000	3.0%
14	Tennessee	92,062,000	2.0%
15	Ohio	88,267,000	1.9%
16	Kansas	87,637,000	1.9%
17	New Jersey	87,357,000	1.9%
18	Kentucky	79,104,000	1.7%
19	Minnesota	69,497,000	1.5%
20	Massachusetts	68,522,000	1.5%
21	Oklahoma	68,420,000	1.5%
22	Arizona	55,954,000	1.2%
23	Louisiana	53,422,000	1.2%
24	Wisconsin	48,071,000	1.0%
25	Connecticut	44,026,000	1.0%
26	Hawaii	41,250,000	0.9%
27	Arkansas	41,240,000	0.9%
28	Mississippi	39,793,000	0.9%
29	Maine	39,279,000	0.9%
30	Indiana	38,509,000	0.8%
31	New Mexico	37,503,000	0.8%
32	Nevada	33,867,000	0.7%
33	Colorado	31,317,000	0.7%
34	Alaska	28,262,000	0.6%
35	Utah	28,174,000	0.6%
36	Missouri	28,026,000	0.6%
37	Maryland	26,863,000	0.6%
38	Nebraska	23,159,000	0.5%
39	Montana	20,570,000	0.4%
40	Vermont	16,894,000	0.4%
41	Delaware	13,385,000	0.3%
42	Oregon	13,306,000	0.3%
43	Iowa	12,709,000	0.3%
44	South Dakota	12,435,000	0.3%
45	New Hampshire	12,239,000	0.3%
46	Rhode Island	10,607,000	0.2%
47	West Virginia	8,624,000	0.2%
48	Idaho	6,609,000	0.1%
49	North Dakota	5,910,000	0.1%
50	Wyoming	1,332,000	0.0%
	District of Columbia*	NA	NA

Source: U.S. Bureau of the Census, Governments Division
"2004 State Government Tax Collections" (http://www.census.gov/govs/www/statetax04.html)
*Not applicable.

Per Capita State Government Alcoholic Beverage Sales Tax Revenue in 2004

National Per Capita = $15.74

ALPHA ORDER

RANK	STATE	PER CAPITA
7	Alabama	$30.32
1	Alaska	42.97
36	Arizona	9.75
22	Arkansas	15.00
39	California	8.73
42	Colorado	6.81
28	Connecticut	12.58
20	Delaware	16.13
3	Florida	34.03
18	Georgia	16.80
4	Hawaii	32.68
47	Idaho	4.74
31	Illinois	11.63
43	Indiana	6.18
48	Iowa	4.30
5	Kansas	32.06
16	Kentucky	19.10
29	Louisiana	11.85
8	Maine	29.87
45	Maryland	4.83
32	Massachusetts	10.69
23	Michigan	14.79
26	Minnesota	13.64
25	Mississippi	13.72
44	Missouri	4.87
12	Montana	22.19
27	Nebraska	13.25
24	Nevada	14.52
37	New Hampshire	9.42
33	New Jersey	10.06
13	New Mexico	19.71
34	New York	9.91
11	North Carolina	24.85
38	North Dakota	9.29
41	Ohio	7.71
15	Oklahoma	19.42
49	Oregon	3.71
17	Pennsylvania	17.86
35	Rhode Island	9.82
2	South Carolina	34.94
19	South Dakota	16.14
21	Tennessee	15.62
10	Texas	26.78
30	Utah	11.64
9	Vermont	27.19
14	Virginia	19.52
6	Washington	31.03
46	West Virginia	4.76
39	Wisconsin	8.73
50	Wyoming	2.63

RANK ORDER

RANK	STATE	PER CAPITA
1	Alaska	$42.97
2	South Carolina	34.94
3	Florida	34.03
4	Hawaii	32.68
5	Kansas	32.06
6	Washington	31.03
7	Alabama	30.32
8	Maine	29.87
9	Vermont	27.19
10	Texas	26.78
11	North Carolina	24.85
12	Montana	22.19
13	New Mexico	19.71
14	Virginia	19.52
15	Oklahoma	19.42
16	Kentucky	19.10
17	Pennsylvania	17.86
18	Georgia	16.80
19	South Dakota	16.14
20	Delaware	16.13
21	Tennessee	15.62
22	Arkansas	15.00
23	Michigan	14.79
24	Nevada	14.52
25	Mississippi	13.72
26	Minnesota	13.64
27	Nebraska	13.25
28	Connecticut	12.58
29	Louisiana	11.85
30	Utah	11.64
31	Illinois	11.63
32	Massachusetts	10.69
33	New Jersey	10.06
34	New York	9.91
35	Rhode Island	9.82
36	Arizona	9.75
37	New Hampshire	9.42
38	North Dakota	9.29
39	California	8.73
39	Wisconsin	8.73
41	Ohio	7.71
42	Colorado	6.81
43	Indiana	6.18
44	Missouri	4.87
45	Maryland	4.83
46	West Virginia	4.76
47	Idaho	4.74
48	Iowa	4.30
49	Oregon	3.71
50	Wyoming	2.63
	District of Columbia*	NA

Source: Morgan Quitno Press using data from U.S. Bureau of the Census, Governments Division
    "2004 State Government Tax Collections" (http://www.census.gov/govs/www/statetax04.html)
*Not applicable.

State Government Total Expenditures in 2003

National Total = $1,359,048,379,000*

RANK	STATE	EXPENDITURES	% of USA
26	Alabama	$18,471,110,000	1.4%
37	Alaska	8,121,540,000	0.6%
23	Arizona	19,606,017,000	1.4%
32	Arkansas	12,084,818,000	0.9%
1	California	204,438,461,000	15.0%
28	Colorado	17,690,925,000	1.3%
22	Connecticut	20,721,194,000	1.5%
45	Delaware	4,857,901,000	0.4%
6	Florida	56,317,331,000	4.1%
13	Georgia	32,526,824,000	2.4%
39	Hawaii	7,611,286,000	0.6%
43	Idaho	5,415,138,000	0.4%
7	Illinois	51,291,090,000	3.8%
18	Indiana	23,089,940,000	1.7%
31	Iowa	13,088,000,000	1.0%
33	Kansas	10,954,011,000	0.8%
24	Kentucky	19,116,816,000	1.4%
25	Louisiana	18,681,314,000	1.4%
41	Maine	6,706,116,000	0.5%
17	Maryland	24,592,128,000	1.8%
11	Massachusetts	32,710,435,000	2.4%
8	Michigan	51,016,280,000	3.8%
15	Minnesota	28,898,514,000	2.1%
30	Mississippi	13,502,885,000	1.0%
19	Missouri	21,566,197,000	1.6%
46	Montana	4,436,890,000	0.3%
40	Nebraska	6,823,849,000	0.5%
38	Nevada	7,816,481,000	0.6%
44	New Hampshire	5,276,466,000	0.4%
9	New Jersey	44,947,598,000	3.3%
34	New Mexico	10,672,603,000	0.8%
2	New York	127,475,233,000	9.4%
10	North Carolina	34,360,977,000	2.5%
49	North Dakota	3,121,369,000	0.2%
5	Ohio	56,392,224,000	4.1%
29	Oklahoma	15,125,090,000	1.1%
27	Oregon	18,005,773,000	1.3%
4	Pennsylvania	57,428,466,000	4.2%
42	Rhode Island	5,976,510,000	0.4%
20	South Carolina	21,039,752,000	1.5%
50	South Dakota	2,898,044,000	0.2%
21	Tennessee	21,021,917,000	1.5%
3	Texas	76,386,043,000	5.6%
35	Utah	10,252,051,000	0.8%
47	Vermont	3,858,957,000	0.3%
14	Virginia	29,129,136,000	2.1%
12	Washington	32,600,336,000	2.4%
36	West Virginia	10,003,729,000	0.7%
16	Wisconsin	27,658,175,000	2.0%
48	Wyoming	3,264,439,000	0.2%

RANK	STATE	EXPENDITURES	% of USA
1	California	$204,438,461,000	15.0%
2	New York	127,475,233,000	9.4%
3	Texas	76,386,043,000	5.6%
4	Pennsylvania	57,428,466,000	4.2%
5	Ohio	56,392,224,000	4.1%
6	Florida	56,317,331,000	4.1%
7	Illinois	51,291,090,000	3.8%
8	Michigan	51,016,280,000	3.8%
9	New Jersey	44,947,598,000	3.3%
10	North Carolina	34,360,977,000	2.5%
11	Massachusetts	32,710,435,000	2.4%
12	Washington	32,600,336,000	2.4%
13	Georgia	32,526,824,000	2.4%
14	Virginia	29,129,136,000	2.1%
15	Minnesota	28,898,514,000	2.1%
16	Wisconsin	27,658,175,000	2.0%
17	Maryland	24,592,128,000	1.8%
18	Indiana	23,089,940,000	1.7%
19	Missouri	21,566,197,000	1.6%
20	South Carolina	21,039,752,000	1.5%
21	Tennessee	21,021,917,000	1.5%
22	Connecticut	20,721,194,000	1.5%
23	Arizona	19,606,017,000	1.4%
24	Kentucky	19,116,816,000	1.4%
25	Louisiana	18,681,314,000	1.4%
26	Alabama	18,471,110,000	1.4%
27	Oregon	18,005,773,000	1.3%
28	Colorado	17,690,925,000	1.3%
29	Oklahoma	15,125,090,000	1.1%
30	Mississippi	13,502,885,000	1.0%
31	Iowa	13,088,000,000	1.0%
32	Arkansas	12,084,818,000	0.9%
33	Kansas	10,954,011,000	0.8%
34	New Mexico	10,672,603,000	0.8%
35	Utah	10,252,051,000	0.8%
36	West Virginia	10,003,729,000	0.7%
37	Alaska	8,121,540,000	0.6%
38	Nevada	7,816,481,000	0.6%
39	Hawaii	7,611,286,000	0.6%
40	Nebraska	6,823,849,000	0.5%
41	Maine	6,706,116,000	0.5%
42	Rhode Island	5,976,510,000	0.4%
43	Idaho	5,415,138,000	0.4%
44	New Hampshire	5,276,466,000	0.4%
45	Delaware	4,857,901,000	0.4%
46	Montana	4,436,890,000	0.3%
47	Vermont	3,858,957,000	0.3%
48	Wyoming	3,264,439,000	0.2%
49	North Dakota	3,121,369,000	0.2%
50	South Dakota	2,898,044,000	0.2%
	District of Columbia**	NA	NA

Source: U.S. Bureau of the Census, Governments Division
    "2003 State Government Finances" (http://www.census.gov/govs/www/state03.html)
*Total expenditures includes all money paid other than for retirement of debt and extension of loans. Includes payments from all sources of funds including current revenues and proceeds from borrowing and prior year fund balances. Includes intergovernmental transfers and expenditures for government owned utilities and other commercial or auxiliary enterprise and insurance trust expenditures. **Not applicable.

Per Capita State Government Total Expenditures in 2003

National Per Capita = $4,682*

RANK	STATE	PER CAPITA
33	Alabama	$4,103
1	Alaska	12,523
47	Arizona	3,515
29	Arkansas	4,433
8	California	5,766
41	Colorado	3,890
6	Connecticut	5,944
7	Delaware	5,940
50	Florida	3,314
45	Georgia	3,719
5	Hawaii	6,098
38	Idaho	3,958
36	Illinois	4,055
44	Indiana	3,726
28	Iowa	4,450
37	Kansas	4,021
25	Kentucky	4,644
32	Louisiana	4,160
15	Maine	5,126
27	Maryland	4,461
16	Massachusetts	5,097
18	Michigan	5,062
9	Minnesota	5,709
24	Mississippi	4,687
43	Missouri	3,771
23	Montana	4,834
40	Nebraska	3,926
48	Nevada	3,487
34	New Hampshire	4,098
14	New Jersey	5,202
10	New Mexico	5,679
2	New York	6,630
35	North Carolina	4,080
22	North Dakota	4,931
21	Ohio	4,933
30	Oklahoma	4,315
20	Oregon	5,054
25	Pennsylvania	4,644
11	Rhode Island	5,556
17	South Carolina	5,074
42	South Dakota	3,790
46	Tennessee	3,599
49	Texas	3,457
31	Utah	4,310
4	Vermont	6,233
39	Virginia	3,945
13	Washington	5,317
12	West Virginia	5,526
19	Wisconsin	5,055
3	Wyoming	6,504

RANK	STATE	PER CAPITA
1	Alaska	$12,523
2	New York	6,630
3	Wyoming	6,504
4	Vermont	6,233
5	Hawaii	6,098
6	Connecticut	5,944
7	Delaware	5,940
8	California	5,766
9	Minnesota	5,709
10	New Mexico	5,679
11	Rhode Island	5,556
12	West Virginia	5,526
13	Washington	5,317
14	New Jersey	5,202
15	Maine	5,126
16	Massachusetts	5,097
17	South Carolina	5,074
18	Michigan	5,062
19	Wisconsin	5,055
20	Oregon	5,054
21	Ohio	4,933
22	North Dakota	4,931
23	Montana	4,834
24	Mississippi	4,687
25	Kentucky	4,644
25	Pennsylvania	4,644
27	Maryland	4,461
28	Iowa	4,450
29	Arkansas	4,433
30	Oklahoma	4,315
31	Utah	4,310
32	Louisiana	4,160
33	Alabama	4,103
34	New Hampshire	4,098
35	North Carolina	4,080
36	Illinois	4,055
37	Kansas	4,021
38	Idaho	3,958
39	Virginia	3,945
40	Nebraska	3,926
41	Colorado	3,890
42	South Dakota	3,790
43	Missouri	3,771
44	Indiana	3,726
45	Georgia	3,719
46	Tennessee	3,599
47	Arizona	3,515
48	Nevada	3,487
49	Texas	3,457
50	Florida	3,314

District of Columbia**   NA

Source: Morgan Quitno Press using data from U.S. Bureau of the Census, Governments Division
"2003 State Government Finances" (http://www.census.gov/govs/www/state03.html)
*Total expenditures includes all money paid other than for retirement of debt and extension of loans. Includes payments from all sources of funds including current revenues and proceeds from borrowing and prior year fund balances. Includes intergovernmental transfers and expenditures for government owned utilities and other commercial or auxiliary enterprise and insurance trust expenditures. **Not applicable.

State Government Direct General Expenditures in 2003

National Total = $781,771,632,000*

ALPHA ORDER

RANK	STATE	EXPENDITURES	% of USA
24	Alabama	$12,935,939,000	1.7%
38	Alaska	6,020,106,000	0.8%
26	Arizona	10,566,299,000	1.4%
32	Arkansas	7,870,774,000	1.0%
1	California	88,689,213,000	11.3%
27	Colorado	10,126,189,000	1.3%
17	Connecticut	14,854,536,000	1.9%
43	Delaware	3,472,830,000	0.4%
5	Florida	35,757,033,000	4.6%
11	Georgia	20,274,641,000	2.6%
36	Hawaii	6,726,471,000	0.9%
44	Idaho	3,310,379,000	0.4%
6	Illinois	30,584,441,000	3.9%
18	Indiana	14,534,463,000	1.9%
31	Iowa	8,272,117,000	1.1%
34	Kansas	6,918,163,000	0.9%
23	Kentucky	13,163,981,000	1.7%
25	Louisiana	11,993,962,000	1.5%
39	Maine	5,020,929,000	0.6%
15	Maryland	16,430,692,000	2.1%
10	Massachusetts	21,434,822,000	2.7%
9	Michigan	24,670,395,000	3.2%
16	Minnesota	15,765,455,000	2.0%
30	Mississippi	8,428,937,000	1.1%
21	Missouri	13,978,118,000	1.8%
46	Montana	2,979,125,000	0.4%
40	Nebraska	4,709,034,000	0.6%
42	Nevada	4,056,876,000	0.5%
45	New Hampshire	3,308,698,000	0.4%
8	New Jersey	25,862,371,000	3.3%
35	New Mexico	6,762,454,000	0.9%
2	New York	60,950,522,000	7.8%
12	North Carolina	20,072,171,000	2.6%
48	North Dakota	2,291,420,000	0.3%
7	Ohio	29,364,281,000	3.8%
29	Oklahoma	9,910,338,000	1.3%
28	Oregon	10,058,653,000	1.3%
4	Pennsylvania	36,309,010,000	4.6%
41	Rhode Island	4,198,292,000	0.5%
22	South Carolina	13,528,974,000	1.7%
49	South Dakota	2,148,132,000	0.3%
19	Tennessee	14,433,892,000	1.8%
3	Texas	49,470,591,000	6.3%
33	Utah	7,011,274,000	0.9%
47	Vermont	2,655,732,000	0.3%
14	Virginia	17,936,632,000	2.3%
13	Washington	19,235,437,000	2.5%
37	West Virginia	6,452,888,000	0.8%
20	Wisconsin	14,335,257,000	1.8%
50	Wyoming	1,928,693,000	0.2%

RANK ORDER

RANK	STATE	EXPENDITURES	% of USA
1	California	$88,689,213,000	11.3%
2	New York	60,950,522,000	7.8%
3	Texas	49,470,591,000	6.3%
4	Pennsylvania	36,309,010,000	4.6%
5	Florida	35,757,033,000	4.6%
6	Illinois	30,584,441,000	3.9%
7	Ohio	29,364,281,000	3.8%
8	New Jersey	25,862,371,000	3.3%
9	Michigan	24,670,395,000	3.2%
10	Massachusetts	21,434,822,000	2.7%
11	Georgia	20,274,641,000	2.6%
12	North Carolina	20,072,171,000	2.6%
13	Washington	19,235,437,000	2.5%
14	Virginia	17,936,632,000	2.3%
15	Maryland	16,430,692,000	2.1%
16	Minnesota	15,765,455,000	2.0%
17	Connecticut	14,854,536,000	1.9%
18	Indiana	14,534,463,000	1.9%
19	Tennessee	14,433,892,000	1.8%
20	Wisconsin	14,335,257,000	1.8%
21	Missouri	13,978,118,000	1.8%
22	South Carolina	13,528,974,000	1.7%
23	Kentucky	13,163,981,000	1.7%
24	Alabama	12,935,939,000	1.7%
25	Louisiana	11,993,962,000	1.5%
26	Arizona	10,566,299,000	1.4%
27	Colorado	10,126,189,000	1.3%
28	Oregon	10,058,653,000	1.3%
29	Oklahoma	9,910,338,000	1.3%
30	Mississippi	8,428,937,000	1.1%
31	Iowa	8,272,117,000	1.1%
32	Arkansas	7,870,774,000	1.0%
33	Utah	7,011,274,000	0.9%
34	Kansas	6,918,163,000	0.9%
35	New Mexico	6,762,454,000	0.9%
36	Hawaii	6,726,471,000	0.9%
37	West Virginia	6,452,888,000	0.8%
38	Alaska	6,020,106,000	0.8%
39	Maine	5,020,929,000	0.6%
40	Nebraska	4,709,034,000	0.6%
41	Rhode Island	4,198,292,000	0.5%
42	Nevada	4,056,876,000	0.5%
43	Delaware	3,472,830,000	0.4%
44	Idaho	3,310,379,000	0.4%
45	New Hampshire	3,308,698,000	0.4%
46	Montana	2,979,125,000	0.4%
47	Vermont	2,655,732,000	0.3%
48	North Dakota	2,291,420,000	0.3%
49	South Dakota	2,148,132,000	0.3%
50	Wyoming	1,928,693,000	0.2%
	District of Columbia**	NA	NA

Source: U.S. Bureau of the Census, Governments Division
   "2003 State Government Finances" (http://www.census.gov/govs/www/state03.html)
*Direct general expenditures include expenditures for current operations, assistance and subsidies, interest on debt and capital outlay. Excludes intergovernmental transfers, expenditures for government owned utilities and other commercial or auxiliary enterprise and insurance trust expenditures.
**Not applicable.

338

Per Capita State Government Direct General Expenditures in 2003

National Per Capita = $2,693*

ALPHA ORDER

RANK	STATE	PER CAPITA
25	Alabama	$2,873
1	Alaska	9,283
49	Arizona	1,894
24	Arkansas	2,887
36	California	2,501
47	Colorado	2,226
4	Connecticut	4,261
5	Delaware	4,246
48	Florida	2,104
45	Georgia	2,318
2	Hawaii	5,389
41	Idaho	2,420
42	Illinois	2,418
44	Indiana	2,346
28	Iowa	2,812
35	Kansas	2,539
15	Kentucky	3,198
31	Louisiana	2,671
8	Maine	3,838
20	Maryland	2,981
12	Massachusetts	3,340
38	Michigan	2,448
18	Minnesota	3,115
23	Mississippi	2,926
39	Missouri	2,444
14	Montana	3,246
30	Nebraska	2,709
50	Nevada	1,810
33	New Hampshire	2,570
19	New Jersey	2,993
10	New Mexico	3,598
16	New York	3,170
43	North Carolina	2,383
9	North Dakota	3,620
34	Ohio	2,569
26	Oklahoma	2,828
27	Oregon	2,823
22	Pennsylvania	2,936
6	Rhode Island	3,903
13	South Carolina	3,263
29	South Dakota	2,809
37	Tennessee	2,471
46	Texas	2,239
21	Utah	2,948
3	Vermont	4,290
40	Virginia	2,429
17	Washington	3,137
11	West Virginia	3,564
32	Wisconsin	2,620
7	Wyoming	3,843

RANK ORDER

RANK	STATE	PER CAPITA
1	Alaska	$9,283
2	Hawaii	5,389
3	Vermont	4,290
4	Connecticut	4,261
5	Delaware	4,246
6	Rhode Island	3,903
7	Wyoming	3,843
8	Maine	3,838
9	North Dakota	3,620
10	New Mexico	3,598
11	West Virginia	3,564
12	Massachusetts	3,340
13	South Carolina	3,263
14	Montana	3,246
15	Kentucky	3,198
16	New York	3,170
17	Washington	3,137
18	Minnesota	3,115
19	New Jersey	2,993
20	Maryland	2,981
21	Utah	2,948
22	Pennsylvania	2,936
23	Mississippi	2,926
24	Arkansas	2,887
25	Alabama	2,873
26	Oklahoma	2,828
27	Oregon	2,823
28	Iowa	2,812
29	South Dakota	2,809
30	Nebraska	2,709
31	Louisiana	2,671
32	Wisconsin	2,620
33	New Hampshire	2,570
34	Ohio	2,569
35	Kansas	2,539
36	California	2,501
37	Tennessee	2,471
38	Michigan	2,448
39	Missouri	2,444
40	Virginia	2,429
41	Idaho	2,420
42	Illinois	2,418
43	North Carolina	2,383
44	Indiana	2,346
45	Georgia	2,318
46	Texas	2,239
47	Colorado	2,226
48	Florida	2,104
49	Arizona	1,894
50	Nevada	1,810
	District of Columbia**	NA

*Source: Morgan Quitno Press using data from U.S. Bureau of the Census, Governments Division
"2003 State Government Finances" (http://www.census.gov/govs/www/state03.html)*
*Direct general expenditures include expenditures for current operations, assistance and subsidies, interest on debt and capital outlay. Excludes intergovernmental transfers, expenditures for government owned utilities and other commercial or auxiliary enterprise and insurance trust expenditures.
**Not applicable.

State Government Debt Outstanding in 2003

National Total = $697,929,028,000*

RANK	STATE	DEBT	% of USA
27	Alabama	$6,284,640,000	0.9%
29	Alaska	5,829,798,000	0.8%
32	Arizona	5,554,020,000	0.8%
42	Arkansas	3,295,143,000	0.5%
1	California	95,209,988,000	13.6%
21	Colorado	8,921,416,000	1.3%
7	Connecticut	22,490,115,000	3.2%
36	Delaware	4,358,281,000	0.6%
9	Florida	21,993,221,000	3.2%
22	Georgia	8,890,184,000	1.3%
30	Hawaii	5,652,531,000	0.8%
44	Idaho	2,602,620,000	0.4%
4	Illinois	46,688,761,000	6.7%
18	Indiana	11,853,847,000	1.7%
37	Iowa	4,279,448,000	0.6%
47	Kansas	2,471,939,000	0.4%
25	Kentucky	7,108,634,000	1.0%
20	Louisiana	9,773,279,000	1.4%
35	Maine	4,417,481,000	0.6%
16	Maryland	12,950,949,000	1.9%
3	Massachusetts	48,478,722,000	6.9%
8	Michigan	22,478,857,000	3.2%
24	Minnesota	7,150,401,000	1.0%
39	Mississippi	4,166,614,000	0.6%
14	Missouri	13,855,016,000	2.0%
43	Montana	2,879,317,000	0.4%
48	Nebraska	2,135,502,000	0.3%
40	Nevada	3,604,272,000	0.5%
31	New Hampshire	5,594,078,000	0.8%
5	New Jersey	33,608,678,000	4.8%
34	New Mexico	4,601,117,000	0.7%
2	New York	91,634,857,000	13.1%
17	North Carolina	12,141,890,000	1.7%
49	North Dakota	1,599,233,000	0.2%
10	Ohio	21,054,220,000	3.0%
26	Oklahoma	6,747,020,000	1.0%
23	Oregon	7,463,722,000	1.1%
6	Pennsylvania	24,330,327,000	3.5%
28	Rhode Island	6,189,389,000	0.9%
19	South Carolina	10,990,201,000	1.6%
45	South Dakota	2,566,542,000	0.4%
41	Tennessee	3,496,139,000	0.5%
13	Texas	14,616,237,000	2.1%
33	Utah	5,064,112,000	0.7%
46	Vermont	2,532,071,000	0.4%
15	Virginia	13,530,190,000	1.9%
12	Washington	14,620,855,000	2.1%
38	West Virginia	4,260,461,000	0.6%
11	Wisconsin	14,801,308,000	2.1%
50	Wyoming	1,111,385,000	0.2%

RANK	STATE	DEBT	% of USA
1	California	$95,209,988,000	13.6%
2	New York	91,634,857,000	13.1%
3	Massachusetts	48,478,722,000	6.9%
4	Illinois	46,688,761,000	6.7%
5	New Jersey	33,608,678,000	4.8%
6	Pennsylvania	24,330,327,000	3.5%
7	Connecticut	22,490,115,000	3.2%
8	Michigan	22,478,857,000	3.2%
9	Florida	21,993,221,000	3.2%
10	Ohio	21,054,220,000	3.0%
11	Wisconsin	14,801,308,000	2.1%
12	Washington	14,620,855,000	2.1%
13	Texas	14,616,237,000	2.1%
14	Missouri	13,855,016,000	2.0%
15	Virginia	13,530,190,000	1.9%
16	Maryland	12,950,949,000	1.9%
17	North Carolina	12,141,890,000	1.7%
18	Indiana	11,853,847,000	1.7%
19	South Carolina	10,990,201,000	1.6%
20	Louisiana	9,773,279,000	1.4%
21	Colorado	8,921,416,000	1.3%
22	Georgia	8,890,184,000	1.3%
23	Oregon	7,463,722,000	1.1%
24	Minnesota	7,150,401,000	1.0%
25	Kentucky	7,108,634,000	1.0%
26	Oklahoma	6,747,020,000	1.0%
27	Alabama	6,284,640,000	0.9%
28	Rhode Island	6,189,389,000	0.9%
29	Alaska	5,829,798,000	0.8%
30	Hawaii	5,652,531,000	0.8%
31	New Hampshire	5,594,078,000	0.8%
32	Arizona	5,554,020,000	0.8%
33	Utah	5,064,112,000	0.7%
34	New Mexico	4,601,117,000	0.7%
35	Maine	4,417,481,000	0.6%
36	Delaware	4,358,281,000	0.6%
37	Iowa	4,279,448,000	0.6%
38	West Virginia	4,260,461,000	0.6%
39	Mississippi	4,166,614,000	0.6%
40	Nevada	3,604,272,000	0.5%
41	Tennessee	3,496,139,000	0.5%
42	Arkansas	3,295,143,000	0.5%
43	Montana	2,879,317,000	0.4%
44	Idaho	2,602,620,000	0.4%
45	South Dakota	2,566,542,000	0.4%
46	Vermont	2,532,071,000	0.4%
47	Kansas	2,471,939,000	0.4%
48	Nebraska	2,135,502,000	0.3%
49	North Dakota	1,599,233,000	0.2%
50	Wyoming	1,111,385,000	0.2%
	District of Columbia**	NA	NA

Source: U.S. Bureau of the Census, Governments Division
   "2003 State Government Finances" (http://www.census.gov/govs/www/state03.html)
*Includes short-term, long-term, full faith and credit, nonguaranteed and public debt for private purposes.
**Not applicable.

Per Capita State Government Debt Outstanding in 2003

National Per Capita = $2,404*

ALPHA ORDER				RANK ORDER		
RANK	STATE	PER CAPITA		RANK	STATE	PER CAPITA
42	Alabama	$1,396		1	Alaska	$8,990
1	Alaska	8,990		2	Massachusetts	7,554
47	Arizona	996		3	Connecticut	6,452
45	Arkansas	1,209		4	Rhode Island	5,754
16	California	2,685		5	Delaware	5,329
30	Colorado	1,962		6	New York	4,766
3	Connecticut	6,452		7	Hawaii	4,529
5	Delaware	5,329		8	New Hampshire	4,345
43	Florida	1,294		9	Vermont	4,090
46	Georgia	1,016		10	New Jersey	3,890
7	Hawaii	4,529		11	Illinois	3,691
33	Idaho	1,902		12	Maine	3,377
11	Illinois	3,691		13	South Dakota	3,357
32	Indiana	1,913		14	Montana	3,137
38	Iowa	1,455		15	Wisconsin	2,705
48	Kansas	907		16	California	2,685
36	Kentucky	1,727		17	South Carolina	2,650
26	Louisiana	2,176		18	North Dakota	2,526
12	Maine	3,377		19	New Mexico	2,448
23	Maryland	2,349		20	Missouri	2,423
2	Massachusetts	7,554		21	Washington	2,385
24	Michigan	2,230		22	West Virginia	2,353
41	Minnesota	1,413		23	Maryland	2,349
39	Mississippi	1,446		24	Michigan	2,230
20	Missouri	2,423		25	Wyoming	2,214
14	Montana	3,137		26	Louisiana	2,176
44	Nebraska	1,229		27	Utah	2,129
37	Nevada	1,608		28	Oregon	2,095
8	New Hampshire	4,345		29	Pennsylvania	1,968
10	New Jersey	3,890		30	Colorado	1,962
19	New Mexico	2,448		31	Oklahoma	1,925
6	New York	4,766		32	Indiana	1,913
40	North Carolina	1,442		33	Idaho	1,902
18	North Dakota	2,526		34	Ohio	1,842
34	Ohio	1,842		35	Virginia	1,833
31	Oklahoma	1,925		36	Kentucky	1,727
28	Oregon	2,095		37	Nevada	1,608
29	Pennsylvania	1,968		38	Iowa	1,455
4	Rhode Island	5,754		39	Mississippi	1,446
17	South Carolina	2,650		40	North Carolina	1,442
13	South Dakota	3,357		41	Minnesota	1,413
50	Tennessee	598		42	Alabama	1,396
49	Texas	661		43	Florida	1,294
27	Utah	2,129		44	Nebraska	1,229
9	Vermont	4,090		45	Arkansas	1,209
35	Virginia	1,833		46	Georgia	1,016
21	Washington	2,385		47	Arizona	996
22	West Virginia	2,353		48	Kansas	907
15	Wisconsin	2,705		49	Texas	661
25	Wyoming	2,214		50	Tennessee	598
					District of Columbia**	NA

Source: Morgan Quitno Press using data from U.S. Bureau of the Census, Governments Division
"2003 State Government Finances" (http://www.census.gov/govs/www/state03.html)
*Includes short-term, long-term, full faith and credit, nonguaranteed and public debt for private purposes.
**Not applicable.

State Government Full-Time Equivalent Employees in 2004

National Total = 4,187,648 FTE Employees*

ALPHA ORDER

RANK	STATE	EMPLOYEES	% of USA
19	Alabama	85,647	2.0%
40	Alaska	24,657	0.6%
25	Arizona	66,026	1.6%
32	Arkansas	54,005	1.3%
1	California	393,057	9.4%
26	Colorado	65,652	1.6%
28	Connecticut	58,648	1.4%
41	Delaware	24,254	0.6%
4	Florida	183,265	4.4%
11	Georgia	121,526	2.9%
31	Hawaii	56,540	1.4%
42	Idaho	23,198	0.6%
8	Illinois	133,672	3.2%
17	Indiana	90,404	2.2%
33	Iowa	53,291	1.3%
36	Kansas	43,787	1.0%
21	Kentucky	79,481	1.9%
16	Louisiana	90,600	2.2%
43	Maine	21,720	0.5%
15	Maryland	90,682	2.2%
18	Massachusetts	88,051	2.1%
9	Michigan	132,825	3.2%
23	Minnesota	74,543	1.8%
30	Mississippi	56,968	1.4%
14	Missouri	90,730	2.2%
46	Montana	18,571	0.4%
38	Nebraska	33,662	0.8%
39	Nevada	25,279	0.6%
45	New Hampshire	19,955	0.5%
6	New Jersey	149,374	3.6%
34	New Mexico	49,286	1.2%
3	New York	246,385	5.9%
10	North Carolina	132,110	3.2%
47	North Dakota	17,754	0.4%
7	Ohio	136,041	3.2%
27	Oklahoma	64,094	1.5%
29	Oregon	57,423	1.4%
5	Pennsylvania	161,089	3.8%
44	Rhode Island	20,158	0.5%
22	South Carolina	75,603	1.8%
49	South Dakota	13,201	0.3%
20	Tennessee	81,905	2.0%
2	Texas	268,172	6.4%
35	Utah	48,900	1.2%
48	Vermont	13,922	0.3%
12	Virginia	119,317	2.8%
13	Washington	112,738	2.7%
37	West Virginia	37,583	0.9%
24	Wisconsin	69,834	1.7%
50	Wyoming	12,063	0.3%

RANK ORDER

RANK	STATE	EMPLOYEES	% of USA
1	California	393,057	9.4%
2	Texas	268,172	6.4%
3	New York	246,385	5.9%
4	Florida	183,265	4.4%
5	Pennsylvania	161,089	3.8%
6	New Jersey	149,374	3.6%
7	Ohio	136,041	3.2%
8	Illinois	133,672	3.2%
9	Michigan	132,825	3.2%
10	North Carolina	132,110	3.2%
11	Georgia	121,526	2.9%
12	Virginia	119,317	2.8%
13	Washington	112,738	2.7%
14	Missouri	90,730	2.2%
15	Maryland	90,682	2.2%
16	Louisiana	90,600	2.2%
17	Indiana	90,404	2.2%
18	Massachusetts	88,051	2.1%
19	Alabama	85,647	2.0%
20	Tennessee	81,905	2.0%
21	Kentucky	79,481	1.9%
22	South Carolina	75,603	1.8%
23	Minnesota	74,543	1.8%
24	Wisconsin	69,834	1.7%
25	Arizona	66,026	1.6%
26	Colorado	65,652	1.6%
27	Oklahoma	64,094	1.5%
28	Connecticut	58,648	1.4%
29	Oregon	57,423	1.4%
30	Mississippi	56,968	1.4%
31	Hawaii	56,540	1.4%
32	Arkansas	54,005	1.3%
33	Iowa	53,291	1.3%
34	New Mexico	49,286	1.2%
35	Utah	48,900	1.2%
36	Kansas	43,787	1.0%
37	West Virginia	37,583	0.9%
38	Nebraska	33,662	0.8%
39	Nevada	25,279	0.6%
40	Alaska	24,657	0.6%
41	Delaware	24,254	0.6%
42	Idaho	23,198	0.6%
43	Maine	21,720	0.5%
44	Rhode Island	20,158	0.5%
45	New Hampshire	19,955	0.5%
46	Montana	18,571	0.4%
47	North Dakota	17,754	0.4%
48	Vermont	13,922	0.3%
49	South Dakota	13,201	0.3%
50	Wyoming	12,063	0.3%
	District of Columbia**	NA	NA

Source: U.S. Bureau of the Census, Governments Division
    "2004 State Government Employment and Payroll" (http://www.census.gov/govs/www/apesst04.html)
*As of March 2004.
**Not applicable.

Rate of State Government Full-Time Equivalent Employees in 2004

National Rate = 143 State Government Employees per 10,000 Population*

ALPHA ORDER

RANK ORDER

RANK	STATE	RATE		RANK	STATE	RATE
16	Alabama	189		1	Hawaii	448
2	Alaska	375		2	Alaska	375
46	Arizona	115		3	Delaware	292
12	Arkansas	196		4	North Dakota	279
47	California	110		5	New Mexico	259
36	Colorado	143		6	Wyoming	238
24	Connecticut	168		7	Vermont	224
3	Delaware	292		8	West Virginia	207
49	Florida	105		9	Utah	202
39	Georgia	136		10	Louisiana	201
1	Hawaii	448		11	Montana	200
25	Idaho	166		12	Arkansas	196
49	Illinois	105		12	Mississippi	196
35	Indiana	145		14	Nebraska	193
20	Iowa	180		15	Kentucky	192
28	Kansas	160		16	Alabama	189
15	Kentucky	192		17	Rhode Island	187
10	Louisiana	201		18	Oklahoma	182
26	Maine	165		18	Washington	182
27	Maryland	163		20	Iowa	180
38	Massachusetts	137		20	South Carolina	180
40	Michigan	131		22	New Jersey	172
34	Minnesota	146		23	South Dakota	171
12	Mississippi	196		24	Connecticut	168
31	Missouri	158		25	Idaho	166
11	Montana	200		26	Maine	165
14	Nebraska	193		27	Maryland	163
48	Nevada	108		28	Kansas	160
33	New Hampshire	154		28	Oregon	160
22	New Jersey	172		30	Virginia	159
5	New Mexico	259		31	Missouri	158
42	New York	128		32	North Carolina	155
32	North Carolina	155		33	New Hampshire	154
4	North Dakota	279		34	Minnesota	146
44	Ohio	119		35	Indiana	145
18	Oklahoma	182		36	Colorado	143
28	Oregon	160		37	Tennessee	139
41	Pennsylvania	130		38	Massachusetts	137
17	Rhode Island	187		39	Georgia	136
20	South Carolina	180		40	Michigan	131
23	South Dakota	171		41	Pennsylvania	130
37	Tennessee	139		42	New York	128
44	Texas	119		43	Wisconsin	127
9	Utah	202		44	Ohio	119
7	Vermont	224		44	Texas	119
30	Virginia	159		46	Arizona	115
18	Washington	182		47	California	110
8	West Virginia	207		48	Nevada	108
43	Wisconsin	127		49	Florida	105
6	Wyoming	238		49	Illinois	105
					District of Columbia**	NA

Source: Morgan Quitno Press using data from U.S. Bureau of the Census, Governments Division
    "2004 State Government Employment and Payroll" (http://www.census.gov/govs/www/apesst04.html)
*Full-time equivalent as of March 2004.
**Not applicable.

Average Annual Earnings of Full-Time State Government Employees in 2004

National Average = $46,135*

ALPHA ORDER				RANK ORDER		
RANK	STATE	EARNINGS		RANK	STATE	EARNINGS
27	Alabama	$41,666		1	California	$61,155
12	Alaska	49,790		2	Connecticut	57,185
28	Arizona	41,351		3	New Jersey	55,978
42	Arkansas	37,558		4	New York	53,962
1	California	61,155		5	Minnesota	53,826
6	Colorado	53,367		6	Colorado	53,367
2	Connecticut	57,185		7	Iowa	52,591
20	Delaware	44,315		8	Massachusetts	51,722
32	Florida	40,764		9	Michigan	51,381
35	Georgia	39,994		10	Wisconsin	50,870
29	Hawaii	41,240		11	Rhode Island	50,551
33	Idaho	40,411		12	Alaska	49,790
13	Illinois	49,117		13	Illinois	49,117
34	Indiana	40,265		14	Washington	47,623
7	Iowa	52,591		15	Maryland	46,716
25	Kansas	41,881		16	Ohio	46,682
31	Kentucky	40,811		17	Pennsylvania	46,648
37	Louisiana	39,452		18	Nevada	46,041
22	Maine	42,691		19	Vermont	44,416
15	Maryland	46,716		20	Delaware	44,315
8	Massachusetts	51,722		21	Oregon	43,966
9	Michigan	51,381		22	Maine	42,691
5	Minnesota	53,826		23	Virginia	42,181
47	Mississippi	36,145		24	New Hampshire	41,971
50	Missouri	35,454		25	Kansas	41,881
38	Montana	38,541		26	Texas	41,688
46	Nebraska	36,631		27	Alabama	41,666
18	Nevada	46,041		28	Arizona	41,351
24	New Hampshire	41,971		29	Hawaii	41,240
3	New Jersey	55,978		30	Utah	41,203
48	New Mexico	36,131		31	Kentucky	40,811
4	New York	53,962		32	Florida	40,764
36	North Carolina	39,673		33	Idaho	40,411
41	North Dakota	37,784		34	Indiana	40,265
16	Ohio	46,682		35	Georgia	39,994
43	Oklahoma	37,447		36	North Carolina	39,673
21	Oregon	43,966		37	Louisiana	39,452
17	Pennsylvania	46,648		38	Montana	38,541
11	Rhode Island	50,551		39	South Dakota	38,522
45	South Carolina	36,976		40	Wyoming	38,449
39	South Dakota	38,522		41	North Dakota	37,784
44	Tennessee	37,270		42	Arkansas	37,558
26	Texas	41,688		43	Oklahoma	37,447
30	Utah	41,203		44	Tennessee	37,270
19	Vermont	44,416		45	South Carolina	36,976
23	Virginia	42,181		46	Nebraska	36,631
14	Washington	47,623		47	Mississippi	36,145
49	West Virginia	35,912		48	New Mexico	36,131
10	Wisconsin	50,870		49	West Virginia	35,912
40	Wyoming	38,449		50	Missouri	35,454

District of Columbia**   NA

Source: Morgan Quitno Press using data from U.S. Bureau of the Census, Governments Division
  "2004 State Government Employment and Payroll" (http://www.census.gov/govs/www/apesst04.html)
*March 2004 full-time payroll (multiplied by 12) divided by full-time employees.
**Not applicable.

Local Government Total Revenue in 2002

National Total = $1,083,129,289,000*

ALPHA ORDER

RANK	STATE	REVENUE	% of USA
23	Alabama	$14,528,407,000	1.3%
43	Alaska	2,865,836,000	0.3%
19	Arizona	19,577,677,000	1.8%
36	Arkansas	6,282,481,000	0.6%
1	California	174,135,840,000	16.1%
21	Colorado	17,834,584,000	1.6%
27	Connecticut	11,093,817,000	1.0%
46	Delaware	2,052,474,000	0.2%
4	Florida	60,028,305,000	5.5%
10	Georgia	29,981,862,000	2.8%
49	Hawaii	1,739,130,000	0.2%
39	Idaho	3,839,122,000	0.4%
5	Illinois	46,218,059,000	4.3%
17	Indiana	20,291,207,000	1.9%
28	Iowa	9,743,415,000	0.9%
30	Kansas	9,304,200,000	0.9%
29	Kentucky	9,712,391,000	0.9%
24	Louisiana	13,553,512,000	1.3%
40	Maine	3,622,932,000	0.3%
20	Maryland	17,926,912,000	1.7%
13	Massachusetts	23,427,030,000	2.2%
8	Michigan	36,227,548,000	3.3%
15	Minnesota	21,132,704,000	2.0%
33	Mississippi	7,998,135,000	0.7%
22	Missouri	16,310,154,000	1.5%
45	Montana	2,295,758,000	0.2%
34	Nebraska	7,586,580,000	0.7%
32	Nevada	8,669,627,000	0.8%
41	New Hampshire	3,518,061,000	0.3%
9	New Jersey	32,488,448,000	3.0%
37	New Mexico	5,530,047,000	0.5%
2	New York	108,835,726,000	10.0%
11	North Carolina	27,473,194,000	2.5%
48	North Dakota	1,766,959,000	0.2%
6	Ohio	42,137,842,000	3.9%
31	Oklahoma	9,182,122,000	0.8%
25	Oregon	13,183,449,000	1.2%
7	Pennsylvania	40,613,964,000	3.7%
42	Rhode Island	2,876,539,000	0.3%
26	South Carolina	12,136,093,000	1.1%
47	South Dakota	1,987,339,000	0.2%
18	Tennessee	20,001,089,000	1.8%
3	Texas	71,361,737,000	6.6%
35	Utah	7,462,279,000	0.7%
50	Vermont	1,668,473,000	0.2%
14	Virginia	22,754,847,000	2.1%
12	Washington	26,002,743,000	2.4%
38	West Virginia	3,938,604,000	0.4%
16	Wisconsin	20,375,718,000	1.9%
44	Wyoming	2,502,335,000	0.2%

RANK ORDER

RANK	STATE	REVENUE	% of USA
1	California	$174,135,840,000	16.1%
2	New York	108,835,726,000	10.0%
3	Texas	71,361,737,000	6.6%
4	Florida	60,028,305,000	5.5%
5	Illinois	46,218,059,000	4.3%
6	Ohio	42,137,842,000	3.9%
7	Pennsylvania	40,613,964,000	3.7%
8	Michigan	36,227,548,000	3.3%
9	New Jersey	32,488,448,000	3.0%
10	Georgia	29,981,862,000	2.8%
11	North Carolina	27,473,194,000	2.5%
12	Washington	26,002,743,000	2.4%
13	Massachusetts	23,427,030,000	2.2%
14	Virginia	22,754,847,000	2.1%
15	Minnesota	21,132,704,000	2.0%
16	Wisconsin	20,375,718,000	1.9%
17	Indiana	20,291,207,000	1.9%
18	Tennessee	20,001,089,000	1.8%
19	Arizona	19,577,677,000	1.8%
20	Maryland	17,926,912,000	1.7%
21	Colorado	17,834,584,000	1.6%
22	Missouri	16,310,154,000	1.5%
23	Alabama	14,528,407,000	1.3%
24	Louisiana	13,553,512,000	1.3%
25	Oregon	13,183,449,000	1.2%
26	South Carolina	12,136,093,000	1.1%
27	Connecticut	11,093,817,000	1.0%
28	Iowa	9,743,415,000	0.9%
29	Kentucky	9,712,391,000	0.9%
30	Kansas	9,304,200,000	0.9%
31	Oklahoma	9,182,122,000	0.8%
32	Nevada	8,669,627,000	0.8%
33	Mississippi	7,998,135,000	0.7%
34	Nebraska	7,586,580,000	0.7%
35	Utah	7,462,279,000	0.7%
36	Arkansas	6,282,481,000	0.6%
37	New Mexico	5,530,047,000	0.5%
38	West Virginia	3,938,604,000	0.4%
39	Idaho	3,839,122,000	0.4%
40	Maine	3,622,932,000	0.3%
41	New Hampshire	3,518,061,000	0.3%
42	Rhode Island	2,876,539,000	0.3%
43	Alaska	2,865,836,000	0.3%
44	Wyoming	2,502,335,000	0.2%
45	Montana	2,295,758,000	0.2%
46	Delaware	2,052,474,000	0.2%
47	South Dakota	1,987,339,000	0.2%
48	North Dakota	1,766,959,000	0.2%
49	Hawaii	1,739,130,000	0.2%
50	Vermont	1,668,473,000	0.2%
	District of Columbia	7,351,982,000	0.7%

Source: U.S. Bureau of the Census, Governments Division
"State and Local Government Finances: 2002 Census" (http://www.census.gov/govs/www/estimate02.html)
Total revenue includes all money received from external sources. This includes taxes, intergovernmental transfers and insurance trust revenue and revenue from government owned utilities and other commercial or auxiliary enterprise.

Per Capita Local Government Total Revenue in 2002

National Per Capita = $3,762*

<table>
<tr><td colspan="3">ALPHA ORDER</td><td colspan="3">RANK ORDER</td></tr>
<tr><td>RANK</td><td>STATE</td><td>PER CAPITA</td><td>RANK</td><td>STATE</td><td>PER CAPITA</td></tr>
<tr><td>28</td><td>Alabama</td><td>$3,242</td><td>1</td><td>New York</td><td>$5,683</td></tr>
<tr><td>4</td><td>Alaska</td><td>4,472</td><td>2</td><td>Wyoming</td><td>5,013</td></tr>
<tr><td>17</td><td>Arizona</td><td>3,599</td><td>3</td><td>California</td><td>4,977</td></tr>
<tr><td>48</td><td>Arkansas</td><td>2,320</td><td>4</td><td>Alaska</td><td>4,472</td></tr>
<tr><td>3</td><td>California</td><td>4,977</td><td>5</td><td>Nebraska</td><td>4,394</td></tr>
<tr><td>9</td><td>Colorado</td><td>3,965</td><td>6</td><td>Washington</td><td>4,286</td></tr>
<tr><td>30</td><td>Connecticut</td><td>3,207</td><td>7</td><td>Minnesota</td><td>4,205</td></tr>
<tr><td>45</td><td>Delaware</td><td>2,546</td><td>8</td><td>Nevada</td><td>3,998</td></tr>
<tr><td>17</td><td>Florida</td><td>3,599</td><td>9</td><td>Colorado</td><td>3,965</td></tr>
<tr><td>19</td><td>Georgia</td><td>3,511</td><td>10</td><td>New Jersey</td><td>3,788</td></tr>
<tr><td>50</td><td>Hawaii</td><td>1,409</td><td>11</td><td>Wisconsin</td><td>3,745</td></tr>
<tr><td>36</td><td>Idaho</td><td>2,858</td><td>12</td><td>Oregon</td><td>3,742</td></tr>
<tr><td>14</td><td>Illinois</td><td>3,672</td><td>13</td><td>Ohio</td><td>3,693</td></tr>
<tr><td>24</td><td>Indiana</td><td>3,295</td><td>14</td><td>Illinois</td><td>3,672</td></tr>
<tr><td>22</td><td>Iowa</td><td>3,320</td><td>15</td><td>Massachusetts</td><td>3,653</td></tr>
<tr><td>21</td><td>Kansas</td><td>3,430</td><td>16</td><td>Michigan</td><td>3,607</td></tr>
<tr><td>47</td><td>Kentucky</td><td>2,375</td><td>17</td><td>Arizona</td><td>3,599</td></tr>
<tr><td>32</td><td>Louisiana</td><td>3,027</td><td>17</td><td>Florida</td><td>3,599</td></tr>
<tr><td>37</td><td>Maine</td><td>2,792</td><td>19</td><td>Georgia</td><td>3,511</td></tr>
<tr><td>25</td><td>Maryland</td><td>3,294</td><td>20</td><td>Tennessee</td><td>3,453</td></tr>
<tr><td>15</td><td>Massachusetts</td><td>3,653</td><td>21</td><td>Kansas</td><td>3,430</td></tr>
<tr><td>16</td><td>Michigan</td><td>3,607</td><td>22</td><td>Iowa</td><td>3,320</td></tr>
<tr><td>7</td><td>MInnesota</td><td>4,205</td><td>23</td><td>North Carolina</td><td>3,305</td></tr>
<tr><td>38</td><td>Mississippi</td><td>2,789</td><td>24</td><td>Indiana</td><td>3,295</td></tr>
<tr><td>35</td><td>Missouri</td><td>2,872</td><td>25</td><td>Maryland</td><td>3,294</td></tr>
<tr><td>46</td><td>Montana</td><td>2,521</td><td>25</td><td>Pennsylvania</td><td>3,294</td></tr>
<tr><td>5</td><td>Nebraska</td><td>4,394</td><td>27</td><td>Texas</td><td>3,285</td></tr>
<tr><td>8</td><td>Nevada</td><td>3,998</td><td>28</td><td>Alabama</td><td>3,242</td></tr>
<tr><td>40</td><td>New Hampshire</td><td>2,758</td><td>29</td><td>Utah</td><td>3,217</td></tr>
<tr><td>10</td><td>New Jersey</td><td>3,788</td><td>30</td><td>Connecticut</td><td>3,207</td></tr>
<tr><td>33</td><td>New Mexico</td><td>2,981</td><td>31</td><td>Virginia</td><td>3,128</td></tr>
<tr><td>1</td><td>New York</td><td>5,683</td><td>32</td><td>Louisiana</td><td>3,027</td></tr>
<tr><td>23</td><td>North Carolina</td><td>3,305</td><td>33</td><td>New Mexico</td><td>2,981</td></tr>
<tr><td>39</td><td>North Dakota</td><td>2,788</td><td>34</td><td>South Carolina</td><td>2,956</td></tr>
<tr><td>13</td><td>Ohio</td><td>3,693</td><td>35</td><td>Missouri</td><td>2,872</td></tr>
<tr><td>43</td><td>Oklahoma</td><td>2,632</td><td>36</td><td>Idaho</td><td>2,858</td></tr>
<tr><td>12</td><td>Oregon</td><td>3,742</td><td>37</td><td>Maine</td><td>2,792</td></tr>
<tr><td>25</td><td>Pennsylvania</td><td>3,294</td><td>38</td><td>Mississippi</td><td>2,789</td></tr>
<tr><td>42</td><td>Rhode Island</td><td>2,691</td><td>39</td><td>North Dakota</td><td>2,788</td></tr>
<tr><td>34</td><td>South Carolina</td><td>2,956</td><td>40</td><td>New Hampshire</td><td>2,758</td></tr>
<tr><td>44</td><td>South Dakota</td><td>2,613</td><td>41</td><td>Vermont</td><td>2,706</td></tr>
<tr><td>20</td><td>Tennessee</td><td>3,453</td><td>42</td><td>Rhode Island</td><td>2,691</td></tr>
<tr><td>27</td><td>Texas</td><td>3,285</td><td>43</td><td>Oklahoma</td><td>2,632</td></tr>
<tr><td>29</td><td>Utah</td><td>3,217</td><td>44</td><td>South Dakota</td><td>2,613</td></tr>
<tr><td>41</td><td>Vermont</td><td>2,706</td><td>45</td><td>Delaware</td><td>2,546</td></tr>
<tr><td>31</td><td>Virginia</td><td>3,128</td><td>46</td><td>Montana</td><td>2,521</td></tr>
<tr><td>6</td><td>Washington</td><td>4,286</td><td>47</td><td>Kentucky</td><td>2,375</td></tr>
<tr><td>49</td><td>West Virginia</td><td>2,182</td><td>48</td><td>Arkansas</td><td>2,320</td></tr>
<tr><td>11</td><td>Wisconsin</td><td>3,745</td><td>49</td><td>West Virginia</td><td>2,182</td></tr>
<tr><td>2</td><td>Wyoming</td><td>5,013</td><td>50</td><td>Hawaii</td><td>1,409</td></tr>
<tr><td></td><td></td><td></td><td></td><td>District of Columbia</td><td>13,021</td></tr>
</table>

Source: Morgan Quitno Press using data from U.S. Bureau of the Census, Governments Division
"State and Local Government Finances: 2002 Census" (http://www.census.gov/govs/www/estimate02.html)
*Total revenue includes all money received from external sources. This includes taxes, intergovernmental transfers and insurance trust revenue and revenue from government owned utilities and other commercial or auxiliary enterprise.

Local Government Revenue from the Federal Government in 2002

National Total = $42,952,953,000

<table>
<tr><td colspan="4">ALPHA ORDER</td><td colspan="4">RANK ORDER</td></tr>
<tr><th>RANK</th><th>STATE</th><th>REVENUE</th><th>% of USA</th><th>RANK</th><th>STATE</th><th>REVENUE</th><th>% of USA</th></tr>
<tr><td>23</td><td>Alabama</td><td>$468,396,000</td><td>1.1%</td><td>1</td><td>California</td><td>$7,406,307,000</td><td>17.2%</td></tr>
<tr><td>35</td><td>Alaska</td><td>237,927,000</td><td>0.6%</td><td>2</td><td>New York</td><td>3,988,632,000</td><td>9.3%</td></tr>
<tr><td>11</td><td>Arizona</td><td>843,767,000</td><td>2.0%</td><td>3</td><td>Pennsylvania</td><td>2,340,945,000</td><td>5.5%</td></tr>
<tr><td>36</td><td>Arkansas</td><td>235,303,000</td><td>0.5%</td><td>4</td><td>Illinois</td><td>2,267,759,000</td><td>5.3%</td></tr>
<tr><td>1</td><td>California</td><td>7,406,307,000</td><td>17.2%</td><td>5</td><td>Texas</td><td>2,242,455,000</td><td>5.2%</td></tr>
<tr><td>24</td><td>Colorado</td><td>462,320,000</td><td>1.1%</td><td>6</td><td>Florida</td><td>2,170,757,000</td><td>5.1%</td></tr>
<tr><td>28</td><td>Connecticut</td><td>353,702,000</td><td>0.8%</td><td>7</td><td>Ohio</td><td>1,535,372,000</td><td>3.6%</td></tr>
<tr><td>49</td><td>Delaware</td><td>68,174,000</td><td>0.2%</td><td>8</td><td>Michigan</td><td>1,301,791,000</td><td>3.0%</td></tr>
<tr><td>6</td><td>Florida</td><td>2,170,757,000</td><td>5.1%</td><td>9</td><td>Massachusetts</td><td>1,114,919,000</td><td>2.6%</td></tr>
<tr><td>13</td><td>Georgia</td><td>816,408,000</td><td>1.9%</td><td>10</td><td>Virginia</td><td>857,422,000</td><td>2.0%</td></tr>
<tr><td>38</td><td>Hawaii</td><td>182,564,000</td><td>0.4%</td><td>11</td><td>Arizona</td><td>843,767,000</td><td>2.0%</td></tr>
<tr><td>46</td><td>Idaho</td><td>90,801,000</td><td>0.2%</td><td>12</td><td>Washington</td><td>825,648,000</td><td>1.9%</td></tr>
<tr><td>4</td><td>Illinois</td><td>2,267,759,000</td><td>5.3%</td><td>13</td><td>Georgia</td><td>816,408,000</td><td>1.9%</td></tr>
<tr><td>25</td><td>Indiana</td><td>397,067,000</td><td>0.9%</td><td>14</td><td>Oregon</td><td>812,374,000</td><td>1.9%</td></tr>
<tr><td>32</td><td>Iowa</td><td>305,920,000</td><td>0.7%</td><td>15</td><td>Minnesota</td><td>805,798,000</td><td>1.9%</td></tr>
<tr><td>41</td><td>Kansas</td><td>134,528,000</td><td>0.3%</td><td>16</td><td>North Carolina</td><td>774,670,000</td><td>1.8%</td></tr>
<tr><td>31</td><td>Kentucky</td><td>311,778,000</td><td>0.7%</td><td>17</td><td>New Jersey</td><td>713,715,000</td><td>1.7%</td></tr>
<tr><td>22</td><td>Louisiana</td><td>490,383,000</td><td>1.1%</td><td>18</td><td>Maryland</td><td>667,582,000</td><td>1.6%</td></tr>
<tr><td>47</td><td>Maine</td><td>83,672,000</td><td>0.2%</td><td>19</td><td>Missouri</td><td>635,228,000</td><td>1.5%</td></tr>
<tr><td>18</td><td>Maryland</td><td>667,582,000</td><td>1.6%</td><td>20</td><td>Wisconsin</td><td>542,810,000</td><td>1.3%</td></tr>
<tr><td>9</td><td>Massachusetts</td><td>1,114,919,000</td><td>2.6%</td><td>21</td><td>Tennessee</td><td>526,322,000</td><td>1.2%</td></tr>
<tr><td>8</td><td>Michigan</td><td>1,301,791,000</td><td>3.0%</td><td>22</td><td>Louisiana</td><td>490,383,000</td><td>1.1%</td></tr>
<tr><td>15</td><td>Minnesota</td><td>805,798,000</td><td>1.9%</td><td>23</td><td>Alabama</td><td>468,396,000</td><td>1.1%</td></tr>
<tr><td>34</td><td>Mississippi</td><td>251,080,000</td><td>0.6%</td><td>24</td><td>Colorado</td><td>462,320,000</td><td>1.1%</td></tr>
<tr><td>19</td><td>Missouri</td><td>635,228,000</td><td>1.5%</td><td>25</td><td>Indiana</td><td>397,067,000</td><td>0.9%</td></tr>
<tr><td>39</td><td>Montana</td><td>171,837,000</td><td>0.4%</td><td>26</td><td>Oklahoma</td><td>369,168,000</td><td>0.9%</td></tr>
<tr><td>37</td><td>Nebraska</td><td>193,444,000</td><td>0.5%</td><td>27</td><td>New Mexico</td><td>363,985,000</td><td>0.8%</td></tr>
<tr><td>29</td><td>Nevada</td><td>351,747,000</td><td>0.8%</td><td>28</td><td>Connecticut</td><td>353,702,000</td><td>0.8%</td></tr>
<tr><td>44</td><td>New Hampshire</td><td>107,307,000</td><td>0.2%</td><td>29</td><td>Nevada</td><td>351,747,000</td><td>0.8%</td></tr>
<tr><td>17</td><td>New Jersey</td><td>713,715,000</td><td>1.7%</td><td>30</td><td>Utah</td><td>346,512,000</td><td>0.8%</td></tr>
<tr><td>27</td><td>New Mexico</td><td>363,985,000</td><td>0.8%</td><td>31</td><td>Kentucky</td><td>311,778,000</td><td>0.7%</td></tr>
<tr><td>2</td><td>New York</td><td>3,988,632,000</td><td>9.3%</td><td>32</td><td>Iowa</td><td>305,920,000</td><td>0.7%</td></tr>
<tr><td>16</td><td>North Carolina</td><td>774,670,000</td><td>1.8%</td><td>33</td><td>South Carolina</td><td>304,781,000</td><td>0.7%</td></tr>
<tr><td>42</td><td>North Dakota</td><td>133,845,000</td><td>0.3%</td><td>34</td><td>Mississippi</td><td>251,080,000</td><td>0.6%</td></tr>
<tr><td>7</td><td>Ohio</td><td>1,535,372,000</td><td>3.6%</td><td>35</td><td>Alaska</td><td>237,927,000</td><td>0.6%</td></tr>
<tr><td>26</td><td>Oklahoma</td><td>369,168,000</td><td>0.9%</td><td>36</td><td>Arkansas</td><td>235,303,000</td><td>0.5%</td></tr>
<tr><td>14</td><td>Oregon</td><td>812,374,000</td><td>1.9%</td><td>37</td><td>Nebraska</td><td>193,444,000</td><td>0.5%</td></tr>
<tr><td>3</td><td>Pennsylvania</td><td>2,340,945,000</td><td>5.5%</td><td>38</td><td>Hawaii</td><td>182,564,000</td><td>0.4%</td></tr>
<tr><td>43</td><td>Rhode Island</td><td>128,929,000</td><td>0.3%</td><td>39</td><td>Montana</td><td>171,837,000</td><td>0.4%</td></tr>
<tr><td>33</td><td>South Carolina</td><td>304,781,000</td><td>0.7%</td><td>40</td><td>West Virginia</td><td>151,770,000</td><td>0.4%</td></tr>
<tr><td>45</td><td>South Dakota</td><td>104,908,000</td><td>0.2%</td><td>41</td><td>Kansas</td><td>134,528,000</td><td>0.3%</td></tr>
<tr><td>21</td><td>Tennessee</td><td>526,322,000</td><td>1.2%</td><td>42</td><td>North Dakota</td><td>133,845,000</td><td>0.3%</td></tr>
<tr><td>5</td><td>Texas</td><td>2,242,455,000</td><td>5.2%</td><td>43</td><td>Rhode Island</td><td>128,929,000</td><td>0.3%</td></tr>
<tr><td>30</td><td>Utah</td><td>346,512,000</td><td>0.8%</td><td>44</td><td>New Hampshire</td><td>107,307,000</td><td>0.2%</td></tr>
<tr><td>50</td><td>Vermont</td><td>46,094,000</td><td>0.1%</td><td>45</td><td>South Dakota</td><td>104,908,000</td><td>0.2%</td></tr>
<tr><td>10</td><td>Virginia</td><td>857,422,000</td><td>2.0%</td><td>46</td><td>Idaho</td><td>90,801,000</td><td>0.2%</td></tr>
<tr><td>12</td><td>Washington</td><td>825,648,000</td><td>1.9%</td><td>47</td><td>Maine</td><td>83,672,000</td><td>0.2%</td></tr>
<tr><td>40</td><td>West Virginia</td><td>151,770,000</td><td>0.4%</td><td>48</td><td>Wyoming</td><td>74,236,000</td><td>0.2%</td></tr>
<tr><td>20</td><td>Wisconsin</td><td>542,810,000</td><td>1.3%</td><td>49</td><td>Delaware</td><td>68,174,000</td><td>0.2%</td></tr>
<tr><td>48</td><td>Wyoming</td><td>74,236,000</td><td>0.2%</td><td>50</td><td>Vermont</td><td>46,094,000</td><td>0.1%</td></tr>
<tr><td></td><td></td><td></td><td></td><td></td><td>District of Columbia</td><td>2,840,094,000</td><td>6.6%</td></tr>
</table>

Source: U.S. Bureau of the Census, Governments Division
"State and Local Government Finances: 2002 Census" (http://www.census.gov/govs/www/estimate02.html)

Per Capita Local Government Revenue from the Federal Government in 2002

National Per Capita = $149

ALPHA ORDER

RANK	STATE	PER CAPITA
29	Alabama	$105
1	Alaska	371
13	Arizona	155
39	Arkansas	87
3	California	212
31	Colorado	103
33	Connecticut	102
40	Delaware	85
20	Florida	130
35	Georgia	96
16	Hawaii	148
47	Idaho	68
9	Illinois	180
48	Indiana	64
30	Iowa	104
50	Kansas	50
44	Kentucky	76
27	Louisiana	110
48	Maine	64
22	Maryland	123
10	Massachusetts	174
20	Michigan	130
12	Minnesota	160
38	Mississippi	88
25	Missouri	112
8	Montana	189
25	Nebraska	112
11	Nevada	162
41	New Hampshire	84
43	New Jersey	83
6	New Mexico	196
5	New York	208
36	North Carolina	93
4	North Dakota	211
19	Ohio	135
28	Oklahoma	106
2	Oregon	231
7	Pennsylvania	190
23	Rhode Island	121
46	South Carolina	74
17	South Dakota	138
37	Tennessee	91
31	Texas	103
14	Utah	149
45	Vermont	75
24	Virginia	118
18	Washington	136
41	West Virginia	84
34	Wisconsin	100
14	Wyoming	149

RANK ORDER

RANK	STATE	PER CAPITA
1	Alaska	$371
2	Oregon	231
3	California	212
4	North Dakota	211
5	New York	208
6	New Mexico	196
7	Pennsylvania	190
8	Montana	189
9	Illinois	180
10	Massachusetts	174
11	Nevada	162
12	Minnesota	160
13	Arizona	155
14	Utah	149
14	Wyoming	149
16	Hawaii	148
17	South Dakota	138
18	Washington	136
19	Ohio	135
20	Florida	130
20	Michigan	130
22	Maryland	123
23	Rhode Island	121
24	Virginia	118
25	Missouri	112
25	Nebraska	112
27	Louisiana	110
28	Oklahoma	106
29	Alabama	105
30	Iowa	104
31	Colorado	103
31	Texas	103
33	Connecticut	102
34	Wisconsin	100
35	Georgia	96
36	North Carolina	93
37	Tennessee	91
38	Mississippi	88
39	Arkansas	87
40	Delaware	85
41	New Hampshire	84
41	West Virginia	84
43	New Jersey	83
44	Kentucky	76
45	Vermont	75
46	South Carolina	74
47	Idaho	68
48	Indiana	64
48	Maine	64
50	Kansas	50

District of Columbia	5,030

Source: Morgan Quitno Press using data from U.S. Bureau of the Census, Governments Division
"State and Local Government Finances: 2002 Census" (http://www.census.gov/govs/www/estimate02.html)

Local Government Own Source Revenue in 2002

National Total = $597,359,026,000*

ALPHA ORDER

RANK	STATE	REVENUE	% of USA
24	Alabama	$7,766,941,000	1.3%
43	Alaska	1,553,499,000	0.3%
22	Arizona	9,204,534,000	1.5%
36	Arkansas	2,510,189,000	0.4%
1	California	80,774,173,000	13.5%
17	Colorado	11,763,511,000	2.0%
25	Connecticut	7,153,250,000	1.2%
49	Delaware	929,807,000	0.2%
4	Florida	37,852,976,000	6.3%
9	Georgia	17,498,894,000	2.9%
47	Hawaii	1,205,888,000	0.2%
38	Idaho	2,159,682,000	0.4%
5	Illinois	27,476,964,000	4.6%
14	Indiana	12,097,291,000	2.0%
28	Iowa	5,664,348,000	0.9%
29	Kansas	5,349,760,000	0.9%
30	Kentucky	5,128,532,000	0.9%
23	Louisiana	7,952,593,000	1.3%
37	Maine	2,406,261,000	0.4%
15	Maryland	11,935,202,000	2.0%
16	Massachusetts	11,780,598,000	2.0%
10	Michigan	16,019,366,000	2.7%
18	Minnesota	10,622,483,000	1.8%
33	Mississippi	4,158,391,000	0.7%
20	Missouri	9,898,104,000	1.7%
45	Montana	1,237,301,000	0.2%
34	Nebraska	3,683,534,000	0.6%
32	Nevada	4,955,774,000	0.8%
40	New Hampshire	2,108,625,000	0.4%
8	New Jersey	21,086,619,000	3.5%
39	New Mexico	2,120,722,000	0.4%
2	New York	64,188,511,000	10.7%
11	North Carolina	14,153,243,000	2.4%
48	North Dakota	1,012,587,000	0.2%
6	Ohio	24,126,655,000	4.0%
31	Oklahoma	5,007,411,000	0.8%
27	Oregon	6,593,163,000	1.1%
7	Pennsylvania	23,124,362,000	3.9%
42	Rhode Island	1,754,401,000	0.3%
26	South Carolina	6,864,467,000	1.1%
46	South Dakota	1,210,750,000	0.2%
21	Tennessee	9,576,098,000	1.6%
3	Texas	45,417,533,000	7.6%
35	Utah	3,541,807,000	0.6%
50	Vermont	627,952,000	0.1%
12	Virginia	13,479,767,000	2.3%
13	Washington	12,876,698,000	2.2%
41	West Virginia	1,958,659,000	0.3%
19	Wisconsin	10,256,485,000	1.7%
44	Wyoming	1,450,423,000	0.2%

RANK ORDER

RANK	STATE	REVENUE	% of USA
1	California	$80,774,173,000	13.5%
2	New York	64,188,511,000	10.7%
3	Texas	45,417,533,000	7.6%
4	Florida	37,852,976,000	6.3%
5	Illinois	27,476,964,000	4.6%
6	Ohio	24,126,655,000	4.0%
7	Pennsylvania	23,124,362,000	3.9%
8	New Jersey	21,086,619,000	3.5%
9	Georgia	17,498,894,000	2.9%
10	Michigan	16,019,366,000	2.7%
11	North Carolina	14,153,243,000	2.4%
12	Virginia	13,479,767,000	2.3%
13	Washington	12,876,698,000	2.2%
14	Indiana	12,097,291,000	2.0%
15	Maryland	11,935,202,000	2.0%
16	Massachusetts	11,780,598,000	2.0%
17	Colorado	11,763,511,000	2.0%
18	Minnesota	10,622,483,000	1.8%
19	Wisconsin	10,256,485,000	1.7%
20	Missouri	9,898,104,000	1.7%
21	Tennessee	9,576,098,000	1.6%
22	Arizona	9,204,534,000	1.5%
23	Louisiana	7,952,593,000	1.3%
24	Alabama	7,766,941,000	1.3%
25	Connecticut	7,153,250,000	1.2%
26	South Carolina	6,864,467,000	1.1%
27	Oregon	6,593,163,000	1.1%
28	Iowa	5,664,348,000	0.9%
29	Kansas	5,349,760,000	0.9%
30	Kentucky	5,128,532,000	0.9%
31	Oklahoma	5,007,411,000	0.8%
32	Nevada	4,955,774,000	0.8%
33	Mississippi	4,158,391,000	0.7%
34	Nebraska	3,683,534,000	0.6%
35	Utah	3,541,807,000	0.6%
36	Arkansas	2,510,189,000	0.4%
37	Maine	2,406,261,000	0.4%
38	Idaho	2,159,682,000	0.4%
39	New Mexico	2,120,722,000	0.4%
40	New Hampshire	2,108,625,000	0.4%
41	West Virginia	1,958,659,000	0.3%
42	Rhode Island	1,754,401,000	0.3%
43	Alaska	1,553,499,000	0.3%
44	Wyoming	1,450,423,000	0.2%
45	Montana	1,237,301,000	0.2%
46	South Dakota	1,210,750,000	0.2%
47	Hawaii	1,205,888,000	0.2%
48	North Dakota	1,012,587,000	0.2%
49	Delaware	929,807,000	0.2%
50	Vermont	627,952,000	0.1%
	District of Columbia	4,082,242,000	0.7%

Source: U.S. Bureau of the Census, Governments Division
   "State and Local Government Finances: 2002 Census" (http://www.census.gov/govs/www/estimate02.html)
*Own source revenue includes taxes, current charges and miscellaneous general revenue. Excluded are intergovernmental transfers, insurance trust revenue and revenue from government owned utilities and other commercial or auxiliary enterprise.

Per Capita Local Government Own Source Revenue in 2002

National Per Capita = $2,075*

<table>
<tr><td colspan="3">ALPHA ORDER</td><td colspan="3">RANK ORDER</td></tr>
<tr><td>RANK</td><td>STATE</td><td>PER CAPITA</td><td>RANK</td><td>STATE</td><td>PER CAPITA</td></tr>
<tr><td>29</td><td>Alabama</td><td>$1,733</td><td>1</td><td>New York</td><td>$3,352</td></tr>
<tr><td>5</td><td>Alaska</td><td>2,424</td><td>2</td><td>Wyoming</td><td>2,906</td></tr>
<tr><td>31</td><td>Arizona</td><td>1,692</td><td>3</td><td>Colorado</td><td>2,615</td></tr>
<tr><td>50</td><td>Arkansas</td><td>927</td><td>4</td><td>New Jersey</td><td>2,458</td></tr>
<tr><td>6</td><td>California</td><td>2,309</td><td>5</td><td>Alaska</td><td>2,424</td></tr>
<tr><td>3</td><td>Colorado</td><td>2,615</td><td>6</td><td>California</td><td>2,309</td></tr>
<tr><td>16</td><td>Connecticut</td><td>2,068</td><td>7</td><td>Nevada</td><td>2,286</td></tr>
<tr><td>45</td><td>Delaware</td><td>1,153</td><td>8</td><td>Florida</td><td>2,269</td></tr>
<tr><td>8</td><td>Florida</td><td>2,269</td><td>9</td><td>Maryland</td><td>2,193</td></tr>
<tr><td>17</td><td>Georgia</td><td>2,049</td><td>10</td><td>Illinois</td><td>2,183</td></tr>
<tr><td>49</td><td>Hawaii</td><td>977</td><td>11</td><td>Nebraska</td><td>2,134</td></tr>
<tr><td>36</td><td>Idaho</td><td>1,608</td><td>12</td><td>Washington</td><td>2,122</td></tr>
<tr><td>10</td><td>Illinois</td><td>2,183</td><td>13</td><td>Minnesota</td><td>2,114</td></tr>
<tr><td>19</td><td>Indiana</td><td>1,964</td><td>13</td><td>Ohio</td><td>2,114</td></tr>
<tr><td>20</td><td>Iowa</td><td>1,930</td><td>15</td><td>Texas</td><td>2,091</td></tr>
<tr><td>18</td><td>Kansas</td><td>1,972</td><td>16</td><td>Connecticut</td><td>2,068</td></tr>
<tr><td>44</td><td>Kentucky</td><td>1,254</td><td>17</td><td>Georgia</td><td>2,049</td></tr>
<tr><td>27</td><td>Louisiana</td><td>1,776</td><td>18</td><td>Kansas</td><td>1,972</td></tr>
<tr><td>24</td><td>Maine</td><td>1,854</td><td>19</td><td>Indiana</td><td>1,964</td></tr>
<tr><td>9</td><td>Maryland</td><td>2,193</td><td>20</td><td>Iowa</td><td>1,930</td></tr>
<tr><td>26</td><td>Massachusetts</td><td>1,837</td><td>21</td><td>Wisconsin</td><td>1,885</td></tr>
<tr><td>38</td><td>Michigan</td><td>1,595</td><td>22</td><td>Pennsylvania</td><td>1,876</td></tr>
<tr><td>13</td><td>Minnesota</td><td>2,114</td><td>23</td><td>Oregon</td><td>1,871</td></tr>
<tr><td>41</td><td>Mississippi</td><td>1,450</td><td>24</td><td>Maine</td><td>1,854</td></tr>
<tr><td>28</td><td>Missouri</td><td>1,743</td><td>25</td><td>Virginia</td><td>1,853</td></tr>
<tr><td>43</td><td>Montana</td><td>1,359</td><td>26</td><td>Massachusetts</td><td>1,837</td></tr>
<tr><td>11</td><td>Nebraska</td><td>2,134</td><td>27</td><td>Louisiana</td><td>1,776</td></tr>
<tr><td>7</td><td>Nevada</td><td>2,286</td><td>28</td><td>Missouri</td><td>1,743</td></tr>
<tr><td>33</td><td>New Hampshire</td><td>1,653</td><td>29</td><td>Alabama</td><td>1,733</td></tr>
<tr><td>4</td><td>New Jersey</td><td>2,458</td><td>30</td><td>North Carolina</td><td>1,703</td></tr>
<tr><td>46</td><td>New Mexico</td><td>1,143</td><td>31</td><td>Arizona</td><td>1,692</td></tr>
<tr><td>1</td><td>New York</td><td>3,352</td><td>32</td><td>South Carolina</td><td>1,672</td></tr>
<tr><td>30</td><td>North Carolina</td><td>1,703</td><td>33</td><td>New Hampshire</td><td>1,653</td></tr>
<tr><td>37</td><td>North Dakota</td><td>1,598</td><td>33</td><td>Tennessee</td><td>1,653</td></tr>
<tr><td>13</td><td>Ohio</td><td>2,114</td><td>35</td><td>Rhode Island</td><td>1,641</td></tr>
<tr><td>42</td><td>Oklahoma</td><td>1,436</td><td>36</td><td>Idaho</td><td>1,608</td></tr>
<tr><td>23</td><td>Oregon</td><td>1,871</td><td>37</td><td>North Dakota</td><td>1,598</td></tr>
<tr><td>22</td><td>Pennsylvania</td><td>1,876</td><td>38</td><td>Michigan</td><td>1,595</td></tr>
<tr><td>35</td><td>Rhode Island</td><td>1,641</td><td>39</td><td>South Dakota</td><td>1,592</td></tr>
<tr><td>32</td><td>South Carolina</td><td>1,672</td><td>40</td><td>Utah</td><td>1,527</td></tr>
<tr><td>39</td><td>South Dakota</td><td>1,592</td><td>41</td><td>Mississippi</td><td>1,450</td></tr>
<tr><td>33</td><td>Tennessee</td><td>1,653</td><td>42</td><td>Oklahoma</td><td>1,436</td></tr>
<tr><td>15</td><td>Texas</td><td>2,091</td><td>43</td><td>Montana</td><td>1,359</td></tr>
<tr><td>40</td><td>Utah</td><td>1,527</td><td>44</td><td>Kentucky</td><td>1,254</td></tr>
<tr><td>48</td><td>Vermont</td><td>1,019</td><td>45</td><td>Delaware</td><td>1,153</td></tr>
<tr><td>25</td><td>Virginia</td><td>1,853</td><td>46</td><td>New Mexico</td><td>1,143</td></tr>
<tr><td>12</td><td>Washington</td><td>2,122</td><td>47</td><td>West Virginia</td><td>1,085</td></tr>
<tr><td>47</td><td>West Virginia</td><td>1,085</td><td>48</td><td>Vermont</td><td>1,019</td></tr>
<tr><td>21</td><td>Wisconsin</td><td>1,885</td><td>49</td><td>Hawaii</td><td>977</td></tr>
<tr><td>2</td><td>Wyoming</td><td>2,906</td><td>50</td><td>Arkansas</td><td>927</td></tr>
<tr><td></td><td></td><td></td><td></td><td>District of Columbia</td><td>7,230</td></tr>
</table>

Source: Morgan Quitno Press using data from U.S. Bureau of the Census, Governments Division
    "State and Local Government Finances: 2002 Census" (http://www.census.gov/govs/www/estimate02.html)
*Own source revenue includes taxes, current charges and miscellaneous general revenue. Excluded are intergovernmental transfers, insurance trust revenue and revenue from government owned utilities and other commercial or auxiliary enterprise.

Local Government Tax Revenue in 2002

National Total = $369,730,209,000

ALPHA ORDER

RANK ORDER

RANK	STATE	TAX REVENUE	% of USA		RANK	STATE	TAX REVENUE	% of USA
28	Alabama	$3,209,062,000	0.9%		1	New York	$45,615,975,000	12.3%
43	Alaska	980,404,000	0.3%		2	California	42,668,690,000	11.5%
21	Arizona	5,943,001,000	1.6%		3	Texas	30,318,113,000	8.2%
40	Arkansas	1,234,805,000	0.3%		4	Florida	19,488,212,000	5.3%
2	California	42,668,690,000	11.5%		5	Illinois	19,094,806,000	5.2%
15	Colorado	6,976,853,000	1.9%		6	New Jersey	16,299,990,000	4.4%
20	Connecticut	6,092,141,000	1.6%		7	Ohio	16,034,775,000	4.3%
49	Delaware	513,498,000	0.1%		8	Pennsylvania	15,491,083,000	4.2%
4	Florida	19,488,212,000	5.3%		9	Georgia	10,286,233,000	2.8%
9	Georgia	10,286,233,000	2.8%		10	Virginia	9,350,097,000	2.5%
45	Hawaii	818,886,000	0.2%		11	Massachusetts	9,072,844,000	2.5%
42	Idaho	1,020,020,000	0.3%		12	Maryland	9,053,005,000	2.4%
5	Illinois	19,094,806,000	5.2%		13	Michigan	8,780,132,000	2.4%
18	Indiana	6,786,047,000	1.8%		14	North Carolina	7,039,053,000	1.9%
27	Iowa	3,324,163,000	0.9%		15	Colorado	6,976,853,000	1.9%
29	Kansas	3,166,614,000	0.9%		16	Washington	6,884,936,000	1.9%
30	Kentucky	2,806,067,000	0.8%		17	Wisconsin	6,796,085,000	1.8%
24	Louisiana	4,825,129,000	1.3%		18	Indiana	6,786,047,000	1.8%
35	Maine	1,914,316,000	0.5%		19	Missouri	6,394,500,000	1.7%
12	Maryland	9,053,005,000	2.4%		20	Connecticut	6,092,141,000	1.6%
11	Massachusetts	9,072,844,000	2.5%		21	Arizona	5,943,001,000	1.6%
13	Michigan	8,780,132,000	2.4%		22	Minnesota	5,232,373,000	1.4%
22	Minnesota	5,232,373,000	1.4%		23	Tennessee	5,176,087,000	1.4%
36	Mississippi	1,794,817,000	0.5%		24	Louisiana	4,825,129,000	1.3%
19	Missouri	6,394,500,000	1.7%		25	Oregon	3,839,550,000	1.0%
47	Montana	692,451,000	0.2%		26	South Carolina	3,663,909,000	1.0%
33	Nebraska	2,323,819,000	0.6%		27	Iowa	3,324,163,000	0.9%
32	Nevada	2,487,235,000	0.7%		28	Alabama	3,209,062,000	0.9%
37	New Hampshire	1,701,841,000	0.5%		29	Kansas	3,166,614,000	0.9%
6	New Jersey	16,299,990,000	4.4%		30	Kentucky	2,806,067,000	0.8%
39	New Mexico	1,249,559,000	0.3%		31	Oklahoma	2,729,209,000	0.7%
1	New York	45,615,975,000	12.3%		32	Nevada	2,487,235,000	0.7%
14	North Carolina	7,039,053,000	1.9%		33	Nebraska	2,323,819,000	0.6%
48	North Dakota	611,456,000	0.2%		34	Utah	2,100,760,000	0.6%
7	Ohio	16,034,775,000	4.3%		35	Maine	1,914,316,000	0.5%
31	Oklahoma	2,729,209,000	0.7%		36	Mississippi	1,794,817,000	0.5%
25	Oregon	3,839,550,000	1.0%		37	New Hampshire	1,701,841,000	0.5%
8	Pennsylvania	15,491,083,000	4.2%		38	Rhode Island	1,494,635,000	0.4%
38	Rhode Island	1,494,635,000	0.4%		39	New Mexico	1,249,559,000	0.3%
26	South Carolina	3,663,909,000	1.0%		40	Arkansas	1,234,805,000	0.3%
44	South Dakota	864,852,000	0.2%		41	West Virginia	1,089,593,000	0.3%
23	Tennessee	5,176,087,000	1.4%		42	Idaho	1,020,020,000	0.3%
3	Texas	30,318,113,000	8.2%		43	Alaska	980,404,000	0.3%
34	Utah	2,100,760,000	0.6%		44	South Dakota	864,852,000	0.2%
50	Vermont	446,653,000	0.1%		45	Hawaii	818,886,000	0.2%
10	Virginia	9,350,097,000	2.5%		46	Wyoming	723,966,000	0.2%
16	Washington	6,884,936,000	1.9%		47	Montana	692,451,000	0.2%
41	West Virginia	1,089,593,000	0.3%		48	North Dakota	611,456,000	0.2%
17	Wisconsin	6,796,085,000	1.8%		49	Delaware	513,498,000	0.1%
46	Wyoming	723,966,000	0.2%		50	Vermont	446,653,000	0.1%
						District of Columbia	3,227,909,000	0.9%

Source: U.S. Bureau of the Census, Governments Division
   "State and Local Government Finances: 2002 Census" (http://www.census.gov/govs/www/estimate02.html)

Per Capita Local Government Tax Revenue in 2002

National Per Capita = $1,284

ALPHA ORDER

RANK ORDER

RANK	STATE	PER CAPITA		RANK	STATE	PER CAPITA
43	Alabama	$716		1	New York	$2,382
6	Alaska	1,530		2	New Jersey	1,900
29	Arizona	1,093		3	Connecticut	1,761
50	Arkansas	456		4	Maryland	1,664
19	California	1,220		5	Colorado	1,551
5	Colorado	1,551		6	Alaska	1,530
3	Connecticut	1,761		7	Illinois	1,517
47	Delaware	637		8	Maine	1,475
21	Florida	1,168		9	Wyoming	1,450
20	Georgia	1,205		10	Massachusetts	1,415
46	Hawaii	663		11	Ohio	1,405
41	Idaho	759		12	Rhode Island	1,398
7	Illinois	1,517		13	Texas	1,396
28	Indiana	1,102		14	Nebraska	1,346
26	Iowa	1,133		15	New Hampshire	1,334
22	Kansas	1,167		16	Virginia	1,285
44	Kentucky	686		17	Pennsylvania	1,257
31	Louisiana	1,078		18	Wisconsin	1,249
8	Maine	1,475		19	California	1,220
4	Maryland	1,664		20	Georgia	1,205
10	Massachusetts	1,415		21	Florida	1,168
37	Michigan	874		22	Kansas	1,167
32	Minnesota	1,041		23	Nevada	1,147
48	Mississippi	626		24	South Dakota	1,137
27	Missouri	1,126		25	Washington	1,135
40	Montana	760		26	Iowa	1,133
14	Nebraska	1,346		27	Missouri	1,126
23	Nevada	1,147		28	Indiana	1,102
15	New Hampshire	1,334		29	Arizona	1,093
2	New Jersey	1,900		30	Oregon	1,090
45	New Mexico	674		31	Louisiana	1,078
1	New York	2,382		32	Minnesota	1,041
38	North Carolina	847		33	North Dakota	965
33	North Dakota	965		34	Utah	906
11	Ohio	1,405		35	Tennessee	894
39	Oklahoma	782		36	South Carolina	892
30	Oregon	1,090		37	Michigan	874
17	Pennsylvania	1,257		38	North Carolina	847
12	Rhode Island	1,398		39	Oklahoma	782
36	South Carolina	892		40	Montana	760
24	South Dakota	1,137		41	Idaho	759
35	Tennessee	894		42	Vermont	724
13	Texas	1,396		43	Alabama	716
34	Utah	906		44	Kentucky	686
42	Vermont	724		45	New Mexico	674
16	Virginia	1,285		46	Hawaii	663
25	Washington	1,135		47	Delaware	637
49	West Virginia	604		48	Mississippi	626
18	Wisconsin	1,249		49	West Virginia	604
9	Wyoming	1,450		50	Arkansas	456

District of Columbia 5,717

Source: Morgan Quitno Press using data from U.S. Bureau of the Census, Governments Division
"State and Local Government Finances: 2002 Census" (http://www.census.gov/govs/www/estimate02.html)

Local Government Total Expenditures in 2002

National Total = $1,140,082,069,000*

ALPHA ORDER

RANK	STATE	EXPENDITURES	% of USA
23	Alabama	$14,642,380,000	1.3%
42	Alaska	3,050,573,000	0.3%
19	Arizona	20,404,462,000	1.8%
36	Arkansas	6,122,574,000	0.5%
1	California	181,511,530,000	15.9%
20	Colorado	19,362,907,000	1.7%
27	Connecticut	11,210,683,000	1.0%
46	Delaware	2,126,564,000	0.2%
4	Florida	61,756,340,000	5.4%
10	Georgia	30,960,277,000	2.7%
47	Hawaii	2,077,196,000	0.2%
39	Idaho	3,742,959,000	0.3%
5	Illinois	51,383,691,000	4.5%
18	Indiana	20,687,497,000	1.8%
29	Iowa	9,928,398,000	0.9%
31	Kansas	9,098,054,000	0.8%
28	Kentucky	9,994,903,000	0.9%
25	Louisiana	13,523,445,000	1.2%
41	Maine	3,386,270,000	0.3%
21	Maryland	17,681,972,000	1.6%
13	Massachusetts	25,035,153,000	2.2%
8	Michigan	39,488,545,000	3.5%
15	Minnesota	22,200,217,000	1.9%
33	Mississippi	8,000,042,000	0.7%
22	Missouri	17,266,374,000	1.5%
45	Montana	2,261,591,000	0.2%
34	Nebraska	7,769,254,000	0.7%
32	Nevada	9,054,599,000	0.8%
40	New Hampshire	3,492,652,000	0.3%
9	New Jersey	31,825,746,000	2.8%
37	New Mexico	5,397,453,000	0.5%
2	New York	123,857,251,000	10.9%
11	North Carolina	28,576,966,000	2.5%
49	North Dakota	1,765,565,000	0.2%
7	Ohio	42,720,325,000	3.7%
30	Oklahoma	9,384,439,000	0.8%
24	Oregon	13,916,029,000	1.2%
6	Pennsylvania	43,526,538,000	3.8%
43	Rhode Island	2,893,638,000	0.3%
26	South Carolina	12,373,778,000	1.1%
48	South Dakota	2,011,049,000	0.2%
17	Tennessee	21,127,555,000	1.9%
3	Texas	77,107,740,000	6.8%
35	Utah	7,598,760,000	0.7%
50	Vermont	1,615,701,000	0.1%
14	Virginia	24,033,271,000	2.1%
12	Washington	26,875,362,000	2.4%
38	West Virginia	3,980,177,000	0.3%
16	Wisconsin	22,076,842,000	1.9%
44	Wyoming	2,364,659,000	0.2%

RANK ORDER

RANK	STATE	EXPENDITURES	% of USA
1	California	$181,511,530,000	15.9%
2	New York	123,857,251,000	10.9%
3	Texas	77,107,740,000	6.8%
4	Florida	61,756,340,000	5.4%
5	Illinois	51,383,691,000	4.5%
6	Pennsylvania	43,526,538,000	3.8%
7	Ohio	42,720,325,000	3.7%
8	Michigan	39,488,545,000	3.5%
9	New Jersey	31,825,746,000	2.8%
10	Georgia	30,960,277,000	2.7%
11	North Carolina	28,576,966,000	2.5%
12	Washington	26,875,362,000	2.4%
13	Massachusetts	25,035,153,000	2.2%
14	Virginia	24,033,271,000	2.1%
15	Minnesota	22,200,217,000	1.9%
16	Wisconsin	22,076,842,000	1.9%
17	Tennessee	21,127,555,000	1.9%
18	Indiana	20,687,497,000	1.8%
19	Arizona	20,404,462,000	1.8%
20	Colorado	19,362,907,000	1.7%
21	Maryland	17,681,972,000	1.6%
22	Missouri	17,266,374,000	1.5%
23	Alabama	14,642,380,000	1.3%
24	Oregon	13,916,029,000	1.2%
25	Louisiana	13,523,445,000	1.2%
26	South Carolina	12,373,778,000	1.1%
27	Connecticut	11,210,683,000	1.0%
28	Kentucky	9,994,903,000	0.9%
29	Iowa	9,928,398,000	0.9%
30	Oklahoma	9,384,439,000	0.8%
31	Kansas	9,098,054,000	0.8%
32	Nevada	9,054,500,000	0.8%
33	Mississippi	8,000,042,000	0.7%
34	Nebraska	7,769,254,000	0.7%
35	Utah	7,598,760,000	0.7%
36	Arkansas	6,122,574,000	0.5%
37	New Mexico	5,397,453,000	0.5%
38	West Virginia	3,980,177,000	0.3%
39	Idaho	3,742,959,000	0.3%
40	New Hampshire	3,492,652,000	0.3%
41	Maine	3,386,270,000	0.3%
42	Alaska	3,050,573,000	0.3%
43	Rhode Island	2,893,638,000	0.3%
44	Wyoming	2,364,659,000	0.2%
45	Montana	2,261,591,000	0.2%
46	Delaware	2,126,564,000	0.2%
47	Hawaii	2,077,196,000	0.2%
48	South Dakota	2,011,049,000	0.2%
49	North Dakota	1,765,565,000	0.2%
50	Vermont	1,615,701,000	0.1%
	District of Columbia	7,832,123,000	0.7%

Source: U.S. Bureau of the Census, Governments Division
    "State and Local Government Finances: 2002 Census" (http://www.census.gov/govs/www/estimate02.html)
*Total expenditures includes all money paid other than for retirement of debt and extension of loans. Includes payments from all sources of funds including current revenues and proceeds from borrowing and prior year fund balances. Includes intergovernmental transfers and expenditures for government owned utilities and other commercial or auxiliary enterprise and insurance trust expenditures.

Per Capita Local Government Total Expenditures in 2002

National Per Capita = $3,959*

ALPHA ORDER				RANK ORDER		
RANK	STATE	PER CAPITA		RANK	STATE	PER CAPITA
29	Alabama	$3,268		1	New York	$6,467
3	Alaska	4,760		2	California	5,188
15	Arizona	3,751		3	Alaska	4,760
48	Arkansas	2,261		4	Wyoming	4,737
2	California	5,188		5	Nebraska	4,500
8	Colorado	4,305		6	Washington	4,430
31	Connecticut	3,241		7	Minnesota	4,418
43	Delaware	2,638		8	Colorado	4,305
18	Florida	3,702		9	Nevada	4,176
20	Georgia	3,625		10	Illinois	4,083
50	Hawaii	1,683		11	Wisconsin	4,058
37	Idaho	2,787		12	Oregon	3,950
10	Illinois	4,083		13	Michigan	3,932
25	Indiana	3,359		14	Massachusetts	3,904
24	Iowa	3,383		15	Arizona	3,751
26	Kansas	3,354		16	Ohio	3,744
47	Kentucky	2,444		17	New Jersey	3,710
33	Louisiana	3,021		18	Florida	3,702
45	Maine	2,609		19	Tennessee	3,648
30	Maryland	3,249		20	Georgia	3,625
14	Massachusetts	3,904		21	Texas	3,550
13	Michigan	3,932		22	Pennsylvania	3,531
7	Minnesota	4,418		23	North Carolina	3,438
36	Mississippi	2,790		24	Iowa	3,383
32	Missouri	3,040		25	Indiana	3,359
46	Montana	2,483		26	Kansas	3,354
5	Nebraska	4,500		27	Virginia	3,304
9	Nevada	4,176		28	Utah	3,276
39	New Hampshire	2,738		29	Alabama	3,268
17	New Jersey	3,710		30	Maryland	3,249
35	New Mexico	2,909		31	Connecticut	3,241
1	New York	6,467		32	Missouri	3,040
23	North Carolina	3,438		33	Louisiana	3,021
38	North Dakota	2,786		34	South Carolina	3,014
16	Ohio	3,744		35	New Mexico	2,909
41	Oklahoma	2,690		36	Mississippi	2,790
12	Oregon	3,950		37	Idaho	2,787
22	Pennsylvania	3,531		38	North Dakota	2,786
40	Rhode Island	2,707		39	New Hampshire	2,738
34	South Carolina	3,014		40	Rhode Island	2,707
42	South Dakota	2,645		41	Oklahoma	2,690
19	Tennessee	3,648		42	South Dakota	2,645
21	Texas	3,550		43	Delaware	2,638
28	Utah	3,276		44	Vermont	2,621
44	Vermont	2,621		45	Maine	2,609
27	Virginia	3,304		46	Montana	2,483
6	Washington	4,430		47	Kentucky	2,444
49	West Virginia	2,205		48	Arkansas	2,261
11	Wisconsin	4,058		49	West Virginia	2,205
4	Wyoming	4,737		50	Hawaii	1,683
					District of Columbia	13,871

Source: Morgan Quitno Press using data from U.S. Bureau of the Census, Governments Division
   "State and Local Government Finances: 2002 Census" (http://www.census.gov/govs/www/estimate02.html)
*Total expenditures includes all money paid other than for retirement of debt and extension of loans. Includes payments from all sources of funds including current revenues and proceeds from borrowing and prior year fund balances. Includes intergovernmental transfers and expenditures for government owned utilities and other commercial or auxiliary enterprise and insurance trust expenditures.

Local Government Direct General Expenditures in 2002

National Total = $986,370,919,000*

ALPHA ORDER

ALPHA ORDER

RANK	STATE	EXPENDITURES	% of USA
23	Alabama	$12,540,038,000	1.3%
42	Alaska	2,796,578,000	0.3%
20	Arizona	15,974,835,000	1.6%
35	Arkansas	5,505,043,000	0.6%
1	California	152,078,631,000	15.4%
18	Colorado	16,732,366,000	1.7%
27	Connecticut	10,397,442,000	1.1%
46	Delaware	1,946,439,000	0.2%
4	Florida	53,848,715,000	5.5%
10	Georgia	26,429,788,000	2.7%
48	Hawaii	1,736,240,000	0.2%
39	Idaho	3,586,097,000	0.4%
5	Illinois	44,231,361,000	4.5%
17	Indiana	18,768,549,000	1.9%
28	Iowa	9,077,403,000	0.9%
31	Kansas	8,229,856,000	0.8%
29	Kentucky	8,774,868,000	0.9%
24	Louisiana	12,326,574,000	1.2%
41	Maine	3,287,482,000	0.3%
19	Maryland	16,327,459,000	1.7%
15	Massachusetts	20,160,018,000	2.0%
8	Michigan	35,962,585,000	3.6%
16	Minnesota	19,726,596,000	2.0%
33	Mississippi	7,378,991,000	0.7%
21	Missouri	15,410,183,000	1.6%
45	Montana	2,176,855,000	0.2%
36	Nebraska	5,346,223,000	0.5%
32	Nevada	7,957,046,000	0.8%
40	New Hampshire	3,344,970,000	0.3%
9	New Jersey	30,771,819,000	3.1%
37	New Mexico	4,990,816,000	0.5%
2	New York	103,583,043,000	10.5%
11	North Carolina	24,453,456,000	2.5%
49	North Dakota	1,658,990,000	0.2%
6	Ohio	39,737,123,000	4.0%
30	Oklahoma	8,627,262,000	0.9%
25	Oregon	12,318,327,000	1.2%
7	Pennsylvania	38,951,905,000	3.9%
43	Rhode Island	2,662,827,000	0.3%
26	South Carolina	11,012,645,000	1.1%
47	South Dakota	1,836,811,000	0.2%
22	Tennessee	14,941,037,000	1.5%
3	Texas	66,513,791,000	6.7%
34	Utah	5,888,987,000	0.6%
50	Vermont	1,432,844,000	0.1%
12	Virginia	22,090,390,000	2.2%
14	Washington	20,291,758,000	2.1%
38	West Virginia	3,741,515,000	0.4%
13	Wisconsin	20,407,603,000	2.1%
44	Wyoming	2,219,126,000	0.2%

RANK ORDER

RANK	STATE	EXPENDITURES	% of USA
1	California	$152,078,631,000	15.4%
2	New York	103,583,043,000	10.5%
3	Texas	66,513,791,000	6.7%
4	Florida	53,848,715,000	5.5%
5	Illinois	44,231,361,000	4.5%
6	Ohio	39,737,123,000	4.0%
7	Pennsylvania	38,951,905,000	3.9%
8	Michigan	35,962,585,000	3.6%
9	New Jersey	30,771,819,000	3.1%
10	Georgia	26,429,788,000	2.7%
11	North Carolina	24,453,456,000	2.5%
12	Virginia	22,090,390,000	2.2%
13	Wisconsin	20,407,603,000	2.1%
14	Washington	20,291,758,000	2.1%
15	Massachusetts	20,160,018,000	2.0%
16	Minnesota	19,726,596,000	2.0%
17	Indiana	18,768,549,000	1.9%
18	Colorado	16,732,366,000	1.7%
19	Maryland	16,327,459,000	1.7%
20	Arizona	15,974,835,000	1.6%
21	Missouri	15,410,183,000	1.6%
22	Tennessee	14,941,037,000	1.5%
23	Alabama	12,540,038,000	1.3%
24	Louisiana	12,326,574,000	1.2%
25	Oregon	12,318,327,000	1.2%
26	South Carolina	11,012,645,000	1.1%
27	Connecticut	10,397,442,000	1.1%
28	Iowa	9,077,403,000	0.9%
29	Kentucky	8,774,868,000	0.9%
30	Oklahoma	8,627,262,000	0.9%
31	Kansas	8,229,856,000	0.8%
32	Nevada	7,957,046,000	0.8%
33	Mississippi	7,378,991,000	0.7%
34	Utah	5,888,987,000	0.6%
35	Arkansas	5,505,043,000	0.6%
36	Nebraska	5,346,223,000	0.5%
37	New Mexico	4,990,816,000	0.5%
38	West Virginia	3,741,515,000	0.4%
39	Idaho	3,586,097,000	0.4%
40	New Hampshire	3,344,970,000	0.3%
41	Maine	3,287,482,000	0.3%
42	Alaska	2,796,578,000	0.3%
43	Rhode Island	2,662,827,000	0.3%
44	Wyoming	2,219,126,000	0.2%
45	Montana	2,176,855,000	0.2%
46	Delaware	1,946,439,000	0.2%
47	South Dakota	1,836,811,000	0.2%
48	Hawaii	1,736,240,000	0.2%
49	North Dakota	1,658,990,000	0.2%
50	Vermont	1,432,844,000	0.1%
	District of Columbia	6,179,613,000	0.6%

Source: U.S. Bureau of the Census, Governments Division
"State and Local Government Finances: 2002 Census" (http://www.census.gov/govs/www/estimate02.html)
*Direct general expenditures include expenditures for current operations, assistance and subsidies, interest on debt and capital outlay. Excludes intergovernmental transfers, expenditures for government owned utilities and other commercial or auxiliary enterprise and insurance trust expenditures.

Per Capita Local Government Direct General Expenditures in 2002

National Per Capita = $3,426*

ALPHA ORDER			RANK ORDER		
RANK	STATE	PER CAPITA	RANK	STATE	PER CAPITA
29	Alabama	$2,798	1	New York	$5,409
3	Alaska	4,364	2	Wyoming	4,445
28	Arizona	2,937	3	Alaska	4,364
49	Arkansas	2,033	4	California	4,347
4	California	4,347	5	Minnesota	3,926
7	Colorado	3,720	6	Wisconsin	3,751
25	Connecticut	3,006	7	Colorado	3,720
43	Delaware	2,415	8	Nevada	3,670
15	Florida	3,228	9	New Jersey	3,588
19	Georgia	3,095	10	Michigan	3,581
50	Hawaii	1,406	11	Illinois	3,515
34	Idaho	2,670	12	Oregon	3,496
11	Illinois	3,515	13	Ohio	3,483
22	Indiana	3,048	14	Washington	3,345
20	Iowa	3,093	15	Florida	3,228
24	Kansas	3,034	16	Pennsylvania	3,160
47	Kentucky	2,145	17	Massachusetts	3,144
30	Louisiana	2,753	18	Nebraska	3,097
40	Maine	2,533	19	Georgia	3,095
26	Maryland	3,001	20	Iowa	3,093
17	Massachusetts	3,144	21	Texas	3,062
10	Michigan	3,581	22	Indiana	3,048
5	Minnesota	3,926	23	Virginia	3,037
38	Mississippi	2,573	24	Kansas	3,034
31	Missouri	2,713	25	Connecticut	3,006
45	Montana	2,390	26	Maryland	3,001
18	Nebraska	3,097	27	North Carolina	2,942
8	Nevada	3,670	28	Arizona	2,937
35	New Hampshire	2,622	29	Alabama	2,798
9	New Jersey	3,588	30	Louisiana	2,753
32	New Mexico	2,690	31	Missouri	2,713
1	New York	5,409	32	New Mexico	2,690
27	North Carolina	2,942	33	South Carolina	2,682
36	North Dakota	2,618	34	Idaho	2,670
13	Ohio	3,483	35	New Hampshire	2,622
42	Oklahoma	2,473	36	North Dakota	2,618
12	Oregon	3,496	37	Tennessee	2,579
16	Pennsylvania	3,160	38	Mississippi	2,573
41	Rhode Island	2,491	39	Utah	2,539
33	South Carolina	2,682	40	Maine	2,533
43	South Dakota	2,415	41	Rhode Island	2,491
37	Tennessee	2,579	42	Oklahoma	2,473
21	Texas	3,062	43	Delaware	2,415
39	Utah	2,539	43	South Dakota	2,415
46	Vermont	2,324	45	Montana	2,390
23	Virginia	3,037	46	Vermont	2,324
14	Washington	3,345	47	Kentucky	2,145
48	West Virginia	2,073	48	West Virginia	2,073
6	Wisconsin	3,751	49	Arkansas	2,033
2	Wyoming	4,445	50	Hawaii	1,406

District of Columbia   10,944

Source: Morgan Quitno Press using data from U.S. Bureau of the Census, Governments Division
   "State and Local Government Finances: 2002 Census" (http://www.census.gov/govs/www/estimate02.html)
*Direct general expenditures include expenditures for current operations, assistance and subsidies, interest on debt and capital outlay. Excludes intergovernmental transfers, expenditures for government owned utilities and other commercial or auxiliary enterprise and insurance trust expenditures.

Local Government Debt Outstanding in 2002

National Total = $1,043,904,090,000*

ALPHA ORDER

RANK	STATE	DEBT	% of USA
24	Alabama	$12,651,831,000	1.2%
39	Alaska	3,337,621,000	0.3%
14	Arizona	22,258,843,000	2.1%
35	Arkansas	5,751,659,000	0.6%
1	California	138,036,602,000	13.2%
16	Colorado	21,299,122,000	2.0%
31	Connecticut	6,983,652,000	0.7%
43	Delaware	1,494,267,000	0.1%
4	Florida	70,010,245,000	6.7%
10	Georgia	26,057,766,000	2.5%
40	Hawaii	2,791,939,000	0.3%
45	Idaho	1,440,447,000	0.1%
6	Illinois	46,175,609,000	4.4%
21	Indiana	14,614,998,000	1.4%
33	Iowa	5,781,408,000	0.6%
29	Kansas	10,024,660,000	1.0%
18	Kentucky	19,954,998,000	1.9%
26	Louisiana	11,752,840,000	1.1%
41	Maine	2,024,883,000	0.2%
22	Maryland	13,354,398,000	1.3%
17	Massachusetts	20,106,252,000	1.9%
7	Michigan	32,247,783,000	3.1%
11	Minnesota	25,601,836,000	2.5%
34	Mississippi	5,773,746,000	0.6%
27	Missouri	11,551,697,000	1.1%
47	Montana	1,210,984,000	0.1%
36	Nebraska	5,690,799,000	0.5%
25	Nevada	12,105,157,000	1.2%
42	New Hampshire	1,824,741,000	0.2%
12	New Jersey	25,497,303,000	2.4%
37	New Mexico	4,109,904,000	0.4%
2	New York	107,338,897,000	10.3%
13	North Carolina	22,332,254,000	2.1%
46	North Dakota	1,231,883,000	0.1%
9	Ohio	31,335,000,000	3.0%
32	Oklahoma	6,031,032,000	0.6%
28	Oregon	11,159,367,000	1.1%
5	Pennsylvania	62,826,518,000	6.0%
44	Rhode Island	1,489,112,000	0.1%
23	South Carolina	12,756,903,000	1.2%
48	South Dakota	1,143,217,000	0.1%
19	Tennessee	17,500,115,000	1.7%
3	Texas	98,801,444,000	9.5%
30	Utah	8,520,440,000	0.8%
50	Vermont	743,968,000	0.1%
15	Virginia	21,637,063,000	2.1%
8	Washington	32,008,374,000	3.1%
38	West Virginia	3,547,252,000	0.3%
20	Wisconsin	15,457,196,000	1.5%
49	Wyoming	1,089,978,000	0.1%

RANK ORDER

RANK	STATE	DEBT	% of USA
1	California	$138,036,602,000	13.2%
2	New York	107,338,897,000	10.3%
3	Texas	98,801,444,000	9.5%
4	Florida	70,010,245,000	6.7%
5	Pennsylvania	62,826,518,000	6.0%
6	Illinois	46,175,609,000	4.4%
7	Michigan	32,247,783,000	3.1%
8	Washington	32,008,374,000	3.1%
9	Ohio	31,335,000,000	3.0%
10	Georgia	26,057,766,000	2.5%
11	Minnesota	25,601,836,000	2.5%
12	New Jersey	25,497,303,000	2.4%
13	North Carolina	22,332,254,000	2.1%
14	Arizona	22,258,843,000	2.1%
15	Virginia	21,637,063,000	2.1%
16	Colorado	21,299,122,000	2.0%
17	Massachusetts	20,106,252,000	1.9%
18	Kentucky	19,954,998,000	1.9%
19	Tennessee	17,500,115,000	1.7%
20	Wisconsin	15,457,196,000	1.5%
21	Indiana	14,614,998,000	1.4%
22	Maryland	13,354,398,000	1.3%
23	South Carolina	12,756,903,000	1.2%
24	Alabama	12,651,831,000	1.2%
25	Nevada	12,105,157,000	1.2%
26	Louisiana	11,752,840,000	1.1%
27	Missouri	11,551,697,000	1.1%
28	Oregon	11,159,367,000	1.1%
29	Kansas	10,024,660,000	1.0%
30	Utah	8,520,440,000	0.8%
31	Connecticut	6,983,652,000	0.7%
32	Oklahoma	6,031,032,000	0.6%
33	Iowa	5,781,408,000	0.6%
34	Mississippi	5,773,746,000	0.6%
35	Arkansas	5,751,659,000	0.6%
36	Nebraska	5,690,799,000	0.5%
37	New Mexico	4,109,904,000	0.4%
38	West Virginia	3,547,252,000	0.3%
39	Alaska	3,337,621,000	0.3%
40	Hawaii	2,791,939,000	0.3%
41	Maine	2,024,883,000	0.2%
42	New Hampshire	1,824,741,000	0.2%
43	Delaware	1,494,267,000	0.1%
44	Rhode Island	1,489,112,000	0.1%
45	Idaho	1,440,447,000	0.1%
46	North Dakota	1,231,883,000	0.1%
47	Montana	1,210,984,000	0.1%
48	South Dakota	1,143,217,000	0.1%
49	Wyoming	1,089,978,000	0.1%
50	Vermont	743,968,000	0.1%
	District of Columbia	5,436,087,000	0.5%

Source: U.S. Bureau of the Census, Governments Division
   "State and Local Government Finances: 2002 Census" (http://www.census.gov/govs/www/estimate02.html)
*Includes short-term, long-term, full faith and credit, nonguaranteed and public debt for private purposes.

Per Capita Local Government Debt Outstanding in 2002

National Per Capita = $3,625*

ALPHA ORDER

RANK	STATE	PER CAPITA
26	Alabama	$2,823
4	Alaska	5,208
11	Arizona	4,092
35	Arkansas	2,124
12	California	3,945
8	Colorado	4,735
37	Connecticut	2,019
42	Delaware	1,854
10	Florida	4,197
21	Georgia	3,051
32	Hawaii	2,262
50	Idaho	1,072
15	Illinois	3,669
31	Indiana	2,373
39	Iowa	1,970
13	Kansas	3,695
7	Kentucky	4,879
29	Louisiana	2,625
44	Maine	1,560
30	Maryland	2,454
19	Massachusetts	3,135
17	Michigan	3,211
6	Minnesota	5,095
38	Mississippi	2,013
36	Missouri	2,034
48	Montana	1,330
16	Nebraska	3,296
2	Nevada	5,583
46	New Hampshire	1,430
24	New Jersey	2,973
33	New Mexico	2,215
1	New York	5,605
28	North Carolina	2,687
41	North Dakota	1,944
27	Ohio	2,746
43	Oklahoma	1,729
18	Oregon	3,167
5	Pennsylvania	5,096
47	Rhode Island	1,393
20	South Carolina	3,107
45	South Dakota	1,503
22	Tennessee	3,021
9	Texas	4,548
14	Utah	3,673
49	Vermont	1,207
23	Virginia	2,975
3	Washington	5,276
40	West Virginia	1,965
25	Wisconsin	2,841
34	Wyoming	2,183

RANK ORDER

RANK	STATE	PER CAPITA
1	New York	$5,605
2	Nevada	5,583
3	Washington	5,276
4	Alaska	5,208
5	Pennsylvania	5,096
6	Minnesota	5,095
7	Kentucky	4,879
8	Colorado	4,735
9	Texas	4,548
10	Florida	4,197
11	Arizona	4,092
12	California	3,945
13	Kansas	3,695
14	Utah	3,673
15	Illinois	3,669
16	Nebraska	3,296
17	Michigan	3,211
18	Oregon	3,167
19	Massachusetts	3,135
20	South Carolina	3,107
21	Georgia	3,051
22	Tennessee	3,021
23	Virginia	2,975
24	New Jersey	2,973
25	Wisconsin	2,841
26	Alabama	2,823
27	Ohio	2,746
28	North Carolina	2,687
29	Louisiana	2,625
30	Maryland	2,454
31	Indiana	2,373
32	Hawaii	2,262
33	New Mexico	2,215
34	Wyoming	2,183
35	Arkansas	2,124
36	Missouri	2,034
37	Connecticut	2,019
38	Mississippi	2,013
39	Iowa	1,970
40	West Virginia	1,965
41	North Dakota	1,944
42	Delaware	1,854
43	Oklahoma	1,729
44	Maine	1,560
45	South Dakota	1,503
46	New Hampshire	1,430
47	Rhode Island	1,393
48	Montana	1,330
49	Vermont	1,207
50	Idaho	1,072
	District of Columbia	9,627

Source: Morgan Quitno Press using data from U.S. Bureau of the Census, Governments Division
"State and Local Government Finances: 2002 Census" (http://www.census.gov/govs/www/estimate02.html)
*Includes short-term, long-term, full faith and credit, nonguaranteed and public debt for private purposes.

Local Government Full-Time Equivalent Employees in 2004

National Total = 11,601,136 FTE Employees*

ALPHA ORDER

RANK	STATE	EMPLOYEES	% of USA
23	Alabama	184,985	1.6%
46	Alaska	26,184	0.2%
19	Arizona	204,693	1.8%
33	Arkansas	97,933	0.8%
1	California	1,383,075	11.9%
24	Colorado	182,752	1.6%
31	Connecticut	122,969	1.1%
48	Delaware	23,625	0.2%
4	Florida	641,072	5.5%
8	Georgia	378,779	3.3%
50	Hawaii	14,392	0.1%
40	Idaho	55,112	0.5%
5	Illinois	502,088	4.3%
13	Indiana	239,177	2.1%
30	Iowa	131,261	1.1%
28	Kansas	135,759	1.2%
26	Kentucky	157,736	1.4%
21	Louisiana	191,711	1.7%
39	Maine	55,335	0.5%
22	Maryland	191,680	1.7%
15	Massachusetts	235,016	2.0%
9	Michigan	371,447	3.2%
20	Minnesota	200,524	1.7%
29	Mississippi	131,401	1.1%
16	Missouri	220,476	1.9%
42	Montana	35,701	0.3%
34	Nebraska	81,105	0.7%
37	Nevada	71,097	0.6%
41	New Hampshire	48,529	0.4%
10	New Jersey	345,815	3.0%
36	New Mexico	75,356	0.6%
3	New York	938,009	8.1%
11	North Carolina	321,830	2.8%
49	North Dakota	23,130	0.2%
6	Ohio	487,185	4.2%
27	Oklahoma	136,845	1.2%
32	Oregon	122,394	1.1%
7	Pennsylvania	409,290	3.5%
44	Rhode Island	30,363	0.3%
25	South Carolina	167,401	1.4%
45	South Dakota	30,348	0.3%
14	Tennessee	235,609	2.0%
2	Texas	1,002,992	8.6%
35	Utah	78,695	0.7%
47	Vermont	24,227	0.2%
12	Virginia	291,568	2.5%
18	Washington	210,253	1.8%
38	West Virginia	60,649	0.5%
17	Wisconsin	217,422	1.9%
43	Wyoming	31,470	0.3%

RANK ORDER

RANK	STATE	EMPLOYEES	% of USA
1	California	1,383,075	11.9%
2	Texas	1,002,992	8.6%
3	New York	938,009	8.1%
4	Florida	641,072	5.5%
5	Illinois	502,088	4.3%
6	Ohio	487,185	4.2%
7	Pennsylvania	409,290	3.5%
8	Georgia	378,779	3.3%
9	Michigan	371,447	3.2%
10	New Jersey	345,815	3.0%
11	North Carolina	321,830	2.8%
12	Virginia	291,568	2.5%
13	Indiana	239,177	2.1%
14	Tennessee	235,609	2.0%
15	Massachusetts	235,016	2.0%
16	Missouri	220,476	1.9%
17	Wisconsin	217,422	1.9%
18	Washington	210,253	1.8%
19	Arizona	204,693	1.8%
20	Minnesota	200,524	1.7%
21	Louisiana	191,711	1.7%
22	Maryland	191,680	1.7%
23	Alabama	184,985	1.6%
24	Colorado	182,752	1.6%
25	South Carolina	167,401	1.4%
26	Kentucky	157,736	1.4%
27	Oklahoma	136,845	1.2%
28	Kansas	135,759	1.2%
29	Mississippi	131,401	1.1%
30	Iowa	131,261	1.1%
31	Connecticut	122,969	1.1%
32	Oregon	122,394	1.1%
33	Arkansas	97,933	0.8%
34	Nebraska	81,105	0.7%
35	Utah	78,695	0.7%
36	New Mexico	75,356	0.6%
37	Nevada	71,097	0.6%
38	West Virginia	60,649	0.5%
39	Maine	55,335	0.5%
40	Idaho	55,112	0.5%
41	New Hampshire	48,529	0.4%
42	Montana	35,701	0.3%
43	Wyoming	31,470	0.3%
44	Rhode Island	30,363	0.3%
45	South Dakota	30,348	0.3%
46	Alaska	26,184	0.2%
47	Vermont	24,227	0.2%
48	Delaware	23,625	0.2%
49	North Dakota	23,130	0.2%
50	Hawaii	14,392	0.1%
	District of Columbia	44,671	0.4%

Source: U.S. Bureau of the Census, Governments Division
    "Local Government Employment and Payroll - March 2004" (http://www.census.gov/govs/www/apesloc04.html)
*As of March 2004.

Rate of Local Government Full-Time Equivalent Employees in 2004

National Rate = 395 Local Government Employees per 10,000 Population*

ALPHA ORDER

RANK	STATE	RATE
12	Alabama	409
15	Alaska	398
38	Arizona	357
39	Arkansas	356
27	California	386
17	Colorado	397
40	Connecticut	351
48	Delaware	285
34	Florida	369
8	Georgia	425
50	Hawaii	114
19	Idaho	395
19	Illinois	395
29	Indiana	384
7	Iowa	445
2	Kansas	497
31	Kentucky	381
8	Louisiana	425
11	Maine	421
41	Maryland	345
36	Massachusetts	367
35	Michigan	368
23	Minnesota	393
5	Mississippi	453
30	Missouri	383
28	Montana	385
4	Nebraska	464
47	Nevada	305
33	New Hampshire	374
15	New Jersey	398
18	New Mexico	396
3	New York	487
32	North Carolina	377
37	North Dakota	364
8	Ohio	425
26	Oklahoma	388
42	Oregon	341
45	Pennsylvania	330
49	Rhode Island	281
14	South Carolina	399
22	South Dakota	394
13	Tennessee	400
6	Texas	446
46	Utah	325
24	Vermont	390
24	Virginia	390
43	Washington	339
44	West Virginia	335
19	Wisconsin	395
1	Wyoming	622

RANK ORDER

RANK	STATE	RATE
1	Wyoming	622
2	Kansas	497
3	New York	487
4	Nebraska	464
5	Mississippi	453
6	Texas	446
7	Iowa	445
8	Georgia	425
8	Louisiana	425
8	Ohio	425
11	Maine	421
12	Alabama	409
13	Tennessee	400
14	South Carolina	399
15	Alaska	398
15	New Jersey	398
17	Colorado	397
18	New Mexico	396
19	Idaho	395
19	Illinois	395
19	Wisconsin	395
22	South Dakota	394
23	Minnesota	393
24	Vermont	390
24	Virginia	390
26	Oklahoma	388
27	California	386
28	Montana	385
29	Indiana	384
30	Missouri	383
31	Kentucky	381
32	North Carolina	377
33	New Hampshire	374
34	Florida	369
35	Michigan	368
36	Massachusetts	367
37	North Dakota	364
38	Arizona	357
39	Arkansas	356
40	Connecticut	351
41	Maryland	345
42	Oregon	341
43	Washington	339
44	West Virginia	335
45	Pennsylvania	330
46	Utah	325
47	Nevada	305
48	Delaware	285
49	Rhode Island	281
50	Hawaii	114
	District of Columbia	806

Source: Morgan Quitno Press using data from U.S. Bureau of the Census, Governments Division
    "Local Government Employment and Payroll - March 2004" (http://www.census.gov/govs/www/apesloc04.html)
*Full-time equivalent as of March 2004.

Average Annual Earnings of Full-Time Local Government Employees in 2004

National Average = $43,249*

ALPHA ORDER

RANK	STATE	EARNINGS
42	Alabama	$33,015
8	Alaska	49,300
20	Arizona	42,184
49	Arkansas	29,807
1	California	57,642
17	Colorado	43,550
5	Connecticut	51,314
18	Delaware	43,400
22	Florida	40,369
33	Georgia	35,538
12	Hawaii	45,830
38	Idaho	34,350
13	Illinois	45,452
28	Indiana	37,182
34	Iowa	35,399
37	Kansas	34,615
43	Kentucky	32,788
47	Louisiana	30,456
40	Maine	33,870
9	Maryland	48,752
10	Massachusetts	48,241
11	Michigan	46,492
15	Minnesota	44,399
50	Mississippi	29,651
35	Missouri	35,022
44	Montana	32,628
25	Nebraska	38,353
7	Nevada	49,728
26	New Hampshire	38,110
2	New Jersey	54,324
45	New Mexico	32,587
3	New York	53,407
30	North Carolina	36,987
24	North Dakota	38,949
21	Ohio	41,473
48	Oklahoma	30,219
16	Oregon	44,047
14	Pennsylvania	45,010
6	Rhode Island	50,307
39	South Carolina	34,245
46	South Dakota	32,349
36	Tennessee	34,755
32	Texas	35,578
27	Utah	37,431
31	Vermont	35,881
23	Virginia	39,057
4	Washington	52,855
41	West Virginia	33,152
19	Wisconsin	42,909
29	Wyoming	37,129

RANK ORDER

RANK	STATE	EARNINGS
1	California	$57,642
2	New Jersey	54,324
3	New York	53,407
4	Washington	52,855
5	Connecticut	51,314
6	Rhode Island	50,307
7	Nevada	49,728
8	Alaska	49,300
9	Maryland	48,752
10	Massachusetts	48,241
11	Michigan	46,492
12	Hawaii	45,830
13	Illinois	45,452
14	Pennsylvania	45,010
15	Minnesota	44,399
16	Oregon	44,047
17	Colorado	43,550
18	Delaware	43,400
19	Wisconsin	42,909
20	Arizona	42,184
21	Ohio	41,473
22	Florida	40,369
23	Virginia	39,057
24	North Dakota	38,949
25	Nebraska	38,353
26	New Hampshire	38,110
27	Utah	37,431
28	Indiana	37,182
29	Wyoming	37,129
30	North Carolina	36,987
31	Vermont	35,881
32	Texas	35,578
33	Georgia	35,538
34	Iowa	35,399
35	Missouri	35,022
36	Tennessee	34,755
37	Kansas	34,615
38	Idaho	34,350
39	South Carolina	34,245
40	Maine	33,870
41	West Virginia	33,152
42	Alabama	33,015
43	Kentucky	32,788
44	Montana	32,628
45	New Mexico	32,587
46	South Dakota	32,349
47	Louisiana	30,456
48	Oklahoma	30,219
49	Arkansas	29,807
50	Mississippi	29,651

District of Columbia 56,782

Source: Morgan Quitno Press using data from U.S. Bureau of the Census, Governments Division
   "Local Government Employment and Payroll - March 2004" (http://www.census.gov/govs/www/apesloc04.html)
*March 2004 full-time payroll (multiplied by 12) divided by full-time employees.

XI. HEALTH

Average Medical Malpractice Payment in 2004

National Average = $298,460*

RANK	STATE	AVERAGE PAYMENT
15	Alabama	$346,279
48	Alaska	151,524
18	Arizona	324,558
27	Arkansas	295,465
45	California	185,746
21	Colorado	314,268
4	Connecticut	449,296
5	Delaware	430,490
35	Florida**	241,204
22	Georgia	312,392
3	Hawaii	457,755
17	Idaho	332,220
1	Illinois	516,529
31	Indiana**	274,316
2	Iowa	481,776
46	Kansas**	175,247
42	Kentucky	219,604
49	Louisiana**	139,746
9	Maine	385,403
14	Maryland	349,697
8	Massachusetts	401,886
50	Michigan	137,484
25	Minnesota	305,483
19	Mississippi	323,567
23	Missouri	311,882
32	Montana	272,637
43	Nebraska**	206,885
28	Nevada	291,095
20	New Hampshire	317,647
11	New Jersey	368,672
44	New Mexico**	200,046
7	New York	404,762
12	North Carolina	366,447
6	North Dakota	416,080
26	Ohio	304,287
38	Oklahoma	235,197
24	Oregon	310,527
16	Pennsylvania**	337,579
10	Rhode Island	370,834
36	South Carolina**	239,055
41	South Dakota	223,723
34	Tennessee	244,408
37	Texas	237,989
47	Utah	154,452
40	Vermont	225,570
30	Virginia	283,567
29	Washington	288,207
33	West Virginia	255,506
13	Wisconsin**	365,662
39	Wyoming	225,865

RANK	STATE	AVERAGE PAYMENT
1	Illinois	$516,529
2	Iowa	481,776
3	Hawaii	457,755
4	Connecticut	449,296
5	Delaware	430,490
6	North Dakota	416,080
7	New York	404,762
8	Massachusetts	401,886
9	Maine	385,403
10	Rhode Island	370,834
11	New Jersey	368,672
12	North Carolina	366,447
13	Wisconsin**	365,662
14	Maryland	349,697
15	Alabama	346,279
16	Pennsylvania**	337,579
17	Idaho	332,220
18	Arizona	324,558
19	Mississippi	323,567
20	New Hampshire	317,647
21	Colorado	314,268
22	Georgia	312,392
23	Missouri	311,882
24	Oregon	310,527
25	Minnesota	305,483
26	Ohio	304,287
27	Arkansas	295,465
28	Nevada	291,095
29	Washington	288,207
30	Virginia	283,567
31	Indiana**	274,316
32	Montana	272,637
33	West Virginia	255,506
34	Tennessee	244,408
35	Florida**	241,204
36	South Carolina**	239,055
37	Texas	237,989
38	Oklahoma	235,197
39	Wyoming	225,865
40	Vermont	225,570
41	South Dakota	223,723
42	Kentucky	219,604
43	Nebraska**	206,885
44	New Mexico**	200,046
45	California	185,746
46	Kansas**	175,247
47	Utah	154,452
48	Alaska	151,524
49	Louisiana**	139,746
50	Michigan	137,484
	District of Columbia	408,865

Source: U.S. Department of Health and Human Services, Bureau of Health Professions
"National Practitioner Data Bank, 2004 Annual Report" (http://www.npdb-hipdb.com/annualrpt.html)
*National figure includes U.S. territories and U.S. Armed Forces locations overseas.
**The figures for these states have not been adjusted for payments by state compensation funds and other similar funds. Average payments for these states understate the actual average amounts received by claimants.

Average Annual Single Coverage Health Insurance Premium per Enrolled Employee in 2003
National Average = $3,481*

ALPHA ORDER

RANK	STATE	PREMIUM
47	Alabama	$3,156
1	Alaska	4,011
46	Arizona	3,209
48	Arkansas	3,127
43	California	3,293
13	Colorado	3,645
11	Connecticut	3,676
2	Delaware	3,854
17	Florida	3,592
14	Georgia	3,624
49	Hawaii	3,020
38	Idaho	3,331
9	Illinois	3,692
25	Indiana	3,493
45	Iowa	3,270
31	Kansas	3,401
27	Kentucky	3,437
40	Louisiana	3,317
3	Maine	3,852
28	Maryland	3,427
24	Massachusetts	3,496
12	Michigan	3,671
10	Minnesota	3,679
41	Mississippi	3,305
41	Missouri	3,305
22	Montana	3,506
22	Nebraska	3,506
19	Nevada	3,578
20	New Hampshire	3,563
4	New Jersey	3,814
35	New Mexico	3,361
17	New York	3,592
30	North Carolina	3,411
50	North Dakota	2,999
29	Ohio	3,416
44	Oklahoma	3,285
34	Oregon	3,362
26	Pennsylvania	3,449
7	Rhode Island	3,725
33	South Carolina	3,371
35	South Dakota	3,361
15	Tennessee	3,597
32	Texas	3,400
37	Utah	3,352
16	Vermont	3,596
39	Virginia	3,322
21	Washington	3,520
5	West Virginia	3,809
6	Wisconsin	3,749
8	Wyoming	3,706

RANK ORDER

RANK	STATE	PREMIUM
1	Alaska	$4,011
2	Delaware	3,854
3	Maine	3,852
4	New Jersey	3,814
5	West Virginia	3,809
6	Wisconsin	3,749
7	Rhode Island	3,725
8	Wyoming	3,706
9	Illinois	3,692
10	Minnesota	3,679
11	Connecticut	3,676
12	Michigan	3,671
13	Colorado	3,645
14	Georgia	3,624
15	Tennessee	3,597
16	Vermont	3,596
17	Florida	3,592
17	New York	3,592
19	Nevada	3,578
20	New Hampshire	3,563
21	Washington	3,520
22	Montana	3,506
22	Nebraska	3,506
24	Massachusetts	3,496
25	Indiana	3,493
26	Pennsylvania	3,449
27	Kentucky	3,437
28	Maryland	3,427
29	Ohio	3,416
30	North Carolina	3,411
31	Kansas	3,401
32	Texas	3,400
33	South Carolina	3,371
34	Oregon	3,362
35	New Mexico	3,361
35	South Dakota	3,361
37	Utah	3,352
38	Idaho	3,331
39	Virginia	3,322
40	Louisiana	3,317
41	Mississippi	3,305
41	Missouri	3,305
43	California	3,293
44	Oklahoma	3,285
45	Iowa	3,270
46	Arizona	3,209
47	Alabama	3,156
48	Arkansas	3,127
49	Hawaii	3,020
50	North Dakota	2,999
	District of Columbia	3,740

Source: U.S. Department of Health and Human Services, Agency for Healthcare Research and Quality
"Private-Sector Data by Firm Size and State" (Table II Series, Medical Expenditures Panel Survey, July 2005)
(http://www.meps.ahrq.gov/MEPSDATA/ic/2003/Index203.htm)
*Enrolled employees at private-sector establishments that offer health insurance coverage.

Average Annual Family Coverage Health Insurance Premium per Enrolled Employee in 2003
National Average = $9,249*

ALPHA ORDER			RANK ORDER		
RANK	STATE	PREMIUM	RANK	STATE	PREMIUM
47	Alabama	$8,045	1	Alaska	$10,564
1	Alaska	10,564	2	Delaware	10,499
32	Arizona	8,972	3	Maine	10,308
48	Arkansas	7,977	4	New Jersey	10,168
30	California	9,091	5	Connecticut	10,119
13	Colorado	9,522	6	Minnesota	10,066
5	Connecticut	10,119	7	Massachusetts	9,867
2	Delaware	10,499	8	New Hampshire	9,776
18	Florida	9,331	9	Illinois	9,693
39	Georgia	8,641	10	Wyoming	9,612
49	Hawaii	7,887	11	Texas	9,575
40	Idaho	8,563	12	Wisconsin	9,562
9	Illinois	9,693	13	Colorado	9,522
19	Indiana	9,315	14	Vermont	9,483
44	Iowa	8,436	15	Rhode Island	9,460
34	Kansas	8,907	16	Michigan	9,449
29	Kentucky	9,118	17	New York	9,439
38	Louisiana	8,735	18	Florida	9,331
3	Maine	10,308	19	Indiana	9,315
22	Maryland	9,217	20	New Mexico	9,299
7	Massachusetts	9,867	21	Tennessee	9,261
16	Michigan	9,449	22	Maryland	9,217
6	Minnesota	10,066	23	Washington	9,212
46	Mississippi	8,075	24	Virginia	9,176
31	Missouri	8,984	25	West Virginia	9,164
41	Montana	8,542	26	Nebraska	9,139
26	Nebraska	9,139	27	Ohio	9,136
36	Nevada	8,831	28	Pennsylvania	9,133
8	New Hampshire	9,776	29	Kentucky	9,118
4	New Jersey	10,168	30	California	9,091
20	New Mexico	9,299	31	Missouri	8,984
17	New York	9,439	32	Arizona	8,972
43	North Carolina	8,463	33	South Carolina	8,918
50	North Dakota	7,866	34	Kansas	8,907
27	Ohio	9,136	35	Oregon	8,861
37	Oklahoma	8,739	36	Nevada	8,831
35	Oregon	8,861	37	Oklahoma	8,739
28	Pennsylvania	9,133	38	Louisiana	8,735
15	Rhode Island	9,460	39	Georgia	8,641
33	South Carolina	8,918	40	Idaho	8,563
42	South Dakota	8,499	41	Montana	8,542
21	Tennessee	9,261	42	South Dakota	8,499
11	Texas	9,575	43	North Carolina	8,463
45	Utah	8,349	44	Iowa	8,436
14	Vermont	9,483	45	Utah	8,349
24	Virginia	9,176	46	Mississippi	8,075
23	Washington	9,212	47	Alabama	8,045
25	West Virginia	9,164	48	Arkansas	7,977
12	Wisconsin	9,562	49	Hawaii	7,887
10	Wyoming	9,612	50	North Dakota	7,866
				District of Columbia	10,748

Source: U.S. Department of Health and Human Services, Agency for Healthcare Research and Quality
  "Private-Sector Data by Firm Size and State" (Table II Series, Medical Expenditures Panel Survey, July 2005)
    (http://www.meps.ahrq.gov/MEPSDATA/ic/2003/Index203.htm)
  *Enrolled employees at private-sector establishments that offer health insurance coverage.

Percent of Private-Sector Establishments That Offer Health Insurance: 2003

National Percent = 56.2%

ALPHA ORDER

RANK	STATE	PERCENT
15	Alabama	58.3
42	Alaska	47.0
35	Arizona	52.4
50	Arkansas	42.2
20	California	55.9
34	Colorado	52.6
5	Connecticut	65.3
7	Delaware	61.1
23	Florida	55.3
26	Georgia	54.6
1	Hawaii	86.2
36	Idaho	51.0
24	Illinois	55.0
30	Indiana	53.4
37	Iowa	50.8
28	Kansas	54.5
17	Kentucky	57.5
39	Louisiana	50.0
29	Maine	53.5
10	Maryland	59.9
3	Massachusetts	65.6
7	Michigan	61.1
20	Minnesota	55.9
44	Mississippi	45.9
31	Missouri	53.3
45	Montana	45.1
46	Nebraska	44.7
14	Nevada	58.7
2	New Hampshire	68.8
9	New Jersey	60.8
38	New Mexico	50.5
11	New York	59.7
19	North Carolina	56.5
46	North Dakota	44.7
12	Ohio	59.6
43	Oklahoma	46.4
15	Oregon	58.3
4	Pennsylvania	65.4
6	Rhode Island	63.6
26	South Carolina	54.6
48	South Dakota	44.2
32	Tennessee	53.0
40	Texas	48.7
41	Utah	48.6
25	Vermont	54.9
13	Virginia	59.4
18	Washington	57.1
33	West Virginia	52.8
22	Wisconsin	55.7
49	Wyoming	42.5

RANK ORDER

RANK	STATE	PERCENT
1	Hawaii	86.2
2	New Hampshire	68.8
3	Massachusetts	65.6
4	Pennsylvania	65.4
5	Connecticut	65.3
6	Rhode Island	63.6
7	Delaware	61.1
7	Michigan	61.1
9	New Jersey	60.8
10	Maryland	59.9
11	New York	59.7
12	Ohio	59.6
13	Virginia	59.4
14	Nevada	58.7
15	Alabama	58.3
15	Oregon	58.3
17	Kentucky	57.5
18	Washington	57.1
19	North Carolina	56.5
20	California	55.9
20	Minnesota	55.9
22	Wisconsin	55.7
23	Florida	55.3
24	Illinois	55.0
25	Vermont	54.9
26	Georgia	54.6
26	South Carolina	54.6
28	Kansas	54.5
29	Maine	53.5
30	Indiana	53.4
31	Missouri	53.3
32	Tennessee	53.0
33	West Virginia	52.8
34	Colorado	52.6
35	Arizona	52.4
36	Idaho	51.0
37	Iowa	50.8
38	New Mexico	50.5
39	Louisiana	50.0
40	Texas	48.7
41	Utah	48.6
42	Alaska	47.0
43	Oklahoma	46.4
44	Mississippi	45.9
45	Montana	45.1
46	Nebraska	44.7
46	North Dakota	44.7
48	South Dakota	44.2
49	Wyoming	42.5
50	Arkansas	42.2
	District of Columbia	79.3

Source: U.S. Department of Health and Human Services, Agency for Healthcare Research and Quality
   "Private-Sector Data by Firm Size and State" (Table II Series, Medical Expenditures Panel Survey, July 2005)
   (http://www.meps.ahrq.gov/MEPSDATA/ic/2003/Index203.htm)

Persons Not Covered by Health Insurance in 2004

National Total = 45,820,000 Uninsured

ALPHA ORDER

RANK	STATE	UNINSURED	% of USA
23	Alabama	609,000	1.3%
46	Alaska	110,000	0.2%
13	Arizona	989,000	2.2%
30	Arkansas	448,000	1.0%
1	California	6,710,000	14.6%
18	Colorado	767,000	1.7%
32	Connecticut	407,000	0.9%
43	Delaware	120,000	0.3%
3	Florida	3,479,000	7.6%
6	Georgia	1,513,000	3.3%
43	Hawaii	120,000	0.3%
38	Idaho	212,000	0.5%
5	Illinois	1,764,000	3.8%
14	Indiana	872,000	1.9%
37	Iowa	277,000	0.6%
35	Kansas	297,000	0.6%
26	Kentucky	582,000	1.3%
19	Louisiana	761,000	1.7%
42	Maine	130,000	0.3%
16	Maryland	810,000	1.8%
20	Massachusetts	748,000	1.6%
11	Michigan	1,156,000	2.5%
29	Minnesota	458,000	1.0%
28	Mississippi	489,000	1.1%
21	Missouri	707,000	1.5%
40	Montana	174,000	0.4%
39	Nebraska	197,000	0.4%
31	Nevada	443,000	1.0%
41	New Hampshire	152,000	0.3%
8	New Jersey	1,322,000	2.9%
33	New Mexico	399,000	0.9%
4	New York	2,705,000	5.9%
8	North Carolina	1,322,000	2.9%
48	North Dakota	70,000	0.2%
10	Ohio	1,282,000	2.8%
22	Oklahoma	685,000	1.5%
25	Oregon	591,000	1.3%
7	Pennsylvania	1,454,000	3.2%
43	Rhode Island	120,000	0.3%
24	South Carolina	605,000	1.3%
47	South Dakota	90,000	0.2%
15	Tennessee	828,000	1.8%
2	Texas	5,583,000	12.2%
34	Utah	337,000	0.7%
50	Vermont	69,000	0.2%
12	Virginia	1,061,000	2.3%
17	Washington	793,000	1.7%
36	West Virginia	294,000	0.6%
27	Wisconsin	566,000	1.2%
48	Wyoming	70,000	0.2%

RANK ORDER

RANK	STATE	UNINSURED	% of USA
1	California	6,710,000	14.6%
2	Texas	5,583,000	12.2%
3	Florida	3,479,000	7.6%
4	New York	2,705,000	5.9%
5	Illinois	1,764,000	3.8%
6	Georgia	1,513,000	3.3%
7	Pennsylvania	1,454,000	3.2%
8	New Jersey	1,322,000	2.9%
8	North Carolina	1,322,000	2.9%
10	Ohio	1,282,000	2.8%
11	Michigan	1,156,000	2.5%
12	Virginia	1,061,000	2.3%
13	Arizona	989,000	2.2%
14	Indiana	872,000	1.9%
15	Tennessee	828,000	1.8%
16	Maryland	810,000	1.8%
17	Washington	793,000	1.7%
18	Colorado	767,000	1.7%
19	Louisiana	761,000	1.7%
20	Massachusetts	748,000	1.6%
21	Missouri	707,000	1.5%
22	Oklahoma	685,000	1.5%
23	Alabama	609,000	1.3%
24	South Carolina	605,000	1.3%
25	Oregon	591,000	1.3%
26	Kentucky	582,000	1.3%
27	Wisconsin	566,000	1.2%
28	Mississippi	489,000	1.1%
29	Minnesota	458,000	1.0%
30	Arkansas	448,000	1.0%
31	Nevada	443,000	1.0%
32	Connecticut	407,000	0.9%
33	New Mexico	399,000	0.9%
34	Utah	337,000	0.7%
35	Kansas	297,000	0.6%
36	West Virginia	294,000	0.6%
37	Iowa	277,000	0.6%
38	Idaho	212,000	0.5%
39	Nebraska	197,000	0.4%
40	Montana	174,000	0.4%
41	New Hampshire	152,000	0.3%
42	Maine	130,000	0.3%
43	Delaware	120,000	0.3%
43	Hawaii	120,000	0.3%
43	Rhode Island	120,000	0.3%
46	Alaska	110,000	0.2%
47	South Dakota	90,000	0.2%
48	North Dakota	70,000	0.2%
48	Wyoming	70,000	0.2%
50	Vermont	69,000	0.2%
	District of Columbia	73,000	0.2%

Source: U.S. Bureau of the Census
"Health Insurance Coverage Status by State for All People: 2004"
(http://ferret.bls.census.gov/macro/032005/health/h06_000.htm)

Percent of Population Not Covered by Health Insurance in 2004

National Percent = 15.5% of Population*

ALPHA ORDER

RANK	STATE	PERCENT
29	Alabama	13.5
8	Alaska	18.2
12	Arizona	17.0
14	Arkansas	16.7
7	California	18.4
13	Colorado	16.8
40	Connecticut	10.9
33	Delaware	11.8
6	Florida	18.5
15	Georgia	16.6
49	Hawaii	9.9
10	Idaho	17.3
22	Illinois	14.2
27	Indiana	13.7
48	Iowa	10.1
41	Kansas	10.8
25	Kentucky	13.9
5	Louisiana	18.8
43	Maine	10.6
24	Maryland	14.0
41	Massachusetts	10.8
37	Michigan	11.4
50	Minnesota	8.5
11	Mississippi	17.2
35	Missouri	11.7
9	Montana	17.9
38	Nebraska	11.0
4	Nevada	19.1
43	New Hampshire	10.6
21	New Jersey	14.4
2	New Mexico	21.4
20	New York	15.0
15	North Carolina	16.6
38	North Dakota	11.0
33	Ohio	11.8
3	Oklahoma	19.2
17	Oregon	16.1
36	Pennsylvania	11.5
45	Rhode Island	10.5
26	South Carolina	13.8
32	South Dakota	11.9
31	Tennessee	12.7
1	Texas	25.1
30	Utah	13.4
45	Vermont	10.5
28	Virginia	13.6
22	Washington	14.2
18	West Virginia	15.9
47	Wisconsin	10.4
18	Wyoming	15.9

RANK ORDER

RANK	STATE	PERCENT
1	Texas	25.1
2	New Mexico	21.4
3	Oklahoma	19.2
4	Nevada	19.1
5	Louisiana	18.8
6	Florida	18.5
7	California	18.4
8	Alaska	18.2
9	Montana	17.9
10	Idaho	17.3
11	Mississippi	17.2
12	Arizona	17.0
13	Colorado	16.8
14	Arkansas	16.7
15	Georgia	16.6
15	North Carolina	16.6
17	Oregon	16.1
18	West Virginia	15.9
18	Wyoming	15.9
20	New York	15.0
21	New Jersey	14.4
22	Illinois	14.2
22	Washington	14.2
24	Maryland	14.0
25	Kentucky	13.9
26	South Carolina	13.8
27	Indiana	13.7
28	Virginia	13.6
29	Alabama	13.5
30	Utah	13.4
31	Tennessee	12.7
32	South Dakota	11.9
33	Delaware	11.8
33	Ohio	11.8
35	Missouri	11.7
36	Pennsylvania	11.5
37	Michigan	11.4
38	Nebraska	11.0
38	North Dakota	11.0
40	Connecticut	10.9
41	Kansas	10.8
41	Massachusetts	10.8
43	Maine	10.6
43	New Hampshire	10.6
45	Rhode Island	10.5
45	Vermont	10.5
47	Wisconsin	10.4
48	Iowa	10.1
49	Hawaii	9.9
50	Minnesota	8.5
	District of Columbia	13.5

Source: U.S. Bureau of the Census
   "Income, Poverty and Health Insurance Covered in the United States: 2004"
     (http://www.census.gov/hhes/www/hlthins/hlthin04/hi04t11.pdf)
*Three-year average for 2002 through 2004.

Percent of Population Lacking Access to Primary Care in 2005

National Percent = 11.5% of Population*

ALPHA ORDER

RANK	STATE	PERCENT
3	Alabama	24.6
16	Alaska	14.0
20	Arizona	13.4
31	Arkansas	10.0
30	California	10.1
28	Colorado	10.3
43	Connecticut	6.3
35	Delaware	7.9
11	Florida	15.7
12	Georgia	15.6
48	Hawaii	4.4
10	Idaho	17.9
20	Illinois	13.4
33	Indiana	8.8
32	Iowa	9.7
13	Kansas	15.4
18	Kentucky	13.8
7	Louisiana	21.6
39	Maine	7.3
44	Maryland	6.2
47	Massachusetts	5.1
25	Michigan	11.0
40	Minnesota	7.0
1	Mississippi	30.1
5	Missouri	22.9
9	Montana	20.4
46	Nebraska	5.7
19	Nevada	13.5
45	New Hampshire	5.9
50	New Jersey	2.8
2	New Mexico	28.2
26	New York	10.8
35	North Carolina	7.9
8	North Dakota	20.9
38	Ohio	7.5
14	Oklahoma	15.3
41	Oregon	6.6
42	Pennsylvania	6.4
34	Rhode Island	8.0
15	South Carolina	15.2
4	South Dakota	24.1
24	Tennessee	11.3
22	Texas	12.7
23	Utah	12.6
49	Vermont	3.6
37	Virginia	7.7
27	Washington	10.4
17	West Virginia	13.9
29	Wisconsin	10.2
6	Wyoming	22.5

RANK ORDER

RANK	STATE	PERCENT
1	Mississippi	30.1
2	New Mexico	28.2
3	Alabama	24.6
4	South Dakota	24.1
5	Missouri	22.9
6	Wyoming	22.5
7	Louisiana	21.6
8	North Dakota	20.9
9	Montana	20.4
10	Idaho	17.9
11	Florida	15.7
12	Georgia	15.6
13	Kansas	15.4
14	Oklahoma	15.3
15	South Carolina	15.2
16	Alaska	14.0
17	West Virginia	13.9
18	Kentucky	13.8
19	Nevada	13.5
20	Arizona	13.4
20	Illinois	13.4
22	Texas	12.7
23	Utah	12.6
24	Tennessee	11.3
25	Michigan	11.0
26	New York	10.8
27	Washington	10.4
28	Colorado	10.3
29	Wisconsin	10.2
30	California	10.1
31	Arkansas	10.0
32	Iowa	9.7
33	Indiana	8.8
34	Rhode Island	8.0
35	Delaware	7.9
35	North Carolina	7.9
37	Virginia	7.7
38	Ohio	7.5
39	Maine	7.3
40	Minnesota	7.0
41	Oregon	6.6
42	Pennsylvania	6.4
43	Connecticut	6.3
44	Maryland	6.2
45	New Hampshire	5.9
46	Nebraska	5.7
47	Massachusetts	5.1
48	Hawaii	4.4
49	Vermont	3.6
50	New Jersey	2.8

District of Columbia   27.0

Source: Morgan Quitno Press using data from U.S. Dept. of Health and Human Services, Div. of Shortage Designation
"Selected Statistics on Health Professional Shortage Areas" (as of September 30, 2005)
*Percent of population considered under-served by primary medical practitioners (Family & General Practice doctors, Internists, Ob/Gyns and Pediatricians). An under-served population does not have primary medical care within reasonable economic and geographic bounds.

Physicians in 2004

National Total = 872,267 Physicians*

ALPHA ORDER

RANK	STATE	PHYSICIANS	% of USA
27	Alabama	10,564	1.2%
49	Alaska	1,580	0.2%
22	Arizona	14,012	1.6%
32	Arkansas	6,202	0.7%
1	California	105,766	12.1%
23	Colorado	13,455	1.5%
21	Connecticut	14,044	1.6%
46	Delaware	2,325	0.3%
4	Florida	51,025	5.8%
14	Georgia	21,639	2.5%
39	Hawaii	4,433	0.5%
43	Idaho	2,693	0.3%
6	Illinois	37,908	4.3%
20	Indiana	14,696	1.7%
31	Iowa	6,288	0.7%
29	Kansas	6,870	0.8%
28	Kentucky	10,464	1.2%
24	Louisiana	12,999	1.5%
41	Maine	4,052	0.5%
11	Maryland	25,098	2.9%
8	Massachusetts	31,216	3.6%
10	Michigan	26,999	3.1%
17	Minnesota	15,952	1.8%
33	Mississippi	5,872	0.7%
19	Missouri	15,026	1.7%
45	Montana	2,425	0.3%
37	Nebraska	4,672	0.5%
36	Nevada	4,934	0.6%
42	New Hampshire	3,884	0.4%
9	New Jersey	29,248	3.4%
35	New Mexico	5,169	0.6%
2	New York	81,716	9.4%
12	North Carolina	24,087	2.8%
48	North Dakota	1,716	0.2%
7	Ohio	33,103	3.8%
30	Oklahoma	6,846	0.8%
25	Oregon	10,957	1.3%
5	Pennsylvania	40,832	4.7%
40	Rhode Island	4,141	0.5%
26	South Carolina	10,762	1.2%
47	South Dakota	1,904	0.2%
16	Tennessee	16,863	1.9%
3	Texas	52,060	6.0%
34	Utah	5,643	0.6%
44	Vermont	2,589	0.3%
13	Virginia	22,587	2.6%
15	Washington	18,894	2.2%
38	West Virginia	4,613	0.5%
18	Wisconsin	15,625	1.8%
50	Wyoming	1,094	0.1%

RANK ORDER

RANK	STATE	PHYSICIANS	% of USA
1	California	105,766	12.1%
2	New York	81,716	9.4%
3	Texas	52,060	6.0%
4	Florida	51,025	5.8%
5	Pennsylvania	40,832	4.7%
6	Illinois	37,908	4.3%
7	Ohio	33,103	3.8%
8	Massachusetts	31,216	3.6%
9	New Jersey	29,248	3.4%
10	Michigan	26,999	3.1%
11	Maryland	25,098	2.9%
12	North Carolina	24,087	2.8%
13	Virginia	22,587	2.6%
14	Georgia	21,639	2.5%
15	Washington	18,894	2.2%
16	Tennessee	16,863	1.9%
17	Minnesota	15,952	1.8%
18	Wisconsin	15,625	1.8%
19	Missouri	15,026	1.7%
20	Indiana	14,696	1.7%
21	Connecticut	14,044	1.6%
22	Arizona	14,012	1.6%
23	Colorado	13,455	1.5%
24	Louisiana	12,999	1.5%
25	Oregon	10,957	1.3%
26	South Carolina	10,762	1.2%
27	Alabama	10,564	1.2%
28	Kentucky	10,464	1.2%
29	Kansas	6,870	0.8%
30	Oklahoma	6,846	0.8%
31	Iowa	6,288	0.7%
32	Arkansas	6,202	0.7%
33	Mississippi	5,872	0.7%
34	Utah	5,643	0.6%
35	New Mexico	5,169	0.6%
36	Nevada	4,934	0.6%
37	Nebraska	4,672	0.5%
38	West Virginia	4,613	0.5%
39	Hawaii	4,433	0.5%
40	Rhode Island	4,141	0.5%
41	Maine	4,052	0.5%
42	New Hampshire	3,884	0.4%
43	Idaho	2,693	0.3%
44	Vermont	2,589	0.3%
45	Montana	2,425	0.3%
46	Delaware	2,325	0.3%
47	South Dakota	1,904	0.2%
48	North Dakota	1,716	0.2%
49	Alaska	1,580	0.2%
50	Wyoming	1,094	0.1%
	District of Columbia	4,725	0.5%

Source: American Medical Association (Chicago, Illinois)
     "Physician Characteristics and Distribution in the U.S." (2006 Edition)
*As of December 31, 2004. Total does not include 12,707 physicians in the U.S. territories and possessions, at APO's and FPO's and whose addresses are unknown.

Rate of Physicians in 2004

National Rate = 297 Physicians per 100,000 Population*

ALPHA ORDER

RANK	STATE	RATE
42	Alabama	233
39	Alaska	241
38	Arizona	244
44	Arkansas	225
17	California	295
19	Colorado	292
5	Connecticut	401
25	Delaware	280
18	Florida	293
37	Georgia	245
7	Hawaii	351
50	Idaho	193
16	Illinois	298
40	Indiana	236
46	Iowa	213
35	Kansas	251
34	Kentucky	252
21	Louisiana	288
11	Maine	308
2	Maryland	452
1	Massachusetts	486
28	Michigan	267
10	Minnesota	313
48	Mississippi	202
31	Missouri	261
30	Montana	262
28	Nebraska	267
47	Nevada	211
15	New Hampshire	299
8	New Jersey	336
26	New Mexico	272
3	New York	425
24	North Carolina	282
27	North Dakota	271
20	Ohio	289
49	Oklahoma	194
12	Oregon	305
9	Pennsylvania	329
6	Rhode Island	383
32	South Carolina	256
36	South Dakota	247
22	Tennessee	286
43	Texas	231
40	Utah	236
4	Vermont	417
14	Virginia	303
12	Washington	305
33	West Virginia	254
23	Wisconsin	284
45	Wyoming	216

RANK ORDER

RANK	STATE	RATE
1	Massachusetts	486
2	Maryland	452
3	New York	425
4	Vermont	417
5	Connecticut	401
6	Rhode Island	383
7	Hawaii	351
8	New Jersey	336
9	Pennsylvania	329
10	Minnesota	313
11	Maine	308
12	Oregon	305
12	Washington	305
14	Virginia	303
15	New Hampshire	299
16	Illinois	298
17	California	295
18	Florida	293
19	Colorado	292
20	Ohio	289
21	Louisiana	288
22	Tennessee	286
23	Wisconsin	284
24	North Carolina	282
25	Delaware	280
26	New Mexico	272
27	North Dakota	271
28	Michigan	267
28	Nebraska	267
30	Montana	262
31	Missouri	261
32	South Carolina	256
33	West Virginia	254
34	Kentucky	252
35	Kansas	251
36	South Dakota	247
37	Georgia	245
38	Arizona	244
39	Alaska	241
40	Indiana	236
40	Utah	236
42	Alabama	233
43	Texas	231
44	Arkansas	225
45	Wyoming	216
46	Iowa	213
47	Nevada	211
48	Mississippi	202
49	Oklahoma	194
50	Idaho	193

District of Columbia   854

Source: Morgan Quitno Press using data from American Medical Association (Chicago, Illinois)
       "Physician Characteristics and Distribution in the U.S." (2006 Edition)
*As of December 31, 2004. National rate does not include physicians in the U.S. territories and possessions, at APO's and FPO's and whose addresses are unknown.

Rate of Registered Nurses in 2004

National Rate = 796 Nurses per 100,000 Population*

ALPHA ORDER

RANK	STATE	RATE
28	Alabama	828
33	Alaska	760
50	Arizona	552
39	Arkansas	716
47	California	634
40	Colorado	697
8	Connecticut	966
18	Delaware	891
32	Florida	767
42	Georgia	671
44	Hawaii	665
41	Idaho	694
31	Illinois	771
27	Indiana	829
5	Iowa	1,024
11	Kansas	945
20	Kentucky	882
21	Louisiana	876
4	Maine	1,030
9	Maryland	949
1	Massachusetts	1,183
30	Michigan	811
12	Minnesota	941
22	Mississippi	869
14	Missouri	910
25	Montana	854
7	Nebraska	968
48	Nevada	577
15	New Hampshire	908
16	New Jersey	898
49	New Mexico	562
24	New York	857
29	North Carolina	824
3	North Dakota	1,059
13	Ohio	927
43	Oklahoma	668
34	Oregon	749
6	Pennsylvania	970
9	Rhode Island	949
35	South Carolina	743
2	South Dakota	1,174
17	Tennessee	894
45	Texas	650
46	Utah	638
19	Vermont	885
38	Virginia	720
36	Washington	736
23	West Virginia	862
26	Wisconsin	848
37	Wyoming	727

RANK ORDER

RANK	STATE	RATE
1	Massachusetts	1,183
2	South Dakota	1,174
3	North Dakota	1,059
4	Maine	1,030
5	Iowa	1,024
6	Pennsylvania	970
7	Nebraska	968
8	Connecticut	966
9	Maryland	949
9	Rhode Island	949
11	Kansas	945
12	Minnesota	941
13	Ohio	927
14	Missouri	910
15	New Hampshire	908
16	New Jersey	898
17	Tennessee	894
18	Delaware	891
19	Vermont	885
20	Kentucky	882
21	Louisiana	876
22	Mississippi	869
23	West Virginia	862
24	New York	857
25	Montana	854
26	Wisconsin	848
27	Indiana	829
28	Alabama	828
29	North Carolina	824
30	Michigan	811
31	Illinois	771
32	Florida	767
33	Alaska	760
34	Oregon	749
35	South Carolina	743
36	Washington	736
37	Wyoming	727
38	Virginia	720
39	Arkansas	716
40	Colorado	697
41	Idaho	694
42	Georgia	671
43	Oklahoma	668
44	Hawaii	665
45	Texas	650
46	Utah	638
47	California	634
48	Nevada	577
49	New Mexico	562
50	Arizona	552

District of Columbia   1,422

Source: Morgan Quitno Press using data from U.S. Department of Labor, Bureau of Labor Statistics
    "Occupational Employment and Wages, 2004" (http://www.bls.gov/oes/)
*Does not include self-employed.

Rate of Dentists in 2002

National Rate = 59 Dentists per 100,000 Population*

ALPHA ORDER

RANK	STATE	RATE
46	Alabama	43
7	Alaska	72
38	Arizona	46
48	Arkansas	40
8	California	69
13	Colorado	64
5	Connecticut	77
43	Delaware	45
28	Florida	51
44	Georgia	44
1	Hawaii	82
25	Idaho	54
11	Illinois	65
33	Indiana	48
26	Iowa	53
28	Kansas	51
24	Kentucky	55
38	Louisiana	46
38	Maine	46
6	Maryland	75
1	Massachusetts	82
16	Michigan	60
17	Minnesota	59
48	Mississippi	40
33	Missouri	48
22	Montana	56
14	Nebraska	63
48	Nevada	40
19	New Hampshire	58
3	New Jersey	79
44	New Mexico	44
3	New York	79
46	North Carolina	43
33	North Dakota	48
26	Ohio	53
32	Oklahoma	49
10	Oregon	66
11	Pennsylvania	65
22	Rhode Island	56
38	South Carolina	46
36	South Dakota	47
28	Tennessee	51
36	Texas	47
14	Utah	63
17	Vermont	59
19	Virginia	58
9	Washington	67
38	West Virginia	46
21	Wisconsin	57
28	Wyoming	51

RANK ORDER

RANK	STATE	RATE
1	Hawaii	82
1	Massachusetts	82
3	New Jersey	79
3	New York	79
5	Connecticut	77
6	Maryland	75
7	Alaska	72
8	California	69
9	Washington	67
10	Oregon	66
11	Illinois	65
11	Pennsylvania	65
13	Colorado	64
14	Nebraska	63
14	Utah	63
16	Michigan	60
17	Minnesota	59
17	Vermont	59
19	New Hampshire	58
19	Virginia	58
21	Wisconsin	57
22	Montana	56
22	Rhode Island	56
24	Kentucky	55
25	Idaho	54
26	Iowa	53
26	Ohio	53
28	Florida	51
28	Kansas	51
28	Tennessee	51
28	Wyoming	51
32	Oklahoma	49
33	Indiana	48
33	Missouri	48
33	North Dakota	48
36	South Dakota	47
36	Texas	47
38	Arizona	46
38	Louisiana	46
38	Maine	46
38	South Carolina	46
38	West Virginia	46
43	Delaware	45
44	Georgia	44
44	New Mexico	44
46	Alabama	43
46	North Carolina	43
48	Arkansas	40
48	Mississippi	40
48	Nevada	40

| | District of Columbia | 119 |

Source: Morgan Quitno Press using data from American Dental Association
    "Distribution of Dentists, by Region and State, 2002"
*Professionally active dentists. National rate includes dentists for whom state is not known. National rate does not
include dentists in territories nor dentists in the Armed Forces stationed overseas.

Community Hospitals in 2004

National Total = 4,919 Hospitals*

RANK	STATE	HOSPITALS	% of USA
20	Alabama	108	2.2%
47	Alaska	19	0.4%
30	Arizona	62	1.3%
24	Arkansas	87	1.8%
2	California	361	7.3%
29	Colorado	70	1.4%
42	Connecticut	35	0.7%
50	Delaware	6	0.1%
4	Florida	203	4.1%
8	Georgia	146	3.0%
45	Hawaii	24	0.5%
39	Idaho	39	0.8%
6	Illinois	191	3.9%
18	Indiana	113	2.3%
16	Iowa	115	2.3%
10	Kansas	134	2.7%
21	Kentucky	105	2.1%
12	Louisiana	131	2.7%
40	Maine	37	0.8%
36	Maryland	50	1.0%
28	Massachusetts	78	1.6%
9	Michigan	144	2.9%
11	Minnesota	132	2.7%
22	Mississippi	93	1.9%
15	Missouri	119	2.4%
34	Montana	54	1.1%
25	Nebraska	85	1.7%
43	Nevada	30	0.6%
44	New Hampshire	28	0.6%
27	New Jersey	80	1.6%
40	New Mexico	37	0.8%
3	New York	206	4.2%
16	North Carolina	115	2.3%
38	North Dakota	40	0.8%
7	Ohio	166	3.4%
19	Oklahoma	109	2.2%
32	Oregon	58	1.2%
5	Pennsylvania	197	4.0%
49	Rhode Island	11	0.2%
30	South Carolina	62	1.3%
35	South Dakota	51	1.0%
13	Tennessee	127	2.6%
1	Texas	418	8.5%
37	Utah	43	0.9%
48	Vermont	14	0.3%
23	Virginia	88	1.8%
25	Washington	85	1.7%
33	West Virginia	57	1.2%
14	Wisconsin	121	2.5%
45	Wyoming	24	0.5%

RANK	STATE	HOSPITALS	% of USA
1	Texas	418	8.5%
2	California	361	7.3%
3	New York	206	4.2%
4	Florida	203	4.1%
5	Pennsylvania	197	4.0%
6	Illinois	191	3.9%
7	Ohio	166	3.4%
8	Georgia	146	3.0%
9	Michigan	144	2.9%
10	Kansas	134	2.7%
11	Minnesota	132	2.7%
12	Louisiana	131	2.7%
13	Tennessee	127	2.6%
14	Wisconsin	121	2.5%
15	Missouri	119	2.4%
16	Iowa	115	2.3%
16	North Carolina	115	2.3%
18	Indiana	113	2.3%
19	Oklahoma	109	2.2%
20	Alabama	108	2.2%
21	Kentucky	105	2.1%
22	Mississippi	93	1.9%
23	Virginia	88	1.8%
24	Arkansas	87	1.8%
25	Nebraska	85	1.7%
25	Washington	85	1.7%
27	New Jersey	80	1.6%
28	Massachusetts	78	1.6%
29	Colorado	70	1.4%
30	Arizona	62	1.3%
30	South Carolina	62	1.3%
32	Oregon	58	1.2%
33	West Virginia	57	1.2%
34	Montana	54	1.1%
35	South Dakota	51	1.0%
36	Maryland	50	1.0%
37	Utah	43	0.9%
38	North Dakota	40	0.8%
39	Idaho	39	0.8%
40	Maine	37	0.8%
40	New Mexico	37	0.8%
42	Connecticut	35	0.7%
43	Nevada	30	0.6%
44	New Hampshire	28	0.6%
45	Hawaii	24	0.5%
45	Wyoming	24	0.5%
47	Alaska	19	0.4%
48	Vermont	14	0.3%
49	Rhode Island	11	0.2%
50	Delaware	6	0.1%
	District of Columbia	11	0.2%

Source: American Hospital Association (Chicago, IL)
    "Hospital Statistics" (2006 edition)
Community hospitals are all nonfederal, short-term, general and special hospitals whose facilities and services are available to the public.

Rate of Community Hospitals in 2004

National Rate = 1.7 Community Hospitals per 100,000 Population*

ALPHA ORDER

RANK	STATE	RATE
18	Alabama	2.4
12	Alaska	2.9
43	Arizona	1.1
8	Arkansas	3.2
45	California	1.0
32	Colorado	1.5
45	Connecticut	1.0
50	Delaware	0.7
40	Florida	1.2
29	Georgia	1.6
24	Hawaii	1.9
14	Idaho	2.8
32	Illinois	1.5
27	Indiana	1.8
7	Iowa	3.9
4	Kansas	4.9
17	Kentucky	2.5
12	Louisiana	2.9
14	Maine	2.8
48	Maryland	0.9
40	Massachusetts	1.2
35	Michigan	1.4
16	Minnesota	2.6
8	Mississippi	3.2
23	Missouri	2.1
3	Montana	5.8
4	Nebraska	4.9
38	Nevada	1.3
20	New Hampshire	2.2
48	New Jersey	0.9
24	New Mexico	1.9
43	New York	1.1
38	North Carolina	1.3
2	North Dakota	6.3
35	Ohio	1.4
10	Oklahoma	3.1
29	Oregon	1.6
29	Pennsylvania	1.6
45	Rhode Island	1.0
32	South Carolina	1.5
1	South Dakota	6.6
20	Tennessee	2.2
24	Texas	1.9
27	Utah	1.8
19	Vermont	2.3
40	Virginia	1.2
35	Washington	1.4
10	West Virginia	3.1
20	Wisconsin	2.2
6	Wyoming	4.7

RANK ORDER

RANK	STATE	RATE
1	South Dakota	6.6
2	North Dakota	6.3
3	Montana	5.8
4	Kansas	4.9
4	Nebraska	4.9
6	Wyoming	4.7
7	Iowa	3.9
8	Arkansas	3.2
8	Mississippi	3.2
10	Oklahoma	3.1
10	West Virginia	3.1
12	Alaska	2.9
12	Louisiana	2.9
14	Idaho	2.8
14	Maine	2.8
16	Minnesota	2.6
17	Kentucky	2.5
18	Alabama	2.4
19	Vermont	2.3
20	New Hampshire	2.2
20	Tennessee	2.2
20	Wisconsin	2.2
23	Missouri	2.1
24	Hawaii	1.9
24	New Mexico	1.9
24	Texas	1.9
27	Indiana	1.8
27	Utah	1.8
29	Georgia	1.6
29	Oregon	1.6
29	Pennsylvania	1.6
32	Colorado	1.5
32	Illinois	1.5
32	South Carolina	1.5
35	Michigan	1.4
35	Ohio	1.4
35	Washington	1.4
38	Nevada	1.3
38	North Carolina	1.3
40	Florida	1.2
40	Massachusetts	1.2
40	Virginia	1.2
43	Arizona	1.1
43	New York	1.1
45	California	1.0
45	Connecticut	1.0
45	Rhode Island	1.0
48	Maryland	0.9
48	New Jersey	0.9
50	Delaware	0.7
	District of Columbia	2.0

Source: Morgan Quitno Press using data from American Hospital Association (Chicago, IL)
    "Hospital Statistics" (2006 edition)
*Community hospitals are all nonfederal, short-term, general and special hospitals whose facilities and services are available to the public.

Births in 2004

National Total = 4,115,590 Live Births*

ALPHA ORDER

RANK	STATE	BIRTHS	% of USA
24	Alabama	59,549	1.4%
47	Alaska	10,338	0.3%
13	Arizona	93,672	2.3%
33	Arkansas	38,602	0.9%
1	California	545,071	13.2%
22	Colorado	68,520	1.7%
31	Connecticut	42,099	1.0%
46	Delaware	11,299	0.3%
4	Florida	218,034	5.3%
8	Georgia	138,851	3.4%
40	Hawaii	18,280	0.4%
38	Idaho	22,527	0.5%
5	Illinois	180,934	4.4%
14	Indiana	86,733	2.1%
34	Iowa	38,439	0.9%
32	Kansas	39,581	1.0%
26	Kentucky	54,451	1.3%
23	Louisiana	65,399	1.6%
42	Maine	13,945	0.3%
19	Maryland	74,605	1.8%
17	Massachusetts	78,566	1.9%
9	Michigan	129,768	3.2%
20	Minnesota	70,615	1.7%
30	Mississippi	42,810	1.0%
18	Missouri	77,780	1.9%
44	Montana	11,525	0.3%
37	Nebraska	26,331	0.6%
35	Nevada	35,188	0.9%
41	New Hampshire	14,566	0.4%
11	New Jersey	114,916	2.8%
36	New Mexico	28,386	0.7%
3	New York	250,894	6.1%
10	North Carolina	119,851	2.9%
48	North Dakota	8,189	0.2%
6	Ohio	149,154	3.6%
27	Oklahoma	51,283	1.2%
29	Oregon	45,693	1.1%
7	Pennsylvania	145,768	3.5%
43	Rhode Island	12,778	0.3%
25	South Carolina	56,592	1.4%
45	South Dakota	11,340	0.3%
16	Tennessee	79,641	1.9%
2	Texas	384,389	9.3%
28	Utah	50,669	1.2%
50	Vermont	6,565	0.2%
12	Virginia	103,915	2.5%
15	Washington	81,740	2.0%
39	West Virginia	20,855	0.5%
21	Wisconsin	70,154	1.7%
49	Wyoming	6,807	0.2%

RANK ORDER

RANK	STATE	BIRTHS	% of USA
1	California	545,071	13.2%
2	Texas	384,389	9.3%
3	New York	250,894	6.1%
4	Florida	218,034	5.3%
5	Illinois	180,934	4.4%
6	Ohio	149,154	3.6%
7	Pennsylvania	145,768	3.5%
8	Georgia	138,851	3.4%
9	Michigan	129,768	3.2%
10	North Carolina	119,851	2.9%
11	New Jersey	114,916	2.8%
12	Virginia	103,915	2.5%
13	Arizona	93,672	2.3%
14	Indiana	86,733	2.1%
15	Washington	81,740	2.0%
16	Tennessee	79,641	1.9%
17	Massachusetts	78,566	1.9%
18	Missouri	77,780	1.9%
19	Maryland	74,605	1.8%
20	Minnesota	70,615	1.7%
21	Wisconsin	70,154	1.7%
22	Colorado	68,520	1.7%
23	Louisiana	65,399	1.6%
24	Alabama	59,549	1.4%
25	South Carolina	56,592	1.4%
26	Kentucky	54,451	1.3%
27	Oklahoma	51,283	1.2%
28	Utah	50,669	1.2%
29	Oregon	45,693	1.1%
30	Mississippi	42,810	1.0%
31	Connecticut	42,099	1.0%
32	Kansas	39,581	1.0%
33	Arkansas	38,602	0.9%
34	Iowa	38,439	0.9%
35	Nevada	35,188	0.9%
36	New Mexico	28,386	0.7%
37	Nebraska	26,331	0.6%
38	Idaho	22,527	0.5%
39	West Virginia	20,855	0.5%
40	Hawaii	18,280	0.4%
41	New Hampshire	14,566	0.4%
42	Maine	13,945	0.3%
43	Rhode Island	12,778	0.3%
44	Montana	11,525	0.3%
45	South Dakota	11,340	0.3%
46	Delaware	11,299	0.3%
47	Alaska	10,338	0.3%
48	North Dakota	8,189	0.2%
49	Wyoming	6,807	0.2%
50	Vermont	6,565	0.2%
	District of Columbia	7,932	0.2%

Source: U.S. Department of Health and Human Services, National Center for Health Statistics
   "National Vital Statistics Reports" (Vol. 54, No. 8, December 29, 2005)
*Preliminary data by state of residence.

Birth Rate in 2004

National Rate = 14.0 Live Births per 1,000 Population*

RANK	STATE	RATE
32	Alabama	13.1
5	Alaska	15.8
3	Arizona	16.3
19	Arkansas	14.0
7	California	15.2
10	Colorado	14.9
44	Connecticut	12.0
24	Delaware	13.6
41	Florida	12.5
6	Georgia	15.7
15	Hawaii	14.5
4	Idaho	16.2
18	Illinois	14.2
21	Indiana	13.9
34	Iowa	13.0
15	Kansas	14.5
32	Kentucky	13.1
15	Louisiana	14.5
49	Maine	10.6
28	Maryland	13.4
43	Massachusetts	12.2
38	Michigan	12.8
23	Minnesota	13.8
12	Mississippi	14.7
25	Missouri	13.5
42	Montana	12.4
8	Nebraska	15.1
8	Nevada	15.1
48	New Hampshire	11.2
30	New Jersey	13.2
10	New Mexico	14.9
34	New York	13.0
19	North Carolina	14.0
37	North Dakota	12.9
34	Ohio	13.0
14	Oklahoma	14.6
39	Oregon	12.7
46	Pennsylvania	11.7
45	Rhode Island	11.8
25	South Carolina	13.5
12	South Dakota	14.7
25	Tennessee	13.5
2	Texas	17.1
1	Utah	21.2
49	Vermont	10.6
21	Virginia	13.9
30	Washington	13.2
47	West Virginia	11.5
39	Wisconsin	12.7
28	Wyoming	13.4

RANK	STATE	RATE
1	Utah	21.2
2	Texas	17.1
3	Arizona	16.3
4	Idaho	16.2
5	Alaska	15.8
6	Georgia	15.7
7	California	15.2
8	Nebraska	15.1
8	Nevada	15.1
10	Colorado	14.9
10	New Mexico	14.9
12	Mississippi	14.7
12	South Dakota	14.7
14	Oklahoma	14.6
15	Hawaii	14.5
15	Kansas	14.5
15	Louisiana	14.5
18	Illinois	14.2
19	Arkansas	14.0
19	North Carolina	14.0
21	Indiana	13.9
21	Virginia	13.9
23	Minnesota	13.8
24	Delaware	13.6
25	Missouri	13.5
25	South Carolina	13.5
25	Tennessee	13.5
28	Maryland	13.4
28	Wyoming	13.4
30	New Jersey	13.2
30	Washington	13.2
32	Alabama	13.1
32	Kentucky	13.1
34	Iowa	13.0
34	New York	13.0
34	Ohio	13.0
37	North Dakota	12.9
38	Michigan	12.8
39	Oregon	12.7
39	Wisconsin	12.7
41	Florida	12.5
42	Montana	12.4
43	Massachusetts	12.2
44	Connecticut	12.0
45	Rhode Island	11.8
46	Pennsylvania	11.7
47	West Virginia	11.5
48	New Hampshire	11.2
49	Maine	10.6
49	Vermont	10.6
	District of Columbia	14.3

Source: U.S. Department of Health and Human Services, National Center for Health Statistics
"National Vital Statistics Reports" (Vol. 54, No. 8, December 29, 2005)
*Preliminary data by state of residence.

Births of Low Birthweight as a Percent of All Births in 2004

National Percent = 8.1% of Live Births*

<table>
<tr><td colspan="3">ALPHA ORDER</td><td colspan="3">RANK ORDER</td></tr>
<tr><td>RANK</td><td>STATE</td><td>PERCENT</td><td>RANK</td><td>STATE</td><td>PERCENT</td></tr>
<tr><td>3</td><td>Alabama</td><td>10.4</td><td>1</td><td>Mississippi</td><td>11.6</td></tr>
<tr><td>49</td><td>Alaska</td><td>6.0</td><td>2</td><td>Louisiana</td><td>10.9</td></tr>
<tr><td>35</td><td>Arizona</td><td>7.2</td><td>3</td><td>Alabama</td><td>10.4</td></tr>
<tr><td>5</td><td>Arkansas</td><td>9.3</td><td>4</td><td>South Carolina</td><td>10.2</td></tr>
<tr><td>42</td><td>California</td><td>6.7</td><td>5</td><td>Arkansas</td><td>9.3</td></tr>
<tr><td>10</td><td>Colorado</td><td>9.0</td><td>5</td><td>Georgia</td><td>9.3</td></tr>
<tr><td>31</td><td>Connecticut</td><td>7.8</td><td>5</td><td>Maryland</td><td>9.3</td></tr>
<tr><td>10</td><td>Delaware</td><td>9.0</td><td>8</td><td>Tennessee</td><td>9.2</td></tr>
<tr><td>15</td><td>Florida</td><td>8.5</td><td>8</td><td>West Virginia</td><td>9.2</td></tr>
<tr><td>5</td><td>Georgia</td><td>9.3</td><td>10</td><td>Colorado</td><td>9.0</td></tr>
<tr><td>30</td><td>Hawaii</td><td>7.9</td><td>10</td><td>Delaware</td><td>9.0</td></tr>
<tr><td>40</td><td>Idaho</td><td>6.8</td><td>10</td><td>North Carolina</td><td>9.0</td></tr>
<tr><td>17</td><td>Illinois</td><td>8.4</td><td>13</td><td>Kentucky</td><td>8.6</td></tr>
<tr><td>23</td><td>Indiana</td><td>8.1</td><td>13</td><td>Wyoming</td><td>8.6</td></tr>
<tr><td>36</td><td>Iowa</td><td>7.0</td><td>15</td><td>Florida</td><td>8.5</td></tr>
<tr><td>34</td><td>Kansas</td><td>7.3</td><td>15</td><td>Ohio</td><td>8.5</td></tr>
<tr><td>13</td><td>Kentucky</td><td>8.6</td><td>17</td><td>Illinois</td><td>8.4</td></tr>
<tr><td>2</td><td>Louisiana</td><td>10.9</td><td>18</td><td>Michigan</td><td>8.3</td></tr>
<tr><td>47</td><td>Maine</td><td>6.4</td><td>18</td><td>Missouri</td><td>8.3</td></tr>
<tr><td>5</td><td>Maryland</td><td>9.3</td><td>18</td><td>Virginia</td><td>8.3</td></tr>
<tr><td>31</td><td>Massachusetts</td><td>7.8</td><td>21</td><td>New Jersey</td><td>8.2</td></tr>
<tr><td>18</td><td>Michigan</td><td>8.3</td><td>21</td><td>New York</td><td>8.2</td></tr>
<tr><td>45</td><td>Minnesota</td><td>6.5</td><td>23</td><td>Indiana</td><td>8.1</td></tr>
<tr><td>1</td><td>Mississippi</td><td>11.6</td><td>23</td><td>New Mexico</td><td>8.1</td></tr>
<tr><td>18</td><td>Missouri</td><td>8.3</td><td>25</td><td>Nevada</td><td>8.0</td></tr>
<tr><td>33</td><td>Montana</td><td>7.6</td><td>25</td><td>Oklahoma</td><td>8.0</td></tr>
<tr><td>36</td><td>Nebraska</td><td>7.0</td><td>25</td><td>Pennsylvania</td><td>8.0</td></tr>
<tr><td>25</td><td>Nevada</td><td>8.0</td><td>25</td><td>Rhode Island</td><td>8.0</td></tr>
<tr><td>40</td><td>New Hampshire</td><td>6.8</td><td>25</td><td>Texas</td><td>8.0</td></tr>
<tr><td>21</td><td>New Jersey</td><td>8.2</td><td>30</td><td>Hawaii</td><td>7.9</td></tr>
<tr><td>23</td><td>New Mexico</td><td>8.1</td><td>31</td><td>Connecticut</td><td>7.8</td></tr>
<tr><td>21</td><td>New York</td><td>8.2</td><td>31</td><td>Massachusetts</td><td>7.8</td></tr>
<tr><td>10</td><td>North Carolina</td><td>9.0</td><td>33</td><td>Montana</td><td>7.6</td></tr>
<tr><td>44</td><td>North Dakota</td><td>6.6</td><td>34</td><td>Kansas</td><td>7.3</td></tr>
<tr><td>15</td><td>Ohio</td><td>8.5</td><td>35</td><td>Arizona</td><td>7.2</td></tr>
<tr><td>25</td><td>Oklahoma</td><td>8.0</td><td>36</td><td>Iowa</td><td>7.0</td></tr>
<tr><td>49</td><td>Oregon</td><td>6.0</td><td>36</td><td>Nebraska</td><td>7.0</td></tr>
<tr><td>25</td><td>Pennsylvania</td><td>8.0</td><td>36</td><td>Wisconsin</td><td>7.0</td></tr>
<tr><td>25</td><td>Rhode Island</td><td>8.0</td><td>39</td><td>South Dakota</td><td>6.9</td></tr>
<tr><td>4</td><td>South Carolina</td><td>10.2</td><td>40</td><td>Idaho</td><td>6.8</td></tr>
<tr><td>39</td><td>South Dakota</td><td>6.9</td><td>40</td><td>New Hampshire</td><td>6.8</td></tr>
<tr><td>8</td><td>Tennessee</td><td>9.2</td><td>42</td><td>California</td><td>6.7</td></tr>
<tr><td>25</td><td>Texas</td><td>8.0</td><td>42</td><td>Utah</td><td>6.7</td></tr>
<tr><td>42</td><td>Utah</td><td>6.7</td><td>44</td><td>North Dakota</td><td>6.6</td></tr>
<tr><td>45</td><td>Vermont</td><td>6.5</td><td>45</td><td>Minnesota</td><td>6.5</td></tr>
<tr><td>18</td><td>Virginia</td><td>8.3</td><td>45</td><td>Vermont</td><td>6.5</td></tr>
<tr><td>48</td><td>Washington</td><td>6.2</td><td>47</td><td>Maine</td><td>6.4</td></tr>
<tr><td>8</td><td>West Virginia</td><td>9.2</td><td>48</td><td>Washington</td><td>6.2</td></tr>
<tr><td>36</td><td>Wisconsin</td><td>7.0</td><td>49</td><td>Alaska</td><td>6.0</td></tr>
<tr><td>13</td><td>Wyoming</td><td>8.6</td><td>49</td><td>Oregon</td><td>6.0</td></tr>
<tr><td></td><td></td><td></td><td></td><td>District of Columbia</td><td>11.1</td></tr>
</table>

Source: U.S. Department of Health and Human Services, National Center for Health Statistics
     "National Vital Statistics Reports" (Vol. 54, No. 8, December 29, 2005)
*Preliminary data by state of residence. Births of less than 2,500 grams (5 pounds 8 ounces).

Teenage Birth Rate in 2004

National Rate = 42.0 Live Births per 1,000 Women 15 to 19 Years Old*

ALPHA ORDER

RANK	STATE	RATE
9	Alabama	53.4
25	Alaska	39.4
5	Arizona	60.9
4	Arkansas	61.5
24	California	40.2
15	Colorado	44.4
45	Connecticut	24.7
17	Delaware	44.2
21	Florida	43.0
8	Georgia	54.5
29	Hawaii	36.5
26	Idaho	39.1
22	Illinois	40.7
19	Indiana	43.8
38	Iowa	31.9
23	Kansas	40.6
14	Kentucky	49.2
6	Louisiana	57.5
46	Maine	24.4
37	Maryland	32.9
48	Massachusetts	22.6
33	Michigan	34.7
44	Minnesota	27.2
2	Mississippi	63.6
18	Missouri	44.0
31	Montana	35.9
30	Nebraska	36.3
12	Nevada	52.1
50	New Hampshire	18.1
46	New Jersey	24.4
3	New Mexico	61.6
43	New York	27.3
13	North Carolina	50.1
42	North Dakota	27.6
26	Ohio	39.1
7	Oklahoma	56.5
35	Oregon	33.9
40	Pennsylvania	30.9
36	Rhode Island	33.6
11	South Carolina	52.9
28	South Dakota	38.9
10	Tennessee	53.1
1	Texas	64.2
34	Utah	34.4
49	Vermont	21.1
32	Virginia	35.8
39	Washington	31.5
15	West Virginia	44.4
41	Wisconsin	30.7
20	Wyoming	43.1

RANK ORDER

RANK	STATE	RATE
1	Texas	64.2
2	Mississippi	63.6
3	New Mexico	61.6
4	Arkansas	61.5
5	Arizona	60.9
6	Louisiana	57.5
7	Oklahoma	56.5
8	Georgia	54.5
9	Alabama	53.4
10	Tennessee	53.1
11	South Carolina	52.9
12	Nevada	52.1
13	North Carolina	50.1
14	Kentucky	49.2
15	Colorado	44.4
15	West Virginia	44.4
17	Delaware	44.2
18	Missouri	44.0
19	Indiana	43.8
20	Wyoming	43.1
21	Florida	43.0
22	Illinois	40.7
23	Kansas	40.6
24	California	40.2
25	Alaska	39.4
26	Idaho	39.1
26	Ohio	39.1
28	South Dakota	38.9
29	Hawaii	36.5
30	Nebraska	36.3
31	Montana	35.9
32	Virginia	35.8
33	Michigan	34.7
34	Utah	34.4
35	Oregon	33.9
36	Rhode Island	33.6
37	Maryland	32.9
38	Iowa	31.9
39	Washington	31.5
40	Pennsylvania	30.9
41	Wisconsin	30.7
42	North Dakota	27.6
43	New York	27.3
44	Minnesota	27.2
45	Connecticut	24.7
46	Maine	24.4
46	New Jersey	24.4
48	Massachusetts	22.6
49	Vermont	21.1
50	New Hampshire	18.1

District of Columbia   68.6

Source: Morgan Quitno Press using data from U.S. Dept. of Health and Human Services, Nat'l Center for Health Statistics
  "National Vital Statistics Reports" (Vol. 54, No. 8, December 29, 2005)
*Preliminary data by state of residence.

Births to Unmarried Women as a Percent of All Births in 2004

National Percent = 35.7% of Live Births*

	ALPHA ORDER			RANK ORDER	
RANK	STATE	PERCENT	RANK	STATE	PERCENT
19	Alabama	36.3	1	Louisiana	49.2
28	Alaska	34.6	2	New Mexico	48.9
6	Arizona	42.2	3	Mississippi	48.3
11	Arkansas	38.8	4	Delaware	42.5
29	California	34.4	5	South Carolina	42.3
47	Colorado	27.5	6	Arizona	42.2
40	Connecticut	30.6	7	Florida	41.2
4	Delaware	42.5	8	Nevada	39.6
7	Florida	41.2	9	Georgia	39.2
9	Georgia	39.2	10	Indiana	39.0
32	Hawaii	33.3	11	Arkansas	38.8
49	Idaho	22.6	12	Oklahoma	38.4
20	Illinois	36.2	13	Tennessee	38.2
10	Indiana	39.0	14	New York	37.8
38	Iowa	31.0	15	Ohio	37.4
33	Kansas	32.7	16	Rhode Island	37.3
24	Kentucky	35.4	17	Missouri	36.9
1	Louisiana	49.2	17	North Carolina	36.9
31	Maine	34.0	19	Alabama	36.3
22	Maryland	35.7	20	Illinois	36.2
46	Massachusetts	28.5	21	Texas	35.9
22	Michigan	35.7	22	Maryland	35.7
45	Minnesota	29.0	22	Michigan	35.7
3	Mississippi	48.3	24	Kentucky	35.4
17	Missouri	36.9	25	South Dakota	35.1
30	Montana	34.3	26	West Virginia	34.9
42	Nebraska	30.2	27	Pennsylvania	34.8
8	Nevada	39.6	28	Alaska	34.6
48	New Hampshire	26.5	29	California	34.4
43	New Jersey	30.1	30	Montana	34.3
2	New Mexico	48.9	31	Maine	34.0
14	New York	37.8	32	Hawaii	33.3
17	North Carolina	36.9	33	Kansas	32.7
44	North Dakota	29.9	34	Oregon	32.5
15	Ohio	37.4	35	Vermont	32.3
12	Oklahoma	38.4	36	Wyoming	31.7
34	Oregon	32.5	37	Wisconsin	31.3
27	Pennsylvania	34.8	38	Iowa	31.0
16	Rhode Island	37.3	38	Virginia	31.0
5	South Carolina	42.3	40	Connecticut	30.6
25	South Dakota	35.1	41	Washington	30.4
13	Tennessee	38.2	42	Nebraska	30.2
21	Texas	35.9	43	New Jersey	30.1
50	Utah	17.5	44	North Dakota	29.9
35	Vermont	32.3	45	Minnesota	29.0
38	Virginia	31.0	46	Massachusetts	28.5
41	Washington	30.4	47	Colorado	27.5
26	West Virginia	34.9	48	New Hampshire	26.5
37	Wisconsin	31.3	49	Idaho	22.6
36	Wyoming	31.7	50	Utah	17.5
				District of Columbia	55.5

Source: U.S. Department of Health and Human Services, National Center for Health Statistics
   "National Vital Statistics Reports" (Vol. 54, No. 8, December 29, 2005)
*Preliminary data by state of residence.

Percent of Mothers Receiving Late or No Prenatal Care in 2003

National Percent = 3.5% of Mothers*

ALPHA ORDER				RANK ORDER		
RANK	STATE	PERCENT		RANK	STATE	PERCENT
24	Alabama	3.5		1	New Mexico	8.1
6	Alaska	5.2		2	Arizona	7.3
2	Arizona	7.3		3	Nevada	6.4
15	Arkansas	4.3		4	Washington	5.8
38	California	2.5		5	Pennsylvania	5.6
12	Colorado	4.4		6	Alaska	5.2
48	Connecticut	1.5		7	South Carolina	4.9
12	Delaware	4.4		8	Oklahoma	4.8
32	Florida	2.8		9	New Jersey	4.7
19	Georgia	3.8		9	Texas	4.7
22	Hawaii	3.6		11	New York	4.5
25	Idaho	3.4		12	Colorado	4.4
32	Illinois	2.8		12	Delaware	4.4
19	Indiana	3.8		12	Utah	4.4
44	Iowa	2.0		15	Arkansas	4.3
40	Kansas	2.3		16	Oregon	4.0
37	Kentucky	2.6		17	Maryland	3.9
25	Louisiana	3.4		17	South Dakota	3.9
46	Maine	1.7		19	Georgia	3.8
17	Maryland	3.9		19	Indiana	3.8
44	Massachusetts	2.0		19	Tennessee	3.8
27	Michigan	3.1		22	Hawaii	3.6
42	Minnesota	2.2		22	Virginia	3.6
30	Mississippi	2.9		24	Alabama	3.5
42	Missouri	2.2		25	Idaho	3.4
35	Montana	2.7		25	Louisiana	3.4
32	Nebraska	2.8		27	Michigan	3.1
3	Nevada	6.4		27	Wisconsin	3.1
49	New Hampshire	1.1		29	Ohio	3.0
9	New Jersey	4.7		30	Mississippi	2.9
1	New Mexico	8.1		30	North Carolina	2.9
11	New York	4.5		32	Florida	2.8
30	North Carolina	2.9		32	Illinois	2.8
35	North Dakota	2.7		32	Nebraska	2.8
29	Ohio	3.0		35	Montana	2.7
8	Oklahoma	4.8		35	North Dakota	2.7
16	Oregon	4.0		37	Kentucky	2.6
5	Pennsylvania	5.6		38	California	2.5
49	Rhode Island	1.1		38	Wyoming	2.5
7	South Carolina	4.9		40	Kansas	2.3
17	South Dakota	3.9		40	West Virginia	2.3
19	Tennessee	3.8		42	Minnesota	2.2
9	Texas	4.7		42	Missouri	2.2
12	Utah	4.4		44	Iowa	2.0
47	Vermont	1.6		44	Massachusetts	2.0
22	Virginia	3.6		46	Maine	1.7
4	Washington	5.8		47	Vermont	1.6
40	West Virginia	2.3		48	Connecticut	1.5
27	Wisconsin	3.1		49	New Hampshire	1.1
38	Wyoming	2.5		49	Rhode Island	1.1
					District of Columbia	6.6

Source: U.S. Department of Health and Human Services, National Center for Health Statistics
"National Vital Statistics Reports" (Vol. 54, No. 2, September 8, 2005)
Final data by state of residence. "Late" means care begun in third trimester.

Reported Legal Abortions in 2002

Reporting States' Total = 854,122 Abortions*

ALPHA ORDER

RANK	STATE	ABORTIONS	% of USA
19	Alabama	12,249	1.4%
NA	Alaska**	NA	NA
22	Arizona	10,677	1.3%
32	Arkansas	5,316	0.6%
NA	California**	NA	NA
27	Colorado	7,757	0.9%
17	Connecticut	13,470	1.6%
34	Delaware	4,493	0.5%
2	Florida	87,964	10.3%
7	Georgia	34,091	4.0%
35	Hawaii	3,920	0.5%
45	Idaho	829	0.1%
4	Illinois	46,945	5.5%
21	Indiana	10,937	1.3%
30	Iowa	6,240	0.7%
20	Kansas	11,765	1.4%
39	Kentucky	3,502	0.4%
24	Louisiana	10,451	1.2%
40	Maine	2,315	0.3%
16	Maryland	13,595	1.6%
11	Massachusetts	25,249	3.0%
9	Michigan	29,231	3.4%
15	Minnesota	14,187	1.7%
37	Mississippi	3,605	0.4%
26	Missouri	8,201	1.0%
41	Montana	2,248	0.3%
36	Nebraska	3,775	0.4%
25	Nevada	9,960	1.2%
NA	New Hampshire**	NA	NA
8	New Jersey	32,854	3.8%
33	New Mexico	5,069	0.6%
1	New York	127,983	15.0%
10	North Carolina	29,229	3.4%
44	North Dakota	1,219	0.1%
5	Ohio	35,830	4.2%
29	Oklahoma	6,500	0.8%
18	Oregon	13,172	1.5%
6	Pennsylvania	35,167	4.1%
31	Rhode Island	5,550	0.6%
28	South Carolina	6,657	0.8%
46	South Dakota	826	0.1%
14	Tennessee	17,807	2.1%
3	Texas	79,929	9.4%
38	Utah	3,524	0.4%
43	Vermont	1,635	0.2%
13	Virginia	24,992	2.9%
12	Washington	25,148	2.9%
42	West Virginia	2,049	0.2%
23	Wisconsin	10,489	1.2%
47	Wyoming	10	0.0%

RANK ORDER

RANK	STATE	ABORTIONS	% of USA
1	New York	127,983	15.0%
2	Florida	87,964	10.3%
3	Texas	79,929	9.4%
4	Illinois	46,945	5.5%
5	Ohio	35,830	4.2%
6	Pennsylvania	35,167	4.1%
7	Georgia	34,091	4.0%
8	New Jersey	32,854	3.8%
9	Michigan	29,231	3.4%
10	North Carolina	29,229	3.4%
11	Massachusetts	25,249	3.0%
12	Washington	25,148	2.9%
13	Virginia	24,992	2.9%
14	Tennessee	17,807	2.1%
15	Minnesota	14,187	1.7%
16	Maryland	13,595	1.6%
17	Connecticut	13,470	1.6%
18	Oregon	13,172	1.5%
19	Alabama	12,249	1.4%
20	Kansas	11,765	1.4%
21	Indiana	10,937	1.3%
22	Arizona	10,677	1.3%
23	Wisconsin	10,489	1.2%
24	Louisiana	10,451	1.2%
25	Nevada	9,960	1.2%
26	Missouri	8,201	1.0%
27	Colorado	7,757	0.9%
28	South Carolina	6,657	0.8%
29	Oklahoma	6,500	0.8%
30	Iowa	6,240	0.7%
31	Rhode Island	5,550	0.6%
32	Arkansas	5,316	0.6%
33	New Mexico	5,069	0.6%
34	Delaware	4,493	0.5%
35	Hawaii	3,920	0.5%
36	Nebraska	3,775	0.4%
37	Mississippi	3,605	0.4%
38	Utah	3,524	0.4%
39	Kentucky	3,502	0.4%
40	Maine	2,315	0.3%
41	Montana	2,248	0.3%
42	West Virginia	2,049	0.2%
43	Vermont	1,635	0.2%
44	North Dakota	1,219	0.1%
45	Idaho	829	0.1%
46	South Dakota	826	0.1%
47	Wyoming	10	0.0%
NA	Alaska**	NA	NA
NA	California**	NA	NA
NA	New Hampshire**	NA	NA
	District of Columbia	5,511	0.6%

Source: U.S. Department of Health and Human Services, Centers for Disease Control and Prevention
   "Abortion Surveillance-United States, 2002" (Morbidity and Mortality Weekly Report, Vol. 54, No. SS-7, 11/25/05)
*By state of occurrence. Total is for reporting states only.
**Not reported.

Reported Legal Abortions per 1,000 Live Births in 2002

Reporting States' Ratio = 246 Abortions per 1,000 Live Births*

ALPHA ORDER				RANK ORDER		
RANK	STATE	RATIO		RANK	STATE	RATIO
24	Alabama	208		1	New York	509
NA	Alaska**	NA		2	Rhode Island	430
37	Arizona	122		3	Florida	428
34	Arkansas	142		4	Delaware	405
NA	California**	NA		5	Connecticut	321
39	Colorado	113		6	Washington	318
5	Connecticut	321		7	Massachusetts	313
4	Delaware	405		8	Nevada	306
3	Florida	428		9	Kansas	299
13	Georgia	256		10	Oregon	291
21	Hawaii	224		11	New Jersey	286
46	Idaho	40		12	Illinois	260
12	Illinois	260		13	Georgia	256
35	Indiana	129		13	Vermont	256
29	Iowa	166		15	Virginia	251
9	Kansas	299		16	North Carolina	249
45	Kentucky	65		17	Pennsylvania	246
30	Louisiana	161		18	Ohio	241
28	Maine	171		19	Tennessee	230
26	Maryland	185		20	Michigan	225
7	Massachusetts	313		21	Hawaii	224
20	Michigan	225		22	Texas	215
23	Minnesota	209		23	Minnesota	209
42	Mississippi	87		24	Alabama	208
40	Missouri	109		25	Montana	203
25	Montana	203		26	Maryland	185
33	Nebraska	149		27	New Mexico	183
8	Nevada	306		28	Maine	171
NA	New Hampshire**	NA		29	Iowa	166
11	New Jersey	286		30	Louisiana	161
27	New Mexico	183		31	North Dakota	157
1	New York	509		32	Wisconsin	153
16	North Carolina	249		33	Nebraska	149
31	North Dakota	157		34	Arkansas	142
18	Ohio	241		35	Indiana	129
35	Oklahoma	129		35	Oklahoma	129
10	Oregon	291		37	Arizona	122
17	Pennsylvania	246		37	South Carolina	122
2	Rhode Island	430		39	Colorado	113
37	South Carolina	122		40	Missouri	109
43	South Dakota	77		41	West Virginia	99
19	Tennessee	230		42	Mississippi	87
22	Texas	215		43	South Dakota	77
44	Utah	72		44	Utah	72
13	Vermont	256		45	Kentucky	65
15	Virginia	251		46	Idaho	40
6	Washington	318		NA	Alaska**	NA
41	West Virginia	99		NA	California**	NA
32	Wisconsin	153		NA	New Hampshire**	NA
NA	Wyoming**	NA		NA	Wyoming**	NA
					District of Columbia	735

Source: U.S. Department of Health and Human Services, Centers for Disease Control and Prevention
    "Abortion Surveillance-United States, 2002" (Morbidity and Mortality Weekly Report, Vol. 54, No. SS-7, 11/25/05)
*By state of occurrence. National figure is for reporting states only.
**Not reported.

Infant Deaths in 2003

National Total = 27,477 Infant Deaths*

ALPHA ORDER

RANK	STATE	DEATHS	% of USA
19	Alabama	502	1.8%
45	Alaska	67	0.2%
17	Arizona	591	2.2%
28	Arkansas	333	1.2%
1	California	2,560	9.3%
24	Colorado	416	1.5%
33	Connecticut	222	0.8%
41	Delaware	97	0.4%
4	Florida	1,576	5.7%
7	Georgia	1,158	4.2%
40	Hawaii	139	0.5%
36	Idaho	158	0.6%
5	Illinois	1,361	5.0%
13	Indiana	672	2.4%
34	Iowa	207	0.8%
31	Kansas	261	0.9%
27	Kentucky	341	1.2%
16	Louisiana	596	2.2%
46	Maine	64	0.2%
15	Maryland	645	2.3%
22	Massachusetts	425	1.5%
8	Michigan	1,130	4.1%
29	Minnesota	325	1.2%
22	Mississippi	425	1.5%
18	Missouri	587	2.1%
43	Montana	79	0.3%
39	Nebraska	145	0.5%
35	Nevada	203	0.7%
48	New Hampshire	52	0.2%
14	New Jersey	660	2.4%
37	New Mexico	157	0.6%
3	New York	1,642	6.0%
10	North Carolina	931	3.4%
47	North Dakota	57	0.2%
6	Ohio	1,162	4.2%
26	Oklahoma	378	1.4%
30	Oregon	270	1.0%
9	Pennsylvania	981	3.6%
44	Rhode Island	76	0.3%
20	South Carolina	451	1.6%
42	South Dakota	80	0.3%
12	Tennessee	717	2.6%
2	Texas	2,400	8.7%
32	Utah	252	0.9%
50	Vermont	32	0.1%
11	Virginia	758	2.8%
24	Washington	416	1.5%
38	West Virginia	153	0.6%
20	Wisconsin	451	1.6%
49	Wyoming	46	0.2%

RANK ORDER

RANK	STATE	DEATHS	% of USA
1	California	2,560	9.3%
2	Texas	2,400	8.7%
3	New York	1,642	6.0%
4	Florida	1,576	5.7%
5	Illinois	1,361	5.0%
6	Ohio	1,162	4.2%
7	Georgia	1,158	4.2%
8	Michigan	1,130	4.1%
9	Pennsylvania	981	3.6%
10	North Carolina	931	3.4%
11	Virginia	758	2.8%
12	Tennessee	717	2.6%
13	Indiana	672	2.4%
14	New Jersey	660	2.4%
15	Maryland	645	2.3%
16	Louisiana	596	2.2%
17	Arizona	591	2.2%
18	Missouri	587	2.1%
19	Alabama	502	1.8%
20	South Carolina	451	1.6%
20	Wisconsin	451	1.6%
22	Massachusetts	425	1.5%
22	Mississippi	425	1.5%
24	Colorado	416	1.5%
24	Washington	416	1.5%
26	Oklahoma	378	1.4%
27	Kentucky	341	1.2%
28	Arkansas	333	1.2%
29	Minnesota	325	1.2%
30	Oregon	270	1.0%
31	Kansas	261	0.9%
32	Utah	252	0.9%
33	Connecticut	222	0.8%
34	Iowa	207	0.8%
35	Nevada	203	0.7%
36	Idaho	158	0.6%
37	New Mexico	157	0.6%
38	West Virginia	153	0.6%
39	Nebraska	145	0.5%
40	Hawaii	139	0.5%
41	Delaware	97	0.4%
42	South Dakota	80	0.3%
43	Montana	79	0.3%
44	Rhode Island	76	0.3%
45	Alaska	67	0.2%
46	Maine	64	0.2%
47	North Dakota	57	0.2%
48	New Hampshire	52	0.2%
49	Wyoming	46	0.2%
50	Vermont	32	0.1%
	District of Columbia	70	0.3%

Source: U.S. Department of Health and Human Services, National Center for Health Statistics
   "National Vital Statistics Reports" (Vol. 53, No. 21, June 28, 2005)
*Preliminary data. Deaths under 1 year old by state of residence.

Infant Mortality Rate in 2003

National Rate = 6.7 Infant Deaths per 1,000 Live Births*

ALPHA ORDER

RANK	STATE	RATE
6	Alabama	8.5
27	Alaska	6.7
28	Arizona	6.5
4	Arkansas	8.7
47	California	4.7
34	Colorado	6.0
44	Connecticut	5.1
6	Delaware	8.5
18	Florida	7.4
6	Georgia	8.5
13	Hawaii	7.7
21	Idaho	7.2
16	Illinois	7.5
13	Indiana	7.7
41	Iowa	5.4
29	Kansas	6.4
33	Kentucky	6.2
2	Louisiana	9.2
48	Maine	4.6
6	Maryland	8.5
42	Massachusetts	5.3
5	Michigan	8.6
48	Minnesota	4.6
1	Mississippi	10.1
13	Missouri	7.7
25	Montana	6.9
39	Nebraska	5.6
34	Nevada	6.0
50	New Hampshire	3.6
39	New Jersey	5.6
38	New Mexico	5.7
32	New York	6.3
11	North Carolina	7.9
21	North Dakota	7.2
12	Ohio	7.8
18	Oklahoma	7.4
36	Oregon	5.9
25	Pennsylvania	6.9
37	Rhode Island	5.8
10	South Carolina	8.1
23	South Dakota	7.1
3	Tennessee	9.1
29	Texas	6.4
45	Utah	5.0
46	Vermont	4.9
16	Virginia	7.5
43	Washington	5.2
20	West Virginia	7.3
29	Wisconsin	6.4
24	Wyoming	7.0

RANK ORDER

RANK	STATE	RATE
1	Mississippi	10.1
2	Louisiana	9.2
3	Tennessee	9.1
4	Arkansas	8.7
5	Michigan	8.6
6	Alabama	8.5
6	Delaware	8.5
6	Georgia	8.5
6	Maryland	8.5
10	South Carolina	8.1
11	North Carolina	7.9
12	Ohio	7.8
13	Hawaii	7.7
13	Indiana	7.7
13	Missouri	7.7
16	Illinois	7.5
16	Virginia	7.5
18	Florida	7.4
18	Oklahoma	7.4
20	West Virginia	7.3
21	Idaho	7.2
21	North Dakota	7.2
23	South Dakota	7.1
24	Wyoming	7.0
25	Montana	6.9
25	Pennsylvania	6.9
27	Alaska	6.7
28	Arizona	6.5
29	Kansas	6.4
29	Texas	6.4
29	Wisconsin	6.4
32	New York	6.3
33	Kentucky	6.2
34	Colorado	6.0
34	Nevada	6.0
36	Oregon	5.9
37	Rhode Island	5.8
38	New Mexico	5.7
39	Nebraska	5.6
39	New Jersey	5.6
41	Iowa	5.4
42	Massachusetts	5.3
43	Washington	5.2
44	Connecticut	5.1
45	Utah	5.0
46	Vermont	4.9
47	California	4.7
48	Maine	4.6
48	Minnesota	4.6
50	New Hampshire	3.6
	District of Columbia	9.4

Source: U.S. Department of Health and Human Services, National Center for Health Statistics
"National Vital Statistics Reports" (Vol. 53, No. 21, June 28, 2005)
*Preliminary data. Deaths under 1 year old by state of residence.

Deaths in 2003

National Total = 2,443,908 Deaths*

ALPHA ORDER

RANK	STATE	DEATHS	% of USA
15	Alabama	46,726	1.9%
48	Alaska	3,185	0.1%
19	Arizona	43,496	1.8%
30	Arkansas	27,924	1.1%
NA	California**	NA	NA
26	Colorado	29,542	1.2%
27	Connecticut	29,432	1.2%
44	Delaware	7,070	0.3%
1	Florida	168,607	6.9%
9	Georgia	66,473	2.7%
41	Hawaii	8,987	0.4%
38	Idaho	10,385	0.4%
NA	Illinois**	NA	NA
13	Indiana	56,193	2.3%
29	Iowa	28,000	1.1%
31	Kansas	24,596	1.0%
21	Kentucky	40,236	1.6%
20	Louisiana	42,893	1.8%
37	Maine	12,534	0.5%
18	Maryland	44,500	1.8%
12	Massachusetts	56,297	2.3%
6	Michigan	86,710	3.5%
23	Minnesota	37,636	1.5%
28	Mississippi	28,535	1.2%
14	Missouri	55,569	2.3%
42	Montana	8,467	0.3%
34	Nebraska	15,466	0.6%
33	Nevada	17,864	0.7%
40	New Hampshire	9,691	0.4%
7	New Jersey	73,683	3.0%
35	New Mexico	14,877	0.6%
2	New York	155,852	6.4%
8	North Carolina	73,548	3.0%
45	North Dakota	6,095	0.2%
5	Ohio	108,660	4.4%
24	Oklahoma	35,733	1.5%
25	Oregon	30,934	1.3%
4	Pennsylvania	129,767	5.3%
39	Rhode Island	10,038	0.4%
22	South Carolina	38,111	1.6%
43	South Dakota	7,133	0.3%
11	Tennessee	57,306	2.3%
3	Texas	155,171	6.3%
36	Utah	13,408	0.5%
46	Vermont	5,112	0.2%
10	Virginia	58,415	2.4%
17	Washington	45,964	1.9%
32	West Virginia	21,299	0.9%
16	Wisconsin	46,174	1.9%
47	Wyoming	4,173	0.2%

RANK ORDER

RANK	STATE	DEATHS	% of USA
1	Florida	168,607	6.9%
2	New York	155,852	6.4%
3	Texas	155,171	6.3%
4	Pennsylvania	129,767	5.3%
5	Ohio	108,660	4.4%
6	Michigan	86,710	3.5%
7	New Jersey	73,683	3.0%
8	North Carolina	73,548	3.0%
9	Georgia	66,473	2.7%
10	Virginia	58,415	2.4%
11	Tennessee	57,306	2.3%
12	Massachusetts	56,297	2.3%
13	Indiana	56,193	2.3%
14	Missouri	55,569	2.3%
15	Alabama	46,726	1.9%
16	Wisconsin	46,174	1.9%
17	Washington	45,964	1.9%
18	Maryland	44,500	1.8%
19	Arizona	43,496	1.8%
20	Louisiana	42,893	1.8%
21	Kentucky	40,236	1.6%
22	South Carolina	38,111	1.6%
23	Minnesota	37,636	1.5%
24	Oklahoma	35,733	1.5%
25	Oregon	30,934	1.3%
26	Colorado	29,542	1.2%
27	Connecticut	29,432	1.2%
28	Mississippi	28,535	1.2%
29	Iowa	28,080	1.1%
30	Arkansas	27,924	1.1%
31	Kansas	24,596	1.0%
32	West Virginia	21,299	0.9%
33	Nevada	17,864	0.7%
34	Nebraska	15,466	0.6%
35	New Mexico	14,877	0.6%
36	Utah	13,408	0.5%
37	Maine	12,534	0.5%
38	Idaho	10,385	0.4%
39	Rhode Island	10,038	0.4%
40	New Hampshire	9,691	0.4%
41	Hawaii	8,987	0.4%
42	Montana	8,467	0.3%
43	South Dakota	7,133	0.3%
44	Delaware	7,070	0.3%
45	North Dakota	6,095	0.2%
46	Vermont	5,112	0.2%
47	Wyoming	4,173	0.2%
48	Alaska	3,185	0.1%
NA	California**	NA	NA
NA	Illinois**	NA	NA
	District of Columbia	5,513	0.2%

Source: U.S. Department of Health and Human Services, National Center for Health Statistics
   "National Vital Statistics Reports" (Vol. 53, No. 15, February 28, 2005)
*Preliminary data by state of residence.
**Not available by state but are included in national total.

Age-Adjusted Death Rate in 2003

National Rate = 831.2 Deaths per 100,000 Population*

ALPHA ORDER

RANK	STATE	RATE
3	Alabama	1,001.9
23	Alaska	831.3
33	Arizona	788.9
9	Arkansas	937.6
NA	California**	NA
35	Colorado	785.3
46	Connecticut	729.5
22	Delaware	844.3
39	Florida	775.7
8	Georgia	946.4
48	Hawaii	650.1
29	Idaho	797.5
NA	Illinois**	NA
14	Indiana	898.1
41	Iowa	769.0
26	Kansas	824.0
6	Kentucky	976.9
2	Louisiana	1,007.4
27	Maine	821.9
17	Maryland	852.9
37	Massachusetts	778.8
20	Michigan	850.3
47	Minnesota	713.4
1	Mississippi	1,015.2
13	Missouri	902.4
24	Montana	828.3
31	Nebraska	790.6
11	Nevada	925.0
45	New Hampshire	748.4
30	New Jersey	794.7
25	New Mexico	827.7
44	New York	759.8
12	North Carolina	906.8
42	North Dakota	767.5
15	Ohio	886.2
7	Oklahoma	973.9
28	Oregon	808.9
21	Pennsylvania	849.1
34	Rhode Island	786.6
10	South Carolina	934.8
32	South Dakota	790.5
5	Tennessee	982.1
16	Texas	857.2
36	Utah	782.1
43	Vermont	764.1
18	Virginia	852.8
38	Washington	776.6
4	West Virginia	994.5
40	Wisconsin	772.3
19	Wyoming	850.6

RANK ORDER

RANK	STATE	RATE
1	Mississippi	1,015.2
2	Louisiana	1,007.4
3	Alabama	1,001.9
4	West Virginia	994.5
5	Tennessee	982.1
6	Kentucky	976.9
7	Oklahoma	973.9
8	Georgia	946.4
9	Arkansas	937.6
10	South Carolina	934.8
11	Nevada	925.0
12	North Carolina	906.8
13	Missouri	902.4
14	Indiana	898.1
15	Ohio	886.2
16	Texas	857.2
17	Maryland	852.9
18	Virginia	852.8
19	Wyoming	850.6
20	Michigan	850.3
21	Pennsylvania	849.1
22	Delaware	844.3
23	Alaska	831.3
24	Montana	828.3
25	New Mexico	827.7
26	Kansas	824.0
27	Maine	821.9
28	Oregon	808.9
29	Idaho	797.5
30	New Jersey	794.7
31	Nebraska	790.6
32	South Dakota	790.5
33	Arizona	788.9
34	Rhode Island	786.6
35	Colorado	785.3
36	Utah	782.1
37	Massachusetts	778.8
38	Washington	776.6
39	Florida	775.7
40	Wisconsin	772.3
41	Iowa	769.0
42	North Dakota	767.5
43	Vermont	764.1
44	New York	759.8
45	New Hampshire	748.4
46	Connecticut	729.5
47	Minnesota	713.4
48	Hawaii	650.1
NA	California**	NA
NA	Illinois**	NA
	District of Columbia	968.2

Source: U.S. Department of Health and Human Services, National Center for Health Statistics
     "National Vital Statistics Reports" (Vol. 53, No. 15, February 28, 2005)
*Preliminary data by state of residence. Age-adjusted rates eliminate the distorting effects of the aging of the population.
Rates based on the year 2000 standard population.
**Not available by state but are included in national rate.

Estimated Deaths by Cancer in 2005

National Estimated Total = 570,280 Deaths

ALPHA ORDER

RANK	STATE	DEATHS	% of USA
20	Alabama	10,100	1.8%
50	Alaska	800	0.1%
21	Arizona	9,920	1.7%
32	Arkansas	6,210	1.1%
1	California	56,090	9.8%
29	Colorado	6,680	1.2%
28	Connecticut	7,030	1.2%
46	Delaware	1,580	0.3%
2	Florida	39,960	7.0%
11	Georgia	14,810	2.6%
44	Hawaii	1,990	0.3%
42	Idaho	2,280	0.4%
6	Illinois	24,810	4.4%
14	Indiana	13,250	2.3%
30	Iowa	6,610	1.2%
33	Kansas	5,370	0.9%
23	Kentucky	9,560	1.7%
22	Louisiana	9,670	1.7%
38	Maine	3,220	0.6%
19	Maryland	10,570	1.9%
13	Massachusetts	13,720	2.4%
8	Michigan	20,860	3.7%
24	Minnesota	9,510	1.7%
31	Mississippi	6,220	1.1%
16	Missouri	12,550	2.2%
43	Montana	2,040	0.4%
36	Nebraska	3,460	0.6%
35	Nevada	4,620	0.8%
40	New Hampshire	2,620	0.5%
9	New Jersey	17,860	3.1%
37	New Mexico	3,230	0.6%
3	New York	36,160	6.3%
10	North Carolina	16,830	3.0%
47	North Dakota	1,280	0.2%
7	Ohio	24,790	4.3%
26	Oklahoma	7,670	1.3%
27	Oregon	7,360	1.3%
5	Pennsylvania	29,840	5.2%
41	Rhode Island	2,440	0.4%
25	South Carolina	9,080	1.6%
45	South Dakota	1,620	0.3%
15	Tennessee	12,910	2.3%
4	Texas	36,090	6.3%
39	Utah	2,650	0.5%
48	Vermont	1,260	0.2%
12	Virginia	13,990	2.5%
17	Washington	11,360	2.0%
34	West Virginia	4,650	0.8%
18	Wisconsin	10,940	1.9%
49	Wyoming	990	0.2%

RANK ORDER

RANK	STATE	DEATHS	% of USA
1	California	56,090	9.8%
2	Florida	39,960	7.0%
3	New York	36,160	6.3%
4	Texas	36,090	6.3%
5	Pennsylvania	29,840	5.2%
6	Illinois	24,810	4.4%
7	Ohio	24,790	4.3%
8	Michigan	20,860	3.7%
9	New Jersey	17,860	3.1%
10	North Carolina	16,830	3.0%
11	Georgia	14,810	2.6%
12	Virginia	13,990	2.5%
13	Massachusetts	13,720	2.4%
14	Indiana	13,250	2.3%
15	Tennessee	12,910	2.3%
16	Missouri	12,550	2.2%
17	Washington	11,360	2.0%
18	Wisconsin	10,940	1.9%
19	Maryland	10,570	1.9%
20	Alabama	10,100	1.8%
21	Arizona	9,920	1.7%
22	Louisiana	9,670	1.7%
23	Kentucky	9,560	1.7%
24	Minnesota	9,510	1.7%
25	South Carolina	9,080	1.6%
26	Oklahoma	7,670	1.3%
27	Oregon	7,360	1.3%
28	Connecticut	7,030	1.2%
29	Colorado	6,680	1.2%
30	Iowa	6,610	1.2%
31	Mississippi	6,220	1.1%
32	Arkansas	6,210	1.1%
33	Kansas	5,370	0.9%
34	West Virginia	4,650	0.8%
35	Nevada	4,620	0.8%
36	Nebraska	3,460	0.6%
37	New Mexico	3,230	0.6%
38	Maine	3,220	0.6%
39	Utah	2,650	0.5%
40	New Hampshire	2,620	0.5%
41	Rhode Island	2,440	0.4%
42	Idaho	2,280	0.4%
43	Montana	2,040	0.4%
44	Hawaii	1,990	0.3%
45	South Dakota	1,620	0.3%
46	Delaware	1,580	0.3%
47	North Dakota	1,280	0.2%
48	Vermont	1,260	0.2%
49	Wyoming	990	0.2%
50	Alaska	800	0.1%
	District of Columbia	1,170	0.2%

Source: American Cancer Society
"Cancer Facts & Figures 2005" (Copyright 2005, American Cancer Society)

Estimated Death Rate by Cancer in 2005

National Estimated Rate = 194.2 Deaths per 100,000 Population*

ALPHA ORDER

RANK	STATE	RATE
9	Alabama	222.9
49	Alaska	122.1
41	Arizona	172.7
7	Arkansas	225.6
47	California	156.3
48	Colorado	145.2
27	Connecticut	200.7
35	Delaware	190.3
5	Florida	229.7
43	Georgia	167.7
46	Hawaii	157.6
44	Idaho	163.6
34	Illinois	195.1
19	Indiana	212.4
8	Iowa	223.7
32	Kansas	196.3
4	Kentucky	230.6
17	Louisiana	214.1
2	Maine	244.4
36	Maryland	190.2
18	Massachusetts	213.8
21	Michigan	206.3
39	Minnesota	186.4
16	Mississippi	214.3
12	Missouri	218.1
10	Montana	220.1
29	Nebraska	198.0
30	Nevada	197.9
26	New Hampshire	201.6
22	New Jersey	205.3
42	New Mexico	169.7
37	New York	188.1
31	North Carolina	197.0
25	North Dakota	201.8
14	Ohio	216.3
13	Oklahoma	217.7
23	Oregon	204.8
3	Pennsylvania	240.5
6	Rhode Island	225.8
14	South Carolina	216.3
20	South Dakota	210.1
11	Tennessee	218.8
45	Texas	160.5
50	Utah	110.9
24	Vermont	202.8
38	Virginia	187.5
40	Washington	183.1
1	West Virginia	256.1
28	Wisconsin	198.6
33	Wyoming	195.4

RANK ORDER

RANK	STATE	RATE
1	West Virginia	256.1
2	Maine	244.4
3	Pennsylvania	240.5
4	Kentucky	230.6
5	Florida	229.7
6	Rhode Island	225.8
7	Arkansas	225.6
8	Iowa	223.7
9	Alabama	222.9
10	Montana	220.1
11	Tennessee	218.8
12	Missouri	218.1
13	Oklahoma	217.7
14	Ohio	216.3
14	South Carolina	216.3
16	Mississippi	214.3
17	Louisiana	214.1
18	Massachusetts	213.8
19	Indiana	212.4
20	South Dakota	210.1
21	Michigan	206.3
22	New Jersey	205.3
23	Oregon	204.8
24	Vermont	202.8
25	North Dakota	201.8
26	New Hampshire	201.6
27	Connecticut	200.7
28	Wisconsin	198.6
29	Nebraska	198.0
30	Nevada	197.9
31	North Carolina	197.0
32	Kansas	196.3
33	Wyoming	195.4
34	Illinois	195.1
35	Delaware	190.3
36	Maryland	190.2
37	New York	188.1
38	Virginia	187.5
39	Minnesota	186.4
40	Washington	183.1
41	Arizona	172.7
42	New Mexico	169.7
43	Georgia	167.7
44	Idaho	163.6
45	Texas	160.5
46	Hawaii	157.6
47	California	156.3
48	Colorado	145.2
49	Alaska	122.1
50	Utah	110.9

District of Columbia	211.4

Source: Morgan Quitno Press using data from American Cancer Society
"Cancer Facts & Figures 2005" (Copyright 2005, American Cancer Society)
*Rates calculated using 2004 Census resident population estimates. Not age-adjusted.

Estimated New Cancer Cases in 2005

National Estimated Total = 1,372,910 New Cases*

ALPHA ORDER

RANK	STATE	CASES	% of USA
20	Alabama	24,320	1.8%
50	Alaska	1,930	0.1%
21	Arizona	23,880	1.7%
32	Arkansas	14,950	1.1%
1	California	135,030	9.8%
29	Colorado	16,080	1.2%
28	Connecticut	16,920	1.2%
46	Delaware	3,800	0.3%
2	Florida	96,200	7.0%
11	Georgia	35,650	2.6%
44	Hawaii	4,790	0.3%
42	Idaho	5,490	0.4%
6	Illinois	59,730	4.4%
14	Indiana	31,900	2.3%
30	Iowa	15,910	1.2%
33	Kansas	12,930	0.9%
23	Kentucky	23,020	1.7%
22	Louisiana	23,280	1.7%
38	Maine	7,750	0.6%
19	Maryland	25,450	1.9%
13	Massachusetts	33,030	2.4%
8	Michigan	50,220	3.7%
24	Minnesota	22,890	1.7%
31	Mississippi	14,970	1.1%
16	Missouri	30,210	2.2%
43	Montana	4,910	0.4%
36	Nebraska	8,330	0.6%
35	Nevada	11,120	0.8%
40	New Hampshire	6,310	0.5%
9	New Jersey	43,000	3.1%
37	New Mexico	7,780	0.6%
3	New York	87,050	6.3%
10	North Carolina	40,520	3.0%
47	North Dakota	3,080	0.2%
7	Ohio	59,680	4.3%
26	Oklahoma	18,460	1.3%
27	Oregon	17,720	1.3%
5	Pennsylvania	71,840	5.2%
41	Rhode Island	5,870	0.4%
25	South Carolina	21,860	1.6%
45	South Dakota	3,900	0.3%
15	Tennessee	31,080	2.3%
4	Texas	86,880	6.3%
39	Utah	6,380	0.5%
48	Vermont	3,030	0.2%
12	Virginia	33,680	2.5%
17	Washington	27,350	2.0%
34	West Virginia	11,190	0.8%
18	Wisconsin	26,340	1.9%
49	Wyoming	2,380	0.2%

RANK ORDER

RANK	STATE	CASES	% of USA
1	California	135,030	9.8%
2	Florida	96,200	7.0%
3	New York	87,050	6.3%
4	Texas	86,880	6.3%
5	Pennsylvania	71,840	5.2%
6	Illinois	59,730	4.4%
7	Ohio	59,680	4.3%
8	Michigan	50,220	3.7%
9	New Jersey	43,000	3.1%
10	North Carolina	40,520	3.0%
11	Georgia	35,650	2.6%
12	Virginia	33,680	2.5%
13	Massachusetts	33,030	2.4%
14	Indiana	31,900	2.3%
15	Tennessee	31,080	2.3%
16	Missouri	30,210	2.2%
17	Washington	27,350	2.0%
18	Wisconsin	26,340	1.9%
19	Maryland	25,450	1.9%
20	Alabama	24,320	1.8%
21	Arizona	23,880	1.7%
22	Louisiana	23,280	1.7%
23	Kentucky	23,020	1.7%
24	Minnesota	22,890	1.7%
25	South Carolina	21,860	1.6%
26	Oklahoma	18,460	1.3%
27	Oregon	17,720	1.3%
28	Connecticut	16,920	1.2%
29	Colorado	16,080	1.2%
30	Iowa	15,910	1.2%
31	Mississippi	14,970	1.1%
32	Arkansas	14,950	1.1%
33	Kansas	12,930	0.9%
34	West Virginia	11,190	0.8%
35	Nevada	11,120	0.8%
36	Nebraska	8,330	0.6%
37	New Mexico	7,780	0.6%
38	Maine	7,750	0.6%
39	Utah	6,380	0.5%
40	New Hampshire	6,310	0.5%
41	Rhode Island	5,870	0.4%
42	Idaho	5,490	0.4%
43	Montana	4,910	0.4%
44	Hawaii	4,790	0.3%
45	South Dakota	3,900	0.3%
46	Delaware	3,800	0.3%
47	North Dakota	3,080	0.2%
48	Vermont	3,030	0.2%
49	Wyoming	2,380	0.2%
50	Alaska	1,930	0.1%
	District of Columbia	2,820	0.2%

Source: American Cancer Society
    "Cancer Facts & Figures 2005" (Copyright 2005, American Cancer Society)
*These estimates are offered as a rough guide and should not be regarded as definitive. They are calculated according to the distribution of estimated 2005 cancer deaths by state. Totals do not include basal and squamous cell skin cancers or in situ carcinomas except urinary bladder.

Estimated Rate of New Cancer Cases in 2005

National Estimated Rate = 467.5 New Cases per 100,000 Population*

ALPHA ORDER

RANK	STATE	RATE
9	Alabama	536.8
49	Alaska	294.5
41	Arizona	415.8
7	Arkansas	543.1
47	California	376.2
48	Colorado	349.5
27	Connecticut	482.9
36	Delaware	457.6
5	Florida	553.0
43	Georgia	403.8
46	Hawaii	379.3
44	Idaho	394.0
34	Illinois	469.8
19	Indiana	511.4
8	Iowa	538.5
32	Kansas	472.7
4	Kentucky	555.2
17	Louisiana	515.5
2	Maine	588.3
35	Maryland	457.9
18	Massachusetts	514.8
21	Michigan	496.6
39	Minnesota	448.7
16	Mississippi	515.7
12	Missouri	525.0
10	Montana	529.7
29	Nebraska	476.8
30	Nevada	476.3
25	New Hampshire	485.6
22	New Jersey	494.3
42	New Mexico	408.8
37	New York	452.7
31	North Carolina	474.4
26	North Dakota	485.5
14	Ohio	520.8
13	Oklahoma	523.9
23	Oregon	493.0
3	Pennsylvania	579.1
6	Rhode Island	543.2
15	South Carolina	520.7
20	South Dakota	505.9
11	Tennessee	526.7
45	Texas	386.3
50	Utah	267.1
24	Vermont	487.6
38	Virginia	451.5
40	Washington	440.9
1	West Virginia	616.4
28	Wisconsin	478.1
33	Wyoming	469.9

RANK ORDER

RANK	STATE	RATE
1	West Virginia	616.4
2	Maine	588.3
3	Pennsylvania	579.1
4	Kentucky	555.2
5	Florida	553.0
6	Rhode Island	543.2
7	Arkansas	543.1
8	Iowa	538.5
9	Alabama	536.8
10	Montana	529.7
11	Tennessee	526.7
12	Missouri	525.0
13	Oklahoma	523.9
14	Ohio	520.8
15	South Carolina	520.7
16	Mississippi	515.7
17	Louisiana	515.5
18	Massachusetts	514.8
19	Indiana	511.4
20	South Dakota	505.9
21	Michigan	496.6
22	New Jersey	494.3
23	Oregon	493.0
24	Vermont	487.6
25	New Hampshire	485.6
26	North Dakota	485.5
27	Connecticut	482.9
28	Wisconsin	478.1
29	Nebraska	476.8
30	Nevada	476.3
31	North Carolina	474.4
32	Kansas	472.7
33	Wyoming	469.9
34	Illinois	469.8
35	Maryland	457.9
36	Delaware	457.6
37	New York	452.7
38	Virginia	451.5
39	Minnesota	448.7
40	Washington	440.9
41	Arizona	415.8
42	New Mexico	408.8
43	Georgia	403.8
44	Idaho	394.0
45	Texas	386.3
46	Hawaii	379.3
47	California	376.2
48	Colorado	349.5
49	Alaska	294.5
50	Utah	267.1
	District of Columbia	509.5

Source: Morgan Quitno Press using data from American Cancer Society
"Cancer Facts & Figures 2005" (Copyright 2005, American Cancer Society)
These estimates are offered as a rough guide and should not be regarded as definitive. They are calculated according to the distribution of estimated 2005 cancer deaths by state. Totals do not include basal and squamous cell skin cancers or in situ carcinomas except urinary bladder. Rates calculated using 2004 Census resident population estimates.

Deaths by Accidents in 2002

National Total = 106,742 Deaths*

ALPHA ORDER

RANK	STATE	DEATHS	% of USA
17	Alabama	2,228	2.1%
45	Alaska	346	0.3%
14	Arizona	2,577	2.4%
30	Arkansas	1,311	1.2%
1	California	10,107	9.5%
24	Colorado	1,812	1.7%
31	Connecticut	1,182	1.1%
46	Delaware	292	0.3%
3	Florida	7,396	6.9%
9	Georgia	3,333	3.1%
42	Hawaii	393	0.4%
39	Idaho	611	0.6%
6	Illinois	4,222	4.0%
19	Indiana	2,148	2.0%
34	Iowa	1,093	1.0%
32	Kansas	1,139	1.1%
21	Kentucky	2,090	2.0%
20	Louisiana	2,115	2.0%
41	Maine	511	0.5%
29	Maryland	1,332	1.2%
27	Massachusetts	1,413	1.3%
10	Michigan	3,285	3.1%
23	Minnesota	1,928	1.8%
25	Mississippi	1,642	1.5%
12	Missouri	2,641	2.5%
40	Montana	524	0.5%
37	Nebraska	762	0.7%
36	Nevada	860	0.8%
43	New Hampshire	357	0.3%
13	New Jersey	2,599	2.4%
33	New Mexico	1,105	1.0%
5	New York	4,663	4.4%
8	North Carolina	3,700	3.5%
49	North Dakota	246	0.2%
7	Ohio	4,146	3.9%
26	Oklahoma	1,580	1.5%
28	Oregon	1,397	1.3%
4	Pennsylvania	4,728	4.4%
48	Rhode Island	277	0.3%
22	South Carolina	1,972	1.8%
44	South Dakota	348	0.3%
11	Tennessee	2,744	2.6%
2	Texas	8,232	7.7%
38	Utah	714	0.7%
50	Vermont	240	0.2%
15	Virginia	2,479	2.3%
18	Washington	2,203	2.1%
35	West Virginia	956	0.9%
16	Wisconsin	2,274	2.1%
47	Wyoming	289	0.3%

RANK ORDER

RANK	STATE	DEATHS	% of USA
1	California	10,107	9.5%
2	Texas	8,232	7.7%
3	Florida	7,396	6.9%
4	Pennsylvania	4,728	4.4%
5	New York	4,663	4.4%
6	Illinois	4,222	4.0%
7	Ohio	4,146	3.9%
8	North Carolina	3,700	3.5%
9	Georgia	3,333	3.1%
10	Michigan	3,285	3.1%
11	Tennessee	2,744	2.6%
12	Missouri	2,641	2.5%
13	New Jersey	2,599	2.4%
14	Arizona	2,577	2.4%
15	Virginia	2,479	2.3%
16	Wisconsin	2,274	2.1%
17	Alabama	2,228	2.1%
18	Washington	2,203	2.1%
19	Indiana	2,148	2.0%
20	Louisiana	2,115	2.0%
21	Kentucky	2,090	2.0%
22	South Carolina	1,972	1.8%
23	Minnesota	1,928	1.8%
24	Colorado	1,812	1.7%
25	Mississippi	1,642	1.5%
26	Oklahoma	1,580	1.5%
27	Massachusetts	1,413	1.3%
28	Oregon	1,397	1.3%
29	Maryland	1,332	1.2%
30	Arkansas	1,311	1.2%
31	Connecticut	1,182	1.1%
32	Kansas	1,139	1.1%
33	New Mexico	1,105	1.0%
34	Iowa	1,093	1.0%
35	West Virginia	956	0.9%
36	Nevada	860	0.8%
37	Nebraska	762	0.7%
38	Utah	714	0.7%
39	Idaho	611	0.6%
40	Montana	524	0.5%
41	Maine	511	0.5%
42	Hawaii	393	0.4%
43	New Hampshire	357	0.3%
44	South Dakota	348	0.3%
45	Alaska	346	0.3%
46	Delaware	292	0.3%
47	Wyoming	289	0.3%
48	Rhode Island	277	0.3%
49	North Dakota	246	0.2%
50	Vermont	240	0.2%
	District of Columbia	200	0.2%

Source: U.S. Department of Health and Human Services, National Center for Health Statistics
"National Vital Statistics Reports" (Vol. 53, No. 5, October 12, 2004)
*Final data by state of residence. Includes motor vehicle deaths, poisoning, falls, drowning and other accidents.

Age-Adjusted Death Rate by Accidents in 2002

National Rate = 36.9 Deaths per 100,000 Population*

RANK	STATE	RATE	RANK	STATE	RATE
	ALPHA ORDER			RANK ORDER	
8	Alabama	49.2	1	New Mexico	61.1
2	Alaska	59.0	2	Alaska	59.0
10	Arizona	48.1	3	Mississippi	57.9
13	Arkansas	47.3	3	Wyoming	57.9
44	California	29.9	5	Montana	55.2
19	Colorado	42.8	6	West Virginia	50.7
42	Connecticut	32.5	7	Kentucky	50.5
32	Delaware	35.9	8	Alabama	49.2
20	Florida	41.9	9	South Carolina	48.2
22	Georgia	41.8	10	Arizona	48.1
43	Hawaii	30.4	11	Louisiana	48.0
14	Idaho	46.8	12	Tennessee	47.4
39	Illinois	33.5	13	Arkansas	47.3
38	Indiana	34.8	14	Idaho	46.8
40	Iowa	33.3	15	Missouri	45.3
24	Kansas	40.6	16	North Carolina	45.2
7	Kentucky	50.5	17	Oklahoma	44.6
11	Louisiana	48.0	18	South Dakota	43.3
28	Maine	37.6	19	Colorado	42.8
47	Maryland	25.1	20	Florida	41.9
50	Massachusetts	20.5	20	Nevada	41.9
41	Michigan	32.7	22	Georgia	41.0
29	Minnesota	37.3	23	Nebraska	41.4
3	Mississippi	57.9	24	Kansas	40.6
15	Missouri	45.3	25	Texas	40.1
5	Montana	55.2	26	Wisconsin	39.7
23	Nebraska	41.4	27	Oregon	38.1
20	Nevada	41.9	28	Maine	37.6
46	New Hampshire	28.1	29	Minnesota	37.3
45	New Jersey	29.5	30	Vermont	37.2
1	New Mexico	61.1	31	Washington	36.5
48	New York	23.7	32	Delaware	35.9
16	North Carolina	45.2	33	Ohio	35.6
36	North Dakota	35.0	33	Pennsylvania	35.6
33	Ohio	35.6	33	Utah	35.6
17	Oklahoma	44.6	36	North Dakota	35.0
27	Oregon	38.1	36	Virginia	35.0
33	Pennsylvania	35.6	38	Indiana	34.8
49	Rhode Island	23.1	39	Illinois	33.5
9	South Carolina	48.2	40	Iowa	33.3
18	South Dakota	43.3	41	Michigan	32.7
12	Tennessee	47.4	42	Connecticut	32.5
25	Texas	40.1	43	Hawaii	30.4
33	Utah	35.6	44	California	29.9
30	Vermont	37.2	45	New Jersey	29.5
36	Virginia	35.0	46	New Hampshire	28.1
31	Washington	36.5	47	Maryland	25.1
6	West Virginia	50.7	48	New York	23.7
26	Wisconsin	39.7	49	Rhode Island	23.1
3	Wyoming	57.9	50	Massachusetts	20.5
				District of Columbia	34.5

Source: U.S. Department of Health and Human Services, National Center for Health Statistics
      "National Vital Statistics Reports" (Vol. 53, No. 5, October 12, 2004)
Final data by state of residence. Includes motor vehicle deaths, poisoning, falls, drowning and other accidents.
Age-adjusted rates based on the year 2000 standard population.

Deaths by Cerebrovascular Diseases in 2002

National Total = 162,672 Deaths*

ALPHA ORDER				RANK ORDER			
RANK	STATE	DEATHS	% of USA	RANK	STATE	DEATHS	% of USA
19	Alabama	3,201	2.0%	1	California	17,626	10.8%
50	Alaska	158	0.1%	2	Texas	10,548	6.5%
26	Arizona	2,535	1.6%	3	Florida	10,269	6.3%
28	Arkansas	2,232	1.4%	4	Pennsylvania	8,579	5.3%
1	California	17,626	10.8%	5	New York	7,625	4.7%
31	Colorado	1,915	1.2%	6	Ohio	7,252	4.5%
32	Connecticut	1,861	1.1%	7	Illinois	7,183	4.4%
47	Delaware	405	0.2%	8	Michigan	5,814	3.6%
3	Florida	10,269	6.3%	9	North Carolina	5,259	3.2%
10	Georgia	4,261	2.6%	10	Georgia	4,261	2.6%
39	Hawaii	812	0.5%	11	New Jersey	4,016	2.5%
40	Idaho	736	0.5%	12	Tennessee	3,980	2.4%
7	Illinois	7,183	4.4%	13	Virginia	3,960	2.4%
16	Indiana	3,717	2.3%	14	Missouri	3,885	2.4%
29	Iowa	2,226	1.4%	15	Washington	3,753	2.3%
33	Kansas	1,845	1.1%	16	Indiana	3,717	2.3%
25	Kentucky	2,554	1.6%	17	Massachusetts	3,559	2.2%
24	Louisiana	2,595	1.6%	18	Wisconsin	3,479	2.1%
38	Maine	823	0.5%	19	Alabama	3,201	2.0%
21	Maryland	2,811	1.7%	20	South Carolina	2,822	1.7%
17	Massachusetts	3,559	2.2%	21	Maryland	2,811	1.7%
8	Michigan	5,814	3.6%	22	Minnesota	2,706	1.7%
22	Minnesota	2,706	1.7%	23	Oregon	2,645	1.6%
30	Mississippi	1,926	1.2%	24	Louisiana	2,595	1.6%
14	Missouri	3,885	2.4%	25	Kentucky	2,554	1.6%
42	Montana	639	0.4%	26	Arizona	2,535	1.6%
35	Nebraska	1,103	0.7%	27	Oklahoma	2,427	1.5%
36	Nevada	976	0.6%	28	Arkansas	2,232	1.4%
43	New Hampshire	627	0.4%	29	Iowa	2,226	1.4%
11	New Jersey	4,016	2.5%	30	Mississippi	1,926	1.2%
41	New Mexico	715	0.4%	31	Colorado	1,915	1.2%
5	New York	7,625	4.7%	32	Connecticut	1,861	1.1%
9	North Carolina	5,259	3.2%	33	Kansas	1,845	1.1%
46	North Dakota	469	0.3%	34	West Virginia	1,260	0.8%
6	Ohio	7,252	4.5%	35	Nebraska	1,103	0.7%
27	Oklahoma	2,427	1.5%	36	Nevada	976	0.6%
23	Oregon	2,645	1.6%	37	Utah	903	0.6%
4	Pennsylvania	8,579	5.3%	38	Maine	823	0.5%
44	Rhode Island	605	0.4%	39	Hawaii	812	0.5%
20	South Carolina	2,822	1.7%	40	Idaho	736	0.5%
45	South Dakota	518	0.3%	41	New Mexico	715	0.4%
12	Tennessee	3,980	2.4%	42	Montana	639	0.4%
2	Texas	10,548	6.5%	43	New Hampshire	627	0.4%
37	Utah	903	0.6%	44	Rhode Island	605	0.4%
48	Vermont	335	0.2%	45	South Dakota	518	0.3%
13	Virginia	3,960	2.4%	46	North Dakota	469	0.3%
15	Washington	3,753	2.3%	47	Delaware	405	0.2%
34	West Virginia	1,260	0.8%	48	Vermont	335	0.2%
18	Wisconsin	3,479	2.1%	49	Wyoming	243	0.1%
49	Wyoming	243	0.1%	50	Alaska	158	0.1%
					District of Columbia	279	0.2%

Source: U.S. Department of Health and Human Services, National Center for Health Statistics
"National Vital Statistics Reports" (Vol. 53, No. 5, October 12, 2004)
*Final data by state of residence. Cerebrovascular diseases include stroke and other disorders of the blood vessels of the brain.

Age-Adjusted Death Rate by Cerebrovascular Diseases in 2002

National Rate = 56.2 Deaths per 100,000 Population*

ALPHA ORDER

RANK ORDER

RANK	STATE	RATE		RANK	STATE	RATE
4	Alabama	69.6		1	Arkansas	74.3
31	Alaska	55.1		2	South Carolina	72.7
44	Arizona	47.7		3	Tennessee	70.1
1	Arkansas	74.3		4	Alabama	69.6
24	California	58.0		5	Mississippi	69.5
34	Colorado	54.4		5	Oregon	69.5
47	Connecticut	45.6		7	North Carolina	67.8
41	Delaware	50.4		8	Oklahoma	66.2
45	Florida	46.0		9	Georgia	65.3
9	Georgia	65.3		10	Washington	65.2
17	Hawaii	60.6		11	Kentucky	63.5
20	Idaho	59.4		12	Louisiana	63.0
27	Illinois	57.2		13	Missouri	62.5
18	Indiana	60.1		14	Montana	62.4
25	Iowa	57.9		15	Texas	61.8
19	Kansas	59.5		16	Virginia	61.2
11	Kentucky	63.5		17	Hawaii	60.6
12	Louisiana	63.0		18	Indiana	60.1
37	Maine	53.7		19	Kansas	59.5
30	Maryland	56.7		20	Idaho	59.4
43	Massachusetts	48.1		20	Ohio	59.4
23	Michigan	58.1		22	West Virginia	58.3
39	Minnesota	51.3		23	Michigan	58.1
5	Mississippi	69.5		24	California	58.0
13	Missouri	62.5		25	Iowa	57.9
14	Montana	62.4		26	Wisconsin	57.7
32	Nebraska	54.7		27	Illinois	57.2
28	Nevada	56.8		28	Nevada	56.8
42	New Hampshire	50.1		28	Utah	56.8
48	New Jersey	43.4		30	Maryland	56.7
49	New Mexico	41.5		31	Alaska	55.1
50	New York	37.4		32	Nebraska	54.7
7	North Carolina	67.8		33	North Dakota	54.6
33	North Dakota	54.6		34	Colorado	54.4
20	Ohio	59.4		34	Pennsylvania	54.4
8	Oklahoma	66.2		36	South Dakota	54.2
5	Oregon	69.5		37	Maine	53.7
34	Pennsylvania	54.4		38	Wyoming	51.5
46	Rhode Island	45.8		39	Minnesota	51.3
2	South Carolina	72.7		40	Vermont	50.9
36	South Dakota	54.2		41	Delaware	50.4
3	Tennessee	70.1		42	New Hampshire	50.1
15	Texas	61.8		43	Massachusetts	48.1
28	Utah	56.8		44	Arizona	47.7
40	Vermont	50.9		45	Florida	46.0
16	Virginia	61.2		46	Rhode Island	45.8
10	Washington	65.2		47	Connecticut	45.6
22	West Virginia	58.3		48	New Jersey	43.4
26	Wisconsin	57.7		49	New Mexico	41.5
38	Wyoming	51.5		50	New York	37.4
					District of Columbia	48.7

Source: U.S. Department of Health and Human Services, National Center for Health Statistics
        "National Vital Statistics Reports" (Vol. 53, No. 5, October 12, 2004)
*Final data by state of residence. Cerebrovascular diseases include stroke and other disorders of the blood vessels of the brain. Age-adjusted rates based on the year 2000 standard population.

Deaths by Diseases of the Heart in 2002

National Total = 696,947 Deaths*

ALPHA ORDER

ALPHA ORDER

RANK	STATE	DEATHS	% of USA
17	Alabama	13,197	1.9%
50	Alaska	567	0.1%
24	Arizona	10,852	1.6%
29	Arkansas	8,330	1.2%
1	California	68,797	9.9%
33	Colorado	6,425	0.9%
27	Connecticut	8,815	1.3%
46	Delaware	1,918	0.3%
3	Florida	49,235	7.1%
11	Georgia	17,529	2.5%
43	Hawaii	2,512	0.4%
42	Idaho	2,532	0.4%
7	Illinois	30,821	4.4%
14	Indiana	15,321	2.2%
30	Iowa	8,181	1.2%
32	Kansas	6,680	1.0%
20	Kentucky	11,696	1.7%
22	Louisiana	11,185	1.6%
38	Maine	3,170	0.5%
19	Maryland	12,008	1.7%
16	Massachusetts	14,736	2.1%
8	Michigan	26,659	3.8%
28	Minnesota	8,602	1.2%
26	Mississippi	9,061	1.3%
12	Missouri	16,708	2.4%
44	Montana	1,944	0.3%
36	Nebraska	4,242	0.6%
35	Nevada	4,421	0.6%
41	New Hampshire	2,776	0.4%
9	New Jersey	22,510	3.2%
37	New Mexico	3,360	0.5%
2	New York	56,672	8.1%
10	North Carolina	18,524	2.7%
47	North Dakota	1,623	0.2%
6	Ohio	31,388	4.5%
21	Oklahoma	11,230	1.6%
31	Oregon	7,262	1.0%
5	Pennsylvania	38,852	5.6%
39	Rhode Island	3,109	0.4%
25	South Carolina	9,659	1.4%
45	South Dakota	1,937	0.3%
13	Tennessee	16,226	2.3%
4	Texas	43,452	6.2%
40	Utah	2,977	0.4%
48	Vermont	1,370	0.2%
15	Virginia	14,952	2.1%
23	Washington	11,141	1.6%
34	West Virginia	6,189	0.9%
18	Wisconsin	12,923	1.9%
49	Wyoming	1,005	0.1%

RANK ORDER

RANK	STATE	DEATHS	% of USA
1	California	68,797	9.9%
2	New York	56,672	8.1%
3	Florida	49,235	7.1%
4	Texas	43,452	6.2%
5	Pennsylvania	38,852	5.6%
6	Ohio	31,388	4.5%
7	Illinois	30,821	4.4%
8	Michigan	26,659	3.8%
9	New Jersey	22,510	3.2%
10	North Carolina	18,524	2.7%
11	Georgia	17,529	2.5%
12	Missouri	16,708	2.4%
13	Tennessee	16,226	2.3%
14	Indiana	15,321	2.2%
15	Virginia	14,952	2.1%
16	Massachusetts	14,736	2.1%
17	Alabama	13,197	1.9%
18	Wisconsin	12,923	1.9%
19	Maryland	12,008	1.7%
20	Kentucky	11,696	1.7%
21	Oklahoma	11,230	1.6%
22	Louisiana	11,185	1.6%
23	Washington	11,141	1.6%
24	Arizona	10,852	1.6%
25	South Carolina	9,659	1.4%
26	Mississippi	9,061	1.3%
27	Connecticut	8,815	1.3%
28	Minnesota	8,602	1.2%
29	Arkansas	8,330	1.2%
30	Iowa	8,181	1.2%
31	Oregon	7,262	1.0%
32	Kansas	6,680	1.0%
33	Colorado	6,425	0.9%
34	West Virginia	6,189	0.9%
35	Nevada	4,421	0.6%
36	Nebraska	4,242	0.6%
37	New Mexico	3,360	0.5%
38	Maine	3,170	0.5%
39	Rhode Island	3,109	0.4%
40	Utah	2,977	0.4%
41	New Hampshire	2,776	0.4%
42	Idaho	2,532	0.4%
43	Hawaii	2,512	0.4%
44	Montana	1,944	0.3%
45	South Dakota	1,937	0.3%
46	Delaware	1,918	0.3%
47	North Dakota	1,623	0.2%
48	Vermont	1,370	0.2%
49	Wyoming	1,005	0.1%
50	Alaska	567	0.1%
	District of Columbia	1,666	0.2%

*Source: U.S. Department of Health and Human Services, National Center for Health Statistics
"National Vital Statistics Reports" (Vol. 53, No. 5, October 12, 2004)*
*Final data by state of residence.

Age-Adjusted Death Rate by Diseases of the Heart in 2002

National Rate = 240.8 Deaths per 100,000 Population*

ALPHA ORDER

RANK	STATE	RATE
5	Alabama	285.8
49	Alaska	166.0
39	Arizona	202.9
7	Arkansas	278.7
26	California	225.7
48	Colorado	178.9
31	Connecticut	217.6
23	Delaware	236.0
27	Florida	222.0
12	Georgia	261.8
46	Hawaii	188.3
38	Idaho	203.0
17	Illinois	246.4
16	Indiana	248.4
30	Iowa	219.5
28	Kansas	220.6
4	Kentucky	287.0
10	Louisiana	269.6
36	Maine	208.5
21	Maryland	239.6
40	Massachusetts	201.3
11	Michigan	266.0
50	Minnesota	164.7
1	Mississippi	326.6
9	Missouri	270.3
45	Montana	191.6
33	Nebraska	213.5
18	Nevada	245.1
29	New Hampshire	220.2
20	New Jersey	243.5
42	New Mexico	193.3
8	New York	277.4
24	North Carolina	235.2
40	North Dakota	201.3
13	Ohio	258.2
2	Oklahoma	306.0
44	Oregon	192.3
14	Pennsylvania	250.1
22	Rhode Island	239.1
19	South Carolina	244.4
35	South Dakota	209.7
6	Tennessee	282.4
15	Texas	249.8
47	Utah	185.1
37	Vermont	208.3
25	Virginia	226.8
42	Washington	193.3
3	West Virginia	287.3
32	Wisconsin	216.5
34	Wyoming	210.0

RANK ORDER

RANK	STATE	RATE
1	Mississippi	326.6
2	Oklahoma	306.0
3	West Virginia	287.3
4	Kentucky	287.0
5	Alabama	285.8
6	Tennessee	282.4
7	Arkansas	278.7
8	New York	277.4
9	Missouri	270.3
10	Louisiana	269.6
11	Michigan	266.0
12	Georgia	261.8
13	Ohio	258.2
14	Pennsylvania	250.1
15	Texas	249.8
16	Indiana	248.4
17	Illinois	246.4
18	Nevada	245.1
19	South Carolina	244.4
20	New Jersey	243.5
21	Maryland	239.6
22	Rhode Island	239.1
23	Delaware	236.0
24	North Carolina	235.2
25	Virginia	226.8
26	California	225.7
27	Florida	222.0
28	Kansas	220.6
29	New Hampshire	220.2
30	Iowa	219.5
31	Connecticut	217.6
32	Wisconsin	216.5
33	Nebraska	213.5
34	Wyoming	210.0
35	South Dakota	209.7
36	Maine	208.5
37	Vermont	208.3
38	Idaho	203.0
39	Arizona	202.9
40	Massachusetts	201.3
40	North Dakota	201.3
42	New Mexico	193.3
42	Washington	193.3
44	Oregon	192.3
45	Montana	191.6
46	Hawaii	188.3
47	Utah	185.1
48	Colorado	178.9
49	Alaska	166.0
50	Minnesota	164.7
	District of Columbia	291.7

Source: U.S. Department of Health and Human Services, National Center for Health Statistics
"National Vital Statistics Reports" (Vol. 53, No. 5, October 12, 2004)
Final data by state of residence. Age-adjusted rates based on the year 2000 standard population.

Deaths by Suicide in 2002

National Total = 31,655 Suicides*

ALPHA ORDER

RANK	STATE	SUICIDES	% of USA
22	Alabama	514	1.6%
42	Alaska	132	0.4%
11	Arizona	886	2.8%
30	Arkansas	377	1.2%
1	California	3,228	10.2%
16	Colorado	727	2.3%
37	Connecticut	260	0.8%
50	Delaware	74	0.2%
2	Florida	2,338	7.4%
10	Georgia	909	2.9%
44	Hawaii	120	0.4%
38	Idaho	202	0.6%
7	Illinois	1,145	3.6%
15	Indiana	743	2.3%
35	Iowa	314	1.0%
32	Kansas	345	1.1%
20	Kentucky	540	1.7%
24	Louisiana	499	1.6%
41	Maine	166	0.5%
26	Maryland	477	1.5%
28	Massachusetts	436	1.4%
8	Michigan	1,106	3.5%
25	Minnesota	497	1.6%
33	Mississippi	343	1.1%
17	Missouri	693	2.2%
40	Montana	184	0.6%
39	Nebraska	201	0.6%
29	Nevada	423	1.3%
42	New Hampshire	132	0.4%
19	New Jersey	553	1.7%
31	New Mexico	349	1.1%
6	New York	1,228	3.9%
9	North Carolina	986	3.1%
48	North Dakota	91	0.3%
5	Ohio	1,287	4.1%
23	Oklahoma	501	1.6%
21	Oregon	518	1.6%
4	Pennsylvania	1,341	4.2%
49	Rhode Island	86	0.3%
27	South Carolina	440	1.4%
46	South Dakota	94	0.3%
14	Tennessee	778	2.5%
3	Texas	2,311	7.3%
34	Utah	340	1.1%
47	Vermont	92	0.3%
13	Virginia	799	2.5%
12	Washington	811	2.6%
36	West Virginia	276	0.9%
18	Wisconsin	627	2.0%
45	Wyoming	105	0.3%

RANK ORDER

RANK	STATE	SUICIDES	% of USA
1	California	3,228	10.2%
2	Florida	2,338	7.4%
3	Texas	2,311	7.3%
4	Pennsylvania	1,341	4.2%
5	Ohio	1,287	4.1%
6	New York	1,228	3.9%
7	Illinois	1,145	3.6%
8	Michigan	1,106	3.5%
9	North Carolina	986	3.1%
10	Georgia	909	2.9%
11	Arizona	886	2.8%
12	Washington	811	2.6%
13	Virginia	799	2.5%
14	Tennessee	778	2.5%
15	Indiana	743	2.3%
16	Colorado	727	2.3%
17	Missouri	693	2.2%
18	Wisconsin	627	2.0%
19	New Jersey	553	1.7%
20	Kentucky	540	1.7%
21	Oregon	518	1.6%
22	Alabama	514	1.6%
23	Oklahoma	501	1.6%
24	Louisiana	499	1.6%
25	Minnesota	497	1.6%
26	Maryland	477	1.5%
27	South Carolina	440	1.4%
28	Massachusetts	436	1.4%
29	Nevada	423	1.3%
30	Arkansas	377	1.2%
31	New Mexico	349	1.1%
32	Kansas	345	1.1%
33	Mississippi	343	1.1%
34	Utah	340	1.1%
35	Iowa	314	1.0%
36	West Virginia	276	0.9%
37	Connecticut	260	0.8%
38	Idaho	202	0.6%
39	Nebraska	201	0.6%
40	Montana	184	0.6%
41	Maine	166	0.5%
42	Alaska	132	0.4%
42	New Hampshire	132	0.4%
44	Hawaii	120	0.4%
45	Wyoming	105	0.3%
46	South Dakota	94	0.3%
47	Vermont	92	0.3%
48	North Dakota	91	0.3%
49	Rhode Island	86	0.3%
50	Delaware	74	0.2%
	District of Columbia	31	0.1%

Source: U.S. Department of Health and Human Services, National Center for Health Statistics
     "National Vital Statistics Reports" (Vol. 53, No. 5, October 12, 2004)
*Final data by state of residence.

Age-Adjusted Death Rate by Suicide in 2002

National Rate = 10.9 Deaths per 100,000 Population*

ALPHA ORDER			RANK ORDER		
RANK	STATE	RATE	RANK	STATE	RATE
28	Alabama	11.4	1	Alaska	21.0
1	Alaska	21.0	2	Wyoming	20.7
6	Arizona	16.5	3	Montana	19.9
15	Arkansas	14.0	4	Nevada	19.8
41	California	9.6	5	New Mexico	19.1
7	Colorado	16.2	6	Arizona	16.5
47	Connecticut	7.4	7	Colorado	16.2
44	Delaware	9.0	8	Utah	16.1
16	Florida	13.4	9	Idaho	15.5
32	Georgia	11.0	10	West Virginia	14.8
42	Hawaii	9.5	11	Oregon	14.4
9	Idaho	15.5	12	Oklahoma	14.3
43	Illinois	9.1	13	North Dakota	14.2
23	Indiana	12.1	14	Vermont	14.1
38	Iowa	10.5	15	Arkansas	14.0
20	Kansas	12.6	16	Florida	13.4
19	Kentucky	12.8	17	Washington	13.3
30	Louisiana	11.2	18	Tennessee	13.2
21	Maine	12.3	19	Kentucky	12.8
45	Maryland	8.7	20	Kansas	12.6
48	Massachusetts	6.5	21	Maine	12.3
32	Michigan	11.0	22	South Dakota	12.2
40	Minnesota	9.7	23	Indiana	12.1
23	Mississippi	12.1	23	Mississippi	12.1
23	Missouri	12.1	23	Missouri	12.1
3	Montana	19.9	26	North Carolina	11.8
27	Nebraska	11.7	27	Nebraska	11.7
4	Nevada	19.8	28	Alabama	11.4
39	New Hampshire	10.2	29	Wisconsin	11.3
49	New Jersey	6.3	30	Louisiana	11.2
5	New Mexico	19.1	30	Ohio	11.2
49	New York	6.3	32	Georgia	11.0
26	North Carolina	11.8	32	Michigan	11.0
13	North Dakota	14.2	32	Texas	11.0
30	Ohio	11.2	35	Virginia	10.9
12	Oklahoma	14.3	36	Pennsylvania	10.7
11	Oregon	14.4	37	South Carolina	10.6
36	Pennsylvania	10.7	38	Iowa	10.5
46	Rhode Island	7.9	39	New Hampshire	10.2
37	South Carolina	10.6	40	Minnesota	9.7
22	South Dakota	12.2	41	California	9.6
18	Tennessee	13.2	42	Hawaii	9.5
32	Texas	11.0	43	Illinois	9.1
8	Utah	16.1	44	Delaware	9.0
14	Vermont	14.1	45	Maryland	8.7
35	Virginia	10.9	46	Rhode Island	7.9
17	Washington	13.3	47	Connecticut	7.4
10	West Virginia	14.8	48	Massachusetts	6.5
29	Wisconsin	11.3	49	New Jersey	6.3
2	Wyoming	20.7	49	New York	6.3
				District of Columbia	5.1

Source: U.S. Department of Health and Human Services, National Center for Health Statistics
   "National Vital Statistics Reports" (Vol. 53, No. 5, October 12, 2004)
*Final data by state of residence. Age-adjusted rates based on the year 2000 standard population.

Deaths by AIDS in 2002

National Total = 14,095 Deaths*

ALPHA ORDER

RANK	STATE	DEATHS	% of USA
18	Alabama	190	1.3%
42	Alaska	16	0.1%
21	Arizona	165	1.2%
29	Arkansas	81	0.6%
3	California	1,435	10.2%
25	Colorado	105	0.7%
19	Connecticut	186	1.3%
32	Delaware	70	0.5%
2	Florida	1,719	12.2%
6	Georgia	708	5.0%
37	Hawaii	26	0.2%
45	Idaho	11	0.1%
9	Illinois	490	3.5%
24	Indiana	118	0.8%
36	Iowa	29	0.2%
34	Kansas	37	0.3%
26	Kentucky	98	0.7%
11	Louisiana	364	2.6%
44	Maine	12	0.1%
7	Maryland	610	4.3%
17	Massachusetts	232	1.6%
16	Michigan	240	1.7%
33	Minnesota	53	0.4%
20	Mississippi	185	1.3%
22	Missouri	123	0.9%
46	Montana	8	0.1%
39	Nebraska	21	0.1%
31	Nevada	76	0.5%
43	New Hampshire	13	0.1%
5	New Jersey	762	5.4%
35	New Mexico	35	0.2%
1	New York	1,980	14.0%
10	North Carolina	486	3.4%
50	North Dakota	1	0.0%
15	Ohio	241	1.7%
27	Oklahoma	91	0.6%
27	Oregon	91	0.6%
8	Pennsylvania	497	3.5%
38	Rhode Island	23	0.2%
13	South Carolina	301	2.1%
48	South Dakota	5	0.0%
12	Tennessee	347	2.5%
4	Texas	1,075	7.6%
41	Utah	19	0.1%
46	Vermont	8	0.1%
14	Virginia	261	1.9%
23	Washington	119	0.8%
40	West Virginia	20	0.1%
30	Wisconsin	77	0.5%
49	Wyoming	2	0.0%

RANK ORDER

RANK	STATE	DEATHS	% of USA
1	New York	1,980	14.0%
2	Florida	1,719	12.2%
3	California	1,435	10.2%
4	Texas	1,075	7.6%
5	New Jersey	762	5.4%
6	Georgia	708	5.0%
7	Maryland	610	4.3%
8	Pennsylvania	497	3.5%
9	Illinois	490	3.5%
10	North Carolina	486	3.4%
11	Louisiana	364	2.6%
12	Tennessee	347	2.5%
13	South Carolina	301	2.1%
14	Virginia	261	1.9%
15	Ohio	241	1.7%
16	Michigan	240	1.7%
17	Massachusetts	232	1.6%
18	Alabama	190	1.3%
19	Connecticut	186	1.3%
20	Mississippi	185	1.3%
21	Arizona	165	1.2%
22	Missouri	123	0.9%
23	Washington	119	0.8%
24	Indiana	118	0.8%
25	Colorado	105	0.7%
26	Kentucky	98	0.7%
27	Oklahoma	91	0.6%
27	Oregon	91	0.6%
29	Arkansas	81	0.6%
30	Wisconsin	77	0.5%
31	Nevada	76	0.5%
32	Delaware	70	0.5%
33	Minnesota	53	0.4%
34	Kansas	37	0.3%
35	New Mexico	35	0.2%
36	Iowa	29	0.2%
37	Hawaii	26	0.2%
38	Rhode Island	23	0.2%
39	Nebraska	21	0.1%
40	West Virginia	20	0.1%
41	Utah	19	0.1%
42	Alaska	16	0.1%
43	New Hampshire	13	0.1%
44	Maine	12	0.1%
45	Idaho	11	0.1%
46	Montana	8	0.1%
46	Vermont	8	0.1%
48	South Dakota	5	0.0%
49	Wyoming	2	0.0%
50	North Dakota	1	0.0%
	District of Columbia	233	1.7%

Source: U.S. Department of Health and Human Services, National Center for Health Statistics
   "National Vital Statistics Reports" (Vol. 53, No. 5, October 12, 2004)
*AIDS is Acquired Immunodeficiency Syndrome. It is a specific group of diseases or conditions which are indicative
of severe immunosuppression related to infection with the Human Immunodeficiency Virus (HIV).

Age-Adjusted Death Rate by AIDS in 2002

National Rate = 4.9 Deaths per 100,000 Population*

ALPHA ORDER			RANK ORDER		
RANK	STATE	RATE	RANK	STATE	RATE
14	Alabama	4.3	1	Maryland	10.7
NA	Alaska**	NA	2	Florida	10.4
21	Arizona	3.3	3	New York	10.2
22	Arkansas	3.2	4	Delaware	8.5
15	California	4.2	4	New Jersey	8.5
26	Colorado	2.3	6	Louisiana	8.4
12	Connecticut	5.2	7	Georgia	8.2
4	Delaware	8.5	8	South Carolina	7.4
2	Florida	10.4	9	Mississippi	6.8
7	Georgia	8.2	10	Tennessee	5.9
30	Hawaii	2.1	11	North Carolina	5.8
NA	Idaho**	NA	12	Connecticut	5.2
17	Illinois	3.9	13	Texas	5.1
32	Indiana	2.0	14	Alabama	4.3
39	Iowa	1.0	15	California	4.2
35	Kansas	1.4	16	Pennsylvania	4.0
26	Kentucky	2.3	17	Illinois	3.9
6	Louisiana	8.4	18	Massachusetts	3.5
NA	Maine**	NA	18	Nevada	3.5
1	Maryland	10.7	18	Virginia	3.5
18	Massachusetts	3.5	21	Arizona	3.3
25	Michigan	2.4	22	Arkansas	3.2
39	Minnesota	1.0	23	Oklahoma	2.7
9	Mississippi	6.8	24	Oregon	2.6
28	Missouri	2.2	25	Michigan	2.4
NA	Montana**	NA	26	Colorado	2.3
37	Nebraska	1.3	26	Kentucky	2.3
18	Nevada	3.5	28	Missouri	2.2
NA	New Hampshire**	NA	28	Ohio	2.2
4	New Jersey	8.5	30	Hawaii	2.1
32	New Mexico	2.0	30	Rhode Island	2.1
3	New York	10.2	32	Indiana	2.0
11	North Carolina	5.8	32	New Mexico	2.0
NA	North Dakota**	NA	34	Washington	1.9
28	Ohio	2.2	35	Kansas	1.4
23	Oklahoma	2.7	35	Wisconsin	1.4
24	Oregon	2.6	37	Nebraska	1.3
16	Pennsylvania	4.0	38	West Virginia	1.1
30	Rhode Island	2.1	39	Iowa	1.0
8	South Carolina	7.4	39	Minnesota	1.0
NA	South Dakota**	NA	NA	Alaska**	NA
10	Tennessee	5.9	NA	Idaho**	NA
13	Texas	5.1	NA	Maine**	NA
NA	Utah**	NA	NA	Montana**	NA
NA	Vermont**	NA	NA	New Hampshire**	NA
18	Virginia	3.5	NA	North Dakota**	NA
34	Washington	1.9	NA	South Dakota**	NA
38	West Virginia	1.1	NA	Utah**	NA
35	Wisconsin	1.4	NA	Vermont**	NA
NA	Wyoming**	NA	NA	Wyoming**	NA
				District of Columbia	40.8

Source: U.S. Department of Health and Human Services, National Center for Health Statistics
    "National Vital Statistics Reports" (Vol. 53, No. 5, October 12, 2004)
*AIDS is Acquired Immunodeficiency Syndrome. It is a specific group of diseases or conditions which are indicative
of severe immunosuppression related to infection with the Human Immunodeficiency Virus (HIV). Age-adjusted rates
based on the year 2000 standard population.
**Insufficient data to determine a reliable rate.

AIDS Cases Reported in 2005

National Total = 30,568 New AIDS Cases*

ALPHA ORDER

RANK	STATE	CASES	% of USA
20	Alabama	385	1.3%
43	Alaska	25	0.1%
15	Arizona	473	1.5%
31	Arkansas	173	0.6%
3	California	3,105	10.2%
25	Colorado	260	0.9%
18	Connecticut	423	1.4%
32	Delaware	134	0.4%
2	Florida	3,963	13.0%
5	Georgia	1,701	5.6%
37	Hawaii	92	0.3%
45	Idaho	15	0.0%
6	Illinois	1,504	4.9%
22	Indiana	348	1.1%
38	Iowa	72	0.2%
36	Kansas	94	0.3%
28	Kentucky	198	0.6%
11	Louisiana	650	2.1%
44	Maine	19	0.1%
7	Maryland	1,370	4.5%
13	Massachusetts	561	1.8%
17	Michigan	439	1.4%
30	Minnesota	176	0.6%
24	Mississippi	288	0.9%
23	Missouri	299	1.0%
45	Montana	15	0.0%
41	Nebraska	27	0.1%
26	Nevada	236	0.8%
42	New Hampshire	26	0.1%
9	New Jersey	956	3.1%
34	New Mexico	115	0.4%
1	New York	4,413	14.4%
12	North Carolina	636	2.1%
48	North Dakota	9	0.0%
14	Ohio	518	1.7%
27	Oklahoma	229	0.7%
29	Oregon	193	0.6%
8	Pennsylvania	1,228	4.0%
35	Rhode Island	105	0.3%
19	South Carolina	413	1.4%
47	South Dakota	13	0.0%
10	Tennessee	675	2.2%
4	Texas	2,491	8.1%
39	Utah	55	0.2%
49	Vermont	7	0.0%
16	Virginia	441	1.4%
21	Washington	352	1.2%
40	West Virginia	51	0.2%
33	Wisconsin	120	0.4%
50	Wyoming	3	0.0%

RANK ORDER

RANK	STATE	CASES	% of USA
1	New York	4,413	14.4%
2	Florida	3,963	13.0%
3	California	3,105	10.2%
4	Texas	2,491	8.1%
5	Georgia	1,701	5.6%
6	Illinois	1,504	4.9%
7	Maryland	1,370	4.5%
8	Pennsylvania	1,228	4.0%
9	New Jersey	956	3.1%
10	Tennessee	675	2.2%
11	Louisiana	650	2.1%
12	North Carolina	636	2.1%
13	Massachusetts	561	1.8%
14	Ohio	518	1.7%
15	Arizona	473	1.5%
16	Virginia	441	1.4%
17	Michigan	439	1.4%
18	Connecticut	423	1.4%
19	South Carolina	413	1.4%
20	Alabama	385	1.3%
21	Washington	352	1.2%
22	Indiana	348	1.1%
23	Missouri	299	1.0%
24	Mississippi	288	0.9%
25	Colorado	260	0.9%
26	Nevada	236	0.8%
27	Oklahoma	229	0.7%
28	Kentucky	198	0.6%
29	Oregon	193	0.6%
30	Minnesota	176	0.6%
31	Arkansas	173	0.6%
32	Delaware	134	0.4%
33	Wisconsin	120	0.4%
34	New Mexico	115	0.4%
35	Rhode Island	105	0.3%
36	Kansas	94	0.3%
37	Hawaii	92	0.3%
38	Iowa	72	0.2%
39	Utah	55	0.2%
40	West Virginia	51	0.2%
41	Nebraska	27	0.1%
42	New Hampshire	26	0.1%
43	Alaska	25	0.1%
44	Maine	19	0.1%
45	Idaho	15	0.0%
45	Montana	15	0.0%
47	South Dakota	13	0.0%
48	North Dakota	9	0.0%
49	Vermont	7	0.0%
50	Wyoming	3	0.0%
	District of Columbia	474	1.6%

Source: U.S. Department of Health and Human Services, National Center for Health Statistics
"Morbidity and Mortality Weekly Report" (January 6, 2006, Vol. 54, Nos. 51 & 52)
*Provisional data. AIDS is Acquired Immunodeficiency Syndrome. It is a specific group of diseases or conditions which are indicative of severe immunosuppression related to infection with the Human Immunodeficiency Virus (HIV). National total does not include 814 new cases in Puerto Rico.

AIDS Rate in 2005

National Rate = 10.3 New AIDS Cases Reported per 100,000 Population*

ALPHA ORDER

RANK	STATE	RATE
19	Alabama	8.4
35	Alaska	3.8
20	Arizona	8.0
24	Arkansas	6.2
18	California	8.6
27	Colorado	5.6
7	Connecticut	12.1
5	Delaware	15.9
3	Florida	22.3
4	Georgia	18.7
22	Hawaii	7.2
49	Idaho	1.0
8	Illinois	11.8
29	Indiana	5.5
39	Iowa	2.4
36	Kansas	3.4
32	Kentucky	4.7
6	Louisiana	14.4
46	Maine	1.4
1	Maryland	24.5
17	Massachusetts	8.8
34	Michigan	4.3
36	Minnesota	3.4
12	Mississippi	9.9
31	Missouri	5.2
44	Montana	1.6
45	Nebraska	1.5
14	Nevada	9.8
42	New Hampshire	2.0
10	New Jersey	11.0
25	New Mexico	6.0
2	New York	22.9
21	North Carolina	7.3
46	North Dakota	1.4
33	Ohio	4.5
23	Oklahoma	6.5
30	Oregon	5.3
12	Pennsylvania	9.9
14	Rhode Island	9.8
16	South Carolina	9.7
43	South Dakota	1.7
9	Tennessee	11.3
11	Texas	10.9
40	Utah	2.2
48	Vermont	1.1
26	Virginia	5.8
27	Washington	5.6
38	West Virginia	2.8
40	Wisconsin	2.2
50	Wyoming	0.6

RANK ORDER

RANK	STATE	RATE
1	Maryland	24.5
2	New York	22.9
3	Florida	22.3
4	Georgia	18.7
5	Delaware	15.9
6	Louisiana	14.4
7	Connecticut	12.1
8	Illinois	11.8
9	Tennessee	11.3
10	New Jersey	11.0
11	Texas	10.9
12	Mississippi	9.9
12	Pennsylvania	9.9
14	Nevada	9.8
14	Rhode Island	9.8
16	South Carolina	9.7
17	Massachusetts	8.8
18	California	8.6
19	Alabama	8.4
20	Arizona	8.0
21	North Carolina	7.3
22	Hawaii	7.2
23	Oklahoma	6.5
24	Arkansas	6.2
25	New Mexico	6.0
26	Virginia	5.8
27	Colorado	5.6
27	Washington	5.6
29	Indiana	5.5
30	Oregon	5.3
31	Missouri	5.2
32	Kentucky	4.7
33	Ohio	4.5
34	Michigan	4.3
35	Alaska	3.8
36	Kansas	3.4
36	Minnesota	3.4
38	West Virginia	2.8
39	Iowa	2.4
40	Utah	2.2
40	Wisconsin	2.2
42	New Hampshire	2.0
43	South Dakota	1.7
44	Montana	1.6
45	Nebraska	1.5
46	Maine	1.4
46	North Dakota	1.4
48	Vermont	1.1
49	Idaho	1.0
50	Wyoming	0.6

District of Columbia	86.1

Source: Morgan Quitno Press using data from U.S. Dept. of Health & Human Serv's, National Center for Health Statistics "Morbidity and Mortality Weekly Report" (January 6, 2006, Vol. 54, Nos. 51 & 52)
Provisional data. AIDS is Acquired Immunodeficiency Syndrome. It is a specific group of diseases or conditions which are indicative of severe immunosuppression related to infection with the Human Immunodeficiency Virus (HIV). National rate does not include cases or population in U.S. territories.

Adult Per Capita Alcohol Consumption in 2003

National Per Capita = 2.5 Gallons Consumed per Adult 21 Years and Older*

ALPHA ORDER

RANK	STATE	PER CAPITA
41	Alabama	2.2
9	Alaska	2.9
11	Arizona	2.8
47	Arkansas	2.0
27	California	2.5
6	Colorado	3.0
27	Connecticut	2.5
3	Delaware	3.5
6	Florida	3.0
34	Georgia	2.4
18	Hawaii	2.7
18	Idaho	2.7
18	Illinois	2.7
41	Indiana	2.2
37	Iowa	2.3
41	Kansas	2.2
47	Kentucky	2.0
11	Louisiana	2.8
18	Maine	2.7
34	Maryland	2.4
11	Massachusetts	2.8
34	Michigan	2.4
11	Minnesota	2.8
27	Mississippi	2.5
25	Missouri	2.6
6	Montana	3.0
25	Nebraska	2.6
2	Nevada	4.1
1	New Hampshire	4.6
27	New Jersey	2.5
11	New Mexico	2.8
41	New York	2.2
37	North Carolina	2.3
9	North Dakota	2.9
37	Ohio	2.3
41	Oklahoma	2.2
18	Oregon	2.7
27	Pennsylvania	2.5
18	Rhode Island	2.7
18	South Carolina	2.7
11	South Dakota	2.8
41	Tennessee	2.2
27	Texas	2.5
50	Utah	1.6
11	Vermont	2.8
37	Virginia	2.3
27	Washington	2.5
49	West Virginia	1.9
5	Wisconsin	3.2
4	Wyoming	3.3

RANK ORDER

RANK	STATE	PER CAPITA
1	New Hampshire	4.6
2	Nevada	4.1
3	Delaware	3.5
4	Wyoming	3.3
5	Wisconsin	3.2
6	Colorado	3.0
6	Florida	3.0
6	Montana	3.0
9	Alaska	2.9
9	North Dakota	2.9
11	Arizona	2.8
11	Louisiana	2.8
11	Massachusetts	2.8
11	Minnesota	2.8
11	New Mexico	2.8
11	South Dakota	2.8
11	Vermont	2.8
18	Hawaii	2.7
18	Idaho	2.7
18	Illinois	2.7
18	Maine	2.7
18	Oregon	2.7
18	Rhode Island	2.7
18	South Carolina	2.7
25	Missouri	2.6
25	Nebraska	2.6
27	California	2.5
27	Connecticut	2.5
27	Mississippi	2.5
27	New Jersey	2.5
27	Pennsylvania	2.5
27	Texas	2.5
27	Washington	2.5
34	Georgia	2.4
34	Maryland	2.4
34	Michigan	2.4
37	Iowa	2.3
37	North Carolina	2.3
37	Ohio	2.3
37	Virginia	2.3
41	Alabama	2.2
41	Indiana	2.2
41	Kansas	2.2
41	New York	2.2
41	Oklahoma	2.2
41	Tennessee	2.2
47	Arkansas	2.0
47	Kentucky	2.0
49	West Virginia	1.9
50	Utah	1.6

District of Columbia	4.2

Source: Morgan Quitno Press using data from U.S. Dept. of HHS, National Institute on Alcohol Abuse and Alcoholism "Volume Beverage and Ethanol Consumption for States" (http://www.niaaa.nih.gov/Resources/)

This is apparent consumption of actual alcohol, not entire volume of an alcoholic beverage (e.g. wine is roughly 11% absolute alcohol content). Apparent consumption is based on several sources which together approximate sales but do not actually measure consumption. Accordingly, figures for some states may be skewed by purchases by nonresidents.

Percent of Adults Who Smoke: 2004

National Median = 20.8% of Adults*

RANK	STATE	PERCENT
7	Alabama	24.8
7	Alaska	24.8
44	Arizona	18.5
6	Arkansas	25.5
48	California	14.7
34	Colorado	20.0
46	Connecticut	18.0
11	Delaware	24.3
32	Florida	20.2
36	Georgia	19.9
NA	Hawaii**	NA
47	Idaho	17.4
19	Illinois	22.2
7	Indiana	24.8
25	Iowa	20.8
39	Kansas	19.8
1	Kentucky	27.5
14	Louisiana	23.5
24	Maine	20.9
41	Maryland	19.5
45	Massachusetts	18.4
15	Michigan	23.2
27	Minnesota	20.7
10	Mississippi	24.5
13	Missouri	24.0
28	Montana	20.4
32	Nebraska	20.2
15	Nevada	23.2
22	New Hampshire	21.6
43	New Jersey	18.8
30	New Mexico	20.3
36	New York	19.9
17	North Carolina	23.1
39	North Dakota	19.8
5	Ohio	25.8
4	Oklahoma	26.0
34	Oregon	20.0
18	Pennsylvania	22.7
23	Rhode Island	21.3
11	South Carolina	24.3
30	South Dakota	20.3
3	Tennessee	26.1
28	Texas	20.4
49	Utah	10.4
36	Vermont	19.9
25	Virginia	20.8
42	Washington	19.2
2	West Virginia	26.8
20	Wisconsin	21.9
21	Wyoming	21.7

RANK	STATE	PERCENT
1	Kentucky	27.5
2	West Virginia	26.8
3	Tennessee	26.1
4	Oklahoma	26.0
5	Ohio	25.8
6	Arkansas	25.5
7	Alabama	24.8
7	Alaska	24.8
7	Indiana	24.8
10	Mississippi	24.5
11	Delaware	24.3
11	South Carolina	24.3
13	Missouri	24.0
14	Louisiana	23.5
15	Michigan	23.2
15	Nevada	23.2
17	North Carolina	23.1
18	Pennsylvania	22.7
19	Illinois	22.2
20	Wisconsin	21.9
21	Wyoming	21.7
22	New Hampshire	21.6
23	Rhode Island	21.3
24	Maine	20.9
25	Iowa	20.8
25	Virginia	20.8
27	Minnesota	20.7
28	Montana	20.4
28	Texas	20.4
30	New Mexico	20.3
30	South Dakota	20.3
32	Florida	20.2
32	Nebraska	20.2
34	Colorado	20.0
34	Oregon	20.0
36	Georgia	19.9
36	New York	19.9
36	Vermont	19.9
39	Kansas	19.8
39	North Dakota	19.8
41	Maryland	19.5
42	Washington	19.2
43	New Jersey	18.8
44	Arizona	18.5
45	Massachusetts	18.4
46	Connecticut	18.0
47	Idaho	17.4
48	California	14.7
49	Utah	10.4
NA	Hawaii**	NA

| | District of Columbia | 20.8 |

Source: U.S. Department of Health and Human Services, Centers for Disease Control and Prevention
"2004 Behavioral Risk Factor Surveillance Summary Prevalence Data" (http://apps.nccd.cdc.gov/brfss/)
*Persons 18 and older who have smoked more than 100 cigarettes during their lifetime and who currently smoke everyday or some days.
**Not available.

Percent of Adults Overweight: 2004

National Median = 36.8% of Adults*

ALPHA ORDER

RANK	STATE	PERCENT
41	Alabama	35.8
1	Alaska	38.8
47	Arizona	34.9
32	Arkansas	36.3
6	California	37.9
33	Colorado	36.2
29	Connecticut	36.4
3	Delaware	38.6
23	Florida	36.8
48	Georgia	34.7
NA	Hawaii**	NA
14	Idaho	37.3
28	Illinois	36.5
27	Indiana	36.6
14	Iowa	37.3
11	Kansas	37.5
11	Kentucky	37.5
43	Louisiana	35.6
11	Maine	37.5
49	Maryland	34.6
35	Massachusetts	36.1
46	Michigan	35.4
10	Minnesota	37.6
39	Mississippi	36.0
23	Missouri	36.8
14	Montana	37.3
4	Nebraska	38.5
1	Nevada	38.8
35	New Hampshire	36.1
8	New Jersey	37.7
29	New Mexico	36.4
43	New York	35.6
18	North Carolina	37.1
5	North Dakota	38.3
41	Ohio	35.8
35	Oklahoma	36.1
8	Oregon	37.7
23	Pennsylvania	36.8
20	Rhode Island	37.0
35	South Carolina	36.1
6	South Dakota	37.9
21	Tennessee	36.9
18	Texas	37.1
39	Utah	36.0
43	Vermont	35.6
23	Virginia	36.8
33	Washington	36.2
29	West Virginia	36.4
17	Wisconsin	37.2
21	Wyoming	36.9

RANK ORDER

RANK	STATE	PERCENT
1	Alaska	38.8
1	Nevada	38.8
3	Delaware	38.6
4	Nebraska	38.5
5	North Dakota	38.3
6	California	37.9
6	South Dakota	37.9
8	New Jersey	37.7
8	Oregon	37.7
10	Minnesota	37.6
11	Kansas	37.5
11	Kentucky	37.5
11	Maine	37.5
14	Idaho	37.3
14	Iowa	37.3
14	Montana	37.3
17	Wisconsin	37.2
18	North Carolina	37.1
18	Texas	37.1
20	Rhode Island	37.0
21	Tennessee	36.9
21	Wyoming	36.9
23	Florida	36.8
23	Missouri	36.8
23	Pennsylvania	36.8
23	Virginia	36.8
27	Indiana	36.6
28	Illinois	36.5
29	Connecticut	36.4
29	New Mexico	36.4
29	West Virginia	36.4
32	Arkansas	36.3
33	Colorado	36.2
33	Washington	36.2
35	Massachusetts	36.1
35	New Hampshire	36.1
35	Oklahoma	36.1
35	South Carolina	36.1
39	Mississippi	36.0
39	Utah	36.0
41	Alabama	35.8
41	Ohio	35.8
43	Louisiana	35.6
43	New York	35.6
43	Vermont	35.6
46	Michigan	35.4
47	Arizona	34.9
48	Georgia	34.7
49	Maryland	34.6
NA	Hawaii**	NA
	District of Columbia	33.0

Source: U.S. Department of Health and Human Services, Centers for Disease Control and Prevention
   "2004 Behavioral Risk Factor Surveillance Summary Prevalence Data" (http://apps.nccd.cdc.gov/brfss/)
Persons 18 and older. Does not include obese adults. Overweight is defined as a Body Mass Index (BMI) of 25.0
to 29.9 regardless of sex. BMI is a ratio of height to weight. As an example, a person 5' 8" and weighing 171
pounds has a BMI of 26. See http://www.cdc.gov/nccdphp/dnpa/bmi/bmi-adult.htm.

Percent of Children Aged 19 to 35 Months Fully Immunized in 2004

National Percent = 76.0%*

ALPHA ORDER				RANK ORDER		
RANK	STATE	PERCENT		RANK	STATE	PERCENT
9	Alabama	80.1		1	Connecticut	84.8
46	Alaska	66.4		2	Florida	84.7
34	Arizona	73.0		3	Massachusetts	84.0
7	Arkansas	80.6		4	Georgia	82.0
15	California	78.6		5	Pennsylvania	81.8
32	Colorado	73.4		6	Rhode Island	81.5
1	Connecticut	84.8		7	Arkansas	80.6
10	Delaware	79.9		8	Mississippi	80.4
2	Florida	84.7		9	Alabama	80.1
4	Georgia	82.0		10	Delaware	79.9
11	Hawaii	79.8		11	Hawaii	79.8
39	Idaho	70.4		12	Michigan	79.2
31	Illinois	73.7		13	Tennessee	79.1
42	Indiana	68.2		14	New Mexico	79.0
23	Iowa	76.1		15	California	78.6
47	Kansas	65.8		16	New Hampshire	78.4
22	Kentucky	77.1		17	New York	78.0
40	Louisiana	70.1		17	Wisconsin	78.0
29	Maine	73.8		19	North Carolina	77.8
24	Maryland	76.0		20	Minnesota	77.7
3	Massachusetts	84.0		21	South Carolina	77.2
12	Michigan	79.2		22	Kentucky	77.1
20	Minnesota	77.7		23	Iowa	76.1
8	Mississippi	80.4		24	Maryland	76.0
26	Missouri	75.2		24	West Virginia	76.0
49	Montana	64.5		26	Missouri	75.2
35	Nebraska	72.6		27	New Jersey	74.4
48	Nevada	65.1		28	Virginia	73.9
16	New Hampshire	78.4		29	Maine	73.8
27	New Jersey	74.4		29	Oregon	73.8
14	New Mexico	79.0		31	Illinois	73.7
17	New York	78.0		32	Colorado	73.4
19	North Carolina	77.8		33	South Dakota	73.3
37	North Dakota	71.0		34	Arizona	73.0
38	Ohio	70.6		35	Nebraska	72.6
36	Oklahoma	71.4		36	Oklahoma	71.4
29	Oregon	73.8		37	North Dakota	71.0
5	Pennsylvania	81.8		38	Ohio	70.6
6	Rhode Island	81.5		39	Idaho	70.4
21	South Carolina	77.2		40	Louisiana	70.1
33	South Dakota	73.3		41	Texas	69.3
13	Tennessee	79.1		42	Indiana	68.2
41	Texas	69.3		43	Utah	67.8
43	Utah	67.8		44	Vermont	66.6
44	Vermont	66.6		45	Washington	66.5
28	Virginia	73.9		46	Alaska	66.4
45	Washington	66.5		47	Kansas	65.8
24	West Virginia	76.0		48	Nevada	65.1
17	Wisconsin	78.0		49	Montana	64.5
50	Wyoming	64.1		50	Wyoming	64.1

	District of Columbia	79.5

Source: U.S. Department of Health and Human Services, Centers for Disease Control and Prevention
  "State Vaccination Coverage Levels" (Morbidity and Mortality Weekly Report, Vol. 54, No. 29, July 29, 2005)
  *Fully immunized (4:3:1:3:3:1 series) children received four doses of DTP/DT/DTaP (Diphtheria, Tetanus, Pertussis
(Whooping Cough), Acellular Pertussis), three doses of OPV (Oral Poliovirus Vaccine), one dose of MCV
(Measles-Containing Vaccine), three doses of Hib (Haemophilus influenzae type b), three doses of Hepatitis B
vaccine and one dose of Varicella (chickenpox) vaccine. This differs from previous "fully" immunized tables.

XII. HOUSEHOLDS & HOUSING

Households in 2004

National Total = 109,902,090 Households*

ALPHA ORDER

RANK	STATE	HOUSEHOLDS	% of USA
23	Alabama	1,755,332	1.6%
49	Alaska	228,358	0.2%
19	Arizona	2,131,534	1.9%
31	Arkansas	1,099,086	1.0%
1	California	11,972,158	10.9%
22	Colorado	1,850,238	1.7%
29	Connecticut	1,329,950	1.2%
45	Delaware	310,676	0.3%
4	Florida	6,819,280	6.2%
10	Georgia	3,210,006	2.9%
42	Hawaii	427,673	0.4%
40	Idaho	515,252	0.5%
6	Illinois	4,659,791	4.2%
15	Indiana	2,412,885	2.2%
30	Iowa	1,175,771	1.1%
32	Kansas	1,076,366	1.0%
25	Kentucky	1,647,464	1.5%
24	Louisiana	1,713,680	1.6%
39	Maine	534,412	0.5%
20	Maryland	2,077,900	1.9%
13	Massachusetts	2,435,421	2.2%
8	Michigan	3,923,135	3.6%
21	Minnesota	2,054,900	1.9%
33	Mississippi	1,074,503	1.0%
17	Missouri	2,309,205	2.1%
44	Montana	368,530	0.3%
38	Nebraska	687,456	0.6%
34	Nevada	871,915	0.8%
41	New Hampshire	491,589	0.4%
11	New Jersey	3,134,481	2.9%
37	New Mexico	711,827	0.6%
3	New York	7,087,566	6.4%
9	North Carolina	3,340,330	3.0%
47	North Dakota	262,585	0.2%
7	Ohio	4,514,723	4.1%
28	Oklahoma	1,360,032	1.2%
27	Oregon	1,427,711	1.3%
5	Pennsylvania	4,817,757	4.4%
43	Rhode Island	409,767	0.4%
26	South Carolina	1,611,401	1.5%
46	South Dakota	300,629	0.3%
16	Tennessee	2,314,688	2.1%
2	Texas	7,790,853	7.1%
35	Utah	780,029	0.7%
48	Vermont	249,590	0.2%
12	Virginia	2,846,417	2.6%
14	Washington	2,416,301	2.2%
36	West Virginia	736,954	0.7%
18	Wisconsin	2,172,924	2.0%
50	Wyoming	202,496	0.2%

RANK ORDER

RANK	STATE	HOUSEHOLDS	% of USA
1	California	11,972,158	10.9%
2	Texas	7,790,853	7.1%
3	New York	7,087,566	6.4%
4	Florida	6,819,280	6.2%
5	Pennsylvania	4,817,757	4.4%
6	Illinois	4,659,791	4.2%
7	Ohio	4,514,723	4.1%
8	Michigan	3,923,135	3.6%
9	North Carolina	3,340,330	3.0%
10	Georgia	3,210,006	2.9%
11	New Jersey	3,134,481	2.9%
12	Virginia	2,846,417	2.6%
13	Massachusetts	2,435,421	2.2%
14	Washington	2,416,301	2.2%
15	Indiana	2,412,885	2.2%
16	Tennessee	2,314,688	2.1%
17	Missouri	2,309,205	2.1%
18	Wisconsin	2,172,924	2.0%
19	Arizona	2,131,534	1.9%
20	Maryland	2,077,900	1.9%
21	Minnesota	2,054,900	1.9%
22	Colorado	1,850,238	1.7%
23	Alabama	1,755,332	1.6%
24	Louisiana	1,713,680	1.6%
25	Kentucky	1,647,464	1.5%
26	South Carolina	1,611,401	1.5%
27	Oregon	1,427,711	1.3%
28	Oklahoma	1,360,032	1.2%
29	Connecticut	1,329,950	1.2%
30	Iowa	1,175,771	1.1%
31	Arkansas	1,099,086	1.0%
32	Kansas	1,076,366	1.0%
33	Mississippi	1,074,503	1.0%
34	Nevada	871,915	0.8%
35	Utah	780,029	0.7%
36	West Virginia	736,954	0.7%
37	New Mexico	711,827	0.6%
38	Nebraska	687,456	0.6%
39	Maine	534,412	0.5%
40	Idaho	515,252	0.5%
41	New Hampshire	491,589	0.4%
42	Hawaii	427,673	0.4%
43	Rhode Island	409,767	0.4%
44	Montana	368,530	0.3%
45	Delaware	310,676	0.3%
46	South Dakota	300,629	0.3%
47	North Dakota	262,585	0.2%
48	Vermont	249,590	0.2%
49	Alaska	228,358	0.2%
50	Wyoming	202,496	0.2%
	District of Columbia	248,563	0.2%

Source: U.S. Bureau of the Census
   "2004 American Community Survey" (http://www.census.gov/acs/www/index.html)
*A household includes all persons who occupy a housing unit. A household consists of a single family, one person living alone, two or more families living together, or any other group of related or unrelated persons who share living arrangements.

Persons per Household in 2004

National Rate = 2.60 Persons per Household*

ALPHA ORDER			RANK ORDER		
RANK	STATE	PERSONS	RANK	STATE	PERSONS
24	Alabama	2.51	1	Utah	3.01
5	Alaska	2.78	2	California	2.93
9	Arizona	2.64	3	Hawaii	2.87
41	Arkansas	2.43	4	Texas	2.81
2	California	2.93	5	Alaska	2.78
41	Colorado	2.43	6	New Jersey	2.71
19	Connecticut	2.55	7	Georgia	2.67
16	Delaware	2.59	8	Illinois	2.66
29	Florida	2.49	9	Arizona	2.64
7	Georgia	2.67	9	Idaho	2.64
3	Hawaii	2.87	9	Nevada	2.64
9	Idaho	2.64	12	New York	2.63
8	Illinois	2.66	13	New Mexico	2.62
24	Indiana	2.51	14	Maryland	2.61
44	Iowa	2.42	14	Mississippi	2.61
33	Kansas	2.47	16	Delaware	2.59
39	Kentucky	2.45	17	New Hampshire	2.57
18	Louisiana	2.56	18	Louisiana	2.56
49	Maine	2.39	19	Connecticut	2.55
14	Maryland	2.61	19	Massachusetts	2.55
19	Massachusetts	2.55	21	Virginia	2.54
24	Michigan	2.51	22	Rhode Island	2.53
46	Minnesota	2.41	23	South Carolina	2.52
14	Mississippi	2.61	24	Alabama	2.51
44	Missouri	2.42	24	Indiana	2.51
39	Montana	2.45	24	Michigan	2.51
33	Nebraska	2.47	24	Oklahoma	2.51
9	Nevada	2.64	24	Washington	2.51
17	New Hampshire	2.57	29	Florida	2.49
6	New Jersey	2.71	30	North Carolina	2.48
13	New Mexico	2.62	30	Pennsylvania	2.48
12	New York	2.63	30	Tennessee	2.48
30	North Carolina	2.48	33	Kansas	2.47
50	North Dakota	2.32	33	Nebraska	2.47
33	Ohio	2.47	33	Ohio	2.47
24	Oklahoma	2.51	33	South Dakota	2.47
37	Oregon	2.46	37	Oregon	2.46
30	Pennsylvania	2.48	37	Wisconsin	2.46
22	Rhode Island	2.53	39	Kentucky	2.45
23	South Carolina	2.52	39	Montana	2.45
33	South Dakota	2.47	41	Arkansas	2.43
30	Tennessee	2.48	41	Colorado	2.43
4	Texas	2.81	41	Wyoming	2.43
1	Utah	3.01	44	Iowa	2.42
46	Vermont	2.41	44	Missouri	2.42
21	Virginia	2.54	46	Minnesota	2.41
24	Washington	2.51	46	Vermont	2.41
48	West Virginia	2.40	48	West Virginia	2.40
37	Wisconsin	2.46	49	Maine	2.39
41	Wyoming	2.43	50	North Dakota	2.32
				District of Columbia	2.08

Source: U.S. Bureau of the Census
   "2004 American Community Survey" (http://www.census.gov/acs/www/index.html)
*A household includes all persons who occupy a housing unit. A household consists of a single family, one person living alone, two or more families living together, or any other group of related or unrelated persons who share living arrangements.

Percent of Households with One Person in 2004

National Percent = 26.9% of Households

RANK	STATE	PERCENT
36	Alabama	26.6
48	Alaska	23.1
37	Arizona	26.4
25	Arkansas	27.5
45	California	24.6
17	Colorado	28.0
31	Connecticut	26.8
39	Delaware	26.0
21	Florida	27.7
40	Georgia	25.7
47	Hawaii	24.3
49	Idaho	22.8
14	Illinois	28.1
22	Indiana	27.6
5	Iowa	28.7
5	Kansas	28.7
38	Kentucky	26.2
32	Louisiana	26.7
30	Maine	27.1
27	Maryland	27.3
9	Massachusetts	28.4
17	Michigan	28.0
27	Minnesota	27.3
42	Mississippi	25.5
10	Missouri	28.3
3	Montana	28.9
10	Nebraska	28.3
14	Nevada	28.1
43	New Hampshire	25.2
46	New Jersey	24.5
5	New Mexico	28.7
4	New York	28.8
32	North Carolina	26.7
1	North Dakota	30.4
8	Ohio	28.6
25	Oklahoma	27.5
22	Oregon	27.6
13	Pennsylvania	28.2
19	Rhode Island	27.8
32	South Carolina	26.7
2	South Dakota	29.1
29	Tennessee	27.2
44	Texas	24.7
50	Utah	18.4
32	Vermont	26.7
41	Virginia	25.6
22	Washington	27.6
10	West Virginia	28.3
19	Wisconsin	27.8
14	Wyoming	28.1

RANK	STATE	PERCENT
1	North Dakota	30.4
2	South Dakota	29.1
3	Montana	28.9
4	New York	28.8
5	Iowa	28.7
5	Kansas	28.7
5	New Mexico	28.7
8	Ohio	28.6
9	Massachusetts	28.4
10	Missouri	28.3
10	Nebraska	28.3
10	West Virginia	28.3
13	Pennsylvania	28.2
14	Illinois	28.1
14	Nevada	28.1
14	Wyoming	28.1
17	Colorado	28.0
17	Michigan	28.0
19	Rhode Island	27.8
19	Wisconsin	27.8
21	Florida	27.7
22	Indiana	27.6
22	Oregon	27.6
22	Washington	27.6
25	Arkansas	27.5
25	Oklahoma	27.5
27	Maryland	27.3
27	Minnesota	27.3
29	Tennessee	27.2
30	Maine	27.1
31	Connecticut	26.8
32	Louisiana	26.7
32	North Carolina	26.7
32	South Carolina	26.7
32	Vermont	26.7
36	Alabama	26.6
37	Arizona	26.4
38	Kentucky	26.2
39	Delaware	26.0
40	Georgia	25.7
41	Virginia	25.6
42	Mississippi	25.5
43	New Hampshire	25.2
44	Texas	24.7
45	California	24.6
46	New Jersey	24.5
47	Hawaii	24.3
48	Alaska	23.1
49	Idaho	22.8
50	Utah	18.4
	District of Columbia	46.5

Source: U.S. Bureau of the Census
   "2004 American Community Survey" (http://www.census.gov/acs/www/index.html)
*A household includes all persons who occupy a housing unit. A household consists of a single family, one person living alone, two or more families living together, or any other group of related or unrelated persons who share living arrangements.

Percent of Households Headed by Married Couples in 2004

National Percent = 50.2% of Households

ALPHA ORDER

RANK	STATE	PERCENT
26	Alabama	50.9
15	Alaska	52.2
25	Arizona	51.1
38	Arkansas	49.7
32	California	50.0
36	Colorado	49.8
21	Connecticut	51.7
41	Delaware	48.7
42	Florida	48.3
40	Georgia	49.3
14	Hawaii	52.4
2	Idaho	57.9
31	Illinois	50.2
15	Indiana	52.2
5	Iowa	53.6
7	Kansas	53.0
7	Kentucky	53.0
47	Louisiana	46.9
23	Maine	51.4
44	Maryland	47.8
42	Massachusetts	48.3
28	Michigan	50.4
4	Minnesota	53.8
46	Mississippi	47.3
23	Missouri	51.4
12	Montana	52.5
6	Nebraska	53.3
45	Nevada	47.6
3	New Hampshire	54.5
11	New Jersey	52.8
49	New Mexico	46.0
50	New York	45.9
29	North Carolina	50.3
19	North Dakota	51.8
34	Ohio	49.9
29	Oklahoma	50.3
38	Oregon	49.7
27	Pennsylvania	50.8
48	Rhode Island	46.7
34	South Carolina	49.9
7	South Dakota	53.0
36	Tennessee	49.8
18	Texas	51.9
1	Utah	63.0
19	Vermont	51.8
15	Virginia	52.2
32	Washington	50.0
12	West Virginia	52.5
22	Wisconsin	51.6
7	Wyoming	53.0

RANK ORDER

RANK	STATE	PERCENT
1	Utah	63.0
2	Idaho	57.9
3	New Hampshire	54.5
4	Minnesota	53.8
5	Iowa	53.6
6	Nebraska	53.3
7	Kansas	53.0
7	Kentucky	53.0
7	South Dakota	53.0
7	Wyoming	53.0
11	New Jersey	52.8
12	Montana	52.5
12	West Virginia	52.5
14	Hawaii	52.4
15	Alaska	52.2
15	Indiana	52.2
15	Virginia	52.2
18	Texas	51.9
19	North Dakota	51.8
19	Vermont	51.8
21	Connecticut	51.7
22	Wisconsin	51.6
23	Maine	51.4
23	Missouri	51.4
25	Arizona	51.1
26	Alabama	50.9
27	Pennsylvania	50.8
28	Michigan	50.4
29	North Carolina	50.3
29	Oklahoma	50.3
31	Illinois	50.2
32	California	50.0
32	Washington	50.0
34	Ohio	49.9
34	South Carolina	49.9
36	Colorado	49.8
36	Tennessee	49.8
38	Arkansas	49.7
38	Oregon	49.7
40	Georgia	49.3
41	Delaware	48.7
42	Florida	48.3
42	Massachusetts	48.3
44	Maryland	47.8
45	Nevada	47.6
46	Mississippi	47.3
47	Louisiana	46.9
48	Rhode Island	46.7
49	New Mexico	46.0
50	New York	45.9
	District of Columbia	21.8

Source: U.S. Bureau of the Census
   "2004 American Community Survey" (http://www.census.gov/acs/www/index.html)
*A household includes all persons who occupy a housing unit. A household consists of a single family, one person living alone, two or more families living together, or any other group of related or unrelated persons who share living arrangements.

Percent of Households Headed by Single Mothers in 2004

National Percent = 7.6% of Households*

ALPHA ORDER				RANK ORDER		
RANK	STATE	PERCENT		RANK	STATE	PERCENT
5	Alabama	8.9		1	Louisiana	10.8
29	Alaska	6.9		2	Mississippi	10.6
17	Arizona	7.6		3	Georgia	9.5
6	Arkansas	8.8		4	Rhode Island	9.4
24	California	7.2		5	Alabama	8.9
36	Colorado	6.3		6	Arkansas	8.8
24	Connecticut	7.2		6	New Mexico	8.8
14	Delaware	7.9		8	South Carolina	8.7
21	Florida	7.5		8	Texas	8.7
3	Georgia	9.5		10	North Carolina	8.4
49	Hawaii	5.3		11	Maryland	8.3
36	Idaho	6.3		12	Ohio	8.2
31	Illinois	6.8		13	Tennessee	8.1
29	Indiana	6.9		14	Delaware	7.9
41	Iowa	6.0		14	New York	7.9
42	Kansas	5.9		16	Nevada	7.8
17	Kentucky	7.6		17	Arizona	7.6
1	Louisiana	10.8		17	Kentucky	7.6
26	Maine	7.0		17	Michigan	7.6
11	Maryland	8.3		17	Oklahoma	7.6
26	Massachusetts	7.0		21	Florida	7.5
17	Michigan	7.6		21	Missouri	7.5
44	Minnesota	5.8		21	Virginia	7.5
2	Mississippi	10.6		24	California	7.2
21	Missouri	7.5		24	Connecticut	7.2
48	Montana	5.4		26	Maine	7.0
46	Nebraska	5.6		26	Massachusetts	7.0
16	Nevada	7.8		26	Washington	7.0
35	New Hampshire	6.4		29	Alaska	6.9
34	New Jersey	6.5		29	Indiana	6.9
6	New Mexico	8.8		31	Illinois	6.8
14	New York	7.9		31	Wisconsin	6.8
10	North Carolina	8.4		33	Pennsylvania	6.6
50	North Dakota	4.9		34	New Jersey	6.5
12	Ohio	8.2		35	New Hampshire	6.4
17	Oklahoma	7.6		36	Colorado	6.3
36	Oregon	6.3		36	Idaho	6.3
33	Pennsylvania	6.6		36	Oregon	6.3
4	Rhode Island	9.4		36	South Dakota	6.3
8	South Carolina	8.7		40	West Virginia	6.1
36	South Dakota	6.3		41	Iowa	6.0
13	Tennessee	8.1		42	Kansas	5.9
8	Texas	8.7		42	Wyoming	5.9
45	Utah	5.7		44	Minnesota	5.8
46	Vermont	5.6		45	Utah	5.7
21	Virginia	7.5		46	Nebraska	5.6
26	Washington	7.0		46	Vermont	5.6
40	West Virginia	6.1		48	Montana	5.4
31	Wisconsin	6.8		49	Hawaii	5.3
42	Wyoming	5.9		50	North Dakota	4.9
					District of Columbia	10.2

Source: U.S. Bureau of the Census
   "2004 American Community Survey" (http://www.census.gov/acs/www/index.html)
*No spouse present in household with children under 18 years old.

411

Housing Units in 2004

National Total = 122,671,734 Housing Units*

RANK	STATE	HOUSING UNITS	% of USA
22	Alabama	2,058,951	1.7%
49	Alaska	271,533	0.2%
19	Arizona	2,458,231	2.0%
31	Arkansas	1,233,203	1.0%
1	California	12,804,702	10.4%
23	Colorado	2,010,806	1.6%
29	Connecticut	1,414,433	1.2%
45	Delaware	367,448	0.3%
3	Florida	8,009,427	6.5%
10	Georgia	3,672,677	3.0%
42	Hawaii	482,873	0.4%
40	Idaho	578,774	0.5%
6	Illinois	5,094,186	4.2%
13	Indiana	2,690,619	2.2%
30	Iowa	1,292,976	1.1%
33	Kansas	1,185,114	1.0%
26	Kentucky	1,842,971	1.5%
24	Louisiana	1,919,859	1.6%
39	Maine	676,667	0.6%
20	Maryland	2,250,339	1.8%
14	Massachusetts	2,672,061	2.2%
8	Michigan	4,433,482	3.6%
21	Minnesota	2,212,701	1.8%
32	Mississippi	1,221,240	1.0%
17	Missouri	2,564,340	2.1%
44	Montana	423,262	0.3%
38	Nebraska	757,743	0.6%
34	Nevada	976,446	0.8%
41	New Hampshire	575,671	0.5%
11	New Jersey	3,414,739	2.8%
37	New Mexico	825,540	0.7%
4	New York	7,819,359	6.4%
9	North Carolina	3,860,078	3.1%
48	North Dakota	300,815	0.2%
7	Ohio	4,966,746	4.0%
27	Oklahoma	1,572,756	1.3%
28	Oregon	1,535,381	1.3%
5	Pennsylvania	5,385,729	4.4%
43	Rhode Island	446,305	0.4%
25	South Carolina	1,890,682	1.5%
46	South Dakota	342,620	0.3%
16	Tennessee	2,595,060	2.1%
2	Texas	8,846,728	7.2%
36	Utah	848,737	0.7%
47	Vermont	304,291	0.2%
12	Virginia	3,116,827	2.5%
15	Washington	2,606,623	2.1%
35	West Virginia	866,944	0.7%
18	Wisconsin	2,463,802	2.0%
50	Wyoming	232,637	0.2%

RANK	STATE	HOUSING UNITS	% of USA
1	California	12,804,702	10.4%
2	Texas	8,846,728	7.2%
3	Florida	8,009,427	6.5%
4	New York	7,819,359	6.4%
5	Pennsylvania	5,385,729	4.4%
6	Illinois	5,094,186	4.2%
7	Ohio	4,966,746	4.0%
8	Michigan	4,433,482	3.6%
9	North Carolina	3,860,078	3.1%
10	Georgia	3,672,677	3.0%
11	New Jersey	3,414,739	2.8%
12	Virginia	3,116,827	2.5%
13	Indiana	2,690,619	2.2%
14	Massachusetts	2,672,061	2.2%
15	Washington	2,606,623	2.1%
16	Tennessee	2,595,060	2.1%
17	Missouri	2,564,340	2.1%
18	Wisconsin	2,463,802	2.0%
19	Arizona	2,458,231	2.0%
20	Maryland	2,250,339	1.8%
21	Minnesota	2,212,701	1.8%
22	Alabama	2,058,951	1.7%
23	Colorado	2,010,806	1.6%
24	Louisiana	1,919,859	1.6%
25	South Carolina	1,890,682	1.5%
26	Kentucky	1,842,971	1.5%
27	Oklahoma	1,572,756	1.3%
28	Oregon	1,535,381	1.3%
29	Connecticut	1,414,433	1.2%
30	Iowa	1,292,976	1.1%
31	Arkansas	1,233,203	1.0%
32	Mississippi	1,221,240	1.0%
33	Kansas	1,185,114	1.0%
34	Nevada	976,446	0.8%
35	West Virginia	866,944	0.7%
36	Utah	848,737	0.7%
37	New Mexico	825,540	0.7%
38	Nebraska	757,743	0.6%
39	Maine	676,667	0.6%
40	Idaho	578,774	0.5%
41	New Hampshire	575,671	0.5%
42	Hawaii	482,873	0.4%
43	Rhode Island	446,305	0.4%
44	Montana	423,262	0.3%
45	Delaware	367,448	0.3%
46	South Dakota	342,620	0.3%
47	Vermont	304,291	0.2%
48	North Dakota	300,815	0.2%
49	Alaska	271,533	0.2%
50	Wyoming	232,637	0.2%
	District of Columbia	276,600	0.2%

Source: U.S. Bureau of the Census
    "Housing Unit Estimates" (http://www.census.gov/popest/housing/HU-EST2004.html)
*A housing unit is a house, an apartment, a mobile home, a group of rooms, or a single room that is occupied (or if vacant, is intended for occupancy) as separate living quarters. Separate living quarters are those in which the occupants live and eat separately from any other persons in the building and which have direct access from the outside of the building or through a common hall.

Housing Units per Square Mile in 2004

National Average = 34.7 Housing Units*

ALPHA ORDER			RANK ORDER		
RANK	STATE	HOUSING UNITS	RANK	STATE	HOUSING UNITS
25	Alabama	40.6	1	New Jersey	460.4
50	Alaska	0.5	2	Rhode Island	427.1
37	Arizona	21.6	3	Massachusetts	340.8
33	Arkansas	23.7	4	Connecticut	291.9
12	California	82.1	5	Maryland	230.2
38	Colorado	19.4	6	Delaware	188.0
4	Connecticut	291.9	7	New York	165.6
6	Delaware	188.0	8	Florida	148.5
8	Florida	148.5	9	Ohio	121.3
19	Georgia	63.4	10	Pennsylvania	120.2
16	Hawaii	75.2	11	Illinois	91.6
44	Idaho	7.0	12	California	82.1
11	Illinois	91.6	13	North Carolina	79.2
17	Indiana	75.0	14	Virginia	78.7
34	Iowa	23.1	15	Michigan	78.0
40	Kansas	14.5	16	Hawaii	75.2
22	Kentucky	46.4	17	Indiana	75.0
24	Louisiana	44.1	18	New Hampshire	64.2
36	Maine	21.9	19	Georgia	63.4
5	Maryland	230.2	20	Tennessee	63.0
3	Massachusetts	340.8	21	South Carolina	62.8
15	Michigan	78.0	22	Kentucky	46.4
31	Minnesota	27.8	23	Wisconsin	45.4
32	Mississippi	26.0	24	Louisiana	44.1
27	Missouri	37.2	25	Alabama	40.6
48	Montana	2.9	26	Washington	39.2
42	Nebraska	9.9	27	Missouri	37.2
43	Nevada	8.9	28	West Virginia	36.0
18	New Hampshire	64.2	29	Texas	33.8
1	New Jersey	460.4	30	Vermont	32.9
45	New Mexico	6.8	31	Minnesota	27.8
7	New York	165.6	32	Mississippi	26.0
13	North Carolina	79.2	33	Arkansas	23.7
47	North Dakota	4.4	34	Iowa	23.1
9	Ohio	121.3	35	Oklahoma	22.9
35	Oklahoma	22.9	36	Maine	21.9
39	Oregon	16.0	37	Arizona	21.6
10	Pennsylvania	120.2	38	Colorado	19.4
2	Rhode Island	427.1	39	Oregon	16.0
21	South Carolina	62.8	40	Kansas	14.5
46	South Dakota	4.5	41	Utah	10.3
20	Tennessee	63.0	42	Nebraska	9.9
29	Texas	33.8	43	Nevada	8.9
41	Utah	10.3	44	Idaho	7.0
30	Vermont	32.9	45	New Mexico	6.8
14	Virginia	78.7	46	South Dakota	4.5
26	Washington	39.2	47	North Dakota	4.4
28	West Virginia	36.0	48	Montana	2.9
23	Wisconsin	45.4	49	Wyoming	2.4
49	Wyoming	2.4	50	Alaska	0.5

District of Columbia		4,534.4

Source: Morgan Quitno Press using data from U.S. Bureau of the Census
    "Housing Unit Estimates" (http://www.census.gov/popest/housing/HU-EST2004.html)
*Based on land area. A housing unit is a house, an apartment, a mobile home, a group of rooms, or a single room that is occupied (or if vacant, is intended for occupancy) as separate living quarters. Separate living quarters are those in which the occupants live and eat separately from any other persons in the building and which have direct access from the outside of the building or through a common hall.

Percent of Housing Units That are Owner-Occupied: 2004

National Percent = 67.1% of Housing Units*

ALPHA ORDER

RANK	STATE	PERCENT
11	Alabama	71.9
40	Alaska	65.5
31	Arizona	68.7
40	Arkansas	65.5
49	California	58.6
32	Colorado	68.6
20	Connecticut	69.7
6	Delaware	72.9
14	Florida	70.5
38	Georgia	67.7
48	Hawaii	58.9
10	Idaho	72.4
27	Illinois	69.2
12	Indiana	71.8
4	Iowa	73.8
24	Kansas	69.5
15	Kentucky	70.1
39	Louisiana	66.2
6	Maine	72.9
24	Maryland	69.5
43	Massachusetts	64.6
2	Michigan	74.7
1	Minnesota	75.3
23	Mississippi	69.6
13	Missouri	70.8
33	Montana	68.5
34	Nebraska	68.4
47	Nevada	61.2
9	New Hampshire	72.6
36	New Jersey	68.1
26	New Mexico	69.3
50	New York	55.6
30	North Carolina	69.0
36	North Dakota	68.1
19	Ohio	69.8
35	Oklahoma	68.2
45	Oregon	63.0
8	Pennsylvania	72.8
46	Rhode Island	61.8
20	South Carolina	69.7
29	South Dakota	69.1
16	Tennessee	70.0
42	Texas	65.1
20	Utah	69.7
5	Vermont	73.3
27	Virginia	69.2
44	Washington	64.1
3	West Virginia	74.0
17	Wisconsin	69.9
17	Wyoming	69.9

RANK ORDER

RANK	STATE	PERCENT
1	Minnesota	75.3
2	Michigan	74.7
3	West Virginia	74.0
4	Iowa	73.8
5	Vermont	73.3
6	Delaware	72.9
6	Maine	72.9
8	Pennsylvania	72.8
9	New Hampshire	72.6
10	Idaho	72.4
11	Alabama	71.9
12	Indiana	71.8
13	Missouri	70.8
14	Florida	70.5
15	Kentucky	70.1
16	Tennessee	70.0
17	Wisconsin	69.9
17	Wyoming	69.9
19	Ohio	69.8
20	Connecticut	69.7
20	South Carolina	69.7
20	Utah	69.7
23	Mississippi	69.6
24	Kansas	69.5
24	Maryland	69.5
26	New Mexico	69.3
27	Illinois	69.2
27	Virginia	69.2
29	South Dakota	69.1
30	North Carolina	69.0
31	Arizona	68.7
32	Colorado	68.6
33	Montana	68.5
34	Nebraska	68.4
35	Oklahoma	68.2
36	New Jersey	68.1
36	North Dakota	68.1
38	Georgia	67.7
39	Louisiana	66.2
40	Alaska	65.5
40	Arkansas	65.5
42	Texas	65.1
43	Massachusetts	64.6
44	Washington	64.1
45	Oregon	63.0
46	Rhode Island	61.8
47	Nevada	61.2
48	Hawaii	58.9
49	California	58.6
50	New York	55.6

| | District of Columbia | 43.6 |

Source: U.S. Bureau of the Census
    "2004 American Community Survey" (http://www.census.gov/acs/www/index.html)
*For occupied housing units.

New Housing Units Authorized in 2005

National Total = 2,147,617 Units*

ALPHA ORDER

RANK	STATE	UNITS	% of USA
25	Alabama	30,272	1.4%
49	Alaska	2,877	0.1%
6	Arizona	91,436	4.3%
33	Arkansas	16,625	0.8%
3	California	202,221	9.4%
15	Colorado	46,262	2.2%
37	Connecticut	11,671	0.5%
41	Delaware	7,977	0.4%
1	Florida	285,062	13.3%
4	Georgia	104,659	4.9%
39	Hawaii	9,828	0.5%
29	Idaho	21,767	1.0%
7	Illinois	67,852	3.2%
19	Indiana	37,993	1.8%
32	Iowa	16,733	0.8%
34	Kansas	14,404	0.7%
30	Kentucky	19,943	0.9%
28	Louisiana	21,794	1.0%
40	Maine	8,765	0.4%
22	Maryland	32,276	1.5%
27	Massachusetts	23,840	1.1%
14	Michigan	46,989	2.2%
20	Minnesota	35,877	1.7%
36	Mississippi	12,988	0.6%
24	Missouri	31,278	1.5%
45	Montana	5,068	0.2%
38	Nebraska	10,922	0.5%
13	Nevada	47,038	2.2%
42	New Hampshire	7,699	0.4%
18	New Jersey	38,481	1.8%
35	New Mexico	14,331	0.7%
9	New York	59,386	2.8%
5	North Carolina	100,220	4.7%
46	North Dakota	3,835	0.2%
10	Ohio	55,237	2.6%
31	Oklahoma	18,304	0.9%
23	Oregon	31,864	1.5%
17	Pennsylvania	44,178	2.1%
50	Rhode Island	2,791	0.1%
11	South Carolina	53,755	2.5%
43	South Dakota	5,790	0.3%
16	Tennessee	46,204	2.2%
2	Texas	208,980	9.7%
26	Utah	28,302	1.3%
48	Vermont	3,034	0.1%
8	Virginia	60,956	2.8%
12	Washington	52,784	2.5%
44	West Virginia	5,399	0.3%
21	Wisconsin	35,843	1.7%
47	Wyoming	3,533	0.2%

RANK ORDER

RANK	STATE	UNITS	% of USA
1	Florida	285,062	13.3%
2	Texas	208,980	9.7%
3	California	202,221	9.4%
4	Georgia	104,659	4.9%
5	North Carolina	100,220	4.7%
6	Arizona	91,436	4.3%
7	Illinois	67,852	3.2%
8	Virginia	60,956	2.8%
9	New York	59,386	2.8%
10	Ohio	55,237	2.6%
11	South Carolina	53,755	2.5%
12	Washington	52,784	2.5%
13	Nevada	47,038	2.2%
14	Michigan	46,989	2.2%
15	Colorado	46,262	2.2%
16	Tennessee	46,204	2.2%
17	Pennsylvania	44,178	2.1%
18	New Jersey	38,481	1.8%
19	Indiana	37,993	1.8%
20	Minnesota	35,877	1.7%
21	Wisconsin	35,843	1.7%
22	Maryland	32,276	1.5%
23	Oregon	31,864	1.5%
24	Missouri	31,278	1.5%
25	Alabama	30,272	1.4%
26	Utah	28,302	1.3%
27	Massachusetts	23,840	1.1%
28	Louisiana	21,794	1.0%
29	Idaho	21,767	1.0%
30	Kentucky	19,943	0.9%
31	Oklahoma	18,304	0.9%
32	Iowa	16,733	0.8%
33	Arkansas	16,625	0.8%
34	Kansas	14,404	0.7%
35	New Mexico	14,331	0.7%
36	Mississippi	12,988	0.6%
37	Connecticut	11,671	0.5%
38	Nebraska	10,922	0.5%
39	Hawaii	9,828	0.5%
40	Maine	8,765	0.4%
41	Delaware	7,977	0.4%
42	New Hampshire	7,699	0.4%
43	South Dakota	5,790	0.3%
44	West Virginia	5,399	0.3%
45	Montana	5,068	0.2%
46	North Dakota	3,835	0.2%
47	Wyoming	3,533	0.2%
48	Vermont	3,034	0.1%
49	Alaska	2,877	0.1%
50	Rhode Island	2,791	0.1%
	District of Columbia	2,294	0.1%

Source: U.S. Bureau of the Census
  "New Privately Owned Housing Units Authorized" (http://www.census.gov/const/www/C40/table2.html)
*Preliminary and unadjusted year to date as of December 2005. Includes single and multifamily privately owned units. Based on approximately 19,000 places in the U.S. having building permit systems.

Value of New Housing Units Authorized in 2005

National Total = $326,519,492,000*

ALPHA ORDER

RANK	STATE	VALUE	% of USA
26	Alabama	$4,081,422,000	1.2%
47	Alaska	525,285,000	0.2%
5	Arizona	14,320,408,000	4.4%
35	Arkansas	2,085,863,000	0.6%
2	California	37,158,906,000	11.4%
9	Colorado	8,968,035,000	2.7%
34	Connecticut	2,134,790,000	0.7%
43	Delaware	958,413,000	0.3%
1	Florida	46,143,133,000	14.1%
6	Georgia	13,812,151,000	4.2%
36	Hawaii	2,050,052,000	0.6%
28	Idaho	3,496,700,000	1.1%
7	Illinois	11,041,271,000	3.4%
19	Indiana	5,682,084,000	1.7%
32	Iowa	2,361,660,000	0.7%
37	Kansas	2,039,856,000	0.6%
30	Kentucky	2,511,566,000	0.8%
29	Louisiana	2,672,492,000	0.8%
41	Maine	1,334,015,000	0.4%
24	Maryland	4,653,903,000	1.4%
27	Massachusetts	3,929,637,000	1.2%
14	Michigan	6,805,519,000	2.1%
18	Minnesota	6,180,614,000	1.9%
38	Mississippi	1,535,241,000	0.5%
25	Missouri	4,499,508,000	1.4%
45	Montana	729,620,000	0.2%
39	Nebraska	1,472,941,000	0.5%
17	Nevada	6,371,764,000	2.0%
40	New Hampshire	1,338,543,000	0.4%
22	New Jersey	4,967,480,000	1.5%
33	New Mexico	2,172,830,000	0.7%
13	New York	7,495,867,000	2.3%
4	North Carolina	14,969,373,000	4.6%
49	North Dakota	427,901,000	0.1%
11	Ohio	8,632,275,000	2.6%
31	Oklahoma	2,478,716,000	0.8%
20	Oregon	5,614,115,000	1.7%
15	Pennsylvania	6,631,898,000	2.0%
50	Rhode Island	374,990,000	0.1%
12	South Carolina	7,618,305,000	2.3%
44	South Dakota	731,970,000	0.2%
16	Tennessee	6,406,486,000	2.0%
3	Texas	26,746,585,000	8.2%
23	Utah	4,670,638,000	1.4%
48	Vermont	467,429,000	0.1%
8	Virginia	9,082,722,000	2.8%
10	Washington	8,810,035,000	2.7%
42	West Virginia	959,387,000	0.3%
21	Wisconsin	5,519,502,000	1.7%
46	Wyoming	602,971,000	0.2%

RANK ORDER

RANK	STATE	VALUE	% of USA
1	Florida	$46,143,133,000	14.1%
2	California	37,158,906,000	11.4%
3	Texas	26,746,585,000	8.2%
4	North Carolina	14,969,373,000	4.6%
5	Arizona	14,320,408,000	4.4%
6	Georgia	13,812,151,000	4.2%
7	Illinois	11,041,271,000	3.4%
8	Virginia	9,082,722,000	2.8%
9	Colorado	8,968,035,000	2.7%
10	Washington	8,810,035,000	2.7%
11	Ohio	8,632,275,000	2.6%
12	South Carolina	7,618,305,000	2.3%
13	New York	7,495,867,000	2.3%
14	Michigan	6,805,519,000	2.1%
15	Pennsylvania	6,631,898,000	2.0%
16	Tennessee	6,406,486,000	2.0%
17	Nevada	6,371,764,000	2.0%
18	Minnesota	6,180,614,000	1.9%
19	Indiana	5,682,084,000	1.7%
20	Oregon	5,614,115,000	1.7%
21	Wisconsin	5,519,502,000	1.7%
22	New Jersey	4,967,480,000	1.5%
23	Utah	4,670,638,000	1.4%
24	Maryland	4,653,903,000	1.4%
25	Missouri	4,499,508,000	1.4%
26	Alabama	4,081,422,000	1.2%
27	Massachusetts	3,929,637,000	1.2%
28	Idaho	3,496,700,000	1.1%
29	Louisiana	2,672,492,000	0.8%
30	Kentucky	2,511,566,000	0.8%
31	Oklahoma	2,478,716,000	0.8%
32	Iowa	2,361,660,000	0.7%
33	New Mexico	2,172,830,000	0.7%
34	Connecticut	2,134,790,000	0.7%
35	Arkansas	2,085,863,000	0.6%
36	Hawaii	2,050,052,000	0.6%
37	Kansas	2,039,856,000	0.6%
38	Mississippi	1,535,241,000	0.5%
39	Nebraska	1,472,941,000	0.5%
40	New Hampshire	1,338,543,000	0.4%
41	Maine	1,334,015,000	0.4%
42	West Virginia	959,387,000	0.3%
43	Delaware	958,413,000	0.3%
44	South Dakota	731,970,000	0.2%
45	Montana	729,620,000	0.2%
46	Wyoming	602,971,000	0.2%
47	Alaska	525,285,000	0.2%
48	Vermont	467,429,000	0.1%
49	North Dakota	427,901,000	0.1%
50	Rhode Island	374,990,000	0.1%
	District of Columbia	242,622,000	0.1%

Source: U.S. Bureau of the Census
"New Privately Owned Housing Units Authorized" (http://www.census.gov/const/www/C40/table2.html)
*Preliminary and unadjusted year to date as of December 2005. Includes single and multifamily privately owned units. Based on approximately 19,000 places in the U.S. having building permit systems.

Average Value of New Housing Units in 2005

National Average = $152,038 per Unit*

ALPHA ORDER

RANK	STATE	VALUE
38	Alabama	$134,825
5	Alaska	182,581
17	Arizona	156,617
46	Arkansas	125,465
3	California	183,754
2	Colorado	193,853
4	Connecticut	182,914
48	Delaware	120,147
15	Florida	161,871
40	Georgia	131,973
1	Hawaii	208,593
16	Idaho	160,642
14	Illinois	162,726
24	Indiana	149,556
33	Iowa	141,138
32	Kansas	141,617
45	Kentucky	125,937
47	Louisiana	122,625
21	Maine	152,198
28	Maryland	144,191
13	Massachusetts	164,834
27	Michigan	144,832
9	Minnesota	172,272
49	Mississippi	118,205
30	Missouri	143,855
29	Montana	143,966
37	Nebraska	134,860
35	Nevada	135,460
8	New Hampshire	173,859
41	New Jersey	129,089
22	New Mexico	151,617
44	New York	126,223
25	North Carolina	149,365
50	North Dakota	111,578
18	Ohio	156,277
36	Oklahoma	135,419
7	Oregon	176,190
23	Pennsylvania	150,118
39	Rhode Island	134,357
31	South Carolina	141,723
43	South Dakota	126,420
34	Tennessee	138,657
42	Texas	127,986
12	Utah	165,029
19	Vermont	154,064
26	Virginia	149,005
11	Washington	166,907
6	West Virginia	177,697
20	Wisconsin	153,991
10	Wyoming	170,668

RANK ORDER

RANK	STATE	VALUE
1	Hawaii	$208,593
2	Colorado	193,853
3	California	183,754
4	Connecticut	182,914
5	Alaska	182,581
6	West Virginia	177,697
7	Oregon	176,190
8	New Hampshire	173,859
9	Minnesota	172,272
10	Wyoming	170,668
11	Washington	166,907
12	Utah	165,029
13	Massachusetts	164,834
14	Illinois	162,726
15	Florida	161,871
16	Idaho	160,642
17	Arizona	156,617
18	Ohio	156,277
19	Vermont	154,064
20	Wisconsin	153,991
21	Maine	152,198
22	New Mexico	151,617
23	Pennsylvania	150,118
24	Indiana	149,556
25	North Carolina	149,365
26	Virginia	149,005
27	Michigan	144,832
28	Maryland	144,191
29	Montana	143,966
30	Missouri	143,855
31	South Carolina	141,723
32	Kansas	141,617
33	Iowa	141,138
34	Tennessee	138,657
35	Nevada	135,460
36	Oklahoma	135,419
37	Nebraska	134,860
38	Alabama	134,825
39	Rhode Island	134,357
40	Georgia	131,973
41	New Jersey	129,089
42	Texas	127,986
43	South Dakota	126,420
44	New York	126,223
45	Kentucky	125,937
46	Arkansas	125,465
47	Louisiana	122,625
48	Delaware	120,147
49	Mississippi	118,205
50	North Dakota	111,578
	District of Columbia	105,764

Source: Morgan Quitno Press using data from U.S. Bureau of the Census
    "New Privately Owned Housing Units Authorized" (http://www.census.gov/const/www/C40/table2.html)
*Preliminary and unadjusted year to date as of December 2005. Includes single and multifamily privately owned
units. Based on approximately 19,000 places in the U.S. having building permit systems.

Median Value of Owner-Occupied Housing in 2004

National Median = $151,366*

ALPHA ORDER

RANK	STATE	MEDIAN
45	Alabama	$94,671
15	Alaska	179,304
22	Arizona	145,741
50	Arkansas	79,006
1	California	391,102
10	Colorado	211,740
6	Connecticut	236,559
17	Delaware	171,589
21	Florida	149,291
26	Georgia	136,912
2	Hawaii	364,840
28	Idaho	120,825
18	Illinois	167,711
37	Indiana	110,020
43	Iowa	95,901
39	Kansas	102,458
41	Kentucky	98,438
42	Louisiana	95,910
24	Maine	143,182
9	Maryland	216,529
3	Massachusetts	331,200
23	Michigan	145,177
14	Minnesota	181,135
49	Mississippi	79,023
32	Missouri	117,033
30	Montana	119,319
38	Nebraska	106,656
12	Nevada	202,937
8	New Hampshire	216,639
4	New Jersey	291,294
35	New Mexico	110,788
7	New York	220,981
31	North Carolina	117,771
47	North Dakota	84,354
27	Ohio	122,384
46	Oklahoma	85,060
13	Oregon	181,544
33	Pennsylvania	116,520
5	Rhode Island	240,150
34	South Carolina	113,910
44	South Dakota	95,523
36	Tennessee	110,198
40	Texas	99,858
19	Utah	157,275
20	Vermont	154,318
16	Virginia	179,191
11	Washington	204,719
48	West Virginia	81,826
25	Wisconsin	137,727
29	Wyoming	119,654

RANK ORDER

RANK	STATE	MEDIAN
1	California	$391,102
2	Hawaii	364,840
3	Massachusetts	331,200
4	New Jersey	291,294
5	Rhode Island	240,150
6	Connecticut	236,559
7	New York	220,981
8	New Hampshire	216,639
9	Maryland	216,529
10	Colorado	211,740
11	Washington	204,719
12	Nevada	202,937
13	Oregon	181,544
14	Minnesota	181,135
15	Alaska	179,304
16	Virginia	179,191
17	Delaware	171,589
18	Illinois	167,711
19	Utah	157,275
20	Vermont	154,318
21	Florida	149,291
22	Arizona	145,741
23	Michigan	145,177
24	Maine	143,182
25	Wisconsin	137,727
26	Georgia	136,912
27	Ohio	122,384
28	Idaho	120,825
29	Wyoming	119,654
30	Montana	119,319
31	North Carolina	117,771
32	Missouri	117,033
33	Pennsylvania	116,520
34	South Carolina	113,910
35	New Mexico	110,788
36	Tennessee	110,198
37	Indiana	110,020
38	Nebraska	106,656
39	Kansas	102,458
40	Texas	99,858
41	Kentucky	98,438
42	Louisiana	95,910
43	Iowa	95,901
44	South Dakota	95,523
45	Alabama	94,671
46	Oklahoma	85,060
47	North Dakota	84,354
48	West Virginia	81,826
49	Mississippi	79,023
50	Arkansas	79,006
	District of Columbia	334,702

Source: U.S. Bureau of the Census
    "2004 American Community Survey" (http://www.census.gov/acs/www/index.html)
*Housing units with a mortgage.

Percent Change in House Prices: 2001 to 2005

National Percent Change = 55.3% Increase*

ALPHA ORDER				RANK ORDER		
RANK	STATE	PERCENT CHANGE		RANK	STATE	PERCENT CHANGE
37	Alabama	28.2		1	California	112.8
23	Alaska	45.2		2	Hawaii	102.8
8	Arizona	78.9		3	Florida	99.7
31	Arkansas	31.1		4	Rhode Island	99.2
1	California	112.8		5	Nevada	99.0
36	Colorado	29.3		6	Maryland	92.5
15	Connecticut	63.4		7	New Jersey	81.6
12	Delaware	68.7		8	Arizona	78.9
3	Florida	99.7		9	Virginia	78.8
35	Georgia	29.9		10	New York	71.9
2	Hawaii	102.8		11	New Hampshire	68.8
24	Idaho	42.7		12	Delaware	68.7
25	Illinois	40.7		13	Massachusetts	67.2
50	Indiana	20.6		14	Maine	67.0
42	Iowa	25.7		15	Connecticut	63.4
41	Kansas	25.8		16	Vermont	63.1
38	Kentucky	26.3		17	Pennsylvania	53.1
32	Louisiana	30.8		18	Minnesota	52.8
14	Maine	67.0		19	Oregon	51.2
6	Maryland	92.5		20	Wyoming	49.6
13	Massachusetts	67.2		21	Washington	49.1
45	Michigan	24.4		22	Montana	48.7
18	Minnesota	52.8		23	Alaska	45.2
49	Mississippi	22.8		24	Idaho	42.7
30	Missouri	34.2		25	Illinois	40.7
22	Montana	48.7		26	New Mexico	40.0
47	Nebraska	23.2		27	North Dakota	37.8
5	Nevada	99.0		28	Wisconsin	37.1
11	New Hampshire	68.8		29	West Virginia	35.7
7	New Jersey	81.6		30	Missouri	34.2
26	New Mexico	40.0		31	Arkansas	31.1
10	New York	71.9		32	Louisiana	30.8
43	North Carolina	25.4		32	South Carolina	30.8
27	North Dakota	37.8		32	South Dakota	30.8
48	Ohio	22.9		35	Georgia	29.9
38	Oklahoma	26.3		36	Colorado	29.3
19	Oregon	51.2		37	Alabama	28.2
17	Pennsylvania	53.1		38	Kentucky	26.3
4	Rhode Island	99.2		38	Oklahoma	26.3
32	South Carolina	30.8		40	Tennessee	26.1
32	South Dakota	30.8		41	Kansas	25.8
40	Tennessee	26.1		42	Iowa	25.7
46	Texas	23.5		43	North Carolina	25.4
44	Utah	24.7		44	Utah	24.7
16	Vermont	63.1		45	Michigan	24.4
9	Virginia	78.8		46	Texas	23.5
21	Washington	49.1		47	Nebraska	23.2
29	West Virginia	35.7		48	Ohio	22.9
28	Wisconsin	37.1		49	Mississippi	22.8
20	Wyoming	49.6		50	Indiana	20.6
					District of Columbia	118.9

Source: Office of Federal Housing Enterprise Oversight
   "House Price Index" (http://www.ofheo.gov/HPI.asp)
Single-family house prices. As of September 30, 2005.

Median Monthly Mortgage Payment in 2004

National Median = $1,212*

ALPHA ORDER

RANK	STATE	MORTGAGE
46	Alabama	$872
9	Alaska	1,421
25	Arizona	1,130
49	Arkansas	773
2	California	1,733
13	Colorado	1,355
5	Connecticut	1,603
18	Delaware	1,191
23	Florida	1,143
26	Georgia	1,126
3	Hawaii	1,648
39	Idaho	953
12	Illinois	1,370
35	Indiana	963
41	Iowa	942
32	Kansas	1,013
45	Kentucky	888
43	Louisiana	902
31	Maine	1,020
10	Maryland	1,406
4	Massachusetts	1,645
24	Michigan	1,137
16	Minnesota	1,260
48	Mississippi	843
36	Missouri	954
34	Montana	974
29	Nebraska	1,051
15	Nevada	1,274
7	New Hampshire	1,472
1	New Jersey	1,847
42	New Mexico	935
6	New York	1,525
30	North Carolina	1,028
43	North Dakota	902
28	Ohio	1,090
47	Oklahoma	871
17	Oregon	1,217
27	Pennsylvania	1,114
8	Rhode Island	1,469
33	South Carolina	987
40	South Dakota	952
36	Tennessee	954
20	Texas	1,166
21	Utah	1,164
19	Vermont	1,174
14	Virginia	1,323
11	Washington	1,389
50	West Virginia	769
22	Wisconsin	1,155
36	Wyoming	954

RANK ORDER

RANK	STATE	MORTGAGE
1	New Jersey	$1,847
2	California	1,733
3	Hawaii	1,648
4	Massachusetts	1,645
5	Connecticut	1,603
6	New York	1,525
7	New Hampshire	1,472
8	Rhode Island	1,469
9	Alaska	1,421
10	Maryland	1,406
11	Washington	1,389
12	Illinois	1,370
13	Colorado	1,355
14	Virginia	1,323
15	Nevada	1,274
16	Minnesota	1,260
17	Oregon	1,217
18	Delaware	1,191
19	Vermont	1,174
20	Texas	1,166
21	Utah	1,164
22	Wisconsin	1,155
23	Florida	1,143
24	Michigan	1,137
25	Arizona	1,130
26	Georgia	1,126
27	Pennsylvania	1,114
28	Ohio	1,090
29	Nebraska	1,051
30	North Carolina	1,028
31	Maine	1,020
32	Kansas	1,013
33	South Carolina	987
34	Montana	974
35	Indiana	963
36	Missouri	954
36	Tennessee	954
36	Wyoming	954
39	Idaho	953
40	South Dakota	952
41	Iowa	942
42	New Mexico	935
43	Louisiana	902
43	North Dakota	902
45	Kentucky	888
46	Alabama	872
47	Oklahoma	871
48	Mississippi	843
49	Arkansas	773
50	West Virginia	769
	District of Columbia	1,612

Source: U.S. Bureau of the Census
    "2004 American Community Survey" (http://www.census.gov/acs/www/index.html)
*For owner-occupied housing.

Percent of Home Owners Spending 30% or More of Household Income on Housing Costs: 2004
National Percent = 32.4% of Home Owners*

RANK	STATE	PERCENT
38	Alabama	26.0
37	Alaska	26.1
13	Arizona	33.4
48	Arkansas	22.7
1	California	44.1
7	Colorado	36.3
18	Connecticut	31.2
40	Delaware	25.4
4	Florida	37.9
20	Georgia	31.1
5	Hawaii	37.3
31	Idaho	28.2
12	Illinois	33.8
43	Indiana	24.4
50	Iowa	21.5
45	Kansas	24.1
39	Kentucky	25.6
35	Louisiana	27.3
34	Maine	27.5
32	Maryland	27.9
9	Massachusetts	35.2
25	Michigan	29.3
26	Minnesota	29.2
21	Mississippi	30.7
43	Missouri	24.4
16	Montana	33.0
45	Nebraska	24.1
2	Nevada	38.6
14	New Hampshire	33.3
3	New Jersey	38.4
18	New Mexico	31.2
5	New York	37.3
24	North Carolina	29.7
49	North Dakota	21.6
33	Ohio	27.6
41	Oklahoma	25.0
11	Oregon	35.0
29	Pennsylvania	28.8
8	Rhode Island	35.9
29	South Carolina	28.8
36	South Dakota	26.5
27	Tennessee	29.1
22	Texas	29.9
15	Utah	33.1
17	Vermont	32.2
28	Virginia	29.0
10	Washington	35.1
42	West Virginia	24.7
23	Wisconsin	29.8
45	Wyoming	24.1

RANK	STATE	PERCENT
1	California	44.1
2	Nevada	38.6
3	New Jersey	38.4
4	Florida	37.9
5	Hawaii	37.3
5	New York	37.3
7	Colorado	36.3
8	Rhode Island	35.9
9	Massachusetts	35.2
10	Washington	35.1
11	Oregon	35.0
12	Illinois	33.8
13	Arizona	33.4
14	New Hampshire	33.3
15	Utah	33.1
16	Montana	33.0
17	Vermont	32.2
18	Connecticut	31.2
18	New Mexico	31.2
20	Georgia	31.1
21	Mississippi	30.7
22	Texas	29.9
23	Wisconsin	29.8
24	North Carolina	29.7
25	Michigan	29.3
26	Minnesota	29.2
27	Tennessee	29.1
28	Virginia	29.0
29	Pennsylvania	28.8
29	South Carolina	28.8
31	Idaho	28.2
32	Maryland	27.9
33	Ohio	27.6
34	Maine	27.5
35	Louisiana	27.3
36	South Dakota	26.5
37	Alaska	26.1
38	Alabama	26.0
39	Kentucky	25.6
40	Delaware	25.4
41	Oklahoma	25.0
42	West Virginia	24.7
43	Indiana	24.4
43	Missouri	24.4
45	Kansas	24.1
45	Nebraska	24.1
45	Wyoming	24.1
48	Arkansas	22.7
49	North Dakota	21.6
50	Iowa	21.5
	District of Columbia	33.5

Source: U.S. Bureau of the Census
   "2004 American Community Survey" (http://www.census.gov/acs/www/index.html)
*For owner-occupied housing units with a mortgage.

Existing Home Sales in 2005

National Total = 7,237,000 Homes*

RANK	STATE	HOMES	% of USA		RANK	STATE	HOMES	% of USA
	ALPHA ORDER					**RANK ORDER**		
23	Alabama	125,100	1.7%		1	California	629,500	8.7%
44	Alaska	25,700	0.4%		2	Texas	565,800	7.8%
12	Arizona	211,000	2.9%		3	Florida	556,800	7.7%
29	Arkansas	84,000	1.2%		4	New York	358,000	4.9%
1	California	629,500	8.7%		5	Illinois	326,900	4.5%
21	Colorado	137,100	1.9%		6	Ohio	300,000	4.1%
31	Connecticut	83,500	1.2%		7	Pennsylvania	262,400	3.6%
43	Delaware	26,300	0.4%		8	North Carolina	253,600	3.5%
3	Florida	556,800	7.7%		9	Georgia	251,700	3.5%
9	Georgia	251,700	3.5%		10	Michigan	215,100	3.0%
39	Hawaii	38,400	0.5%		11	New Jersey	214,500	3.0%
40	Idaho	37,400	0.5%		12	Arizona	211,000	2.9%
5	Illinois	326,900	4.5%		13	Virginia	184,900	2.6%
17	Indiana	146,100	2.0%		14	Washington	179,600	2.5%
33	Iowa	76,300	1.1%		15	Tennessee	175,500	2.4%
32	Kansas	80,000	1.1%		16	Massachusetts	162,700	2.2%
27	Kentucky	98,800	1.4%		17	Indiana	146,100	2.0%
30	Louisiana	83,600	1.2%		18	Missouri	145,000	2.0%
41	Maine	35,300	0.5%		19	Minnesota	144,200	2.0%
20	Maryland	139,700	1.9%		20	Maryland	139,700	1.9%
16	Massachusetts	162,700	2.2%		21	Colorado	137,100	1.9%
10	Michigan	215,100	3.0%		22	Wisconsin	131,300	1.8%
19	Minnesota	144,200	2.0%		23	Alabama	125,100	1.7%
35	Mississippi	54,000	0.7%		24	South Carolina	120,600	1.7%
18	Missouri	145,000	2.0%		25	Oregon	110,200	1.5%
42	Montana	26,400	0.4%		26	Oklahoma	108,200	1.5%
37	Nebraska	42,500	0.6%		27	Kentucky	98,800	1.4%
28	Nevada	94,100	1.3%		28	Nevada	94,100	1.3%
NA	New Hampshire**	NA	NA		29	Arkansas	84,000	1.2%
11	New Jersey	214,500	3.0%		30	Louisiana	83,600	1.2%
36	New Mexico	43,300	0.6%		31	Connecticut	83,500	1.2%
4	New York	358,000	4.9%		32	Kansas	80,000	1.1%
8	North Carolina	253,600	3.5%		33	Iowa	76,300	1.1%
47	North Dakota	17,900	0.2%		34	Utah	55,200	0.8%
6	Ohio	300,000	4.1%		35	Mississippi	54,000	0.7%
26	Oklahoma	108,200	1.5%		36	New Mexico	43,300	0.6%
25	Oregon	110,200	1.5%		37	Nebraska	42,500	0.6%
7	Pennsylvania	262,400	3.6%		38	West Virginia	39,400	0.5%
45	Rhode Island	20,800	0.3%		39	Hawaii	38,400	0.5%
24	South Carolina	120,600	1.7%		40	Idaho	37,400	0.5%
46	South Dakota	20,000	0.3%		41	Maine	35,300	0.5%
15	Tennessee	175,500	2.4%		42	Montana	26,400	0.4%
2	Texas	565,800	7.8%		43	Delaware	26,300	0.4%
34	Utah	55,200	0.8%		44	Alaska	25,700	0.4%
NA	Vermont**	NA	NA		45	Rhode Island	20,800	0.3%
13	Virginia	184,900	2.6%		46	South Dakota	20,000	0.3%
14	Washington	179,600	2.5%		47	North Dakota	17,900	0.2%
38	West Virginia	39,400	0.5%		48	Wyoming	14,900	0.2%
22	Wisconsin	131,300	1.8%		NA	New Hampshire**	NA	NA
48	Wyoming	14,900	0.2%		NA	Vermont**	NA	NA
						District of Columbia	10,100	0.1%

Source: National Association of Realtors®, Economics and Research Division
    "Existing Home Sales" (http://www.realtor.org/Research.nsf/Pages/MetroPrice)
*Seasonally adjusted preliminary data as of September 2005. Includes existing houses, apartment condos and
co-ops. Excludes new construction.
**Not available.

Percent Change in Existing Home Sales: 2004 to 2005

National Percent Change = 6.5% Increase*

RANK	STATE (ALPHA ORDER)	PERCENT CHANGE		RANK	STATE (RANK ORDER)	PERCENT CHANGE
12	Alabama	12.0		1	Arkansas	32.1
13	Alaska	11.7		2	Utah	26.6
26	Arizona	7.7		3	Washington	20.0
1	Arkansas	32.1		4	North Dakota	19.3
37	California	4.8		5	South Carolina	18.1
25	Colorado	7.9		6	Oregon	15.5
23	Connecticut	8.3		7	Georgia	14.4
34	Delaware	5.2		8	Texas	13.9
20	Florida	9.0		9	Oklahoma	12.9
7	Georgia	14.4		10	Idaho	12.3
27	Hawaii	7.6		10	Indiana	12.3
10	Idaho	12.3		12	Alabama	12.0
37	Illinois	4.8		13	Alaska	11.7
10	Indiana	12.3		13	North Carolina	11.7
31	Iowa	6.7		15	Massachusetts	11.2
22	Kansas	8.4		16	South Dakota	10.5
18	Kentucky	9.5		17	Tennessee	10.4
39	Louisiana	4.6		18	Kentucky	9.5
35	Maine	5.1		19	Wisconsin	9.4
46	Maryland	(3.0)		20	Florida	9.0
15	Massachusetts	11.2		21	Wyoming	8.8
45	Michigan	(1.7)		22	Kansas	8.4
42	Minnesota	0.7		23	Connecticut	8.3
48	Mississippi	(7.2)		24	Montana	8.2
43	Missouri	0.6		25	Colorado	7.9
24	Montana	8.2		26	Arizona	7.7
41	Nebraska	3.4		27	Hawaii	7.6
44	Nevada	0.3		28	Ohio	7.3
NA	New Hampshire**	NA		29	New York	7.0
40	New Jersey	3.9		30	New Mexico	6.9
30	New Mexico	6.9		31	Iowa	6.7
29	New York	7.0		31	Rhode Island	6.7
13	North Carolina	11.7		33	Pennsylvania	5.8
4	North Dakota	19.3		34	Delaware	5.2
28	Ohio	7.3		35	Maine	5.1
9	Oklahoma	12.9		35	West Virginia	5.1
6	Oregon	15.5		37	California	4.8
33	Pennsylvania	5.8		37	Illinois	4.8
31	Rhode Island	6.7		39	Louisiana	4.6
5	South Carolina	18.1		40	New Jersey	3.9
16	South Dakota	10.5		41	Nebraska	3.4
17	Tennessee	10.4		42	Minnesota	0.7
8	Texas	13.9		43	Missouri	0.6
2	Utah	26.6		44	Nevada	0.3
NA	Vermont**	NA		45	Michigan	(1.7)
47	Virginia	(3.6)		46	Maryland	(3.0)
3	Washington	20.0		47	Virginia	(3.6)
35	West Virginia	5.1		48	Mississippi	(7.2)
19	Wisconsin	9.4		NA	New Hampshire**	NA
21	Wyoming	8.8		NA	Vermont**	NA
					District of Columbia	3.1

Source: National Association of Realtors®, Economics and Research Division
   "Existing Home Sales" (http://www.realtor.org/Research.nsf/Pages/EHSdata)
*Seasonally adjusted preliminary data as of September 2005. Includes existing houses, apartment condos and co-ops. Excludes new construction.
**Not available.

Homeownership Rate in 2004

National Rate = 69.0%*

ALPHA ORDER

RANK	STATE	PERCENT
2	Alabama	78.0
42	Alaska	67.2
40	Arizona	68.7
37	Arkansas	69.1
49	California	59.7
30	Colorado	71.1
26	Connecticut	71.7
3	Delaware	77.3
23	Florida	72.2
32	Georgia	70.9
48	Hawaii	60.6
12	Idaho	73.7
20	Illinois	72.7
7	Indiana	75.8
17	Iowa	73.2
35	Kansas	69.9
14	Kentucky	73.3
33	Louisiana	70.6
10	Maine	74.7
24	Maryland	72.1
46	Massachusetts	63.8
4	Michigan	77.1
5	Minnesota	76.4
11	Mississippi	74.0
21	Missouri	72.4
21	Montana	72.4
29	Nebraska	71.2
44	Nevada	65.7
14	New Hampshire	73.3
39	New Jersey	68.8
28	New Mexico	71.5
50	New York	54.8
36	North Carolina	69.8
34	North Dakota	70.0
18	Ohio	73.1
30	Oklahoma	71.1
38	Oregon	69.0
8	Pennsylvania	74.9
47	Rhode Island	61.5
6	South Carolina	76.2
41	South Dakota	68.5
27	Tennessee	71.6
45	Texas	65.5
8	Utah	74.9
25	Vermont	72.0
13	Virginia	73.4
43	Washington	66.0
1	West Virginia	80.3
14	Wisconsin	73.3
19	Wyoming	72.8

RANK ORDER

RANK	STATE	PERCENT
1	West Virginia	80.3
2	Alabama	78.0
3	Delaware	77.3
4	Michigan	77.1
5	Minnesota	76.4
6	South Carolina	76.2
7	Indiana	75.8
8	Pennsylvania	74.9
8	Utah	74.9
10	Maine	74.7
11	Mississippi	74.0
12	Idaho	73.7
13	Virginia	73.4
14	Kentucky	73.3
14	New Hampshire	73.3
14	Wisconsin	73.3
17	Iowa	73.2
18	Ohio	73.1
19	Wyoming	72.8
20	Illinois	72.7
21	Missouri	72.4
21	Montana	72.4
23	Florida	72.2
24	Maryland	72.1
25	Vermont	72.0
26	Connecticut	71.7
27	Tennessee	71.6
28	New Mexico	71.5
29	Nebraska	71.2
30	Colorado	71.1
30	Oklahoma	71.1
32	Georgia	70.9
33	Louisiana	70.6
34	North Dakota	70.0
35	Kansas	69.9
36	North Carolina	69.8
37	Arkansas	69.1
38	Oregon	69.0
39	New Jersey	68.8
40	Arizona	68.7
41	South Dakota	68.5
42	Alaska	67.2
43	Washington	66.0
44	Nevada	65.7
45	Texas	65.5
46	Massachusetts	63.8
47	Rhode Island	61.5
48	Hawaii	60.6
49	California	59.7
50	New York	54.8
	District of Columbia	45.6

Source: U.S. Bureau of the Census
   "Housing Vacancies and Homeownership, Annual Statistics: 2004"
   (http://www.census.gov/hhes/www/housing/hvs/annual04/ann04t13.html)
*Percent of households occupied by the owner.

Median Monthly Rental Payment in 2004

National Median = $694*

<table>
<tr><td colspan="3">ALPHA ORDER</td><td colspan="3">RANK ORDER</td></tr>
<tr><td>RANK</td><td>STATE</td><td>RENT</td><td>RANK</td><td>STATE</td><td>RENT</td></tr>
<tr><td>45</td><td>Alabama</td><td>$519</td><td>1</td><td>California</td><td>$914</td></tr>
<tr><td>8</td><td>Alaska</td><td>808</td><td>2</td><td>New Jersey</td><td>877</td></tr>
<tr><td>18</td><td>Arizona</td><td>691</td><td>3</td><td>Hawaii</td><td>871</td></tr>
<tr><td>46</td><td>Arkansas</td><td>517</td><td>4</td><td>Massachusetts</td><td>852</td></tr>
<tr><td>1</td><td>California</td><td>914</td><td>5</td><td>Maryland</td><td>837</td></tr>
<tr><td>16</td><td>Colorado</td><td>724</td><td>6</td><td>Connecticut</td><td>811</td></tr>
<tr><td>6</td><td>Connecticut</td><td>811</td><td>7</td><td>New Hampshire</td><td>810</td></tr>
<tr><td>13</td><td>Delaware</td><td>743</td><td>8</td><td>Alaska</td><td>808</td></tr>
<tr><td>11</td><td>Florida</td><td>766</td><td>9</td><td>New York</td><td>796</td></tr>
<tr><td>20</td><td>Georgia</td><td>677</td><td>10</td><td>Nevada</td><td>787</td></tr>
<tr><td>3</td><td>Hawaii</td><td>871</td><td>11</td><td>Florida</td><td>766</td></tr>
<tr><td>35</td><td>Idaho</td><td>566</td><td>12</td><td>Virginia</td><td>757</td></tr>
<tr><td>17</td><td>Illinois</td><td>698</td><td>13</td><td>Delaware</td><td>743</td></tr>
<tr><td>30</td><td>Indiana</td><td>589</td><td>14</td><td>Rhode Island</td><td>740</td></tr>
<tr><td>41</td><td>Iowa</td><td>533</td><td>15</td><td>Washington</td><td>727</td></tr>
<tr><td>33</td><td>Kansas</td><td>567</td><td>16</td><td>Colorado</td><td>724</td></tr>
<tr><td>47</td><td>Kentucky</td><td>503</td><td>17</td><td>Illinois</td><td>698</td></tr>
<tr><td>39</td><td>Louisiana</td><td>540</td><td>18</td><td>Arizona</td><td>691</td></tr>
<tr><td>32</td><td>Maine</td><td>582</td><td>19</td><td>Oregon</td><td>681</td></tr>
<tr><td>5</td><td>Maryland</td><td>837</td><td>20</td><td>Georgia</td><td>677</td></tr>
<tr><td>4</td><td>Massachusetts</td><td>852</td><td>21</td><td>Vermont</td><td>674</td></tr>
<tr><td>25</td><td>Michigan</td><td>628</td><td>22</td><td>Minnesota</td><td>673</td></tr>
<tr><td>22</td><td>Minnesota</td><td>673</td><td>23</td><td>Utah</td><td>662</td></tr>
<tr><td>42</td><td>Mississippi</td><td>529</td><td>24</td><td>Texas</td><td>648</td></tr>
<tr><td>33</td><td>Missouri</td><td>567</td><td>25</td><td>Michigan</td><td>628</td></tr>
<tr><td>44</td><td>Montana</td><td>520</td><td>26</td><td>Pennsylvania</td><td>611</td></tr>
<tr><td>37</td><td>Nebraska</td><td>547</td><td>27</td><td>North Carolina</td><td>610</td></tr>
<tr><td>10</td><td>Nevada</td><td>787</td><td>27</td><td>South Carolina</td><td>610</td></tr>
<tr><td>7</td><td>New Hampshire</td><td>810</td><td>29</td><td>Wisconsin</td><td>609</td></tr>
<tr><td>2</td><td>New Jersey</td><td>877</td><td>30</td><td>Indiana</td><td>589</td></tr>
<tr><td>38</td><td>New Mexico</td><td>546</td><td>31</td><td>Ohio</td><td>587</td></tr>
<tr><td>9</td><td>New York</td><td>796</td><td>32</td><td>Maine</td><td>582</td></tr>
<tr><td>27</td><td>North Carolina</td><td>610</td><td>33</td><td>Kansas</td><td>567</td></tr>
<tr><td>49</td><td>North Dakota</td><td>466</td><td>33</td><td>Missouri</td><td>567</td></tr>
<tr><td>31</td><td>Ohio</td><td>587</td><td>35</td><td>Idaho</td><td>566</td></tr>
<tr><td>43</td><td>Oklahoma</td><td>525</td><td>36</td><td>Tennessee</td><td>564</td></tr>
<tr><td>19</td><td>Oregon</td><td>681</td><td>37</td><td>Nebraska</td><td>547</td></tr>
<tr><td>26</td><td>Pennsylvania</td><td>611</td><td>38</td><td>New Mexico</td><td>546</td></tr>
<tr><td>14</td><td>Rhode Island</td><td>740</td><td>39</td><td>Louisiana</td><td>540</td></tr>
<tr><td>27</td><td>South Carolina</td><td>610</td><td>40</td><td>Wyoming</td><td>534</td></tr>
<tr><td>48</td><td>South Dakota</td><td>493</td><td>41</td><td>Iowa</td><td>533</td></tr>
<tr><td>36</td><td>Tennessee</td><td>564</td><td>42</td><td>Mississippi</td><td>529</td></tr>
<tr><td>24</td><td>Texas</td><td>648</td><td>43</td><td>Oklahoma</td><td>525</td></tr>
<tr><td>23</td><td>Utah</td><td>662</td><td>44</td><td>Montana</td><td>520</td></tr>
<tr><td>21</td><td>Vermont</td><td>674</td><td>45</td><td>Alabama</td><td>519</td></tr>
<tr><td>12</td><td>Virginia</td><td>757</td><td>46</td><td>Arkansas</td><td>517</td></tr>
<tr><td>15</td><td>Washington</td><td>727</td><td>47</td><td>Kentucky</td><td>503</td></tr>
<tr><td>50</td><td>West Virginia</td><td>461</td><td>48</td><td>South Dakota</td><td>493</td></tr>
<tr><td>29</td><td>Wisconsin</td><td>609</td><td>49</td><td>North Dakota</td><td>466</td></tr>
<tr><td>40</td><td>Wyoming</td><td>534</td><td>50</td><td>West Virginia</td><td>461</td></tr>
<tr><td></td><td></td><td></td><td></td><td>District of Columbia</td><td>799</td></tr>
</table>

Source: U.S. Bureau of the Census
  "2004 American Community Survey" (http://www.census.gov/acs/www/index.html)
*For renter-occupied housing.

Percent of Renters Spending 30% or More of Household Income on Rent and Utilities: 2004
National Percent = 44.1% of Renters*

ALPHA ORDER

RANK	STATE	PERCENT
37	Alabama	39.6
47	Alaska	36.3
6	Arizona	47.3
31	Arkansas	40.6
2	California	49.9
7	Colorado	47.0
14	Connecticut	43.2
45	Delaware	37.5
1	Florida	50.5
11	Georgia	43.9
15	Hawaii	42.9
8	Idaho	45.1
18	Illinois	42.5
43	Indiana	37.8
42	Iowa	37.9
41	Kansas	38.1
38	Kentucky	39.5
20	Louisiana	42.3
29	Maine	40.8
30	Maryland	40.7
15	Massachusetts	42.9
13	Michigan	43.4
24	Minnesota	41.7
21	Mississippi	42.0
39	Missouri	39.1
33	Montana	40.2
44	Nebraska	37.6
12	Nevada	43.7
18	New Hampshire	42.5
10	New Jersey	44.8
36	New Mexico	39.7
5	New York	47.4
27	North Carolina	40.9
49	North Dakota	32.1
24	Ohio	41.7
35	Oklahoma	39.9
3	Oregon	47.6
23	Pennsylvania	41.8
9	Rhode Island	45.0
32	South Carolina	40.3
48	South Dakota	34.6
33	Tennessee	40.2
21	Texas	42.0
15	Utah	42.9
40	Vermont	38.5
26	Virginia	41.6
4	Washington	47.5
46	West Virginia	36.7
27	Wisconsin	40.9
50	Wyoming	31.3

RANK ORDER

RANK	STATE	PERCENT
1	Florida	50.5
2	California	49.9
3	Oregon	47.6
4	Washington	47.5
5	New York	47.4
6	Arizona	47.3
7	Colorado	47.0
8	Idaho	45.1
9	Rhode Island	45.0
10	New Jersey	44.8
11	Georgia	43.9
12	Nevada	43.7
13	Michigan	43.4
14	Connecticut	43.2
15	Hawaii	42.9
15	Massachusetts	42.9
15	Utah	42.9
18	Illinois	42.5
18	New Hampshire	42.5
20	Louisiana	42.3
21	Mississippi	42.0
21	Texas	42.0
23	Pennsylvania	41.8
24	Minnesota	41.7
24	Ohio	41.7
26	Virginia	41.6
27	North Carolina	40.9
27	Wisconsin	40.9
29	Maine	40.8
30	Maryland	40.7
31	Arkansas	40.6
32	South Carolina	40.3
33	Montana	40.2
33	Tennessee	40.2
35	Oklahoma	39.9
36	New Mexico	39.7
37	Alabama	39.6
38	Kentucky	39.5
39	Missouri	39.1
40	Vermont	38.5
41	Kansas	38.1
42	Iowa	37.9
43	Indiana	37.8
44	Nebraska	37.6
45	Delaware	37.5
46	West Virginia	36.7
47	Alaska	36.3
48	South Dakota	34.6
49	North Dakota	32.1
50	Wyoming	31.3

| | District of Columbia | 43.5 |

Source: U.S. Bureau of the Census
    "2004 American Community Survey" (http://www.census.gov/acs/www/index.html)
*Based on Renter-occupied units as a percent of household population. Excludes population living in institutions, college dormitories and other group quarters.

State and Local Government Expenditures
For Housing and Community Development in 2002
National Total = $31,610,470,000*

RANK	STATE	EXPENDITURES	% of USA
22	Alabama	$404,362,000	1.3%
33	Alaska	174,734,000	0.6%
26	Arizona	300,456,000	1.0%
34	Arkansas	157,986,000	0.5%
1	California	5,381,446,000	17.0%
20	Colorado	444,818,000	1.4%
21	Connecticut	440,361,000	1.4%
43	Delaware	104,273,000	0.3%
8	Florida	1,179,014,000	3.7%
14	Georgia	740,049,000	2.3%
28	Hawaii	220,877,000	0.7%
49	Idaho	30,690,000	0.1%
3	Illinois	1,787,920,000	5.7%
16	Indiana	589,477,000	1.9%
37	Iowa	151,214,000	0.5%
39	Kansas	138,339,000	0.4%
32	Kentucky	177,744,000	0.6%
24	Louisiana	369,498,000	1.2%
40	Maine	129,589,000	0.4%
13	Maryland	754,354,000	2.4%
7	Massachusetts	1,344,441,000	4.3%
23	Michigan	371,969,000	1.2%
11	Minnesota	763,197,000	2.4%
38	Mississippi	144,524,000	0.5%
19	Missouri	467,040,000	1.5%
46	Montana	82,302,000	0.3%
42	Nebraska	113,011,000	0.4%
29	Nevada	195,174,000	0.6%
36	New Hampshire	154,513,000	0.5%
9	New Jersey	940,573,000	3.0%
44	New Mexico	91,602,000	0.3%
2	New York	3,765,621,000	11.9%
12	North Carolina	760,343,000	2.4%
47	North Dakota	53,484,000	0.2%
6	Ohio	1,448,573,000	4.6%
31	Oklahoma	178,111,000	0.6%
18	Oregon	483,101,000	1.5%
4	Pennsylvania	1,645,075,000	5.2%
35	Rhode Island	155,513,000	0.5%
27	South Carolina	270,075,000	0.9%
48	South Dakota	50,917,000	0.2%
17	Tennessee	496,139,000	1.6%
5	Texas	1,564,490,000	4.9%
30	Utah	179,679,000	0.6%
45	Vermont	90,095,000	0.3%
15	Virginia	702,324,000	2.2%
10	Washington	896,955,000	2.8%
41	West Virginia	113,601,000	0.4%
25	Wisconsin	314,224,000	1.0%
50	Wyoming	8,507,000	0.0%

RANK	STATE	EXPENDITURES	% of USA
1	California	$5,381,446,000	17.0%
2	New York	3,765,621,000	11.9%
3	Illinois	1,787,920,000	5.7%
4	Pennsylvania	1,645,075,000	5.2%
5	Texas	1,564,490,000	4.9%
6	Ohio	1,448,573,000	4.6%
7	Massachusetts	1,344,441,000	4.3%
8	Florida	1,179,014,000	3.7%
9	New Jersey	940,573,000	3.0%
10	Washington	896,955,000	2.8%
11	Minnesota	763,197,000	2.4%
12	North Carolina	760,343,000	2.4%
13	Maryland	754,354,000	2.4%
14	Georgia	740,049,000	2.3%
15	Virginia	702,324,000	2.2%
16	Indiana	589,477,000	1.9%
17	Tennessee	496,139,000	1.6%
18	Oregon	483,101,000	1.5%
19	Missouri	467,040,000	1.5%
20	Colorado	444,818,000	1.4%
21	Connecticut	440,361,000	1.4%
22	Alabama	404,362,000	1.3%
23	Michigan	371,969,000	1.2%
24	Louisiana	369,498,000	1.2%
25	Wisconsin	314,224,000	1.0%
26	Arizona	300,456,000	1.0%
27	South Carolina	270,075,000	0.9%
28	Hawaii	220,877,000	0.7%
29	Nevada	195,174,000	0.6%
30	Utah	179,679,000	0.6%
31	Oklahoma	178,111,000	0.6%
32	Kentucky	177,744,000	0.6%
33	Alaska	174,734,000	0.6%
34	Arkansas	157,986,000	0.5%
35	Rhode Island	155,513,000	0.5%
36	New Hampshire	154,513,000	0.5%
37	Iowa	151,214,000	0.5%
38	Mississippi	144,524,000	0.5%
39	Kansas	138,339,000	0.4%
40	Maine	129,589,000	0.4%
41	West Virginia	113,601,000	0.4%
42	Nebraska	113,011,000	0.4%
43	Delaware	104,273,000	0.3%
44	New Mexico	91,602,000	0.3%
45	Vermont	90,095,000	0.3%
46	Montana	82,302,000	0.3%
47	North Dakota	53,484,000	0.2%
48	South Dakota	50,917,000	0.2%
49	Idaho	30,690,000	0.1%
50	Wyoming	8,507,000	0.0%
	District of Columbia	88,096,000	0.3%

Source: U.S. Bureau of the Census, Governments Division
    "State and Local Government Finances: 2002 Census" (http://www.census.gov/govs/www/estimate02.html)
*Direct general expenditures.

Per Capita State and Local Government Expenditures
For Housing and Community Development in 2002
National Per Capita = $110*

ALPHA ORDER

ALPHA ORDER

RANK	STATE	PER CAPITA
24	Alabama	$90
1	Alaska	273
41	Arizona	55
39	Arkansas	58
5	California	154
20	Colorado	99
15	Connecticut	127
14	Delaware	129
34	Florida	71
27	Georgia	87
4	Hawaii	179
49	Idaho	23
10	Illinois	142
22	Indiana	96
42	Iowa	52
43	Kansas	51
47	Kentucky	43
30	Louisiana	83
19	Maine	100
11	Maryland	139
2	Massachusetts	210
48	Michigan	37
6	Minnesota	152
45	Mississippi	50
31	Missouri	82
24	Montana	90
37	Nebraska	65
24	Nevada	90
17	New Hampshire	121
18	New Jersey	110
46	New Mexico	49
3	New York	197
23	North Carolina	91
29	North Dakota	84
15	Ohio	127
43	Oklahoma	51
12	Oregon	137
13	Pennsylvania	133
9	Rhode Island	145
36	South Carolina	66
35	South Dakota	67
28	Tennessee	86
33	Texas	72
32	Utah	77
8	Vermont	146
21	Virginia	97
7	Washington	148
38	West Virginia	63
39	Wisconsin	58
50	Wyoming	17

RANK ORDER

RANK	STATE	PER CAPITA
1	Alaska	$273
2	Massachusetts	210
3	New York	197
4	Hawaii	179
5	California	154
6	Minnesota	152
7	Washington	148
8	Vermont	146
9	Rhode Island	145
10	Illinois	142
11	Maryland	139
12	Oregon	137
13	Pennsylvania	133
14	Delaware	129
15	Connecticut	127
15	Ohio	127
17	New Hampshire	121
18	New Jersey	110
19	Maine	100
20	Colorado	99
21	Virginia	97
22	Indiana	96
23	North Carolina	91
24	Alabama	90
24	Montana	90
24	Nevada	90
27	Georgia	87
28	Tennessee	86
29	North Dakota	84
30	Louisiana	83
31	Missouri	82
32	Utah	77
33	Texas	72
34	Florida	71
35	South Dakota	67
36	South Carolina	66
37	Nebraska	65
38	West Virginia	63
39	Arkansas	58
39	Wisconsin	58
41	Arizona	55
42	Iowa	52
43	Kansas	51
43	Oklahoma	51
45	Mississippi	50
46	New Mexico	49
47	Kentucky	43
48	Michigan	37
49	Idaho	23
50	Wyoming	17

District of Columbia — 156

Source: Morgan Quitno Press using data from U.S. Bureau of the Census, Governments Division
   "State and Local Government Finances: 2002 Census" (http://www.census.gov/govs/www/estimate02.html)
*Direct general expenditures.

XIII. POPULATION

XIII. POPULATION (continued)

Population in 2005

National Total = 296,410,404*

ALPHA ORDER

RANK	STATE	POPULATION	% of USA
23	Alabama	4,557,808	1.5%
47	Alaska	663,661	0.2%
17	Arizona	5,939,292	2.0%
32	Arkansas	2,779,154	0.9%
1	California	36,132,147	12.2%
22	Colorado	4,665,177	1.6%
29	Connecticut	3,510,297	1.2%
45	Delaware	843,524	0.3%
4	Florida	17,789,864	6.0%
9	Georgia	9,072,576	3.1%
42	Hawaii	1,275,194	0.4%
39	Idaho	1,429,096	0.5%
5	Illinois	12,763,371	4.3%
15	Indiana	6,271,973	2.1%
30	Iowa	2,966,334	1.0%
33	Kansas	2,744,687	0.9%
26	Kentucky	4,173,405	1.4%
24	Louisiana	4,523,628	1.5%
40	Maine	1,321,505	0.4%
19	Maryland	5,600,388	1.9%
13	Massachusetts	6,398,743	2.2%
8	Michigan	10,120,860	3.4%
21	Minnesota	5,132,799	1.7%
31	Mississippi	2,921,088	1.0%
18	Missouri	5,800,310	2.0%
44	Montana	935,670	0.3%
38	Nebraska	1,758,787	0.6%
35	Nevada	2,414,807	0.8%
41	New Hampshire	1,309,940	0.4%
10	New Jersey	8,717,925	2.9%
36	New Mexico	1,928,384	0.7%
3	New York	19,254,630	6.5%
11	North Carolina	8,683,242	2.9%
48	North Dakota	636,677	0.2%
7	Ohio	11,464,042	3.9%
28	Oklahoma	3,547,884	1.2%
27	Oregon	3,641,056	1.2%
6	Pennsylvania	12,429,616	4.2%
43	Rhode Island	1,076,189	0.4%
25	South Carolina	4,255,083	1.4%
46	South Dakota	775,933	0.3%
16	Tennessee	5,962,959	2.0%
2	Texas	22,859,968	7.7%
34	Utah	2,469,585	0.8%
49	Vermont	623,050	0.2%
12	Virginia	7,567,465	2.6%
14	Washington	6,287,759	2.1%
37	West Virginia	1,816,856	0.6%
20	Wisconsin	5,536,201	1.9%
50	Wyoming	509,294	0.2%

RANK ORDER

RANK	STATE	POPULATION	% of USA
1	California	36,132,147	12.2%
2	Texas	22,859,968	7.7%
3	New York	19,254,630	6.5%
4	Florida	17,789,864	6.0%
5	Illinois	12,763,371	4.3%
6	Pennsylvania	12,429,616	4.2%
7	Ohio	11,464,042	3.9%
8	Michigan	10,120,860	3.4%
9	Georgia	9,072,576	3.1%
10	New Jersey	8,717,925	2.9%
11	North Carolina	8,683,242	2.9%
12	Virginia	7,567,465	2.6%
13	Massachusetts	6,398,743	2.2%
14	Washington	6,287,759	2.1%
15	Indiana	6,271,973	2.1%
16	Tennessee	5,962,959	2.0%
17	Arizona	5,939,292	2.0%
18	Missouri	5,800,310	2.0%
19	Maryland	5,600,388	1.9%
20	Wisconsin	5,536,201	1.9%
21	Minnesota	5,132,799	1.7%
22	Colorado	4,665,177	1.6%
23	Alabama	4,557,808	1.5%
24	Louisiana	4,523,628	1.5%
25	South Carolina	4,255,083	1.4%
26	Kentucky	4,173,405	1.4%
27	Oregon	3,641,056	1.2%
28	Oklahoma	3,547,884	1.2%
29	Connecticut	3,510,297	1.2%
30	Iowa	2,966,334	1.0%
31	Mississippi	2,921,088	1.0%
32	Arkansas	2,779,154	0.9%
33	Kansas	2,744,687	0.9%
34	Utah	2,469,585	0.8%
35	Nevada	2,414,807	0.8%
36	New Mexico	1,928,384	0.7%
37	West Virginia	1,816,856	0.6%
38	Nebraska	1,758,787	0.6%
39	Idaho	1,429,096	0.5%
40	Maine	1,321,505	0.4%
41	New Hampshire	1,309,940	0.4%
42	Hawaii	1,275,194	0.4%
43	Rhode Island	1,076,189	0.4%
44	Montana	935,670	0.3%
45	Delaware	843,524	0.3%
46	South Dakota	775,933	0.3%
47	Alaska	663,661	0.2%
48	North Dakota	636,677	0.2%
49	Vermont	623,050	0.2%
50	Wyoming	509,294	0.2%
	District of Columbia	550,521	0.2%

Source: U.S. Bureau of the Census
"Population Estimates" (December 22, 2005, http://www.census.gov/popest/estimates.php)
*Resident population.

Population in 2004

National Total = 293,656,842*

ALPHA ORDER

RANK	STATE	POPULATION	% of USA
23	Alabama	4,525,375	1.5%
47	Alaska	657,755	0.2%
18	Arizona	5,739,879	2.0%
32	Arkansas	2,750,000	0.9%
1	California	35,842,038	12.2%
22	Colorado	4,601,821	1.6%
29	Connecticut	3,498,966	1.2%
45	Delaware	830,069	0.3%
4	Florida	17,385,430	5.9%
9	Georgia	8,918,129	3.0%
42	Hawaii	1,262,124	0.4%
39	Idaho	1,395,140	0.5%
5	Illinois	12,712,016	4.3%
14	Indiana	6,226,537	2.1%
30	Iowa	2,952,904	1.0%
33	Kansas	2,733,697	0.9%
26	Kentucky	4,141,835	1.4%
24	Louisiana	4,506,685	1.5%
40	Maine	1,314,985	0.4%
19	Maryland	5,561,332	1.9%
13	Massachusetts	6,407,382	2.2%
8	Michigan	10,104,206	3.4%
21	Minnesota	5,096,546	1.7%
31	Mississippi	2,900,768	1.0%
17	Missouri	5,759,532	2.0%
44	Montana	926,920	0.3%
38	Nebraska	1,747,704	0.6%
35	Nevada	2,332,898	0.8%
41	New Hampshire	1,299,169	0.4%
10	New Jersey	8,685,166	3.0%
36	New Mexico	1,903,006	0.6%
3	New York	19,280,727	6.6%
11	North Carolina	8,540,468	2.9%
48	North Dakota	636,308	0.2%
7	Ohio	11,450,143	3.9%
28	Oklahoma	3,523,546	1.2%
27	Oregon	3,591,363	1.2%
6	Pennsylvania	12,394,471	4.2%
43	Rhode Island	1,079,916	0.4%
25	South Carolina	4,197,892	1.4%
46	South Dakota	770,621	0.3%
16	Tennessee	5,893,298	2.0%
2	Texas	22,471,549	7.7%
34	Utah	2,420,708	0.8%
49	Vermont	621,233	0.2%
12	Virginia	7,481,332	2.5%
15	Washington	6,207,046	2.1%
37	West Virginia	1,812,548	0.6%
20	Wisconsin	5,503,533	1.9%
50	Wyoming	505,887	0.2%

RANK ORDER

RANK	STATE	POPULATION	% of USA
1	California	35,842,038	12.2%
2	Texas	22,471,549	7.7%
3	New York	19,280,727	6.6%
4	Florida	17,385,430	5.9%
5	Illinois	12,712,016	4.3%
6	Pennsylvania	12,394,471	4.2%
7	Ohio	11,450,143	3.9%
8	Michigan	10,104,206	3.4%
9	Georgia	8,918,129	3.0%
10	New Jersey	8,685,166	3.0%
11	North Carolina	8,540,468	2.9%
12	Virginia	7,481,332	2.5%
13	Massachusetts	6,407,382	2.2%
14	Indiana	6,226,537	2.1%
15	Washington	6,207,046	2.1%
16	Tennessee	5,893,298	2.0%
17	Missouri	5,759,532	2.0%
18	Arizona	5,739,879	2.0%
19	Maryland	5,561,332	1.9%
20	Wisconsin	5,503,533	1.9%
21	Minnesota	5,096,546	1.7%
22	Colorado	4,601,821	1.6%
23	Alabama	4,525,375	1.5%
24	Louisiana	4,506,685	1.5%
25	South Carolina	4,197,892	1.4%
26	Kentucky	4,141,835	1.4%
27	Oregon	3,591,363	1.2%
28	Oklahoma	3,523,546	1.2%
29	Connecticut	3,498,966	1.2%
30	Iowa	2,952,904	1.0%
31	Mississippi	2,900,768	1.0%
32	Arkansas	2,750,000	0.9%
33	Kansas	2,733,697	0.9%
34	Utah	2,420,708	0.8%
35	Nevada	2,332,898	0.8%
36	New Mexico	1,903,006	0.6%
37	West Virginia	1,812,548	0.6%
38	Nebraska	1,747,704	0.6%
39	Idaho	1,395,140	0.5%
40	Maine	1,314,985	0.4%
41	New Hampshire	1,299,169	0.4%
42	Hawaii	1,262,124	0.4%
43	Rhode Island	1,079,916	0.4%
44	Montana	926,920	0.3%
45	Delaware	830,069	0.3%
46	South Dakota	770,621	0.3%
47	Alaska	657,755	0.2%
48	North Dakota	636,308	0.2%
49	Vermont	621,233	0.2%
50	Wyoming	505,887	0.2%
	District of Columbia	554,239	0.2%

Source: U.S. Bureau of the Census
   "Population Estimates" (December 22, 2005, http://www.census.gov/popest/estimates.php)
*Resident population. Revised estimates.

Numerical Population Change: 2004 to 2005

National Total = 2,753,562 Increase*

ALPHA ORDER

RANK	STATE	GAIN/LOSS	% of USA
24	Alabama	32,433	1.2%
42	Alaska	5,906	0.2%
4	Arizona	199,413	7.2%
26	Arkansas	29,154	1.1%
3	California	290,109	10.5%
11	Colorado	63,356	2.3%
36	Connecticut	11,331	0.4%
33	Delaware	13,455	0.5%
1	Florida	404,434	14.7%
5	Georgia	154,447	5.6%
35	Hawaii	13,070	0.5%
21	Idaho	33,956	1.2%
13	Illinois	51,355	1.9%
16	Indiana	45,436	1.7%
34	Iowa	13,430	0.5%
38	Kansas	10,990	0.4%
25	Kentucky	31,570	1.1%
30	Louisiana	16,943	0.6%
41	Maine	6,520	0.2%
18	Maryland	39,056	1.4%
49	Massachusetts	(8,639)	
31	Michigan	16,654	0.6%
19	Minnesota	36,253	1.3%
29	Mississippi	20,320	0.7%
17	Missouri	40,778	1.5%
40	Montana	8,750	0.3%
37	Nebraska	11,083	0.4%
8	Nevada	81,909	3.0%
39	New Hampshire	10,771	0.4%
22	New Jersey	32,759	1.2%
27	New Mexico	25,378	0.9%
50	New York	(26,097)	
6	North Carolina	142,774	5.2%
47	North Dakota	369	0.0%
32	Ohio	13,899	0.5%
28	Oklahoma	24,338	0.9%
14	Oregon	49,693	1.8%
20	Pennsylvania	35,145	1.3%
48	Rhode Island	(3,727)	
12	South Carolina	57,191	2.1%
43	South Dakota	5,312	0.2%
10	Tennessee	69,661	2.5%
2	Texas	388,419	14.1%
15	Utah	48,877	1.8%
46	Vermont	1,817	0.1%
7	Virginia	86,133	3.1%
9	Washington	80,713	2.9%
44	West Virginia	4,308	0.2%
23	Wisconsin	32,668	1.2%
45	Wyoming	3,407	0.1%

RANK ORDER

RANK	STATE	GAIN/LOSS	% of USA
1	Florida	404,434	14.7%
2	Texas	388,419	14.1%
3	California	290,109	10.5%
4	Arizona	199,413	7.2%
5	Georgia	154,447	5.6%
6	North Carolina	142,774	5.2%
7	Virginia	86,133	3.1%
8	Nevada	81,909	3.0%
9	Washington	80,713	2.9%
10	Tennessee	69,661	2.5%
11	Colorado	63,356	2.3%
12	South Carolina	57,191	2.1%
13	Illinois	51,355	1.9%
14	Oregon	49,693	1.8%
15	Utah	48,877	1.8%
16	Indiana	45,436	1.7%
17	Missouri	40,778	1.5%
18	Maryland	39,056	1.4%
19	Minnesota	36,253	1.3%
20	Pennsylvania	35,145	1.3%
21	Idaho	33,956	1.2%
22	New Jersey	32,759	1.2%
23	Wisconsin	32,668	1.2%
24	Alabama	32,433	1.2%
25	Kentucky	31,570	1.1%
26	Arkansas	29,154	1.1%
27	New Mexico	25,378	0.9%
28	Oklahoma	24,338	0.9%
29	Mississippi	20,320	0.7%
30	Louisiana	16,943	0.6%
31	Michigan	16,654	0.6%
32	Ohio	13,899	0.5%
33	Delaware	13,455	0.5%
34	Iowa	13,430	0.5%
35	Hawaii	13,070	0.5%
36	Connecticut	11,331	0.4%
37	Nebraska	11,083	0.4%
38	Kansas	10,990	0.4%
39	New Hampshire	10,771	0.4%
40	Montana	8,750	0.3%
41	Maine	6,520	0.2%
42	Alaska	5,906	0.2%
43	South Dakota	5,312	0.2%
44	West Virginia	4,308	0.2%
45	Wyoming	3,407	0.1%
46	Vermont	1,817	0.1%
47	North Dakota	369	0.0%
48	Rhode Island	(3,727)	
49	Massachusetts	(8,639)	
50	New York	(26,097)	

District of Columbia (3,718)

Source: Morgan Quitno Press using data from U.S. Bureau of the Census
"Population Estimates" (December 22, 2005, http://www.census.gov/popest/estimates.php)
*Resident population from July 1, 2004 to July 1, 2005

Percent Change in Population: 2004 to 2005

National Percent Change = 0.9% Increase*

RANK	STATE	PERCENT CHANGE
24	Alabama	0.7
19	Alaska	0.9
1	Arizona	3.5
17	Arkansas	1.1
21	California	0.8
10	Colorado	1.4
41	Connecticut	0.3
9	Delaware	1.6
4	Florida	2.3
6	Georgia	1.7
18	Hawaii	1.0
3	Idaho	2.4
37	Illinois	0.4
24	Indiana	0.7
35	Iowa	0.5
37	Kansas	0.4
21	Kentucky	0.8
37	Louisiana	0.4
35	Maine	0.5
24	Maryland	0.7
48	Massachusetts	(0.1)
44	Michigan	0.2
24	Minnesota	0.7
24	Mississippi	0.7
24	Missouri	0.7
19	Montana	0.9
33	Nebraska	0.6
1	Nevada	3.5
21	New Hampshire	0.8
37	New Jersey	0.4
13	New Mexico	1.3
48	New York	(0.1)
6	North Carolina	1.7
46	North Dakota	0.1
46	Ohio	0.1
24	Oklahoma	0.7
10	Oregon	1.4
41	Pennsylvania	0.3
50	Rhode Island	(0.3)
10	South Carolina	1.4
24	South Dakota	0.7
15	Tennessee	1.2
6	Texas	1.7
5	Utah	2.0
41	Vermont	0.3
15	Virginia	1.2
13	Washington	1.3
44	West Virginia	0.2
33	Wisconsin	0.6
24	Wyoming	0.7

RANK	STATE	PERCENT CHANGE
1	Arizona	3.5
1	Nevada	3.5
3	Idaho	2.4
4	Florida	2.3
5	Utah	2.0
6	Georgia	1.7
6	North Carolina	1.7
6	Texas	1.7
9	Delaware	1.6
10	Colorado	1.4
10	Oregon	1.4
10	South Carolina	1.4
13	New Mexico	1.3
13	Washington	1.3
15	Tennessee	1.2
15	Virginia	1.2
17	Arkansas	1.1
18	Hawaii	1.0
19	Alaska	0.9
19	Montana	0.9
21	California	0.8
21	Kentucky	0.8
21	New Hampshire	0.8
24	Alabama	0.7
24	Indiana	0.7
24	Maryland	0.7
24	Minnesota	0.7
24	Mississippi	0.7
24	Missouri	0.7
24	Oklahoma	0.7
24	South Dakota	0.7
24	Wyoming	0.7
33	Nebraska	0.6
33	Wisconsin	0.6
35	Iowa	0.5
35	Maine	0.5
37	Illinois	0.4
37	Kansas	0.4
37	Louisiana	0.4
37	New Jersey	0.4
41	Connecticut	0.3
41	Pennsylvania	0.3
41	Vermont	0.3
44	Michigan	0.2
44	West Virginia	0.2
46	North Dakota	0.1
46	Ohio	0.1
48	Massachusetts	(0.1)
48	New York	(0.1)
50	Rhode Island	(0.3)

District of Columbia	(0.7)

Source: Morgan Quitno Press using data from U.S. Bureau of the Census
   "Population Estimates" (December 22, 2005, http://www.census.gov/popest/estimates.php)
*Resident population from July 1, 2004 to July 1, 2005

Population in 2000 Census

National Total = 281,421,906*

<table>
<tr><td colspan="4">ALPHA ORDER</td><td colspan="4">RANK ORDER</td></tr>
<tr><td>RANK</td><td>STATE</td><td>POPULATION</td><td>% of USA</td><td>RANK</td><td>STATE</td><td>POPULATION</td><td>% of USA</td></tr>
<tr><td>23</td><td>Alabama</td><td>4,447,100</td><td>1.6%</td><td>1</td><td>California</td><td>33,871,648</td><td>12.0%</td></tr>
<tr><td>48</td><td>Alaska</td><td>626,932</td><td>0.2%</td><td>2</td><td>Texas</td><td>20,851,820</td><td>7.4%</td></tr>
<tr><td>20</td><td>Arizona</td><td>5,130,632</td><td>1.8%</td><td>3</td><td>New York</td><td>18,976,457</td><td>6.7%</td></tr>
<tr><td>33</td><td>Arkansas</td><td>2,673,400</td><td>0.9%</td><td>4</td><td>Florida</td><td>15,982,378</td><td>5.7%</td></tr>
<tr><td>1</td><td>California</td><td>33,871,648</td><td>12.0%</td><td>5</td><td>Illinois</td><td>12,419,293</td><td>4.4%</td></tr>
<tr><td>24</td><td>Colorado</td><td>4,301,261</td><td>1.5%</td><td>6</td><td>Pennsylvania</td><td>12,281,054</td><td>4.4%</td></tr>
<tr><td>29</td><td>Connecticut</td><td>3,405,565</td><td>1.2%</td><td>7</td><td>Ohio</td><td>11,353,140</td><td>4.0%</td></tr>
<tr><td>45</td><td>Delaware</td><td>783,600</td><td>0.3%</td><td>8</td><td>Michigan</td><td>9,938,444</td><td>3.5%</td></tr>
<tr><td>4</td><td>Florida</td><td>15,982,378</td><td>5.7%</td><td>9</td><td>New Jersey</td><td>8,414,350</td><td>3.0%</td></tr>
<tr><td>10</td><td>Georgia</td><td>8,186,453</td><td>2.9%</td><td>10</td><td>Georgia</td><td>8,186,453</td><td>2.9%</td></tr>
<tr><td>42</td><td>Hawaii</td><td>1,211,537</td><td>0.4%</td><td>11</td><td>North Carolina</td><td>8,049,313</td><td>2.9%</td></tr>
<tr><td>39</td><td>Idaho</td><td>1,293,953</td><td>0.5%</td><td>12</td><td>Virginia</td><td>7,078,515</td><td>2.5%</td></tr>
<tr><td>5</td><td>Illinois</td><td>12,419,293</td><td>4.4%</td><td>13</td><td>Massachusetts</td><td>6,349,097</td><td>2.3%</td></tr>
<tr><td>14</td><td>Indiana</td><td>6,080,485</td><td>2.2%</td><td>14</td><td>Indiana</td><td>6,080,485</td><td>2.2%</td></tr>
<tr><td>30</td><td>Iowa</td><td>2,926,324</td><td>1.0%</td><td>15</td><td>Washington</td><td>5,894,121</td><td>2.1%</td></tr>
<tr><td>32</td><td>Kansas</td><td>2,688,418</td><td>1.0%</td><td>16</td><td>Tennessee</td><td>5,689,283</td><td>2.0%</td></tr>
<tr><td>25</td><td>Kentucky</td><td>4,041,769</td><td>1.4%</td><td>17</td><td>Missouri</td><td>5,595,211</td><td>2.0%</td></tr>
<tr><td>22</td><td>Louisiana</td><td>4,468,976</td><td>1.6%</td><td>18</td><td>Wisconsin</td><td>5,363,675</td><td>1.9%</td></tr>
<tr><td>40</td><td>Maine</td><td>1,274,923</td><td>0.5%</td><td>19</td><td>Maryland</td><td>5,296,486</td><td>1.9%</td></tr>
<tr><td>19</td><td>Maryland</td><td>5,296,486</td><td>1.9%</td><td>20</td><td>Arizona</td><td>5,130,632</td><td>1.8%</td></tr>
<tr><td>13</td><td>Massachusetts</td><td>6,349,097</td><td>2.3%</td><td>21</td><td>Minnesota</td><td>4,919,479</td><td>1.7%</td></tr>
<tr><td>8</td><td>Michigan</td><td>9,938,444</td><td>3.5%</td><td>22</td><td>Louisiana</td><td>4,468,976</td><td>1.6%</td></tr>
<tr><td>21</td><td>Minnesota</td><td>4,919,479</td><td>1.7%</td><td>23</td><td>Alabama</td><td>4,447,100</td><td>1.6%</td></tr>
<tr><td>31</td><td>Mississippi</td><td>2,844,658</td><td>1.0%</td><td>24</td><td>Colorado</td><td>4,301,261</td><td>1.5%</td></tr>
<tr><td>17</td><td>Missouri</td><td>5,595,211</td><td>2.0%</td><td>25</td><td>Kentucky</td><td>4,041,769</td><td>1.4%</td></tr>
<tr><td>44</td><td>Montana</td><td>902,195</td><td>0.3%</td><td>26</td><td>South Carolina</td><td>4,012,012</td><td>1.4%</td></tr>
<tr><td>38</td><td>Nebraska</td><td>1,711,263</td><td>0.6%</td><td>27</td><td>Oklahoma</td><td>3,450,654</td><td>1.2%</td></tr>
<tr><td>35</td><td>Nevada</td><td>1,998,257</td><td>0.7%</td><td>28</td><td>Oregon</td><td>3,421,399</td><td>1.2%</td></tr>
<tr><td>41</td><td>New Hampshire</td><td>1,235,786</td><td>0.4%</td><td>29</td><td>Connecticut</td><td>3,405,565</td><td>1.2%</td></tr>
<tr><td>9</td><td>New Jersey</td><td>8,414,350</td><td>3.0%</td><td>30</td><td>Iowa</td><td>2,926,324</td><td>1.0%</td></tr>
<tr><td>36</td><td>New Mexico</td><td>1,819,046</td><td>0.6%</td><td>31</td><td>Mississippi</td><td>2,844,658</td><td>1.0%</td></tr>
<tr><td>3</td><td>New York</td><td>18,976,457</td><td>6.7%</td><td>32</td><td>Kansas</td><td>2,688,418</td><td>1.0%</td></tr>
<tr><td>11</td><td>North Carolina</td><td>8,049,313</td><td>2.9%</td><td>33</td><td>Arkansas</td><td>2,673,400</td><td>0.9%</td></tr>
<tr><td>47</td><td>North Dakota</td><td>642,200</td><td>0.2%</td><td>34</td><td>Utah</td><td>2,233,169</td><td>0.8%</td></tr>
<tr><td>7</td><td>Ohio</td><td>11,353,140</td><td>4.0%</td><td>35</td><td>Nevada</td><td>1,998,257</td><td>0.7%</td></tr>
<tr><td>27</td><td>Oklahoma</td><td>3,450,654</td><td>1.2%</td><td>36</td><td>New Mexico</td><td>1,819,046</td><td>0.6%</td></tr>
<tr><td>28</td><td>Oregon</td><td>3,421,399</td><td>1.2%</td><td>37</td><td>West Virginia</td><td>1,808,344</td><td>0.6%</td></tr>
<tr><td>6</td><td>Pennsylvania</td><td>12,281,054</td><td>4.4%</td><td>38</td><td>Nebraska</td><td>1,711,263</td><td>0.6%</td></tr>
<tr><td>43</td><td>Rhode Island</td><td>1,048,319</td><td>0.4%</td><td>39</td><td>Idaho</td><td>1,293,953</td><td>0.5%</td></tr>
<tr><td>26</td><td>South Carolina</td><td>4,012,012</td><td>1.4%</td><td>40</td><td>Maine</td><td>1,274,923</td><td>0.5%</td></tr>
<tr><td>46</td><td>South Dakota</td><td>754,844</td><td>0.3%</td><td>41</td><td>New Hampshire</td><td>1,235,786</td><td>0.4%</td></tr>
<tr><td>16</td><td>Tennessee</td><td>5,689,283</td><td>2.0%</td><td>42</td><td>Hawaii</td><td>1,211,537</td><td>0.4%</td></tr>
<tr><td>2</td><td>Texas</td><td>20,851,820</td><td>7.4%</td><td>43</td><td>Rhode Island</td><td>1,048,319</td><td>0.4%</td></tr>
<tr><td>34</td><td>Utah</td><td>2,233,169</td><td>0.8%</td><td>44</td><td>Montana</td><td>902,195</td><td>0.3%</td></tr>
<tr><td>49</td><td>Vermont</td><td>608,827</td><td>0.2%</td><td>45</td><td>Delaware</td><td>783,600</td><td>0.3%</td></tr>
<tr><td>12</td><td>Virginia</td><td>7,078,515</td><td>2.5%</td><td>46</td><td>South Dakota</td><td>754,844</td><td>0.3%</td></tr>
<tr><td>15</td><td>Washington</td><td>5,894,121</td><td>2.1%</td><td>47</td><td>North Dakota</td><td>642,200</td><td>0.2%</td></tr>
<tr><td>37</td><td>West Virginia</td><td>1,808,344</td><td>0.6%</td><td>48</td><td>Alaska</td><td>626,932</td><td>0.2%</td></tr>
<tr><td>18</td><td>Wisconsin</td><td>5,363,675</td><td>1.9%</td><td>49</td><td>Vermont</td><td>608,827</td><td>0.2%</td></tr>
<tr><td>50</td><td>Wyoming</td><td>493,782</td><td>0.2%</td><td>50</td><td>Wyoming</td><td>493,782</td><td>0.2%</td></tr>
<tr><td></td><td></td><td></td><td></td><td></td><td>District of Columbia</td><td>572,059</td><td>0.2%</td></tr>
</table>

Source: U.S. Bureau of the Census
   "First Census 2000 Results" (December 28, 2000, http://www.census.gov/main/www/cen2000.html)
*Resident population as of April 2000 Census.

Population (Resident and Overseas) in 2000

National Total = 281,998,273*

ALPHA ORDER

ALPHA ORDER

RANK ORDER

RANK	STATE	POPULATION	% of USA		RANK	STATE	POPULATION	% of USA
23	Alabama	4,461,130	1.6%		1	California	33,930,798	12.0%
48	Alaska	628,933	0.2%		2	Texas	20,903,994	7.4%
20	Arizona	5,140,683	1.8%		3	New York	19,004,973	6.7%
33	Arkansas	2,679,733	1.0%		4	Florida	16,028,890	5.7%
1	California	33,930,798	12.0%		5	Illinois	12,439,042	4.4%
24	Colorado	4,311,882	1.5%		6	Pennsylvania	12,300,670	4.4%
29	Connecticut	3,409,535	1.2%		7	Ohio	11,374,540	4.0%
45	Delaware	785,068	0.3%		8	Michigan	9,955,829	3.5%
4	Florida	16,028,890	5.7%		9	New Jersey	8,424,354	3.0%
10	Georgia	8,206,975	2.9%		10	Georgia	8,206,975	2.9%
42	Hawaii	1,216,642	0.4%		11	North Carolina	8,067,673	2.9%
39	Idaho	1,297,274	0.5%		12	Virginia	7,100,702	2.5%
5	Illinois	12,439,042	4.4%		13	Massachusetts	6,355,568	2.3%
14	Indiana	6,090,782	2.2%		14	Indiana	6,090,782	2.2%
30	Iowa	2,931,923	1.0%		15	Washington	5,908,684	2.1%
32	Kansas	2,693,824	1.0%		16	Tennessee	5,700,037	2.0%
25	Kentucky	4,049,431	1.4%		17	Missouri	5,606,260	2.0%
22	Louisiana	4,480,271	1.6%		18	Wisconsin	5,371,210	1.9%
40	Maine	1,277,731	0.5%		19	Maryland	5,307,886	1.9%
19	Maryland	5,307,886	1.9%		20	Arizona	5,140,683	1.8%
13	Massachusetts	6,355,568	2.3%		21	Minnesota	4,925,670	1.7%
8	Michigan	9,955,829	3.5%		22	Louisiana	4,400,271	1.6%
21	Minnesota	4,925,670	1.7%		23	Alabama	4,461,130	1.6%
31	Mississippi	2,852,927	1.0%		24	Colorado	4,311,882	1.5%
17	Missouri	5,606,260	2.0%		25	Kentucky	4,049,431	1.4%
44	Montana	905,316	0.3%		26	South Carolina	4,025,061	1.4%
38	Nebraska	1,715,369	0.6%		27	Oklahoma	3,458,819	1.2%
35	Nevada	2,002,032	0.7%		28	Oregon	3,428,543	1.2%
41	New Hampshire	1,238,415	0.4%		29	Connecticut	3,409,535	1.2%
9	New Jersey	8,424,354	3.0%		30	Iowa	2,931,923	1.0%
36	New Mexico	1,823,821	0.6%		31	Mississippi	2,852,927	1.0%
3	New York	19,004,973	6.7%		32	Kansas	2,693,824	1.0%
11	North Carolina	8,067,673	2.9%		33	Arkansas	2,679,733	1.0%
47	North Dakota	643,756	0.2%		34	Utah	2,236,714	0.8%
7	Ohio	11,374,540	4.0%		35	Nevada	2,002,032	0.7%
27	Oklahoma	3,458,819	1.2%		36	New Mexico	1,823,821	0.6%
28	Oregon	3,428,543	1.2%		37	West Virginia	1,813,077	0.6%
6	Pennsylvania	12,300,670	4.4%		38	Nebraska	1,715,369	0.6%
43	Rhode Island	1,049,662	0.4%		39	Idaho	1,297,274	0.5%
26	South Carolina	4,025,061	1.4%		40	Maine	1,277,731	0.5%
46	South Dakota	756,874	0.3%		41	New Hampshire	1,238,415	0.4%
16	Tennessee	5,700,037	2.0%		42	Hawaii	1,216,642	0.4%
2	Texas	20,903,994	7.4%		43	Rhode Island	1,049,662	0.4%
34	Utah	2,236,714	0.8%		44	Montana	905,316	0.3%
49	Vermont	609,890	0.2%		45	Delaware	785,068	0.3%
12	Virginia	7,100,702	2.5%		46	South Dakota	756,874	0.3%
15	Washington	5,908,684	2.1%		47	North Dakota	643,756	0.2%
37	West Virginia	1,813,077	0.6%		48	Alaska	628,933	0.2%
18	Wisconsin	5,371,210	1.9%		49	Vermont	609,890	0.2%
50	Wyoming	495,304	0.2%		50	Wyoming	495,304	0.2%
						District of Columbia	574,096	0.2%

Source: Morgan Quitno Press using data from U.S. Bureau of the Census
"First Census 2000 Results" (December 28, 2000, http://www.census.gov/main/www/cen2000.html)
*This is the total of resident and overseas population. Overseas population includes U.S. military and federal civilian employees (and their dependents living with them) allocated to their home state or the District of Columbia, as reported by the employing federal agencies. This is the same population as that used for congressional apportionment except that the population for the District of Columbia is removed for that purpose.

U.S. Population Living Overseas in 2000

National Total = 576,367*

ALPHA ORDER

ALPHA ORDER

RANK	STATE	OVERSEAS	% of USA
13	Alabama	14,030	2.4%
45	Alaska	2,001	0.3%
21	Arizona	10,051	1.7%
29	Arkansas	6,333	1.1%
1	California	59,150	10.3%
19	Colorado	10,621	1.8%
37	Connecticut	3,970	0.7%
48	Delaware	1,468	0.3%
3	Florida	46,512	8.1%
7	Georgia	20,522	3.6%
33	Hawaii	5,105	0.9%
40	Idaho	3,321	0.6%
8	Illinois	19,749	3.4%
20	Indiana	10,297	1.8%
31	Iowa	5,599	1.0%
32	Kansas	5,406	0.9%
25	Kentucky	7,662	1.3%
16	Louisiana	11,295	2.0%
42	Maine	2,808	0.5%
15	Maryland	11,400	2.0%
28	Massachusetts	6,471	1.1%
11	Michigan	17,385	3.0%
30	Minnesota	6,191	1.1%
23	Mississippi	8,269	1.4%
17	Missouri	11,049	1.9%
41	Montana	3,121	0.5%
36	Nebraska	4,106	0.7%
38	Nevada	3,775	0.7%
43	New Hampshire	2,629	0.5%
22	New Jersey	10,004	1.7%
34	New Mexico	4,775	0.8%
4	New York	28,516	4.9%
10	North Carolina	18,360	3.2%
46	North Dakota	1,556	0.3%
6	Ohio	21,400	3.7%
24	Oklahoma	8,165	1.4%
27	Oregon	7,144	1.2%
9	Pennsylvania	19,616	3.4%
49	Rhode Island	1,343	0.2%
14	South Carolina	13,049	2.3%
44	South Dakota	2,030	0.4%
18	Tennessee	10,754	1.9%
2	Texas	52,174	9.1%
39	Utah	3,545	0.6%
50	Vermont	1,063	0.2%
5	Virginia	22,187	3.8%
12	Washington	14,563	2.5%
35	West Virginia	4,733	0.8%
26	Wisconsin	7,535	1.3%
47	Wyoming	1,522	0.3%

RANK ORDER

RANK	STATE	OVERSEAS	% of USA
1	California	59,150	10.3%
2	Texas	52,174	9.1%
3	Florida	46,512	8.1%
4	New York	28,516	4.9%
5	Virginia	22,187	3.8%
6	Ohio	21,400	3.7%
7	Georgia	20,522	3.6%
8	Illinois	19,749	3.4%
9	Pennsylvania	19,616	3.4%
10	North Carolina	18,360	3.2%
11	Michigan	17,385	3.0%
12	Washington	14,563	2.5%
13	Alabama	14,030	2.4%
14	South Carolina	13,049	2.3%
15	Maryland	11,400	2.0%
16	Louisiana	11,295	2.0%
17	Missouri	11,049	1.9%
18	Tennessee	10,754	1.9%
19	Colorado	10,621	1.8%
20	Indiana	10,297	1.8%
21	Arizona	10,051	1.7%
22	New Jersey	10,004	1.7%
23	Mississippi	8,269	1.4%
24	Oklahoma	8,165	1.4%
25	Kentucky	7,662	1.3%
26	Wisconsin	7,535	1.3%
27	Oregon	7,144	1.2%
28	Massachusetts	6,471	1.1%
29	Arkansas	6,333	1.1%
30	Minnesota	6,191	1.1%
31	Iowa	5,599	1.0%
32	Kansas	5,406	0.9%
33	Hawaii	5,105	0.9%
34	New Mexico	4,775	0.8%
35	West Virginia	4,733	0.8%
36	Nebraska	4,106	0.7%
37	Connecticut	3,970	0.7%
38	Nevada	3,775	0.7%
39	Utah	3,545	0.6%
40	Idaho	3,321	0.6%
41	Montana	3,121	0.5%
42	Maine	2,808	0.5%
43	New Hampshire	2,629	0.5%
44	South Dakota	2,030	0.4%
45	Alaska	2,001	0.3%
46	North Dakota	1,556	0.3%
47	Wyoming	1,522	0.3%
48	Delaware	1,468	0.3%
49	Rhode Island	1,343	0.2%
50	Vermont	1,063	0.2%
	District of Columbia	2,037	0.4%

Source: U.S. Bureau of the Census
"First Census 2000 Results" (December 28, 2000, http://www.census.gov/main/www/cen2000.html)
*Includes overseas U.S. military and federal civilian employees (and their dependents living with them) allocated to their home state or the District of Columbia, as reported by the employing federal agencies.

Population per Square Mile in 2005

National Rate = 83.8 Persons per Square Mile*

ALPHA ORDER

RANK	STATE	RATE
26	Alabama	89.8
50	Alaska	1.2
35	Arizona	52.3
33	Arkansas	53.4
11	California	231.7
37	Colorado	45.0
4	Connecticut	724.5
6	Delaware	431.7
8	Florida	329.9
18	Georgia	156.7
13	Hawaii	198.5
44	Idaho	17.3
12	Illinois	229.6
17	Indiana	174.9
34	Iowa	53.1
40	Kansas	33.5
22	Kentucky	105.0
23	Louisiana	103.8
38	Maine	42.8
5	Maryland	573.0
3	Massachusetts	816.2
16	Michigan	178.2
31	Minnesota	64.5
32	Mississippi	62.3
28	Missouri	84.2
48	Montana	6.4
42	Nebraska	22.9
43	Nevada	22.0
19	New Hampshire	146.1
1	New Jersey	1,175.4
45	New Mexico	15.9
7	New York	407.8
15	North Carolina	178.3
47	North Dakota	9.2
9	Ohio	280.0
36	Oklahoma	51.7
39	Oregon	37.9
10	Pennsylvania	277.3
2	Rhode Island	1,029.8
21	South Carolina	141.3
46	South Dakota	10.2
20	Tennessee	144.7
27	Texas	87.3
41	Utah	30.1
30	Vermont	67.4
14	Virginia	191.1
25	Washington	94.5
29	West Virginia	75.5
24	Wisconsin	101.9
49	Wyoming	5.2

RANK ORDER

RANK	STATE	RATE
1	New Jersey	1,175.4
2	Rhode Island	1,029.8
3	Massachusetts	816.2
4	Connecticut	724.5
5	Maryland	573.0
6	Delaware	431.7
7	New York	407.8
8	Florida	329.9
9	Ohio	280.0
10	Pennsylvania	277.3
11	California	231.7
12	Illinois	229.6
13	Hawaii	198.5
14	Virginia	191.1
15	North Carolina	178.3
16	Michigan	178.2
17	Indiana	174.9
18	Georgia	156.7
19	New Hampshire	146.1
20	Tennessee	144.7
21	South Carolina	141.3
22	Kentucky	105.0
23	Louisiana	103.8
24	Wisconsin	101.9
25	Washington	94.5
26	Alabama	89.8
27	Texas	87.3
28	Missouri	84.2
29	West Virginia	75.5
30	Vermont	67.4
31	Minnesota	64.5
32	Mississippi	62.3
33	Arkansas	53.4
34	Iowa	53.1
35	Arizona	52.3
36	Oklahoma	51.7
37	Colorado	45.0
38	Maine	42.8
39	Oregon	37.9
40	Kansas	33.5
41	Utah	30.1
42	Nebraska	22.9
43	Nevada	22.0
44	Idaho	17.3
45	New Mexico	15.9
46	South Dakota	10.2
47	North Dakota	9.2
48	Montana	6.4
49	Wyoming	5.2
50	Alaska	1.2
	District of Columbia	9,024.9

Source: Morgan Quitno Press using data from U.S. Bureau of the Census
    "Population Estimates" (December 22, 2005, http://www.census.gov/popest/estimates.php)
*Resident population. Based on land area of states.

Population per Square Mile in 2000

National Rate = 79.8 Persons per Square Mile*

ALPHA ORDER

RANK	STATE	RATE
26	Alabama	87.7
50	Alaska	1.1
36	Arizona	45.5
34	Arkansas	51.4
12	California	218.1
37	Colorado	41.7
4	Connecticut	704.2
6	Delaware	402.3
8	Florida	297.6
18	Georgia	142.2
13	Hawaii	188.8
44	Idaho	15.7
11	Illinois	223.8
16	Indiana	169.8
33	Iowa	52.4
40	Kansas	32.9
23	Kentucky	101.9
22	Louisiana	102.6
38	Maine	41.4
5	Maryland	543.5
3	Massachusetts	811.7
15	Michigan	175.3
31	Minnesota	62.0
32	Mississippi	60.7
27	Missouri	81.4
48	Montana	6.2
42	Nebraska	22.3
43	Nevada	18.4
20	New Hampshire	138.3
1	New Jersey	1,136.7
45	New Mexico	15.0
6	New York	402.3
17	North Carolina	165.9
47	North Dakota	9.3
9	Ohio	277.5
35	Oklahoma	50.3
39	Oregon	35.7
10	Pennsylvania	274.1
2	Rhode Island	1,005.5
21	South Carolina	133.6
46	South Dakota	10.0
19	Tennessee	138.4
28	Texas	80.0
41	Utah	27.3
30	Vermont	65.9
14	Virginia	179.5
25	Washington	88.8
29	West Virginia	75.0
24	Wisconsin	98.9
49	Wyoming	5.1

RANK ORDER

RANK	STATE	RATE
1	New Jersey	1,136.7
2	Rhode Island	1,005.5
3	Massachusetts	811.7
4	Connecticut	704.2
5	Maryland	543.5
6	Delaware	402.3
6	New York	402.3
8	Florida	297.6
9	Ohio	277.5
10	Pennsylvania	274.1
11	Illinois	223.8
12	California	218.1
13	Hawaii	188.8
14	Virginia	179.5
15	Michigan	175.3
16	Indiana	169.8
17	North Carolina	165.9
18	Georgia	142.2
19	Tennessee	138.4
20	New Hampshire	138.3
21	South Carolina	133.6
22	Louisiana	102.6
23	Kentucky	101.9
24	Wisconsin	98.9
25	Washington	88.8
26	Alabama	87.7
27	Missouri	81.4
28	Texas	80.0
29	West Virginia	75.0
30	Vermont	65.9
31	Minnesota	62.0
32	Mississippi	60.7
33	Iowa	52.4
34	Arkansas	51.4
35	Oklahoma	50.3
36	Arizona	45.5
37	Colorado	41.7
38	Maine	41.4
39	Oregon	35.7
40	Kansas	32.9
41	Utah	27.3
42	Nebraska	22.3
43	Nevada	18.4
44	Idaho	15.7
45	New Mexico	15.0
46	South Dakota	10.0
47	North Dakota	9.3
48	Montana	6.2
49	Wyoming	5.1
50	Alaska	1.1
	District of Columbia	9,371.2

Source: Morgan Quitno Press using data from U.S. Bureau of the Census
    "Population Estimates" (December 20, 2002, http://eire.census.gov/popest/estimates.php)
*Resident population. Based on land area of states.

Male Population in 2004

National Total = 144,537,408 Males

ALPHA ORDER					RANK ORDER			
RANK	STATE	MALES	% of USA		RANK	STATE	MALES	% of USA
23	Alabama	2,196,208	1.5%		1	California	17,913,717	12.4%
47	Alaska	338,910	0.2%		2	Texas	11,201,268	7.7%
17	Arizona	2,873,663	2.0%		3	New York	9,304,581	6.4%
33	Arkansas	1,348,719	0.9%		4	Florida	8,524,398	5.9%
1	California	17,913,717	12.4%		5	Illinois	6,243,216	4.3%
22	Colorado	2,321,504	1.6%		6	Pennsylvania	6,013,662	4.2%
29	Connecticut	1,700,186	1.2%		7	Ohio	5,580,635	3.9%
45	Delaware	404,676	0.3%		8	Michigan	4,968,663	3.4%
4	Florida	8,524,398	5.9%		9	Georgia	4,365,423	3.0%
9	Georgia	4,365,423	3.0%		10	New Jersey	4,235,853	2.9%
42	Hawaii	630,025	0.4%		11	North Carolina	4,198,851	2.9%
39	Idaho	698,624	0.5%		12	Virginia	3,671,433	2.5%
5	Illinois	6,243,216	4.3%		13	Massachusetts	3,106,345	2.1%
15	Indiana	3,068,975	2.1%		14	Washington	3,094,471	2.1%
30	Iowa	1,454,107	1.0%		15	Indiana	3,068,975	2.1%
32	Kansas	1,358,381	0.9%		16	Tennessee	2,886,284	2.0%
26	Kentucky	2,033,894	1.4%		17	Arizona	2,873,663	2.0%
24	Louisiana	2,193,983	1.5%		18	Missouri	2,810,852	1.9%
40	Maine	643,143	0.4%		19	Wisconsin	2,726,992	1.9%
20	Maryland	2,690,901	1.9%		20	Maryland	2,690,901	1.9%
13	Massachusetts	3,106,345	2.1%		21	Minnesota	2,531,918	1.8%
8	Michigan	4,968,663	3.4%		22	Colorado	2,321,504	1.6%
21	Minnesota	2,531,918	1.8%		23	Alabama	2,196,208	1.5%
31	Mississippi	1,408,733	1.0%		24	Louisiana	2,193,983	1.5%
18	Missouri	2,810,852	1.9%		25	South Carolina	2,045,177	1.4%
44	Montana	462,265	0.3%		26	Kentucky	2,033,894	1.4%
38	Nebraska	863,628	0.6%		27	Oregon	1,786,769	1.2%
35	Nevada	1,188,803	0.8%		28	Oklahoma	1,740,265	1.2%
41	New Hampshire	640,940	0.4%		29	Connecticut	1,700,186	1.2%
10	New Jersey	4,235,853	2.9%		30	Iowa	1,454,107	1.0%
36	New Mexico	936,067	0.6%		31	Mississippi	1,408,733	1.0%
3	New York	9,304,581	6.4%		32	Kansas	1,358,381	0.9%
11	North Carolina	4,198,851	2.9%		33	Arkansas	1,348,719	0.9%
48	North Dakota	316,631	0.2%		34	Utah	1,199,315	0.8%
7	Ohio	5,580,635	3.9%		35	Nevada	1,188,803	0.8%
28	Oklahoma	1,740,265	1.2%		36	New Mexico	936,067	0.6%
27	Oregon	1,786,769	1.2%		37	West Virginia	887,302	0.6%
6	Pennsylvania	6,013,662	4.2%		38	Nebraska	863,628	0.6%
43	Rhode Island	521,215	0.4%		39	Idaho	698,624	0.5%
25	South Carolina	2,045,177	1.4%		40	Maine	643,143	0.4%
46	South Dakota	383,249	0.3%		41	New Hampshire	640,940	0.4%
16	Tennessee	2,886,284	2.0%		42	Hawaii	630,025	0.4%
2	Texas	11,201,268	7.7%		43	Rhode Island	521,215	0.4%
34	Utah	1,199,315	0.8%		44	Montana	462,265	0.3%
49	Vermont	305,802	0.2%		45	Delaware	404,676	0.3%
12	Virginia	3,671,433	2.5%		46	South Dakota	383,249	0.3%
14	Washington	3,094,471	2.1%		47	Alaska	338,910	0.2%
37	West Virginia	887,302	0.6%		48	North Dakota	316,631	0.2%
19	Wisconsin	2,726,992	1.9%		49	Vermont	305,802	0.2%
50	Wyoming	255,056	0.2%		50	Wyoming	255,056	0.2%
						District of Columbia	261,730	0.2%

Source: Morgan Quitno Press using data from U.S. Bureau of the Census
"SC-EST2004-AGESEX_RES - State Characteristic Estimates"
(http://www.census.gov/popest/datasets.html)

Female Population in 2004

National Total = 149,117,996 Females

ALPHA ORDER

RANK	STATE	FEMALES	% of USA
22	Alabama	2,333,974	1.6%
48	Alaska	316,525	0.2%
18	Arizona	2,870,171	1.9%
32	Arkansas	1,403,910	0.9%
1	California	17,980,082	12.1%
24	Colorado	2,279,899	1.5%
28	Connecticut	1,803,418	1.2%
45	Delaware	425,688	0.3%
4	Florida	8,872,763	6.0%
9	Georgia	4,463,960	3.0%
42	Hawaii	632,815	0.4%
39	Idaho	694,638	0.5%
5	Illinois	6,470,418	4.3%
14	Indiana	3,168,594	2.1%
30	Iowa	1,500,344	1.0%
33	Kansas	1,377,121	0.9%
26	Kentucky	2,112,028	1.4%
23	Louisiana	2,321,787	1.6%
40	Maine	674,110	0.5%
19	Maryland	2,867,157	1.9%
13	Massachusetts	3,310,160	2.2%
8	Michigan	5,143,957	3.4%
21	Minnesota	2,569,040	1.7%
31	Mississippi	1,494,233	1.0%
17	Missouri	2,943,766	2.0%
44	Montana	464,600	0.3%
38	Nebraska	883,586	0.6%
35	Nevada	1,145,968	0.8%
41	New Hampshire	658,560	0.4%
10	New Jersey	4,463,026	3.0%
36	New Mexico	967,222	0.6%
3	New York	9,922,507	6.7%
11	North Carolina	4,342,370	2.9%
47	North Dakota	317,735	0.2%
7	Ohio	5,878,376	3.9%
29	Oklahoma	1,783,288	1.2%
27	Oregon	1,807,817	1.2%
6	Pennsylvania	6,392,630	4.3%
43	Rhode Island	559,417	0.4%
25	South Carolina	2,152,891	1.4%
46	South Dakota	387,634	0.3%
16	Tennessee	3,014,678	2.0%
2	Texas	11,288,754	7.6%
34	Utah	1,189,724	0.8%
49	Vermont	315,592	0.2%
12	Virginia	3,788,394	2.5%
15	Washington	3,109,317	2.1%
37	West Virginia	928,052	0.6%
20	Wisconsin	2,782,034	1.9%
50	Wyoming	251,473	0.2%

RANK ORDER

RANK	STATE	FEMALES	% of USA
1	California	17,980,082	12.1%
2	Texas	11,288,754	7.6%
3	New York	9,922,507	6.7%
4	Florida	8,872,763	6.0%
5	Illinois	6,470,418	4.3%
6	Pennsylvania	6,392,630	4.3%
7	Ohio	5,878,376	3.9%
8	Michigan	5,143,957	3.4%
9	Georgia	4,463,960	3.0%
10	New Jersey	4,463,026	3.0%
11	North Carolina	4,342,370	2.9%
12	Virginia	3,788,394	2.5%
13	Massachusetts	3,310,160	2.2%
14	Indiana	3,168,594	2.1%
15	Washington	3,109,317	2.1%
16	Tennessee	3,014,678	2.0%
17	Missouri	2,943,766	2.0%
18	Arizona	2,870,171	1.9%
19	Maryland	2,867,157	1.9%
20	Wisconsin	2,782,034	1.9%
21	Minnesota	2,569,040	1.7%
22	Alabama	2,333,974	1.6%
23	Louisiana	2,321,787	1.6%
24	Colorado	2,279,899	1.5%
25	South Carolina	2,152,891	1.4%
26	Kentucky	2,112,028	1.4%
27	Oregon	1,807,817	1.2%
28	Connecticut	1,803,418	1.2%
29	Oklahoma	1,783,288	1.2%
30	Iowa	1,500,344	1.0%
31	Mississippi	1,494,233	1.0%
32	Arkansas	1,403,910	0.9%
33	Kansas	1,377,121	0.9%
34	Utah	1,189,724	0.8%
35	Nevada	1,145,968	0.8%
36	New Mexico	967,222	0.6%
37	West Virginia	928,052	0.6%
38	Nebraska	883,586	0.6%
39	Idaho	694,638	0.5%
40	Maine	674,110	0.5%
41	New Hampshire	658,560	0.4%
42	Hawaii	632,815	0.4%
43	Rhode Island	559,417	0.4%
44	Montana	464,600	0.3%
45	Delaware	425,688	0.3%
46	South Dakota	387,634	0.3%
47	North Dakota	317,735	0.2%
48	Alaska	316,525	0.2%
49	Vermont	315,592	0.2%
50	Wyoming	251,473	0.2%
	District of Columbia	291,793	0.2%

Source: Morgan Quitno Press using data from U.S. Bureau of the Census
"SC-EST2004-AGESEX_RES - State Characteristic Estimates"
(http://www.census.gov/popest/datasets.html)

Male to Female Ratio in 2004

National Ratio = 96.9 Males per 100 Females

<table>
<tr><td colspan="3">ALPHA ORDER</td><td colspan="3">RANK ORDER</td></tr>
<tr><td>RANK</td><td>STATE</td><td>RATIO</td><td>RANK</td><td>STATE</td><td>RATIO</td></tr>
<tr><td>45</td><td>Alabama</td><td>94.1</td><td>1</td><td>Alaska</td><td>107.1</td></tr>
<tr><td>1</td><td>Alaska</td><td>107.1</td><td>2</td><td>Nevada</td><td>103.7</td></tr>
<tr><td>7</td><td>Arizona</td><td>100.1</td><td>3</td><td>Colorado</td><td>101.8</td></tr>
<tr><td>32</td><td>Arkansas</td><td>96.1</td><td>4</td><td>Wyoming</td><td>101.4</td></tr>
<tr><td>9</td><td>California</td><td>99.6</td><td>5</td><td>Utah</td><td>100.8</td></tr>
<tr><td>3</td><td>Colorado</td><td>101.8</td><td>6</td><td>Idaho</td><td>100.6</td></tr>
<tr><td>43</td><td>Connecticut</td><td>94.3</td><td>7</td><td>Arizona</td><td>100.1</td></tr>
<tr><td>38</td><td>Delaware</td><td>95.1</td><td>8</td><td>North Dakota</td><td>99.7</td></tr>
<tr><td>32</td><td>Florida</td><td>96.1</td><td>9</td><td>California</td><td>99.6</td></tr>
<tr><td>19</td><td>Georgia</td><td>97.8</td><td>9</td><td>Hawaii</td><td>99.6</td></tr>
<tr><td>9</td><td>Hawaii</td><td>99.6</td><td>11</td><td>Montana</td><td>99.5</td></tr>
<tr><td>6</td><td>Idaho</td><td>100.6</td><td>11</td><td>Washington</td><td>99.5</td></tr>
<tr><td>30</td><td>Illinois</td><td>96.5</td><td>13</td><td>Texas</td><td>99.2</td></tr>
<tr><td>23</td><td>Indiana</td><td>96.9</td><td>14</td><td>South Dakota</td><td>98.9</td></tr>
<tr><td>23</td><td>Iowa</td><td>96.9</td><td>15</td><td>Oregon</td><td>98.8</td></tr>
<tr><td>16</td><td>Kansas</td><td>98.6</td><td>16</td><td>Kansas</td><td>98.6</td></tr>
<tr><td>31</td><td>Kentucky</td><td>96.3</td><td>16</td><td>Minnesota</td><td>98.6</td></tr>
<tr><td>42</td><td>Louisiana</td><td>94.5</td><td>18</td><td>Wisconsin</td><td>98.0</td></tr>
<tr><td>37</td><td>Maine</td><td>95.4</td><td>19</td><td>Georgia</td><td>97.8</td></tr>
<tr><td>47</td><td>Maryland</td><td>93.9</td><td>20</td><td>Nebraska</td><td>97.7</td></tr>
<tr><td>48</td><td>Massachusetts</td><td>93.8</td><td>21</td><td>Oklahoma</td><td>97.6</td></tr>
<tr><td>29</td><td>Michigan</td><td>96.6</td><td>22</td><td>New Hampshire</td><td>97.3</td></tr>
<tr><td>16</td><td>Minnesota</td><td>98.6</td><td>23</td><td>Indiana</td><td>96.9</td></tr>
<tr><td>43</td><td>Mississippi</td><td>94.3</td><td>23</td><td>Iowa</td><td>96.9</td></tr>
<tr><td>36</td><td>Missouri</td><td>95.5</td><td>23</td><td>Vermont</td><td>96.9</td></tr>
<tr><td>11</td><td>Montana</td><td>99.5</td><td>23</td><td>Virginia</td><td>96.9</td></tr>
<tr><td>20</td><td>Nebraska</td><td>97.7</td><td>27</td><td>New Mexico</td><td>96.8</td></tr>
<tr><td>2</td><td>Nevada</td><td>103.7</td><td>28</td><td>North Carolina</td><td>96.7</td></tr>
<tr><td>22</td><td>New Hampshire</td><td>97.3</td><td>29</td><td>Michigan</td><td>96.6</td></tr>
<tr><td>40</td><td>New Jersey</td><td>94.9</td><td>30</td><td>Illinois</td><td>96.5</td></tr>
<tr><td>27</td><td>New Mexico</td><td>96.8</td><td>31</td><td>Kentucky</td><td>96.3</td></tr>
<tr><td>48</td><td>New York</td><td>93.8</td><td>32</td><td>Arkansas</td><td>96.1</td></tr>
<tr><td>28</td><td>North Carolina</td><td>96.7</td><td>32</td><td>Florida</td><td>96.1</td></tr>
<tr><td>8</td><td>North Dakota</td><td>99.7</td><td>34</td><td>Tennessee</td><td>95.7</td></tr>
<tr><td>40</td><td>Ohio</td><td>94.9</td><td>35</td><td>West Virginia</td><td>95.6</td></tr>
<tr><td>21</td><td>Oklahoma</td><td>97.6</td><td>36</td><td>Missouri</td><td>95.5</td></tr>
<tr><td>15</td><td>Oregon</td><td>98.8</td><td>37</td><td>Maine</td><td>95.4</td></tr>
<tr><td>45</td><td>Pennsylvania</td><td>94.1</td><td>38</td><td>Delaware</td><td>95.1</td></tr>
<tr><td>50</td><td>Rhode Island</td><td>93.2</td><td>39</td><td>South Carolina</td><td>95.0</td></tr>
<tr><td>39</td><td>South Carolina</td><td>95.0</td><td>40</td><td>New Jersey</td><td>94.9</td></tr>
<tr><td>14</td><td>South Dakota</td><td>98.9</td><td>40</td><td>Ohio</td><td>94.9</td></tr>
<tr><td>34</td><td>Tennessee</td><td>95.7</td><td>42</td><td>Louisiana</td><td>94.5</td></tr>
<tr><td>13</td><td>Texas</td><td>99.2</td><td>43</td><td>Connecticut</td><td>94.3</td></tr>
<tr><td>5</td><td>Utah</td><td>100.8</td><td>43</td><td>Mississippi</td><td>94.3</td></tr>
<tr><td>23</td><td>Vermont</td><td>96.9</td><td>45</td><td>Alabama</td><td>94.1</td></tr>
<tr><td>23</td><td>Virginia</td><td>96.9</td><td>45</td><td>Pennsylvania</td><td>94.1</td></tr>
<tr><td>11</td><td>Washington</td><td>99.5</td><td>47</td><td>Maryland</td><td>93.9</td></tr>
<tr><td>35</td><td>West Virginia</td><td>95.6</td><td>48</td><td>Massachusetts</td><td>93.8</td></tr>
<tr><td>18</td><td>Wisconsin</td><td>98.0</td><td>48</td><td>New York</td><td>93.8</td></tr>
<tr><td>4</td><td>Wyoming</td><td>101.4</td><td>50</td><td>Rhode Island</td><td>93.2</td></tr>
<tr><td></td><td></td><td></td><td></td><td>District of Columbia</td><td>89.7</td></tr>
</table>

Source: Morgan Quitno Press using data from U.S. Bureau of the Census
"SC-EST2004-AGESEX_RES - State Characteristic Estimates"
(http://www.census.gov/popest/datasets.html)

White Population in 2004

National Total = 236,057,761 White Persons*

ALPHA ORDER

RANK	STATE	WHITES	% of USA
25	Alabama	3,234,762	1.4%
49	Alaska	463,616	0.2%
16	Arizona	5,032,701	2.1%
33	Arkansas	2,238,490	0.9%
1	California	27,710,227	11.7%
21	Colorado	4,154,464	1.8%
26	Connecticut	2,983,059	1.3%
45	Delaware	625,117	0.3%
4	Florida	14,022,447	5.9%
11	Georgia	5,862,978	2.5%
50	Hawaii	334,752	0.1%
39	Idaho	1,331,057	0.6%
6	Illinois	10,101,163	4.3%
13	Indiana	5,529,707	2.3%
29	Iowa	2,806,633	1.2%
31	Kansas	2,444,815	1.0%
22	Kentucky	3,746,921	1.6%
27	Louisiana	2,896,096	1.2%
40	Maine	1,277,026	0.5%
23	Maryland	3,583,210	1.5%
12	Massachusetts	5,581,053	2.4%
8	Michigan	8,232,138	3.5%
20	Minnesota	4,583,418	1.9%
35	Mississippi	1,780,313	0.8%
18	Missouri	4,915,696	2.1%
43	Montana	844,461	0.4%
38	Nebraska	1,609,056	0.7%
34	Nevada	1,927,086	0.8%
41	New Hampshire	1,249,579	0.5%
9	New Jersey	6,690,290	2.8%
37	New Mexico	1,612,343	0.7%
3	New York	14,216,281	6.0%
10	North Carolina	6,332,037	2.7%
47	North Dakota	586,336	0.2%
7	Ohio	9,768,243	4.1%
30	Oklahoma	2,770,299	1.2%
24	Oregon	3,266,596	1.4%
5	Pennsylvania	10,693,313	4.5%
42	Rhode Island	962,437	0.4%
28	South Carolina	2,868,094	1.2%
44	South Dakota	683,768	0.3%
19	Tennessee	4,762,789	2.0%
2	Texas	18,725,559	7.9%
32	Utah	2,241,072	0.9%
46	Vermont	602,311	0.3%
14	Virginia	5,502,331	2.3%
15	Washington	5,290,018	2.2%
36	West Virginia	1,727,793	0.7%
17	Wisconsin	4,966,500	2.1%
48	Wyoming	480,064	0.2%

RANK ORDER

RANK	STATE	WHITES	% of USA
1	California	27,710,227	11.7%
2	Texas	18,725,559	7.9%
3	New York	14,216,281	6.0%
4	Florida	14,022,447	5.9%
5	Pennsylvania	10,693,313	4.5%
6	Illinois	10,101,163	4.3%
7	Ohio	9,768,243	4.1%
8	Michigan	8,232,138	3.5%
9	New Jersey	6,690,290	2.8%
10	North Carolina	6,332,037	2.7%
11	Georgia	5,862,978	2.5%
12	Massachusetts	5,581,053	2.4%
13	Indiana	5,529,707	2.3%
14	Virginia	5,502,331	2.3%
15	Washington	5,290,018	2.2%
16	Arizona	5,032,701	2.1%
17	Wisconsin	4,966,500	2.1%
18	Missouri	4,915,696	2.1%
19	Tennessee	4,762,789	2.0%
20	Minnesota	4,583,418	1.9%
21	Colorado	4,154,464	1.8%
22	Kentucky	3,746,921	1.6%
23	Maryland	3,583,210	1.5%
24	Oregon	3,266,596	1.4%
25	Alabama	3,234,762	1.4%
26	Connecticut	2,983,059	1.3%
27	Louisiana	2,896,096	1.2%
28	South Carolina	2,868,094	1.2%
29	Iowa	2,806,633	1.2%
30	Oklahoma	2,770,299	1.2%
31	Kansas	2,444,815	1.0%
32	Utah	2,241,072	0.9%
33	Arkansas	2,238,490	0.9%
34	Nevada	1,927,086	0.8%
35	Mississippi	1,780,313	0.8%
36	West Virginia	1,727,793	0.7%
37	New Mexico	1,612,343	0.7%
38	Nebraska	1,609,056	0.7%
39	Idaho	1,331,057	0.6%
40	Maine	1,277,026	0.5%
41	New Hampshire	1,249,579	0.5%
42	Rhode Island	962,437	0.4%
43	Montana	844,461	0.4%
44	South Dakota	683,768	0.3%
45	Delaware	625,117	0.3%
46	Vermont	602,311	0.3%
47	North Dakota	586,336	0.2%
48	Wyoming	480,064	0.2%
49	Alaska	463,616	0.2%
50	Hawaii	334,752	0.1%
	District of Columbia	207,246	0.1%

Source: U.S. Bureau of the Census
    "Race and Hispanic Origin" (http://www.census.gov/popest/states/asrh/SC-EST2004-04.html)
*"White" is defined by Census as a person having origins in any of the original peoples of Europe, North Africa, or the Middle East. There are 197,840,821 non-Hispanic whites. Census states "Race is a self-identification data item in which respondents choose the race or races with which they most closely identify."

Percent of Population White in 2004

National Percent = 80.4% White*

ALPHA ORDER

RANK	STATE	PERCENT
43	Alabama	71.4
44	Alaska	70.7
21	Arizona	87.6
32	Arkansas	81.3
37	California	77.2
14	Colorado	90.3
27	Connecticut	85.1
39	Delaware	75.3
34	Florida	80.6
46	Georgia	66.4
50	Hawaii	26.5
4	Idaho	95.5
35	Illinois	79.5
19	Indiana	88.7
6	Iowa	95.0
17	Kansas	89.4
13	Kentucky	90.4
48	Louisiana	64.1
1	Maine	96.9
47	Maryland	64.5
22	Massachusetts	87.0
31	Michigan	81.4
16	Minnesota	89.9
49	Mississippi	61.3
24	Missouri	85.4
11	Montana	91.1
10	Nebraska	92.1
30	Nevada	82.5
3	New Hampshire	96.2
38	New Jersey	76.9
28	New Mexico	84.7
41	New York	73.9
40	North Carolina	74.1
9	North Dakota	92.4
26	Ohio	85.2
36	Oklahoma	78.6
12	Oregon	90.9
23	Pennsylvania	86.2
18	Rhode Island	89.1
45	South Carolina	68.3
19	South Dakota	88.7
33	Tennessee	80.7
29	Texas	83.3
8	Utah	93.8
1	Vermont	96.9
42	Virginia	73.8
25	Washington	85.3
5	West Virginia	95.2
15	Wisconsin	90.2
7	Wyoming	94.8

RANK ORDER

RANK	STATE	PERCENT
1	Maine	96.9
1	Vermont	96.9
3	New Hampshire	96.2
4	Idaho	95.5
5	West Virginia	95.2
6	Iowa	95.0
7	Wyoming	94.8
8	Utah	93.8
9	North Dakota	92.4
10	Nebraska	92.1
11	Montana	91.1
12	Oregon	90.9
13	Kentucky	90.4
14	Colorado	90.3
15	Wisconsin	90.2
16	Minnesota	89.9
17	Kansas	89.4
18	Rhode Island	89.1
19	Indiana	88.7
19	South Dakota	88.7
21	Arizona	87.6
22	Massachusetts	87.0
23	Pennsylvania	86.2
24	Missouri	85.4
25	Washington	85.3
26	Ohio	85.2
27	Connecticut	85.1
28	New Mexico	84.7
29	Texas	83.3
30	Nevada	82.5
31	Michigan	81.4
32	Arkansas	81.3
33	Tennessee	80.7
34	Florida	80.6
35	Illinois	79.5
36	Oklahoma	78.6
37	California	77.2
38	New Jersey	76.9
39	Delaware	75.3
40	North Carolina	74.1
41	New York	73.9
42	Virginia	73.8
43	Alabama	71.4
44	Alaska	70.7
45	South Carolina	68.3
46	Georgia	66.4
47	Maryland	64.5
48	Louisiana	64.1
49	Mississippi	61.3
50	Hawaii	26.5

District of Columbia — 37.4

Source: Morgan Quitno Press using data from U.S. Bureau of the Census
"Race and Hispanic Origin" (http://www.census.gov/popest/states/asrh/SC-EST2004-04.html)
*"White" is defined by Census as a person having origins in any of the original peoples of Europe, North Africa, or the Middle East. Non-Hispanic whites comprise 67.4% of the total population. Census states "Race is a self-identification data item in which respondents choose the race or races with which they most closely identify."

Black Population in 2004

National Total = 37,502,320 Black Persons*

ALPHA ORDER

RANK	STATE	BLACKS	% of USA
16	Alabama	1,194,396	3.2%
41	Alaska	23,842	0.1%
29	Arizona	203,233	0.5%
22	Arkansas	434,395	1.2%
5	California	2,436,678	6.5%
30	Colorado	189,159	0.5%
23	Connecticut	352,272	0.9%
32	Delaware	169,251	0.5%
2	Florida	2,726,160	7.3%
4	Georgia	2,612,936	7.0%
40	Hawaii	28,105	0.1%
45	Idaho	7,863	0.0%
6	Illinois	1,926,010	5.1%
20	Indiana	548,269	1.5%
35	Iowa	67,596	0.2%
33	Kansas	161,305	0.4%
25	Kentucky	310,996	0.8%
9	Louisiana	1,492,298	4.0%
44	Maine	9,560	0.0%
8	Maryland	1,615,036	4.3%
21	Massachusetts	434,545	1.2%
11	Michigan	1,450,583	3.9%
28	Minnesota	211,628	0.6%
17	Mississippi	1,068,990	2.9%
19	Missouri	661,233	1.8%
50	Montana	3,471	0.0%
34	Nebraska	74,815	0.2%
31	Nevada	176,167	0.5%
43	New Hampshire	12,263	0.0%
14	New Jersey	1,259,839	3.4%
39	New Mexico	44,749	0.1%
1	New York	3,361,053	9.0%
7	North Carolina	1,861,416	5.0%
47	North Dakota	4,583	0.0%
12	Ohio	1,362,446	3.6%
26	Oklahoma	272,224	0.7%
37	Oregon	64,117	0.2%
13	Pennsylvania	1,304,439	3.5%
36	Rhode Island	65,958	0.2%
15	South Carolina	1,232,732	3.3%
46	South Dakota	6,006	0.0%
18	Tennessee	991,435	2.6%
3	Texas	2,633,219	7.0%
42	Utah	22,534	0.1%
49	Vermont	3,704	0.0%
10	Virginia	1,482,963	4.0%
27	Washington	216,484	0.6%
38	West Virginia	58,094	0.2%
24	Wisconsin	327,626	0.9%
48	Wyoming	4,448	0.0%

RANK ORDER

RANK	STATE	BLACKS	% of USA
1	New York	3,361,053	9.0%
2	Florida	2,726,160	7.3%
3	Texas	2,633,219	7.0%
4	Georgia	2,612,936	7.0%
5	California	2,436,678	6.5%
6	Illinois	1,926,010	5.1%
7	North Carolina	1,861,416	5.0%
8	Maryland	1,615,036	4.3%
9	Louisiana	1,492,298	4.0%
10	Virginia	1,482,963	4.0%
11	Michigan	1,450,583	3.9%
12	Ohio	1,362,446	3.6%
13	Pennsylvania	1,304,439	3.5%
14	New Jersey	1,259,839	3.4%
15	South Carolina	1,232,732	3.3%
16	Alabama	1,194,396	3.2%
17	Mississippi	1,068,990	2.9%
18	Tennessee	991,435	2.6%
19	Missouri	661,233	1.8%
20	Indiana	548,269	1.5%
21	Massachusetts	434,545	1.2%
22	Arkansas	434,395	1.2%
23	Connecticut	352,272	0.9%
24	Wisconsin	327,626	0.9%
25	Kentucky	310,996	0.8%
26	Oklahoma	272,224	0.7%
27	Washington	216,484	0.6%
28	Minnesota	211,628	0.6%
29	Arizona	203,233	0.5%
30	Colorado	189,159	0.5%
31	Nevada	176,167	0.5%
32	Delaware	169,251	0.5%
33	Kansas	161,305	0.4%
34	Nebraska	74,815	0.2%
35	Iowa	67,596	0.2%
36	Rhode Island	65,958	0.2%
37	Oregon	64,117	0.2%
38	West Virginia	58,094	0.2%
39	New Mexico	44,749	0.1%
40	Hawaii	28,105	0.1%
41	Alaska	23,842	0.1%
42	Utah	22,534	0.1%
43	New Hampshire	12,263	0.0%
44	Maine	9,560	0.0%
45	Idaho	7,863	0.0%
46	South Dakota	6,006	0.0%
47	North Dakota	4,583	0.0%
48	Wyoming	4,448	0.0%
49	Vermont	3,704	0.0%
50	Montana	3,471	0.0%
	District of Columbia	319,196	0.9%

Source: U.S. Bureau of the Census
    "Race and Hispanic Origin" (http://www.census.gov/popest/states/asrh/SC-EST2004-04.html)
"Black" is defined by Census as a person having origins in any of the Black racial groups of Africa. Census states "Race is a self-identification data item in which respondents choose the race or races with which they most closely identify."

Percent of Population Black in 2004

National Percent = 12.8% Black*

ALPHA ORDER

RANK	STATE	PERCENT
6	Alabama	26.4
34	Alaska	3.6
35	Arizona	3.5
12	Arkansas	15.8
26	California	6.8
32	Colorado	4.1
21	Connecticut	10.1
8	Delaware	20.4
13	Florida	15.7
3	Georgia	29.6
40	Hawaii	2.2
48	Idaho	0.6
14	Illinois	15.1
22	Indiana	8.8
39	Iowa	2.3
29	Kansas	5.9
24	Kentucky	7.5
2	Louisiana	33.0
46	Maine	0.7
5	Maryland	29.1
26	Massachusetts	6.8
16	Michigan	14.3
32	Minnesota	4.1
1	Mississippi	36.8
19	Missouri	11.5
50	Montana	0.4
31	Nebraska	4.3
24	Nevada	7.5
42	New Hampshire	0.9
15	New Jersey	14.5
38	New Mexico	2.4
10	New York	17.5
7	North Carolina	21.8
46	North Dakota	0.7
17	Ohio	11.9
23	Oklahoma	7.7
41	Oregon	1.8
20	Pennsylvania	10.5
28	Rhode Island	6.1
4	South Carolina	29.4
45	South Dakota	0.8
11	Tennessee	16.8
18	Texas	11.7
42	Utah	0.9
48	Vermont	0.6
9	Virginia	19.9
35	Washington	3.5
37	West Virginia	3.2
29	Wisconsin	5.9
42	Wyoming	0.9

RANK ORDER

RANK	STATE	PERCENT
1	Mississippi	36.8
2	Louisiana	33.0
3	Georgia	29.6
4	South Carolina	29.4
5	Maryland	29.1
6	Alabama	26.4
7	North Carolina	21.8
8	Delaware	20.4
9	Virginia	19.9
10	New York	17.5
11	Tennessee	16.8
12	Arkansas	15.8
13	Florida	15.7
14	Illinois	15.1
15	New Jersey	14.5
16	Michigan	14.3
17	Ohio	11.9
18	Texas	11.7
19	Missouri	11.5
20	Pennsylvania	10.5
21	Connecticut	10.1
22	Indiana	8.8
23	Oklahoma	7.7
24	Kentucky	7.5
24	Nevada	7.5
26	California	6.8
26	Massachusetts	6.8
28	Rhode Island	6.1
29	Kansas	5.9
29	Wisconsin	5.9
31	Nebraska	4.3
32	Colorado	4.1
32	Minnesota	4.1
34	Alaska	3.6
35	Arizona	3.5
35	Washington	3.5
37	West Virginia	3.2
38	New Mexico	2.4
39	Iowa	2.3
40	Hawaii	2.2
41	Oregon	1.8
42	New Hampshire	0.9
42	Utah	0.9
42	Wyoming	0.9
45	South Dakota	0.8
46	Maine	0.7
46	North Dakota	0.7
48	Idaho	0.6
48	Vermont	0.6
50	Montana	0.4

	District of Columbia	57.7

Source: Morgan Quitno Press using data from U.S. Bureau of the Census
    "Race and Hispanic Origin" (http://www.census.gov/popest/states/asrh/SC-EST2004-04.html)
*"Black" is defined by Census as a person having origins in any of the Black racial groups of Africa. Census states "Race is a self-identification data item in which respondents choose the race or races with which they most closely identify."

Hispanic Population in 2004

National Total = 41,322,070 Hispanics*

RANK	STATE	HISPANICS	% of USA
38	Alabama	98,388	0.2%
43	Alaska	32,386	0.1%
6	Arizona	1,608,698	3.9%
33	Arkansas	120,820	0.3%
1	California	12,442,626	30.1%
8	Colorado	878,803	2.1%
18	Connecticut	371,818	0.9%
41	Delaware	48,153	0.1%
3	Florida	3,304,832	8.0%
10	Georgia	598,322	1.4%
37	Hawaii	99,830	0.2%
32	Idaho	123,900	0.3%
5	Illinois	1,774,551	4.3%
21	Indiana	269,267	0.7%
36	Iowa	104,119	0.3%
26	Kansas	220,288	0.5%
39	Kentucky	77,055	0.2%
31	Louisiana	124,222	0.3%
48	Maine	12,476	0.0%
20	Maryland	297,717	0.7%
14	Massachusetts	494,188	1.2%
17	Michigan	375,041	0.9%
27	Minnesota	179,303	0.4%
40	Mississippi	49,075	0.1%
29	Missouri	148,201	0.4%
45	Montana	21,841	0.1%
34	Nebraska	119,975	0.3%
11	Nevada	531,929	1.3%
44	New Hampshire	27,500	0.1%
7	New Jersey	1,294,422	3.1%
9	New Mexico	823,352	2.0%
4	New York	3,076,697	7.4%
13	North Carolina	517,617	1.3%
49	North Dakota	9,755	0.0%
23	Ohio	252,269	0.6%
25	Oklahoma	223,005	0.5%
19	Oregon	343,278	0.8%
15	Pennsylvania	475,552	1.2%
35	Rhode Island	111,823	0.3%
30	South Carolina	130,432	0.3%
46	South Dakota	15,093	0.0%
28	Tennessee	167,025	0.4%
2	Texas	7,781,211	18.8%
22	Utah	253,073	0.6%
50	Vermont	6,414	0.0%
16	Virginia	426,152	1.0%
12	Washington	526,667	1.3%
47	West Virginia	14,621	0.0%
24	Wisconsin	237,200	0.6%
42	Wyoming	33,830	0.1%

RANK	STATE	HISPANICS	% of USA
1	California	12,442,626	30.1%
2	Texas	7,781,211	18.8%
3	Florida	3,304,832	8.0%
4	New York	3,076,697	7.4%
5	Illinois	1,774,551	4.3%
6	Arizona	1,608,698	3.9%
7	New Jersey	1,294,422	3.1%
8	Colorado	878,803	2.1%
9	New Mexico	823,352	2.0%
10	Georgia	598,322	1.4%
11	Nevada	531,929	1.3%
12	Washington	526,667	1.3%
13	North Carolina	517,617	1.3%
14	Massachusetts	494,188	1.2%
15	Pennsylvania	475,552	1.2%
16	Virginia	426,152	1.0%
17	Michigan	375,041	0.9%
18	Connecticut	371,818	0.9%
19	Oregon	343,278	0.8%
20	Maryland	297,717	0.7%
21	Indiana	269,267	0.7%
22	Utah	253,073	0.6%
23	Ohio	252,269	0.6%
24	Wisconsin	237,200	0.6%
25	Oklahoma	223,005	0.5%
26	Kansas	220,288	0.5%
27	Minnesota	179,303	0.4%
28	Tennessee	167,025	0.4%
29	Missouri	148,201	0.4%
30	South Carolina	130,432	0.3%
31	Louisiana	124,222	0.3%
32	Idaho	123,900	0.3%
33	Arkansas	120,820	0.3%
34	Nebraska	119,975	0.3%
35	Rhode Island	111,823	0.3%
36	Iowa	104,119	0.3%
37	Hawaii	99,830	0.2%
38	Alabama	98,388	0.2%
39	Kentucky	77,055	0.2%
40	Mississippi	49,075	0.1%
41	Delaware	48,153	0.1%
42	Wyoming	33,830	0.1%
43	Alaska	32,386	0.1%
44	New Hampshire	27,500	0.1%
45	Montana	21,841	0.1%
46	South Dakota	15,093	0.0%
47	West Virginia	14,621	0.0%
48	Maine	12,476	0.0%
49	North Dakota	9,755	0.0%
50	Vermont	6,414	0.0%
	District of Columbia	47,258	0.1%

Source: U.S. Bureau of the Census
"Race and Hispanic Origin" (http://www.census.gov/popest/states/asrh/SC-EST2004-04.html)
*Persons of Hispanic origin may be of any race. Census states "Race is a self-identification data item in which respondents choose the race or races with which they most closely identify."

Percent of Population Hispanic in 2004

National Percent = 14.1% Hispanic*

ALPHA ORDER

RANK	STATE	PERCENT
41	Alabama	2.2
28	Alaska	4.9
4	Arizona	28.0
29	Arkansas	4.4
2	California	34.7
6	Colorado	19.1
11	Connecticut	10.6
25	Delaware	5.8
7	Florida	19.0
21	Georgia	6.8
18	Hawaii	7.9
15	Idaho	8.9
10	Illinois	14.0
30	Indiana	4.3
34	Iowa	3.5
17	Kansas	8.1
45	Kentucky	1.9
37	Louisiana	2.8
49	Maine	0.9
27	Maryland	5.4
19	Massachusetts	7.7
33	Michigan	3.7
34	Minnesota	3.5
46	Mississippi	1.7
39	Missouri	2.6
40	Montana	2.4
20	Nebraska	6.9
5	Nevada	22.8
43	New Hampshire	2.1
9	New Jersey	14.9
1	New Mexico	43.3
8	New York	16.0
24	North Carolina	6.1
47	North Dakota	1.5
41	Ohio	2.2
23	Oklahoma	6.3
14	Oregon	9.5
32	Pennsylvania	3.8
13	Rhode Island	10.3
36	South Carolina	3.1
44	South Dakota	2.0
37	Tennessee	2.8
3	Texas	34.6
11	Utah	10.6
48	Vermont	1.0
26	Virginia	5.7
16	Washington	8.5
50	West Virginia	0.8
30	Wisconsin	4.3
22	Wyoming	6.7

RANK ORDER

RANK	STATE	PERCENT
1	New Mexico	43.3
2	California	34.7
3	Texas	34.6
4	Arizona	28.0
5	Nevada	22.8
6	Colorado	19.1
7	Florida	19.0
8	New York	16.0
9	New Jersey	14.9
10	Illinois	14.0
11	Connecticut	10.6
11	Utah	10.6
13	Rhode Island	10.3
14	Oregon	9.5
15	Idaho	8.9
16	Washington	8.5
17	Kansas	8.1
18	Hawaii	7.9
19	Massachusetts	7.7
20	Nebraska	6.9
21	Georgia	6.8
22	Wyoming	6.7
23	Oklahoma	6.3
24	North Carolina	6.1
25	Delaware	5.8
26	Virginia	5.7
27	Maryland	5.4
28	Alaska	4.9
29	Arkansas	4.4
30	Indiana	4.3
30	Wisconsin	4.3
32	Pennsylvania	3.8
33	Michigan	3.7
34	Iowa	3.5
34	Minnesota	3.5
36	South Carolina	3.1
37	Louisiana	2.8
37	Tennessee	2.8
39	Missouri	2.6
40	Montana	2.4
41	Alabama	2.2
41	Ohio	2.2
43	New Hampshire	2.1
44	South Dakota	2.0
45	Kentucky	1.9
46	Mississippi	1.7
47	North Dakota	1.5
48	Vermont	1.0
49	Maine	0.9
50	West Virginia	0.8

District of Columbia   8.5

Source: Morgan Quitno Press using data from U.S. Bureau of the Census
    "Race and Hispanic Origin" (http://www.census.gov/popest/states/asrh/SC-EST2004-04.html)
*Persons of Hispanic origin may be of any race. Census states "Race is a self-identification data item in which respondents choose the race or races with which they most closely identify."

Asian Population in 2004

National Total = 12,326,216 Asians*

ALPHA ORDER

RANK ORDER

RANK	STATE	ASIANS	% of USA
34	Alabama	36,798	0.3%
35	Alaska	29,783	0.2%
19	Arizona	122,933	1.0%
38	Arkansas	25,907	0.2%
1	California	4,326,126	35.1%
21	Colorado	116,483	0.9%
22	Connecticut	107,762	0.9%
41	Delaware	21,466	0.2%
8	Florida	351,975	2.9%
13	Georgia	229,741	1.9%
5	Hawaii	527,546	4.3%
43	Idaho	14,166	0.1%
6	Illinois	504,618	4.1%
25	Indiana	73,013	0.6%
32	Iowa	42,378	0.3%
28	Kansas	56,859	0.5%
33	Kentucky	36,986	0.3%
27	Louisiana	61,803	0.5%
44	Maine	10,854	0.1%
12	Maryland	257,876	2.1%
10	Massachusetts	294,701	2.4%
14	Michigan	220,019	1.8%
15	Minnesota	172,312	1.4%
42	Mississippi	21,409	0.2%
24	Missouri	74,585	0.6%
48	Montana	5,044	0.0%
37	Nebraska	26,746	0.2%
18	Nevada	128,470	1.0%
40	New Hampshire	21,824	0.2%
4	New Jersey	607,108	4.9%
39	New Mexico	24,025	0.2%
2	New York	1,249,166	10.1%
17	North Carolina	148,299	1.2%
49	North Dakota	4,150	0.0%
16	Ohio	159,094	1.3%
29	Oklahoma	53,846	0.4%
20	Oregon	121,880	1.0%
11	Pennsylvania	266,757	2.2%
36	Rhode Island	28,763	0.2%
31	South Carolina	44,385	0.4%
47	South Dakota	5,208	0.0%
26	Tennessee	71,115	0.6%
3	Texas	717,986	5.8%
30	Utah	44,608	0.4%
46	Vermont	6,311	0.1%
9	Virginia	329,529	2.7%
7	Washington	387,757	3.1%
45	West Virginia	10,238	0.1%
23	Wisconsin	105,769	0.9%
50	Wyoming	3,255	0.0%

RANK	STATE	ASIANS	% of USA
1	California	4,326,126	35.1%
2	New York	1,249,166	10.1%
3	Texas	717,986	5.8%
4	New Jersey	607,108	4.9%
5	Hawaii	527,546	4.3%
6	Illinois	504,618	4.1%
7	Washington	387,757	3.1%
8	Florida	351,975	2.9%
9	Virginia	329,529	2.7%
10	Massachusetts	294,701	2.4%
11	Pennsylvania	266,757	2.2%
12	Maryland	257,876	2.1%
13	Georgia	229,741	1.9%
14	Michigan	220,019	1.8%
15	Minnesota	172,312	1.4%
16	Ohio	159,094	1.3%
17	North Carolina	148,299	1.2%
18	Nevada	128,470	1.0%
19	Arizona	122,933	1.0%
20	Oregon	121,880	1.0%
21	Colorado	116,483	0.9%
22	Connecticut	107,762	0.9%
23	Wisconsin	105,769	0.9%
24	Missouri	74,585	0.6%
25	Indiana	73,013	0.6%
26	Tennessee	71,115	0.6%
27	Louisiana	61,803	0.5%
28	Kansas	56,859	0.5%
29	Oklahoma	53,846	0.4%
30	Utah	44,608	0.4%
31	South Carolina	44,385	0.4%
32	Iowa	42,378	0.3%
33	Kentucky	36,986	0.3%
34	Alabama	36,798	0.3%
35	Alaska	29,783	0.2%
36	Rhode Island	28,763	0.2%
37	Nebraska	26,746	0.2%
38	Arkansas	25,907	0.2%
39	New Mexico	24,025	0.2%
40	New Hampshire	21,824	0.2%
41	Delaware	21,466	0.2%
42	Mississippi	21,409	0.2%
43	Idaho	14,166	0.1%
44	Maine	10,854	0.1%
45	West Virginia	10,238	0.1%
46	Vermont	6,311	0.1%
47	South Dakota	5,208	0.0%
48	Montana	5,044	0.0%
49	North Dakota	4,150	0.0%
50	Wyoming	3,255	0.0%
	District of Columbia	16,784	0.1%

Source: U.S. Bureau of the Census
   "Race and Hispanic Origin" (http://www.census.gov/popest/states/asrh/SC-EST2004-04.html)
*Census states "Race is a self-identification data item in which respondents choose the race or races with which they most closely identify."

Percent of Population Asian in 2004

National Percent = 4.2% Asian*

ALPHA ORDER				RANK ORDER		

RANK	STATE	PERCENT		RANK	STATE	PERCENT
43	Alabama	0.8		1	Hawaii	41.8
9	Alaska	4.5		2	California	12.1
22	Arizona	2.1		3	New Jersey	7.0
41	Arkansas	0.9		4	New York	6.5
2	California	12.1		5	Washington	6.3
19	Colorado	2.5		6	Nevada	5.5
15	Connecticut	3.1		7	Maryland	4.6
17	Delaware	2.6		7	Massachusetts	4.6
24	Florida	2.0		9	Alaska	4.5
17	Georgia	2.6		10	Virginia	4.4
1	Hawaii	41.8		11	Illinois	4.0
39	Idaho	1.0		12	Minnesota	3.4
11	Illinois	4.0		12	Oregon	3.4
36	Indiana	1.2		14	Texas	3.2
31	Iowa	1.4		15	Connecticut	3.1
22	Kansas	2.1		16	Rhode Island	2.7
41	Kentucky	0.9		17	Delaware	2.6
31	Louisiana	1.4		17	Georgia	2.6
43	Maine	0.8		19	Colorado	2.5
7	Maryland	4.6		20	Michigan	2.2
7	Massachusetts	4.6		20	Pennsylvania	2.2
20	Michigan	2.2		22	Arizona	2.1
12	Minnesota	3.4		22	Kansas	2.1
45	Mississippi	0.7		24	Florida	2.0
34	Missouri	1.3		25	Utah	1.9
50	Montana	0.5		25	Wisconsin	1.9
29	Nebraska	1.5		27	New Hampshire	1.7
6	Nevada	5.5		27	North Carolina	1.7
27	New Hampshire	1.7		29	Nebraska	1.5
3	New Jersey	7.0		29	Oklahoma	1.5
34	New Mexico	1.3		31	Iowa	1.4
4	New York	6.5		31	Louisiana	1.4
27	North Carolina	1.7		31	Ohio	1.4
45	North Dakota	0.7		34	Missouri	1.3
31	Ohio	1.4		34	New Mexico	1.3
29	Oklahoma	1.5		36	Indiana	1.2
12	Oregon	3.4		36	Tennessee	1.2
20	Pennsylvania	2.2		38	South Carolina	1.1
16	Rhode Island	2.7		39	Idaho	1.0
38	South Carolina	1.1		39	Vermont	1.0
45	South Dakota	0.7		41	Arkansas	0.9
36	Tennessee	1.2		41	Kentucky	0.9
14	Texas	3.2		43	Alabama	0.8
25	Utah	1.9		43	Maine	0.8
39	Vermont	1.0		45	Mississippi	0.7
10	Virginia	4.4		45	North Dakota	0.7
5	Washington	6.3		45	South Dakota	0.7
48	West Virginia	0.6		48	West Virginia	0.6
25	Wisconsin	1.9		48	Wyoming	0.6
48	Wyoming	0.6		50	Montana	0.5
					District of Columbia	3.0

Source: Morgan Quitno Press using data from U.S. Bureau of the Census
   "Race and Hispanic Origin" (http://www.census.gov/popest/states/asrh/SC-EST2004-04.html)
*Census states "Race is a self-identification data item in which respondents choose the race or races with which they most closely identify."

American Indian Population in 2004

National Total = 2,824,751 American Indians*

ALPHA ORDER

RANK	STATE	INDIANS	% of USA
29	Alabama	23,095	0.8%
7	Alaska	103,617	3.7%
2	Arizona	288,918	10.2%
32	Arkansas	19,555	0.7%
1	California	416,646	14.7%
15	Colorado	52,334	1.9%
41	Connecticut	11,812	0.4%
48	Delaware	3,263	0.1%
10	Florida	73,606	2.6%
22	Georgia	27,457	1.0%
46	Hawaii	4,299	0.2%
31	Idaho	19,891	0.7%
18	Illinois	38,997	1.4%
35	Indiana	17,532	0.6%
42	Iowa	10,338	0.4%
26	Kansas	26,193	0.9%
43	Kentucky	9,220	0.3%
23	Louisiana	27,331	1.0%
44	Maine	7,454	0.3%
34	Maryland	17,860	0.6%
33	Massachusetts	18,404	0.7%
12	Michigan	60,462	2.1%
14	Minnesota	59,411	2.1%
39	Mississippi	13,448	0.5%
25	Missouri	26,493	0.9%
13	Montana	59,514	2.1%
37	Nebraska	16,562	0.6%
19	Nevada	33,045	1.2%
49	New Hampshire	3,214	0.1%
24	New Jersey	26,625	0.9%
4	New Mexico	192,135	6.8%
8	New York	103,443	3.7%
6	North Carolina	110,198	3.9%
20	North Dakota	33,032	1.2%
27	Ohio	26,025	0.9%
3	Oklahoma	283,844	10.0%
17	Oregon	49,138	1.7%
30	Pennsylvania	21,900	0.8%
45	Rhode Island	6,366	0.2%
38	South Carolina	15,677	0.6%
11	South Dakota	66,535	2.4%
36	Tennessee	17,005	0.6%
5	Texas	153,353	5.4%
21	Utah	32,191	1.1%
50	Vermont	2,326	0.1%
28	Virginia	24,314	0.9%
9	Washington	101,384	3.6%
47	West Virginia	3,729	0.1%
16	Wisconsin	51,463	1.8%
40	Wyoming	12,224	0.4%

RANK ORDER

RANK	STATE	INDIANS	% of USA
1	California	416,646	14.7%
2	Arizona	288,918	10.2%
3	Oklahoma	283,844	10.0%
4	New Mexico	192,135	6.8%
5	Texas	153,353	5.4%
6	North Carolina	110,198	3.9%
7	Alaska	103,617	3.7%
8	New York	103,443	3.7%
9	Washington	101,384	3.6%
10	Florida	73,606	2.6%
11	South Dakota	66,535	2.4%
12	Michigan	60,462	2.1%
13	Montana	59,514	2.1%
14	Minnesota	59,411	2.1%
15	Colorado	52,334	1.9%
16	Wisconsin	51,463	1.8%
17	Oregon	49,138	1.7%
18	Illinois	38,997	1.4%
19	Nevada	33,045	1.2%
20	North Dakota	33,032	1.2%
21	Utah	32,191	1.1%
22	Georgia	27,457	1.0%
23	Louisiana	27,331	1.0%
24	New Jersey	26,625	0.9%
25	Missouri	26,493	0.9%
26	Kansas	26,193	0.9%
27	Ohio	26,025	0.9%
28	Virginia	24,314	0.9%
29	Alabama	23,095	0.8%
30	Pennsylvania	21,900	0.8%
31	Idaho	19,891	0.7%
32	Arkansas	19,555	0.7%
33	Massachusetts	18,404	0.7%
34	Maryland	17,860	0.6%
35	Indiana	17,532	0.6%
36	Tennessee	17,005	0.6%
37	Nebraska	16,562	0.6%
38	South Carolina	15,677	0.6%
39	Mississippi	13,448	0.5%
40	Wyoming	12,224	0.4%
41	Connecticut	11,812	0.4%
42	Iowa	10,338	0.4%
43	Kentucky	9,220	0.3%
44	Maine	7,454	0.3%
45	Rhode Island	6,366	0.2%
46	Hawaii	4,299	0.2%
47	West Virginia	3,729	0.1%
48	Delaware	3,263	0.1%
49	New Hampshire	3,214	0.1%
50	Vermont	2,326	0.1%
	District of Columbia	1,873	0.1%

Source: U.S. Bureau of the Census
"Race and Hispanic Origin" (http://www.census.gov/popest/states/asrh/SC-EST2004-04.html)
*Includes Alaska Native populations. Census states "Race is a self-identification data item in which respondents choose the race or races with which they most closely identify."

449

Percent of Population American Indian in 2004

National Percent = 1.0% American Indian*

ALPHA ORDER		
RANK	**STATE**	**PERCENT**
27	Alabama	0.5
1	Alaska	15.8
7	Arizona	5.0
21	Arkansas	0.7
15	California	1.2
17	Colorado	1.1
35	Connecticut	0.3
31	Delaware	0.4
31	Florida	0.4
35	Georgia	0.3
35	Hawaii	0.3
10	Idaho	1.4
35	Illinois	0.3
35	Indiana	0.3
35	Iowa	0.3
18	Kansas	1.0
46	Kentucky	0.2
23	Louisiana	0.6
23	Maine	0.6
35	Maryland	0.3
35	Massachusetts	0.3
23	Michigan	0.6
15	Minnesota	1.2
27	Mississippi	0.5
27	Missouri	0.5
5	Montana	6.4
19	Nebraska	0.9
10	Nevada	1.4
46	New Hampshire	0.2
35	New Jersey	0.3
2	New Mexico	10.1
27	New York	0.5
13	North Carolina	1.3
6	North Dakota	5.2
46	Ohio	0.2
4	Oklahoma	8.1
10	Oregon	1.4
46	Pennsylvania	0.2
23	Rhode Island	0.6
31	South Carolina	0.4
3	South Dakota	8.6
35	Tennessee	0.3
21	Texas	0.7
13	Utah	1.3
31	Vermont	0.4
35	Virginia	0.3
9	Washington	1.6
46	West Virginia	0.2
19	Wisconsin	0.9
8	Wyoming	2.4

RANK ORDER		
RANK	**STATE**	**PERCENT**
1	Alaska	15.8
2	New Mexico	10.1
3	South Dakota	8.6
4	Oklahoma	8.1
5	Montana	6.4
6	North Dakota	5.2
7	Arizona	5.0
8	Wyoming	2.4
9	Washington	1.6
10	Idaho	1.4
10	Nevada	1.4
10	Oregon	1.4
13	North Carolina	1.3
13	Utah	1.3
15	California	1.2
15	Minnesota	1.2
17	Colorado	1.1
18	Kansas	1.0
19	Nebraska	0.9
19	Wisconsin	0.9
21	Arkansas	0.7
21	Texas	0.7
23	Louisiana	0.6
23	Maine	0.6
23	Michigan	0.6
23	Rhode Island	0.6
27	Alabama	0.5
27	Mississippi	0.5
27	Missouri	0.5
27	New York	0.5
31	Delaware	0.4
31	Florida	0.4
31	South Carolina	0.4
31	Vermont	0.4
35	Connecticut	0.3
35	Georgia	0.3
35	Hawaii	0.3
35	Illinois	0.3
35	Indiana	0.3
35	Iowa	0.3
35	Maryland	0.3
35	Massachusetts	0.3
35	New Jersey	0.3
35	Tennessee	0.3
35	Virginia	0.3
46	Kentucky	0.2
46	New Hampshire	0.2
46	Ohio	0.2
46	Pennsylvania	0.2
46	West Virginia	0.2
	District of Columbia	0.3

Source: Morgan Quitno Press using data from U.S. Bureau of the Census
    "Race and Hispanic Origin" (http://www.census.gov/popest/states/asrh/SC-EST2004-04.html)
*Includes Alaska Native populations. Census states "Race is a self-identification data item in which respondents choose the race or races with which they most closely identify."

Mixed Race Population in 2004

National Total = 4,438,754 Mixed Race*

ALPHA ORDER

RANK	STATE	MIXED RACE	% of USA
30	Alabama	39,419	0.9%
35	Alaska	30,809	0.7%
15	Arizona	85,665	1.9%
33	Arkansas	31,997	0.7%
1	California	854,988	19.3%
19	Colorado	82,478	1.9%
27	Connecticut	46,051	1.0%
46	Delaware	10,814	0.2%
5	Florida	209,028	4.7%
14	Georgia	89,503	2.0%
3	Hawaii	253,792	5.7%
39	Idaho	18,645	0.4%
10	Illinois	134,784	3.0%
23	Indiana	66,215	1.5%
37	Iowa	26,231	0.6%
28	Kansas	44,460	1.0%
29	Kentucky	39,872	0.9%
31	Louisiana	36,666	0.8%
45	Maine	11,900	0.3%
20	Maryland	80,757	1.8%
18	Massachusetts	82,579	1.9%
7	Michigan	145,648	3.3%
22	Minnesota	71,520	1.6%
40	Mississippi	17,962	0.4%
21	Missouri	72,800	1.6%
43	Montana	13,864	0.3%
38	Nebraska	18,859	0.4%
24	Nevada	57,970	1.3%
44	New Hampshire	12,100	0.3%
13	New Jersey	108,283	2.4%
36	New Mexico	27,616	0.6%
2	New York	279,269	6.3%
16	North Carolina	83,487	1.9%
50	North Dakota	6,020	0.1%
9	Ohio	139,647	3.1%
8	Oklahoma	140,406	3.2%
17	Oregon	83,225	1.9%
12	Pennsylvania	114,680	2.6%
41	Rhode Island	15,833	0.4%
32	South Carolina	34,897	0.8%
47	South Dakota	9,086	0.2%
25	Tennessee	55,689	1.3%
4	Texas	235,411	5.3%
34	Utah	31,266	0.7%
48	Vermont	6,576	0.1%
11	Virginia	115,214	2.6%
6	Washington	179,956	4.1%
42	West Virginia	15,075	0.3%
26	Wisconsin	55,512	1.3%
49	Wyoming	6,180	0.1%

RANK ORDER

RANK	STATE	MIXED RACE	% of USA
1	California	854,988	19.3%
2	New York	279,269	6.3%
3	Hawaii	253,792	5.7%
4	Texas	235,411	5.3%
5	Florida	209,028	4.7%
6	Washington	179,956	4.1%
7	Michigan	145,648	3.3%
8	Oklahoma	140,406	3.2%
9	Ohio	139,647	3.1%
10	Illinois	134,784	3.0%
11	Virginia	115,214	2.6%
12	Pennsylvania	114,680	2.6%
13	New Jersey	108,283	2.4%
14	Georgia	89,503	2.0%
15	Arizona	85,665	1.9%
16	North Carolina	83,487	1.9%
17	Oregon	83,225	1.9%
18	Massachusetts	82,579	1.9%
19	Colorado	82,478	1.9%
20	Maryland	80,757	1.8%
21	Missouri	72,800	1.6%
22	Minnesota	71,520	1.6%
23	Indiana	66,215	1.5%
24	Nevada	57,970	1.3%
25	Tennessee	55,689	1.3%
26	Wisconsin	55,512	1.3%
27	Connecticut	46,051	1.0%
28	Kansas	44,460	1.0%
29	Kentucky	39,872	0.9%
30	Alabama	39,419	0.9%
31	Louisiana	36,666	0.8%
32	South Carolina	34,897	0.8%
33	Arkansas	31,997	0.7%
34	Utah	31,266	0.7%
35	Alaska	30,809	0.7%
36	New Mexico	27,616	0.6%
37	Iowa	26,231	0.6%
38	Nebraska	18,859	0.4%
39	Idaho	18,645	0.4%
40	Mississippi	17,962	0.4%
41	Rhode Island	15,833	0.4%
42	West Virginia	15,075	0.3%
43	Montana	13,864	0.3%
44	New Hampshire	12,100	0.3%
45	Maine	11,900	0.3%
46	Delaware	10,814	0.2%
47	South Dakota	9,086	0.2%
48	Vermont	6,576	0.1%
49	Wyoming	6,180	0.1%
50	North Dakota	6,020	0.1%
	District of Columbia	8,050	0.2%

Source: U.S. Bureau of the Census
"Race and Hispanic Origin" (http://www.census.gov/popest/states/asrh/SC-EST2004-04.html)
*Census states "Race is a self-identification data item in which respondents choose the race or races with which they most closely identify." The 2000 Census was the first to allow respondents to identify themselves as one or more races.

451

Percent of Population of Mixed Race in 2004

National Percent = 1.5% Mixed Race*

RANK	STATE	PERCENT
40	Alabama	0.9
2	Alaska	4.7
10	Arizona	1.5
25	Arkansas	1.2
6	California	2.4
8	Colorado	1.8
19	Connecticut	1.3
19	Delaware	1.3
25	Florida	1.2
35	Georgia	1.0
1	Hawaii	20.1
19	Idaho	1.3
31	Illinois	1.1
31	Indiana	1.1
40	Iowa	0.9
9	Kansas	1.6
35	Kentucky	1.0
47	Louisiana	0.8
40	Maine	0.9
10	Maryland	1.5
19	Massachusetts	1.3
17	Michigan	1.4
17	Minnesota	1.4
50	Mississippi	0.6
19	Missouri	1.3
10	Montana	1.5
31	Nebraska	1.1
5	Nevada	2.5
40	New Hampshire	0.9
25	New Jersey	1.2
10	New Mexico	1.5
10	New York	1.5
35	North Carolina	1.0
40	North Dakota	0.9
25	Ohio	1.2
3	Oklahoma	4.0
7	Oregon	2.3
40	Pennsylvania	0.9
10	Rhode Island	1.5
47	South Carolina	0.8
25	South Dakota	1.2
40	Tennessee	0.9
35	Texas	1.0
19	Utah	1.3
10	Virginia	1.5
4	Washington	2.9
47	West Virginia	0.8
35	Wisconsin	1.0
25	Wyoming	1.2

RANK	STATE	PERCENT
1	Hawaii	20.1
2	Alaska	4.7
3	Oklahoma	4.0
4	Washington	2.9
5	Nevada	2.5
6	California	2.4
7	Oregon	2.3
8	Colorado	1.8
9	Kansas	1.6
10	Arizona	1.5
10	Maryland	1.5
10	Montana	1.5
10	New Mexico	1.5
10	New York	1.5
10	Rhode Island	1.5
10	Virginia	1.5
17	Michigan	1.4
17	Minnesota	1.4
19	Connecticut	1.3
19	Delaware	1.3
19	Idaho	1.3
19	Massachusetts	1.3
19	Missouri	1.3
19	Utah	1.3
25	Arkansas	1.2
25	Florida	1.2
25	New Jersey	1.2
25	Ohio	1.2
25	South Dakota	1.2
25	Wyoming	1.2
31	Illinois	1.1
31	Indiana	1.1
31	Nebraska	1.1
31	Vermont	1.1
35	Georgia	1.0
35	Kentucky	1.0
35	North Carolina	1.0
35	Texas	1.0
35	Wisconsin	1.0
40	Alabama	0.9
40	Iowa	0.9
40	Maine	0.9
40	New Hampshire	0.9
40	North Dakota	0.9
40	Pennsylvania	0.9
40	Tennessee	0.9
47	Louisiana	0.8
47	South Carolina	0.8
47	West Virginia	0.8
50	Mississippi	0.6
	District of Columbia	1.5

Source: Morgan Quitno Press using data from U.S. Bureau of the Census
   "Race and Hispanic Origin" (http://www.census.gov/popest/states/asrh/SC-EST2004-04.html)
*Census states "Race is a self-identification data item in which respondents choose the race or races with which they most closely identify." The 2000 Census was the first to allow respondents to identify themselves as one or more races.

Projected State Population in 2030

National Total = 363,584,435

ALPHA ORDER

RANK	STATE	POPULATION	% of USA
24	Alabama	4,874,243	1.3%
46	Alaska	867,674	0.2%
10	Arizona	10,712,397	2.9%
32	Arkansas	3,240,208	0.9%
1	California	46,444,861	12.8%
22	Colorado	5,792,357	1.6%
30	Connecticut	3,688,630	1.0%
45	Delaware	1,012,658	0.3%
3	Florida	28,685,769	7.9%
8	Georgia	12,017,838	3.3%
41	Hawaii	1,466,046	0.4%
37	Idaho	1,969,624	0.5%
5	Illinois	13,432,892	3.7%
18	Indiana	6,810,108	1.9%
34	Iowa	2,955,172	0.8%
35	Kansas	2,940,084	0.8%
27	Kentucky	4,554,998	1.3%
26	Louisiana	4,802,633	1.3%
42	Maine	1,411,097	0.4%
16	Maryland	7,022,251	1.9%
17	Massachusetts	7,012,009	1.9%
11	Michigan	10,694,172	2.9%
20	Minnesota	6,306,130	1.7%
33	Mississippi	3,092,410	0.9%
19	Missouri	6,430,173	1.8%
44	Montana	1,044,898	0.3%
38	Nebraska	1,820,247	0.5%
28	Nevada	4,282,102	1.2%
40	New Hampshire	1,646,471	0.5%
13	New Jersey	9,802,440	2.7%
36	New Mexico	2,099,708	0.6%
4	New York	19,477,429	5.4%
7	North Carolina	12,227,739	3.4%
49	North Dakota	606,566	0.2%
9	Ohio	11,550,528	3.2%
29	Oklahoma	3,913,251	1.1%
25	Oregon	4,833,918	1.3%
6	Pennsylvania	12,768,184	3.5%
43	Rhode Island	1,152,941	0.3%
23	South Carolina	5,148,569	1.4%
47	South Dakota	800,462	0.2%
15	Tennessee	7,380,634	2.0%
2	Texas	33,317,744	9.2%
31	Utah	3,485,367	1.0%
48	Vermont	711,867	0.2%
12	Virginia	9,825,019	2.7%
14	Washington	8,624,801	2.4%
39	West Virginia	1,719,959	0.5%
21	Wisconsin	6,150,764	1.7%
50	Wyoming	522,979	0.1%

RANK ORDER

RANK	STATE	POPULATION	% of USA
1	California	46,444,861	12.8%
2	Texas	33,317,744	9.2%
3	Florida	28,685,769	7.9%
4	New York	19,477,429	5.4%
5	Illinois	13,432,892	3.7%
6	Pennsylvania	12,768,184	3.5%
7	North Carolina	12,227,739	3.4%
8	Georgia	12,017,838	3.3%
9	Ohio	11,550,528	3.2%
10	Arizona	10,712,397	2.9%
11	Michigan	10,694,172	2.9%
12	Virginia	9,825,019	2.7%
13	New Jersey	9,802,440	2.7%
14	Washington	8,624,801	2.4%
15	Tennessee	7,380,634	2.0%
16	Maryland	7,022,251	1.9%
17	Massachusetts	7,012,009	1.9%
18	Indiana	6,810,108	1.9%
19	Missouri	6,430,173	1.8%
20	Minnesota	6,306,130	1.7%
21	Wisconsin	6,150,764	1.7%
22	Colorado	5,792,357	1.6%
23	South Carolina	5,148,569	1.4%
24	Alabama	4,874,243	1.3%
25	Oregon	4,833,918	1.3%
26	Louisiana	4,802,633	1.3%
27	Kentucky	4,554,998	1.3%
28	Nevada	4,282,102	1.2%
29	Oklahoma	3,913,251	1.1%
30	Connecticut	3,688,630	1.0%
31	Utah	3,485,367	1.0%
32	Arkansas	3,240,208	0.9%
33	Mississippi	3,092,410	0.9%
34	Iowa	2,955,172	0.8%
35	Kansas	2,940,084	0.8%
36	New Mexico	2,099,708	0.6%
37	Idaho	1,969,624	0.5%
38	Nebraska	1,820,247	0.5%
39	West Virginia	1,719,959	0.5%
40	New Hampshire	1,646,471	0.5%
41	Hawaii	1,466,046	0.4%
42	Maine	1,411,097	0.4%
43	Rhode Island	1,152,941	0.3%
44	Montana	1,044,898	0.3%
45	Delaware	1,012,658	0.3%
46	Alaska	867,674	0.2%
47	South Dakota	800,462	0.2%
48	Vermont	711,867	0.2%
49	North Dakota	606,566	0.2%
50	Wyoming	522,979	0.1%
	District of Columbia	433,414	0.1%

Source: U.S. Bureau of the Census
   "State Interim Population Projections: 2004-2030 "
   (http://www.census.gov/population/www/projections/projectionsagesex.html)

Projected Percent Change in Population: 2000 to 2030

National Projected Percent Change = 29.2% Increase*

ALPHA ORDER

RANK	STATE	PERCENT CHANGE
35	Alabama	9.6
12	Alaska	38.4
2	Arizona	108.8
21	Arkansas	21.2
13	California	37.1
14	Colorado	34.7
38	Connecticut	8.3
18	Delaware	29.2
3	Florida	79.5
8	Georgia	46.8
22	Hawaii	21.0
6	Idaho	52.2
39	Illinois	8.2
31	Indiana	12.0
48	Iowa	1.0
36	Kansas	9.4
30	Kentucky	12.7
41	Louisiana	7.5
32	Maine	10.7
16	Maryland	32.6
33	Massachusetts	10.4
40	Michigan	7.6
20	Minnesota	28.2
37	Mississippi	8.7
27	Missouri	14.9
25	Montana	15.8
42	Nebraska	6.4
1	Nevada	114.3
15	New Hampshire	33.2
24	New Jersey	16.5
26	New Mexico	15.4
46	New York	2.6
7	North Carolina	51.9
50	North Dakota	(5.5)
47	Ohio	1.7
29	Oklahoma	13.4
10	Oregon	41.3
45	Pennsylvania	4.0
34	Rhode Island	10.0
19	South Carolina	28.3
43	South Dakota	6.0
17	Tennessee	29.7
4	Texas	59.8
5	Utah	56.1
23	Vermont	16.9
11	Virginia	38.8
9	Washington	46.3
49	West Virginia	(4.9)
28	Wisconsin	14.7
44	Wyoming	5.9

RANK ORDER

RANK	STATE	PERCENT CHANGE
1	Nevada	114.3
2	Arizona	108.8
3	Florida	79.5
4	Texas	59.8
5	Utah	56.1
6	Idaho	52.2
7	North Carolina	51.9
8	Georgia	46.8
9	Washington	46.3
10	Oregon	41.3
11	Virginia	38.8
12	Alaska	38.4
13	California	37.1
14	Colorado	34.7
15	New Hampshire	33.2
16	Maryland	32.6
17	Tennessee	29.7
18	Delaware	29.2
19	South Carolina	28.3
20	Minnesota	28.2
21	Arkansas	21.2
22	Hawaii	21.0
23	Vermont	16.9
24	New Jersey	16.5
25	Montana	15.8
26	New Mexico	15.4
27	Missouri	14.9
28	Wisconsin	14.7
29	Oklahoma	13.4
30	Kentucky	12.7
31	Indiana	12.0
32	Maine	10.7
33	Massachusetts	10.4
34	Rhode Island	10.0
35	Alabama	9.6
36	Kansas	9.4
37	Mississippi	8.7
38	Connecticut	8.3
39	Illinois	8.2
40	Michigan	7.6
41	Louisiana	7.5
42	Nebraska	6.4
43	South Dakota	6.0
44	Wyoming	5.9
45	Pennsylvania	4.0
46	New York	2.6
47	Ohio	1.7
48	Iowa	1.0
49	West Virginia	(4.9)
50	North Dakota	(5.5)
	District of Columbia	(24.2)

Source: U.S. Bureau of the Census
"State Interim Population Projections: 2004-2030 "
(http://www.census.gov/population/www/projections/projectionsagesex.html)

Projected Percent of State Population Under Age 18 in 2030

National Percent = 23.6%

<table>
<tr><td colspan="3">ALPHA ORDER</td><td colspan="3">RANK ORDER</td></tr>
<tr><th>RANK</th><th>STATE</th><th>PERCENT</th><th>RANK</th><th>STATE</th><th>PERCENT</th></tr>
<tr><td>27</td><td>Alabama</td><td>22.8</td><td>1</td><td>Utah</td><td>30.4</td></tr>
<tr><td>2</td><td>Alaska</td><td>28.7</td><td>2</td><td>Alaska</td><td>28.7</td></tr>
<tr><td>14</td><td>Arizona</td><td>24.3</td><td>3</td><td>Texas</td><td>27.0</td></tr>
<tr><td>17</td><td>Arkansas</td><td>24.2</td><td>4</td><td>Georgia</td><td>26.2</td></tr>
<tr><td>21</td><td>California</td><td>23.8</td><td>5</td><td>Colorado</td><td>25.3</td></tr>
<tr><td>5</td><td>Colorado</td><td>25.3</td><td>6</td><td>North Carolina</td><td>25.2</td></tr>
<tr><td>32</td><td>Connecticut</td><td>22.3</td><td>7</td><td>Nevada</td><td>25.1</td></tr>
<tr><td>41</td><td>Delaware</td><td>21.6</td><td>8</td><td>Nebraska</td><td>25.1</td></tr>
<tr><td>46</td><td>Florida</td><td>20.1</td><td>9</td><td>Oklahoma</td><td>25.0</td></tr>
<tr><td>4</td><td>Georgia</td><td>26.2</td><td>10</td><td>Indiana</td><td>25.0</td></tr>
<tr><td>35</td><td>Hawaii</td><td>22.2</td><td>11</td><td>Idaho</td><td>24.7</td></tr>
<tr><td>11</td><td>Idaho</td><td>24.7</td><td>12</td><td>South Dakota</td><td>24.5</td></tr>
<tr><td>16</td><td>Illinois</td><td>24.3</td><td>13</td><td>Maryland</td><td>24.5</td></tr>
<tr><td>10</td><td>Indiana</td><td>25.0</td><td>14</td><td>Arizona</td><td>24.3</td></tr>
<tr><td>31</td><td>Iowa</td><td>22.4</td><td>15</td><td>Tennessee</td><td>24.3</td></tr>
<tr><td>18</td><td>Kansas</td><td>24.1</td><td>16</td><td>Illinois</td><td>24.3</td></tr>
<tr><td>30</td><td>Kentucky</td><td>22.6</td><td>17</td><td>Arkansas</td><td>24.2</td></tr>
<tr><td>19</td><td>Louisiana</td><td>23.9</td><td>18</td><td>Kansas</td><td>24.1</td></tr>
<tr><td>50</td><td>Maine</td><td>18.1</td><td>19</td><td>Louisiana</td><td>23.9</td></tr>
<tr><td>13</td><td>Maryland</td><td>24.5</td><td>20</td><td>Minnesota</td><td>23.9</td></tr>
<tr><td>38</td><td>Massachusetts</td><td>22.0</td><td>21</td><td>California</td><td>23.8</td></tr>
<tr><td>29</td><td>Michigan</td><td>22.8</td><td>22</td><td>Virginia</td><td>23.6</td></tr>
<tr><td>20</td><td>Minnesota</td><td>23.9</td><td>23</td><td>Missouri</td><td>23.3</td></tr>
<tr><td>25</td><td>Mississippi</td><td>23.0</td><td>24</td><td>Oregon</td><td>23.1</td></tr>
<tr><td>23</td><td>Missouri</td><td>23.3</td><td>25</td><td>Mississippi</td><td>23.0</td></tr>
<tr><td>45</td><td>Montana</td><td>20.1</td><td>26</td><td>Ohio</td><td>22.9</td></tr>
<tr><td>8</td><td>Nebraska</td><td>25.1</td><td>27</td><td>Alabama</td><td>22.8</td></tr>
<tr><td>7</td><td>Nevada</td><td>25.1</td><td>28</td><td>Washington</td><td>22.8</td></tr>
<tr><td>42</td><td>New Hampshire</td><td>21.6</td><td>29</td><td>Michigan</td><td>22.8</td></tr>
<tr><td>37</td><td>New Jersey</td><td>22.2</td><td>30</td><td>Kentucky</td><td>22.6</td></tr>
<tr><td>40</td><td>New Mexico</td><td>21.7</td><td>31</td><td>Iowa</td><td>22.4</td></tr>
<tr><td>34</td><td>New York</td><td>22.2</td><td>32</td><td>Connecticut</td><td>22.3</td></tr>
<tr><td>6</td><td>North Carolina</td><td>25.2</td><td>33</td><td>South Carolina</td><td>22.2</td></tr>
<tr><td>44</td><td>North Dakota</td><td>21.2</td><td>34</td><td>New York</td><td>22.2</td></tr>
<tr><td>26</td><td>Ohio</td><td>22.9</td><td>35</td><td>Hawaii</td><td>22.2</td></tr>
<tr><td>9</td><td>Oklahoma</td><td>25.0</td><td>36</td><td>Wisconsin</td><td>22.2</td></tr>
<tr><td>24</td><td>Oregon</td><td>23.1</td><td>37</td><td>New Jersey</td><td>22.2</td></tr>
<tr><td>43</td><td>Pennsylvania</td><td>21.5</td><td>38</td><td>Massachusetts</td><td>22.0</td></tr>
<tr><td>39</td><td>Rhode Island</td><td>21.9</td><td>39</td><td>Rhode Island</td><td>21.9</td></tr>
<tr><td>33</td><td>South Carolina</td><td>22.2</td><td>40</td><td>New Mexico</td><td>21.7</td></tr>
<tr><td>12</td><td>South Dakota</td><td>24.5</td><td>41</td><td>Delaware</td><td>21.6</td></tr>
<tr><td>15</td><td>Tennessee</td><td>24.3</td><td>42</td><td>New Hampshire</td><td>21.6</td></tr>
<tr><td>3</td><td>Texas</td><td>27.0</td><td>43</td><td>Pennsylvania</td><td>21.5</td></tr>
<tr><td>1</td><td>Utah</td><td>30.4</td><td>44</td><td>North Dakota</td><td>21.2</td></tr>
<tr><td>47</td><td>Vermont</td><td>19.5</td><td>45</td><td>Montana</td><td>20.1</td></tr>
<tr><td>22</td><td>Virginia</td><td>23.6</td><td>46</td><td>Florida</td><td>20.1</td></tr>
<tr><td>28</td><td>Washington</td><td>22.8</td><td>47</td><td>Vermont</td><td>19.5</td></tr>
<tr><td>49</td><td>West Virginia</td><td>18.9</td><td>48</td><td>Wyoming</td><td>19.1</td></tr>
<tr><td>36</td><td>Wisconsin</td><td>22.2</td><td>49</td><td>West Virginia</td><td>18.9</td></tr>
<tr><td>48</td><td>Wyoming</td><td>19.1</td><td>50</td><td>Maine</td><td>18.1</td></tr>
<tr><td></td><td></td><td></td><td></td><td>District of Columbia</td><td>23.2</td></tr>
</table>

Source: U.S. Bureau of the Census
  "State Interim Population Projections: 2004-2030 "
  (http://www.census.gov/population/www/projections/projectionsagesex.html)

Projected Percent of State Population Age 65 and Older in 2030

National Percent = 19.7%

ALPHA ORDER

RANK	STATE	PERCENT
20	Alabama	21.3
49	Alaska	14.7
14	Arizona	22.1
25	Arkansas	20.3
43	California	17.8
46	Colorado	16.5
16	Connecticut	21.5
9	Delaware	23.5
1	Florida	27.1
47	Georgia	15.9
13	Hawaii	22.3
38	Idaho	18.3
42	Illinois	18.0
41	Indiana	18.1
12	Iowa	22.4
27	Kansas	20.2
30	Kentucky	19.8
31	Louisiana	19.7
2	Maine	26.5
45	Maryland	17.6
21	Massachusetts	20.9
32	Michigan	19.5
35	Minnesota	18.9
23	Mississippi	20.5
26	Missouri	20.2
5	Montana	25.8
22	Nebraska	20.6
37	Nevada	18.6
17	New Hampshire	21.4
29	New Jersey	20.0
4	New Mexico	26.4
28	New York	20.1
44	North Carolina	17.8
6	North Dakota	25.1
24	Ohio	20.4
33	Oklahoma	19.4
39	Oregon	18.2
11	Pennsylvania	22.6
18	Rhode Island	21.4
15	South Carolina	22.0
10	South Dakota	23.1
34	Tennessee	19.2
48	Texas	15.6
50	Utah	13.2
8	Vermont	24.4
36	Virginia	18.8
40	Washington	18.1
7	West Virginia	24.8
19	Wisconsin	21.3
3	Wyoming	26.5

RANK ORDER

RANK	STATE	PERCENT
1	Florida	27.1
2	Maine	26.5
3	Wyoming	26.5
4	New Mexico	26.4
5	Montana	25.8
6	North Dakota	25.1
7	West Virginia	24.8
8	Vermont	24.4
9	Delaware	23.5
10	South Dakota	23.1
11	Pennsylvania	22.6
12	Iowa	22.4
13	Hawaii	22.3
14	Arizona	22.1
15	South Carolina	22.0
16	Connecticut	21.5
17	New Hampshire	21.4
18	Rhode Island	21.4
19	Wisconsin	21.3
20	Alabama	21.3
21	Massachusetts	20.9
22	Nebraska	20.6
23	Mississippi	20.5
24	Ohio	20.4
25	Arkansas	20.3
26	Missouri	20.2
27	Kansas	20.2
28	New York	20.1
29	New Jersey	20.0
30	Kentucky	19.8
31	Louisiana	19.7
32	Michigan	19.5
33	Oklahoma	19.4
34	Tennessee	19.2
35	Minnesota	18.9
36	Virginia	18.8
37	Nevada	18.6
38	Idaho	18.3
39	Oregon	18.2
40	Washington	18.1
41	Indiana	18.1
42	Illinois	18.0
43	California	17.8
44	North Carolina	17.8
45	Maryland	17.6
46	Colorado	16.5
47	Georgia	15.9
48	Texas	15.6
49	Alaska	14.7
50	Utah	13.2
	District of Columbia	13.4

Source: U.S. Bureau of the Census
  "State Interim Population Projections: 2004-2030 "
  (http://www.census.gov/population/www/projections/projectionsagesex.html)

Median Age in 2004

National Median = 36.2 Years Old

ALPHA ORDER

RANK	STATE	MEDIAN AGE
22	Alabama	37.0
48	Alaska	33.4
46	Arizona	34.1
29	Arkansas	36.6
45	California	34.2
43	Colorado	34.5
8	Connecticut	38.9
16	Delaware	37.5
5	Florida	39.3
47	Georgia	34.0
13	Hawaii	38.0
44	Idaho	34.3
39	Illinois	35.4
38	Indiana	35.7
13	Iowa	38.0
34	Kansas	36.1
19	Kentucky	37.3
40	Louisiana	35.2
1	Maine	40.7
28	Maryland	36.8
11	Massachusetts	38.1
29	Michigan	36.6
29	Minnesota	36.6
42	Mississippi	34.9
19	Missouri	37.3
4	Montana	39.6
35	Nebraska	36.0
41	Nevada	35.1
7	New Hampshire	39.2
15	New Jersey	37.8
37	New Mexico	35.8
19	New York	37.3
35	North Carolina	36.0
9	North Dakota	38.8
16	Ohio	37.5
32	Oklahoma	36.5
22	Oregon	37.0
5	Pennsylvania	39.3
11	Rhode Island	38.1
26	South Carolina	36.9
22	South Dakota	37.0
22	Tennessee	37.0
49	Texas	32.9
50	Utah	28.0
2	Vermont	40.4
26	Virginia	36.9
33	Washington	36.4
3	West Virginia	40.3
16	Wisconsin	37.5
10	Wyoming	38.4

RANK ORDER

RANK	STATE	MEDIAN AGE
1	Maine	40.7
2	Vermont	40.4
3	West Virginia	40.3
4	Montana	39.6
5	Florida	39.3
5	Pennsylvania	39.3
7	New Hampshire	39.2
8	Connecticut	38.9
9	North Dakota	38.8
10	Wyoming	38.4
11	Massachusetts	38.1
11	Rhode Island	38.1
13	Hawaii	38.0
13	Iowa	38.0
15	New Jersey	37.8
16	Delaware	37.5
16	Ohio	37.5
16	Wisconsin	37.5
19	Kentucky	37.3
19	Missouri	37.3
19	New York	37.3
22	Alabama	37.0
22	Oregon	37.0
22	South Dakota	37.0
22	Tennessee	37.0
26	South Carolina	36.9
26	Virginia	36.9
28	Maryland	36.8
29	Arkansas	36.6
29	Michigan	36.6
29	Minnesota	36.6
32	Oklahoma	36.5
33	Washington	36.4
34	Kansas	36.1
35	Nebraska	36.0
35	North Carolina	36.0
37	New Mexico	35.8
38	Indiana	35.7
39	Illinois	35.4
40	Louisiana	35.2
41	Nevada	35.1
42	Mississippi	34.9
43	Colorado	34.5
44	Idaho	34.3
45	California	34.2
46	Arizona	34.1
47	Georgia	34.0
48	Alaska	33.4
49	Texas	32.9
50	Utah	28.0
	District of Columbia	35.8

Source: U.S. Bureau of the Census
"2004 American Community Survey" (http://www.census.gov/acs/www/index.html)

Population Under 5 Years Old in 2004

National Total = 20,071,268

ALPHA ORDER

RANK	STATE	POPULATION	% of USA
24	Alabama	296,100	1.5%
47	Alaska	49,758	0.2%
13	Arizona	449,904	2.2%
33	Arkansas	185,555	0.9%
1	California	2,633,972	13.1%
20	Colorado	339,079	1.7%
30	Connecticut	213,048	1.1%
44	Delaware	53,781	0.3%
4	Florida	1,091,292	5.4%
8	Georgia	679,064	3.4%
40	Hawaii	88,759	0.4%
38	Idaho	103,482	0.5%
5	Illinois	890,545	4.4%
14	Indiana	430,557	2.1%
34	Iowa	180,839	0.9%
32	Kansas	188,782	0.9%
26	Kentucky	266,614	1.3%
23	Louisiana	323,991	1.6%
42	Maine	67,628	0.3%
18	Maryland	374,578	1.9%
15	Massachusetts	395,662	2.0%
9	Michigan	619,842	3.2%
22	Minnesota	332,024	1.7%
31	Mississippi	208,354	1.0%
19	Missouri	371,469	1.9%
45	Montana	52,510	0.3%
37	Nebraska	122,049	0.6%
35	Nevada	169,018	0.8%
41	New Hampshire	72,678	0.4%
11	New Jersey	581,467	2.9%
36	New Mexico	133,366	0.7%
3	New York	1,246,045	6.2%
10	North Carolina	600,113	3.0%
48	North Dakota	35,754	0.2%
6	Ohio	730,035	3.6%
27	Oklahoma	242,240	1.2%
29	Oregon	226,069	1.1%
7	Pennsylvania	719,125	3.6%
43	Rhode Island	61,538	0.3%
25	South Carolina	280,272	1.4%
46	South Dakota	51,720	0.3%
17	Tennessee	384,704	1.9%
2	Texas	1,842,808	9.2%
28	Utah	232,793	1.2%
49	Vermont	31,181	0.2%
12	Virginia	498,386	2.5%
16	Washington	387,403	1.9%
39	West Virginia	101,109	0.5%
21	Wisconsin	338,310	1.7%
50	Wyoming	30,867	0.2%

RANK ORDER

RANK	STATE	POPULATION	% of USA
1	California	2,633,972	13.1%
2	Texas	1,842,808	9.2%
3	New York	1,246,045	6.2%
4	Florida	1,091,292	5.4%
5	Illinois	890,545	4.4%
6	Ohio	730,035	3.6%
7	Pennsylvania	719,125	3.6%
8	Georgia	679,064	3.4%
9	Michigan	649,842	3.2%
10	North Carolina	600,113	3.0%
11	New Jersey	581,467	2.9%
12	Virginia	498,386	2.5%
13	Arizona	449,904	2.2%
14	Indiana	430,557	2.1%
15	Massachusetts	395,662	2.0%
16	Washington	387,403	1.9%
17	Tennessee	384,704	1.9%
18	Maryland	374,578	1.9%
19	Missouri	371,469	1.9%
20	Colorado	339,079	1.7%
21	Wisconsin	338,310	1.7%
22	Minnesota	332,024	1.7%
23	Louisiana	323,991	1.6%
24	Alabama	296,100	1.5%
25	South Carolina	280,272	1.4%
26	Kentucky	266,614	1.3%
27	Oklahoma	242,240	1.2%
28	Utah	232,793	1.2%
29	Oregon	226,069	1.1%
30	Connecticut	213,048	1.1%
31	Mississippi	208,354	1.0%
32	Kansas	188,782	0.9%
33	Arkansas	185,555	0.9%
34	Iowa	180,839	0.9%
35	Nevada	169,018	0.8%
36	New Mexico	133,366	0.7%
37	Nebraska	122,049	0.6%
38	Idaho	103,482	0.5%
39	West Virginia	101,109	0.5%
40	Hawaii	88,759	0.4%
41	New Hampshire	72,678	0.4%
42	Maine	67,628	0.3%
43	Rhode Island	61,538	0.3%
44	Delaware	53,781	0.3%
45	Montana	52,510	0.3%
46	South Dakota	51,720	0.3%
47	Alaska	49,758	0.2%
48	North Dakota	35,754	0.2%
49	Vermont	31,181	0.2%
50	Wyoming	30,867	0.2%
	District of Columbia	35,029	0.2%

Source: U.S. Bureau of the Census
   "Table ST-EST2004-01res - Annual Estimates of the Resident Population" (February 25, 2005)
   (http://www.census.gov/popest/states/asrh/SC-est2004-01.html)

Percent of Population Under 5 Years Old in 2004

National Percent = 6.8% of Population

RANK	STATE	PERCENT
26	Alabama	6.5
5	Alaska	7.6
3	Arizona	7.8
20	Arkansas	6.7
8	California	7.3
6	Colorado	7.4
39	Connecticut	6.1
26	Delaware	6.5
35	Florida	6.3
4	Georgia	7.7
12	Hawaii	7.0
6	Idaho	7.4
12	Illinois	7.0
17	Indiana	6.9
39	Iowa	6.1
17	Kansas	6.9
32	Kentucky	6.4
9	Louisiana	7.2
49	Maine	5.1
20	Maryland	6.7
37	Massachusetts	6.2
32	Michigan	6.4
26	Minnesota	6.5
9	Mississippi	7.2
26	Missouri	6.5
44	Montana	5.7
12	Nebraska	7.0
9	Nevada	7.2
46	New Hampshire	5.6
20	New Jersey	6.7
12	New Mexico	7.0
26	New York	6.5
12	North Carolina	7.0
46	North Dakota	5.6
32	Ohio	6.4
17	Oklahoma	6.9
35	Oregon	6.3
43	Pennsylvania	5.8
44	Rhode Island	5.7
20	South Carolina	6.7
20	South Dakota	6.7
26	Tennessee	6.5
2	Texas	8.2
1	Utah	9.7
50	Vermont	5.0
20	Virginia	6.7
37	Washington	6.2
46	West Virginia	5.6
39	Wisconsin	6.1
39	Wyoming	6.1

RANK	STATE	PERCENT
1	Utah	9.7
2	Texas	8.2
3	Arizona	7.8
4	Georgia	7.7
5	Alaska	7.6
6	Colorado	7.4
6	Idaho	7.4
8	California	7.3
9	Louisiana	7.2
9	Mississippi	7.2
9	Nevada	7.2
12	Hawaii	7.0
12	Illinois	7.0
12	Nebraska	7.0
12	New Mexico	7.0
12	North Carolina	7.0
17	Indiana	6.9
17	Kansas	6.9
17	Oklahoma	6.9
20	Arkansas	6.7
20	Maryland	6.7
20	New Jersey	6.7
20	South Carolina	6.7
20	South Dakota	6.7
20	Virginia	6.7
26	Alabama	6.5
26	Delaware	6.5
26	Minnesota	6.5
26	Missouri	6.5
26	New York	6.5
26	Tennessee	6.5
32	Kentucky	6.4
32	Michigan	6.4
32	Ohio	6.4
35	Florida	6.3
35	Oregon	6.3
37	Massachusetts	6.2
37	Washington	6.2
39	Connecticut	6.1
39	Iowa	6.1
39	Wisconsin	6.1
39	Wyoming	6.1
43	Pennsylvania	5.8
44	Montana	5.7
44	Rhode Island	5.7
46	New Hampshire	5.6
46	North Dakota	5.6
46	West Virginia	5.6
49	Maine	5.1
50	Vermont	5.0

	District of Columbia	6.3

Source: Morgan Quitno Press using data from U.S. Bureau of the Census
"Table ST-EST2004-01res - Annual Estimates of the Resident Population" (February 25, 2005)
(http://www.census.gov/popest/states/asrh/SC-est2004-01.html)

Population 5 to 17 Years Old in 2004

National Total = 53,206,730

ALPHA ORDER				RANK ORDER			
RANK	STATE	POPULATION	% of USA	RANK	STATE	POPULATION	% of USA
24	Alabama	798,433	1.5%	1	California	6,962,491	13.1%
47	Alaska	138,471	0.3%	2	Texas	4,423,971	8.3%
15	Arizona	1,097,356	2.1%	3	New York	3,326,318	6.3%
34	Arkansas	490,995	0.9%	4	Florida	2,911,998	5.5%
1	California	6,962,491	13.1%	5	Illinois	2,347,605	4.4%
23	Colorado	839,810	1.6%	6	Pennsylvania	2,117,884	4.0%
28	Connecticut	625,740	1.2%	7	Ohio	2,049,177	3.9%
45	Delaware	139,725	0.3%	8	Michigan	1,883,597	3.5%
4	Florida	2,911,998	5.5%	9	Georgia	1,653,503	3.1%
9	Georgia	1,653,503	3.1%	10	New Jersey	1,574,592	3.0%
42	Hawaii	209,934	0.4%	11	North Carolina	1,518,379	2.9%
39	Idaho	268,929	0.5%	12	Virginia	1,306,514	2.5%
5	Illinois	2,347,605	4.4%	13	Indiana	1,169,738	2.2%
13	Indiana	1,169,738	2.2%	14	Washington	1,098,617	2.1%
32	Iowa	499,598	0.9%	15	Arizona	1,097,356	2.1%
33	Kansas	494,709	0.9%	16	Massachusetts	1,068,527	2.0%
26	Kentucky	713,573	1.3%	17	Maryland	1,020,230	1.9%
22	Louisiana	840,970	1.6%	18	Missouri	1,013,073	1.9%
41	Maine	214,501	0.4%	19	Tennessee	1,006,585	1.9%
17	Maryland	1,020,230	1.9%	20	Wisconsin	969,676	1.8%
16	Massachusetts	1,068,527	2.0%	21	Minnesota	908,256	1.7%
8	Michigan	1,883,597	3.5%	22	Louisiana	840,970	1.6%
21	Minnesota	908,256	1.7%	23	Colorado	839,810	1.6%
30	Mississippi	541,215	1.0%	24	Alabama	798,433	1.5%
18	Missouri	1,013,073	1.9%	25	South Carolina	744,428	1.4%
44	Montana	155,583	0.3%	26	Kentucky	713,573	1.3%
37	Nebraska	312,517	0.6%	27	Oregon	626,288	1.2%
35	Nevada	434,578	0.8%	28	Connecticut	625,740	1.2%
40	New Hampshire	232,316	0.4%	29	Oklahoma	617,630	1.2%
10	New Jersey	1,574,592	3.0%	30	Mississippi	541,215	1.0%
36	New Mexico	358,921	0.7%	31	Utah	507,321	1.0%
3	New York	3,326,318	6.3%	32	Iowa	499,598	0.9%
11	North Carolina	1,518,379	2.9%	33	Kansas	494,709	0.9%
49	North Dakota	103,201	0.2%	34	Arkansas	490,995	0.9%
7	Ohio	2,049,177	3.9%	35	Nevada	434,578	0.8%
29	Oklahoma	617,630	1.2%	36	New Mexico	358,921	0.7%
27	Oregon	626,288	1.2%	37	Nebraska	312,517	0.6%
6	Pennsylvania	2,117,884	4.0%	38	West Virginia	283,532	0.5%
43	Rhode Island	182,275	0.3%	39	Idaho	268,929	0.5%
25	South Carolina	744,428	1.4%	40	New Hampshire	232,316	0.4%
46	South Dakota	139,154	0.3%	41	Maine	214,501	0.4%
19	Tennessee	1,006,585	1.9%	42	Hawaii	209,934	0.4%
2	Texas	4,423,971	8.3%	43	Rhode Island	182,275	0.3%
31	Utah	507,321	1.0%	44	Montana	155,583	0.3%
48	Vermont	103,713	0.2%	45	Delaware	139,725	0.3%
12	Virginia	1,306,514	2.5%	46	South Dakota	139,154	0.3%
14	Washington	1,098,617	2.1%	47	Alaska	138,471	0.3%
38	West Virginia	283,532	0.5%	48	Vermont	103,713	0.2%
20	Wisconsin	969,676	1.8%	49	North Dakota	103,201	0.2%
50	Wyoming	86,065	0.2%	50	Wyoming	86,065	0.2%
					District of Columbia	74,518	0.1%

Source: U.S. Bureau of the Census
   "Table ST-EST2004-01res - Annual Estimates of the Resident Population" (February 25, 2005)
   (http://www.census.gov/popest/states/asrh/SC-est2004-01.html)

Percent of Population 5 to 17 Years Old in 2004

National Percent = 18.1% of Population

<table>
<tr><td colspan="3">ALPHA ORDER</td><td colspan="3">RANK ORDER</td></tr>
<tr><th>RANK</th><th>STATE</th><th>PERCENT</th><th>RANK</th><th>STATE</th><th>PERCENT</th></tr>
<tr><td>29</td><td>Alabama</td><td>17.6</td><td>1</td><td>Utah</td><td>21.2</td></tr>
<tr><td>2</td><td>Alaska</td><td>21.1</td><td>2</td><td>Alaska</td><td>21.1</td></tr>
<tr><td>6</td><td>Arizona</td><td>19.1</td><td>3</td><td>Texas</td><td>19.7</td></tr>
<tr><td>24</td><td>Arkansas</td><td>17.8</td><td>4</td><td>California</td><td>19.4</td></tr>
<tr><td>4</td><td>California</td><td>19.4</td><td>5</td><td>Idaho</td><td>19.3</td></tr>
<tr><td>16</td><td>Colorado</td><td>18.3</td><td>6</td><td>Arizona</td><td>19.1</td></tr>
<tr><td>20</td><td>Connecticut</td><td>17.9</td><td>7</td><td>New Mexico</td><td>18.9</td></tr>
<tr><td>42</td><td>Delaware</td><td>16.8</td><td>8</td><td>Indiana</td><td>18.8</td></tr>
<tr><td>44</td><td>Florida</td><td>16.7</td><td>9</td><td>Georgia</td><td>18.7</td></tr>
<tr><td>9</td><td>Georgia</td><td>18.7</td><td>10</td><td>Louisiana</td><td>18.6</td></tr>
<tr><td>47</td><td>Hawaii</td><td>16.6</td><td>10</td><td>Michigan</td><td>18.6</td></tr>
<tr><td>5</td><td>Idaho</td><td>19.3</td><td>10</td><td>Mississippi</td><td>18.6</td></tr>
<tr><td>14</td><td>Illinois</td><td>18.5</td><td>10</td><td>Nevada</td><td>18.6</td></tr>
<tr><td>8</td><td>Indiana</td><td>18.8</td><td>14</td><td>Illinois</td><td>18.5</td></tr>
<tr><td>40</td><td>Iowa</td><td>16.9</td><td>15</td><td>Maryland</td><td>18.4</td></tr>
<tr><td>17</td><td>Kansas</td><td>18.1</td><td>16</td><td>Colorado</td><td>18.3</td></tr>
<tr><td>36</td><td>Kentucky</td><td>17.2</td><td>17</td><td>Kansas</td><td>18.1</td></tr>
<tr><td>10</td><td>Louisiana</td><td>18.6</td><td>17</td><td>New Jersey</td><td>18.1</td></tr>
<tr><td>48</td><td>Maine</td><td>16.3</td><td>17</td><td>South Dakota</td><td>18.1</td></tr>
<tr><td>15</td><td>Maryland</td><td>18.4</td><td>20</td><td>Connecticut</td><td>17.9</td></tr>
<tr><td>44</td><td>Massachusetts</td><td>16.7</td><td>20</td><td>Nebraska</td><td>17.9</td></tr>
<tr><td>10</td><td>Michigan</td><td>18.6</td><td>20</td><td>New Hampshire</td><td>17.9</td></tr>
<tr><td>24</td><td>Minnesota</td><td>17.8</td><td>20</td><td>Ohio</td><td>17.9</td></tr>
<tr><td>10</td><td>Mississippi</td><td>18.6</td><td>24</td><td>Arkansas</td><td>17.8</td></tr>
<tr><td>29</td><td>Missouri</td><td>17.6</td><td>24</td><td>Minnesota</td><td>17.8</td></tr>
<tr><td>42</td><td>Montana</td><td>16.8</td><td>24</td><td>North Carolina</td><td>17.8</td></tr>
<tr><td>20</td><td>Nebraska</td><td>17.9</td><td>27</td><td>South Carolina</td><td>17.7</td></tr>
<tr><td>10</td><td>Nevada</td><td>18.6</td><td>27</td><td>Washington</td><td>17.7</td></tr>
<tr><td>20</td><td>New Hampshire</td><td>17.9</td><td>29</td><td>Alabama</td><td>17.6</td></tr>
<tr><td>17</td><td>New Jersey</td><td>18.1</td><td>29</td><td>Missouri</td><td>17.6</td></tr>
<tr><td>7</td><td>New Mexico</td><td>18.9</td><td>29</td><td>Wisconsin</td><td>17.6</td></tr>
<tr><td>35</td><td>New York</td><td>17.3</td><td>32</td><td>Oklahoma</td><td>17.5</td></tr>
<tr><td>24</td><td>North Carolina</td><td>17.8</td><td>32</td><td>Virginia</td><td>17.5</td></tr>
<tr><td>48</td><td>North Dakota</td><td>16.3</td><td>34</td><td>Oregon</td><td>17.4</td></tr>
<tr><td>20</td><td>Ohio</td><td>17.9</td><td>35</td><td>New York</td><td>17.3</td></tr>
<tr><td>32</td><td>Oklahoma</td><td>17.5</td><td>36</td><td>Kentucky</td><td>17.2</td></tr>
<tr><td>34</td><td>Oregon</td><td>17.4</td><td>37</td><td>Pennsylvania</td><td>17.1</td></tr>
<tr><td>37</td><td>Pennsylvania</td><td>17.1</td><td>37</td><td>Tennessee</td><td>17.1</td></tr>
<tr><td>40</td><td>Rhode Island</td><td>16.9</td><td>39</td><td>Wyoming</td><td>17.0</td></tr>
<tr><td>27</td><td>South Carolina</td><td>17.7</td><td>40</td><td>Iowa</td><td>16.9</td></tr>
<tr><td>17</td><td>South Dakota</td><td>18.1</td><td>40</td><td>Rhode Island</td><td>16.9</td></tr>
<tr><td>37</td><td>Tennessee</td><td>17.1</td><td>42</td><td>Delaware</td><td>16.8</td></tr>
<tr><td>3</td><td>Texas</td><td>19.7</td><td>42</td><td>Montana</td><td>16.8</td></tr>
<tr><td>1</td><td>Utah</td><td>21.2</td><td>44</td><td>Florida</td><td>16.7</td></tr>
<tr><td>44</td><td>Vermont</td><td>16.7</td><td>44</td><td>Massachusetts</td><td>16.7</td></tr>
<tr><td>32</td><td>Virginia</td><td>17.5</td><td>44</td><td>Vermont</td><td>16.7</td></tr>
<tr><td>27</td><td>Washington</td><td>17.7</td><td>47</td><td>Hawaii</td><td>16.6</td></tr>
<tr><td>50</td><td>West Virginia</td><td>15.6</td><td>48</td><td>Maine</td><td>16.3</td></tr>
<tr><td>29</td><td>Wisconsin</td><td>17.6</td><td>48</td><td>North Dakota</td><td>16.3</td></tr>
<tr><td>39</td><td>Wyoming</td><td>17.0</td><td>50</td><td>West Virginia</td><td>15.6</td></tr>
<tr><td></td><td></td><td></td><td></td><td>District of Columbia</td><td>13.5</td></tr>
</table>

Source: Morgan Quitno Press using data from U.S. Bureau of the Census
   "Table ST-EST2004-01res - Annual Estimates of the Resident Population" (February 25, 2005)
   (http://www.census.gov/popest/states/asrh/SC-est2004-01.html)

Population 18 Years Old and Older in 2004

National Total = 220,377,406

ALPHA ORDER				RANK ORDER			
RANK	STATE	POPULATION	% of USA	RANK	STATE	POPULATION	% of USA
22	Alabama	3,435,649	1.6%	1	California	26,297,336	11.9%
49	Alaska	467,206	0.2%	2	Texas	16,223,243	7.4%
19	Arizona	4,196,574	1.9%	3	New York	14,654,725	6.6%
32	Arkansas	2,076,079	0.9%	4	Florida	13,393,871	6.1%
1	California	26,297,336	11.9%	5	Pennsylvania	9,569,283	4.3%
23	Colorado	3,422,514	1.6%	6	Illinois	9,475,484	4.3%
28	Connecticut	2,664,816	1.2%	7	Ohio	8,679,799	3.9%
45	Delaware	636,858	0.3%	8	Michigan	7,579,181	3.4%
4	Florida	13,393,871	6.1%	9	New Jersey	6,542,820	3.0%
10	Georgia	6,496,816	2.9%	10	Georgia	6,496,816	2.9%
42	Hawaii	964,147	0.4%	11	North Carolina	6,422,729	2.9%
40	Idaho	1,020,851	0.5%	12	Virginia	5,654,927	2.6%
6	Illinois	9,475,484	4.3%	13	Massachusetts	4,952,316	2.2%
15	Indiana	4,637,274	2.1%	14	Washington	4,717,768	2.1%
30	Iowa	2,274,014	1.0%	15	Indiana	4,637,274	2.1%
33	Kansas	2,052,011	0.9%	16	Tennessee	4,509,673	2.0%
26	Kentucky	3,165,735	1.4%	17	Missouri	4,370,076	2.0%
24	Louisiana	3,350,809	1.5%	18	Wisconsin	4,201,040	1.9%
39	Maine	1,035,124	0.5%	19	Arizona	4,196,574	1.9%
20	Maryland	4,163,250	1.9%	20	Maryland	4,163,250	1.9%
13	Massachusetts	4,952,316	2.2%	21	Minnesota	3,860,678	1.8%
8	Michigan	7,579,181	3.4%	22	Alabama	3,435,649	1.6%
21	Minnesota	3,860,678	1.8%	23	Colorado	3,422,514	1.6%
31	Mississippi	2,153,397	1.0%	24	Louisiana	3,350,809	1.5%
17	Missouri	4,370,076	2.0%	25	South Carolina	3,173,368	1.4%
44	Montana	718,772	0.3%	26	Kentucky	3,165,735	1.4%
38	Nebraska	1,312,648	0.6%	27	Oregon	2,742,229	1.2%
34	Nevada	1,731,175	0.8%	28	Connecticut	2,664,816	1.2%
41	New Hampshire	994,506	0.5%	29	Oklahoma	2,663,683	1.2%
9	New Jersey	6,542,820	3.0%	30	Iowa	2,274,014	1.0%
37	New Mexico	1,411,002	0.6%	31	Mississippi	2,153,397	1.0%
3	New York	14,654,725	6.6%	32	Arkansas	2,076,079	0.9%
11	North Carolina	6,422,729	2.9%	33	Kansas	2,052,011	0.9%
47	North Dakota	495,411	0.2%	34	Nevada	1,731,175	0.8%
7	Ohio	8,679,799	3.9%	35	Utah	1,648,925	0.7%
29	Oklahoma	2,663,683	1.2%	36	West Virginia	1,430,713	0.6%
27	Oregon	2,742,229	1.2%	37	New Mexico	1,411,002	0.6%
5	Pennsylvania	9,569,283	4.3%	38	Nebraska	1,312,648	0.6%
43	Rhode Island	836,819	0.4%	39	Maine	1,035,124	0.5%
25	South Carolina	3,173,368	1.4%	40	Idaho	1,020,851	0.5%
46	South Dakota	580,009	0.3%	41	New Hampshire	994,506	0.5%
16	Tennessee	4,509,673	2.0%	42	Hawaii	964,147	0.4%
2	Texas	16,223,243	7.4%	43	Rhode Island	836,819	0.4%
35	Utah	1,648,925	0.7%	44	Montana	718,772	0.3%
48	Vermont	486,500	0.2%	45	Delaware	636,858	0.3%
12	Virginia	5,654,927	2.6%	46	South Dakota	580,009	0.3%
14	Washington	4,717,768	2.1%	47	North Dakota	495,411	0.2%
36	West Virginia	1,430,713	0.6%	48	Vermont	486,500	0.2%
18	Wisconsin	4,201,040	1.9%	49	Alaska	467,206	0.2%
50	Wyoming	389,597	0.2%	50	Wyoming	389,597	0.2%
					District of Columbia	443,976	0.2%

Source: U.S. Bureau of the Census
"Table ST-EST2004-01res - Annual Estimates of the Resident Population" (February 25, 2005)
(http://www.census.gov/popest/states/asrh/SC-est2004-01.html)

Percent of Population 18 Years Old and Older in 2004

National Percent = 75.0% of Population

RANK	STATE	PERCENT
23	Alabama	75.8
49	Alaska	71.3
47	Arizona	73.1
29	Arkansas	75.4
45	California	73.3
38	Colorado	74.4
20	Connecticut	76.1
12	Delaware	76.7
9	Florida	77.0
44	Georgia	73.6
16	Hawaii	76.3
45	Idaho	73.3
37	Illinois	74.5
39	Indiana	74.3
9	Iowa	77.0
34	Kansas	75.0
14	Kentucky	76.4
40	Louisiana	74.2
2	Maine	78.6
35	Maryland	74.9
7	Massachusetts	77.2
35	Michigan	74.9
25	Minnesota	75.7
40	Mississippi	74.2
22	Missouri	75.9
5	Montana	77.5
33	Nebraska	75.1
42	Nevada	74.1
13	New Hampshire	76.5
30	New Jersey	75.2
42	New Mexico	74.1
19	New York	76.2
30	North Carolina	75.2
4	North Dakota	78.1
25	Ohio	75.7
27	Oklahoma	75.6
16	Oregon	76.3
8	Pennsylvania	77.1
6	Rhode Island	77.4
27	South Carolina	75.6
30	South Dakota	75.2
14	Tennessee	76.4
48	Texas	72.1
50	Utah	69.0
3	Vermont	78.3
23	Virginia	75.8
21	Washington	76.0
1	West Virginia	78.8
16	Wisconsin	76.3
11	Wyoming	76.9

RANK	STATE	PERCENT
1	West Virginia	78.8
2	Maine	78.6
3	Vermont	78.3
4	North Dakota	78.1
5	Montana	77.5
6	Rhode Island	77.4
7	Massachusetts	77.2
8	Pennsylvania	77.1
9	Florida	77.0
9	Iowa	77.0
11	Wyoming	76.9
12	Delaware	76.7
13	New Hampshire	76.5
14	Kentucky	76.4
14	Tennessee	76.4
16	Hawaii	76.3
16	Oregon	76.3
16	Wisconsin	76.3
19	New York	76.2
20	Connecticut	76.1
21	Washington	76.0
22	Missouri	75.9
23	Alabama	75.8
23	Virginia	75.8
25	Minnesota	75.7
25	Ohio	75.7
27	Oklahoma	75.6
27	South Carolina	75.6
29	Arkansas	75.4
30	New Jersey	75.2
30	North Carolina	75.2
30	South Dakota	75.2
33	Nebraska	75.1
34	Kansas	75.0
35	Maryland	74.9
35	Michigan	74.9
37	Illinois	74.5
38	Colorado	74.4
39	Indiana	74.3
40	Louisiana	74.2
40	Mississippi	74.2
42	Nevada	74.1
42	New Mexico	74.1
44	Georgia	73.6
45	California	73.3
45	Idaho	73.3
47	Arizona	73.1
48	Texas	72.1
49	Alaska	71.3
50	Utah	69.0

District of Columbia   80.2

Source: Morgan Quitno Press using data from U.S. Bureau of the Census
   "Table ST-EST2004-01res - Annual Estimates of the Resident Population" (February 25, 2005)
   (http://www.census.gov/popest/states/asrh/SC-est2004-01.html)

463

Population 18 to 24 Years Old in 2004

National Total = 29,245,102

ALPHA ORDER

RANK	STATE	POPULATION	% of USA
24	Alabama	455,878	1.6%
48	Alaska	73,960	0.3%
19	Arizona	570,795	2.0%
34	Arkansas	279,818	1.0%
1	California	3,596,126	12.3%
23	Colorado	456,691	1.6%
32	Connecticut	310,612	1.1%
46	Delaware	83,684	0.3%
4	Florida	1,549,324	5.3%
9	Georgia	901,607	3.1%
40	Hawaii	126,248	0.4%
39	Idaho	156,734	0.5%
5	Illinois	1,260,365	4.3%
14	Indiana	632,427	2.2%
30	Iowa	316,404	1.1%
33	Kansas	299,476	1.0%
26	Kentucky	412,635	1.4%
22	Louisiana	503,192	1.7%
41	Maine	124,451	0.4%
21	Maryland	521,202	1.8%
15	Massachusetts	598,047	2.0%
8	Michigan	996,571	3.4%
20	Minnesota	530,997	1.8%
29	Mississippi	323,150	1.1%
16	Missouri	589,309	2.0%
44	Montana	99,049	0.3%
37	Nebraska	190,767	0.7%
35	Nevada	209,851	0.7%
42	New Hampshire	122,278	0.4%
12	New Jersey	743,937	2.5%
36	New Mexico	206,085	0.7%
3	New York	1,825,192	6.2%
10	North Carolina	828,100	2.8%
47	North Dakota	76,665	0.3%
7	Ohio	1,127,662	3.9%
27	Oklahoma	385,439	1.3%
28	Oregon	350,458	1.2%
6	Pennsylvania	1,185,180	4.1%
43	Rhode Island	112,484	0.4%
25	South Carolina	428,864	1.5%
45	South Dakota	86,646	0.3%
17	Tennessee	575,689	2.0%
2	Texas	2,400,474	8.2%
31	Utah	312,896	1.1%
49	Vermont	62,080	0.2%
11	Virginia	748,049	2.6%
13	Washington	634,717	2.2%
38	West Virginia	172,806	0.6%
18	Wisconsin	574,901	2.0%
50	Wyoming	57,231	0.2%

RANK ORDER

RANK	STATE	POPULATION	% of USA
1	California	3,596,126	12.3%
2	Texas	2,400,474	8.2%
3	New York	1,825,192	6.2%
4	Florida	1,549,324	5.3%
5	Illinois	1,260,365	4.3%
6	Pennsylvania	1,185,180	4.1%
7	Ohio	1,127,662	3.9%
8	Michigan	996,571	3.4%
9	Georgia	901,607	3.1%
10	North Carolina	828,100	2.8%
11	Virginia	748,049	2.6%
12	New Jersey	743,937	2.5%
13	Washington	634,717	2.2%
14	Indiana	632,427	2.2%
15	Massachusetts	598,047	2.0%
16	Missouri	589,309	2.0%
17	Tennessee	575,689	2.0%
18	Wisconsin	574,901	2.0%
19	Arizona	570,795	2.0%
20	Minnesota	530,997	1.8%
21	Maryland	521,202	1.8%
22	Louisiana	503,192	1.7%
23	Colorado	456,691	1.6%
24	Alabama	455,878	1.6%
25	South Carolina	428,864	1.5%
26	Kentucky	412,635	1.4%
27	Oklahoma	385,439	1.3%
28	Oregon	350,458	1.2%
29	Mississippi	323,150	1.1%
30	Iowa	316,404	1.1%
31	Utah	312,896	1.1%
32	Connecticut	310,612	1.1%
33	Kansas	299,476	1.0%
34	Arkansas	279,818	1.0%
35	Nevada	209,851	0.7%
36	New Mexico	206,085	0.7%
37	Nebraska	190,767	0.7%
38	West Virginia	172,806	0.6%
39	Idaho	156,734	0.5%
40	Hawaii	126,248	0.4%
41	Maine	124,451	0.4%
42	New Hampshire	122,278	0.4%
43	Rhode Island	112,484	0.4%
44	Montana	99,049	0.3%
45	South Dakota	86,646	0.3%
46	Delaware	83,684	0.3%
47	North Dakota	76,665	0.3%
48	Alaska	73,960	0.3%
49	Vermont	62,080	0.2%
50	Wyoming	57,231	0.2%
	District of Columbia	57,899	0.2%

Source: U.S. Bureau of the Census
"Table ST-EST2004-01res - Annual Estimates of the Resident Population" (February 25, 2005)
(http://www.census.gov/popest/states/asrh/SC-est2004-01.html)

Percent of Population 18 to 24 Years Old in 2004

National Percent = 10.0% of Population

ALPHA ORDER

RANK	STATE	PERCENT
24	Alabama	10.1
3	Alaska	11.3
32	Arizona	9.9
19	Arkansas	10.2
27	California	10.0
32	Colorado	9.9
48	Connecticut	8.9
24	Delaware	10.1
48	Florida	8.9
19	Georgia	10.2
27	Hawaii	10.0
5	Idaho	11.2
32	Illinois	9.9
24	Indiana	10.1
13	Iowa	10.7
9	Kansas	10.9
27	Kentucky	10.0
7	Louisiana	11.1
43	Maine	9.4
43	Maryland	9.4
46	Massachusetts	9.3
32	Michigan	9.9
16	Minnesota	10.4
7	Mississippi	11.1
19	Missouri	10.2
13	Montana	10.7
9	Nebraska	10.9
47	Nevada	9.0
43	New Hampshire	9.4
50	New Jersey	8.6
12	New Mexico	10.8
41	New York	9.5
38	North Carolina	9.7
2	North Dakota	12.1
36	Ohio	9.8
9	Oklahoma	10.9
38	Oregon	9.7
40	Pennsylvania	9.6
16	Rhode Island	10.4
19	South Carolina	10.2
5	South Dakota	11.2
36	Tennessee	9.8
13	Texas	10.7
1	Utah	13.1
27	Vermont	10.0
27	Virginia	10.0
19	Washington	10.2
41	West Virginia	9.5
16	Wisconsin	10.4
3	Wyoming	11.3

RANK ORDER

RANK	STATE	PERCENT
1	Utah	13.1
2	North Dakota	12.1
3	Alaska	11.3
3	Wyoming	11.3
5	Idaho	11.2
5	South Dakota	11.2
7	Louisiana	11.1
7	Mississippi	11.1
9	Kansas	10.9
9	Nebraska	10.9
9	Oklahoma	10.9
12	New Mexico	10.8
13	Iowa	10.7
13	Montana	10.7
13	Texas	10.7
16	Minnesota	10.4
16	Rhode Island	10.4
16	Wisconsin	10.4
19	Arkansas	10.2
19	Georgia	10.2
19	Missouri	10.2
19	South Carolina	10.2
19	Washington	10.2
24	Alabama	10.1
24	Delaware	10.1
24	Indiana	10.1
27	California	10.0
27	Hawaii	10.0
27	Kentucky	10.0
27	Vermont	10.0
27	Virginia	10.0
32	Arizona	9.9
32	Colorado	9.9
32	Illinois	9.9
32	Michigan	9.9
36	Ohio	9.8
36	Tennessee	9.8
38	North Carolina	9.7
38	Oregon	9.7
40	Pennsylvania	9.6
41	New York	9.5
41	West Virginia	9.5
43	Maine	9.4
43	Maryland	9.4
43	New Hampshire	9.4
46	Massachusetts	9.3
47	Nevada	9.0
48	Connecticut	8.9
48	Florida	8.9
50	New Jersey	8.6

	District of Columbia	10.5

Source: Morgan Quitno Press using data from U.S. Bureau of the Census
"Table ST-EST2004-01res - Annual Estimates of the Resident Population" (February 25, 2005)
(http://www.census.gov/popest/states/asrh/SC-est2004-01.html)

Population 25 to 44 Years Old in 2004

National Total = 84,140,590

ALPHA ORDER

RANK	STATE	POPULATION	% of USA
23	Alabama	1,253,740	1.5%
47	Alaska	182,955	0.2%
17	Arizona	1,630,429	1.9%
33	Arkansas	745,046	0.9%
1	California	10,793,157	12.8%
22	Colorado	1,425,841	1.7%
28	Connecticut	973,944	1.2%
44	Delaware	238,132	0.3%
4	Florida	4,671,734	5.6%
9	Georgia	2,755,988	3.3%
42	Hawaii	341,359	0.4%
39	Idaho	376,582	0.4%
5	Illinois	3,703,357	4.4%
15	Indiana	1,733,724	2.1%
31	Iowa	787,033	0.9%
32	Kansas	746,056	0.9%
25	Kentucky	1,189,512	1.4%
24	Louisiana	1,239,938	1.5%
41	Maine	350,442	0.4%
18	Maryland	1,605,417	1.9%
13	Massachusetts	1,910,811	2.3%
8	Michigan	2,819,898	3.4%
21	Minnesota	1,471,584	1.7%
30	Mississippi	796,095	0.9%
19	Missouri	1,596,315	1.9%
45	Montana	234,483	0.3%
38	Nebraska	473,637	0.6%
34	Nevada	710,299	0.8%
40	New Hampshire	364,920	0.4%
11	New Jersey	2,511,298	3.0%
36	New Mexico	501,746	0.6%
3	New York	5,626,026	6.7%
10	North Carolina	2,531,063	3.0%
48	North Dakota	165,758	0.2%
7	Ohio	3,147,813	3.7%
29	Oklahoma	958,067	1.1%
27	Oregon	1,016,650	1.2%
6	Pennsylvania	3,294,379	3.9%
43	Rhode Island	305,401	0.4%
26	South Carolina	1,179,222	1.4%
46	South Dakota	198,636	0.2%
16	Tennessee	1,714,986	2.0%
2	Texas	6,673,546	7.9%
35	Utah	690,645	0.8%
49	Vermont	164,655	0.2%
12	Virginia	2,188,434	2.6%
14	Washington	1,815,067	2.2%
37	West Virginia	478,437	0.6%
20	Wisconsin	1,535,043	1.8%
50	Wyoming	130,452	0.2%

RANK ORDER

RANK	STATE	POPULATION	% of USA
1	California	10,793,157	12.8%
2	Texas	6,673,546	7.9%
3	New York	5,626,026	6.7%
4	Florida	4,671,734	5.6%
5	Illinois	3,703,357	4.4%
6	Pennsylvania	3,294,379	3.9%
7	Ohio	3,147,813	3.7%
8	Michigan	2,819,898	3.4%
9	Georgia	2,755,988	3.3%
10	North Carolina	2,531,063	3.0%
11	New Jersey	2,511,298	3.0%
12	Virginia	2,188,434	2.6%
13	Massachusetts	1,910,811	2.3%
14	Washington	1,815,067	2.2%
15	Indiana	1,733,724	2.1%
16	Tennessee	1,714,986	2.0%
17	Arizona	1,630,429	1.9%
18	Maryland	1,605,417	1.9%
19	Missouri	1,596,315	1.9%
20	Wisconsin	1,535,043	1.8%
21	Minnesota	1,471,584	1.7%
22	Colorado	1,425,841	1.7%
23	Alabama	1,253,740	1.5%
24	Louisiana	1,239,938	1.5%
25	Kentucky	1,189,512	1.4%
26	South Carolina	1,179,222	1.4%
27	Oregon	1,016,650	1.2%
28	Connecticut	973,944	1.2%
29	Oklahoma	958,067	1.1%
30	Mississippi	796,095	0.9%
31	Iowa	787,033	0.9%
32	Kansas	746,056	0.9%
33	Arkansas	745,046	0.9%
34	Nevada	710,299	0.8%
35	Utah	690,645	0.8%
36	New Mexico	501,746	0.6%
37	West Virginia	478,437	0.6%
38	Nebraska	473,637	0.6%
39	Idaho	376,582	0.4%
40	New Hampshire	364,920	0.4%
41	Maine	350,442	0.4%
42	Hawaii	341,359	0.4%
43	Rhode Island	305,401	0.4%
44	Delaware	238,132	0.3%
45	Montana	234,483	0.3%
46	South Dakota	198,636	0.2%
47	Alaska	182,955	0.2%
48	North Dakota	165,758	0.2%
49	Vermont	164,655	0.2%
50	Wyoming	130,452	0.2%
	District of Columbia	190,838	0.2%

Source: Morgan Quitno Press using data from U.S. Bureau of the Census
"SC-EST2004-AGESEX_RES - State Characteristic Estimates"
(http://www.census.gov/popest/datasets.html)

Percent of Population 25 to 44 Years Old in 2004

National Percent = 28.7% of Population

ALPHA ORDER

RANK	STATE	PERCENT
29	Alabama	27.7
24	Alaska	27.9
19	Arizona	28.4
36	Arkansas	27.1
4	California	30.1
2	Colorado	31.0
27	Connecticut	27.8
17	Delaware	28.7
40	Florida	26.9
1	Georgia	31.2
38	Hawaii	27.0
38	Idaho	27.0
11	Illinois	29.1
27	Indiana	27.8
41	Iowa	26.6
34	Kansas	27.3
17	Kentucky	28.7
31	Louisiana	27.5
41	Maine	26.6
13	Maryland	28.9
5	Massachusetts	29.8
24	Michigan	27.9
16	Minnesota	28.8
33	Mississippi	27.4
29	Missouri	27.7
50	Montana	25.3
36	Nebraska	27.1
3	Nevada	30.4
22	New Hampshire	28.1
13	New Jersey	28.9
45	New Mexico	26.4
8	New York	29.3
7	North Carolina	29.6
47	North Dakota	26.1
31	Ohio	27.5
35	Oklahoma	27.2
20	Oregon	28.3
41	Pennsylvania	26.6
20	Rhode Island	28.3
22	South Carolina	28.1
48	South Dakota	25.8
11	Tennessee	29.1
6	Texas	29.7
13	Utah	28.9
44	Vermont	26.5
8	Virginia	29.3
8	Washington	29.3
45	West Virginia	26.4
24	Wisconsin	27.9
48	Wyoming	25.8

RANK ORDER

RANK	STATE	PERCENT
1	Georgia	31.2
2	Colorado	31.0
3	Nevada	30.4
4	California	30.1
5	Massachusetts	29.8
6	Texas	29.7
7	North Carolina	29.6
8	New York	29.3
8	Virginia	29.3
8	Washington	29.3
11	Illinois	29.1
11	Tennessee	29.1
13	Maryland	28.9
13	New Jersey	28.9
13	Utah	28.9
16	Minnesota	28.8
17	Delaware	28.7
17	Kentucky	28.7
19	Arizona	28.4
20	Oregon	28.3
20	Rhode Island	28.3
22	New Hampshire	28.1
22	South Carolina	28.1
24	Alaska	27.9
24	Michigan	27.9
24	Wisconsin	27.9
27	Connecticut	27.8
27	Indiana	27.8
29	Alabama	27.7
29	Missouri	27.7
31	Louisiana	27.5
31	Ohio	27.5
33	Mississippi	27.4
34	Kansas	27.3
35	Oklahoma	27.2
36	Arkansas	27.1
36	Nebraska	27.1
38	Hawaii	27.0
38	Idaho	27.0
40	Florida	26.9
41	Iowa	26.6
41	Maine	26.6
41	Pennsylvania	26.6
44	Vermont	26.5
45	New Mexico	26.4
45	West Virginia	26.4
47	North Dakota	26.1
48	South Dakota	25.8
48	Wyoming	25.8
50	Montana	25.3

District of Columbia 34.5

Source: Morgan Quitno Press using data from U.S. Bureau of the Census
*   "SC-EST2004-AGESEX_RES - State Characteristic Estimates"*
*   (http://www.census.gov/popest/datasets.html)*

Population 45 to 64 Years Old in 2004

National Total = 70,697,729

ALPHA ORDER

ALPHA ORDER

RANK	STATE	POPULATION	% of USA
22	Alabama	1,128,072	1.6%
48	Alaska	168,404	0.2%
20	Arizona	1,263,279	1.8%
32	Arkansas	670,109	0.9%
1	California	8,085,096	11.4%
23	Colorado	1,089,011	1.5%
28	Connecticut	906,567	1.3%
45	Delaware	206,081	0.3%
4	Florida	4,245,230	6.0%
11	Georgia	1,992,139	2.8%
42	Hawaii	324,532	0.5%
41	Idaho	328,840	0.5%
6	Illinois	2,991,133	4.2%
15	Indiana	1,499,113	2.1%
30	Iowa	737,438	1.0%
33	Kansas	651,900	0.9%
26	Kentucky	1,044,261	1.5%
24	Louisiana	1,080,035	1.5%
39	Maine	370,480	0.5%
18	Maryland	1,401,888	2.0%
13	Massachusetts	1,589,115	2.2%
8	Michigan	2,516,117	3.6%
21	Minnesota	1,242,918	1.8%
31	Mississippi	681,285	1.0%
17	Missouri	1,418,760	2.0%
44	Montana	258,691	0.4%
38	Nebraska	416,441	0.6%
34	Nevada	548,946	0.8%
40	New Hampshire	350,636	0.5%
9	New Jersey	2,161,444	3.1%
36	New Mexico	473,697	0.7%
3	New York	4,710,691	6.7%
10	North Carolina	2,031,317	2.9%
49	North Dakota	159,817	0.2%
7	Ohio	2,879,408	4.1%
29	Oklahoma	855,737	1.2%
27	Oregon	915,300	1.3%
5	Pennsylvania	3,193,221	4.5%
43	Rhode Island	268,347	0.4%
25	South Carolina	1,044,890	1.5%
46	South Dakota	185,234	0.3%
16	Tennessee	1,480,945	2.1%
2	Texas	4,932,613	7.0%
37	Utah	437,673	0.6%
47	Vermont	179,003	0.3%
12	Virginia	1,871,523	2.6%
14	Washington	1,564,839	2.2%
35	West Virginia	501,116	0.7%
19	Wisconsin	1,375,528	1.9%
50	Wyoming	140,801	0.2%

RANK ORDER

RANK	STATE	POPULATION	% of USA
1	California	8,085,096	11.4%
2	Texas	4,932,613	7.0%
3	New York	4,710,691	6.7%
4	Florida	4,245,230	6.0%
5	Pennsylvania	3,193,221	4.5%
6	Illinois	2,991,133	4.2%
7	Ohio	2,879,408	4.1%
8	Michigan	2,516,117	3.6%
9	New Jersey	2,161,444	3.1%
10	North Carolina	2,031,317	2.9%
11	Georgia	1,992,139	2.8%
12	Virginia	1,871,523	2.6%
13	Massachusetts	1,589,115	2.2%
14	Washington	1,564,839	2.2%
15	Indiana	1,499,113	2.1%
16	Tennessee	1,480,945	2.1%
17	Missouri	1,418,760	2.0%
18	Maryland	1,401,888	2.0%
19	Wisconsin	1,375,528	1.9%
20	Arizona	1,263,279	1.8%
21	Minnesota	1,242,918	1.8%
22	Alabama	1,128,072	1.6%
23	Colorado	1,089,011	1.5%
24	Louisiana	1,080,035	1.5%
25	South Carolina	1,044,890	1.5%
26	Kentucky	1,044,261	1.5%
27	Oregon	915,300	1.3%
28	Connecticut	906,567	1.3%
29	Oklahoma	855,737	1.2%
30	Iowa	737,438	1.0%
31	Mississippi	681,285	1.0%
32	Arkansas	670,109	0.9%
33	Kansas	651,900	0.9%
34	Nevada	548,946	0.8%
35	West Virginia	501,116	0.7%
36	New Mexico	473,697	0.7%
37	Utah	437,673	0.6%
38	Nebraska	416,441	0.6%
39	Maine	370,480	0.5%
40	New Hampshire	350,636	0.5%
41	Idaho	328,840	0.5%
42	Hawaii	324,532	0.5%
43	Rhode Island	268,347	0.4%
44	Montana	258,691	0.4%
45	Delaware	206,081	0.3%
46	South Dakota	185,234	0.3%
47	Vermont	179,003	0.3%
48	Alaska	168,404	0.2%
49	North Dakota	159,817	0.2%
50	Wyoming	140,801	0.2%
	District of Columbia	128,068	0.2%

Source: U.S. Bureau of the Census
"Table ST-EST2004-01res - Annual Estimates of the Resident Population" (February 25, 2005)
(http://www.census.gov/popest/states/asrh/SC-est2004-01.html)

Percent of Population 45 to 64 Years Old in 2004

National Percent = 24.1% of Population

ALPHA ORDER

RANK	STATE	PERCENT
21	Alabama	24.9
8	Alaska	25.7
48	Arizona	22.0
33	Arkansas	24.3
47	California	22.5
41	Colorado	23.7
7	Connecticut	25.9
25	Delaware	24.8
31	Florida	24.4
46	Georgia	22.6
8	Hawaii	25.7
42	Idaho	23.6
43	Illinois	23.5
35	Indiana	24.0
19	Iowa	25.0
38	Kansas	23.8
12	Kentucky	25.2
37	Louisiana	23.9
2	Maine	28.1
12	Maryland	25.2
25	Massachusetts	24.8
21	Michigan	24.9
31	Minnesota	24.4
43	Mississippi	23.5
29	Missouri	24.7
3	Montana	27.9
38	Nebraska	23.8
43	Nevada	23.5
6	New Hampshire	27.0
25	New Jersey	24.8
21	New Mexico	24.9
30	New York	24.5
38	North Carolina	23.8
12	North Dakota	25.2
16	Ohio	25.1
33	Oklahoma	24.3
11	Oregon	25.5
8	Pennsylvania	25.7
25	Rhode Island	24.8
21	South Carolina	24.9
35	South Dakota	24.0
16	Tennessee	25.1
49	Texas	21.9
50	Utah	18.3
1	Vermont	28.8
16	Virginia	25.1
12	Washington	25.2
5	West Virginia	27.6
19	Wisconsin	25.0
4	Wyoming	27.8

RANK ORDER

RANK	STATE	PERCENT
1	Vermont	28.8
2	Maine	28.1
3	Montana	27.9
4	Wyoming	27.8
5	West Virginia	27.6
6	New Hampshire	27.0
7	Connecticut	25.9
8	Alaska	25.7
8	Hawaii	25.7
8	Pennsylvania	25.7
11	Oregon	25.5
12	Kentucky	25.2
12	Maryland	25.2
12	North Dakota	25.2
12	Washington	25.2
16	Ohio	25.1
16	Tennessee	25.1
16	Virginia	25.1
19	Iowa	25.0
19	Wisconsin	25.0
21	Alabama	24.9
21	Michigan	24.9
21	New Mexico	24.9
21	South Carolina	24.9
25	Delaware	24.8
25	Massachusetts	24.8
25	New Jersey	24.8
25	Rhode Island	24.8
29	Missouri	24.7
30	New York	24.5
31	Florida	24.4
31	Minnesota	24.4
33	Arkansas	24.3
33	Oklahoma	24.3
35	Indiana	24.0
35	South Dakota	24.0
37	Louisiana	23.9
38	Kansas	23.8
38	Nebraska	23.8
38	North Carolina	23.8
41	Colorado	23.7
42	Idaho	23.6
43	Illinois	23.5
43	Mississippi	23.5
43	Nevada	23.5
46	Georgia	22.6
47	California	22.5
48	Arizona	22.0
49	Texas	21.9
50	Utah	18.3

	District of Columbia	23.1

Source: Morgan Quitno Press using data from U.S. Bureau of the Census
"Table ST-EST2004-01res - Annual Estimates of the Resident Population" (February 25, 2005)
(http://www.census.gov/popest/states/asrh/SC-est2004-01.html)

Population 65 Years Old and Older in 2004

National Total = 36,293,985

RANK	STATE	POPULATION	% of USA
22	Alabama	597,959	1.6%
50	Alaska	41,887	0.1%
17	Arizona	732,071	2.0%
31	Arkansas	381,106	1.1%
1	California	3,822,957	10.5%
29	Colorado	450,971	1.2%
26	Connecticut	473,693	1.3%
46	Delaware	108,961	0.3%
2	Florida	2,927,583	8.1%
12	Georgia	847,082	2.3%
40	Hawaii	172,008	0.5%
41	Idaho	158,695	0.4%
7	Illinois	1,520,629	4.2%
14	Indiana	772,010	2.1%
30	Iowa	433,139	1.2%
32	Kansas	354,579	1.0%
25	Kentucky	519,327	1.4%
23	Louisiana	527,644	1.5%
39	Maine	189,751	0.5%
20	Maryland	634,743	1.7%
11	Massachusetts	854,343	2.4%
8	Michigan	1,246,595	3.4%
21	Minnesota	615,179	1.7%
33	Mississippi	352,867	1.0%
15	Missouri	765,692	2.1%
44	Montana	126,549	0.3%
36	Nebraska	231,803	0.6%
35	Nevada	262,079	0.7%
42	New Hampshire	156,672	0.4%
9	New Jersey	1,126,141	3.1%
37	New Mexico	229,474	0.6%
3	New York	2,492,816	6.9%
10	North Carolina	1,032,249	2.8%
47	North Dakota	93,171	0.3%
6	Ohio	1,524,916	4.2%
27	Oklahoma	464,440	1.3%
28	Oregon	459,821	1.3%
5	Pennsylvania	1,896,503	5.2%
43	Rhode Island	150,587	0.4%
24	South Carolina	520,392	1.4%
45	South Dakota	109,493	0.3%
16	Tennessee	738,053	2.0%
4	Texas	2,216,610	6.1%
38	Utah	207,711	0.6%
48	Vermont	80,762	0.2%
13	Virginia	846,921	2.3%
19	Washington	703,145	1.9%
34	West Virginia	278,354	0.8%
18	Wisconsin	715,568	2.0%
49	Wyoming	61,113	0.2%

RANK	STATE	POPULATION	% of USA
1	California	3,822,957	10.5%
2	Florida	2,927,583	8.1%
3	New York	2,492,816	6.9%
4	Texas	2,216,610	6.1%
5	Pennsylvania	1,896,503	5.2%
6	Ohio	1,524,916	4.2%
7	Illinois	1,520,629	4.2%
8	Michigan	1,246,595	3.4%
9	New Jersey	1,126,141	3.1%
10	North Carolina	1,032,249	2.8%
11	Massachusetts	854,343	2.4%
12	Georgia	847,082	2.3%
13	Virginia	846,921	2.3%
14	Indiana	772,010	2.1%
15	Missouri	765,692	2.1%
16	Tennessee	738,053	2.0%
17	Arizona	732,071	2.0%
18	Wisconsin	715,568	2.0%
19	Washington	703,145	1.9%
20	Maryland	634,743	1.7%
21	Minnesota	615,179	1.7%
22	Alabama	597,959	1.6%
23	Louisiana	527,644	1.5%
24	South Carolina	520,392	1.4%
25	Kentucky	519,327	1.4%
26	Connecticut	473,693	1.3%
27	Oklahoma	464,440	1.3%
28	Oregon	459,821	1.3%
29	Colorado	450,971	1.2%
30	Iowa	433,139	1.2%
31	Arkansas	381,106	1.1%
32	Kansas	354,579	1.0%
33	Mississippi	352,867	1.0%
34	West Virginia	278,354	0.8%
35	Nevada	262,079	0.7%
36	Nebraska	231,803	0.6%
37	New Mexico	229,474	0.6%
38	Utah	207,711	0.6%
39	Maine	189,751	0.5%
40	Hawaii	172,008	0.5%
41	Idaho	158,695	0.4%
42	New Hampshire	156,672	0.4%
43	Rhode Island	150,587	0.4%
44	Montana	126,549	0.3%
45	South Dakota	109,493	0.3%
46	Delaware	108,961	0.3%
47	North Dakota	93,171	0.3%
48	Vermont	80,762	0.2%
49	Wyoming	61,113	0.2%
50	Alaska	41,887	0.1%
	District of Columbia	67,171	0.2%

Source: U.S. Bureau of the Census
"Table ST-EST2004-01res - Annual Estimates of the Resident Population" (February 25, 2005)
(http://www.census.gov/popest/states/asrh/SC-est2004-01.html)

Percent of Population 65 Years Old and Older in 2004

National Percent = 12.4% of Population

ALPHA ORDER				RANK ORDER		
RANK	**STATE**	**PERCENT**		**RANK**	**STATE**	**PERCENT**
17	Alabama	13.2		1	Florida	16.8
50	Alaska	6.4		2	Pennsylvania	15.3
26	Arizona	12.7		2	West Virginia	15.3
9	Arkansas	13.8		4	Iowa	14.7
45	California	10.7		4	North Dakota	14.7
47	Colorado	9.8		6	Maine	14.4
12	Connecticut	13.5		7	South Dakota	14.2
19	Delaware	13.1		8	Rhode Island	13.9
1	Florida	16.8		9	Arkansas	13.8
48	Georgia	9.6		10	Montana	13.7
11	Hawaii	13.6		11	Hawaii	13.6
40	Idaho	11.4		12	Connecticut	13.5
38	Illinois	12.0		13	Massachusetts	13.3
29	Indiana	12.4		13	Missouri	13.3
4	Iowa	14.7		13	Nebraska	13.3
20	Kansas	13.0		13	Ohio	13.3
27	Kentucky	12.5		17	Alabama	13.2
39	Louisiana	11.7		17	Oklahoma	13.2
6	Maine	14.4		19	Delaware	13.1
40	Maryland	11.4		20	Kansas	13.0
13	Massachusetts	13.3		20	New York	13.0
31	Michigan	12.3		20	Vermont	13.0
33	Minnesota	12.1		20	Wisconsin	13.0
32	Mississippi	12.2		24	New Jersey	12.9
13	Missouri	13.3		25	Oregon	12.8
10	Montana	13.7		26	Arizona	12.7
13	Nebraska	13.3		27	Kentucky	12.5
44	Nevada	11.2		27	Tennessee	12.5
33	New Hampshire	12.1		29	Indiana	12.4
24	New Jersey	12.9		29	South Carolina	12.4
33	New Mexico	12.1		31	Michigan	12.3
20	New York	13.0		32	Mississippi	12.2
33	North Carolina	12.1		33	Minnesota	12.1
4	North Dakota	14.7		33	New Hampshire	12.1
13	Ohio	13.3		33	New Mexico	12.1
17	Oklahoma	13.2		33	North Carolina	12.1
25	Oregon	12.8		33	Wyoming	12.1
2	Pennsylvania	15.3		38	Illinois	12.0
8	Rhode Island	13.9		39	Louisiana	11.7
29	South Carolina	12.4		40	Idaho	11.4
7	South Dakota	14.2		40	Maryland	11.4
27	Tennessee	12.5		40	Virginia	11.4
46	Texas	9.9		43	Washington	11.3
49	Utah	8.7		44	Nevada	11.2
20	Vermont	13.0		45	California	10.7
40	Virginia	11.4		46	Texas	9.9
43	Washington	11.3		47	Colorado	9.8
2	West Virginia	15.3		48	Georgia	9.6
20	Wisconsin	13.0		49	Utah	8.7
33	Wyoming	12.1		50	Alaska	6.4
					District of Columbia	12.1

Source: Morgan Quitno Press using data from U.S. Bureau of the Census
"Table ST-EST2004-01res - Annual Estimates of the Resident Population" (February 25, 2005)
(http://www.census.gov/popest/states/asrh/SC-est2004-01.html)

Population 85 Years Old and Older in 2004

National Total = 4,859,631

ALPHA ORDER				RANK ORDER			
RANK	STATE	POPULATION	% of USA	RANK	STATE	POPULATION	% of USA
25	Alabama	66,170	1.4%	1	California	514,013	10.6%
50	Alaska	3,502	0.1%	2	Florida	379,572	7.8%
19	Arizona	85,886	1.8%	3	New York	353,883	7.3%
32	Arkansas	47,842	1.0%	4	Pennsylvania	290,886	6.0%
1	California	514,013	10.6%	5	Texas	245,992	5.1%
29	Colorado	55,636	1.1%	6	Illinois	219,387	4.5%
22	Connecticut	82,075	1.7%	7	Ohio	208,433	4.3%
47	Delaware	13,259	0.3%	8	Michigan	175,067	3.6%
2	Florida	379,572	7.8%	9	New Jersey	162,808	3.4%
18	Georgia	95,273	2.0%	10	Massachusetts	136,125	2.8%
39	Hawaii	25,344	0.5%	11	North Carolina	120,640	2.5%
42	Idaho	22,478	0.5%	12	Wisconsin	111,027	2.3%
6	Illinois	219,387	4.5%	13	Indiana	104,873	2.2%
13	Indiana	104,873	2.2%	14	Washington	103,259	2.1%
23	Iowa	72,373	1.5%	15	Virginia	102,561	2.1%
30	Kansas	55,055	1.1%	16	Missouri	100,379	2.1%
28	Kentucky	59,024	1.2%	17	Minnesota	98,215	2.0%
26	Louisiana	60,321	1.2%	18	Georgia	95,273	2.0%
40	Maine	25,091	0.5%	19	Arizona	85,886	1.8%
21	Maryland	82,752	1.7%	20	Tennessee	83,725	1.7%
10	Massachusetts	136,125	2.8%	21	Maryland	82,752	1.7%
8	Michigan	175,067	3.6%	22	Connecticut	82,075	1.7%
17	Minnesota	98,215	2.0%	23	Iowa	72,373	1.5%
33	Mississippi	39,632	0.8%	24	Oregon	69,898	1.4%
16	Missouri	100,379	2.1%	25	Alabama	66,170	1.4%
44	Montana	18,233	0.4%	26	Louisiana	60,321	1.2%
34	Nebraska	35,910	0.7%	27	South Carolina	59,451	1.2%
41	Nevada	24,000	0.5%	28	Kentucky	59,024	1.2%
43	New Hampshire	21,723	0.4%	29	Colorado	55,636	1.1%
9	New Jersey	162,808	3.4%	30	Kansas	55,055	1.1%
36	New Mexico	26,817	0.6%	31	Oklahoma	54,305	1.1%
3	New York	353,883	7.3%	32	Arkansas	47,842	1.0%
11	North Carolina	120,640	2.5%	33	Mississippi	39,632	0.8%
46	North Dakota	16,413	0.3%	34	Nebraska	35,910	0.7%
7	Ohio	208,433	4.3%	35	West Virginia	32,535	0.7%
31	Oklahoma	54,305	1.1%	36	New Mexico	26,817	0.6%
24	Oregon	69,898	1.4%	37	Rhode Island	26,290	0.5%
4	Pennsylvania	290,886	6.0%	38	Utah	25,700	0.5%
37	Rhode Island	26,290	0.5%	39	Hawaii	25,344	0.5%
27	South Carolina	59,451	1.2%	40	Maine	25,091	0.5%
45	South Dakota	17,658	0.4%	41	Nevada	24,000	0.5%
20	Tennessee	83,725	1.7%	42	Idaho	22,478	0.5%
5	Texas	245,992	5.1%	43	New Hampshire	21,723	0.4%
38	Utah	25,700	0.5%	44	Montana	18,233	0.4%
48	Vermont	11,478	0.2%	45	South Dakota	17,658	0.4%
15	Virginia	102,561	2.1%	46	North Dakota	16,413	0.3%
14	Washington	103,259	2.1%	47	Delaware	13,259	0.3%
35	West Virginia	32,535	0.7%	48	Vermont	11,478	0.2%
12	Wisconsin	111,027	2.3%	49	Wyoming	7,374	0.2%
49	Wyoming	7,374	0.2%	50	Alaska	3,502	0.1%
					District of Columbia	9,288	0.2%

Source: U.S. Bureau of the Census
"Table ST-EST2004-01res - Annual Estimates of the Resident Population" (February 25, 2005)
(http://www.census.gov/popest/states/asrh/SC-est2004-01.html)

Percent of Population 85 Years Old and Older in 2004

National Percent = 1.7% of Population

ALPHA ORDER				RANK ORDER		
RANK	STATE	PERCENT		RANK	STATE	PERCENT
31	Alabama	1.5		1	North Dakota	2.6
50	Alaska	0.5		2	Iowa	2.4
31	Arizona	1.5		2	Rhode Island	2.4
22	Arkansas	1.7		4	Connecticut	2.3
36	California	1.4		4	Pennsylvania	2.3
45	Colorado	1.2		4	South Dakota	2.3
4	Connecticut	2.3		7	Florida	2.2
29	Delaware	1.6		8	Massachusetts	2.1
7	Florida	2.2		8	Nebraska	2.1
46	Georgia	1.1		10	Hawaii	2.0
10	Hawaii	2.0		10	Kansas	2.0
29	Idaho	1.6		10	Montana	2.0
22	Illinois	1.7		10	Wisconsin	2.0
22	Indiana	1.7		14	Maine	1.9
2	Iowa	2.4		14	Minnesota	1.9
10	Kansas	2.0		14	New Jersey	1.9
36	Kentucky	1.4		14	Oregon	1.9
44	Louisiana	1.3		18	New York	1.8
14	Maine	1.9		18	Ohio	1.8
31	Maryland	1.5		18	Vermont	1.8
8	Massachusetts	2.1		18	West Virginia	1.8
22	Michigan	1.7		22	Arkansas	1.7
14	Minnesota	1.9		22	Illinois	1.7
36	Mississippi	1.4		22	Indiana	1.7
22	Missouri	1.7		22	Michigan	1.7
10	Montana	2.0		22	Missouri	1.7
8	Nebraska	2.1		22	New Hampshire	1.7
49	Nevada	1.0		22	Washington	1.7
22	New Hampshire	1.7		29	Delaware	1.6
14	New Jersey	1.9		29	Idaho	1.6
36	New Mexico	1.4		31	Alabama	1.5
18	New York	1.8		31	Arizona	1.5
36	North Carolina	1.4		31	Maryland	1.5
1	North Dakota	2.6		31	Oklahoma	1.5
18	Ohio	1.8		31	Wyoming	1.5
31	Oklahoma	1.5		36	California	1.4
14	Oregon	1.9		36	Kentucky	1.4
4	Pennsylvania	2.3		36	Mississippi	1.4
2	Rhode Island	2.4		36	New Mexico	1.4
36	South Carolina	1.4		36	North Carolina	1.4
4	South Dakota	2.3		36	South Carolina	1.4
36	Tennessee	1.4		36	Tennessee	1.4
46	Texas	1.1		36	Virginia	1.4
46	Utah	1.1		44	Louisiana	1.3
18	Vermont	1.8		45	Colorado	1.2
36	Virginia	1.4		46	Georgia	1.1
22	Washington	1.7		46	Texas	1.1
18	West Virginia	1.8		46	Utah	1.1
10	Wisconsin	2.0		49	Nevada	1.0
31	Wyoming	1.5		50	Alaska	0.5
					District of Columbia	1.7

Source: Morgan Quitno Press using data from U.S. Bureau of the Census
"Table ST-EST2004-01res - Annual Estimates of the Resident Population" (February 25, 2005)
(http://www.census.gov/popest/states/asrh/SC-est2004-01.html)

Percent of Native Population Born in Their State of Residence: 2004

National Percent = 67.5%

ALPHA ORDER		
RANK	STATE	PERCENT
9	Alabama	75.8
47	Alaska	42.3
49	Arizona	41.0
31	Arkansas	63.1
19	California	70.7
44	Colorado	46.1
30	Connecticut	63.2
41	Delaware	50.6
48	Florida	41.2
29	Georgia	63.7
20	Hawaii	69.3
43	Idaho	49.3
6	Illinois	76.1
11	Indiana	74.1
8	Iowa	75.9
31	Kansas	63.1
10	Kentucky	74.7
2	Louisiana	81.8
24	Maine	68.4
38	Maryland	54.9
7	Massachusetts	76.0
3	Michigan	80.5
11	Minnesota	74.1
14	Mississippi	73.8
22	Missouri	68.5
38	Montana	54.9
18	Nebraska	71.2
50	Nevada	28.1
45	New Hampshire	44.7
28	New Jersey	65.0
35	New Mexico	56.7
1	New York	82.5
26	North Carolina	67.1
15	North Dakota	73.3
5	Ohio	77.4
33	Oklahoma	62.8
41	Oregon	50.6
4	Pennsylvania	80.3
25	Rhode Island	67.9
34	South Carolina	61.5
21	South Dakota	68.6
27	Tennessee	66.3
16	Texas	71.8
22	Utah	68.5
37	Vermont	55.4
36	Virginia	55.7
40	Washington	52.4
17	West Virginia	71.7
13	Wisconsin	74.0
46	Wyoming	43.5

RANK ORDER		
RANK	STATE	PERCENT
1	New York	82.5
2	Louisiana	81.8
3	Michigan	80.5
4	Pennsylvania	80.3
5	Ohio	77.4
6	Illinois	76.1
7	Massachusetts	76.0
8	Iowa	75.9
9	Alabama	75.8
10	Kentucky	74.7
11	Indiana	74.1
11	Minnesota	74.1
13	Wisconsin	74.0
14	Mississippi	73.8
15	North Dakota	73.3
16	Texas	71.8
17	West Virginia	71.7
18	Nebraska	71.2
19	California	70.7
20	Hawaii	69.3
21	South Dakota	68.6
22	Missouri	68.5
22	Utah	68.5
24	Maine	68.4
25	Rhode Island	67.9
26	North Carolina	67.1
27	Tennessee	66.3
28	New Jersey	65.0
29	Georgia	63.7
30	Connecticut	63.2
31	Arkansas	63.1
31	Kansas	63.1
33	Oklahoma	62.8
34	South Carolina	61.5
35	New Mexico	56.7
36	Virginia	55.7
37	Vermont	55.4
38	Maryland	54.9
38	Montana	54.9
40	Washington	52.4
41	Delaware	50.6
41	Oregon	50.6
43	Idaho	49.3
44	Colorado	46.1
45	New Hampshire	44.7
46	Wyoming	43.5
47	Alaska	42.3
48	Florida	41.2
49	Arizona	41.0
50	Nevada	28.1
	District of Columbia	46.9

Source: U.S. Bureau of the Census
"2004 American Community Survey" (http://www.census.gov/acs/www/index.html)

Domestic Migration of Population: 2004 to 2005

National Net Migration = 0 People*

ALPHA ORDER

RANK	STATE	NET MIGRATION
14	Alabama	12,994
33	Alaska	(2,831)
2	Arizona	123,704
13	Arkansas	14,503
50	California	(239,417)
19	Colorado	5,497
43	Connecticut	(14,319)
17	Delaware	7,197
1	Florida	262,511
6	Georgia	46,437
32	Hawaii	(1,864)
11	Idaho	19,812
48	Illinois	(79,525)
21	Indiana	5,061
35	Iowa	(3,215)
39	Kansas	(9,998)
15	Kentucky	10,754
41	Louisiana	(12,849)
25	Maine	3,321
42	Maryland	(13,289)
47	Massachusetts	(60,053)
45	Michigan	(47,900)
38	Minnesota	(8,448)
27	Mississippi	942
16	Missouri	8,283
18	Montana	5,929
36	Nebraska	(3,286)
4	Nevada	55,715
23	New Hampshire	4,600
46	New Jersey	(56,989)
20	New Mexico	5,138
49	New York	(232,638)
3	North Carolina	66,383
34	North Dakota	(2,908)
44	Ohio	(39,976)
26	Oklahoma	1,070
9	Oregon	24,329
37	Pennsylvania	(5,078)
40	Rhode Island	(10,243)
8	South Carolina	31,556
28	South Dakota	828
7	Tennessee	38,792
5	Texas	51,067
22	Utah	4,970
31	Vermont	(453)
12	Virginia	14,889
10	Washington	24,072
24	West Virginia	4,250
30	Wisconsin	38
29	Wyoming	550

RANK ORDER

RANK	STATE	NET MIGRATION
1	Florida	262,511
2	Arizona	123,704
3	North Carolina	66,383
4	Nevada	55,715
5	Texas	51,067
6	Georgia	46,437
7	Tennessee	38,792
8	South Carolina	31,556
9	Oregon	24,329
10	Washington	24,072
11	Idaho	19,812
12	Virginia	14,889
13	Arkansas	14,503
14	Alabama	12,994
15	Kentucky	10,754
16	Missouri	8,283
17	Delaware	7,197
18	Montana	5,929
19	Colorado	5,497
20	New Mexico	5,138
21	Indiana	5,061
22	Utah	4,970
23	New Hampshire	4,600
24	West Virginia	4,250
25	Maine	3,321
26	Oklahoma	1,070
27	Mississippi	942
28	South Dakota	828
29	Wyoming	550
30	Wisconsin	38
31	Vermont	(453)
32	Hawaii	(1,864)
33	Alaska	(2,831)
34	North Dakota	(2,908)
35	Iowa	(3,215)
36	Nebraska	(3,286)
37	Pennsylvania	(5,078)
38	Minnesota	(8,448)
39	Kansas	(9,998)
40	Rhode Island	(10,243)
41	Louisiana	(12,849)
42	Maryland	(13,289)
43	Connecticut	(14,319)
44	Ohio	(39,976)
45	Michigan	(47,900)
46	New Jersey	(56,989)
47	Massachusetts	(60,053)
48	Illinois	(79,525)
49	New York	(232,638)
50	California	(239,417)
	District of Columbia	(9,913)

Source: U.S. Bureau of the Census
   "Components of Population Change" (http://www.census.gov/popest/datasets.html)
*From July 1, 2004 to July 1, 2005. Includes armed forces residing in each state. Net Domestic Migration is the difference between domestic inmigration to an area and domestic outmigration from it during the period. Domestic inmigration and outmigration consist of moves where both the origins and destinations are within the United States (excluding Puerto Rico).

Net International Migration: 2004 to 2005

National Net = 1,049,526 Immigrants*

ALPHA ORDER					RANK ORDER			
RANK	**STATE**	**IMMIGRANTS**	**% of USA**		**RANK**	**STATE**	**IMMIGRANTS**	**% of USA**
34	Alabama	4,418	0.4%		1	California	232,700	22.2%
43	Alaska	1,330	0.1%		2	Texas	109,467	10.4%
8	Arizona	27,626	2.6%		3	New York	108,811	10.4%
36	Arkansas	3,652	0.3%		4	Florida	87,222	8.3%
1	California	232,700	22.2%		5	Illinois	53,597	5.1%
14	Colorado	18,815	1.8%		6	New Jersey	47,392	4.5%
17	Connecticut	12,524	1.2%		7	Georgia	32,582	3.1%
41	Delaware	1,865	0.2%		8	Arizona	27,626	2.6%
4	Florida	87,222	8.3%		9	North Carolina	27,355	2.6%
7	Georgia	32,582	3.1%		10	Massachusetts	26,515	2.5%
30	Hawaii	5,699	0.5%		11	Virginia	25,552	2.4%
39	Idaho	2,427	0.2%		12	Washington	22,837	2.2%
5	Illinois	53,597	5.1%		13	Michigan	19,915	1.9%
22	Indiana	9,062	0.9%		14	Colorado	18,815	1.8%
32	Iowa	4,795	0.5%		15	Maryland	18,251	1.7%
28	Kansas	6,427	0.6%		16	Pennsylvania	16,668	1.6%
31	Kentucky	4,885	0.5%		17	Connecticut	12,524	1.2%
37	Louisiana	3,644	0.3%		18	Ohio	12,332	1.2%
44	Maine	883	0.1%		19	Oregon	11,706	1.1%
15	Maryland	18,251	1.7%		20	Minnesota	11,317	1.1%
10	Massachusetts	26,515	2.5%		21	Nevada	10,892	1.0%
13	Michigan	19,915	1.9%		22	Indiana	9,062	0.9%
20	Minnesota	11,317	1.1%		23	Tennessee	8,421	0.8%
40	Mississippi	2,005	0.2%		24	Utah	8,179	0.8%
26	Missouri	7,171	0.7%		25	Wisconsin	7,372	0.7%
50	Montana	405	0.0%		26	Missouri	7,171	0.7%
35	Nebraska	3,729	0.4%		27	South Carolina	6,545	0.6%
21	Nevada	10,892	1.0%		28	Kansas	6,427	0.6%
42	New Hampshire	1,809	0.2%		29	Oklahoma	6,285	0.6%
6	New Jersey	47,392	4.5%		30	Hawaii	5,699	0.5%
33	New Mexico	4,737	0.5%		31	Kentucky	4,885	0.5%
3	New York	108,811	10.4%		32	Iowa	4,795	0.5%
9	North Carolina	27,355	2.6%		33	New Mexico	4,737	0.5%
46	North Dakota	703	0.1%		34	Alabama	4,418	0.4%
18	Ohio	12,332	1.2%		35	Nebraska	3,729	0.4%
29	Oklahoma	6,285	0.6%		36	Arkansas	3,652	0.3%
19	Oregon	11,706	1.1%		37	Louisiana	3,644	0.3%
16	Pennsylvania	16,668	1.6%		38	Rhode Island	3,140	0.3%
38	Rhode Island	3,140	0.3%		39	Idaho	2,427	0.2%
27	South Carolina	6,545	0.6%		40	Mississippi	2,005	0.2%
45	South Dakota	706	0.1%		41	Delaware	1,865	0.2%
23	Tennessee	8,421	0.8%		42	New Hampshire	1,809	0.2%
2	Texas	109,467	10.4%		43	Alaska	1,330	0.1%
24	Utah	8,179	0.8%		44	Maine	883	0.1%
47	Vermont	684	0.1%		45	South Dakota	706	0.1%
11	Virginia	25,552	2.4%		46	North Dakota	703	0.1%
12	Washington	22,837	2.2%		47	Vermont	684	0.1%
48	West Virginia	613	0.1%		48	West Virginia	613	0.1%
25	Wisconsin	7,372	0.7%		49	Wyoming	424	0.0%
49	Wyoming	424	0.0%		50	Montana	405	0.0%
						District of Columbia	3,435	0.3%

Source: U.S. Bureau of the Census
   "Components of Population Change" (http://www.census.gov/popest/datasets.html)
*From July 1, 2004 to July 1, 2005. Net International Migration is the difference between migration to an area from
outside the United States (immigration) and migration from the area to outside the United States (emigration) during
the period. Includes legal immigration and estimates of undocumented immigration.

Percent of Population Foreign Born: 2004

National Percent = 12.0% of Population*

ALPHA ORDER

RANK	STATE	PERCENT
44	Alabama	2.5
23	Alaska	6.1
8	Arizona	14.4
37	Arkansas	3.6
1	California	26.8
15	Colorado	9.7
12	Connecticut	11.6
20	Delaware	7.6
6	Florida	17.9
19	Georgia	8.4
4	Hawaii	18.5
26	Idaho	5.9
10	Illinois	13.3
33	Indiana	3.9
40	Iowa	3.1
29	Kansas	4.8
46	Kentucky	2.4
43	Louisiana	2.9
41	Maine	3.0
14	Maryland	11.0
9	Massachusetts	13.7
23	Michigan	6.1
23	Minnesota	6.1
49	Mississippi	1.3
39	Missouri	3.2
48	Montana	1.6
27	Nebraska	4.9
5	Nevada	18.0
27	New Hampshire	4.9
3	New Jersey	18.8
17	New Mexico	9.2
2	New York	21.0
22	North Carolina	6.5
44	North Dakota	2.5
38	Ohio	3.5
31	Oklahoma	4.4
17	Oregon	9.2
30	Pennsylvania	4.7
11	Rhode Island	12.3
33	South Carolina	3.9
47	South Dakota	1.7
36	Tennessee	3.8
7	Texas	15.1
21	Utah	7.0
33	Vermont	3.9
16	Virginia	9.5
13	Washington	11.3
50	West Virginia	0.8
32	Wisconsin	4.1
41	Wyoming	3.0

RANK ORDER

RANK	STATE	PERCENT
1	California	26.8
2	New York	21.0
3	New Jersey	18.8
4	Hawaii	18.5
5	Nevada	18.0
6	Florida	17.9
7	Texas	15.1
8	Arizona	14.4
9	Massachusetts	13.7
10	Illinois	13.3
11	Rhode Island	12.3
12	Connecticut	11.6
13	Washington	11.3
14	Maryland	11.0
15	Colorado	9.7
16	Virginia	9.5
17	New Mexico	9.2
17	Oregon	9.2
19	Georgia	8.4
20	Delaware	7.6
21	Utah	7.0
22	North Carolina	6.5
23	Alaska	6.1
23	Michigan	6.1
23	Minnesota	6.1
26	Idaho	5.9
27	Nebraska	4.9
27	New Hampshire	4.9
29	Kansas	4.8
30	Pennsylvania	4.7
31	Oklahoma	4.4
32	Wisconsin	4.1
33	Indiana	3.9
33	South Carolina	3.9
33	Vermont	3.9
36	Tennessee	3.8
37	Arkansas	3.6
38	Ohio	3.5
39	Missouri	3.2
40	Iowa	3.1
41	Maine	3.0
41	Wyoming	3.0
43	Louisiana	2.9
44	Alabama	2.5
44	North Dakota	2.5
46	Kentucky	2.4
47	South Dakota	1.7
48	Montana	1.6
49	Mississippi	1.3
50	West Virginia	0.8

| District of Columbia | | 13.1 |

Source: U.S. Bureau of the Census
      "2004 American Community Survey" (http://www.census.gov/acs/www/index.html)
*"Foreign born" are persons not born in the United States, Puerto Rico, a U.S. Island Area or abroad of American parent or parents.

Percent of Population Speaking a Language Other Than English in 2004

National Percent = 18.7%*

RANK	STATE	PERCENT
48	Alabama	3.4
19	Alaska	12.7
7	Arizona	25.4
38	Arkansas	5.6
1	California	41.3
14	Colorado	16.1
13	Connecticut	18.9
21	Delaware	11.1
9	Florida	24.3
22	Georgia	11.0
8	Hawaii	24.4
23	Idaho	10.6
10	Illinois	20.4
25	Indiana	8.9
41	Iowa	5.4
30	Kansas	8.0
45	Kentucky	4.2
31	Louisiana	7.7
35	Maine	7.4
16	Maryland	13.8
12	Massachusetts	19.5
25	Michigan	8.9
24	Minnesota	10.2
49	Mississippi	2.5
43	Missouri	5.2
47	Montana	3.6
29	Nebraska	8.2
6	Nevada	25.5
31	New Hampshire	7.7
5	New Jersey	26.6
2	New Mexico	36.4
4	New York	27.3
27	North Carolina	8.7
39	North Dakota	5.5
36	Ohio	5.9
33	Oklahoma	7.5
17	Oregon	12.9
28	Pennsylvania	8.5
11	Rhode Island	19.8
42	South Carolina	5.3
45	South Dakota	4.2
39	Tennessee	5.5
3	Texas	32.0
20	Utah	12.1
43	Vermont	5.2
18	Virginia	12.8
15	Washington	15.2
50	West Virginia	2.1
33	Wisconsin	7.5
36	Wyoming	5.9

RANK	STATE	PERCENT
1	California	41.3
2	New Mexico	36.4
3	Texas	32.0
4	New York	27.3
5	New Jersey	26.6
6	Nevada	25.5
7	Arizona	25.4
8	Hawaii	24.4
9	Florida	24.3
10	Illinois	20.4
11	Rhode Island	19.8
12	Massachusetts	19.5
13	Connecticut	18.9
14	Colorado	16.1
15	Washington	15.2
16	Maryland	13.8
17	Oregon	12.9
18	Virginia	12.8
19	Alaska	12.7
20	Utah	12.1
21	Delaware	11.1
22	Georgia	11.0
23	Idaho	10.6
24	Minnesota	10.2
25	Indiana	8.9
25	Michigan	8.9
27	North Carolina	8.7
28	Pennsylvania	8.5
29	Nebraska	8.2
30	Kansas	8.0
31	Louisiana	7.7
31	New Hampshire	7.7
33	Oklahoma	7.5
33	Wisconsin	7.5
35	Maine	7.4
36	Ohio	5.9
36	Wyoming	5.9
38	Arkansas	5.6
39	North Dakota	5.5
39	Tennessee	5.5
41	Iowa	5.4
42	South Carolina	5.3
43	Missouri	5.2
43	Vermont	5.2
45	Kentucky	4.2
45	South Dakota	4.2
47	Montana	3.6
48	Alabama	3.4
49	Mississippi	2.5
50	West Virginia	2.1
	District of Columbia	16.2

Source: U.S. Bureau of the Census
   "2004 American Community Survey" (http://www.census.gov/acs/www/index.html)
*Population five years old and older.

Percent of Population Speaking Spanish at Home in 2004

National Percent = 11.5%*

ALPHA ORDER

RANK	STATE	PERCENT
38	Alabama	2.0
33	Alaska	3.0
4	Arizona	19.8
26	Arkansas	4.0
3	California	27.6
10	Colorado	11.7
11	Connecticut	8.9
23	Delaware	5.3
6	Florida	17.9
17	Georgia	6.5
46	Hawaii	1.3
14	Idaho	7.2
9	Illinois	11.9
28	Indiana	3.9
35	Iowa	2.7
25	Kansas	4.5
38	Kentucky	2.0
37	Louisiana	2.5
48	Maine	0.9
19	Maryland	5.6
16	Massachusetts	6.8
35	Michigan	2.7
30	Minnesota	3.5
43	Mississippi	1.6
38	Missouri	2.0
44	Montana	1.5
22	Nebraska	5.4
5	Nevada	18.7
42	New Hampshire	1.8
8	New Jersey	13.3
1	New Mexico	29.2
7	New York	13.5
19	North Carolina	5.6
47	North Dakota	1.2
41	Ohio	1.9
24	Oklahoma	4.7
14	Oregon	7.2
31	Pennsylvania	3.3
12	Rhode Island	8.7
32	South Carolina	3.2
44	South Dakota	1.5
33	Tennessee	3.0
2	Texas	27.7
13	Utah	7.9
49	Vermont	0.8
21	Virginia	5.5
18	Washington	6.2
49	West Virginia	0.8
29	Wisconsin	3.6
26	Wyoming	4.0

RANK ORDER

RANK	STATE	PERCENT
1	New Mexico	29.2
2	Texas	27.7
3	California	27.6
4	Arizona	19.8
5	Nevada	18.7
6	Florida	17.9
7	New York	13.5
8	New Jersey	13.3
9	Illinois	11.9
10	Colorado	11.7
11	Connecticut	8.9
12	Rhode Island	8.7
13	Utah	7.9
14	Idaho	7.2
14	Oregon	7.2
16	Massachusetts	6.8
17	Georgia	6.5
18	Washington	6.2
19	Maryland	5.6
19	North Carolina	5.6
21	Virginia	5.5
22	Nebraska	5.4
23	Delaware	5.3
24	Oklahoma	4.7
25	Kansas	4.5
26	Arkansas	4.0
26	Wyoming	4.0
28	Indiana	3.9
29	Wisconsin	3.6
30	Minnesota	3.5
31	Pennsylvania	3.3
32	South Carolina	3.2
33	Alaska	3.0
33	Tennessee	3.0
35	Iowa	2.7
35	Michigan	2.7
37	Louisiana	2.5
38	Alabama	2.0
38	Kentucky	2.0
38	Missouri	2.0
41	Ohio	1.9
42	New Hampshire	1.8
43	Mississippi	1.6
44	Montana	1.5
44	South Dakota	1.5
46	Hawaii	1.3
47	North Dakota	1.2
48	Maine	0.9
49	Vermont	0.8
49	West Virginia	0.8
	District of Columbia	9.1

Source: U.S. Bureau of the Census
"2004 American Community Survey" (http://www.census.gov/acs/www/index.html)
*Population five years old and older.

Marriages in 2004

National Total = 2,223,822 Marriages*

ALPHA ORDER

RANK	STATE	MARRIAGES	% of USA
16	Alabama	42,536	1.9%
47	Alaska	5,594	0.3%
21	Arizona	37,882	1.7%
22	Arkansas	36,806	1.7%
2	California	172,302	7.7%
27	Colorado	33,826	1.5%
34	Connecticut	20,240	0.9%
48	Delaware	5,095	0.2%
3	Florida	156,370	7.0%
9	Georgia	68,897	3.1%
30	Hawaii	28,843	1.3%
37	Idaho	14,997	0.7%
6	Illinois	77,845	3.5%
15	Indiana	48,354	2.2%
33	Iowa	20,455	0.9%
35	Kansas	19,072	0.9%
23	Kentucky	36,391	1.6%
24	Louisiana	36,282	1.6%
41	Maine	11,234	0.5%
20	Maryland	38,318	1.7%
17	Massachusetts	41,549	1.9%
13	Michigan	61,932	2.8%
28	Minnesota	30,359	1.4%
36	Mississippi	17,705	0.8%
18	Missouri	40,824	1.8%
44	Montana	6,946	0.3%
40	Nebraska	12,489	0.6%
4	Nevada	145,763	6.6%
42	New Hampshire	10,383	0.5%
14	New Jersey	50,662	2.3%
38	New Mexico	14,067	0.6%
5	New York	130,813	5.9%
11	North Carolina	62,235	2.8%
50	North Dakota	4,424	0.2%
7	Ohio	75,287	3.4%
32	Oklahoma	22,812	1.0%
29	Oregon	29,040	1.3%
8	Pennsylvania	73,599	3.3%
43	Rhode Island	8,243	0.4%
25	South Carolina	34,546	1.6%
45	South Dakota	6,485	0.3%
10	Tennessee	67,104	3.0%
1	Texas	178,512	8.0%
31	Utah	23,796	1.1%
46	Vermont	5,835	0.3%
12	Virginia	61,990	2.8%
19	Washington	40,169	1.8%
39	West Virginia	13,621	0.6%
26	Wisconsin	34,056	1.5%
49	Wyoming	4,740	0.2%

RANK ORDER

RANK	STATE	MARRIAGES	% of USA
1	Texas	178,512	8.0%
2	California	172,302	7.7%
3	Florida	156,370	7.0%
4	Nevada	145,763	6.6%
5	New York	130,813	5.9%
6	Illinois	77,845	3.5%
7	Ohio	75,287	3.4%
8	Pennsylvania	73,599	3.3%
9	Georgia	68,897	3.1%
10	Tennessee	67,104	3.0%
11	North Carolina	62,235	2.8%
12	Virginia	61,990	2.8%
13	Michigan	61,932	2.8%
14	New Jersey	50,662	2.3%
15	Indiana	48,354	2.2%
16	Alabama	42,536	1.9%
17	Massachusetts	41,549	1.9%
18	Missouri	40,824	1.8%
19	Washington	40,169	1.8%
20	Maryland	38,318	1.7%
21	Arizona	37,882	1.7%
22	Arkansas	36,806	1.7%
23	Kentucky	36,391	1.6%
24	Louisiana	36,282	1.6%
25	South Carolina	34,546	1.6%
26	Wisconsin	34,056	1.5%
27	Colorado	33,826	1.5%
28	Minnesota	30,359	1.4%
29	Oregon	29,040	1.3%
30	Hawaii	28,843	1.3%
31	Utah	23,796	1.1%
32	Oklahoma	22,812	1.0%
33	Iowa	20,455	0.9%
34	Connecticut	20,240	0.9%
35	Kansas	19,072	0.9%
36	Mississippi	17,705	0.8%
37	Idaho	14,997	0.7%
38	New Mexico	14,067	0.6%
39	West Virginia	13,621	0.6%
40	Nebraska	12,489	0.6%
41	Maine	11,234	0.5%
42	New Hampshire	10,383	0.5%
43	Rhode Island	8,243	0.4%
44	Montana	6,946	0.3%
45	South Dakota	6,485	0.3%
46	Vermont	5,835	0.3%
47	Alaska	5,594	0.3%
48	Delaware	5,095	0.2%
49	Wyoming	4,740	0.2%
50	North Dakota	4,424	0.2%
	District of Columbia	2,497	0.1%

*Source: U.S. Department of Health and Human Services, National Center for Health Statistics
"National Vital Statistics Reports" (Vol. 53, No. 21, June 28, 2005)*

Provisional data by state of occurrence.

Marriage Rate in 2004

National Rate = 7.6 Marriages per 1,000 Population*

ALPHA ORDER

RANK	STATE	RATE
7	Alabama	9.4
12	Alaska	8.5
36	Arizona	6.6
3	Arkansas	13.4
50	California	4.8
26	Colorado	7.4
48	Connecticut	5.8
42	Delaware	6.1
10	Florida	9.0
22	Georgia	7.7
2	Hawaii	22.9
5	Idaho	10.7
42	Illinois	6.1
21	Indiana	7.8
33	Iowa	6.9
31	Kansas	7.0
11	Kentucky	8.8
17	Louisiana	8.1
12	Maine	8.5
33	Maryland	6.9
38	Massachusetts	6.5
42	Michigan	6.1
46	Minnesota	6.0
42	Mississippi	6.1
29	Missouri	7.1
24	Montana	7.5
29	Nebraska	7.1
1	Nevada	62.5
19	New Hampshire	8.0
48	New Jersey	5.8
26	New Mexico	7.4
35	New York	6.8
28	North Carolina	7.3
31	North Dakota	7.0
36	Ohio	6.6
38	Oklahoma	6.5
17	Oregon	8.1
47	Pennsylvania	5.9
23	Rhode Island	7.6
16	South Carolina	8.2
14	South Dakota	8.4
4	Tennessee	11.4
20	Texas	7.9
6	Utah	9.8
7	Vermont	9.4
15	Virginia	8.3
38	Washington	6.5
24	West Virginia	7.5
41	Wisconsin	6.2
7	Wyoming	9.4

RANK ORDER

RANK	STATE	RATE
1	Nevada	62.5
2	Hawaii	22.9
3	Arkansas	13.4
4	Tennessee	11.4
5	Idaho	10.7
6	Utah	9.8
7	Alabama	9.4
7	Vermont	9.4
7	Wyoming	9.4
10	Florida	9.0
11	Kentucky	8.8
12	Alaska	8.5
12	Maine	8.5
14	South Dakota	8.4
15	Virginia	8.3
16	South Carolina	8.2
17	Louisiana	8.1
17	Oregon	8.1
19	New Hampshire	8.0
20	Texas	7.9
21	Indiana	7.8
22	Georgia	7.7
23	Rhode Island	7.6
24	Montana	7.5
24	West Virginia	7.5
26	Colorado	7.4
26	New Mexico	7.4
28	North Carolina	7.3
29	Missouri	7.1
29	Nebraska	7.1
31	Kansas	7.0
31	North Dakota	7.0
33	Iowa	6.9
33	Maryland	6.9
35	New York	6.8
36	Arizona	6.6
36	Ohio	6.6
38	Massachusetts	6.5
38	Oklahoma	6.5
38	Washington	6.5
41	Wisconsin	6.2
42	Delaware	6.1
42	Illinois	6.1
42	Michigan	6.1
42	Mississippi	6.1
46	Minnesota	6.0
47	Pennsylvania	5.9
48	Connecticut	5.8
48	New Jersey	5.8
50	California	4.8
	District of Columbia	4.5

Source: Morgan Quitno Press using data from U.S. Dept. of Health and Human Services, Nat'l Center for Health Statistics "National Vital Statistics Reports" (Vol. 53, No. 21, June 28, 2005)

*Provisional data by state of occurrence.

Estimated Median Age of Men at First Marriage: 2003

National Median = 26.7 Years*

ALPHA ORDER			RANK ORDER		
RANK	**STATE**	**YEARS**	**RANK**	**STATE**	**YEARS**
44	Alabama	25.5	1	Massachusetts	29.1
40	Alaska	25.7	2	Connecticut	28.9
29	Arizona	26.1	2	New York	28.9
47	Arkansas	25.0	4	New Jersey	28.6
9	California	27.2	5	Hawaii	27.8
24	Colorado	26.4	5	Vermont	27.8
2	Connecticut	28.9	7	Pennsylvania	27.6
14	Delaware	27.0	7	Rhode Island	27.6
11	Florida	27.1	9	California	27.2
26	Georgia	26.3	9	New Hampshire	27.2
5	Hawaii	27.8	11	Florida	27.1
49	Idaho	24.6	11	Maryland	27.1
14	Illinois	27.0	11	Michigan	27.1
29	Indiana	26.1	14	Delaware	27.0
33	Iowa	25.9	14	Illinois	27.0
44	Kansas	25.5	14	Virginia	27.0
46	Kentucky	25.3	17	North Dakota	26.9
31	Louisiana	26.0	17	Wisconsin	26.9
19	Maine	26.6	19	Maine	26.6
11	Maryland	27.1	19	Minnesota	26.6
1	Massachusetts	29.1	19	Ohio	26.6
11	Michigan	27.1	19	Oregon	26.6
19	Minnesota	26.6	23	Washington	26.5
36	Mississippi	25.8	24	Colorado	26.4
36	Missouri	25.8	24	South Carolina	26.4
28	Montana	26.2	26	Georgia	26.3
31	Nebraska	26.0	26	Nevada	26.3
26	Nevada	26.3	28	Montana	26.2
9	New Hampshire	27.2	29	Arizona	26.1
4	New Jersey	28.6	29	Indiana	26.1
33	New Mexico	25.9	31	Louisiana	26.0
2	New York	28.9	31	Nebraska	26.0
36	North Carolina	25.8	33	Iowa	25.9
17	North Dakota	26.9	33	New Mexico	25.9
19	Ohio	26.6	33	West Virginia	25.9
48	Oklahoma	24.9	36	Mississippi	25.8
19	Oregon	26.6	36	Missouri	25.8
7	Pennsylvania	27.6	36	North Carolina	25.8
7	Rhode Island	27.6	36	South Dakota	25.8
24	South Carolina	26.4	40	Alaska	25.7
36	South Dakota	25.8	40	Tennessee	25.7
40	Tennessee	25.7	40	Texas	25.7
40	Texas	25.7	40	Wyoming	25.7
50	Utah	23.9	44	Alabama	25.5
5	Vermont	27.8	44	Kansas	25.5
14	Virginia	27.0	46	Kentucky	25.3
23	Washington	26.5	47	Arkansas	25.0
33	West Virginia	25.9	48	Oklahoma	24.9
17	Wisconsin	26.9	49	Idaho	24.6
40	Wyoming	25.7	50	Utah	23.9
				District of Columbia	30.1

Source: U.S. Census Bureau, American Community Survey
   "Indicators of Marriage and Fertility in the United States: 2000-2003
*Four-year average: 2000-2003.

Estimated Median Age of Women at First Marriage: 2003

National Median = 25.1 Years*

ALPHA ORDER				RANK ORDER		
RANK	STATE	YEARS		RANK	STATE	YEARS
41	Alabama	23.8		1	Massachusetts	27.4
45	Alaska	22.8		2	New York	27.0
28	Arizona	24.5		3	Rhode Island	26.7
45	Arkansas	22.8		4	Connecticut	26.4
16	California	25.2		4	New Jersey	26.4
32	Colorado	24.4		6	Pennsylvania	25.9
4	Connecticut	26.4		6	Vermont	25.9
13	Delaware	25.5		8	Maryland	25.8
16	Florida	25.2		9	Hawaii	25.7
32	Georgia	24.4		9	New Hampshire	25.7
9	Hawaii	25.7		11	Maine	25.6
45	Idaho	22.8		11	Michigan	25.6
13	Illinois	25.5		13	Delaware	25.5
32	Indiana	24.4		13	Illinois	25.5
28	Iowa	24.5		13	Wisconsin	25.5
32	Kansas	24.4		16	California	25.2
45	Kentucky	22.8		16	Florida	25.2
24	Louisiana	24.8		16	Minnesota	25.2
11	Maine	25.6		16	Ohio	25.2
8	Maryland	25.8		16	South Carolina	25.2
1	Massachusetts	27.4		21	North Dakota	25.0
11	Michigan	25.6		21	Virginia	25.0
16	Minnesota	25.2		23	Washington	24.9
24	Mississippi	24.8		24	Louisiana	24.8
26	Missouri	24.7		24	Mississippi	24.8
28	Montana	24.5		26	Missouri	24.7
32	Nebraska	24.4		27	Oregon	24.6
42	Nevada	23.7		28	Arizona	24.5
9	New Hampshire	25.7		28	Iowa	24.5
4	New Jersey	26.4		28	Montana	24.5
32	New Mexico	24.4		28	North Carolina	24.5
2	New York	27.0		32	Colorado	24.4
28	North Carolina	24.5		32	Georgia	24.4
21	North Dakota	25.0		32	Indiana	24.4
16	Ohio	25.2		32	Kansas	24.4
49	Oklahoma	22.7		32	Nebraska	24.4
27	Oregon	24.6		32	New Mexico	24.4
6	Pennsylvania	25.9		38	South Dakota	24.3
3	Rhode Island	26.7		39	Tennessee	24.0
16	South Carolina	25.2		40	West Virginia	23.9
38	South Dakota	24.3		41	Alabama	23.8
39	Tennessee	24.0		42	Nevada	23.7
43	Texas	23.5		43	Texas	23.5
50	Utah	21.9		44	Wyoming	23.3
6	Vermont	25.9		45	Alaska	22.8
21	Virginia	25.0		45	Arkansas	22.8
23	Washington	24.9		45	Idaho	22.8
40	West Virginia	23.9		45	Kentucky	22.8
13	Wisconsin	25.5		49	Oklahoma	22.7
44	Wyoming	23.3		50	Utah	21.9
					District of Columbia	29.9

Source: U.S. Census Bureau, American Community Survey
    "Indicators of Marriage and Fertility in the United States: 2000-2003
*Four-year average: 2000-2003.

Divorces in 2004

Reporting States' Total = 879,128 Divorces*

ALPHA ORDER

RANK	STATE	DIVORCES	% of USA
14	Alabama	22,405	2.5%
41	Alaska	2,829	0.3%
13	Arizona	24,403	2.8%
20	Arkansas	16,874	1.9%
NA	California**	NA	NA
17	Colorado	20,230	2.3%
28	Connecticut	10,942	1.2%
40	Delaware	3,108	0.4%
1	Florida	82,662	9.4%
NA	Georgia**	NA	NA
NA	Hawaii**	NA	NA
34	Idaho	6,922	0.8%
8	Illinois	33,076	3.8%
NA	Indiana**	NA	NA
33	Iowa	8,305	0.9%
31	Kansas	9,102	1.0%
16	Kentucky	20,298	2.3%
NA	Louisiana**	NA	NA
36	Maine	5,677	0.6%
18	Maryland	17,802	2.0%
25	Massachusetts	14,148	1.6%
7	Michigan	34,701	3.9%
24	Minnesota	14,235	1.6%
27	Mississippi	13,077	1.5%
15	Missouri	21,700	2.5%
38	Montana	3,516	0.4%
35	Nebraska	5,962	0.7%
22	Nevada	14,828	1.7%
37	New Hampshire	5,131	0.6%
12	New Jersey	25,981	3.0%
32	New Mexico	8,829	1.0%
3	New York	57,830	6.6%
6	North Carolina	35,926	4.1%
45	North Dakota	1,979	0.2%
4	Ohio	40,770	4.6%
19	Oklahoma	17,146	2.0%
23	Oregon	14,774	1.7%
5	Pennsylvania	36,692	4.2%
39	Rhode Island	3,287	0.4%
26	South Carolina	13,448	1.5%
44	South Dakota	2,364	0.3%
10	Tennessee	28,858	3.3%
2	Texas	81,324	9.3%
29	Utah	9,811	1.1%
43	Vermont	2,442	0.3%
9	Virginia	29,411	3.3%
11	Washington	26,674	3.0%
30	West Virginia	9,148	1.0%
21	Wisconsin	16,802	1.9%
42	Wyoming	2,656	0.3%

RANK ORDER

RANK	STATE	DIVORCES	% of USA
1	Florida	82,662	9.4%
2	Texas	81,324	9.3%
3	New York	57,830	6.6%
4	Ohio	40,770	4.6%
5	Pennsylvania	36,692	4.2%
6	North Carolina	35,926	4.1%
7	Michigan	34,701	3.9%
8	Illinois	33,076	3.8%
9	Virginia	29,411	3.3%
10	Tennessee	28,858	3.3%
11	Washington	26,674	3.0%
12	New Jersey	25,981	3.0%
13	Arizona	24,403	2.8%
14	Alabama	22,405	2.5%
15	Missouri	21,700	2.5%
16	Kentucky	20,298	2.3%
17	Colorado	20,230	2.3%
18	Maryland	17,802	2.0%
19	Oklahoma	17,146	2.0%
20	Arkansas	16,874	1.9%
21	Wisconsin	16,802	1.9%
22	Nevada	14,828	1.7%
23	Oregon	14,774	1.7%
24	Minnesota	14,235	1.6%
25	Massachusetts	14,148	1.6%
26	South Carolina	13,448	1.5%
27	Mississippi	13,077	1.5%
28	Connecticut	10,942	1.2%
29	Utah	9,811	1.1%
30	West Virginia	9,148	1.0%
31	Kansas	9,102	1.0%
32	New Mexico	8,829	1.0%
33	Iowa	8,305	0.9%
34	Idaho	6,922	0.8%
35	Nebraska	5,962	0.7%
36	Maine	5,677	0.6%
37	New Hampshire	5,131	0.6%
38	Montana	3,516	0.4%
39	Rhode Island	3,287	0.4%
40	Delaware	3,108	0.4%
41	Alaska	2,829	0.3%
42	Wyoming	2,656	0.3%
43	Vermont	2,442	0.3%
44	South Dakota	2,364	0.3%
45	North Dakota	1,979	0.2%
NA	California**	NA	NA
NA	Georgia**	NA	NA
NA	Hawaii**	NA	NA
NA	Indiana**	NA	NA
NA	Louisiana**	NA	NA
	District of Columbia	1,043	0.1%

Source: U.S. Department of Health and Human Services, National Center for Health Statistics
    "National Vital Statistics Reports" (Vol. 53, No. 21, June 28, 2005)
*Provisional data by state of occurrence. National total is only for reporting states.
**Not available.

Divorce Rate in 2004

Reporting States' Rate = 3.0 Divorces per 1,000 Population*

ALPHA ORDER

RANK	STATE	RATE
4	Alabama	5.0
14	Alaska	4.3
14	Arizona	4.3
2	Arkansas	6.1
NA	California**	NA
13	Colorado	4.4
34	Connecticut	3.1
26	Delaware	3.7
10	Florida	4.8
NA	Georgia**	NA
NA	Hawaii**	NA
4	Idaho	5.0
44	Illinois	2.6
NA	Indiana**	NA
42	Iowa	2.8
31	Kansas	3.3
7	Kentucky	4.9
NA	Louisiana**	NA
14	Maine	4.3
32	Maryland	3.2
45	Massachusetts	2.2
29	Michigan	3.4
42	Minnesota	2.8
12	Mississippi	4.5
24	Missouri	3.8
24	Montana	3.8
29	Nebraska	3.4
1	Nevada	6.4
21	New Hampshire	3.9
38	New Jersey	3.0
11	New Mexico	4.6
38	New York	3.0
18	North Carolina	4.2
34	North Dakota	3.1
27	Ohio	3.6
7	Oklahoma	4.9
19	Oregon	4.1
38	Pennsylvania	3.0
38	Rhode Island	3.0
32	South Carolina	3.2
34	South Dakota	3.1
7	Tennessee	4.9
27	Texas	3.6
19	Utah	4.1
21	Vermont	3.9
21	Virginia	3.9
14	Washington	4.3
4	West Virginia	5.0
34	Wisconsin	3.1
3	Wyoming	5.3

RANK ORDER

RANK	STATE	RATE
1	Nevada	6.4
2	Arkansas	6.1
3	Wyoming	5.3
4	Alabama	5.0
4	Idaho	5.0
4	West Virginia	5.0
7	Kentucky	4.9
7	Oklahoma	4.9
7	Tennessee	4.9
10	Florida	4.8
11	New Mexico	4.6
12	Mississippi	4.5
13	Colorado	4.4
14	Alaska	4.3
14	Arizona	4.3
14	Maine	4.3
14	Washington	4.3
18	North Carolina	4.2
19	Oregon	4.1
19	Utah	4.1
21	New Hampshire	3.9
21	Vermont	3.9
21	Virginia	3.9
24	Missouri	3.8
24	Montana	3.8
26	Delaware	3.7
27	Ohio	3.6
27	Texas	3.6
29	Michigan	3.4
29	Nebraska	3.4
31	Kansas	3.3
32	Maryland	3.2
32	South Carolina	3.2
34	Connecticut	3.1
34	North Dakota	3.1
34	South Dakota	3.1
34	Wisconsin	3.1
38	New Jersey	3.0
38	New York	3.0
38	Pennsylvania	3.0
38	Rhode Island	3.0
42	Iowa	2.8
42	Minnesota	2.8
44	Illinois	2.6
45	Massachusetts	2.2
NA	California**	NA
NA	Georgia**	NA
NA	Hawaii**	NA
NA	Indiana**	NA
NA	Louisiana**	NA

District of Columbia   1.9

Source: Morgan Quitno Press using data from U.S. Dept. of Health and Human Services, Nat'l Center for Health Statistics
    "National Vital Statistics Reports" (Vol. 53, No. 21, June 28, 2005)
*Provisional data by state of occurrence. National rate is only for reporting states.
**Not available.

Average Family Size in 2004

National Average = 3.18 Persons per Family

RANK	STATE	PERSONS
28	Alabama	3.05
5	Alaska	3.32
12	Arizona	3.22
44	Arkansas	2.95
1	California	3.55
38	Colorado	3.01
17	Connecticut	3.13
15	Delaware	3.15
28	Florida	3.05
11	Georgia	3.23
2	Hawaii	3.48
20	Idaho	3.09
6	Illinois	3.31
24	Indiana	3.08
41	Iowa	2.98
32	Kansas	3.04
44	Kentucky	2.95
18	Louisiana	3.12
50	Maine	2.88
13	Maryland	3.19
14	Massachusetts	3.17
20	Michigan	3.09
44	Minnesota	2.95
16	Mississippi	3.14
41	Missouri	2.98
38	Montana	3.01
32	Nebraska	3.04
8	Nevada	3.27
20	New Hampshire	3.09
8	New Jersey	3.27
10	New Mexico	3.25
7	New York	3.28
40	North Carolina	3.00
49	North Dakota	2.89
32	Ohio	3.04
25	Oklahoma	3.07
36	Oregon	3.02
26	Pennsylvania	3.06
19	Rhode Island	3.11
28	South Carolina	3.05
28	South Dakota	3.05
35	Tennessee	3.03
4	Texas	3.40
3	Utah	3.46
48	Vermont	2.90
26	Virginia	3.06
20	Washington	3.09
47	West Virginia	2.94
36	Wisconsin	3.02
41	Wyoming	2.98

RANK	STATE	PERSONS
1	California	3.55
2	Hawaii	3.48
3	Utah	3.46
4	Texas	3.40
5	Alaska	3.32
6	Illinois	3.31
7	New York	3.28
8	Nevada	3.27
8	New Jersey	3.27
10	New Mexico	3.25
11	Georgia	3.23
12	Arizona	3.22
13	Maryland	3.19
14	Massachusetts	3.17
15	Delaware	3.15
16	Mississippi	3.14
17	Connecticut	3.13
18	Louisiana	3.12
19	Rhode Island	3.11
20	Idaho	3.09
20	Michigan	3.09
20	New Hampshire	3.09
20	Washington	3.09
24	Indiana	3.08
25	Oklahoma	3.07
26	Pennsylvania	3.06
26	Virginia	3.06
28	Alabama	3.05
28	Florida	3.05
28	South Carolina	3.05
28	South Dakota	3.05
32	Kansas	3.04
32	Nebraska	3.04
32	Ohio	3.04
35	Tennessee	3.03
36	Oregon	3.02
36	Wisconsin	3.02
38	Colorado	3.01
38	Montana	3.01
40	North Carolina	3.00
41	Iowa	2.98
41	Missouri	2.98
41	Wyoming	2.98
44	Arkansas	2.95
44	Kentucky	2.95
44	Minnesota	2.95
47	West Virginia	2.94
48	Vermont	2.90
49	North Dakota	2.89
50	Maine	2.88
	District of Columbia	3.04

Source: U.S. Bureau of the Census
   "2004 American Community Survey" (http://www.census.gov/acs/www/index.html)

Seats in the U.S. House of Representatives in 2006

National Total = 435 Seats*

ALPHA ORDER

RANK	STATE	SEATS	% of USA
22	Alabama	7	1.6%
44	Alaska	1	0.2%
18	Arizona	8	1.8%
31	Arkansas	4	0.9%
1	California	53	12.2%
22	Colorado	7	1.6%
27	Connecticut	5	1.1%
44	Delaware	1	0.2%
4	Florida	25	5.7%
9	Georgia	13	3.0%
39	Hawaii	2	0.5%
39	Idaho	2	0.5%
5	Illinois	19	4.4%
14	Indiana	9	2.1%
27	Iowa	5	1.1%
31	Kansas	4	0.9%
25	Kentucky	6	1.4%
22	Louisiana	7	1.6%
39	Maine	2	0.5%
18	Maryland	8	1.8%
13	Massachusetts	10	2.3%
8	Michigan	15	3.4%
18	Minnesota	8	1.8%
31	Mississippi	4	0.9%
14	Missouri	9	2.1%
44	Montana	1	0.2%
34	Nebraska	3	0.7%
34	Nevada	3	0.7%
39	New Hampshire	2	0.5%
9	New Jersey	13	3.0%
34	New Mexico	3	0.7%
3	New York	29	6.7%
9	North Carolina	13	3.0%
44	North Dakota	1	0.2%
7	Ohio	18	4.1%
27	Oklahoma	5	1.1%
27	Oregon	5	1.1%
5	Pennsylvania	19	4.4%
39	Rhode Island	2	0.5%
25	South Carolina	6	1.4%
44	South Dakota	1	0.2%
14	Tennessee	9	2.1%
2	Texas	32	7.4%
34	Utah	3	0.7%
44	Vermont	1	0.2%
12	Virginia	11	2.5%
14	Washington	9	2.1%
34	West Virginia	3	0.7%
18	Wisconsin	8	1.8%
44	Wyoming	1	0.2%

RANK ORDER

RANK	STATE	SEATS	% of USA
1	California	53	12.2%
2	Texas	32	7.4%
3	New York	29	6.7%
4	Florida	25	5.7%
5	Illinois	19	4.4%
5	Pennsylvania	19	4.4%
7	Ohio	18	4.1%
8	Michigan	15	3.4%
9	Georgia	13	3.0%
9	New Jersey	13	3.0%
9	North Carolina	13	3.0%
12	Virginia	11	2.5%
13	Massachusetts	10	2.3%
14	Indiana	9	2.1%
14	Missouri	9	2.1%
14	Tennessee	9	2.1%
14	Washington	9	2.1%
18	Arizona	8	1.8%
18	Maryland	8	1.8%
18	Minnesota	8	1.8%
18	Wisconsin	8	1.8%
22	Alabama	7	1.6%
22	Colorado	7	1.6%
22	Louisiana	7	1.6%
25	Kentucky	6	1.4%
25	South Carolina	6	1.4%
27	Connecticut	5	1.1%
27	Iowa	5	1.1%
27	Oklahoma	5	1.1%
27	Oregon	5	1.1%
31	Arkansas	4	0.9%
31	Kansas	4	0.9%
31	Mississippi	4	0.9%
34	Nebraska	3	0.7%
34	Nevada	3	0.7%
34	New Mexico	3	0.7%
34	Utah	3	0.7%
34	West Virginia	3	0.7%
39	Hawaii	2	0.5%
39	Idaho	2	0.5%
39	Maine	2	0.5%
39	New Hampshire	2	0.5%
39	Rhode Island	2	0.5%
44	Alaska	1	0.2%
44	Delaware	1	0.2%
44	Montana	1	0.2%
44	North Dakota	1	0.2%
44	South Dakota	1	0.2%
44	Vermont	1	0.2%
44	Wyoming	1	0.2%
	District of Columbia**	0	0.0%

Source: U.S. Bureau of the Census
    "Congressional Apportionment" (http://www.census.gov/population/www/censusdata/apportionment.html)
*This table shows the number of seats after reapportionment of the 2000 Census. This apportionment became effective with the Congress elected in November 2002 and that took office in January 2003.
**The District of Columbia has one non-voting delegate. Each state has two members in the U.S. Senate.

Estimated Population per U.S. House Seat in 2006

National Rate = 680,138 Persons per House Member*

ALPHA ORDER			RANK ORDER		
RANK	STATE	RATE	RANK	STATE	RATE
36	Alabama	651,115	1	Montana	935,670
31	Alaska	663,661	2	Delaware	843,524
6	Arizona	742,412	3	Utah	823,195
20	Arkansas	694,789	4	Nevada	804,936
24	California	681,739	5	South Dakota	775,933
29	Colorado	666,454	6	Arizona	742,412
14	Connecticut	702,059	7	Mississippi	730,272
2	Delaware	843,524	8	Oregon	728,211
11	Florida	711,595	9	Idaho	714,548
17	Georgia	697,890	10	Texas	714,374
42	Hawaii	637,597	11	Florida	711,595
9	Idaho	714,548	12	Oklahoma	709,577
26	Illinois	671,756	13	South Carolina	709,181
18	Indiana	696,886	14	Connecticut	702,059
47	Iowa	593,267	15	Maryland	700,049
23	Kansas	686,172	16	Washington	698,640
19	Kentucky	695,568	17	Georgia	697,890
37	Louisiana	646,233	18	Indiana	696,886
33	Maine	660,753	19	Kentucky	695,568
15	Maryland	700,049	20	Arkansas	694,789
41	Massachusetts	639,874	21	Wisconsin	602,025
25	Michigan	074,724	22	Virginia	687,951
40	Minnesota	641,600	23	Kansas	686,172
7	Mississippi	730,272	24	California	681,739
38	Missouri	644,479	25	Michigan	674,724
1	Montana	935,670	26	Illinois	671,756
48	Nebraska	586,262	27	New Jersey	670,610
4	Nevada	804,936	28	North Carolina	667,942
34	New Hampshire	654,970	29	Colorado	666,454
27	New Jersey	670,610	30	New York	663,953
39	New Mexico	642,795	31	Alaska	663,661
30	New York	663,953	32	Tennessee	662,551
28	North Carolina	667,942	33	Maine	660,753
44	North Dakota	636,677	34	New Hampshire	654,970
43	Ohio	636,891	35	Pennsylvania	654,190
12	Oklahoma	709,577	36	Alabama	651,115
8	Oregon	728,211	37	Louisiana	646,233
35	Pennsylvania	654,190	38	Missouri	644,479
49	Rhode Island	538,095	39	New Mexico	642,795
13	South Carolina	709,181	40	Minnesota	641,600
5	South Dakota	775,933	41	Massachusetts	639,874
32	Tennessee	662,551	42	Hawaii	637,597
10	Texas	714,374	43	Ohio	636,891
3	Utah	823,195	44	North Dakota	636,677
45	Vermont	623,050	45	Vermont	623,050
22	Virginia	687,951	46	West Virginia	605,619
16	Washington	698,640	47	Iowa	593,267
46	West Virginia	605,619	48	Nebraska	586,262
21	Wisconsin	692,025	49	Rhode Island	538,095
50	Wyoming	509,294	50	Wyoming	509,294

District of Columbia**   NA

Source: Morgan Quitno Press using data from U.S. Bureau of the Census
    "Congressional Apportionment" (http://www.census.gov/population/www/censusdata/apportionment.html)
National rate does not include population of the District of Columbia. D.C. has one non-voting delegate. Each state has two members in the U.S. Senate. This table is based only on U.S. Representatives and not U.S. Senate members. This table reflects reapportionment resulting from the 2000 census.
***Not applicable.*

State Legislators in 2006

National Total = 7,382 Legislators*

ALPHA ORDER

RANK	STATE	LEGISLATORS	% of USA
27	Alabama	140	1.9%
49	Alaska	60	0.8%
43	Arizona	90	1.2%
30	Arkansas	135	1.8%
35	California	120	1.6%
42	Colorado	100	1.4%
9	Connecticut	187	2.5%
48	Delaware	62	0.8%
18	Florida	160	2.2%
3	Georgia	236	3.2%
46	Hawaii	76	1.0%
39	Idaho	105	1.4%
13	Illinois	177	2.4%
19	Indiana	150	2.0%
19	Iowa	150	2.0%
17	Kansas	165	2.2%
29	Kentucky	138	1.9%
25	Louisiana	144	2.0%
10	Maine	186	2.5%
8	Maryland	188	2.5%
6	Massachusetts	200	2.7%
23	Michigan	148	2.0%
5	Minnesota	201	2.7%
14	Mississippi	174	2.4%
7	Missouri	197	2.7%
19	Montana	150	2.0%
50	Nebraska	49	0.7%
47	Nevada	63	0.9%
1	New Hampshire	424	5.7%
35	New Jersey	120	1.6%
38	New Mexico	112	1.5%
4	New York	212	2.9%
15	North Carolina	170	2.3%
26	North Dakota	141	1.9%
32	Ohio	132	1.8%
22	Oklahoma	149	2.0%
43	Oregon	90	1.2%
2	Pennsylvania	253	3.4%
37	Rhode Island	113	1.5%
15	South Carolina	170	2.3%
39	South Dakota	105	1.4%
32	Tennessee	132	1.8%
11	Texas	181	2.5%
41	Utah	104	1.4%
12	Vermont	180	2.4%
27	Virginia	140	1.9%
24	Washington	147	2.0%
31	West Virginia	134	1.8%
32	Wisconsin	132	1.8%
43	Wyoming	90	1.2%

RANK ORDER

RANK	STATE	LEGISLATORS	% of USA
1	New Hampshire	424	5.7%
2	Pennsylvania	253	3.4%
3	Georgia	236	3.2%
4	New York	212	2.9%
5	Minnesota	201	2.7%
6	Massachusetts	200	2.7%
7	Missouri	197	2.7%
8	Maryland	188	2.5%
9	Connecticut	187	2.5%
10	Maine	186	2.5%
11	Texas	181	2.5%
12	Vermont	180	2.4%
13	Illinois	177	2.4%
14	Mississippi	174	2.4%
15	North Carolina	170	2.3%
15	South Carolina	170	2.3%
17	Kansas	165	2.2%
18	Florida	160	2.2%
19	Indiana	150	2.0%
19	Iowa	150	2.0%
19	Montana	150	2.0%
22	Oklahoma	149	2.0%
23	Michigan	148	2.0%
24	Washington	147	2.0%
25	Louisiana	144	2.0%
26	North Dakota	141	1.9%
27	Alabama	140	1.9%
27	Virginia	140	1.9%
29	Kentucky	138	1.9%
30	Arkansas	135	1.8%
31	West Virginia	134	1.8%
32	Ohio	132	1.8%
32	Tennessee	132	1.8%
32	Wisconsin	132	1.8%
35	California	120	1.6%
35	New Jersey	120	1.6%
37	Rhode Island	113	1.5%
38	New Mexico	112	1.5%
39	Idaho	105	1.4%
39	South Dakota	105	1.4%
41	Utah	104	1.4%
42	Colorado	100	1.4%
43	Arizona	90	1.2%
43	Oregon	90	1.2%
43	Wyoming	90	1.2%
46	Hawaii	76	1.0%
47	Nevada	63	0.9%
48	Delaware	62	0.8%
49	Alaska	60	0.8%
50	Nebraska	49	0.7%
	District of Columbia**	NA	NA

Source: National Conference of State Legislatures (Denver, CO)
   "2006 Partisan Composition of State Legislatures"
      (http://www.ncsl.org/ncsldb/elect98/partcomp.cfm?yearsel=2006)
There are 1,971 state senators (including Nebraska's 49 unicameral seats) and 5,411 state house members.
**Not applicable.*

Population per State Legislator in 2006

National Rate = 40,079 Population per Legislator*

ALPHA ORDER				RANK ORDER		
RANK	STATE	RATE		RANK	STATE	RATE
22	Alabama	32,556		1	California	301,101
42	Alaska	11,061		2	Texas	126,298
9	Arizona	65,992		3	Florida	111,187
32	Arkansas	20,586		4	New York	90,824
1	California	301,101		5	Ohio	86,849
13	Colorado	46,652		6	New Jersey	72,649
34	Connecticut	18,772		7	Illinois	72,109
40	Delaware	13,605		8	Michigan	68,384
3	Florida	111,187		9	Arizona	65,992
19	Georgia	38,443		10	Virginia	54,053
37	Hawaii	16,779		11	North Carolina	51,078
39	Idaho	13,610		12	Pennsylvania	49,129
7	Illinois	72,109		13	Colorado	46,652
17	Indiana	41,813		14	Tennessee	45,174
33	Iowa	19,776		15	Washington	42,774
38	Kansas	16,634		16	Wisconsin	41,941
25	Kentucky	30,242		17	Indiana	41,813
24	Louisiana	31,414		18	Oregon	40,456
45	Maine	7,105		19	Georgia	38,443
26	Maryland	29,789		20	Nevada	38,330
23	Massachusetts	31,994		21	Nebraska	35,894
8	Michigan	68,384		22	Alabama	32,556
28	Minnesota	25,536		23	Massachusetts	31,994
36	Mississippi	16,788		24	Louisiana	31,414
27	Missouri	29,443		25	Kentucky	30,242
46	Montana	6,238		26	Maryland	29,789
21	Nebraska	35,894		27	Missouri	29,443
20	Nevada	38,330		28	Minnesota	25,536
50	New Hampshire	3,089		29	South Carolina	25,030
6	New Jersey	72,649		30	Oklahoma	23,811
35	New Mexico	17,218		31	Utah	23,746
4	New York	90,824		32	Arkansas	20,586
11	North Carolina	51,078		33	Iowa	19,776
48	North Dakota	4,515		34	Connecticut	18,772
5	Ohio	86,849		35	New Mexico	17,218
30	Oklahoma	23,811		36	Mississippi	16,788
18	Oregon	40,456		37	Hawaii	16,779
12	Pennsylvania	49,129		38	Kansas	16,634
43	Rhode Island	9,524		39	Idaho	13,610
29	South Carolina	25,030		40	Delaware	13,605
44	South Dakota	7,390		41	West Virginia	13,559
14	Tennessee	45,174		42	Alaska	11,061
2	Texas	126,298		43	Rhode Island	9,524
31	Utah	23,746		44	South Dakota	7,390
49	Vermont	3,461		45	Maine	7,105
10	Virginia	54,053		46	Montana	6,238
15	Washington	42,774		47	Wyoming	5,659
41	West Virginia	13,559		48	North Dakota	4,515
16	Wisconsin	41,941		49	Vermont	3,461
47	Wyoming	5,659		50	New Hampshire	3,089
				District of Columbia**		NA

Source: Morgan Quitno Press using data from National Conference of State Legislatures (Denver, CO)
        "2006 Partisan Composition of State Legislatures"
        (http://www.ncsl.org/ncsldb/elect98/partcomp.cfm?yearsel=2006)
*There are 1,971 state senators (including Nebraska's 49 unicameral seats) and 5,411 state house members.
National rate does not include population for the District of Columbia.
**Not applicable.

490

Registered Voters in 2004

National Total = 142,070,000

ALPHA ORDER

RANK	STATE	REGISTERED	% of USA
22	Alabama	2,418,000	1.7%
49	Alaska	334,000	0.2%
21	Arizona	2,485,000	1.7%
33	Arkansas	1,328,000	0.9%
1	California	14,193,000	10.0%
24	Colorado	2,307,000	1.6%
29	Connecticut	1,695,000	1.2%
46	Delaware	415,000	0.3%
4	Florida	8,219,000	5.8%
11	Georgia	3,948,000	2.8%
44	Hawaii	497,000	0.3%
41	Idaho	663,000	0.5%
6	Illinois	6,437,000	4.5%
18	Indiana	3,031,000	2.1%
30	Iowa	1,674,000	1.2%
32	Kansas	1,338,000	0.9%
26	Kentucky	2,231,000	1.6%
23	Louisiana	2,413,000	1.7%
39	Maine	824,000	0.6%
20	Maryland	2,676,000	1.9%
12	Massachusetts	3,483,000	2.5%
8	Michigan	5,364,000	3.8%
17	Minnesota	3,080,000	2.2%
31	Mississippi	1,510,000	1.1%
14	Missouri	3,336,000	2.3%
43	Montana	519,000	0.4%
38	Nebraska	918,000	0.6%
35	Nevada	965,000	0.7%
40	New Hampshire	716,000	0.5%
10	New Jersey	4,085,000	2.9%
36	New Mexico	936,000	0.7%
3	New York	8,624,000	6.1%
9	North Carolina	4,292,000	3.0%
47	North Dakota	412,000	0.3%
7	Ohio	6,003,000	4.2%
28	Oklahoma	1,781,000	1.3%
27	Oregon	2,049,000	1.4%
5	Pennsylvania	6,481,000	4.6%
42	Rhode Island	522,000	0.4%
25	South Carolina	2,238,000	1.6%
45	South Dakota	425,000	0.3%
19	Tennessee	2,739,000	1.9%
2	Texas	9,681,000	6.8%
34	Utah	1,141,000	0.8%
48	Vermont	354,000	0.2%
13	Virginia	3,441,000	2.4%
16	Washington	3,133,000	2.2%
37	West Virginia	935,000	0.7%
15	Wisconsin	3,225,000	2.3%
50	Wyoming	265,000	0.2%

RANK ORDER

RANK	STATE	REGISTERED	% of USA
1	California	14,193,000	10.0%
2	Texas	9,681,000	6.8%
3	New York	8,624,000	6.1%
4	Florida	8,219,000	5.8%
5	Pennsylvania	6,481,000	4.6%
6	Illinois	6,437,000	4.5%
7	Ohio	6,003,000	4.2%
8	Michigan	5,364,000	3.8%
9	North Carolina	4,292,000	3.0%
10	New Jersey	4,085,000	2.9%
11	Georgia	3,948,000	2.8%
12	Massachusetts	3,483,000	2.5%
13	Virginia	3,441,000	2.4%
14	Missouri	3,336,000	2.3%
15	Wisconsin	3,225,000	2.3%
16	Washington	3,133,000	2.2%
17	Minnesota	3,080,000	2.2%
18	Indiana	3,031,000	2.1%
19	Tennessee	2,739,000	1.9%
20	Maryland	2,676,000	1.9%
21	Arizona	2,485,000	1.7%
22	Alabama	2,418,000	1.7%
23	Louisiana	2,413,000	1.7%
24	Colorado	2,307,000	1.6%
25	South Carolina	2,238,000	1.6%
26	Kentucky	2,231,000	1.6%
27	Oregon	2,049,000	1.4%
28	Oklahoma	1,781,000	1.3%
29	Connecticut	1,695,000	1.2%
30	Iowa	1,674,000	1.2%
31	Mississippi	1,510,000	1.1%
32	Kansas	1,338,000	0.9%
33	Arkansas	1,328,000	0.9%
34	Utah	1,141,000	0.8%
35	Nevada	965,000	0.7%
36	New Mexico	936,000	0.7%
37	West Virginia	935,000	0.7%
38	Nebraska	918,000	0.6%
39	Maine	824,000	0.6%
40	New Hampshire	716,000	0.5%
41	Idaho	663,000	0.5%
42	Rhode Island	522,000	0.4%
43	Montana	519,000	0.4%
44	Hawaii	497,000	0.3%
45	South Dakota	425,000	0.3%
46	Delaware	415,000	0.3%
47	North Dakota	412,000	0.3%
48	Vermont	354,000	0.2%
49	Alaska	334,000	0.2%
50	Wyoming	265,000	0.2%
	District of Columbia	293,000	0.2%

Source: U.S. Bureau of the Census
"Voting and Registration" (Table 4c, http://www.census.gov/population/www/socdemo/voting.html)

Percent of Eligible Voters Reported Registered in 2004

National Percent = 72.1%*

ALPHA ORDER

RANK	STATE	PERCENT
21	Alabama	74.2
9	Alaska	77.0
37	Arizona	70.8
43	Arkansas	68.4
42	California	68.6
21	Colorado	74.2
38	Connecticut	70.3
33	Delaware	71.6
32	Florida	71.7
46	Georgia	67.3
50	Hawaii	58.4
39	Idaho	69.9
20	Illinois	74.5
44	Indiana	68.3
7	Iowa	78.4
28	Kansas	72.3
16	Kentucky	75.1
17	Louisiana	75.0
4	Maine	81.8
26	Maryland	72.7
8	Massachusetts	77.5
18	Michigan	74.7
2	Minnesota	84.5
24	Mississippi	73.7
5	Missouri	81.2
14	Montana	75.5
14	Nebraska	75.5
48	Nevada	65.3
12	New Hampshire	75.6
25	New Jersey	73.1
30	New Mexico	72.0
45	New York	67.5
27	North Carolina	72.5
1	North Dakota	89.3
28	Ohio	72.3
31	Oklahoma	71.9
6	Oregon	78.8
33	Pennsylvania	71.6
36	Rhode Island	71.3
19	South Carolina	74.6
10	South Dakota	76.8
49	Tennessee	64.4
40	Texas	69.5
11	Utah	75.7
12	Vermont	75.6
41	Virginia	69.2
21	Washington	74.2
47	West Virginia	67.1
3	Wisconsin	82.1
33	Wyoming	71.6

RANK ORDER

RANK	STATE	PERCENT
1	North Dakota	89.3
2	Minnesota	84.5
3	Wisconsin	82.1
4	Maine	81.8
5	Missouri	81.2
6	Oregon	78.8
7	Iowa	78.4
8	Massachusetts	77.5
9	Alaska	77.0
10	South Dakota	76.8
11	Utah	75.7
12	New Hampshire	75.6
12	Vermont	75.6
14	Montana	75.5
14	Nebraska	75.5
16	Kentucky	75.1
17	Louisiana	75.0
18	Michigan	74.7
19	South Carolina	74.6
20	Illinois	74.5
21	Alabama	74.2
21	Colorado	74.2
21	Washington	74.2
24	Mississippi	73.7
25	New Jersey	73.1
26	Maryland	72.7
27	North Carolina	72.5
28	Kansas	72.3
28	Ohio	72.3
30	New Mexico	72.0
31	Oklahoma	71.9
32	Florida	71.7
33	Delaware	71.6
33	Pennsylvania	71.6
33	Wyoming	71.6
36	Rhode Island	71.3
37	Arizona	70.8
38	Connecticut	70.3
39	Idaho	69.9
40	Texas	69.5
41	Virginia	69.2
42	California	68.6
43	Arkansas	68.4
44	Indiana	68.3
45	New York	67.5
46	Georgia	67.3
47	West Virginia	67.1
48	Nevada	65.3
49	Tennessee	64.4
50	Hawaii	58.4
	District of Columbia	75.2

Source: U.S. Bureau of the Census
   "Voting and Registration" (Table 4c, http://www.census.gov/population/www/socdemo/voting.html)
As a percent of citizen population 18 and older.

Persons Voting in 2004

National Total = 125,736,000

<table>
<tr><td colspan="4">ALPHA ORDER</td><td colspan="4">RANK ORDER</td></tr>
<tr><td>RANK</td><td>STATE</td><td>VOTERS</td><td>% of USA</td><td>RANK</td><td>STATE</td><td>VOTERS</td><td>% of USA</td></tr>
<tr><td>24</td><td>Alabama</td><td>2,060,000</td><td>1.6%</td><td>1</td><td>California</td><td>12,807,000</td><td>10.2%</td></tr>
<tr><td>49</td><td>Alaska</td><td>293,000</td><td>0.2%</td><td>2</td><td>Texas</td><td>7,950,000</td><td>6.3%</td></tr>
<tr><td>21</td><td>Arizona</td><td>2,239,000</td><td>1.8%</td><td>3</td><td>New York</td><td>7,698,000</td><td>6.1%</td></tr>
<tr><td>33</td><td>Arkansas</td><td>1,140,000</td><td>0.9%</td><td>4</td><td>Florida</td><td>7,372,000</td><td>5.9%</td></tr>
<tr><td>1</td><td>California</td><td>12,807,000</td><td>10.2%</td><td>5</td><td>Pennsylvania</td><td>5,845,000</td><td>4.6%</td></tr>
<tr><td>22</td><td>Colorado</td><td>2,097,000</td><td>1.7%</td><td>6</td><td>Illinois</td><td>5,672,000</td><td>4.5%</td></tr>
<tr><td>29</td><td>Connecticut</td><td>1,524,000</td><td>1.2%</td><td>7</td><td>Ohio</td><td>5,485,000</td><td>4.4%</td></tr>
<tr><td>45</td><td>Delaware</td><td>385,000</td><td>0.3%</td><td>8</td><td>Michigan</td><td>4,818,000</td><td>3.8%</td></tr>
<tr><td>4</td><td>Florida</td><td>7,372,000</td><td>5.9%</td><td>9</td><td>New Jersey</td><td>3,693,000</td><td>2.9%</td></tr>
<tr><td>11</td><td>Georgia</td><td>3,332,000</td><td>2.6%</td><td>10</td><td>North Carolina</td><td>3,639,000</td><td>2.9%</td></tr>
<tr><td>44</td><td>Hawaii</td><td>433,000</td><td>0.3%</td><td>11</td><td>Georgia</td><td>3,332,000</td><td>2.6%</td></tr>
<tr><td>41</td><td>Idaho</td><td>585,000</td><td>0.5%</td><td>12</td><td>Virginia</td><td>3,134,000</td><td>2.5%</td></tr>
<tr><td>6</td><td>Illinois</td><td>5,672,000</td><td>4.5%</td><td>13</td><td>Massachusetts</td><td>3,085,000</td><td>2.5%</td></tr>
<tr><td>18</td><td>Indiana</td><td>2,598,000</td><td>2.1%</td><td>14</td><td>Wisconsin</td><td>3,010,000</td><td>2.4%</td></tr>
<tr><td>30</td><td>Iowa</td><td>1,522,000</td><td>1.2%</td><td>15</td><td>Minnesota</td><td>2,887,000</td><td>2.3%</td></tr>
<tr><td>32</td><td>Kansas</td><td>1,188,000</td><td>0.9%</td><td>16</td><td>Washington</td><td>2,851,000</td><td>2.3%</td></tr>
<tr><td>25</td><td>Kentucky</td><td>1,930,000</td><td>1.5%</td><td>17</td><td>Missouri</td><td>2,815,000</td><td>2.2%</td></tr>
<tr><td>23</td><td>Louisiana</td><td>2,067,000</td><td>1.6%</td><td>18</td><td>Indiana</td><td>2,598,000</td><td>2.1%</td></tr>
<tr><td>39</td><td>Maine</td><td>736,000</td><td>0.6%</td><td>19</td><td>Maryland</td><td>2,413,000</td><td>1.9%</td></tr>
<tr><td>19</td><td>Maryland</td><td>2,413,000</td><td>1.9%</td><td>20</td><td>Tennessee</td><td>2,319,000</td><td>1.8%</td></tr>
<tr><td>13</td><td>Massachusetts</td><td>3,085,000</td><td>2.5%</td><td>21</td><td>Arizona</td><td>2,239,000</td><td>1.8%</td></tr>
<tr><td>8</td><td>Michigan</td><td>4,818,000</td><td>3.8%</td><td>22</td><td>Colorado</td><td>2,097,000</td><td>1.7%</td></tr>
<tr><td>15</td><td>Minnesota</td><td>2,887,000</td><td>2.3%</td><td>23</td><td>Louisiana</td><td>2,067,000</td><td>1.6%</td></tr>
<tr><td>31</td><td>Mississippi</td><td>1,263,000</td><td>1.0%</td><td>24</td><td>Alabama</td><td>2,060,000</td><td>1.6%</td></tr>
<tr><td>17</td><td>Missouri</td><td>2,815,000</td><td>2.2%</td><td>25</td><td>Kentucky</td><td>1,930,000</td><td>1.5%</td></tr>
<tr><td>42</td><td>Montana</td><td>482,000</td><td>0.4%</td><td>26</td><td>Oregon</td><td>1,924,000</td><td>1.5%</td></tr>
<tr><td>38</td><td>Nebraska</td><td>793,000</td><td>0.6%</td><td>27</td><td>South Carolina</td><td>1,899,000</td><td>1.5%</td></tr>
<tr><td>35</td><td>Nevada</td><td>871,000</td><td>0.7%</td><td>28</td><td>Oklahoma</td><td>1,541,000</td><td>1.2%</td></tr>
<tr><td>40</td><td>New Hampshire</td><td>677,000</td><td>0.5%</td><td>29</td><td>Connecticut</td><td>1,524,000</td><td>1.2%</td></tr>
<tr><td>9</td><td>New Jersey</td><td>3,693,000</td><td>2.9%</td><td>30</td><td>Iowa</td><td>1,522,000</td><td>1.2%</td></tr>
<tr><td>36</td><td>New Mexico</td><td>837,000</td><td>0.7%</td><td>31</td><td>Mississippi</td><td>1,263,000</td><td>1.0%</td></tr>
<tr><td>3</td><td>New York</td><td>7,698,000</td><td>6.1%</td><td>32</td><td>Kansas</td><td>1,188,000</td><td>0.9%</td></tr>
<tr><td>10</td><td>North Carolina</td><td>3,639,000</td><td>2.9%</td><td>33</td><td>Arkansas</td><td>1,140,000</td><td>0.9%</td></tr>
<tr><td>47</td><td>North Dakota</td><td>330,000</td><td>0.3%</td><td>34</td><td>Utah</td><td>1,022,000</td><td>0.8%</td></tr>
<tr><td>7</td><td>Ohio</td><td>5,485,000</td><td>4.4%</td><td>35</td><td>Nevada</td><td>871,000</td><td>0.7%</td></tr>
<tr><td>28</td><td>Oklahoma</td><td>1,541,000</td><td>1.2%</td><td>36</td><td>New Mexico</td><td>837,000</td><td>0.7%</td></tr>
<tr><td>26</td><td>Oregon</td><td>1,924,000</td><td>1.5%</td><td>37</td><td>West Virginia</td><td>798,000</td><td>0.6%</td></tr>
<tr><td>5</td><td>Pennsylvania</td><td>5,845,000</td><td>4.6%</td><td>38</td><td>Nebraska</td><td>793,000</td><td>0.6%</td></tr>
<tr><td>43</td><td>Rhode Island</td><td>467,000</td><td>0.4%</td><td>39</td><td>Maine</td><td>736,000</td><td>0.6%</td></tr>
<tr><td>27</td><td>South Carolina</td><td>1,899,000</td><td>1.5%</td><td>40</td><td>New Hampshire</td><td>677,000</td><td>0.5%</td></tr>
<tr><td>46</td><td>South Dakota</td><td>378,000</td><td>0.3%</td><td>41</td><td>Idaho</td><td>585,000</td><td>0.5%</td></tr>
<tr><td>20</td><td>Tennessee</td><td>2,319,000</td><td>1.8%</td><td>42</td><td>Montana</td><td>482,000</td><td>0.4%</td></tr>
<tr><td>2</td><td>Texas</td><td>7,950,000</td><td>6.3%</td><td>43</td><td>Rhode Island</td><td>467,000</td><td>0.4%</td></tr>
<tr><td>34</td><td>Utah</td><td>1,022,000</td><td>0.8%</td><td>44</td><td>Hawaii</td><td>433,000</td><td>0.3%</td></tr>
<tr><td>48</td><td>Vermont</td><td>316,000</td><td>0.3%</td><td>45</td><td>Delaware</td><td>385,000</td><td>0.3%</td></tr>
<tr><td>12</td><td>Virginia</td><td>3,134,000</td><td>2.5%</td><td>46</td><td>South Dakota</td><td>378,000</td><td>0.3%</td></tr>
<tr><td>16</td><td>Washington</td><td>2,851,000</td><td>2.3%</td><td>47</td><td>North Dakota</td><td>330,000</td><td>0.3%</td></tr>
<tr><td>37</td><td>West Virginia</td><td>798,000</td><td>0.6%</td><td>48</td><td>Vermont</td><td>316,000</td><td>0.3%</td></tr>
<tr><td>14</td><td>Wisconsin</td><td>3,010,000</td><td>2.4%</td><td>49</td><td>Alaska</td><td>293,000</td><td>0.2%</td></tr>
<tr><td>50</td><td>Wyoming</td><td>247,000</td><td>0.2%</td><td>50</td><td>Wyoming</td><td>247,000</td><td>0.2%</td></tr>
<tr><td></td><td></td><td></td><td></td><td></td><td>District of Columbia</td><td>270,000</td><td>0.2%</td></tr>
</table>

Source: U.S. Bureau of the Census
   "Voting and Registration" (Table 4c, http://www.census.gov/population/www/socdemo/voting.html)

Percent of Eligible Population Reported Voting in 2004

National Percent = 63.8%

ALPHA ORDER

RANK	STATE	PERCENT
33	Alabama	63.2
13	Alaska	67.6
31	Arizona	63.8
44	Arkansas	58.7
38	California	61.9
15	Colorado	67.5
33	Connecticut	63.2
19	Delaware	66.4
28	Florida	64.3
48	Georgia	56.8
50	Hawaii	50.8
40	Idaho	61.6
22	Illinois	65.6
45	Indiana	58.6
7	Iowa	71.3
29	Kansas	64.2
25	Kentucky	65.0
29	Louisiana	64.2
4	Maine	73.1
22	Maryland	65.6
9	Massachusetts	68.6
17	Michigan	67.1
1	Minnesota	79.2
39	Mississippi	61.7
10	Missouri	68.5
8	Montana	70.2
24	Nebraska	65.3
43	Nevada	58.9
5	New Hampshire	71.5
21	New Jersey	66.0
27	New Mexico	64.4
42	New York	60.2
41	North Carolina	61.4
5	North Dakota	71.5
20	Ohio	66.1
37	Oklahoma	62.3
3	Oregon	74.0
26	Pennsylvania	64.5
32	Rhode Island	63.7
33	South Carolina	63.2
11	South Dakota	68.3
49	Tennessee	54.6
47	Texas	57.1
12	Utah	67.8
16	Vermont	67.3
36	Virginia	63.1
13	Washington	67.6
46	West Virginia	57.2
2	Wisconsin	76.6
18	Wyoming	66.9

RANK ORDER

RANK	STATE	PERCENT
1	Minnesota	79.2
2	Wisconsin	76.6
3	Oregon	74.0
4	Maine	73.1
5	New Hampshire	71.5
5	North Dakota	71.5
7	Iowa	71.3
8	Montana	70.2
9	Massachusetts	68.6
10	Missouri	68.5
11	South Dakota	68.3
12	Utah	67.8
13	Alaska	67.6
13	Washington	67.6
15	Colorado	67.5
16	Vermont	67.3
17	Michigan	67.1
18	Wyoming	66.9
19	Delaware	66.4
20	Ohio	66.1
21	New Jersey	66.0
22	Illinois	65.6
22	Maryland	65.6
24	Nebraska	65.3
25	Kentucky	65.0
26	Pennsylvania	64.5
27	New Mexico	64.4
28	Florida	64.3
29	Kansas	64.2
29	Louisiana	64.2
31	Arizona	63.8
32	Rhode Island	63.7
33	Alabama	63.2
33	Connecticut	63.2
33	South Carolina	63.2
36	Virginia	63.1
37	Oklahoma	62.3
38	California	61.9
39	Mississippi	61.7
40	Idaho	61.6
41	North Carolina	61.4
42	New York	60.2
43	Nevada	58.9
44	Arkansas	58.7
45	Indiana	58.6
46	West Virginia	57.2
47	Texas	57.1
48	Georgia	56.8
49	Tennessee	54.6
50	Hawaii	50.8

| | District of Columbia | 69.2 |

Source: U.S. Bureau of the Census
   "Voting and Registration" (Table 4c, http://www.census.gov/population/www/socdemo/voting.html)
*As a percent of citizen population 18 and older.

XIV. SOCIAL WELFARE

Poverty Rate in 2004

National Rate = 12.4% of Population in Poverty*

ALPHA ORDER				RANK ORDER		
RANK	STATE	PERCENT		RANK	STATE	PERCENT
7	Alabama	15.5		1	Mississippi	17.7
43	Alaska	9.2		2	Arkansas	17.6
14	Arizona	13.8		3	New Mexico	17.5
2	Arkansas	17.6		4	Louisiana	17.0
15	California	13.2		5	Texas	16.4
36	Colorado	9.8		6	West Virginia	16.1
44	Connecticut	8.8		7	Alabama	15.5
47	Delaware	8.5		8	Kentucky	15.4
19	Florida	12.3		9	Tennessee	14.9
22	Georgia	12.0		10	North Carolina	14.8
39	Hawaii	9.7		11	New York	14.4
29	Idaho	10.5		12	Montana	14.3
17	Illinois	12.5		13	South Carolina	14.0
32	Indiana	10.2		14	Arizona	13.8
39	Iowa	9.7		15	California	13.2
28	Kansas	10.7		16	Oklahoma	12.6
8	Kentucky	15.4		17	Illinois	12.5
4	Louisiana	17.0		17	South Dakota	12.5
20	Maine	12.2		19	Florida	12.3
46	Maryland	8.6		20	Maine	12.2
36	Massachusetts	9.8		21	Michigan	12.1
21	Michigan	12.1		22	Georgia	12.0
49	Minnesota	7.0		23	Oregon	11.7
1	Mississippi	17.7		23	Washington	11.7
26	Missouri	10.9		25	Rhode Island	11.3
12	Montana	14.3		26	Missouri	10.9
35	Nebraska	9.9		27	Ohio	10.8
32	Nevada	10.2		28	Kansas	10.7
50	New Hampshire	5.7		29	Idaho	10.5
48	New Jersey	8.2		30	Pennsylvania	10.4
3	New Mexico	17.5		31	North Dakota	10.3
11	New York	14.4		32	Indiana	10.2
10	North Carolina	14.8		32	Nevada	10.2
31	North Dakota	10.3		32	Wisconsin	10.2
27	Ohio	10.8		35	Nebraska	9.9
16	Oklahoma	12.6		36	Colorado	9.8
23	Oregon	11.7		36	Massachusetts	9.8
30	Pennsylvania	10.4		36	Virginia	9.8
25	Rhode Island	11.3		39	Hawaii	9.7
13	South Carolina	14.0		39	Iowa	9.7
17	South Dakota	12.5		41	Utah	9.6
9	Tennessee	14.9		41	Wyoming	9.6
5	Texas	16.4		43	Alaska	9.2
41	Utah	9.6		44	Connecticut	8.8
44	Vermont	8.8		44	Vermont	8.8
36	Virginia	9.8		46	Maryland	8.6
23	Washington	11.7		47	Delaware	8.5
6	West Virginia	16.1		48	New Jersey	8.2
32	Wisconsin	10.2		49	Minnesota	7.0
41	Wyoming	9.6		50	New Hampshire	5.7
					District of Columbia	16.8

Source: U.S. Bureau of the Census
   "Income, Poverty and Health Insurance Coverage in the United States: 2004"
      (http://www.census.gov/prod/2005pubs/p60-229.pdf)
*Three-year average: 2002-2004. The poverty threshold for a family of four (two children) in 2004 was $19,157.

Percent of Senior Citizens Living in Poverty in 2004

National Percent = 9.4%*

ALPHA ORDER

RANK	STATE	PERCENT
10	Alabama	11.9
50	Alaska	3.4
41	Arizona	7.5
5	Arkansas	12.8
32	California	7.8
38	Colorado	7.6
45	Connecticut	6.6
43	Delaware	7.2
15	Florida	9.7
4	Georgia	13.2
25	Hawaii	8.3
43	Idaho	7.2
24	Illinois	8.4
42	Indiana	7.3
32	Iowa	7.8
27	Kansas	8.2
6	Kentucky	12.6
2	Louisiana	14.7
16	Maine	9.5
32	Maryland	7.8
20	Massachusetts	8.7
31	Michigan	7.9
36	Minnesota	7.7
1	Mississippi	15.2
16	Missouri	9.5
19	Montana	8.8
36	Nebraska	7.7
47	Nevada	6.4
25	New Hampshire	8.3
27	New Jersey	8.2
10	New Mexico	11.9
13	New York	11.3
12	North Carolina	11.6
14	North Dakota	10.9
38	Ohio	7.6
18	Oklahoma	9.1
45	Oregon	6.6
29	Pennsylvania	8.1
23	Rhode Island	8.5
3	South Carolina	13.3
21	South Dakota	8.6
9	Tennessee	12.0
7	Texas	12.5
49	Utah	5.4
32	Vermont	7.8
21	Virginia	8.6
29	Washington	8.1
8	West Virginia	12.1
38	Wisconsin	7.6
48	Wyoming	6.1

RANK ORDER

RANK	STATE	PERCENT
1	Mississippi	15.2
2	Louisiana	14.7
3	South Carolina	13.3
4	Georgia	13.2
5	Arkansas	12.8
6	Kentucky	12.6
7	Texas	12.5
8	West Virginia	12.1
9	Tennessee	12.0
10	Alabama	11.9
10	New Mexico	11.9
12	North Carolina	11.6
13	New York	11.3
14	North Dakota	10.9
15	Florida	9.7
16	Maine	9.5
16	Missouri	9.5
18	Oklahoma	9.1
19	Montana	8.8
20	Massachusetts	8.7
21	South Dakota	8.6
21	Virginia	8.6
23	Rhode Island	8.5
24	Illinois	8.4
25	Hawaii	8.3
25	New Hampshire	8.3
27	Kansas	8.2
27	New Jersey	8.2
29	Pennsylvania	8.1
29	Washington	8.1
31	Michigan	7.9
32	California	7.8
32	Iowa	7.8
32	Maryland	7.8
32	Vermont	7.8
36	Minnesota	7.7
36	Nebraska	7.7
38	Colorado	7.6
38	Ohio	7.6
38	Wisconsin	7.6
41	Arizona	7.5
42	Indiana	7.3
43	Delaware	7.2
43	Idaho	7.2
45	Connecticut	6.6
45	Oregon	6.6
47	Nevada	6.4
48	Wyoming	6.1
49	Utah	5.4
50	Alaska	3.4

| | District of Columbia | 14.4 |

Source: U.S. Bureau of the Census
   "2004 American Community Survey" (http://www.census.gov/acs/www/index.html)
*People 65 years and older living with incomes below the poverty level.

Percent of Children Living in Poverty in 2004

National Percent = 18.1%*

ALPHA ORDER

ALPHA ORDER

RANK	STATE	PERCENT
7	Alabama	23.2
47	Alaska	10.4
16	Arizona	19.6
4	Arkansas	25.3
19	California	18.5
33	Colorado	14.2
49	Connecticut	10.1
34	Delaware	13.6
23	Florida	17.2
11	Georgia	20.9
34	Hawaii	13.6
17	Idaho	19.1
27	Illinois	16.5
32	Indiana	14.4
42	Iowa	12.1
44	Kansas	11.6
5	Kentucky	24.6
2	Louisiana	29.5
26	Maine	16.7
45	Maryland	11.0
41	Massachusetts	12.2
23	Michigan	17.2
48	Minnesota	10.2
1	Mississippi	30.8
29	Missouri	15.8
18	Montana	18.7
39	Nebraska	12.7
19	Nevada	18.5
50	New Hampshire	9.4
43	New Jersey	11.7
3	New Mexico	27.0
15	New York	20.3
10	North Carolina	21.5
30	North Dakota	14.8
22	Ohio	18.0
14	Oklahoma	20.5
21	Oregon	18.3
27	Pennsylvania	16.5
12	Rhode Island	20.7
9	South Carolina	22.5
31	South Dakota	14.5
13	Tennessee	20.6
8	Texas	22.6
38	Utah	13.1
46	Vermont	10.9
40	Virginia	12.6
25	Washington	16.9
6	West Virginia	24.0
34	Wisconsin	13.6
34	Wyoming	13.6

RANK ORDER

RANK	STATE	PERCENT
1	Mississippi	30.8
2	Louisiana	29.5
3	New Mexico	27.0
4	Arkansas	25.3
5	Kentucky	24.6
6	West Virginia	24.0
7	Alabama	23.2
8	Texas	22.6
9	South Carolina	22.5
10	North Carolina	21.5
11	Georgia	20.9
12	Rhode Island	20.7
13	Tennessee	20.6
14	Oklahoma	20.5
15	New York	20.3
16	Arizona	19.6
17	Idaho	19.1
18	Montana	18.7
19	California	18.5
19	Nevada	18.5
21	Oregon	18.3
22	Ohio	18.0
23	Florida	17.2
23	Michigan	17.2
25	Washington	16.9
26	Maine	16.7
27	Illinois	16.5
27	Pennsylvania	16.5
29	Missouri	15.8
30	North Dakota	14.8
31	South Dakota	14.5
32	Indiana	14.4
33	Colorado	14.2
34	Delaware	13.6
34	Hawaii	13.6
34	Wisconsin	13.6
34	Wyoming	13.6
38	Utah	13.1
39	Nebraska	12.7
40	Virginia	12.6
41	Massachusetts	12.2
42	Iowa	12.1
43	New Jersey	11.7
44	Kansas	11.6
45	Maryland	11.0
46	Vermont	10.9
47	Alaska	10.4
48	Minnesota	10.2
49	Connecticut	10.1
50	New Hampshire	9.4
	District of Columbia	33.7

Source: U.S. Bureau of the Census
"2004 American Community Survey" (http://www.census.gov/acs/www/index.html)
*Children 17 and under living in families with incomes below the poverty level.

Percent of Families Living in Poverty in 2004

National Percent = 10.1%*

ALPHA ORDER				RANK ORDER		
RANK	STATE	PERCENT		RANK	STATE	PERCENT
8	Alabama	13.1		1	Mississippi	17.6
48	Alaska	5.5		2	New Mexico	15.9
16	Arizona	10.9		3	Louisiana	14.9
4	Arkansas	14.1		4	Arkansas	14.1
17	California	10.5		4	West Virginia	14.1
30	Colorado	8.6		6	Kentucky	13.9
45	Connecticut	6.2		7	Texas	13.5
38	Delaware	7.6		8	Alabama	13.1
25	Florida	9.1		9	South Carolina	12.5
11	Georgia	12.0		10	North Carolina	12.1
34	Hawaii	7.9		11	Georgia	12.0
14	Idaho	11.1		11	Oklahoma	12.0
26	Illinois	9.0		13	Tennessee	11.6
34	Indiana	7.9		14	Idaho	11.1
42	Iowa	6.8		14	New York	11.1
42	Kansas	6.8		16	Arizona	10.9
6	Kentucky	13.9		17	California	10.5
3	Louisiana	14.9		17	Montana	10.5
23	Maine	9.5		19	Oregon	10.4
46	Maryland	5.8		19	Rhode Island	10.4
41	Massachusetts	7.1		21	Nevada	10.0
26	Michigan	9.0		21	Ohio	10.0
50	Minnesota	5.3		23	Maine	9.5
1	Mississippi	17.6		24	Washington	9.4
29	Missouri	8.7		25	Florida	9.1
17	Montana	10.5		26	Illinois	9.0
36	Nebraska	7.7		26	Michigan	9.0
21	Nevada	10.0		28	Pennsylvania	8.9
48	New Hampshire	5.5		29	Missouri	8.7
44	New Jersey	6.5		30	Colorado	8.6
2	New Mexico	15.9		31	South Dakota	8.4
14	New York	11.1		32	Utah	8.2
10	North Carolina	12.1		33	North Dakota	8.0
33	North Dakota	8.0		34	Hawaii	7.9
21	Ohio	10.0		34	Indiana	7.9
11	Oklahoma	12.0		36	Nebraska	7.7
19	Oregon	10.4		36	Wyoming	7.7
28	Pennsylvania	8.9		38	Delaware	7.6
19	Rhode Island	10.4		38	Wisconsin	7.6
9	South Carolina	12.5		40	Virginia	7.2
31	South Dakota	8.4		41	Massachusetts	7.1
13	Tennessee	11.6		42	Iowa	6.8
7	Texas	13.5		42	Kansas	6.8
32	Utah	8.2		44	New Jersey	6.5
47	Vermont	5.6		45	Connecticut	6.2
40	Virginia	7.2		46	Maryland	5.8
24	Washington	9.4		47	Vermont	5.6
4	West Virginia	14.1		48	Alaska	5.5
38	Wisconsin	7.6		48	New Hampshire	5.5
36	Wyoming	7.7		50	Minnesota	5.3
					District of Columbia	16.9

Source: Morgan Quitno Press using data from U.S. Bureau of the Census
"2004 American Community Survey" (http://www.census.gov/acs/www/index.html)
*Families living with incomes below the poverty level.

Percent of Female-Headed Families with Children Living in Poverty in 2004

National Percent = 37.6%*

ALPHA ORDER

RANK	STATE	PERCENT
8	Alabama	46.2
50	Alaska	20.4
38	Arizona	32.9
5	Arkansas	48.0
34	California	34.2
34	Colorado	34.2
42	Connecticut	30.0
38	Delaware	32.9
40	Florida	32.5
15	Georgia	42.6
44	Hawaii	29.0
13	Idaho	43.4
25	Illinois	37.9
27	Indiana	37.4
34	Iowa	34.2
46	Kansas	28.3
4	Kentucky	48.7
2	Louisiana	49.7
10	Maine	44.4
49	Maryland	22.1
32	Massachusetts	35.1
27	Michigan	37.4
48	Minnesota	25.5
1	Mississippi	52.9
37	Missouri	33.3
9	Montana	45.4
23	Nebraska	38.6
29	Nevada	36.0
47	New Hampshire	26.6
45	New Jersey	28.8
3	New Mexico	49.3
26	New York	37.5
11	North Carolina	44.0
12	North Dakota	43.5
19	Ohio	40.6
14	Oklahoma	42.7
18	Oregon	41.6
24	Pennsylvania	38.0
7	Rhode Island	46.3
16	South Carolina	42.3
22	South Dakota	38.7
17	Tennessee	42.1
21	Texas	39.9
31	Utah	35.4
43	Vermont	29.1
41	Virginia	30.6
33	Washington	34.9
6	West Virginia	47.5
30	Wisconsin	35.5
19	Wyoming	40.6

RANK ORDER

RANK	STATE	PERCENT
1	Mississippi	52.9
2	Louisiana	49.7
3	New Mexico	49.3
4	Kentucky	48.7
5	Arkansas	48.0
6	West Virginia	47.5
7	Rhode Island	46.3
8	Alabama	46.2
9	Montana	45.4
10	Maine	44.4
11	North Carolina	44.0
12	North Dakota	43.5
13	Idaho	43.4
14	Oklahoma	42.7
15	Georgia	42.6
16	South Carolina	42.3
17	Tennessee	42.1
18	Oregon	41.6
19	Ohio	40.6
19	Wyoming	40.6
21	Texas	39.9
22	South Dakota	38.7
23	Nebraska	38.6
24	Pennsylvania	38.0
25	Illinois	37.9
26	New York	37.5
27	Indiana	37.4
27	Michigan	37.4
29	Nevada	36.0
30	Wisconsin	35.5
31	Utah	35.4
32	Massachusetts	35.1
33	Washington	34.9
34	California	34.2
34	Colorado	34.2
34	Iowa	34.2
37	Missouri	33.3
38	Arizona	32.9
38	Delaware	32.9
40	Florida	32.5
41	Virginia	30.6
42	Connecticut	30.0
43	Vermont	29.1
44	Hawaii	29.0
45	New Jersey	28.8
46	Kansas	28.3
47	New Hampshire	26.6
48	Minnesota	25.5
49	Maryland	22.1
50	Alaska	20.4
	District of Columbia	40.6

Source: Morgan Quitno Press using data from U.S. Bureau of the Census
  "2004 American Community Survey" (http://www.census.gov/acs/www/index.html)
*Households headed by females with own children under 18 years living with them with incomes below the poverty
level as a percent of all such female-headed households.

State and Local Government Expenditures for Public Welfare Programs in 2002

National Total = $279,597,690,000*

<table>
<tr><td colspan="4">ALPHA ORDER</td><td colspan="4">RANK ORDER</td></tr>
<tr><th>RANK</th><th>STATE</th><th>EXPENDITURES</th><th>% of USA</th><th>RANK</th><th>STATE</th><th>EXPENDITURES</th><th>% of USA</th></tr>
<tr><td>23</td><td>Alabama</td><td>$4,161,953,000</td><td>1.5%</td><td>1</td><td>California</td><td>$35,559,242,000</td><td>12.7%</td></tr>
<tr><td>43</td><td>Alaska</td><td>1,034,937,000</td><td>0.4%</td><td>2</td><td>New York</td><td>32,503,209,000</td><td>11.6%</td></tr>
<tr><td>27</td><td>Arizona</td><td>3,286,119,000</td><td>1.2%</td><td>3</td><td>Texas</td><td>14,903,225,000</td><td>5.3%</td></tr>
<tr><td>32</td><td>Arkansas</td><td>2,592,774,000</td><td>0.9%</td><td>4</td><td>Pennsylvania</td><td>14,486,426,000</td><td>5.2%</td></tr>
<tr><td>1</td><td>California</td><td>35,559,242,000</td><td>12.7%</td><td>5</td><td>Florida</td><td>12,500,047,000</td><td>4.5%</td></tr>
<tr><td>30</td><td>Colorado</td><td>2,823,132,000</td><td>1.0%</td><td>6</td><td>Ohio</td><td>12,278,304,000</td><td>4.4%</td></tr>
<tr><td>25</td><td>Connecticut</td><td>3,471,835,000</td><td>1.2%</td><td>7</td><td>Illinois</td><td>9,861,010,000</td><td>3.5%</td></tr>
<tr><td>48</td><td>Delaware</td><td>659,394,000</td><td>0.2%</td><td>8</td><td>Michigan</td><td>9,837,380,000</td><td>3.5%</td></tr>
<tr><td>5</td><td>Florida</td><td>12,500,047,000</td><td>4.5%</td><td>9</td><td>North Carolina</td><td>7,657,145,000</td><td>2.7%</td></tr>
<tr><td>14</td><td>Georgia</td><td>6,159,345,000</td><td>2.2%</td><td>10</td><td>Minnesota</td><td>7,473,369,000</td><td>2.7%</td></tr>
<tr><td>40</td><td>Hawaii</td><td>1,141,298,000</td><td>0.4%</td><td>11</td><td>New Jersey</td><td>6,608,168,000</td><td>2.4%</td></tr>
<tr><td>42</td><td>Idaho</td><td>1,034,938,000</td><td>0.4%</td><td>12</td><td>Tennessee</td><td>6,458,267,000</td><td>2.3%</td></tr>
<tr><td>7</td><td>Illinois</td><td>9,861,010,000</td><td>3.5%</td><td>13</td><td>Washington</td><td>6,198,479,000</td><td>2.2%</td></tr>
<tr><td>18</td><td>Indiana</td><td>5,312,531,000</td><td>1.9%</td><td>14</td><td>Georgia</td><td>6,159,345,000</td><td>2.2%</td></tr>
<tr><td>31</td><td>Iowa</td><td>2,682,250,000</td><td>1.0%</td><td>15</td><td>Massachusetts</td><td>5,731,241,000</td><td>2.0%</td></tr>
<tr><td>35</td><td>Kansas</td><td>2,002,967,000</td><td>0.7%</td><td>16</td><td>Wisconsin</td><td>5,559,624,000</td><td>2.0%</td></tr>
<tr><td>19</td><td>Kentucky</td><td>4,816,404,000</td><td>1.7%</td><td>17</td><td>Missouri</td><td>5,519,734,000</td><td>2.0%</td></tr>
<tr><td>26</td><td>Louisiana</td><td>3,362,348,000</td><td>1.2%</td><td>18</td><td>Indiana</td><td>5,312,531,000</td><td>1.9%</td></tr>
<tr><td>36</td><td>Maine</td><td>1,791,700,000</td><td>0.6%</td><td>19</td><td>Kentucky</td><td>4,816,404,000</td><td>1.7%</td></tr>
<tr><td>20</td><td>Maryland</td><td>4,737,003,000</td><td>1.7%</td><td>20</td><td>Maryland</td><td>4,737,003,000</td><td>1.7%</td></tr>
<tr><td>15</td><td>Massachusetts</td><td>5,731,241,000</td><td>2.0%</td><td>21</td><td>Virginia</td><td>4,673,802,000</td><td>1.7%</td></tr>
<tr><td>8</td><td>Michigan</td><td>9,837,380,000</td><td>3.5%</td><td>22</td><td>South Carolina</td><td>4,373,722,000</td><td>1.6%</td></tr>
<tr><td>10</td><td>Minnesota</td><td>7,473,369,000</td><td>2.7%</td><td>23</td><td>Alabama</td><td>4,161,953,000</td><td>1.5%</td></tr>
<tr><td>28</td><td>Mississippi</td><td>3,236,353,000</td><td>1.2%</td><td>24</td><td>Oregon</td><td>4,045,141,000</td><td>1.4%</td></tr>
<tr><td>17</td><td>Missouri</td><td>5,519,734,000</td><td>2.0%</td><td>25</td><td>Connecticut</td><td>3,471,835,000</td><td>1.2%</td></tr>
<tr><td>46</td><td>Montana</td><td>670,968,000</td><td>0.2%</td><td>26</td><td>Louisiana</td><td>3,362,348,000</td><td>1.2%</td></tr>
<tr><td>37</td><td>Nebraska</td><td>1,702,873,000</td><td>0.6%</td><td>27</td><td>Arizona</td><td>3,286,119,000</td><td>1.2%</td></tr>
<tr><td>41</td><td>Nevada</td><td>1,120,376,000</td><td>0.4%</td><td>28</td><td>Mississippi</td><td>3,236,353,000</td><td>1.2%</td></tr>
<tr><td>44</td><td>New Hampshire</td><td>1,029,934,000</td><td>0.4%</td><td>29</td><td>Oklahoma</td><td>3,191,774,000</td><td>1.1%</td></tr>
<tr><td>11</td><td>New Jersey</td><td>6,608,168,000</td><td>2.4%</td><td>30</td><td>Colorado</td><td>2,823,132,000</td><td>1.0%</td></tr>
<tr><td>34</td><td>New Mexico</td><td>2,076,797,000</td><td>0.7%</td><td>31</td><td>Iowa</td><td>2,682,250,000</td><td>1.0%</td></tr>
<tr><td>2</td><td>New York</td><td>32,503,209,000</td><td>11.6%</td><td>32</td><td>Arkansas</td><td>2,592,774,000</td><td>0.9%</td></tr>
<tr><td>9</td><td>North Carolina</td><td>7,657,145,000</td><td>2.7%</td><td>33</td><td>West Virginia</td><td>2,139,275,000</td><td>0.8%</td></tr>
<tr><td>47</td><td>North Dakota</td><td>663,785,000</td><td>0.2%</td><td>34</td><td>New Mexico</td><td>2,076,797,000</td><td>0.7%</td></tr>
<tr><td>6</td><td>Ohio</td><td>12,278,304,000</td><td>4.4%</td><td>35</td><td>Kansas</td><td>2,002,967,000</td><td>0.7%</td></tr>
<tr><td>29</td><td>Oklahoma</td><td>3,191,774,000</td><td>1.1%</td><td>36</td><td>Maine</td><td>1,791,700,000</td><td>0.6%</td></tr>
<tr><td>24</td><td>Oregon</td><td>4,045,141,000</td><td>1.4%</td><td>37</td><td>Nebraska</td><td>1,702,873,000</td><td>0.6%</td></tr>
<tr><td>4</td><td>Pennsylvania</td><td>14,486,426,000</td><td>5.2%</td><td>38</td><td>Rhode Island</td><td>1,666,668,000</td><td>0.6%</td></tr>
<tr><td>38</td><td>Rhode Island</td><td>1,666,668,000</td><td>0.6%</td><td>39</td><td>Utah</td><td>1,595,137,000</td><td>0.6%</td></tr>
<tr><td>22</td><td>South Carolina</td><td>4,373,722,000</td><td>1.6%</td><td>40</td><td>Hawaii</td><td>1,141,298,000</td><td>0.4%</td></tr>
<tr><td>49</td><td>South Dakota</td><td>604,844,000</td><td>0.2%</td><td>41</td><td>Nevada</td><td>1,120,376,000</td><td>0.4%</td></tr>
<tr><td>12</td><td>Tennessee</td><td>6,458,267,000</td><td>2.3%</td><td>42</td><td>Idaho</td><td>1,034,938,000</td><td>0.4%</td></tr>
<tr><td>3</td><td>Texas</td><td>14,903,225,000</td><td>5.3%</td><td>43</td><td>Alaska</td><td>1,034,937,000</td><td>0.4%</td></tr>
<tr><td>39</td><td>Utah</td><td>1,595,137,000</td><td>0.6%</td><td>44</td><td>New Hampshire</td><td>1,029,934,000</td><td>0.4%</td></tr>
<tr><td>45</td><td>Vermont</td><td>756,815,000</td><td>0.3%</td><td>45</td><td>Vermont</td><td>756,815,000</td><td>0.3%</td></tr>
<tr><td>21</td><td>Virginia</td><td>4,673,802,000</td><td>1.7%</td><td>46</td><td>Montana</td><td>670,968,000</td><td>0.2%</td></tr>
<tr><td>13</td><td>Washington</td><td>6,198,479,000</td><td>2.2%</td><td>47</td><td>North Dakota</td><td>663,785,000</td><td>0.2%</td></tr>
<tr><td>33</td><td>West Virginia</td><td>2,139,275,000</td><td>0.8%</td><td>48</td><td>Delaware</td><td>659,394,000</td><td>0.2%</td></tr>
<tr><td>16</td><td>Wisconsin</td><td>5,559,624,000</td><td>2.0%</td><td>49</td><td>South Dakota</td><td>604,844,000</td><td>0.2%</td></tr>
<tr><td>50</td><td>Wyoming</td><td>381,266,000</td><td>0.1%</td><td>50</td><td>Wyoming</td><td>381,266,000</td><td>0.1%</td></tr>
<tr><td></td><td></td><td></td><td></td><td></td><td>District of Columbia</td><td>1,462,362,000</td><td>0.5%</td></tr>
</table>

Source: U.S. Bureau of the Census, Governments Division
   "State and Local Government Finances: 2002 Census" (http://www.census.gov/govs/www/estimate02.html)
*Direct general expenditures. Includes funds for cash assistance programs, medical and other vendor payments, welfare institutions and other public welfare programs.

500

Per Capita State and Local Government Expenditures
For Public Welfare Programs in 2002
National Per Capita = $971*

RANK	STATE	PER CAPITA
25	Alabama	$929
2	Alaska	1,615
49	Arizona	604
24	Arkansas	958
19	California	1,016
48	Colorado	628
20	Connecticut	1,004
33	Delaware	818
41	Florida	749
44	Georgia	721
26	Hawaii	924
37	Idaho	771
36	Illinois	784
32	Indiana	863
29	Iowa	914
42	Kansas	738
8	Kentucky	1,178
40	Louisiana	751
5	Maine	1,381
31	Maryland	871
30	Massachusetts	894
22	Michigan	980
4	Minnesota	1,487
11	Mississippi	1,129
23	Missouri	972
43	Montana	737
21	Nebraska	986
50	Nevada	517
34	New Hampshire	807
38	New Jersey	770
12	New Mexico	1,119
1	New York	1,697
27	North Carolina	921
16	North Dakota	1,047
14	Ohio	1,076
28	Oklahoma	915
10	Oregon	1,148
9	Pennsylvania	1,175
3	Rhode Island	1,559
15	South Carolina	1,065
35	South Dakota	795
13	Tennessee	1,115
46	Texas	686
45	Utah	688
6	Vermont	1,228
47	Virginia	643
17	Washington	1,022
7	West Virginia	1,185
17	Wisconsin	1,022
39	Wyoming	764

RANK	STATE	PER CAPITA
1	New York	$1,697
2	Alaska	1,615
3	Rhode Island	1,559
4	Minnesota	1,487
5	Maine	1,381
6	Vermont	1,228
7	West Virginia	1,185
8	Kentucky	1,178
9	Pennsylvania	1,175
10	Oregon	1,148
11	Mississippi	1,129
12	New Mexico	1,119
13	Tennessee	1,115
14	Ohio	1,076
15	South Carolina	1,065
16	North Dakota	1,047
17	Washington	1,022
17	Wisconsin	1,022
19	California	1,016
20	Connecticut	1,004
21	Nebraska	986
22	Michigan	980
23	Missouri	972
24	Arkansas	958
25	Alabama	929
26	Hawaii	924
27	North Carolina	921
28	Oklahoma	915
29	Iowa	914
30	Massachusetts	894
31	Maryland	871
32	Indiana	863
33	Delaware	818
34	New Hampshire	807
35	South Dakota	795
36	Illinois	784
37	Idaho	771
38	New Jersey	770
39	Wyoming	764
40	Louisiana	751
41	Florida	749
42	Kansas	738
43	Montana	737
44	Georgia	721
45	Utah	688
46	Texas	686
47	Virginia	643
48	Colorado	628
49	Arizona	604
50	Nevada	517

District of Columbia	2,590

Source: Morgan Quitno Press using data from U.S. Bureau of the Census, Governments Division
  "State and Local Government Finances: 2002 Census" (http://www.census.gov/govs/www/estimate02.html)
*Direct general expenditures. Includes funds for cash assistance programs, medical and other vendor payments, welfare institutions and other public welfare programs.

State and Local Government Spending for Public Welfare Programs As a Percent of All State and Local Government Expenditures in 2002
National Percent = 16.2%*

ALPHA ORDER

RANK	STATE	PERCENT
21	Alabama	16.9
44	Alaska	12.3
42	Arizona	13.0
10	Arkansas	19.8
30	California	15.1
48	Colorado	10.4
33	Connecticut	14.3
44	Delaware	12.3
32	Florida	14.4
36	Georgia	13.7
34	Hawaii	13.8
29	Idaho	15.2
39	Illinois	13.4
23	Indiana	16.2
27	Iowa	15.6
37	Kansas	13.5
3	Kentucky	22.3
34	Louisiana	13.8
2	Maine	22.5
31	Maryland	14.9
37	Massachusetts	13.5
23	Michigan	16.2
6	Minnesota	21.4
7	Mississippi	21.0
12	Missouri	19.0
41	Montana	13.3
18	Nebraska	17.5
50	Nevada	9.5
23	New Hampshire	16.2
46	New Jersey	12.2
15	New Mexico	18.2
8	New York	20.2
19	North Carolina	17.2
20	North Dakota	17.1
14	Ohio	18.3
16	Oklahoma	17.6
16	Oregon	17.6
10	Pennsylvania	19.8
1	Rhode Island	24.7
13	South Carolina	18.4
27	South Dakota	15.6
3	Tennessee	22.3
39	Texas	13.4
43	Utah	12.4
9	Vermont	19.9
47	Virginia	11.9
26	Washington	16.0
5	West Virginia	21.7
22	Wisconsin	16.4
49	Wyoming	9.9

RANK ORDER

RANK	STATE	PERCENT
1	Rhode Island	24.7
2	Maine	22.5
3	Kentucky	22.3
3	Tennessee	22.3
5	West Virginia	21.7
6	Minnesota	21.4
7	Mississippi	21.0
8	New York	20.2
9	Vermont	19.9
10	Arkansas	19.8
10	Pennsylvania	19.8
12	Missouri	19.0
13	South Carolina	18.4
14	Ohio	18.3
15	New Mexico	18.2
16	Oklahoma	17.6
16	Oregon	17.6
18	Nebraska	17.5
19	North Carolina	17.2
20	North Dakota	17.1
21	Alabama	16.9
22	Wisconsin	16.4
23	Indiana	16.2
23	Michigan	16.2
23	New Hampshire	16.2
26	Washington	16.0
27	Iowa	15.6
27	South Dakota	15.6
29	Idaho	15.2
30	California	15.1
31	Maryland	14.9
32	Florida	14.4
33	Connecticut	14.3
34	Hawaii	13.8
34	Louisiana	13.8
36	Georgia	13.7
37	Kansas	13.5
37	Massachusetts	13.5
39	Illinois	13.4
39	Texas	13.4
41	Montana	13.3
42	Arizona	13.0
43	Utah	12.4
44	Alaska	12.3
44	Delaware	12.3
46	New Jersey	12.2
47	Virginia	11.9
48	Colorado	10.4
49	Wyoming	9.9
50	Nevada	9.5

	District of Columbia	23.7

Source: Morgan Quitno Press using data from U.S. Bureau of the Census, Governments Division
"State and Local Government Finances: 2002 Census" (http://www.census.gov/govs/www/estimate02.html)
*As a percent of direct general expenditures. Includes funds for cash assistance programs, medical and other vendor payments, welfare institutions and other public welfare programs.

Social Security (OASDI) Payments in 2004

National Total = $493,078,000,000*

ALPHA ORDER

RANK	STATE	PAYMENTS	% of USA
20	Alabama	$8,697,000,000	1.8%
50	Alaska	618,000,000	0.1%
19	Arizona	9,282,000,000	1.9%
31	Arkansas	5,228,000,000	1.1%
1	California	45,788,000,000	9.3%
29	Colorado	5,822,000,000	1.2%
26	Connecticut	6,642,000,000	1.3%
45	Delaware	1,618,000,000	0.3%
2	Florida	34,976,000,000	7.1%
11	Georgia	11,958,000,000	2.4%
42	Hawaii	2,039,000,000	0.4%
41	Idaho	2,202,000,000	0.4%
7	Illinois	20,456,000,000	4.1%
13	Indiana	11,259,000,000	2.3%
30	Iowa	5,689,000,000	1.2%
33	Kansas	4,745,000,000	1.0%
23	Kentucky	7,656,000,000	1.6%
25	Louisiana	7,121,000,000	1.4%
39	Maine	2,548,000,000	0.5%
22	Maryland	8,076,000,000	1.6%
14	Massachusetts	11,195,000,000	2.3%
8	Michigan	19,067,000,000	3.9%
21	Minnesota	8,080,000,000	1.6%
32	Mississippi	5,092,000,000	1.0%
15	Missouri	10,686,000,000	2.2%
44	Montana	1,653,000,000	0.3%
36	Nebraska	2,963,000,000	0.6%
35	Nevada	3,594,000,000	0.7%
40	New Hampshire	2,327,000,000	0.5%
9	New Jersey	15,777,000,000	3.2%
37	New Mexico	2,871,000,000	0.6%
3	New York	33,354,000,000	6.8%
10	North Carolina	14,779,000,000	3.0%
47	North Dakota	1,125,000,000	0.2%
6	Ohio	20,609,000,000	4.2%
28	Oklahoma	6,234,000,000	1.3%
27	Oregon	6,437,000,000	1.3%
5	Pennsylvania	25,893,000,000	5.3%
43	Rhode Island	2,007,000,000	0.4%
24	South Carolina	7,538,000,000	1.5%
46	South Dakota	1,340,000,000	0.3%
16	Tennessee	10,679,000,000	2.2%
4	Texas	28,664,000,000	5.8%
38	Utah	2,710,000,000	0.5%
48	Vermont	1,117,000,000	0.2%
12	Virginia	11,381,000,000	2.3%
18	Washington	9,833,000,000	2.0%
34	West Virginia	4,189,000,000	0.8%
17	Wisconsin	10,000,000,000	2.0%
49	Wyoming	856,000,000	0.2%

RANK ORDER

RANK	STATE	PAYMENTS	% of USA
1	California	$45,788,000,000	9.3%
2	Florida	34,976,000,000	7.1%
3	New York	33,354,000,000	6.8%
4	Texas	28,664,000,000	5.8%
5	Pennsylvania	25,893,000,000	5.3%
6	Ohio	20,609,000,000	4.2%
7	Illinois	20,456,000,000	4.1%
8	Michigan	19,067,000,000	3.9%
9	New Jersey	15,777,000,000	3.2%
10	North Carolina	14,779,000,000	3.0%
11	Georgia	11,958,000,000	2.4%
12	Virginia	11,381,000,000	2.3%
13	Indiana	11,259,000,000	2.3%
14	Massachusetts	11,195,000,000	2.3%
15	Missouri	10,686,000,000	2.2%
16	Tennessee	10,679,000,000	2.2%
17	Wisconsin	10,000,000,000	2.0%
18	Washington	9,833,000,000	2.0%
19	Arizona	9,282,000,000	1.9%
20	Alabama	8,697,000,000	1.8%
21	Minnesota	8,080,000,000	1.6%
22	Maryland	8,076,000,000	1.6%
23	Kentucky	7,656,000,000	1.6%
24	South Carolina	7,538,000,000	1.5%
25	Louisiana	7,121,000,000	1.4%
26	Connecticut	6,642,000,000	1.3%
27	Oregon	6,437,000,000	1.3%
28	Oklahoma	6,234,000,000	1.3%
29	Colorado	5,822,000,000	1.2%
30	Iowa	5,689,000,000	1.2%
31	Arkansas	5,228,000,000	1.1%
32	Mississippi	5,092,000,000	1.0%
33	Kansas	4,745,000,000	1.0%
34	West Virginia	4,189,000,000	0.8%
35	Nevada	3,594,000,000	0.7%
36	Nebraska	2,963,000,000	0.6%
37	New Mexico	2,871,000,000	0.6%
38	Utah	2,710,000,000	0.5%
39	Maine	2,548,000,000	0.5%
40	New Hampshire	2,327,000,000	0.5%
41	Idaho	2,202,000,000	0.4%
42	Hawaii	2,039,000,000	0.4%
43	Rhode Island	2,007,000,000	0.4%
44	Montana	1,653,000,000	0.3%
45	Delaware	1,618,000,000	0.3%
46	South Dakota	1,340,000,000	0.3%
47	North Dakota	1,125,000,000	0.2%
48	Vermont	1,117,000,000	0.2%
49	Wyoming	856,000,000	0.2%
50	Alaska	618,000,000	0.1%
	District of Columbia	653,000,000	0.1%

Source: Social Security Administration
    "Social Security Bulletin, Annual Statistical Supplement 2005"
    (http://www.ssa.gov/policy/docs/statcomps/supplement/2005/)
*"OASDI" is Old Age, Survivors and Disability Insurance. National total includes $7,915,000,000 in payments to recipients in U.S. territories and foreign countries.

Per Capita Social Security (OASDI) Payments in 2004

National Per Capita = $1,652*

<table>
<tr><td colspan="3">ALPHA ORDER</td><td colspan="3">RANK ORDER</td></tr>
<tr><th>RANK</th><th>STATE</th><th>PER CAPITA</th><th>RANK</th><th>STATE</th><th>PER CAPITA</th></tr>
<tr><td>7</td><td>Alabama</td><td>$1,922</td><td>1</td><td>West Virginia</td><td>$2,311</td></tr>
<tr><td>50</td><td>Alaska</td><td>940</td><td>2</td><td>Pennsylvania</td><td>2,089</td></tr>
<tr><td>34</td><td>Arizona</td><td>1,617</td><td>3</td><td>Florida</td><td>2,012</td></tr>
<tr><td>8</td><td>Arkansas</td><td>1,901</td><td>4</td><td>Delaware</td><td>1,949</td></tr>
<tr><td>46</td><td>California</td><td>1,277</td><td>5</td><td>Maine</td><td>1,938</td></tr>
<tr><td>48</td><td>Colorado</td><td>1,265</td><td>6</td><td>Iowa</td><td>1,927</td></tr>
<tr><td>9</td><td>Connecticut</td><td>1,898</td><td>7</td><td>Alabama</td><td>1,922</td></tr>
<tr><td>4</td><td>Delaware</td><td>1,949</td><td>8</td><td>Arkansas</td><td>1,901</td></tr>
<tr><td>3</td><td>Florida</td><td>2,012</td><td>9</td><td>Connecticut</td><td>1,898</td></tr>
<tr><td>45</td><td>Georgia</td><td>1,341</td><td>10</td><td>Michigan</td><td>1,887</td></tr>
<tr><td>35</td><td>Hawaii</td><td>1,616</td><td>11</td><td>Rhode Island</td><td>1,858</td></tr>
<tr><td>40</td><td>Idaho</td><td>1,578</td><td>12</td><td>Missouri</td><td>1,855</td></tr>
<tr><td>36</td><td>Illinois</td><td>1,609</td><td>13</td><td>Kentucky</td><td>1,848</td></tr>
<tr><td>17</td><td>Indiana</td><td>1,808</td><td>14</td><td>New Jersey</td><td>1,817</td></tr>
<tr><td>6</td><td>Iowa</td><td>1,927</td><td>14</td><td>Wisconsin</td><td>1,817</td></tr>
<tr><td>29</td><td>Kansas</td><td>1,736</td><td>16</td><td>Tennessee</td><td>1,812</td></tr>
<tr><td>13</td><td>Kentucky</td><td>1,848</td><td>17</td><td>Indiana</td><td>1,808</td></tr>
<tr><td>39</td><td>Louisiana</td><td>1,580</td><td>18</td><td>Ohio</td><td>1,800</td></tr>
<tr><td>5</td><td>Maine</td><td>1,938</td><td>19</td><td>Vermont</td><td>1,798</td></tr>
<tr><td>44</td><td>Maryland</td><td>1,452</td><td>20</td><td>South Carolina</td><td>1,796</td></tr>
<tr><td>27</td><td>Massachusetts</td><td>1,747</td><td>21</td><td>Oregon</td><td>1,792</td></tr>
<tr><td>10</td><td>Michigan</td><td>1,007</td><td>22</td><td>New Hampshire</td><td>1,791</td></tr>
<tr><td>37</td><td>Minnesota</td><td>1,585</td><td>23</td><td>Montana</td><td>1,783</td></tr>
<tr><td>26</td><td>Mississippi</td><td>1,755</td><td>24</td><td>Oklahoma</td><td>1,769</td></tr>
<tr><td>12</td><td>Missouri</td><td>1,855</td><td>25</td><td>North Dakota</td><td>1,768</td></tr>
<tr><td>23</td><td>Montana</td><td>1,783</td><td>26</td><td>Mississippi</td><td>1,755</td></tr>
<tr><td>32</td><td>Nebraska</td><td>1,695</td><td>27</td><td>Massachusetts</td><td>1,747</td></tr>
<tr><td>41</td><td>Nevada</td><td>1,541</td><td>28</td><td>South Dakota</td><td>1,739</td></tr>
<tr><td>22</td><td>New Hampshire</td><td>1,791</td><td>29</td><td>Kansas</td><td>1,736</td></tr>
<tr><td>14</td><td>New Jersey</td><td>1,817</td><td>30</td><td>New York</td><td>1,730</td></tr>
<tr><td>43</td><td>New Mexico</td><td>1,509</td><td>30</td><td>North Carolina</td><td>1,730</td></tr>
<tr><td>30</td><td>New York</td><td>1,730</td><td>32</td><td>Nebraska</td><td>1,695</td></tr>
<tr><td>30</td><td>North Carolina</td><td>1,730</td><td>33</td><td>Wyoming</td><td>1,692</td></tr>
<tr><td>25</td><td>North Dakota</td><td>1,768</td><td>34</td><td>Arizona</td><td>1,617</td></tr>
<tr><td>18</td><td>Ohio</td><td>1,800</td><td>35</td><td>Hawaii</td><td>1,616</td></tr>
<tr><td>24</td><td>Oklahoma</td><td>1,769</td><td>36</td><td>Illinois</td><td>1,609</td></tr>
<tr><td>21</td><td>Oregon</td><td>1,792</td><td>37</td><td>Minnesota</td><td>1,585</td></tr>
<tr><td>2</td><td>Pennsylvania</td><td>2,089</td><td>38</td><td>Washington</td><td>1,584</td></tr>
<tr><td>11</td><td>Rhode Island</td><td>1,858</td><td>39</td><td>Louisiana</td><td>1,580</td></tr>
<tr><td>20</td><td>South Carolina</td><td>1,796</td><td>40</td><td>Idaho</td><td>1,578</td></tr>
<tr><td>28</td><td>South Dakota</td><td>1,739</td><td>41</td><td>Nevada</td><td>1,541</td></tr>
<tr><td>16</td><td>Tennessee</td><td>1,812</td><td>42</td><td>Virginia</td><td>1,521</td></tr>
<tr><td>47</td><td>Texas</td><td>1,276</td><td>43</td><td>New Mexico</td><td>1,509</td></tr>
<tr><td>49</td><td>Utah</td><td>1,120</td><td>44</td><td>Maryland</td><td>1,452</td></tr>
<tr><td>19</td><td>Vermont</td><td>1,798</td><td>45</td><td>Georgia</td><td>1,341</td></tr>
<tr><td>42</td><td>Virginia</td><td>1,521</td><td>46</td><td>California</td><td>1,277</td></tr>
<tr><td>38</td><td>Washington</td><td>1,584</td><td>47</td><td>Texas</td><td>1,276</td></tr>
<tr><td>1</td><td>West Virginia</td><td>2,311</td><td>48</td><td>Colorado</td><td>1,265</td></tr>
<tr><td>14</td><td>Wisconsin</td><td>1,817</td><td>49</td><td>Utah</td><td>1,120</td></tr>
<tr><td>33</td><td>Wyoming</td><td>1,692</td><td>50</td><td>Alaska</td><td>940</td></tr>
<tr><td></td><td></td><td></td><td></td><td>District of Columbia</td><td>1,178</td></tr>
</table>

Source: Morgan Quitno Press using data from Social Security Administration
"Social Security Bulletin, Annual Statistical Supplement 2005"
(http://www.ssa.gov/policy/docs/statcomps/supplement/2005/)
"OASDI" is Old Age, Survivors and Disability Insurance. National per capita does not include payments or population in U.S. territories and foreign countries.

Social Security (OASDI) Monthly Payments in 2004

National Total = $41,591,855,000*

ALPHA ORDER					RANK ORDER			
RANK	STATE	PAYMENTS	% of USA		RANK	STATE	PAYMENTS	% of USA
20	Alabama	$722,714,000	1.7%		1	California	$3,876,601,000	9.3%
50	Alaska	51,917,000	0.1%		2	Florida	2,985,634,000	7.2%
19	Arizona	794,247,000	1.9%		3	New York	2,821,845,000	6.8%
31	Arkansas	436,581,000	1.0%		4	Texas	2,406,126,000	5.8%
1	California	3,876,601,000	9.3%		5	Pennsylvania	2,180,687,000	5.2%
29	Colorado	493,571,000	1.2%		6	Ohio	1,723,337,000	4.1%
26	Connecticut	566,578,000	1.4%		7	Illinois	1,722,772,000	4.1%
45	Delaware	137,822,000	0.3%		8	Michigan	1,603,478,000	3.9%
2	Florida	2,985,634,000	7.2%		9	New Jersey	1,341,270,000	3.2%
11	Georgia	1,004,376,000	2.4%		10	North Carolina	1,251,605,000	3.0%
42	Hawaii	175,645,000	0.4%		11	Georgia	1,004,376,000	2.4%
41	Idaho	187,314,000	0.5%		12	Virginia	959,592,000	2.3%
7	Illinois	1,722,772,000	4.1%		13	Indiana	950,014,000	2.3%
13	Indiana	950,014,000	2.3%		14	Massachusetts	946,394,000	2.3%
30	Iowa	480,250,000	1.2%		15	Missouri	898,963,000	2.2%
33	Kansas	401,416,000	1.0%		16	Tennessee	895,689,000	2.2%
24	Kentucky	632,483,000	1.5%		17	Wisconsin	850,099,000	2.0%
25	Louisiana	582,293,000	1.4%		18	Washington	837,606,000	2.0%
39	Maine	213,717,000	0.5%		19	Arizona	794,247,000	1.9%
22	Maryland	681,245,000	1.6%		20	Alabama	722,714,000	1.7%
14	Massachusetts	946,394,000	2.3%		21	Minnesota	686,336,000	1.7%
8	Michigan	1,603,478,000	3.9%		22	Maryland	681,245,000	1.6%
21	Minnesota	686,336,000	1.7%		23	South Carolina	635,980,000	1.5%
32	Mississippi	422,221,000	1.0%		24	Kentucky	632,483,000	1.5%
15	Missouri	808,963,000	2.2%		25	Louisiana	582,293,000	1.4%
44	Montana	139,775,000	0.3%		26	Connecticut	566,578,000	1.4%
36	Nebraska	251,213,000	0.6%		27	Oregon	548,081,000	1.3%
35	Nevada	307,626,000	0.7%		28	Oklahoma	522,890,000	1.3%
40	New Hampshire	197,646,000	0.5%		29	Colorado	493,571,000	1.2%
9	New Jersey	1,341,270,000	3.2%		30	Iowa	480,250,000	1.2%
37	New Mexico	243,013,000	0.6%		31	Arkansas	436,581,000	1.0%
3	New York	2,821,845,000	6.8%		32	Mississippi	422,221,000	1.0%
10	North Carolina	1,251,605,000	3.0%		33	Kansas	401,416,000	1.0%
48	North Dakota	94,123,000	0.2%		34	West Virginia	343,345,000	0.8%
6	Ohio	1,723,337,000	4.1%		35	Nevada	307,626,000	0.7%
28	Oklahoma	522,890,000	1.3%		36	Nebraska	251,213,000	0.6%
27	Oregon	548,081,000	1.3%		37	New Mexico	243,013,000	0.6%
5	Pennsylvania	2,180,687,000	5.2%		38	Utah	230,695,000	0.6%
43	Rhode Island	170,040,000	0.4%		39	Maine	213,717,000	0.5%
23	South Carolina	635,980,000	1.5%		40	New Hampshire	197,646,000	0.5%
46	South Dakota	113,123,000	0.3%		41	Idaho	187,314,000	0.5%
16	Tennessee	895,689,000	2.2%		42	Hawaii	175,645,000	0.4%
4	Texas	2,406,126,000	5.8%		43	Rhode Island	170,040,000	0.4%
38	Utah	230,695,000	0.6%		44	Montana	139,775,000	0.3%
47	Vermont	94,676,000	0.2%		45	Delaware	137,822,000	0.3%
12	Virginia	959,592,000	2.3%		46	South Dakota	113,123,000	0.3%
18	Washington	837,606,000	2.0%		47	Vermont	94,676,000	0.2%
34	West Virginia	343,345,000	0.8%		48	North Dakota	94,123,000	0.2%
17	Wisconsin	850,099,000	2.0%		49	Wyoming	72,944,000	0.2%
49	Wyoming	72,944,000	0.2%		50	Alaska	51,917,000	0.1%
						District of Columbia	54,878,000	0.1%

Source: Social Security Administration
"Social Security Bulletin, Annual Statistical Supplement 2005"
(http://www.ssa.gov/policy/docs/statcomps/supplement/2005/)
For December 2004. "OASDI" is Old Age, Survivors and Disability Insurance. National total includes
$646,000,000 in payments to recipients in U.S. territories and foreign countries.

Social Security (OASDI) Beneficiaries in 2004

National Total = 47,707,380*

Source: Social Security Administration
   "Social Security Bulletin, Annual Statistical Supplement 2005"
   (http://www.ssa.gov/policy/docs/statcomps/supplement/2005/)
*For December 2004. "OASDI" is Old Age, Survivors and Disability Insurance. National total includes 1,172,210 beneficiaries in U.S. territories and foreign countries.

Average Monthly Social Security (OASDI) Payment in 2004

National Average = $880 Each Month per Beneficiary*

ALPHA ORDER

RANK	STATE	AVERAGE BENEFIT
43	Alabama	$817
42	Alaska	818
16	Arizona	894
48	Arkansas	799
25	California	879
28	Colorado	864
2	Connecticut	970
5	Delaware	926
21	Florida	883
35	Georgia	843
23	Hawaii	882
32	Idaho	854
7	Illinois	915
7	Indiana	915
24	Iowa	880
13	Kansas	898
45	Kentucky	806
49	Louisiana	788
46	Maine	805
15	Maryland	895
17	Massachusetts	887
3	Michigan	934
19	Minnesota	886
50	Mississippi	774
30	Missouri	859
37	Montana	842
27	Nebraska	865
11	Nevada	903
12	New Hampshire	902
1	New Jersey	979
47	New Mexico	800
4	New York	927
33	North Carolina	853
41	North Dakota	820
21	Ohio	883
39	Oklahoma	839
14	Oregon	896
9	Pennsylvania	907
17	Rhode Island	887
34	South Carolina	847
44	South Dakota	809
40	Tennessee	837
38	Texas	840
25	Utah	879
30	Vermont	859
29	Virginia	861
6	Washington	917
35	West Virginia	843
9	Wisconsin	907
20	Wyoming	884

RANK ORDER

RANK	STATE	AVERAGE BENEFIT
1	New Jersey	$979
2	Connecticut	970
3	Michigan	934
4	New York	927
5	Delaware	926
6	Washington	917
7	Illinois	915
7	Indiana	915
9	Pennsylvania	907
9	Wisconsin	907
11	Nevada	903
12	New Hampshire	902
13	Kansas	898
14	Oregon	896
15	Maryland	895
16	Arizona	894
17	Massachusetts	887
17	Rhode Island	887
19	Minnesota	886
20	Wyoming	884
21	Florida	883
21	Ohio	883
23	Hawaii	882
24	Iowa	880
25	California	879
25	Utah	879
27	Nebraska	865
28	Colorado	864
29	Virginia	861
30	Missouri	859
30	Vermont	859
32	Idaho	854
33	North Carolina	853
34	South Carolina	847
35	Georgia	843
35	West Virginia	843
37	Montana	842
38	Texas	840
39	Oklahoma	839
40	Tennessee	837
41	North Dakota	820
42	Alaska	818
43	Alabama	817
44	South Dakota	809
45	Kentucky	806
46	Maine	805
47	New Mexico	800
48	Arkansas	799
49	Louisiana	788
50	Mississippi	774
	District of Columbia	766

Source: Morgan Quitno Press using data from Social Security Administration
    "Social Security Bulletin, Annual Statistical Supplement 2005"
      (http://www.ssa.gov/policy/docs/statcomps/supplement/2005/)
*As of December 2004. "OASDI" is Old Age, Survivors and Disability Insurance. National average does not include
beneficiaries or payments in U.S. territories or foreign countries.

Social Security Supplemental Security Income Beneficiaries in 2004

National Total = 6,987,845 Beneficiaries*

<table>
<tr><td colspan="4">ALPHA ORDER</td><td colspan="4">RANK ORDER</td></tr>
<tr><td>RANK</td><td>STATE</td><td>BENEFICIARIES</td><td>% of USA</td><td>RANK</td><td>STATE</td><td>BENEFICIARIES</td><td>% of USA</td></tr>
<tr><td>14</td><td>Alabama</td><td>163,002</td><td>2.3%</td><td>1</td><td>California</td><td>1,183,002</td><td>16.9%</td></tr>
<tr><td>48</td><td>Alaska</td><td>10,781</td><td>0.2%</td><td>2</td><td>New York</td><td>626,593</td><td>9.0%</td></tr>
<tr><td>23</td><td>Arizona</td><td>94,400</td><td>1.4%</td><td>3</td><td>Texas</td><td>472,347</td><td>6.8%</td></tr>
<tr><td>26</td><td>Arkansas</td><td>87,928</td><td>1.3%</td><td>4</td><td>Florida</td><td>412,970</td><td>5.9%</td></tr>
<tr><td>1</td><td>California</td><td>1,183,002</td><td>16.9%</td><td>5</td><td>Pennsylvania</td><td>316,917</td><td>4.5%</td></tr>
<tr><td>31</td><td>Colorado</td><td>54,131</td><td>0.8%</td><td>6</td><td>Illinois</td><td>255,624</td><td>3.7%</td></tr>
<tr><td>33</td><td>Connecticut</td><td>51,536</td><td>0.7%</td><td>7</td><td>Ohio</td><td>245,401</td><td>3.5%</td></tr>
<tr><td>44</td><td>Delaware</td><td>13,452</td><td>0.2%</td><td>8</td><td>Michigan</td><td>219,337</td><td>3.1%</td></tr>
<tr><td>4</td><td>Florida</td><td>412,970</td><td>5.9%</td><td>9</td><td>Georgia</td><td>199,898</td><td>2.9%</td></tr>
<tr><td>9</td><td>Georgia</td><td>199,898</td><td>2.9%</td><td>10</td><td>North Carolina</td><td>195,654</td><td>2.8%</td></tr>
<tr><td>39</td><td>Hawaii</td><td>22,251</td><td>0.3%</td><td>11</td><td>Kentucky</td><td>179,438</td><td>2.6%</td></tr>
<tr><td>42</td><td>Idaho</td><td>20,993</td><td>0.3%</td><td>12</td><td>Louisiana</td><td>169,549</td><td>2.4%</td></tr>
<tr><td>6</td><td>Illinois</td><td>255,624</td><td>3.7%</td><td>13</td><td>Massachusetts</td><td>169,205</td><td>2.4%</td></tr>
<tr><td>22</td><td>Indiana</td><td>96,191</td><td>1.4%</td><td>14</td><td>Alabama</td><td>163,002</td><td>2.3%</td></tr>
<tr><td>34</td><td>Iowa</td><td>42,618</td><td>0.6%</td><td>15</td><td>Tennessee</td><td>160,521</td><td>2.3%</td></tr>
<tr><td>35</td><td>Kansas</td><td>38,476</td><td>0.6%</td><td>16</td><td>New Jersey</td><td>150,151</td><td>2.1%</td></tr>
<tr><td>11</td><td>Kentucky</td><td>179,438</td><td>2.6%</td><td>17</td><td>Virginia</td><td>134,531</td><td>1.9%</td></tr>
<tr><td>12</td><td>Louisiana</td><td>169,549</td><td>2.4%</td><td>18</td><td>Mississippi</td><td>125,180</td><td>1.8%</td></tr>
<tr><td>37</td><td>Maine</td><td>31,641</td><td>0.5%</td><td>19</td><td>Missouri</td><td>116,131</td><td>1.7%</td></tr>
<tr><td>24</td><td>Maryland</td><td>92,776</td><td>1.3%</td><td>20</td><td>Washington</td><td>111,895</td><td>1.6%</td></tr>
<tr><td>13</td><td>Massachusetts</td><td>169,205</td><td>2.4%</td><td>21</td><td>South Carolina</td><td>105,223</td><td>1.5%</td></tr>
<tr><td>8</td><td>Michigan</td><td>219,337</td><td>3.1%</td><td>22</td><td>Indiana</td><td>96,191</td><td>1.4%</td></tr>
<tr><td>29</td><td>Minnesota</td><td>70,745</td><td>1.0%</td><td>23</td><td>Arizona</td><td>94,400</td><td>1.4%</td></tr>
<tr><td>18</td><td>Mississippi</td><td>125,180</td><td>1.8%</td><td>24</td><td>Maryland</td><td>92,776</td><td>1.3%</td></tr>
<tr><td>19</td><td>Missouri</td><td>116,131</td><td>1.7%</td><td>25</td><td>Wisconsin</td><td>90,026</td><td>1.3%</td></tr>
<tr><td>43</td><td>Montana</td><td>14,558</td><td>0.2%</td><td>26</td><td>Arkansas</td><td>87,928</td><td>1.3%</td></tr>
<tr><td>40</td><td>Nebraska</td><td>22,100</td><td>0.3%</td><td>27</td><td>Oklahoma</td><td>77,100</td><td>1.1%</td></tr>
<tr><td>36</td><td>Nevada</td><td>32,129</td><td>0.5%</td><td>28</td><td>West Virginia</td><td>75,982</td><td>1.1%</td></tr>
<tr><td>45</td><td>New Hampshire</td><td>13,029</td><td>0.2%</td><td>29</td><td>Minnesota</td><td>70,745</td><td>1.0%</td></tr>
<tr><td>16</td><td>New Jersey</td><td>150,151</td><td>2.1%</td><td>30</td><td>Oregon</td><td>58,842</td><td>0.8%</td></tr>
<tr><td>32</td><td>New Mexico</td><td>51,656</td><td>0.7%</td><td>31</td><td>Colorado</td><td>54,131</td><td>0.8%</td></tr>
<tr><td>2</td><td>New York</td><td>626,593</td><td>9.0%</td><td>32</td><td>New Mexico</td><td>51,656</td><td>0.7%</td></tr>
<tr><td>10</td><td>North Carolina</td><td>195,654</td><td>2.8%</td><td>33</td><td>Connecticut</td><td>51,536</td><td>0.7%</td></tr>
<tr><td>49</td><td>North Dakota</td><td>7,966</td><td>0.1%</td><td>34</td><td>Iowa</td><td>42,618</td><td>0.6%</td></tr>
<tr><td>7</td><td>Ohio</td><td>245,401</td><td>3.5%</td><td>35</td><td>Kansas</td><td>38,476</td><td>0.6%</td></tr>
<tr><td>27</td><td>Oklahoma</td><td>77,100</td><td>1.1%</td><td>36</td><td>Nevada</td><td>32,129</td><td>0.5%</td></tr>
<tr><td>30</td><td>Oregon</td><td>58,842</td><td>0.8%</td><td>37</td><td>Maine</td><td>31,641</td><td>0.5%</td></tr>
<tr><td>5</td><td>Pennsylvania</td><td>316,917</td><td>4.5%</td><td>38</td><td>Rhode Island</td><td>29,703</td><td>0.4%</td></tr>
<tr><td>38</td><td>Rhode Island</td><td>29,703</td><td>0.4%</td><td>39</td><td>Hawaii</td><td>22,251</td><td>0.3%</td></tr>
<tr><td>21</td><td>South Carolina</td><td>105,223</td><td>1.5%</td><td>40</td><td>Nebraska</td><td>22,100</td><td>0.3%</td></tr>
<tr><td>47</td><td>South Dakota</td><td>12,469</td><td>0.2%</td><td>41</td><td>Utah</td><td>21,646</td><td>0.3%</td></tr>
<tr><td>15</td><td>Tennessee</td><td>160,521</td><td>2.3%</td><td>42</td><td>Idaho</td><td>20,993</td><td>0.3%</td></tr>
<tr><td>3</td><td>Texas</td><td>472,347</td><td>6.8%</td><td>43</td><td>Montana</td><td>14,558</td><td>0.2%</td></tr>
<tr><td>41</td><td>Utah</td><td>21,646</td><td>0.3%</td><td>44</td><td>Delaware</td><td>13,452</td><td>0.2%</td></tr>
<tr><td>46</td><td>Vermont</td><td>12,915</td><td>0.2%</td><td>45</td><td>New Hampshire</td><td>13,029</td><td>0.2%</td></tr>
<tr><td>17</td><td>Virginia</td><td>134,531</td><td>1.9%</td><td>46</td><td>Vermont</td><td>12,915</td><td>0.2%</td></tr>
<tr><td>20</td><td>Washington</td><td>111,895</td><td>1.6%</td><td>47</td><td>South Dakota</td><td>12,469</td><td>0.2%</td></tr>
<tr><td>28</td><td>West Virginia</td><td>75,982</td><td>1.1%</td><td>48</td><td>Alaska</td><td>10,781</td><td>0.2%</td></tr>
<tr><td>25</td><td>Wisconsin</td><td>90,026</td><td>1.3%</td><td>49</td><td>North Dakota</td><td>7,966</td><td>0.1%</td></tr>
<tr><td>50</td><td>Wyoming</td><td>5,645</td><td>0.1%</td><td>50</td><td>Wyoming</td><td>5,645</td><td>0.1%</td></tr>
<tr><td></td><td></td><td></td><td></td><td></td><td>District of Columbia</td><td>20,856</td><td>0.3%</td></tr>
</table>

Source: Social Security Administration
"Social Security Bulletin, Annual Statistical Supplement 2005"
(http://www.ssa.gov/policy/docs/statcomps/supplement/2005/)

*For December 2004. National total includes 735 beneficiaries in U.S. territories or otherwise not distributed by state. The SSI program provides income support to persons age 65 and older and blind or disabled adults and children.

Average Monthly Social Security Supplemental Security Income Payment: 2004

National Average = $428.29 Each Month per Beneficiary*

ALPHA ORDER				RANK ORDER		
RANK	STATE	AVERAGE BENEFIT		RANK	STATE	AVERAGE BENEFIT
38	Alabama	$374.41		1	California	$559.10
26	Alaska	386.74		2	New York	460.63
13	Arizona	405.51		3	Massachusetts	437.64
47	Arkansas	360.67		4	Pennsylvania	437.48
1	California	559.10		5	Hawaii	436.54
32	Colorado	381.02		6	Rhode Island	429.75
14	Connecticut	404.29		7	Illinois	426.76
23	Delaware	391.49		8	Michigan	424.10
20	Florida	394.73		9	Washington	423.16
39	Georgia	371.79		10	Ohio	417.72
5	Hawaii	436.54		11	New Jersey	414.80
30	Idaho	382.87		12	Maryland	408.08
7	Illinois	426.76		13	Arizona	405.51
17	Indiana	397.55		14	Connecticut	404.29
40	Iowa	369.78		15	West Virginia	401.34
29	Kansas	383.60		16	Minnesota	397.97
22	Kentucky	392.43		17	Indiana	397.55
24	Louisiana	390.90		18	Nevada	396.43
45	Maine	363.59		19	Oregon	395.38
12	Maryland	408.08		20	Florida	394.73
3	Massachusetts	437.64		21	Utah	394.04
8	Michigan	424.10		22	Kentucky	392.43
16	Minnesota	397.97		23	Delaware	391.49
41	Mississippi	369.42		24	Louisiana	390.90
28	Missouri	385.96		25	Vermont	387.02
34	Montana	376.56		26	Alaska	386.74
44	Nebraska	367.53		27	Wisconsin	386.42
18	Nevada	396.43		28	Missouri	385.96
36	New Hampshire	376.51		29	Kansas	383.60
11	New Jersey	414.80		30	Idaho	382.87
33	New Mexico	377.14		31	Oklahoma	382.12
2	New York	460.63		32	Colorado	381.02
48	North Carolina	358.55		33	New Mexico	377.14
50	North Dakota	337.26		34	Montana	376.56
10	Ohio	417.72		34	Tennessee	376.56
31	Oklahoma	382.12		36	New Hampshire	376.51
19	Oregon	395.38		37	Virginia	375.38
4	Pennsylvania	437.48		38	Alabama	374.41
6	Rhode Island	429.75		39	Georgia	371.79
42	South Carolina	368.74		40	Iowa	369.78
49	South Dakota	352.51		41	Mississippi	369.42
34	Tennessee	376.56		42	South Carolina	368.74
46	Texas	362.37		43	Wyoming	367.55
21	Utah	394.04		44	Nebraska	367.53
25	Vermont	387.02		45	Maine	363.59
37	Virginia	375.38		46	Texas	362.37
9	Washington	423.16		47	Arkansas	360.67
15	West Virginia	401.34		48	North Carolina	358.55
27	Wisconsin	386.42		49	South Dakota	352.51
43	Wyoming	367.55		50	North Dakota	337.26
					District of Columbia	430.42

Source: Social Security Administration
  "Social Security Bulletin, Annual Statistical Supplement 2005"
    (http://www.ssa.gov/policy/docs/statcomps/supplement/2005/)

*As of December 2004. National average includes payments to beneficiaries in U.S. territories and foreign countries. The SSI program provides income support to persons age 65 and older and blind or disabled adults and children

Medicare Enrollees in 2004

National Total = 41,729,000 Enrollees*

ALPHA ORDER

RANK	STATE	ENROLLEES	% of USA
20	Alabama	733,000	1.8%
50	Alaska	50,000	0.1%
19	Arizona	754,000	1.8%
31	Arkansas	461,000	1.1%
1	California	4,142,000	9.9%
29	Colorado	506,000	1.2%
27	Connecticut	525,000	1.3%
45	Delaware	123,000	0.3%
2	Florida	2,980,000	7.1%
11	Georgia	995,000	2.4%
42	Hawaii	178,000	0.4%
41	Idaho	184,000	0.4%
7	Illinois	1,678,000	4.0%
16	Indiana	889,000	2.1%
30	Iowa	485,000	1.2%
33	Kansas	397,000	1.0%
23	Kentucky	660,000	1.6%
24	Louisiana	629,000	1.5%
38	Maine	231,000	0.6%
22	Maryland	685,000	1.6%
12	Massachusetts	969,000	2.3%
8	Michigan	1,466,000	3.5%
21	Minnesota	687,000	1.6%
32	Mississippi	446,000	1.1%
14	Missouri	896,000	2.1%
44	Montana	145,000	0.3%
36	Nebraska	259,000	0.6%
35	Nevada	287,000	0.7%
40	New Hampshire	186,000	0.4%
10	New Jersey	1,226,000	2.9%
37	New Mexico	256,000	0.6%
3	New York	2,779,000	6.7%
9	North Carolina	1,234,000	3.0%
47	North Dakota	103,000	0.2%
6	Ohio	1,740,000	4.2%
26	Oklahoma	529,000	1.3%
27	Oregon	525,000	1.3%
5	Pennsylvania	2,120,000	5.1%
43	Rhode Island	173,000	0.4%
25	South Carolina	623,000	1.5%
45	South Dakota	123,000	0.3%
15	Tennessee	891,000	2.1%
4	Texas	2,450,000	5.9%
39	Utah	227,000	0.5%
48	Vermont	94,000	0.2%
13	Virginia	966,000	2.3%
18	Washington	795,000	1.9%
34	West Virginia	351,000	0.8%
17	Wisconsin	814,000	2.0%
49	Wyoming	69,000	0.2%

RANK ORDER

RANK	STATE	ENROLLEES	% of USA
1	California	4,142,000	9.9%
2	Florida	2,980,000	7.1%
3	New York	2,779,000	6.7%
4	Texas	2,450,000	5.9%
5	Pennsylvania	2,120,000	5.1%
6	Ohio	1,740,000	4.2%
7	Illinois	1,678,000	4.0%
8	Michigan	1,466,000	3.5%
9	North Carolina	1,234,000	3.0%
10	New Jersey	1,226,000	2.9%
11	Georgia	995,000	2.4%
12	Massachusetts	969,000	2.3%
13	Virginia	966,000	2.3%
14	Missouri	896,000	2.1%
15	Tennessee	891,000	2.1%
16	Indiana	889,000	2.1%
17	Wisconsin	814,000	2.0%
18	Washington	795,000	1.9%
19	Arizona	754,000	1.8%
20	Alabama	733,000	1.8%
21	Minnesota	687,000	1.6%
22	Maryland	685,000	1.6%
23	Kentucky	660,000	1.6%
24	Louisiana	629,000	1.5%
25	South Carolina	623,000	1.5%
26	Oklahoma	529,000	1.3%
27	Connecticut	525,000	1.3%
27	Oregon	525,000	1.3%
29	Colorado	506,000	1.2%
30	Iowa	485,000	1.2%
31	Arkansas	461,000	1.1%
32	Mississippi	446,000	1.1%
33	Kansas	397,000	1.0%
34	West Virginia	351,000	0.8%
35	Nevada	287,000	0.7%
36	Nebraska	259,000	0.6%
37	New Mexico	256,000	0.6%
38	Maine	231,000	0.6%
39	Utah	227,000	0.5%
40	New Hampshire	186,000	0.4%
41	Idaho	184,000	0.4%
42	Hawaii	178,000	0.4%
43	Rhode Island	173,000	0.4%
44	Montana	145,000	0.3%
45	Delaware	123,000	0.3%
45	South Dakota	123,000	0.3%
47	North Dakota	103,000	0.2%
48	Vermont	94,000	0.2%
49	Wyoming	69,000	0.2%
50	Alaska	50,000	0.1%
	District of Columbia	74,000	0.2%

Source: U.S. Department of Health and Human Services, Centers for Medicare and Medicaid Services
"Annual Statistical Supplement 2005" (http://www.ssa.gov/policy/docs/statcomps/supplement/2005/)
*Includes aged and disabled enrollees. Total includes 933,000 enrollees in Puerto Rico and other outlying areas, foreign countries or whose address is unknown.

Percent of Population Enrolled in Medicare in 2004

National Percent = 13.9% of Population*

ALPHA ORDER

RANK STATE   PERCENT

RANK	STATE	PERCENT
7	Alabama	16.2
50	Alaska	7.6
40	Arizona	13.1
5	Arkansas	16.8
45	California	11.6
47	Colorado	11.0
19	Connecticut	15.0
21	Delaware	14.8
3	Florida	17.1
46	Georgia	11.2
32	Hawaii	14.1
38	Idaho	13.2
38	Illinois	13.2
30	Indiana	14.3
6	Iowa	16.4
26	Kansas	14.5
11	Kentucky	15.9
34	Louisiana	14.0
2	Maine	17.6
43	Maryland	12.3
16	Massachusetts	15.1
26	Michigan	14.5
36	Minnesota	13.5
14	Mississippi	15.4
12	Missouri	15.6
12	Montana	15.6
21	Nebraska	14.8
43	Nevada	12.3
30	New Hampshire	14.3
32	New Jersey	14.1
36	New Mexico	13.5
28	New York	14.4
28	North Carolina	14.4
7	North Dakota	16.2
15	Ohio	15.2
19	Oklahoma	15.0
25	Oregon	14.6
3	Pennsylvania	17.1
9	Rhode Island	16.0
21	South Carolina	14.8
9	South Dakota	16.0
16	Tennessee	15.1
48	Texas	10.9
49	Utah	9.4
16	Vermont	15.1
41	Virginia	12.9
42	Washington	12.8
1	West Virginia	19.4
21	Wisconsin	14.8
35	Wyoming	13.6

RANK ORDER

RANK STATE   PERCENT

RANK	STATE	PERCENT
1	West Virginia	19.4
2	Maine	17.6
3	Florida	17.1
3	Pennsylvania	17.1
5	Arkansas	16.8
6	Iowa	16.4
7	Alabama	16.2
7	North Dakota	16.2
9	Rhode Island	16.0
9	South Dakota	16.0
11	Kentucky	15.9
12	Missouri	15.6
12	Montana	15.6
14	Mississippi	15.4
15	Ohio	15.2
16	Massachusetts	15.1
16	Tennessee	15.1
16	Vermont	15.1
19	Connecticut	15.0
19	Oklahoma	15.0
21	Delaware	14.8
21	Nebraska	14.8
21	South Carolina	14.8
21	Wisconsin	14.8
25	Oregon	14.6
26	Kansas	14.5
26	Michigan	14.5
28	New York	14.4
28	North Carolina	14.4
30	Indiana	14.3
30	New Hampshire	14.3
32	Hawaii	14.1
32	New Jersey	14.1
34	Louisiana	14.0
35	Wyoming	13.6
36	Minnesota	13.5
36	New Mexico	13.5
38	Idaho	13.2
38	Illinois	13.2
40	Arizona	13.1
41	Virginia	12.9
42	Washington	12.8
43	Maryland	12.3
43	Nevada	12.3
45	California	11.6
46	Georgia	11.2
47	Colorado	11.0
48	Texas	10.9
49	Utah	9.4
50	Alaska	7.6

District of Columbia   13.4

Source: MQ Press using data from U.S. Dept of Health & Human Services, Centers for Medicare and Medicaid Services "Annual Statistical Supplement 2005" (http://www.ssa.gov/policy/docs/statcomps/supplement/2005/)
*Includes aged and disabled enrollees. National rate includes only residents of the 50 states and the District of Columbia.

Medicare Benefit Payments in 2001

National Total = $245,186,000,000*

ALPHA ORDER					RANK ORDER			
RANK	STATE	BENEFITS	% of USA		RANK	STATE	BENEFITS	% of USA
19	Alabama	$4,058,221,000	1.7%		1	California	$26,919,858,000	11.0%
50	Alaska	254,145,000	0.1%		2	Florida	19,935,116,000	8.1%
22	Arizona	3,777,161,000	1.5%		3	New York	19,402,963,000	7.9%
32	Arkansas	2,354,085,000	1.0%		4	Texas	15,104,941,000	6.2%
1	California	26,919,858,000	11.0%		5	Pennsylvania	13,731,756,000	5.6%
30	Colorado	2,526,949,000	1.0%		6	Ohio	10,139,407,000	4.1%
24	Connecticut	3,463,305,000	1.4%		7	Illinois	10,072,716,000	4.1%
44	Delaware	753,991,000	0.3%		8	New Jersey	9,305,846,000	3.8%
2	Florida	19,935,116,000	8.1%		9	Michigan	9,227,281,000	3.8%
12	Georgia	5,486,318,000	2.2%		10	Massachusetts	6,651,188,000	2.7%
43	Hawaii	798,513,000	0.3%		11	North Carolina	6,299,915,000	2.6%
42	Idaho	834,950,000	0.3%		12	Georgia	5,486,318,000	2.2%
7	Illinois	10,072,716,000	4.1%		13	Missouri	5,009,583,000	2.0%
16	Indiana	4,773,470,000	1.9%		14	Tennessee	4,847,107,000	2.0%
31	Iowa	2,368,591,000	1.0%		15	Virginia	4,797,871,000	2.0%
33	Kansas	2,071,216,000	0.8%		16	Indiana	4,773,470,000	1.9%
23	Kentucky	3,600,612,000	1.5%		17	Maryland	4,674,796,000	1.9%
18	Louisiana	4,454,101,000	1.8%		18	Louisiana	4,454,101,000	1.8%
37	Maine	1,118,964,000	0.5%		19	Alabama	4,058,221,000	1.7%
17	Maryland	4,674,796,000	1.9%		20	Wisconsin	3,948,015,000	1.6%
10	Massachusetts	6,651,188,000	2.7%		21	Washington	3,862,966,000	1.6%
9	Michigan	9,227,201,000	3.8%		22	Arizona	3,777,161,000	1.5%
26	Minnesota	3,373,029,000	1.4%		23	Kentucky	3,600,612,000	1.5%
28	Mississippi	2,604,168,000	1.1%		24	Connecticut	3,463,305,000	1.4%
13	Missouri	5,009,583,000	2.0%		25	South Carolina	3,429,335,000	1.4%
45	Montana	658,649,000	0.3%		26	Minnesota	3,373,029,000	1.4%
36	Nebraska	1,325,208,000	0.5%		27	Oklahoma	3,043,503,000	1.2%
35	Nevada	1,495,977,000	0.6%		28	Mississippi	2,604,168,000	1.1%
41	New Hampshire	878,715,000	0.4%		29	Oregon	2,595,888,000	1.1%
8	New Jersey	9,305,846,000	3.8%		30	Colorado	2,526,949,000	1.0%
38	New Mexico	1,106,938,000	0.5%		31	Iowa	2,368,591,000	1.0%
3	New York	19,402,963,000	7.9%		32	Arkansas	2,354,085,000	1.0%
11	North Carolina	6,299,915,000	2.6%		33	Kansas	2,071,216,000	0.8%
48	North Dakota	479,025,000	0.2%		34	West Virginia	1,906,516,000	0.8%
6	Ohio	10,139,407,000	4.1%		35	Nevada	1,495,977,000	0.6%
27	Oklahoma	3,043,503,000	1.2%		36	Nebraska	1,325,208,000	0.5%
29	Oregon	2,595,888,000	1.1%		37	Maine	1,118,964,000	0.5%
5	Pennsylvania	13,731,756,000	5.6%		38	New Mexico	1,106,938,000	0.5%
39	Rhode Island	1,070,422,000	0.4%		39	Rhode Island	1,070,422,000	0.4%
25	South Carolina	3,429,335,000	1.4%		40	Utah	1,004,074,000	0.4%
46	South Dakota	540,327,000	0.2%		41	New Hampshire	878,715,000	0.4%
14	Tennessee	4,847,107,000	2.0%		42	Idaho	834,950,000	0.3%
4	Texas	15,104,941,000	6.2%		43	Hawaii	798,513,000	0.3%
40	Utah	1,004,074,000	0.4%		44	Delaware	753,991,000	0.3%
47	Vermont	480,466,000	0.2%		45	Montana	658,649,000	0.3%
15	Virginia	4,797,871,000	2.0%		46	South Dakota	540,327,000	0.2%
21	Washington	3,862,966,000	1.6%		47	Vermont	480,466,000	0.2%
34	West Virginia	1,906,516,000	0.8%		48	North Dakota	479,025,000	0.2%
20	Wisconsin	3,948,015,000	1.6%		49	Wyoming	338,211,000	0.1%
49	Wyoming	338,211,000	0.1%		50	Alaska	254,145,000	0.1%
						District of Columbia	568,988,000	0.2%

Source: U.S. Department of Health and Human Services, Centers for Medicare and Medicaid Services
"2004 Medicare and Medicaid Statistical Supplement" (http://new.cms.hhs.gov/MedicareMedicaidStatSupp)
*Revised figures for fiscal year 2001. Includes payments to aged and disabled enrollees. Total includes
$1,661,000,000 in payments to enrollees in Puerto Rico and other outlying areas.

Medicare Payments per Enrollee in 2001

National Rate = $6,223*

ALPHA ORDER

RANK	STATE	PER ENROLLEE
21	Alabama	$5,833
22	Alaska	5,831
29	Arizona	5,418
31	Arkansas	5,328
7	California	6,828
32	Colorado	5,316
8	Connecticut	6,722
9	Delaware	6,592
5	Florida	6,972
20	Georgia	5,866
47	Hawaii	4,742
44	Idaho	4,934
14	Illinois	6,164
27	Indiana	5,567
43	Iowa	4,963
33	Kansas	5,300
25	Kentucky	5,714
2	Louisiana	7,354
39	Maine	5,100
4	Maryland	7,147
6	Massachusetts	6,941
12	Michigan	6,543
38	Minnesota	5,117
15	Mississippi	6,143
23	Missouri	5,776
46	Montana	4,758
36	Nebraska	5,207
18	Nevada	5,901
41	New Hampshire	5,085
1	New Jersey	7,730
49	New Mexico	4,641
3	New York	7,158
28	North Carolina	5,442
48	North Dakota	4,652
17	Ohio	5,952
16	Oklahoma	5,955
35	Oregon	5,216
10	Pennsylvania	6,558
13	Rhode Island	6,238
19	South Carolina	5,895
50	South Dakota	4,503
24	Tennessee	5,743
11	Texas	6,557
45	Utah	4,764
30	Vermont	5,343
34	Virginia	5,268
37	Washington	5,173
26	West Virginia	5,616
42	Wisconsin	5,016
40	Wyoming	5,095

RANK ORDER

RANK	STATE	PER ENROLLEE
1	New Jersey	$7,730
2	Louisiana	7,354
3	New York	7,158
4	Maryland	7,147
5	Florida	6,972
6	Massachusetts	6,941
7	California	6,828
8	Connecticut	6,722
9	Delaware	6,592
10	Pennsylvania	6,558
11	Texas	6,557
12	Michigan	6,543
13	Rhode Island	6,238
14	Illinois	6,164
15	Mississippi	6,143
16	Oklahoma	5,955
17	Ohio	5,952
18	Nevada	5,901
19	South Carolina	5,895
20	Georgia	5,866
21	Alabama	5,833
22	Alaska	5,831
23	Missouri	5,776
24	Tennessee	5,743
25	Kentucky	5,714
26	West Virginia	5,616
27	Indiana	5,567
28	North Carolina	5,442
29	Arizona	5,418
30	Vermont	5,343
31	Arkansas	5,328
32	Colorado	5,316
33	Kansas	5,300
34	Virginia	5,268
35	Oregon	5,216
36	Nebraska	5,207
37	Washington	5,173
38	Minnesota	5,117
39	Maine	5,100
40	Wyoming	5,095
41	New Hampshire	5,085
42	Wisconsin	5,016
43	Iowa	4,963
44	Idaho	4,934
45	Utah	4,764
46	Montana	4,758
47	Hawaii	4,742
48	North Dakota	4,652
49	New Mexico	4,641
50	South Dakota	4,503
	District of Columbia	7,683

Source: MQ Press using data from U.S. Dept of Health & Human Services, Centers for Medicare and Medicaid Services "2004 Medicare and Medicaid Statistical Supplement" (http://new.cms.hhs.gov/MedicareMedicaidStatSupp)

*Revised figures for fiscal year 2001. Includes payments to aged and disabled enrollees. National rate does not include payments or enrollees in Puerto Rico and other outlying areas.

Enrollment in Medicare Prescription Drug Plans as of January 13, 2006

National Total = 23,750,661 Enrollees*

RANK	STATE	ENROLLEES	% of USA
20	Alabama	414,447	1.7%
47	Alaska	41,672	0.2%
16	Arizona	478,718	2.0%
31	Arkansas	246,218	1.0%
1	California	2,988,048	12.6%
25	Colorado	338,317	1.4%
29	Connecticut	269,524	1.1%
44	Delaware	76,771	0.3%
2	Florida	1,821,446	7.7%
14	Georgia	543,280	2.3%
37	Hawaii	153,481	0.6%
43	Idaho	83,794	0.4%
7	Illinois	951,888	4.0%
18	Indiana	425,075	1.8%
34	Iowa	167,802	0.7%
36	Kansas	158,170	0.7%
24	Kentucky	350,979	1.5%
22	Louisiana	373,127	1.6%
38	Maine	125,401	0.5%
19	Maryland	414,608	1.7%
11	Massachusetts	583,733	2.5%
8	Michigan	861,203	3.6%
27	Minnesota	286,900	1.2%
30	Mississippi	246,594	1.0%
15	Missouri	499,351	2.1%
45	Montana	53,030	0.2%
41	Nebraska	107,943	0.5%
32	Nevada	187,044	0.8%
42	New Hampshire	84,113	0.4%
10	New Jersey	685,260	2.9%
35	New Mexico	163,973	0.7%
3	New York	1,494,830	6.3%
9	North Carolina	778,838	3.3%
49	North Dakota	34,227	0.1%
6	Ohio	1,067,476	4.5%
26	Oklahoma	288,828	1.2%
28	Oregon	272,885	1.1%
5	Pennsylvania	1,141,114	4.8%
40	Rhode Island	108,269	0.5%
23	South Carolina	372,920	1.6%
48	South Dakota	41,588	0.2%
13	Tennessee	559,114	2.4%
4	Texas	1,411,470	5.9%
39	Utah	116,163	0.5%
46	Vermont	48,793	0.2%
12	Virginia	572,184	2.4%
17	Washington	432,183	1.8%
33	West Virginia	184,556	0.8%
21	Wisconsin	373,467	1.6%
50	Wyoming	28,410	0.1%

RANK	STATE	ENROLLEES	% of USA
1	California	2,988,048	12.6%
2	Florida	1,821,446	7.7%
3	New York	1,494,830	6.3%
4	Texas	1,411,470	5.9%
5	Pennsylvania	1,141,114	4.8%
6	Ohio	1,067,476	4.5%
7	Illinois	951,888	4.0%
8	Michigan	861,203	3.6%
9	North Carolina	778,838	3.3%
10	New Jersey	685,260	2.9%
11	Massachusetts	583,733	2.5%
12	Virginia	572,184	2.4%
13	Tennessee	559,114	2.4%
14	Georgia	543,280	2.3%
15	Missouri	499,351	2.1%
16	Arizona	478,718	2.0%
17	Washington	432,183	1.8%
18	Indiana	425,075	1.8%
19	Maryland	414,608	1.7%
20	Alabama	414,447	1.7%
21	Wisconsin	373,467	1.6%
22	Louisiana	373,127	1.6%
23	South Carolina	372,920	1.6%
24	Kentucky	350,979	1.5%
25	Colorado	338,317	1.4%
26	Oklahoma	288,828	1.2%
27	Minnesota	286,900	1.2%
28	Oregon	272,885	1.1%
29	Connecticut	269,524	1.1%
30	Mississippi	246,594	1.0%
31	Arkansas	246,218	1.0%
32	Nevada	187,044	0.8%
33	West Virginia	184,556	0.8%
34	Iowa	167,802	0.7%
35	New Mexico	163,973	0.7%
36	Kansas	158,170	0.7%
37	Hawaii	153,481	0.6%
38	Maine	125,401	0.5%
39	Utah	116,163	0.5%
40	Rhode Island	108,269	0.5%
41	Nebraska	107,943	0.5%
42	New Hampshire	84,113	0.4%
43	Idaho	83,794	0.4%
44	Delaware	76,771	0.3%
45	Montana	53,030	0.2%
46	Vermont	48,793	0.2%
47	Alaska	41,672	0.2%
48	South Dakota	41,588	0.2%
49	North Dakota	34,227	0.1%
50	Wyoming	28,410	0.1%
	District of Columbia	49,451	0.2%

*Source: U.S. Department of Health and Human Services, Centers for Medicare and Medicaid Services
"State-by-State Prescription Drug Enrollment" (http://new.cms.hhs.gov/apps/media/?media=pressr)
Press release dated January 19, 2006. National total includes 191,985 enrollees in U.S. territories.

Percent of Population Age 65 and Older Enrolled in Medicare Prescription Drug Plans in 2006
National Percent = 64.9%*

ALPHA ORDER

RANK	STATE	PERCENT
15	Alabama	69.3
1	Alaska	99.5
22	Arizona	65.4
25	Arkansas	64.6
3	California	78.2
6	Colorado	75.0
37	Connecticut	56.9
12	Delaware	70.5
29	Florida	62.2
26	Georgia	64.1
2	Hawaii	89.2
41	Idaho	52.8
28	Illinois	62.6
39	Indiana	55.1
48	Iowa	38.7
46	Kansas	44.6
18	Kentucky	67.6
11	Louisiana	70.7
21	Maine	66.1
23	Maryland	65.3
17	Massachusetts	68.3
16	Michigan	69.1
43	Minnesota	46.6
14	Mississippi	69.9
24	Missouri	65.2
47	Montana	41.9
43	Nebraska	46.6
10	Nevada	71.4
40	New Hampshire	53.7
32	New Jersey	60.9
9	New Mexico	71.5
35	New York	60.0
5	North Carolina	75.5
50	North Dakota	36.7
13	Ohio	70.0
29	Oklahoma	62.2
36	Oregon	59.3
34	Pennsylvania	60.2
7	Rhode Island	71.9
8	South Carolina	71.7
49	South Dakota	38.0
4	Tennessee	75.8
27	Texas	63.7
38	Utah	55.9
33	Vermont	60.4
18	Virginia	67.6
31	Washington	61.5
20	West Virginia	66.3
42	Wisconsin	52.2
45	Wyoming	46.5

RANK ORDER

RANK	STATE	PERCENT
1	Alaska	99.5
2	Hawaii	89.2
3	California	78.2
4	Tennessee	75.8
5	North Carolina	75.5
6	Colorado	75.0
7	Rhode Island	71.9
8	South Carolina	71.7
9	New Mexico	71.5
10	Nevada	71.4
11	Louisiana	70.7
12	Delaware	70.5
13	Ohio	70.0
14	Mississippi	69.9
15	Alabama	69.3
16	Michigan	69.1
17	Massachusetts	68.3
18	Kentucky	67.6
18	Virginia	67.6
20	West Virginia	66.3
21	Maine	66.1
22	Arizona	65.4
23	Maryland	65.3
24	Missouri	65.2
25	Arkansas	64.6
26	Georgia	64.1
27	Texas	63.7
28	Illinois	62.6
29	Florida	62.2
29	Oklahoma	62.2
31	Washington	61.5
32	New Jersey	60.9
33	Vermont	60.4
34	Pennsylvania	60.2
35	New York	60.0
36	Oregon	59.3
37	Connecticut	56.9
38	Utah	55.9
39	Indiana	55.1
40	New Hampshire	53.7
41	Idaho	52.8
42	Wisconsin	52.2
43	Minnesota	46.6
43	Nebraska	46.6
45	Wyoming	46.5
46	Kansas	44.6
47	Montana	41.9
48	Iowa	38.7
49	South Dakota	38.0
50	North Dakota	36.7
	District of Columbia	73.6

Source: MQ Press using data from U.S. Dept of Health and Human Services, Centers for Medicare and Medicaid Services "State-by-State Prescription Drug Enrollment" (http://new.cms.hhs.gov/apps/media/?media=pressr)
*Press release dated January 19, 2006. National percent does not include enrollees in U.S. territories. Calculated with 2004 population data.

Medicaid Enrollment in 2004

National Total = 44,596,338 Enrollees*

ALPHA ORDER

RANK	STATE	ENROLLEES	% of USA
20	Alabama	800,177	1.8%
45	Alaska	99,439	0.2%
13	Arizona	992,055	2.2%
26	Arkansas	612,953	1.4%
1	California	6,454,112	14.5%
31	Colorado	407,565	0.9%
32	Connecticut	405,311	0.9%
43	Delaware	137,017	0.3%
4	Florida	2,237,376	5.0%
9	Georgia	1,340,174	3.0%
38	Hawaii	198,010	0.4%
41	Idaho	171,483	0.4%
5	Illinois	1,770,800	4.0%
18	Indiana	827,034	1.9%
34	Iowa	294,470	0.7%
35	Kansas	268,065	0.6%
23	Kentucky	686,813	1.5%
15	Louisiana	944,438	2.1%
36	Maine	266,098	0.6%
22	Maryland	705,914	1.6%
14	Massachusetts	973,233	2.2%
8	Michigan	1,350,343	3.0%
27	Minnesota	561,892	1.3%
24	Mississippi	644,210	1.4%
12	Missouri	1,001,999	2.2%
48	Montana	85,175	0.2%
37	Nebraska	200,512	0.4%
42	Nevada	170,109	0.4%
47	New Hampshire	97,178	0.2%
21	New Jersey	774,217	1.7%
30	New Mexico	416,092	0.9%
2	New York	3,952,005	8.9%
11	North Carolina	1,125,624	2.5%
50	North Dakota	53,104	0.1%
6	Ohio	1,661,388	3.7%
28	Oklahoma	530,480	1.2%
29	Oregon	423,275	0.9%
7	Pennsylvania	1,656,762	3.7%
40	Rhode Island	181,215	0.4%
17	South Carolina	849,049	1.9%
46	South Dakota	99,151	0.2%
10	Tennessee	1,336,691	3.0%
3	Texas	2,756,776	6.2%
39	Utah	192,163	0.4%
44	Vermont	130,372	0.3%
25	Virginia	641,359	1.4%
16	Washington	940,693	2.1%
33	West Virginia	299,788	0.7%
19	Wisconsin	804,769	1.8%
49	Wyoming	59,657	0.1%

RANK ORDER

RANK	STATE	ENROLLEES	% of USA
1	California	6,454,112	14.5%
2	New York	3,952,005	8.9%
3	Texas	2,756,776	6.2%
4	Florida	2,237,376	5.0%
5	Illinois	1,770,800	4.0%
6	Ohio	1,661,388	3.7%
7	Pennsylvania	1,656,762	3.7%
8	Michigan	1,350,343	3.0%
9	Georgia	1,340,174	3.0%
10	Tennessee	1,336,691	3.0%
11	North Carolina	1,125,624	2.5%
12	Missouri	1,001,999	2.2%
13	Arizona	992,055	2.2%
14	Massachusetts	973,233	2.2%
15	Louisiana	944,438	2.1%
16	Washington	940,693	2.1%
17	South Carolina	849,049	1.9%
18	Indiana	827,034	1.9%
19	Wisconsin	804,769	1.8%
20	Alabama	800,177	1.8%
21	New Jersey	774,217	1.7%
22	Maryland	705,914	1.6%
23	Kentucky	686,813	1.5%
24	Mississippi	644,210	1.4%
25	Virginia	641,359	1.4%
26	Arkansas	612,953	1.4%
27	Minnesota	561,892	1.3%
28	Oklahoma	530,480	1.2%
29	Oregon	423,275	0.9%
30	New Mexico	416,092	0.9%
31	Colorado	407,565	0.9%
32	Connecticut	405,311	0.9%
33	West Virginia	299,788	0.7%
34	Iowa	294,470	0.7%
35	Kansas	268,065	0.6%
36	Maine	266,098	0.6%
37	Nebraska	200,512	0.4%
38	Hawaii	198,010	0.4%
39	Utah	192,163	0.4%
40	Rhode Island	181,215	0.4%
41	Idaho	171,483	0.4%
42	Nevada	170,109	0.4%
43	Delaware	137,017	0.3%
44	Vermont	130,372	0.3%
45	Alaska	99,439	0.2%
46	South Dakota	99,151	0.2%
47	New Hampshire	97,178	0.2%
48	Montana	85,175	0.2%
49	Wyoming	59,657	0.1%
50	North Dakota	53,104	0.1%
	District of Columbia	139,595	0.3%

Source: U.S. Department of Health and Human Services, Centers for Medicare and Medicaid Services
"Medicaid Managed Care State Enrollment" (http://new.cms.hhs.gov/MedicaidDataSourcesGenInfo/)
*Unduplicated enrollment as of December 31, 2004. National total includes 868,158 Medicaid enrollees in Puerto Rico and the Virgin Islands.

Percent of Population Enrolled in Medicaid in 2004

National Percent = 14.9% of Population*

ALPHA ORDER				RANK ORDER		
RANK	**STATE**	**PERCENT**		**RANK**	**STATE**	**PERCENT**
11	Alabama	17.7		1	Tennessee	22.7
21	Alaska	15.1		2	Arkansas	22.3
13	Arizona	17.3		3	Mississippi	22.2
2	Arkansas	22.3		4	New Mexico	21.9
10	California	18.0		5	Louisiana	21.0
44	Colorado	8.9		5	Vermont	21.0
38	Connecticut	11.6		7	New York	20.5
16	Delaware	16.5		8	Maine	20.2
31	Florida	12.9		8	South Carolina	20.2
23	Georgia	15.0		10	California	18.0
18	Hawaii	15.7		11	Alabama	17.7
34	Idaho	12.3		12	Missouri	17.4
26	Illinois	13.9		13	Arizona	17.3
29	Indiana	13.3		14	Rhode Island	16.8
41	Iowa	10.0		15	Kentucky	16.6
42	Kansas	9.8		16	Delaware	16.5
15	Kentucky	16.6		16	West Virginia	16.5
5	Louisiana	21.0		18	Hawaii	15.7
8	Maine	20.2		19	Massachusetts	15.2
33	Maryland	12.7		19	Washington	15.2
19	Massachusetts	15.2		21	Alaska	15.1
27	Michigan	13.4		21	Oklahoma	15.1
40	Minnesota	11.0		23	Georgia	15.0
3	Mississippi	22.2		24	Wisconsin	14.6
12	Missouri	17.4		25	Ohio	14.5
43	Montana	9.2		26	Illinois	13.9
39	Nebraska	11.5		27	Michigan	13.4
50	Nevada	7.3		27	Pennsylvania	13.4
49	New Hampshire	7.5		29	Indiana	13.3
44	New Jersey	8.9		30	North Carolina	13.2
4	New Mexico	21.9		31	Florida	12.9
7	New York	20.5		31	South Dakota	12.9
30	North Carolina	13.2		33	Maryland	12.7
47	North Dakota	8.3		34	Idaho	12.3
25	Ohio	14.5		34	Texas	12.3
21	Oklahoma	15.1		36	Oregon	11.8
36	Oregon	11.8		36	Wyoming	11.8
27	Pennsylvania	13.4		38	Connecticut	11.6
14	Rhode Island	16.8		39	Nebraska	11.5
8	South Carolina	20.2		40	Minnesota	11.0
31	South Dakota	12.9		41	Iowa	10.0
1	Tennessee	22.7		42	Kansas	9.8
34	Texas	12.3		43	Montana	9.2
48	Utah	7.9		44	Colorado	8.9
5	Vermont	21.0		44	New Jersey	8.9
46	Virginia	8.6		46	Virginia	8.6
19	Washington	15.2		47	North Dakota	8.3
16	West Virginia	16.5		48	Utah	7.9
24	Wisconsin	14.6		49	New Hampshire	7.5
36	Wyoming	11.8		50	Nevada	7.3
					District of Columbia	25.2

Source: MQ Press using data from U.S. Dept of Health & Human Services, Centers for Medicare and Medicaid Services
    "Medicaid Managed Care State Enrollment" (http://new.cms.hhs.gov/MedicaidDataSourcesGenInfo/)
*Unduplicated enrollment as of December 31, 2004. National percent does not include recipients or population in
U.S. territories.

Estimated Medicaid Expenditures in 2004

National Total = $259,736,000,000*

ALPHA ORDER					RANK ORDER			

RANK	STATE	EXPENDITURES	% of USA
26	Alabama	$3,634,000,000	1.4%
46	Alaska	638,000,000	0.2%
17	Arizona	5,007,000,000	1.9%
28	Arkansas	2,760,000,000	1.1%
1	California	29,129,000,000	11.2%
30	Colorado	2,700,000,000	1.0%
16	Connecticut	5,444,000,000	2.1%
45	Delaware	728,000,000	0.3%
5	Florida	12,159,000,000	4.7%
15	Georgia	5,500,000,000	2.1%
43	Hawaii	911,000,000	0.4%
42	Idaho	928,000,000	0.4%
7	Illinois	11,590,000,000	4.5%
21	Indiana	4,378,000,000	1.7%
33	Iowa	2,124,000,000	0.8%
36	Kansas	1,727,000,000	0.7%
23	Kentucky	4,009,000,000	1.5%
19	Louisiana	4,772,000,000	1.8%
35	Maine	1,772,000,000	0.7%
20	Maryland	4,713,000,000	1.8%
12	Massachusetts	5,856,000,000	2.3%
8	Michigan	8,450,000,000	3.3%
18	Minnesota	4,983,000,000	1.9%
27	Mississippi	3,175,000,000	1.2%
14	Missouri	5,725,000,000	2.2%
47	Montana	634,000,000	0.2%
38	Nebraska	1,317,000,000	0.5%
40	Nevada	1,172,000,000	0.5%
41	New Hampshire	1,080,000,000	0.4%
9	New Jersey	7,538,000,000	2.9%
32	New Mexico	2,287,000,000	0.9%
2	New York	27,562,000,000	10.6%
11	North Carolina	7,011,000,000	2.7%
49	North Dakota	508,000,000	0.2%
6	Ohio	12,073,000,000	4.6%
31	Oklahoma	2,395,000,000	0.9%
29	Oregon	2,704,000,000	1.0%
4	Pennsylvania	14,375,000,000	5.5%
37	Rhode Island	1,568,000,000	0.6%
25	South Carolina	3,808,000,000	1.5%
48	South Dakota	557,000,000	0.2%
10	Tennessee	7,246,000,000	2.8%
3	Texas	14,903,000,000	5.7%
39	Utah	1,265,000,000	0.5%
44	Vermont	795,000,000	0.3%
24	Virginia	3,896,000,000	1.5%
13	Washington	5,783,000,000	2.2%
34	West Virginia	1,923,000,000	0.7%
22	Wisconsin	4,148,000,000	1.6%
50	Wyoming	368,000,000	0.1%

RANK	STATE	EXPENDITURES	% of USA
1	California	$29,129,000,000	11.2%
2	New York	27,562,000,000	10.6%
3	Texas	14,903,000,000	5.7%
4	Pennsylvania	14,375,000,000	5.5%
5	Florida	12,159,000,000	4.7%
6	Ohio	12,073,000,000	4.6%
7	Illinois	11,590,000,000	4.5%
8	Michigan	8,458,000,000	3.3%
9	New Jersey	7,538,000,000	2.9%
10	Tennessee	7,246,000,000	2.8%
11	North Carolina	7,011,000,000	2.7%
12	Massachusetts	5,856,000,000	2.3%
13	Washington	5,783,000,000	2.2%
14	Missouri	5,725,000,000	2.2%
15	Georgia	5,500,000,000	2.1%
16	Connecticut	5,444,000,000	2.1%
17	Arizona	5,007,000,000	1.9%
18	Minnesota	4,983,000,000	1.9%
19	Louisiana	4,772,000,000	1.8%
20	Maryland	4,713,000,000	1.8%
21	Indiana	4,378,000,000	1.7%
22	Wisconsin	4,148,000,000	1.6%
23	Kentucky	4,009,000,000	1.5%
24	Virginia	3,896,000,000	1.5%
25	South Carolina	3,808,000,000	1.5%
26	Alabama	3,634,000,000	1.4%
27	Mississippi	3,175,000,000	1.2%
28	Arkansas	2,760,000,000	1.1%
29	Oregon	2,704,000,000	1.0%
30	Colorado	2,700,000,000	1.0%
31	Oklahoma	2,395,000,000	0.9%
32	New Mexico	2,287,000,000	0.9%
33	Iowa	2,124,000,000	0.8%
34	West Virginia	1,923,000,000	0.7%
35	Maine	1,772,000,000	0.7%
36	Kansas	1,727,000,000	0.7%
37	Rhode Island	1,568,000,000	0.6%
38	Nebraska	1,317,000,000	0.5%
39	Utah	1,265,000,000	0.5%
40	Nevada	1,172,000,000	0.5%
41	New Hampshire	1,080,000,000	0.4%
42	Idaho	928,000,000	0.4%
43	Hawaii	911,000,000	0.4%
44	Vermont	795,000,000	0.3%
45	Delaware	728,000,000	0.3%
46	Alaska	638,000,000	0.2%
47	Montana	634,000,000	0.2%
48	South Dakota	557,000,000	0.2%
49	North Dakota	508,000,000	0.2%
50	Wyoming	368,000,000	0.1%
	District of Columbia**	NA	NA

Source: National Association of State Budget Officers
   "2003 State Expenditure Report" (http://www.nasbo.org/publications/PDFs/2003ExpendReport.pdf)
*Estimates for fiscal year 2004.
**Not available.

Percent Change in Medicaid Expenditures: 2003 to 2004

National Percent Change = 6.6% Increase*

ALPHA ORDER

RANK	STATE	PERCENT CHANGE
41	Alabama	1.8
50	Alaska	(18.8)
2	Arizona	23.7
10	Arkansas	11.9
47	California	(2.3)
8	Colorado	14.6
33	Connecticut	5.0
21	Delaware	8.7
9	Florida	12.4
13	Georgia	11.5
4	Hawaii	17.1
20	Idaho	8.8
3	Illinois	21.1
16	Indiana	10.6
49	Iowa	(12.8)
25	Kansas	6.9
32	Kentucky	5.1
24	Louisiana	7.2
39	Maine	3.5
5	Maryland	15.8
23	Massachusetts	8.0
27	Michigan	6.3
36	Minnesota	3.8
31	Mississippi	5.3
45	Missouri	0.6
14	Montana	11.2
40	Nebraska	2.2
43	Nevada	1.0
45	New Hampshire	0.6
42	New Jersey	1.1
11	New Mexico	11.8
19	New York	8.9
34	North Carolina	4.0
27	North Dakota	6.3
12	Ohio	11.6
44	Oklahoma	0.8
48	Oregon	(4.3)
30	Pennsylvania	5.5
22	Rhode Island	8.1
37	South Carolina	3.7
1	South Dakota	30.4
29	Tennessee	5.6
18	Texas	9.9
6	Utah	15.4
7	Vermont	15.1
25	Virginia	6.9
38	Washington	3.6
16	West Virginia	10.6
35	Wisconsin	3.9
15	Wyoming	10.8

RANK ORDER

RANK	STATE	PERCENT CHANGE
1	South Dakota	30.4
2	Arizona	23.7
3	Illinois	21.1
4	Hawaii	17.1
5	Maryland	15.8
6	Utah	15.4
7	Vermont	15.1
8	Colorado	14.6
9	Florida	12.4
10	Arkansas	11.9
11	New Mexico	11.8
12	Ohio	11.6
13	Georgia	11.5
14	Montana	11.2
15	Wyoming	10.0
16	Indiana	10.6
16	West Virginia	10.6
18	Texas	9.9
19	New York	8.9
20	Idaho	8.8
21	Delaware	8.7
22	Rhode Island	8.1
23	Massachusetts	8.0
24	Louisiana	7.2
25	Kansas	6.9
25	Virginia	6.9
27	Michigan	6.3
27	North Dakota	6.3
29	Tennessee	5.6
30	Pennsylvania	5.5
31	Mississippi	5.3
32	Kentucky	5.1
33	Connecticut	5.0
34	North Carolina	4.0
35	Wisconsin	3.9
36	Minnesota	3.8
37	South Carolina	3.7
38	Washington	3.6
39	Maine	3.5
40	Nebraska	2.2
41	Alabama	1.8
42	New Jersey	1.1
43	Nevada	1.0
44	Oklahoma	0.8
45	Missouri	0.6
45	New Hampshire	0.6
47	California	(2.3)
48	Oregon	(4.3)
49	Iowa	(12.8)
50	Alaska	(18.8)
	District of Columbia**	NA

Source: National Association of State Budget Officers
   "2003 State Expenditure Report" (http://www.nasbo.org/publications/PDFs/2003ExpendReport.pdf)
*Estimates for fiscal year 2004.
**Not available.

Percent of Population Receiving Public Aid in 2004

National Percent = 4.0% of Population*

RANK	STATE	PERCENT		RANK	STATE	PERCENT
9	Alabama	4.7		1	California	6.4
20	Alaska	3.6		2	Kentucky	6.2
22	Arizona	3.5		3	West Virginia	6.0
17	Arkansas	3.9		4	Tennessee	5.9
1	California	6.4		5	Mississippi	5.6
47	Colorado	2.0		6	Rhode Island	5.4
38	Connecticut	2.7		7	New Mexico	5.2
26	Delaware	3.2		8	New York	5.0
28	Florida	3.1		9	Alabama	4.7
24	Georgia	3.4		9	Louisiana	4.7
22	Hawaii	3.5		11	Pennsylvania	4.6
48	Idaho	1.8		12	Maine	4.4
37	Illinois	2.8		13	Massachusetts	4.3
20	Indiana	3.6		13	Michigan	4.3
33	Iowa	2.9		15	Vermont	4.0
28	Kansas	3.1		15	Washington	4.0
2	Kentucky	6.2		17	Arkansas	3.9
9	Louisiana	4.7		18	Ohio	3.8
12	Maine	4.4		19	Missouri	3.7
38	Maryland	2.7		20	Alaska	3.6
13	Massachusetts	4.3		20	Indiana	3.6
13	Michigan	4.3		22	Arizona	3.5
33	Minnesota	2.9		22	Hawaii	3.5
5	Mississippi	5.6		24	Georgia	3.4
19	Missouri	3.7		24	South Carolina	3.4
33	Montana	2.9		26	Delaware	3.2
40	Nebraska	2.6		26	North Carolina	3.2
45	Nevada	2.1		28	Florida	3.1
45	New Hampshire	2.1		28	Kansas	3.1
32	New Jersey	3.0		28	Oklahoma	3.1
7	New Mexico	5.2		28	Texas	3.1
8	New York	5.0		32	New Jersey	3.0
26	North Carolina	3.2		33	Iowa	2.9
42	North Dakota	2.4		33	Minnesota	2.9
18	Ohio	3.8		33	Montana	2.9
28	Oklahoma	3.1		33	Oregon	2.9
33	Oregon	2.9		37	Illinois	2.8
11	Pennsylvania	4.6		38	Connecticut	2.7
6	Rhode Island	5.4		38	Maryland	2.7
24	South Carolina	3.4		40	Nebraska	2.6
42	South Dakota	2.4		41	Wisconsin	2.5
4	Tennessee	5.9		42	North Dakota	2.4
28	Texas	3.1		42	South Dakota	2.4
49	Utah	1.4		44	Virginia	2.2
15	Vermont	4.0		45	Nevada	2.1
44	Virginia	2.2		45	New Hampshire	2.1
15	Washington	4.0		47	Colorado	2.0
3	West Virginia	6.0		48	Idaho	1.8
41	Wisconsin	2.5		49	Utah	1.4
50	Wyoming	1.2		50	Wyoming	1.2
					District of Columbia	11.6

ALPHA ORDER

RANK ORDER

Source: Morgan Quitno Press using data from U.S. Social Security Administration and
    U.S. Department of Health and Human Services
*As of December 2004. Includes recipients of Temporary Assistance to Needy Families (TANF) and/or Supplemental
Security Income payments.

Recipients of Temporary Assistance to Needy Families (TANF) Payments: 2005

National Total = 4,547,143 Monthly Recipients*

ALPHA ORDER

RANK	STATE	RECIPIENTS	% of USA
21	Alabama	48,117	1.1%
43	Alaska	13,342	0.3%
13	Arizona	98,165	2.2%
40	Arkansas	18,845	0.4%
1	California	1,092,422	24.0%
28	Colorado	38,060	0.8%
27	Connecticut	39,812	0.9%
45	Delaware	12,296	0.3%
11	Florida	104,503	2.3%
16	Georgia	87,979	1.9%
39	Hawaii	20,713	0.5%
49	Idaho	3,446	0.1%
14	Illinois	97,736	2.1%
9	Indiana	124,007	2.7%
26	Iowa	42,942	0.9%
24	Kansas	45,269	1.0%
17	Kentucky	75,375	1.7%
29	Louisiana	37,009	0.8%
36	Maine	25,876	0.6%
20	Maryland	54,658	1.2%
12	Massachusetts	103,921	2.3%
4	Michigan	216,726	4.8%
18	Minnesota	73,880	1.6%
31	Mississippi	33,795	0.7%
15	Missouri	97,352	2.1%
44	Montana	12,894	0.3%
37	Nebraska	23,300	0.5%
41	Nevada	15,531	0.3%
42	New Hampshire	14,333	0.3%
10	New Jersey	105,044	2.3%
25	New Mexico	44,476	1.0%
2	New York	322,681	7.1%
19	North Carolina	65,919	1.4%
47	North Dakota	7,242	0.2%
7	Ohio	180,165	4.0%
35	Oklahoma	26,448	0.6%
23	Oregon	46,354	1.0%
3	Pennsylvania	253,763	5.6%
34	Rhode Island	27,157	0.6%
30	South Carolina	34,955	0.8%
48	South Dakota	5,871	0.1%
6	Tennessee	185,246	4.1%
5	Texas	195,944	4.3%
38	Utah	23,016	0.5%
46	Vermont	11,459	0.3%
32	Virginia	28,126	0.6%
8	Washington	140,461	3.1%
33	West Virginia	27,219	0.6%
22	Wisconsin	46,749	1.0%
50	Wyoming	545	0.0%

RANK ORDER

RANK	STATE	RECIPIENTS	% of USA
1	California	1,092,422	24.0%
2	New York	322,681	7.1%
3	Pennsylvania	253,763	5.6%
4	Michigan	216,726	4.8%
5	Texas	195,944	4.3%
6	Tennessee	185,246	4.1%
7	Ohio	180,165	4.0%
8	Washington	140,461	3.1%
9	Indiana	124,007	2.7%
10	New Jersey	105,044	2.3%
11	Florida	104,503	2.3%
12	Massachusetts	103,921	2.3%
13	Arizona	98,165	2.2%
14	Illinois	97,736	2.1%
15	Missouri	97,352	2.1%
16	Georgia	87,979	1.9%
17	Kentucky	75,375	1.7%
18	Minnesota	73,880	1.6%
19	North Carolina	65,919	1.4%
20	Maryland	54,658	1.2%
21	Alabama	48,117	1.1%
22	Wisconsin	46,749	1.0%
23	Oregon	46,354	1.0%
24	Kansas	45,269	1.0%
25	New Mexico	44,476	1.0%
26	Iowa	42,942	0.9%
27	Connecticut	39,812	0.9%
28	Colorado	38,060	0.8%
29	Louisiana	37,009	0.8%
30	South Carolina	34,955	0.8%
31	Mississippi	33,795	0.7%
32	Virginia	28,126	0.6%
33	West Virginia	27,219	0.6%
34	Rhode Island	27,157	0.6%
35	Oklahoma	26,448	0.6%
36	Maine	25,876	0.6%
37	Nebraska	23,300	0.5%
38	Utah	23,016	0.5%
39	Hawaii	20,713	0.5%
40	Arkansas	18,845	0.4%
41	Nevada	15,531	0.3%
42	New Hampshire	14,333	0.3%
43	Alaska	13,342	0.3%
44	Montana	12,894	0.3%
45	Delaware	12,296	0.3%
46	Vermont	11,459	0.3%
47	North Dakota	7,242	0.2%
48	South Dakota	5,871	0.1%
49	Idaho	3,446	0.1%
50	Wyoming	545	0.0%
	District of Columbia	41,916	0.9%

Source: U.S. Department of Health and Human Services, Administration for Children and Families
    "TANF Caseload Data" (http://www.acf.hhs.gov/programs/ofa/caseload/caseloadindex.htm)
*As of March 2005. Welfare reform replaced the Aid to Families with Dependent Children program (AFDC) with
Temporary Assistance to Needy Families (TANF) as of July 1, 1997. National total includes 54,083 recipients in
U.S. territories (41,910 in Puerto Rico).

Percent Change in TANF Recipients: 2004 to 2005

National Percent Change = 5.0% Decrease*

RANK	STATE	PERCENT CHANGE
4	Alabama	7.3
34	Alaska	(10.2)
38	Arizona	(15.3)
40	Arkansas	(16.2)
13	California	(1.3)
14	Colorado	(1.4)
28	Connecticut	(7.2)
11	Delaware	(1.2)
27	Florida	(6.7)
50	Georgia	(29.8)
33	Hawaii	(8.8)
31	Idaho	(7.3)
2	Illinois	10.4
25	Indiana	(6.0)
21	Iowa	(3.9)
6	Kansas	4.0
22	Kentucky	(4.0)
37	Louisiana	(14.8)
23	Maine	(4.6)
32	Maryland	(7.5)
16	Massachusetts	(2.3)
7	Michigan	0.9
43	Minnesota	(17.0)
45	Mississippi	(19.4)
19	Missouri	(3.4)
35	Montana	(12.0)
40	Nebraska	(16.2)
49	Nevada	(26.1)
7	New Hampshire	0.9
15	New Jersey	(1.6)
18	New Mexico	(3.2)
24	New York	(5.2)
36	North Carolina	(13.2)
28	North Dakota	(7.2)
20	Ohio	(3.6)
47	Oklahoma	(20.5)
3	Oregon	10.1
1	Pennsylvania	11.1
42	Rhode Island	(16.6)
26	South Carolina	(6.6)
10	South Dakota	(0.7)
17	Tennessee	(2.6)
46	Texas	(19.5)
11	Utah	(1.2)
28	Vermont	(7.2)
5	Virginia	5.4
9	Washington	(0.6)
48	West Virginia	(21.9)
38	Wisconsin	(15.3)
44	Wyoming	(17.5)

RANK	STATE	PERCENT CHANGE
1	Pennsylvania	11.1
2	Illinois	10.4
3	Oregon	10.1
4	Alabama	7.3
5	Virginia	5.4
6	Kansas	4.0
7	Michigan	0.9
7	New Hampshire	0.9
9	Washington	(0.6)
10	South Dakota	(0.7)
11	Delaware	(1.2)
11	Utah	(1.2)
13	California	(1.3)
14	Colorado	(1.4)
15	New Jersey	(1.6)
16	Massachusetts	(2.3)
17	Tennessee	(2.6)
18	New Mexico	(3.2)
19	Missouri	(3.4)
20	Ohio	(3.6)
21	Iowa	(3.9)
22	Kentucky	(4.0)
23	Maine	(4.6)
24	New York	(5.2)
25	Indiana	(6.0)
26	South Carolina	(6.6)
27	Florida	(6.7)
28	Connecticut	(7.2)
28	North Dakota	(7.2)
28	Vermont	(7.2)
31	Idaho	(7.3)
32	Maryland	(7.5)
33	Hawaii	(8.8)
34	Alaska	(10.2)
35	Montana	(12.0)
36	North Carolina	(13.2)
37	Louisiana	(14.8)
38	Arizona	(15.3)
38	Wisconsin	(15.3)
40	Arkansas	(16.2)
40	Nebraska	(16.2)
42	Rhode Island	(16.6)
43	Minnesota	(17.0)
44	Wyoming	(17.5)
45	Mississippi	(19.4)
46	Texas	(19.5)
47	Oklahoma	(20.5)
48	West Virginia	(21.9)
49	Nevada	(26.1)
50	Georgia	(29.8)

District of Columbia (4.5)

Source: Morgan Quitno Press using data from U.S. Dept. of HHS, Administration for Children and Families "TANF Caseload Data" (http://www.acf.hhs.gov/programs/ofa/caseload/caseloadindex.htm)
*March 2004 to March 2005. Welfare reform replaced the Aid to Families with Dependent Children program (AFDC) with Temporary Assistance to Needy Families (TANF) as of July 1, 1997. National percent includes recipients in U.S. territories.

TANF Work Participation Rates in 2004

National Rate = 32.0%*

ALPHA ORDER				RANK ORDER		
RANK	STATE	PERCENT		RANK	STATE	PERCENT
19	Alabama	37.9		1	Montana	92.7
15	Alaska	43.6		2	Kansas	88.0
37	Arizona	25.5		3	Wyoming	77.8
34	Arkansas	27.3		4	Hawaii	70.5
44	California	23.1		5	Ohio	65.2
23	Colorado	34.7		6	Wisconsin	61.3
42	Connecticut	24.3		7	Massachusetts	60.0
45	Delaware	22.1		8	South Dakota	54.8
17	Florida	40.4		9	South Carolina	53.7
40	Georgia	24.8		10	Tennessee	50.6
4	Hawaii	70.5		11	Virginia	50.1
16	Idaho	41.0		12	Iowa	50.0
14	Illinois	46.1		13	New Mexico	46.2
33	Indiana	30.0		14	Illinois	46.1
12	Iowa	50.0		15	Alaska	43.6
2	Kansas	88.0		16	Idaho	41.0
18	Kentucky	38.1		17	Florida	40.4
21	Louisiana	35.4		18	Kentucky	38.1
29	Maine	32.1		19	Alabama	37.9
48	Maryland	16.0		20	New York	37.8
7	Massachusetts	60.0		21	Louisiana	35.4
41	Michigan	24.5		21	Washington	35.4
35	Minnesota	26.8		23	Colorado	34.7
46	Mississippi	21.0		24	New Jersey	34.6
47	Missouri	19.5		25	Nebraska	34.5
1	Montana	92.7		25	Nevada	34.5
25	Nebraska	34.5		27	Texas	34.2
25	Nevada	34.5		28	Oklahoma	33.2
32	New Hampshire	30.2		29	Maine	32.1
24	New Jersey	34.6		29	Oregon	32.1
13	New Mexico	46.2		31	North Carolina	31.4
20	New York	37.8		32	New Hampshire	30.2
31	North Carolina	31.4		33	Indiana	30.0
38	North Dakota	25.3		34	Arkansas	27.3
5	Ohio	65.2		35	Minnesota	26.8
28	Oklahoma	33.2		36	Utah	26.2
29	Oregon	32.1		37	Arizona	25.5
50	Pennsylvania	7.1		38	North Dakota	25.3
43	Rhode Island	23.7		39	Vermont	24.9
9	South Carolina	53.7		40	Georgia	24.8
8	South Dakota	54.8		41	Michigan	24.5
10	Tennessee	50.6		42	Connecticut	24.3
27	Texas	34.2		43	Rhode Island	23.7
36	Utah	26.2		44	California	23.1
39	Vermont	24.9		45	Delaware	22.1
11	Virginia	50.1		46	Mississippi	21.0
21	Washington	35.4		47	Missouri	19.5
49	West Virginia	11.7		48	Maryland	16.0
6	Wisconsin	61.3		49	West Virginia	11.7
3	Wyoming	77.8		50	Pennsylvania	7.1
					District of Columbia	18.2

Source: U.S. Department of Health and Human Services, Administration for Children and Families

"Table 1A: TANF Work Participation Rates" (http://www.acf.hhs.gov/programs/ofa/particip/2004/table01a.htm)
For fiscal year 2004. Percent of parents in TANF families who work for at least 30 hours per week, or 20 hours per week if they have children under age six. Welfare reform replaced the Aid to Families with Dependent Children program (AFDC) with Temporary Assistance to Needy Families (TANF) as of July 1, 1997. National average includes recipients in U.S. territories.

Average Monthly TANF Assistance per Recipient in 2004

National Average = $165.89*

ALPHA ORDER				RANK ORDER		
RANK	STATE	PER RECIPIENT		RANK	STATE	PER RECIPIENT
43	Alabama	$84.10		1	New York	$261.34
4	Alaska	239.00		2	California	261.33
31	Arizona	120.68		3	Massachusetts	241.00
40	Arkansas	101.53		4	Alaska	239.00
2	California	261.33		5	New Hampshire	217.19
26	Colorado	133.89		6	Vermont	212.30
8	Connecticut	206.43		7	Hawaii	208.99
37	Delaware	109.50		8	Connecticut	206.43
28	Florida	126.73		9	Wisconsin	189.37
42	Georgia	95.93		10	Oregon	183.55
7	Hawaii	208.99		11	Washington	174.16
12	Idaho	164.43		12	Idaho	164.43
50	Illinois	61.94		13	Rhode Island	163.67
46	Indiana	76.44		14	New Jersey	159.22
27	Iowa	132.58		15	Utah	157.98
32	Kansas	118.04		16	South Dakota	153.78
36	Kentucky	111.03		17	Michigan	149.95
34	Louisiana	113.96		18	Maryland	149.68
25	Maine	135.45		19	Ohio	144.51
18	Maryland	149.68		20	Nebraska	140.82
3	Massachusetts	241.00		21	North Dakota	139.64
17	Michigan	149.95		22	Minnesota	138.04
22	Minnesota	138.04		23	West Virginia	137.98
48	Mississippi	66.59		24	Nevada	136.23
41	Missouri	98.80		25	Maine	135.45
30	Montana	121.20		26	Colorado	133.89
20	Nebraska	140.82		27	Iowa	132.58
24	Nevada	136.23		28	Florida	126.73
5	New Hampshire	217.19		29	Pennsylvania	123.50
14	New Jersey	159.22		30	Montana	121.20
33	New Mexico	116.54		31	Arizona	120.68
1	New York	261.34		32	Kansas	118.04
39	North Carolina	104.86		33	New Mexico	116.54
21	North Dakota	139.64		34	Louisiana	113.96
19	Ohio	144.51		35	Wyoming	111.23
44	Oklahoma	80.89		36	Kentucky	111.03
10	Oregon	183.55		37	Delaware	109.50
29	Pennsylvania	123.50		38	Virginia	107.24
13	Rhode Island	163.67		39	North Carolina	104.86
47	South Carolina	70.20		40	Arkansas	101.53
16	South Dakota	153.78		41	Missouri	98.80
49	Tennessee	63.91		42	Georgia	95.93
45	Texas	80.11		43	Alabama	84.10
15	Utah	157.98		44	Oklahoma	80.89
6	Vermont	212.30		45	Texas	80.11
38	Virginia	107.24		46	Indiana	76.44
11	Washington	174.16		47	South Carolina	70.20
23	West Virginia	137.98		48	Mississippi	66.59
9	Wisconsin	189.37		49	Tennessee	63.91
35	Wyoming	111.23		50	Illinois	61.94
					District of Columbia	130.73

Source: U.S. Department of Health and Human Services, Administration for Children and Families
   "Average Monthly Amount of Assistance" (http://www.ssa.gov/policy/docs/statcomps/supplement/2005/9g.html)
*For fiscal year 2004.   Welfare reform replaced the Aid to Families with Dependent Children program
(AFDC) with Temporary Assistance to Needy Families (TANF) as of July 1, 1997. National average includes
recipients in U.S. territories.

Food Stamp Benefits in 2005

National Total = $28,562,543,462*

ALPHA ORDER

RANK	STATE	BENEFITS	% of USA
16	Alabama	$616,090,009	2.2%
43	Alaska	80,405,244	0.3%
14	Arizona	633,808,912	2.2%
25	Arkansas	401,286,262	1.4%
2	California	2,311,835,904	8.1%
29	Colorado	313,224,564	1.1%
33	Connecticut	223,194,713	0.8%
45	Delaware	65,229,058	0.2%
4	Florida	1,596,664,564	5.6%
9	Georgia	1,047,842,395	3.7%
37	Hawaii	155,976,093	0.5%
41	Idaho	102,970,484	0.4%
5	Illinois	1,400,091,866	4.9%
15	Indiana	626,608,340	2.2%
34	Iowa	219,761,890	0.8%
35	Kansas	179,999,844	0.6%
17	Kentucky	611,490,522	2.1%
10	Louisiana	978,765,504	3.4%
36	Maine	162,202,784	0.6%
27	Maryland	320,133,493	1.1%
26	Massachusetts	363,033,709	1.3%
8	Michigan	1,098,817,352	3.8%
30	Minnesota	275,123,010	1.0%
21	Mississippi	462,961,820	1.6%
13	Missouri	735,757,569	2.6%
42	Montana	89,231,197	0.3%
40	Nebraska	119,540,826	0.4%
39	Nevada	128,901,489	0.5%
47	New Hampshire	50,569,118	0.2%
24	New Jersey	437,423,007	1.5%
32	New Mexico	251,414,424	0.9%
3	New York	2,135,860,430	7.5%
12	North Carolina	856,161,978	3.0%
49	North Dakota	44,674,426	0.2%
6	Ohio	1,156,822,631	4.1%
23	Oklahoma	439,598,807	1.5%
22	Oregon	455,943,437	1.6%
7	Pennsylvania	1,104,711,263	3.9%
44	Rhode Island	78,517,688	0.3%
18	South Carolina	565,811,046	2.0%
46	South Dakota	61,477,144	0.2%
11	Tennessee	941,638,149	3.3%
1	Texas	2,656,263,589	9.3%
38	Utah	141,217,600	0.5%
48	Vermont	44,999,412	0.2%
20	Virginia	499,708,150	1.7%
19	Washington	539,048,283	1.9%
31	West Virginia	258,050,316	0.9%
28	Wisconsin	316,951,818	1.1%
50	Wyoming	26,976,298	0.1%

RANK ORDER

RANK	STATE	BENEFITS	% of USA
1	Texas	$2,656,263,589	9.3%
2	California	2,311,835,904	8.1%
3	New York	2,135,869,438	7.5%
4	Florida	1,596,664,564	5.6%
5	Illinois	1,400,091,866	4.9%
6	Ohio	1,156,822,631	4.1%
7	Pennsylvania	1,104,711,263	3.9%
8	Michigan	1,098,817,352	3.8%
9	Georgia	1,047,842,395	3.7%
10	Louisiana	978,765,504	3.4%
11	Tennessee	941,638,149	3.3%
12	North Carolina	856,161,978	3.0%
13	Missouri	735,757,569	2.6%
14	Arizona	633,808,912	2.2%
15	Indiana	626,600,340	2.2%
16	Alabama	616,090,009	2.2%
17	Kentucky	611,490,522	2.1%
18	South Carolina	565,811,046	2.0%
19	Washington	539,048,283	1.9%
20	Virginia	499,708,150	1.7%
21	Mississippi	462,961,820	1.6%
22	Oregon	455,943,437	1.6%
23	Oklahoma	439,598,807	1.5%
24	New Jersey	437,423,007	1.5%
25	Arkansas	401,286,262	1.4%
26	Massachusetts	363,033,709	1.3%
27	Maryland	320,133,493	1.1%
28	Wisconsin	316,951,818	1.1%
29	Colorado	313,224,564	1.1%
30	Minnesota	275,123,010	1.0%
31	West Virginia	258,050,316	0.9%
32	New Mexico	251,414,424	0.9%
33	Connecticut	223,194,713	0.8%
34	Iowa	219,761,890	0.8%
35	Kansas	179,999,844	0.6%
36	Maine	162,202,784	0.6%
37	Hawaii	155,976,093	0.5%
38	Utah	141,217,600	0.5%
39	Nevada	128,901,489	0.5%
40	Nebraska	119,540,826	0.4%
41	Idaho	102,970,484	0.4%
42	Montana	89,231,197	0.3%
43	Alaska	80,405,244	0.3%
44	Rhode Island	78,517,688	0.3%
45	Delaware	65,229,058	0.2%
46	South Dakota	61,477,144	0.2%
47	New Hampshire	50,569,118	0.2%
48	Vermont	44,999,412	0.2%
49	North Dakota	44,674,426	0.2%
50	Wyoming	26,976,298	0.1%
	District of Columbia	103,295,526	0.4%

*Source: U.S. Department of Agriculture, Food, Nutrition and Consumer Services
  "Food Stamp Program: Benefits" (http://www.fns.usda.gov/pd/fsfybft.htm)*
Preliminary for year ending December 21, 2005. National total includes $74,450,497 to U.S. territories. Costs are for benefits only and exclude administrative expenditures.

Monthly Food Stamp Recipients in 2005

National Total = 25,682,561 Recipients*

ALPHA ORDER

RANK	STATE	RECIPIENTS	% of USA
15	Alabama	558,596	2.2%
46	Alaska	55,567	0.2%
17	Arizona	550,291	2.1%
25	Arkansas	373,764	1.5%
2	California	1,990,919	7.8%
31	Colorado	245,926	1.0%
34	Connecticut	204,146	0.8%
44	Delaware	61,586	0.2%
4	Florida	1,381,804	5.4%
9	Georgia	921,427	3.6%
40	Hawaii	93,548	0.4%
41	Idaho	93,441	0.4%
5	Illinois	1,158,271	4.5%
16	Indiana	556,285	2.2%
33	Iowa	206,696	0.8%
35	Kansas	177,782	0.7%
14	Kentucky	570,277	2.2%
11	Louisiana	807,896	3.1%
36	Maine	152,910	0.6%
28	Maryland	288,943	1.1%
26	Massachusetts	368,122	1.4%
6	Michigan	1,047,594	4.1%
30	Minnesota	259,937	1.0%
24	Mississippi	391,485	1.5%
13	Missouri	766,425	3.0%
42	Montana	80,870	0.3%
39	Nebraska	117,415	0.5%
38	Nevada	121,707	0.5%
47	New Hampshire	52,310	0.2%
23	New Jersey	392,416	1.5%
32	New Mexico	240,637	0.9%
3	New York	1,754,861	6.8%
12	North Carolina	799,769	3.1%
49	North Dakota	42,204	0.2%
8	Ohio	1,007,225	3.9%
22	Oklahoma	424,402	1.7%
21	Oregon	429,358	1.7%
7	Pennsylvania	1,042,809	4.1%
43	Rhode Island	76,085	0.3%
18	South Carolina	521,125	2.0%
45	South Dakota	56,095	0.2%
10	Tennessee	849,703	3.3%
1	Texas	2,451,197	9.5%
37	Utah	133,263	0.5%
48	Vermont	45,218	0.2%
20	Virginia	488,481	1.9%
19	Washington	508,472	2.0%
29	West Virginia	262,442	1.0%
27	Wisconsin	345,748	1.3%
50	Wyoming	25,482	0.1%

RANK ORDER

RANK	STATE	RECIPIENTS	% of USA
1	Texas	2,451,197	9.5%
2	California	1,990,919	7.8%
3	New York	1,754,861	6.8%
4	Florida	1,381,804	5.4%
5	Illinois	1,158,271	4.5%
6	Michigan	1,047,594	4.1%
7	Pennsylvania	1,042,809	4.1%
8	Ohio	1,007,225	3.9%
9	Georgia	921,427	3.6%
10	Tennessee	849,703	3.3%
11	Louisiana	807,896	3.1%
12	North Carolina	799,769	3.1%
13	Missouri	766,425	3.0%
14	Kentucky	570,277	2.2%
15	Alabama	558,596	2.2%
16	Indiana	556,285	2.2%
17	Arizona	550,291	2.1%
18	South Carolina	521,125	2.0%
19	Washington	508,472	2.0%
20	Virginia	488,481	1.9%
21	Oregon	429,358	1.7%
22	Oklahoma	424,402	1.7%
23	New Jersey	392,416	1.5%
24	Mississippi	391,485	1.5%
25	Arkansas	373,764	1.5%
26	Massachusetts	368,122	1.4%
27	Wisconsin	345,748	1.3%
28	Maryland	288,943	1.1%
29	West Virginia	262,442	1.0%
30	Minnesota	259,937	1.0%
31	Colorado	245,926	1.0%
32	New Mexico	240,637	0.9%
33	Iowa	206,696	0.8%
34	Connecticut	204,146	0.8%
35	Kansas	177,782	0.7%
36	Maine	152,910	0.6%
37	Utah	133,263	0.5%
38	Nevada	121,707	0.5%
39	Nebraska	117,415	0.5%
40	Hawaii	93,548	0.4%
41	Idaho	93,441	0.4%
42	Montana	80,870	0.3%
43	Rhode Island	76,085	0.3%
44	Delaware	61,586	0.2%
45	South Dakota	56,095	0.2%
46	Alaska	55,567	0.2%
47	New Hampshire	52,310	0.2%
48	Vermont	45,218	0.2%
49	North Dakota	42,204	0.2%
50	Wyoming	25,482	0.1%
	District of Columbia	88,799	0.3%

Source: U.S. Department of Agriculture, Food, Nutrition and Consumer Services
    "Food Stamp Program: Number of Persons Participating" (http://www.fns.usda.gov/pd/fsfypart.htm)
*Preliminary for fiscal year 2005. National total includes 40,827 recipients in U.S. territories.

Average Monthly Food Stamp Benefit per Recipient in 2005

National Average = $92.68 per Recipient*

ALPHA ORDER

RANK	STATE	PER RECIPIENT
18	Alabama	$91.91
2	Alaska	120.58
10	Arizona	95.98
24	Arkansas	89.47
8	California	96.77
3	Colorado	106.14
21	Connecticut	91.11
33	Delaware	88.26
9	Florida	96.29
12	Georgia	94.77
1	Hawaii	138.95
19	Idaho	91.83
6	Illinois	100.73
13	Indiana	93.87
27	Iowa	88.60
44	Kansas	84.37
25	Kentucky	89.36
5	Louisiana	100.96
29	Maine	88.40
16	Maryland	92.33
46	Massachusetts	82.18
38	Michigan	87.41
37	Minnesota	88.20
7	Mississippi	98.55
49	Missouri	80.00
17	Montana	91.95
43	Nebraska	84.84
33	Nevada	88.26
48	New Hampshire	80.56
14	New Jersey	92.89
39	New Mexico	87.07
4	New York	101.43
26	North Carolina	89.21
36	North Dakota	88.21
11	Ohio	95.71
40	Oklahoma	86.32
28	Oregon	88.49
32	Pennsylvania	88.28
41	Rhode Island	86.00
22	South Carolina	90.48
20	South Dakota	91.33
15	Tennessee	92.35
23	Texas	90.31
31	Utah	88.31
45	Vermont	82.93
42	Virginia	85.25
30	Washington	88.34
47	West Virginia	81.94
50	Wisconsin	76.39
35	Wyoming	88.22

RANK ORDER

RANK	STATE	PER RECIPIENT
1	Hawaii	$138.95
2	Alaska	120.58
3	Colorado	106.14
4	New York	101.43
5	Louisiana	100.96
6	Illinois	100.73
7	Mississippi	98.55
8	California	96.77
9	Florida	96.29
10	Arizona	95.98
11	Ohio	95.71
12	Georgia	94.77
13	Indiana	93.87
14	New Jersey	92.89
15	Tennessee	92.35
16	Maryland	92.33
17	Montana	91.95
18	Alabama	91.91
19	Idaho	91.83
20	South Dakota	91.33
21	Connecticut	91.11
22	South Carolina	90.48
23	Texas	90.31
24	Arkansas	89.47
25	Kentucky	89.36
26	North Carolina	89.21
27	Iowa	88.60
28	Oregon	88.49
29	Maine	88.40
30	Washington	88.34
31	Utah	88.31
32	Pennsylvania	88.28
33	Delaware	88.26
33	Nevada	88.26
35	Wyoming	88.22
36	North Dakota	88.21
37	Minnesota	88.20
38	Michigan	87.41
39	New Mexico	87.07
40	Oklahoma	86.32
41	Rhode Island	86.00
42	Virginia	85.25
43	Nebraska	84.84
44	Kansas	84.37
45	Vermont	82.93
46	Massachusetts	82.18
47	West Virginia	81.94
48	New Hampshire	80.56
49	Missouri	80.00
50	Wisconsin	76.39
	District of Columbia	96.94

Source: U.S. Department of Agriculture, Food, Nutrition and Consumer Services
   "Food Stamp Program: Average Monthly Benefit per Person" (http://www.fns.usda.gov/pd/fsavgben.htm)
*Preliminary for fiscal year 2005. National average includes recipients in U.S. territories.

Percent of Population Receiving Food Stamps in 2005

National Percent = 8.7%*

ALPHA ORDER

RANK	STATE	PERCENT
9	Alabama	12.3
24	Alaska	8.4
17	Arizona	9.3
5	Arkansas	13.4
42	California	5.5
44	Colorado	5.3
40	Connecticut	5.8
28	Delaware	7.3
27	Florida	7.8
16	Georgia	10.2
28	Hawaii	7.3
36	Idaho	6.5
19	Illinois	9.1
21	Indiana	8.9
33	Iowa	7.0
36	Kansas	6.5
4	Kentucky	13.7
1	Louisiana	17.9
13	Maine	11.6
45	Maryland	5.2
40	Massachusetts	5.8
15	Michigan	10.4
46	Minnesota	5.1
5	Mississippi	13.4
7	Missouri	13.2
23	Montana	8.6
34	Nebraska	6.7
47	Nevada	5.0
50	New Hampshire	4.0
49	New Jersey	4.5
8	New Mexico	12.5
19	New York	9.1
18	North Carolina	9.2
35	North Dakota	6.6
22	Ohio	8.8
11	Oklahoma	12.0
12	Oregon	11.8
24	Pennsylvania	8.4
32	Rhode Island	7.1
10	South Carolina	12.2
31	South Dakota	7.2
3	Tennessee	14.2
14	Texas	10.7
43	Utah	5.4
28	Vermont	7.3
36	Virginia	6.5
26	Washington	8.1
2	West Virginia	14.4
39	Wisconsin	6.2
47	Wyoming	5.0

RANK ORDER

RANK	STATE	PERCENT
1	Louisiana	17.9
2	West Virginia	14.4
3	Tennessee	14.2
4	Kentucky	13.7
5	Arkansas	13.4
5	Mississippi	13.4
7	Missouri	13.2
8	New Mexico	12.5
9	Alabama	12.3
10	South Carolina	12.2
11	Oklahoma	12.0
12	Oregon	11.8
13	Maine	11.6
14	Texas	10.7
15	Michigan	10.4
16	Georgia	10.2
17	Arizona	9.3
18	North Carolina	9.2
19	Illinois	9.1
19	New York	9.1
21	Indiana	8.9
22	Ohio	8.8
23	Montana	8.6
24	Alaska	8.4
24	Pennsylvania	8.4
26	Washington	8.1
27	Florida	7.8
28	Delaware	7.3
28	Hawaii	7.3
28	Vermont	7.3
31	South Dakota	7.2
32	Rhode Island	7.1
33	Iowa	7.0
34	Nebraska	6.7
35	North Dakota	6.6
36	Idaho	6.5
36	Kansas	6.5
36	Virginia	6.5
39	Wisconsin	6.2
40	Connecticut	5.8
40	Massachusetts	5.8
42	California	5.5
43	Utah	5.4
44	Colorado	5.3
45	Maryland	5.2
46	Minnesota	5.1
47	Nevada	5.0
47	Wyoming	5.0
49	New Jersey	4.5
50	New Hampshire	4.0

| | District of Columbia | 16.1 |

Source: Morgan Quitno Press using data from U.S. Department of Agriculture, Food, Nutrition and Consumer Services "Food Stamp Program: Number of Persons Participating" (http://www.fns.usda.gov/pd/fsfypart.htm)
Preliminary data for fiscal year 2005. National rate does not include recipients in U.S. territories.

528

Percent of Households Receiving Food Stamps in 2005

National Percent = 10.2% of Households*

ALPHA ORDER

RANK	STATE	PERCENT
13	Alabama	12.7
29	Alaska	8.9
21	Arizona	10.3
8	Arkansas	13.9
42	California	6.6
48	Colorado	5.8
32	Connecticut	8.1
31	Delaware	8.4
26	Florida	9.6
17	Georgia	11.7
19	Hawaii	11.1
38	Idaho	7.2
18	Illinois	11.2
23	Indiana	9.9
33	Iowa	7.6
36	Kansas	7.3
5	Kentucky	14.9
1	Louisiana	18.6
7	Maine	14.6
44	Maryland	6.3
38	Massachusetts	7.2
16	Michigan	12.0
46	Minnesota	6.1
6	Mississippi	14.8
11	Missouri	12.9
27	Montana	9.4
36	Nebraska	7.3
44	Nevada	6.3
49	New Hampshire	5.1
47	New Jersey	6.0
10	New Mexico	13.1
11	New York	12.9
21	North Carolina	10.3
38	North Dakota	7.2
23	Ohio	9.9
13	Oklahoma	12.7
4	Oregon	15.3
25	Pennsylvania	9.8
30	Rhode Island	8.5
9	South Carolina	13.6
35	South Dakota	7.5
2	Tennessee	16.2
15	Texas	12.1
41	Utah	6.8
28	Vermont	9.0
33	Virginia	7.6
20	Washington	10.4
3	West Virginia	15.5
42	Wisconsin	6.6
49	Wyoming	5.1

RANK ORDER

RANK	STATE	PERCENT
1	Louisiana	18.6
2	Tennessee	16.2
3	West Virginia	15.5
4	Oregon	15.3
5	Kentucky	14.9
6	Mississippi	14.8
7	Maine	14.6
8	Arkansas	13.9
9	South Carolina	13.6
10	New Mexico	13.1
11	Missouri	12.9
11	New York	12.9
13	Alabama	12.7
13	Oklahoma	12.7
15	Texas	12.1
16	Michigan	12.0
17	Georgia	11.7
18	Illinois	11.2
19	Hawaii	11.1
20	Washington	10.4
21	Arizona	10.3
21	North Carolina	10.3
23	Indiana	9.9
23	Ohio	9.9
25	Pennsylvania	9.8
26	Florida	9.6
27	Montana	9.4
28	Vermont	9.0
29	Alaska	8.9
30	Rhode Island	8.5
31	Delaware	8.4
32	Connecticut	8.1
33	Iowa	7.6
33	Virginia	7.6
35	South Dakota	7.5
36	Kansas	7.3
36	Nebraska	7.3
38	Idaho	7.2
38	Massachusetts	7.2
38	North Dakota	7.2
41	Utah	6.8
42	California	6.6
42	Wisconsin	6.6
44	Maryland	6.3
44	Nevada	6.3
46	Minnesota	6.1
47	New Jersey	6.0
48	Colorado	5.8
49	New Hampshire	5.1
49	Wyoming	5.1

	District of Columbia	17.8

Source: Morgan Quitno Press using data from U.S. Department of Agriculture, Food, Nutrition and Consumer Services
    "Food Stamp Program: Number of Persons Participating" (http://www.fns.usda.gov/pd/fsfypart.htm)
*Food stamp program households are for fiscal year 2005. Percent calculated using 2004 estimated total households. National percent excludes households in U.S. territories.

Average Monthly Participants in Women, Infants and Children (WIC) Special Nutrition Program in 2005
National Total = 8,110,944 Participants*

ALPHA ORDER

RANK	STATE	PARTICIPANTS	% of USA
22	Alabama	120,123	1.5%
41	Alaska	26,868	0.3%
11	Arizona	179,928	2.2%
29	Arkansas	92,970	1.1%
1	California	1,338,889	16.5%
30	Colorado	84,857	1.0%
35	Connecticut	51,308	0.6%
46	Delaware	19,507	0.2%
4	Florida	373,188	4.6%
7	Georgia	274,407	3.4%
40	Hawaii	32,516	0.4%
39	Idaho	37,294	0.5%
6	Illinois	276,399	3.4%
16	Indiana	135,011	1.7%
33	Iowa	68,346	0.8%
31	Kansas	69,665	0.9%
20	Kentucky	124,778	1.5%
18	Louisiana	129,024	1.6%
42	Maine	23,801	0.3%
24	Maryland	112,727	1.4%
23	Massachusetts	116,422	1.4%
9	Michigan	231,076	2.8%
19	Minnesota	127,020	1.6%
28	Mississippi	95,174	1.2%
17	Missouri	131,968	1.6%
45	Montana	21,443	0.3%
38	Nebraska	41,130	0.5%
37	Nevada	48,453	0.6%
47	New Hampshire	16,998	0.2%
14	New Jersey	148,926	1.8%
34	New Mexico	64,808	0.8%
3	New York	484,510	6.0%
10	North Carolina	230,870	2.8%
49	North Dakota	14,593	0.2%
5	Ohio	276,997	3.4%
21	Oklahoma	121,367	1.5%
27	Oregon	103,947	1.3%
8	Pennsylvania	242,767	3.0%
43	Rhode Island	22,778	0.3%
26	South Carolina	110,287	1.4%
44	South Dakota	21,579	0.3%
13	Tennessee	159,410	2.0%
2	Texas	904,581	11.2%
32	Utah	69,025	0.9%
48	Vermont	16,097	0.2%
15	Virginia	142,090	1.8%
12	Washington	159,760	2.0%
36	West Virginia	49,063	0.6%
25	Wisconsin	112,321	1.4%
50	Wyoming	13,011	0.2%

RANK ORDER

RANK	STATE	PARTICIPANTS	% of USA
1	California	1,338,889	16.5%
2	Texas	904,581	11.2%
3	New York	484,510	6.0%
4	Florida	373,188	4.6%
5	Ohio	276,997	3.4%
6	Illinois	276,399	3.4%
7	Georgia	274,407	3.4%
8	Pennsylvania	242,767	3.0%
9	Michigan	231,076	2.8%
10	North Carolina	230,870	2.8%
11	Arizona	179,928	2.2%
12	Washington	159,760	2.0%
13	Tennessee	159,410	2.0%
14	New Jersey	148,926	1.8%
15	Virginia	142,090	1.8%
16	Indiana	135,011	1.7%
17	Missouri	131,968	1.6%
18	Louisiana	129,024	1.6%
19	Minnesota	127,020	1.6%
20	Kentucky	124,778	1.5%
21	Oklahoma	121,367	1.5%
22	Alabama	120,123	1.5%
23	Massachusetts	116,422	1.4%
24	Maryland	112,727	1.4%
25	Wisconsin	112,321	1.4%
26	South Carolina	110,287	1.4%
27	Oregon	103,947	1.3%
28	Mississippi	95,174	1.2%
29	Arkansas	92,970	1.1%
30	Colorado	84,857	1.0%
31	Kansas	69,665	0.9%
32	Utah	69,025	0.9%
33	Iowa	68,346	0.8%
34	New Mexico	64,808	0.8%
35	Connecticut	51,308	0.6%
36	West Virginia	49,063	0.6%
37	Nevada	48,453	0.6%
38	Nebraska	41,130	0.5%
39	Idaho	37,294	0.5%
40	Hawaii	32,516	0.4%
41	Alaska	26,868	0.3%
42	Maine	23,801	0.3%
43	Rhode Island	22,778	0.3%
44	South Dakota	21,579	0.3%
45	Montana	21,443	0.3%
46	Delaware	19,507	0.2%
47	New Hampshire	16,998	0.2%
48	Vermont	16,097	0.2%
49	North Dakota	14,593	0.2%
50	Wyoming	13,011	0.2%
	District of Columbia	16,481	0.2%

Source: U.S. Department of Agriculture, Food, Nutrition and Consumer Services
"WIC Program: Total Participation" (http://www.fns.usda.gov/pd/wifypart.htm)
*Preliminary data for fiscal year 2005. National total includes 224,386 participants in outlying areas not shown separately (Puerto Rico has 205,789 participants).

Average Monthly Benefit per Participant in Women, Infant and Children (WIC) Special Nutrition Program in 2005
National Average = $37.50*

ALPHA ORDER				RANK ORDER		
RANK	STATE	AVERAGE BENEFIT		RANK	STATE	AVERAGE BENEFIT
4	Alabama	$44.51		1	Hawaii	$52.32
2	Alaska	45.82		2	Alaska	45.82
19	Arizona	36.97		3	New York	44.72
24	Arkansas	35.55		4	Alabama	44.51
14	California	38.51		5	Louisiana	42.67
34	Colorado	33.50		6	Tennessee	42.23
7	Connecticut	42.15		7	Connecticut	42.15
39	Delaware	32.95		8	North Dakota	42.08
13	Florida	38.53		9	Washington	41.81
20	Georgia	36.77		10	Illinois	41.25
1	Hawaii	52.32		11	Vermont	40.89
47	Idaho	30.64		12	Mississippi	38.89
10	Illinois	41.25		13	Florida	38.53
40	Indiana	32.80		14	California	38.51
38	Iowa	32.96		15	Kentucky	38.40
36	Kansas	33.04		16	North Carolina	38.03
15	Kentucky	38.40		17	New Jersey	37.81
5	Louisiana	42.67		18	South Carolina	37.37
49	Maine	27.69		19	Arizona	36.97
44	Maryland	31.43		20	Georgia	36.77
29	Massachusetts	34.48		21	Oregon	36.39
31	Michigan	34.42		22	West Virginia	36.19
28	Minnesota	35.05		23	Rhode Island	36.15
12	Mississippi	38.89		24	Arkansas	35.55
41	Missouri	32.77		25	Nebraska	35.37
27	Montana	35.08		26	New Mexico	35.14
25	Nebraska	35.37		27	Montana	35.08
45	Nevada	31.04		28	Minnesota	35.05
46	New Hampshire	30.71		29	Massachusetts	34.48
17	New Jersey	37.81		30	Virginia	34.46
26	New Mexico	35.14		31	Michigan	34.42
3	New York	44.72		32	Ohio	34.15
16	North Carolina	38.03		33	Wisconsin	34.02
8	North Dakota	42.08		34	Colorado	33.50
32	Ohio	34.15		35	Pennsylvania	33.25
42	Oklahoma	32.53		36	Kansas	33.04
21	Oregon	36.39		37	South Dakota	33.00
35	Pennsylvania	33.25		38	Iowa	32.96
23	Rhode Island	36.15		39	Delaware	32.95
18	South Carolina	37.37		40	Indiana	32.80
37	South Dakota	33.00		41	Missouri	32.77
6	Tennessee	42.23		42	Oklahoma	32.53
43	Texas	31.73		43	Texas	31.73
50	Utah	27.48		44	Maryland	31.43
11	Vermont	40.89		45	Nevada	31.04
30	Virginia	34.46		46	New Hampshire	30.71
9	Washington	41.81		47	Idaho	30.64
22	West Virginia	36.19		48	Wyoming	29.23
33	Wisconsin	34.02		49	Maine	27.69
48	Wyoming	29.23		50	Utah	27.48
					District of Columbia	42.69

Source: U.S. Department of Agriculture, Food, Nutrition and Consumer Services
   "WIC Program: Average Benefit per Person per Month" (http://www.fns.usda.gov/pd/wifyavgfd$.htm)
*Preliminary data for fiscal year 2005. National average includes outlying areas and Indian reservations not shown separately.

Percent of Public Elementary and Secondary School Students Eligible for Free or Reduced-Price Meals in 2004
Reporting States Percent = 39.8%*

ALPHA ORDER

RANK	STATE	PERCENT
6	Alabama	50.5
43	Alaska	27.3
13	Arizona	45.1
7	Arkansas	49.8
9	California	47.9
33	Colorado	30.2
46	Connecticut	25.4
25	Delaware	33.8
12	Florida	46.0
11	Georgia	46.4
15	Hawaii	42.5
19	Idaho	37.0
20	Illinois	36.9
23	Indiana	34.4
36	Iowa	30.0
18	Kansas	37.4
NA	Kentucky**	NA
2	Louisiana	61.4
35	Maine	30.1
30	Maryland	31.4
44	Massachusetts	27.2
20	Michigan	32.5
39	Minnesota	28.2
1	Mississippi	64.3
17	Missouri	38.0
26	Montana	33.7
24	Nebraska	33.9
26	Nevada	33.7
47	New Hampshire	16.3
45	New Jersey	26.9
3	New Mexico	58.2
NA	New York**	NA
14	North Carolina	44.5
38	North Dakota	28.3
37	Ohio	29.5
4	Oklahoma	53.0
16	Oregon	40.1
40	Pennsylvania	28.1
22	Rhode Island	35.0
5	South Carolina	51.0
30	South Dakota	31.4
NA	Tennessee**	NA
10	Texas	46.7
29	Utah	32.1
42	Vermont	27.4
33	Virginia	30.2
21	Washington	35.5
8	West Virginia	49.3
41	Wisconsin	27.7
32	Wyoming	30.6

RANK ORDER

RANK	STATE	PERCENT
1	Mississippi	64.3
2	Louisiana	61.4
3	New Mexico	58.2
4	Oklahoma	53.0
5	South Carolina	51.0
6	Alabama	50.5
7	Arkansas	49.8
8	West Virginia	49.3
9	California	47.9
10	Texas	46.7
11	Georgia	46.4
12	Florida	46.0
13	Arizona	45.1
14	North Carolina	44.5
15	Hawaii	42.5
16	Oregon	40.1
17	Missouri	38.0
18	Kansas	37.4
19	Idaho	37.0
20	Illinois	36.9
21	Washington	35.5
22	Rhode Island	35.0
23	Indiana	34.4
24	Nebraska	33.9
25	Delaware	33.8
26	Montana	33.7
26	Nevada	33.7
28	Michigan	32.5
29	Utah	32.1
30	Maryland	31.4
30	South Dakota	31.4
32	Wyoming	30.6
33	Colorado	30.2
33	Virginia	30.2
35	Maine	30.1
36	Iowa	30.0
37	Ohio	29.5
38	North Dakota	28.3
39	Minnesota	28.2
40	Pennsylvania	28.1
41	Wisconsin	27.7
42	Vermont	27.4
43	Alaska	27.3
44	Massachusetts	27.2
45	New Jersey	26.9
46	Connecticut	25.4
47	New Hampshire	16.3
NA	Kentucky**	NA
NA	New York**	NA
NA	Tennessee**	NA

District of Columbia 51.4

Source: Morgan Quitno Press using data from U.S. Department of Education, National Center for Education Statistics "Common Core of Data (CCD) Database" (http://nces.ed.gov/ccd/)
*Preliminary data for school year 2003-2004. National percent is only for reporting states.
**Not available.

Child Support Collections in 2004

National Total = $21,603,562,250*

ALPHA ORDER

RANK	STATE	COLLECTIONS	% of USA
28	Alabama	$226,484,276	1.0%
40	Alaska	82,112,657	0.4%
25	Arizona	247,704,782	1.1%
34	Arkansas	144,740,929	0.7%
1	California	2,177,842,511	10.1%
29	Colorado	217,200,793	1.0%
27	Connecticut	226,642,739	1.0%
44	Delaware	63,647,137	0.3%
7	Florida	982,706,031	4.5%
15	Georgia	465,376,601	2.2%
41	Hawaii	80,829,473	0.4%
37	Idaho	110,889,809	0.5%
13	Illinois	511,215,349	2.4%
17	Indiana	442,638,880	2.0%
23	Iowa	280,399,263	1.3%
35	Kansas	142,711,660	0.7%
21	Kentucky	322,100,896	1.5%
24	Louisiana	279,621,377	1.3%
39	Maine	99,549,245	0.5%
19	Maryland	427,575,362	2.0%
18	Massachusetts	439,874,829	2.0%
4	Michigan	1,414,387,902	6.5%
11	Minnesota	567,377,338	2.6%
30	Mississippi	182,008,930	0.8%
16	Missouri	449,718,615	2.1%
50	Montana	45,000,554	0.2%
33	Nebraska	153,576,166	0.7%
38	Nevada	107,714,631	0.5%
42	New Hampshire	79,608,466	0.4%
8	New Jersey	861,917,778	4.0%
43	New Mexico	66,398,704	0.3%
6	New York	1,312,113,067	6.1%
12	North Carolina	527,372,864	2.4%
45	North Dakota	57,670,079	0.3%
2	Ohio	1,636,418,913	7.6%
32	Oklahoma	154,022,936	0.7%
22	Oregon	298,280,030	1.4%
5	Pennsylvania	1,370,957,279	6.3%
47	Rhode Island	54,654,636	0.3%
26	South Carolina	235,648,240	1.1%
46	South Dakota	55,767,437	0.3%
20	Tennessee	382,290,366	1.8%
3	Texas	1,502,575,692	7.0%
36	Utah	140,596,546	0.7%
48	Vermont	48,680,441	0.2%
14	Virginia	495,051,082	2.3%
9	Washington	591,198,936	2.7%
31	West Virginia	158,469,493	0.7%
10	Wisconsin	588,915,411	2.7%
49	Wyoming	48,600,954	0.2%

RANK ORDER

RANK	STATE	COLLECTIONS	% of USA
1	California	$2,177,842,511	10.1%
2	Ohio	1,636,418,913	7.6%
3	Texas	1,502,575,692	7.0%
4	Michigan	1,414,387,902	6.5%
5	Pennsylvania	1,370,957,279	6.3%
6	New York	1,312,113,067	6.1%
7	Florida	982,706,031	4.5%
8	New Jersey	861,917,778	4.0%
9	Washington	591,198,936	2.7%
10	Wisconsin	588,915,411	2.7%
11	Minnesota	567,377,338	2.6%
12	North Carolina	527,372,864	2.4%
13	Illinois	511,215,349	2.4%
14	Virginia	495,051,082	2.3%
15	Georgia	465,376,601	2.2%
16	Missouri	449,718,615	2.1%
17	Indiana	442,638,880	2.0%
18	Massachusetts	439,874,829	2.0%
19	Maryland	427,575,362	2.0%
20	Tennessee	382,290,366	1.8%
21	Kentucky	322,100,896	1.5%
22	Oregon	298,280,030	1.4%
23	Iowa	280,399,263	1.3%
24	Louisiana	279,621,377	1.3%
25	Arizona	247,704,782	1.1%
26	South Carolina	235,648,240	1.1%
27	Connecticut	226,642,739	1.0%
28	Alabama	226,484,276	1.0%
29	Colorado	217,200,793	1.0%
30	Mississippi	182,008,930	0.8%
31	West Virginia	158,469,493	0.7%
32	Oklahoma	154,022,936	0.7%
33	Nebraska	153,576,166	0.7%
34	Arkansas	144,740,929	0.7%
35	Kansas	142,711,660	0.7%
36	Utah	140,596,546	0.7%
37	Idaho	110,889,809	0.5%
38	Nevada	107,714,631	0.5%
39	Maine	99,549,245	0.5%
40	Alaska	82,112,657	0.4%
41	Hawaii	80,829,473	0.4%
42	New Hampshire	79,608,466	0.4%
43	New Mexico	66,398,704	0.3%
44	Delaware	63,647,137	0.3%
45	North Dakota	57,670,079	0.3%
46	South Dakota	55,767,437	0.3%
47	Rhode Island	54,654,636	0.3%
48	Vermont	48,680,441	0.2%
49	Wyoming	48,600,954	0.2%
50	Montana	45,000,554	0.2%
	District of Columbia	44,704,165	0.2%

Source: U.S. Department of Health and Human Services, Office of Child Support Enforcement
"Child Support Enforcement" (http://www.acf.hhs.gov/programs/cse/pubs/2005/reports/preliminary_data/)
*Fiscal year 2004. Total does not include $257,696,626 collected in U.S. territories.

XV. TRANSPORTATION

Federal Highway Funding in 2006

National Total = $35,043,420,950*

ALPHA ORDER

RANK	STATE	FUNDS	% of USA
16	Alabama	$694,784,250	2.0%
32	Alaska	406,704,436	1.2%
18	Arizona	619,650,916	1.8%
29	Arkansas	454,922,751	1.3%
1	California	3,240,610,040	9.2%
28	Colorado	459,424,206	1.3%
27	Connecticut	491,337,727	1.4%
50	Delaware	151,076,213	0.4%
4	Florida	1,653,805,090	4.7%
7	Georgia	1,212,858,135	3.5%
48	Hawaii	167,510,522	0.5%
40	Idaho	264,199,668	0.8%
8	Illinois	1,137,198,215	3.2%
13	Indiana	834,016,431	2.4%
33	Iowa	395,789,672	1.1%
35	Kansas	379,138,835	1.1%
20	Kentucky	604,109,177	1.7%
24	Louisiana	553,868,804	1.6%
46	Maine	187,030,218	0.5%
23	Maryland	555,697,834	1.6%
19	Massachusetts	607,800,575	1.7%
9	Michigan	1,057,665,835	3.0%
25	Minnesota	538,915,049	1.5%
30	Mississippi	428,995,185	1.2%
14	Missouri	823,398,900	2.3%
36	Montana	339,067,668	1.0%
39	Nebraska	265,325,731	0.8%
42	Nevada	247,490,977	0.7%
49	New Hampshire	167,436,943	0.5%
11	New Jersey	896,731,944	2.6%
37	New Mexico	337,280,379	1.0%
3	New York	1,669,815,477	4.8%
10	North Carolina	964,231,584	2.8%
44	North Dakota	223,782,535	0.6%
6	Ohio	1,227,434,172	3.5%
26	Oklahoma	533,696,389	1.5%
31	Oregon	422,864,224	1.2%
5	Pennsylvania	1,632,727,878	4.7%
45	Rhode Island	200,060,259	0.6%
22	South Carolina	556,714,940	1.6%
41	South Dakota	248,863,964	0.7%
15	Tennessee	760,909,393	2.2%
2	Texas	2,756,982,966	7.9%
38	Utah	268,806,448	0.8%
47	Vermont	172,200,831	0.5%
12	Virginia	887,793,125	2.5%
21	Washington	593,326,168	1.7%
34	West Virginia	385,734,514	1.1%
17	Wisconsin	679,766,537	1.9%
43	Wyoming	238,329,133	0.7%

RANK ORDER

RANK	STATE	FUNDS	% of USA
1	California	$3,240,610,040	9.2%
2	Texas	2,756,982,966	7.9%
3	New York	1,669,815,477	4.8%
4	Florida	1,653,805,090	4.7%
5	Pennsylvania	1,632,727,878	4.7%
6	Ohio	1,227,434,172	3.5%
7	Georgia	1,212,858,135	3.5%
8	Illinois	1,137,198,215	3.2%
9	Michigan	1,057,665,835	3.0%
10	North Carolina	964,231,584	2.8%
11	New Jersey	896,731,944	2.6%
12	Virginia	887,793,125	2.5%
13	Indiana	834,016,431	2.4%
14	Missouri	823,398,900	2.3%
15	Tennessee	760,909,393	2.2%
16	Alabama	694,784,250	2.0%
17	Wisconsin	679,766,537	1.9%
18	Arizona	619,650,916	1.8%
19	Massachusetts	607,800,575	1.7%
20	Kentucky	604,109,177	1.7%
21	Washington	593,326,168	1.7%
22	South Carolina	556,714,940	1.6%
23	Maryland	555,697,834	1.6%
24	Louisiana	553,868,804	1.6%
25	Minnesota	538,915,049	1.5%
26	Oklahoma	533,696,389	1.5%
27	Connecticut	491,337,727	1.4%
28	Colorado	459,424,206	1.3%
29	Arkansas	454,922,751	1.3%
30	Mississippi	428,995,185	1.2%
31	Oregon	422,864,224	1.2%
32	Alaska	406,704,436	1.2%
33	Iowa	395,789,672	1.1%
34	West Virginia	385,734,514	1.1%
35	Kansas	379,138,835	1.1%
36	Montana	339,067,668	1.0%
37	New Mexico	337,280,379	1.0%
38	Utah	268,806,448	0.8%
39	Nebraska	265,325,731	0.8%
40	Idaho	264,199,668	0.8%
41	South Dakota	248,863,964	0.7%
42	Nevada	247,490,977	0.7%
43	Wyoming	238,329,133	0.7%
44	North Dakota	223,782,535	0.6%
45	Rhode Island	200,060,259	0.6%
46	Maine	187,030,218	0.5%
47	Vermont	172,200,831	0.5%
48	Hawaii	167,510,522	0.5%
49	New Hampshire	167,436,943	0.5%
50	Delaware	151,076,213	0.4%
	District of Columbia	150,060,022	0.4%

Source: U.S. Department of Transportation, Federal Highway Administration
"FHWA Apportionment" (http://www.fhwa.dot.gov/reauthorization/rta-000-1664ar.xls)
*Fiscal Year 2006 apportionments. National total includes $295,478,067 not shown by state.

Per Capita Federal Highway Funding in 2006

National Per Capita = $118*

ALPHA ORDER

RANK	STATE	PER CAPITA
13	Alabama	$152
1	Alaska	613
40	Arizona	104
12	Arkansas	164
48	California	90
44	Colorado	98
20	Connecticut	140
10	Delaware	179
47	Florida	93
22	Georgia	134
25	Hawaii	131
9	Idaho	185
49	Illinois	89
23	Indiana	133
23	Iowa	133
21	Kansas	138
17	Kentucky	145
31	Louisiana	122
18	Maine	142
43	Maryland	99
45	Massachusetts	95
38	Michigan	105
38	Minnesota	105
16	Mississippi	147
18	Missouri	142
3	Montana	362
14	Nebraska	151
42	Nevada	102
28	New Hampshire	128
41	New Jersey	103
11	New Mexico	175
50	New York	87
35	North Carolina	111
4	North Dakota	351
37	Ohio	107
15	Oklahoma	150
34	Oregon	116
25	Pennsylvania	131
8	Rhode Island	186
25	South Carolina	131
5	South Dakota	321
28	Tennessee	128
32	Texas	121
36	Utah	109
6	Vermont	276
33	Virginia	117
46	Washington	94
7	West Virginia	212
30	Wisconsin	123
2	Wyoming	468

RANK ORDER

RANK	STATE	PER CAPITA
1	Alaska	$613
2	Wyoming	468
3	Montana	362
4	North Dakota	351
5	South Dakota	321
6	Vermont	276
7	West Virginia	212
8	Rhode Island	186
9	Idaho	185
10	Delaware	179
11	New Mexico	175
12	Arkansas	164
13	Alabama	152
14	Nebraska	151
15	Oklahoma	150
16	Mississippi	147
17	Kentucky	145
18	Maine	142
18	Missouri	142
20	Connecticut	140
21	Kansas	138
22	Georgia	134
23	Indiana	133
23	Iowa	133
25	Hawaii	131
25	Pennsylvania	131
25	South Carolina	131
28	New Hampshire	128
28	Tennessee	128
30	Wisconsin	123
31	Louisiana	122
32	Texas	121
33	Virginia	117
34	Oregon	116
35	North Carolina	111
36	Utah	109
37	Ohio	107
38	Michigan	105
38	Minnesota	105
40	Arizona	104
41	New Jersey	103
42	Nevada	102
43	Maryland	99
44	Colorado	98
45	Massachusetts	95
46	Washington	94
47	Florida	93
48	California	90
49	Illinois	89
50	New York	87

| | District of Columbia | 273 |

Source: Morgan Quitno Press using data from U.S. Department of Transportation, Federal Highway Administration
"FHWA Apportionment" (http://www.fhwa.dot.gov/reauthorization/rta-000-1664ar.xls)
*Fiscal Year 2006 apportionments. Rates calculated with July 2005 population estimates.

Public Road and Street Mileage in 2004

National Total = 3,981,521 Miles*

ALPHA ORDER

RANK	STATE	MILES	% of USA
18	Alabama	95,486	2.4%
47	Alaska	14,108	0.4%
34	Arizona	58,113	1.5%
17	Arkansas	98,607	2.5%
2	California	169,793	4.3%
22	Colorado	87,094	2.2%
44	Connecticut	21,144	0.5%
49	Delaware	6,043	0.2%
10	Florida	119,525	3.0%
11	Georgia	116,915	2.9%
50	Hawaii	4,318	0.1%
35	Idaho	47,101	1.2%
3	Illinois	138,626	3.5%
19	Indiana	94,597	2.4%
12	Iowa	113,836	2.9%
4	Kansas	135,017	3.4%
26	Kentucky	77,365	1.9%
33	Louisiana	60,943	1.5%
43	Maine	22,748	0.6%
41	Maryland	30,810	0.8%
39	Massachusetts	35,782	0.9%
0	Michigan	122,381	3.1%
5	Minnesota	131,937	3.3%
27	Mississippi	74,127	1.9%
6	Missouri	125,923	3.2%
29	Montana	69,450	1.7%
20	Nebraska	93,246	2.3%
40	Nevada	33,976	0.9%
45	New Hampshire	15,627	0.4%
37	New Jersey	38,121	1.0%
32	New Mexico	64,005	1.6%
14	New York	113,343	2.8%
16	North Carolina	102,666	2.6%
23	North Dakota	86,781	2.2%
7	Ohio	124,752	3.1%
15	Oklahoma	112,713	2.8%
31	Oregon	65,861	1.7%
9	Pennsylvania	120,622	3.0%
48	Rhode Island	6,419	0.2%
30	South Carolina	66,249	1.7%
24	South Dakota	83,548	2.1%
21	Tennessee	88,989	2.2%
1	Texas	303,176	7.6%
36	Utah	42,712	1.1%
46	Vermont	14,370	0.4%
28	Virginia	71,534	1.8%
25	Washington	81,218	2.0%
38	West Virginia	37,012	0.9%
13	Wisconsin	113,699	2.9%
42	Wyoming	27,594	0.7%

RANK ORDER

RANK	STATE	MILES	% of USA
1	Texas	303,176	7.6%
2	California	169,793	4.3%
3	Illinois	138,626	3.5%
4	Kansas	135,017	3.4%
5	Minnesota	131,937	3.3%
6	Missouri	125,923	3.2%
7	Ohio	124,752	3.1%
8	Michigan	122,381	3.1%
9	Pennsylvania	120,622	3.0%
10	Florida	119,525	3.0%
11	Georgia	116,915	2.9%
12	Iowa	113,836	2.9%
13	Wisconsin	113,699	2.9%
14	New York	113,343	2.8%
15	Oklahoma	112,713	2.8%
16	North Carolina	102,666	2.6%
17	Arkansas	98,607	2.5%
18	Alabama	95,486	2.4%
19	Indiana	94,597	2.4%
20	Nebraska	93,246	2.3%
21	Tennessee	88,989	2.2%
22	Colorado	87,094	2.2%
23	North Dakota	86,781	2.2%
24	South Dakota	83,548	2.1%
25	Washington	81,218	2.0%
26	Kentucky	77,365	1.9%
27	Mississippi	74,127	1.9%
28	Virginia	71,534	1.8%
29	Montana	69,450	1.7%
30	South Carolina	66,249	1.7%
31	Oregon	65,861	1.7%
32	New Mexico	64,005	1.6%
33	Louisiana	60,943	1.5%
34	Arizona	58,113	1.5%
35	Idaho	47,101	1.2%
36	Utah	42,712	1.1%
37	New Jersey	38,121	1.0%
38	West Virginia	37,012	0.9%
39	Massachusetts	35,782	0.9%
40	Nevada	33,976	0.9%
41	Maryland	30,810	0.8%
42	Wyoming	27,594	0.7%
43	Maine	22,748	0.6%
44	Connecticut	21,144	0.5%
45	New Hampshire	15,627	0.4%
46	Vermont	14,370	0.4%
47	Alaska	14,108	0.4%
48	Rhode Island	6,419	0.2%
49	Delaware	6,043	0.2%
50	Hawaii	4,318	0.1%
	District of Columbia	1,499	0.0%

Source: U.S. Department of Transportation, Federal Highway Administration
    "Highway Statistics 2004" (Table HM-10) (http://www.fhwa.dot.gov/policy/ohpi/hss/index.htm)
*Does not include 15,935 miles of roads and streets in Puerto Rico.

Percent of Public Road and Street Mileage Federally-Funded in 2004

National Percent = 24.3% of Public Road and Street Mileage*

ALPHA ORDER

RANK	STATE	PERCENT
21	Alabama	25.1
4	Alaska	30.8
38	Arizona	21.8
41	Arkansas	21.4
2	California	32.0
44	Colorado	20.1
6	Connecticut	28.9
25	Delaware	24.5
39	Florida	21.6
17	Georgia	26.4
1	Hawaii	35.9
35	Idaho	22.5
22	Illinois	25.0
29	Indiana	23.5
34	Iowa	22.7
20	Kansas	25.4
50	Kentucky	17.8
40	Louisiana	21.5
8	Maine	28.0
24	Maryland	24.8
3	Massachusetts	31.1
12	Michigan	27.4
27	Minnesota	23.9
7	Mississippi	28.7
26	Missouri	24.1
42	Montana	21.0
36	Nebraska	21.9
48	Nevada	18.9
36	New Hampshire	21.9
15	New Jersey	27.1
49	New Mexico	17.9
32	New York	23.1
44	North Carolina	20.1
42	North Dakota	21.0
32	Ohio	23.1
8	Oklahoma	28.0
13	Oregon	27.3
31	Pennsylvania	23.2
14	Rhode Island	27.2
18	South Carolina	26.3
28	South Dakota	23.6
46	Tennessee	19.6
19	Texas	25.8
47	Utah	19.4
16	Vermont	26.9
5	Virginia	29.7
29	Washington	23.5
11	West Virginia	27.7
22	Wisconsin	25.0
10	Wyoming	27.8

RANK ORDER

RANK	STATE	PERCENT
1	Hawaii	35.9
2	California	32.0
3	Massachusetts	31.1
4	Alaska	30.8
5	Virginia	29.7
6	Connecticut	28.9
7	Mississippi	28.7
8	Maine	28.0
8	Oklahoma	28.0
10	Wyoming	27.8
11	West Virginia	27.7
12	Michigan	27.4
13	Oregon	27.3
14	Rhode Island	27.2
15	New Jersey	27.1
16	Vermont	26.9
17	Georgia	26.4
18	South Carolina	26.3
19	Texas	25.8
20	Kansas	25.4
21	Alabama	25.1
22	Illinois	25.0
22	Wisconsin	25.0
24	Maryland	24.8
25	Delaware	24.5
26	Missouri	24.1
27	Minnesota	23.9
28	South Dakota	23.6
29	Indiana	23.5
29	Washington	23.5
31	Pennsylvania	23.2
32	New York	23.1
32	Ohio	23.1
34	Iowa	22.7
35	Idaho	22.5
36	Nebraska	21.9
36	New Hampshire	21.9
38	Arizona	21.8
39	Florida	21.6
40	Louisiana	21.5
41	Arkansas	21.4
42	Montana	21.0
42	North Dakota	21.0
44	Colorado	20.1
44	North Carolina	20.1
46	Tennessee	19.6
47	Utah	19.4
48	Nevada	18.9
49	New Mexico	17.9
50	Kentucky	17.8

| | District of Columbia | 30.2 |

Source: Morgan Quitno Press using data from U.S. Department of Transportation, Federal Highway Administration
"Highway Statistics 2004" (Table HM-15) (http://www.fhwa.dot.gov/policy/ohpi/hss/index.htm)
*National percent does not include federally-funded highway miles in Puerto Rico.

Interstate Highway Mileage in 2004

National Total = 46,572 Miles*

ALPHA ORDER

RANK	STATE	MILES	% of USA
24	Alabama	904	1.9%
16	Alaska	1,082	2.3%
13	Arizona	1,168	2.5%
35	Arkansas	656	1.4%
2	California	2,458	5.3%
19	Colorado	956	2.1%
45	Connecticut	346	0.7%
50	Delaware	41	0.1%
7	Florida	1,471	3.2%
8	Georgia	1,244	2.7%
49	Hawaii	55	0.1%
36	Idaho	612	1.3%
3	Illinois	2,169	4.7%
12	Indiana	1,169	2.5%
28	Iowa	782	1.7%
26	Kansas	874	1.9%
30	Kentucky	762	1.6%
25	Louisiana	903	1.9%
44	Maine	367	0.8%
42	Maryland	481	1.0%
37	Massachusetts	573	1.2%
9	Michigan	1,243	2.7%
22	Minnesota	914	2.0%
33	Mississippi	685	1.5%
11	Missouri	1,181	2.5%
10	Montana	1,192	2.6%
41	Nebraska	482	1.0%
39	Nevada	560	1.2%
47	New Hampshire	235	0.5%
43	New Jersey	431	0.9%
18	New Mexico	1,000	2.1%
5	New York	1,674	3.6%
17	North Carolina	1,046	2.2%
38	North Dakota	571	1.2%
6	Ohio	1,574	3.4%
21	Oklahoma	931	2.0%
32	Oregon	728	1.6%
4	Pennsylvania	1,757	3.8%
48	Rhode Island	71	0.2%
27	South Carolina	844	1.8%
34	South Dakota	678	1.5%
15	Tennessee	1,105	2.4%
1	Texas	3,233	6.9%
20	Utah	940	2.0%
46	Vermont	320	0.7%
14	Virginia	1,116	2.4%
29	Washington	764	1.6%
40	West Virginia	555	1.2%
31	Wisconsin	743	1.6%
23	Wyoming	913	2.0%

RANK ORDER

RANK	STATE	MILES	% of USA
1	Texas	3,233	6.9%
2	California	2,458	5.3%
3	Illinois	2,169	4.7%
4	Pennsylvania	1,757	3.8%
5	New York	1,674	3.6%
6	Ohio	1,574	3.4%
7	Florida	1,471	3.2%
8	Georgia	1,244	2.7%
9	Michigan	1,243	2.7%
10	Montana	1,192	2.6%
11	Missouri	1,181	2.5%
12	Indiana	1,169	2.5%
13	Arizona	1,168	2.5%
14	Virginia	1,116	2.4%
15	Tennessee	1,105	2.4%
16	Alaska	1,082	2.3%
17	North Carolina	1,046	2.2%
18	New Mexico	1,000	2.1%
19	Colorado	956	2.1%
20	Utah	940	2.0%
21	Oklahoma	931	2.0%
22	Minnesota	914	2.0%
23	Wyoming	913	2.0%
24	Alabama	904	1.0%
25	Louisiana	903	1.9%
26	Kansas	874	1.9%
27	South Carolina	844	1.8%
28	Iowa	782	1.7%
29	Washington	764	1.6%
30	Kentucky	762	1.6%
31	Wisconsin	743	1.6%
32	Oregon	728	1.6%
33	Mississippi	685	1.5%
34	South Dakota	678	1.5%
35	Arkansas	656	1.4%
36	Idaho	612	1.3%
37	Massachusetts	573	1.2%
38	North Dakota	571	1.2%
39	Nevada	560	1.2%
40	West Virginia	555	1.2%
41	Nebraska	482	1.0%
42	Maryland	481	1.0%
43	New Jersey	431	0.9%
44	Maine	367	0.8%
45	Connecticut	346	0.7%
46	Vermont	320	0.7%
47	New Hampshire	235	0.5%
48	Rhode Island	71	0.2%
49	Hawaii	55	0.1%
50	Delaware	41	0.1%
	District of Columbia	13	0.0%

Source: U.S. Department of Transportation, Federal Highway Administration
"Highway Statistics 2004" (Table HM-15) (http://www.fhwa.dot.gov/policy/ohpi/hss/index.htm)
**Does not include 265 miles of highway in Puerto Rico that are part of the interstate system.*

Toll Road Mileage in 2003

National Total = 4,722 Miles

ALPHA ORDER					RANK ORDER			

RANK	STATE	MILES	% of USA		RANK	STATE	MILES	% of USA
22	Alabama	6	0.1%		1	Florida	657	13.9%
27	Alaska	0	0.0%		2	Oklahoma	597	12.6%
27	Arizona	0	0.0%		3	New York	575	12.2%
27	Arkansas	0	0.0%		4	Pennsylvania	508	10.8%
15	California	96	2.0%		5	Ohio	392	8.3%
19	Colorado	48	1.0%		6	New Jersey	356	7.5%
27	Connecticut	0	0.0%		7	Illinois	282	6.0%
18	Delaware	49	1.0%		8	Kentucky	249	5.3%
1	Florida	657	13.9%		9	Kansas	236	5.0%
22	Georgia	6	0.1%		10	Indiana	157	3.3%
27	Hawaii	0	0.0%		11	Texas	146	3.1%
27	Idaho	0	0.0%		12	Massachusetts	136	2.9%
7	Illinois	282	6.0%		13	Maine	106	2.2%
10	Indiana	157	3.3%		14	New Hampshire	97	2.1%
27	Iowa	0	0.0%		15	California	96	2.0%
9	Kansas	236	5.0%		16	West Virginia	87	1.8%
8	Kentucky	249	5.3%		17	Virginia	65	1.4%
25	Louisiana	2	0.0%		18	Delaware	49	1.0%
13	Maine	106	2.2%		19	Colorado	48	1.0%
27	Maryland	0	0.0%		20	South Carolina	24	0.5%
12	Massachusetts	136	2.9%		21	Vermont	12	0.3%
27	Michigan	0	0.0%		22	Alabama	6	0.1%
27	Minnesota	0	0.0%		22	Georgia	6	0.1%
27	Mississippi	0	0.0%		22	Nevada	6	0.1%
27	Missouri	0	0.0%		25	Louisiana	2	0.0%
27	Montana	0	0.0%		26	Utah	1	0.0%
27	Nebraska	0	0.0%		27	Alaska	0	0.0%
22	Nevada	6	0.1%		27	Arizona	0	0.0%
14	New Hampshire	97	2.1%		27	Arkansas	0	0.0%
6	New Jersey	356	7.5%		27	Connecticut	0	0.0%
27	New Mexico	0	0.0%		27	Hawaii	0	0.0%
3	New York	575	12.2%		27	Idaho	0	0.0%
27	North Carolina	0	0.0%		27	Iowa	0	0.0%
27	North Dakota	0	0.0%		27	Maryland	0	0.0%
5	Ohio	392	8.3%		27	Michigan	0	0.0%
2	Oklahoma	597	12.6%		27	Minnesota	0	0.0%
27	Oregon	0	0.0%		27	Mississippi	0	0.0%
4	Pennsylvania	508	10.8%		27	Missouri	0	0.0%
27	Rhode Island	0	0.0%		27	Montana	0	0.0%
20	South Carolina	24	0.5%		27	Nebraska	0	0.0%
27	South Dakota	0	0.0%		27	New Mexico	0	0.0%
27	Tennessee	0	0.0%		27	North Carolina	0	0.0%
11	Texas	146	3.1%		27	North Dakota	0	0.0%
26	Utah	1	0.0%		27	Oregon	0	0.0%
21	Vermont	12	0.3%		27	Rhode Island	0	0.0%
17	Virginia	65	1.4%		27	South Dakota	0	0.0%
27	Washington	0	0.0%		27	Tennessee	0	0.0%
16	West Virginia	87	1.8%		27	Washington	0	0.0%
27	Wisconsin	0	0.0%		27	Wisconsin	0	0.0%
27	Wyoming	0	0.0%		27	Wyoming	0	0.0%
						District of Columbia	0	0.0%

Source: U.S. Department of Transportation, Bureau of Transportation Statistics
   "State Transportation Statistics 2004" (http://www.bts.gov/)

Rural Road and Street Mileage in 2004

National Total = 3,000,247 Rural Miles*

ALPHA ORDER					RANK ORDER			
RANK	STATE	MILES	% of USA		RANK	STATE	MILES	% of USA
20	Alabama	73,963	2.5%		1	Texas	219,728	7.3%
44	Alaska	12,013	0.4%		2	Kansas	124,158	4.1%
35	Arizona	36,058	1.2%		3	Minnesota	115,645	3.9%
9	Arkansas	87,744	2.9%		4	Missouri	107,593	3.6%
13	California	83,655	2.8%		5	Iowa	102,875	3.4%
22	Colorado	68,630	2.3%		6	Illinois	101,075	3.4%
47	Connecticut	6,138	0.2%		7	Oklahoma	97,601	3.3%
48	Delaware	3,184	0.1%		8	Wisconsin	91,719	3.1%
34	Florida	41,256	1.4%		9	Arkansas	87,744	2.9%
15	Georgia	80,503	2.7%		10	Nebraska	87,325	2.9%
49	Hawaii	2,182	0.1%		11	Michigan	86,820	2.9%
33	Idaho	42,480	1.4%		12	North Dakota	84,935	2.8%
6	Illinois	101,075	3.4%		13	California	83,655	2.8%
19	Indiana	73,998	2.5%		14	South Dakota	81,105	2.7%
5	Iowa	102,875	3.4%		15	Georgia	80,503	2.7%
2	Kansas	124,158	4.1%		16	Ohio	80,273	2.7%
25	Kentucky	65,387	2.2%		17	North Carolina	77,986	2.6%
32	Louisiana	46,128	1.5%		18	Pennsylvania	76,206	2.5%
40	Maine	20,107	0.7%		19	Indiana	73,998	2.5%
41	Maryland	13,915	0.5%		20	Alabama	73,963	2.5%
45	Massachusetts	7,926	0.3%		21	New York	72,117	2.4%
11	Michigan	86,820	2.9%		22	Colorado	68,630	2.3%
3	Minnesota	115,645	3.9%		23	Tennessee	67,928	2.3%
26	Mississippi	63,507	2.1%		24	Montana	66,697	2.2%
4	Missouri	107,593	3.6%		25	Kentucky	65,387	2.2%
24	Montana	66,697	2.2%		26	Mississippi	63,507	2.1%
10	Nebraska	87,325	2.9%		27	Washington	61,093	2.0%
38	Nevada	28,250	0.9%		28	New Mexico	56,048	1.9%
43	New Hampshire	12,593	0.4%		29	South Carolina	55,562	1.9%
46	New Jersey	6,970	0.2%		30	Oregon	53,502	1.8%
28	New Mexico	56,048	1.9%		31	Virginia	50,308	1.7%
21	New York	72,117	2.4%		32	Louisiana	46,128	1.5%
17	North Carolina	77,986	2.6%		33	Idaho	42,480	1.4%
12	North Dakota	84,935	2.8%		34	Florida	41,256	1.4%
16	Ohio	80,273	2.7%		35	Arizona	36,058	1.2%
7	Oklahoma	97,601	3.3%		36	West Virginia	33,820	1.1%
30	Oregon	53,502	1.8%		37	Utah	32,295	1.1%
18	Pennsylvania	76,206	2.5%		38	Nevada	28,250	0.9%
50	Rhode Island	1,227	0.0%		39	Wyoming	25,046	0.8%
29	South Carolina	55,562	1.9%		40	Maine	20,107	0.7%
14	South Dakota	81,105	2.7%		41	Maryland	13,915	0.5%
23	Tennessee	67,928	2.3%		42	Vermont	12,973	0.4%
1	Texas	219,728	7.3%		43	New Hampshire	12,593	0.4%
37	Utah	32,295	1.1%		44	Alaska	12,013	0.4%
42	Vermont	12,973	0.4%		45	Massachusetts	7,926	0.3%
31	Virginia	50,308	1.7%		46	New Jersey	6,970	0.2%
27	Washington	61,093	2.0%		47	Connecticut	6,138	0.2%
36	West Virginia	33,820	1.1%		48	Delaware	3,184	0.1%
8	Wisconsin	91,719	3.1%		49	Hawaii	2,182	0.1%
39	Wyoming	25,046	0.8%		50	Rhode Island	1,227	0.0%
						District of Columbia	0	0.0%

Source: U.S. Department of Transportation, Federal Highway Administration
"Highway Statistics 2004" (Table HM-10) (http://www.fhwa.dot.gov/policy/ohpi/hss/index.htm)
*Does not include 3,199 miles of rural roads and streets in Puerto Rico.

Urban Road and Street Mileage in 2004

National Total = 981,274 Urban Miles*

ALPHA ORDER

ALPHA ORDER

RANK	STATE	MILES	% of USA
15	Alabama	21,523	2.2%
48	Alaska	2,095	0.2%
13	Arizona	22,055	2.2%
30	Arkansas	10,863	1.1%
1	California	86,138	8.8%
20	Colorado	18,464	1.9%
25	Connecticut	15,006	1.5%
42	Delaware	2,859	0.3%
3	Florida	78,269	8.0%
8	Georgia	36,412	3.7%
47	Hawaii	2,136	0.2%
39	Idaho	4,621	0.5%
7	Illinois	37,551	3.8%
18	Indiana	20,599	2.1%
29	Iowa	10,961	1.1%
31	Kansas	10,859	1.1%
28	Kentucky	11,978	1.2%
26	Louisiana	14,815	1.5%
44	Maine	2,641	0.3%
22	Maryland	16,895	1.7%
11	Massachusetts	27,856	2.8%
9	Michigan	35,561	3.6%
23	Minnesota	16,292	1.7%
33	Mississippi	10,620	1.1%
21	Missouri	18,330	1.9%
43	Montana	2,753	0.3%
36	Nebraska	5,921	0.6%
37	Nevada	5,726	0.6%
41	New Hampshire	3,034	0.3%
10	New Jersey	31,151	3.2%
35	New Mexico	7,957	0.8%
6	New York	41,226	4.2%
12	North Carolina	24,680	2.5%
49	North Dakota	1,846	0.2%
4	Ohio	44,479	4.5%
24	Oklahoma	15,112	1.5%
27	Oregon	12,359	1.3%
5	Pennsylvania	44,416	4.5%
38	Rhode Island	5,192	0.5%
32	South Carolina	10,687	1.1%
46	South Dakota	2,443	0.2%
17	Tennessee	21,061	2.1%
2	Texas	83,448	8.5%
34	Utah	10,417	1.1%
50	Vermont	1,397	0.1%
16	Virginia	21,226	2.2%
19	Washington	20,125	2.1%
40	West Virginia	3,192	0.3%
14	Wisconsin	21,980	2.2%
45	Wyoming	2,548	0.3%

RANK ORDER

RANK	STATE	MILES	% of USA
1	California	86,138	8.8%
2	Texas	83,448	8.5%
3	Florida	78,269	8.0%
4	Ohio	44,479	4.5%
5	Pennsylvania	44,416	4.5%
6	New York	41,226	4.2%
7	Illinois	37,551	3.8%
8	Georgia	36,412	3.7%
9	Michigan	35,561	3.6%
10	New Jersey	31,151	3.2%
11	Massachusetts	27,856	2.8%
12	North Carolina	24,680	2.5%
13	Arizona	22,055	2.2%
14	Wisconsin	21,980	2.2%
15	Alabama	21,523	2.2%
16	Virginia	21,226	2.2%
17	Tennessee	21,061	2.1%
18	Indiana	20,599	2.1%
19	Washington	20,125	2.1%
20	Colorado	18,464	1.9%
21	Missouri	18,330	1.9%
22	Maryland	16,895	1.7%
23	Minnesota	16,292	1.7%
24	Oklahoma	15,112	1.5%
25	Connecticut	15,006	1.5%
26	Louisiana	14,815	1.5%
27	Oregon	12,359	1.3%
28	Kentucky	11,978	1.2%
29	Iowa	10,961	1.1%
30	Arkansas	10,863	1.1%
31	Kansas	10,859	1.1%
32	South Carolina	10,687	1.1%
33	Mississippi	10,620	1.1%
34	Utah	10,417	1.1%
35	New Mexico	7,957	0.8%
36	Nebraska	5,921	0.6%
37	Nevada	5,726	0.6%
38	Rhode Island	5,192	0.5%
39	Idaho	4,621	0.5%
40	West Virginia	3,192	0.3%
41	New Hampshire	3,034	0.3%
42	Delaware	2,859	0.3%
43	Montana	2,753	0.3%
44	Maine	2,641	0.3%
45	Wyoming	2,548	0.3%
46	South Dakota	2,443	0.2%
47	Hawaii	2,136	0.2%
48	Alaska	2,095	0.2%
49	North Dakota	1,846	0.2%
50	Vermont	1,397	0.1%
	District of Columbia	1,499	0.2%

Source: U.S. Department of Transportation, Federal Highway Administration
   "Highway Statistics 2004" (Table HM-10) (http://www.fhwa.dot.gov/policy/ohpi/hss/index.htm)
*Does not include 12,736 miles of urban roads and streets in Puerto Rico.

Bridges in 2004

National Total = 591,750 Bridges*

ALPHA ORDER

RANK	STATE	BRIDGES	% of USA
15	Alabama	15,648	2.6%
47	Alaska	1,187	0.2%
30	Arizona	7,119	1.2%
23	Arkansas	12,456	2.1%
6	California	23,823	4.0%
27	Colorado	8,182	1.4%
38	Connecticut	4,167	0.7%
49	Delaware	850	0.1%
24	Florida	11,469	1.9%
17	Georgia	14,461	2.4%
48	Hawaii	1,099	0.2%
39	Idaho	4,047	0.7%
3	Illinois	25,727	4.3%
11	Indiana	18,171	3.1%
5	Iowa	24,902	4.2%
4	Kansas	25,525	4.3%
19	Kentucky	13,500	2.3%
20	Louisiana	13,362	2.3%
44	Maine	2,371	0.4%
34	Maryland	5,064	0.9%
36	Massachusetts	4,954	0.8%
25	Michigan	10,818	1.8%
22	Minnesota	13,026	2.2%
14	Mississippi	16,838	2.8%
7	Missouri	23,791	4.0%
35	Montana	5,043	0.9%
16	Nebraska	15,455	2.6%
46	Nevada	1,611	0.3%
45	New Hampshire	2,357	0.4%
32	New Jersey	6,484	1.1%
40	New Mexico	3,839	0.6%
13	New York	17,301	2.9%
12	North Carolina	17,340	2.9%
37	North Dakota	4,507	0.8%
2	Ohio	27,907	4.7%
8	Oklahoma	23,312	3.9%
29	Oregon	7,261	1.2%
9	Pennsylvania	22,253	3.8%
50	Rhode Island	749	0.1%
26	South Carolina	9,201	1.6%
33	South Dakota	5,961	1.0%
10	Tennessee	19,688	3.3%
1	Texas	48,950	8.3%
42	Utah	2,805	0.5%
43	Vermont	2,690	0.5%
21	Virginia	13,160	2.2%
28	Washington	7,543	1.3%
31	West Virginia	6,881	1.2%
18	Wisconsin	13,611	2.3%
41	Wyoming	3,033	0.5%

RANK ORDER

RANK	STATE	BRIDGES	% of USA
1	Texas	48,950	8.3%
2	Ohio	27,907	4.7%
3	Illinois	25,727	4.3%
4	Kansas	25,525	4.3%
5	Iowa	24,902	4.2%
6	California	23,823	4.0%
7	Missouri	23,791	4.0%
8	Oklahoma	23,312	3.9%
9	Pennsylvania	22,253	3.8%
10	Tennessee	19,688	3.3%
11	Indiana	18,171	3.1%
12	North Carolina	17,340	2.9%
13	New York	17,301	2.9%
14	Mississippi	16,838	2.8%
15	Alabama	15,648	2.6%
16	Nebraska	15,455	2.6%
17	Georgia	14,461	2.4%
18	Wisconsin	13,611	2.3%
19	Kentucky	13,500	2.3%
20	Louisiana	13,362	2.3%
21	Virginia	13,160	2.2%
22	Minnesota	13,026	2.2%
23	Arkansas	12,456	2.1%
24	Florida	11,469	1.9%
25	Michigan	10,818	1.8%
26	South Carolina	9,201	1.6%
27	Colorado	8,182	1.4%
28	Washington	7,543	1.3%
29	Oregon	7,261	1.2%
30	Arizona	7,119	1.2%
31	West Virginia	6,881	1.2%
32	New Jersey	6,484	1.1%
33	South Dakota	5,961	1.0%
34	Maryland	5,064	0.9%
35	Montana	5,043	0.9%
36	Massachusetts	4,954	0.8%
37	North Dakota	4,507	0.8%
38	Connecticut	4,167	0.7%
39	Idaho	4,047	0.7%
40	New Mexico	3,839	0.6%
41	Wyoming	3,033	0.5%
42	Utah	2,805	0.5%
43	Vermont	2,690	0.5%
44	Maine	2,371	0.4%
45	New Hampshire	2,357	0.4%
46	Nevada	1,611	0.3%
47	Alaska	1,187	0.2%
48	Hawaii	1,099	0.2%
49	Delaware	850	0.1%
50	Rhode Island	749	0.1%
	District of Columbia	251	0.0%

Source: U.S. Department of Transportation, Federal Highway Administration
"Deficient Bridges by State and Highway System, 2004" (http://www.fhwa.dot.gov/bridge/deficient.htm)
*As of December 2004. Includes federal-aid and nonfederal-aid system bridges. National total does not include 2,135 bridges in Puerto Rico.

Deficient Bridges in 2004

National Total = 157,269 Deficient Bridges*

ALPHA ORDER

RANK	STATE	BRIDGES	% of USA
12	Alabama	4,679	3.0%
48	Alaska	353	0.2%
43	Arizona	717	0.5%
20	Arkansas	3,132	2.0%
7	California	6,668	4.2%
34	Colorado	1,387	0.9%
35	Connecticut	1,363	0.9%
50	Delaware	122	0.1%
28	Florida	2,118	1.3%
22	Georgia	2,948	1.9%
45	Hawaii	513	0.3%
41	Idaho	730	0.5%
14	Illinois	4,361	2.8%
17	Indiana	4,016	2.6%
6	Iowa	6,958	4.4%
9	Kansas	5,900	3.8%
16	Kentucky	4,104	2.6%
15	Louisiana	4,324	2.7%
39	Maine	843	0.5%
33	Maryland	1,479	0.9%
24	Massachusetts	2,546	1.6%
21	Michigan	3,121	2.0%
31	Minnesota	1,633	1.0%
11	Mississippi	4,697	3.0%
4	Missouri	8,244	5.2%
36	Montana	1,074	0.7%
18	Nebraska	3,975	2.5%
49	Nevada	198	0.1%
40	New Hampshire	788	0.5%
25	New Jersey	2,370	1.5%
42	New Mexico	724	0.5%
8	New York	6,552	4.2%
10	North Carolina	5,196	3.3%
37	North Dakota	1,062	0.7%
5	Ohio	7,102	4.5%
3	Oklahoma	8,757	5.6%
30	Oregon	1,848	1.2%
2	Pennsylvania	9,404	6.0%
47	Rhode Island	405	0.3%
27	South Carolina	2,130	1.4%
32	South Dakota	1,490	0.9%
13	Tennessee	4,499	2.9%
1	Texas	10,195	6.5%
46	Utah	506	0.3%
38	Vermont	954	0.6%
19	Virginia	3,348	2.1%
29	Washington	2,056	1.3%
23	West Virginia	2,555	1.6%
26	Wisconsin	2,339	1.5%
44	Wyoming	629	0.4%

RANK ORDER

RANK	STATE	BRIDGES	% of USA
1	Texas	10,195	6.5%
2	Pennsylvania	9,404	6.0%
3	Oklahoma	8,757	5.6%
4	Missouri	8,244	5.2%
5	Ohio	7,102	4.5%
6	Iowa	6,958	4.4%
7	California	6,668	4.2%
8	New York	6,552	4.2%
9	Kansas	5,900	3.8%
10	North Carolina	5,196	3.3%
11	Mississippi	4,697	3.0%
12	Alabama	4,679	3.0%
13	Tennessee	4,499	2.9%
14	Illinois	4,361	2.8%
15	Louisiana	4,324	2.7%
16	Kentucky	4,104	2.6%
17	Indiana	4,016	2.6%
18	Nebraska	3,975	2.5%
19	Virginia	3,348	2.1%
20	Arkansas	3,132	2.0%
21	Michigan	3,121	2.0%
22	Georgia	2,948	1.9%
23	West Virginia	2,555	1.6%
24	Massachusetts	2,546	1.6%
25	New Jersey	2,370	1.5%
26	Wisconsin	2,339	1.5%
27	South Carolina	2,130	1.4%
28	Florida	2,118	1.3%
29	Washington	2,056	1.3%
30	Oregon	1,848	1.2%
31	Minnesota	1,633	1.0%
32	South Dakota	1,490	0.9%
33	Maryland	1,479	0.9%
34	Colorado	1,387	0.9%
35	Connecticut	1,363	0.9%
36	Montana	1,074	0.7%
37	North Dakota	1,062	0.7%
38	Vermont	954	0.6%
39	Maine	843	0.5%
40	New Hampshire	788	0.5%
41	Idaho	730	0.5%
42	New Mexico	724	0.5%
43	Arizona	717	0.5%
44	Wyoming	629	0.4%
45	Hawaii	513	0.3%
46	Utah	506	0.3%
47	Rhode Island	405	0.3%
48	Alaska	353	0.2%
49	Nevada	198	0.1%
50	Delaware	122	0.1%
	District of Columbia	157	0.1%

Source: U.S. Department of Transportation, Federal Highway Administration
"Deficient Bridges by State and Highway System, 2004" (http://www.fhwa.dot.gov/bridge/deficient.htm)
*As of December 2004. Includes federal-aid and nonfederal-aid system bridges. National total does not include 1,049 deficient bridges in Puerto Rico. Bridges classified as deficient are either functionally obsolete or structurally deficient and are not necessarily unsafe.

Deficient Bridges as a Percent of Total Bridges in 2004

National Percent = 26.6% of Bridges are Deficient*

ALPHA ORDER			RANK ORDER		
RANK	STATE	PERCENT	RANK	STATE	PERCENT
17	Alabama	29.9	1	Rhode Island	54.1
18	Alaska	29.7	2	Massachusetts	51.4
50	Arizona	10.1	3	Hawaii	46.7
29	Arkansas	25.1	4	Pennsylvania	42.3
21	California	28.0	5	New York	37.9
45	Colorado	17.0	6	Oklahoma	37.6
13	Connecticut	32.7	7	West Virginia	37.1
47	Delaware	14.4	8	New Jersey	36.6
41	Florida	18.5	9	Maine	35.6
39	Georgia	20.4	10	Vermont	35.5
3	Hawaii	46.7	11	Missouri	34.7
42	Idaho	18.0	12	New Hampshire	33.4
45	Illinois	17.0	13	Connecticut	32.7
35	Indiana	22.1	14	Louisiana	32.4
22	Iowa	27.9	15	Kentucky	30.4
32	Kansas	23.1	16	North Carolina	30.0
15	Kentucky	30.4	17	Alabama	29.9
14	Louisiana	32.4	18	Alaska	29.7
9	Maine	35.6	19	Maryland	29.2
19	Maryland	29.2	20	Michigan	28.9
2	Massachusetts	51.4	21	California	28.0
20	Michigan	28.9	22	Iowa	27.9
48	Minnesota	12.5	22	Mississippi	27.9
22	Mississippi	27.9	24	Washington	27.3
11	Missouri	34.7	25	Nebraska	25.7
36	Montana	21.3	26	Oregon	25.5
25	Nebraska	25.7	27	Ohio	25.4
49	Nevada	12.3	27	Virginia	25.4
12	New Hampshire	33.4	29	Arkansas	25.1
8	New Jersey	36.6	30	South Dakota	25.0
40	New Mexico	18.9	31	North Dakota	23.6
5	New York	37.9	32	Kansas	23.1
16	North Carolina	30.0	32	South Carolina	23.1
31	North Dakota	23.6	34	Tennessee	22.9
27	Ohio	25.4	35	Indiana	22.1
6	Oklahoma	37.6	36	Montana	21.3
26	Oregon	25.5	37	Texas	20.8
4	Pennsylvania	42.3	38	Wyoming	20.7
1	Rhode Island	54.1	39	Georgia	20.4
32	South Carolina	23.1	40	New Mexico	18.9
30	South Dakota	25.0	41	Florida	18.5
34	Tennessee	22.9	42	Idaho	18.0
37	Texas	20.8	42	Utah	18.0
42	Utah	18.0	44	Wisconsin	17.2
10	Vermont	35.5	45	Colorado	17.0
27	Virginia	25.4	45	Illinois	17.0
24	Washington	27.3	47	Delaware	14.4
7	West Virginia	37.1	48	Minnesota	12.5
44	Wisconsin	17.2	49	Nevada	12.3
38	Wyoming	20.7	50	Arizona	10.1
				District of Columbia	62.5

Source: Morgan Quitno Press using data from U.S. Department of Transportation, Federal Highway Administration
    "Deficient Bridges by State and Highway System, 2004" (http://www.fhwa.dot.gov/bridge/deficient.htm)
*As of December 2004. Includes federal-aid and nonfederal-aid system bridges. National percent does not include
bridges in Puerto Rico. Bridges classified as deficient are either functionally obsolete or structurally deficient and
are not necessarily unsafe.

Vehicle-Miles of Travel in 2004

National Total = 2,963,513,000,000 Miles

ALPHA ORDER

RANK	STATE	MILES	% of USA
17	Alabama	59,035,000,000	2.0%
50	Alaska	4,990,000,000	0.2%
18	Arizona	57,336,000,000	1.9%
30	Arkansas	31,648,000,000	1.1%
1	California	328,917,000,000	11.1%
26	Colorado	45,891,000,000	1.5%
31	Connecticut	31,608,000,000	1.1%
44	Delaware	9,301,000,000	0.3%
3	Florida	196,444,000,000	6.6%
5	Georgia	112,620,000,000	3.8%
43	Hawaii	9,725,000,000	0.3%
40	Idaho	14,729,000,000	0.5%
7	Illinois	109,135,000,000	3.7%
13	Indiana	72,713,000,000	2.5%
32	Iowa	31,538,000,000	1.1%
33	Kansas	29,172,000,000	1.0%
24	Kentucky	47,322,000,000	1.6%
27	Louisiana	44,607,000,000	1.5%
39	Maine	14,948,000,000	0.5%
21	Maryland	55,284,000,000	1.9%
22	Massachusetts	54,771,000,000	1.8%
9	Michigan	103,326,000,000	3.5%
19	Minnesota	56,570,000,000	1.9%
28	Mississippi	39,431,000,000	1.3%
15	Missouri	68,994,000,000	2.3%
42	Montana	11,207,000,000	0.4%
38	Nebraska	19,171,000,000	0.6%
37	Nevada	19,354,000,000	0.7%
41	New Hampshire	13,216,000,000	0.4%
12	New Jersey	72,844,000,000	2.5%
35	New Mexico	23,942,000,000	0.8%
4	New York	137,898,000,000	4.7%
10	North Carolina	95,903,000,000	3.2%
49	North Dakota	7,594,000,000	0.3%
6	Ohio	111,654,000,000	3.8%
25	Oklahoma	46,443,000,000	1.6%
29	Oregon	35,598,000,000	1.2%
8	Pennsylvania	108,070,000,000	3.6%
47	Rhode Island	8,473,000,000	0.3%
23	South Carolina	49,551,000,000	1.7%
46	South Dakota	8,784,000,000	0.3%
14	Tennessee	70,943,000,000	2.4%
2	Texas	231,008,000,000	7.8%
34	Utah	24,696,000,000	0.8%
48	Vermont	7,855,000,000	0.3%
11	Virginia	78,877,000,000	2.7%
20	Washington	55,673,000,000	1.9%
36	West Virginia	20,302,000,000	0.7%
16	Wisconsin	60,399,000,000	2.0%
45	Wyoming	9,261,000,000	0.3%

RANK ORDER

RANK	STATE	MILES	% of USA
1	California	328,917,000,000	11.1%
2	Texas	231,008,000,000	7.8%
3	Florida	196,444,000,000	6.6%
4	New York	137,898,000,000	4.7%
5	Georgia	112,620,000,000	3.8%
6	Ohio	111,654,000,000	3.8%
7	Illinois	109,135,000,000	3.7%
8	Pennsylvania	108,070,000,000	3.6%
9	Michigan	103,326,000,000	3.5%
10	North Carolina	95,903,000,000	3.2%
11	Virginia	78,877,000,000	2.7%
12	New Jersey	72,844,000,000	2.5%
13	Indiana	72,713,000,000	2.5%
14	Tennessee	70,943,000,000	2.4%
15	Missouri	68,994,000,000	2.3%
16	Wisconsin	60,399,000,000	2.0%
17	Alabama	59,035,000,000	2.0%
18	Arizona	57,336,000,000	1.9%
19	Minnesota	56,570,000,000	1.9%
20	Washington	55,673,000,000	1.9%
21	Maryland	55,284,000,000	1.9%
22	Massachusetts	54,771,000,000	1.8%
23	South Carolina	49,551,000,000	1.7%
24	Kentucky	47,322,000,000	1.6%
25	Oklahoma	46,443,000,000	1.6%
26	Colorado	45,891,000,000	1.5%
27	Louisiana	44,607,000,000	1.5%
28	Mississippi	39,431,000,000	1.3%
29	Oregon	35,598,000,000	1.2%
30	Arkansas	31,648,000,000	1.1%
31	Connecticut	31,608,000,000	1.1%
32	Iowa	31,538,000,000	1.1%
33	Kansas	29,172,000,000	1.0%
34	Utah	24,696,000,000	0.8%
35	New Mexico	23,942,000,000	0.8%
36	West Virginia	20,302,000,000	0.7%
37	Nevada	19,354,000,000	0.7%
38	Nebraska	19,171,000,000	0.6%
39	Maine	14,948,000,000	0.5%
40	Idaho	14,729,000,000	0.5%
41	New Hampshire	13,216,000,000	0.4%
42	Montana	11,207,000,000	0.4%
43	Hawaii	9,725,000,000	0.3%
44	Delaware	9,301,000,000	0.3%
45	Wyoming	9,261,000,000	0.3%
46	South Dakota	8,784,000,000	0.3%
47	Rhode Island	8,473,000,000	0.3%
48	Vermont	7,855,000,000	0.3%
49	North Dakota	7,594,000,000	0.3%
50	Alaska	4,990,000,000	0.2%
	District of Columbia	3,742,000,000	0.1%

Source: U.S. Department of Transportation, Federal Highway Administration
  "Highway Statistics 2004" (Table VM-2) (http://www.fhwa.dot.gov/policy/ohpi/hss/index.htm)

Highway Fatalities in 2004

National Total = 42,636 Fatalities

ALPHA ORDER					RANK ORDER			
RANK	STATE	FATALITIES	% of USA		RANK	STATE	FATALITIES	% of USA
12	Alabama	1,154	2.7%		1	California	4,120	9.7%
47	Alaska	101	0.2%		2	Texas	3,583	8.4%
13	Arizona	1,150	2.7%		3	Florida	3,244	7.6%
24	Arkansas	704	1.7%		4	Georgia	1,634	3.8%
1	California	4,120	9.7%		5	North Carolina	1,557	3.7%
25	Colorado	665	1.6%		6	New York	1,493	3.5%
37	Connecticut	291	0.7%		7	Pennsylvania	1,490	3.5%
46	Delaware	134	0.3%		8	Illinois	1,356	3.2%
3	Florida	3,244	7.6%		9	Tennessee	1,288	3.0%
4	Georgia	1,634	3.8%		10	Ohio	1,286	3.0%
45	Hawaii	142	0.3%		11	Michigan	1,159	2.7%
38	Idaho	260	0.6%		12	Alabama	1,154	2.7%
8	Illinois	1,356	3.2%		13	Arizona	1,150	2.7%
17	Indiana	947	2.2%		14	Missouri	1,130	2.7%
35	Iowa	390	0.9%		15	South Carolina	1,046	2.5%
31	Kansas	461	1.1%		16	Kentucky	964	2.3%
16	Kentucky	964	2.3%		17	Indiana	947	2.2%
19	Louisiana	904	2.1%		18	Virginia	925	2.2%
42	Maine	194	0.5%		19	Louisiana	904	2.1%
26	Maryland	643	1.5%		20	Mississippi	900	2.1%
30	Massachusetts	476	1.1%		21	Wisconsin	792	1.9%
11	Michigan	1,159	2.7%		22	Oklahoma	774	1.8%
27	Minnesota	567	1.3%		23	New Jersey	731	1.7%
20	Mississippi	900	2.1%		24	Arkansas	704	1.7%
14	Missouri	1,130	2.7%		25	Colorado	665	1.6%
40	Montana	229	0.5%		26	Maryland	643	1.5%
39	Nebraska	254	0.6%		27	Minnesota	567	1.3%
34	Nevada	395	0.9%		28	Washington	563	1.3%
43	New Hampshire	171	0.4%		29	New Mexico	521	1.2%
23	New Jersey	731	1.7%		30	Massachusetts	476	1.1%
29	New Mexico	521	1.2%		31	Kansas	461	1.1%
6	New York	1,493	3.5%		32	Oregon	456	1.1%
5	North Carolina	1,557	3.7%		33	West Virginia	411	1.0%
48	North Dakota	100	0.2%		34	Nevada	395	0.9%
10	Ohio	1,286	3.0%		35	Iowa	390	0.9%
22	Oklahoma	774	1.8%		36	Utah	296	0.7%
32	Oregon	456	1.1%		37	Connecticut	291	0.7%
7	Pennsylvania	1,490	3.5%		38	Idaho	260	0.6%
50	Rhode Island	83	0.2%		39	Nebraska	254	0.6%
15	South Carolina	1,046	2.5%		40	Montana	229	0.5%
41	South Dakota	197	0.5%		41	South Dakota	197	0.5%
9	Tennessee	1,288	3.0%		42	Maine	194	0.5%
2	Texas	3,583	8.4%		43	New Hampshire	171	0.4%
36	Utah	296	0.7%		44	Wyoming	164	0.4%
49	Vermont	98	0.2%		45	Hawaii	142	0.3%
18	Virginia	925	2.2%		46	Delaware	134	0.3%
28	Washington	563	1.3%		47	Alaska	101	0.2%
33	West Virginia	411	1.0%		48	North Dakota	100	0.2%
21	Wisconsin	792	1.9%		49	Vermont	98	0.2%
44	Wyoming	164	0.4%		50	Rhode Island	83	0.2%
						District of Columbia	43	0.1%

Source: U.S. Department of Transportation, National Highway Safety Administration
"Traffic Safety Facts 2004" (http://www-nrd.nhtsa.dot.gov/pdf/nrd-30/NCSA/TSF2004/809915.pdf)

Highway Fatality Rate in 2004

National Rate = 1.44 Fatalities per 100 Million Vehicle-Miles of Travel

ALPHA ORDER

RANK	STATE	RATE
13	Alabama	1.95
10	Alaska	2.02
12	Arizona	2.01
3	Arkansas	2.22
35	California	1.25
24	Colorado	1.45
49	Connecticut	0.92
26	Delaware	1.44
18	Florida	1.65
24	Georgia	1.45
23	Hawaii	1.46
15	Idaho	1.77
37	Illinois	1.24
31	Indiana	1.30
37	Iowa	1.24
21	Kansas	1.58
6	Kentucky	2.04
9	Louisiana	2.03
31	Maine	1.30
41	Maryland	1.16
50	Massachusetts	0.87
43	Michigan	1.12
46	Minnesota	1.00
1	Mississippi	2.28
19	Missouri	1.64
6	Montana	2.04
28	Nebraska	1.32
6	Nevada	2.04
33	New Hampshire	1.29
46	New Jersey	1.00
4	New Mexico	2.18
44	New York	1.08
20	North Carolina	1.62
28	North Dakota	1.32
42	Ohio	1.15
17	Oklahoma	1.67
34	Oregon	1.28
27	Pennsylvania	1.38
48	Rhode Island	0.98
5	South Carolina	2.11
2	South Dakota	2.24
14	Tennessee	1.82
22	Texas	1.55
39	Utah	1.20
35	Vermont	1.25
40	Virginia	1.17
45	Washington	1.01
10	West Virginia	2.02
30	Wisconsin	1.31
15	Wyoming	1.77

RANK ORDER

RANK	STATE	RATE
1	Mississippi	2.28
2	South Dakota	2.24
3	Arkansas	2.22
4	New Mexico	2.18
5	South Carolina	2.11
6	Kentucky	2.04
6	Montana	2.04
6	Nevada	2.04
9	Louisiana	2.03
10	Alaska	2.02
10	West Virginia	2.02
12	Arizona	2.01
13	Alabama	1.95
14	Tennessee	1.82
15	Idaho	1.77
15	Wyoming	1.77
17	Oklahoma	1.67
18	Florida	1.65
19	Missouri	1.64
20	North Carolina	1.62
21	Kansas	1.58
22	Texas	1.55
23	Hawaii	1.46
24	Colorado	1.45
24	Georgia	1.45
26	Delaware	1.44
27	Pennsylvania	1.38
28	Nebraska	1.32
28	North Dakota	1.32
30	Wisconsin	1.31
31	Indiana	1.30
31	Maine	1.30
33	New Hampshire	1.29
34	Oregon	1.28
35	California	1.25
35	Vermont	1.25
37	Illinois	1.24
37	Iowa	1.24
39	Utah	1.20
40	Virginia	1.17
41	Maryland	1.16
42	Ohio	1.15
43	Michigan	1.12
44	New York	1.08
45	Washington	1.01
46	Minnesota	1.00
46	New Jersey	1.00
48	Rhode Island	0.98
49	Connecticut	0.92
50	Massachusetts	0.87

	District of Columbia	1.15

Source: Morgan Quitno Press using data from U.S. Department of Transportation, National Highway Safety Admin
"Traffic Safety Facts 2004" (http://www-nrd.nhtsa.dot.gov/pdf/nrd-30/NCSA/TSFAnn/TSF2004.pdf)

Percent of Traffic Fatalities That Were Speeding-Related: 2004

National Percent = 30.9%*

<table>
<tr><td colspan="3">ALPHA ORDER</td><td colspan="3">RANK ORDER</td></tr>
<tr><td>RANK</td><td>STATE</td><td>PERCENT</td><td>RANK</td><td>STATE</td><td>PERCENT</td></tr>
<tr><td>8</td><td>Alabama</td><td>44.0</td><td>1</td><td>Rhode Island</td><td>54.2</td></tr>
<tr><td>17</td><td>Alaska</td><td>37.6</td><td>2</td><td>Hawaii</td><td>47.2</td></tr>
<tr><td>22</td><td>Arizona</td><td>35.3</td><td>3</td><td>Vermont</td><td>46.9</td></tr>
<tr><td>48</td><td>Arkansas</td><td>14.8</td><td>4</td><td>Maine</td><td>46.4</td></tr>
<tr><td>26</td><td>California</td><td>32.4</td><td>5</td><td>Pennsylvania</td><td>44.4</td></tr>
<tr><td>15</td><td>Colorado</td><td>38.3</td><td>6</td><td>South Carolina</td><td>44.3</td></tr>
<tr><td>24</td><td>Connecticut</td><td>33.7</td><td>7</td><td>Montana</td><td>44.1</td></tr>
<tr><td>28</td><td>Delaware</td><td>31.3</td><td>8</td><td>Alabama</td><td>44.0</td></tr>
<tr><td>46</td><td>Florida</td><td>17.0</td><td>9</td><td>Missouri</td><td>43.7</td></tr>
<tr><td>43</td><td>Georgia</td><td>20.5</td><td>10</td><td>Illinois</td><td>43.4</td></tr>
<tr><td>2</td><td>Hawaii</td><td>47.2</td><td>11</td><td>Oklahoma</td><td>40.7</td></tr>
<tr><td>33</td><td>Idaho</td><td>28.1</td><td>12</td><td>Washington</td><td>40.1</td></tr>
<tr><td>10</td><td>Illinois</td><td>43.4</td><td>13</td><td>Texas</td><td>39.8</td></tr>
<tr><td>32</td><td>Indiana</td><td>28.2</td><td>14</td><td>Wyoming</td><td>39.0</td></tr>
<tr><td>50</td><td>Iowa</td><td>8.2</td><td>15</td><td>Colorado</td><td>38.3</td></tr>
<tr><td>35</td><td>Kansas</td><td>26.7</td><td>16</td><td>Maryland</td><td>37.8</td></tr>
<tr><td>44</td><td>Kentucky</td><td>20.3</td><td>17</td><td>Alaska</td><td>37.6</td></tr>
<tr><td>37</td><td>Louisiana</td><td>24.0</td><td>18</td><td>New Mexico</td><td>37.4</td></tr>
<tr><td>4</td><td>Maine</td><td>46.4</td><td>19</td><td>Wisconsin</td><td>37.2</td></tr>
<tr><td>16</td><td>Maryland</td><td>37.8</td><td>20</td><td>North Carolina</td><td>36.0</td></tr>
<tr><td>25</td><td>Massachusetts</td><td>33.2</td><td>20</td><td>South Dakota</td><td>36.0</td></tr>
<tr><td>40</td><td>Michigan</td><td>21.5</td><td>22</td><td>Arizona</td><td>35.3</td></tr>
<tr><td>36</td><td>Minnesota</td><td>25.4</td><td>23</td><td>Nevada</td><td>34.2</td></tr>
<tr><td>45</td><td>Mississippi</td><td>19.2</td><td>24</td><td>Connecticut</td><td>33.7</td></tr>
<tr><td>9</td><td>Missouri</td><td>43.7</td><td>25</td><td>Massachusetts</td><td>33.2</td></tr>
<tr><td>7</td><td>Montana</td><td>44.1</td><td>26</td><td>California</td><td>32.4</td></tr>
<tr><td>47</td><td>Nebraska</td><td>16.5</td><td>27</td><td>Oregon</td><td>31.8</td></tr>
<tr><td>23</td><td>Nevada</td><td>34.2</td><td>28</td><td>Delaware</td><td>31.3</td></tr>
<tr><td>37</td><td>New Hampshire</td><td>24.0</td><td>29</td><td>New York</td><td>31.1</td></tr>
<tr><td>49</td><td>New Jersey</td><td>8.8</td><td>29</td><td>Utah</td><td>31.1</td></tr>
<tr><td>18</td><td>New Mexico</td><td>37.4</td><td>31</td><td>West Virginia</td><td>29.0</td></tr>
<tr><td>29</td><td>New York</td><td>31.1</td><td>32</td><td>Indiana</td><td>28.2</td></tr>
<tr><td>20</td><td>North Carolina</td><td>36.0</td><td>33</td><td>Idaho</td><td>28.1</td></tr>
<tr><td>39</td><td>North Dakota</td><td>23.0</td><td>34</td><td>Virginia</td><td>27.4</td></tr>
<tr><td>41</td><td>Ohio</td><td>21.2</td><td>35</td><td>Kansas</td><td>26.7</td></tr>
<tr><td>11</td><td>Oklahoma</td><td>40.7</td><td>36</td><td>Minnesota</td><td>25.4</td></tr>
<tr><td>27</td><td>Oregon</td><td>31.8</td><td>37</td><td>Louisiana</td><td>24.0</td></tr>
<tr><td>5</td><td>Pennsylvania</td><td>44.4</td><td>37</td><td>New Hampshire</td><td>24.0</td></tr>
<tr><td>1</td><td>Rhode Island</td><td>54.2</td><td>39</td><td>North Dakota</td><td>23.0</td></tr>
<tr><td>6</td><td>South Carolina</td><td>44.3</td><td>40</td><td>Michigan</td><td>21.5</td></tr>
<tr><td>20</td><td>South Dakota</td><td>36.0</td><td>41</td><td>Ohio</td><td>21.2</td></tr>
<tr><td>42</td><td>Tennessee</td><td>20.9</td><td>42</td><td>Tennessee</td><td>20.9</td></tr>
<tr><td>13</td><td>Texas</td><td>39.8</td><td>43</td><td>Georgia</td><td>20.5</td></tr>
<tr><td>29</td><td>Utah</td><td>31.1</td><td>44</td><td>Kentucky</td><td>20.3</td></tr>
<tr><td>3</td><td>Vermont</td><td>46.9</td><td>45</td><td>Mississippi</td><td>19.2</td></tr>
<tr><td>34</td><td>Virginia</td><td>27.4</td><td>46</td><td>Florida</td><td>17.0</td></tr>
<tr><td>12</td><td>Washington</td><td>40.1</td><td>47</td><td>Nebraska</td><td>16.5</td></tr>
<tr><td>31</td><td>West Virginia</td><td>29.0</td><td>48</td><td>Arkansas</td><td>14.8</td></tr>
<tr><td>19</td><td>Wisconsin</td><td>37.2</td><td>49</td><td>New Jersey</td><td>8.8</td></tr>
<tr><td>14</td><td>Wyoming</td><td>39.0</td><td>50</td><td>Iowa</td><td>8.2</td></tr>
<tr><td></td><td></td><td></td><td></td><td>District of Columbia</td><td>46.5</td></tr>
</table>

Source: Morgan Quitno Press using data from U.S. Department of Transportation, National Highway Traffic Safety Admin. "Traffic Safety Facts 2004" (http://www-nrd.nhtsa.dot.gov/pdf/nrd-30/NCSA/TSF2004/809915.pdf)
*A speeding-related crash is if the driver was charged with a speeding-related offense or if an officer indicated that racing, driving too fast for conditions, or exceeding the posted speed limit was a contributing factor in the crash.

Percent of Vehicles Involved in Fatal Crashes That Were Large Trucks: 2004

National Percent = 8.3%*

ALPHA ORDER

RANK	STATE	PERCENT
19	Alabama	8.7
17	Alaska	9.2
40	Arizona	6.7
7	Arkansas	10.0
40	California	6.7
40	Colorado	6.7
43	Connecticut	6.5
15	Delaware	9.3
30	Florida	7.8
8	Georgia	9.9
50	Hawaii	2.1
23	Idaho	8.6
27	Illinois	8.0
3	Indiana	12.3
5	Iowa	10.9
2	Kansas	13.6
15	Kentucky	9.3
30	Louisiana	7.8
36	Maine	7.0
19	Maryland	8.7
45	Massachusetts	6.3
39	Michigan	6.8
26	Minnesota	8.1
34	Mississippi	7.4
11	Missouri	9.7
46	Montana	5.5
4	Nebraska	11.6
48	Nevada	5.2
46	New Hampshire	5.5
27	New Jersey	8.0
17	New Mexico	9.2
44	New York	6.4
24	North Carolina	8.4
12	North Dakota	9.6
10	Ohio	9.8
12	Oklahoma	9.6
27	Oregon	8.0
8	Pennsylvania	9.9
49	Rhode Island	4.3
33	South Carolina	7.5
35	South Dakota	7.2
25	Tennessee	8.2
19	Texas	8.7
36	Utah	7.0
14	Vermont	9.4
30	Virginia	7.8
38	Washington	6.9
6	West Virginia	10.8
19	Wisconsin	8.7
1	Wyoming	22.6

RANK ORDER

RANK	STATE	PERCENT
1	Wyoming	22.6
2	Kansas	13.6
3	Indiana	12.3
4	Nebraska	11.6
5	Iowa	10.9
6	West Virginia	10.8
7	Arkansas	10.0
8	Georgia	9.9
8	Pennsylvania	9.9
10	Ohio	9.8
11	Missouri	9.7
12	North Dakota	9.6
12	Oklahoma	9.6
14	Vermont	9.4
15	Delaware	9.3
15	Kentucky	9.3
17	Alaska	9.2
17	New Mexico	9.2
19	Alabama	8.7
19	Maryland	8.7
19	Texas	8.7
19	Wisconsin	8.7
23	Idaho	8.6
24	North Carolina	8.4
25	Tennessee	8.2
26	Minnesota	8.1
27	Illinois	8.0
27	New Jersey	8.0
27	Oregon	8.0
30	Florida	7.8
30	Louisiana	7.8
30	Virginia	7.8
33	South Carolina	7.5
34	Mississippi	7.4
35	South Dakota	7.2
36	Maine	7.0
36	Utah	7.0
38	Washington	6.9
39	Michigan	6.8
40	Arizona	6.7
40	California	6.7
40	Colorado	6.7
43	Connecticut	6.5
44	New York	6.4
45	Massachusetts	6.3
46	Montana	5.5
46	New Hampshire	5.5
48	Nevada	5.2
49	Rhode Island	4.3
50	Hawaii	2.1

	District of Columbia	7.1

Source: U.S. Department of Transportation, National Highway Safety Administration
   "Traffic Safety Facts 2004" (http://www-nrd.nhtsa.dot.gov/pdf/nrd-30/NCSA/TSF2004/809907.pdf)
*Large trucks are those with gross vehicle weight greater than 10,000 pounds. In 2004, 4,862 large trucks were involved in fatal crashes and 74% of these were combination trucks.

Rate of Young Drivers Involved in Fatal Crashes in 2003

National Rate = 63.4 per 100,000 Licensed Young Drivers*

ALPHA ORDER

RANK	STATE	RATE
18	Alabama	71.1
39	Alaska	54.1
5	Arizona	86.0
13	Arkansas	76.8
36	California	55.5
16	Colorado	72.4
49	Connecticut	35.2
1	Delaware	98.7
3	Florida	90.2
9	Georgia	84.0
26	Hawaii	59.1
25	Idaho	59.5
40	Illinois	51.5
24	Indiana	59.9
38	Iowa	54.5
33	Kansas	56.3
7	Kentucky	84.7
6	Louisiana	85.2
35	Maine	56.0
30	Maryland	56.6
48	Massachusetts	35.7
42	Michigan	49.4
31	Minnesota	56.5
4	Mississippi	87.7
11	Missouri	81.9
8	Montana	84.6
43	Nebraska	48.9
10	Nevada	83.0
50	New Hampshire	31.3
47	New Jersey	37.4
21	New Mexico	67.0
46	New York	39.5
2	North Carolina	97.1
27	North Dakota	59.0
37	Ohio	55.2
23	Oklahoma	61.1
34	Oregon	56.1
20	Pennsylvania	67.3
19	Rhode Island	68.1
15	South Carolina	74.0
29	South Dakota	57.1
17	Tennessee	72.3
14	Texas	75.7
45	Utah	43.3
41	Vermont	49.7
32	Virginia	56.4
44	Washington	48.3
12	West Virginia	78.4
28	Wisconsin	57.7
22	Wyoming	61.9

RANK ORDER

RANK	STATE	RATE
1	Delaware	98.7
2	North Carolina	97.1
3	Florida	90.2
4	Mississippi	87.7
5	Arizona	86.0
6	Louisiana	85.2
7	Kentucky	84.7
8	Montana	84.6
9	Georgia	84.0
10	Nevada	83.0
11	Missouri	81.9
12	West Virginia	78.4
13	Arkansas	76.8
14	Texas	75.7
15	South Carolina	74.0
16	Colorado	72.4
17	Tennessee	72.3
18	Alabama	71.1
19	Rhode Island	68.1
20	Pennsylvania	67.3
21	New Mexico	67.0
22	Wyoming	61.9
23	Oklahoma	61.1
24	Indiana	59.9
25	Idaho	59.5
26	Hawaii	59.1
27	North Dakota	59.0
28	Wisconsin	57.7
29	South Dakota	57.1
30	Maryland	56.6
31	Minnesota	56.5
32	Virginia	56.4
33	Kansas	56.3
34	Oregon	56.1
35	Maine	56.0
36	California	55.5
37	Ohio	55.2
38	Iowa	54.5
39	Alaska	54.1
40	Illinois	51.5
41	Vermont	49.7
42	Michigan	49.4
43	Nebraska	48.9
44	Washington	48.3
45	Utah	43.3
46	New York	39.5
47	New Jersey	37.4
48	Massachusetts	35.7
49	Connecticut	35.2
50	New Hampshire	31.3

	District of Columbia	139.8

*Source: U.S. Department of Transportation, National Highway Traffic Safety Administration
"Crash-Stats" (December 2004, http://www-nrd.nhtsa.dot.gov/pdf/nrd-30/NCSA/RNotes/2004/809820.pdf)*
Drivers 15 to 20 years old.

Safety Belt Usage Rate in 2005

National Rate = 82.0% Use Safety Belts*

ALPHA ORDER				RANK ORDER		
RANK	**STATE**	**PERCENT**		**RANK**	**STATE**	**PERCENT**
23	Alabama	81.8		1	Hawaii	95.3
32	Alaska	78.4		2	Washington	95.2
4	Arizona	94.2		3	Nevada	94.8
45	Arkansas	68.3		4	Arizona	94.2
7	California	92.5		5	Oregon	93.3
29	Colorado	79.2		6	Michigan	92.9
24	Connecticut	81.6		7	California	92.5
19	Delaware	83.8		8	Maryland	91.1
40	Florida	73.9		9	Texas	89.9
24	Georgia	81.6		10	New Mexico	89.5
1	Hawaii	95.3		11	Utah	86.9
36	Idaho	76.0		12	North Carolina	86.7
13	Illinois	86.0		13	Illinois	86.0
26	Indiana	81.2		13	New Jersey	86.0
15	Iowa	85.9		15	Iowa	85.9
43	Kansas	69.0		16	New York	85.0
46	Kentucky	66.7		17	West Virginia	84.9
33	Louisiana	77.7		18	Vermont	84.7
37	Maine	75.8		19	Delaware	83.8
8	Maryland	91.1		20	Pennsylvania	83.3
47	Massachusetts	64.8		21	Oklahoma	83.1
6	Michigan	92.9		22	Minnesota	82.6
22	Minnesota	82.6		23	Alabama	81.8
48	Mississippi	60.8		24	Connecticut	81.6
34	Missouri	77.4		24	Georgia	81.6
28	Montana	80.0		26	Indiana	81.2
29	Nebraska	79.2		27	Virginia	80.4
3	Nevada	94.8		28	Montana	80.0
NA	New Hampshire**	NA		29	Colorado	79.2
13	New Jersey	86.0		29	Nebraska	79.2
10	New Mexico	89.5		31	Ohio	78.7
16	New York	85.0		32	Alaska	78.4
12	North Carolina	86.7		33	Louisiana	77.7
35	North Dakota	76.3		34	Missouri	77.4
31	Ohio	78.7		35	North Dakota	76.3
21	Oklahoma	83.1		36	Idaho	76.0
5	Oregon	93.3		37	Maine	75.8
20	Pennsylvania	83.3		38	Rhode Island	74.7
38	Rhode Island	74.7		39	Tennessee	74.4
42	South Carolina	69.7		40	Florida	73.9
44	South Dakota	68.8		41	Wisconsin	73.3
39	Tennessee	74.4		42	South Carolina	69.7
9	Texas	89.9		43	Kansas	69.0
11	Utah	86.9		44	South Dakota	68.8
18	Vermont	84.7		45	Arkansas	68.3
27	Virginia	80.4		46	Kentucky	66.7
2	Washington	95.2		47	Massachusetts	64.8
17	West Virginia	84.9		48	Mississippi	60.8
41	Wisconsin	73.3		NA	New Hampshire**	NA
NA	Wyoming**	NA		NA	Wyoming**	NA
					District of Columbia	88.8

Source: U.S. Department of Transportation, National Highway Traffic Safety Administration
   "Safety Belt Use in 2005" (http://www-nrd.nhtsa.dot.gov/pdf/nrd-30/NCSA/RNotes/2005/809932.pdf)
*National estimate is from the National Occupant Protection Use Survey (NOPUS) using a different methodology.
**Not available.

Percent of Passenger Car Occupant Fatalities
Where Victim Used a Seat Belt in 2004
National Percent = 41.5% of Passenger Car Occupant Fatalities*

ALPHA ORDER

RANK	STATE	PERCENT
16	Alabama	42.4
25	Alaska	39.1
35	Arizona	34.6
42	Arkansas	28.8
5	California	52.7
15	Colorado	42.5
19	Connecticut	40.9
4	Delaware	52.9
29	Florida	38.2
23	Georgia	40.0
26	Hawaii	39.0
13	Idaho	45.4
14	Illinois	42.9
20	Indiana	40.7
17	Iowa	42.0
34	Kansas	35.1
39	Kentucky	33.4
36	Louisiana	34.2
32	Maine	36.8
6	Maryland	52.2
42	Massachusetts	28.8
0	Michigan	51.4
18	Minnesota	41.8
50	Mississippi	22.5
44	Missouri	28.5
48	Montana	26.9
38	Nebraska	33.6
11	Nevada	48.1
41	New Hampshire	30.1
10	New Jersey	48.6
21	New Mexico	40.4
6	New York	52.2
12	North Carolina	47.8
45	North Dakota	28.0
24	Ohio	39.6
21	Oklahoma	40.4
1	Oregon	63.6
37	Pennsylvania	34.1
46	Rhode Island	27.7
49	South Carolina	26.2
47	South Dakota	27.1
40	Tennessee	33.2
3	Texas	53.3
26	Utah	39.0
9	Vermont	50.0
26	Virginia	39.0
2	Washington	54.3
30	West Virginia	37.7
33	Wisconsin	36.5
30	Wyoming	37.7

RANK ORDER

RANK	STATE	PERCENT
1	Oregon	63.6
2	Washington	54.3
3	Texas	53.3
4	Delaware	52.9
5	California	52.7
6	Maryland	52.2
6	New York	52.2
8	Michigan	51.4
9	Vermont	50.0
10	New Jersey	48.6
11	Nevada	48.1
12	North Carolina	47.8
13	Idaho	45.4
14	Illinois	42.9
15	Colorado	42.5
16	Alabama	42.4
17	Iowa	42.0
18	Minnesota	41.8
19	Connecticut	40.9
20	Indiana	40.7
21	New Mexico	40.4
21	Oklahoma	40.4
23	Georgia	40.0
24	Ohio	39.6
25	Alaska	39.1
26	Hawaii	39.0
26	Utah	39.0
26	Virginia	39.0
29	Florida	38.2
30	West Virginia	37.7
30	Wyoming	37.7
32	Maine	36.8
33	Wisconsin	36.5
34	Kansas	35.1
35	Arizona	34.6
36	Louisiana	34.2
37	Pennsylvania	34.1
38	Nebraska	33.6
39	Kentucky	33.4
40	Tennessee	33.2
41	New Hampshire	30.1
42	Arkansas	28.8
42	Massachusetts	28.8
44	Missouri	28.5
45	North Dakota	28.0
46	Rhode Island	27.7
47	South Dakota	27.1
48	Montana	26.9
49	South Carolina	26.2
50	Mississippi	22.5
	District of Columbia	33.3

Source: U.S. Department of Transportation, National Highway Safety Administration
"Traffic Safety Facts 2004" (http://www-nrd.nhtsa.dot.gov/pdf/nrd-30/NCSA/TSFAnn/TSF2004.pdf)
*Only those fatalities where seat belts are known to have been used are counted.

Fatalities in Alcohol-Related Crashes in 2004

National Total = 16,694 Fatalities*

ALPHA ORDER

RANK	STATE	FATALITIES	% of USA
13	Alabama	442	2.6%
50	Alaska	31	0.2%
14	Arizona	435	2.6%
24	Arkansas	276	1.7%
1	California	1,643	9.8%
26	Colorado	259	1.6%
35	Connecticut	127	0.8%
46	Delaware	51	0.3%
3	Florida	1,222	7.3%
8	Georgia	525	3.1%
43	Hawaii	65	0.4%
38	Idaho	93	0.6%
5	Illinois	604	3.6%
21	Indiana	299	1.8%
36	Iowa	110	0.7%
33	Kansas	148	0.9%
20	Kentucky	308	1.8%
16	Louisiana	414	2.5%
42	Maine	70	0.4%
22	Maryland	286	1.7%
29	Massachusetts	203	1.2%
15	Michigan	430	2.6%
31	Minnesota	184	1.1%
19	Mississippi	341	2.0%
12	Missouri	449	2.7%
37	Montana	106	0.6%
39	Nebraska	92	0.6%
32	Nevada	152	0.9%
44	New Hampshire	59	0.4%
25	New Jersey	270	1.6%
28	New Mexico	211	1.3%
6	New York	587	3.5%
7	North Carolina	553	3.3%
48	North Dakota	39	0.2%
10	Ohio	492	2.9%
23	Oklahoma	278	1.7%
30	Oregon	199	1.2%
4	Pennsylvania	614	3.7%
47	Rhode Island	42	0.3%
11	South Carolina	464	2.8%
40	South Dakota	86	0.5%
9	Tennessee	519	3.1%
2	Texas	1,642	9.8%
41	Utah	72	0.4%
49	Vermont	32	0.2%
17	Virginia	359	2.2%
27	Washington	246	1.5%
34	West Virginia	136	0.8%
18	Wisconsin	358	2.1%
44	Wyoming	59	0.4%

RANK ORDER

RANK	STATE	FATALITIES	% of USA
1	California	1,643	9.8%
2	Texas	1,642	9.8%
3	Florida	1,222	7.3%
4	Pennsylvania	614	3.7%
5	Illinois	604	3.6%
6	New York	587	3.5%
7	North Carolina	553	3.3%
8	Georgia	525	3.1%
9	Tennessee	519	3.1%
10	Ohio	492	2.9%
11	South Carolina	464	2.8%
12	Missouri	449	2.7%
13	Alabama	442	2.6%
14	Arizona	435	2.6%
15	Michigan	430	2.6%
16	Louisiana	414	2.5%
17	Virginia	359	2.2%
18	Wisconsin	358	2.1%
19	Mississippi	341	2.0%
20	Kentucky	308	1.8%
21	Indiana	299	1.8%
22	Maryland	286	1.7%
23	Oklahoma	278	1.7%
24	Arkansas	276	1.7%
25	New Jersey	270	1.6%
26	Colorado	259	1.6%
27	Washington	246	1.5%
28	New Mexico	211	1.3%
29	Massachusetts	203	1.2%
30	Oregon	199	1.2%
31	Minnesota	184	1.1%
32	Nevada	152	0.9%
33	Kansas	148	0.9%
34	West Virginia	136	0.8%
35	Connecticut	127	0.8%
36	Iowa	110	0.7%
37	Montana	106	0.6%
38	Idaho	93	0.6%
39	Nebraska	92	0.6%
40	South Dakota	86	0.5%
41	Utah	72	0.4%
42	Maine	70	0.4%
43	Hawaii	65	0.4%
44	New Hampshire	59	0.4%
44	Wyoming	59	0.4%
46	Delaware	51	0.3%
47	Rhode Island	42	0.3%
48	North Dakota	39	0.2%
49	Vermont	32	0.2%
50	Alaska	31	0.2%
	District of Columbia	18	0.1%

Source: U.S. Department of Transportation, National Highway Safety Administration
    "Traffic Safety Facts 2004" (http://www-nrd.nhtsa.dot.gov/pdf/nrd-30/NCSA/TSF2004/809905.pdf)
*Drivers with Blood Alcohol Content (BAC) of .01 or more. "Legally Drunk" BAC differs from state to state but is often .08 or higher.

Fatalities in Alcohol-Related Crashes
As a Percent of All Highway Fatalities in 2004
National Percent = 39% of Highway Fatalities*

ALPHA ORDER

RANK	STATE	PERCENT
26	Alabama	38
48	Alaska	31
26	Arizona	38
20	Arkansas	39
16	California	40
20	Colorado	39
9	Connecticut	44
26	Delaware	38
26	Florida	38
42	Georgia	32
2	Hawaii	46
34	Idaho	36
6	Illinois	45
42	Indiana	32
49	Iowa	28
42	Kansas	32
42	Kentucky	32
2	Louisiana	46
34	Maine	36
6	Maryland	45
14	Massachusetts	43
32	Michigan	37
42	Minnesota	32
26	Mississippi	38
16	Missouri	40
2	Montana	46
34	Nebraska	36
20	Nevada	39
39	New Hampshire	35
32	New Jersey	37
16	New Mexico	40
20	New York	39
39	North Carolina	35
20	North Dakota	39
26	Ohio	38
34	Oklahoma	36
9	Oregon	44
15	Pennsylvania	41
1	Rhode Island	50
9	South Carolina	44
9	South Dakota	44
16	Tennessee	40
2	Texas	46
50	Utah	24
42	Vermont	32
20	Virginia	39
9	Washington	44
41	West Virginia	33
6	Wisconsin	45
34	Wyoming	36

RANK ORDER

RANK	STATE	PERCENT
1	Rhode Island	50
2	Hawaii	46
2	Louisiana	46
2	Montana	46
2	Texas	46
6	Illinois	45
6	Maryland	45
6	Wisconsin	45
9	Connecticut	44
9	Oregon	44
9	South Carolina	44
9	South Dakota	44
9	Washington	44
14	Massachusetts	43
15	Pennsylvania	41
16	California	40
16	Missouri	40
16	New Mexico	40
16	Tennessee	40
20	Arkansas	39
20	Colorado	39
20	Nevada	39
20	New York	39
20	North Dakota	39
20	Virginia	39
26	Alabama	38
26	Arizona	38
26	Delaware	38
26	Florida	38
26	Mississippi	38
26	Ohio	38
32	Michigan	37
32	New Jersey	37
34	Idaho	36
34	Maine	36
34	Nebraska	36
34	Oklahoma	36
34	Wyoming	36
39	New Hampshire	35
39	North Carolina	35
41	West Virginia	33
42	Georgia	32
42	Indiana	32
42	Kansas	32
42	Kentucky	32
42	Minnesota	32
42	Vermont	32
48	Alaska	31
49	Iowa	28
50	Utah	24

District of Columbia	41

Source: U.S. Department of Transportation, National Highway Safety Administration
"Traffic Safety Facts 2004" (http://www-nrd.nhtsa.dot.gov/pdf/nrd-30/NCSA/TSF2004/809905.pdf)
*Drivers with Blood Alcohol Content (BAC) of .01 or more. "Legally Drunk" BAC differs from state to state but is often .08 or higher.

Licensed Drivers in 2004

National Total = 198,888,912 Licensed Drivers

ALPHA ORDER				RANK ORDER			
RANK	STATE	DRIVERS	% of USA	RANK	STATE	DRIVERS	% of USA
20	Alabama	3,613,138	18.2%	1	California	22,761,088	114.4%
48	Alaska	482,532	2.4%	2	Texas	14,543,528	73.1%
19	Arizona	3,783,927	19.0%	3	Florida	13,146,357	66.1%
33	Arkansas	1,862,430	9.4%	4	New York	11,246,675	56.5%
1	California	22,761,088	114.4%	5	Pennsylvania	8,430,142	42.4%
22	Colorado	3,205,054	16.1%	6	Illinois	8,057,683	40.5%
27	Connecticut	2,694,574	13.5%	7	Ohio	7,675,007	38.6%
47	Delaware	533,943	2.7%	8	Michigan	7,103,404	35.7%
3	Florida	13,146,357	66.1%	9	North Carolina	6,122,137	30.8%
11	Georgia	5,793,143	29.1%	10	New Jersey	5,799,532	29.2%
42	Hawaii	843,876	4.2%	11	Georgia	5,793,143	29.1%
41	Idaho	942,983	4.7%	12	Virginia	5,112,523	25.7%
6	Illinois	8,057,683	40.5%	13	Massachusetts	4,645,857	23.4%
14	Indiana	4,521,329	22.7%	14	Indiana	4,521,329	22.7%
30	Iowa	2,003,723	10.1%	15	Washington	4,504,581	22.6%
31	Kansas	1,979,746	10.0%	16	Tennessee	4,247,884	21.4%
26	Kentucky	2,823,454	14.2%	17	Missouri	4,047,652	20.4%
23	Louisiana	3,169,627	15.9%	18	Wisconsin	3,910,188	19.7%
40	Maine	984,829	5.0%	19	Arizona	3,783,927	19.0%
21	Maryland	3,594,251	18.1%	20	Alabama	3,613,138	18.2%
13	Massachusetts	4,645,857	23.4%	21	Maryland	3,594,251	18.1%
8	Michigan	7,103,404	35.7%	22	Colorado	3,205,054	16.1%
24	Minnesota	3,083,007	15.5%	23	Louisiana	3,169,627	15.9%
32	Mississippi	1,896,008	9.5%	24	Minnesota	3,083,007	15.5%
17	Missouri	4,047,652	20.4%	25	South Carolina	2,972,369	14.9%
44	Montana	712,880	3.6%	26	Kentucky	2,823,454	14.2%
36	Nebraska	1,315,819	6.6%	27	Connecticut	2,694,574	13.5%
35	Nevada	1,548,097	7.8%	28	Oregon	2,625,856	13.2%
39	New Hampshire	985,775	5.0%	29	Oklahoma	2,369,621	11.9%
10	New Jersey	5,799,532	29.2%	30	Iowa	2,003,723	10.1%
38	New Mexico	1,271,365	6.4%	31	Kansas	1,979,746	10.0%
4	New York	11,246,675	56.5%	32	Mississippi	1,896,008	9.5%
9	North Carolina	6,122,137	30.8%	33	Arkansas	1,862,430	9.4%
49	North Dakota	461,780	2.3%	34	Utah	1,582,599	8.0%
7	Ohio	7,675,007	38.6%	35	Nevada	1,548,097	7.8%
29	Oklahoma	2,369,621	11.9%	36	Nebraska	1,315,819	6.6%
28	Oregon	2,625,856	13.2%	37	West Virginia	1,292,036	6.5%
5	Pennsylvania	8,430,142	42.4%	38	New Mexico	1,271,365	6.4%
43	Rhode Island	741,841	3.7%	39	New Hampshire	985,775	5.0%
25	South Carolina	2,972,369	14.9%	40	Maine	984,829	5.0%
45	South Dakota	563,298	2.8%	41	Idaho	942,983	4.7%
16	Tennessee	4,247,884	21.4%	42	Hawaii	843,876	4.2%
2	Texas	14,543,528	73.1%	43	Rhode Island	741,841	3.7%
34	Utah	1,582,599	8.0%	44	Montana	712,880	3.6%
46	Vermont	550,462	2.8%	45	South Dakota	563,298	2.8%
12	Virginia	5,112,523	25.7%	46	Vermont	550,462	2.8%
15	Washington	4,504,581	22.6%	47	Delaware	533,943	2.7%
37	West Virginia	1,292,036	6.5%	48	Alaska	482,532	2.4%
18	Wisconsin	3,910,188	19.7%	49	North Dakota	461,780	2.3%
50	Wyoming	380,180	1.9%	50	Wyoming	380,180	1.9%
					District of Columbia	349,122	1.8%

Source: U.S. Department of Transportation, Federal Highway Administration
   "Highway Statistics 2004" (Table DL-1C) (http://www.fhwa.dot.gov/policy/ohpi/hss/index.htm)

Licensed Drivers per 1,000 Driving Age Population in 2004

National Ratio = 870 Licensed Drivers

ALPHA ORDER				RANK ORDER		
RANK	STATE	RATIO		RANK	STATE	RATIO
2	Alabama	1,014		1	Vermont	1,090
3	Alaska	985		2	Alabama	1,014
30	Arizona	869		3	Alaska	985
31	Arkansas	865		4	Connecticut	976
45	California	833		5	Nebraska	965
22	Colorado	903		6	Montana	955
4	Connecticut	976		7	New Hampshire	954
48	Delaware	810		8	Florida	949
8	Florida	949		9	Indiana	939
36	Georgia	859		9	Wyoming	939
44	Hawaii	846		11	South Dakota	933
27	Idaho	887		12	Kansas	929
47	Illinois	820		13	Oregon	925
9	Indiana	939		14	North Carolina	921
41	Iowa	850		14	Washington	921
12	Kansas	929		16	Maine	918
34	Kentucky	862		16	Utah	918
19	Louisiana	909		18	Tennessee	910
16	Maine	918		19	Louisiana	909
46	Maryland	832		20	Massachusetts	907
20	Massachusetts	907		21	South Carolina	904
23	Michigan	902		22	Colorado	903
49	Minnesota	769		23	Michigan	902
43	Mississippi	847		24	North Dakota	899
26	Missouri	893		25	Wisconsin	896
6	Montana	955		26	Missouri	893
5	Nebraska	965		27	Idaho	887
33	Nevada	864		28	West Virginia	875
7	New Hampshire	954		29	Virginia	873
39	New Jersey	855		30	Arizona	869
31	New Mexico	865		31	Arkansas	865
50	New York	741		31	New Mexico	865
14	North Carolina	921		33	Nevada	864
24	North Dakota	899		34	Kentucky	862
40	Ohio	852		35	Texas	861
37	Oklahoma	858		36	Georgia	859
13	Oregon	925		37	Oklahoma	858
41	Pennsylvania	850		38	Rhode Island	857
38	Rhode Island	857		39	New Jersey	855
21	South Carolina	904		40	Ohio	852
11	South Dakota	933		41	Iowa	850
18	Tennessee	910		41	Pennsylvania	850
35	Texas	861		43	Mississippi	847
16	Utah	918		44	Hawaii	846
1	Vermont	1,090		45	California	833
29	Virginia	873		46	Maryland	832
14	Washington	921		47	Illinois	820
28	West Virginia	875		48	Delaware	810
25	Wisconsin	896		49	Minnesota	769
9	Wyoming	939		50	New York	741
					District of Columbia	769

Source: U.S. Department of Transportation, Federal Highway Administration
"Highway Statistics 2004" (Table DL-1C) (http://www.fhwa.dot.gov/policy/ohpi/hss/index.htm)

Motor Vehicle Registrations in 2004

National Total = 237,242,616 Motor Vehicles*

ALPHA ORDER					RANK ORDER			
RANK	STATE	VEHICLES	% of USA		RANK	STATE	VEHICLES	% of USA
20	Alabama	4,507,751	1.9%		1	California	31,399,596	13.2%
48	Alaska	659,981	0.3%		2	Texas	16,906,714	7.1%
22	Arizona	3,776,114	1.6%		3	Florida	15,057,473	6.3%
34	Arkansas	1,917,503	0.8%		4	New York	11,098,785	4.7%
1	California	31,399,596	13.2%		5	Ohio	10,636,290	4.5%
32	Colorado	2,023,292	0.9%		6	Pennsylvania	9,821,267	4.1%
28	Connecticut	3,041,592	1.3%		7	Illinois	9,231,541	3.9%
46	Delaware	711,039	0.3%		8	Michigan	8,398,621	3.5%
3	Florida	15,057,473	6.3%		9	Georgia	7,882,365	3.3%
9	Georgia	7,882,365	3.3%		10	Virginia	6,497,426	2.7%
43	Hawaii	947,412	0.4%		11	New Jersey	6,224,256	2.6%
38	Idaho	1,344,124	0.6%		12	North Carolina	6,198,470	2.6%
7	Illinois	9,231,541	3.9%		13	Washington	5,535,236	2.3%
14	Indiana	5,524,752	2.3%		14	Indiana	5,524,752	2.3%
24	Iowa	3,369,431	1.4%		15	Massachusetts	5,456,267	2.3%
30	Kansas	2,346,522	1.0%		16	Tennessee	5,034,662	2.1%
25	Kentucky	3,319,034	1.4%		17	Missouri	4,812,096	2.0%
23	Louisiana	3,766,793	1.6%		18	Wisconsin	4,705,069	2.0%
41	Maine	1,068,064	0.5%		19	Minnesota	4,593,349	1.9%
21	Maryland	4,119,664	1.7%		20	Alabama	4,507,751	1.9%
15	Massachusetts	5,456,267	2.3%		21	Maryland	4,119,664	1.7%
8	Michigan	8,398,621	3.5%		22	Arizona	3,776,114	1.6%
19	Minnesota	4,593,349	1.9%		23	Louisiana	3,766,793	1.6%
33	Mississippi	1,964,488	0.8%		24	Iowa	3,369,431	1.4%
17	Missouri	4,812,096	2.0%		25	Kentucky	3,319,034	1.4%
42	Montana	1,008,701	0.4%		26	South Carolina	3,257,072	1.4%
35	Nebraska	1,689,072	0.7%		27	Oklahoma	3,150,989	1.3%
39	Nevada	1,281,424	0.5%		28	Connecticut	3,041,592	1.3%
40	New Hampshire	1,178,312	0.5%		29	Oregon	3,003,227	1.3%
11	New Jersey	6,224,256	2.6%		30	Kansas	2,346,522	1.0%
36	New Mexico	1,542,964	0.7%		31	Utah	2,084,424	0.9%
4	New York	11,098,785	4.7%		32	Colorado	2,023,292	0.9%
12	North Carolina	6,198,470	2.6%		33	Mississippi	1,964,488	0.8%
47	North Dakota	700,882	0.3%		34	Arkansas	1,917,503	0.8%
5	Ohio	10,636,290	4.5%		35	Nebraska	1,689,072	0.7%
27	Oklahoma	3,150,989	1.3%		36	New Mexico	1,542,964	0.7%
29	Oregon	3,003,227	1.3%		37	West Virginia	1,396,420	0.6%
6	Pennsylvania	9,821,267	4.1%		38	Idaho	1,344,124	0.6%
45	Rhode Island	807,995	0.3%		39	Nevada	1,281,424	0.5%
26	South Carolina	3,257,072	1.4%		40	New Hampshire	1,178,312	0.5%
44	South Dakota	841,167	0.4%		41	Maine	1,068,064	0.5%
16	Tennessee	5,034,662	2.1%		42	Montana	1,008,701	0.4%
2	Texas	16,906,714	7.1%		43	Hawaii	947,412	0.4%
31	Utah	2,084,424	0.9%		44	South Dakota	841,167	0.4%
50	Vermont	523,212	0.2%		45	Rhode Island	807,995	0.3%
10	Virginia	6,497,426	2.7%		46	Delaware	711,039	0.3%
13	Washington	5,535,236	2.3%		47	North Dakota	700,882	0.3%
37	West Virginia	1,396,420	0.6%		48	Alaska	659,981	0.3%
18	Wisconsin	4,705,069	2.0%		49	Wyoming	640,914	0.3%
49	Wyoming	640,914	0.3%		50	Vermont	523,212	0.2%
						District of Columbia	238,802	0.1%

Source: U.S. Department of Transportation, Federal Highway Administration
   "Highway Statistics 2004" (Table MV-1) (http://www.fhwa.dot.gov/policy/ohpi/hss/index.htm)
Includes automobiles, trucks and buses. Does not include motorcycles.

Motor Vehicles per Driving Age Population in 2004

National Rate = 1.04 Motor Vehicles*

ALPHA ORDER				RANK ORDER		
RANK	STATE	RATE		RANK	STATE	RATE
7	Alabama	1.27		1	Wyoming	1.58
5	Alaska	1.35		2	Iowa	1.43
47	Arizona	0.87		3	South Dakota	1.39
45	Arkansas	0.89		4	North Dakota	1.36
13	California	1.15		5	Alaska	1.35
50	Colorado	0.57		5	Montana	1.35
20	Connecticut	1.10		7	Alabama	1.27
23	Delaware	1.08		8	Idaho	1.26
22	Florida	1.09		9	Nebraska	1.24
12	Georgia	1.17		10	Utah	1.21
38	Hawaii	0.95		11	Ohio	1.18
8	Idaho	1.26		12	Georgia	1.17
41	Illinois	0.94		13	California	1.15
13	Indiana	1.15		13	Indiana	1.15
2	Iowa	1.43		13	Minnesota	1.15
20	Kansas	1.10		16	New Hampshire	1.14
33	Kentucky	1.01		16	Oklahoma	1.14
23	Louisiana	1.08		18	Washington	1.13
34	Maine	1.00		19	Virginia	1.11
38	Maryland	0.95		20	Connecticut	1.10
27	Massachusetts	1.07		20	Kansas	1.10
27	Michigan	1.07		22	Florida	1.09
13	Minnesota	1.15		23	Delaware	1.08
46	Mississippi	0.88		23	Louisiana	1.08
29	Missouri	1.06		23	Tennessee	1.08
5	Montana	1.35		23	Wisconsin	1.08
9	Nebraska	1.24		27	Massachusetts	1.07
49	Nevada	0.71		27	Michigan	1.07
16	New Hampshire	1.14		29	Missouri	1.06
44	New Jersey	0.92		29	Oregon	1.06
31	New Mexico	1.05		31	New Mexico	1.05
48	New York	0.73		32	Vermont	1.04
42	North Carolina	0.93		33	Kentucky	1.01
4	North Dakota	1.36		34	Maine	1.00
11	Ohio	1.18		34	Texas	1.00
16	Oklahoma	1.14		36	Pennsylvania	0.99
29	Oregon	1.06		36	South Carolina	0.99
36	Pennsylvania	0.99		38	Hawaii	0.95
42	Rhode Island	0.93		38	Maryland	0.95
36	South Carolina	0.99		38	West Virginia	0.95
3	South Dakota	1.39		41	Illinois	0.94
23	Tennessee	1.08		42	North Carolina	0.93
34	Texas	1.00		42	Rhode Island	0.93
10	Utah	1.21		44	New Jersey	0.92
32	Vermont	1.04		45	Arkansas	0.89
19	Virginia	1.11		46	Mississippi	0.88
18	Washington	1.13		47	Arizona	0.87
38	West Virginia	0.95		48	New York	0.73
23	Wisconsin	1.08		49	Nevada	0.71
1	Wyoming	1.58		50	Colorado	0.57
					District of Columbia	0.53

*Source: Morgan Quitno Press using data from U.S. Department of Transportation, Federal Highway Administration
"Highway Statistics 2004" (Table MV-1) (http://www.fhwa.dot.gov/policy/ohpi/hss/index.htm)
Persons age 16 and older. Motor Vehicles include automobiles, trucks and buses. Motorcycles are not included.

Average Travel Time to Work in 2004

National Average = 24.7 Minutes*

ALPHA ORDER			RANK ORDER		
RANK	**STATE**	**MINUTES**	**RANK**	**STATE**	**MINUTES**
18	Alabama	23.8	1	New York	30.6
44	Alaska	18.0	2	Maryland	29.7
21	Arizona	23.4	3	New Jersey	29.4
37	Arkansas	20.8	4	Illinois	27.7
5	California	27.1	5	California	27.1
20	Colorado	23.5	6	Georgia	26.8
15	Connecticut	24.0	7	Virginia	26.5
23	Delaware	23.2	8	Massachusetts	26.4
11	Florida	25.4	9	Hawaii	25.8
6	Georgia	26.8	10	West Virginia	25.6
9	Hawaii	25.8	11	Florida	25.4
41	Idaho	19.7	12	Pennsylvania	25.1
4	Illinois	27.7	13	Washington	24.8
33	Indiana	21.8	14	New Hampshire	24.6
43	Iowa	18.2	15	Connecticut	24.0
44	Kansas	18.0	16	Louisiana	23.9
27	Kentucky	22.7	16	North Carolina	23.9
16	Louisiana	23.9	18	Alabama	23.8
31	Maine	21.9	18	Texas	23.8
2	Maryland	29.7	20	Colorado	23.5
8	Massachusetts	26.4	21	Arizona	23.4
26	Michigan	22.9	22	Missouri	23.3
30	Minnesota	22.3	23	Delaware	23.2
34	Mississippi	21.7	23	Tennessee	23.2
22	Missouri	23.3	25	Rhode Island	23.1
48	Montana	16.3	26	Michigan	22.9
47	Nebraska	16.5	27	Kentucky	22.7
28	Nevada	22.6	28	Nevada	22.6
14	New Hampshire	24.6	29	South Carolina	22.4
3	New Jersey	29.4	30	Minnesota	22.3
40	New Mexico	20.1	31	Maine	21.9
1	New York	30.6	31	Ohio	21.9
16	North Carolina	23.9	33	Indiana	21.8
50	North Dakota	15.4	34	Mississippi	21.7
31	Ohio	21.9	35	Oregon	21.4
42	Oklahoma	19.5	35	Vermont	21.4
35	Oregon	21.4	37	Arkansas	20.8
12	Pennsylvania	25.1	38	Utah	20.7
25	Rhode Island	23.1	39	Wisconsin	20.6
29	South Carolina	22.4	40	New Mexico	20.1
49	South Dakota	15.8	41	Idaho	19.7
23	Tennessee	23.2	42	Oklahoma	19.5
18	Texas	23.8	43	Iowa	18.2
38	Utah	20.7	44	Alaska	18.0
35	Vermont	21.4	44	Kansas	18.0
7	Virginia	26.5	46	Wyoming	17.3
13	Washington	24.8	47	Nebraska	16.5
10	West Virginia	25.6	48	Montana	16.3
39	Wisconsin	20.6	49	South Dakota	15.8
46	Wyoming	17.3	50	North Dakota	15.4
				District of Columbia	28.0

Source: U.S. Bureau of the Census
"2004 American Community Survey" (http://www.census.gov/acs/www/)
*Workers 16 and older not working at home.

Percent of Commuters Who Drive to Work Alone: 2004

National Percent = 77.7%*

ALPHA ORDER				RANK ORDER		
RANK	STATE	PERCENT		RANK	STATE	PERCENT
1	Alabama	85.4		1	Alabama	85.4
48	Alaska	68.8		2	Michigan	84.6
36	Arizona	76.0		3	Ohio	84.5
6	Arkansas	83.4		4	Tennessee	83.9
40	California	75.4		5	Kansas	83.6
32	Colorado	77.5		6	Arkansas	83.4
19	Connecticut	81.6		7	Oklahoma	83.3
16	Delaware	82.0		8	New Hampshire	83.2
20	Florida	81.0		9	Kentucky	83.1
27	Georgia	79.9		10	Rhode Island	82.7
49	Hawaii	68.4		11	Indiana	82.6
38	Idaho	75.6		11	South Carolina	82.6
43	Illinois	74.8		13	Mississippi	82.5
11	Indiana	82.6		14	Louisiana	82.3
26	Iowa	80.3		15	Missouri	82.2
5	Kansas	83.6		16	Delaware	82.0
9	Kentucky	83.1		17	North Carolina	81.7
14	Louisiana	82.3		17	West Virginia	81.7
24	Maine	80.5		19	Connecticut	81.6
44	Maryland	74.3		20	Florida	81.0
37	Massachusetts	75.9		20	Nebraska	81.0
2	Michigan	84.6		22	Wisconsin	80.7
28	Minnesota	79.2		23	New Mexico	80.6
13	Mississippi	82.5		24	Maine	80.5
15	Missouri	82.2		24	Texas	80.5
42	Montana	74.9		26	Iowa	80.3
20	Nebraska	81.0		27	Georgia	79.9
32	Nevada	77.5		28	Minnesota	79.2
8	New Hampshire	83.2		29	Virginia	78.7
47	New Jersey	73.5		30	Pennsylvania	78.5
23	New Mexico	80.6		31	North Dakota	78.3
50	New York	56.3		32	Colorado	77.5
17	North Carolina	81.7		32	Nevada	77.5
31	North Dakota	78.3		32	South Dakota	77.5
3	Ohio	84.5		35	Vermont	76.5
7	Oklahoma	83.3		36	Arizona	76.0
45	Oregon	73.8		37	Massachusetts	75.9
30	Pennsylvania	78.5		38	Idaho	75.6
10	Rhode Island	82.7		39	Wyoming	75.5
11	South Carolina	82.6		40	California	75.4
32	South Dakota	77.5		41	Washington	75.3
4	Tennessee	83.9		42	Montana	74.9
24	Texas	80.5		43	Illinois	74.8
45	Utah	73.8		44	Maryland	74.3
35	Vermont	76.5		45	Oregon	73.8
29	Virginia	78.7		45	Utah	73.8
41	Washington	75.3		47	New Jersey	73.5
17	West Virginia	81.7		48	Alaska	68.8
22	Wisconsin	80.7		49	Hawaii	68.4
39	Wyoming	75.5		50	New York	56.3
				District of Columbia		40.5

Source: U.S. Bureau of the Census
   "2004 American Community Survey" (http://www.census.gov/acs/www/)
*Workers 16 and older who traveled to work by car, truck or van.

Percent of Commuters Who Drive to Work in Carpools: 2004

National Percent = 10.1%*

ALPHA ORDER

RANK	STATE	PERCENT
30	Alabama	9.7
3	Alaska	13.8
2	Arizona	14.4
16	Arkansas	10.9
10	California	11.3
28	Colorado	9.9
48	Connecticut	7.8
35	Delaware	9.2
24	Florida	10.1
7	Georgia	11.7
1	Hawaii	16.4
5	Idaho	12.5
30	Illinois	9.7
25	Indiana	10.0
32	Iowa	9.6
41	Kansas	8.6
17	Kentucky	10.7
28	Louisiana	9.9
38	Maine	9.1
19	Maryland	10.3
50	Massachusetts	7.2
41	Michigan	8.6
35	Minnesota	9.2
10	Mississippi	11.3
39	Missouri	9.0
19	Montana	10.3
41	Nebraska	8.6
13	Nevada	11.2
46	New Hampshire	8.1
44	New Jersey	8.5
13	New Mexico	11.2
48	New York	7.8
8	North Carolina	11.5
40	North Dakota	8.8
47	Ohio	7.9
35	Oklahoma	9.2
10	Oregon	11.3
33	Pennsylvania	9.4
33	Rhode Island	9.4
17	South Carolina	10.7
25	South Dakota	10.0
23	Tennessee	10.2
8	Texas	11.5
4	Utah	13.6
25	Vermont	10.0
13	Virginia	11.2
19	Washington	10.3
19	West Virginia	10.3
45	Wisconsin	8.3
6	Wyoming	12.4

RANK ORDER

RANK	STATE	PERCENT
1	Hawaii	16.4
2	Arizona	14.4
3	Alaska	13.8
4	Utah	13.6
5	Idaho	12.5
6	Wyoming	12.4
7	Georgia	11.7
8	North Carolina	11.5
8	Texas	11.5
10	California	11.3
10	Mississippi	11.3
10	Oregon	11.3
13	Nevada	11.2
13	New Mexico	11.2
13	Virginia	11.2
16	Arkansas	10.9
17	Kentucky	10.7
17	South Carolina	10.7
19	Maryland	10.3
19	Montana	10.3
19	Washington	10.3
19	West Virginia	10.3
23	Tennessee	10.2
24	Florida	10.1
25	Indiana	10.0
25	South Dakota	10.0
25	Vermont	10.0
28	Colorado	9.9
28	Louisiana	9.9
30	Alabama	9.7
30	Illinois	9.7
32	Iowa	9.6
33	Pennsylvania	9.4
33	Rhode Island	9.4
35	Delaware	9.2
35	Minnesota	9.2
35	Oklahoma	9.2
38	Maine	9.1
39	Missouri	9.0
40	North Dakota	8.8
41	Kansas	8.6
41	Michigan	8.6
41	Nebraska	8.6
44	New Jersey	8.5
45	Wisconsin	8.3
46	New Hampshire	8.1
47	Ohio	7.9
48	Connecticut	7.8
48	New York	7.8
50	Massachusetts	7.2
	District of Columbia	8.7

Source: U.S. Bureau of the Census
"2004 American Community Survey" (http://www.census.gov/acs/www/)
*Workers 16 and older who traveled to work by car, truck or van.

Percent of Commuters Who Travel to Work by Public Transportation: 2004

National Percent = 4.6%*

ALPHA ORDER				RANK ORDER		
RANK	STATE	PERCENT		RANK	STATE	PERCENT
42	Alabama	0.5		1	New York	25.1
32	Alaska	1.0		2	New Jersey	10.7
21	Arizona	1.8		3	Maryland	8.3
45	Arkansas	0.4		3	Massachusetts	8.3
8	California	4.8		5	Illinois	8.0
16	Colorado	2.5		6	Hawaii	5.5
10	Connecticut	3.9		7	Pennsylvania	5.0
18	Delaware	2.1		8	California	4.8
23	Florida	1.7		9	Washington	4.3
18	Georgia	2.1		10	Connecticut	3.9
6	Hawaii	5.5		11	Nevada	3.8
28	Idaho	1.2		12	Oregon	3.7
5	Illinois	8.0		13	Virginia	3.5
37	Indiana	0.8		14	Minnesota	2.9
32	Iowa	1.0		15	Utah	2.6
48	Kansas	0.2		16	Colorado	2.5
32	Kentucky	1.0		17	Rhode Island	2.2
21	Louisiana	1.8		18	Delaware	2.1
40	Maine	0.6		18	Georgia	2.1
3	Maryland	8.3		20	Wisconsin	1.9
3	Massachusetts	8.3		21	Arizona	1.8
35	Michigan	0.9		21	Louisiana	1.8
14	Minnesota	2.9		23	Florida	1.7
48	Mississippi	0.2		24	Ohio	1.5
27	Missouri	1.4		24	Texas	1.5
42	Montana	0.5		24	Wyoming	1.5
40	Nebraska	0.6		27	Missouri	1.4
11	Nevada	3.8		28	Idaho	1.2
38	New Hampshire	0.7		28	New Mexico	1.2
2	New Jersey	10.7		30	Vermont	1.1
28	New Mexico	1.2		30	West Virginia	1.1
1	New York	25.1		32	Alaska	1.0
35	North Carolina	0.9		32	Iowa	1.0
45	North Dakota	0.4		32	Kentucky	1.0
24	Ohio	1.5		35	Michigan	0.9
45	Oklahoma	0.4		35	North Carolina	0.9
12	Oregon	3.7		37	Indiana	0.8
7	Pennsylvania	5.0		38	New Hampshire	0.7
17	Rhode Island	2.2		38	Tennessee	0.7
42	South Carolina	0.5		40	Maine	0.6
48	South Dakota	0.2		40	Nebraska	0.6
38	Tennessee	0.7		42	Alabama	0.5
24	Texas	1.5		42	Montana	0.5
15	Utah	2.6		42	South Carolina	0.5
30	Vermont	1.1		45	Arkansas	0.4
13	Virginia	3.5		45	North Dakota	0.4
9	Washington	4.3		45	Oklahoma	0.4
30	West Virginia	1.1		48	Kansas	0.2
20	Wisconsin	1.9		48	Mississippi	0.2
24	Wyoming	1.5		48	South Dakota	0.2
					District of Columbia	33.6

Source: U.S. Bureau of the Census
"2004 American Community Survey" (http://www.census.gov/acs/www/)
*Workers 16 and older.

Annual Miles per Vehicle in 2004

National Annual Average = 12,491 Miles*

ALPHA ORDER			RANK ORDER		
RANK	STATE	MILES	RANK	STATE	MILES
21	Alabama	13,096	1	Colorado	22,681
50	Alaska	7,561	2	Mississippi	20,072
7	Arizona	15,184	3	Arkansas	16,505
3	Arkansas	16,505	4	New Mexico	15,517
43	California	10,475	5	North Carolina	15,472
1	Colorado	22,681	6	South Carolina	15,213
45	Connecticut	10,392	7	Arizona	15,184
22	Delaware	13,081	8	Nevada	15,104
23	Florida	13,046	9	Vermont	15,013
14	Georgia	14,288	10	Oklahoma	14,739
46	Hawaii	10,265	11	West Virginia	14,539
39	Idaho	10,958	12	Wyoming	14,450
33	Illinois	11,822	13	Missouri	14,338
20	Indiana	13,161	14	Georgia	14,288
49	Iowa	9,360	15	Kentucky	14,258
25	Kansas	12,432	16	Tennessee	14,091
15	Kentucky	14,258	17	Maine	13,995
32	Louisiana	11,842	18	Texas	13,664
17	Maine	13,995	19	Maryland	13,420
19	Maryland	13,420	20	Indiana	13,161
48	Massachusetts	10,038	21	Alabama	13,096
28	Michigan	12,303	22	Delaware	13,081
27	Minnesota	12,316	23	Florida	13,046
2	Mississippi	20,072	24	Wisconsin	12,837
13	Missouri	14,338	25	Kansas	12,432
37	Montana	11,110	26	New York	12,425
35	Nebraska	11,350	27	Minnesota	12,316
8	Nevada	15,104	28	Michigan	12,303
36	New Hampshire	11,216	29	Virginia	12,140
34	New Jersey	11,703	30	Oregon	11,853
4	New Mexico	15,517	31	Utah	11,848
26	New York	12,425	32	Louisiana	11,842
5	North Carolina	15,472	33	Illinois	11,822
40	North Dakota	10,835	34	New Jersey	11,703
41	Ohio	10,497	35	Nebraska	11,350
10	Oklahoma	14,739	36	New Hampshire	11,216
30	Oregon	11,853	37	Montana	11,110
38	Pennsylvania	11,004	38	Pennsylvania	11,004
42	Rhode Island	10,486	39	Idaho	10,958
6	South Carolina	15,213	40	North Dakota	10,835
44	South Dakota	10,443	41	Ohio	10,497
16	Tennessee	14,091	42	Rhode Island	10,486
18	Texas	13,664	43	California	10,475
31	Utah	11,848	44	South Dakota	10,443
9	Vermont	15,013	45	Connecticut	10,392
29	Virginia	12,140	46	Hawaii	10,265
47	Washington	10,058	47	Washington	10,058
11	West Virginia	14,539	48	Massachusetts	10,038
24	Wisconsin	12,837	49	Iowa	9,360
12	Wyoming	14,450	50	Alaska	7,561
				District of Columbia	15,670

Source: Morgan Quitno Press using data from U.S. Department of Transportation, Federal Highway Administration
"Highway Statistics 2004" (Tables MV-1 and VM-2) (http://www.fhwa.dot.gov/policy/ohpi/hss/index.htm)
*Includes automobiles, trucks, buses and motorcycles.

Average Miles per Gallon in 2004

National Average = 17.0 Miles per Gallon*

ALPHA ORDER

RANK	STATE	MILES PER GALLON
14	Alabama	17.7
50	Alaska	10.2
31	Arizona	16.5
36	Arkansas	15.9
12	California	17.8
14	Colorado	17.7
44	Connecticut	15.2
3	Delaware	19.5
1	Florida	20.0
20	Georgia	17.5
2	Hawaii	19.9
18	Idaho	17.6
28	Illinois	16.6
32	Indiana	16.4
46	Iowa	14.9
22	Kansas	17.2
42	Kentucky	15.3
39	Louisiana	15.6
23	Maine	17.1
20	Maryland	17.5
27	Massachusetts	16.9
14	Michigan	17.7
23	Minnesota	17.1
9	Mississippi	18.1
28	Missouri	16.6
35	Montana	16.1
37	Nebraska	15.8
49	Nevada	13.8
34	New Hampshire	16.3
48	New Jersey	14.0
25	New Mexico	17.0
3	New York	19.5
12	North Carolina	17.8
39	North Dakota	15.6
28	Ohio	16.6
7	Oklahoma	18.9
18	Oregon	17.6
32	Pennsylvania	16.4
3	Rhode Island	19.5
42	South Carolina	15.3
44	South Dakota	15.2
14	Tennessee	17.7
39	Texas	15.6
10	Utah	17.9
6	Vermont	19.4
38	Virginia	15.7
25	Washington	17.0
10	West Virginia	17.9
8	Wisconsin	18.8
47	Wyoming	14.4

RANK ORDER

RANK	STATE	MILES PER GALLON
1	Florida	20.0
2	Hawaii	19.9
3	Delaware	19.5
3	New York	19.5
3	Rhode Island	19.5
6	Vermont	19.4
7	Oklahoma	18.9
8	Wisconsin	18.8
9	Mississippi	18.1
10	Utah	17.9
10	West Virginia	17.9
12	California	17.8
12	North Carolina	17.8
14	Alabama	17.7
14	Colorado	17.7
14	Michigan	17.7
14	Tennessee	17.7
18	Idaho	17.6
18	Oregon	17.6
20	Georgia	17.5
20	Maryland	17.5
22	Kansas	17.2
23	Maine	17.1
23	Minnesota	17.1
25	New Mexico	17.0
25	Washington	17.0
27	Massachusetts	16.9
28	Illinois	16.6
28	Missouri	16.6
28	Ohio	16.6
31	Arizona	16.5
32	Indiana	16.4
32	Pennsylvania	16.4
34	New Hampshire	16.3
35	Montana	16.1
36	Arkansas	15.9
37	Nebraska	15.8
38	Virginia	15.7
39	Louisiana	15.6
39	North Dakota	15.6
39	Texas	15.6
42	Kentucky	15.3
42	South Carolina	15.3
44	Connecticut	15.2
44	South Dakota	15.2
46	Iowa	14.9
47	Wyoming	14.4
48	New Jersey	14.0
49	Nevada	13.8
50	Alaska	10.2

District of Columbia	23.0

Source: Morgan Quitno Press using data from U.S. Department of Transportation, Federal Highway Administration "Highway Statistics 2004" (http://www.fhwa.dot.gov/policy/ohpi/hss/index.htm)
*Total vehicle-miles for 2004 divided by total highway motor-fuel use. Includes gasoline, gasohol, diesel and other "special fuels."

Airports in 2004

National Total = 13,715 Airports*

RANK	STATE	AIRPORTS	% of USA
32	Alabama	182	1.3%
5	Alaska	508	3.7%
29	Arizona	198	1.4%
27	Arkansas	229	1.7%
3	California	537	3.9%
23	Colorado	250	1.8%
46	Connecticut	55	0.4%
48	Delaware	32	0.2%
7	Florida	485	3.5%
17	Georgia	335	2.4%
49	Hawaii	31	0.2%
28	Idaho	202	1.5%
2	Illinois	593	4.3%
6	Indiana	496	3.6%
25	Iowa	235	1.7%
14	Kansas	370	2.7%
37	Kentucky	144	1.0%
24	Louisiana	241	1.8%
39	Maine	100	0.7%
35	Maryland	153	1.1%
43	Massachusetts	77	0.6%
13	Michigan	379	2.8%
12	Minnesota	385	2.8%
30	Mississippi	189	1.4%
10	Missouri	403	2.9%
26	Montana	234	1.7%
22	Nebraska	267	1.9%
40	Nevada	98	0.7%
47	New Hampshire	52	0.4%
38	New Jersey	119	0.9%
36	New Mexico	149	1.1%
11	New York	400	2.9%
19	North Carolina	305	2.2%
20	North Dakota	292	2.1%
4	Ohio	511	3.7%
15	Oklahoma	344	2.5%
16	Oregon	342	2.5%
8	Pennsylvania	467	3.4%
50	Rhode Island	10	0.1%
33	South Carolina	158	1.2%
34	South Dakota	156	1.1%
30	Tennessee	189	1.4%
1	Texas	1,415	10.3%
40	Utah	98	0.7%
45	Vermont	61	0.4%
21	Virginia	288	2.1%
18	Washington	332	2.4%
44	West Virginia	72	0.5%
9	Wisconsin	451	3.3%
42	Wyoming	94	0.7%

RANK	STATE	AIRPORTS	% of USA
1	Texas	1,415	10.3%
2	Illinois	593	4.3%
3	California	537	3.9%
4	Ohio	511	3.7%
5	Alaska	508	3.7%
6	Indiana	496	3.6%
7	Florida	485	3.5%
8	Pennsylvania	467	3.4%
9	Wisconsin	451	3.3%
10	Missouri	403	2.9%
11	New York	400	2.9%
12	Minnesota	385	2.8%
13	Michigan	379	2.8%
14	Kansas	370	2.7%
15	Oklahoma	344	2.5%
16	Oregon	342	2.5%
17	Georgia	335	2.4%
18	Washington	332	2.4%
19	North Carolina	305	2.2%
20	North Dakota	292	2.1%
21	Virginia	288	2.1%
22	Nebraska	267	1.9%
23	Colorado	250	1.8%
24	Louisiana	241	1.8%
25	Iowa	235	1.7%
26	Montana	234	1.7%
27	Arkansas	229	1.7%
28	Idaho	202	1.5%
29	Arizona	198	1.4%
30	Mississippi	189	1.4%
30	Tennessee	189	1.4%
32	Alabama	182	1.3%
33	South Carolina	158	1.2%
34	South Dakota	156	1.1%
35	Maryland	153	1.1%
36	New Mexico	149	1.1%
37	Kentucky	144	1.0%
38	New Jersey	119	0.9%
39	Maine	100	0.7%
40	Nevada	98	0.7%
40	Utah	98	0.7%
42	Wyoming	94	0.7%
43	Massachusetts	77	0.6%
44	West Virginia	72	0.5%
45	Vermont	61	0.4%
46	Connecticut	55	0.4%
47	New Hampshire	52	0.4%
48	Delaware	32	0.2%
49	Hawaii	31	0.2%
50	Rhode Island	10	0.1%
	District of Columbia	2	0.0%

Source: U.S. Department of Transportation, Bureau of Transportation Statistics
   "State Transportation Statistics 2004" (http://www.bts.gov/)
*This table comprises all U.S. public use and private use airports. There are 5,286 public use facilities of which
628 are certified for air carrier operations. Public use facilities are open to the public with no prior authorization or
permission required. Private use facilities are not open to the general public and include medical, law
enforcement, corporate, and other such facilities.

Airport Enplanements in 2004

National Total = 697,296,854 Enplanements*

RANK	STATE	ENPLANEMENTS	% of USA
35	Alabama	2,681,749	0.4%
29	Alaska	4,520,907	0.6%
11	Arizona	21,858,678	3.1%
39	Arkansas	1,763,768	0.3%
1	California	83,932,216	12.0%
9	Colorado	22,346,426	3.2%
30	Connecticut	3,366,197	0.5%
50	Delaware	0	0.0%
3	Florida	62,481,440	9.0%
5	Georgia	42,481,909	6.1%
17	Hawaii	15,534,070	2.2%
38	Idaho	1,771,574	0.3%
4	Illinois	46,541,871	6.7%
28	Indiana	4,975,818	0.7%
40	Iowa	1,604,479	0.2%
44	Kansas	785,208	0.1%
19	Kentucky	13,203,073	1.9%
26	Louisiana	5,986,980	0.9%
43	Maine	1,088,955	0.2%
23	Maryland	10,176,670	1.5%
18	Massachusetts	13,266,494	1.9%
12	Michigan	19,912,250	2.9%
14	Minnesota	17,875,544	2.6%
42	Mississippi	1,186,737	0.2%
20	Missouri	11,815,944	1.7%
41	Montana	1,420,763	0.2%
36	Nebraska	2,143,437	0.3%
7	Nevada	22,805,430	3.3%
37	New Hampshire	2,006,555	0.3%
15	New Jersey	16,349,649	2.3%
33	New Mexico	3,140,897	0.5%
6	New York	39,160,350	5.6%
13	North Carolina	19,122,421	2.7%
47	North Dakota	608,585	0.1%
21	Ohio	10,964,858	1.6%
31	Oklahoma	3,204,106	0.5%
25	Oregon	7,201,565	1.0%
10	Pennsylvania	22,241,189	3.2%
34	Rhode Island	2,746,191	0.4%
32	South Carolina	3,170,991	0.5%
46	South Dakota	626,063	0.1%
22	Tennessee	10,829,305	1.6%
2	Texas	63,950,483	9.2%
24	Utah	8,946,644	1.3%
45	Vermont	630,112	0.1%
8	Virginia	22,782,714	3.3%
16	Washington	16,124,519	2.3%
48	West Virginia	386,427	0.1%
27	Wisconsin	5,189,882	0.7%
49	Wyoming	384,761	0.1%

RANK	STATE	ENPLANEMENTS	% of USA
1	California	83,932,216	12.0%
2	Texas	63,950,483	9.2%
3	Florida	62,481,440	9.0%
4	Illinois	46,541,871	6.7%
5	Georgia	42,481,909	6.1%
6	New York	39,160,350	5.6%
7	Nevada	22,805,430	3.3%
8	Virginia	22,782,714	3.3%
9	Colorado	22,346,426	3.2%
10	Pennsylvania	22,241,189	3.2%
11	Arizona	21,858,678	3.1%
12	Michigan	19,912,250	2.9%
13	North Carolina	19,122,421	2.7%
14	Minnesota	17,875,544	2.6%
15	New Jersey	16,349,649	2.3%
16	Washington	16,124,519	2.3%
17	Hawaii	15,534,070	2.2%
18	Massachusetts	13,266,494	1.9%
19	Kentucky	13,203,073	1.9%
20	Missouri	11,815,944	1.7%
21	Ohio	10,964,858	1.6%
22	Tennessee	10,829,305	1.6%
23	Maryland	10,176,670	1.5%
24	Utah	8,946,644	1.3%
25	Oregon	7,201,565	1.0%
26	Louisiana	5,986,980	0.9%
27	Wisconsin	5,189,882	0.7%
28	Indiana	4,975,818	0.7%
29	Alaska	4,520,907	0.6%
30	Connecticut	3,366,197	0.5%
31	Oklahoma	3,204,106	0.5%
32	South Carolina	3,170,991	0.5%
33	New Mexico	3,140,897	0.5%
34	Rhode Island	2,746,191	0.4%
35	Alabama	2,681,749	0.4%
36	Nebraska	2,143,437	0.3%
37	New Hampshire	2,006,555	0.3%
38	Idaho	1,771,574	0.3%
39	Arkansas	1,763,768	0.3%
40	Iowa	1,604,479	0.2%
41	Montana	1,420,763	0.2%
42	Mississippi	1,186,737	0.2%
43	Maine	1,088,955	0.2%
44	Kansas	785,208	0.1%
45	Vermont	630,112	0.1%
46	South Dakota	626,063	0.1%
47	North Dakota	608,585	0.1%
48	West Virginia	386,427	0.1%
49	Wyoming	384,761	0.1%
50	Delaware	0	0.0%
	District of Columbia	0	0.0%

Source: U.S. Department of Transportation, Federal Aviation Administration
"Enplanements by Carrier Type" (http://www.faa.gov/arp/planning/stats/)
National total does not include U.S. territories. Figures are for commercial service airports.

Inland Waterway Mileage in 2004

National Total = 29,627 Miles*

ALPHA ORDER				RANK ORDER			
RANK	STATE	MILES	% of USA	RANK	STATE	MILES	% of USA
6	Alabama	1,270	4.3%	1	Alaska	5,497	18.6%
1	Alaska	5,497	18.6%	2	Louisiana	2,823	9.5%
40	Arizona	0	0.0%	3	Arkansas	1,860	6.3%
3	Arkansas	1,860	6.3%	4	Kentucky	1,591	5.4%
26	California	286	1.0%	5	Florida	1,540	5.2%
40	Colorado	0	0.0%	6	Alabama	1,270	4.3%
32	Connecticut	117	0.4%	7	North Carolina	1,152	3.9%
34	Delaware	99	0.3%	8	Illinois	1,095	3.7%
5	Florida	1,540	5.2%	9	Washington	1,057	3.6%
14	Georgia	721	2.4%	10	Missouri	1,033	3.5%
40	Hawaii	0	0.0%	11	Tennessee	946	3.2%
33	Idaho	111	0.4%	12	Mississippi	873	2.9%
8	Illinois	1,095	3.7%	13	Texas	834	2.8%
24	Indiana	353	1.2%	14	Georgia	721	2.4%
19	Iowa	492	1.7%	15	West Virginia	682	2.3%
31	Kansas	120	0.4%	16	Oregon	681	2.3%
4	Kentucky	1,591	5.4%	17	Virginia	674	2.3%
2	Louisiana	2,823	9.5%	18	Maryland	532	1.8%
37	Maine	73	0.2%	19	Iowa	492	1.7%
18	Maryland	532	1.8%	20	South Carolina	482	1.6%
35	Massachusetts	90	0.3%	21	Ohio	444	1.5%
40	Michigan	0	0.0%	22	New York	394	1.3%
28	Minnesota	258	0.9%	23	New Jersey	360	1.2%
12	Mississippi	873	2.9%	24	Indiana	353	1.2%
10	Missouri	1,033	3.5%	25	Nebraska	318	1.1%
40	Montana	0	0.0%	26	California	286	1.0%
25	Nebraska	318	1.1%	27	Pennsylvania	259	0.9%
40	Nevada	0	0.0%	28	Minnesota	258	0.9%
39	New Hampshire	8	0.0%	29	Wisconsin	231	0.8%
23	New Jersey	360	1.2%	30	Oklahoma	150	0.5%
40	New Mexico	0	0.0%	31	Kansas	120	0.4%
22	New York	394	1.3%	32	Connecticut	117	0.4%
7	North Carolina	1,152	3.9%	33	Idaho	111	0.4%
40	North Dakota	0	0.0%	34	Delaware	99	0.3%
21	Ohio	444	1.5%	35	Massachusetts	90	0.3%
30	Oklahoma	150	0.5%	36	South Dakota	75	0.3%
16	Oregon	681	2.3%	37	Maine	73	0.2%
27	Pennsylvania	259	0.9%	38	Rhode Island	39	0.1%
38	Rhode Island	39	0.1%	39	New Hampshire	8	0.0%
20	South Carolina	482	1.6%	40	Arizona	0	0.0%
36	South Dakota	75	0.3%	40	Colorado	0	0.0%
11	Tennessee	946	3.2%	40	Hawaii	0	0.0%
13	Texas	834	2.8%	40	Michigan	0	0.0%
40	Utah	0	0.0%	40	Montana	0	0.0%
40	Vermont	0	0.0%	40	Nevada	0	0.0%
17	Virginia	674	2.3%	40	New Mexico	0	0.0%
9	Washington	1,057	3.6%	40	North Dakota	0	0.0%
15	West Virginia	682	2.3%	40	Utah	0	0.0%
29	Wisconsin	231	0.8%	40	Vermont	0	0.0%
40	Wyoming	0	0.0%	40	Wyoming	0	0.0%
					District of Columbia	7	0.0%

Source: U.S. Department of Transportation, Bureau of Transportation Statistics
    "State Transportation Statistics 2004" (http://www.bts.gov/)
*Waterway mileage was determined by including the length of channels 1) with a controlling draft of nine feet or greater, 2) with commercial cargo traffic reported for 1998 and 1999, but 3) were not offshore. Channels within major bays are included (e.g., Chesapeake Bay, San Francisco Bay, Puget Sound, Long Island Sound, and major sounds and straits in southeastern Alaska). Channels in the Great Lakes are not included.

Percent of Recreational Boating Accidents Involving Alcohol: 2004

National Percent = 11.9% of Accidents*

RANK	STATE	PERCENT	RANK	STATE	PERCENT
20	Alabama	14.3	1	Vermont	40.0
24	Alaska	11.5	2	South Dakota	37.5
9	Arizona	24.7	3	Idaho	37.1
30	Arkansas	9.1	4	Wyoming	33.3
39	California	6.1	5	Iowa	31.3
27	Colorado	10.5	6	Oklahoma	29.1
32	Connecticut	8.6	7	Illinois	27.8
23	Delaware	12.5	8	Montana	25.0
43	Florida	5.2	9	Arizona	24.7
28	Georgia	10.2	10	Missouri	23.8
48	Hawaii	0.0	11	Nebraska	22.2
3	Idaho	37.1	12	Michigan	21.7
7	Illinois	27.8	13	Indiana	19.6
13	Indiana	19.6	14	Kansas	19.4
5	Iowa	31.3	14	Washington	19.4
14	Kansas	19.4	16	Minnesota	19.3
38	Kentucky	6.5	17	Nevada	18.5
24	Louisiana	11.5	18	Wisconsin	17.8
19	Maine	17.1	19	Maine	17.1
37	Maryland	6.7	20	Alabama	14.3
36	Massachusetts	7.3	20	North Carolina	14.3
12	Michigan	21.7	22	Virginia	14.0
16	Minnesota	19.3	23	Delaware	12.5
32	Mississippi	8.6	24	Alaska	11.5
10	Missouri	23.8	24	Louisiana	11.5
8	Montana	25.0	26	Tennessee	11.0
11	Nebraska	22.2	27	Colorado	10.5
17	Nevada	18.5	28	Georgia	10.2
42	New Hampshire	5.7	29	New Mexico	9.5
47	New Jersey	3.2	30	Arkansas	9.1
29	New Mexico	9.5	31	New York	9.0
31	New York	9.0	32	Connecticut	8.6
20	North Carolina	14.3	32	Mississippi	8.6
48	North Dakota	0.0	32	Ohio	8.6
32	Ohio	8.6	35	Texas	8.2
6	Oklahoma	29.1	36	Massachusetts	7.3
40	Oregon	6.0	37	Maryland	6.7
43	Pennsylvania	5.2	38	Kentucky	6.5
45	Rhode Island	4.9	39	California	6.1
40	South Carolina	6.0	40	Oregon	6.0
2	South Dakota	37.5	40	South Carolina	6.0
26	Tennessee	11.0	42	New Hampshire	5.7
35	Texas	8.2	43	Florida	5.2
46	Utah	3.6	43	Pennsylvania	5.2
1	Vermont	40.0	45	Rhode Island	4.9
22	Virginia	14.0	46	Utah	3.6
14	Washington	19.4	47	New Jersey	3.2
48	West Virginia	0.0	48	Hawaii	0.0
18	Wisconsin	17.8	48	North Dakota	0.0
4	Wyoming	33.3	48	West Virginia	0.0
				District of Columbia	66.7

Source: Morgan Quitno Press using data from United States Coast Guard
  "Boating Statistics 2004" (http://www.uscgboating.org/statistics/accident_stats.htm)
*Alcohol involvement in a boating accident includes any accident in which alcoholic beverages are consumed in the boat and the investigating official has determined that the operator was impaired or affected while operating the boat.

Railroad Mileage Operated in 2004

National Total = 140,806 Miles of Railroad*

ALPHA ORDER

RANK	STATE	MILES	% of USA
17	Alabama	3,332	2.4%
46	Alaska	506	0.4%
35	Arizona	1,815	1.3%
25	Arkansas	2,692	1.9%
3	California	5,796	4.1%
28	Colorado	2,530	1.8%
45	Connecticut	543	0.4%
48	Delaware	228	0.2%
24	Florida	2,840	2.0%
7	Georgia	4,779	3.4%
50	Hawaii	0	0.0%
37	Idaho	1,529	1.1%
2	Illinois	7,338	5.2%
9	Indiana	4,192	3.0%
11	Iowa	3,946	2.8%
6	Kansas	4,936	3.5%
26	Kontucky	2,640	1.9%
23	Louisiana	2,971	2.1%
40	Maine	1,148	0.8%
43	Maryland	759	0.5%
41	Massachusetts	1,097	0.8%
13	Michigan	3,590	2.5%
8	Minnesota	4,589	3.3%
29	Mississippi	2,481	1.8%
10	Missouri	4,122	2.9%
18	Montana	3,269	2.3%
15	Nebraska	3,478	2.5%
39	Nevada	1,202	0.9%
47	New Hampshire	421	0.3%
42	New Jersey	917	0.7%
36	New Mexico	1,703	1.2%
14	New York	3,553	2.5%
19	North Carolina	3,250	2.3%
12	North Dakota	3,593	2.6%
4	Ohio	5,179	3.7%
21	Oklahoma	3,228	2.3%
29	Oregon	2,481	1.8%
5	Pennsylvania	5,060	3.6%
49	Rhode Island	102	0.1%
31	South Carolina	2,300	1.6%
34	South Dakota	1,837	1.3%
27	Tennessee	2,609	1.9%
1	Texas	10,246	7.3%
38	Utah	1,452	1.0%
44	Vermont	568	0.4%
20	Virginia	3,236	2.3%
22	Washington	3,179	2.3%
32	West Virginia	2,258	1.6%
16	Wisconsin	3,400	2.4%
33	Wyoming	1,862	1.3%

RANK ORDER

RANK	STATE	MILES	% of USA
1	Texas	10,246	7.3%
2	Illinois	7,338	5.2%
3	California	5,796	4.1%
4	Ohio	5,179	3.7%
5	Pennsylvania	5,060	3.6%
6	Kansas	4,936	3.5%
7	Georgia	4,779	3.4%
8	Minnesota	4,589	3.3%
9	Indiana	4,192	3.0%
10	Missouri	4,122	2.9%
11	Iowa	3,946	2.8%
12	North Dakota	3,593	2.6%
13	Michigan	3,590	2.5%
14	New York	3,553	2.5%
15	Nebraska	3,478	2.5%
16	Wisconsin	3,400	2.4%
17	Alabama	3,332	2.4%
18	Montana	3,269	2.3%
19	North Carolina	3,250	2.3%
20	Virginia	3,236	2.3%
21	Oklahoma	3,228	2.3%
22	Washington	3,179	2.3%
23	Louisiana	2,971	2.1%
24	Florida	2,840	2.0%
25	Arkansas	2,692	1.9%
26	Kentucky	2,640	1.9%
27	Tennessee	2,609	1.9%
28	Colorado	2,530	1.8%
29	Mississippi	2,481	1.8%
29	Oregon	2,481	1.8%
31	South Carolina	2,300	1.6%
32	West Virginia	2,258	1.6%
33	Wyoming	1,862	1.3%
34	South Dakota	1,837	1.3%
35	Arizona	1,815	1.3%
36	New Mexico	1,703	1.2%
37	Idaho	1,529	1.1%
38	Utah	1,452	1.0%
39	Nevada	1,202	0.9%
40	Maine	1,148	0.8%
41	Massachusetts	1,097	0.8%
42	New Jersey	917	0.7%
43	Maryland	759	0.5%
44	Vermont	568	0.4%
45	Connecticut	543	0.4%
46	Alaska	506	0.4%
47	New Hampshire	421	0.3%
48	Delaware	228	0.2%
49	Rhode Island	102	0.1%
50	Hawaii	0	0.0%
	District of Columbia	24	0.0%

Source: Association of American Railroads
  "Railroads and States 2004" (www.aar.org/PubCommon/Documents/AboutTheIndustry/RRState_Rankings.pdf)
Includes Class I and non-Class I miles. Excludes trackage rights. Synonymous with route-miles, so that a mile of single track is counted the same as a mile of double track.

XVI. SOURCES

ACT, Inc.
500 ACT Drive, P.O. Box 168
Iowa City, IA 52243-0168
319-337-1000
www.act.org

Administration for Children and Families
U.S. Dept. of Health and Human Services
370 L'Enfant Promenade, SW
Washington, DC 20447
202-401-9215
www.acf.dhhs.gov

American Cancer Society, Inc.
1599 Clifton Road, NE
Atlanta, GA 30329-4251
800-227-2345
www.cancer.org

American Dental Association
211 E. Chicago Ave.
Chicago, IL 60611-2678
312-440-2500
www.ada.org

American Hospital Association
One North Franklin
Chicago, IL 60606-3421
312-422-3000
www.aha.org

American Medical Association
515 North State Street
Chicago, IL 60610
800-621-8335
www.ama-assn.org

Association of American Railroads
50 F Street, NW
Washington, DC 20001-1564
202-639-2100
www.aar.org

Bureau of the Census
4700 Silver Hill Road
Washington, DC 20233-0001
301-457-2800
www.census.gov

Bureau of Economic Analysis
U.S. Department of Commerce
1441 L Street, NW
Washington, DC 20230
202-606-9900
www.bea.doc.gov

Bureau of Justice Statistics
U.S. Department of Justice
810 Seventh St., NW
Washington, DC 20531
202-307-0765
www.ojp.usdoj.gov/bjs/

Bureau of Labor Statistics
U.S.Department of Labor
2 Massachusetts Ave., NE.
Washington, DC 20212-0001
202-691-5200
www.bls.gov/iif/

Bureau of Transportation Statistics
U.S. Department of Transportation
400 7th Street, SW, room 3103
Washington DC 20590
800-853-1351
www.bts.gov

Centers for Disease Control and Prevention
1600 Clifton Road
Atlanta, GA 30333
800-311-3435
www.cdc.gov

Centers for Medicare and Medicaid Services
7500 Security Boulevard
Baltimore, MD 21244-1850
877-267-2323
www.cms.gov

College Board
The College Board
45 Columbus Avenue
New York, NY 10023
212-713-8000
www.collegeboard.com

Economic Research Service
U.S. Department of Agriculture
1800 M Street, NW
Washington, DC 20036-5831
202-694-5050
www.ers.usda.gov

Energy Information Administration
1000 Independence Avenue, SW
Washington, DC 20585
202-586-8800
www.eia.doe.gov

Environmental Protection Agency
Ariel Rios Building
1200 Pennsylvania Ave, NW
Washington, DC 20464
202-272-0167
www.epa.gov

Federal Bureau of Investigation
935 Pennsylvania Avenue, NW
Washington, DC 20535
202-324-3000
www.fbi.gov

Federal Election Commission
999 E Street, NW
Washington, DC 20463
800-424-9530
www.fec.gov

Federal Highway Administration
400 7th Street, SW
Washington, DC 20590
202-366-0660
www.fhwa.dot.gov

Federation of Tax Administrators
444 North Capitol St., NW, Ste 348
Washington, DC 20001
202-624-5890
www.taxadmin.org

XVI. SOURCES (continued)

Food and Nutrition Service
U.S. Department of Agriculture
3101 Park Center Drive, Room 926
Alexandria, VA 22302
703-305-2062
www.fns.usda.gov/fns/

General Services Administration
1800 F Street, NW
Washington, DC 20405
202-501-0705
www.gsa.gov

Health Resources and Services Administration
Bureau of Health Professions
Division of Practitioner Data Banks
7519 Standish Place, Ste. 300
Rockville MD 20857
800-767-6732
www.npdb-hipdb.com

Internal Revenue Service
U.S. Department of the Treasury
1111 Constitution Avenue, NW
Washington, DC 20224
800-829-1040
www.irs.gov

Medical Expenditure Panel Survey
Agency for Healthcare Research and Quality
540 Gaither Road
Rockville MD 20850
301-427-1656
www.meps.ahrq.gov

National Agricultural Statistics Service
Room 5829, South
Washington, DC 20250
800-727-9540
www.usda.gov/nass

National Assembly of State Arts Agencies
1029 Vermont Ave., NW 2nd Fl
Washington, DC 20005
202-347-6352
www.nasaa-arts.org

National Association of Realtors
430 N. Michigan Ave
Chicago, IL 60611
800-874-6500
www.realtor.org

National Association of State Park Directors
8829 Woodyhill Road
Raleigh, NC 27613
919-971-9300
www.naspd.org

National Center for Education Statistics
U.S. Department of Education
1990 K Street, NW
Washington, DC 20006
202-502-7300
http://nces.ed.gov

National Center for Health Statistics
U.S. Department of Health and Human Services
3311 Toledo Road
Hyattsville, MD 20782-2003
301-458-4000
www.cdc.gov/nchs/

National Conference of State Legislatures
770 E. First Place
Denver, CO 80230
303-346-7700
www.ncsl.org

National Education Association
1201 16th Street, NW
Washington, DC 20036-3290
202-833-4000
www.nea.org

National Highway Traffic Safety Admin.
U.S. Department of Transportation
400 7th Street, SW
Washington, DC 20590
202-366-9550
www.nhtsa.dot.gov

National Institute on Alcohol Abuse And Alcoholism
5635 Fishers Lane, MSC 9304
Bethesda, MD 20892-9304
301-443-9970
www.niaaa.nih.gov/

National Oceanic & Atmospheric Admin.
U.S. Department of Commerce
14th Street & Constitution Ave., NW. Rm 6217
Washington, DC 20230
202-482-6090
www.noaa.gov

National Weather Service
Storm Prediction Center
1313 Halley Circle
Norman, OK 73069
405-579-0771
www.spc.noaa.gov

Social Security Administration
Windsor Park Building
6401 Security Boulevard
Baltimore, MD 21235
800-772-1213 (information)
www.ssa.gov

Tax Foundation
1900 M Street, NW
Ste 550
Washington, DC 20036
202-464-6200
www.taxfoundation.org

U.S. Department of Defense
The Pentagon
Washington, DC 20301
703-697-5737
www.defenselink.mil

U.S. Department of Veterans Affairs
810 Vermont Avenue, NW
Washington, DC 20420
202-273-5700
www.va.gov

U.S. Geological Survey
12201 Sunrise Valley Drive
Reston, VA 20192
1-888-275-8747
www.usgs.gov

XVII. INDEX

XVII. INDEX (continued)

XVII. INDEX (continued)

XVII. INDEX (continued)

CHAPTER INDEX

HOW TO USE THIS INDEX

Place left thumb on the outer edge of this page. To locate the desired entry, fold back the remaining page edges and align the index edge mark with the appropriate page edge mark.

Other books by Morgan Quitno Press:

- *State Trends*
- *Health Care State Rankings*
- *Crime State Rankings*
- *City Crime Rankings*
- *Education State Rankings*

Call toll free: 1-800-457-0742 or
visit us at www.statestats.com